SOMETHING ABOUT THE AUTHOR®

Something about
the Author *was named
an*"**Outstanding
Reference Source,**"
*the highest honor given
by the American
Library Association
Reference and Adult
Services Division.*

ISSN 0276-816X

something ABOUT THE AUTHOR®

Facts and Pictures about Authors
and Illustrators of Books for Young People

volume 195

GALE
CENGAGE Learning™

Detroit • New York • San Francisco • New Haven, Conn • Waterville, Maine • London

Something about the Author, Volume 195

Project Editor: Lisa Kumar

Editorial: Dana Ferguson, Amy Elisabeth Fuller, Michelle Kazensky, Jennifer Mossman, Joseph Palmisano, Mary Ruby, Marie Toft

Permissions: Jennifer Altschul, Margaret Chamberlain, Jhanay Williams

Imaging and Multimedia: Leitha Etheridge-Sims, John Watkins

Composition and Electronic Capture: Amy Darga

Manufacturing: Drew Kalasky

Product Manager: Janet Witalec

For product information and technology assistance, contact us at
Gale Customer Support, 1-800-877-4253.
For permission to use material from this text or product,
submit all requests online at **www.cengage.com/permissions.**
Further permissions questions can be emailed to
permissionrequest@cengage.com

Since this page cannot legibly accommodate all copyright notices, the acknowledgments constitute an extension of the copyright notice.

While every effort has been made to ensure the reliability of the information presented in this publication, Gale, a part of Cengage Learning, does not guarantee the accuracy of the data contained herein. Gale accepts no payment for listing; and inclusion in the publication of any organization, agency, institution, publication, service, or individual does not imply endorsement of the editors or publisher. Errors brought to the attention of the publisher and verified to the satisfaction of the publisher will be corrected in future editions.

EDITORIAL DATA PRIVACY POLICY: Does this publication contain information about you as an individual? If so, for more information about our editorial data privacy policies, please see our Privacy Statement at www.gale.cengage.com.

Gale
27500 Drake Rd.
Farmington Hills, MI, 48331-3535

LIBRARY OF CONGRESS CATALOG CARD NUMBER 62-52046

ISBN-13: 978-1-4144-2167-4
ISBN-10: 1-4144-2167-2

ISSN 0276-816X

This title is also available as an e-book.
ISBN-13: 978-1-4144-5741-3
ISBN-10: 1-4144-5741-3
Contact your Gale, Cengage Learning sales representative for ordering information.

Printed in the United States of America
1 2 3 4 5 6 7 13 12 11 10 09

Contents

Authors in Forthcoming Volumes ix

Introduction xi

SATA Product Advisory Board xiii

Illustrations Index 223

Author Index 255

A

Alexander, Sue 1933-2008
Obituary Notice 1

B

Baker, Deirdre 1955- 1

Bang-Campbell, Monika 1975(?)- 2

Berlin, Eric 4

Blair, Mary 1911-1978 5

Blume, Judy 1938- 6

Bogue, Gary 1938- 13

Bogue, Gary L.
See Bogue, Gary 13

Bowsher, Melodie 14

C

Carlton, Susan 1960- 16

Carwell, L'Ann
See McKissack, Patricia C. 134

Castillo, Lauren 17

Catalanotto, Peter 1959- 18

Christiana, David 1960- 25

Condon, Ken 27

Cornwell, Autumn 29

Couvillon, Jacques 1978- 30

Cuyler, Margery 1948- 31

Cuyler, Margery Stuyvesant
See Cuyler, Margery 31

D

Deans, Karen 38

DeLaCroix, Alice 1940- 40

DeMijohn, Thom
See Disch, Thomas M. 44

DeVita, James 41

Dijkstra, Lida 1961- 42

Disch, Thomas M. 1940-2008
Obituary Notice 44

Disch, Thomas Michael
See Disch, Thomas M. 44

Disch, Tom
See Disch, Thomas M. 44

Dong-Sung, Kim 1970- 45

Dong-Sung Kim
See Dong-Sung, Kim

Draper, Sharon M. 1948- 45

F

Fardell, John 1967- 51

Feinstein, John 1956- 52

Fischer, Scott M. 1971- 56

Fishbone, Greg R. 1970- 57

Fisher, Cynthia 58

Fletcher, Ralph 1953- 59

Friend, David Michael 1975- 65

G

Gable, Brian 1949- 67

Glenn, John W. 69

Goossens, Philippe 1963- 69

Greif, Jean-Jacques 1944- 72

Griffin, Adele 1970- 73

H

Hargrave, Leonie
  See Disch, Thomas M. 44

Harris, Bob
  See Harris, Robert J. 79

Harris, Robert J. 1955- 79

Hastings, Victor
  See Disch, Thomas M. 44

Horowitz, Anthony 1955- 81

Hubery, Julia 86

J

James, Gordon C. 1973- 88

K

Katz, Karen 1947- 89

Knye, Cassandra
  See Disch, Thomas M. 44

L

Lamba, Marie 93

Levine, Gail Carson 1947- 94

Lewin, Ted 1935- 97

Lyons, Mary E. 1947- 104

Lyons, Mary Evelyn
  See Lyons, Mary E. 104

M

Maass, Robert 124

Macdonald, Guy 124

Maland, Nick 125

Mason, Prue 127

McKinley, Robin 1952- 128

McKissack, Patricia C. 1944- 134

Meunier, Brian 1954- 143

Michaels, Jamie 144

N

Nielsen, Susin 1964- 146

Nielsen-Fernlund, Susin
  See Nielsen, Susin 146

Nuzum, K.A. 147

P

Palen, Debbie 1964- 147

Pelletier, Andrew T. 149

Pelletier, Andrew Thomas
  See Pelletier, Andrew T. 149

Pickering, Jimmy 151

Pohrt, Tom 1953- 152

Powers, Jessica
  See Powers, J.L. 155

Powers, Jessica Lynn
  See Powers, J.L. 155

Powers, J.L. 1974- 155

Puybaret, Eric 1976- 155

R

Ratner, Sue Lynn
  See Alexander, Sue 1

Reilly, Joan 157

Rylant, Cynthia 1954- 157

S

Salisbury, Graham 1944- 169

Schembri, Pamela 1969- 174

Sheppard, Kate 175

Sierra, Judy 1945- 177

Sniegoski, Thomas E. 183

Sniegoski, Tom
  See Sniegoski, Thomas E. 183

Spinelli, Jerry 1941- 185

Steffensmeier, Alexander 1977- 190

Stein, Mathilde 1969- 191

Stevenson, James 1929- 192

Stower, Adam 199

T

Thach, James Otis 1969- 201

Titlebaum, Ellen 202

Todd, Chuck 202

Trewellard, J.M. 203

Trewellard, Juliet
  See Trewellard, J.M. 203

U

Uhlig, Richard 1970- 205

V

van Straaten, Harmen 1961- 206

Varon, Sara 207

Vaught, Susan 1965- 209

W

Wallace, Daisy
  See Cuyler, Margery 31

Walsh, Marissa 1972- 211

Walsh, Marissa "Mitzy"
  See Walsh, Marissa 211

Willis, Jeanne 1959- 212

Wohnoutka, Mike 217

Y

Yarrow, Peter 1938- 219

Authors in Forthcoming Volumes

Below are some of the authors and illustrators that will be featured in upcoming volumes of *SATA*. These include new entries on the swiftly rising stars of the field, as well as completely revised and updated entries (indicated with *) on some of the most notable and best-loved creators of books for children.

*Jon Agee ▌ Agee is an author and illustrator of children's books such as *The Incredible Painting of Felix Clousseau, The Return of Freddy LeGrand, Nothing,* and *The Retired Kid.* His fascination with language has inspired Agee to create a series of books on wordplay as well as the books and lyrics for two musicals produced Off-Off Broadway. A cartoonist, he has also had several of his original comics published in the *New Yorker.*

Suzanne Crowley ▌ A Texas native, Crowley set her young-adult novel *The Very Ordered Existence of Merilee Marvelous* in the Lone Star State. The novel, which has received several Best Book honors, introduces a highly intelligent but obsessively compulsive thirteen year old who overcomes her innate shyness through her friendship with a boy with an unusual interest: dragons.

Carmen Agra Deedy ▌ Award-winning writer and storyteller Deedy is the author of *The Yellow Star: The Legend of King Christian X of Denmark,* which recounts the fictional but often-repeated story of the king of Denmark's courage in proclaiming solidarity with Jews during the German occupation of his country. Deedy also taps her Cuban heritage in picture books such as *Martina the Beautiful Cockroach,* which retells a traditional Latin-American folktale.

*Andy Griffiths ▌ Griffiths is an Australian children's writer who began his publishing career in middle school. Writing full time while raising his own children, he is best known for quirky stories and the brand of sophomoric humor that salts his "Just!" books. Featuring cartoon art by Terry Denton, the humorous "Just!" series includes such boy-friendly titles as *Just Annoying!, Just Stupid!,* and *Just Disgusting!*

Hal Iggulden ▌ Theatre director Iggulden joined his older brother, British educator and writer Conn Iggulden, to compile *The Dangerous Book for Boys.* Tapping into the nostalgia surrounding childhoods of an earlier, less-technological age, the Igguldens' best-seller appeared on bookstore shelves in the brothers' native England in 2006 and quickly jumped the Atlantic. Including everything from how to tie knots to the use of a Swiss Army knife, *The Dangerous Book for Boys* has spawned a series of similar guides and sparked some controversy for its all-boy focus.

James Kochalka ▌ Kochalka is a celebrated alternative cartoonist who is best known for the daily comic strip *American Elf.* His graphic novels *Fantastic Butterflies* and *Monkey vs. Robot* are aimed at adults, while children are the intended audience of picture books such as *Peanutbutter and Jeremy* and *Squirrelly Gray. Johnny Boo: The Best Little Ghost in the World!,* another work for young readers, centers on an amiable ghoul and a friendly cyclops, while *Pinky and Stinky* focuses on a pair of pigs that crash on the moon while on their way to Pluto.

Kim LaFave ▌ A highly regarded illustrator from Canada, LaFave provides the artwork for picture-book texts by Sarah Ellis and Nicola I. Campbell, among other writers. He has received the Governor General's Literary Award, the Ruth Schwartz Children's Book Award, and the Amelia Frances Howard-Gibbon Award, among other honors, for his book illustrations. Among LaFave's works are illustrations for *Bats about Baseball,* by Jean Little and Claire Mackay, and *Gregory and Alexander,* by William Barringer.

*Sharelle Byars Moranville ▌ Moranville completed her first young-adult novel, *Over the River,* while she was a college student, and her native midwest has been the setting for her more-recent teen fiction. In *A Higher Geometry* Moranville sets her story in the midst of the cold war, as a fifteen year old is torn between her desire to study mathematics and the expectations of her parents that she become a wife and mother. *The Snows,* another teen novel, focuses on the sixteenth year of four different young people representing succeeding generations of the Snow family.

Norbert Rosing ▌ Born in Germany, internationally known photographer Rosing is recognized for his stunning images of wildlife. A frequent contributor to *National Geographic* and other magazines, he has traveled throughout Africa, Germany, and the Canadian Arctic to capture pictures of muskoxen, walruses, snow foxes, and, most famously, polar bears. In addition to illuminating books such as *The World of the Polar Bear,* Rosing's photographs of polar bears have appeared in books and periodicals, as well as on calendars and postcards.

Cat Urbigkit ▌ Urbigkit is a journalist and photographer whose work reflects her lifelong love of the Western prairie where she makes her home. She shares the culture of this area with young readers in photo-essays included in the picture books *Brave Dogs, Gentle Dogs, A Young Shepherd,* and *Cattle Kids: A Year on the Western Range.* Urbigkit focuses on her own son in *The Shepherd's Trail,* a photo-essay depicting how sheep are raised, herded, and sheared on the ranches of the Rocky Mountain states.

Introduction

Something about the Author (*SATA*) is an ongoing reference series that examines the lives and works of authors and illustrators of books for children. *SATA* includes not only well-known writers and artists but also less prominent individuals whose works are just coming to be recognized. This series is often the only readily available information source on emerging authors and illustrators. You'll find *SATA* informative and entertaining, whether you are a student, a librarian, an English teacher, a parent, or simply an adult who enjoys children's literature.

What's Inside *SATA*

SATA provides detailed information about authors and illustrators who span the full time range of children's literature, from early figures like John Newbery and L. Frank Baum to contemporary figures like Judy Blume and Richard Peck. Authors in the series represent primarily English-speaking countries, particularly the United States, Canada, and the United Kingdom. Also included, however, are authors from around the world whose works are available in English translation. The writings represented in *SATA* include those created intentionally for children and young adults as well as those written for a general audience and known to interest younger readers. These writings cover the entire spectrum of children's literature, including picture books, humor, folk and fairy tales, animal stories, mystery and adventure, science fiction and fantasy, historical fiction, poetry and nonsense verse, drama, biography, and nonfiction. Obituaries are also included in *SATA* and are intended not only as death notices but also as concise overviews of people's lives and work. Additionally, each edition features newly revised and updated entries for a selection of *SATA* listees who remain of interest to today's readers and who have been active enough to require extensive revisions of their earlier biographies.

Autobiography Feature

Beginning with Volume 103, many volumes of *SATA* feature one or more specially commissioned autobiographical essays. These unique essays, averaging about ten thousand words in length and illustrated with an abundance of personal photos, present an entertaining and informative first-person perspective on the lives and careers of prominent authors and illustrators profiled in *SATA*.

Two Convenient Indexes

In response to suggestions from librarians, *SATA* indexes no longer appear in every volume but are included in alternate (odd-numbered) volumes of the series, beginning with Volume 57.

SATA continues to include two indexes that cumulate with each alternate volume: the Illustrations Index, arranged by the name of the illustrator, gives the number of the volume and page where the illustrator's work appears in the current volume as well as all preceding volumes in the series; the Author Index gives the number of the volume in which a person's biographical sketch, autobiographical essay, or obituary appears in the current volume as well as all preceding volumes in the series.

These indexes also include references to authors and illustrators who appear in *Gale's Yesterday's Authors of Books for Children, Children's Literature Review,* and *Something about the Author Autobiography Series.*

Easy-to-Use Entry Format

Whether you're already familiar with the *SATA* series or just getting acquainted, you will want to be aware of the kind of information that an entry provides. In every *SATA* entry the editors attempt to give as complete a picture of the person's life and work as possible. A typical entry in *SATA* includes the following clearly labeled information sections:

PERSONAL: date and place of birth and death, parents' names and occupations, name of spouse, date of marriage, names of children, educational institutions attended, degrees received, religious and political affiliations, hobbies and other interests.

ADDRESSES: complete home, office, electronic mail, and agent addresses, whenever available.

CAREER: name of employer, position, and dates for each career post; art exhibitions; military service; memberships and offices held in professional and civic organizations.

MEMBER: professional, civic, and other association memberships and any official posts held.

AWARDS, HONORS: literary and professional awards received.

WRITINGS: title-by-title chronological bibliography of books written and/or illustrated, listed by genre when known; lists of other notable publications, such as plays, screenplays, and periodical contributions.

ADAPTATIONS: a list of films, television programs, plays, CD-ROMs, recordings, and other media presentations that have been adapted from the author's work.

WORK IN PROGRESS: description of projects in progress.

SIDELIGHTS: a biographical portrait of the author or illustrator's development, either directly from the biographee—and often written specifically for the *SATA* entry—or gathered from diaries, letters, interviews, or other published sources.

BIOGRAPHICAL AND CRITICAL SOURCES: cites sources quoted in "Sidelights" along with references for further reading.

EXTENSIVE ILLUSTRATIONS: photographs, movie stills, book illustrations, and other interesting visual materials supplement the text.

How a *SATA* Entry Is Compiled

SATA editors examine a wide variety of published sources to gather information for an entry. Biographical and bibliographic sources are consulted, as are book reviews, feature articles, published interviews, and material sometimes obtained from the biographee's family, publishers, agent, or other associates. Whenever possible, the author or illustrator is sent a copy of the entry to check for accuracy and completeness.

Entries that have not been verified by the biographees or their representatives are marked with an asterisk (*).

Contact the Editor

We encourage our readers to examine the entire *SATA* series. Please write and tell us if we can make *SATA* even more helpful to you. Give your comments and suggestions to the editor:

Editor
Something about the Author
Gale, Cengage Learning
27500 Drake Rd.
Farmington Hills MI 48331-3535

Toll-free: 800-877-GALE
Fax: 248-699-8070

Something about the Author Product Advisory Board

The editors of *Something about the Author* are dedicated to maintaining a high standard of excellence by publishing comprehensive, accurate, and highly readable entries on a wide array of writers for children and young adults. In addition to the quality of the content, the editors take pride in the graphic design of the series, which is intended to be orderly yet inviting, allowing readers to utilize the pages of *SATA* easily and with efficiency. Despite the longevity of the *SATA* print series, and the success of its format, we are mindful that the vitality of a literary reference product is dependent on its ability to serve its users over time. As literature, and attitudes about literature, constantly evolve, so do the reference needs of students, teachers, scholars, journalists, researchers, and book club members. To be certain that we continue to keep pace with the expectations of our customers, the editors of *SATA* listen carefully to their comments regarding the value, utility, and quality of the series. Librarians, who have firsthand knowledge of the needs of library users, are a valuable resource for us. The *Something about the Author* Product Advisory Board, made up of school, public, and academic librarians, is a forum to promote focused feedback about *SATA* on a regular basis. The nine-member advisory board includes the following individuals, whom the editors wish to thank for sharing their expertise:

SOMETHING ABOUT THE AUTHOR

ALEXANDER, Sue 1933-2008
(Sue Lynn Ratner)

OBITUARY NOTICE—

See index for *SATA* sketch: Born August 20, 1933, in Tucson, AZ; died July 3, 2008, in West Hills, CA. Children's author and educator. Alexander devoted her entire career to encouraging children to become lifelong readers. She accomplished this primarily through the many children's books that she wrote between 1973 and 2001. Alexander covered a wide range of subject matter—from fantasy, as in the "Witch, Goblin, and Ghost" series (1976-85) to fact, as in *Behold the Trees* (2001), a story of Israel—from the streets of her Chicago childhood, as in *Sara's City* (1996) to the sandy deserts of *Nadia the Willful* (1983). The common theme in all of her books, she once wrote, is the importance of feelings, and she was credited with a special gift for exploring the feelings of childhood. Alexander published more than two dozen books, featuring "world-famous Muriel," "Marc the magnificent," and other characters that piqued the curiosity of children over the years. She also worked diligently to encourage other writers in their quest for success. Alexander was a founding member of the professional organization now known as the Society of Children's Book Writers and Illustrators (SCBWI), which created the Sue Alexander Most Promising New Work Award in her honor at the Los Angeles chapter in 1996. She taught classes for aspiring picture-book writers at the University of California in Los An-

geles, and she was an enthusiastic contributor to the *Los Angeles Times* "Kids' Reading Page" as recently as 2007. Alexander received many awards and other recognitions during her lifetime, including the Dorothy C. McKenzie Award of the Southern California Council of Literature for Children and Young People and the Golden Kite Award from her organizational alma mater, SCBWI. One of her most celebrated books was *Lila on the Landing* (1987), the story of an urban childhood and a young girl who triumphs over the loneliness and rejection that too often afflict young people who do not quite fit into their peer group. Alexander also wrote *One More Time, Mama* (1999), about the lasting bond between mother and child.

OBITUARIES AND OTHER SOURCES:

PERIODICALS

Chicago Tribune, July 20, 2008, sec. 4, p. 5.
Los Angeles Times, July 14, 2008, p. B7.

*　　*　　*

BAKER, Deirdre 1955-

Personal

Born 1955, in Haney, British Columbia, Canada; married; children: two daughters. *Education:* University of Victoria, B.A. (English literature); University of Toronto, M.A. (medieval studies), Ph.D. (medieval studies); Pontifical Institute for Mediaeval Studies, licentiate in mediaeval studies.

Addresses

Home—Toronto, Ontario, Canada. *Office*—Department of English, University of Toronto, 170 St. George St., Toronto, Ontario M5R 2M8, Canada. *E-mail*—df. baker@utoronto.ca.

Career

Writer and educator. *Toronto Star,* Toronto, Ontario, Canada, children's book reviewer, 1998—; *Horn Book,* Boston, MA, children's book reviewer. University of Toronto, assistant professor of English; has also taught teaching religion, medieval literature, and children's literature at universities in Canada and the United States.

Awards, Honors

Book of the Year for Children nomination, Canadian Library Association, *Globe & Mail* Top Ten Children's Books designation, and *Quill & Quire* Most Significant Books of the Year designation, all 2007, and Best Books for Older Children and Teens selection, Cooperative Children's Book Center, 2008, all for *Becca at Sea.*

Writings

(With Ken Setterington) *A Guide to Canadian Children's Books in English,* illustrated by Kady MacDonald Denton, McClelland & Stewart (Toronto, Ontario, Canada), 2003.
Becca at Sea (novel), Groundwood Books (Toronto, Ontario, Canada), 2007.

Contributor of essays to books, including *Scribner's Dictionary of the Middle Ages,* 1983, and *Horn Book Guide to Children's Books,* Candlewick Press, 2008. Contributor of articles and reviews to periodicals, including *Children's Literature in Education, New Outlook, Medieval Studies,* and *Books in Canada.*

Sidelights

Canadian author and educator Deirdre Baker, a reviewer for both *Horn Book* magazine and the *Toronto Star,* has also earned critical acclaim for her debut novel *Becca at Sea.* With her expertise in children's literature, Baker has also cowritten the highly regarded reference work *A Guide to Canadian Children's Books in English.* "Children's literature is a large, vital part of our literary tradition," Baker remarked in the *University of Toronto Bulletin.* "Its impact . . . is even more significant than that of adult literature, since the children's stories we imbibe in childhood go into the programming of our literary hard drives along with our mother tongue. It is worth studying if only for that reason."

Becca at Sea centers on an intelligent and feisty ten year old and her adventures at her grandmother's island home off the coast of British Columbia. During her visits, Becca must deal with an assortment of eccentric relatives, including absent-minded Aunt Fifi and troublesome older cousins Alicia and Lucy. The girl also learns much about the natural world while tending her grandmother's garden, discovering a pearl-filled oyster, and helping to save a baby seal that has become separated from its mother. "The riotous yet harmonious life of seabirds, fish, and mammals mirrors the energy and unpredictability of Becca's relationships with her family," wrote *Quill & Quire* reviewer Joanne Findon in a review of Baker's novel. Writing that the "charming" and "beautifully written" novel contains "passages [that] are almost lyrical," Kristin Butcher concluded in the *Canadian Review of Materials* that *Becca at Sea* "embodies innocence, understanding, compassion, morality, and humor." Baker's work also drew praise from *Horn Book* contributor Joanna Rudge Long, who noted that the author's "dialogue is true-to-life, witty, and intelligent. Each episode enriches the portrait of Becca's memorable extended family with delightfully preposterous, yet insightful, detail."

Biographical and Critical Sources

PERIODICALS

Books in Canada, April, 2003, Jeffrey Canton, review of *A Guide to Canadian Children's Books in English,* p. 41.
Canadian Review of Materials, September 5, 2003, review of *A Guide to Canadian Children's Books in English;* August 31, 2007, Kristin Butcher, review of *Becca at Sea.*
Horn Book, January-February, 2008, Joanna Rudge Long, review of *Becca at Sea,* p. 81.
Kirkus Reviews, August 1, 2007, review of *Becca at Sea.*
Quill & Quire, May, 2003, Kenneth Oppel, review of *A Guide to Canadian Children's Books in English;* September, 2007, Joanne Findon, review of *Becca at Sea.*
School Library Journal, September, 2003, Robyn Walker, review of *A Guide to Canadian Children's Books in English,* p. 243.

ONLINE

University of Toronto Bulletin Online, http://www.news. utoronto.ca/ (September 25, 2007), Deirdre Baker, "Not a Childish Pursuit: Children's Literature a Vital Part of Our Literary Tradition."

*   *   *

BANG-CAMPBELL, Monika 1975(?)-

Personal

Born c. 1975; daughter of Richard H. Campbell (an acoustics engineer) and Molly Bang (an author and illustrator). *Education:* Wheaton College, B.A.; Boston University, M.A. (clinical social work).

Addresses

Home—Cape Cod, MA.

Career

Educator, sailor, and writer.

Writings

CHAPTER BOOKS

Little Rat Sets Sail, illustrated by mother, Molly Bang, Harcourt (San Diego, CA), 2002.
Little Rat Rides, illustrated by Molly Bang, Harcourt (San Diego, CA), 2004.
Little Rat Makes Music, illustrated by Molly Bang, Harcourt (San Diego, CA), 2007.

Sidelights

A professional sailor based near Boston, Massachusetts, Monika Bang-Campbell joins her mother, well-known author and illustrator Molly Bang, in creating the "Little

Monika Bang-Campbell teams up with her artist mom Molly Bang to create the picture book **Little Rat Rides.** (Illustration copyright © 2004 by Molly Bang. Reproduced by permission of Houghton Mifflin Harcourt Publishing Company.)

Rat" chapter-book series. In the first series installment, *Little Rat Sets Sail,* Bang-Campbell draws on her extensive experience as a sailor to add authenticity to the little rat's adventures. In *Little Rat Sets Sail* Bang-Campbell writes "with a remarkable understanding of childhood feelings," according to Martha V. Parravano in *Horn Book,* and her story finds Little Rat terrified of the water. Unfortunately, the rat's parents have just signed her up for a summer of sailing lessons. Instructor Buzzy Bear allows Little Rat to sail with him until her fears subside, and she then happily learns about sailing terms and tactics. The more knowledge Little Rat gains about sailing, the less afraid she becomes. Parravano noted that Bang-Campbell "captures the joys of sailing while presenting it from the point of view of a reluctant participant." Also giving *Little Rat Sets Sail* a favorable review, a *Publishers Weekly* critic described the chapter book as "a breezy junket for aspiring skippers and confirmed landlubbers alike."

Little Rat's adventures continue in *Little Rat Rides* and *Little Rat Makes Music,* two further mother-daughter collaborations. Having overcome her fear of water, Little Rat must now face a fear of horses in *Little Rat Rides,* but when she learns to communicate with Pee Wee the pony, she earns a ribbon at a local horse show. In *Little Rat Makes Music* the young rodent dreams of becoming a virtuoso violinist, but when she picks up the instrument, she learns that practicing is boring and playing is harder than she thought. "Little Rat's second outing should earn her a whole new stable of fans," concluded Jennifer M. Brabander in a *Horn Book* review of *Little Rat Rides,* while in *School Library Journal* Joy Fleishhacker noted that the author "skillfully captures" the young rat's feelings "as she takes on a new challenge, and [gains] . . . the self-assurance that comes with success." Reviewing the text of *Little Rat Makes Music,* which like other books in the series is divided into eight chapters, *Horn Book* critic Lolly Robinson wrote that Bang-Campbell "sets a matter-of-fact tone that allows her flashes of humor to shine more brightly."

Bang-Campbell once told *SATA:* "I have sailed on boats since I was little and have continued my sailing career into adulthood. I am a professional sailor aboard tall ships that run educational programs for students ranging from middle school to adults.

"I received my master's degree in clinical social work from Boston University. Integrating the art of traditional sail to an educational curriculum enhances the students' learning experience."

Biographical and Critical Sources

PERIODICALS

Booklist, April 1, 2002, Kathy Broderick, review of *Little Rat Sets Sail,* p. 1326; May 1, 2004, Gillian Engberg, review of *Little Rat Rides,* p. 1561.

Bulletin of the Center for Children's Books, May, 2002, review of *Little Rat Sets Sail,* p. 307; April, 2004, Deborah Stevenson, review of *Little Rat Rides,* p. 315; September, 2007, Deborah Stevenson, review of *Little Rat Makes Music,* p. 6.

Horn Book, July-August, 2002, Martha V. Parravano, review of *Little Rat Sets Sail,* p. 452; May-June, 2004, Jennifer M. Brabander, review of *Little Rat Rides,* p. 325; November-December, 2007, Lolly Robinson, review of *Little Rat Makes Music,* p. 673.

Kirkus Reviews, March 1, 2004, review of *Little Rat Rides,* p. 218; July 1, 2007, review of *Little Rat Makes Music.*

Publishers Weekly, January 7, 2002, review of *Little Rat Sets Sail,* p. 65.

School Library Journal, June, 2002, Lynda S. Poling, review of *Little Rat Sets Sail,* p. 80; May, 2004, Joy Fleishhacker, review of *Little Rat Rides,* p. 101; September, 2007, Erika Qualls, review of *Little Rat Makes Music,* p. 156.

ONLINE

Harcourt Web site, http://www.harcourtbooks.com/ (March 30, 2003), interview with Molly Bang and Bang-Campbell.*

*　　*　　*

BERLIN, Eric

Personal

Married; wife's name Janinne (a homemaker); children: Alexander, Lea. *Education:* State University of New York at Albany, degree, 1990; attended Juilliard School, 1993-94.

Addresses

Home—Milford, CT. *E-mail*—ericberlin@gmail.com.

Career

Writer, publisher, and puzzle creator. *PC Magazine,* editorial researcher, 1990-92; Mecklermedia, editor, 1995-97; Uproar, game designer, 1998-2000; Skillgames, game designer, 2000-01; Vtech, producer, 2002-03; Penny Publications, assistant publisher, 2004—.

Member

National Puzzlers' League.

Writings

The Puzzling World of Winston Breen (novel), Putnam (New York, NY), 2007.

The Potato Chip Puzzles (novel), Putnam (New York, NY), 2008.

PLAYS

Babes and Brides: Two One-act Plays (contains *The Line That's Picked Up 1,000 Babes* and *The Midnight Moonlight Wedding Chapel*), Samuel French (New York, NY), 1993.

Sidelights

Eric Berlin, a former playwright and game designer, is the author of the young-adult mystery *The Puzzling World of Winston Breen.* Berlin, a graduate of the Juilliard School's playwriting program, also creates crossword puzzles for the *New York Times,* among others. In addition, he works as an assistant publisher for Penny Publications, which produces dozen of puzzle magazines.

The Puzzling World of Winston Breen was inspired by Ellen Raskin's puzzle-mystery masterpiece *The Westing Game,* winner of a Newbery medal. Berlin's novel focuses on Winston Breen, a puzzle-loving twelve year old whose birthday gift to his younger sister—a decorative antique box with a secret compartment containing wooden tiles—leads to a treasure hunt involving the local town librarian, a policeman, and two enigmatic strangers. "It was important to me that the puzzles be seamlessly integrated into the story—it wouldn't do to have them shoehorned in whether they made sense or not," the author explained on the *Ficlets* Web log. Berlin added, "I really wanted to capture the joy and agony of what it's like to be a puzzle person—the frustration of getting stuck, the inability to think one's way out of a corner . . . and the great big AHA! that makes it all worthwhile."

The Puzzling World of Winston Breen garnered strong reviews. In *School Library Journal* Connie Tyrrell Burns described the work as a "delightfully clever mystery," and Jennifer Mattson, writing in *Booklist,* noted that "Berlin's puzzles are challenging yet satisfying, but they're also backed by a lot of storytelling flair."

Biographical and Critical Sources

PERIODICALS

Booklist, November 15, 2007, Jennifer Mattson, review of *The Puzzling World of Winston Breen,* p. 58.

Bulletin of the Center for Children's Books, November, 2007, Deborah Stevenson, review of *The Puzzling World of Winston Breen,* p. 129.

Kirkus Reviews, August 1, 2007, review of *The Puzzling World of Winston Breen.*

School Library Journal, November, 2007, Connie Tyrrell Burns, review of *The Puzzling World of Winston Breen,* p. 116.

ONLINE

Eric Berlin Web log, http://www.ericberlin.com (October 31, 2008).

Ficlets Web log, http://ficlets.com/blog/ (October 8, 2007), "The Big Idea: Eric Berlin."

Winston Breen Web site, http://www.winstonbreen.com/ (October 31, 2008).

*   *   *

BLAIR, Mary 1911-1978

Personal

Born October 21, 1911, in McAlester, OK; died of a cerebral hemorrhage, July 26, 1978, in Soquel, CA; married Lee Everett Blair (an artist; deceased), 1934. *Education:* San Jose State College, degree; Chouinard Art Institute, degree, 1933.

Career

Animator, illustrator, and artist. Ub Iwerks studio, animator; Metro-Goldwyn-Mayer, Hollywood, CA, animator; Walt Disney Studios, animator, art supervisor, and concept artist, 1940-53, member of Disney touring expedition to South America, 1941; freelance graphic designer and illustrator. Film credits include: (art supervisor) *Saludos Amigos;* (art supervisor) *The Three Caballeros;* (art supervisor) *Make Mine Music;* (artist) *Song of the South,* 1946; (artist) *Melody Time;* (artist) *Dear to My Heart;* (artist) *The Adventures of Ichabod and Mr. Toad;* (concept artist and color stylist) *Cinderella,* 1950; (concept artist) *Alice in Wonderland,* 1951; and (color stylist) *Peter Pan,* 1953. Other works included "It's a Small World" pavilion, 1964 New York World's Fair. *Exhibitions:* Mural installations include Tomorrowland Promenade, Disneyland, 1967 (covered over, 1987); and Disney's Contemporary Resort Hotel, Walt Disney World, 1971.

Awards, Honors

Named Disney Legend, 1991; Winsor McCay Award, ASIFA-Hollywood, 1996.

Illustrator

Ruth Krauss, *I Can Fly,* Simon & Schuster (New York, NY), 1950, reprinted, Western Pub. Co. (Racine, WI), 1992.

Baby's House, Simon & Schuster (New York, NY), 1950.

Ruth Krauss, *The Up and Down Book,* Golden Press (New York, NY), 1964, reprinted, Golden Books (New York, NY), 2004.

Cynthia Rylant, reteller, *Walt Disney's Cinderella* (includes concept art from the Disney film), Disney/Hyperion (New York, NY), 2007.

Jon Scieszka, reteller, *Walt Disney's Alice in Wonderland* (includes concept art from the Disney film), Disney Press (New York, NY), 2008.

Sidelights

Born in Oklahoma in 1911, artist and animator Mary Blair is best remembered for her contributions to classic films by Walt Disney Company. Considered a significant influence within 1950s animation, Blair's modernist concept art—the paintings that mapped out the look of each scene for Disney animators—defined the look of such classic films as *Peter Pan, Cinderella,* and *Alice and Wonderland.* In addition, she also designed the characters for Disneyland's popular "It's a Small World" exhibit. According to *School Library Journal* critic Marian Drabkin, Blair's work for the film *Cinderella* is "spare and impressionistic, reflecting trends in the art of animation during the 1950s."

In addition to appearing in film, Blair's concept art for Disney has been adapted for the picture-book format in *Walt Disney's Cinderella,* with a text by Cynthia Rylant, and *Walt Disney's Alice in Wonderland,* with a story by Jon Scieszka. In addition, her vibrantly colored illustrations appear in Ruth Krauss's classic "Golden Books" titles *I Can Fly* and *The Up and Down House,* both of which have remained in print since first appearing in the mid-twentieth century. In a review of *Walt Disney's Alice in Wonderland,* Joy Fleishhacker wrote in *School Library Journal* that Blair's "stunning concept art . . . shaped the look of the Disney animated film" upon which Scieszka's text is based. The artist's "whimsical style and exuberant palette" was groundbreaking within film animation, observed a *Publishers Weekly* critic in a review of *Walt Disney's Cinderella* before predicting that the book "will find its way onto collectors' shelves."

Biographical and Critical Sources

BOOKS

Canemaker, John, *The Art and Flair of Mary Blair,* Disney Editions (New York, NY), 2003.

PERIODICALS

Horn Book, September, 2003, review of *I Can Fly,* p. 569; January-February, 2008, Christine M. Heppermann, review of *Walt Disney's Cinderella,* p. 100; September-October, 2008, Monica Edinger, review of *Walt Disney's Alice in Wonderland,* p. 573.

Kirkus Reviews, July 1, 2007, review of *Walt Disney's Cinderella;* August 1, 2008, review of *Walt Disney's Alice in Wonderland.*

Publishers Weekly, July 15, 2007, review of *Walt Disney's Cinderella,* p. 163.

School Library Journal, February, 2008, Marian Drabkin, review of *Walt Disney's Cinderella,* p. 96; October, 2008, Joy Fleishhacker, review of *Walt Disney's Alice in Wonderland,* p. 124.

ONLINE

Disney Legends Web site, http://legends.disney.go.com/ (November 15, 2008).*

BLUME, Judy 1938-

Personal

Born February 12, 1938, in Elizabeth, NJ; daughter of Rudolph (a dentist) and Esther Sussman; married John M. Blume (an attorney), August 15, 1959 (divorced, 1975); married George Cooper (a writer), June 6, 1987; children: (first marriage) Randy Lee (daughter), Lawrence Andrew; Amanda (stepdaughter). *Education:* New York University, B.A., 1961. *Religion:* Jewish.

Addresses

Home—Key West, FL, and New York, NY. *Office*—c/o Tashmoo Productions, 1841 Broadway, Ste. 711A, New York, NY 10023. *Agent*—Suzanne Gluck, William Morris Agency, 1325 Avenue of the Americas, New York, NY 10022. *E-mail*—JudyB@judyblume.com.

Career

Writer of juvenile and adult fiction. Founder and trustee of KIDS Fund, 1981.

Member

Society of Children's Book Writers and Illustrators (member of board), Authors Guild (member of council), National Coalition against Censorship (council of advisors), Key West Literary Seminar (member of board).

Awards, Honors

Best Books for Children selection, *New York Times,* 1970, Nene Award, Hawaii Association of School Librarians/Hawaii Library Association, 1975, Young Hoosier Book Award, Association for Indiana Media Educators, 1976, and North Dakota Children's Choice Award, Children's Round Table of the North Dakota Library Association, 1979, all for *Are You There God? It's Me, Margaret;* Charlie May Swann Children's Book Award, Arkansas Elementary School Council, 1972, Young Readers Choice Award, Pacific Northwest Library Association, and Sequoyah Children's Book Award, Oklahoma Library Association, both 1975, Arizona Young Readers Award, Arizona State University/University of Arizona—Tempe, Massachusetts Children's Book Award, Education Department of Salem State College, Georgia Children's Book Award, College of Education of the University of Georgia, and South Carolina Children's Book Award, South Carolina Association of School Librarians, all 1977, Rhode Island Library Association Award, 1978, North Dakota Children's Choice Award, Children's Round Table of the North Dakota Library Association, and West Australian Young Readers' Book Award, Library Association of Australia, both 1980, and United States Army in Europe Kinderbuch Award and Great Stone Face Award, New Hampshire Library Council, both 1981, all for *Tales of a Fourth Grade Nothing;* Outstanding Books of the Year selection, *New York Times,* 1974, Arizona Young

Readers Award, and Young Readers Choice Award, Pacific Northwest Library Association, both 1977, and North Dakota Children's Choice Award, Children's Round Table of the North Dakota Library Association, 1983, all for *Blubber;* South Carolina Children's Book Award, South Carolina Association of School Librarians, 1978, for *Otherwise Known as Sheila the Great;* Michigan Young Reader's Award, 1980, for *Freckle Juice;* Texas Bluebonnet list, 1980, CRABery Award, Michigan Young Reader's Award, Michigan Council of Teachers, and International Reading Association Children's Choice Award, all 1981, Buckeye Children's Book Award, State Library of Ohio, Nene Award, Sue Hefley Book Award, Louisiana Association of School Libraries, United States Army in Europe Kinderbuch Award, West Australian Young Readers' Book Award, Library Association of Australia, North Dakota Children's Choice Award, Children's Round Table of the North Dakota Library Association, Colorado Children's Book Award, University of Colorado, Georgia Children's Book Award, Tennessee Children's Choice Book Award, Texas Bluebonnet Award, Texas Association of School Librarians and the Children's Round Table, and Utah Children's Book Award, Children's Literature Association of Utah, all 1982, Northern Territory Young Readers' Book Award, Young Readers Choice Award, Pacific Northwest Library Association, Garden State Children's Book Award, Iowa Children's Choice Award, Iowa Educational Media Association, Arizona Young Readers' Award, Young Reader Medal, California Reading Association, and Young Hoosier Book Award, Association for Indiana Media Educators, all 1983, Land of Enchantment Book Award, 1984, and Sunshine State Young Reader's Award, Florida Association for Media in Education, 1985, all for *Superfudge;* CRABery Award, 1982, Dorothy Canfield Fisher Children's Book Award, Vermont Department of Libraries and the Vermont Congress of Parents and Teachers, Buckeye Children's Book Award, State Library of Ohio, Young Reader Medal, California Reading Association, and American Book Award finalist, Association of American Publishers, all 1983, and Blue Spruce Colorado Young-Adult Book Award, Colorado Library Association, and Iowa Children's Choice Award, Iowa Educational Media Association, both 1985, all for *Tiger Eyes;* Children's Books of the Year selection, Child Study Association of America, 1985, for *The Pain and the Great One;* Best Books for Young Adults selection, American Library Association (ALA), 1986, for *Letters to Judy;* Young Reader Medal, California Reading Association, Iowa Children's Choice Award, Nene Award, Nevada Young Readers Award, Nevada Library Association, Sunshine State Young Reader's Award, Pennsylvania Young Reader's Award, Pennsylvania School Librarians Association, and Michigan Readers Choice Award, all 1993, all for *Fudge-a-Mania;* Parent's Choice Award, 1993, for *Here's to You, Rachel Robinson.* Golden Archer Award, 1974; Today's Woman Award, Council of Cerebral Palsy Auxiliary, Nassau County, 1981; Outstanding Mother Award, 1982; Eleanor Roosevelt Humanitarian Award, Favorite Author—Children's Choice

Award, Milner Award, Friends of the Atlanta Public Library, for children's favorite living author, and Jeremiah Ludington Memorial Award, all 1983; Carl Sandburg Freedom to Read Award, Chicago Public Library, 1984; Civil Liberties Award, Atlanta American Civil Liberties Union, and John Rock Award, Center for Population Options, both 1986; D.H.L., Kean College, 1987; Excellence in the Field of Literature Award, New Jersey Education Association, 1987; South Australian Youth Media Award for Best Author, South Australian Association for Media Education, 1988; Most Admired Author, Heroes of Young America Poll, 1989; National Hero Award, Big Brothers/Big Sisters, 1992; Dean's Award, Columbia University College of Physicians and Surgeons, 1993; Margaret A. Edwards Award for Outstanding Literature for Young Adults, ALA, 1996, for lifetime achievement writing for teens; honorary D.F.A., Mount Holyoke College, 2003; Medal for Distinguished Contribution to American Letters, National Book Foundation, 2004.

Writings

CHILDREN'S FICTION; EXCEPT AS NOTED

The One in the Middle Is the Green Kangaroo, illustrated by Lois Axeman, Reilly & Lee (Chicago, IL), 1969, revised edition, illustrated by Amy Aitken, Bradbury (Scarsdale, NY), 1981, reprinted, Dell Yearling (New York, NY), 2004, revised edition, illustrated by Irene Trivas, 1991.
Iggie's House, Bradbury (Englewood Cliffs, NJ), 1970, reprinted, Dell Yearling (New York, NY), 2004.
Are You There God? It's Me, Margaret, Bradbury (Englewood Cliffs, NJ), 1970, reprinted, Dell Yearling (New York, NY), 2004.
Then Again, Maybe I Won't, Bradbury (Scarsdale, NY), 1971.
Freckle Juice, Four Winds (New York, NY), 1971.
Tales of a Fourth Grade Nothing, illustrated by Roy Doty, Dutton (New York, NY), 1972, reprinted, Puffin (New York, NY), 2003.
Otherwise Known as Sheila the Great, Dutton (New York, NY), 1972, reprinted, Puffin (New York, NY), 2003.
It's Not the End of the World, Bradbury (Scarsdale, NY), 1972.
Deenie, Bradbury (Scarsdale, NY), 1973.
Blubber, Bradbury (Scarsdale, NY), 1974, reprinted, Dell Yearling (New York, NY), 2004.
Forever . . ., (young-adult novel), Bradbury (Scarsdale, NY), 1975, reprinted, Simon Pulse (New York, NY), 2007.
Starring Sally J. Freedman as Herself, Bradbury (Scarsdale, NY), 1977, reprinted, Dell Yearling (New York, NY), 2004.
Superfudge, Dutton (New York, NY), 1980, reprinted, Puffin (New York, NY), 2003.
Tiger Eyes (young-adult novel), Bradbury (Scarsdale, NY), 1981.

The Pain and the Great One, Bradbury (Scarsdale, NY), 1984.
Just as Long as We're Together, Orchard Books (New York, NY), 1987.
Fudge-a-Mania, Dutton (New York, NY), 1990.
Here's to You, Rachel Robinson, Orchard Books (New York, NY), 1993.
Double Fudge, Scholastic (New York, NY), 2002.
A Judy Blume Collection (contains *Deenie, It's Not the End of the World,* and *Then Again, Maybe I Won't*), Atheneum (New York, NY), 2003.
BFF*: Two Novels by Judy Blume (contains *Just as Long as We're Together* and *Here's to You, Rachel Robinson*), Random House (New York, NY), 2007.
Soupy Saturdays with the Pain and the Great One, illustrated by James Stevenson, Delacorte (New York, NY), 2007.
Cool Zone with the Pain and the Great One, illustrated by James Stevenson, Delacorte (New York, NY), 2008.
Going, Going, Gone! with the Pain and the Great One, illustrated by James Stevenson, Delacorte (New York, NY), 2008.

Contributor to *Free to Be . . . You and Me,* by Marlo Thomas and friends, 1973, expanded edition published by Running Press, 2008.

OTHER

Wifey (adult novel), Putnam (New York, NY), 1978, reprinted, 2004.
Smart Women (adult novel), Putnam (New York, NY), 1983, reprinted, 2004.
Letters to Judy: What Your Kids Wish They Could Tell You (nonfiction), Putnam (New York, NY), 1986.
The Judy Blume Memory Book (limited edition), Dell (New York, NY), 1988.
(And producer with son, Lawrence Blume) *Otherwise Known as Sheila the Great* (screenplay; adapted from her novel), Barr Films, 1988.
Summer Sisters (adult novel), Delacorte (New York, NY), 1998.
(Editor) *Places I Never Meant to Be: Original Stories by Censored Writers,* Simon & Schuster (New York, NY), 1999.

Contributor to *Author Talk: Conversations with Judy Blume (and Others),* Simon & Schuster (New York, NY), 2000.

Some of Blume's papers are housed in the Kerlan Collection, University of Minnesota.

Adaptations

Forever . . . was adapted as a television film broadcast by Columbia Broadcasting System (CBS), 1978; *Freckle Juice* was adapted as an animated film by Barr Films, 1987; the "Fudge" books were adapted by American Broadcasting Companies (ABC) as a television series, 1994-96, and on CBS, 1997; *Tales of a Fourth Grade*

Nothing was adapted as a play; *Wifey* was produced by Audio Book in 1979. Listening Library has adapted various Blume books along with teacher's guides, including *Freckle Juice*, 1982; *Blubber*, 1983; *The One in the Middle Is the Green Kangaroo*, 1983; and *Deenie*, 1983. Audiobooks adapted by Listening Library include *Are You There God? It's Me, Margaret*, 1985; *It's Not the End of the World*, 1985; and *The Pain and the Great One*, 1985. Blume books adapted for audio by Ingram include *Superfudge*, 1992; *Fudge-a-Mania*, 1993; *Tales of a Fourth Grade Nothing*, 1996; *Are You There God? It's Me, Margaret*, 1997; and *Otherwise Known as Sheila the Great*, 1997.

Sidelights

"For several generations of former adolescents, Judy Blume is the reason flashlights were invented," observed *Entertainment Weekly* contributor Rebecca Ascher Walsh. "From the 'Fudge' books to *Are You There God? It's Me, Margaret* to *Forever . . .*, Blume has expertly guided huddling insomniac masses through the confusion of childhood and teenage hell into young adulthood." Since she published her first book in 1969, Blume has become one of the most popular and controversial authors for children. Her accessible, humorous style and direct, sometimes explicit treatment of youthful concerns have won her many fans—as well as critics who sometimes seek to censor her work. Nevertheless, Blume has continued to produce works that are, according to critics, both entertaining and thought-provoking. "Judy Blume has a knack for knowing what children think about and an honest, highly amusing way of writing about it," Jean Van Leeuwen stated in the *New York Times Book Review*. The author has also garnered countless honors for her work; in 1996 she won the Margaret A. Edwards Award for Outstanding Literature for Young Adults, and in 2004 Blume received the National Book Foundation's Medal for Distinguished Contribution to American Letters.

Many critics attribute Blume's popularity to her ability to discuss openly, realistically, and compassionately the subjects that concern her readers. Her books for younger children, such as *Tales of a Fourth Grade Nothing*, *Blubber*, *Otherwise Known as Sheila the Great*, and *Soupy Saturdays with the Pain and the Great One*, deal with problems of sibling rivalry, establishing self-confidence, and social ostracism. Books for older readers, such as *Are You There God? It's Me, Margaret*, *Deenie*, and *Just as Long as We're Together*, consider matters of divorce, friendship, family breakups, and sexual development (including menstruation and masturbation), while *Forever . . .* specifically deals with a young woman's first love and first sexual experience. Whatever the situation, however, Blume's characters confront their feelings of confusion as a start to resolving their problems. In *Are You There God? It's Me, Margaret*, for instance, the young protagonist examines her thoughts about religion and speculates about becoming a woman. The result is a book that uses "sensi-

tivity and humor" in capturing "the joys, fears, and uncertainty that surround a young girl approaching adolescence," Lavinia Russ wrote in *Publishers Weekly*.

Born in New Jersey, in 1938, Blume and her older brother grew up in a home full of books. Her father, a dentist, nurtured her imagination; her mother, quieter and more introspective, encouraged her young daughter in a growing love of books and reading. Beginning in the third grade, Blume, her mother, and her brother went to live in Florida for two years in hopes of improving her brother's heath, and she was separated from her father during this time. The outgoing Blume began taking dance classes as a young child and generally excelled at school, attending an all-girls high school where she sang in the chorus and worked on the school newspaper as a features editor. Graduating from high school, she went on to Boston University for a year until a bout of mononucleosis forced her to drop out. Blume subsequently enrolled at New York University, where she graduated in 1961, majoring in early childhood education. During her sophomore year of college, she met her first husband, John M. Blume, a lawyer, and the couple

Cover of Judy Blume's award-winning novel Are You There God? It's Me, Margaret, *featuring artwork by Lori Earley.* (Bantam Books, 1986. Used by permission of Random House Children's Books, a division of Random House, Inc.)

was married during Blume's junior year. Shortly after graduation, Blume had her first child, Randy Lee, and two years later Randy was joined by brother Lawrence Andrew.

Deciding she needed a creative outlet, Blume began making up children's stories as she went about her housework, even illustrating them in crayon. Her early stories were rejected by magazines, and then, coming upon a brochure for a New York University class in writing for children and young adults, she enrolled. As part of the coursework, she wrote what became her first publication, *The One in the Middle Is the Green Kangaroo,* a picture book about an in-between child. The following semester, Blume took the class once more time, writing the initial draft for her second publication, *Iggie's House,* a children's novel about racial prejudice. *The One in the Middle* was published in 1969, and was called "satisfying" by Zena Sutherland in a review for *Bulletin of the Center for Children's Books.*

Blume's first two books did not give, however, any indication of the direction she would go with her third, *Are You There God? It's Me, Margaret.* In 1967, S.E. Hinton, a schoolgirl herself at the time, revolutionized the world of young-adult literature with her hard-hitting and gritty *The Outsiders,* a novel about class rivalry in an Oklahoma high school. However, until Blume's 1970 publication of *Are You There God?,* the literature for younger adolescents had generally gone along its well-worn pathway of simplistic plots and happy endings. With *Are You There God?,* Blume broke publishing taboos by writing about such topics as a girl's menstrual cycle and first bra. Based on many of Blume's own adolescent experiences, the novel tells the tale of Margaret Simon and her family, who move to the suburbs in New Jersey. There Margaret has to make new friends, and she is beset by such worries as the arrival of her period and the size of her breasts. She is also concerned about religion; born to a Christian mother and Jewish father, Margaret is confused where she fits and thus starts visiting different churches and talking directly with God. Most reviewers praised the book's humor but decried Blume's focus on what were once unmentionables. Ann Evans, writing in the *Times Literary Supplement,* for example, found that Blume focuses too much on Margaret's body and that her "private talks with God are insufferably self-conscious and arch." A critic for *Kirkus Reviews* also complained that "there's danger in the preoccupation with the physical signs of puberty." Children did not read the reviews; they read the book. And read it and read it. When it appeared in paperback in 1974, *Are You There God? It's Me, Margaret* attracted readers in the hundreds of thousands, and Blume began getting the deluge of letters from young readers that has persisted over the decades, thanking her for letting them know they were not alone in such thoughts.

Blume repeated the favor for young male readers with *Then Again, Maybe I Won't,* published in 1971. Here Vic is like Margaret; he has just moved to a new town. He is also worried about the changes that are taking place with his body; he has uncontrollable erections and worries about wet dreams. Vick's family has also undergone a change, recently becoming more affluent. *Then Again, Maybe I Won't* was not as popular as *Are You There God?,* but it broke similar ground in juvenile literature, making formerly taboo topics part of the subject matter of children's literature.

More problem books dating from Blume's early career include *It's Not the End of the World,* in which the twelve-year-old protagonist learns to cope with her parents' separation and divorce; *Deenie,* in which a beautiful thirteen-year-old girl, whose mother desperately wants her to become a model, is diagnosed with the spinal disease scoliosis; and *Blubber,* about childhood cruelty as expressed in taunting an overweight girl. Blume's work continued to stir up the critics and invite parental condemnation if not outright attempts—in many schools successful—at censorship. In *Deenie,* for example, the young girl thinks at first that her disease has been brought on by her masturbation. Despite such concerns, *School Library Journal* critic Melinda Schroeder called *Deenie* a "compelling" novel.

Blume's least-controversial and most popular series fiction, the "Fudge" books, encompasses five interrelated stories that span thirty years of writing and start off with *Tales of a Fourth Grade Nothing.* That book details the trials and tribulations of Peter Warren Hatcher and his younger brother, Fudge. The brothers live in an apartment in Manhattan and undergo the usual sibling rivalry. At one point, young Fudge—rambunctious and often in trouble—swallows his older brother's turtle. This book became the third best-selling children's book of all time, with over six million copies sold. *Otherwise Known as Sheila the Great,* a spin-off of *Tales of a Fourth Grade Nothing,* focuses on Peter's nemesis as she tries to deal with summer camp.

Blume returns to the brothers in *Superfudge,* in which the Hatcher family is joined by a baby sister, Tootsie, who complicates the boy's lives. The family has also moved to Princeton, New Jersey, and Fudge is ready to enter kindergarten. *Superfudge* became Blume's best-selling hardcover edition, receiving much praise by critics. Writing in the *Washington Post Book World,* Brigitte Weeks lauded Blume's ability to create "good clean fun," while *School Library Journal* critic Pamela D. Pollack commented that "no one knows the byways of the under-twelves better than Blume." *Fudge-a-Mania* continues the saga with a reunion of all the characters in a summer house in Maine. Even when Blume returns to familiar characters, as she does in this novel and others in the series, her sequels "expand on the original and enrich it, so that [the] stories . . . add up to one long and much more wonderful story," Van Leeuwen remarked in her *New York Times Book Review* article about *Fudge-a-Mania.*

THE NEW YORK TIMES BESTSELLER

"Compulsively readable... her powers are prodigious."
—*The New York Times Book Review*

Judy Blume

SUMMER SISTERS

Cover of Blume's young-adult novel Summer Sisters. (Dell Publishing, 1998. Used by permission of Dell Publishing, a division of Random House, Inc.)

In 2002, to satisfy the wishes of her grandchild, Blume returned once again to Peter and Fudge, writing *Double Fudge*. In this installment, Fudge is about to begin school and is obsessed with money. His parents take him to visit the Bureau of Engraving and Printing in Washington, DC, where the family accidentally runs into distant cousins from Hawaii. The Howie Hatcher clan includes twin daughters Fauna and Flora and a younger brother who has the same name as Fudge: Farley Drexel Hatcher. "Peter's wry reactions to the sometimes outsize goings-on, Fudge's inimitable antics and the characters' rousing repartée contribute to the sprightly clip of this cheerful read," wrote a reviewer for *Publishers Weekly*. In *Booklist* Gillian Engberg commended Blume on her "humor and pitch-perfect ear for sibling rivalry and family dynamics [that] will have readers giggling with recognition."

A more-recent series of humorous tales was inspired by characters from one of Blume's early picture books. First published in 1984, *The Pain and the Great One*

focuses on the relationship between a pair of squabbling siblings: third-grader Abigail, dubbed "The Great One" by her pesky younger brother, Jake, whom she refers to as "The Pain." Zena Sutherland, writing in the *Bulletin of the Center for Children's Books*, praised the "insight and wit" of that tale. Some two decades later, Blume resurrected the duo in the chapter book *Soupy Saturdays with the Pain and the Great One*, illustrated by James Stevenson. The vignettes concern Jake's attempt to deodorize his aunt's foul-smelling dog and Abigail's efforts to host the perfect sleepover, and the pair also join forces to find a clever solution to Jake's fear of the barber. "Blume fills the duo's narratives with playful bickering, banter and baiting, while slyly and satisfyingly revealing their mutual affection," a critic in *Publishers Weekly* remarked. The siblings' adventures continue in *Cool Zone with the Pain and the Great One*, which addresses a host of childhood concerns, and *Going, Going, Gone! with the Pain and the Great One*, which focuses on a series of trips. According to *Booklist* contributor Ilene Cooper, "Blume gets right to the heart of children's concerns and relationships."

One way in which Blume achieves a close affinity with her readers is through her consistent use of first-person narratives. As R.A. Siegal explained in the *Lion and the Unicorn*, "Through this technique she succeeds in establishing intimacy and identification between character and audience. All her books read like diaries or journals and the reader is drawn in by the narrator's self-revelations." In *Just as Long as We're Together*, for instance, the twelve-year-old heroine "tells her story in simple, real kid language," noted Mitzi Myers in the *Los Angeles Times*, "inviting readers to identify with her dilemmas over girlfriends and boyfriends and that most basic of all teen problems: 'Sometimes I feel grown up and other times I feel like a little kid.'" Stephanie, Alison, and Rachel are the three characters of that title, but Stephanie takes center stage, as her parents split up and she begins to put on weight. More problems ensue as she starts to have problems with her friends, partly because of a new friendship Stephanie is forming with Alison. The girls make a return engagement—this time with the focus on Rachel—in *Here's to You, Rachel Robinson*, a book "filled with intelligence and humor and real understanding of the human condition," according to Claire Rosser in *Kliatt*. In this novel, Rachel's brother, Charles, is expelled from boarding school, much to the chagrin of Rachel's mother, a newly appointed judge. Reviewing both novels, *Kliatt* critic Sherri Forgash Ginsberg concluded that Blume's books "are truly pure enjoyment."

Although Blume's work is consistently in favor with readers, it has frequently been the target of criticism. Some commentators have charged that the author's readable style, with its focus on mundane detail, lacks the depth to deal with the complex issues that she raises. In a *Times Literary Supplement* review of *Just as Long as We're Together*, for example, Jan Dalley claimed that Blume's work "is all very professionally achieved, as one would expect from this highly successful author, but Blume's concoctions are unvaryingly smooth, bland, and glutinous." As Beryl Lieff Benderly noted, however, the author's readability sometimes masks what the critic calls her "enormous skill as a novelist" in a *Washington Post Book World* review of the same book. "While apparently presenting the bright, slangy, surface details of life in an upper-middle class suburban junior high school," Benderly added, Blume is "really plumbing the meaning of honesty, friendship, loyalty, secrecy, individuality, and the painful, puzzling question of what we owe those we love."

Other reviewers have taken exception to Blume's tendency to avoid resolving fictional dilemmas in a straightforward fashion, for her protagonists rarely finish dealing with all their difficulties by the end of the book. Many critics, however, think that it is to Blume's credit that she does not settle every problem for her readers. Robert Lipsyte, writing in the *Nation,* maintained that "Blume explores the feelings of children in a nonjudgmental way. The immediate resolution of a problem is never as important as what the protagonist . . . will learn about herself by confronting her life." Lipsyte explained that "the young reader gains from the emotional adventure story both by observing another youngster in a realistic situation and by finding a reference from which to start a discussion with a friend or parent or teacher. For many children, talking about a Blume story is a way to expose their own fears about menstruation or masturbation or death."

Even more disturbing to some adults are Blume's treatment of mature issues and her use of frank language. "Menstruation, wet dreams, masturbation, all the things that are whispered about in real school halls" are the subjects of Blume's books, related interviewer Sandy Rovner in the *Washington Post.* As a result, Blume's works have frequently been the targets of censorship, and Blume herself has become an active crusader for freedom of expression. As she related to *Instructor* contributor Judy Freeman, "I felt alone and frightened when my books first came under attack. I felt angry. But for many years now I've felt sad—sad for the kids—because banning a book sends such a negative message. It says to them, 'There's something in this book we don't want you to know about, something we don't want to discuss with you.'" To answer those who would censor her work for its explicitness, Blume replied: "The way to instill values in children is to talk about difficult issues and bring them out in the open, not to restrict their access to books that may help them deal with their problems and concerns," she said in a Toronto *Globe and Mail* interview with Isabel Vincent.

Blume realizes that the controversial nature of her work receives the most attention, and that causes concern for her beyond any censorship attempts. As the author explained to *New York Times Magazine* contributor Joyce Maynard: "What I worry about is that an awful lot of people, looking at my example, have gotten the idea

that what sells is teenage sex, and they'll exploit it. I don't believe that sex is why kids like my books. The impression I get, from letter after letter [I receive], is that a great many kids don't communicate with their parents. They feel alone in the world. Sometimes, reading books that deal with other kids who feel the same things they do makes them feel less alone." The volume of Blume's fan mail seems to reinforce the fact that her readers are looking for contact with an understanding adult. Hundreds of letters arrive each week not only praising her books but also asking her for advice or information. As Blume remarked to Steinberg in *Publishers Weekly,* "I have a wonderful, intimate relationship with kids. It's rare and lovely. They feel that they know me and that I know them."

In 1986, Blume collected a number of letters from her readers and published them, along with some of her own comments, as *Letters to Judy: What Your Kids Wish They Could Tell You.* The resulting book, aimed at both children and adults, "is an effort to break the silence, to show parents that they can talk without looking foolish, to show children that parents are human and remember what things were like when they were young, and to show everyone that however trivial the problem may seem it's worth trying to sort it out," wrote *New Statesman* contributor Adèlè Geras. "If parents and children alike read 'Letters to Judy,'" advice columnist Elizabeth Winship likewise observed in the *New York Times Book Review,* "it might well help them to ease into genuine conversation. The book is not a how-to manual, but one compassionate and popular author's way to help parents see life through their children's eyes, and feel it through their hearts and souls." Blume feels so strongly about the lack of communication between children and their parents that she has used the royalties from *Letters to Judy,* among other projects, to help endow the KIDS Fund, which she established in 1981. Each year, the fund contributes its income to various nonprofit organizations set up to help young people communicate with their parents.

Like other critics, *Washington Post Book World* contributor Carolyn Banks commended Blume not only for her honest approach to issues, but for her "artistic integrity." "She's never content to rest on her laurels, writing the same book over and over as so many successful writers do," Banks noted. For instance, *Tiger Eyes,* the story of Davey, a girl whose father is killed in a robbery, is "a lesson on how the conventions of a genre can best be put to use," Lipsyte claimed. While the author uses familiar situations and characters, showing Davey dealing with an annoying younger sibling, a move far from home, and a new family situation, "the story deepens, takes turns," the critic continued, particularly when Davey's family moves in with an uncle who works for a nuclear weapons plant. The result, Lipsyte stated, is Blume's "finest book—ambitious, absorbing, smoothly written, emotionally engaging and subtly political." Walter Clemons noted in a *Newsweek* review of *Tiger Eyes:* "No wonder teen-agers love Judy

Blume's novels: . . . [her] delicate sense of character, eye for social detail and clear access to feelings touches even a hardened older reader. Her intended younger audience gets a first-rate novel written directly to them."

Blume's adult novel *Summer Sisters* does not deal with such hard-hitting themes as *Tiger Eyes,* but in this work the author proves that she remains, as Cooper put it, a "pithy writer." Although the book, like *Wifey* and *Smart Women,* was published as an adult title, because most of the action focuses on a pair of friends in the adolescence and teenage years, *Summer Sisters* "could just as easily have been on a YA list," according to Cooper. Set during a series of summers on Martha's Vineyard, the book follows the fortunes of Vix Weaver and Caitlin Somers through the 1970s and 1980s. Vix is the daughter of middle-class parents from Santa Fe, New Mexico, while Caitlin moves in a more upscale crowd. During the summer of their sixth-grade year, Caitlin invites Vix to share her house on the Vineyard, and during subsequent summers spent together the two form a strong bond through shared adventures and sexual awakenings. A reviewer for *Publishers Weekly* felt that this "portrait of an unlikely yet enduring friendship as it changes over time . . . will remind readers why they read Blume's books when they were young: she finds a provocative theme and spins an involving story."

"Blume is concerned [with describing] characters surviving, finding themselves, growing in understanding, coming to terms with life," John Gough noted in *School Librarian.* While the solutions her characters find and the conclusions they make "may not be original or profound," the critic continued, ". . . neither are they trivial. The high sales of Blume's books are testimony to the fact that what she has to say is said well and is well worth saying." "Many of today's children have found a source of learning in Judy Blume," Goldberger contended. "She speaks to children, and, in spite of loud protests, her voice is clear to them."

Though she has numerous books to her credit, Blume continues to find the writing process a challenge. As she admitted to Melissa Whitworth in the London *Telegraph,* "After each book I get panicky, I don't love the reviews. I don't like going through all that, and you would think that, after almost 40 years of writing, I'd have got the hang of it. You can never grow complacent about it because it's always new, it's always exciting and it's always like the first time."

Biographical and Critical Sources

BOOKS

Children's Literature Review, Gale (Detroit, MI), Volume 2, 1976, Volume 15, 1988, Volume 69, 2001.

Contemporary Literary Criticism, Gale (Detroit, MI), Volume 12, 1980, Volume 30, 1984.

Dictionary of Literary Biography, Volume 52: *American Writers for Children since 1960: Fiction,* Gale (Detroit, MI), 1986, pp. 30-38.

Fisher, Emma, and Justin Wintle, *The Pied Pipers,* Paddington Press (New York, NY), 1975.

Gleasner, Diana, *Breakthrough: Women in Writing,* Walker (New York, NY), 1980.

Lee, Betsey, *Judy Blume's Story,* Dillon Press (Minneapolis, MN), 1981.

Newsmakers 1998, Issue 4, Gale (Detroit, MI), 1998.

St. James Guide to Young-Adult Writers, 2nd edition, St. James Press (Detroit, MI), 1999.

Weidt, Maryann, *Presenting Judy Blume,* Twayne (Boston, MI), 1989.

PERIODICALS

Booklist, March 15, 1998, Ilene Cooper, review of *Summer Sisters,* p. 1179; June 1, 1999, Sally Estes, review of *Places I Never Meant to Be,* p. 1812; September 15, 2002, Gillian Engberg, "Fudge Is Back!," p. 235; August, 2007, Ilene Cooper, review of *Soupy Saturdays with the Pain and the Great One,* p. 78; March 1, 2008, Ilene Cooper, review of *Cool Zone with the Pain and the Great One,* p. 67; October 15, 2008, Ilene Cooper, review of *Going, Going, Gone! with the Pain and the Great One,* p. 36.

Bulletin of the Center for Children's Books, April, 1970, Zena Sutherland, review of *The One in the Middle Is the Green Kangaroo,* p. 125; May, 1975, Zena Sutherland, review of *The Pain and the Great One,* p. 40; November, 1984, Zena Sutherland, review of *The One in the Middle Is the Green Kangaroo,* p. 125; October, 1993, Roger Sutton, review of *Here's To You, Rachel Robinson,* p. 39.

Chicago Tribune, March 15, 1985, Peter Gorner, interview with Blume, sec. 2, pp. 1-2.

Commentary, March, 1980, Naomi Decter, "Judy Blume's Children," pp. 65-67.

Entertainment Weekly, October 11, 2002, Rebecca Ascher Walsh, "The 'Fudge' Report," p. 77.

Globe and Mail (Toronto, Ontario, Canada), November 17, 1990, Isabel Vincent, "A Heroine for Children," p. C10.

Instructor, May-June, 2005, Judy Freeman, "Talking with Judy Blume," p. 37.

Kirkus Reviews, October 1, 1970, review of *Are You There God? It's Me, Margaret,* p. 1093; September 1, 2002, review of *Double Fudge,* p. 1304; July 1, 2008, review of *Going, Going, Gone! with the Pain and the Great One.*

Kliatt, January, 1995, Sherri Forgash Ginsberg, reviews of *Just as Long as We're Together* and *Here's to You, Rachel Robinson,* p. 4; January, 1996, Claire Rosser, review of *Here's to You, Rachel Robinson,* p. 4.

Library Journal, April 15, 1998, Michele Leber, review of *Summer Sisters,* p. 111.

Lion and the Unicorn, fall, 1978, R.A. Siegal, "Are You There God? It's Me, Me, Me!," pp. 72-77.

Los Angeles Times, December 26, 1987, Mitzi Myers, "An Optimistic World according to Blume."

Ms., July-August, 1998, Carolyn Mackler, "Judy Blume on Sex, the Suburbs, and *Summer Sisters,*" pp. 89-90.

Nation, November 21, 1981, Robert Lipsyte, "A Bridge of Words," pp. 551-553.

Newsletter on Intellectual Freedom, May, 1981, Judith M. Goldberger, "Judy Blume: Target of the Censor," pp. 57, 61-62, 81-82.

New Statesman, October 24, 1986, Adélè Geras, "Help!," pp. 28-29.

Newsweek, October 9, 1978, Linda Bird Francke, "Growing up with Judy," pp. 99-101; December 7, 1981, Walter Clemons, review of *Tiger Eyes,* pp. 101-104.

New Yorker, December 5, 1983, Faith McNulty, "Children's Books for Christmas," pp. 191-201.

New York Times Book Review, January 16, 1972, Dorothy M. Broderick, "Growing Time," p. 8; November 23, 1980, Natalie Babbitt, review of *Superfudge,* pp. 36-37; June 8, 1986, Elizabeth Winship, "Taking Adolescents Seriously," p. 12; November 11, 1990, Jean Van Leeuwen, "Peter's Pesky Little Brother," p. 29; November 16, 1997, Mark Oppenheimer, "Why Judy Bloom Endures," pp. 44-45.

New York Times Magazine, December 3, 1978, Joyce Maynard, "Coming of Age with Judy Blume!," p. 80.

People, October 16, 1978, John Neary, interview with Blume, pp. 47-48; December 28, 1998, "Judy Blume: The Queen of Preteen Fiction Hits Home with Her Grown-up Fans," p. 80.

Publishers Weekly, January 11, 1971, Lavinia Russ, review of *Are You There God? It's Me, Margaret,* pp. 62-63; April 17, 1978, Sybil Steinberg, "PW Interviews: Judy Blume," pp. 6-7; March 30, 1998, review of *Summer Sisters,* p. 66; August, 1999, review of *Places I Never Meant to Be,* p. 152; March 4, 2002, "In Full Blume," p. 82; March 18, 2002, John F. Baker, "Judy Blume Moves 'Fudge,'" p. 16; June 24, 2002, review of *Double Fudge,* p. 57; August 12, 2002, Sally Lodge, "The Return of Fudge," p. 150; June 18, 2007, review of *Soupy Saturdays with the Pain and the Great One,* p. 53.

School Librarian, May, 1987, John Gough, "Growth, Survival, and Style in the Novels of Judy Blume," pp. 100-106.

School Library Journal, January, 1972, Alice Adkins, review of *Freckle Juice,* p. 50; May, 1974, Melinda Schroeder, review of *Deenie,* p. 53; August, 1980, Pamela D. Pollack, review of *Superfudge,* pp. 60-61; June, 1996, Carolyn Caywood, "Deja Views," p. 62; June, 1998, Mary Alice Giarda, review of *Summer Sisters,* p. 175; August, 1999, Cindy Darling Codell, review of *Places I Never Meant to Be,* p. 152; September, 2002, Terrie Dorio, review of *Double Fudge,* p. 181; August, 2007, Laura Lutz, review of *Soupy Saturdays with the Pain and the Great One,* p. 77; June, 2008, Maryann H. Owen, review of *Cool Zone with the Pain and the Great One,* p. 96; September, 2008, Kathleen Meulen, review of *Going, Going, Gone! with the Pain and the Great One,* p. 138.

Telegraph (London, England), March 2, 2008, Melissa Whitworth, "Judy Blume's Lessons in Love."

Times Educational Supplement, September 20, 2002, Michael Thorn, "Whizz-Kids Revisited," p. 14.

Times Literary Supplement, April 7, 1978, Ann Evans, review of *Are You There God? It's Me, Margaret,* p. 383; January 29-February 4, 1988, Jan Dalley, "The Great American Feast," p. 119.

U.S. News and World Report, October 14, 2002, Vicky Hallett, "She Can't Say Farewell to Fudge," p. 12.

Washington Post, November 3, 1981, Sandy Rovner, interview with Blume.

Washington Post Book World, November 9, 1982, Brigitte Weeks, "The Return of Peter Hatcher," p. 12; February 12, 1984, Carolyn Banks, "A Hot Time in the Hot Tub Tonight," p. 3; April 27, 1986, Phyllis Theroux, "Judy Blume Listens to Her Young Readers," pp. 3-4; November 8, 1987, Beryl Lieff Benderly, "Judy Blume: Junior High Blues," p. 19.

Writer's Digest, November, 2001, Karen Struckel Brogan, "Judy Blume," pp. 30-31.

ONLINE

Judy Blume Home Page, http://www.judyblume.com (December 1, 2008).

Judy Blume Web log, http://www.judyblume.com/blog.php (December 1, 2008).*

*   *   *

BOGUE, Gary 1938- (Gary L. Bogue)

Personal

Born 1938.

Addresses

Office—P.O. 8099, Walnut Creek, CA 94596-8099. *E-mail*—garybug@infionline.net.

Career

Naturalist and writer. Lindsay Wildlife Museum, Walnut Creek, CA, curator, 1967-79; Contra Costa Newspapers, Walnut Creek, columnist, beginning 1970; Animal Rescue Foundation, Oakland, CA, executive director, 1992-93.

Member

International Wildlife Rehabilitation Council (founder and former president), Western Interpreters Association (cofounder and former president).

Writings

FOR CHILDREN

The Raccoon Next Door, illustrated by Chuck Todd, Heyday Books (Berkeley, CA), 2003.

There's an Opossum in My Backyard, illustrated by Chuck Todd, Heyday Books (Berkeley, CA), 2007.

OTHER

(With Dave Garcelon) *Raptor Rehabilitation* (textbook), Lindsay Wildlife Museum (Walnut Creek, CA), 1972.

It's a Wild Life, Lesher Communications (Walnut Creek, CA), 1989.

Isis, Lesher Communications (Walnut Creek, CA), 1989.

Author of "Pets and Wildlife" Web log.

Sidelights

As curator of Walnut Creek, California's Lindsay Wildlife Museum, from the late 1960s to 1979, writer, educator, and naturalist Gary Bogue developed and oversaw one of the country's first wildlife rescue and rehabilitation centers. Among its many successes under Bogue's direction, the museum rehabilitated a native mountain lion and then successfully returned the creature to the wild—a first in North America. The Lindsay Wildlife Museum introduces patrons to hundreds of species of wild birds, as well as many of the mammals, snakes, and other reptiles native to the western United States.

In addition to writing several books that relate to his work in wildlife rehabilitation and education, Bogue has also teamed up with artist Chuck Todd to create the picture books *The Raccoon Next Door* and *There's an Opossum in My Backyard.* In the latter title, young readers join Nathan Green and his parents in watching a baby marsupial learn to survive a year in the boy's backyard, amid a world bustling with the activity of snakes, owls, and other woodland creatures. Predicting that young readers "will enjoy the story" in *There's an Opossum in My Backyard,* Susan E. Murray added in *School Library Journal* that Bogue's picture book "does a terrific job" introducing animal facts and demonstrating how to observe wildlife while not interfering with nature. In *Booklist* Ilene Cooper noted the inclusion of useful information and a Web site listing, adding that Todd's watercolor illustrations for *There's an Opossum in My Backyard* "convey . . . a constant energy and vigor" to supplement Bogue's text.

Biographical and Critical Sources

PERIODICALS

Booklist, August, 2007, Ilene Cooper, review of *There's an Opossum in My Backyard,* p. 86.

Kirkus Reviews, July 15, 2007, review of *There's an Opossum in My Backyard.*

School Library Journal, February, 2008, Susan E. Murray, review of *There's an Opossum in My Backyard,* p. 83.

ONLINE

Contra Costa Times Online, http://www.contracostatimes.com/ (November 15, 2008), "Gary Bogue."

Gary Bogue: Pets and Wildlife Web Log, http://ibabuzz.com/garybogue/ (November 15, 2008).*

*   *   *

BOGUE, Gary L.
See BOGUE, Gary

*   *   *

BOWSHER, Melodie

Personal

Born in Dodge City, KS; children: Mia, Luca. *Education:* Kansas State University, B.A.

Addresses

Home—San Francisco, CA. *Agent*—Kirby Kim, Vigliano Associates, 405 Park Ave., Ste. 1700, New York, NY 10022. *E-mail*—lostandfoundauthor@gmail.com.

Career

Wall Street Journal, Dallas, TX, former reporter; has also worked in corporate communications in San Francisco, CA, and as a freelance business writer.

Awards, Honors

First-place award for investigative reporting, William Randolph Hearst Foundation.

Writings

My Lost and Found Life (novel), Bloomsbury Children's Books (New York, NY), 2006.

Sidelights

Journalist Melodie Bowsher's debut novel, *My Lost and Found Life,* tells the story of seventeen-year-old Ashley. Once rich and spoiled, Ashley is brought down to a more common economic level by her mother's misbehavior. "Debut author Bowsher has a great concept," commented a *Kirkus Reviews* critic. A homecoming queen and straight-A student with a prestigious college in her future, wealthy and popular Ashley finds her perfect lifestyle rapidly slipping away when her mother is accused of embezzling millions of dollars and then disappears. Abruptly poor and homeless, unsure of her mother's whereabouts, and shunned by the bright rich kids who used to be her friends, Ashley is forced to move into a grubby camper behind a gas station and take a job in the local coffee shop. Though her material existence has been diminished, Ashley soon finds that there are advantages to her new situation, including romance with the devilishly handsome Patrick and a new perspective on people from a side of life she has never known before. A *Children's Bookwatch* reviewer called *My Lost and Found Life* a "warm coming of age story," while *Booklist* reviewer Hazel Rochman remarked that "readers will be caught up in the riches-to-rags turnaround in a materialistic world."

Biographical and Critical Sources

PERIODICALS

Booklist, November 15, 2006, Hazel Rochman, review of *My Lost and Found Life,* p. 57.

Children's Bookwatch, October, 2006, "Bloomsbury," review of *My Lost and Found Life.*

Kirkus Reviews, September 1, 2006, review of *My Lost and Found Life,* p. 900.

ONLINE

Melodie Bowsher Home Page, http://www.melodiebowsher.com (April 2, 2007).

C-D

CARLTON, Susan 1960-

Personal

Born January 3, 1960; married; children: two daughters. *Education:* Attended college in Oregon; Columbia University, degree.

Addresses

Home—MA. *E-mail*—susan@susancarlton.com.

Career

Magazine writer and editor.

Writings

(With Coco Myers) *The Nanny Book: The Smart Parent's Guide to Hiring, Firing, and Every Sticky Situation in Between,* St. Martin's Press (New York, NY), 1999.
Lobsterland (novel), Holt (New York, NY), 2007.

Contributing editor for *Mademoiselle* magazine. Contributor to periodicals, including *Parents, Parenting, Seventeen, Self,* and *Mirabella.*

Sidelights

A contributor to such publications as *Parenting, Seventeen,* and *Mirabella,* Susan Carlton is also the author of *Lobsterland,* her debut young-adult novel. The work centers on an intelligent, frustrated sixteen-year-old girl living off the coast of Maine. "I started with the idea that we all feel, at some point, trapped in the wrong place and the wrong family," Carlton stated in discussing *Lobsterland* on her home page. "A small island in Maine seemed the perfect backdrop for fermenting that sense of desperation and for hatching an elaborate escape plan."

Lobsterland concerns Charlotte, the harried eldest child in a dysfunctional family. Charlotte must care for her younger brother and sister while her mother medicates

Cover of Susan Carlton's young-adult novel Lobsterland, *featuring artwork by Martha Rich.* (Illustration copyright © 2007 by Martha Rich. Reprinted by permission of Henry Holt and Company, LLC.)

herself with pills and her father, who may be wanted by federal authorities, spends his time playing computer games. The desperately unhappy teen, who also suspects that her boyfriend has been cheating on her, decides to leave her island home and enroll at boarding school. As Charlotte races to fill out application forms, her literate, biting responses to a series of essay questions "evoke a realistic picture of a girl who yearns for independence but secretly fears letting go of the familiar," noted a contributor in *Publishers Weekly.* Deborah Stevenson, writing in the *Bulletin of the Center for Children's Books,* observed of *Lobsterland* that "readers will revel in Charlotte's sharp, funny company."

Biographical and Critical Sources

PERIODICALS

Bulletin of the Center for Children's Books, November, 2007, Deborah Stevenson, review of *Lobsterland,* p. 133.
Kirkus Reviews, July 15, 2007, review of *Lobsterland.*
Publishers Weekly, September 24, 2007, review of *Lobsterland,* p. 74.
School Library Journal, Heather E. Miller, review of *Lobsterland,* p. 120.

ONLINE

Susan Carlton Home Page, http://www.susancarlton.com (October 31, 2008).*

*   *   *

CARWELL, L'Ann
See McKISSACK, Patricia C.

*   *   *

CASTILLO, Lauren

Personal
Born in Long Island, NY. *Education:* Maryland Institute College of Art, B.F.A., 2003; School of Visual Arts, M.F.A., 2005.

Addresses
Home—Brooklyn, NY. *E-mail*—info@laurencastillo.com.

Career
Children's book illustrator. Henry Holt Books for Young Readers, New York, NY, assistant art director.

Illustrator
Emily Jenkins, *What Happens on Wednesdays,* Farrar, Straus & Giroux (New York, NY), 2007.
Linda Stanek, *The Pig and Miss Prudence,* Star Bright Books (New York, NY), 2008.
Tracey E. Fern, *Buffalo Music,* Clarion Books (New York, NY), 2008.
Kate Banks, *That's Papa's Way,* Farrar, Straus & Giroux (New York, NY), 2009.
Elizabeth Partridge, *Big Cat Pepper,* Bloomsbury (New York, NY), 2009.

Sidelights
As children's book illustrator Lauren Castillo noted on her home page, her multicultural heritage exposed her to a "potpourri of cultural traditions" at a young age. "I was surrounded by Spanish paintings, patterned walls and tapestries, old Armenian textiles, ornate furniture, beautiful ceramics, and, of course, lots and lots and lots of books—so many rich visuals that helped to expand and mold my visual vocabulary," Castillo recalled. "I looked forward to weekend trips to my grandparents' houses. Those trips always meant storytelling, which stretched my imagination toward the entire world."

Castillo, who cites Norman Rockwell, Richard Scarry, and Tomie DePaola among her creative influences, landed her first illustration assignment shortly after graduating with a master's degree from New York City's School of Visual Arts. That work, Emily Jenkins's *What Happens on Wednesdays,* centers on the quiet, familiar activities of a young girl, including naptime and a visit to the local library. According to *School Library Journal* contributor Amy Lilien-Harper, "Castillo's slightly impressionistic mixed-media illustrations give viewers a real feel for the youngster's Brooklyn neighborhood." The book's images also drew praise from a *Publishers Weekly* reviewer who wrote that Castillo "shows real skill with color, punctuating urban grays and browns with the girl's red clothes." In *Booklist* Jennifer Mattson noted that the artist illustrates "rich elements, such as a gorgeously patterned bedspread, in a manner consistent with a child's intense but often selective memory for details."

Castillo also provided the illustrations for *Buffalo Music,* a picture book by Tracey E. Fern that offers a fictionalized portrait of nineteenth-century conservationist Mary Ann Goodnight. Fern's story centers on Molly and her efforts to nurture a pair of orphaned buffalo calves. "Castillo's smudgy illustrations . . . invest both Molly and the buffalo calves with enormous personality," observed a critic in an appraisal of *Buffalo Music* for *Kirkus Reviews.*

Biographical and Critical Sources

PERIODICALS

Booklist, October 15, 2007, Jennifer Mattson, review of *What Happens on Wednesdays,* p. 47; April 15, 2008, Hazel Rochman, review of *Buffalo Music,* p. 57.

Kirkus Reviews, July 1, 2007, review of *What Happens on Wednesdays;* April 1, 2008, review of *Buffalo Music.*
Publishers Weekly, August 27, 2007, review of *What Happens on Wednesdays,* p. 88.
School Library Journal, August, 2007, Amy Lilien-Harper, review of *What Happens on Wednesdays,* p. 82; May, 2008, Grace Oliff, review of *The Pig and Miss Prudence,* p. 109.

ONLINE

Lauren Castillo Home Page, http://www.laurencastillo. com (October 31, 2008).
Lauren Castillo Web log, http://www.laurencastillo. blogspot.com (October 31, 2008).
Macmillan Web log, http://us.macmillan.com/ (October 31, 2008), "Lauren Castillo."
Seven Impossible Things before Breakfast Web site, http:// blaine.org/sevenimpossiblethings/ (April 16, 2008), Emily Jenkins, interview with Castillo.

*   *   *

CATALANOTTO, Peter 1959-

Personal

Surname is pronounced "KA-ta-la-NOT-to"; born March 21, 1959, in Brooklyn, NY; son of Anthony (a printer) and Ella Virginia (a homemaker) Catalanotto; married Jo-Ann Carrie Maynard (a photographer), August 8, 1989; children: Chelsea. *Education:* Pratt Institute, B.F. A., 1981. *Hobbies and other interests:* Basketball, reading.

Addresses

Home—Doylestown, PA.

Career

Illustrator and author of children's books. Freelance illustrator, 1982-87; freelance writer and illustrator of children's books, beginning 1987. *Exhibitions:* Work exhibited at Mazza Collection, Findlay, OH; and at Keene State Gallery, Keene, NH. Included in permanent collection at Elizabeth Stone Gallery, Birmingham, MI, then Alexandria, VA.

Awards, Honors

Most Promising New Artist designation, *Publishers Weekly,* 1989; Best Book for Teens designation, American Library Association, 1990, for *Soda Jerk* by Cynthia Rylant; Keystone Book designation, 1991, for *Cecil's Story* by George Ella Lyon; Best Book designation, *Publishers Weekly,* 1992, for *Who Came down the Road?* by Lyon; Carolyn Field Award, 1993, for *Dreamplace* by Lyon; Best Book designation, *Booklist,* 1999, for *Letter to the Lake* by Susan Marie Swanson; Best Books designation, *Booklinks,* 1999, both for *Dad and Me* and *Book,* by Lyon.

Peter Catalanotto (Reproduced by permission.)

Writings

SELF-ILLUSTRATED

Dylan's Day Out, Orchard Books (New York, NY), 1989, reprinted, Southpaw Books (Maplewood, NJ), 2006.
Mr. Mumble, Orchard Books (New York, NY), 1990, reprinted, Southpaw Books (Maplewood, NJ), 2006.
Christmas Always . . . , Orchard Books (New York, NY), 1991.
The Painter, Orchard Books (New York, NY), 1995.
Dad and Me, DK Publishing (New York, NY), 1999.
Emily's Art, Atheneum Books for Young Readers (New York, NY), 2001.
Matthew A, B, C, Atheneum Books for Young Readers (New York, NY), 2002.
Daisy 1, 2, 3, Atheneum Books for Young Readers (New York, NY), 2003.
Kitten Red, Yellow, Blue, Atheneum Books for Young Readers (New York, NY), 2005.
Ivan the Terrier, Atheneum Books for Young Readers (New York, NY), 2007.

"SECOND-GRADE FRIENDS" SERIES; AND ILLUSTRATOR

(With Pamela Schembri) *The Secret Lunch Special,* Henry Holt (New York, NY), 2006.
(With Pamela Schembri) *No More Pumpkins,* Henry Holt (New York, NY), 2007.
(With Pamela Schembri) *The Veterans Day Visitor,* Henry Holt (New York, NY), 2008.

ILLUSTRATOR

Cynthia Rylant, *All I See,* Orchard Books (New York, NY), 1988.

Cynthia Rylant, *Soda Jerk* (poems), Orchard Books (New York, NY), 1990.

George Ella Lyon, *Cecil's Story,* Orchard Books (New York, NY), 1991.

George Ella Lyon, *Who Came down the Road?,* Orchard Books (New York, NY), 1992.

Cynthia Rylant, *An Angel for Solomon Singer,* Orchard Books (New York, NY), 1992.

George Ella Lyon, *Dreamplace,* Orchard Books (New York, NY), 1993.

SuAnn Kiser, *The Catspring Somersault Flying One-handed Flip-Flop,* Orchard Books (New York, NY), 1993.

Susan Patron, *Dark Cloud Strong Breeze,* Orchard Books (New York, NY), 1994.

George Ella Lyon, *Mama Is a Miner,* Orchard Books (New York, NY), 1994.

Megan McDonald, *My House Has Stars,* Orchard Books (New York, NY), 1996.

George Ella Lyon, *A Day at Damp Camp,* Orchard Books (New York, NY), 1996.

Angela Johnson, *The Rolling Store,* Orchard Books (New York, NY), 1997.

Susan Marie Swanson, *Getting Used to the Dark,* Orchard Books (New York, NY), 1997.

Susi G. Fowler, *Circle of Thanks,* Scholastic (New York, NY), 1998.

Marie Bradby, *The Longest Wait,* Orchard Books (New York, NY), 1998.

Susan Marie Swanson, *Letter to the Lake,* DK Publishing (New York, NY), 1998.

Gilda Berger, *Celebrate!,* Scholastic (New York, NY), 1998.

George Ella Lyon, *Book,* DK Publishing (New York, NY), 1999.

Katharine Kenah, *The Dream Shop,* HarperCollins (New York, NY), 2002.

Liz Rosenberg, *We Wanted You,* Roaring Brook Press (Brookfield, CT), 2002.

Mary Pope Osborne, *Happy Birthday, America,* Roaring Brook Press (Brookfield, CT), 2003.

George Ella Lyon, *Mother to Tigers,* Atheneum Books for Young Readers (New York, NY), 2003.

Joanne Ryder, *My Mother's Voice,* HarperCollins (New York, NY), 2006.

George Ella Lyon, *No Dessert Forever!,* Atheneum Books for Young Readers (New York, NY), 2006.

Coleen M. Paratore, *Catching the Sun,* Charlesbridge (Watertown, MA), 2008.

George Ella Lyon, *Sleepsong,* Atheneum Books for Young Readers (New York, NY), 2009.

Sidelights

Peter Catalanotto is an author and illustrator of children's books whose work was described by a *Kirkus Reviews* critic as "explosively joyful and expressive." In both his self-illustrated titles and the books he has il-

lustrated for other authors, Catalanotto has built an impressive and distinctive body of award-winning work, teaming up with authors such as Cynthia Rylant and George Ella Lyon. As an essayist noted in *Children's Books and Their Creators,* "the imagery throughout Catalanotto's evanescent watercolors encases emotions and reflects ruminations while enhancing the texts and adding new dimensions to the stories." As the author/illustrator stated in an essay for the *Something about the Author Autobiography Series* (*SAAS*), "I think the most successful picture books are when the words and pictures are wed to create something bigger and better than when separate."

"I grew up in a household in East Northport, Long Island, where four of the five children went to art schools in New York City," Catalanotto once told *SATA.* "I remember when I started school I was amazed to learn everybody didn't draw like my family." Catalanotto was, he admitted, a "shy child. Although I had a lot of friends, I most enjoyed solitude, reading, doing jigsaw puzzles, or spending endless hours drawing. Comic book characters were my favorite things to draw, especially 'Spider-Man.'"

After graduating from high school, Catalanotto enrolled at Pratt Institute, where he took classes in illustration, drawing, and painting. "It was at Pratt that I developed the watercolor technique I still use today," he added. "I think it's important for an artist to find a medium that

Peter Catalanotto captures the playful relationship between a father and son in his picture book Dad and Me. (DK Publishing, 1999. Copyright © 1999 by Peter Catalanotto. Reproduced by permission.)

Catalanotto's light-filled artwork is a hallmark of self-illustrated picture books such as his The Painter. (Copyright © 1999 by Peter Catalanotto. Reproduced by permission of Orchard Books, an imprint of Scholastic, Inc.)

suits his/her personality. Watercolor allows me to stop and start without a lot of preparation. I can be loose or tight with my style with washes and rendering."

Graduation from Pratt in 1981, Catalanotto worked for newspapers, working predominately in black and white. Soon he started getting assignments from magazines such as *Reader's Digest, Family Circle, Woman's Day,* and *Redbook.* A job painting young-adult book jackets in 1984 led to an illustration project and his first picture-book project, *All I See* by Cynthia Rylant. "I became enamored with the process of creating paintings for an entire story," Catalanotto recalled. "The research included spending time on a lake, since this was the setting for the story. I spent thirteen hours in a rowboat, sketching and photographing the lake at all angles and times of the day. Seasick and sunburned, I started my sketches."

Catalanotto's first self-illustrated picture book, *Dylan's Day Out,* is done in black and white and details the adventures of a Dalmatian with a serious case of cabin fever. The book was well received and inspired Catalanotto to pursue further solo efforts in addition to the illustration work he was doing for other writers. His second solo title, *Mr. Mumble,* was inspired by his own shyness, "a feeling I think most people, especially children, can relate to," he noted. In *Christmas Always . . .* he tells a story of a girl who gets more visitors than she expects on Christmas Eve. "When my parents would

have parties on Christmas Eve," Catalanotto recalled, "I was always sent to bed long before the party ended. This story is simply what I wished happened to me, instead of being in that bedroom all by myself."

Catalanotto's critically acclaimed picture book *The Painter* tells the story of a little girl whose father is a busy painter. She is forbidden to enter his studio, and outside of the studio he is usually too busy to give her his full attention. Finally, however, the pair works out a solution, and the girl is rewarded for her patience after dinner with entrance to the studio where she paints her own family portrait. The book was in part inspired by Catalanotto's own child, Chelsea, for whom his studio was off limits because it contained tools that were potentially harmful to a toddler. A *Publishers Weekly* critic remarked that *The Painter* "subtly attests to the joy inherent in the creation of both life and art," while in *Kirkus Reviews* a contributor wrote that Catalanotto's "loose fluid style focuses on important details" and results in a book that "is simply and beautifully done."

Another busy and distracted dad is at the heart of Catalanotto's *Dad and Me*. Tommy is looking forward to sharing the good news of Gemini IV—the first U.S. space walk—with his father. Rushing home from school, the boy dons a colander as a space helmet, but after he is reprimanded for wearing the colander at dinner, Tommy is sent to his room by his father. Finally, the boy re-connects with his father by giving his dad a newspaper photo of the astronaut with a photograph of his own face inserted in it. A *Kirkus Reviews* critic commented that in *Dad and Me* "Catalanotto's watercolors deftly capture both Tommy's disappointment and his longing for adventure," while a *Publishers Weekly* contributor called the book's watercolor images "breathtaking."

Creativity is the focus of *Emily's Art,* a self-illustrated book inspired by Catalanotto's conversations with students at school presentations. In the story, Emily draws things the way she sees them. For example, to represent her mother's business in one picture, she draws her mother in several places while other family members remain in one place. When she draws her dog, she draws him with large ears, because he is a good listener. She submits the picture of her dog to a school competition. When the judge sees it and thinks Emily has painted a rabbit, the judge praises her, but when Emily explains it is her dog, the judge no longer likes her painting and gives someone else first place. "Catalanotto subtly conveys the value of creating art for art's sake in this tender picture book," wrote a reviewer for *Publishers Weekly*. Marta Segal, writing in *Booklist,* called Catalanotto's illustrations for *Emily's Art* "stunning," while Wendy Lukehart concluded in *School Library Journal* that the "creative and heartfelt book is a masterpiece."

A rambunctious Jack Russell terrier is the star of *Ivan the Terrier,* a fanciful story featuring Catalanotto's gouache and watercolor art. In the story a narrator attempts to tell four traditional bedtime tales, but each effort is derailed when the energetic puppy inserts himself into the story. He startles the three Billy goats gruff, chases the three bears, discombobulates the three pigs, and distracts the gingerbread boy, until it finally becomes sleepy itself. The artist/storyteller exhibits a "keen understanding of terrier behavior and design," wrote a *Kirkus Reviews* writer, and in *Booklist* Ilene Cooper observed that in *Ivan the Terrier* Catalanotto "mixes the soft-edged fairy-tale world with a heady realism" in his humorous tale. Reviewing the imaginative picture book, *School Library Journal* critic Linda L. Walkins concluded of *Ivan the Terrier* that the dog's "expressive countenance will make readers chuckle and chortle with delight." In *Publishers Weekly* a reviewer wrote that the book's ingredients—"a dearth of words, a plethora of familiar storybook characters and a delicious pun in the title"—add up to a book sure to be "read-aloud favorite."

Catalanotto turns to the concept book with *Matthew A, B, C, Daisy 1, 2, 3,* and *Kitten Red, Yellow, Blue.* Illustrated with cartoon art, *Matthew A, B, C* centers on an entire classroom full of students named Matthew. Luckily, each Matthew has a last name beginning with a different letter, and that letter corresponds to a specific trait the boy has. For example, Matthew A. is affectionate, while Matthew N. is nearly naked, wearing only "briefs and a superhero cape" explained Christine M.

Hepperman in *Horn Book.* In *School Library Journal,* Jody McCoy predicted that *Matthew A, B, C* will appeal to "Catalanotto's fans and those with a soft spot in their hearts for the quirky."

Set in a dog training school, *Daisy 1, 2, 3* features twenty Dalmatians, all named Daisy, and each has a particular talent or trait that corresponds to a number. For example, Daisy 2 wears two name tags, Daisy 3 plays three different musical instruments, and Daisy 20 has fooled twenty fleas. *Kitten Red, Yellow, Blue* uses a similar strategy to teach youngsters about color. In the book a mama cat has sixteen kittens, and each kitten goes to live with someone who has a color matching the color of that kitten's fur. For example, the red kitten goes to live with a firefighter, the orange kitten lives with a basketball player, and the brown kitten's owner delivers parcels. Carolyn Phelan noted in *Booklist* that *Daisy 1, 2, 3* has "plenty of visual humor," and Blair Christolon wrote in *School Library Journal* that Catalanotto's "canines exude winning personalities." According to a critic for *Kirkus Reviews,* in *Kitten Red, Yellow, Blue* Catalanotto "renders each lively, humorous scene in neutral tones," and closes his story with a "chromatic bash" as all the kittens are reunited.

In addition to picture books, Catalanotto turns to beginning readers in the "Second Grade Friends" books, a joint project with writer Pamela Schembri. In *No More Pumpkins* Emily and her class have studied pumpkins, made pumpkin art, and written pumpkin stories. Even

Catalanotto's self-illustrated **Ivan the Terrier** *follows the hijinks of a frisky pup.* (Copyright © 2007 Peter Catalanotto. Reprinted with the permission of Atheneum Books for Young Readers, an imprint of Simon & Schuster Children's Publishing Division.)

though the orange squash has lost its charm, after her carved Jack o' lantern is damaged by friend Vinni just before the class open house, Emily is hurt and confused until she understands the feelings that prompted her friend's act. Comparing the series to popular beginning readers by Barbara Park and Patricia Reilly Giff, *School Library Journal* critic Kelly Roth added that Catalanotto's ink-wash illustrations for *No More Pumpkins* are

Daisy the Dalmatian presents a simple lesson in counting in Catalanotto's self-illustrated **Daisy 1, 2, 3.** (Copyright © 2003 Peter Catalanotto. Reprinted with the permission of Atheneum Books for Young Readers, an imprint of Simon & Schuster Children's Publishing Division.)

"well done and expressive." Other volumes in the series include *The Secret Lunch Special* and *The Veterans Day Visitor,* the last described by *Horn Book* critic Robin L. Smith as a "welcome addition" to classroom discussions of the contributions of U.S. servicemen and women.

In addition to his original stories, Catalanotto has continued to do illustration work for other authors. As he explained at *VisitingAuthors.com,* "When I illustrate another writer's text, I want to extend the words by adding new ideas into the art. . . . I enjoy illustrating stories that are ethereal, airy, and emotional, not locked into a specific time and place."

Beginning an ongoing collaboration with writer Lyon, *Cecil's Story* contains a powerful, yet simple poem about a boy whose father goes off to fight in the U.S. Civil War. In *Who Came down the Road?* Lyon's story finds a curious boy and his mother discovering a pathway through the woods. Though the mother and son are contemporary, the people who have used the road before—whom the mother speculates about as they walk along—come from epochs as distant as the Civil War and the age of the mastodon. To illustrate Lyon's text for *Dreamplace,* Catalanotto traveled to Colorado to see Mesa Verde and the Anasazi Indian cliff dwellings. As he explained in *SAAS,* "The spirit of the Anasazi people . . . haunted me as I painted their stories. I walked in the same place as my characters." A *Publishers Weekly* acknowledged the artist's efforts, writing that *Dreamplace* provides "an atmospheric, shimmering glance" back in time highlighted by "Catalanotto's extraordinary watercolors."

Other collaborations with Lyon include *Mother to Tiger, Sleepsong,* and *No Dessert Forever!,* the last which follows the temper tantrum of an angry young girl. *Mother to Tigers* focuses on Helen Martini, who, with husband Fred Martini, started the first nursery at the Bronx Zoo in 1944. Fred Martini was a zookeeper, and when he began bringing home baby animals for extra care, Helen had a lot of love to give to the baby animals. Through her care, many newborns were given the chance to survive into adulthood. "Catalanotto adds a bold graphic dimension to the story," noted Margaret Bush in her review of *Mother to Tigers* for *School Library Journal.* A contributor to *Publishers Weekly* wrote that the book's "watercolor paintings are drenched in sunlight while charcoals and chalks on brown paper reinforce the 1940s context," and a *Kirkus* reviewer cited as "especially breathtaking" Catalanotto's paintings of "lion and tiger faces."

Reviewing SuAnn Kiser's *The Catspring Somersault Flying One-handed Flip-Flop,* a contributor to *Publishers Weekly* described Catalanotto's "sun-drenched watercolors . . . as lush and complex as ever." The artist depicts children of many different cultures in Megan McDonald's *My House Has Stars* in "watercolor paintings in soft, misty colors" that "reflect the awesome quality of the universe as viewed by youngsters throughout the world," according to Sally R. Dow in *School Library Journal.* Reviewing Susan Marie Swanson's *Letter to the Lake,* a *Publishers Weekly* reviewer enjoyed Catalanotto's "exquisite paintings," while *Booklist* reviewer Shelle Rosenfeld called the same work a "fine and visually astonishing book about the power of dreaming and memories."

The Longest Wait, a picture book by Marie Bradby, details the effects of a blizzard on an African-American family living in pre-industrial America. Also featuring a realistic setting, Liz Rosenberg's *We Wanted You* follows a young child from his adoption until he leaves his loving parents' home to attend college. Here Judith Constantinides complimented Catalanotto's "glowing illustrations" in her review for *School Library Journal,* and a reviewer for *Publishers Weekly* wrote that the "radiant paintings" in *We Wanted You* "form a kind of treasured photo album."

Working with Mary Pope Osborne, Catalanotto brings to life a home-town America setting in his artwork for *Happy Birthday, America,* while in Coleen M. Paratore's *Catching the Sun* his watercolor art enriches a story about a young boy's early-morning walk along the beach. Julie Cummins, in her *Booklist* review of *Happy Birthday, America,* commented that Catalanotto's choice of color "lends a candlelike glow to scenes," while a critic for *Kirkus Reviews* maintained that the picture book's "watercolor illustrations invoke summer." In another *Kirkus Reviews* appraisal, a critic wrote that the "muted watercolor illustrations" in *Catching the Sun* contribute to a story that is "warm and winning," while *School Library Journal* reviewer Susan Weitz dubbed the same picture book "peacefully illustrated" with art that is "always tranquil, [and] sometimes surprising in perspective and beauty."

"I feel very lucky that my job is something I love to do," Catalanotto concluded in *SAAS.* "My work is a constant challenge, and I grow as a writer and artist with every book. The most important thing I want children to know when I visit their school is this: if you love to write and draw, you can do it for life!"

Biographical and Critical Sources

BOOKS

Silvey, Anita, editor *Children's Books and Their Creators,* Houghton (Boston, MA), 1995, p. 125.
Something about the Author Autobiography Series, Volume 25, Gale (Detroit, MI), 1998, pp. 37-52.

PERIODICALS

Booklist, November 1, 1996, Carolyn Phelan, review of *My House Has Stars,* p. 508; April 15, 1998, Shelle Rosenfeld, review of *Letter to the Lake,* p. 1454; Sep-

A family's July 4th celebration is the focus of Happy Birthday America, *which pairs Catalanotto's art with a text by Mary Pope Osborne.* (Illustration © 2003 by Peter Catalanotto. All rights reserved. Reprinted by permission of Henry Holt and Company, LLC.)

tember 15, 1998, Shelle Rosenfeld, review of *Circle of Thanks,* p. 236; December 1, 1998, Linda Perkins, review of *The Longest Wait,* pp. 669-670; July, 2001, Marta Segal, review of *Emily's Art,* p. 2018; July 2002, Ilene Cooper, review of *Matthew A, B, C,* p. 1854; May 1, 2003, Julie Cummins, review of *Happy Birthday, America,* p. 1605; November 1, 2003, Carolyn Phelan, review of *Daisy 1, 2, 3,* p. 500; February 15, 2005, Gillian Engberg, review of *Kitten Red, Yellow, Blue,* p. 1984; September 1, 2006, Carolyn Phelan, review of *The Secret Lunch Special,* p. 134; August, 2007, Ilene Cooper, review of *Ivan the Terrier,* p. 81; August, 2007, Carolyn Phelan, review of *No More Pumpkins,* p. 62.

Five Owls, September-October, 1995, Cassie Whetstone, review of *The Painter,* p. 10.

Horn Book, May-June, 1994, Nancy Vasilakis, review of *Dark Cloud Strong Breeze,* p. 318; July-August, 2002, Christine M. Heppermann, review of *Matthew A, B, C,* p. 441; May-June, 2003, Betty Carter, review of *Mother to Tigers,* p. 369; September-October, 2006, Robin Smith, review of *The Secret Lunch Special,* p. 575; November-December, 2007, Tanya D. Auger, review of *Ivan the Terrier,* p. 664; September-October, 2008, Robin L. Smith, review of *The Veterans Day Visitor,* p. 579.

Kirkus Reviews, August 15, 1995, review of *The Painter,* p. 1186; July 15, 1999, review of *Dad and Me,* p.

1131; January 15, 2002, review of *We Wanted You,* p. 108; February 1, 2003, review of *Mother to Tigers,* p. 236; April 15, 2003, review of *Happy Birthday, America,* p. 609; October 15, 2003, review of *Daisy 1, 2 3,* p. 1269; January 1, 2005, review of *Kitten Red, Yellow, Blue,* p. 50; July 1, 2007, review of *No More Pumpkins;* September 1, 2007, review of *Ivan the Terrier;* December 15, 2007, review of *Catching the Sun.*

Publishers Weekly, September 29, 1989, review of *Dylan's Day Out,* p. 65; July 13, 1990, review of *Mr. Mumble,* p. 53; January 25, 1993, review of *Dreamplace,* p. 86; July 26, 1993, review of *The Catspring Somersault Flying One-handed Flip-Flop,* p. 70; August 21, 1995, review of *The Painter,* p. 64; August 26, 1996, review of *My House Has Stars,* p. 97; April 20, 1998, review of *Letter to the Lake,* p. 65; September 21, 1998, review of *The Longest Wait,* p. 83; October 19, 1998, review of *Circle of Thanks,* p. 79; August 19, 1999, review of *Dad and Me,* p. 351; June 18, 2001, review of *My House Has Stars,* p. 83; July 2, 2001, review of *Emily's Art,* p. 75; October 15, 2001, review of *Circle of Thanks,* p. 74; December 10, 2001, review of *The Dream Shop,* p. 70; February 25, 2002, review of *We Wanted You,* p. 66; May 20, 2002, review of *Matthew A, B, C,* p. 64; December 23, 2002, review of *Mother to Tigers,* p. 71; November 6, 2006, review of *No Dessert Forever!,* p. 61; July 16, 2007, review of *Ivan the Terrier,* p. 162.

School Library Journal, September, 1990, Susan Powers, review of *Mr. Mumble,* p. 196; October, 1996, Sally R. Dow, review of *My House Has Stars,* pp. 102-103; May, 1998, Tana Elias, review of *Letter to the Lake,* p. 126; December, 1998, Pam Gosner, review of *Circle of Thanks,* p. 82; June, 1999, Miriam Lang Budin, review of *Book,* p. 119; June, 2001, Wendy Lukehart, review of *Emily's Art,* p. 105; April, 2002, Judith Constantinides, review of *We Wanted You,* p. 121; June, 2002, Jody McCoy, review of *Matthew A.B. C.,* p. 91; March, 2003, Margaret Bush, review of *Mother to Tigers,* p. 220; December, 2003, Blair Christolon, review of *Daisy 1, 2, 3,* p. 111; March, 2005, Corina Austin, review of *Kitten Red, Yellow, Blue,* p. 168; September, 2007, Linda L. Walkins, review of *Ivan the Terrier,* and Kelly Roth, review of *No More Pumpkins,* both p. 160; June, 2008, Susan Weitz, review of *Catching the Sun,* p. 113.

ONLINE

SimonSays.com, http://www.simonsays.com/ (April 21, 2005), "Peter Catalanotto."

VisitingAuthors.com, http://www.visitingauthors.com/ (November 17, 2008), "Peter Catalanotto."*

*　　　*　　　*

CHRISTIANA, David 1960-

Personal

Born April 18, 1960; married to Kristy Atwood. *Education:* Tyler School of Art, B.F.A.; Syracuse University, M.F.A.

Addresses

Home and office—13990 N. Sutherland Tr., Tucson, AZ 85739. *Office*—School of Art, Art Building, Rm. 207B, University of Arizona, Tucson, AZ 85721-0002. *E-mail*—drchristiana@aol.com; davidc@email.arizona. edu.

Career

Artist and educator. University of Arizona, Tucson, associate professor of art. *Exhibitions:* Work exhibited in shows at galleries, including at Society of Illustrators, New York, NY, 1994, 1995, 1996, 1997; Tohono Chul Gallery, Tucson, AZ, 1995; Northern Arizona University Art Museum, Flagstaff, 1996; Boehm Gallery, Palomar College, San Marcos, CA, 1997; and (solo exhibition) Reality Room, Washington, DC, 1998.

Member

Society of Illustrators.

Writings

SELF-ILLUSTRATED

Drawer in a Drawer, Farrar, Straus & Giroux (New York, NY), 1990.

White Nineteens, Farrar, Straus & Giroux (New York, NY), 1992.

A Tooth Fairy's Tale, Farrar, Straus & Giroux (New York, NY), 1994.

The First Snow, Farrar, Straus & Giroux (New York, NY), 1996.

O Come, All Ye Faithful, Simon & Schuster (New York, NY), 2003.

ILLUSTRATOR

Alvin Schwartz, reteller, *Fat Man in a Fur Coat, and Other Bear Stories,* Farrar, Straus & Giroux (New York, NY), 1984.

Alvin Schwartz, reteller, *Tales of Trickery from the Land of Spoof,* Farrar, Straus & Giroux (New York, NY), 1985.

Rex Benedict, *Run for Your Sweet Life,* Farrar, Straus & Giroux (New York, NY), 1986.

Elizabeth Muskopf, *The Revenge of Jeremiah Plum,* Holt (New York, NY), 1987.

Alvin Schwartz, reteller, *Gold and Silver, Silver and Gold: Tales of Hidden Treasure,* Farrar, Straus & Giroux (New York, NY), 1988.

Brian J. Heinz, *The Alley Cat,* Delacorte (New York, NY), 1993.

Jane Yolen, *Good Griselle,* Harcourt Brace (San Diego, CA), 1994.

Joy Cowley, *The Mouse Bride,* Scholastic (New York, NY), 1995.

Eve Bunting, *I Am the Mummy Heb-Nefert,* Harcourt Brace (San Diego, CA), 1997.

Jane Yolen, *The Book of Fairy Holidays,* Blue Sky Press (New York, NY), 1998.

Susan Pearson, *Silver Morning,* Harcourt Brace (San Diego, CA), 1998.

Nancy Willard, *The Tale I Told Sasha,* Little, Brown (Boston, MA), 1999.

Patricia Lee Gauch, *Poppy's Puppet,* Holt (New York, NY), 1999.

Susan Campbell Bartoletti, *The Christmas Promise,* Holt (New York, NY), 2001.

Catherine Ann Cullen, *The Magical, Mystical, Marvelous Coat,* Little, Brown (Boston, MA), 2001.

Lauren Thompson, *One Starry Night,* Simon & Schuster (New York, NY), 2002.

K.P. Bath, *The Secret of Castle Cant: Being an Account of the Remarkable Adventures of Lucy Wickwright, Maidservant and Spy,* Little, Brown (Boston, MA), 2004.

Gail Carson Levine, *Fairy Dust and the Quest for the Egg,* Disney Press (New York, NY), 2005.

Gail Carson Levine, *Fairy Haven and the Quest for the Wand,* Disney Press (New York, NY), 2007.

Contributor to periodicals, including *Print, Communication Arts,* and *Applied Arts.*

Sidelights

David Christiana, a painter and professor of art, has illustrated more than twenty children's books, including Nancy Willard's *The Tale I Told Sasha* and Catherine

Ann Cullen's *The Magical, Mystical, Marvelous Coat.* Christiana's work has also appeared in such publications as *Print* and *Applied Arts,* and his paintings have been exhibited internationally.

In *The First Snow,* a self-illustrated tale, Christiana presents a fable about the changing of the seasons. When Mother Nature, as a young girl, prevents winter from appearing one year, the planet's vegetation grows lush and wildly out of control. Winter then enlists the help of Aunt Arctica to persuade Mother Nature that his chilly touch is needed. According to Susan Dove Lempke, writing in *Booklist,* the author/illustrator's "whimsical story is paired with swirling paintings," and *Horn Book* critic Lolly Robinson stated that "Christiana's watercolor-and-pencil illustrations resemble [nineteenth-century illustrator] Arthur Rackham's drawings in design and variety of line." A popular Christmas Carol is the inspiration for *O Come, All Ye Faithful,* another self-illustrated work. Here Christiana's gouache paintings "provide a flesh yet fittingly respectful look at the Nativity," a *Publishers Weekly* contributor wrote.

Christiana has also enjoyed successful collaborations with several highly regarded children's authors. He teams with Eve Bunting for *I Am the Mummy Heb-Nefert,* in which a female mummy wistfully recounts her life in ancient Egypt. Christiana's watercolors "superbly capture the contrast between the breathtaking beauty of the young woman . . . and the frighteningly wizened mummy," noted Lempke of this work. In *The Tale I Told Sasha,* Willard offers an imaginative story of a young girl who discovers a dreamlike world. Critics praised the combination of Willard's text and Christiana's illustrations. In *Booklist,* GraceAnne A. DeCandido observed that the book's "pages draw the attention again and again, as connections between the poem and the pictures insinuate themselves and the perspectives shimmer and re-form," and a *Publishers Weekly* contributor noted that the illustrator's "fey, dreamy watercolors of a surreal landscape match the poem's fantastical mood while preserving its ambiguities."

Another tale of magic, *Poppy's Puppet* by Patricia Lee Gauch, concerns a toymaker's gift for creating beautiful and lively marionettes from simple pieces of wood. "Christiana's watercolor paintings clothe the story in an appealing combination of gossamer and homespun," Carolyn Phelan remarked in *Booklist,* and a *Publishers Weekly* reviewer stated that Gauch's narrative "gains a measure of mystery and magic from the ethereal illustrations." Set during the Great Depression, Susan Campbell Bartoletti's *The Christmas Promise* focuses on a homeless young girl and her father. "Christiana's art is quite astounding here, filling oversized pages with haunting images," wrote a critic in *Kirkus Reviews.* In *The Magical, Mystical, Marvelous Coat* a youngster helps a variety of fanciful creatures by offering them the magical buttons from her overcoat. According to Linda Ludke in *School Library Journal,* "Christiana's watercolor illustrations are stylized and slightly haunting with dark, shadowy backgrounds, unconventional perspectives, and gaunt figures with angular features."

Christiana has also illustrated a pair of works by Gail Carson Levine that are set in Peter Pan's Neverland. Reviewing *Fairy Dust and the Quest for the Egg* in *School Library Journal,* Elizabeth Bird remarked that "Christiana's lush, full-color illustrations are breathtaking." The illustrator's work in *Fairy Haven and the Quest for the Wand* garnered praise from *School Library Journal* critic Pat Leach, who stated that his "watercolors convey a nostalgic tone; their soft colors reflect the feel of fantasy."

David Christiana's evocative crayon and ink wash images capture the emotions of the young heroine in Susan Campbell Bartoletti's **The Christmas Promise.** (Illustration copyright © 2001 by David Christiana. Reproduced by permission of Scholastic, Inc.)

Biographical and Critical Sources

PERIODICALS

Booklist, February 1, 1997, Susan Dove Lempke, review of *The First Snow,* p. 945; May 15, 1997, Susan Dove Lempke, review of *I Am the Mummy Heb-Nefert,* p. 1576; March 15, 1998, Ilene Cooper, review of *Silver Morning,* p. 1250; June 1, 1999, GraceAnne A. DeCandido, review of *The Tale I Told Sasha,* p. 1826;

Christiana plays with perspective in his illustrations for Joy Cowley's **The Mouse Bride.** (Illustration copyright © 1995 by David Christiana. Reproduced by permission of Scholastic, Inc.)

September 15, 1999, Carolyn Phelan, review of *Poppy's Puppet,* p. 267; September 15, 2001, GraceAnne A. DeCandido, review of *The Christmas Promise,* p. 234; December 15, 2001, Lauren Peterson, review of *The Magical, Mystical, Marvelous Coat,* p. 738; August, 2005, Jennifer Mattson, review of *Fairy Dust and the Quest for the Egg,* p. 2023; January 1, 2008, Jennifer Mattson, review of *Fairy Haven and the Quest for the Wand,* p. 76.

Horn Book, March-April, 1997, Lolly Robinson, review of *The First Snow,* p. 191.

Kirkus Reviews, August 1, 2001, review of *The Magical, Mystical, Marvelous Coat,* p. 1120; October 15, 2001, review of *The Christmas Promise,* p. 1480; November 1, 2003, review of *O Come, All Ye Faithful,* p. 1315; August 1, 2005, review of *Fairy Dust and the Quest For the Egg,* p. 853; July 1, 2007, review of *Fairy Haven and the Quest for the Wand.*

Publishers Weekly, April 16, 1999, review of *The Tale I Told Sasha,* p. 82; July 19, 1999, review of *Poppy's Puppet,* p. 194; September 3, 2001, review of *The Magical, Mystical, Marvelous Coat,* p. 87; September 24, 2001, review of *The Christmas Promise,* p. 53; September 22, 2003, review of *O Come, All Ye Faithful,* p. 68; August 29, 2005, review of *Fairy Dust and the Quest for the Egg,* p. 56.

School Library Journal, October, 2001, review of *The Christmas Promise,* p. 62; December, 2001, Linda Ludke, review of *The Magical, Mystical, Marvelous Coat,* p. 97; October, 2003, Eva Mitnick, review of *O Come, All Ye Faithful,* p. 69; October, 2005, Elizabeth Bird, review of *Fairy Dust and the Quest for the Egg,* p. 119; November, 2007, Pat Leach, review of *Fairy Haven and the Quest for the Wand,* p. 94.

ONLINE

David Christiana Home Page, http://www.davidchristiana. com (October 31, 2008).

University of Arizona Web site, http://www.arizona.edu/ (October 31, 2008), "David Christiana."*

*   *   *

CONDON, Ken

Personal

Married; children: one daughter. *Education:* Art Institute of Boston, degree.

Addresses

Office—126 Ashfield Mt. Rd., Ashfield, MA 01330. *E-mail*—ken@kencondon.com.

Career

Illustrator, 1981—. Clients include Traveler's Insurance, Fidelity Investments, Cooper's & Lybrand, Hewlett Packard, and Ameritech.

Member

Western Massachusetts Illustrators Guild.

Illustrator

Jane Yolen, editor, *Sky Scrape/City Scape: Poems of City Life,* Boyds Mills Press (Honesdale, PA), 1996.

Allan A. De Fina, *When a City Leans against the Sky* (poems), Boyds Mills Press (Honesdale, PA), 1997.

Monica Gunning, *America, My New Home* (poems), Boyds Mills Press (Honesdale, PA), 2004.

Andrea Cheng, *Tire Mountain,* Boyds Mills Press (Honesdale, PA), 2007.

Contributor of illustrations to periodicals, including *New York Times, Washington Post, Fortune, Runner's World,* and *Parenting.*

Sidelights

A graduate of the Art Institute of Boston, Ken Condon has been a freelance illustrator since 1981. His work has appeared in such publications as the *New York Times*

Ken Condon captures the majesty of a nation's treasured monument in his artwork for Monica Gunning's **America, My New Home.** (Boyds Mills Press, Inc., 2004. Illustration © 2004 by Ken Condon. Reprinted by permission.)

and the *Washington Post,* and his clients include Fidelity Investments, Hewlett Packard, and Ameritech, among others.

Condon has also illustrated a number of well-received picture books for young readers. His debut effort, *Sky Scrape/City Scape: Poems of City Life,* is a collection edited by Jane Yolen that contains twenty-five poems about crowds, subways, neon signs, and other facets of urban living. The anthology includes Carl Sandburg's "Prayers of Steel," Lilian Moore's "Pigeons," and Norma Farber's "Manhattan Lullaby," as well as poems by Langston Hughes, Judith Thurman, and Felice Holman. To create the artwork for the volume, Condon utilized a variety of media, including charcoal, gouache, oil stick, oil pastel, and chalk pastel. According to *Booklist* contributor Hazel Rochman, the "rousing illustrations" in *Sky Scrape/City Scape,* "filled with light and color, express the rumble and rush of city life."

Condon has also created illustrations for Monica Gunning's *America, My New Home,* another collection of poems. A native of Jamaica, Gunning moved to the United States as a teenager in the 1950s; her work describes the experiences of an immigrant youngster who has come to live in North America. The often-overwhelmed young girl, while confused by the unfamiliar sights and sounds of the city, also finds herself enthralled by such wonders as the Statue of Liberty, the Lincoln Memorial, and the Metropolitan Museum of Art. "Condon's bright, upbeat urban scenes clearly show that the child does miss home," observed Rochman, and Lee Bock noted in *School Library Journal* that the illustrator's "rendering of buildings is skillful as are his portraits, which often merely suggest facial features." "Complemented by colorful chalk-and-oil pastels, the poems speak to anyone new to this country," observed a critic in a *Kirkus Reviews* appraisal of *America, My New Home.*

A boy helps his family find a peaceful resolution to its conflict in *Tire Mountain,* a picture book by Andrea Cheng that also features Condon's art. Although Aaron loves the location of his home, which sits next to his father's tire shop, the youngster's mother has grown tired of the noise and smell. When Aaron's mom begins looking for a tidy new house in the suburbs, her son becomes upset at the thought of leaving his favorite play area: the mountain of used tires behind the tire store. After he discovers an empty lot nearby, Aaron devises a perfect solution to his dilemma. Condon's artwork drew praise from several critics, a contributor in *Kirkus Reviews* remarking that the book's "detailed illustrations are realistically depictive of the city and done in subtle chalky hues." In the words of a *Publishers Weekly* reviewer, Condon's "warm colors and mural-like qualities feel absolutely right. It's a kid's-eye view of the world, where physical presences offer rock-solid comfort."

A child's ability to find fun anywhere is the focus of Condon's art for **Tire Mountain,** *a picture book by Andrea Cheng.* (Boyds Mills Press, 2007. Illustration © 2007 by Ken Condon. All rights reserved. Reproduced by permission.)

Biographical and Critical Sources

PERIODICALS

Booklist, May 15, 1996, Hazel Rochman, review of *Sky Scrape/City Scape: Poems of City Life,* p. 1587; November 15, 2004, Hazel Rochman, review of *America, My New Home,* p. 575.

Kirkus Reviews, November 15, 2004, review of *America, My New Home,* p. 1089; July 1, 2007, review of *Tire Mountain.*

Publishers Weekly, August 20, 2007, review of *Tire Mountain,* p. 67.

School Library Journal, December, 2004, Lee Bock, review of *America, My New Home,* p. 130.

ONLINE

Western Massachusetts Illustrators Guild Web site, http://www.wmig.org/ (October 31, 2008), "Ken Condon."*

*   *   *

CORNWELL, Autumn

Personal

Daughter of missionaries; married; husband's name J.C. (a visual effects artist); children: Dexter. *Education:* Attended college in California. *Hobbies and other interests:* Traveling.

Addresses

Home—Los Angeles, CA. *Agent*—Rosemary Stimola, Stimola Literary Studio, 306 Chase Ct., Edgewater, NJ 07020. *E-mail*—autumn@autumncornwell.com.

Career

Writer. Has also worked in the television and film industry.

Member

Society of Children's Book Writers and Illustrators.

Writings

Carpe Diem (novel), Feiwel and Friends (New York, NY), 2007.

Sidelights

A dedicated world traveler, Autumn Cornwell was inspired to write her young-adult novel *Carpe Diem* while visiting Southeast Asia. "The adventures and mishaps I experienced in Malaysia, Cambodia, and Laos lent themselves to the story of a girl transformed by travel," the author remarked in an interview on the *Ya Ya Yas* Web log. "How would a sheltered American teen who'd never left the state she was born in react to being plucked from Washington State and plopped into a land of temples and squat toilets?"

Cornwell's zest for travel began at a young age; she spent part of her childhood in New Papua with her missionary parents. In an interview with Jen Garsee on the *Class of 2k7* Web log, the author recalled those adventurous times: "I ate guavas from our own trees, played in waist-high mud on river banks, visited tribes of reformed headhunters and cannibals, lived through an 8.0 earthquake, cavorted outside during monsoons, almost drowned three times, watched my sister fall into an open sewer in Jakarta, kept my own pet fruit bat—and loved (almost) every single minute of it."

Cornwell's debut work of fiction, *Carpe Diem,* focuses on sixteen-year-old Vassar Spore, an ambitious honors student who finds—to her great surprise—that she will be spending the summer backpacking through the jungles of Southeast Asia with her bohemian grandmother. Once there, Vassar braves the extreme and unfamiliar conditions, learns the truth behind a old family secret, and discovers hidden strengths she never knew she had. In her interview, Cornwell described writing her novel as a "journey of transformation. Vassar's physical journey mirrors her interior journey. She's forced to deal with issues like 'fish out of water' and how rugged travel brings out the 'Extreme You'—the real self with all its flaws, idiosyncrasies, and prejudices."

Carpe Diem garnered praise from several critics. A contributor in *Kirkus Reviews* called the work "a witty coming-of-age adventure," and Vicki Reutter, writing in *School Library Journal,* stated that Cornwell's "well-crafted story maintains its page-turning pace while adding small doses of cultural insight and humor." In *Publishers Weekly,* a critic observed that "the exotic settings and the wacky predicaments will exercise a strong enough grip to hold readers' imaginations."

Biographical and Critical Sources

PERIODICALS

Booklist, August, 1007, Michael Cart, review of *Carpe Diem,* p. 63.
Publishers Weekly, September 3, 2007, review of *Carpe Diem,* p. 60.
School Library Journal, November, 2007, Vicki Reutter, review of *Carpe Diem,* p. 118.

ONLINE

Autumn Cornwell Home Page, http://www.autumncornwell.com (October 31, 2008).
Class of 2k7 Web log, http://community.livejournal.com/classof2k7/ (December 22, 2007), Jen Garsee, interview with Cornwell.
Class of 2k7 Web site, http://classof2k7.com/ (October 31, 2008), "Autumn Cornwell."
Ya Ya Yas Web log, http://theyayayas.wordpress.com/ (November 6, 2007), "Winter Blog Blast Tour: Autumn Cornwell."*

* * *

COUVILLON, Jacques 1978-

Personal

Born 1978, in Cow Island, LA; son of Andrew (a farmer) and Julia (a teacher) Couvillon. *Education:* University of Louisiana, B.A; University of Connecticut, M.B.A.

Addresses

Home—Vermilion Parish, LA. *E-mail*—cowgarcon@gmail.com.

Career

Writer. Worked in retail management and marketing, c. 1990s. Has also worked as a caterer, hotel desk clerk, tie salesperson, secretary, and nanny.

Member

Authors Guild, Authors League.

Writings

The Chicken Dance (novel), Bloomsbury (New York, NY), 2007.

Biographical and Critical Sources

PERIODICALS

Guardian (London, England), April 19, 2008, Philip Ardagh, "Fowl Deeds Will Rise," review of *The Chicken Dance*, p. 20.
Kirkus Reviews, July 15, 2007, review of *The Chicken Dance.*
School Library Journal, November, 2007, Steven Engelfried, review of *The Chicken Dance,* p. 118.

ONLINE

Jacques Couvillon Home Page, http://www.jacquescouvillon.com (October 15, 2008).
Jacques Couvillon Web log, http://www.mynameisjacques.blogspot.com (October 15, 2008).
That Other Paper Online, http://thatotherpaper.com/austin/ (December 9, 2007), Nicole Haddad, "Jacques Couvillon: What's Funnier than a Chicken Farm?"

* * *

CUYLER, Margery 1948-
(Margery Stuyvesant Cuyler, Daisy Wallace)

Personal

Born December 31, 1948, in Princeton, NJ; daughter of Lewis Baker and Margery Pepperell Cuyler; married John Newman Hewson Perkins (a psychoanalyst), August 23, 1979; children Thomas, Timothy. *Education:* Sarah Lawrence College, B.A., 1970.

Addresses

Home—Princeton, NJ. *E-mail*—margery.cuyler@verizon.net.

Career

Publisher, editor, and author of children's books. Atlantic Monthly Press, Boston, MA, assistant to editor of children's books, 1970-71; Walker & Co., New York, NY, editor of children's books, 1972-74; Holiday House, New York, NY, vice president and editor-in-chief of children's books, 1974-95; Henry Holt & Co., New York, NY, vice president and associate publisher, Books for Young Readers, 1996-97; Golden Books Family Entertainment, vice president and director of trade publishing, 1997-99; Windslow Press, New York, NY, vice president and editor-in-chief, beginning 1999; Marshall Cavendish, Tarrytown, NY, currently director of trade publishing. Lecturer on children's book editing, Rutgers University, 1974, New School for Social Research, 1975, and Vassar College, 1984. Board member, Women's National Book Association and Children's Book Council, 1980-82. Library trustee and member of alumnae board, Sarah Lawrence College

Awards, Honors

Children's Choice designation, International Reading Association/Children's Book Council, for *The Trouble with Soap* and *Witch Poems;* New Jersey Institute of Technology Author's Award, 1988, for *Fat Santa.*

Writings

PICTURE BOOKS

Jewish Holidays, illustrated by Lisa C. Wesson, Holt (New York, NY), 1978.
The All-around Pumpkin Book, illustrated by Corbett Jones, Holt (New York, NY), 1980.
The All-around Christmas Book, illustrated by Corbett Jones, Holt (New York, NY), 1982.
Sir William and the Pumpkin Monster, illustrated by Marcia Winborn, Holt (New York, NY), 1984.
Freckles and Willie, illustrated by Marcia Winborn, Holt (New York, NY), 1986.
Fat Santa, illustrated by Marcia Winborn, Holt (New York, NY), 1987.
Freckles and Jane, illustrated by Leslie Holt Morrill, Holt (New York, NY), 1989.
Shadow's Baby, illustrated by Ellen Weiss, Clarion (New York, NY), 1989.
Baby Dot, illustrated by Ellen Weiss, Clarion (New York, NY), 1990.
Daisy's Crazy Thanksgiving, illustrated by Robin Kramer, Holt (New York, NY), 1990.
That's Good! That's Bad!, illustrated by David Catrow, Holt (New York, NY), 1991.
The Christmas Snowman, illustrated by Johanna Westerman, Arcade, 1992.
Buddy Bear and the Bad Guys, illustrated by Janet Stevens, Clarion (New York, NY), 1993.
The Biggest, Best Snowman, illustrated by Will Hillenbrand, Scholastic (New York, NY), 1998.
From Here to There, illustrated by Yu Cha Pak, Henry Holt (New York, NY), 1999.
One Hundredth-Day Worries, illustrated by Arthur Howard, Simon & Schuster (New York, NY), 2000.
Road Signs: A Harey Race with a Tortoise: An Aesop Fable Adapted, illustrated by Steve Haskamp, Winslow Press, 2000.
Stop, Drop, and Roll: Fire Safety, illustrated by Arthur Howard, Simon & Schuster (New York, NY), 2001.
Skeleton Hiccups, illustrated by S.D. Schindler, Margaret K. McElderry Books (New York, NY), 2002.

That's Good! That's Bad! in the Grand Canyon, illustrated by David Catrow, Henry Holt (New York, NY), 2002.

Ah-choo!, illustrated by Bruce McNally, Scholastic (New York, NY), 2002.

Please Say Please!: Penguin's Guide to Manners, illustrated by Will Hillenbrand, Scholastic (New York, NY), 2004.

Big Friends, illustrated by Ezra Tucker, Walker & Co. (New York, NY), 2004.

The Bumpy Little Pumpkin, illustrated by Will Hillenbrand, Scholastic (New York, NY), 2005.

Groundhog Stays up Late, illustrated by Jean Cassels, Walker & Co. (New York, NY), 2005.

Please Play Safe!: Penguin's Guide to Playground Safety, illustrated by Will Hillenbrand, Scholastic (New York, NY), 2006.

That's Good! That's Bad! in Washington, DC, illustrated by Michael Garland, Henry Holt (New York, NY), 2007.

Kindness Is Cooler, Mrs. Ruler, illustrated by Sachiko Yohikawa, Simon & Schuster (New York, NY), 2007.

Hooray for Reading Day!, illustrated by Arthur Howard, Simon & Schuster (New York, NY), 2008.

Monster Mess!, illustrated by S.D. Schindler, Margaret K. McElderry Books (New York, NY), 2008.

(Adaptor) *We're Going on a Lion Hunt,* illustrated by Joe Mathieu, Marshall Cavendish (Tarrytown, NY), 2008.

Princess Bess Gets Dressed, illustrated by Heather Maione, Simon & Schuster (New York, NY), 2009.

Bullies Never Win, illustrated by Arthur Howard, Simon & Schuster (New York, NY), 2009.

BEGINNING READERS

The Trouble with Soap, Dutton (New York, NY), 1982.

Weird Wolf, illustrated by Dirk Zimmer, Holt (New York, NY), 1989.

Invisible in the Third Grade, illustrated by Mirko Gabler, Holt (New York, NY), 1995.

The Battlefield Ghost, illustrated by Arthur Howard, Scholastic (New York, NY), 1999.

FOR CHILDREN; EDITOR, UNDER PSEUDONYM DAISY WALLACE

Monster Poems, illustrated by Kay Chorao, Holiday House (New York, NY), 1976.

Witch Poems, illustrated by Trina Schart Hyman, Holiday House (New York, NY), 1976.

Giant Poems, illustrated by Margot Tomes, Holiday House (New York, NY), 1978.

Ghost Poems, illustrated by Tomie De Paola, Holiday House (New York, NY), 1979.

Fairy Poems, illustrated by Trina Schart Hyman, Holiday House (New York, NY), 1980.

Adaptations

Several of Cuyler's books have been adapted as audiobooks, including *That's Good! That's Bad!, The Biggest, Best Snowman,* and *One Hundredth-Day Worries.*

Sidelights

Margery Cuyler was already an experienced editor of children's books for New York City-based publisher Holiday House when she decided to try her hand at writing. While she once admitted to *SATA* that her passion has been for editing children's books, she has come to love writing as well, "since it exercises my imagination in a more personal and introspective fashion." In addition to authoring a wide range of both nonfiction and fiction picture books, including *Freckles and Willie, Fat Santa, Skeleton Hiccups,* and *Groundhog Stays up Late,* Cuyler has also written chapter books for more talented readers.

Born in Princeton, New Jersey, Cuyler was raised in a large family and grew up in the oldest house in town, part of a family that included four siblings and an equal number of cousins who had joined Cuyler's family after their own mother died. After graduating from high school, she attended Sarah Lawrence College, earning her bachelor's degree in 1970. From there, it was a quick move to Boston to work for Atlantic Monthly Press before Cuyler returned to New York City and found a job with Holiday House. Cuyler found Holiday House to be the perfect fit with her own career aspirations; beginning there in 1974, she served as its editor-in-chief for children's fiction for many years before ex-

Margery Cuyler's chapter book **Invisible in the Third Grade** *features amusing pen-and-ink illustrations by Mirko Gabler.* (Henry Holt and Company, 1995. Illustration copyright © 1995 by Mirko Gabler. All rights reserved. Reproduced by permission.)

panding her career opportunities at other publishers, among them Henry Holt, Golden Books, and Winslow Press.

For Cuyler's first self-penned work, *Jewish Holidays,* she relied on the generous assistance of Jewish friends to get her facts straight. Her second picture book, *The All-around Pumpkin Book,* was written in three days, and was inspired by a dream. "I woke up . . . at two in the morning and I started writing," she told interviewer Jim Roginski in *Behind the Covers: Interviews with Authors and Illustrators of Books for Children and Young Adults.* Visualizing all the illustrations in her mind, she quickly made a dummy of the book, sketched out the pictures as she imagined them, and then added the text. Following the entire life span of the typical Halloween Jack-o'-lantern, from seed to garden to its ultimate destiny as a holiday decoration or pumpkin pie, the book was described by Ethel L. Heins in *Horn Book* as "a compendium of fascinating and practical facts," as well as a list of nontraditional uses for the fall squash. "Here's a way to stretch Halloween all around the year," commented Barbara Elleman in her *Booklist* appraisal of *The All-around Pumpkin Book.*

In *The All-around Christmas Book* Cuyler uses much the same format as *The All-around Pumpkin Book.* After presenting the story of the Nativity, she includes a discussion of folklore, crafts, recipes, games, and other information about the Christian holiday, both in its religious and secular manifestations. The wide variety of celebrations undertaken by many different cultures around the world is explored, with answers to such questions as where the tradition of decorating trees came from and an explanation of the history of advent wreaths. Praising the information presented, a *Publishers Weekly* reviewer termed the work "a treasure of holiday lore."

Although her earliest books were nonfiction, Cuyler has more recently focused on creating entertaining picture books for preschoolers and children in the early grades. In *Shadow's Baby,* a little dog is determined to take care of the new baby in his house, but when the infant grows older and wants to play with other things, the attentive Shadow gets in the way. Fortunately, the dog's owner realizes that Shadow feels useless with nothing to care for; the introduction of a new puppy into the home provides a ready solution. Ann A. Flowers, reviewing the book for *Horn Book,* called *Shadow's Baby* "as warm and affectionate as a puppy," while a *Publishers Weekly* critic commended Cuyler's "sensitivity to the feelings of all involved" in this warmhearted story.

Although Cuyler admits to being a cat owner, dogs and their human companions figure prominently in several of her stories, including her tales about Freckles the dog and Willie, the teenage boy. In *Freckles and Willie,* Freckles feels forlorn when Willie starts to spend most of his time with a girl named Jane; the girl, for her part, is obviously not a person of character—she dislikes dogs and makes Willie keep Freckles away from her

when she is around. Ultimately, Willie realizes where his true loyalty lies, and boy and dog are once again the best of friends—"a nice lesson in relationships and loyalty," according to a *Publishers Weekly* critic. However, despite her mistake in bringing a jar of flea powder to Freckles's birthday party, Jane redeems herself in *Freckles and Jane,* as Freckles gets the stuck-up teen out of a tight situation involving a German shepherd on the loose and finally wins her affection. A *Kirkus Reviews* commentator dubbed *Freckles and Jane* "a satisfying 'here and now' story."

With *Fat Santa,* Cuyler returns to the subject of Christmas. Molly is determined to wait up for Santa's arrival; she settles into a comfortable chair and listens to Christmas carols on her headphones while she waits. Awakened out of a semi-sleep in the wee hours of the morning by a cloud of ash, the girl realizes that Santa has gotten stuck in the chimney! After his rescue, the jolly man exhibits some caution and convinces Molly to don his red jacket and make the rest of his gift-giving rounds. Praising the book's energy, *Bulletin of the Center for Children's Books* contributor Betsy Hearne cited *Fat Santa* as "a holiday picture book that will be easy for children to listen to, look at, and like." In *Booklist* Phillis Wilson pointed out that "the open end works in this well-constructed plot," while a *Publishers Weekly* critic praised Cuyler for "amiably captur[ing]" the spirit of Christmas Eve.

Cuyler focuses on another holiday in *Daisy's Crazy Thanksgiving.* Here Daisy begs to be excused from her parents' busy restaurant to join her grandparents for the holiday dinner, only to discover pandemonium in a house full of eccentric relatives, a menagerie of pet animals, and an absentminded Granny who has forgotten to turn on the oven for the turkey. "No getting around the success of the story's wacky humor," observed *Booklist* reviewer Denise Wilms, the critic going on to dub Cuyler's book "offbeat and, intermittently, very funny."

A more serious story is at the center of *From Here to There,* which helps young children gain perspective on their role as part of the larger world. In the book, Maria Mendoza introduces herself, at first within the context of her role in her family, then to her neighborhood, state, country, and beyond, Cuyler's concept-driven text is enhanced by "gorgeously rendered" watercolor and pastel illustrations by Yu Cha Pak, according to a *Publishers Weekly* critic. Praising *From Here to There* as a "heartfelt picture book," the *Publishers Weekly* reviewer added that Cuyler and Pak's work takes readers on an "enlightening journey" that serves as "both a meditation on humanity's small place in the universe and a celebration of each person's immutable individuality."

Skeleton Hiccups also contains a seasonal theme as it relates the efforts of a frustrated skeleton that cannot rid itself of the hiccups. Unfortunately, when you are a skeleton, the tried-and-true remedy of getting the hiccups scared out of you does not work; the most frightening "boo!" of Skeleton's best friend Ghost is nothing to be startled about, and drinking water while hanging its head upside down just leaks the liquid out of Skeleton's empty eye sockets. Praising the quirky artwork contributed by S.D. Schindler, *Booklist* reviewer Jeanette Larson called *Skeleton Hiccups* "a treat for children who can laugh at the slightly macabre," and *Horn Book* contributor Joanna Rudge Long predicted that Cuyler's simple text, with its "hic, hic, hic" refrain, is "sure to have kids giggling and joining in."

Groundhog Day is the holiday at the core of *Groundhog Stays up Late,* an updated Aesop's tale that features artwork by Jean Cassels. Here Roly-poly Groundhog wants to play with his friends in the fall, and he puts off preparing his burrow for winter. When the snows come, Groundhog's playmates snuggle down for a long nap while he goes hungry, until he finds a way to trick them into thinking it is time for a spring feast. Although Groundhog ultimately snoozes through his appointed appearance when spring really does arrive, the playful creature does not learn his lesson, and the closing pages

Will Hillenbrand contributes entertaining art to Cuyler's well-mannered picture book **Please Say Please!** (Illustration © 2004 by Will Hellenbrand. Reprinted by permission of Scholastic, Inc.)

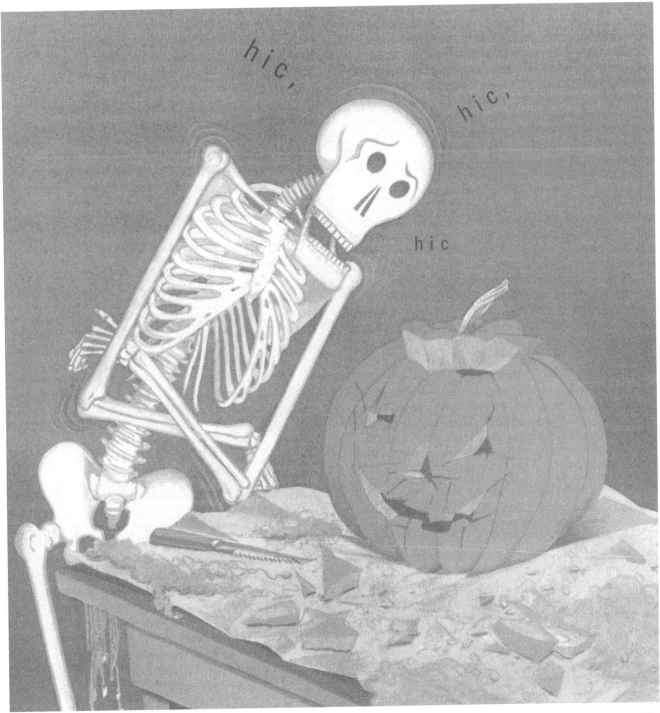

***Cuyler presents a Halloween story with a twist in* Skeleton Hiccups, *featuring artwork by S.D. Schindler.* (Illustration © 2002 by S.D. Schindler. Reproduced by permission of Margaret K. McElderry Books, an imprint of Simon & Schuster Children's Publishing Division.)

of the book find Groundhog as before, spending the fall playing rather than preparing for winter. In *School Library Journal* Linda L. Walkins praised Cassels' art, writing that "the colors and textures of the changing seasons are beautifully portrayed" in *Groundhog Stays up Late*. Cuyler's accompanying text "bubbles with comic winks," wrote a *Publishers Weekly* reviewer, and its rhythm "will encourage even antsy youngsters to snuggle." "Children who like to test limits will identify with" Cuyler's impractical hero, concluded *Booklist*

contributor Kay Weisman, the critic adding that the upbeat ending of *Groundhog Stays up Late* will entertain Groundhog Day story-hour audiences.

That's Good! That's Bad!, Cuyler's story of a little boy traveling by balloon in a wild trip over a zoo, successfully combines sound effects, a large format, and plenty of opportunity for audience participation where "kids will enjoy the push-me-pull-me tension," according to Roger Sutton in his review for the *Bulletin of the Center for Children's Books*. In a sequel, *That's Good!*

Road Signs, *a picture book by Cuyler, features child-friendly illustrations by Steve Haskamp.* (Winslow Press Children, 2000. Illustration © 2000 by Steve Haskamp. To further explore the theme of this book through activities, games and links all over the world, please go to: www.readandclick.com. For educators: This book has been included in the Read&Click&Learn Curriculum Learning System's virtual library. All rights reserved. Reproduced by permission.)

That's Bad! in the Grand Canyon, the boy joins his grandmother for a trip to the Grand Canyon, where he again encounters good and bad in a series of adventures, while *That's Good! That's Bad! in Washington, DC* finds him in the nation's capital. *School Library Journal* contributor Marian Drabkin noted that, with its humorous plot and singsongy text, *That's Good! That's Bad! in the Grand Canyon* "begs to be read aloud" and would be a "natural for storytime," and Wendy Lukehart noted in the same periodical that "the sound effects and refrain" in Cuyler's text for *That's Good! That's Bad! in Washington, DC* "allow plenty of opportunities for audience participation."

Cuyler takes her readers to school along with a young girl named Jessica in *One Hundredth-Day Worries* and *Stop, Drop, and Roll: Fire Safety.* In *One Hundredth-Day Worries* readers worry right along with Jessica as she tackles the first weeks of school in Mr. Martin's class, and in *Stop, Drop, and Roll* she is nervous about messing up her role in a school-wide demonstration for Fire Prevention Week. In *Stop, Drop, and Roll* Cuyler "humorously driv[es] . . . home basic fire-safety tips

for children to follow," according to *Booklist* critic Annie Ayres. Another kindergarten classroom is the focus of *Kindness Is Cooler, Mrs. Ruler,* which emphasizes the reward to be found in good behavior via Cuyler's rhyming text and cartoon art by Sachiko Yoshikawa. The story features "the same enthusiasm, counting practice, and humor" that characterized *One Hundredth-Day Worries,* concluded Weisman in *Booklist.*

Teaming up with artist Will Hillenbrand, Cuyler presents a quirky slant on etiquette books with both *Please Say Please!: Penguin's Guide to Manners* and its companion volume, *Please Play Safe!: Penguin's Guide to Playground Safety.* In *Please Say Please!* Penguin plans a wonderful dinner for his friends and dresses the part, but is disappointed when guests Giraffe, Pig, and Elephant show that their table manners are not up to par with the fancy feast. Playtime manners and safety concerns are addressed in *Please Play Safe!,* in which Penguin and his friends survive some near misses on the playground. In *Publishers Weekly* a critic cited Cuyler for the "simple, crisp text" she creates for *Please Say Please!,* while Christine M. Heppermann dubbed the book "a natural read-aloud, with a generous helping of onomatopoeia." Writing that Cuyler "covers all the bases" in her focus on sharing, playing games, and proper use of playground equipment, a *Kirkus Reviews* writer added that in *Please Play Safe!* Hillenbrand's ink-and-crayon cartoon art "masterfully portrays facial expressions." In *Booklist* Ilene Cooper described the playground guide as "activity-filled," noting that it "cleverly plays on young children's burgeoning sense of irony."

Cuyler's first novel, *The Trouble with Soap,* was written after she attended a writer's conference in her capacity as editor. "I sat around for two weeks listening to people read their stuff," she told interviewer Roginski. "Then I started writing." *The Trouble with Soap* is based on its author's own experiences as a not-so-model child. In the novel, thirteen-year-old Lucinda Sokoloff—a.k.a Soap—is suspended from school due to her excessive zeal in playing practical jokes. After an incident involving a roll of plastic wrap and the toilets in the boys' lavatory cause her to be shipped off to Miss Pringle's Private School for Girls along with partner-in-crime and narrator Laurie Endersby, Soap rejects the snobbish students in favor of her own company. Laurie, on the other hand, desperately wants to be accepted by the in-crowd at her new school, and she ultimately tells a painful secret about Soap's father as a way of gaining that acceptance. A *Publishers Weekly* writer observed that *The Trouble with Soap* is completely unlike any of Cuyler's former works and "displays impressive versatility."

"I wanted to write about what it is that makes twelve- and thirteen-year-old kids so sensitive to peer pressure," Cuyler explained to Roginski of her decision to write books for older readers. "Why do they care so much about what other kids think of them? They're really imprisoned by collective values—how they think, how they dress, how they look at the world. It's a very conformist way of living. It's hard to be outside the collective spirit at that age and yet my character Soap is. That fascinates me because the whole key of life is to break through the walls that parents and society build around you, to be an individual, to express yourself."

Cuyler has followed *The Trouble with Soap* with several more novels for young people, including *Invisible in the Third Grade, Weird Wolf,* and *The Battlefield Ghost.* In *Weird Wolf* her protagonist again has trouble fitting in with his friends. It is not so much that nine-year-old Harry Walpole is unpopular, but he has a terribly embarrassing problem: he turns into a wolf when the moon is full. As inconvenient as this is—it gets increasingly difficult to come up with excuses for being caught running around naked outside at sunrise—Harry is fortunate that his blood lust only extends to hamburgers. A research trip to the library results in several possible cures for his problem, and one of them actually works, in a book critics praised as appropriately seductive for even the most reluctant of readers. Indeed, *Weird*

Wolf is "destined for greatness in the opinion of werewolf-crazy eight year olds," noted Kathryn Pierson in a review for the *Bulletin of the Center for Children's Books.*

The Battlefield Ghost marks a bit of a departure for Cuyler, because the story mixes historical fact with fiction. Actually, the book was inspired by the author's interest in her home town of Princeton, where she lives in the same colonial-era house where she grew up. In the story, John and his sister move into what their new Princeton neighbors claim is a house haunted by the spirits of the 1777 Battle of Princeton. After a series of uncanny but not terribly frightening hauntings, the children learn that their home is haunted by a Hessian mercenary soldier who was killed while fighting for the British. When they discover that the soldier is wandering the area in search of his long-dead horse, John and his sister figure out how to put the spirit to rest in a novel that *Booklist* reviewer Jean Franklin praised as a "fast read" that "offers a nice blend of realism and the supernatural." A *Publishers Weekly* contributor also praised Cuyler for presenting the history of the battle in an entertaining fashion, noting that in addition to providing historical notes, *The Battlefield Ghost* ends with a "vivid, ghostly reenactment on the battlefield."

Biographical and Critical Sources

BOOKS

Roginski, Jim, *Behind the Covers: Interviews with Authors and Illustrators of Books for Children and Young Adults,* Libraries Unlimited (Littleton, CO), 1985, pp. 51-58.

PERIODICALS

Booklist, July 15, 1980, Barbara Elleman, review of *The All-around Pumpkin Book,* p. 1674; November 1, 1987, Phillis Wilson, review of *Fat Santa,* p. 474; October 1, 1990, Denise Wilms, review of *Daisy's Crazy Thanksgiving,* p. 338; December 1, 1991, Deborah Abbott, review of *That's Good! That's Bad! in the Grand Canyon,* pp. 702-703; December 15, 1998, Lauren Peterson, review of *The Biggest, Best Snowman,* p. 754; June 1, 1999, Susan Dove Lempke, review of *From Here to There,* p. 1838; November 1, 1999, GraceAnne A. DeCandido, review of *One Hundredth-Day Worries,* p. 537; November 15, 1999, Jean Franklin, review of *The Battlefield Ghost,* p. 626; December 1, 2000, Michael Cart, review of *Road Signs: A Harey Race with a Tortoise,* p. 717; September 15, 2001, Annie Ayres, review of *Stop, Drop, and Roll: Fire Safety,* p. 230; September 15, 2002, John Peters, review of *Skeleton Hiccups,* p. 245; February 1, 2004, Karin Snelson, review of *Please Say Please!: Penguin's Guide to Manners,* p. 980; April 15, 2004, Hazel Rochman, review of *Big Friends,* p. 1445; September 1, 2005, Gillian Engberg, review of *The Bumpy Little Pumpkin,* p. 143; August 1, 2006, Ilene Cooper, review of *Please Play Safe!: Penguin's Guide to Playground Safety,* p. 84; May 15, 2007, Kay Weisman, review of *Kindness Is Cooler, Mrs. Ruler,* p. 52.

Bulletin of the Center for Children's Books, January, 1979, Zena Sutherland, review of *Jewish Holidays,* p. 77; November, 1987, Betsy Hearne, review of *Fat Santa,* p. 46; January, 1990, Kathryn Pierson, review of *Weird Wolf,* pp. 107-108; December, 1991, Roger Sutton, review of *That's Good! That's Bad! in the Grand Canyon,* p. 87; November, 2001, review of *Stop, Drop, and Roll,* p. 98; September, 2002, review of *Skeleton Hiccups,* p. 11; April 15, 2004, Hope Morrison, review of *Big Friends,* p. 1445; December 1, 2005, Kay Weisman, review of *Groundhog Stays up Late,* p. 53.

Horn Book, October, 1980, Ethel L. Heins, review of *The All-around Pumpkin Book,* p. 534; January, 1990, Ann A. Flowers, review of *Shadow's Baby,* p. 50; September-October, 2002, Joanna Rudge Long, review of *Skeleton Hiccups,* p. 549; May-June, 2004, Christine M. Hepperman, review of *Please Say Please!,* p. 310; July-August, 2006, Bridget T. McCaffrey, review of *Please Play Safe!,* p. 423.

Kirkus Reviews, November 1, 1989, review of *Freckles and Jane,* p. 602; March 15, 2002, review of *That's Good! That's Bad! in the Grand Canyon,* p. 408; April 1, 2004, reviews of *Skeleton Hiccups, Big Friends,* and *Please Say Please!,* p. 327; July 1, 2005, review of *The Bumpy Little Pumpkin,* p. 733; October 15, 2005, review of *Groundhog Stays up Late,* p. 1134; July 1, 2006, review of *Please Play Safe!,* p. 676; June 1, 2007, review of *Kindness Is Cooler, Mrs. Ruler;* July 1, 2007, review of *That's Good! That's Bad! in Washington, DC.*

Publishers Weekly, May 28, 1982, review of *The Trouble with Soap,* p. 72; September 17, 1982, review of *The All-around Christmas Book,* p. 115; April 25, 1986, review of *Freckles and Willie,* p. 78; October 13, 1989, review of *Shadow's Baby,* p. 51; October 30, 1987, review of *Fat Santa,* p. 70; November 9, 1998, review of *The Biggest, Best Snowman,* p. 75; March 15, 1999, review of *From Here to There,* p. 56; September 27, 1999, review of *The Battlefield Ghost,* p. 106; December 13, 1999, review of *One Hundredth-Day Worries,* p. 81; July 10, 2000, review of *Road Signs,* p. 62; September 23, 2002, review of *Skeleton Hiccups,* p. 22; April 19, 2004, review of *Please Say Please!,* p. 59; August 1, 2005, review of *The Bumpy Little Pumpkin,* p. 64; November 14, 2005, review of *Groundhog Stays up Late,* p. 67.

School Library Journal, January, 1979, Joan C. Feldman, review of *Jewish Holidays,* p. 41; September, 2000, Louise L. Sherman, review of *Road Signs,* p. 193; April, 2001, Teresa Bateman, review of *One Hundredth-Day Worries,* p. 74; October, 2001, Roxanne Burg, review of *Stop, Drop, and Roll,* p. 113; June, 2002, Marian Drabkin, review of *That's Good! That's Bad! in the Grand Canyon,* p. 92; October, 2002, Piper L. Nyman, review of *Skeleton Hiccups,* p. 100; April, 2004, Mary N. Oluonye, review of *Big Friends,* and Janet Blair, review of *Please Say Please!,*

both p. 109; August, 2005, Kara Schaff Dean, review of *The Bumpy Little Pumpkin,* p. 87; December, 2005, Linda L. Walkins, review of *Groundhog Stays up Late,* p. 107; August, 2006, Maura Breshahan, review of *Please Play Safe!,* p. 78; June, 2007, Barbara Katz, review of *Kindness Is Cooler, Mrs. Ruler,* p. 96; September, 2007, Wendy Lukehart, review of *That's Good! That's Bad! in Washington, DC,* p. 161.

ONLINE

Margery Cuyler Home Page, http://www.margerycuyler.com (November 28, 2008).*

*   *   *

CUYLER, Margery Stuyvesant
See CUYLER, Margery

*   *   *

DEANS, Karen

Personal

Born in Atlanta, GA; married; children: three. *Education:* American University (Paris, France), degree.

Addresses

Home—Bethesda, MD. *E-mail*—karendeans@woodentile.com.

Career

Muralist, illustrator, fine artist, and author.

Member

Children's Book Guild.

Writings

Playing to Win: The Story of Althea Gibson, illustrated by Elbrite Brown, Holiday House (New York, NY), 2007.

Sidelights

Karen Deans, a muralist and fine artist, is the author of *Playing to Win: The Story of Althea Gibson,* her debut picture book. The idea for the work came to Deans as she searched for biographies of African-American heroes with her school-aged daughter. Spotting a work about legendary tennis pro Arthur Ashe, Deans, a former competitive tennis player herself, recalled her childhood fascination with Gibson, the first black player to win the U.S. Nationals and Wimbledon. As the author stated in an essay on the Children's Book Guild Web site, "I saw an opportunity that connected with my sensibilities and seemed to be waving a flag and shouting 'Write Me! Write Me!'"

In *Playing to Win,* Deans recounts Gibson's often difficult life, from her birth into a family of poor sharecroppers in South Carolina to her rebellious childhood in Harlem, where her energies were first channeled into athletics. Dean also notes Gibson's struggles against discrimination, which she experienced as one of the few minorities playing a sport dominated by whites. "Gibson's missteps both academically and athletically receive mention, lending depth to the scale of her eventual victories," remarked a critic in *Kirkus Reviews.* Judy Chichinski, writing in *School Library Journal,* praised the combination of Deans's narrative and Elbrite Brown's artwork in *Playing to Win,* writing that "the multimedia illustrations are well matched to the power and fluidity of the text."

Biographical and Critical Sources

PERIODICALS

Booklist, September 1, 2007, Carolyn Phelan, review of *Playing to Win: The Story of Althea Gibson,* p. 137.

Kirkus Reviews, July 15, 2007, review of *Playing to Win.*

Publishers Weekly, August 27, 2007, review of *Playing to Win,* p. 89.

School Library Journal, September, 2007, Judy Chichinski, review of *Playing to Win,* p. 182.

ONLINE

Children's Book Guild Web site, http://www.childrens bookguild.org/ (February 1, 2005), Karen Deans, "Blazing Trails for Each Other."

Karen Deans Home Page, http://www.woodentile.com (October 15, 2008).*

Karen Deans' high-energy picture book **Playing to Win** *features brightly colored artwork by Elbrite Brown.* (Illustration copyright © 2007 by Elbrite Brown. All rights reserved. Reproduced by permission of Holiday House, Inc.)

DeLaCROIX, Alice 1940-

Personal

Born 1940, in IN; married; children: two children. *Education:* Purdue University, M.A. *Hobbies and other interests:* Animals, gardening.

Addresses

Home—Penfield, NY.

Career

Educator and author. Purdue University, Purdue, IN, instructor.

Writings

Mattie's Whisper, illustrated by John Dyess, Caroline House (Honesdale, PA), 1992.

The Hero of Third Grade, illustrated by Cynthia Fisher, Holiday House (New York, NY), 2002.

Cover of Alice DeLaCroix's humorous chapter book How to Survive a Totally Boring Summer, *featuring artwork by Cynthia Fisher.* (Illustration copyright © 2007 by Cynthia Fisher. Reproduced by permission of Holiday House, Inc.)

How to Survive a Totally Boring Summer, illustrated by Cynthia Fisher, Holiday House (New York, NY), 2007.

Contributor of stories to periodicals, including *Highlights for Children,* and to the anthology *Bruce Coville's Book of Magic II.*

Sidelights

Alice DeLaCroix became interested in writing children's books while raising her own two children, and she had her first novel, *Mattie's Whisper,* published in 1992. A contributor to *Highlights for Children,* DeLaCroix has also introduced readers to a likeable third grader named Randall in her chapter books *The Hero of Third Grade* and *How to Survive a Totally Boring Summer.*

In *The Hero of Third Grade* Randall's parents have just divorced, and he now finds himself living with his mom in a new town and starting a new school part way through the academic year. When Gordo, the bully in Randall's new third-grade class, decides to make the boy his new target, the beleaguered Randall decides that to model his reaction on those of the eighteenth-century fictional French hero the Scarlet Pimpernel. Acting meek in public and strong in secret, Randall does several good deeds, and along the way, he gains self-confidence. Praising DeLaCroix for creating realistic third-grade characters and relationships, *School Library Journal* critic Elaine E. Knight described *The Hero of Third Grade* as a "humorous . . . book with a quiet message about courage and individuality." In *Booklist,* Connie Fletcher also enjoyed the chapter book, dubbing DeLaCroix's story "funny" and "ingenious," with "a wonderful sense of pacing."

Randall returns in *How to Survive a Totally Boring Summer,* where the challenge is to survive a potentially bleak summer in his new hometown of Rushville. Fortunately, Randall has best friends Max and Tara to help him, and the trio form the Checkmate Squad. Hoping to teach chess to the town's masses, the newly minted fourth graders hatch ambitious plans to take over Rushport park's chess tables for gaming, and even host classes for those unfamiliar with the game. As the summer passes, the new friends Randall makes keep his summer far from boring and even interject a mystery or two into his school vacation. In *School Library Journal* Kelly Roth recommended *How to Survive a Totally Boring Summer* as "a positive story about inclusion and kindness." In addition to enjoying Cynthia Fisher's illustrations, Shelle Rosenfeld commented in *Booklist* that DeLaCroix's "lively novel highlights community building and the rewards of . . . cross-generational relationships."

Biographical and Critical Sources

PERIODICALS

Booklist, January 1, 2003, Connie Fletcher, review of *The Hero of Third Grade,* p. 888; August, 2007, Shelle

Rosenfeld, review of *How to Survive a Totally Boring Summer,* p. 73.

Bulletin of the Center for Children's Books, November, 2002, review of *The Hero of Third Grade,* p. 102.

Kirkus Reviews, October 15, 2002, review of *The Hero of Third Grade,* p. 1528; July 1, 2007, review of *How to Survive a Totally Boring Summer.*

School Library Journal, June, 1992, Carolyn Noah, review of *Mattie's Whisper,* p. 112; December, 2002, Elaine E. Knight, review of *The Hero of Third Grade,* p. 86; July, 2007, Kelly Roth, review of *How to Survive a Totally Boring Summer,* p. 73.*

*   *   *

DeMIJOHN, Thom
See DISCH, Thomas M.

*   *   *

DeVITA, James

Personal

Born in North Babylon, NY; married; children: one son, one daughter. *Education:* Suffolk County Community College, A.A., 1983; University of Wisconsin—Milwaukee, degree, 1987.

Addresses

Home—Spring Green, WI. *Office*—American Players Theatre, P.O. Box 819, Spring Green, WI 53588. *E-mail*—jibvii@charter.net.

Career

Novelist, playwright, and actor. First Stage Children's Theater, Milwaukee, WI, resident playwright; American Players Theater, Spring Green, WI, actor, 1995—; also performed in Australia, Japan, and Germany. Worked as a first mate on charter boats, Long Island, NY; volunteer with Spring Green, WI, Emergency Medical Service.

Awards, Honors

Shubert Fendrich Memorial Playwriting Contest, for *Looking Glass Land;* Distinguished Play Award, American Alliance of Theater and Education; Intellectual Freedom Award, Council of Teachers of English/Language Arts; National Endowment for the Arts fellowship; Chorpenning Award, American Alliance for Theater and Education, 2007, for body of work for young audiences.

Writings

NOVELS

Blue, Laura Geringer Books (New York, NY), 2001.
The Silenced, Eos (New York, NY), 2007.

PLAYS

The Christmas Angel, Dramatic Publishing (Woodstock, IL), 1998.

Excavating Mom, Dramatic Publishing (Woodstock, IL), 1999.

The Swiss Family Robinson (based on the novel by Johann David Wyss), Eldridge Publishing (Tallahassee, FL), 2002.

The Three Musketeers (based on *The Three Guardsmen* by Alexandré Dumas), Baker's Plays (Quincy, MA), 2002.

The Rose of Treason: A Fictional Dramatization Based on the True Story of Sophie Scholl and the White Rose, Anchorage Press Plays (Louisville, KY), 2003.

Dickens in America, produced in Milwaukee, WI, 2006.

Henry IV: The Making of a King, produced in Spring Green, WI, 2008.

(And director) *The Desert Queen,* produced in Spring Green, WI, 2008.

Also author of *Waiting for Vern, Zero Tolerance, Bambi: A Life in the Woods, A Little House Christmas, Treasure Island, Looking Glass Land, Arthur: The Boy Who Would Be King, Wonderland!, Huck Finn, Tom Sawyer, Trials: The Story of Joan of Arc, Beth,* and *A Midnight Cry: The Underground Railroad to Freedom.*

Sidelights

Award-winning playwright James DeVita is the author of the young-adult novels *Blue* and *The Silenced.* A professional actor for more than twenty years, DeVita has toured throughout the United States as well as in Germany, Japan, and Australia. He also serves as the resident playwright at First Stage Children's Theater in Milwaukee, Wisconsin, and is a member of the acting company at the American Players Theater in Spring Green, Wisconsin. DeVita has written a number of plays for young audiences, including *Looking Glass Land,* based on Lewis Carroll's classic story, and *Trials: The Story of Joan of Arc.*

DeVita's debut novel, *Blue,* is a middle-grade fantasy about a boy who undergoes a bizarre transformation. Morgan lives an uneventful life with his dull parents until one fateful night when a talking marlin appears to him in a dream. Soon, scales begin to appear on Morgan's body, and he develops a sudden taste for anchovies. After his parents rush him to the hospital, the boy is submerged in a huge tank which allows doctors to study Morgan's budding dorsal fin. When surgery is planned to remove the growth, a group of strange, human-marlin hybrids invade the hospital and attempt to rescue the boy.

Reviewing *Blue,* Michael Cart wrote in *Booklist* that DeVita "handles the Kafkaesque details of Morgan's metamorphosis with humor and conviction." Some critics questioned the motivation behind the protagonist's ready acceptance of his new condition, *School Library*

Journal critic Alison Follos remarking that "there's never any driving cause that explains his need for such a dramatic transformation."

DeVita's second novel, *The Silenced*, was inspired by a study of Sophie Scholl, the young woman who organized one of the first resistance movements in Nazi Germany. (DeVita also wrote about Scholl in a play titled *The Rose of Treason*.) In a *Curb* online interview with Sarah Fortin, the writer remarked that *The Silenced* is "ripe with parallels to many modern-day political issues." "A lot of people think I'm writing about what happened in our country and the world in the last six, seven years," he added. "What really is frightening is I wrote about something that happened 60 years ago or more. And that we're drawing parallels to that, I think is scary."

Set in a dystopian future society ruled by the Zero Tolerance Party, *The Silenced* centers on teenaged Marena, who lives with her father and brother behind the walls of a "social readaptation community." While attending a youth training facility designed to reeducate citizens, Marena slowly begins to recapture memories of her mother, a revolutionary who was forcibly removed from their home years earlier by the authorities. Along with Dex, her boyfriend, and Eric, a defiant newcomer, Marena forms the White Rose, a resistance movement, to combat government oppression.

A critic for *Kirkus Reviews* praised DeVita's novel, calling *The Silenced* "tautly plotted," and Eric Norton, writing in *School Library Journal*, noted that "young adults will certainly empathize with the characters' conflicts between self-expression and a desire to fit in." "Gripping suspense combined with satisfyingly capable teen characters make this a good YA read," concluded Kathleen Isaacs in her *Booklist* review of *The Silenced*.

Biographical and Critical Sources

PERIODICALS

Booklist, April 15, 2001, Michael Cart, review of *Blue*, p. 1557; June 1, 2007, Kathleen Isaacs, review of *The Silenced*, p. 62.
Kirkus Reviews, July 1, 2007, review of *The Silenced*.
Kliatt, July 1, 2007, Myrna Marler, review of *The Silenced*, p. 10.
Milwaukee Journal-Sentinel, November 18, 2006, Damien Jacques, "A Tale of 3 Plays: For Dickens Fans, It Is the Best of Times"; June 9, 2008, Damien Jacques, "Tactical Move: APT Actor, Director Join Forces to Create a Stronger, Single Piece from 2-Part *Henry IV*."
Publishers Weekly, April 16, 2001, review of *Blue*, p. 66.
School Library Journal, May, 2001, Alison Follos, review of *Blue*, p. 149; September, 2007, Eric Norton, review of *The Silenced*, p. 194.

ONLINE

American Players Theater Web site, http://www.playinthe woods.org/ (October 15, 2008), "James DeVita."
Curb Web site, http://www.journalism.wisc.edu/ (September 21, 2007), Sarah Fortin, "Making It Write: James DeVita Authors Change."*

*   *   *

DIJKSTRA, Lida 1961-

Personal

Born July 15, 1961, in Heerenveen, Friesland, Netherlands; married; children: Ingeborg. *Education:* Reinwardt Academie, H.B.O. (museum work); Leiden University, degree (archaeology).

Addresses

Home—Friesland, Netherlands. *E-mail*—lidadijkstra@ hetnet.nl.

Career

Children's book author, beginning 1992. Formerly worked as an art conservator and in museum work.

Awards, Honors

Rely Jorritsma prize, 1999; International Board on Books for Young People Award Honor listee, and Vlag en Wimpel award honorable mention, Griffeljury, both 2002, both for *Wachten op Apollo*; Simke Kloosterman-prijs, 2004, for Frisian translation of *Muisje mihn meisje*, 2007, for *Lederwyntsje*; Leespluim, 2008, for *Eén muisje kan geen optocht zihn*.

Writings

Sjoerd Stiensma syn reis troch de tiid (title means "Sjoerd Stiensma Travels through Time"), Afûk (Netherlands), 1994.
De billebiter, Friese Pers Boekerij (Netherlands), 1995.
De skat fan jonker Jan, Afûk (Netherlands), 1996.
Pake past op Dideldeinstsje, Afûk (Netherlands), 1997.
Gevaar voor graaf Max, Bekadidact (Baarn, Netherlands), 1997.
Poppennact, Maretak (Assen, Netherlands), 1998.
Leaverikjes, Friese Pers Boekerij (Netherlands), 1998.
Sinto de Saurus, Bekadidact (Baarn, Netherlands), 1999.
Vlieg naar de zon, Pip, Maretak (Assen, Netherlands), 2000.
Sim loopt weg, Maretak (Assen, Netherlands), 2000.
Konig Kind, Maretak (Assen, Netherlands), 2000.
Wolken fan wol (title means "Waiting for Apollo"; based on Ovid's *Metamorphoses*), illustrated by Martijn van der Linden, 2000, translated into Dutch as *Wachten op Apollo* Lemniscaat (Rotterdam, Netherlands), 2001.

Praat maar met Duif, Maretak (Assen, Netherlands), 2001.

Pootjes, pootjes, puf, puf, Maretak (Assen, Netherlands), 2001.

Het kinderhotel van juffrouw Kummel, Maretak (Assen, Netherlands), 2002.

Ootje, illustrated by Marijke Klompmaker, Lemniscaat (Rotterdam, Netherlands), 2002.

Pip is op Snoes, Maretak (Assen, Netherlands), 2002.

Maan en de Pixies, Maretak (Assen, Netherlands), 2002.

Ootje weer, illustrated by Marijke Klompmaker, Lemniscaat (Rotterdam, Netherlands), 2003.

Pin wil geen prik, Maretak (Assen, Netherlands), 2003.

Muisje mihn meisje, illustrated by Piet Grobler, Lemniscaat (Rotterdam, Netherlands), 2004, translated as *Little Mouse,* Lemniscaat (Asheville, NC), 2003.

Geeske en de cirkel van drie, illustrated by Harmen van Straaten, Lemniscaat (Rotterdam, Netherlands), 2004.

Stoppen!, Maretak (Assen, Netherlands), 2005.

Tien kleine heksje, illustrated by Jung Hee Spetter, Lemniscaat (Rotterdam, Netherlands), 2005.

Rollebollebom, illustrated by Marijke Klompmaker, Gottmer (Haarlem, Netherlands), 2006.

Slaap lekker, prinses, Maretak (Assen, Netherlands), 2006.

Schattig, illustrated by Marije Tolman, Lemniscaat (Rotterdam, Netherlands), 2006, translated as *Cute,* Lemniscaat (Asheville, NC), 2007.

Juffrouw Kummel en de kikkerprins, Maretak (Assen, Netherlands), 2007.

Eén muisje kan geen optocht zijn, illustrated by Noëlle Smit, Gottmer (Haarlem, Netherlands), 2007.

Spiegelspreuk, illustrated by Roelof van der Schans, Aed Livwerd (Netherlands), 2007.

Kom van die peer, mier!, Maretak (Assen, Netherlands), 2008.

Aangeboden: 2 schoolhond, Maretak (Assen, Netherlands), 2008.

Ik wil geen broertje!, illustrated by Noëlle Smit, Gottmer (Haarlem, Netherlands), 2008.

Sidelights

Lida Dijkstra is a Dutch author whose work has proved popular enough with young readers to merit an English translation. Born in Friesland, she enrolled at Leiden University with the dream of becoming an art historian and museum curator. After the birth of her daughter, however, Dijkstra began writing stories in her native Friesian as well as in Dutch. Her first published picture book, 1994's *Sjoerd Stiensma syn rys troch de tiid,* is the imaginative story of a young girl who travels through time. In 1999 Dijkstra was honored with the first of several awards for her writing: the Rely Jorritsma prize for a short story for adult readers. Her highly praised and ambitious adaptation of six stories from Ovid's *Metamorphoses,* published in Dutch as *Wachten op Apollo,* was included on the International

One of Norwegian writer Lida Dijkstra's most popular stories for children, **Cute,** *features artwork by Marije Tolman.* (Lemniscaat, 2006. Illustration copyright © 2006 by Marije Tolman. All rights reserved. Reproduced by permission of Boyds Mills Press.)

Board on Books for Young People Honors List and 2002, in addition to receiving other honors.

Several of Dijkstra's book have been translated into English and published with the illustrations created for their Dutch or Frisian text. In *Cute* illustrator Marije Tolman brings to life Dijkstra's story about a young rabbit named Toby who is weary of being called "cute." Hoping to gain a grown-up appearance, Toby gets a pierced ear and a tattoo, and addresses his family and friends with tough-guy bravado. However, when he tries to impress observers with his skill on a motorbike, Toby meets the beautiful, long-eared Tara, who is more impressed with cuteness than toughness.

Another English translation, *Little Mouse,* was originally published as *Muisje mihn meisje* and features art by Piet Grobler. The book was described by *School Library Journal* contributor Robin L. Gibson as an "engaging retelling" of the folk story "The Mouse Bride." Dijkstra's version of the story finds an orphaned mouse raised by a hermit owl. When the mouse comes of age to be married, she and the wise old owl go in search of the strongest possible husband on earth, only to learn that strength is not always found in things of great size. Reviewing *Little Mouse* in *Publishers Weekly,* a critic wrote that "Dijkstra's brisk, straightforward text and familiar elements" provide a story with timeless appeal while "the giddy glee emanating from Grobler's artwork . . . makes the story magic."

Biographical and Critical Sources

PERIODICALS

Booklist, January 1, 2005, Ilene Cooper, review of *Little Mouse,* p. 868.

Bulletin of the Center for Children's Books, February, 2005, Deborah Stevenson, review of *Little Mouse,* p. 249.

Kirkus Reviews, October 1, 2004, review of *Little Mouse,* p. 959; July 1, 2004, review of *Cute.*

Publishers Weekly, January 10, 2005, review of *Little Mouse,* p. 55.

School Library Journal, February, 2005, Robin L. Gibson, review of *Little Mouse,* p. 96; September, 2007, Maryann H. Owen, review of *Cute,* p. 162.

ONLINE

Foundation for the Production and Translation of Dutch Literature Web site, http://www.nlpvf.nl/ (November 15, 2008), Lida Dijkstra.

Lemniscaat Web site, http://www.lemniscaatkrant.nl/ (November 15, 2008), "Lida Dijkstra."

Lida Dijkstra Home Page, http://home.hetnet.nl/~lidadijkstra (November 15, 2008).*

DISCH, Thomas M. 1940-2008
(Thom DeMijohn, a joint pseudonym, Thomas Michael Disch, Tom Disch, Leonie Hargrave, Victor Hastings, Cassandra Knye, a joint pseudonym)

OBITUARY NOTICE—

See index for *SATA* sketch: Born February 2, 1940, in Des Moines, IA; died of a self-inflicted gunshot wound, July 5, 2008, in New York, NY. Novelist, short-story writer, poet, critic, children's writer, playwright, librettist, editor, and author. Among the prominent judges of science fiction, Disch was respected as one of America's most talented authors of speculative fiction, as he insisted upon calling it. Yet he was better known in England than his homeland and was most often recognized on both sides of the Atlantic for his children's stories. One of them, *The Brave Little Toaster: A Bedtime Story for Small Appliances* (1986), won a British science-fiction award and nominations for both the Hugo Award of the World Science Fiction Convention and the Nebula Award from the Science Fiction and Fantasy Writers of America. It was later adapted as a popular animated film. Disch's adult novels and short stories were not for everyone, for they were often dark and troubling, bleak and foreboding, verging on horror or crossing altogether into the gothic genre, such as his novel *The Priest* (1994). However, critics praised the author for his imagination, social conscience, and especially his literary approach to a genre often considered escapist or frivolous. He employed surrealist "new wave" elements in work like the novel *On Wings of Song* (1979), for which he received a John W. Campbell Memorial Award from the World Science Fiction Convention and an American Book Award nomination. Disch was, in fact, a highly versatile author. He wrote mainstream fiction, poetry, plays and opera librettos, and also worked as a theater and arts critic for periodicals ranging from the *Nation* to the *New York Daily News.* He published under a variety of pseudonyms and worked with other authors under joint pseudonyms, and he edited anthologies of writings by his colleagues and other authors whose work he admired. His short stories, which are often the lifeblood of science-fiction writers, appeared in magazines from *Amazing Stories* to *Harper's* to *Playboy.* Disch also wrote award-winning nonfiction such as *The Dreams Our Stuff Is Made Of: How Science Fiction Conquered the World* (1998), which received a Hugo Award in the nonfiction category. Disch never stopped writing; his satirical novel *The Word of God; or, Holy Writ Rewritten* (2008) was published only days before his unexpected death.

OBITUARIES AND OTHER SOURCES:

BOOKS

Contemporary Poets, 7th edition, Gale (Detroit, MI), 2001.

St. James Guide to Horror, Ghost, and Gothic Writers, St. James Press (Detroit, MI), 1998.

St. James Guide to Science-Fiction Writers, 4th edition, St. James Press (Detroit, MI), 1996.

PERIODICALS

Chicago Tribune, July 9, 2008, sec. 2, p. 9.
Los Angeles Times, July 8, 2008, p. B6.
New York Times, July 8, 2008, p. A19.
Times (London, England), July 18, 2008, p. 58.

*   *   *

DISCH, Thomas Michael
See DISCH, Thomas M.

*   *   *

DISCH, Tom
See DISCH, Thomas M.

*   *   *

DONG-SUNG, Kim 1970-
(Dong-Sung Kim)

Personal
Born 1970, in Korea.

Addresses
Home—Korea.

Career
Illustrator and artist.

Illustrator
Long Long Time Ago: Korean Folk Tales, Hollym International (Elizabeth, NJ), 1997.

Tae-Joon Lee, *Waiting for Mama* (new edition; bilingual English-Hangeul), translated by Eun Hee Cheun, afterword by Andreas Schirmer, North-South Books (New York, NY), 2007.

Biographical and Critical Sources

PERIODICALS

Kirkus Reviews, July 15, 2007, review of *Waiting for Mama.*
School Library Journal, September, 2007, Mary Hazelton, review of *Waiting for Mama,* p. 168.*

DONG-SUNG KIM
See DONG-SUNG, Kim

*   *   *

DRAPER, Sharon M. 1948-

Personal
Born August 21, 1948, in Cleveland, OH; daughter of Victor D. (a hotel manager) and Catherine (an administrative assistant) Mills; married Larry E. Draper (an educator); children: Wendy, Damon, Crystal, Cory. *Ethnicity:* "African American." *Education:* Pepperdine University, B.A., 1971; Miami University (Oxford, OH), M.A. *Hobbies and other interests:* Reading; "I won't read junk; there's no time to waste on poorly written books."

Addresses
Office—P.O. Box 36551, Cincinnati, OH 45236. *E-mail*—drapersharon@mac.com.

Career
Public speaker, poet, educator, and author. Walnut Hills High School, Cincinnati, OH, English teacher and head of department, 1972-2005; Mayerson Academy, associate; former Duncanson artist-in-residence at Taft Museum. Member of board, National Commission on Teaching and America's Future; member, National Board for Professional Teaching Standards. Lecturer and presenter at schools and other venues. Guest on radio and television programs.

Member
International Reading Association, American Federation of Teachers, National Board for Professional Teaching Standards (member of board of directors, 1995—), National Council of Teachers of English, Top Ladies of Distinction, Links, Inc., Ohio Council of Teachers of English Language Arts, Conference on English Leadership, Delta Kappa Gamma, Phi Delta Kappa, Women's City Club.

Awards, Honors
First prize, *Ebony* Literary Contest, 1991, for short story "One Small Torch"; Coretta Scott King Genesis Award, American Library Association (ALA), Best Book for Young Adults designation, ALA, Best Books designation, Children's Book Council (CBC)/Bank Street College, Books for the Teen Age selection, New York Public Library, and Notable Trade Book in the Field of Social Studies designation, National Council for the Social Studies, all 1995, all for *Tears of a Tiger,* and all 1998, all for *Forged by Fire;* named Outstanding High School English Language Arts Educator, Ohio Council of Teachers of English Language Arts, 1995;

Sharon M. Draper (Reproduced by permission.)

Midwest regional winner, National Council of Negro Women Excellence in Teaching Award, 1996; Ohio Governor's Educational Leadership Award, 1996; named National Teacher of the Year, 1997; ALA Best Book designation, International Reading Association (IRA) Notable Book designation, and Books for the Teen Age selection, New York Public Library, all 2000, all for *Romiette and Julio;* IRA Children's Choice designation, 2001, and IRA Young-Adult Choice selection, 2003, both for *Darkness before Dawn;* CBC Notable Social Studies Trade Book designation, and named among ALA Top Ten Sports Books for Youth, both 2003, both for *Double Dutch;* Coretta Scott King Honor Book designation, and Books for the Teen Age designation, New York Public Library, both 2004, and IRA Young-Adult Choice designation, 2005, all for *The Battle of Jericho;* Coretta Scott King Award, Notable Social Studies Trade Book designation, CBC/National Council of Social Studies, Heartland Award, IRA Notable Book for a Global Society designation, NAACP Image Award nomination, and Ohioana Award for Young Adult Literature, all 2007, all for *Copper Sun;* Coretta Scott King Honor Book designation, 2008, for *November Blues;* Milken Family Foundation National Educator Award; named YWCA Career Woman of Achievement; Dean's Award, Howard University School of Education; Pepperdine

University Distinguished Alumnus Award; Marva Collins Education Excellence Award; named Ohio State Department of Education Pioneer in Education. Honorary degrees include D.H.L, College of Mount Saint Joseph, and D.H., Cincinnati State University.

Writings

FOR YOUNG ADULTS

Tears of a Tiger ("Hazelwood High Trilogy"), Simon & Schuster (New York, NY), 1994.
Forged by Fire ("Hazelwood High Trilogy"), Simon & Schuster (New York, NY), 1997.
Romiette and Julio, Simon & Schuster (New York, NY), 1999.
Jazzimagination, Scholastic (New York, NY), 1999.
Darkness before Dawn ("Hazelwood High Trilogy"), Simon & Schuster (New York, NY), 2001.
Double Dutch, Simon & Schuster (New York, NY), 2002.
The Battle of Jericho ("Jericho" trilogy), Simon & Schuster (New York, NY), 2003.
Copper Sun, Atheneum (New York, NY), 2006.
November Blues ("Jericho" trilogy), Atheneum (New York, NY), 2007.
Fire from the Rock, Dutton (New York, NY), 2007.
Sassy: Little Sister Is Not My Name, Scholastic (New York, NY), 2009.
Just Another Hero ("Jericho" trilogy), Atheneum (New York, NY), 2009.

"ZIGGY AND THE BLACK DINOSAURS" SERIES; FOR CHILDREN

The Buried Bones Mystery, Just Us Books (East Orange, NJ), 1994.
Lost in the Tunnel of Time, illustrated by Jesse Joshua Watson, Just Us Books (East Orange, NJ), 1996.
Shadows of Caesar's Creek, illustrated by Jesse Joshua Watson, Just Us Books (East Orange, NJ), 1997.
The Space Camp Adventure, illustrated by Jesse Joshua Watson, Aladdin (New York, NY), 2006.
The Backyard Animal Show, illustrated by Jesse Joshua Watson, Aladdin (New York, NY), 2006.
Stars and Sparks on Stage, illustrated by Jesse Joshua Watson, Aladdin (New York, NY), 2006.

OTHER

Teaching from the Heart: Reflections, Encouragement, and Inspiration, Heinemann (Portsmouth, NH), 2000.
Not Quite Burned out but Crispy around the Edges: Inspiration, Laughter, and Encouragement for Teachers, Heinemann (Portsmouth, NH), 2001.
(Coauthor) Sampson, Davis, George Jenkins, and Rameck Hunt, *We Beat the Street: How a Friendship Pact Led to Success,* Dutton (New York, NY), 2005.

Also author of *Let the Circle Be Unbroken* (children's poetry), and *Buttered Bones* (poetry for adults). Contributor of poems and short stories to literary magazines; contributor of essay "The Touch of a Teacher" to *What Governors Need to Know about Education,* Center for Policy Research of the National Governor's Association.

Adaptations

All Draper's books have been recorded on audiocassette by Recorded Books, including *Double Dutch,* read by Patricia R. Floyd, 2002; *The Battle of Jericho,* read by J.D. Jackson, 203; *Romiette and Julio* and *Darkness before Dawn,* both read by Sisi Aisha Johnson, 2003; and *Copper Sun,* read by Myra Lucretia Taylor, 2006.

Sidelights

Sharon M. Draper is a nationally award-winning teacher and writer whose books include *Forged by Fire, Romiette and Julio, Darkness before Dawn,* the Coretta Scott King Award-winning *Copper Sun,* and the easy-reading "Ziggy and the Black Dinosaurs" mystery series. Reading, teaching, and writing are all connected for Draper, who wanted to be a teacher since childhood. As she once told an interviewer, "I was an avid reader. I read every single book in the elementary school library, all of them. I did not plan to be a writer until much, much later. I tell students all the time that in order to be a good writer it is necessary first to be a good reader. You need some information in your head. Reading is input. Writing is output. You can't write without input."

Born in Cleveland, Ohio, Draper was the eldest of three children raised in a family where education was a given. The question was not "would you attend college, it was where and to study what," Draper explained in her interview. She entered Cleveland Public Schools in the 1950s, inspired by a home where she was surrounded by books. Her mother read stories, poems, fairytales, and nursery rhymes to Draper and her siblings from the time they were very young. She recalled a teacher who once "gave me O's for outstanding, saying an A wasn't good enough." A fifth-grade teacher introduced Draper and her fellow students to poetry by Langston Hughes and Robert Frost, and they also read and loved Shakespeare. "We didn't know we weren't supposed to be able to do that in fifth grade. She gave it to us and we loved it," Draper said. "It was part of making me the teacher I am today."

Draper attended Pepperdine University as a National Merit scholar, majoring in English. Upon graduation in 1971, she returned to Ohio where she married and assumed a teaching position in the Cincinnati Public Schools. Her many years teaching public school has given her some definite ideas on the reading habits of teens. "I know what kids like—what they will read, and what they won't. Although I have nothing against Charles Dickens, many teenagers would rather gag than

read him. Dickens wrote for his contemporaries—young people of a hundred and fifty years ago. American students might need to know about the world of London in the 1860s, but they would much rather read about their own world first. Not only will they read about recognizable experiences with pleasure, but they will also be encouraged to write as well."

According to an essayist in the *St. James Guide to Young-Adult Writers,* "Draper's works address the problems African Americans face in a predominantly white society, specifically stereotyping of black males. They also examine the dynamics of African American families and communities. Her . . . fiction is energetic and intense, as characters become self aware and attain emotional growth. She often creates mystery plots as a means for characters to be introspective and explore their identities. She sets her books in Cincinnati where she lives and teaches, suggesting a familiarity with her characters and community that enhances their realism."

Draper's first young-adult novel, and the first volume in her "Hazelwood High" trilogy, *Tears of a Tiger* recounts

Cover of Draper's young-adult novel Tears of a Tiger, *featuring artwork by Kelynn Adler.* (Aladdin Paperbacks, 1996. Cover illustration © 1996 by Kelynn Alder. All rights reserved. Reproduced by permission of Kelynn Alder.)

the story of Andy Jackson, a black youth who struggles to make sense of the death of his best friend, Robert, in an automobile accident in which Andy was the driver. The two teens had been drinking beer with their friends Tyrone and B.J. in celebration of a victory by their high-school basketball team. Tyrone and B.J. are able to move past the awful pain caused by the accident, Tyrone by finding support from his girlfriend Rhonda, and B.J. through religion. Andy, however, is wracked with guilt, grief, and pain that do not subside with time.

In *Tears of a Tiger* Draper depicts the difficulties in healing emotionally through the character of Andy, and through him she also addresses the institutional attitudes confronting young black males. In one episode, for example, teachers discuss how Andy's grief cannot be all that serious since he is African American. The teen also internalizes ideas about himself that prevent him from realizing his full capabilities; for example, he believes he cannot be successful academically because he is a basketball player. Merri Monks, writing in *Booklist,* observed that "Andy's perceptions of the racism directed toward young black males—by teachers, guidance counselors, and clerks in shopping malls—will be recognized by African American YAs." Draper's use of news stories, journal entries, homework assignments, and letters give the novel an immediacy that adds to its power.

Kathy Fritts, reviewing *Tears of a Tiger* for *School Library Journal,* pointed out that in Draper's "moving novel" "the characters' voices are strong, vivid, and ring true," while Monks remarked that the work's "characters and their experiences will captivate teen readers." In *Publishers Weekly,* a reviewer concluded of *Tears of a Tiger* that "the combination of raw energy and intense emotions should stimulate readers," and Dorothy M. Broderick wrote in *Voice of Youth Advocates:* "Suffice to say, not only is Draper an author to watch for, but that this is as compelling a novel as any published in the last two decades." Roger Sutton, reviewing *Tears of a Tiger* for the *Bulletin of the Center for Children's Books,* stated that, "rather than a tidy summary of suicide symptoms and 'ways to help,' readers instead get a grave portrait of unceasing despair and a larger picture of how young African-American men like Andy get lost in a system that will not trust or reach out to them." *Tears of a Tiger* received several honors, including the Coretta Scott King Genesis Award.

Forged by Fire, the sequel to *Tears of a Tiger,* is also grounded in socially relevant themes. Child sexual abuse and drug addiction replace suicide and racism, yet both books reach a tragic finality. Draper wrote *Forged by Fire*'s first chapter as a short story, "One Small Torch," which she published in *Ebony.* The novel went on to win Draper her second Coretta Scott King Award.

A minor character in *Tears of a Tiger,* Gerald Nickelby, is the focus of *Forged by Fire.* At age three Gerald was burned in a fire after being left alone by his mother,

Cover of Draper's novel **Forged by Fire,** *featuring cover art by John Clapp.* (Aladdin Paperbacks, 1998. Cover illustration copyright © 1998 by John Clapp. Reproduced by permission of John Clapp.)

Monique. Following his hospital stay, Gerald goes to live with Aunt Queen, a loving and supportive woman. Six years later, following Aunt Queen's death, Monique reenters her son's life. Monique has married Jordan Sparks, the father of Angel, Gerald's new half-sister. Gerald soon learns that Sparks has sexually abused Angel and through the testimony of the children, Sparks is sent to prison. When Sparks returns six years later, Monique, who indulges too much in drugs, lets him return to family life where he once again attempts to sexually harm his young daughter.

Tom S. Hurlburt, reviewing *Forged by Fire* for *School Library Journal,* wrote that although there is "no all's-well ending, . . . readers will have hope for Gerald and Angel, who have survived a number of gut-wrenching ordeals by relying on their constant love and caring for one another." Candace Smith, writing in *Booklist,* concluded that "Draper faces some big issues (abuse, death, drugs)" in her novel "and provides concrete options and a positive African American role model in Gerald."

In *Darkness before Dawn,* which concludes the "Hazelwood High" trilogy, Draper tells the story of high schooler Keisha Montgomery, who has just lost her ex-boyfriend to suicide and must now deal with an overly aggressive track coach. Debbie Carton, reviewing the novel for *Booklist,* wrote that "the graduation scene, in which class president Keisha gives the closing speech, is moving and triumphant, showing Draper and her vibrant characters at their best." While Angela J. Reynolds observed in *School Library Journal* that "readers may be overwhelmed by the soap-opera feel of this issue-laden world," Odette Cornwall concluded in the *Journal of Adolescent and Adult Literacy* that "not only did Draper make Keisha real, but she also wove many prominent social issues faced by young adults today into the story line."

Draper begins another series with *The Battle of Jericho.* Here readers meet sixteen-year-old cousins Josh and Jericho Prescott as they decide to pledge the popular Warriors of Distinction fraternity at Frederick Douglass High. During pledge week the Warriors' hazing gets out of control, with tragic results. Although Ilene Cooper wrote in *Booklist* that the characters' dialogue sounds "stilted" due to Draper's decision to avoid profanity, *The Battle of Jericho* involves "a timely scenario" that finds "middle-class African American kids . . . put into a situation that many young people face": the need to fit in, no matter what the cost. Draper effectively "conveys the seductive power of teen clubs and the dangers of hazing rituals in this timely novel," concluded a *Publishers Weekly* contributor.

A sequel to *The Battle of Jericho, November Blues,* examines the aftermath of Josh's tragic death, as Jericho and Josh's girlfriend, November Nelson, attempt to come to terms with life without him. For November, a promising high-school senior, their brief relationship has left her pregnant with Josh's child and a decision that will decide the course of her future. Anne Rouyer predicted in her *School Library Journal* review that teens will appreciate Draper's "accurate and sympathetic portrayal of urban teens" and "the straightforward way that the author presents the issues they face." *November Blues* "is well-plotted, realistic and matter-of-fact," noted a *Kirkus Reviews* writer, the critic adding that Draper's characters "are well-drawn" and "likeable." "Along with the serious issues, teens will appreciate the fast, funny contemporary dialogue . . . ," wrote *Booklist* critic Hazel Rochman, "and also the view of the [perfect] girl who . . . screws up big time."

One of several stand-alone novels by Draper, *Double Dutch* concerns a group of eighth graders with serious problems. Delia is unable to read and does not want anyone to find out; her friend Randy fears that his father has deserted the family; and the violent Tolliver twins scare their new classmates. "Draper adeptly paints a convincing portrayal of how young people think, act, feel, and interact with one another," Connie Tyrrell

Burns commented in *School Library Journal.* A critic for *Kirkus Reviews* found that "Delia and her friends are delightful, and the reader is rooting for them all the way."

One of Draper's most acclaimed novels, *Copper Sun,* finds fifteen-year-old Amari taken from her home amid the Ewe people and sold into slavery by brutal African slavers. Through Draper's compelling description, readers share the horrors of the Middle Passage with the frightened young teen, and discover the indignities of life as a slave when Amari's boat lands in the Carolinas. Bought by a plantation owner, the young woman serves her master's teenage son until events prompt her to escape south to Florida and freedom. While KaaVonia Hinton observed in *Kliatt* that Draper does not shy away from depicting the more-violent aspects of slavery, such as torture, murder, and sexual aggression, *Copper Sun* will inspire "discussions about early African culture and sensibility, acts of resistance executed by slaves . . . , and abolitionist efforts." In *School Library Journal* Gerry Larson called the award-winning novel an "action-packed, multifaceted, character-rich story [that] describes the shocking realities of the slave trade and plantation life while portraying the perseverance, resourcefulness, and triumph of the human spirit."

Draper focuses on more-recent history in *Fire from the Rock,* which is set in the midst of the civil rights movement of the twentieth century. In the story, set in Little Rock, Arkansas, in 1957, Sylvia Patterson has been an honor student in her all-black junior high school. As a freshman, she is now selected as one of the nine students to be transferred to all-white Central High School in response to the Supreme Court's mandate to integrate the nation's public schools. Concerned more with academic success than with crusading, Sylvia fears the move, and her experiences as one of the Little Rock Nine are recounted in both a narrative and diary entries. "With stirring complexity, Draper personalizes the civil rights struggle beyond slogans and politics," wrote Rochman in a review of *Fire from the Rock,* while a *Kirkus Reviews* writer dubbed the story "compelling." Noting the many historical aspects of the novel, Hinton wrote in her *Kliatt* review that the author "skillfully portrays the attitude and climate of late 1950s Arkansas and of the United States in general," thereby presenting the mixed view toward integration that existed on both sides of the racial divide.

In her "Ziggy and the Black Dinosaurs" series Draper mixes interesting characters with elements of African-American history and folklore. Ziggy and his three friends, who call themselves the Black Dinosaurs, begin their adventures in *Ziggy and the Black Dinosaurs.* In *Lost in the Tunnel of Time,* Ziggy and friends take a field trip to the Ohio River and learn about the Underground Railroad and the tunnels the slaves used to escape the South. In the third volume, *Shadows of Caesar's Creek,* Draper makes connections between African Americans and Native Americans. Other titles featuring

Ziggy and the Black Dinosaurs include *The Buried Bones Mystery, The Space Camp Adventure,* and *The Backyard Animal Show,* all featuring artwork by Jesse Joshua Watson. Reviewing *The Space Camp Adventure,* in which Ziggy and company attend space camp at the Alabama Space Center, Elaine E. Knight wrote in *School Library Journal* that Draper incorporates "considerable humor and even a light touch of mystery" into her easy-reading, science-themed story.

Draper once commented: "I feel very blessed that I have had so much success in such a short time. I hope that my books can continue to make a difference in the lives of young people." In a statement posted on her home page, Draper proclaimed: "I approach the world with the eyes of an artist, the ears of a musician, and the soul of a writer. I see rainbows where others see only rain, and possibilities when others see only problems."

Biographical and Critical Sources

BOOKS

Contemporary Black Biography, Gale (Detroit, MI), Volume 16, 1998.
Hinton, KaaVonia, *Sharon M. Draper: Embracing Literacy,* Scarecrow Press (Metuchen, NJ), 2008.
St. James Guide to Young-Adult Writers, 2nd edition, St. James Press (Detroit, MI), 1999.

PERIODICALS

Booklist, November 1, 1994, Merri Monks, review of *Tears of a Tiger,* p. 492; February 15, 1997, Candace Smith, review of *Forged by Fire,* pp. 1016-1017; January 1, 2001, Debbie Carton, review of *Darkness before Dawn,* p. 939; June 1, 2003, Ilene Cooper, review of *The Battle of Jericho,* p. 1761; August, 2007, Hazel Rochman, review of *Fire from the Rock,* p. 63; October 15, 2007, Hazel Rochman, review of *November Blues,* p. 44.
Bulletin of the Center for Children's Books, January, 1995, review of *Tears of a Tiger,* p. 164; June, 1997, review of *Forged by Fire,* p. 355; October, 2002, review of *Double Dutch,* p. 54; July, 2003, review of *The Battle of Jericho,* p. 444; April, 2006, Karen Coats, review of *Copper Sun,* p. 348; September, 2007, Karen Coats, review of *Fire from the Rock,* p. 18.
Christian Science Monitor, May 5, 1997, David Holmstrom, "America's Top Teacher Gives Tough Assignments—And Plenty of Support," p. 12.

Journal of Adolescent and Adult Literacy, April, 2002, Arina Zonnenberg, review of *Romiette and Julio,* p. 660, and Odette Cornwall, review of *Darkness before Dawn,* p. 661.
Kirkus Reviews, June 1, 2002, review of *Double Dutch,* p. 804; June 1, 2003, review of *The Battle of Jericho,* p. 802; July 15, 2007, review of *Fire from the Rock;* October 1, 2007, review of *November Blues.*
Kliatt, July, 1998, Jean Palmer, review of *Forged by Fire,* p. 10; July, 2002, Claire Rosser, review of *Double Dutch,* p. 9; November, 2003, Nancy C. Chaplin, review of *Darkness before Dawn,* p. 46; January, 2006, KaaVonia Hinton, review of *Copper Sun;* July, 2007, KaaVonia Hinton, review of *Fire from the Rock,* p. 12.
Ohioana, 2002, Virginia Schaefer Horvath, review *Darkness before Dawn.*
Publishers Weekly, January 15, 1996, review of *Tears of a Tiger,* p. 463; March 25, 1996, review of *Lost in the Tunnel of Time,* p. 85; December 16, 1996, review of *Forged by Fire,* p. 61; June 17, 2002, review of *Double Dutch,* p. 66; June 9, 2003, review of *The Battle of Jericho,* p. 53.
School Library Journal, September, 1999, Jane Halsall, review of *Romiette and Julio,* p. 222; February, 2001, Angela J. Reynolds, review of *Darkness before Dawn,* p. 117; June, 2002, Connie Tyrrell Burns, review of *Double Dutch,* p. 137; June 9, 2003, review of *The Battle of Jericho,* p. 53; January, 2006, Gerry Larson, review of *Copper Sun,* p. 130; January, 2007, Elaine E. Knight, review of *The Space Camp Adventure,* p. 92; November, 2007, Anne Rouyer, review of *November Blues,* p. 120.
USA Today, April 17, 1997, "An 'A' for Creativity: Variety Is on Teacher of the Year's Lesson Plan," p. D4.
Voice of Youth Advocates, February, 1995, review of *Tears of a Tiger,* p. 338; June, 1997, review of *Forged by Fire,* p. 108; December, 1999, Deborah L. Dubois, review of *Romiette and Julio;* August, 2001, review of *Darkness before Dawn,* p. 200; August, 2002, review of *Double Dutch,* p. 191; August, 2007, Robbie L. Flowers, review of *Fire from the Rock,* p. 238.

ONLINE

Ohio Department of Education Web site, http://school improvement.ode.ohio.gov/ (June 5, 1998), "Sharon Draper."
Sharon M. Draper Home Page, http://sharondraper.com (November 24, 2008).
Teaching Books Web site, http://www.teachingbooks.net/ (November 24, 2008), "Sharon M. Draper."

F

FARDELL, John 1967-

Personal

Born July 10, 1967; married; wife's name Jenny; children: Josh, Connor.

Addresses

Home and office—Edinburgh, Scotland.

Career

Cartoonist, illustrator, puppeteer, and author. Creator of comic strips, including "Ferdinand the Foodie," "The Modern Parents" and "The Critics," for *Viz* magazine; creator of comic strip "Hanover Square" for *Property Week*.

Writings

FANTASY NOVELS

(And illustrator) *The Seven Professors of the Far North,* Putnam (New York, NY), 2005.
(And illustrator) *The Flight of the Silver Turtle,* Putnam (New York, NY), 2006.

Contributor of comic strips and cartoons to periodicals, including the *Independent, Evening Standard, New Statesman, Glasgow Herald,* and the *List.*

Sidelights

John Fardell, a writer, illustrator, and cartoonist, is the author of the highly regarded fantasy novels *The Seven Professors of the Far North* and *The Flight of the Silver Turtle.* The British-born Fardell, who lives in Edinburgh, Scotland, is the creator of such popular comic strips as "The Modern Parents," "The Critics," and "Hanover Square," and his work appears regularly in the adult comic magazine *Viz.* "I've been a cartoonist for considerably longer than I've been a writer, though my cartoon and comic strip work has always involved a lot of writing and idea-generating," Fardell told *Books from Scotland* Web site interviewer Anna Gibbons. "Also, for many years before starting to write children's novels, I'd tried writing and illustrating picture book ideas."

Fardell began work on his first novel after a chance meeting with Suzy Jenvey, a children's book editor who enjoyed his work for *Viz.* As Fardell related to Tom Maxwell in an interview for *Scotsman.com:* "She asked me if I had any ideas for a children's book and I said: 'Yes, lots.' Whether it's true or not, that's what you say when you're self-employed and someone offers you an opportunity."

Published in 2005, his novel *The Seven Professors of the Far North* concerns three youngsters who join forces to combat an evil mastermind. While the parents of eleven-year-old Sam Carnabie attend a conference, Sam stays with madcap inventor Professor Ampersand and the professor's great-nephew Ben and great-niece Zara. During his visit, Sam learns that Ampersand and six colleagues had once attempted to create the world's greatest university at Nordberg, a remote island in the Arctic Ocean. Their hopes were dashed, however, when the scientists uncovered a series of horrible experiments conducted by the villainous Professor Murdo. Thirty-five years later Murdo has resurfaced, and his henchmen now kidnap Ampersand and the other six professors. Sam, Ben, and Zara must now journey to the frozen north to rescue their friends and halt Murdo's latest scheme, which threatens the entire human race.

Fardell's debut novel earned strong reviews. A critic in *Publishers Weekly* described *The Seven Professors of the Far North* as a "lightning-paced, skillfully stream-lined caper," and *Booklist* contributor Todd Morning remarked that the tale "offers plenty of humor and suspense for adventure fans." According to B. Allison Gray, writing in *School Library Journal,* Fardell's "inventive, funny, suspenseful, and exciting book will appeal to most readers, especially fans of [Roald] Dahl and [J.K.] Rowling."

Sam, Ben, Zara, and Professor Ampersand return in *The Flight of the Silver Turtle,* a sequel to *The Seven Professors of the Far North.* When the professor and his young charges agree to help a friend construct an experimental aircraft named the *Silver Turtle,* their movements are tracked by Noctarma, a secret paramilitary organization. The children are placed in peril when the leader of Noctarma believes that they have discovered the secret of antigravity. "The writing is consistently upbeat and energetic," noted *School Library Journal* contributor Elizabeth Bird of Fardell's second novel, and a critic in *Kirkus Reviews* stated that in *The Flight of the Silver Turtle* "the action is swift, and the James Bondian gadgets abound."

Biographical and Critical Sources

PERIODICALS

Booklist, January 1, 2006, Todd Morning, review of *The Seven Professors of the Far North,* p. 99.

Kirkus Reviews, August 1, 2005, review of *The Seven Professors of the Far North,* p. 847; September 15, 2006, review of *The Flight of the Silver Turtle,* p. 952.

Property Week, August 4, 2006, Ian Wall, "Seventh Heaven," review of *The Seven Professors of the Far North,* p. 37.

Publishers Weekly, October 17, 2005, review of *The Seven Professors of the Far North,* p. 69.

School Library Journal, December, 2005, B. Allison Gray, review of *The Seven Professors of the Far North,* p. 146; October, 2006, Elizabeth Bird, review of *The Flight of the Silver Turtle,* p. 154.

Teacher Librarian, October, 2006, Betty Winslow, "Dreams and Journeys," review of *The Seven Professors of the Far North,* p. 46.

ONLINE

Books from Scotland, http://www.booksfromscotland.com/ (March 30, 2007), Anna Gibbons, interview with Fardell.

Guardian Unlimited, http://books.guardian.co.uk/ (July 23, 2006), Phil Hogan, "Snot, Snogs and a Tumour with Humour," review of *The Flight of the Silver Turtle.*

KidsReads.com, http://www.kidsreads.com/ (January 5, 2009), Paula Jolin, review of *The 7 Professors of the Far North.*

Scotsman.com, http://www.scotsman.com/ (March 8, 2006), Tom Maxwell, "Drawing up a World of Fun and Adventure."*

*   *   *

FEINSTEIN, John 1956-

Personal

Surname pronounced "Fine-steen"; born July 28, 1956, in New York, NY; son of Martin (an opera director) and Berwile (a college professor) Feinstein; married; wife's name Mary Clare; children: Daniel. *Education:* Duke University, B.A., 1977 (one source says 1978). *Politics:* Democrat. *Religion:* Jewish.

Addresses

Home—Potomac, MD; Shelter Island, NY.

Career

Washington Post, Washington, DC, sportswriter, 1977-88, 1992—; special contributor to *Sports Illustrated,* 1988-90; sportswriter for *National Sports Daily,* 1990-91; contributor to America Online, 2000—, *Golf Digest,* 2003—, and *Golf World,* 2003—. Commentator for National Public Radio's *Morning Edition,* 1988—, *Sporting News* Radio, 1992—, and ESPN. Visiting professor of journalism at Duke University.

Member

U.S. Basketball Writer's Association, U.S. Tennis Writer's Association (vice president), National Sportscasters and Sportswriters Association, Newspaper Guild.

Awards, Honors

Awards from U.S. Basketball Writer's Association, 1981, 1982, 1983, 1984, 1985; Best Sports Stories Award, National Sportscasters and Sportswriters Association, 1982, 1985, 1986; DC Writer of the Year award, 1985; Best Event Coverage Award, Associated Press Sports Editors, 1985.

Writings

NONFICTION

A Season on the Brink: A Year with Bob Knight and the Indiana Hoosiers, Macmillan (New York, NY), 1986.

A Season Inside: One Year in College Basketball, Villard Books (New York, NY), 1988.

Forever's Team, Villard Books (New York, NY), 1990.

Hard Courts: Real Life on the Professional Tennis Tours, Villard Books (New York, NY), 1991.

Play Ball: The Life and Troubled Times of Major League Baseball, Villard Books (New York, NY), 1993.

A Good Walk Spoiled: Days and Nights on the PGA Tour, Little, Brown (Boston, MA), 1995.

A Civil War, Army vs. Navy: A Year inside College Football's Purest Rivalry, Little, Brown (Boston, MA), 1996.

(Editor) *The Best American Sports Writing 1996,* Houghton (Boston, MA), 1997.

A March to Madness: The View from the Floor in the Atlantic Coast Conference, Little, Brown (Boston, MA), 1998 with new afterword, 1999.

The First Coming: Tiger Woods, Master or Martyr?, Ballantine (New York, NY), 1998.

The Majors: In Pursuit of Golf's Holy Grail, Little, Brown (Boston, MA), 1999.

The Last Amateurs: Playing for Glory and Honor in Division 1 Basketball's Least-known League, Little, Brown (Boston, MA), 2000.

The Punch: One Night, Two Lives, and the Fight That Changed Basketball Forever, Little, Brown (Boston, MA), 2002.

Open: Inside the Ropes at Bethpage Black, Little, Brown (Boston, MA), 2003.

Caddy for Life: The Bruce Edwards Story, Little, Brown (New York, NY), 2004.

(With Red Auerbach) *Let Me Tell You a Story: A Lifetime in the Game,* Little, Brown (New York, NY), 2004.

Next Man Up: A Year behind the Lines in Today's NFL, Little, Brown (Boston, MA), 2005.

Last Dance: Behind the Scenes at the Final Four, Little, Brown (Boston, MA), 2006.

Tales from Q School: Inside Golf's Fifth Major, Little, Brown (Boston, MA), 2007.

Living on the Black: Two Pitchers, Two Teams, One Season to Remember, Little, Brown (Boston, MA), 2008.

Contributor to periodicals, including *Sporting News, Basketball Times, Outlook,* and *Eastern Basketball.*

FICTION

Running Mates, Villard Books (New York, NY), 1992.

Winter Games, Little, Brown (Boston, MA), 1995.

Last Shot: A Final Four Mystery, Knopf (New York, NY), 2005.

Vanishing Act, Knopf (New York, NY), 2006.

Cover-up: Mystery at the Super Bowl, Knopf (New York, NY), 2007.

Adaptations

A Good Walk Spoiled: Days and Nights on the PGA Tour was adapted as an audiobook, Time Warner AudioBooks, 1998. *A Season on the Brink* was filmed as a made-for-TV movie starring Brian Dennehy, ESPN, 2002. *Last Shot* was adapted as an audiobook, performed by the author.

Sidelights

John Feinstein is an award-winning sportswriter whose work has appeared in such publications as the *Washington Post* and *Sports Illustrated.* Feinstein has also penned several nonfiction works that present a behind-the-scenes look at professional and college sports, including *Tales from Q School: Inside Golf's Fifth Major* and *Next Man Up: A Year behind the Lines in Today's NFL.* In addition, he has created a series of well-received mystery novels featuring a pair of teenaged reporters.

Feinstein gained national attention with his best-seller *A Season on the Brink: A Year with Bob Knight and the Indiana Hoosiers.* The book recounts Indiana University's 1985-86 basketball season, from the first organizational meetings to the team's surprising loss to Cleveland State University in the first round of the National Collegiate Athletic Association (NCAA) basketball tournament. Feinstein wrote the book after enjoying unusually close access to coach Bobby Knight and Knight's team's practices, meetings, and game-time huddles over the course of an entire season. (Many reporters have tried unsuccessfully to get the kind of intimate coverage Feinstein was allowed.) When *A Season on the Brink* was published, it quickly sold out of its initial printing of 17,000 copies and appeared on the *New York Times* best-seller list, where it was number one for seventeen weeks. Impressive sales of *A Season on the Brink* reflect the widespread interest in Indiana's legendary basketball coach. Kim Gagne wrote in the *Atlanta Journal-Constitution* that "Feinstein offers an insider's perspective that brings the reader to an appreciation of both the genius and the madness of" Knight.

Feinstein has written a number of other books on college hoops. *A Season Inside: One Year in College Basketball* details the 1987-88 basketball season, during which Feinstein attended 104 games. He recounts the highs and lows of the year and provides an inside look at such prominent university coaches as Dean Smith of North Carolina, John Thompson of Georgetown, and Larry Brown of Kansas, the school that ultimately won the 1988 NCAA championship. According to *Washington Post* contributor Robert D. Novak, in the book "Feinstein has attempted a tour de force and pretty well pulled it off. He has managed to convey the excitement, intrigue, confrontation, hysteria and sheer intoxication of college basketball." *Forever's Team* is perhaps Feinstein's most personal work: it concerns the 1978-79 basketball team from Duke University, his alma mater. In *Last Dance: Behind the Scenes at the Final Four,* the author presents a look at one of America's premier sporting events. "The anecdotes are entertaining, and the insights into the tournament's logistics fascinating," wrote *Booklist* contributor Wes Lukowsky.

In *Hard Courts: Real Life on the Professional Tennis Tours* Feinstein demystifies the glamour surrounding the world of professional tennis. He spent a year on the pro tennis circuit, getting to know the famous and not-so-famous players, their families, and their agents. More than one hundred interviews form the text, which presents professional tennis in a distinctly unflattering light. As Julie Cart wrote in the *New York Times,* Feinstein shows he has "rare insight into the professional tennis tour. *Hard Courts* peels back layer after layer of surface gloss and undeniable glamour to expose the machinations of players' agents, the power of television and the wheeling and dealing of unscrupulous promoters. The picture is not pretty." Feinstein takes a similar approach in *A Good Walk Spoiled: Days and Nights on the PGA Tour,* spending a year on the Professional Golfers' Association (PGA) tour to learn what life is like for golf insiders. He found golf a stark contrast to many other professional sports; golfers generally really do play by the rules, live quiet lives, and go to bed early. Michael Bamberger stated in the *New York Times Book Review* that Feinstein "has proved himself to be a dependable, thorough and honest reporter." The author revisited the golf world several years later with *The Majors: In Pursuit of Golf's Holy Grail.*

According to a *Kirkus Reviews* contributor, Feinstein "revisits an important National Basketball Association incident and ably dramatizes how it changed the participants and the league forever" in *The Punch: One Night, Two Lives, and the Fight That Changed Basketball Forever.* Retelling the story of Los Angeles Lakers forward Kermit Washington, who punched and broke the jaw of Houston Rocket All-Star Rudy Tomjanovich during a fight on the basketball court, Feinstein explains how the incident—which left Washington suspended and struggling to regain his reputation and brought Tomjanovich close to death—played out in both players' careers. Neither player was able to return to his promising status of their pre-fight careers.

In a completely different sports story, Feinstein retells the life of Bruce Edwards, professional caddy for legendary golfer Tom Watson, in *Caddy for Life: The Bruce Edwards Story.* Edwards served as a caddy for Watson for over forty years, and his life reveals parts of the golf industry known only to insiders. Edwards was diagnosed with Lou Gehrig's disease in 2003, and Feinstein covers the caddy's struggle with the disease. *Caddy for Life* "will thoroughly entertain golf fans," promised a critic for *Publishers Weekly.* Larry R. Little, writing in *School Library Journal* commented that readers will appreciate the "unique insight into a caddy's dedicated life on the P.G.A. tour." In *Tales from Q School,* Feinstein chronicles the action at the PGA 2005 qualifying tournaments, where more than 1,000 aspiring pros vied for only thirty available spots on the tour. Reviewing the work in *Booklist,* Bill Ott called Feinstein's account "compelling," adding, "The subject is made to order for his slices-of-life approach."

Feinstein turned his attention to the National Football League (NFL) for *Next Man Up,* "one of the most compelling portraits of NFL life ever written," observed Charles Hirshberg in *Sports Illustrated.* Granted complete access to the Baltimore Ravens' players and personnel, Feinstein provides an in-depth look at the team's 2004 season, focusing not only on game strategy but also on the intense pressures that drove the managers, coaches, and players. According to a contributor in *Publishers Weekly,* the author "persuasively argues that pro football is the most dramatic American sport," and Ott stated: "Football has never seemed as personal as it does here, in one of Feinstein's most involving books." Professional baseball is the subject of *Living on the Black: Two Pitchers, Two Teams, One Season to Remember,* in which Feinstein follows Tom Glavine of the New York Mets and Mike Mussina of the New York Yankees through the 2007 season. According to

Lukowsky, here the author "guides readers into a world with which fans have only surface familiarity, revealing in the process multiple substrata of nuance and meaning."

In addition to his nonfiction work, Feinstein has also penned several mysteries. His first, *Running Mates,* is a political thriller involving the assassination of Maryland's governor. An investigative reporter looking into the case discovers a surprising alliance between a right-wing extremist and a radical feminist who may have had the governor killed so that his female lieutenant-governor would come to power. A *Publishers Weekly* reviewer voiced praise for *Running Mates,* stating: "A strong, surprising resolution caps this thriller that delivers on its promise despite its protagonist's occasionally larger-than-life heroism and incredible luck."

In *Winter Games,* Feinstein's second mystery, a burned-out reporter returns to his hometown seeking peace and quiet, but discovers that the place is in an uproar because of a superstar on the high-school basketball team. The recruiting frenzy surrounding the young sports figure leads to the death of an assistant coach. *Winter Games* is, in the opinion of a *Publishers Weekly* commentator, a "dark portrayal of murder and rampant corruption on the college courts."

Feinstein combined his love of mystery novels and his expertise in sportswriting in his first novel for teens, *Last Shot: A Final Four Mystery.* Teen writers Stevie Thomas and Susan Carol Anderson, both aspiring journalists, have won an award in a sportswriting competition and are allowed to cover the NCAA Final Four game along with professional journalists. The two begin as rivals, but when they uncover a blackmail plot against one of the players, the pair become a team, working to uncover the mystery and get the scoop, "ultimately weaseling themselves into the bad guys' lair in classic Hardy Boys' fashion," Ott pointed out in *Booklist.* "This story . . . breaks new ground for teens, focusing primarily on the influential role of media in promoting college basketball," praised Gerry Larson, who reviewed *Last Shot* for *School Library Journal.* According to a critic in *Kirkus Reviews,* "Feinstein uses simple prose, lively dialogue, and authentic details" to bring the Final Four game to life for his readers. A *Publishers Weekly* critic praised the mystery aspect, noting that "the author's plotting entails some fancy footwork that will keep readers on their toes." With his experience as a commentator for National Public Radio, Feinstein performed the audiobook version of *Last Shot* himself.

Stevie and Susan Carol make a return appearance in *Vanishing Act,* a mystery set at the U.S. Open tennis championship in New York City. While covering the event, the thirteen-year-old reporters investigate the disappearance of Nadia Symanova, a beautiful Russian star, and learn that Susan Carol's uncle may be involved in the kidnapping. Critics noted that *Vanishing Act* would appeal to a variety of readers; Gillian Engberg, writing in *Booklist,* remarked that "sports fans will be fascinated by the insider's view of the tournament," and *School Library Journal* contributor D. Maria LaRocco observed that "the mystery maintains a genuine level of suspense throughout the story."

In *Cover-up: Mystery at the Super Bowl,* Feinstein's third work featuring the intrepid teen reporters, Stevie and Susan Carol uncover a scandal on the eve of the big game. While Susan serves as the co-anchor of *Kid-Sports,* a cable television show, Stevie writes human interest stories for the *Herald;* they join forces to unravel a conspiracy hiding the fact that several players failed a steroid test. Leah Krippner praised the novel in *School Library Journal,* stating that "the teens are well crafted and the villains are extraordinary," *Booklist* reviewer Betty Carter commented of *Cover-up* that "Feinstein's ease with the sports milieu create[s] a glamorous background" for his tale.

Biographical and Critical Sources

PERIODICALS

Atlanta Journal-Constitution, March 1, 1987, Kim Gagne, review of *A Season on the Brink.*

Booklist, March 15, 1992, Mary Carroll, review of *Running Mates,* p. 1340; April 1, 1993, Wes Lukowsky, review of *Play Ball: The Life and Troubled Times of Major League Baseball,* p. 1386; May 15, 1995, Bill Ott, review of *A Good Walk Spoiled: Days and Nights on the PGA Tour,* p. 1626; November 1, 1995, Wes Lukowsky, review of *Winter Games,* p. 457; October 1, 1996, Bill Ott, review of *The Best American Sports Writing 1996,* p. 316; November 15, 1996, Wes Lukowsky, review of *A Civil War, Army vs. Navy: A Year inside College Football's Purest Rivalry,* p. 565; November 15, 1997, Wes Lukowsky, review of *A March to Madness: The View from the Floor in the Atlantic Coast Conference,* p. 522; September 1, 1998, Bill Ott, review of *A March to Madness,* p. 55; March 1, 1999, Bill Ott, review of *The Majors: In Pursuit of Golf's Holy Grail,* p. 1100; September 15, 2000, Wes Lukowsky, review of *The Last Amateurs: Playing for Glory and Honor in Division I, Basketball's Least-Known League,* p. 186; July, 2002, Wes Lukowsky, review of *The Punch: One Night, Two Lives, and the Fight That Changed Basketball Forever,* p. 1794; May 1, 2003, Bill Ott, review of *Open: Inside the Ropes at Bethpage Black,* p. 1506; April 15, 2004, Gilbert Taylor, review of *Caddy for Life: The Bruce Edwards Story,* p. 1402; February 1, 2005, Bill Ott, review of *Last Shot: A Final Four Mystery,* p. 954; October 15, 2005, Bill Ott, review of *Next Man Up: A Year behind the Lines in the NFL,* p. 4; January 1, 2006, Wes Lukowsky, review of *Last Dance: Behind the Scenes at the Final Four,* p. 21; September 1, 2006, Gillian Engberg, review of *Vanishing Act,* p. 115; April 15, 2007, Bill Ott, review of *Tales from Q School: Inside Golf's Fifth Major,* p. 4; September 1, 2007, Bill Ott, review of *Cover-up: Mystery at the Super Bowl,* p. 131; May 1, 2008, Wes Lukowsky, review of *Living on the Black: Two Pitchers, Two Teams, One Season to Remember,* p. 5.*

Business Week, April 5, 1993, David Greising, review of *Play Ball: The Life and Troubled Times of Major League Baseball,* p. 8.

Christian Science Monitor, August 23, 1991, Gregory M. Lamb, review of *Hard Courts: Real Life on the Professional Tennis Tours,* p. 12; April 23, 1993, Charles Fountain, review of *Play Ball,* p. 11; October 4, 1995, Keith Henderson, review of *A Good Walk Spoiled,* p. 15; December 6, 1996, Ross Atkin, review of *A Civil War, Army vs. Navy,* p. 13.

Commentary, September, 1993, Jay P. Lefkowitz, review of *Play Ball,* p. 61.

Economist, February 15, 1997, review of *The Best American Sports Writing 1996,* p. 15.

Globe & Mail (Toronto, Ontario, Canada), April 10, 1999, review of *The Majors,* p. D11.

Horn Book, September-October, 2007, Betty Carter, review of *Cover-up,* p. 574.

Kirkus Reviews, November 15, 1997, review of *A March to Madness,* p. 1683; March 15, 1999, review of *The Majors,* p. 426; September 15, 2002, review of *The Punch,* p. 1363; January 1, 2005, review of *Last Shot,* p. 51.

Kliatt, September, 1997, review of *A Good Walk Spoiled,* p. 7.

Library Journal, May 1, 1993, Albert Spencer, review of *Play Ball,* p. 92; May 15, 1995, Terry Madden, review of *A Good Walk Spoiled,* p. 76; November 1, 1995, Rex E. Klett, review of *Winter Games,* p. 109; October 1, 1996, review of *A Civil War, Army vs. Navy,* p. 87; January, 1998, William O. Scheeren, review of *A March to Madness,* p. 109; April 15, 1999, Peter Ward, review of *The Majors,* p. 105; November 1, 2002, Jim Burns, review of *The Punch,* p. 97; April 15, 2004, Larry R. Little, review of *Caddy for Life,* p. 93.

Library Media Connection, April-May, 2005, Ruth Cox Clark, review of *Last Shot,* p. 77.

New York Times, August 25, 1991, Julie Cart, review of *Hard Courts;* December 22, 1991, Michael Kornfeld, review of *Hard Courts;* February 11, 1996, Charley Rosen, review of *Winter Games;* December 24, 1997, Richard Bernstein, review of *A March to Madness;* December 12, 2000, Michiko Kakutani, review of *The Last Amateurs,* p. B7.

New York Times Book Review, May 10, 1992, Marilyn Stasio, review of *Running Mates,* p. 23; April 4, 1993, Roger Noll, review of *Play Ball,* p. 24; June 11, 1995, Michael Bamberger, review of *A Good Walk Spoiled;* February 11, 1996, Charley Rosen, review of *Winter Games,* p. 22; November 3, 1996, Michael Lichtenstein, review of *A Civil War, Army vs. Navy,* p. 18; March 22, 1998, David Davis, review of *A March to Madness,* p. 16; February 28, 1999, review of *A March to Madness,* p. 24; May 2, 1999, Dave Anderson, review of *The Majors,* p. 16.

People, June 19, 1995, Tony Chiu, review of *A Good Walk Spoiled,* p. 36; March 16, 1998, Alex Tresniowski, review of *A March to Madness,* p. 34.

Publishers Weekly, March 2, 1992, review of *Running Mates,* p. 52; April 24, 1995, review of *A Good Walk Spoiled,* p. 52; September 25, 1995, review of *Winter Games,* p. 46; September 16, 1996, review of *A Civil War, Army vs. Navy,* p. 61; October 14, 1996, review of *The Best American Sports Writing 1996,* p. 78; December 1, 1997, review of *A March to Madness,* p. 38; March 22, 1998, David Davis, review of *A March to Madness,* p. 16; March 29, 1999, review of *The Majors,* p. 76; October 23, 2000, review of *The Last Amateurs,* p. 71; April 28, 2003, review of *Open,* p. 60; April 5, 2004, review of *Caddy for Life,* p. 58; April 19, 2004, Daisy Maryles, "Remembering the Caddy," p. 18; January 24, 2005, review of *Last Shot,* p. 244; August 15, 2005, review of *Next Man Up,* p. 53; January 9, 2006, review of *Last Dance,* p. 50; August 7, 2006, review of *Vanishing Act,* p. 59.

School Library Journal, January, 1992, Dino Vretos, review of *Hard Courts,* p. 145; August, 1993, Judy Sokoll, review of *Play Ball,* p. 206; January, 2005, Gerry Larson, review of *Last Shot,* p. 128; October, 2006, D. Maria LaRocco, review of *Vanishing Act,* p. 154; December, 2007, Leah Krippner, review of *Cover-up,* p. 126.

Sporting News, July 3, 1995, Steve Gietschier, review of *A Good Walk Spoiled,* p. 7; November 18, 1996, Steve Gietschier, review of *A Civil War, Army vs. Navy,* p. 8.

Sports Illustrated, October 14, 1991, Ron Fimrite, review of *Hard Courts,* p. 8; February 23, 1998, Charles Hirshberg, review of *A March to Madness,* p. A27; March 22, 1999, Walter Bingham, review of *The Majors,* p. R26; November 13, 2000, Charles Hirshberg, review of *The Last Amateur,* p. R16; November 14, 2005, Charles Hirshberg, "Stress Management: John Feinstein's Season with the Baltimore Ravens Gives an Intimate Look at the Pressure of NFL Life," p. Z4.

Time, September 2, 1991, John Skow, review of *Hard Courts,* p. 69.

Voice of Youth Advocates, April, 1998, review of *Winter Games,* p. 41.

Wall Street Journal, April 23, 1993, Frederick C. Klein, review of *Play Ball,* p. A12; July 26, 1995, Frederick C. Klein, *A Good Walk Spoiled,* p. A10; April 9, 1999, review of *The Majors,* p. W10; November 10, 2000, Larry Platt, review of *The Last Amateurs,* p. W8.

Washington Monthly, December, 2000, David Plotz, review of *The Last Amateurs,* p. 52.

Washington Post, November 28, 1988, Robert D. Novak, review of *A Season Inside.*

ONLINE

National Public Radio Web site, http://www.npr.org/ (November 1, 2008) "John Feinstein."

Random House Web site, http://www.randomhouse/ (November 1, 2008) interview with Feinstein.*

FISCHER, Scott M. 1971-

Personal

Born 1971; married; wife's name Teresa Nicole Fischer (a painter); children: one daughter. *Education:* Savannah College of Art and Design, B.A., 1994.

Addresses

Home and office—344 Stebbins St., Belchertown, MA 01007. *Agent*—Eddie Gamarra, Gotham Group, 9255 Sunset Blvd., Ste. 515, Los Angeles, CA 90069. *E-mail*—fisch@fischart.com.

Career

Painter, illustrator, author, and musician. Has designed trading cards for Magic the Gathering and Dungeons & Dragons game series. Amherst College, Amherst, MA, instructor at illustration master class, 2008. Musical recordings include children's songs. *Exhibitions:* Works exhibited at iO Gallery, Cornwall Bridge, CT, 2008.

Illustrator

SELF-ILLUSTRATED

Twinkle, Simon & Schuster (New York, NY), 2007.

ILLUSTRATOR

Geraldine McCaughrean, *Peter Pan in Scarlet* (U.S. edition; British edition illustrated by David Wyatt), Margaret K. McElderry Books (New York, NY), 2006.

Rich Michelson, *Animals Anonymous* (poems), Simon & Schuster (New York, NY), 2008.

ILLUSTRATOR; "SECRETS OF DRIPPING FANG" SERIES

Dan Greenburg, *The Onts,* Harcourt (Orlando, FL), 2005.

Dan Greenburg, *Treachery and Betrayal at Jolly Days,* Harcourt (Orlando, FL), 2006.

Dan Greenburg, *The Vampire's Curse,* Harcourt (Orlando, FL), 2006.

Dan Greenburg, *Fall of the House of Mandible,* Harcourt (Orlando, FL), 2006.

Dan Greenburg, *The Shluffmuffin Boy Is History,* Harcourt (Orlando, FL), 2006.

Dan Greenburg, *Attack of the Giant Octopus,* Harcourt (Orlando, FL), 2007.

Dan Greenburg, *Please Don't Eat the Children,* Harcourt (Orlando, FL), 2007.

Dan Greenburg, *When Bad Snakes Attack Good Children,* Harcourt (Orlando, FL), 2007.

Sidelights

Scott M. Fischer, an artist best known for his paintings featuring science-fiction and fantasy themes, has also created the original self-illustrated children's book

Twinkle. As an illustrator, Fischer has also contributed illustrations to Dan Greenburg's popular "Secrets of Dripping Fang" series of middle-grade novels, and he provided the artwork for the U.S. edition of Geraldine McCaughrean's highly anticipated *Peter Pan in Scarlet,* an officially sanctioned sequel to J.M. Barrie's classic novel *Peter Pan.* In addition, Fischer, who has designed trading cards based on the Magic the Gathering and Dungeons & Dragons role-playing games, also writes and performs his own songs for children.

In *Twinkle,* Fischer offers a unique interpretation of the children's tune, "Twinkle, Twinkle Little Star." The work centers on two youngsters—a blue-haired alien who jets into space aboard a sailing ship and an Earth-born lad who reaches the heavens via his balloon-assisted tricycle. After an encounter with a meteor shower leaves both children stranded, they cobble together a vessel from the debris and head off together. Readers follow the friends' parallel journeys, which begin at opposite ends of the book, by flipping the work back and forth; the travelers meet in the middle of the story. According to a contributor in *Publishers Weekly,* Fischer's "digitally rendered pictures have the slightly smeared textures and bouncy colors of graffiti, and there are plenty of nifty details." In *Kirkus Reviews* a contributor praised the "intense colors and high-energy action" of Fischer's artwork.

Greenburg's "Secrets of Dripping Fang" series follows the misfortunes of the ten-year-old Shluffmuffin twins—Wally and Cheyenne—after they arrive at the despicable Jolly Days Orphanage following the tragic deaths of their father, who drowned in a porta-potty, and mother, who was attacked by bunnies. After Wally and Cheyenne are adopted by the repulsive Mandible sisters and taken to a mansion in Dripping Fang Forest, they discover a terrible secret: the Mandibles are actually giant ants bent on conquering the planet. Reviewing the first volume of the "Secrets of Dripping Fang" series, *The Onts,* for *School Library Journal,* Elaine E. Knight stated that Fischer's "eerie black-and-white drawings complement the heavily tongue-in-cheek plot."

Fischer's silhouette ink drawings grace the interior of *Peter Pan in Scarlet,* "an exquisitely rendered, magical return to Neverland," according to *Horn Book* contributor Lissa Paul. Commissioned by trustees of the Great Ormond Street Hospital to mark the centenary of Barrie's 1904 play, the book was written by McCaughrean after she won an intense, worldwide competition involving more than 200 authors. Set in 1926, the novel examines themes of memory, loss, and identity. *Peter Pan in Scarlet* proved to be a worthy successor to Barrie's tale, according to several reviewers, and Fischer's pen-and-ink artwork also drew praise. As Farida S. Dowler remarked in *School Library Journal,* the book's illustrations "add to the enjoyment of the story."

Biographical and Critical Sources

PERIODICALS

Booklist, November 15, 2006, Gillian Engberg, "Trouble in Neverland," p. 42.
Horn Book, January-February, 2007, Lissa Paul, review of *Peter Pan in Scarlet,* p. 51.
Kirkus Reviews, October 15, 2006, review of *Peter Pan in Scarlet,* p. 1074; July 1, 2007, review of *Twinkle.*
Publishers Weekly, October 3, 2005, review of *The Onts,* p. 70; August 13, 2007, review of *Twinkle,* p. 66.
School Library Journal, December, 2005, Elaine E. Knight, review of *The Onts,* p. 112; June, 2006, Walter Minkel, review of *Treachery and Betrayal at Jolly Days,* p. 156; December, 2006, Farida S. Dowler, review of *Peter Pan in Scarlet,* p. 150; September, 2007, Martha Simpson, review of *Twinkle,* p. 164.

ONLINE

Scott M. Fischer Home Page, http://www.fischart.com (October 15, 2008).*

*   *   *

FISHBONE, Greg R. 1970-

Personal

Born August 12, 1970, in MA; married; children: one daughter. *Education:* University of Pennsylvania, B.A., 1992; Temple University, J.D., 1995.

Addresses

Office—Waltham, MA. *E-mail*—greg@gfishbone.com.

Career

Attorney, author, and illustrator. Class of 2k7 (online authors collective), founder.

Member

Society of Children's Book Writers and Illustrators (webmaster and assistant regional coordinator for New England regions, 2001—).

Writings

(Self-illustrated) *The Penguins of Doom,* Blooming Tree Press (Austin, TX), 2007.

Former editor and contributor to *Event Horizon.*

Biographical and Critical Sources

PERIODICALS

Kirkus Reviews, July 1, 2007, review of *The Penguins of Doom.*

Greg R. Fishbone

School Library Journal, December, 2007, Carol Schene, review of *The Penguins of Doom,* p. 128.

ONLINE

Class of 2k7 Web site, http://classof2k7.com/ (October 15, 2008), "Greg R. Fishbone."

Greg R. Fishbone Home Page, http://gfishbone.com (October 15, 2008).

Greg R. Fishbone Web log, http://tem2.livejournal.com/ (October 15, 2008).

*   *   *

FISHER, Cynthia

Personal

Female. *Education:* University of Maine, B.S., 1980; attended Greenfield Community College, 1986-87; attended Art Institute of Boston, 1987-89.

Addresses

Office—Big Bang Mosaics, 15 Forgette Rd., Charlemont, MA 01339. *E-mail*—cindy@bigbangmosaics.com.

Career

Artist and illustrator. Freelance illustrator, 1989—; Big Bang Mosaics, Buckland, MA, founder. Teacher of mosaic art at Ashfield Summer Arts Program, Ashfield, MA, Snow Farm New England Craft Program, Haydenville, MA, Brookfield Craft Center, Brookfield, CT, and Worcester Art Museum, Worcester, MA. Peace Corps volunteer in the Philippines, 1980-82, for U.S. Park Service, 1983, and for U.S. Forest Service, 1983-86. *Exhibitions:* Work exhibited at The Art Bank, Shelburne, MA, 2002; Forbes Library Gallery, Northampton, MA, 2003; Museo Italoamericano, San Francisco, CA, 2004; Higgins Art Gallery, Cape Cod Community College, West Barnstable, MA, 2004; Whistler House Museum of Art, Lowell, MA, 2004; Slater Concourse Gallery, Tufts University, Medford, MA, 2006; High Risk Gallery, Chicago, IL, 2006; Great Falls Discovery Center, Turner's Falls, MA, 2006; Worcester Art Museum, Worcester, MA, 2007; Somerville Museum, Somerville, MA, 2007; U.S. Fish & Wildlife Gallery, Hadley, MA, 2008; and (solo exhibit) Jones Library, Amherst, MA, 2008.

Illustrator

Anne Fine, *The Chicken Gave It to Me,* Joy Street Books (Boston, MA), 1993.

Constance Hiser, *Night of the Werepoodle,* Holiday House (New York, NY), 1994.

Julie Anne Peters, *B.J.'s Billion Dollar Bet,* Little, Brown (Boston, MA), 1994.

Melvin Berger, *All about Sound,* Scholastic (New York, NY), 1994.

Dick King-Smith, *The School Mouse,* Hyperion (New York, NY), 1995.

David A. Adler, *Calculator Riddles,* Holiday House (New York, NY), 1995.

Peggy Parish, *Be Ready at Eight,* Simon & Schuster (New York, NY), 1996.

Nancy White Carlstrom, *Ten Christmas Sheep,* Eerdmans (Grand Rapids, MI), 1996.

David A. Adler, *Easy Math Puzzles,* Holiday House (New York, NY), 1997.

Laurie Lawlor, *The Biggest Pest on Eighth Avenue,* Holiday House (New York, NY), 1997.

Laurie Lawlor, *The Worst Kid Who Ever Lived on Eighth Avenue,* Holiday House (New York, NY), 1998.

Betty Miles, *The Sky Is Falling,* Simon & Schuster (New York, NY), 1998.

Elvira Woodruff, *Can You Guess Where We're Going?,* Holiday House (New York, NY), 1998.

Judy Cox, *Third Grade Pet,* Holiday House (New York, NY), 1998.

Natasha Wing, *The Night before Halloween,* Grosset & Dunlap (New York, NY), 1999.

Anne Schreiber, *One Stormy Night,* Scholastic (New York, NY), 1999.

Judith Bauer, *A Squeak, a Squeal, and a Screech!,* Scholastic (New York, NY), 1999.

Joan Holub, *The Spooky Sleepover,* Grosset & Dunlop (New York, NY), 1999.

Barbara deRubertis, *Deena's Lucky Penny,* Kane Press (New York, NY), 1999.

Lee Bennett Hopkins, compiler, *Dino-roars,* Golden Books (New York, NY), 1999.

Judy Cox, *Mean, Mean Maureen Green,* Holiday House (New York, NY), 2000.

Anne Schreiber, *Brent's B-day Party,* Scholastic (New York, NY), 2000.

David F. Marx, *Baby in the House,* Children's Press (New York, NY), 2000.

Alice DeLaCroix, *The Hero of Third Grade,* Holiday House (New York, NY), 2002.

Jane Schoenberg, *My Bodyworks: Songs about Your Bones, Muscles, Heart, and More!,* Crocodile Books (New York, NY), 2005.

Alice DeLaCroix, *How to Survive a Totally Boring Summer,* Holiday House (New York, NY), 2007.

Sidelights

Cynthia Fisher, a mosaic artist and illustrator based in Massachusetts, has illustrated more than two dozen children's books, including Judy Cox's *Mean, Mean Maureen Green* and Alice DeLaCroix's *The Hero of Third Grade.* In one of Fisher's early efforts, *The School Mouse* by Dick King-Smith, a young rodent with a love of learning prevents the other mice in her family from eating the poison left behind by exterminators. The animal characters "are hilariously embellished in Fisher's imaginative illustrations," observed a critic in *Publishers Weekly.*

Mean, Mean Maureen Green centers on third-grader Lilley, who dreads the thought of riding the school bus with Maureen Green, a notorious bully. Lilley also attempts to conquer her fear of riding her new bike without using training wheels. According to *School Library Journal* reviewer Kay Bowes, Fisher's "black-and-white cartoons add a touch of humor and capture the intent of the characters" in Cox's story.

Fisher has also provided the artwork for a pair of works by DeLaCroix. In *The Hero of Third Grade,* young Randall is inspired by the romantic French fictional hero the Scarlet Pimpernel to perform good deeds for his new classmates. *Booklist* contributor Connie Fletcher stated that the illustrator's "comical pen-and-ink drawings capture the intrigue and chaos of a grade-school classroom." Randall starts a chess club once school lets out in *How to Survive a Totally Boring Summer.* Here "Fisher's illustrations . . . include clever touches such as Randall's 'I love chess' shirt," noted Kelly Roth in *School Library Journal.*

Biographical and Critical Sources

PERIODICALS

Booklist, October 15, 1995, Lauren Peterson, review of *The School Mouse,* p. 404; November 1, 1995, Carolyn Phelan, review of *Calculator Riddles,* p. 466; May 1, 1998, Ilene Cooper, review of *The Worst Kid Who Ever Lived on Eighth Avenue,* p. 1524; December 1, 1999, Gillian Engberg, review of *Mean, Mean Maureen Green,* p. 703, and Carolyn Phelan, review of *Deena's Lucky Penny,* p. 716; January 1, 2003, Connie Fletcher, review of *The Hero of the Third Grade,* p. 888; August, 2007, Shelle Rosenfeld, review of *How to Survive a Totally Boring Summer,* p. 73.

Publishers Weekly, September 11, 1995, review of *The School Mouse,* p. 86; November 10, 1997, review of *The Biggest Pest on Eighth Avenue,* p. 73; December 14, 1998, review of *Third Grade Pet,* p. 76.

School Library Journal, March, 2000, Kay Bowes, review of *Mean, Mean Maureen Green,* p. 192; December, 2002, Elaine E. Knight, review of *The Hero of Third Grade,* p. 86; July, 2007, Kelly Roth, review of *How to Survive a Totally Boring Summer,* p. 73.

ONLINE

Cynthia Fisher Web site, http://www.bigbangmosaics.com (October 15, 2008).*

*   *   *

FLETCHER, Ralph 1953-

Personal

Born March 17, 1953; son of Ralph (a textbook publisher) and Jean Fletcher; married JoAnn Portalupi (a professor), May, 1989; children: Taylor Curtis, Adam Curtis, Robert, Joseph. *Education:* Dartmouth College, B.A., 1975; Columbia University, M.F.A., 1983. *Politics:* Democrat.

Addresses

Home—Durham, NH. *Office*—Arrowpoint 17, Inc., P.O. Box 8, South Hadley, MA 01075. *E-mail*—fletcher17@ earthlink.net.

Career

Educational consultant, 1985—; author, 1990—.

Awards, Honors

Christopher Medal, 2002, for *Uncle Daddy.*

Writings

JUVENILE FICTION

Fig Pudding, Clarion (New York, NY), 1995.
Spider Boy, Clarion (New York, NY), 1997.
Twilight Comes Twice, illustrated by Kate Kiesler, Clarion (New York, NY), 1997.
Flying Solo, Clarion (New York, NY), 1998.
Tommy Trouble and the Magic Marble, Holt (New York, NY), 2000.

Ralph Fletcher (Reproduced by permission.)

Grandpa Never Lies, illustrated by Harvey Stevenson, Clarion (New York, NY), 2000.

The Circus Surprise, illustrated by Vladimir Vagin, Clarion (New York, NY), 2001.

Uncle Daddy, Holt (New York, NY), 2001.

Have You Been to the Beach Lately?, illustrated by Andrea Sperling, Orchard (New York, NY), 2001.

Hello, Harvest Moon, illustrated by Kate Kiesler, Clarion (New York, NY), 2003.

Moving Day, illustrated by Jennifer Emery, Wordsong (Honesdale, PA), 2006.

The One O'Clock Chop, Holt (New York, NY), 2007.

The Sandman, illustrated by Richard Cowdrey, Holt (New York, NY), 2008.

Fig Pudding has been translated into Dutch, German, and French.

JUVENILE NONFICTION

A Writer's Notebook: Unlocking the Writer within You, Avon (New York, NY), 1996.

Live Writing: Breathing Life into Your Words, Avon (New York, NY), 1999.

How Writers Work: Finding a Process That Works for You, HarperCollins (New York, NY), 2000.

Poetry Matters: Writing a Poem from the Inside Out, HarperCollins (New York, NY), 2002.

Marshfield Dreams: When I Was a Kid (memoir), Holt (New York, NY), 2005.

How to Write Your Life Story, HarperCollins (New York, NY), 2007.

POETRY

Water Planet: Poems about Water, Arrowhead Books (Paramus, NJ), 1991.

I Am Wings: Poems about Love (also see below), photographs by Joe Baker, Atheneum (New York, NY), 1994.

Buried Alive: The Elements of Love (also see below), photographs by Andrew Moore, Atheneum (New York, NY), 1996.

Ordinary Things: Poems from a Walk in Early Spring, illustrated by Walter Lyon Krudop, Atheneum (New York, NY), 1997.

Room Enough for Love (contains *I Am Wings* and *Buried Alive*), Aladdin (New York, NY), 1998.

Relatively Speaking: Poems about Family, Orchard (New York, NY), 1999.

A Writing Kind of Day: Poems for Young Poets, illustrated by April Ward, Wordsong (Honesdale, PA), 2005.

OTHER

Walking Trees: Teaching Teachers in the New York City Schools, Heinemann (Portsmouth, NH), 1991, published as *Walking Trees: Portraits of Teachers and Children in the Culture of Schools,* Heinemann (Portsmouth, NH), 1995.

What a Writer Needs, Heinemann (Portsmouth, NH), 1993.

Breathing In, Breathing Out: Keeping a Writer's Notebook, Heinemann (Portsmouth, NH), 1996.

(With JoAnn Portalupi) *Craft Lessons: Teaching Writing K-8,* Stenhouse (Portland, ME), 1998, 2nd edition, 2007.

(With JoAnn Portalupi) *Nonfiction Craft Lessons: Teaching Information Writing K-8,* Stenhouse (Portland, ME), 2001.

(With JoAnn Portalupi) *Writing Workshop: The Essential Guide,* Heinemann (Portsmouth, NH), 2001.

(With JoAnn Portalupi) *Teaching the Qualities of Writing: Ideas, Design, Language, Presentation,* Heinemann (Portsmouth, NH), 2004.

(With JoAnn Portalupi) *Lessons for the Writer's Notebook* (curriculum guide), Heinemann (Portsmouth, NH), 2005.

Boy Writers: Reclaiming Their Voices, Stenhouse Publishers (Portland, ME), 2006.

Contributor to periodicals, including *Redbook, People, Cosmopolitan,* and the *Wall Street Journal.*

Sidelights

Ralph Fletcher is the author of a number of well-received volumes of fiction and poetry for young readers, including *Uncle Daddy,* and *Moving Day.* An educational consultant, he has also written extensively on the craft of writing, penning such titles as *Poetry Matters: Writing a Poem from the Inside Out* and *How to Write Your Life Story.* "Most writers specialize in one particular kind of writing," Fletcher stated on his home page. "Not me. I have published novels, poetry collections, nonfiction, books for teachers and picture books. I find that each form comes with its own particular pleasures and challenges."

Fletcher's first published titles appeared in the early 1990s, but it was his 1994 volume of poetry for young adults, *I Am Wings: Poems about Love,* that garnered him solid reviews and established him as a popular writer with adolescent readers. *I Am Wings* consists of several short, unrhymed poems coupled with black-and-white photographs of teenagers by Joe Baker. The poems chronicle a romance, told by a boy named Lee. Divided into two sections, "Falling In" and "Falling Out," Fletcher's verse attempts to capture the gamut of feelings that many young teens struggle with and find bewildering: the crush, the kiss, the betrayal. It is written in the vernacular of teen speech, and for this Fletcher won recurrent praise from reviewers for creating accessible verse for an age group that is usually not expected to gravitate toward poetry. Diane Tuccillo reviewed *I Am Wings* for *Voice of Youth Advocates* and found the verse "romantic and pensive, but not mushy."

Fletcher's next book of poetry, *Ordinary Things: Poems from a Walk in Early Spring,* was also geared toward teen readers, consisting of thirty-three brief poems with pencil drawings by Walter Lyon Krudop. The verses serve as a tutorial for the reader on how to leave the house and become an observer of the magic of nature. "Fletcher reminds young people that such a walk can be mind-clearing and therapeutic," remarked Sharon Korbeck in *School Library Journal.*

Fletcher returns to the subject of love, but ties in observations of the natural world outside with the inner turmoil of ardor in *Buried Alive: The Elements of Love.* Interspersing poetry with photographs and sectioned into four parts—Earth, Water, Fire, and Air—Fletcher's thirty-one poems each recount a tale of love or love's woe: the magic of mutual attraction; a secret crush on the baby-sitter; a gay girl ostracized but still proud, though her yearbook contains no signatures. A *Kirkus Reviews* critic praised Fletcher for creating "articulate, intense poems that treat the subject of love with dignity and compassion." *School Library Journal* reviewer Marjorie Lewis wrote that *Buried Alive,* as a whole, puts Fletcher "a step above" some of the other poets who write for adolescents. "Plainspeaking but lyrical, Fletcher makes poetry accessible while still keeping it, well, poetry," commented Roger Sutton in a review of the work for *Bulletin of the Center for Children's Books.*

The humorous and astute observations of an eleven-year-old boy spending a day along the shore comprise *Have You Been to the Beach Lately?,* a collection of thirty-three poems. Very little escapes the narrator's at-

tention, including the foolish antics of a group of teenagers and a chubby baby with a wet diaper. According to Lauralyn Persson, writing in *School Library Journal,* Fletcher's "simple language and conversational tone are just right for capturing the emotions of a child on the edge of adolescence." *Moving Day,* another poetry collection, details the emotions of twelve-year-old Fletch, who is preparing to move to a new state with his family. Noting the gamut of books that examine a youngster's adjustment to a new home, *School Library Journal* critic Mary Jean Smith remarked that "few focus in such depth on what was left behind."

A youngster chronicles the trials and triumphs of everyday life in *A Writing Kind of Day: Poems for Young Poets.* The more than two dozen free-verse poems examine such varied topics as homework, road kill, haiku, and a grandmother's battle with senility. "What emerges is a picture of a young writer at work, looking closely at the world," noted *School Library Journal* contributor Lee Bock. In the words of *Booklist* reviewer Jennifer Mattson, the collection "demonstrates how poems can transform the daily experiences of a child's life into dead-on truth bombs."

Fletcher has also penned a number of works for young readers, including *Twilight Comes Twice,* a picture book told in verse. Illustrated by Kate Kiesler with drawings

Cover of Fletcher's middle-grade novel **Flying Solo,** *featuring artwork by Ben Caldwell.* (Jacket illustration copyright © 1998 by Ben Caldwell. Reprinted by permission of Clarion Books, an imprint of Houghton Mifflin Harcourt Publishing Company. All rights reserved.)

of a young girl and her dog out for a walk, the work is structured around a twenty-four-hour period. Fletcher begins with the coming of night in a somewhat rural, though still populated, setting and picks up again with the arrival of daylight, hence the title. Observations of commuters, children playing, and animals and their activities are recorded in the verse. A *Publishers Weekly* reviewer found the work somewhat "cerebral," but granted that "both art and text are filled with sumptuous detail." A *Kirkus Reviews* contributor termed *Twilight Comes Twice* "a quietly alluring mood piece" that might entice "readers to move beyond the page" and explore dusk and dawn's special quietness for themselves.

Another notable book from Fletcher is *Hello, Harvest Moon,* a companion volume to *Twilight Comes Twice.* The work, noted a *Kirkus Reviews* contributor, "makes peaceful reading either in season, or on any moonlit night." *Hello Harvest Moon* traces the path of a single night, from the rising to the setting of the moon. Many people observe the light of the moon as they go about their lives; a girl and her cat play by it, a pilot flies by it, luna moths dance under it, and turtle hatchlings follow its reflection to the sea. Fletcher describes all of these activities with "lyrical, child-friendly images [which] will linger in readers' minds," remarked a *Publishers Weekly* contributor.

In *Grandpa Never Lies,* a girl recounts special times with her grandparents, who invite the youngster to their cabin to hunt fossils, drink hot chocolate, and listen to Grandpa's imaginative stories. After her grandmother suddenly dies, however, the girl and her grandpa help each other cope with the loss. Despite its somber theme, *Grandpa Never Lies* "is an upbeat, joyous story of an intergenerational relationship," noted Lauren Peterson in *Booklist.* A familiar childhood predicament is the subject of *The Circus Surprise.* When Nick becomes separated from his parents while visiting the Big Top, a friendly clown lends assistance to the frightened boy. "Fletcher's text is by turns reassuring and practical in tone," observed a *Publishers Weekly* reviewer. Fletcher explores the origins of a fabled individual in *The Sandman,* a "charming and comforting bedtime tale," wrote Ian Chipman in *Booklist.* The work centers on Tor, a wee fellow who discovers that dust from a dragon's scale cures his insomnia. "Fletcher's smoothly written story flows in a thoroughly plausible way," Persson stated.

Fletcher is also the author of several acclaimed novels for late-elementary readers. The first of these was *Fig Pudding,* published in 1995 to excellent reviews. Its narrator is Cliff Abernathy, III, the oldest of six children in a pleasant and close-knit family. Fletcher structures the narrative around a year in the life of the Abernathy family, beginning at Christmas one year and ending with the subsequent holiday season. Each chapter revolves around a family member, and through Cliff's tale, which encompasses everything from daily events to the tragic death of a sibling, readers come to know

the characters and their very different personalities. "Written with humor, perception, and a clarity of language, the book resonates with laughter and sorrow," declared Alice Casey Smith in a review of *Fig Pudding* for *School Library Journal.* Chris Sherman, assessing the work for *Booklist,* termed the hero of Fletcher's story "a sympathetic and thoughtful narrator." The author writes about the tragedy and the way in which the family deals with its grief "with remarkable restraint and understatement," noted a *Publishers Weekly* reviewer.

Fletcher introduces yet another likable kid in *Spider Boy.* Seventh-grader Bobby loves his pet tarantulas and is fascinated by spiders in general. This never seemed to be a problem until Bobby's family leaves Illinois and moves halfway across the country. Bobby is suddenly known as the new kid in school with the bizarre hobby. Furthermore, his beloved tarantula Thelma has stopped eating, probably because of the stress of the move. So has Bobby, who still keeps his wristwatch set on Illinois time. Coming to terms with the bully at school, who derisively names Bobby "Spider Boy" and then is responsible for the death of one of his tarantulas, is the great trial of Bobby's life and one that resonates with the novel's intended audience. Candace Smith, writing in *Booklist* called *Spider Boy* an "appealing story" in which, Smith wrote, "Fletcher portrays the new-kid-on-the-block syndrome honestly by making Bobby a sympathetic but not perfect character." A *Kirkus Reviews* contributor said of the book: "Creating and guiding a winning cast with a light, sure hand, Fletcher puts a fine, fresh spin on a familiar premise."

A former educator, Fletcher drew upon his classroom experiences to depict a common fantasy among younger students in *Flying Solo.* When their substitute teacher fails to show up, a classroom of smart sixth graders seizes the opportunity and takes charge of the class curriculum for a day, while struggling to keep others at school in the dark regarding the situation. Fletcher introduces a host of students as lead characters, each with their own personal travail to resolve: Bastian is moving to Hawaii with his family the next day and must decide whether he will leave his dog with a family here or force it to undergo a long period of quarantine; Rachel has not spoken since a classmate who had a crush on her died several months earlier; Sean, a boy with a troubled family life, has a crush on Rachel now; Karen emerges as a natural leader, while Jessica shows herself as too uptight to learn from the experience of taking on responsibility for the first time. In the end, each student learns how to rely upon, trust, and forgive one another. The author, noted Kathleen Squires in *Booklist,* "expertly balances a wide variety of emotions, giving readers a story that is by turns sad, poignant, and funny." Writing in *Horn Book,* Susan P. Bloom stated that Fletcher's "kaleidoscopic novel is more thoughtful and poignant than most school stories, while still appropriately leavened with comic moments."

Another novel by Fletcher is *Uncle Daddy,* described as "a reassuring picture of forgiveness and acceptance within a family" by *School Library Journal* reviewer Heide Piehler. Ever since his father abandoned the family without warning when he was three years old, Rivers has been raised by his mother and his great-uncle, a man whom the boy calls "Uncle Daddy." Then, six years later, when Rivers is nine, his father returns. Although Fletcher avoids the clichés that readers might have expected from this situation—for example, Rivers's father and Uncle Daddy do not try to force the boy to choose between them—Rivers still faces a difficult adjustment. "With uncomplicated sentences and plenty of dialogue, Fletcher makes Rivers's dilemma immediate and real," commented a *Horn Book* critic.

Set in 1973, *The One O'Clock Chop* centers on fourteen-year-old Matt, a Long Island resident who takes a job as a clam digger so he can earn enough to buy his own boat. While dealing with his conflicted emotions about his father's remarriage, Matt falls in love with his exotic cousin, Jazzy, who comes to visit for the summer. "Fletcher's insight into Matt and his

Cover of Fletcher's novel Uncle Daddy, *featuring artwork by Andy* *Newman.* (Henry Holt and Company, 2001. Reprinted by permission of Henry Holt and Company, LLC.)

boat dreams fly off the page with a solid resonance," a contributor noted in *Kirkus Reviews.* "Writing with his customary sensitivity and flair for language," observed a *Publishers Weekly* contributor, "Fletcher turns a coming-of-age story into a rich, affecting read."

Fletcher has also written several nonfiction works focused on the writing process, including *Breathing In, Breathing Out: Keeping a Writer's Notebook.* He begins the book by positing that it is not altogether necessary for a writer to keep such a journal, and then moves on to provide guidelines for those who decide they would like to. He explains such a tool can help one learn to write without fear of judgment, and thus develop a clear voice. Such journals are also excellent ways for writers to find their inspiration, and Fletcher provides examples of how insignificant details, rhetorical questions, lists of oddities, and even the conversations of strangers can spark fire to the creative process. Compared to most "how-to" works for aspiring writers, "this one is refreshingly varied and undogmatic in its approach," noted Jeffrey Cooper in *Kliatt.*

Poetry Matters, a guide for middle-grade students, is written in a similar style. Described as "chatty, but never condescending" by *Booklist* critic Hazel Rochman, *Poetry Matters* "packs in a wealth of information without a word of jargon." In addition to writing about the components of poetry—images, rhythm, voice— Fletcher also includes interviews with three other children's poets. His points are illustrated with numerous excerpts from his own and others' works, which "embody the author's advice by showing how writing techniques actually function in poems," explained Kristen Oravec in *School Library Journal.*

Hoping to nurture young writers, Fletcher has also produced other books geared specifically to budding authors—*A Writer's Notebook: Unlocking the Writer within You* and *Live Writing: Breathing Life into Your Words* among them. *A Writer's Notebook* offers realistic advice on how to keep notes and use them to create stories and poems. *Live Writing* instructs young writers on how to use words, imagination, ideas, and a love of books to create written works that "live and breathe." In *How to Write Your Life Story,* Fletcher offers advice for young people who wish to write an autobiography or memoir. According to *Booklist* critic Ilene Cooper, aspiring writers "will be pleased with the suggestions Fletcher makes in his easy style."

Fletcher shares his own life story in *Marshfield Dreams: When I Was a Kid,* "a dreamy reminiscence of growing up in the 1950s and 1960s," observed Anne O'Malley in *Booklist.* Fletcher grew up in a large Catholic family in the small Massachusetts town of Marshfield, where he explored the woods near his home, helped raise chicks, and, much to his embarrassment, learned from a classmate that his mother was going to have another baby. Writing in *School Library Journal,* Alison Follos praised the memoir's "sagacious eloquence and gentle

Cover of Fletcher's nonfiction guide **How to Write Your Life Story,** *featuring artwork by Ian Nagy.* (Cover art © 2007 by Ian Nagy. Used by permission of HarperCollins Children's Books, a division of HarperCollins Publishers.)

humor," and a *Kirkus Reviews* critic stated that *Marshfield Dreams* "will open readers' eyes to the bonds of a peerless time and simpler lifestyle."

"I've always treasured books," Fletcher once told *SATA.* "Books opened my eyes. They moved me from the inside out. At some point, I dreamed of becoming a writer. Today, when I write, I'm trying to put the reader through a powerful experience. I want to move my readers in the same way other authors have moved me with their books." On his home page, Fletcher noted that "becoming a writer is . . . a dream that has come true. I love to write. I love getting up every morning and mucking around in sentences, playing with stories, trying to build my city of words."

Biographical and Critical Sources

PERIODICALS

Audubon, November-December, 2001, Christopher Camuto, review of *Twilight Comes Twice,* p. 86.

Booklist, March 15, 1994, Hazel Rochman, review of *I Am Wings: Poems about Love,* p. 1345; May 15, 1995, Chris Sherman, review of *Fig Pudding,* p. 1645; May 1, 1996, Hazel Rochman, review of *Buried Alive: The Elements of Love,* p. 1500; April 15, 1997, Karen Morgan, review of *Ordinary Things: Poems from a Walk in Early Spring,* pp. 1421-1422; June 1-15, 1997, Candace Smith, review of *Spider Boy,* p. 1702; October 15, 1997, Stephanie Zvirin, review of *Twilight Comes Twice,* p. 414; August, 1998, Kathleen Squires, review of *Flying Solo,* p. 1998; July, 1999, Susan Dove Lempke, review of *Relatively Speaking: Poems about Family,* p. 1940; August, 2000, Todd Morning, review of *Tommy Trouble and the Magic Marble,* p. 2138; December 15, 2000, Lauren Peterson, review of *Grandpa Never Lies,* p. 825; May 15, 2002, Hazel Rochman, review of *Poetry Matters: Writing a Poem from the Inside Out,* p. 1593; March 15, 2005, Jennifer Mattson, review of *A Writing Kind of Day: Poems for Young Poets,* p. 1290; October 1, 2005, Anne O'Malley, review of *Marshfield Dreams: When I Was a Kid,* p. 51; October 1, 2007, Ilene Cooper, review of *How to Write Your Life Story,* p. 51; September 15, 2007, Stephanie Zvirin, review of *The One O'Clock Chop,* p. 74; July 1, 2008, Ian Chipman, review of *The Sandman,* p. 73.

Bulletin of the Center for Children's Books, July-August, 1996, Roger Sutton, review of *Buried Alive,* pp. 370-371.

Educational Leadership, March, 1991, Brenda Miller Power, review of *Walking Trees: Teaching Teachers in the New York City Schools,* pp. 84-85.

English Journal, April, 1993, Tom Romano, review of *What a Writer Needs,* pp. 93-94.

Horn Book, July-August, 1994, Nancy Vasilakis, review of *I Am Wings,* pp. 466-467; July-August, 1997, Elizabeth S. Watson, review of *Spider Boy,* pp. 454-455; November-December, 1998, Susan P. Bloom, review of *Flying Solo,* pp. 728-729; July, 2001, review of *Uncle Daddy,* p. 450.

Kirkus Reviews, April 15, 1996, review of *Buried Alive,* p. 601; March 15, 1997, review of *Spider Boy,* p. 460; September 1, 1997, review of *Twilight Comes Twice,* p. 1388; February 15, 2002, review of *Poetry Matters,* pp. 254-255; September 15, 2003, review of *Hello, Harvest Moon,* p. 1174; August 15, 2005, review of *Marshfield Dreams,* p. 913; November 15, 2006, review of *Moving Day,* p. 1173; July 1, 2007, review of *The One O'Clock Chop.*

Kliatt, September, 1997, Jeffrey Cooper, review of *Breathing In, Breathing Out: Keeping a Writer's Notebook,* p. 25.

Language Arts, April, 1992, review of *Walking Trees,* p. 304; March, 1994, review of *What a Writer Needs,* p. 230; May, 2003, Junko Yokota, Mingshui Cai, and Theresa Kubasak, review of *Poetry Matters,* p. 396.

Library Journal, November 15, 1990, Nancy E. Zuwiyya, review of *Walking Trees,* p. 78.

Publishers Weekly, April 24, 1995, review of *Fig Pudding,* p. 72; October 27, 1997, review of *Twilight Comes Twice,* p. 75; May 3, 1999, review of *Relatively Speaking,* p. 78; April 23, 2001, review of *The Circus Sur-*

prise, p. 77; September 15, 2003, review of *Hello, Harvest Moon,* pp. 63-64; August 6, 2007, review of *The One O'Clock Chop,* p. 189.

Reading Teacher, December, 1997, Bonita L. Wilcox, review of *Breathing In, Breathing Out,* pp. 350-353.

School Library Journal, June, 1994, Judy Greenfield, review of *I Am Wings,* p. 154; July, 1995, Alice Casey Smith, review of *Fig Pudding,* p. 78; May, 1996, Marjorie Lewis, review of *Buried Alive,* p. 138; May, 1997, Sharon Korbeck, review of *Ordinary Things,* p. 144; July, 1997, Adele Greenlee, review of *Spider Boy,* p. 93; October, 1997, Virginia Golodetz, review of *Twilight Comes Twice,* p. 95; October, 1998, July Siebecker, review of *Flying Solo,* p. 135; April, 1999, Kristen Oravec, review of *Relatively Speaking,* p. 146; November, 1999, Ginny Harrell, review of *Fig Pudding,* p. 64; September, 2000, Steve Clancy, review of *Tommy Trouble and the Magic Marble,* p. 196; November, 2000, Alicia Eames, review of *Grandpa Never Lies,* p. 119; December, 2000, Timothy Capehart, review of *How Writers Work: Finding a Process That Works for You,* p. 160; May, 2001, Heide Piehler, review of *Uncle Daddy,* p. 149; June, 2001, Bina Williams, review of *The Circus Surprise,* p. 112; August, 2001, Lauralyn Persson, review of *Have You Been to the Beach Lately?,* p. 194; February, 2002, Kristen Oravec, review of *Poetry Matters,* p. 143; September, 2003, Shawn Brommer, review of *Hello, Harvest Moon,* p. 178; April, 2005, Lee Bock, review of *A Writing Kind of Day,* p. 150; September, 2005, Alison Follos, review of *Marshfield Dreams,* p. 222; December, 2006, Mary Jean Smith, review of *Moving Day,* p. 98; November, 2007, Debbie Whitbeck, review of *How to Write Your Life Story,* p. 144; May, 2008, Lauralyn Persson, review of *The Sandman,* p. 98.

Voice of Youth Advocates, June, 1994, Diane Tuccillo, review of *I Am Wings,* pp. 106-107.

ONLINE

Ralph Fletcher Home Page, http://www.ralphfletcher.com (December 1, 2008).*

*　　*　　*

FRIEND, David Michael 1975-

Personal

Born December 14, 1975, in Wadsworth, IL; son of Richard William Friend, Jr., and Karen Kucera Friend. *Education:* Parsons School of Design, B.F.A.; attended School of Visual Arts (New York, NY).

Addresses

Home—New York, NY. *E-mail*—david.michael.friend@ dmfriend.com.

Career

Illustrator, animator, designer, puppeteer, and art director. Has worked on multimedia projects for Sesame Workshop, Nickelodeon, Jim Henson Productions, Dis-

ney, American Girl, *Saturday Night Live,* and Cartoon Network. Cofounder, with Gretchen Van Lente, of Drama of Works (puppet theater group), 1996. Creator of puppet shows, including *The Typist, Pertussis, Lunatic,* and *The Bident of Angels;* contributor to puppet performances *Doctor Faustus, The Ballad of Phineas P. Gage,* and *Curiouser and Curiouser.* Director and artistic designer of *Moonfishing* (short film). Resident artist at HERE Arts Center, New York, NY, 2007—.

Awards, Honors

Starr Foundation Award, Society of Illustrators, 1996; grants from Jim Henson Foundation, 2000, 2002, 2008.

Illustrator

Alice Low, *Blueberry Mouse,* Mondo (New York, NY), 2004.

J.T. Petty, *The Squampkin Patch: A Nasselrogt Adventure,* Simon & Schuster (New York, NY), 2006.

J.T. Petty, *The Scrivener Bees* ("Clemency Pogue" series), Simon & Schuster (New York, NY), 2007.

Richard W. Friend III, *Daniel and the Great Bearded One* (graphic novel), Mondo (New York, NY), 2007.

Sidelights

David Michael Friend is an animator and illustrator whose darkly humorous work has been televised on the Cartoon Network, Nickelodeon, and *Saturday Night Live.* A freelance art director based in New York City, Friend cofounded the puppet theater group Drama of Works, and he has contributed to a number of theater and film pieces featuring his puppet creations. In addition, Friend has provided the artwork for a number of picture books, including *The Scrivener Bees* by J.T. Perry.

Blueberry Mouse with a text by Alice Low, was Friend's first children's-book project. The book centers on a friendly creature that cannot stop nibbling away at its home, which is made of blueberry pie. "This story in rhyme becomes a feast for the eyes," remarked *School Library Journal* contributor Wanda Meyers-Hines, the critic also praising the "rich colors" Friend uses in his artwork.

Friend and Petty began their creative collaboration with *The Squampkin Patch: A Nasselrogt Adventure,* which follows the adventures of siblings Milton and Chloe Nasselrogt. The two children face a challenge when they discover a confectioner's sinister plot to grow deadly squampkins: squash-pumpkin hybrids. A critic in *Kirkus Reviews* predicted that "readers will note how the illustrations . . . progress throughout [the book] from sprout to monstrous vegetables."

In *The Scrivener Bees,* Clemency Pogue attempts to stop Inky Mess, a changeling, from taking control of Make Believe. Remarking on Friend's artwork for Petty's story, a *Kirkus Reviews* contributor wrote that the book's illustrations "underscore Inky's haunting dark side and bring life to the tale's fantastical creatures."

Biographical and Critical Sources

PERIODICALS

Kirkus Reviews, August 15, 2006, review of *The Squampkin Patch: A Nasselrogt Adventure,* p. 850; July 1, 2007, review of *The Scrivener Bees.*

School Library Journal, May, 2004, Wanda Meyers-Hines, review of *Blueberry Mouse,* p. 118; July, 2006, Caitlin Augusta, review of *The Squampkin Patch,* p. 110; August, 2007, Sheila Fiscus, review of *The Scrivener Bees,* p. 124.

ONLINE

David Michael Friend Home Page, http://www.dmfriend. com (October 15, 2008).

HERE Arts Center Web site, http://www.here.org/ (October 15, 2008), "David Michael Friend."*

G

GABLE, Brian 1949-

Personal
Born 1949, in Saskatoon, Saskatchewan, Canada. *Education:* University of Saskatchewan, B.F.A.; University of Toronto, B.Ed., 1971.

Addresses
Home—Toronto, Ontario, Canada. *E-mail*—bgable@ globeandmail.ca.

Career
Illustrator and cartoonist. Art teacher in Brockville, Ontario, Canada; freelance cartoonist, beginning 1977; *Regina Leader-Post,* Regina, Saskatchewan, Canada, cartoonist, beginning 1980; *Globe and Mail,* Toronto, Ontario, currently editorial cartoonist.

Awards, Honors
National Newspaper Award (Canada), 1986, 1995, 2001, 2005.

Illustrator

FOR CHILDREN

Diane L. Burns and Peter and Connie Roop, *Backyard Beasties: Jokes to Snake You Smile,* Carolrhoda (Minneapolis, MN), 2004.

Peter and Connie Roop, *Holiday Howlers: Jokes for Punny Parties,* Carolrhoda (Minneapolis, MN), 2004.

Sam Schultz, *Don't Kid Yourself: Relatively Great (Family) Jokes,* Carolrhoda (Minneapolis, MN), 2004.

Sam Schultz, *Game-Day Gigglers: Winning Jokes to Score Some Laughs,* Carolrhoda (Minneapolis, MN), 2004.

Sam Schultz, *Monster Mayhem: Jokes to Scare You Silly!,* Carolrhoda (Minneapolis, MN), 2004.

Sam Schultz, *Schoolyard Snickers: Classy Jokes That Make the Grade,* Carolrhoda (Minneapolis, MN), 2004.

June Swanson, *Punny Places: Jokes to Make You Mappy,* Carolrhoda (Minneapolis, MN), 2004.

Rick Walton, *Foul Play: Sports Jokes That Won't Strike Out,* Carolrhoda (Minneapolis, MN), 2005.

Rick and Ann Walton, *Magical Mischief: Jokes That Shock and Maze,* Carolrhoda (Minneapolis, MN), 2005.

Rick and Ann Walton, *Real Classy: Silly School Jokes,* Carolrhoda (Minneapolis, MN), 2005.

Sharon Friedman, *Grin and Bear It: Zoo Jokes to Make You Roar,* Carolrhoda (Minneapolis, MN), 2005.

Diane L. Burns, *Horsing Around: Jokes to Make You Smile,* Carolrhoda (Minneapolis, MN), 2005.

Sam Schultz, *Ivan to Make You Laugh: Jokes and Novel, Nifty, and Notorious Names,* Carolrhoda (Minneapolis, MN), 2005.

Scott K. Peterson, *Let the Fun Begin: Wacky What-Do-You-Get Jokes, Playful Puns, and More,* Carolrhoda (Minneapolis, MN), 2005.

Rick Walton, *The Sky's the Limit: Naturally Funny Jokes,* Carolrhoda (Minneapolis, MN), 2005.

FOR CHILDREN; "WORDS ARE CATEGORICAL" SERIES

Brian P. Cleary, *Under, Over, by the Clover: What Is a Preposition?,* Millbrook Press (Minneapolis, MN), 2002.

Brian P. Cleary, *Dearly, Nearly, Insincerely: What Is an Adverb?,* Carolrhoda (Minneapolis, MN), 2003.

Brian P. Cleary, *I and You and Don't Forget Who: What Is a Pronoun?,* Millbrook Press (Minneapolis, MN), 2004.

Brian P. Cleary, *How Much Can a Bare Bear Bear?: What Are Homonyms and Homophones?,* Millbrook Press (Minneapolis, MN), 2005.

Brian P. Cleary, *Pitch and Throw, Grasp and Know: What Is a Synonym?,* Millbrook Press (Minneapolis, MN), 2005.

Brian P. Cleary, *A Lime, a Mime, a Pool of Slime: More about Nouns,* Millbrook Press (Minneapolis, MN), 2006.

Brian P. Cleary, *Stop and Go, Yes and No: What Is an Antonym?,* Millbrook Press (Minneapolis, MN), 2006.

Brian P. Cleary, *Quirky, Jerky, Extra-Perky: More about Adjectives,* Millbrook Press (Minneapolis, MN), 2007.

Brian P. Cleary, *Slide and Slurp, Scratch and Burp: More about Verbs,* Millbrook Press (Minneapolis, MN), 2007.

Brian P. Cleary, *Lazily, Crazily, Just a Bit Nasally: More about Adverbs,* Millbrook Press (Minneapolis, MN), 2008.

FOR CHILDREN; "MATH IS CATEGORICAL" SERIES

Brian P. Cleary, *The Mission of Addition,* Millbrook Press (Minneapolis, MN), 2005.

Brian P. Cleary, *The Action of Subtraction,* Millbrook Press (Minneapolis, MN), 2006.

Brian P. Cleary, *On the Scale: A Weighty Tale,* Lerner (Minneapolis, MN), 2008.

Brian P. Cleary, *Stroll and Walk, Babble and Talk: More about Synonyms,* Millbrook Press (Minneapolis, MN), 2008.

Brian P. Cleary, *Straight and Curvy, Meek and Nervy: More about Antonyms,* Millbrook Press (Minneapolis, MN), 2009.

OTHER

Gable: The Editorial Cartoons of Brian Gable, Western Producer Prairie Books (Saskatoon, Saskatchewan, Canada), 1987.

***Book cover illustration by Brian Gable from* Stop and Go, Yes and No, *written by Brian P. Cleary.** (Illustrations copyright © 2006 by Lerner Publishing Group, Inc. Reproduced by Millbrook Press, Inc., a division of Lerner Publishing Group. All rights reserved. No part of this text excerpt may be used or reproduced in any manner whatsoever without the prior written permission of Lerner Publishing Group, Inc.)*

Another Day, Another Doom: Brian Gable's Cartoon Commentary, introduction by Jeffrey Simpson, Greystone Books (Vancouver, British Columbia, Canada), 1995.

John Allemang, *Poetic Justice: Satirical Verse from the Globe & Mail,* Firefly Books (Richmond Hill, Ontario, Canada), 2006.

Contributor of cartoons to newspapers, including *Brockville Recorder and Times.* Contributor of essays to periodicals, including *Literary Review of Canada.*

Sidelights

Known to his fellow Canadians on the strength of the many editorial cartoons he has contributed to the Toronto *Globe and Mail,* artist Brian Gable has also won a younger following through his collaboration with children's-book author Brian P. Cleary on the "Words Are CATegorical" series. Cleary's humorous books about the intricacies and inconsistencies of English grammar, which include such titles as *How Much Can a Bare Bear Bear?: What Are Homonyms and Homophones?, A Lime, a Mime, a Pool of Slime: More about Nouns,* and *Pitch and Throw, Grasp and Know: What Is a Synonym?,* have earned the praise of teachers and critics alike.

Born and raised in Saskatchewan, Gable studied fine arts at the University of Saskatchewan and also earned a degree in education at the University of Toronto. Originally intending to be a teacher, he found a greater satisfaction in creating editorial cartoons, and he began his freelance career in the mid-1970s. As the editorial cartoonist for the *Globe and Mail,* Gable has been honored with several prestigious National Newspaper Awards in his native Canada.

While Gable's editorial cartoons often feature caricatures of presidents, prime ministers, and other current movers and shakers, in his work with Cleary he is allowed to range more widely, creating what Hazel Rochman described in *Booklist* as "wild cartoon scenarios" featuring loosely drawn animal characters. "The energy and sheer razzmatazz of the text and graphics [in *Dearly, Nearly, Insincerely: What Is an Adverb?*] will have young grammarians entranced," asserted Dona Ratterree in her *School Library Journal* review of one Gable-Cleary collaboration, while in *Booklist* Carolyn Phelan praised *Lazily, Crazily, Just a Bit Nasally: More about Adverbs* for luring readers into its pages with "comical line drawings zapped with color." "Cleary's often-goofy examples" of peoples, places, and things in *A Lime, a Mime, a Pool of Slime* are paired with "wildly colored, cartoonlike drawings [that] have a zany edge," Phelan also noted, while in the same periodical, Rochman described *Pitch and Throw, Grasp and Know* as a "fun" way to convey to young readers "the message that words are not boring."

In addition to his work in children's picture books, Gable has also collected his most popular editorial cartoons in the books *Gable: The Editorial Cartoons of Brian Gable* and *Another Day, Another Doom: Brian*

Illustration of a gardener watching peas grow from Cleary and Gable's collaborative work about adverbs: **Dearly, Nearly, Insincerely.** (Illustration copyright © 2003 by Brian Gable. Reprinted with the permission of Carolrhoda Books, a division of Lerner Publishing Group, Inc. All rights reserved. No part of this text excerpt may be used or reproduced in any manner whatsoever without the prior written permission of Lerner Publishing Group, Inc.)

Gable's Cartoon Commentary. His political-based art is also included in *Poetic Justice: Satirical Verse from the Globe & Mail,* a book collecting the verses of journalism colleague John Allemang.

Biographical and Critical Sources

PERIODICALS

Booklist, March 1, 2002, GraceAnne A. DeCandido, review of *Under, Over, by the Clover: What Is a Preposition?,* p. 1132; May 1, 2004, Carolyn Phelan, review of *I and You and Don't Forget Who: What Is a Pronoun?,* p. 1560; February 1, 2005, Hazel Rochman, review of *Pitch and Throw, Grasp and Know: What Is a Synonym?,* p. 956; January 1, 2007, Carolyn Phelan, review of *A Lime, a Mime, a Pool of Slime: More about Nouns,* p. 112; August, 2007, Carolyn Phelan, review of *Quirky, Jerky, Extra Perky: More about Adjectives,* p. 89; April 15, 2008, Carolyn Phelan, review of *Lazily, Crazily, Just a Bit Nasally: More about Adverbs,* p. 44.

Kirkus Reviews, March 1, 2002, review of *Under, Over, by the Clover,* p. 331; February 1, 2003, review of *Dearly, Nearly, Insincerely: What Is an Adverb?,* p. 227.

School Library Journal, March, 2003, Dona Ratterree, review of *Dearly, Nearly, Insincerely,* p. 216; July, 2004, Lisa Gangemi Kropp, review of *I and You and Don't Forget Who,* p. 91; March, 2005, Gloria Koster, review of *Pitch and Throw, Grasp and Know,* p. 191; October, 2005, Barbara Auerbach, review of *The Mission of Addition,* p. 136; November, 2005, Maura Bresnahan, review of *How Much Can a Bare Bear Bear?: What Are Homonyms and Homophones?,* p. 112; June, 2006, Kathleen Muelen, review of *Stop and Go, Yes and No: What Is an Antonym?,* p. 134; November, 2006, Jayne Damron, review of *A Lime, a Mime, a Pool of Slime,* and Erlene Bishop Killeen, review of *The Action of Subtraction,* p. 118; December, 2007, Laura Lutz, review of *Quirky, Jerky, Extra Perky,* p. 106; April, 2008, Jayne Damron, review of *Lazily, Crazily, Just a Bit Nasally,* p. 129.

ONLINE

Association of Canadian Editorial Cartoonists Web site, http://www.canadiancartoonist.com/ (December 15, 2008), "Brian Gable."*

*   *   *

GLENN, John W.

Personal

Male.

Addresses

Home—Maplewood, NJ.

Career

Editor and freelance writer.

Writings

(With Marc Aronson) *The World Made New: Why the Age of Exploration Happened and How It Changed the World,* National Geographic (Washington, DC), 2007.

Biographical and Critical Sources

PERIODICALS

Booklist, September 15, 2007, Carolyn Phelan, review of *The World Made New: Why the Age of Exploration Happened and How It Changed the World,* p. 65.

Kirkus Reviews, July 1, 2007, review of *The World Made New.*

*   *   *

GOOSSENS, Philippe 1963-

Personal

Born 1963, in Belgium. *Education:* Attended Institut Saint-Luc.

Addresses

Home—Brussels, Belgium.

Career

Illustrator, animator, and commercial artist. *Exhibition:* Work included in Bologna Book Fair, 2004.

Illustrator

PICTURE BOOKS

Thierry Robberecht, *Ik kan weer lachen*, Clavis (Amsterdam, Netherlands), 2000, translated as *Stolen Smile*, Random House (New York, NY), 2002.

Thierry Robberecht, *Toen papa köning was*, Clavis (Amsterdam, Netherlands), 2001.

Thierry Robberecht, *Eva in het land van de verloren zusjes*, Clavis (Amsterdam, Netherlands), 2002.

Maria C.P. Van Velzen, *De verrekijker*, Clavis (Amsterdam, Netherlands), 2003.

Thierry Robberecht, *Boze Draak*, Clavis (Amsterdam, Belgium), 2003, translated as *Angry Dragon*, Clarion (New York, NY), 2004.

Hermann Moers, *Axel und Bibi*, Nord-Süd, 2003 translated by Kathryn Grell as *Rufus and Max*, North-South Books (New York, NY), 2003.

Thierry Robberecht, *Het meisje dat terung in mama's buik wilde*, Clavis (Amsterdam, Belgium), 2004 translated as *Back into Mommy's Tummy*, Clarion (New York, NY), 2005.

Heinz Janisch, *Cleo in der Klemme*, Nord-Süd, 2005.

Heinz Janisch, *Help!*, Vier Windstreken, 2005.

Thierry Robberecht, *Sarah en haar spookjes*, Clavis (Amsterdam, Netherlands), 2006, translated as *Sarah's Little Ghosts*, Clarion (New York, NY), 2007.

Thierry Robberecht, *Harold*, Clavis (Amsterdam, Netherlands), 2007.

Thierry Robberecht, *Mijn kerstopa*, Clavis (Amsterdam, Netherlands), 2008.

PICTURE BOOKS; "BENNO/SAM" SERIES

Thierry Robberecht, *Benno is nooit bang*, Clavis (Hasselt, Belgium), 2005, translated as *Sam Is Never Scared*, Clarion (New York, NY), 2006.

Thierry Robberecht, *Benno Buitengewoon*, Clavis (Amsterdam, Netherlands), 2005, translated as *Sam Tells Stories*, Clarion (New York, NY), 2007.

Thierry Robberecht, *Benno Bloost*, Clavis (Amsterdam, Netherlands), 2006, translated as *Sam's New Friend*, Clarion (New York, NY), 2007.

Thierry Robberecht, *Benno buitenspel*, Clavis (Amsterdam, Netherlands), 2006, translated as *Sam Is Not a Loser*, Clarion (New York, NY), 2008.

Thierry Robberecht, *Benno en zijn broertje* (title means "Benno and His Brother"), Clavis (Amsterdam, Netherlands), 2008.

Thierry Robberecht, *Benno is jarig* (title means "Beno Has His Birthday"), Clavis (Amsterdam, Netherlands), 2008.

Books featuring Goossens' artwork have been translated into French, Spanish, German, Greek, Italian, Slovenian, Korean, and Taiwanese.

Sidelights

Since studying art at the Institute Saint Luc in Brussels, Philippe Goossens has gained popularity in his native Belgium as a result of his collaboration with popular children's book author Thierry Robberecht. Goossens' illustrations for Robberecht's *Boze Draak* were exhibited at the prestigious Bologna Book Fair in 2004, and books featuring his work have been published in thirteen countries, including France, Italy, South Korea, Greece, Germany, and Spain. *Ik kan weer lachen*, the duo's first picture-book collaboration, was also the first to reach English-speaking readers under the title *Stolen Smile*. Paired with a story about a girl who decides not to smile after being teased by a school bully, Goossens' brightly colored, highly textured paintings feature "a technique well suited for a story that unfolds on that emotional crucible otherwise known as the blacktop," in the opinion of a *Publishers Weekly* reviewer.

In reviews of the Belgian picture-book team's more-recent work, critics consistently remark on Goossens' art; in a review of Robberecht's *Angry Dragon*, for instance, *Booklist* contributor Jennifer Mattson noted that the illustrator's "distinctly European, stylized artwork visually reproduces the intense emotions" of Robberecht's story. Working with Hermann Moers on *Rufus and Max*, another Belgian import, Goossens "plays interestingly with perspective," according to *School Library Journal* critic Shelley B. Sutherland, "and the overall effect is delightful." One of the mens' most imaginative collaborations, *Back into Mommy's Tummy*, features what Hazel Rochman dubbed a "mischievous take on the elemental sibling rivalry scenario." Holly T. Sneeringer, appraising the same book, noted in *School Library Journal* that in *Back into Mommy's Tummy* the illustrator's "imagined view of the world adds humor and lightness to real anxieties that many children encounter but are often unable to express," while a *Kirkus Reviews* writer called the picture book "engagingly silly yet compassionate."

Benno is nooit bang, the first book in Robberecht and Goossens' popular board-book series, was released in English as *Sam Is Never Scared*, and the name of their main character changes from Benno to Sam in translation. When readers meet Sam in *Sam Is Never Scared*, the young wolf believes he is the bravest of his comrades, and he calls friend Max a scaredy-cat. However, Sam's bravado disappears when he sees a spider, and soon Max is shown to be the brave one. Praising *Sam Is Never Scared* in *School Library Journal*, Piper L. Nyman wrote that "Goossens's bright-hued, fuzzy-edged oil illustrations exude charm and the exuberance of the animal characters" in Robberecht's tale, while a *Kirkus Reviews* contributor maintained that his simplistic oil paintings "suit the youngest listeners, with close-ups on the characters and few distracting details."

Other books in the "Sam" series include *Sam Is Not a Loser, Sam's New Friend*, and *Sam Tells Stories*. In *Sam Is Not a Loser*, which finds the young wolf faced with playing a losing soccer match against a far older team, "the characters are appealingly drawn," according to

School Library Journal contributor Amy Lilien-Harper. *Sam's New Friend*, which finds the young pup upset when he must share his bedroom with a little white kitten whose parents are divorcing, features what Rochman described as "clear, bright pictures [that] show both the bonding and the heartfelt feelings." Goossens' illustrations for *Sam Tells Stories* "are uncluttered, with strong, simple shapes and muted colors," in the opinion of *School Library Journal* reviewer Susan E. Murray, and a *Kirkus Reviews* writer concluded of the work that

Philippe Goossens joins author Thierry Robberecht in capturing the adventures of an endearing young character in **Sam Is Never Scared.**

the illustrator "hit[s] the mark again, keeping the focus on the characters and their feelings, while downplaying distracting details."

Biographical and Critical Sources

PERIODICALS

Booklist, January 1, 2005, Jennifer Mattson, review of *Angry Dragon,* p. 874; December 1, 2005, Hazel Rochman, review of *Back into Mommy's Tummy,* p. 56; September 1, 2006, Julie Cummins, review of *Sam Is Never Scared,* p. 140; February 15, 2008, Hazel Rochman, review of *Sam's New Friend,* p. 87.

Horn Book, January-February, 2005, Martha V. Parravano, review of *Angry Dragon,* p. 83.

Kirkus Reviews, September 1, 2004, review of *Angry Dragon,* p. 873; October 15, 2005, review of *Back into Mommy's Tummy,* p. 1145; August 15, 2006, review of *Sam Is Never Scared,* p. 850; June 15, 2007, review of *Sam Tells Stories;* September 15, 2007, review of *Sarah's Little Ghosts.*

Publishers Weekly, November 4, 2002, review of *Stolen Smile,* p. 83.

School Library Journal, January, 2003, Leslie Barban, review of *Stolen Smile,* p. 110; September, 2003, Shelley B. Sutherland, review of *Rufus and Max,* p. 185; December, 2004, Maria B. Salvadore, review of *Angry Dragon,* p. 118; February, 2006, Holly T. Sneeringer, review of *Back into Mommy's Tummy,* p. 108; October, 2006, Piper L. Nyman, review of *Sam Is Never Scared,* p. 124; November, 2007, Susan E. Murray, review of *Sam Tells Stories,* and Susan Moorhead, review of *Sarah's Little Ghosts,* both p. 99; February, 2008, Maryann H. Owen, review of *Sam's New Friend,* p. 95; May, 2008, Amy Lilien-Harper, review of *Sam Is Not a Loser,* p. 107.

ONLINE

Clavis Web site, http://www.clavisbook.com/ (December 15, 2008), "Philippe Goossens."*

*   *   *

GREIF, Jean-Jacques 1944-

Personal

Born September 23, 1944, in Paris, France; son of Lonek Greif (a doctor) and Malvina Zien; married; wife's name Katia; children: two sons, one daughter. *Education:* Attended École Polytechnique, 1964-66.

Addresses

Home—Paris, France. *E-mail*—greifjj@aol.com.

Career

Worked variously as an artist, advertising executive, copywriter, and freelance writer. *Marie Claire,* Paris, France, journalist, 1975—; founder and teacher at a small, experimental high school, Paris, France, 1982-87.

Writings

YOUNG-ADULT NOVELS

Ring de la mort, École des loisirs (Paris, France), 1998, translated as *The Fighter,* Bloomsbury (New York, NY), 2006.

Une nouvelle vie, Malvina (title means "A New Life, Malvina"; children's book), École des loisirs (Paris, France), 2000.

Lonek le hussard, École des loisirs (Paris, France), 2000.

Sans accent, École des loisirs (Paris, France), 2001.

Nine Eleven, École des loisirs (Paris, France), 2002.

OTHER

Les ordinateurs et les robots, (title means "Computers and Robots"; nonfiction children's book), Hachette jeunesse (Paris, France), 1987.

Moi, Marilyn (title means "I, Marilyn"; biographical novel), École des loisirs (Paris, France), 1998.

Jeanne d'Arc (title means "Joan of Arc"; children's book), École des loisirs (Paris, France), 1999.

Einstein: l'homme qui chevauchait la lumière, (biography), Archipel (Paris, France), 2005.

Also author of biographical novels about Beethoven and Mozart; author of numerous computer manuals.

Sidelights

French writer and journalist Jean-Jacques Greif began his career in 1969 as an advertising account executive and moved on to work as a copywriter when he realized he could actually earn money by writing. In 1975, he took a position as a staff writer for *Marie Claire* magazine in Paris, and he continued there while writing computer books, children's books, and young-adult novels.

Several of Greif's books are inspired by his parents, Lonek and Malvina, who escaped from Poland prior to World War II to avoid persecution as Jews. Both worked as part of the French Resistance and were arrested by the Nazis. Lonek spent one year in the Auschwitz concentration camp, and his friend's experiences there inspired *The Fighter,* the first of Greif's young-adult novels to be published in English.

The Fighter tells the story of Moshe, a fourteen-year-old Polish boy who emigrates from Warsaw to Paris in 1929. Moshe finds his new life as an amateur boxer thrown into upheaval when the Nazis invade the city and he is sent to Auschwitz. Hazel Rochman, writing for *Booklist,* commented that *The Fighter* "may be too much for some readers." However, Rita Soltan, in a review for *School Library Journal,* found Greif's effort to be "tough, realistic reading with some raw language."

Biographical and Critical Sources

PERIODICALS

Booklist, October 1, 2006, Hazel Rochman, review of *The Fighter,* p. 48.
Horn Book, November-December, 2006, Martha V. Parravano, review of *The Fighter,* p. 712.
Kirkus Reviews, August 15, 2006, review of *The Fighter,* p. 841.
School Library Journal, December, 2006, Rita Soltan, review of *The Fighter,* p. 140.

ONLINE

Jean-Jacques Greif Home Page, http://www.jjgreif.com (April 14, 2007).

*   *   *

GRIFFIN, Adele 1970-

Personal

Born July 29, 1970, in Philadelphia, PA; daughter of John Berg (a business manager) and Priscilla Sands (a school principal); married Erich Paul Mauff (an investment banker); children: Priscilla. *Education:* University of Pennsylvania, B.A., 1993. *Politics:* Democrat. *Hobbies and other interests:* Movies.

Addresses

Home—New York, NY. *Office*—215 Park Ave. S., New York, NY 10003. *Agent*—Charlotte Sheedy, c/o Sterling Lord Literistic, 65 Bleecker St., New York, NY 10012. *E-mail*—adele@adelegriffin.net.

Career

Writer. Clarion Books, New York, NY, assistant editor, 1996-98, freelance manuscript reader, 1996-99.

Member

PEN, WGA, Society of Children's Book Writers and Illustrators, Young Penn Alum, Friends of the New York Public Library, 92nd Street Young Men's Christian Association (YMCA) of New York.

Awards, Honors

National Book Award nomination, National Book Foundation, and Notable Book citation, American Library Association (ALA), both 1997, both for *Sons of Lib-*

Adele Griffin (Photo by John Berg. Courtesy of Adele Griffin.)

erty; Books for the Teen Age designation, New York Public Library, and *Parenting* magazine award, both 1997, both for *Split Just Right;* Blue Ribbon designation, *Bulletin of the Center for Children's Books,* Best Books designation, *Publishers Weekly* and *School Library Journal,* Notable Book citation, and Best Books for Young Adults citation, both ALA, and 100 Titles for Reading and Sharing inclusion, New York Public Library, all 1998, all for *The Other Shepards;* Best Books designation, ALA and *Publishers Weekly,* both 2001, both for *Amandine;* National Book Award nomination, and *Kirkus Reviews* Best Book of the Year honor, both 2004, both for *Where I Want to Be.*

Writings

NOVELS

Rainy Season, Houghton Mifflin (Boston, MA), 1996.
Split Just Right, Hyperion (New York, NY), 1997.
Sons of Liberty, Hyperion (New York, NY), 1997.
The Other Shepards, Hyperion (New York, NY), 1998.
Dive, Hyperion (New York, NY), 1999.
Amandine, Hyperion (New York, NY), 2001.
Hannah, Divided, Hyperion (New York, NY), 2002.
Overnight, G.P. Putnam's Sons (New York, NY), 2003.
Where I Want to Be, G.P. Putnam's Sons (New York, NY), 2004.
My Almost Epic Summer, G.P. Putnam's Sons (New York, NY), 2006.

"WITCH TWINS" NOVEL SERIES

Witch Twins, Hyperion (New York, NY), 2001.
Witch Twins at Camp Bliss, Hyperion (New York, NY), 2002.
Witch Twins and Melody Malady, illustrated by Jacqueline Rogers, Hyperion (New York, NY), 2003.

Witch Twins and the Ghost of Glenn Bly, illustrated by Jacqueline Rogers, Hyperion (New York, NY), 2004.

"VAMPIRE ISLAND" NOVEL SERIES

Vampire Island, G.P. Putnam's Sons (New York, NY), 2007.

The Knaveheart's Curse, G.P. Putnam's Sons (New York, NY), 2008.

V Is for . . . Vampire, G.P. Putnam's Sons (New York, NY), 2009.

Adaptations

Where I Want to Be was adapted as an audiobook, read by Ruth Ann Phimister and Jenny Ikeda, Recorded Books, 2005. *My Almost Epic Summer* was adapted as an audiobook, read by Jessica Almasy, Recorded Books, 2006.

Sidelights

In her fiction, Adele Griffin explores teen behavior in all its variety, good and bad. Some of her teen novels, such as *Overnight* and *Amandine,* offer realistic portraits of manipulative, selfish young women and the friends they attract, while others, including *Dive, Hannah, Divided,* and *Where I Want to Be,* introduce unconventional young people coming to terms with their uniqueness. On the lighter side, Griffin's "Witch Twins" books wrap lessons on sibling rivalry and cooperation around stories of magic, spell-casting, and the supernatural, while the "Vampire Island" novels follow a family of school-aged veggie vampires. According to Ilene Cooper in *Booklist,* "Griffin elevates every genre she writes," whether it be fantasy or straight realistic fiction.

Griffin's well-received debut novel, *Rainy Season,* was lauded in a *Publishers Weekly* review as "ambitiously conceived and sharply observed." The story follows Lane Beck, a fearful twelve year old, and her belligerently bold younger brother Charlie through a single transformative day. The Beck family is living on an army base in the Panama Canal Zone in 1977, as resentment of U.S. imperialism is at its peak. Griffin's setting contributes danger and suspense to her story, and she discusses the history and politics relevant to the Canal Zone in an author's note. In anticipation of a battle with the children living on the opposite side of the Canal Zone, Lane and Charlie Beck and their friends begin building a fort. The political tensions escalating outside the Beck home are paralleled by tensions within the family: Lane is prone to panic attacks while her brother Charlie is becoming a bully, but both children's problems are deliberately ignored by their parents. Ultimately, Lane's concern for her brother forces her to break the family's pathological silence, a silence grounded in the grief they feel over older sister Emily's recent death in a car accident.

Reviewing *Rainy Season* for *School Library Journal,* Lucinda Lockwood commented favorably on Griffin's "evocative" writing, as well as on the author's ability to "capture the setting and the nuances of adolescent relationships." A *Publishers Weekly* critic commended the way Griffin "unfolds the events of the day and lets the reader make sense of them," revealing the nature of the tragedy "without resorting to melodrama or otherwise manipulating the characterizations." Del Negro concluded of the novel that certain images in *Rainy Season* "will remain with readers long after the book is closed."

Griffin tackles divorce and a girl's experience of life without her father in *Split Just Right.* A well-grounded fourteen year old who enjoys writing, Dandelion "Danny" Finzimer lives with her flamboyant, single, part-time waitress/actress/drama-teacher mom. With no memory of her father, Danny is unsure whether she should trust her mother's view of him and longs to learn about—or perhaps even meet—him. By way of a mix-up, Danny does get to meet her father, and in the process discovers much about her parents, her work as a burgeoning writer, and the line between fact and fiction. *School Library Journal* contributor Carol A. Edwards asserted that in *Split Just Right* Griffin "takes one of the most tired plots in current fiction and gives it

Cover of Griffin's middle-grade novel **Hannah, Divided.** (Hyperion Books for Children, 2002. Reprinted with permission of Hyperion Books for Children. All rights reserved.)

fresh zip." In *Booklist* Cooper praised the book for successfully tackling "a number of interesting issues, including class distinction and family relationships."

In *Sons of Liberty* Griffin returns to the serious tone of her first novel, examining the complicated issues faced by members of a dysfunctional family via the life of seventh-grader Rock Kindle. Rock has always looked up to his father, and in imitation of the older man's behavior he has become a bully. In contrast, older brother Cliff has lost patience with their father's warped sense of militancy, which prescribes regular doses of humiliation and such bizarre punishments as waking the boys up in the middle of the night to do chores and calisthenics. When the family shatters, no longer able to stand the strain, Rock is forced to choose between loyalty to his father and loyalty to his newly discovered sense of self. A *Publishers Weekly* contributor praised Griffin's use of "pointedly jarring dialogue" and her "keen ear for adolescent jargon." *Horn Book* reviewer Kitty Flynn credited the development of Rock's character in *Sons of Liberty* with providing "the tension in what could have been a superficial treatment of the issues."

The Other Shepards features a supernatural teen romance involving Holland and her obsessive-compulsive sister Geneva. The two teen girls live in a world haunted by the memory of three older siblings who died before the sisters were even born. In the guise of Annie, a mural painter, the spirit of the older sister breathes color into the Shepard family. A *Publishers Weekly* critic wrote that Griffin "spins a taut story of two girls . . . who must confront the unknown in order to liberate themselves. . . . Griffin's story offers a resounding affirmation that fears are to be faced, not denied, and life is to be lived, not mourned." Praising the novel's realistic characters, Cooper concluded her assessment of *The Other Shepards* by asserting: "Carefully crafted both in plot and language, this book shows the heights that popular literature can scale."

Dive explores the difference between family ties forged by biology and those crafted from circumstance. When his irresponsible mother deserts the family, eleven-year-old Ben elects to stay with his responsible and reliable stepfather, Lyle. Ben's brother, Dustin, is more inclined to engage in daring behavior, and the teen chafes under Lyle's rules. The brothers must sort out their problematic relationship after Dustin suffers a serious injury in a diving accident. Nancy Vasilakis, reviewing *Dive* for *Horn Book,* called Griffin's novel "a wrenching tale of a young man struggling to find his voice in an unpredictable world."

Griffin tackles the difficult subject of teen friendships in the novels *Amandine* and *Overnight,* both which frankly confront the way some teenaged girls seek to manipulate their peers and to exert power. Delia, the insecure narrator of *Amandine,* is drawn into an obsessive friendship with dramatic, artistic Amandine. When Amand-

Teens are transported into a world of suspense in Griffin's middle-grade novel The Other Shepards, *featuring artwork by Jim Carroll.*
(Cover art © 1997 by Jim Carroll. Reprinted with permission of Hyperion Books for Children. All rights reserved.)

ine's behavior toward another girl takes a dangerous turn, Delia tries to break away. Only then does she discover the full force of Amandine's wrath. According to Anita L. Burkam in *Horn Book,* "Amandine's controlling nature and Delia's weak complicity are believably and subtly developed." Cooper wrote of the novel that Griffin "takes well-worn stereotypes . . . and . . . makes them seem much more: more real, more vulnerable, more scary." *School Library Journal* contributor Alison Follos called *Amandine* "a powerful story with real characters."

Overnight "once again penetrates the cruelty inherent in female cliques," according to a *Publishers Weekly* critic. Here Griffin introduces readers to the "Lucky Seven," a tightly knit group of girls who gather for a sleepover on Friday the thirteenth. Certain rifts have developed amongst the girls, and these conflicts become noticeable when one of their number, Gray, disappears during the party. Group leader Martha is ready to assert her control, even if it means putting Gray's life in jeopardy. B. Allison Gray, reviewing *Overnight* for *School Library Journal,* deemed the novel an "insightful version of the universal story of ostracism and manipulation among preteens." A *Publishers Weekly* critic wrote that Griffin "expertly captures the pettiness of the Lucky Seven."

Set in Depression-era Pennsylvania, *Hannah, Divided* centers on Hannah Bennett, a thirteen-year-old farm girl who also happens to be a math genius and an obsessive-compulsive who counts everything. Hannah loves living on a farm, helping her family with the chores, and attending a one-room school with children she has known all her life. With the help of a wealthy Philadelphia patron, Hannah travels to the big city to try to win a math scholarship. Once there, she is torn between her homesickness and her burning desire to work with numbers, even in an alien place full of automobiles, loud music, and strangers. Griffin's "portrait of a child struggling with symptoms of obsessive-compulsive disorder is sensitive and convincing," declared Barbara Scotto in *School Library Journal*, the critic dubbing *Hannah, Divided* "a novel well worth savoring." In *Publishers Weekly* a critic praised the way Griffin "makes inventive use of a third-person narration to demonstrate Hannah's computer-like brain and quirky personality." As *Booklist* reviewer Cooper concluded: "In other hands, this might have been a problem novel. Here it is a celebration."

Fourteen-year-old Irene, the main character in *My Almost Epic Summer*, is looking forward to her first year in high school. While working as a babysitter to Evan and Lainie, Irene becomes fascinated by Starla, the lifeguard at the pool where the children swim. The teen's world gets more interesting when she attracts the attention of Starla's ex-boyfriend; meanwhile, young Lainie idolizes Irene in turn, while Irene's mother needs consoling when her relationship with her current beau goes south in a novel that *Horn Book* critic Jeannine M. Chapman dubbed "funny" and "thoughtfully layered." Praising *My Almost Epic Summer* as "delightful," *Kliatt* critic Claire Rosser added that the novel "borders on being a farce" due to Irene's witty observations, while in *Booklist* Cooper concluded that Griffin's "characters . . . are all neatly, if not broadly drawn, and readers will have lots of fun" spending time between the pages. *My Almost Epic Summer* is a coming-of-age novel that features "vivid scenes, believable dilemmas, and satisfyingly human characters," according to *School Library Journal* contributor Roxanne Myers Spencer.

Nominated for a National Book Award, *Where I Want to Be* features a story salted with the supernatural, as sisters Lily and Jane Culvert are separated by death. Sixteen-year-old Lily was happy-go-lucky until older sister Jane succumbed to mental illness and committed suicide by walking in front of a car. In the novel's dual narratives, readers learn that Jane's spirit must continue to relive a single day from her childhood, while Lily cannot recover from the guilt she feels following her sister's death until she is aided by boyfriend Caleb. Noting that the sisters are portrayed as complex but fascinating individuals, Cooper added that "Griffin artfully dabs details on her canvas, then overlays . . . a super-

Cover of Griffin's amusing teen novel My Almost Epic Summer, *featuring artwork by Kristina Duewell.* (Cover illustration © 2006 by Alli Arnold. Reproduced by permission of Speak, a division of Penguin Putnam Books for Young Readers.)

natural patina that will immediately draw in" her novel's intended teen readership. In *School Library Journal*, Crystal Faris described *Where I Want to Be* as a "well-crafted blend of reality and otherworldliness" that is "thoughtful, unique, and ultimately life-affirming."

Griffin turns to younger readers in her "Witch Twins" series, which introduces ten-year-old twins Claire and Luna. Although they look alike, Claire and Luna are distinct individuals with unique personalities. They must keep their magic a secret from most of their family members, with the exception of Grandy, the grandmother from whom they have inherited their witchy talents. Series opener *Witch Twins* revolves around Claire and Luna's attempts to break up their father's impending marriage to a woman named Fluffy. "Griffin's modern tale bursts with everyday enchantment," noted Catherine T. Quattlebaum in her *School Library Journal* review of *Witch Twins*. The critic also lauded the work for its "breezy mixture of otherworldly witchcraft and ordinary activities."

Sixth-grade twins Claire and Luna attend summer camp in *Witch Twins at Camp Bliss,* once again proving their independence by pursuing different courses from the moment they arrive. Claire must overcome a rival to win the coveted "Camp Bliss Girl" trophy, and Luna cannot find the magic dust given to her by her grandmother. In *Witch Twins and Melody Malady* the girls get an opportunity to meet their film-star idol Melody Malady, but tensions erupt when Melody becomes friends with Claire, leaving Luna in the company of Melody's brainy but quiet sister, Dolores. A trip to a Scottish castle is the focus of *Witch Twins and the Ghost of Glenn Bly,* as Claire and Luna help put to rest the ghostly but harmless Sir Percival. In *School Library Journal,* Debbie Whitbeck observed that in *Witch Twins at Camp Bliss* Griffin "keeps the characters true to their personalities," and *Booklist* critic Diane Foote enjoyed the story's "satisfying and convincing happy ending." "Fans of the series will enjoy this offering," maintained Linda B. Zeilstra in a *School Library Journal* appraisal of *Witch Twins and Melody Malady,* while Karin Snelson dubbed the series "ebullient" and "quirky" in her *Booklist* review of the third "Witch Twins" installment.

Also designed for upper-elementary-grade readers, Griffin's "Vampire Island" books focus on the Livingstones, a family of vegetarian fruit-bat vampires that has given up immortality and relocated from Europe to New York City. In *Vampire Island* thirteen-year-old Lexington, eleven-year-old Madison, and nine-year-old Hudson try to fit in with their new schoolmates, although their Old-World mannerisms and odd craving for fruit make them stand out. In *The Knaveheart's Curse,* when a blood-drinking vampire comes to town and behaves in the classic vampire vein, Maddy must find help in order to fight the threat to their new neighbors. Praising Griffin's text as "clever and descriptive," *School Library Journal* contributor Christi Voth dubbed *Vampire Island* "a fun, light twist on the horror genre," while in *Booklist* Debbie Carton described the book as a "friendly vampire story" in which "fang-in-cheek jokes carry the swiftly moving plot."

Griffin once told *SATA:* "One of my most treasured childhood memories is the excitement I felt going book shopping before summer vacation. I looked forward to our family's annual visit to New York City and trip to Brentano's, where I was allowed to purchase as many books as I wanted, a joyful extravagance. I knew what I liked: stories about princesses, tough heroines who, defying all odds, would rise from a garret or cottage adjacent to the requisite bog to become a mogul—usually of a department store. I did *not* like science fiction, fantasy, or books about boys.

"While my books are not science fiction or fantasy, I do like to write about both girls *and* boys. (Perhaps age and marriage have helped with that particular aversion.) The voices in my writing are those of the children I have listened to hear and have strained to remember, voices that speak from the secret world we too soon leave. My goal, as I continue my career, is to write books for all young people, even boys, who look forward to a trip to the library or bookstore with great joy, and who are companioned by the friendship of a favorite book."

Biographical and Critical Sources

PERIODICALS

Booklist, June 1 and 15, 1997, Ilene Cooper, review of *The Other Shepards,* pp. 1702-1703; September 15, 1997, Carolyn Phelan, review of *Sons of Liberty,* p. 235; August, 1998, Ilene Cooper, review of *The Other Shepards,* p. 1999; April 15, 2001, Ilene Cooper, review of *Witch Twins,* p. 1552; September 15, 2001, Ilene Cooper, review of *Amandine,* p. 226; July, 2002, Diane Foote, review of *Witch Twins at Camp Bliss,* p. 1844; October 1, 2002, Ilene Cooper, review of *Hannah, Divided,* p. 323; September 15, 2003, Karin Snelson, review of *Witch Twins and Melody Malady,* p. 236; February 15, 2005, Ilene Cooper, review of *Where I Want to Be,* p. 1078; February 15, 2006, Ilene Cooper, review of *My Almost Epic Summer,* p. 91; August, 2007, Debbie Carton, review of *Vampire Island,* p. 78.

Bulletin of the Center for Children's Books, February, 1997, Janice M. Del Negro, review of *Rainy Season,* p. 207; September, 1997, Janice Del Negro, review of *Split Just Right,* p. 11.

Horn Book, March-April, 1997, Nancy Vasilakis, review of *Rainy Season,* p. 198; July-August, 1997, Nancy Vasilakis, review of *Split Just Right,* p. 455; January-February, 1998, Kitty Flynn, review of *Sons of Liberty,* p. 72; November, 1999, Nancy Vasilakis, review of *Dive,* p. 739; September, 2001, Anita L. Burkam, review of *Witch Twins,* p. 583; November-December, 2001, Anita L. Burkam, review of *Amandine,* p. 748; November-December, 2002, Susan P. Bloom, review of *Hannah, Divided,* p. 323; March-April, 2005, Christine M. Heppermann, review of *Where I Want to Be,* p. 202; May-June, 2006, Jeannine M. Chapman, review of *My Almost Epic Summer,* p. 318.

Kirkus Review, August 15, 2001, review of *Amandine,* p. 1213; May 15, 2002, review of *Witch Twins at Camp Bliss,* p. 733; September 1, 2002, review of *Hannah, Divided,* p. 1309; February 1, 2003, review of *Overnight,* p. 229; March 1, 2005, Adele Griffin, review of *Where I Want to Be,* p. 297; March 15, 2006, Adele Griffin, review of *My Almost Epic Summer,* p. 291; July 1, 2007, Adele Griffin, review of *Vampire Island.*

Kliatt, March, 2004, Courtney Lewis, review of *Amandine,* p. 19; March, 2006, Claire Rosser, review of *My Almost Epic Summer,* p. 10.

Plain Dealer (Cleveland, OH), April 13, 2003, Cheryl Stritzel McCarthy, "A Transplanted Savant Finds She Has Much to Learn off the Farm," p. J11.

Publishers Weekly, October 14, 1996, review of *Rainy Season,* p. 84; December 16, 1996, Elizabeth Devereaux, "Flying Starts," p. 32; September 8, 1997, review of *Sons of Liberty,* p. 77; September 21, 1998, review of *The Other Shepards,* p. 86; July 2, 2001, review of *Witch Twins,* p. 76; August 20, 2001, review of *Amandine,* p. 81; August 26, 2002, review of *Hannah, Divided,* p. 69; December 16, 2002, review of *Overnight,* p. 68; March 21, 2005, review of *Where I Want to Be,* p. 52; March 13, 2006, review of *My Almost Epic Summer,* p. 67; August 20, 2007, review of *Vampire Island,* p. 69.

San Francisco Chronicle, April 25, 1999, Susan Faust, "Haunting Novel Is Not Your Average Ghost Story," p. 9.

School Library Journal, November, 1996, Lucinda Lockwood, review of *Rainy Season,* pp. 104-105; June, 1997, Carol A. Edwards, review of *Split Just Right,* p. 117; July, 2001, Catherine T. Quattlebaum, review of *Witch Twins,* p. 82; November, 2001, Alison Follos, review of *Amandine,* p. 158; June, 2002, Debbie Whitbeck, review of *Witch Twins at Camp Bliss,* p. 96; December, 2002, Barbara Scotto, review of *Hannah, Divided,* p. 138; February, 2003, B. Allison Gray, review of *Overnight,* p. 141; July, 2003, Linda B. Zeilstra, review of *Witch Twins and Melody Malady,* p. 96; October, 2004, Tina Zubak, review of *Witch Twins and the Ghost of Glenn Bly,* p. 114; April, 2005, Crystal Faris, review of *Where I Want to Be,* p. 130; April, 2006, Roxanne Myers Spencer, review of *My Almost Epic Summer,* p. 140; August, 2007, Christi Voth, review of *Vampire Island,* p. 118.

ONLINE

Adele Griffin Home Page, http://www.adelegriffin.net (December 1, 2008).

Embracing the Child Web site, http://www.embracingthe child.org/ (November 1, 2002), interview with Griffin.

H

HARGRAVE, Leonie
See DISCH, Thomas M.

*   *   *

HARRIS, Bob
See HARRIS, Robert J.

*   *   *

HARRIS, Robert J. 1955-
(Bob Harris)

Personal

Born 1955, in Dundee, Scotland; married Deborah Turner; children: three sons. *Education:* St. Andrews University. degree. *Hobbies and other interests:* Blues and jazz music, reading, playing board games, watching Fred Astaire movies, football (soccer).

Addresses

Home—St. Andrews, Scotland. *E-mail*—bob@harris-authors.com.

Career

Author. Worked variously as a bartender, salesman, nurse, and actor. Creator of *Talisman* (fantasy board game).

Writings

"SCOTTISH QUARTET" HISTORICAL NOVELS; FOR YOUNG ADULTS

(With Jane Yolen) *Queen's Own Fool,* Philomel (New York, NY), 2000.

(With Jane Yolen) *Girl in a Cage,* Philomel (New York, NY), 2002.
(With Jane Yolen) *Prince across the Water,* Philomel (New York, NY), 2004.
(With Jane Yolen) *The Rogues,* Philomel (New York, NY), 2007.

"YOUNG HEROES" NOVEL SERIES

(With Jane Yolen) *Odysseus in the Serpent Maze,* HarperCollins (New York, NY), 2001.
(With Jane Yolen) *Hippolyta and the Curse of the Amazons,* HarperCollins (New York, NY), 2002.
(With Jane Yolen) *Atalanta and the Arcadian Beast,* HarperCollins (New York, NY), 2003.
(With Jane Yolen) *Jason and the Gorgon's Blood,* HarperCollins (New York, NY), 2004.

'YOUNG LEGENDS" NOVEL SERIES

Leonardo and the Death Machine, HarperCollins (London, England), 2005.
Will Shakespeare and the Pirate's Fire, HarperCollins (London, England), 2006.

OTHER

(As Bob Harris; with Alan Mcfadzean) *The Queen's Heid* (radio play), produced on BBC Radio Scotland, 2005.
(As Bob Harris; with Alan Mcfadzean) *The Knox Factor* (radio play), produced on BBC Radio Scotland, 2008.

Contributor to anthologies, including *Tales of the Knights Templar,* edited by Katherine Kurtz, Warner Books (New York, NY), 1995; *In the Shadow of the Gargoyle,* edited by Nancy Kilpatrick and Thomas S. Roche, Ace Books (New York, NY), 1998; and *Ribbiting Tales,* edited by Nancy Springer, Philomel Books (New York, NY), 2000. Contributor to periodicals, including *Asimov's Science Fiction.*

Sidelights

Robert J. Harris, who developed the best-selling fantasy board game Talisman, has written several novels in collaboration with celebrated children's author Jane Yolen. Born in Dundee, Scotland, Harris developed an early interest in both science fiction and fantasy, and this interest influences his work today. "I aim to write well-plotted novels with strong characters and lively dialogue," Harris stated on his home page. "I want each story to be a page-turning adventure filled with mysteries that will draw the reader on."

Harris and Yolen first joined forces on the "Scottish Quartet" series of historical novels that focuses on the history of Scotland. Narrated by Nicola Ambruzzi, an orphaned court jester, *Queen's Own Fool* examines the life of Mary, Queen of Scots, the sixteenth-century royal who claimed the crowns of four nations during her reign and who was imprisoned for nearly two decades by her cousin, Elizabeth I of England. "Yolen and Harris do an excellent job of weaving historical information into the story," remarked *School Library Journal* contributor Cheri Estes, and *Kliatt* reviewer Claire Rosser praised Harris's "gifts of plotting and characterizations."

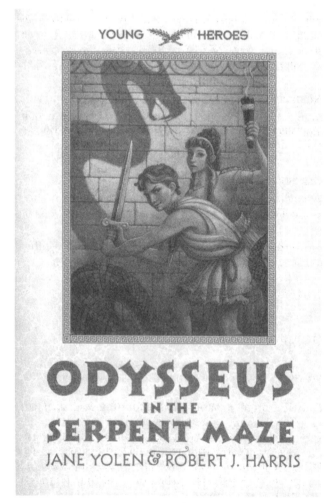

Robert J. Harris teams up with Jane Yolen to retell an exciting myth in **Odysseus in the Serpent Maze,** *featuring artwork by Hala Wittwer.*
(Cover art copyright © 2001 by Hala Wittwer. Cover copyright © 2002 by HarperCollins Publishers, Inc. Reproduced by permission of the illustrator.)

In *Girl in a Cage,* another "Scottish Quartet" novel, Harris and Yolen tell the story of Marjorie Bruce, the eldest daughter of Robert the Bruce, king of the Scots. At age eleven, Marjorie was taken prisoner by enemies of her father and held in England for eight years. Readers "will welcome this . . . tale of a strong-minded young woman coming of age," noted a critic in *Kirkus Reviews.*

A thirteen-year-old Highlander fights for Bonnie Prince Charlie at the pivotal Battle of Culloden in *Prince across the Water,* called "a spirited historical adventure" by *Booklist* critic Carolyn Phelan. *Prince across the Water* concerns Duncan, who leaves his family farm to join his cousin and other clansmen in the last great Jacobite uprising. *Horn Book* critic Anita L. Burkam called the novel "a well-told story set in an intriguing era that will leave readers mulling over thoughts of war and peace." In *The Rogues,* the fourth and final work in the series, tenant farmer Roddy Macallan is rescued from certain death by outlaw Alan Dunbar, a man who then serves as Roddy's mentor. Harris and Yolen "deftly weave historical facts into their action-packed adventure," observed Cheri Dobbs in a *School Library Journal* review of *The Rogues.*

Harris and Yolen also teamed on the "Young Heroes" novel series, which draws on Greek mythology. In *Odysseus in the Serpent Maze* the epic hero is depicted as a brash, adventurous thirteen year old who battles the deadly beasts in Crete's famed labyrinth. *Booklist* critic Gillian Engberg complimented the tale's "cliffhanger chapter endings, snappy humor, and breakneck adventure." In this novel an Amazon princess undertakes a dangerous mission in *Hippolyta and the Curse of the Amazons,* described as "a detailed, compelling story" by Beth L. Meister in *School Library Journal.* According to a *Kirkus Reviews* critic, the authors of *Hippolyta and the Curse of the Amazons* provide "accurate details from both history and myth that will give readers a taste of what the classical stories themselves have to offer."

In *Atalanta and the Arcadian Beast,* another "Young Heroes" novel, Harris and Yolen's twelve-year-old protagonist sets out after the winged creature that killed her father, accompanied by boastful and skillful Orion the hunter. "Atalanta is a strong female hero," Angela J. Reynolds remarked in *School Library Journal,* "and her adventures will thrill readers." Jason, the future leader of the Argonauts, battles evil centaurs as he undertakes a perilous quest in the collaborators' novel *Jason and the Gorgon's Blood.* "There is plenty of action to keep mythology enthusiasts happy," Reynolds noted of the myth-based work.

Biographical and Critical Sources

PERIODICALS

Booklist, April 15, 2001, Gillian Engberg, review of *Odysseus in the Serpent Maze,* p. 1561; February 1, 2003,

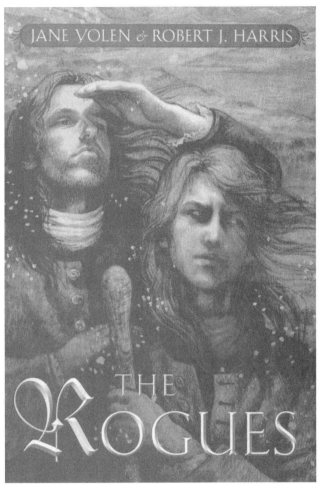

Cover of Harris's historical novel The Rogues, *featuring artwork by Yvonne Gilbert.* (Jacket art © 2007 by Yvonne Gilbert. Reproduced by permission of Philomel Books, a division of Penguin Putnam Books for Young Readers.)

John Peters, review of *Atalanta and the Arcadian Beast,* p. 996; November 15, 2004, Carolyn Phelan, review of *Prince across the Water,* p. 585; September 15, 2007, Anne O'Malley, review of *The Rogues,* p. 63.

Horn Book, November-December, 2004, Anita L. Burkam, review of *Prince across the Water,* p. 720.

Kirkus Reviews, January 1, 2002, review of *Hippolyta and the Curse of the Amazons,* p. 54; August 15, 2002, review of *Girl in a Cage,* p. 1240; February 1, 2003, review of *Atalanta and the Arcadian Beast,* p. 244; September 15, 2004, review of *Prince across the Water,* p. 923.

Kliatt, November, 2000, Claire Rosser, review of *Queen's Own Fool.*

New York Times Book Review, Jane Resh Thomas, "Off with Her Head," review of *Queen's Own Fool,* p. 58.

School Library Journal, June, 2000, Cheri Estes, review of *Queen's Own Fool,* p. 156; July, 2001, Angela J. Reynolds, review of *Odysseus in the Serpent Maze,* p. 116; March, 2002, Beth L. Meister, review of *Hippolyta and the Curse of the Amazons,* p. 240; October, 2002, Starr E. Smith, review of *Girl in a Cage,* p. 178; February, 2003, Angela J. Reynolds, review of *Atalanta and the Arcadian Beast,* p. 150; February,

2004, Angela J. Reynolds, review of *Jason and the Gorgon's Blood,* p. 154; December, 2004, Kimberly Monaghan, review of *Prince across the Water,* p. 154; September, 2007, Cheri Dobbs, review of *The Rogues,* p. 212.

ONLINE

Robert J. Harris Home Page, http://www.harris-authors. com (October 15, 2008).*

* * *

HASTINGS, Victor
See DISCH, Thomas M.

* * *

HOROWITZ, Anthony 1955-

Personal

Born April 5, 1955, in Stanmore, Middlesex, England; son of Mark (a businessman) and Joyce Horowitz; married Jill Green (a television producer), April 15, 1988; children: Nicholas, Cassian (sons). *Education:* University of York, B.A., 1979.

Addresses

Home—London, England. *Agent*—Peters, Fraser & Dunlop, 34-43 Russell St., London WC2B 5HP, England. *E-mail*—ajh13w@aol.com.

Career

Novelist and screenwriter. Also worked in advertising as a copywriter.

Awards, Honors

Red House Children's Book Award, 2003, for *Skeleton Key;* Rebecca Caudill Young Readers' Book Award, 2004, for *Stormbreaker.*

Writings

NOVELS

Enter Frederick K. Bower, Arlington (London, England), 1979.

The Sinister Secret of Frederick K. Bower, illustrated by John Woodgate, Arlington (London, England), 1979.

Misha the Magician and the Mysterious Amulet, illustrated by John Woodgate, Arlington (London, England), 1981.

The Kingfisher Book of Myths and Legend, illustrated by Frances Mosley, Kingfisher (London, England), 1985, published as *Myths and Mythology,* Little Simon (New York, NY), 1985.

(Adaptor) *Adventurer* (based on a television script by Richard Carpenter), Corgi (London, England), 1986.

(Adaptor with Robin May) Richard Carpenter, *Robin of Sherwood: The Hooded Man* (based on a television play), Puffin (Harmondsworth, England), 1986, published as *The Complete Adventures of Robin of Sherwood*, Puffin (Harmondsworth, England), 1990.

Groosham Grange (also see below), illustrated by Cathy Simpson, Methuen (London, England), 1988, Philomel (New York, NY), 2008.

Starting Out (play), Oberon (London, England), 1990.

Groosham Grange II: The Unholy Grail, Methuen (London, England), 1991, published as *The Unholy Grail: A Tale of Groosham Grange* (also see below), Walker (London, England), 1999.

The Puffin Book of Horror Stories, illustrated by Daniel Payne, Viking (London, England), 1994.

Granny, Walker (London, England), 1994.

(Editor and contributor) *Death Walks Tonight: Horrifying Stories*, Puffin (New York, NY), 1996.

The Switch, Walker (London, England), 1996.

The Devil and His Boy, Walker (London, England), 1998, Puffin (New York, NY), 2001.

Horowitz Horror: Nine Nasty Stories to Chill You to the Bone, Orchard (London, England), 1999.

Groosham Grange; and, The Unholy Grail: Two Stories in One, Walker (London, England), 2000.

Mindgame (play), Oberon (London, England), 2000.

More Horowitz Horror: Eight Sinister Stories You'll Wish You Never Read, Orchard (London, England), 2000, published as *More Horowitz Horror: Stories You'll Wish You'd Never Read*, Philomel (New York, NY), 2006.

Myths and Legends, Kingfisher (Boston, MA), 2007.

"PENTAGRAM" SERIES

The Devil's Door-Bell, Holt (New York, NY), 1983.

The Night of the Scorpion, Pacer (New York, NY), 1984.

The Silver Citadel, Berkley (New York, NY), 1986.

Day of the Dragon, Methuen (London, England), 1989.

"DIAMOND BROTHERS" SERIES

The Falcon's Malteser (also see below), Grafton (London, England), 1986, Philomel (New York, NY), 2004, published as *Just Ask for Diamond*, Lions (London, England), 1998.

Public Enemy Number Two (also see below), Dragon (London, England), 1987, Philomel (New York, NY), 2004.

South by South East, Walker (London, England), 1991, Puffin Books, 2005.

I Know What You Did Last Wednesday, Walker (London, England), 2002.

The French Confection [and] *Public Enemy Number Two* (omnibus), 2002.

The Blurred Man (bound with *The Falcon's Malteser*), Walker (London, England), 2002.

The French Confection (also see below), Walker (London, England), 2003.

Three of Diamonds, Puffin Books (New York, NY), 2005.

The Greek Who Stole Christmas, 2007.

"ALEX RIDER" SERIES; FOR YOUNG ADULTS

Stormbreaker (also see below), Walker (London, England), 2000, Puffin (New York, NY), 2001.

Point Blanc, Walker (London, England), 2001, published as *Point Blank*, Philomel (New York, NY), 2002.

Skeleton Key, Walker (London, England), 2002, Philomel (New York, NY), 2003.

Eagle Strike, Walker (London, England), 2003, Philomel (New York, NY), 2004.

Alex Rider Pack (omnibus), Walker (London, England), 2003.

Scorpia, Walker (London, England), 2004.

Ark Angel, Walker (London, England), 2005.

Alex Rider: The Gadgets, Philomel (New York, NY), 2006.

Stormbreaker (screenplay; adaptation of his novel of the same name), 2006.

Snakehead, Philomel (New York, NY), 2007.

The Mission Files, Walker (London, England), 2008.

The Alex Rider Collection, Puffin Books (Harmondsworth, England), 2008.

"POCKET HOROWITZ" SERIES

The Night Bus, Orchard (London, England), 2002.

Twist Cottage, Orchard (London, England), 2002.

Burnt, Orchard (London, England), 2002.

Scared, Orchard (London, England), 2002.

Killer Camera, Orchard (London, England), 2002.

The Phone Goes Dead, Orchard (London, England), 2002.

"POWER OF FIVE" SERIES

Raven's Gate, Scholastic Press (New York, NY), 2005.

Evil Star, Scholastic Press (New York, NY), 2006.

Nightrise, Scholastic Press (New York, NY), 2007.

Necropolis City of the Dead, Walker (London, England), 2008.

OTHER

Also author of *Stormbreaker* (screenplay), adapted from his novel, Entertainment Film Distributors/Weinstein Company, 2006. Creator and contributor to television series *Midsomer Murders, Murder in Mind*, and *Foyle's War*, Contributor of scripts to television series *Heroes and Villains*, British Broadcasting System (BBC) 1; and to *Agatha Christie's Poirot, Crime Traveller*, and *The Saint*. Also author of stage play *Mind Game*, produced in London's West End.

Books by Horowitz have been translated into Spanish, French, German, Danish, Swedish, Hebrew, Japanese, Flemish, Italian, and other languages, and published in Braille editions.

Adaptations

The Little Soldier, The Moor, and *The Legend*, original television scripts by Horowitz, were adapted into books by Royston Drake, Carnival, 1989. *Stormbreaker* was adapted for audiocassette, Listening Library, 2001. *The Gathering* was adapted for film by Dimension Films, 2003, and adapted as a graphic novel by Antony Johnston, illustrated by Kanako Damerum and Yuzuru Takasaki, Walker (London, England), 2006. *Point Blanc* was adapted by Johnston as the graphic novel *Point Blank,* illustrated by Damerum and Takasaki, Walker, 2007.

Sidelights

Anthony Horowitz first established his reputation in England as a writer and editor of horror stories for a young-adult audience. The editor of *The Puffin Book of Horror Stories,* Horowitz has also entertained—and frightened—his readers with such chilling books as *Death Walks Tonight: Horrifying Stories* and the novels *Scared* and *Twist Cottage.* U.S. readers were introduced to Horowitz through his popular series of books featuring protagonist Alex Rider, the teenage nephew of a former British secret agent, who finds himself thrust into a series of daring adventures. "There are times when a grade-B adventure is just the ticket for a bored teenager," maintained *Booklist* reviewer Jean Franklin, "especially if it offers plenty of slam-bang action, spying, and high-tech gadgets." According to Franklin, the "Alex Rider" novels provide just that. Horowitz has also created other series that are popular with readers in England and the United States, including the "Diamond Brothers" novels, about a pair of brothers who are also detectives, and the "Power of Five" stories, which focus on five teens whose mission is to save the world from evil.

The action-packed "Alex Rider" series has much the same sensibility as Ian Fleming's "James Bond" novel series for adults, about a British superspy. Like the Bond series, Alex's adventures are frequently life threatening. Alex, like Bond, remains cool and resourceful, making good use of the high-tech gadgetry provided for him by his superiors.

The fourteen-year-old spy makes his debut in *Stormbreaker.* Alex, an orphan, has been raised by his Uncle Ian. When his uncle dies in a car crash, the incident is ruled an accident, but Alex discovers bullet holes in the body of the wrecked car, and he begins to ask questions about what really led to Ian's death. His curiosity regarding his uncle's death ultimately almost gets him killed, and he soon discovers that Ian had been an agent for British Intelligence. With this information, the teen decides that joining the agency himself might be the best way to stay alive. Leaving prep school for two weeks of intensive training as an MI6 agent, Alex is given a collection of spy gadgets and sent on his first assignment: to infiltrate a training group run by demented inventor Herod Sayles, who is trying to wipe out Great Britain's children by using biological weapons introduced through an in-school computer system known as "Stormbreaker."

Noting that "satirical names abound . . . and the hard-boiled language is equally outrageous," a *Publishers Weekly* reviewer nonetheless wrote that "these exaggerations only add to the fun" for readers. *Stormbreaker* was deemed "an excellent choice for reluctant readers" by *School Library Journal* contributor Lynn Bryant, due to its "short cliff-hanger chapters and its breathless pace."

In *Point Blanc,* the second installment in the "Alex Rider" series, the teen operative enrolls at an exclusive prep school called Point Blanc, located in the French Alps and designed to house the young black sheep in Britain's wealthiest families. Run by a South African named Dr. Grief, the school has surprisingly good luck in making these rich teen troublemakers toe the line. After Alex, now trapped at the school, discovers that brainwashing by Grief is only one of the ways these young men are controlled, he begins to worry about his own safety. Fortunately, as a *Kirkus Reviews* critic assured readers, "Horowitz devises a string of miraculous circumstances that keeps Alex alive and spying throughout." Propelled by hidden passages, frightening medical experiments, and a protagonist who barely stays one step away from death, *Point Blanc* was described by Franklin as a "non-stop thriller" in her *Booklist* review.

In *Scorpia,* Alex must try to bring down a powerful international crime organization created by an international network of ruthless, greedy assassins and spies. The crime ring known as Scorpia—its name is an acronym for "sabotage, corruption, intelligence, and assassination"—has become involved in international power plays and is now responsible for a tenth of all terrorist activity in the world. Scorpia's newest venture, "Invisible Sword," involves severing the powerful alliance between the United States and Great Britain by using biological weapons to wipe out all the twelve-and thirteen year olds in Great Britain. Alex's activities eventually bring him face to face with the head of Scorpia, the evil Mrs. Rothman, and with some chilling facts about his father. According to a reviewer for *KidsReads* online, *Scorpia* is "the most heartstopping adventure yet in this action-filled series, with an ending that will surprise you and a cliffhanger that will astound you!"

In *Ark Angel,* Alex is involved in espionage surrounding a luxury hotel being constructed in outer space, while *Snakehead* finds him once again working against the Scorpia network. Having regained power, Scorpia is now planning to assassinate eight high-profile individuals, including a former U.S. president and a pop star. The plot of *Snakehead* also involves Major Winston Yu, the head of a criminal network called *shetou,* or "snakehead." Alex, having been rescued from outer space, is asked to go undercover as a refugee as part of a plan to learn more about Snakehead. The depiction of poverty and exploited children is starkly portrayed in *Snakehead,* and Horowitz's novel was highly recommended by Amanda Craig in the London *Times.* According to

Craig, this installment in the "Alex Rider" series "goes deeper than any previous book, either by Horowitz or his rivals in the spy kids trade, in its vivid portrayal of pure evil."

Many of Horowitz's books feature young teens who find their mundane lives suddenly turned upside down by an evil force. Such is the case in *The Devil's Door-Bell,* one of Horowitz's first novels for young readers. Published in 1983 as the first segment in the "Pentagram" series, it tells the story of thirteen-year-old Martin Hopkins, whose parents' tragic death forces him into the care of a foster mother named Elvira. In her company, Martin goes to live on her country farm in Yorkshire, England. Upset at being newly orphaned and nervous over Elvira's strange demeanor and intimations that Martin's time will also soon be up, the teen realizes that his suspicions are not just due to stress: Elvira is actually a witch, and her coven is planning something that will cause him harm. A clue left by a murdered friend leads Martin and journalist friend Richard Cole to an ancient circle of stones known as the "Devil's Door-Bell" where Elvira's plans to unleash a malevolent supernatural horror energized by a nearby nuclear power station are revealed. Calling *The Devil's Door-Bell* "a satisfyingly scary book," *School Library Journal* contributor Anne Connor added that Horowitz creates a "chilling atmosphere of horror" despite the novel's "sketchy characterization . . . and . . . unbelievable plot."

The "Pentagram" series continues with *The Night of the Scorpion,* as Martin and Richard must close a portal into hell after a mysterious explosion almost kills a group of Martin's classmates. This time the pair travel to Peru, where their efforts to battle the demons known as the Old Ones are thwarted by human accomplices who arrest Richard as soon as he gets off the plane. Left alone in a strange country, Martin meets another boy named Pedro, a descendant of the Incas who, like Martin, is destined to do battle with the Old Ones. "Horowitz packs enough suspense and violence into the story to satisfy the most avid thriller fans," according to a *Publishers Weekly* contributor, while *English Journal* reviewer Regina Cowin noted that "the reader is drawn into this story of ancient mysticism just as inexorably as Martin and Pedro are drawn into" their battle against ancient evil. Other "Pentagram" novels include *The Silver Citadel* and *Day of the Dragon.*

Another Horowitz novel involving time travel is *The Devil and His Boy.* Set in Elizabethan England, this work finds a servant boy named Tom Falconer thrust into an alien world after he is ordered to accompany a friend of his master's to London, only to have his companion murdered along the way. Befriended by a pickpocket named Moll, Tom joins a troupe of thespians and suddenly finds himself enmeshed in political intrigue and drawn into the illegal activities of some of his new friends. Cast in a play titled "The Devil and His Boy" which is being produced by the secretive Dr.

Mobius, Tom winds up in the lap of the queen of England herself. "Horowitz paints his characters . . . with broad strokes and keeps the melodramatic story moving at a rapid clip," wrote *School Library Journal* contributor Barbara Scotto, the critic dubbing *The Devil and His Boy* a "rollicking good tale that is mostly based on historical fact." Ilene Cooper also cited the historical basis of the novel, adding that, "to his credit, [Horowitz] does not try to pretty up Elizabethan life for his audience. . . . Dirty and disfigured characters are described in detail."

Horowitz returns to contemporary times in his "Diamond Brothers" books. Here the author recounts the adventures of Tim and Nick Simple, teenaged brothers who become involved in mysteries. In the first novel of the series, *South by South East,* the brothers become entangled in a twisted adventure involving an assassin, the international art world, and M16. *Public Enemy Number Two* and *The Falcon's Malteser* continue the brothers' adventures, while *Three of Diamonds* presents three shorter tales "full of clever puns and deadpan comments," according to Kay Weisman in *Booklist.*

Mystical powers are at the heart of Horowitz's "Power of Five" saga, which includes the books *Raven's Gate, Evil Star, Nightrise,* and *Necropolis City of the Dead.* In *Evil Star* the action takes place in Peru, where a gate to another world exists; this gate may be exploited by a greedy businessman to turn some ancient, malevolent spirits loose on the world. Special individuals with psychic powers must battle these spirits: the Old Ones which are reprised from *The Night of the Scorpion.* Reviewing *Evil Star* for *Kliatt,* Paula Rohrlick described it as filled with "lots of action, horror and suspense," and she dubbed *Nightrise* "as exciting and over-the-top" as the "Alex Rider" series. Lynn Evarts, reviewing the "Power of Five" books for *School Library Review,* credited Horowitz with "masterfully" mixing suspense and fantasy.

In addition to his series fiction and stand-alone novels, Horowitz has published a number of short-story collections, both as editor and sole author. Reading only the titles of *Horowitz Horror: Nine Nasty Stories to Chill You to the Bone* and its sequel, *More Horowitz Horror: Eight Sinister Stories You'll Wish You Never Read,* readers can consider themselves forewarned. "None will disappoint readers with an appetite for ghoulish happenings," predicted *School Librarian* reviewer Peter Hollindale in praise of several stories in the second of the two books. The critic also commended Horowitz's creative use of irony, subtlety, and "creepy and surprising variants on familiar themes."

Writing children's books is only one of several areas where Horowitz has used his writing talents; the other is in authoring series and segments for British television, an activity that has helped Horowitz imbue his fiction with a strong cinematic sense and draw even reluctant readers into his tales of horror and suspense. He frequently includes film references in his books, particularly in his "Diamond Brothers" books. Series titles *The Falcon's Malteser, Public Enemy Number Two,* and *South by South East* are references to classic films. Calling these books "rattling good yarns," Jo Goodman observed in her *Magpies* review that "*South by South East* contains, amongst others, the windmill scene from [Alfred Hitchcock's film] *Foreign Correspondent* and the crop duster from *North by Northwest.*" The *Falcon's Malteser* references the classic film *The Maltese Falcon* starring Humphrey Bogart, while *Public Enemy Number Two* is a take-off on the gangster film *Public Enemy Number One.*

Discussing the immense popularity of his works with London *Evening Standard* contributor Joyce Lynn, Horowitz stated that "the main key to my success is longevity, or survival. For 25 years I've been sustaining 10-hour days writing books, TV, theatre, films, but it's only in the past four years that I've achieved overnight success with Alex Rider—*Stormbreaker* being the 'breakout' book." Though Horowitz insists there are no particular messages in his novels, he told Glasgow *Sunday Herald* interviewer Stephen Phelan: "I do get that sense that children, and all people, can resolve their problems though books. They have a wonderful vicarious quality about them. And in that way, yes, I would like to think I'm holding up a torch for the idea that reading is a good thing."

Biographical and Critical Sources

BOOKS

Abrams, Dennis, *Anthony Horowitz,* Chelsea House (New York, NY), 2006.

PERIODICALS

Booklist, January 1, 2000, Ilene Cooper, review of *The Devil and His Boy,* p. 922; September 1, 2001, Kelly Milner Halls, review of *Stormbreaker,* p. 97; April 1, 2002, Jean Franklin, review of *Point Blanc,* p. 1319; February 1, 2005, Frances Bradburn, review of *Scorpia,* p. 955; May 15, 2005, Kay Weisman, review of *Three of Diamonds,* p. 1658; July 1, 2005, Ilene Cooper, review of *Raven's Gate,* p. 1923; December 1, 2005, John Peters, review of *South by South East,* p. 47; April 1, 2006, Kay Weisman, review of *Alex Rider: The Gadgets,* p. 40; April 15, 2006, Stephanie Zvirin, review of *Ark Angel,* p. 42; June 1, 2006, Stephanie Zvirin, review of *Evil Star,* p. 71; September 15, 2007, Kay Weisman, review of *Snakehead,* p. 61; July 1, 2008, Ian Chipman, review of *Groosham Grange,* p. 66.

Bookseller, February 18, 2005, review of *Ark Angel,* p. 36; May 20, 2005, Caroline Horn, "The Horror of Horowitz," p. 22; February 17, 2006, review of *Evil Star,* p. 32.

Daily Mail (London, England), July 23, 2005, Mary Riddell, "Hope and Gory," interview with Horowitz, p. 16.

Daily Telegraph (London, England), March 30, 2005, Sarah Crompton, "'I Knew That Alex Was Special from the First,'" interview with Horowitz, p. 16; April 7, 2007, Christopher Middleton, interview with Horowitz; October 27, 2007, Christopher Middleton, "True Grit And Gruesome Goings-on . . . Alex Rider Is Back with a Vengeance."

English Journal, October, 1985, review of *The Night of the Scorpion,* p. 82.

Evening Standard (London, England), March 29, 2004, Katie Campbell, "Teenage Action Hero," interview with Horowitz, p. 39; April 14, 2005, Joyce Lynn, "My Prep School Headmaster Was a Sadistic Brute," interview with Horowitz, p. 55; July 6, 2006, Fiona Maddocks, "The Teenage Spy Who Is Whipping up a Storm," p. 30.

Guardian (London, England), April 9, 2005, Philip Ardagh, review of *Ark Angel.*

Independent (London, England), July 31, 2002, Robert Hanks, "The New Kid on the Block," interview with Horowitz, p. 6; August 13, 2004, Barry Forshaw, "Growing up in Public," interview with Horowitz, p. 18.

Kirkus Reviews, March 15, 2001, review of *Stormbreaker,* p. 410; February 15, 2002, review of *Point Blanc,* p. 258; June 1, 2005, review of *Raven's Gate,* p. 637; June 1, 2006, review of *Evil Star,* p. 574; July 1, 2007, review of *Nightrise;* July 1, 2008, review of *Groosham Grange.*

Kliatt, March 1, 2005, Paula Rohrlick, review of *Scorpia,* p. 12; July 1, 2005, Paula Rohrlick, review of *Raven's Gate,* p. 12; March 1, 2006, Paula Rohrlick, review of *Ark Angel,* p. 12; May 1, 2006, Paula Rohrlick, review of *Evil Star,* p. 10; July 1, 2006, Miles Klein, review of *Eagle Strike,* p. 46; September 1, 2006, Janet Julian, review of *Ark Angel,* p. 52; May 1, 2007, Paula Rohrlick, review of *Nightrise,* p. 13; November 1, 2007, Paula Rohrlick, review of *Snakehead,* p. 10.

Magpies, March, 2001, Jo Goodman, "So You Want to Be a Private Investigator?," pp. 14-15.

New Statesman, April 30, 2001, Andrew Billen, "A Few Twists Too Far," p. 49.

Observer (London, England), April 10, 2005, Kate Kellaway, "The Observer Profile: Anthony Horowitz," p. 27.

Publishers Weekly, March 1, 1985, review of *The Night of the Scorpion,* p. 81; May 21, 2001, review of *Stormbreaker,* p. 109; May 13, 2002, review of *Point Blanc,* p. 72; June 20, 2005, review of *Raven's Gate,* p. 78.

School Librarian, summer, 2001, Peter Hollindale, review of *More Horowitz Horror: Eight Sinister Stories You'll Wish You Never Read,* p. 102.

School Library Journal, April, 1984, Anne Connor, review of *The Devil's Door-Bell,* p. 124; July, 1994, Mary Jo Drungil, review of *Myths and Legends,* p. 124; April, 2000, Barbara Scotto, review of *The Devil and His Boy,* p. 136; June, 2001, Lynn Bryant, review of *Stormbreaker,* p. 150; March, 2002, review of *Point Blank,* p. 232; March, 2005, Delia Fritz, review of

Scorpia, p. 212; May, 2005, Angela M. Boccuzzi-Reichert, review of *Three of Diamonds,* p. 130; July, 2005, Lynn Evarts, review of *Raven's Gate,* p. 104; December, 2005, Alice DiNizo, review of *South by South East,* p. 148; April, 2006, Lynn Evarts, review of *The Gadgets,* p. 140; April, 2006, Heather E. Miller, review of *Ark Angel,* p. 140; July, 2006, Morgan Johnson-Doyle, review of *Evil Star,* p. 106; January, 2008, Lynn Evarts, review of *Nightrise,* p. 120; January, 2008, Tim Wadham, review of *Snakehead,* p. 120; September, 2008, Lynn Evarts, review of *Groosham Grange,* p. 186.

Spectator, February 11, 1995, Ian Hislop, "Last of a Kind," p. 47.

Sunday Herald (Glasgow, Scotland), Stephan Phelan, "Boys' Own Stories: He Created Plucky Teen Agent Alex Rider," p. 16.

Times (London, England), November 9, 2007, Amanda Craig, "Deeper and Darker for Alex Rider," review of *Snakehead.*

Voice of Youth Advocates, April, 2000, review of *The Devil and His Boy,* p. 35.

ONLINE

Anthony Horowitz Home Page, http://www.anthonyhorowitz.com (October 15, 2008).

Australian Broadcasting Corporation Web site, http://www.abc.net.au/ (August 1, 2008), interview with Horowitz.

CBBC Newsround, http://news.bbc.co.uk/ (June 9, 2004), review of *Scorpia.*

KidsReads Web site, http://www.kidsreads.com/ (August 1, 2008), review of *Scorpia;* Tom Donadio, review of *Ark Angel* and *Snakehead.**

*   *   *

HUBERY, Julia

Personal

Born in Stamford, Lincolnshire, England; married; children: three children. *Education:* Attended college. *Hobbies and other interests:* Pottery.

Addresses

Home—Gosport, Hampshire, England.

Career

Children's book writer. Formerly worked as an architect.

Writings

The Naughtiest Piglet, illustrated by John Bendall-Brunello, Gullane Children's (London, England), 2004.

Raffi's Surprise, illustrated by Mei Matsuoka, Simon & Schuster (London, England), 2006, published as *A Friend for All Seasons,* Atheneum (New York, NY), 2007.

A Christmas Wish, illustrated by Sophy Williams, Little Tiger Press (London, England), 2008.

Come Home, Little Brave, illustrated by Julie Monks, Orchard Books (London, England), 2008.

Wishmoley and the Little Piece of Sky, illustrated by Mary McQuillan, Scholastic (London, England), 2009.

Sidelights

Julia Hubery worked as an architect for several years before turning to writing. Inspired by her own three children, she has created several picture-book stories featuring simple texts. In her first, *The Naughtiest Pig,* one naughty piglet constantly strays away from Mother Pig, causing great worry among the family. With a penchant for getting into mischief, the frisky piglet soon finds that Horse, Cow, and other farm animals are also worried, because the foolish creature is heading for trouble. Her story *A Christmas Wish* is brought to life with pastel artwork by Sophy Williams and chronicles the day Gemma and Ty accidentally break a beloved Christmas tree decoration—the sparkly snow deer—and unleash a special holiday magic.

Another young animal is the star of *Raffi's Surprise,* a picture book by Hubery that was published in the United States as *A Friend for All Seasons.* In the story, a young raccoon lives in Old Father Oak, where the leaves prove enticing as they change from green to gold in autumn. When the oak leaves start to fall, however, the raccoon worries about the tree until his mother explains the change of seasons. Praising the mixed-media illustrations Mei Hatsuoka contributes to Hubery's story, Hazel Rochman noted in *Booklist* that *A Friend for All Seasons* "offers a fun way to tell the hibernation story," and a *Kirkus Reviews* writer deemed the book "a gentle tale with a nifty lesson."

Discussing her writing process on the Little Tiger Press Web site, Hubery commented: "As I work part-time and have three children, I have to grab the writing time whenever I can and hope the ideas flow. I nearly always have a few texts bubbling along, so my writing day varies. Sometimes I'll play with new ideas, maybe a picture or a sentence, to see if anything comes. Other times I'll prod and stir my half-way texts to see if I can move them on. Inspiration likes to strike in awkward places, like on the way to work—so I have to scrabble for a pen and scribble it down to play with later."

Biographical and Critical Sources

PERIODICALS

Booklist, July 1, 2007, Hazel Rochman, review of *A Friend for All Seasons,* p. 65.

Kirkus Reviews, July 15, 2007, review of *A Friend for All Seasons.*

School Library Journal, August, 2007, Marianne Saccardi, review of *A Friend for All Seasons,* p. 82.

ONLINE

Little Tiger Press Web site, http://www.littletigerpress.com/ (November 28, 2008), "Julia Hubery."*

J-L

JAMES, Gordon C. 1973-

Personal

Born 1973, in Washington, DC. *Education:* School of Visual Arts, B.F.A., 1995. *Hobbies and other interests:* Figurative drawing and painting, spending time with family.

Addresses

E-mail—contact@gordoncjames.com.

Career

Painter and children's book illustrator. Hallmark Cards, Kansas City, MO, artist and designer, 1997-2001. Artist-in-residence, McColl Center for the Arts, 2003; University of North Carolina at Charlotte, adjunct professor of art, 2006. *Exhibitions:* Work included in permanent collections at Hallmark Cards Illustration Archive, Kansas City, MO; Prince George's County (MD) Public Schools; and Paul R. Jones Collection, University of Delaware. Work included in exhibits at School of Visual Arts, New York, NY, 1994; Hallmark Cards Black History Month Exhibition, Kansas City, 1997; El Dorado Gallery, Kansas City, 1998; Artists of the Greater Washington Urban League exhibit, Washington, DC, 2001; National Press Building, Washington, DC, 2002; and National Black Fine Art Show, Puck Building, New York, NY, 2003.

Member

Oil Painters of America, Portrait Society of America.

Awards, Honors

International Artist Magazine Challenge finalist; Best Portfolio Award, Portrait Society of America, 2003.

Illustrator

Patricia C. McKissack, *Abby Takes a Stand* ("Scraps of Time" series), Viking (New York, NY), 2005.

Patricia C. McKissack, *Away West* ("Scraps of Time" series), Viking (New York, NY), 2006.

Patricia C. McKissack, *A Song for Harlem* ("Scraps of Time" series), Viking (New York, NY), 2007.

David A. Adler, *Campy: The Story of Roy Campanella,* Viking (New York, NY), 2007.

Patricia C. McKissack, *The Homerun King* ("Scraps of Time" series), Viking (New York, NY), 2008.

Sidelights

Inspired by artists such as John Singer Sargent, Nicholai Fechin, and Henry Ossawa Tanner, Gordon C. James has enjoyed a successful career as a painter and illustrator. James has provided the art for a number of children's titles, including books in Patricia C. McKissack's "Scraps of Time" series of chapter books for young readers.

The "Scraps of Time" series explores the history of an African-American family. In *Abby Takes a Stand,* cousins Mattie Rae, Aggie, and Trey Webster find an old restaurant menu while exploring in their grandmother's attic. The discovery of the menu prompts the elderly woman, named Abby, to recall a turbulent episode from 1960. As a youngster, Abby was denied entry into a circus-themed restaurant at a local department store because of the color of her skin. Abby's humiliation stirred her to action, and she became a proponent of civil rights as a member of the Flyer Brigade, which advocated civil disobedience, including sit-ins. "This accessible, lively, and heartfelt chapter book reads like a memoir," noted *Horn Book* contributor Robin Smith in a review of *Abby Takes a Stand.* James's illustrations also drew praise, *School Library Journal* critic Mary N. Oluonye citing the "liberal sprinkling of Gordon's expressive black-and-white drawings," and Ilene Cooper writing in *Booklist* that his artwork "adds to the ambience of the time."

In *Away West,* the second installment in the chapter-book series, the Webster children find a memento belonging to their ancestor, Everett Turner. Born after the

Gordon C. James evokes the energy that made Roy Campanella a baseball hero in his work for David A. Adler's **Campy.** (Viking, 2007. Reproduced by permission of Viking, a division of Penguin Putnam Books for Young Readers.)

U.S. Civil War, Turner flees the South by stowing away on a riverboat bound for St. Louis, where he learns to work with horses. Turner eventually settles in Nicodemus, Kansas, a town founded by former slaves. As their grandmother narrates Everett's tale, the two youngsters learn about the contributions of the black soldiers who served in the Union Army during the War between the States. "Short chapters, simple sentences, and James' pencil sketches make this an appealing choice for newly independent readers," wrote Kay Weisman in *Booklist.* James also illustrated *A Song for Harlem,* the third offering in McKissack's "Scraps of Time" series. Set in 1928, the story centers on the literary triumphs of Lilly Belle Turner, who studied with celebrated author Zora Neale Huston. Lilly Belle also faces a crisis of conscience when her friend and classmate plagiarizes an article from a prominent magazine.

In addition to his collaboration with McKissack, James also provided artwork for *Campy: The Story of Roy Campanella,* a biography by David A. Adler. Campanella, who helped break the color line in major league baseball, played catcher for the Brooklyn Dodgers from 1948 to 1957. His career ended abruptly after he was severely injured in an automobile accident. Noted for his spirited play, "Campy" led his team to five World Series appearances and was named the National League's Most Valuable Player three times and was elected to the Hall of Fame in 1969. According to Bill Ott in *Booklist,* "James delivers evocative illustrations

in [a] soft-focus, pastel-heavy style," and a *Kirkus Reviews* critic stated that the artist's "compelling oils present a beautifully lit, softly focused view of the events" detailed in Adler's biography.

Biographical and Critical Sources

PERIODICALS

Booklist, May 15, 2005, Ilene Cooper, review of *Abby Takes a Stand,* p. 1675; April 15, 2006, Kay Weisman, review of *Away West,* p. 59; February 1, 2007, Bill Ott, review of *Campy: The Story of Roy Campanella,* p. 59; August, 2007, Carolyn Phelan, review of *A Song for Harlem,* p. 62.

Horn Book, September-October, 2005, Robin Smith, review of *Abby Takes a Stand,* p. 585.

Kirkus Reviews, May 15, 2005, review of *Abby Takes a Stand,* p. 593; February 1, 2007, review of *Campy,* p. 119; July 1, 2007, review of *A Song for Harlem.*

School Library Journal, July, 2005, Mary N. Oluonye, review of *Abby Takes a Stand,* p. 78; May, 2006, Pat Leach, review of *Away West,* p. 94; September, 2007, Donna Atmur, review of *A Song for Harlem,* p. 171.

ONLINE

Gordon C. James Home Page, http://www.gjamespaintings.addr.com (October 15, 2008).*

*   *   *

KATZ, Karen 1947-

Personal

Born September 16, 1947, in Newark, NJ; daughter of Alex (a furniture manufacturer) and Muriel (a homemaker) Katz; married Gary Richards (a writer), 1999; children: Lena. *Education:* Tyler School of Art, degree. 1969; Yale School of Art and Architecture, M.F.A., 1971.

Addresses

Home—New York, NY. *E-mail*—karen@karenkatz.com.

Career

Author and illustrator of children's books. Has also worked as a costume designer, quilt maker, fabric artist, graphic designer, and toy designer. *Exhibitions:* Work exhibited at Society of Illustrators Picture Book show, 1999, 2002, and Children's Museum of Arts, New York, NY, 1999.

Awards, Honors

Smithsonian, People, and *Parent Guide* magazines Best Books designation, all 1997, all for *Over the Moon;* Bill Martin, Jr. Picture Book Award nomination, Florida

Karen Katz (Photo by Gary Richards. Courtesy of Karen Katz.)

Reading Association Award nomination, and *Child* magazine Best Book designation, all 2000, all for *The Colors of Us;* National Parenting Publications Gold Award, and *Child* magazine Best Book designation, both 2001, and Bank Street School Books Committee Best Book designation, 2002, all for *Counting Kisses;* Oppenheim Toy Portfolio Gold Seal Award, 2002, for *Counting Kisses* and *Twelve Hats for Lena;* Dollywood Foundation Imagination Library Award, 2004, for *I Can Share!;* National Parenting Publications Award, 2005, for *Ten Tiny Tickles;* National Parenting Publications Award, 2005, for *Daddy Hugs 1 2 3;* National Parenting Publications Award, 2006, for *Mommy Hugs.*

Writings

SELF-ILLUSTRATED

Over the Moon: An Adoption Tale, Holt (New York, NY), 1997.
The Colors of Us, Holt (New York, NY), 1999.
Where Is Baby's Belly Button?, Little Simon (New York, NY), 2000.
In Grandmother's Arms, Scholastic (New York, NY), 2001.
Counting Kisses, Margaret K. McElderry (New York, NY), 2001.
Where Is Baby's Mommy?, Little Simon (New York, NY), 2001.
Excuse Me!, Grosset & Dunlap (New York, NY), 2002.
Grandma and Me, Little Simon (New York, NY), 2002.

Twelve Hats for Lena: A Book of Months, Margaret K. McElderry (New York, NY), 2002.
No Biting!, Grosset & Dunlap (New York, NY), 2002.
My First Kwanzaa, Holt (New York, NY), 2003.
Daddy and Me, Simon & Schuster (New York, NY), 2003.
Counting Christmas, Margaret K. McElderry (New York, NY), 2003.
Grandpa and Me, Little Simon (New York, NY), 2004.
What Does Baby Say?, Little Simon (New York, NY), 2004.
My First Chinese New Year, Holt (New York, NY), 2004.
No Hitting!, Grosset & Dunlap (New York, NY), 2004.
I Can Share!, Grosset & Dunlap (New York, NY), 2004.
Ten Tiny Tickles, Margaret K. McElderry (New York, NY), 2005.
A Potty for Me!, Little Simon (New York, NY), 2005.
Daddy Hugs 1 2 3, Margaret K. McElderry (New York, NY), 2005.
Mommy Hugs, Margaret K. McElderry (New York, NY), 2006.
Best-ever Big Brother, Grosset & Dunlap (New York, NY), 2006.
Can You Say Peace?, Holt (New York, NY), 2006.
Where Is Baby's Pumpkin?, Little Simon (New York, NY), 2006.
Best-ever Big Sister, Grosset & Dunlap (New York, NY), 2006.
Wiggle Your Toes, paper engineering by Gene Vosough, Little Simon (New York, NY), 2006.
My First Ramadan, Holt (New York, NY), 2007.
Peek-a-Baby, Little Simon (New York, NY), 2007.
Where Is Baby's Dreidel?, Little Simon (New York, NY), 2007.
Ten Tiny Babies, Margaret K. McElderry (New York, NY), 2008.
Princess Baby, Schwartz & Wade (New York, NY), 2008.

ILLUSTRATOR

Marion Dane Bauer, *Toes, Ears, and Nose!,* Little Simon (New York, NY), 2003.
Anastasia Suen, *Subway,* Viking (New York, NY), 2004.
Jayne C. Shelton, *In Grandma's Arms,* Scholastic (New York, NY), 2007.
Margaret Wise Brown, *A Child's Good Morning Book,* HarperCollins (New York, NY), 2009.

Sidelights

Karen Katz has written and illustrated dozens of picture books and lift-the-flap books for young readers. Katz, a graduate of the Yale School of Art and Architecture, is the author of such works as *Over the Moon: An Adoption Tale, Grandpa and Me,* and *Princess Baby.* For her efforts, she has earned a number of National Parenting Publications Awards, as well as several other honors.

Published in 1997, Katz's debut picture book *Over the Moon* was inspired by events from her own life. As she stated on the *Random House* Web site, "After my husband and I adopted our daughter from Guatemala, I decided I wanted to illustrate children's books. I had been a graphic designer for many years. For nine months, I painted pictures of kids and anything that looked like it could be in a children's book. Then I put together a portfolio to show." Katz later met with Laura Godwin, a senior editor who encouraged her to write a book about adoption. "That was the beginning of my career," Katz noted. "I was very lucky to meet someone who had great vision and was willing to trust in my potential."

Marked by elements of fantasy, *Over the Moon* follows a couple's journey to a distant land to adopt the tiny baby they both had seen in their dreams. "Bold colors and lively patterns swirl across the pages," noted *Booklist* critic Stephanie Zvirin, and a *Publishers Weekly* reviewer praised the "contagious exuberance" of Katz's "playfully stylized collage, gouache and colored pencil illustrations, which display a vibrant palette and all the energy of a flamenco dance."

The Colors of Us is another picture-book tribute to Katz's daughter. In the work, a young girl wants to use brown paint for her self-portrait. The girl's mother, an artist, takes her daughter for a walk through their neighborhood, pointing out the many different shades of brown skin on the people they meet. In the words of *Booklist* contributor Hazel Rochman, Katz's illustrations "celebrate the delicious colors of the individual people, all brown, and each one different."

Counting Kisses, a "delightfully simple, interactive story," according to *Childhood Education* reviewer Susan A. Miller, appeared in 2001. In this book a fussy baby is coaxed to sleep by a series of kisses from her mother and father, her grandmother, her older sister, and even the family pets. "With buoyant cartoons rendered in a bouquet of vibrant pastel tones, Katz creates a book as irresistible as a baby's smile," observed a contributor in *Publishers Weekly.* In another family-centered work, *Counting Christmas,* a family prepares lights, presents, and cookies for their holiday celebration. "The collage, gouache, and colored-pencil illustrations are cheery and have a nice textural feel," wrote Linda Israelson in *School Library Journal.*

A young girl creates a different style of headgear for each month of the year in *Twelve Hats for Lena: A Book of Months.* January's stocking cap is adorned with pictures of snowmen and sleds; March's hat is decorated with shamrocks. When December arrives, Lena cannot decide which holiday to emphasize, so she designs an oversized headpiece that includes symbols from Hanukkah, Kwanzaa, and Christmas. "Katz's mixed-media artwork, primarily a combination of gouache and collage, has a kicky brightness that refreshes such traditional subjects as valentines, a spring flower garden, [and] American flags," remarked a contributor in *Publishers Weekly.*

Katz looks at holiday celebrations in *My First Kwanzaa* and *My First Chinese New Year.* In the former, a pre-

schooler discusses the seven underlying principles of Kwanzaa. Katz's text and illustrations "combine to convey the wider sense of community that is the essence of the holiday," stated Rochman. In the latter, a young girl makes an altar to honor her ancestors, enjoys a meal with her relatives, and attends a parade in Chinatown. Katz "introduces readers to the traditions and importance of this holiday," noted a reviewer in *Publishers Weekly.* A number of critics offered praise for Katz's collage and mixed-media illustrations; a contributor in *Kirkus Reviews* remarked that the pictures "capture the excitement that surrounds the celebration." In a later work, *My First Ramadan,* Katz looks at the traditional holiday through the eyes of a young Muslim boy. "Children will appreciate the warm, personal narrative," Rochman observed.

To celebrate the United Nations International Day of Peace, Katz offered the self-illustrated title *Can You Say Peace?,* "a simple, buoyantly illustrated look at the wonderful variety of lifestyles across the globe and the similarities of children everywhere," remarked Shelley B. Sutherland in *School Library Journal.* The work depicts children from a host of nations, including India, France, and Mexico, who teach readers how to say "peace" in their native languages. While complimenting the "vibrantly colored patterns" and "soothing rhythmic lines" in Katz's illustrations, a *Kirkus Reviews* contributor stated that this "primer on nonviolence works in its simplicity." As Katz once remarked to *SATA,* "I am . . . fascinated by people from all over the world—what they look like, how they live, and the differences that make us all unique."

Katz once told *SATA:* "I am fascinated by babies and little kids. The simplest words and gestures can make them laugh. Sometimes while I'm standing in line at the supermarket and watching kids sitting in grocery carts, my best ideas are born." *Daddy Hugs 1 2 3* focuses on the warm relationship between a father and his infant. Describing the collage, gouache, and colored-pencil illustrations, *School Library Journal* reviewer Rachael Vilmar noted that the pictures "are made up of Katz's signature patterned objects and cutesy round-headed figures." In a companion volume, *Mommy Hugs,* Katz follows a baby and her mother through a busy day. "The sunny pictures capture familiar activities," remarked Linda Ludke in *School Library Journal.*

In the counting book *Ten Tiny Tickles,* a baby's caregivers, including her parents, siblings, and grandparents, gently touch and tickle the infant as they bathe, diaper, and dress her. Katz's "illustrations depict loving family members with round faces, happy smiles, and rosy cheeks," Maryann H. Owen stated in *School Library Journal.* A set of playful babies wriggle their toes, splash in the tub, and cuddle before bedtime in *Ten Tiny Babies,* a companion counting book that employs rhyming couplets to describe infants' boundless energy. In the words of a *Publishers Weekly* contributor, the work "is a solid addition to Katz's extensive oeuvre of adorableness." In *Princess Baby,* a toddler who has grown tired of such nicknames as "Cupcake" and "Giggly Goose" dons a shiny crown and fabulous jewels to firmly establish her identity. Here Katz's artwork "supports the book's messages about children's rich fantasy life and their desire to assert themselves," commented Abby Nolan in *Booklist.*

In addition to her self-illustrated titles, Katz has provided artwork for a number of books by other authors, including *Subway* by Anastasia Suen. A work told in verse, *Subway* depicts a young girl's trip uptown with her mother. "Katz creates a merry metropolis that is both multicolored and multicultural," remarked a critic in *Publishers Weekly,* and *Booklist* contributor Gillian Engberg noted that the "jelly-bean colors in the artwork extend the sense of sunny excitement."

Katz once told *SATA:* "I have always loved to paint and experiment with pattern, texture, collage, and color. I have always been interested in folk art from around the world, Indian miniatures, Mexican ceramics, fabrics, Marc Chagall, Henri Matisse, children's art, and primitive painting. My careers have included costume design, quilt making, fabric artistry, and graphic design. Looking back, I can see that all of these passions and career choices have had a part in influencing me to become a children's book author and illustrator.

"When an idea for a story pops into my head, I ask these questions: Will a child want to read this book? Will parents want to read this book with their children? Will this book make a child laugh? Will this book make a parent and child feel something? Is there something visual here that will hold a child's interest? Will a child see something in a different way after reading this book? If the answer to any of those questions is 'yes,' then I know I'm on the right track.

"I am very lucky to get to do what I do. Everyday I go into my studio and have fun. Don't get me wrong: some days are very frustrating. Sometimes the colors are all wrong and the words don't sound right, but after I work at it for a while . . . and try to do it a different way . . . and think . . . and change the words or colors . . . and try some more . . . suddenly, there it is—a great page of writing or a great illustration. And nothing is more satisfying than that."

Biographical and Critical Sources

PERIODICALS

Booklist, September 1, 1997, Stephanie Zvirin, review of *Over the Moon: An Adoption Tale,* p. 133; September 15, 1999, Hazel Rochman, review of *The Colors of Us,* p. 268; February 1, 2001, Lauren Peterson, review of *Counting Kisses,* p. 1056; September 1, 2003, Hazel Rochman, review of *My First Kwanzaa,* p. 134;

November 1, 2003, Hazel Rochman, review of *Counting Christmas,* p. 501; February 1, 2004, Gillian Engberg, review of *Subway,* p. 982; February 1, 2005, Linda Perkins, review of *My First Chinese New Year,* p. 965; July, 2005, Ilene Cooper, review of *Ten Tiny Tickles,* p. 1929; February 15, 2006, Ilene Cooper, review of *Mommy Hugs,* p. 102; May 15, 2006, Hazel Rochman, review of *Can You Say Peace?,* p. 50; June 1, 2007, Hazel Rochman, review of *My First Ramadan,* p. 83; January 1, 2008, Abby Nolan, review of *Princess Baby,* p. 95; July 1, 2008, Hazel Rochman, review of *Ten Tiny Babies,* p. 74.

Childhood Education, spring, 2002, review of *Counting Kisses,* p. 173.

Kirkus Reviews, August 1, 2002, review of *Twelve Hats for Lena: A Book of Months,* p. 1134; November 1, 2003, review of *My First Kwanzaa,* p. 1317; November 15, 2004, review of *My First Chinese New Year,* p. 1090; June 1, 2006, review of *Can You Say Peace?,* p. 575.

Publishers Weekly, August 4, 1997, review of *Over the Moon,* p. 73; June 5, 2000, review of *Where Is Baby's Belly Button?,* p. 96; November 27, 2000, review of *Counting Kisses,* p. 75; April 29, 2002, review of *Grandma and Me,* p. 73; July 15, 2002, review of *Twelve Hats for Lena,* p. 72; September 22, 2003, review of *Counting Christmas,* p. 69; February 2, 2004, review of *Subway,* p. 75; December 20, 2004, review of *My First Chinese New Year,* p. 61; June 25, 2007, review of *My First Ramadan,* p. 63; December 17, 2007, review of *Princess Baby,* p. 50; June 23, 2008, review of *Ten Tiny Babies,* p. 53.

School Library Journal, February, 2001, Kathleen Kelly MacMillan, review of *Counting Kisses,* p. 102; October, 2002, Joy Fleishhacker, review of *Twelve Hats for Lena,* p. 114; October, 2003, Linda Israelson, review of *Counting Christmas,* p. 64, and Virginia Walter, review of *My First Kwanzaa,* p. 64; December, 2004, Rachel G. Payne, review of *My First Chinese New Year,* p. 112; February, 2004, Margaret R. Tassia, review of *Subway,* p. 124; June, 2005, Rachael Vilmar, review of *Daddy Hugs 1 2 3,* p. 118; July, 2005, Maryann H. Owen, review of *Ten Tiny Tickles,* p. 75; April, 2006, Linda Ludke, review of *Mommy Hugs,* p. 110; September, 2006, Shelley B. Sutherland, review of *Can You Say Peace?,* p. 174; August, 2007, Kristin Anderson, review of *My First Ramadan,* p. 82; March, 2008, Blair Christolon, review of *Princess Baby,* p. 168; September, 2008, Linda Ludke, review of *Ten Tiny Babies,* p. 151.

ONLINE

Karen Katz Home Page, http://www.karenkatz.com (December 1, 2008).

Random House Web site, http://www.randomhouse.com/ (December 1, 2008), "Author Spotlight: Karen Katz."*

*   *   *

KNYE, Cassandra
See DISCH, Thomas M.

LAMBA, Marie

Personal

Born in Flushing, NY; married Baldev Lamba (a landscape architect); children: two daughters. *Education:* University of Pennsylvania, B.A., 1984; attended College of St. Paul and St. Mary. *Hobbies and other interests:* Girl Scouts.

Addresses

Home—Doylestown, PA. *E-mail*—marielamba@hotmail.com.

Career

Freelance writer and novelist. Has also worked as a publishers assistant, promotion manager, freelance editor, and in public relations.

Member

Society of Children's Book Writers and Illustrators.

Writings

What I Meant . . . (novel), Random House (New York, NY), 2007.
What I Said . . . (novel), Random House (New York, NY), 2008.

Contributor to periodicals, including *Writer's Digest, Garden Design, Sports International,* and *Your Home.*

Sidelights

Marie Lamba is a freelance writer whose work has appeared in such publications as *Garden Design* and *Your Home.* In 2007, after more than a decade of writing fiction, her young-adult novel *What I Meant . . .* was published.

Set in Lamba's home town of Doylestown, Pennsylvania, *What I Meant . . .* focuses on fifteen-year-old Sangeet Jumnal, the daughter of an Italian-American mother and an East Indian father. Sang's troubles begin when her best friend, Gina, inexplicably stops talking to her, and she is later stood up by her classmate and secret crush Jason. Things get worse when Sang's widowed aunt moves into the family home and items begin disappearing. When her aunt places the blame on Sang, the teen must defend her honor. Writing in *Booklist,* Hazel Rochman praised "Sang's hilarious, angry, hip narrative about her diverse family and friends," and a *Kirkus Reviews* critic deemed *What I Meant . . .* "realistic and well-paced." "The teen's family life and struggles will resonate with readers of all backgrounds," concluded *School Library Journal* reviewer Cara von Wrangel Kinsey of Lamba's fiction debut.

Biographical and Critical Sources

PERIODICALS

Booklist, July 1, 2007, Hazel Rochman, review of *What I Meant . . .,* 52.
Kirkus Reviews, July 1, 2007, review of *What I Meant . . . .*
Publishers Weekly, July 23, Hazel Rochman, review of *What I Meant . . .,* p. 69.
School Library Journal, November, 2007, Cara von Wrangel Kinsey, review of *What I Meant . . .,* p. 128.

ONLINE

Asians of Mixed Race Web site, http://www.asiansofmixedrace.com/ (December 1, 2007), Frank Y Pak Agostinelli, interview with Lamba.
Marie Lamba Home Page, http://www.marielamba.com (October 15, 2008).
Marie Lamba Web log, http://marielamba.wordpress.com (October 15, 2008).*

Cover of Marie Lamba's What I Meant . . ., *a young-adult novel featuring artwork by Cindy Revell.* (Jacket Illustration copyright © 2007 by Cindy Revell. Used by permission of Random House Children's Books, a division of Random House, Inc.)

LEVINE, Gail Carson 1947-

Personal

Born September 17, 1947, in New York, NY; daughter of David (owner of a commercial art studio) and Sylvia (a teacher) Carson; married David Levine (a software developer), September 2, 1967. *Education:* City College of the City University of New York, B.A., 1969.

Addresses

Home—Brewster, NY.

Career

Children's book author. New York State Department of Labor, New York, NY, employment interviewer, 1970-82; New York State Department of Commerce, New York, NY, administrative assistant, 1982-86; New York State Department of Social Services, New York, NY, welfare administrator, 1986-96; New York State Department of Labor, New York, NY, welfare administrator, 1986—.

Awards, Honors

Best Books for Young Adults designation, and Quick Picks for Young Adults citations, American Library Association (ALA), and Newbery Honor Book, ALA, all 1998, all for *Ella Enchanted.*

Writings

Ella Enchanted, HarperCollins (New York, NY), 1997.
The Wish, HarperCollins (New York, NY), 1999.
The Princess Test, HarperCollins (New York, NY), 1999.
Princess Sonora and the Long Sleep, HarperCollins (New York, NY), 1999.
The Fairy's Mistake, HarperCollins (New York, NY), 1999.
Dave at Night, HarperCollins (New York, NY), 1999.
Cinderellis and the Glass Hill, HarperCollins (New York, NY), 2000.
The Two Princesses of Bamarre, HarperCollins (New York, NY), 2001.
For Biddle's Sake, HarperCollins (New York, NY), 2002.
The Fairy's Return, HarperCollins (New York, NY), 2002.
Betsy Who Cried Wolf, illustrated by Scott Nash, HarperCollins (New York, NY), 2002.
The Princess Tales, HarperCollins (New York, NY), 2003.
Fairy Dust and the Quest for the Egg, illustrated by David Christiana, Disney Press (New York, NY), 2005.
Writing Magic: Creating Stories That Fly, HarperCollins (New York, NY), 2006.
The Fairy's Return and Other Princess Tales, illustrated by Mark Elliott, HarperCollins (New York, NY), 2006.
Fairest, HarperCollins (New York, NY), 2006.
Fairy Haven and the Quest for the Wand, illustrated by David Christiana, Disney Press (New York, NY), 2007.

Gail Carson Levine (Reproduced by permission.)

Ever, HarperCollins (New York, NY), 2008.

Also author of script for children's musical *Space-napped,* produced in Brooklyn, NY.

Adaptations

Ella Enchanted was adapted for film by Miramax, 2004; *The Two Princesses of Bamarre* was optioned for film by Miramax; many of Levine's books have been adapted for audiocassette by Listening Library, including *Dave at Night,* 2000, *The Two Princesses of Bamarre,* 2001, and *Fairy Dust and the Quest for the Egg,* 2005.

Sidelights

While Gail Carson Levine writes fairy tales featuring princesses, dragons, elves, and fairies, hers are modern renditions of traditional themes. Although she sometimes bases her novels on such familiar stories as *Cinderella* or *Sleeping Beauty,* and adopts characters from J.M. Barrie's childhood classic *Peter Pan,* the heroes and heroines in books such as *Ella Enchanted, The Princess Tales,* and *Fairy Dust and the Quest for the Egg* are decidedly modern in their outlook.

Levine was raised in New York City, in a family that valued books and reading. As she once told *SATA:* "My father was interested in writing, and my mother wrote full-length plays in rhyme for her students to perform. Both of them had an absolute reverence for creativity and creative people, a reverence that they passed along to my sister and me."

Levine did not originally intend to be a writer. "It was painting that brought me to writing in earnest for children," she explained. "I took a class in writing and illustrating children's books and found that I was much more interested in the writing than in the illustrating."

The story that would evolve into the Newbery honor book *Ella Enchanted* actually had its start in a writing class. "I had to write something and couldn't think of a plot, so I decided to write a Cinderella story because it already had a plot! Then, when I thought about Cinderella's character, I realized she was too much of a goody-two-shoes for me, and I would hate her before I finished ten pages. That's when I came up with the curse: she's only good because she has to be, and she is in constant rebellion."

Ella Enchanted focuses on a girl who is cursed at birth: she is unable to disobey the commands of other people, no matter what they are. When the condition becomes too much to bear, Ella runs away in search of the thoughtless fairy who originally cursed her. Her journey leads only to a job as a scullery maid for her new stepmother, where she finally overcomes her curse. Anne Deifendeifer, writing in *Horn Book,* observed that Levine's "expert characterization and original ideas enliven this novelization of *Cinderella.*"

With the success of *Ella Enchanted,* Levine realized that she had designed a winning concept that appealed to young fantasy fans. In another early fairy-tale update, *The Princess Test,* she updates Hans Christian Andersen's "The Princess and the Pea," In Levine's version of Andersen's tale, the familiar tale is turned on its head as a blacksmith's daughter proves that she is as delicate and sensitive as any girl of royal blood. A *Horn Book* contributor wrote that "fans of funny fairy tales will have some laughs" over Levine's book, while a critic for *Publishers Weekly* maintained that the author's heroines "defy fairy-tale stereotypes." Levine's "Princess Tales" series continues with *The Fairy Mistake, The Fairy's Return,* and *For Biddle's Sake,* the last a reworking of the Rapunzel story that a *Kirkus Reviews* writer described as containing "deliriously funny and well-wrought prose, [and] full of sly wit and clever asides."

In *Dave at Night,* Levine turns to her own family history, drawing inspiration from her father's experiences growing up in an orphanage in New York City during the 1920s. Dave Carlos lives at the Hebrew Home for Boys because his father died in an accident and his mother is unable to raise him alone. Each night, the rebellious boy climbs over the orphanage wall and explores the nearby streets of Harlem, where he befriends an elderly fortune teller, listens to jazz music, and learns how to dance the Charleston. Eventually, Dave discovers his artistic talents and, more importantly, the value of his orphan friends. "Dave's excursions into the noise and excitement of long-ago Harlem nights will linger in the memory," predicted a critic for *Horn Book.*

In *The Wish,* Levine gives a modern-day story a fairy-tale twist. Wilma Sturtz is an eighth-grader in New York City. Her two best friends have left her school and Wilma is feeling lonely and unwanted. When she gives up her seat on the bus to an eccentric old woman, the woman grants her one wish: to be the most popular student at her school. Very soon Wilma is invited to parties and dances, but the wish only lasts until the end of the school year. Will anyone still be her friend after

that? Renee Steinberg, writing in *School Library Journal,* called *The Wish* "an enjoyable, thought-provoking, and absorbing selection." "The fun is watching the nerdy girl, with whom readers will identify, blossom into a self-assured kid," commented Ilene Cooper in *Booklist.*

The Two Princesses of Bamarre is set in a fairy-tale kingdom where Princess Addie and Princess Meryl live in the castle of their father, the king. While Meryl is an independent girl, Addie is less so. When Meryl comes down with a serious illness called the Gray Death, however, Addie takes it upon herself to discover the cure and save her sister's life. Donna Miller, writing in *Book Report,* called *The Two Princesses of Bamarre* "a lively tale with vivid characters and an exciting plot," while *Kliatt* reviewer Claire Rosser predicted that the "fanciful" story will appeal to "younger YAs who love high fantasy."

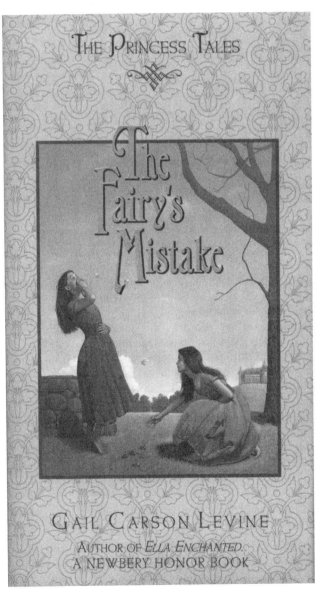

Cover of Levine's imaginative adaptation **The Fairy's Mistake,** *featuring artwork by Mark Elliott.* (Jacket art copyright © 1999 by Mark Elliott. Used by permission of HarperCollins Children's Books, a division of HarperCollins Publishers.)

Cover of Levine's fantasy novel **Fairest***, featuring artwork by Larry Rostant.* (Cover art copyright © 2006 by Larry Rostant. Used by permission of Harper-Collins Children's Books, a division of HarperCollins Publishers.)

Described as a "visionary rendering of the Snow White tale" by a *Publishers Weekly* contributor, *Fairest* focuses on Aza, a homely and awkward fifteen year old. Aza cherishes her one beautiful quality: her melodious voice. In fact, Aza is able to throw her voice, and mimic almost anything, and this talent draws the attention of the queen of Ayortha. When the homely girl is hidden behind the throne and her voice used to increase the queen's prestige, the ruse is discovered and Aza is forced to flee, finding her true strength in the process. Noting that Levine's novel probes "the real-life problems of living in an appearance-obsessed society," *School Library Journal* critic Melissa Christy Buron dubbed *Fairest* "a distinguished contribution" to Levine's body of work, and the *Publishers Weekly* reviewer ranked the novel as one that "may . . . even surpass . . . *Ella Enchanted.*"

Levine moves to the realm of myth in *Ever*, which focuses on immortal gods. Olus, the god of the winds, is fascinated by humans and wishes to live among them. On Earth, he meets and falls in love with Kezi, a young rug weaver whose father has bargained with the family god Admat to trade the life of his dying wife for any-

one who wishes the family well. Kezi prevents this sacrifice from happening by giving the wish herself, thus dooming herself unless Olus can arrange with the illusive Admat to make her immortal. In the novel, Levine depicts "the classic quest . . . young people must accomplish in order to live as they choose," according to *Kliatt* critic Janis Flint-Ferguson, while *Horn Book* reviewer Anita L. Burkam cited *Ever* for presenting readers with a "fascinating quandary" about the nature of religious faith.

The rural folk-tale world becomes the backdrop of the picture book *Betsy Who Cried Wolf*, as Levine turns from the stories of Europe to the simple tales of Aesop. In her variant of "The Boy Who Cried Wolf," an eight-year-old girl strives to excel at her task of shepherding. A cagey old wolf named Zimmo, who may have dipped into the pages of Aesop, decides to outsmart the girl by provoking her into raising the alarm, then disappearing without a trace. When Betsy draws nearby farmers two times, with no wolf to be found, she realizes that Zimmo would likely be satisfied with a good meal rather than a tough old ewe, in a story that a *Kirkus Reviews* critic dubbed "a delightful tale" featuring "especially funny" art by Scott Nash. In *Publishers Weekly* a critic described the story as a "perky, girl-centric take" on the Aesop classic, and predicted that "kids may well cheer [Betsy's] . . . courage and can-do spirit."

In both *Fairy Dust and the Quest for the Egg* and *Fairy Haven and the Quest for the Wand* Levine teams up with Disney, adapting characters from Disney's classic animated versions of *Peter Pan, Bambi,* and other films into stories for elementary-grade readers. Tinker Bell, the feisty fairy from *Peter Pan,* is the star of *Fairy Dust and the Quest for the Egg,* which takes readers on a tour of a newly envisioned Never Land. Here Never Land is an island where the mild climate is sustained by a magical bird known as Mother Dove. Mother Dove sits on a magic egg, and her annual molt provides Tink and other Never Land fairies with the valuable fairy dust. When Mother Dove becomes ill, new fairy Prilla must undertake a quest in order to save the magic bird, meeting up with Peter Pan, Captain Hook, and other characters along the way. Another quest, this time for a magic but unpredictable wand, is the focus of *Fairy Haven and the Quest for the Wand,* as Tink and others hope to stop a flood that threatens to destroy their island home. While several critics noted that the many characters make the two books difficult to follow, *Booklist* critic Jennifer Mattson cited the "lavish visual element" created by artist David Christiana as "a major draw of the Disney Fairies series." Reviewing *Fairy Dust and the Quest for the Egg,* Mattson described it as "the kind of lovable, illustrated chapter book that high production costs have all but driven out of existence."

Levine once told *SATA:* "As a child I loved fairy tales because the story, the what-comes-next, is paramount. As an adult I am fascinated by their logic and illogic. Ella's magic book gave me the chance to answer a question that always plagued me about *The Shoemaker and the Elves:* why the elves abandon the shoemaker. I came up with one answer, but many are possible—and I think the real solution goes to the heart of gratitude and recognition, an example of the depth in fairy tales. Levine goes into greater detail regarding her views of folk and fairy tales in her book *Writing Magic: Creating Stories That Fly,* which inspires preteen writer with writing exercises, encouragement, and other useful creative how-to's.

Levine's advice to aspiring writers? "Suspend judgment of your work and keep writing. Take advantage of the wonderful community of writers for children, who are always ready with helpful criticism and support in the struggle to succeed. And be patient: writing and glaciers advance at about the same pace!"

Biographical and Critical Sources

BOOKS

McGinty, Alice B., *Meet Gail Carson Levine,* Rosen Publishing (New York, NY), 2003.

PERIODICALS

Booklist, November 15, 1999, Susan Dove Lempke, review of *Princess Sonora and the Long Sleep,* p. 627; April 1, 2000, Ilene Cooper, review of *The Wish,* p. 1462, and Anna Rich, review of *Dave at Night,* p. 1494; April 15, 2001, Carolyn Phelan, review of *The Two Princesses of Bamarre,* p. 1558; August, 2002, Carolyn Phelan, review of *The Fairy's Return,* p. 1964; August, 2005, Jennifer Mattson, review of *Fairy Dust and the Quest for the Egg,* p. 2023; July 1, 2006, Gillian Engberg, review of *Fairest,* p. 56; December 1, 2006, Ilene Cooper, review of *Writing Magic: Creating Stories That Fly,* p. 45; January 1, 2008, Jennifer Mattson, review of *Fairy Haven and the Quest for the Wand,* p. 76.

Book Report, September-October, 2001, Donna Miller, review of *The Two Princesses of Bamarre,* p. 63.

Horn Book, May-June, 1997, Anne Deifendeifer, review of *Ella Enchanted,* p. 325; May, 1999, reviews of *The Fairy's Mistake* and *The Princess Test,* p. 332; January, 2000, review of *Dave at Night,* p. 78; May, 2001, review of *The Two Princesses of Bamarre,* p. 330; May-June, 2008, Anita L. Burkham, review of *Ever,* p. 319.

Journal of Adolescent and Adult Literacy, November, 2002, review of *The Wish,* p. 218.

Kirkus Reviews, April 15, 2002, review of *Betsy Who Cried Wolf,* p. 574; September 15, 2002, review of *For Biddle's Sake,* p. 1393; August 1, 2005, review of *Fairy Dust and the Quest for the Egg,* p. 853; August 1, 2006, review of *Fairest,* p. 790; July 1, 2007, review of *Fairy Haven and the Quest for the Wand;* April 1, 2008, review of *Ever.*

Kliatt, March, 2004, Claire Rosser, review of *The Two Princesses of Bamarre,* p. 26; September, 2005, Erin Darr, review of *The Wish,* p. 28; September, 2006, Claire Rosser, review of *Fairest,* p. 14; January, 2007, Anthony Pucci, review of *Writing Magic,* p. 35; May, 2008, Janis Flint-Ferguson, review of *Ever,* p. 12.

Publishers Weekly, February 15, 1999, reviews of *The Fairy's Mistake* and *The Princess Test,* p. 108; November 1, 1999, review of *Dave at Night,* p. 58; April 24, 2000, review of *The Wish,* p. 91; May 7, 2001, review of *The Two Princesses of Bamarre,* p. 248; May 6, 2002, review of *Betsy Who Cried Wolf,* p. 57; August 29, 2005, review of *Fairy Dust and the Quest for the Egg,* p. 56; July 24, 2006, review of *Fairest,* p. 58.

School Library Journal, May, 2000, Renee Steinberg, review of *The Wish,* p. 173; May, 2001, Kit Vaughan, review of *The Two Princesses of Bamarre,* p. 155; June, 2002, Grace Oliff, review of *Betsy Who Cried Wolf,* p. 98; September, 2002, Eva Mitnick, review of *For Biddle's Sake,* p. 198; October, 2005, Elizabeth Bird, review of *Fairy Dust and the Quest for the Egg,* p. 119; September, 2006, Melissa Christy Buron, review of *Fairest,* p. 209; February, 2007, Beth Gallego, review of *Writing Magic,* p. 142; November, 2007, Pat Leach, review of *Fairy Haven and the Quest for the Wand,* p. 94.

ONLINE

Cynthia Leitich Smith Web site, http://www.cynthia leitichsmith.com/ (May 6, 2005), interview with Levine.

HarperCollins Web site, http://www.harperchildrens.com/ (November 26, 2008), "Gale Carson Levine."

OTHER

Good Conversation!: A Talk with Gail Carson Levine (video), Tim Podell Productions, 2001.*

* * *

LEWIN, Ted 1935-

Personal

Born May 6, 1935, in Buffalo, NY; son of Sidney (a retail jeweler) and Berenece (a homemaker) Lewin; married Betsy Reilly (an author and illustrator of children's books), 1963. *Education:* Pratt Institute of Art, B.F.A., 1956. *Hobbies and other interests:* Photography, painting, and watching birds.

Addresses

Home—Brooklyn, NY. *E-mail*—betsyandted@aol.com.

Career

Professional wrestler, 1952-65; artist and freelance illustrator, 1956—. *Exhibitions:* Solo exhibit at Laboratory of Ornithology, Cornell University, 1978, and Cen-

Ted Lewin (Reproduced by permission.)

tral Park 200 Gallery, New York, NY, 1994; joint exhibition with Betsy Lewin at National Center for Children's Illustrated Literature, Abilene, TX, 2002. *Military service:* U.S. Army, 1958.

Awards, Honors

Mark Twain Award, 1981, for *Soup for President;* Sandburg Award, 1985, for *The Search for Grissi;* Book Can Develop Empathy award, 1990, for *Faithful Elephants;* Great Stone Face award, 1991, for *The Secret of the Indian;* Boston Globe/Horn Book Award, 1991, for *Judy Scuppernong;* Hungry Mind Award, 1993, for *Sami and the Time of the Troubles;* Caldecott Honor Book, American Library Association (ALA), 1993, for *Peppe the Lamplighter;* Notable Children's Trade Book in the Field of Social Studies designation, National Council for the Social Studies (NCSS)/Children's Book Council (CBC), 1997, for *American Too;* Best Books of the Year selection, Bank Street College, and Notable Children's Trade Book in the Field of Social Studies designation, NCSS/CBC, 1998, both for *Fair!;* Best Books of the Year selection, Bank Street College, and Notable Children's Trade Book in the Field of Social Studies designation, NCSS/CBC, 1998, both for *Ali, Child of the Desert;* Big Crit award for excellence in design, *Critique* magazine, 1998, for signage at Central Park Children's Zoo; Parents' Choice Award, 1999, for *Nilo and the Tortoise;* Top-of-the-List Youth picture book honor, *Booklist,* 1999, for *Barn Savers;* Notable Children's Trade Book in the Field of Social Studies designation, NCSS/CBC, 1999, for *The Storytellers;* Notable Book for Children designation, *Smithsonian* magazine,

1999, and Outstanding Science Trade Books for Children designation, National Science Teachers Association (NSTA)/CBC, 2000, both for *Gorilla Walk;* Alumni Achievement Award, Pratt Institute, 2000; John Burroughs Award, American Museum of Natural History, and Outstanding Trade Books for Children Award designation, NSTA/CBC, both 2000, both for *Elephant Quest.*

Writings

SELF-ILLUSTRATED

World within a World—Everglades, Dodd (New York, NY), 1976.
World within a World—Baja, Dodd (New York, NY), 1978.
World within a World—Pribilofs, Dodd (New York, NY), 1980.
Tiger Trek, Macmillan (New York, NY), 1990.
When the Rivers Go Home, Macmillan (New York, NY), 1992.
Amazon Boy, Macmillan (New York, NY), 1993.
I Was a Teenage Professional Wrestler (memoir), Orchard Books (New York, NY), 1993.
The Reindeer People, Macmillan (New York, NY), 1994.
Sacred River, Houghton (Boston, MA), 1995.
Market!, Lothrop, Lee (New York, NY), 1996.
Fair!, Lothrop, Lee (New York, NY), 1997.
The Storytellers, Lothrop, Lee (New York, NY), 1998.
Touch and Go: Travels of a Children's Book Illustrator, Lothrop, Lee (New York, NY), 1999.
(With wife, Betsy Lewin) *Gorilla Walk,* Lothrop, Lee (New York, NY), 1999.
Nilo and the Tortoise, Scholastic (New York, NY), 1999.
(With Betsy Lewin) *Elephant Quest,* Morrow (New York, NY), 2000.
Red Legs: A Drummer Boy of the Civil War, HarperCollins (New York, NY), 2001.
Big Jimmy's Kum Kau Chinese Take-Out, HarperCollins (New York, NY), 2001.
Tooth and Claw: Animal Adventures in the Wild, HarperCollins (New York, NY), 2003.
Lost City: The Discovery of Machu Picchu, Philomel Books (New York, NY), 2003.
(With Betsy Lewin) *Top to Bottom Down Under,* HarperCollins (New York, NY), 2005.
How Much?: Visiting Markets around the World, HarperCollins (New York, NY), 2006.
At Gleason's Gym, Roaring Brook Press (New Milford, CT), 2007.
(With Betsy Lewin) *Horse Song: The Naadam of Mongolia,* Lee & Low (New York, NY), 2008.

ILLUSTRATOR

Jack McClellan, Millard Black, and Sid Norris, adapters, *A Blind Man Can!,* Houghton Mifflin (Boston, MA), 1968.

Wyatt Blassingame, *The Look-It-up Book of Presidents,* Random House (New York, NY), 1968.

Jack McClellan, Millard Black, and Sheila Flume Taylor, *Up, out, and Over!,* Houghton Mifflin (Boston, MA), 1969.

George S. Trow, *Meet Robert E. Lee,* Random House (New York, NY), 1969.

Margaret T. Burroughs, *Jasper, the Drummin' Boy,* Follett (New York, NY), 1970.

Janet H. Ervin, *More than Half Way There,* Follett (New York, NY), 1970.

Donald W. Cox, *Pioneers of Ecology,* Hammond, 1971.

Nellie Burchardt, *A Surprise for Carlotta,* Franklin Watts (New York, NY), 1971.

Darrell A. Rolerson, *Mr. Big Britches,* Dodd (New York, NY), 1971.

Gene Smith, *The Visitor,* Cowles, 1971.

Betty Horvath, *Not Enough Indians,* Franklin Watts (New York, NY), 1971.

Maurine H. Gee, *Chicano, Amigo,* Morrow (New York, NY), 1972.

Rose Blue, *Grandma Didn't Wave Back,* Franklin Watts (New York, NY), 1972.

Michael Capizzi, *Getting It All Together,* Delacorte (New York, NY), 1972.

Rose Blue, *A Month of Sundays,* Franklin Watts (New York, NY), 1972.

Rita Micklish, *Sugar Bee,* Delacorte (New York, NY), 1972.

Darrell A. Rolerson, *In Sheep's Clothing,* Dodd (New York, NY), 1972.

Rose Blue, *Nikki 108,* Franklin Watts (New York, NY), 1972.

Charlotte Gantz, *Boy with Three Names,* Houghton Mifflin (Boston, MA), 1973.

William MacKellar, *The Ghost of Grannoch Moor,* Dodd (New York, NY), 1973.

Marjorie M. Prince, *The Cheese Stands Alone,* Houghton Mifflin (Boston, MA), 1973.

Marian Rumsey, *Lion on the Run,* Morrow (New York, NY), 1973.

Darrell A. Rolerson, *A Boy Called Plum,* Dodd (New York, NY), 1974.

Jean Slaughter Doty, *Gabriel,* Macmillan (New York, NY), 1974.

Gene Smith, *The Hayburners,* Delacorte (New York, NY), 1974.

Matt Christopher, *Earthquake,* Little, Brown (Boston, MA), 1975.

Patricia Beatty, *Rufus, Red Rufus,* Morrow (New York, NY), 1975.

Charles Ferry, *Up in Sister Bay,* Houghton Mifflin (Boston, MA), 1975.

Jean Slaughter Doty, *Winter Pony,* Macmillan (New York, NY), 1975.

S.T. Tung, *One Small Dog,* Dodd (New York, NY), 1975.

Rose Blue, *The Preacher's Kid,* Franklin Watts (New York, NY), 1975.

Scott O'Dell, *Zia,* Houghton Mifflin (Boston, MA), 1976.

Lynne Martin, *Puffin, Bird of the Open Seas,* Morrow (New York, NY), 1976.

Laurence Pringle, *Listen to the Crows,* Crowell (New York, NY), 1976.

Patricia Edwards Clyne, *Ghostly Animals of America,* Dodd (New York, NY), 1977.

Mildred Teal, *Bird of Passage,* Little, Brown (Boston, MA), 1977.

Marian Rumsey, *Carolina Hurricane,* Morrow (New York, NY), 1977.

Nigel Gray, *The Deserter,* Harper (New York, NY), 1977.

Robert Newton Peck, *Patooie,* Knopf (New York, NY), 1977.

Philippa Pearce, *The Shadow-Cage, and Other Tales of the Supernatural,* Crowell (New York, NY), 1977.

Helen Hill, Agnes Perkins, and Alethea Helbig, editors, *Straight on till Morning: Poems of the Imaginary World,* Crowell (New York, NY), 1977.

Rose Blue, *The Thirteenth Year: A Bar Mitzvah Story,* Franklin Watts (New York, NY), 1977.

Leslie Norris, *Merlin and the Snake's Egg: Poems,* Viking (New York, NY), 1978.

William MacKellar, *The Silent Bells,* Dodd (New York, NY), 1978.

Robert Newton Peck, *Soup for President,* Knopf (New York, NY), 1978.

William MacKellar, *The Witch of Glen Gowrie,* Dodd (New York, NY), 1978.

Anne E. Crompton, *A Woman's Place,* Little, Brown (Boston, MA), 1978.

Margaret Goff Clark, *Barney and the UFO,* Dodd (New York, NY), 1979.

Patricia Edwards Clyne, *Strange and Supernatural Animals,* Dodd (New York, NY), 1979.

Robert Newton Peck, *Hub,* Knopf (New York, NY), 1979.

David Stemple, *High Ridge Gobbler: A Story of the American Wild Turkey,* Collins (New York, NY), 1979.

Jean Slaughter Doty, *Can I Get There by Candlelight?,* Macmillan (New York, NY), 1980.

Rose Blue, *My Mother, the Witch,* McGraw (New York, NY), 1980.

Margaret Goff Clark, *Barney in Space,* Dodd (New York, NY), 1981.

Francine Jacobs, *Bermuda Petrel: The Bird That Would Not Die,* Morrow (New York, NY), 1981.

Mark Twain, *The Adventures of Tom Sawyer,* Wanderer Books, 1982.

Margaret Goff Clark, *Barney on Mars,* Dodd (New York, NY), 1983.

Eleanor Clymer, *The Horse in the Attic,* Bradbury Press (New York, NY), 1983.

Priscilla Homola, *The Willow Whistle,* Dodd (New York, NY), 1983.

Enid Bagnold, *National Velvet,* Morrow (New York, NY), 1985.

R.R. Knudson, *Babe Didrikson, Athlete of the Century,* Viking Kestrel (New York, NY), 1985.

Mary Francis Shura, *The Search for Grissi,* Dodd (New York, NY), 1985.

Frances Wosmek, *A Brown Bird Singing,* Lothrop, Lee (New York, NY), 1986.

Patricia Reilly Giff, *Mother Teresa, Sister to the Poor,* Viking Kestrel (New York, NY), 1986.

Elizabeth Simpson Smith, *A Dolphin Goes to School: The Story of Squirt, a Trained Dolphin,* Morrow (New York, NY), 1986.

Scott O'Dell, *The Serpent Never Sleeps: A Novel of Jamestown and Pocahontas,* Houghton Mifflin (Boston, MA), 1987.

Susan Saunders, *Margaret Mead: The World Was Her Family,* Viking Kestrel (New York, NY), 1987.

Kathleen V. Kudlinski, *Rachel Carson: Pioneer of Ecology,* Viking Kestrel (New York, NY), 1988.

Yukio Tsuchiya, *Faithful Elephants: A True Story of Animals, People, and War,* translated by Tomoko Tsuchiya Dykes, Houghton Mifflin (Boston, MA), 1988.

Lynne Reid Banks, *The Secret of the Indian,* Doubleday (New York, NY), 1989.

Bruce Coville, editor, *Herds of Thunder, Manes of Gold: A Collection of Horse Stories and Poems,* Doubleday (New York, NY), 1989.

Leon Garfield, *Young Nick and Jubilee,* Delacorte (New York, NY), 1989.

Florence Parry Heide and Judith Heide Gilliland, *The Day of Ahmed's Secret,* Lothrop, Lee (New York, NY), 1990.

Scott O'Dell, *Island of the Blue Dolphins,* Houghton Mifflin (Boston, MA), 1990.

Gregory Patent, *Shanghai Passage,* Clarion (New York, NY), 1990.

Brenda Seabrooke, *Judy Scuppernong,* Cobblehill Books (New York, NY), 1990.

Jane Yolen, *Bird Watch: A Book of Poetry,* Philomel Books (New York, NY), 1990.

Margaret Hodges, *Brother Francis and the Friendly Beasts,* Scribner (New York, NY), 1991.

Megan McDonald, *The Potato Man,* Orchard Books (New York, NY), 1991.

Frances Ward Weller, *I Wonder If I'll See a Whale,* Philomel Books (New York, NY), 1991.

Corinne Demas Bliss, *Matthew's Meadow,* Harcourt (San Diego, CA), 1992.

Florence Parry Heide and Judith Heide Gilliland, *Sami and the Time of the Troubles,* Clarion (New York, NY), 1992.

Megan McDonald, *The Great Pumpkin Switch,* Orchard Books (New York, NY), 1992.

Frances Ward Weller, *Matthew Wheelock's Wall,* Macmillan (New York, NY), 1992.

Elisa Bartone, *Peppe the Lamplighter,* Lothrop, Lee (New York, NY), 1993.

Ann Herbert Scott, *Cowboy Country,* Clarion (New York, NY), 1993.

Sheldon Oberman, *The Always Prayer Shawl,* Boyds Mills Press (Honesdale, PA), 1993.

Louise Borden, *Just in Time for Christmas,* Scholastic (New York, NY), 1994.

Jan Slepian, *Lost Moose,* Putnam (New York, NY), 1995.

Mary Kay Kroeger and Louise Borden, *Paperboy,* Houghton Mifflin (Boston, MA), 1996.

Jane Yolen, *Sea Watch: A Book of Poetry,* Putnam (New York, NY), 1996.

Megan McDonald, *The Great Pumpkin Switch,* Orchard Books (New York, NY), 1996.

Elisa Bartone, *American Too,* Lothrop, Lee (New York, NY), 1996.

Jonathan London, *Ali, Child of the Desert,* Lothrop, Lee (New York, NY), 1997.

Jane Yolen, *The Originals,* Putnam (New York, NY), 1997.

Sheldon Oberman, *The Always Prayer Shawl,* Puffin Books (New York, NY), 1997.

Linda Oatman High, *Barn Savers,* Boyds Mills Press (Honesdale, PA), 1999.

Louise Borden, *A. Lincoln and Me,* Scholastic (New York, NY), 1999.

Faith McNulty, *How Whales Walked into the Sea,* Scholastic (New York, NY), 1999.

Corinne Demas Bliss, *The Disappearing Island,* Simon and Schuster (New York, NY), 2000.

Edward Grimm, *The Doorman,* Orchard Books (New York, NY), 2000.

Linda Oatman High, *Winter Shoes for Shadow Horse,* Boyds Mills Press (Honesdale, PA), 2001.

Tony Johnston, *Sunsets of the West,* Putnam (New York, NY), 2002.

Linda Oatman High, *The Girl on the High-diving Horse: An Adventure in Atlantic City,* Philomel Books (New York, NY), 2003.

T.A. Barron, *High as a Hawk: A Brave Girl's Historic Climb,* Philomel Books (New York, NY), 2004.

Ralph Helfer, *The World's Greatest Elephant,* Philomel Books (New York, NY), 2006.

Eve Bunting, *One Green Apple,* Clarion (New York, NY), 2006.

Dori Chaconas, *Pennies in a Jar,* Peachtree (Atlanta, GA), 2007.

Illustrations have also appeared in periodicals, including *Boy's Life, Ladies' Home Journal, Seventeen,* and *Reader's Digest.*

Sidelights

Author and illustrator Ted Lewin was inspired in his career by his lifelong love of nature. "I am a deeply concerned environmentalist and conservationist," Lewin once noted, adding that he travels "to wilderness areas around the world for both graphic and literary material." Married to fellow author/illustrator and sometime collaborator Betsy Lewin, Ted Lewin has written and illustrated many books for children and young adults, among them *Gorilla Walk, Tiger Trek, Lost City: The Discovery of Machu Picchu,* and *At Gleason's Gym.* As an author, he has been praised for the poetic quality he brings to his texts, and his plots draw from his extensive knowledge of and concern for wildlife and its habitats throughout the world.

As an illustrator, Lewin's work is characterized by its realistic detail, and his award-winning paintings have enhanced the texts of a wide variety of writers. Praising Lewin's watercolor art for Tony Johnston's *Sunsets of the West,* a *Kirkus Reviews* writer noted that the illustrator's paintings feature "characters and scenery . . . infused with life," while *School Library Journal* writer Rosalyn Pierini wrote that "prairie and mountain vistas are well served by Lewin's majestic, detailed paintings." Ralph Helfer's *The World's Greatest Elephant,* a true story of a circus elephant named Modoc who befriends a lonely orphan, is brought to life by Lewin in what *Booklist* critic Hazel Rochman described as "stunning . . . depictions of the bond between the lifelong friends, the exhilarating public performances, the wrenching partings, and the loving reunion years later."

As a young boy growing up in upstate New York, Lewin always had dreams of becoming an artist. "Not a policeman, fireman, or doctor—an artist," he recalled in his autobiography, *I Was a Teenage Professional Wrestler.* "I remember working first with a metal-armed copying toy I got for Christmas, then the Magic-Pad, on which you could pull up a flap and make whatever you'd drawn disappear." With the encouragement of his family, Lewin practiced drawing by copying photographs, illustrations from children's books, and even a portrait of President Harry S Truman, for which he received a personal letter from the White House.

By the time Lewin graduated from high school, he had made plans to study art at Pratt Institute in Brooklyn. Because paying for school and living expenses would be expensive, he established the secondary career that would help support him for almost fifteen years: professional wrestling. Lewin had attended professional matches with his family for many years, and his older

brother Donn had become a wrestler after serving in the U.S. Marines during World War II. With the aid of his brother and the many contacts his family had made in the sport over the years, the seventeen year old began wrestling during summers and at night during the school year. In his autobiography, Lewin recalled his dual life, alternating between art classes and wrestling matches: "Every day I had classes in two-dimensional design, three-dimensional design, and figure drawing. Around me, the light-filled, high-ceilinged studio would be electric with concentrated effort. . . . I would see a great play of light and shadow—in a sense, not so different from what I'd seen in the charged, dramatic atmosphere of a wrestling arena. The medium was different, that's all."

"More a series of vignettes than an autobiography," as *Bulletin of the Center for Children's Books* writer Deborah Stevenson described it, *I Was a Teenage Professional Wrestler* details Lewin's involvement with the sport and provides portraits—written and painted—of the many wrestlers he met during his career. "It is a fascinating story that leaves the reader wanting to learn more about both Lewin and the other wrestlers," noted Patrick Jones in the *Voice of Youth Advocates.* In recreating a different era, Lewin describes the wrestlers "quite masterfully in words, then he brings them to life with old black and white photographs, drawings and paintings." *School Library Journal* contributor Todd Morning likewise praised Lewin's "surprisingly funny and affectionate" remembrances, as well as the author's combination of "vivid" artwork and human stories. "The artist's sensibility and eye for detail are always in evidence," the critic concluded. "His talent in this realm is truly formidable."

After earning his bachelor of fine arts degree, Lewin continued wrestling as he slowly built a career as a freelance artist. He began with magazine work, and by the late 1960s obtained his first assignments illustrating children's books. In 1976 Lewin debuted his series, "World within a World," which focuses on wildlife in several regions visited by the author; the series has received high praise for both Lewin's text and the illustrations. The first volume in the series, concerning the Everglades, is based on observations of the plant and animal life in the area made by Lewin over a five-year period. The volume on Baja, California, describes elephant seals and details the annual migration of the California gray whales. Of the volume on the Pribilof Islands, which highlights the precarious fate of the seals who bear and raise their young on these Alaskan coastal islands, a reviewer from *Booklist* called Lewin's prose "elegant and uncompromising," adding that "the evocation of this small corner of the world is strong."

Many of Lewin's self-authored books are inspired by the many trips he has made while exploring planet Earth. He depicts a trip made on the back of an elephant through one of India's national parks in *Tiger Trek,* while other travel books include *The Reindeer*

Lewin's illustration projects include artwork for **Matthew's Meadow** *by* **Corinne Demas Bliss.** (Illustration © 1992 by Ted Lewin Ltd. Reproduced by permission of Harcourt, Inc.)

Using warm tones, Lewin gives a nostalgic light to his paintings for Linda Oatman High's picture book Winter Shoes for Shadow Horse. (Boyds Mill Press, 2001. Illustration © 2001 by Ted Lewin. Reproduced by permission.)

People, Sacred River, and *Tooth and Claw: Animal Adventures in the Wild.* Joan McGrath, reviewing *Tiger Trek* for *School Library Journal,* found the book "gorgeous" and "far above the ordinary." A similar journey is documented in *When the Rivers Go Home,* which describes Lewin's trip through a large swamp in central Brazil called the Pantanal. *When the Rivers Go Home* also received praise for its watercolor paintings, a *Kirkus Reviews* writer describing Lewin's work as "lovely" and "evocative." In *Amazon Boy* Lewin's "light-filled pictures, dense with detail, reinforce the theme that the riches of the rain forest must be protected," according to *School Library Journal* contributor Kathleen Odean.

In *The Reindeer People* Lewin introduces readers to Ola, a Sami reindeer herdsman from Lapland, a remote area north of the Arctic Circle. In addition to describing Ola's unique line of work—herding reindeer—the book also describes favorite pastimes of the Sami people—racing reindeer—and a traditional wedding blended with contemporary flavor. "The author's highly descriptive prose is as luxurious as a reindeer coat, and his finely detailed, snapshot-style watercolors will engage readers of any age," enthused a *Publishers Weekly* reviewer. Describing *Sacred River,* based on a trip Lewin made to India, *Horn Book* contributor Maria B. Salvadore wrote that the author's "descriptive, fluid, and straightforward

text combines with richly detailed full-color illustrations to describe a pilgrimage to the Ganges River in the Indian city of Benares."

Together with his wife, Lewin has traveled the world, and in a series of books the couple recounts their many adventures. *Gorilla Walk,* a chronicle of a 1997 trip to Uganda to view the mountain gorillas, was praised for its "handsome paintings and carefully focused text" by *Horn Book* critic Margaret A. Bush, the critic adding that the Lewins "offer . . . intriguing glimpses of both the rarely seen animals and the ambiguities of ecotourism." *Elephant Quest* also take the couple to Africa, while in *Top to Bottom Down Under* they explore the vast continent of Australia, ranging from Kakadu National Park to Australia's Kangaroo Island. Another volume, *Horse Song: The Naadam of Mongolia,* profiles a young jockey racing horses at the outer reaches of Asia. Illustrated with Lewin's paintings and his wife's field sketches, *Top to Bottom Down Under* was praised by *School Library Journal* contributor Patricia Manning as an "eye-catching and informative . . . treat for animal lovers and adventurers alike." Citing Lewin's "striking, realistic" watercolors and noting the inclusion of animal facts, *Booklist* reviewer Karin Snelson also lauded the work, noting that *Top to Bottom Down Under* allows readers to accompany the creative couple on a "contagiously cheerful Aussie expedition."

A perusal of the adventurous author/illustrator's *Tooth and Claw* prompted *Horn Book* critic Danielle J. Ford to exclaim: "Thank goodness Ted Lewin has survived" his travels. Calling Lewin a "gifted storyteller," Ford praised the author's presentation of fourteen "suspenseful, often terrifying, and sometimes quite funny experiences" Lewin and his fellow travelers have had during a life of globe-hopping. Lewin comes face to face with North American grizzly bears, Bengal tigers, African snakes and other grassland creatures, Florida bull sharks, and many other creatures, all told in a travelogue format. Ford praised the work as "outstanding nature storytelling," while in *Kirkus Reviews* a critic explained that, by hauling a rucksack full of drawing supplies with him, Lewin was able to highlight his "fascinating" stories with his "typically wonderful drawings" and "on-site photographs." Echoing other praise, *School Library Journal* critic Pam Spencer Holley noted that *Tooth and Claw* will serve children as "a great read-aloud" for budding naturalists or "simply as a good adventure story."

In addition to narrative accounts, Lewin sometimes weaves his experiences into picture-book texts, such as *Market!* and *Fair!* In *Market!* he creates "paintings so vivid you can almost smell the market scents," according to Susan Dove Lempke in *Booklist.* In the book Lewin describes the various people, products, and atmosphere of six markets—from New York City to Nepal. Similar in focus, *Fair!* presents the many scenes and flavors of a typical country fair, including animal and food contests, games, rides, and fireworks. A *Kirkus Reviews* critic described *Fair!* as a "pulsing, panoramic examination of a summertime ritual," and a *Publishers Weekly* reviewer asserted that "this visit to the fair [is] worth the price of admission." Lewin's fascination with the Galapagos Islands provided him with the setting for his fictional tale *Nilo and the Tortoise,* about a young boy who is stranded on one of the islands. In *Booklist* Stephanie Zvirin noted that Lewin's pictures once again are the main attraction of the book, capturing "the remoteness and beauty of the exotic place and some of its distinctive wildlife."

Several of Lewin's books focus on history, among them *Red Legs: A Drummer Boy of the Civil War* and *Lost City: The Discovery of Machu Picchu.* In *Red Legs* a nine-year-old boy accompanies his father to the reenactment of a U.S. Civil War battle, and plays the part of Stephen Benjamin Bertow, a young drummer boy who died during the fight. Noting Lewin's "brief yet stirring text" and evocative watercolors, a *Publishers Weekly* reviewer wrote that the book expresses a "true passion for history" that might inspire similar enthusiasm in young readers. The fascinating story of the discovery of an ancient Incan city also proves arresting in Lewin's book about Hiram Bingham's 1911 jungle adventure. Based on Bingham's account, *Lost City* follows the explorer' path through the Andes, linking his tale to the dreams of a young Quechua boy that anticipate Bingham's arrival. Lewin "balances a compelling visual chronicle with sure storytelling," according to a *Publishers Weekly* critic, while in *Horn Book* Bush called Bingham's "tortuous journey richly rewarded is a good adventure story" brought to life by Lewin's "evocative" watercolor art.

Working from photos he shoots during his travels and then projects onto a screen in his studio, Lewin manages to retain much of the original realism and force of scenes he has witnessed firsthand. A steady producer, he maintains a disciplined work regimen as well. His day begins at eight in the morning and continues without break into the afternoon. While he is at work in the upstairs of his New York brownstone, his wife, Betsy, works in her studio downstairs. In addition to creating the artwork for his own books, Lewin has also illustrated the texts of numerous other writers, among them *Peppe the Lamplighter* by Elisa Bartone, *Paperboy* by Mary Kay Kroeger, and Louise Borden, and *Sea Watch: A Book of Poetry* by Jane Yolen.

A Caldecott honor book, *Peppe the Lamplighter* focuses on a young Italian immigrant living in New York City who takes a job lighting gas lamps to help support his family. "Lewin's masterly watercolors express the swirling energy of the crowded streets as well as the intimate feelings and interactions of individual people," Rochman observed in *Booklist.* Lewin also illustrated *American Too,* in which Bartone continues the young immigrant's adventures in his new country. *Paperboy,* "filled with carefully detailed watercolors," according to *Horn Book* contributor Elizabeth S. Watson, features Willie Brinkman, a young paperboy living in Cincinnati

in 1927. After boxing hero Jack Dempsey loses a major prizefight, Willie honors his commitment to sell newspapers despite his and the neighborhood's shock and disappointment. Rochman, writing in *Booklist,* declared that the artist's watercolor illustrations are "more exuberant than the artwork in Lewin's Caldecott Honor Book, *Peppe the Lamplighter.*" For his contribution to *Sea Watch, Booklist* reviewer Lauren Peterson noted that "Lewin's trademark watercolors, fresh, realistic, and beautifully rendered, nicely complement the poetry."

Also set in New York City, *At Gleason's Gym* transports readers to the place where famous pugilists such as Muhammad Ali and Jake La Motta once trained. In Lewin's self-illustrated story, a nine-year-old statewide champion boxer named Sugar Boy Younan weighs in at just over 100 pounds. Helped by his father, Sugar Boy works daily at the historic Brooklyn gym in the hopes that he too will achieve a similar measure of fame in the ring. In both pencil drawings and watercolor paintings, Lewin captures the energy of the place, and "sets the scene in fittingly staccato prose," according to a *Publishers Weekly* writer. Calling the book a "glorious tribute" to the many athletes who train at the gym, *Booklist* critic Ilene Cooper cited *At Gleason's Gym* for "text that is both moving and informative and . . . vibrant artwork so realistic that readers can practically smell the sweat."

About his career, Lewin once commented: "There are still so many stories out there waiting to be found and so many manuscripts by wonderful authors to take me on journeys I might never have made myself."

Biographical and Critical Sources

BOOKS

Lewin, Ted, *I Was a Teenage Professional Wrestler,* Orchard Books (New York, NY), 1993.

Silvey, Anita, editor, *Children's Books and Their Creators,* Houghton (Boston, MA), 1995.

Something about the Author Autobiography Series, Volume 25, Gale (Detroit, MI), 1998.

PERIODICALS

Booklist, January 1, 1981, review of *World within a World—Pribilofs,* p. 625; April 15, 1993, Hazel Rochman, review of *Peppe the Lamplighter,* p. 1522; December 15, 1993, Stephanie Zvirin, review of *The Always Prayer Shawl,* p. 750; October 1, 1994, Julie Corsaro, review of *The Reindeer People,* p. 322; June 1, 1995, Hazel Rochman, review of *Sacred River,* p. 1778; March 15, 1996, Hazel Rochman, review of *Paperboy,* p. 1269; April 15, 1996, Susan Dove Lempke, review of *Market!,* p. 1444; June 1, 1996, Lauren Peterson, review of *Sea Watch: A Book of Poetry,* p.

1716; August, 1996, Hazel Rochman, review of *American Too,* p. 1903; February 1, 1998, Hazel Rochman, review of *The Originals,* p. 917; April, 1998, Susan Dove Lempke, review of *The Storytellers,* p. 1332; May 31, 1999, Stephanie Zvirin, review of *Nilo and the Tortoise,* p. 93; January 1, 2002, Cynthia Turnquest, *Big Jimmy's Kum Kau Chinese Take Out,* p. 866; June 1, 2002, Carolyn Phelan, review of *Sunsets of the West,* p. 1738; January 1, 2003, Carolyn Phelan, review of *Tooth and Claw: Animal Adventures in the West,* p. 882; July, 2003, Gillian Engberg, review of *Lost City: The Discovery of Machu Picchu,* p. 1895; March 1, 2004, Ilene Cooper, review of *As High as a Hawk: A Brave Girl's Historic Climb,* p. 1204; January 1, 2005, Karin Snelson, review of *Top to Bottom Down Under,* p. 866; February 1, 2006, Hazel Rochman, review of *The World's Greatest Elephant,* p. 48, and Carolyn Phelan, review of *How Much? Visiting Markets around the World,* p. 52; June 1, 2006, Jennifer Mattson, review of *One Green Apple,* p. 74; September 1, 2007, Ilene Cooper, review of *At Gleason's Gym,* p. 133; May 1, 2008, Gillian Engberg, review of *Horse Song: The Naadam of Mongolia,* p. 88.

Bulletin of the Center for Children's Books, June, 1993, Deborah Stevenson, review of *I Was a Teenage Professional Wrestler,* pp. 321-322; April, 1998, Betsy Hearne, review of *The Storytellers,* p. 286; January, 2002, review of *Big Jimmy's Kum Kau Chinese Take Out,* p. 177; September, 2003, Elizabeth Bush, review of *Lost City,* p. 23.

Horn Book, May-June, 1993, Margaret A. Bush, review of *Amazon Boy,* pp. 320-321; January-February 1996, Maria B. Salvadore, review of *Sacred River,* p. 99; September-October, 1996, Elizabeth S. Watson, review of *Paperboy,* p. 581; November-December, 1999, Margaret A. Bush, review of *Gorilla Walk,* p. 758; January 2001, review of *Elephant Quest,* p. 111; March-April, Danielle J. Ford, review of *Tooth and Claw,* p. 226; September-October, 2003, Margaret A. Bush, review of *Lost City,* p. 631.

Kirkus Reviews, February 15, 1992, review of *When the Rivers Go Home,* pp. 257-258; July 1, 1997, review of *Fair!,* p. 1031; May 15, 1999, review of *Touch and Go,* p. 803; May 15, 2002, review of *Sunsets of the West,* p. 734; February 2, 2003, review of *Tooth and Claw,* p. 235; March 15, 2003, review of *The Girl on the High-diving Horse: An Adventure in Atlantic City,* p. 468; June 1, 2003, review of *Lost City,* p. 807; April 1, 2004, review of *High as a Hawk,* p. 324; February 15, 2005, review of *Top to Bottom Down Under,* p. 231; February 1, 2006, review of *The World's Greatest Elephant,* p. 132; June 1, 2006, review of *One Green Apple,* p. 569; August 15, 2007, review of *Pennies in a Jar.*

Publishers Weekly, August 10, 1990, review of *The Day of Ahmed's Secret,* p. 444; October 26, 1990, review of *Bird Watch,* p. 71; April 17, 1993, review of *Peppe the Lamplighter,* p. 61; April 26, 1993, review of *Amazon Boy,* p. 78; October 24, 1994, review of *The Reindeer People,* p. 61; August 7, 1995, review of *Sacred River,* p. 460; April 29, 1996, review of *Market!,* p. 72; June 9, 1997, review of *Fair!,* p. 45; June 19, 2000, review of *The Disappearing Island,* p. 79; September 4, 2000, review of *The Doorman,* p. 107; December 11, 2000, review of *A. Lincoln and Me,* p. 86; March 19, 2001, review of *Paperboy,* p. 102; June 18, 2001, review of *Red Legs: A Drummer Boy of the Civil War,* p. 81; February 25, 2002, review of *Big Jimmy's Kum Kau Chinese Take Out,* p. 68; May 13, 2002, review of *Sunsets of the West,* p. 70; January 13, 2003, review of *The Girl on the High-diving Horse,* p. 60; June 2, 2003, review of *Lost City,* p. 51; June 21, 2004, review of *High as a Hawk,* p. 62; April 10, 2006, review of *The World's Greatest Elephant,* p. 71; July 23, 2007, review of *At Gleason's Gym* p. 68; September 17, 2007, review of *Pennies in a Jar,* p. 54.

School Library Journal, March, 1990, Joan McGrath, review of *Tiger Trek,* p. 208; June, 1993, Kathleen Odean, review of *Amazon Boy,* pp. 80, 83; July, 1993, Barbara Peklo Abrahams, review of *Peppe the Lamplighter,* p. 56; July, 1993, Todd Morning, review of *I Was a Teenage Professional Wrestler,* p. 108; July, 1997, Jackie Hechtkopf, review of *Fair!,* p. 85; July, 2000, Kate McClelland, review of *The Disappearing Island,* p. 70; October 2000, Marianne Saccardi, review of *The Doorman,* p. 126; April, 2002, John Peters, review of *Big Jimmy's Kum Kau Chinese Take Out,* p. 114; July, 2002, Rosalyn Pierini, review of *Sunsets of the West,* p. 94; February, 2003, Carol Schene, review of *The Girl on the High-diving Horse,* p. 112; May, 2003, Pam Spencer Holley, review of *Tooth and Claw,* p. 173; June, 2003, Daryl Grabarek, review of *Lost City,* p. 163; November, 2003, Carol Fazioli, review of *I Was a Teenage Professional Wrestler,* p. 83; May, 2004, Laurie Edwards, review of *High as a Hawk,* p. 101; March, 2005, Patricia Manning, review of *Top to Bottom Down Under,* p. 196; January, 2006, Carol L. MacKay, review of *How Much?,* p. 120; February, 2006, Margaret Bush, review of *The World's Greatest Elephant,* p. 120; June, 2006, Marianne Saccardi, review of *One Green Apple,* p. 107.

Social Education, January, 2001, Barbara J. Holt, review of *Faithful Elephants: A True Story of Animals, People, and War,* p. S9.

Voice of Youth Advocates, October, 1993, Patrick Jones, review of *I Was a Teenage Professional Wrestler,* p. 247.

ONLINE

Ted Lewin Home Page, http://www.tedlewin.com (November 28, 2008).*

*   *   *

LYONS, Mary E. 1947-
(Mary Evelyn Lyons)

Personal

Born November 28, 1947, in Macon, GA; daughter of Joseph and Evelyn Lyons; married Paul Collinge (owner of a used and rare bookstore). *Education:* Appalachian

Mary E. Lyons (Reproduced by permission.)

State University, B.S., 1970, M.S., 1972; University of Virginia, doctoral study. *Hobbies and other interests:* Playing Irish penny whistle and banjo with the group The Chicken Heads.

Addresses

Home—Charlottesville, VA.

Career

Writer. Reading teacher at elementary and middle schools in North Carolina and in Charlottesville, VA, and school librarian at elementary, middle, and high schools, Charlottesville. Instructor in writing at University of Virginia.

Awards, Honors

Best Books for Young Adults designation, American Library Association (ALA), and Carter G. Woodson Book Award, National Council for the Social Studies (NCSS), both 1991, both for *Sorrow's Kitchen;* Teacher Scholar Award, National Endowment for the Humanities, 1991-92; Notable Children's Trade Book in the Field of Social Studies designation, NCSS/Children's Book Council (CBC), 1992, for *Raw Head, Bloody Bones,* 1994,

for *Stitching Stars,* and 1996, for *Keeping Secrets;* ALA Best Books for Young Adults designation, and Golden Kite Award for fiction, Society of Children's Book Writers and Illustrators, both 1992, Jane Addams Children's Book Award Honor designation, 1993, and Parents' Choice Award, 1996, all for *Letters from a Slave Girl;* ALA Notable Book designation, 1993, and Carter G. Woodson Award, 1994, both for *Starting Home;* Books for the Teen Age designation, New York Public Library, 1995, for *Deep Blues;* Carter G. Woodson Elementary Merit Book designation, 1995, for *Master of Mahogany;* Jefferson Cup Series Award, Virginia Library Association, 1996, for "African-American Artists and Artisans" series; Joan Sugarman Honor Book Award, Washington Independent Writers, and New York Public Library One Hundred Books for Reading and Sharing inclusion, both 2002, both for *Dear Ellen Bee;* Parents' Choice Gold Award, and Aesop Award, American Folklore Association, both 2005, and Big Read for Little Readers Designated Juvenile Title, Virginia Center for the Book, 2008-09, all for *Roy Makes a Car;* three Virginia Foundation for the Humanities fellowships.

Writings

FOR YOUNG PEOPLE

Sorrow's Kitchen: The Life and Folklore of Zora Neale Hurston, Scribner (New York, NY), 1990.
(Editor) *Raw Head, Bloody Bones: African-American Tales of the Supernatural,* Scribner (New York, NY), 1991.
Letters from a Slave Girl: The Story of Harriet Jacobs, Scribner (New York, NY), 1992.
The Butter Tree: Tales of Bruh Rabbit, illustrated by Mireille Vautier, Holt (New York, NY), 1995.
Keeping Secrets: The Girlhood Diaries of Seven Working Writers, Holt (New York, NY), 1995.
The Poison Place (novel), Atheneum (New York, NY), 1997.
(With Muriel M. Branch) *Dear Ellen Bee: A Civil War Scrapbook of Two Union Spies,* Atheneum (New York, NY), 2000.
Knockabeg: A Famine Tale, Houghton Mifflin (Boston, MA), 2001.
(Editor) *Feed the Children First: Memories of the Great Hunger,* Atheneum (New York, NY), 2002.
(Adaptor) *Roy Makes a Car* (based on a story collected by Zora Neale Hurston), illustrated by Terry Widener, Atheneum (New York, NY), 2005.
(With William Fash) *The Ancient American World* (nonfiction), Oxford University Press (New York, NY), 2005.
Letters from a Slave Boy: The Story of Joseph Jacobs, Atheneum (New York, NY), 2007.

"AFRICAN-AMERICAN ARTISTS AND ARTISANS" SERIES

Starting Home: The Story of Horace Pippin, Painter, Scribner (New York, NY), 1993.

Stitching Stars: The Story Quilts of Harriet Powers, Scribner (New York, NY), 1993.

Master of Mahogany: Tom Day, Free Black Cabinetmaker, Scribner (New York, NY), 1994.

Deep Blues: Bill Traylor, Self-Taught Artist, Scribner (New York, NY), 1994.

Painting Dreams: Minnie Evans, Visionary Artist, Houghton Mifflin (Boston, MA), 1996.

Catching the Fire: Philip Simmons, Blacksmith, photographs by Mannie Garcia, Houghton Mifflin (Boston, MA), 1997.

(Editor) *Talking with Tebé: Clementine Hunter, Memory Artist,* Houghton (Boston, MA), 1998.

Sidelights

Mary E. Lyons is Southern born and her Southern sensibility is clearly evident in her many award-winning historical and biographical works for children. In her fiction and nonfiction titles, Lyons explores the lives of marginalized people in history, from women to African Americans to impoverished Irish during the potato famine. Her "African-American Artists and Artisans" nonfiction series is geared for middle-grade readers, and older teens are the audience for her biography of folklorist Zora Neale Hurston as well as of *Keeping Secrets: The Girlhood Diaries of Seven Women Writers.* The writings of two young slaves are fictionalized in the companion volumes *Letters from a Slave Girl: The Story of Harriet Jacobs* and *Letters from a Slave Boy: The Story of Joseph Jacobs.* Based on actual historical figures, both titles focus on the lives of a mother and son in the antebellum years of the early 1800s. Lyons's other fiction for young adults includes the novel *The Poison Place, Dear Ellen Bee: The Civil War Scrapbook of Two Union Spies,* and *Knockabeg: A Famine Tale.*

Lyons was born in Macon, Georgia, and moved often during her childhood. "We followed my father in his work," the author recalled, "and by the time I was eleven, I had already lived in five Southern states and eight Southern towns. . . . I didn't know it at the time, but reading provided an instant escape. If I felt uncomfortable in a strange neighborhood or new school, I glued myself to a book and forgot it all." This somewhat rootless childhood has inspired the author to center much of her writing around her Southern origins.

After graduating from college, Lyons found her first teaching job in an inner-city school located in the middle of a housing project; the doors were locked most of the time for security. Lyons, who had been a mediocre science student, was assigned to teach science to her predominately black students. After one year she returned to college to earn a master's degree in reading so that she might be a better teacher. She taught in public schools for the next seventeen years before leaving the classroom to retrain as a school librarian. Her classroom and library experience led Lyons to write her first publication.

"Life has a weird way of sending us what we need to complete ourselves," Lyons later noted. "When I was a reading teacher, I discovered that my eighth-grade classes enjoyed stories by women writers and African American writers. They especially loved the humorous folktales collected by Zora Neale Hurston. There was no biography of her in the school library for the students to read, so I wrote my first book, *Sorrow's Kitchen: The Life and Folklore of Zora Neale Hurston.*"

Part biography, part introduction to the works of Hurston, *Sorrow's Kitchen* traces the writer's life from her childhood in Eatonville, Florida, at the turn of the twentieth century through her fight to become educated, her participation in the Harlem Renaissance, and finally to her work collecting and preserving the folklore of both her native South and of the West Indies. Researching and writing the book was a challenge for Lyons, "I had to relearn everything I had studied years before in high school and college," the author noted. "World War I, the Depression, World War II, the civil rights movement. This time I studied with Zora in mind." In *Booklist* Hazel Rochman observed that the "strength of Lyons's book is that she includes long excerpts from Hurston's works, set off within each chapter by a handsome border design." Elizabeth S. Watson, writing in *Horn Book,* called *Sorrow's Kitchen* "fascinating, enlightening, stimulating, and satisfying," and also cited Lyons's use of extended quotes from Hurston's writing.

Lyons uses Hurston's writings as a springboard for several books, including *Raw Head, Bloody Bones: African-American Tales of the Supernatural* and *Roy Makes a Car. Raw Head, Bloody Bones* incorporates some of the stories and tales Hurston collected during the 1930s as part of the Florida Federal Writers' Project. Several of the fifteen tales of ghosts and demons included in the collection are cast in the Gullah dialect spoken by the African-American inhabitants of the South Carolina and Georgia coasts, where Lyons lived as a child. In her *Booklist* review of *Raw Head, Bloody Bones,* Denia Hester warned that the "timid and faint-hearted" should beware; Lyons's "collection of African-American tales is a bone chiller" as well as "a scary good read." A critic in *Publishers Weekly* observed that the tales "derive their bewitching quality from the rhythms of the spoken word and the dancelike quality of early African American speech," both of which combine to "provide a quixotic contrast to the often gruesome subject matter."

Based on one of Hurston's collected tales, *Roy Makes a Car* introduces a mechanic named Roy Tyle, who is known far and wide for working magic with automobiles. When Roy makes the claim that he can construct a car that cannot break down, he comes through on his promise and sells the car for lots of money. A flying car is his next creation, and when Roy rides this winged auto up into the heavens, God becomes the mechanic's business partner in the hopes that the car will be useful to the angels. In her *School Library Journal* review of the picture book, Carolyn Janssen asserted that Lyons tells her story "with the ease of a seasoned storyteller," producing a book the critic dubbed "Southern storytelling at its best." In *Kirkus Reviews* a contributor noted that Terry Widener's illustrations are reminiscent of the Depression-era artwork of Thomas Hart Benton, while a *Publishers Weekly* critic described Lyons's version of Hurston's tale as "turbocharge[d]" with "brisk pacing and plenty of colloquialisms."

Letters from a Slave Girl is an account of the early life of Harriet Ann Jacobs, a slave who later fled to the North and became, through her writings, an important voice in the abolitionist movement. In researching Jacobs's life, Lyons relied heavily on the woman's autobiography, and she recreates Jacobs's life from age twelve to twenty-nine in letters Jacobs might have written. The fictional letters detail the loss of Jacobs's mother and the forced separation of her family after the death of one owner. There is a letter to her dead father after she is denied permission to attend his funeral; another letter addresses the man she loves and explains that she has decided to accept the attentions of a relatively kind white man in order to escape those of her brutal master. Jacobs ran away from her owners and hid for seven years in a crawl space under the eaves of her grandmother's cabin, eventually escaping to the North in 1842. A *Kirkus Reviews* critic noted that the narrative voice "Lyons creates for Harriet—a luminous character, gentle and resolute—is graceful and direct," while a *Horn Book* reviewer dubbed *Letters from a Slave Girl* "historical fiction at its best." A *Publishers Weekly* contributor also found much to praise in the book, describing it as a "searing epistolary work" that "stirringly celebrates the strength of the human spirit."

The life of Jacobs's son, Joseph Jacobs, is transformed into fictional diary entries and a series of imagined letters in *Letters from a Slave Boy.* After his mother escapes in 1835, five-year-old Joseph is left with his great until he runs away in 1843. Able to pass for white and with rudimentary reading skills, he embarks on a series of adventures that move him from work as a printer's apprentice in Boston to a crew member on a whaling ship. An adventurer at heart, Joseph then joins the rush to California, and his search for the gold needed to buy his family's freedom ultimately takes him to Australia. According to *Horn Book* contributor Betty Carter, *Letters from a Slave Boy* gives readers "a glimpse of America in the nineteenth century—not only the yearning for a better life but also the prejudice toward minorities." In *Horn Book* Paula Rohrlick called the work a "fine historical novel," and Carolyn Janssen noted in her *School Library Journal* that in *Letters from a Slave Boy* Lyons's use of "dialect and spelling give authenticity" to the boy's story "without making the text difficult to read and understand."

In her "African-American Artists and Artisans" series, Lyons details the lives of several creative black Americans, some of whom were overlooked during their lifetimes. Series opener *Starting Home* features self-taught painter Horace Pippin, whose works include many scenes from World War I, where he fought as part of the first U.S. all-black regiment to fight overseas. Wounded in the war and left unable to lift his right hand above shoulder level, Pippin went on to become a highly renowned folk artist. Focusing on a former slave named Harriet Powers, *Stitching the Stars* describes the life and career of the woman who "wrote" stories in quilts with needle and thread. (Slaves were forbidden to read or write.) Powers's two story quilts are now on display at the Museum of American History and are considered priceless examples of folk art. Reviewing both titles for *Booklist,* Rochman noted that "Lyons's sensitive commentary will draw middle-grade readers to look at the paintings and photographs." Describing *Stitching Stars* in the *Bulletin of the Center for Children's Books,* Deborah Stevenson remarked that "Lyons's lively writing stitches concepts together with smoothness and clarity" to produce "an unusual take on history and a reminder of the democratic possibilities of art."

In *Master of Mahogany: Tom Day, Free Black Cabinetmaker* and *Catching the Fire: Philip Simmons, Blacksmith,* Lyons tells the stories of a cabinetmaker and a blacksmith, respectively. Born of free parents in 1801, Thomas Day became one of the most successful cabinetmakers in pre-Civil War North Carolina, and his works have become collector's items. In *Master of Mahogany,* "Lyons does an excellent job of piecing together the sketchy details of Day's life, of which little is known," wrote a *Horn Book* reviewer. In *Catching the Fire,* Lyons presents the life and work of Philip Simmons, a blacksmith whose gates, fences, and railings decorate the city of Charleston, South Carolina, where Simmons has lived most of his life. Based on personal interviews with Simmons and those who have worked with him, the book was dubbed "an engrossing biography" by a *Kirkus Reviews* critic and "engaging" by a reviewer in *Horn Book.* Stevenson concluded that *Catching the Fire* would be "useful not only as an introduction to a gifted professional craftsman, but also a reminder of how unexpected things can become art when executed with authority."

Other visual artists are profiled in books such as *Deep Blues: Bill Traylor, Self-Taught Artist; Painting Dreams: Minnie Evans, Visionary Artist;* and *Talking with Tebé: Clementine Hunter, Memory Artist.* In *Deep Blues,* Lyons details the life and works of a man who was born into slavery in Alabama in 1856 and who did not begin painting until he was eighty years old. Traylor's works are now acclaimed and exhibited throughout the United States. A critic in *Horn Book* noted that "Lyons's perceptive commentary . . . points out possible connections between Traylor's life as a farmer and the subject matter of his works."

Minnie Evans, the subject of *Painting Dreams,* was forty-three years old when she began to draw, and she based her pictures on dreams that had haunted her all her life. Born into poverty and untrained as an artist, Evans did not let this stop her, nor would she be stopped by her family and friends who thought she was crazy. "Lyons has brought us the life and work of an African American folk artist who succeeded despite community prejudice," commented Rochman. In *Talking with Tebé*, Lyons presents the art of Clementine Hunter, called Tebé, whose work portrays the life of a southern laborer. This story is told through Hunter's own words, which Lyons gathered from magazine and newspaper articles and tape-recorded interviews.

Other books by Lyons include *Keeping Secrets, The Butter Tree: Tales of Bruh Rabbit,* and *The Poison Place.* In the first of these titles, Lyons blends her own commentary with excerpts from the girlhood diaries of seven nineteenth-century women writers: Louisa May Alcott, Charlotte Forten, Sarah Jane Foster, Kate Chopin, Alice Dunbar-Nelson, Ida B. Wells, and Charlotte Perkins Gilman. She demonstrates how keeping a diary helped each of these young writers develop a public voice. A critic in *Kirkus Reviews* noted that "Lyons writes with style and feeling, creating a strong sense of each individual life story, even as she gives us a social history of what it was like to be a woman at that time." A *Horn Book* reviewer called *Keeping Secrets* "a fascinating look at the public and private lives" of these writers that explores "issues of femininity, social expectations, family, and racism."

In a somewhat lighter vein, Lyons retells African American trickster tales in *The Butter Tree.* These six tales from South Carolina involve the usual scenario of a small animal tricking a much larger one, and as a critic in *Publishers Weekly* noted, "undoubtedly helped the enslaved originators of these tales endure their own oppression." "Bruh" as well as "brer" is a variant of "brother," an indication that the slaves held this wily rabbit close to their hearts. In *Horn Book* Maeve Visser Knoth noted that "Lyons's skilled retellings are brief and uncluttered, recalling the oral tradition. She uses few adjectives, yet her language is colorful and evokes regional flavor."

Begun in 1989 with the scrap of an idea, Lyons's novel *The Poison Place* uses historical fact as its background, detailing the lives of two men. One is Charles Willson Peale, the eighteenth-century portraitist and founder of the first museum of natural history in the United States, the Peale Museum in Philadelphia. The other is Moses Williams, Peale's former slave, who became a silhouette cutter and the first black professional artist in post-revolutionary America. The novel is told through the voice of Williams on a nighttime tour with his young daughter through the museum. Williams's own struggle for survival is contrasted to Peale's story and that of his museum. As Rachelle M. Bilz noted in *Voice of Youth Advocates,* "Moses's lifelong quest for freedom is intertwined with the Peale family's success and failure." Through the narrator's revelations, the reader is led to

wonder how much responsibility Peale himself had in the eventual poisoning of his own son, a taxidermist in the museum who died from the arsenic he used in his work. Bilz concluded that the novel was "fast paced and well written . . . sure to appeal to historical fiction fans." A contributor in *Kirkus Reviews* called *The Poison Place* "a riveting work of historical fiction."

Inspired by the stories of her Irish forbears, Lyons deals with the Irish Potato Famine of the nineteenth century in two books: the novel *Knockabeg: A Famine Tale* and the nonfiction *Feed the Children First: Memories of the Great Hunger. Knockabeg* mixes creatures and characters from Irish folklore with real-life characters. The fairy folk known as the Nuckelavees have put a curse on Ireland's potatoes, causing a famine and a war between the fairies and the mortals. A critic for *Publishers Weekly* found that "the action shifts between (and often intersects) both worlds, detailing the impact of famine on the human community as well as the wounded faeries' war stories when they return to heal the residents of Knockabeg." Kit Vaughan, writing in *School Library Journal,* concluded: "Don't expect an entirely happy ending in this story, which includes some gruesome descriptions of the effects of the potato famine on the mortals of Knockabeg."

Feed the Children First is a collection of comments made by descendants of Irish men and women who lived through a devastating potato famine in Ireland. Their accounts include descriptions of the many deaths that occurred—almost one-quarter of the population perished—as well as remembrances of the voyages many of them made to start new lives in North America. Diane S. Marton, writing in *School Library Journal,* found that these firsthand accounts "bear witness not only to unbearable suffering, but also to the humanity, dignity, and endurance of a people." "The personal voices and images in this collection bring the horror of the Irish potato famine very close," added Rochman, and Margaret A. Bush concluded in *Horn Book* that *Feed the Children First* serves as "a powerful introduction to Ireland's history and to the human devastation of a country in extreme poverty."

Lyons continues to pen historical fiction and to write for young readers. "I can't imagine writing for anyone besides young people," the author once stated. "They like to be told the truth and can handle complexities that adults can't." She also maintains contact with her audience by frequent visits to schools. "Teachers often expect a black author to show up because so many of my books have dealt with African-American issues. I'm always flattered that people assume I'm black; I hope it means I'm doing my job as a writer. But now I consider myself not only a writer of black history or of women's history, but increasingly as a historian of the South." For Lyons this means giving a voice to those who have not been heard before. "Many people I write about have never had a chance to speak for themselves," she explained. "In articles already written about them, you don't really hear their voices. I want to let my subjects tell their own stories in a form accessible to young readers."

Biographical and Critical Sources

BOOKS

St. James Guide to Children's Writers, 5th edition, St. James Press (Detroit, MI), 1999.

PERIODICALS

Booklist, December 15, 1990, Hazel Rochman, review of *Sorrow's Kitchen: The Life and Folklore of Zora Neale Hurston,* p. 866; January 1, 1992, Denia Hester, review of *Raw Head, Bloody Bones: African-American Tales of the Supernatural,* pp. 830-831; November 15, 1993, Hazel Rochman, review of *Starting Home: The Story of Horace Pippin, Painter* and *Stitching Stars: The Story Quilts of Harriet Powers,* pp. 618-619; October 1, 1994, Ilene Cooper, review of *Master of Mahogany: Tom Day, Free Black Cabinetmaker,* p. 322; November 15, 1994, Hazel Rochman, review of *Deep Blues: Bill Traylor, Self-Taught Artist,* p. 598; July, 1996, Hazel Rochman, review of *Painting Dreams: Minnie Evans, Visionary Artist,* pp. 1825-1826; September 1, 1997, Carolyn Phelan, review of *Catching the Fire: Philip Simmons, Blacksmith,* p. 117; December 1, 1997, Randy Meyer, review of *The Poison Place,* p. 616; November 1, 2000, Carolyn Phelan, review of *Dear Ellen Bee: A Civil War Scrapbook of Two Union Spies,* p. 540; December 15, 2001, Hazel Rochman, review of *Feed the Children First: Irish Memories of the Great Hunger,* p. 725; January 1, 2007, Carolyn Phelan, review of *Letters from a Slave Boy: The Story of Joseph Jacobs,* p. 83.

Bulletin of the Center for Children's Books, December, 1993, Deborah Stevenson, review of *Stitching Stars,* p. 128; October, 1997, Deborah Stevenson, review of *Catching the Fire,* p. 57; September, 2001, review of *Knockabeg: A Famine Tale,* p. 26; May, 2007, Karen Coats, review of *Letters from a Slave Boy,* p. 375.

Horn Book, March-April, 1991, Elizabeth S. Watson, review of *Sorrow's Kitchen,* p. 216; November, 1992, review of *Letters from a Slave Girl: The Story of Harriet Jacobs,* p. 729; March-April, 1994, Ellen Fader, review of *Starting Home,* and Ellen Fader, review of *Stitching Stars,* p. 219; November, 1994, review of *Master of Mahogany,* p. 750; March, 1995, review of

Deep Blues, p. 221; September, 1995, review of *Keeping Secrets: The Girlhood Diaries of Seven Women Writers* and Maeve Visser Knoth, review of *The Butter Tree: Tales of Bruh Rabbit,* p. 614; September-October, 1997, review of *Catching the Fire,* p. 592; September-October, 1998, Susan P. Bloom, review of *Talking with Tebé: Clementine Hunter, Memory Artist,* p. 620; March-April, 2002, Margaret A. Bush, review of *Feed the Children First,* p. 229; March-April, 2005, Barbara Bader, review of *Roy Makes a Car,* p. 211; March-April, 2007, Betty Carter, review of *Letters from a Slave Boy,* p. 197.

Kirkus Reviews, November 1, 1992, review of *Letters from a Slave Girl,* p. 1380; June 1, 1995, review of *Keeping Secrets;* July 1, 1997, review of *Catching the Fire;* October 1, 1997, review of *The Poison Place;* December 15, 2004, review of *Roy Makes a Car,* p. 1204; November 15, 2006, review of *Letters from a Slave Boy,* p. 15.

Kliatt, January, 2007, Paula Rohrlick, review of *Letters from a Slave Boy,* p. 1176.

Publishers Weekly, October 25, 1991, review of *Raw Head, Bloody Bones,* p. 69; October 26, 1992, review of *Letters from a Slave Girl,* pp. 72-73; February 20, 1995, review of *The Butter Tree,* p. 206; September 18, 2000, review of *Dear Ellen Bee,* p. 112; July 23, 2001, review of *Knockabeg,* p. 78; December 10, 2001, review of *Feed the Children First,* p. 71; January 24, 2005, review of *Roy Makes a Car,* p. 243.

Reading Today, April, 2001, Lynne T. Burke, review of *Dear Ellen Bee,* p. 32.

School Library Journal, February, 1994, Maria B. Salvadore, reviews of *Starting Home* and *Stitching Stars,* p. 113; October, 1994, Joanne Kelleher, review of *Master of Mahogany,* p. 136; January, 1995, p. 127; September, 1997, Margaret C. Howell, review of *Catching the Fire,* p. 233; November, 1997, Sally Margolis, review of *The Poison Place,* p. 120; September, 1998, Judith Constantinides, review of *Talking with Tebé,* p. 221; October, 2000, Patricia B. McGee, review of *Dear Ellen Bee,* p. 164; September, 2001, Kit Vaughan, review of *Knockabeg,* p. 226; March, 2002, Diane S. Marton, review of *Feed the Children First,* p. 254; February, 2005, Carolyn Janssen, review of *Roy Makes a Car,* p. 106; February, 2007, Carolyn Janssen, review of *Letters from a Slave Boy,* p. 122.

Voice of Youth Advocates, December, 1997, Rachelle M. Bilz, review of *The Poison Place,* p. 318.

ONLINE

Mary Lyons Home Page, http://www.lyonsdenbooks.com (June 10, 2008).

Autobiography Feature

Mary E. Lyons

Lyons contributed the following autobiographical essay to *SATA:*

Childhood

Most people are surprised to learn that I was a remedial reader in the first grade. It wasn't my fault. Really, it wasn't. I had only been in this world for five years when I started school. With no year of kindergarten under my little belt, I wasn't quite ready to enter the land of reading. Besides, I was too busy dreaming about the party for my upcoming sixth birthday and talking to imaginary playmates named Kerchief and Johnny.

My mother drilled me with flash cards. My father told me I could have anything I wanted, if only I would move up from the Crows to the Swans, or whatever the good nuns at Holy Family Catholic School in Miami, Florida, called reading groups back then. Anything I wanted! I worked hard for weeks and must have made progress. When reward time rolled around, I announced that I wanted a . . . chocolate milkshake.

I no longer remember that particular milkshake (it was one of many to come), but I still remember the first word I learned to read: LOOK. Those four letters grabbed me by the hand and haven't let go since. They've led me through thousands of books written by other people and twenty that I've written myself.

The stories in my first-grade reading books were about cardboard children named John and Jean. They had perma-freeze smiles and owned an ugly dog called Spot. John and Jean led very dull lives. Mostly they called their dog: "Here, Spot, here! Come here!"

Mary E. Lyons, age six, and her sister, Eileen, age three, Miami, FL, 1954 (Copyright © 2008 by Mary E. Lyons. Reproduced by permission.)

As I went up through the grades, each teacher assigned a new reading book on the first day of school. It was supposed to last all year, but before the day was over, I read the book from cover to cover. That left 179 school days to sit through vocabulary and comprehension drills on stories I'd already read.

It's no wonder that whenever we moved to a new town, I read my way through the school library. And though my family didn't own many books, there was always something in the house to read: magazines, newspapers, and an ever-changing menu of public library books.

I spent my third-grade year in Savannah, Georgia. That's when I won a school contest and the first book I ever owned: *Nancy Drew and the Secret of the Old Clock.* Nancy was a cool detective who wore a long skirt with a matching jacket. Thanks to her, I learned words like "cloche" (she wore one on her head) and "roadster" (she drove one). The sophistication of the terms appealed to me. They also taught me how to use the rest of a sentence to figure out the general meaning of an unfamiliar word.

Third grade wasn't my finest year. The lay (non-nun) teacher at Cathedral Catholic School was young and inexperienced. One day she walked off the job for good, leaving a wild group of kids to run the classroom on their own. That didn't last long. Within an hour, the principal took over. One substitute teacher after another for the rest of the year meant that I didn't learn to write in cursive. By the time we moved to Orangeburg, South Carolina, I was a remedial writer.

Come to think of it, fourth grade wasn't a banner year either. I suppose I was tired of moving by then. Things didn't go so well at Ellis Avenue Elementary, the public school in Orangeburg. One report card suggested that I work on my table manners in the cafeteria. I should also stop talking so much in class (that last bit might sound familiar to some of you).

My fourth-grade teacher gathered her long straight hair into a bun and was a cold sort of person. I remember only two things that she said to me personally: "Didn't you learn to write in cursive in third grade?" and "Is it true that you Caflics (Catholics) worship fire?"

This was my first encounter with religious ignorance. It was also the first time I realized I was an outsider. I had been born in the South, yet I was outside of it as a Catholic, and a cursive-less one to boot. There were so few Catholics in the South at the time that the Church called it missionary country.

Two field trips stand out as highlights of my fourth-grade year: one to a turkey farm and one to a farm where we students picked cotton. I bet the bun-headed teacher would be surprised to know that the cotton-picking trip became part of the introduction to my book *Talking with Tebè: Clementine Hunter, Memory Artist.*

The author, her older brother, Joe, and their father, Joseph E. Lyons (1919-1982), c. 1950 (Copyright © 2008 by Mary E. Lyons. Reproduced by permission.)

School mattered during my two years in South Carolina. School always matters. But home was where I had fun and where my younger sister and I invented pretend worlds. A full bathtub of water was a swimming pool in a swank Paris hotel. A neighbor's side garden was an enchanted forest. Dinner leftovers became gourmet dishes when we turned our shared bedroom into a restaurant (I was the waiter, my sister was the polite customer). Glasses of water thrown on our bedroom floor made the hardwood as slick as an Olympic ice-skating rink. This last was my idea. We ruined the finish on the floor. What was I thinking?

About once a week, we kids walked with Dad to the corner newsstand. The tiny shop was my source for "Katie Keene" comic books and a pulp series about a girl named Donna Parker. Donna had a perfect pageboy hairstyle, wore perfect shirtwaist dresses, and lived in a perfect house.

I also adored the *Classics Illustrated.* These were comic-book versions of grown-up novels such as *The Count of Monte Cristo* by Alexandré Dumas and *Jane Eyre* by Charlotte Brontë. You'd think I'd like present-day graphic novels, but the illustrations and texts seem thin compared to the *Classics Illustrated* of my childhood.

Occasionally I dipped into *The Book House.* My mother bought this set of literature books for my older brother when he was a toddler. The fairy tale volume was my favorite. I still have the set, complete with crayon marks, torn pages, and end papers where I practiced writing my name in cursive.

In the fifth grade, my parents let me subscribe to the *Weekly Reader* Book Club. Receiving a book in the mail with my name on the package was the greatest thing ever. The first title was *Wild Geese Flying* by Cornelia Meigs. I loved the book, though I can't remember a thing about it now—only that it came in the mail like a Christmas present.

During the fifth grade, I faced censorship for the first time. Unfortunately, my mother was the censor. I came home from school with a biography of Martin Luther, a leader of the Protestant Reformation. I didn't care one way or the other about Martin Luther. The book was just one that I grabbed off of the shelf, the way that kids do when the bell is about to ring, and the teacher is shoving the class out the library door.

Maybe the book brought back bad memories for Mom. A Southerner, she had grown up with neighborhood Protestant kids throwing rocks at her while screaming "Catholic!" And I guess she was afraid that reading a book about a Protestant would be a sin. That seems crazy, but some of what she did was just right. She was

The author's mother, Evelyn Rea Lyons (1916-2006) (Copyright © 2008 by Mary E. Lyons. Reproduced by permission.)

a parent taking an interest in her child's reading. She made me return the book. But she didn't march down to the school and demand that the librarian yank it from the collection so other kids couldn't read it. That happens much too often nowadays.

By my sixth-grade year, we were living in Charlotte, North Carolina, and my childhood wandering was over. (I lived in Charlotte until I finished high school.) The library in my Catholic elementary school was the size of a regular classroom—big but not big enough. After reading all the books with Newbery stars on them— *Rifles for Watie* was a favorite—I read historical fiction for adults that my older brother bought through *his* book club. I especially remember *Hawaii* by James Michener and *Exodus,* a novel about Israel by Leon Uris. Though I only partly understood the themes of these grown-up books, they affected me deeply.

For the first time, I was reading about outsiders. I couldn't have expressed it this way at the time, but the books made me realize something I've always remembered. Outsiders exist only in the minds of other people. The native people of Hawaii weren't outsiders until missionaries arrived in the nineteenth century and treated them that way. Jews weren't outsiders until Adolf Hitler—among many others down through the centuries, including Catholics—defined them as such.

Some events in *Hawaii* are based on actual history. In the book, as in real life, thousands of native people died from diseases that missionaries brought to the islands. Reading about the mass deaths upset me so much that I wrote a long essay. It wasn't a school assignment, and it wasn't a diary entry (those were mostly about boys). I wrote it just for me. Writing the words was similar to shedding tears. I felt better afterward, the way you do after a good cry.

High School

When I was a junior, I transferred to Myers Park High School in Charlotte. I suppose that other Catholic teenagers were doing the same, because the clerk behind the school office counter rolled her eyes and shook her head when my father registered me. Standing behind a counter often gives people a sense of authority they don't have. "Too many Catholics coming here," she mumbled.

Unsettled by her irritation, we stood tongue-tied as she assigned me to a general-level English class. In my insulated Catholic-school world, I was the same as everyone else: an excellent reader with college-level standardized test scores. But advanced? For all Dad and I knew, I was below average compared to public-school kids. Besides, I was a girl, and advanced classes weren't supposed to matter for girls back then.

The teachers in my junior and senior year English classes usually called on the cute boys. I soon learned not to raise my hand, even when I wanted to answer

The author's sister, Eileen, and their younger brother, Pat, Charlotte, North Carolina, 1962 (Copyright © 2008 by Mary E. Lyons. Reproduced by permission.)

questions about Jane Austen's *Pride and Prejudice* or Nathaniel Hawthorne's *The Scarlet Letter.* To this day, I'm uninterested in works by these writers. Hearing their names brings back memories of conversations that were closed to me.

Still, I had some sensational teachers in Catholic school and at Myers Park. Despite the snotty clerk, who I hope has gone to her just rewards along with Miss Bun Head, I reveled in the freedom and space of public high school. The campus was spread out like a small college, with grassy areas between the buildings.

The well-stocked library became my refuge during lunch hour. My taste for historical fiction grew. I gorged on books by the Brontë sisters, Edna Ferber, Thomas Costain, Victoria Holt, and Mary Stewart. Like many teens, I went through an Edgar Allan Poe phase, and I wept bitterly over the end of Margaret Mitchell's *Gone with the Wind.* I'm still convinced that Rhett will sweep Scarlett into his arms and carry her up the mansion staircase again.

After a time, it seemed that there were no good books left to read. That's when an interested teacher or librarian might have made a difference in my reading life. He

or she could have guided me toward more-challenging literature. By some standards, my high-school reading left a lot to be desired. I lurched from one mediocre adult book to another, reading an average of one per day. If I chose a title that I would think of now as quality literature, it was by accident.

No matter. The main thing was that I read and read and read. My speaking vocabulary became so broad that my best friend made fun of me for using what she called fifty-cent words (I mispronounced some of them, but she didn't know that). Her teasing embarrassed me. I would have felt better if I'd known that those fifty-cent words were a valuable currency. I would spend them again and again when I became a writer years later.

Reading was my apprenticeship for writing. There's no other way to do it. If you want to be a writer one day, and you're reading this essay on a printed page, you're lucky. If you're reading it on a screen, you might be in trouble. Here's why. Recently I discovered some research about reading on a computer screen. The light reflects back onto the reader's eye and slows down the reading speed, whatever it is, by one third.

Think about what this means. Reading makes a child smarter without even trying. If reading on a screen slows down your speed, then reading on a screen will make you less smart. It's that simple.

I feel fortunate to have childhood memories of bound books, not digital scraps of information on the Internet. Books were one of the best things in a childhood that, overall, could have been better. I yearned for piano lessons. That never happened, but I learned to play old-time banjo and Irish penny whistle as an adult. Much more portable! I passionately wanted braces but had to wait until I was grown and could pay for them myself. Life, like teeth, slowly straightens itself out after a while.

Moving from one strange town to another as a child made it easier for me to take risks as an adult. More important, something else was going on as I roamed the South with my family. My young mind was taking memory pictures of the landscape. My young ears were recording a remarkable variety of Southern stories and accents. I tucked the sights and sounds away until I was the writer I never planned to be.

College

Appalachian State University is in Boone, North Carolina—the "Hub of the Holiday Highlands," they used to call it. The college sits in a skinny valley surrounded by mountains. Some of the lower hills run slap up against the back of campus buildings.

Local people call the tallest hill Howard's Knob. Go west on Main Street to Mast's General Store, take a right, and you're at the bottom of Howard's Knob. Continue up the steep incline, and you're in Junaluska, Boone's African American neighborhood in 1967.

As part of ASU's teacher-in-training requirement, I tutored a bright, sweet girl who lived in Junaluska. The Appalachia area was especially poor in those days, and substandard housing was a familiar sight in Boone. The first time I walked my student home, I wasn't surprised to see that she lived in a weathered plank cabin perched dangerously on the mountainside.

What surprised me was that town officials deliberately kept Junaluska outside the city limits. The girl's family lived without sanitation services, trash pickup, and running water. The meanness of those town limits appalled me.

I asked around and learned that Junaluska's residents might be descendants of the few slaves who lived in the area before the U.S. Civil War. That was the beginning of my deep curiosity about black history.

ASU offered a black history course. This was unusual for any college those days, especially one with only one black student at the time (she went on to become a college president). I had to take other history classes first—prerequisites, they're called. I completed the required courses, but the black history course was a disappointment. The professor broke his ankle and couldn't manage the steps to the third-floor classroom. We students were left with static-y taped lectures, and I was still thirsty for black history.

My curiosity deepened after I dropped out of college for a semester to earn tuition money. By complete accident, I ended up working as a secretary for a job counseling service in nearby Hickory, North Carolina. Nervous about race riots, town officials financed the service shortly after the assassination of the Rev. Martin Luther King, Jr. The counseling office was meant to be a place where African Americans could take racial concerns and also get help finding a job.

The permanent staff was African American. Eager to serve clients of all races, they wanted a white face at the reception desk. I was the white face. I will tell you flat out that I didn't have the experience or maturity to handle that position, though racism was all around me when I was growing up. The poisonous "n" word floated through conversations I overhead as a child. "Whites Only" drinking fountains were a common sight in Savannah. I have a vivid fifth-grade memory of seeing white members of the Catholic congregation in Orangeburg leave our dollhouse-sized church when a black family approached the communion rail.

But mostly segregated schools in Charlotte meant that I had little reason to discuss race with anyone. One black student attended my Catholic school. Shy but popular, she was president of the freshman class. One black student integrated Myers Park High School without incident while I was there. Even though the civil-rights struggle was raging through the South, it passed over my head. I wasn't prepared for the racism I experienced personally in Hickory. "Personally" is the key word. You don't know what it's like until it happens to you.

As a student at Appalachia State University, Boone, North Carolina, 1970 (Copyright © 2008 by Mary E. Lyons. Reproduced by permission.)

The functionally illiterate white people who came to our office needed help filling out job applications. I was happy to assist. But when they realized that the interviewer who would help them find a job was black, they balked. One man spat on me. Others insulted my coworkers. My boss was ten years older in age than I was and about one hundred years wiser. If not for his gentle guidance, I would have started a race riot all on my own.

My roommate and I shared an apartment that caught fire while we were at work one dreary winter day. The fire imploded, so nothing burned, but all the mirrors and windows cracked, and smoke damage was extensive. Our apartment neighbors were students at Lenoir-Rhyne College in Hickory. They graciously let us camp out on their floor until they learned where I worked. That was the end of their southern hospitality.

My coworkers worried that the fire was related to recent Ku Klux Klan activity in the area. (It wasn't. Apparently my roommate or I had left a cigarette burning in an ashtray on the sofa.) They found us a temporary home with a welcoming black family.

My experience with white hostility and black generosity in Hickory changed me. Compared to the civil-rights workers of that decade, I risked nothing and contributed nothing. I was merely a sheltered young woman who was fortunate to witness reality for six months.

One semester later I was back in the comforting rhythm of college life and education courses. If you were an elementary education major at Appalachian State University, the first thing you learned was to postpone Beulah Campbell's REALLY HARD children's literature course as long as possible. I thought I'd be clever and take it in summer school. Foolish me. It's not easy to read and review one hundred children's books in a four-week-long class.

I don't remember my final grade, but I do remember Miss Campbell's charming stories about the children's book authors she met over the years. Her excitement as she talked about them, her pride as she showed us her signed, first-edition books—this was teaching at its best. When teachers are excited, students catch the fever, too.

I also had some clunker teachers. During my freshman year, a history professor accused me of plagiarizing a research paper because it was too well written. One of my English professors openly harassed his female students in class with off-color remarks.

But most ASU teachers were so dedicated that I can only think that my college degree was a deal. Room, board, and tuition totaled about $1,500 per year. The low fees were a gift, because like many ASU students at the time, I financed my college education with federal government loans and work-study grants. I was the first woman to graduate from college on either side of my family, and I paid for most of it myself. I'm more proud of that than any book I've written.

When I graduated from ASU, I had something that most education schools don't require these days: a solid background in history and literature. I also knew, or thought I knew, how to teach elementary-level music, physical education, health, math, art, reading, and handwriting, both print and *cursive*.

I almost didn't learn how to teach science because I dropped out of the science teaching methods class three times (it always met at the impossible hour of 8 a.m.). I finally completed the course. This was a great relief, not because I wanted to teach science—I couldn't imagine such a thing—but because ASU required it for graduation. And I had to graduate. I had already signed a contract to teach in Georgia.

Teaching

With Junaluska and Hickory still on my mind, I asked the school system in Georgia to let me teach in one of their all-black schools. My assigned K-8 school was in a forgotten corner of the city, surrounded by low-income housing projects. The building was large but ugly. The principal, I found out later, had a brain tumor and

couldn't think straight. Teachers had no access to the supply closet, so the school secretary doled out mimeograph paper sheet by sheet. We lined up for it every morning, looking rather like people in the bread lines of the Great Depression years.

The school had no library. My classroom had no textbooks. This was a sad thing for everyone, especially inexperienced me. Unbelievably, I was the seventh-grade science teacher. My supplies consisted of one cracked aquarium and a few Petri dishes. What I wrote on the blackboard each day served as the textbook. I bought the chalk and eraser.

My African-American colleagues were immensely helpful, and my students were witty and talented. Years of living in Boone had mixed my Southern Piedmont drawl with an Appalachian mountain twang. The students spoke with a lyrical, lightning-fast, Deep South accent. We simply couldn't understand one another, a situation that led to much giggling for all of us. Finally I appointed an interpreter who proudly translated when necessary.

Oh, the teaching I could have done, if only I had known the rich background of what some scholars call "Black English." Twenty years later, I remembered those Deep South children when I compiled stories for *Raw Head, Bloody Bones: African American Tales of the Supernatural*. I'm sure they would have been interested in the African origins of Black English. Together we would have shivered and tittered over these tales told in the storytellers' original voices.

The following year I returned to the hills of ASU and earned a master's degree in reading education. My fellow students were a companionable, noncompetitive lot. Best of all, I redeemed my lousy undergraduate performance by graduating with all A's.

After four years as a Title I reading teacher in North Carolina, I packed my bags and set out for the University of Virginia in Charlottesville. When I left, I had a cast the size of a truck muffler on my broken right arm. I should have seen it as a bad omen, because the next two years in a doctoral degree program at UVA left me discouraged. The university had recently graduated its first female students, but the professors in my department still complained openly about the good old days when only men attended the school. I soon realized that I wasn't tough enough to survive their dismissive attitude toward women.

Not all of those two years was a loss. I learned the value of teaching reading skills with literature instead of reading series and workbooks. But I was broke, and most of the coursework bored me. It was time for the next step in my life: a return to classroom teaching.

That first year back in the classroom was a killer. It was as if I'd never taught before. Every day I instructed restless sixth-, seventh-, and eighth-grade children: a to-tal of ninety students in six classes that met daily. Most of the seventh graders were still stuck at a third-grade reading level. One class of eighth graders could read at about a sixth-grade level—they just didn't want to. Some had never read one entire book in their lives.

I tried to lure my students into the world of reading pleasure with a variety of teaching materials—reading kits, plays, paperback books, poetry units, literature readers. Most middle-school literature readers in those days featured stories by Mark Twain, Edgar Allan Poe, Hart Crane, Stephen Crane, Washington Irving, and other BMWs (boring male writers).

Some people call these the classic American writers, but there's another reason why their names keep rising like Lazarus in the school curricula. Their works are old enough to be copyright free. Educational publishers reprint them without paying permission fees. Then they pass some of the savings on to teachers. This means that school systems can buy multiple classroom copies at a budget rate. Literature by writers such as Washington Irving may or may not be classic. It's certainly cheap.

One gorgeous fall day, many of my eighth graders were falling asleep as they read a short version of Irving's short story, "The Legend of Sleepy Hollow." I looked around the classroom. One half of the students were girls. One third of the students were African American. I was doing my teacherly duty by preparing them to study longer works by the same writers in high school. But what was the point of classic literature if it made my students dislike reading even more?

While their heads drooped over Irving's text, I took an inventory of my teaching materials. Later I calculated the percentage of literature by women and African Americans. The figures were astonishingly low. Women: 5 percent. African American: .5 percent.

Maybe, I thought, I could continue to teach comprehension and vocabulary skills with the so-called classics but add to the mix. That was the same year I met my husband-to-be. For the next few years, I scoured the shelves of his used and rare bookstore, Heartwood Books. I also spent every weekend reading in the University of Virginia library.

My goal was to find literature by women, including women of color. The selections had to be on an accessible reading level with themes that would interest eighth graders. My final list of fifty stories and book excerpts included works by Kate Chopin, Rebecca Harding Davis, Charlotte Perkins Gilman, Zora Neale Hurston, Harriet Jacobs, Leslie Silko, Alice Walker, and Anzia Yezierska.

My students left middle school knowing more about women and minority writers than the teachers who would instruct them in high school. The word "multi-cultural" hadn't been invented then. Without knowing it, I had created a multicultural literature curriculum. And without knowing it, I had tilled the earth for a writing career.

Writing: The Beginning

Zora Neale Hurston (1891-1960) was an African-American folklorist, writer, and anthropologist. She published three collections of folklore, three novels, an autobiography, short stories, and plays. For what I called my "Women Writers Unit," I chose brief selections of her collected folklore. "The Black Cat Bone" and "How to Eat Fish" were big hits, especially with the boys. When I told them that this successful writer of the 1930s and 1940s ended up dying alone and poor in a charity home, they wanted to read a biography about her. No such book existed, and her autobiography would have been tough going for most of them.

The same happened with Harriet Jacobs's narrative, *Incidents in the Life of a Slave Girl*. Like Hurston's autobiography, Jacobs's entire book was too big a bite for my students. I chose an excerpt in which she wrote about her life as an enslaved child. "Are there more stories like that?" my students asked after reading it. "Stories about slave girls?"

Well, no, not in our school library, not in 1980. It seems hard to believe now, but the only books I could find were a dog-eared copy of *Tituba of Salem Village* by

Lyons and her husband, Paul Collinge, in 1987 (Copyright © 2008 by Mary E. Lyons. Reproduced by permission.)

Ann Petry (a splendid book, by the way), and a short biography of Harriet Tubman. The first title was too long for my students. The second was falling apart.

A few years later, I won a grant from the Education School at the University of Virginia. I used the money to write and print classroom copies of a short biography of Zora Neale Hurston. The booklets were like little textbooks, with discussion questions and vocabulary exercises at the end. "You should try and get that published," a teacher on my team commented.

The idea had never occurred to me. With her casual remark as encouragement, I learned everything I could about the business side of children's books: publishers, editors, and how to write a query letter. By 1988, I was writing to companies that published nonfiction for children. Sending the letters was a "let's jump off this cliff and see what happens" adventure.

I already knew that professors of women's studies classes at the college level were teaching Hurston. And I knew that Alice Walker, author of *The Color Purple,* had written a widely read essay about finding Hurston's grave. I had no clue that the subject of Hurston was hot and getting hotter in the publishing and theater worlds of New York.

I soon received a reply from a major publisher of children's books. They were interested in my idea for an anthology of Hurston's works and suggested that I add biographical material between the selections. An assistant editor at the company discussed early drafts of the manuscript with me for the next nine months. I will always be grateful for her help with what I call "getting the teacher out" of my writing.

In the end, the assistant editor's boss wanted a book focusing on Hurston's love life. Anyone who studies Zora Neale Hurston knows that she was deliberately private about her romances. I simply didn't have enough information to write about that aspect of her life. And I didn't want to. Alice Walker erected a stone over Hurston's grave that says "Genius of the South." For my students, Hurston's retelling of African-American folklore was her genius.

After sending another round of letters, I heard from the editor of Scribner's Books for Young Readers in July of 1989. Within a few weeks, she sent me the contract for my first book, *Sorrow's Kitchen: The Life and Folklore of Zora Neale Hurston.* The book was published in the fall of 1990. This was the same school year that I worked as an elementary-school librarian. It was also the same year that I won the National Endowment for the Humanities Teacher-Scholar Award for Virginia. Those were exciting but upsetting months.

The success of *Sorrow's Kitchen* still seems ridiculous for a writer's first book. Librarians and other people who review children's books liked it. It won three awards. *USA Today* newspaper and *Ms.* magazine reviewed it.

One day in the school library, I found myself wiping a first grader's nose with a tissue in my left hand while talking on the phone in my right hand with a public radio interviewer. Local and state newspapers called for interviews. A regional public television station featured me on a program about writers. I had my first book signing at a children's book store, where a teacher sniped, "Who would have thought it?"

No kidding. I'd been a little Dixie gypsy who had moved every two years or so as a child. A remedial reader in the first grade, a remedial writer in the fourth. Now I was an ordinary school teacher and librarian. Just who did I think I was? I wasn't sure, but I didn't have much time to ponder the question.

I had almost completed *Raw Head, Bloody Bones* and knew that Scribner would publish it in 1991. I was also researching the life of Harriet Jacobs so that I could write *Letters from a Slave Girl: The Story of Harriet Jacobs.*

A class of learning-disabled children who visited the library each week loved hearing me read Julius Lester's *Tales of Uncle Remus* books aloud. I started writing an easy reader called *The Butter Tree: Tales of Bruh Rabbit* so that this class and other children could enjoy B'rer Rabbit stories on their own.

Finally, I wanted to research a series of ten books about artists and artisans. I learned about most of the artists from John Michael Vlach's 1979 book, *The Afro-American Tradition in Decorative Arts.* Their names were and still are famous in the field of folk art, but no one had written children's books about them. Once again, I saw a hole on the school library shelf that needed filling. But first I had to find out if young people liked the art. During that year as an elementary-school librarian, I shared slides of artwork with students while telling them about the artists.

One book published, three baking in the oven, and ten at the recipe stage—I was a very busy cook. The NEH Teacher Scholar award came just in time. It would give me a paid leave of absence for the upcoming 1991-92 school year so that I could devote myself to reading, writing, and study. Colleges call such a year a sabbatical, and they routinely schedule them for professors. For a public-school teacher, a paid sabbatical year is an almost-unheard-of opportunity.

I was thrilled. I had already turned every weekend and holiday into a reading marathon, but I still didn't have enough time. More than twenty years had passed since I tried to learn black history in college. With a year off from teaching, I could finally catch up with what I needed and longed to know.

So much to look forward to! What could possibly be upsetting about it? Before writing this paragraph, I've brewed a fresh pot of tea and thought over the answer.

Sometime during that year, my sister sent me a bottle cap. Teacup in hand, I've just gone to the closet and fetched it. A quote by British writer Oscar Wilde is printed on the inside. "Anybody can sympathize with the sufferings of a friend," he wrote, "but it requires a very fine nature to sympathize with a friend's success."

My sister was trying to comfort me, because the truth is, not everyone was pleased with the publication of *Sorrow's Kitchen* or the Teacher-Scholar award. My mother and husband were proud, of course, along with treasured friends and acquaintances. Elderly ladies brought flowers to me at school—not because they knew me, but because professional success had been off limits to them as young women. They wanted to make sure that I felt congratulated.

For some reason, the administrators and a few teachers in the Charlottesville school system were disturbed. It was okay for me to teach black literature and history in the classroom. It definitely wasn't okay for me to write a book about it. Around that time, I came across Rita Mae Brown's 1988 book, *Starting from Scratch: A Different Kind of Writers' Manual.* "Don't ever tell anyone you're a writer," she advises. "They'll think that you think you're better than they are."

I don't understand why some adults in the field of education are resentful of published writers. As nearly as I can tell, the same folks don't feel that way about musicians or painters. But it has proven true for me many times over. I don't always follow Brown's advice. Still, knowing that the same problem plagued her has heartened me through my writing years.

Letters from a Slave Girl and *Letters from a Slave Boy*

Children's book writers will tell you that correspondence from young readers is one of the best parts of the job. Most frequently, kids ask about my first historical novel, *Letters from a Slave Girl.*

Here's a quote from a typical letter: "When you wrote about Harriet and her feelings it seemed like you knew exactly what she felt and I was wondering if I could have a tip or two about learning how to do that without actually meeting the person."

Here's my answer: "Early one morning after I started writing the book, I sat quietly in my living room with a yellow legal pad. I listed the things Harriet and I had in common. She was from North Carolina, and I spent my later childhood years there. She had a younger brother, and so did I. She had a strict grandmother. My parents weren't terribly strict about boys, but it seemed that way when I was Harriet's age. If I had become pregnant as Harriet did, I would have had a hard time telling them.

"Most important, I remembered the job I had at a local department store when I was a sixteen year old. I was assigned to the Men's Department. The assistant man-ager was probably in his thirties, which seemed ancient. A lecherous fellow, he never whispered filthy words in my ear, as Doctor Norcom did to Harriet, but he made sly sexual comments meant to embarrass me. I felt ashamed, though that was silly. He was the one who should have been ashamed. And I never told my parents, just as Harriet didn't tell her grandmother about Doctor Norcom.

"The second thing that helped me understand Harriet was transcribing the real letters she wrote long after she grew up. It was a tough job, because they were on microfilm. I printed them out at the library and brought them home but couldn't read her scratchy writing. For days I sat with a tape recorder, painstakingly figuring out each sentence and speaking it into the microphone. It was like deciphering a secret code. I'd fill in four or five words, then use context clues to decode the rest of the sentence. By the time I finished, I felt as if Harriet's emotions had entered my brain in some magical way."

The letters in *Letters from a Slave Girl* are fictional and came from my head. I hope that after reading the novel, young people go on to read Harriet Jacobs's narrative, because she and her family are one of the most important in the history of slavery in our country.

Oddly, though, Harriet Jacobs hasn't become a household name. Most people recognize the name of her counterpart, Frederick Douglass. Like Jacobs, he was an escaped slave. The two knew each other in Rochester, New York, when Jacobs worked for a time on the second floor of the building where Douglass ran his *North Star* newspaper. Both were abolitionists, and both wrote about their enslavement. Yet most adults haven't heard of Jacobs.

That's why it pleases me that young readers know about her through *Letters from a Slave Girl.* Although the book was almost chosen for a major children's literature award in 1993, a few years later a member of the committee told me that it didn't win because of the sexual aspect of the story. Though my text is subtle, Norcom's sexual threats toward Jacobs made the committee members twitch. Naturally my first reaction was disappointment. Who doesn't want to win their book to win an award?!

My second reaction was horror. Like the assistant manager of my teen years, Norcom harassed Jacobs, not the other way around. Yet this slaveholder still controls Harriet Jacobs 150 years after throwing her down the steps of her grandmother's cottage. Why? Because we allow it. What *he* did was shameful, so we avoid *her.*

Joy Hakim, author of the popular "Story of Us" history textbook series for middle schoolers, spoke at the Virginia Festival of the Book in 1995. I asked her why she didn't include Harriet Jacobs in her series. "Because of the sex," she said.

The answer surprised me. There is nothing in Jacobs's narrative that we would call "sex." It's true that she described Norcom's threats and had two children by another white man, hoping to discourage Norcom. But her text is as modest as she was. We do Harriet Jacobs a great disservice if we believe that these events define her entire life.

To escape from Norcom, Jacobs hid under the eaves of her grandmother's roof for seven years so that she could remain near her children. The decision required emotional and physical courage that we can barely comprehend.

After she fled to the North, she risked public embarrassment to write a book that she hoped would help end slavery. During the U.S. Civil War, she taught freed slaves in Alexandria, Virginia, and Savannah, Georgia. After the war, she returned to her birthplace of Edenton, North Carolina, and helped elderly friends living in poverty. Why should we let two slaveholding men overshadow a woman who lived her entire life with integrity?

A few years back, a television special written by African Americans devoted a thirty-minute segment to Harriet Jacobs. Otherwise, she's almost invisible outside of college literature and history courses.

It isn't fair. That's one reason why I wrote *Letters from a Slave Boy: The Story of Joseph Jacobs.* I wanted to keep Harriet Jacobs's story alive, and I wanted to answer another frequent question from young readers: "Whatever happened to her son, Joseph?"

The format of *Letters from a Slave Boy* is the same as *Letters from a Slave Girl.* I created fictional letters inspired by real letters that Joseph wrote to his mother from the California and Australia gold fields. As far as I know, his letters are now lost, but the real Harriet mentioned them in her real letters.

I have high hopes for my books when I send them out into the world, the way that parents have hopes for children who leave the nest of home. The real Joseph Jacobs was a child of mixed racial heritage who passed for white at least twice in his life. More than two million mixed-race children now live in the United States. My hope is that reading about the fictional Joseph will help young readers who are frustrated when people rudely ask, "What are you?"

Artists and Artisans

I wrote *Letters from a Slave Girl* at the Virginia Center for the Humanities in Charlottesville. My little slanted-roof office was on the second floor of the building. It was private and quiet, but my childhood habit of making pretend worlds started working *too* well. I felt so cooped up in the small office that sometimes it seemed as if I were Harriet, hiding under a roof in a space the

size of two coffins. I had to get myself—and her—out of there! Maybe that's why I finished the first draft of the book in five short weeks.

Almost immediately I started research for the first title in my "African-American Artists and Artisans" series. I began with Horace Pippin. During World War I, Pippin was in the first African-American regiment to serve overseas. While fighting in France, he spent two days in a trench, wounded in the right shoulder and arm. Unable to move when a dead soldier fell on top of him, Pippin was finally rescued and taken to a field hospital. After the war, he taught himself to paint with his pain-free left hand.

Pippin's story and how he painted his life into his art fascinates students. I wrote about him in *Starting Home: The Story of Horace Pippin, Painter.* Young people are also delighted by the droll dogs and cats drawn by Bill Traylor, a street artist born enslaved on an Alabama plantation. Those same drawings appear in *Deep Blues: Bill Traylor, Self-Taught Artist.* When I show Clementine Hunter's painting of a child dangling upside down from a pecan tree, kids laugh out loud. That picture appears in *Talking with Tebé.* Children usually gasp at Minnie Evans's colorful drawings of her dreams. Ms. Evans's abstract designs disturb some adults, but young people see things in art that grownups can't, so I decided to write *Painting Dreams: Minnie Evans, Visionary Artist.*

Slides of artisans' work impress my young audiences most of all. *Master of Mahogany: Thomas Day, Free Black Cabinetmaker* is about a successful businessman working in North Carolina before the Civil War. *Stitching Stars: The Story Quilts of Harriet Powers* tells how an illiterate Georgia quilter wrote her favorite stories using cloth, needle, and thread instead of paper, pen, and ink. *Catching the Fire: Philip Simmons, Blacksmith* describes how a South Carolina blacksmith learned to beat wrought iron into intricate shapes.

People who write for children never know where their words will end up. Sometimes adults like the books as much as young readers but for different reasons. Three years ago I heard from a woman whose grandfather grew up with Minnie Evans in Wrightsville Beach, North Carolina. The woman was a lonely teenager when she first met Evans in 1968 and now had a grown son fighting in the Iraq war.

After reading *Painting Dreams,* she wrote me a thank-you letter. "I cried for my son in Fallujah [Iraq]," she said. "I cried for the years I missed my grandfather, but mostly I cried for Minnie. She was my rock that I went to with my troubles, never thinking she had any of her own. She was like my own fairy godmother, not with material things, but with a golden angel's heart."

Each title in the "African-American Artists and Artisans" series was a heap o' trouble. I stopped after seven books, knowing that I couldn't afford the expense of researching the last three. But when I hear from people who love the art and the artists, I'm glad that my efforts have made a difference. A royalty check from a publisher can help pay the mortgage; a letter from a reader pays the heart. Children's book writers need both.

Strong Bones

Research is like marrow. It builds the invisible bones that hold up every book I write. Before writing, I first read everything that other people have written on the subject. These printed books and articles are secondary sources of information. They tell me what others—usually scholars—think is true. Sometimes I agree with them. For instance, did Horace Pippin die after a lifetime of drinking alcohol to dull the pain in his shoulder? The evidence I found in secondary sources suggested that this was accurate.

Just as often, I find misleading evidence in a secondary source. While writing *Letters from a Slave Boy,* I read a biography of Harriet Jacobs. The author wrote that Harriet's son, Joseph, mined for gold on Muiron Island. This made no sense. Muiron Island is off the west coast of Australia, and the Australian gold rush took place on the eastern side of the continent.

Patrick Lyons, the author's grandfather, was born in Ireland in 1869
(Copyright © 2008 by Mary E. Lyons. Reproduced by permission.)

The author of the biography had found her information in one of Harriet Jacobs's letters, but I already knew that it's easy to misread nineteenth-century handwriting. I ordered a photocopy of the letter and read it myself. My husband also read it. He noticed that Harriet had written the words "Mormon Island," not Muiron Island. Mormon Island was a gold mining town in California. My husband's discovery changed the entire ending of *Letters from a Slave Boy.*

Harriet's letter is an example of what we call a primary source of information. The best historians depend on primary sources for proving facts. A primary source can be a photograph, letter, painting, scrapbook, cracked plate, tombstone, or even an old house. Any authentic piece of history is a primary source as long as you're looking at the original. A handwritten page from the United States' 1790 census is a primary source. A scan of that page on the Internet is a secondary source.

While compiling *Feed the Children First: Irish Memories of the Great Famine,* I found a 125-year-old family letter hiding in a box in my mother's apartment. A relative in Ireland wrote it after his son immigrated to America to escape those hungry times. The letter inspired me as I wrote the introduction to the book. I included a picture of it at the end, along with a photograph taken of my Irish grandfather around 1900.

Sometimes a primary source lights a fire that I can't put out until I write a book about it. This happened when I discovered that Moses Williams cut the two eighteenth-century silhouettes I had owned for years. Williams was the first professional African-American artist in the United States. He was also the enslaved assistant of Charles Willson Peale, founder of a museum in Philadelphia. My novel *The Poison Place* imagines how Moses freed himself from slavery and from Peale's tangled relationship with his own son.

Primary sources inspired Muriel Branch and me to collaborate on *Dear Ellen Bee: A Civil War Scrapbook of Two Union Spies.* This work of historical fiction is based on two real Southerners—one black, one white—who worked as spies in Richmond, Virginia. Muriel and I knew that the white woman, Elizabeth Van Lew, kept a scrapbook, but some of the pages had disappeared. Mary Elizabeth Bowser, her freed slave, may have kept one, too. It was probably thrown away. Van Lew also kept a diary. Much of it rotted when she buried it for safekeeping during the U.S. Civil War. We wanted to imagine what these missing primary sources might have revealed about the bossy "Miss Bet," as we called her, and "Liza," the let-me-think-for-myself child whom she freed.

Dear Ellen Bee is similar to real scrapbooks that girls kept during the Civil-War era. It's a combination of diary entries, letters to and from the main characters, and scrapbook ephemera such as newspaper clippings, broadsides, a train ticket, valentine, and bookmark. Muriel and I wrote some of the text with the same secret codes that Elizabeth Van Lew's spy ring actually used when sending information to Union generals during the war.

Travel can be the best primary source of all, so I make multiple trips when researching a book. *Knockabeg: A Famine Tale* took me to a village on the west coast of Ireland and archives at the University College, Dublin. In the archives, I read 1930s interviews that Irish sixth graders conducted with descendants of 1840s famine survivors.

While reading the interviews, I discovered that some nineteenth-century Irish thought of faeries in the same way that people now think of angels, and that faeries helped a few lucky families survive the famine. I wove those details into *Knockabeg,* which describes the Great Famine from the faeries' point of view.

The Poison Place took me twice to Philadelphia, Pennsylvania. That's where I saw the exact spot that Moses Williams cut silhouettes in Charles Willson Peale's museum of natural history (now Independence Hall). In Goshen, New York, I counted the number of steps that Horace Pippin walked to school when he was a boy. In Edenton, North Carolina, I climbed the same thirty-seven steps that Harriet Jacobs climbed when she slaved for James Norcom at his plantation house.

For *Letters from a Slave Boy,* I toured the school that the real Joseph Jacobs probably attended in Boston. A walk through Sutter's Mill in California let me imagine the rough-and-tumble poker game that my character of Joseph plays with a slave catcher. The book I'm writing now has led me three times to Norfolk, Virginia, and once to the Delmarva Peninsula.

Interviews that I conduct on research trips are a crucial primary source of information. I couldn't have written any of the books in the artists and artisans series without the help of others. Many people who knew Minnie Evans in Wilmington, North Carolina, shared their special memories with me, including her son and granddaughter. Philip Simmons met with me for hours at a time. He described his life as a child on a South Carolina sea island and his work as a blacksmith in Charleston.

Scholars and experts often read my work and make suggestions or discuss my subject with me. Professor John Michael Vlach shared his thoughts about Harriet Powers's quilts. Furniture curator Jonathan Prown answered my questions about Thomas Day's nineteenth-century furniture. Southern folk-art dealers were extremely helpful when I wrote *Deep Blues* and *Talking with Tebé.*

Almost all of the people I meet on research trips enrich my books and my life, though I seldom see any of them again. Black or white, northern or southern, wealthy or living in modest homes—it doesn't matter. People who are willing to help a children's book writer are people with big hearts.

Which Book Is My Favorite?, and Other Questions

I hear the question "Which book is your favorite?" often. It's hard to answer. Right now, three of my titles are favorites because they're the newest. I've heard through the grapevine that *Letters from a Slave Boy* is helping readers sort out their feelings about skin color. *Roy Makes a Car* is a picture book based on a folktale collected by Zora Neale Hurston. I've seen it bring smiles to the faces of people from ages three to sixty-three.

Writing *Ancient American World* with William Fash of Harvard University gave me a chance to learn more about the ancient civilizations that led up to the Maya, Aztec, and Inca cultures. Some new fact amazed me every day while writing the book.

Do you think that people of the Aztec empire invented chocolate? I did, and I sure was wrong. Do you think that everyone living south of the US border speaks Spanish? More than one million people in Mexico speak the ancient language of Nahuatl. Six million people in Central America speak one of thirty-nine Mayan dialects. Eight million Peruvians still speak the ancient language of Quechua.

When you hear the word "America" do you think of the United States? America means North America, including the United States and Canada. But it also means Mexico, Central America, and South America. Many cultures, many languages, many people: all living on two continents called the Americas.

Interview with Mary E. Lyons

What's the best thing about writing children's books? It seems weird, but I love coming up with an idea for a book, then dashing off a quick outline to see how I might organize the chapters. I also like revising. It's satisfying to untangle words and ideas until the text is just right. That doesn't last long. It never reads as well the next morning. Then I revise again.

What's the worst thing about writing children's books? Constant worry about how to pay expenses, including ever-rising health insurance premiums. Most people involved in children's books—editors, librarians, school teachers, professors of children's literature—receive a paycheck and some form of health insurance. The writers who make their jobs possible get neither. Instead, the publisher sends them royalty payments. This ranges from five to ten to twelve percent of the cover price of a book. I never know how much the royalty checks will be, and they only come twice a year.

The author researching a book in Ireland, 1999 (Copyright © 2008 by Mary E. Lyons. Reproduced by permission.)

Favorite hangout? Our step-down living room is on the back of the house and opens onto a patio. Beyond is a steep ravine and woods with 100-foot-tall oak trees. Writing on the patio is like writing in a tree house. In the winter, I'm inside, lolling on my chaise by a roaring fire.

Most overrated thing about children's books? Young-adult novels. I'm a hard reader to please, I guess, because I was reading adult novels by seventh grade. What I think doesn't matter, though, because I'm a grown-up. What young adults think of their books is much more important. That said, I suggest that young readers challenge themselves and try hard books, too. None of us ever get better at anything by always taking the easy road. If you want your brain to grow, move beyond series books, fantasy, science fiction, and sports. Try something completely different every now and then. Otherwise you'll turn into a reading vegetable.

People would be surprised to know. . .? I used to watch *The Young and the Restless* every day. This embarrassed me until Toni Morrison, a Nobel Prize winner for literature, admitted that she watched it. A soap opera was a great way for me to relax after hours of difficult writing. Also, my mother and I shared lots of laughs about the plot and characters. I gave up watching the show after she died in 2006.

Proudest accomplishment? Marrying my husband twenty-five years ago.

What would you change about yourself? I'd stop smoking. To do that, I'd have to stop writing. I can't write without cigarettes. Don't ever start smoking!

People find most annoying about you: Smoking. Also, arguing that tobacco isn't a fossil fuel. Gasoline is. A car produces one pound of particulate matter for every twenty-five miles it's driven. Smoking is terrible for your health, but it isn't causing catastrophic climate changes.

Whom do you admire? Nineteenth-century abolitionists such as William Chaplin and William Stills. They risked their lives to help enslaved people escape.

Favorite book? My favorite recent children's book is *A Single Shard* by Linda Sue Park. It's permanently on the reading list for the writing course I teach at the University of Virginia. At the moment, my favorite book for adults is *1491* by Charles C. Mann.

Subject that causes you to rant? The high percentage of male artists who receive the annual Caldecott Award and Honor awards for the best-illustrated children's books. The numbers have been rising steadily since 1990. I don't get it. Do men really create better art? Or do award committees unconsciously perceive that men create superior art? The November 11, 2007 edition of the *New York Times Book Review* is a perfect example. It lists the ten best illustrated books for the year. Eight of the illustrators are men. Two are women.

Biggest 21st-century thrill? iTunes.

Biggest 21st-century creep-out? The 2000 and 2004 U.S. presidential elections and electronic voting machines with no paper trail.

What do you drive? A 1998 Toyota Camry.

In your car CD player right now? Jazz by Stephane Grappelli, Ella Fitzgerald, John Coltrane, and Johnny Hartman. Rock by Neil Young and Sinead O'Connor.

Never-miss television shows? *American Experience* and *Masterpiece Theater.*

Next journey? Alexandria, Virginia, to take photographs for my upcoming book.

Most trouble you got into as a teen? Going to an unchaperoned mid-week slumber party in high school and cutting classes the next day. The hostess girl was sick, and her parents were out of town. I reasoned that the rest of us should stay home from school and take care of her. It was a noble thought, but the school counselor didn't believe me. Thankfully, my parents did.

Regret? Not traveling through Europe after I finished college.

Favorite comfort food? Potato dishes of any sort.

Always in your refrigerator? Lemons. I couldn't cook without them.

Favorite cartoon? Almost any cartoon in the *New Yorker* magazine.

Describe a perfect day? The setting would be a suite with a balcony at a beachfront hotel in late September. After reading a well-written book in the morning, I'd swim laps in the pool. Then I'd have a chocolate milkshake served poolside, followed by a walk on the beach with my husband. In the afternoon, I'd take a long soak with lavender bath salts in a huge tub. That evening, my husband and I would order a room service dinner and dance to "La Vie en Rose."

Favorite Fantasy? To be a boot-stomping singer like Emmy Lou Harris.

Who'd play you in a movie? British actress Dame Judy Dench.

Most embarrassing moment? Getting myself dressed in first grade and forgetting to put on underwear.

Best writing advice you ever got? Newbery Honor Award winner David Kherdian once told me that every book is the one you think you can't write. In other words, lack of confidence can be a good thing.

Favorite bumper sticker? "I haven't been the same since that house fell on my sister."

*   *   *

LYONS, Mary Evelyn
   See LYONS, Mary E.

M

MAASS, Robert

Personal

Male. *Hobbies and other interests:* Fishing.

Addresses

Home—Brooklyn, NY.

Career

Still photographer, writer, and documentary filmmaker. Freelance editorial photographer for clients, including *Newsweek* magazine and New York City Department of Environmental Protection. Films include *Gotham Fish Tales.*

Awards, Honors

Fort Meyers Beach Film Festival Award for Best Documentary, for *Gotham Fish Tales.*

Writings

AND PHOTOGRAPHER

Fire Fighters, Scholastic (New York, NY), 1989.
When Autumn Comes, Henry Holt (New York, NY), 1990.
When Summer Comes, Henry Holt (New York, NY), 1993.
When Winter Comes, Henry Holt (New York, NY), 1993.
When Spring Comes, Henry Holt (New York, NY), 1994.
UN Ambassador: A Behind-the-Scenes Look at Madeleine Albright's World, Walker & Co. (New York, NY), 1995.
Tugboats, Henry Holt (New York, NY), 1997.
Garden, Henry Holt (New York, NY), 1998.
Garbage, Henry Holt (New York, NY), 2000.
Little Trucks with Big Jobs, Henry Holt (New York, NY), 2007.

PHOTOGRAPHER

Maxine B. Rosenberg, *Mommy's in the Hospital Having a Baby,* Clarion (New York, NY), 1997.

Biographical and Critical Sources

PERIODICALS

Booklist, June 1, 1994, Deborah Abbott, review of *When Spring Comes,* p. 1827; November 15, 1995, Julie Corsaro, review of *UN Ambassador: A Behind-the-Scenes Look at Madeleine Albright's World,* p. 556; April 1, 1997, Stephanie Zvirin, review of *Mommy's in the Hospital Having a Baby,* p. 1336; June 1, 1998, Susan Dove Lempke, review of *Garden,* p. 1772; May 1, 2000, Carolyn Phelan, review of *Garbage,* p. 1674; August, 2007, Ilene Cooper, review of *Little Trucks with Big Jobs,* p. 78.
Horn Book, July-August, 1998, Ellen Fader, review of *Garden,* p. 515.
Kirkus Reviews, July 15, 2007, review of *Little Trucks with Big Jobs.*
Publishers Weekly, October 26, 1990, review of *When Autumn Comes,* p. 68.
School Library Journal, May, 2000, Kathy Piehl, review of *Garbage,* p. 163; August, 2007, Linda Ludke, review of *Little Trucks with Big Jobs,* p. 102.

ONLINE

Gotham Fish Tales Web site, http://www.tothamfishtales. com/ (November 28, 2008), "Robert Maass."*

*   *   *

MACDONALD, Guy

Personal

Born in England.

Addresses

Home—Kent, England.

Career

Writer.

Writings

(With Dominique Enright) *The Boys' Book: How to Be the Best at Everything* (expanded edition of *How to Be the Best at Everything*), illustrated by Niki Catlow, Buster Books (London, England), 2006, Scholastic (New York, NY), 2007.

Children's Miscellany, Volume 3, Buster Books (London, England), 2003, published as *Even More Children's Miscellany: Smart, Silly, and Strange Information That's Essential to Know,* Chronicle Books (San Francisco, CA), 2008.

My Brilliant Body: Everything You Ever Wanted to Know about Your Own Body, illustrated by Paul Cemmick, Barrons Educational (Hauppauge, NY), 2008.

Sidelights

One of Guy Macdonald's tasks as a freelance writer has been adapting British author Dominique Enright's popular childhood guidebook, *The Boys' Book: How to Be the Best at Everything,* for U.S. readers. A scan of the book's chapter titles tip off readers as to the wealth of instruction provided: everything from how to fight off crocodiles or survive a zombie attack to information on how to build a fire, read a compass, get rid of hiccups, and fool friends using only toothpicks. The coauthors' how-to advice, augmented by Niki Catlow's amusing art, range from "benign . . . to outrageous . . . to outrageously exaggerated," according to *School Library Journal* critic Baran Elaine Black in her review of Enright and Macdonald's book. In *Kirkus Reviews* a contributor deemed *The Boys' Book* "worth picking up for all those lads . . . eager to learn" the various intriguingly off-beat skills offered.

Together with its companion volume, *The Girls' Book: How to Be the Best at Everything, The Boys' Book* was ranked as "jokier and more kid friendly" than similar how-to books by Roger Sutton in *Horn Book.* As a sequel, Macdonald also teamed up with Catlow to produce *Even More Children's Miscellany: Smart, Silly, and Strange Information That's Essential to Know.* In this further installment in the "How to" series, Macdonald includes instructions as to how to talk like a pirate, as well as riddles, puzzles, and a host of useless but amazing facts about snakes, burps, and other boy magnets.

Biographical and Critical Sources

PERIODICALS

Horn Book, September-October, 2007, Roger Sutton, review of *The Boys' Book: How to Be the Best at Everything,* p. 596.

Kirkus Reviews, July 15, 2007, review of *The Boys' Book.*

School Library Journal, September, 2007, Elaine Baran Black, review of *The Boys' Book,* p. 216.

Voice of Youth Advocates, October, 2007, Pam Carlson, review of *The Boys' Book,* p. 363.*

*   *   *

MALAND, Nick

Personal

Born in England; married; children: Eloise, Aldo (son). *Education:* London University, B.A. (English and drama), 1981.

Addresses

Home—North London, England; France. *Agent*—Eunice McMullen Children's Literary Agent, Ltd., Low Ibbotsholme Cottage, Off Bridge La., Troutbeck Bridge, Windermere, Cumbria LA23 1HU, England.

Career

Illustrator. Formerly worked in London theatre as an actor and director; freelance commercial illustrator and editorial cartoonist.

Awards, Honors

Mother Goose Award shortlist, 1996, for *Welcome Night;* Children's Book Award, 1998, for *Brave Whale* by Alan Temperley; *Parenting* magazine award, 1997, for *Big Blue Whale* by Nicola Davies; Victoria & Albert Museum Illustration Award, 2003, for *You've Got Dragons* by Kathryn Cave; British Society of Illustrators Silver Medal, and Stockport Children's Book Award, both 2005, both for *Snip Snap!* by Mara Bergman; British Book Trust Early Years Award shortlist, 2007, for *Oliver Who Would Not Sleep!* by Bergman.

Illustrator

Richard Brown and Kate Ruttle, selectors, *Welcome Night* (poetry), Cambridge University Press (Cambridge, England), 1996.

Nicola Davies, *Big Blue Whale,* Candlewick Press (Cambridge, MA), 1997.

Tony Mitton, *The Seal Hunter,* Scholastic (London, England), 1998.

Berlie Doherty, *The Forsaken Mermen and Other Story Poems,* Hodder Children's (London, England), 1998.

Alan Temperley, *The Brave Whale,* Scholastic (London, England), 1999.

William Mayne, *Imogen and the Ark,* Hodder Children's (London, England), 1999.

Kathryn Cave, *The Boy Who Became an Eagle,* Dorling Kindersley (New York, NY), 2000.

Kathryn Cave, *You've Got Dragons,* Hodder Children's (London, England), 2002, Peachtree (Atlanta, GA), 2003.

Pauline Stewart, *Sunshine Showers and Four o'Clock,* Bodley Head (London, England), 2000.

Kathryn Cave, *The Brave Little Grork,* Hodder Children's (London, England), 2002.

Kathryn Cave, *Friends,* Hodder Children's (London, England), 2004, published as *That's What Friends Do,* Hyperion (New York, NY), 2004.

Mara Bergman, *Snip Snap! What's That?,* Greenwillow Books (New York, NY), 2005.

Angela McAllister, *A Place for Middle,* Hodder Children's (London, England), 2007.

Mij Kelly, *Giants,* Hodder Children's (London, England), 2007.

Pippa Goodhart, *Glog,* Walker Books (London, England), 2007.

Mara Bergman, *Oliver Who Would Not Sleep!,* Alfred A. Levine (New York, NY), 2007.

Mara Bergman, *Yum! Yum! What Fun!,* Greenwillow Books (New York, NY), 2009.

Contributor of cartoons to periodicals, including *Times Educational Supplement,* London *Times,* London *Observer, Guardian,* and *Independent.*

Adaptations

Big Blue Whale was adapted as an audio version by Random House, 2008.

Sidelights

After graduating from college in the early 1980s, British artist and illustrator Nick Maland embarked on a career in the dramatic arts, acting and directing for London's "fringe" theatre. Eventually, however, his interests turned to drawing, and he has since become well known for the editorial cartoons he creates for such major London newspapers as the *Times, Observer, Guardian,* and *Independent.* Maland is also well know to younger people as the illustrator of picture books by Kathryn Cave, Mara Bergman, and Nicole Davies, several of which have garnered praise from critics and recognition from juries for major awards. Maland lives with his family in London, where he also shares studio space with fellow children's book illustrator Sam Childs.

One of Maland's early works, *Big Blue Whale* by Davies, introduces young children to one of the biggest creatures to ever live on Earth, showing how magical the whale is. The illustrator's pen-and-ink and watercolor art, featuring ocean tones, has what *Horn Book* contributor Ellen Fader described as a "flowing quality" that pairs well with Davies' "brisk . . . storytelling." In his work for Cave's *You've Got Dragons,* a story that addresses and mollifies youngsters' worries, he creates "toothy but disarmingly tubby dragons" that a *Kirkus Review* critic asserted will entertain rather than frighten young children. In *Publishers Weekly* a reviewer described Maland's illustrations as "energetic," adding that they "demonstrate a wide array of perspectives and dashes of silliness." Calling the book "reassuring," GraceAnne A. DeCandido also enjoyed Maland's "cheerful" images, with their pastel tones and concluded that *You've Got Dragons* is "a great choice for the walking worried."

Maland earned a Silver Medal from England's prestigious Society of Illustrators for *Snip Snap! What's That?,* one of several picture-book collaborations with writer Bergman. Called an "offbeat fantasy" by *Booklist* contributor Carolyn Phelan, *Snip Snap!* follows a toothy alligator as it emerges from the sewer, strolls up a city street, enters an apartment building, and barges into the home of three startled children. As rendered by the artist, the story's "big, scaly intruder positively exudes toothy menace," according to a *Kirkus Reviews* writer, although a *Publishers Weekly* writer explained that "the goofy gothic mood" embodied in Maland's "etching-like pictures and melodramatic characterizations" is countered by the illustrator's use of warm-toned watercolor hues that "give . . . strong hint that the children are not on the menu." In depicting the ultimate victory experienced by the youngsters as they frighten the 'gator away, Maland's "expressive" ink-and-watercolor illustrations bring the story to life "with wit and style," Phelan added.

Together with *Snip Snap!, Oliver Who Would Not Sleep!* is one of the books featuring Maland's art that has been released in both the United Kingdom and the United States. Bolstered by what a *Kirkus Reviews* contributor described as "whimsically detailed watercolor and line illustrations," Bergman's text for the book describes the travails of young Oliver Donnington Rimington-Sneep, a boy whose battle to fall asleep in a room full of fun toys is captured in a sing-song rhyme. Reviewing Maland's artwork for *Oliver Who Would Not Sleep!,* Kara Schaff Dean wrote in *School Library Journal* that his "fanciful" images help make the book "an excellent selection for pajama storytimes."

Biographical and Critical Sources

PERIODICALS

Booklist, September 1, 1997, Ellen Mandel, review of *Big Blue Whale,* p. 128; October 15, 2003, GraceAnne A. DeCandido, review of *You've Got Dragons,* p. 416; March 1, 2005, Carolyn Phelan, review of *Snip Snap! What's That?,* p. 1201.

Horn Book, May-June, 1997, Ellen Fader, review of *Big Blue Whale,* p. 338.

Kirkus Reviews, August 15, 2003, review of *You've Got Dragons,* p. 1070; April 1, 2005, review of *Snip Snap!,* p. 413; August 1, 2007, review of *Oliver Who Would Not Sleep!*

Publishers Weekly, October 20, 2003, review of *You've Got Dragons,* p. 54; May 9, 2005, review of *Snip Snap!,* p. 68.

School Library Journal, December, 2003, Steven Engelfried, review of *You've Got Dragons,* p. 111; November, 2004, Martha Topol, review of *That's What Friends Do,* p. 94; June, 2005, Linda Ludke, review of *Snip Snap!,* p. 104; September, 2007, Kara Schaff Dean, review of *Oliver Who Would Not Sleep!,* p. 157.

ONLINE

Hodder Children's Web site, http://www.hodderchildrens. co.uk/ (December 15, 2008), "Nick Maland."*

* * *

MASON, Prue

Personal

Born in Australia; married to a pilot. *Education:* Earned CELTA (certificate in English-language teaching to adults). *Hobbies and other interests:* Flying, reading, gardening, walking.

Addresses

Home—Maleny, Queensland, Australia. *E-mail*—prue mason@bigpond.com.

Career

Writer and educator. Former flight attendant on a private airplane piloted by her husband; wrote for a children's publication in Dubai, United Arab Emirates, 1990-2001; owner of writers' retreat and guesthouse in Queensland, Australia. Science and technology editor for an Australian children's magazine published by Scholastic, beginning 1996. Also teaches English as a second language.

Awards, Honors

Queensland Premier's Literary Award, 2005, and Notable Social Studies Trade Book for Young People selection, National Council for the Social Studies/Children's Book Council, and Best Books of the Year selection, Bank Street College of Education, both 2007, all for *Camel Rider.*

Writings

Camel Rider (novel), Puffin (Camberwell, Victoria, Australia), 2004, Charlesbridge (Watertown, MA), 2007.

Contributor to an Australian magazine published by Pearson Education, beginning 1997.

Sidelights

Prue Mason is the author of *Camel Rider,* a young-adult novel based on the author's experiences living in Dubai, United Arab Emirates, during the 1990s. Born in Australia, Mason traveled the world as a flight attendant with her husband, a professional pilot. After moving to the Gulf region of the Middle East, Mason began working for a children's newspaper, writing columns about astronomy, astrology, and technology. She also penned

Prue Mason (Reproduced by permission.)

an advice column for Indian, Pakistani, and Arab teenagers. In a comment for the Charlesbridge publishers Web site, Mason observed: "After having lived and made friends with people from other nationalities, I know that no culture is better than another; we just do things differently."

The idea for *Camel Rider* came to Mason in a dream about a young boy lost in the desert. Shortly after that, she read a newspaper article describing the plight of camel jockeys—children who are enslaved and forced to race camels. "It was as if there were two different worlds living side by side," she remarked on the Charlesbridge Web site. "I began to wonder what would happen if these two worlds met each other." Her novel *Camel Rider* centers on Adam, a twelve-year-old Australia living in the fictional Middle-eastern city of Abudai. When war erupts and foreigners begin fleeing the city, Adam is separated from his neighbors and becomes stranded in the desert. There he finds Walid, a young camel rider who has been left for dead by his slave owners. As the boys fight for survival, they learn to overcome their differences. "The alternating first-person voices, set off typographically, reveal the depth of the boys' cultural differences and their growing ability to communicate," observed *School Library Journal* contributor Kathleen Isaacs. In the words of a *Kirkus Reviews* critic, *Camel Rider* will "open readers' eyes to a way of life they'll hardly believe actually exists."

Asked what message she hoped to impart in *Camel Rider,* Mason explained: "I hope readers realize that,

Cover of Mason's adventure-filled novel Camel Rider. (Jacket design by David Altheim, copyright © 2004 by Penguin Group (Australia). All rights reserved. Jacket photographs courtesy of Steven Wilkes and Philip Lee Harvey/Getty Images. Reproduced by permission of Penguin Books (Australia) and Getty Images.)

while there are differences in the way we think about things, deep down there is a common, shared humanity. If we can learn to respect the differences between us, then we might finally learn how we can all survive in this world. I know it's a bit of a heavy message but I can't help but think that these are desperate times and the messages can no longer be so subtle."

Biographical and Critical Sources

PERIODICALS

Booklist, September 1, 2007, Jennifer Mattson, review of *Camel Rider,* p. 113.

Kirkus Reviews, July 1, 2007, review of *Camel Rider.*

Publishers Weekly, June 25, 2007, review of *Camel Rider,* p. 60.

School Library Journal, July, 2007, Kathleen Isaacs, review of *Camel Rider,* p. 106.

ONLINE

Booked Out Speakers Agency Web site, http://www. bookedout.com.au/ (November 1, 2008), "Prue Mason."

Charlesbridge Web site, http://www.charlesbridge.com/ (November 1, 2008), essay by Mason.

Prue Mason Home Page, http://www.pruemason.com (November 1, 2008).

Writers.net, http://www.writers.net/ (November 1, 2008), "Prue Mason."*

*   *   *

McKINLEY, Robin 1952-

Personal

Born November 16, 1952, in Warren, OH; daughter of William (in the U.S. Navy and Merchant Marines) and Jeanne Carolyn (a teacher) McKinley; married Peter Dickinson (an author), January 3, 1992. *Education:* Attended Dickinson College, 1970-72; Bowdoin College, B.A. (summa cum laude), 1975. *Hobbies and other interests:* Gardening, horses, walking, travel, many kinds of music, and life as an expatriate and the English-American culture chasm.

Addresses

Home—Hampshire, England. *E-mail*—nuraddin@robin mckinley.com.

Career

Writer, 1975—. Ward & Paul (stenographic reporting firm), Washington, DC, editor and transcriber, 1972-73; Research Associates, Brunswick, ME, research assistant, 1976-77; bookstore clerk in Maine, 1978; teacher and counselor at private secondary school in Natick, MA, 1978-79; Little, Brown, Inc., Boston, MA, editorial assistant, 1979-81; barn manager on a horse farm, Holliston, MA, 1981-82; Books of Wonder, New York, NY, clerk, 1983; freelance reader, copy-and line-editor, general all-purpose publishing dogsbody, 1983-91.

Awards, Honors

Horn Book Honor Book designation, 1978, for *Beauty,* 1985, for *The Hero and the Crown,* 1988, for *The Outlaws of Sherwood,* and 1995, for *Knot in the Grain;* Best Books for the Teen Age citation, New York Public Library, 1980, 1981, and 1982, all for *Beauty;* Best Young-Adult Books citation, American Library Association (ALA), 1982, and Newbery Honor Book designation, ALA, 1983, both for *The Blue Sword;* Newbery Medal, and ALA Notable Book designation, both 1985, both for *The Hero and the Crown;* World Fantasy Award for best anthology, 1986, for *Imaginary Lands;* Best Books for the Teen Age citation and ALA Best Adult Book for the Teen Age designation, both 1994, both for

Deerskin; Mythopoeic Award for Adult Literature, 2003, for _Sunshine._ D.H.L., Bowdoin College, 1986, Wilson College, 1996.

Writings

FICTION

Beauty: A Retelling of the Story of Beauty and the Beast, Harper (New York, NY), 1978.

The Door in the Hedge (short stories), Greenwillow (New York, NY), 1981.

The Blue Sword, Greenwillow (New York, NY), 1982, reprinted, Ace Books (New York, NY), 2007.

The Hero and the Crown, Greenwillow (New York, NY), 1984, reprinted, Ace Books (New York, NY), 2007.

(Editor and contributor) _Imaginary Lands_ (short stories; includes "The Stone Fey"), Greenwillow (New York, NY), 1985.

The Outlaws of Sherwood, Greenwillow (New York, NY), 1988, reprinted, Firebird (New York, NY), 2002.

My Father Is in the Navy (picture book), illustrated by Martine Gourbault, Greenwillow (New York, NY), 1992.

Rowan (picture book), illustrated by Donna Ruff, Greenwillow (New York, NY), 1992.

Deerskin (adult fantasy), Putnam (New York, NY), 1993.

A Knot in the Grain and Other Stories, Greenwillow (New York, NY), 1994.

Rose Daughter, Greenwillow (New York, NY), 1997.

Stone Fey, illustrated by John Clapp, Harcourt (San Diego, CA), 1998.

Spindle's End, Putnam (New York, NY), 2000.

(With husband, Peter Dickinson) _Water: Tales of Elemental Spirits,_ Putnam (New York, NY), 2002.

Sunshine (adult novel), Berkeley Books (New York, NY), 2003.

Dragonhaven, Putnam (New York, NY), 2007.

Chalice, Putnam (New York, NY), 2008.

Contributor to anthologies, including _Elsewhere II,_ edited by Terri Windling and Mark Arnold, Ace Books, 1982; _Elsewhere III,_ edited by Windling and Arnold, Ace Books, 1984; and _Faery,_ edited by Windling, Ace Books, 1985. Also contributor of book reviews to numerous periodicals. Author of column, "In the Country," for _New England Monthly,_ 1987-88.

ADAPTER

Rudyard Kipling, _Tales from the Jungle Book,_ Random House (New York, NY), 1985.

Anna Sewell, _Black Beauty,_ illustrated by Susan Jeffers, Random House (New York, NY), 1986.

George MacDonald, _The Light Princess,_ illustrated by Katie Thamer Treherne, Harcourt (San Diego, CA), 1988.

Adaptations

Random House recorded _The Blue Sword_ (1994), and _The Hero and the Crown_ (1986) on audiocassette.

Sidelights

Robin McKinley is the award-winning author of novels, short stories, and picture books that mine the world of fantasy and fairy tales. Her renditions of classic fairy tales have a feminist twist; no weak-kneed damsels in distress, McKinley's protagonists are females who do things rather than "waiting limply to be rescued by the hero," as the author explained on her home page. McKinley's self-sufficient heroines "are intelligent, loyal, and courageous—eager and not afraid to cross the physical and psychological barriers that lie between them and the fulfillment of their destinies," according to Hilary S. Crew in _Twentieth-Century Children's Writers._ In novels such as _Beauty: A Retelling of the Story of Beauty and the Beast, The Blue Sword, The Hero and the Crown, Rose Daughter, Spindle's End,_ and _Chalice,_ she fills her fantasy realms with realistic detail and powerful characters, attracting readers both young and old. McKinley has also collaborated with writer husband Peter Dickinson on the story collection _Water:_

Cover of Robin McKinley's fantasy novel **The Blue Sword,** _featuring an illustration by Kirk Reinert._ (Ace Books, 1987. Copyright © 1982 by Robin McKinley. All rights reserved. Reproduced by permission of Penguin Putnam, Inc.)

Tales of Elemental Spirits, which John Peters explained in *School Library Journal* features six "masterfully written stories" that, with their "distinct, richly detailed casts and settings," will "excite, enthrall, and move even the pickiest readers."

Although she now makes her home in the United Kingdom, McKinley was born in the United States and "grew up a military brat and an only child [who] decided early on that books were much more reliable friends than people," as she wrote on her home page. Moving every two years, from California to Japan to New York, she found comfort in fictional worlds. "Writing has always been the other side of reading for me," McKinley further commented. "It never occurred to me not to make up stories." However, as a young girl, she also had identity issues. "I despised myself for being a girl," she once told *SATA,* "and ipso facto being someone who stayed at home and was boring, and started trying to tell myself stories about girls who did things and had adventures."

"Once I got old enough to realize that authorship existed as a thing one might aspire to, I knew it was for me," McKinley recalled on her home page. "I even majored in English literature in college, a good indication of my fine bold disdain for anything so trivial as earning a living." She saw herself as a writer in the J.R.R. Tolkien or H. Rider Haggard vein, but unlike those authors, she was "going to tell breathtaking stories about *girls* who had adventures." McKinley's first publication, written only a few years after her graduation from Bowdoin, was inspired by viewing a television adaptation of "Beauty and the Beast." She was so disappointed with what she saw that she began to write a version of the classic fairy tale herself.

Beauty won praise from readers and critics alike. According to Michael Malone in the *New York Times Book Review,* the novel is "much admired not only for its feminism but for the density of detail in the retelling." "It's simply a filling out of the story, with a few alterations," wrote a *Kirkus Reviews* critic. Beauty—or Honour, as the heroine in McKinley's version is named—is an awkward child, not a beauty, and her "evil sisters" are caring and kind. Critics have also praised McKinley's handling of fantasy in the medieval setting. "The aura of magic around the Beast and his household comes surprisingly to life," commented a *Choice* critic. The winner of several literary awards, *Beauty* instantly established McKinley as a powerful new voice in young-adult literature and it has remained one of the author's most-popular novels.

Years after publishing *Beauty,* McKinley returns to the fairy tale that novel was based on in *Rose Daughter.* Over 300 pages in length, *Rose Daughter* has "a more mystical, darker edge," according to Estes. In the novel, readers learn about the early family life and personalities of the three sisters: the acerbic Jeweltongue; Lionheart, a physically daring girl; and the title character,

Cover of McKinley's novel **Rose Daughter.** (The Berkley Publishing Group, 1977. Reproduced by permission of The Berkley Publishing Group, a division of Penguin Putnam Books for Young Readers and Getty Images.)

Beauty. Unlike the original tale of "Beauty and the Beast," the relationship between the three sisters is loving rather than hostile. Although the girls have been raised in the city by their wealthy and widowed father, when he loses his business they relocate to a rural cottage where new hardships bring the family closer together.

One central element of *Rose Daughter* is the flower of the title: at the sisters' new country home roses are extremely difficult to cultivate. Beauty discovers, while working in her garden, that she possesses a skill for raising the beautiful flower. She also finds herself plagued by disturbing dreams of a dark corridor, a memory of her mother, and the heavy scent of roses. The Beast in this novel is a legendary local figure, a tragic hero who is half man. When Beauty journeys to his castle and begins tending the magic roses in his garden, other flora and fauna return to the Beast's former wasteland. A romance develops between the two, and Beauty's tenderness toward the Beast eventually unlocks the curse that has beset him. "As before, McKinley takes the essentials of the traditional tale and embellishes them with vivid and quirky particulars," declared a contributor for *Publishers Weekly*. Jennifer Fakolt, reviewing *Rose Daughter* for *Voice of Youth Advocates*, asserted that the author "has captured the timelessness of the traditional tale and breathed into it passion and new life appropriate to the story's own 'universal themes' of love and regeneration," while a *Publishers Weekly* reviewer concluded that McKinley's "heady mix of fairy tale, magic and romance has the power to exhilarate."

Prior to writing *Beauty*, McKinley had begun work on several stories set in a fictional world she has named Damar. As she once explained to *SATA*, "I had begun . . . to realize that there was more than one story to tell about Damar, that in fact it seemed to be a whole history, volumes and volumes of the stuff, and this terrified me. I had plots and characters multiplying like mice and running in all directions." The first "Damar" book to appear was her story collection *The Door in the Hedge*, which was published in the late 1970s. *The Blue Sword*, a novel published in 1982. The hero in this second "Damar" book is Harry Crewe, a young woman who must forge her identity and battle an evil force at the same time. After Harry is kidnapped, she learns from her kidnappers how to ride a horse and battle as a true warrior. While she struggles in the tradition of the legendary female hero of Damar, Aerin, the teen becomes a hero in her own right.

Although *The Blue Door* is set in a fantasy world—Damar was characterized as "pseudo-Victorian" by Darrell Schweitzer in *Science Fiction Review*—critics have found Harry to be a heroine contemporary readers may well understand. Like *Beauty*, *The Blue Sword* earned McKinley both recognition and praise. It also earned a Newbery Honor Book designation. In *Booklist* Sally Estes described the novel as "a zesty, romantic heroic fantasy with . . . a grounding in reality that enhances the tale's verve as a fantasy."

In *The Hero and the Crown*, the next "Damar" novel, readers are taken back in time to learn the story of Aerin, the legendary warrior woman Harry so reveres. As McKinley once explained to *SATA*, "I recognized that there were specific connections between Harry and Aerin, and I deliberately wrote their stories in reverse chronological order because one of the things I'm fooling around with is the idea of heroes: real heroes as opposed to the legends that are told of them afterwards. Aerin is one of her country's greatest heroes, and by the time Harry comes along, Harry is expected—or Harry thinks she is—to live up to her. When you go back and find out about Aerin in *The Hero and the Crown*, you discover that she wasn't this mighty invincible figure. . . . She had a very hard and solitary time [because] of her early fate."

When readers first meet Aerin in *The Hero and the Crown*, she is graceless and clumsy; it takes her a long time to turn herself into a true warrior, and she suffers many traumas in the process. Yet she is also clever and

courageous, bravely battling and killing the dragons that are threatening Damar. Merri Rosenberg asserted in the *New York Times Book Review* that in *The Hero and the Crown* McKinley "created an utterly engrossing fantasy, replete with a fairly mature romantic subplot as well as adventure." According to *Horn Book* contributor Mary M. Burns, *The Hero and the Crown* is "as richly detailed and elegant as a medieval tapestry. . . . Vibrant, witty, compelling, the story is the stuff of which true dreams are made." Writing in the *New Statesman*, Gillian Wilce cited the novel's "completeness, [and] its engaging imagination," while *Wilson Library Bulletin* contributor Frances Bradburn called McKinley's novel a "marvelous tale of excitement and female ingenuity."

Upon winning the coveted Newbery Medal in 1985 for *The Hero and the Crown*, McKinley shared her feelings with *SATA*: "The Newbery award is supposed to be the peak of your career as a writer for children or young adults. I was rather young to receive it; and it is a little disconcerting to feel—okay, you've done it; that's it, you should retire now." Far from retiring, however, McKinley has continued to write retellings of traditional favorites as well as original novels and stories. She has returned, on occasion to Damar, as she does in *A Knot in the Grain and Other Stories*. The tales in this collection, according to *Bulletin of the Center for Children's Books* critic Betsy Hearne, bear "McKinley's signature blend of the magical and the mundane in the shape of heroines" who triumph and find love despite the obstacles they face. They also demonstrate McKinley's "remarkable ability to evoke wonder and belief," asserted *Horn Book* contributor Ann A. Flowers. A reviewer for *Publishers Weekly* called *A Knot in the Grain* a "thrilling, satisfying and thought-provoking collection."

Also set in the world of Damar, McKinley's short story "The Stone Fey" first appeared in *Imaginary Lands* and was republished as an illustrated book with artwork by John Clapp. In the story Maddy, a shepherdess, falls in love with a Stone Fey, a fairy with skin the color of stone. Entranced by her new love, Maddy drifts away from the people and things she loves until she realizes that the fey can not return her love. A contributor for *Publishers Weekly* noted that, "while staying true to her penchant for presenting strong female protagonists, . . . McKinley strikes a softer note with this deeply romantic yet ultimately clear-eyed love story." In *Booklist* Carolyn Phelan deemed *The Stone Fey* a "haunting story," and Virginia Golodetz described McKinley's writing in *School Library Journal* as "passionate."

The Outlaws of Sherwood exhibits McKinley's talent for revising and reviving traditional tales. Instead of concentrating on Robin Hood—or glorifying him—this novel focuses on other members in Robin's band of outlaws and provides carefully wrought details about their daily lives: how they get dirty and sick, and how they manage their outlaw affairs. Robin is not portrayed as the bold, handsome marksman and sword handler readers may remember from traditional versions of the "Robin Hood" story. Instead, he is nervous, a poor shot, and even reluctant to form his band of merry men. Not surprisingly, McKinley's merry men include merry *women* among their number. "The young women are allowed to be angry, frankly sexual, self willed—and even to outshoot the men, who don't seem to mind," observed *Washington Post Book World* reviewer Michele Landsberg in discussing the author's alteration of the well-known story. In another characteristic revisioning by McKinley, Maid Marian stands out as a brilliant, beautiful leader and an amazingly talented archer. *The Outlaws of Sherwood* is "romantic and absorbing . . . [and] the perfect adolescent daydream where happiness is found in being young and among friends," concluded Shirley Wilton in her review of the book for *Voice of Youth Advocates*.

The adult novel *Deerskin* also demonstrates McKinley's talent for creating new tales out of the foundations of old ones. As Hearne noted, *Deerskin* presents a "darker

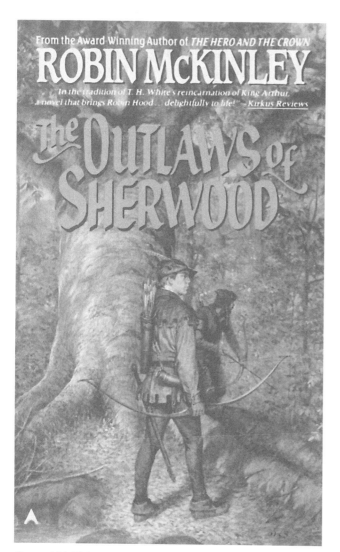

Cover of McKinley's novel **The Outlaws of Sherwood,** *featuring artwork by Darrell Sweet.* (Ace Books, 1989. Copyright © 1988 by Robin McKinley. All rights reserved. Reproduced by permission of Penguin Putnam, Inc.)

side of fairy tales." Based on Perrault's "Donkeyskin," a story in which a king assaults his own daughter after his queen dies, the novel relates how a beautiful princess is raped by her father after the death of her mother. This "is also a dog story," Hearne reminded readers: Princess Lissar survives the brutal attack and heals emotionally because of her relationship with her dog, Ash. "Written with deep passion and power, *Deerskin* is an almost unbearably intense portrait of a severely damaged young woman. . . . There is also romance, humor, and sheer delight," commented Christy Tyson in *Voice of Youth Advocates*. In *School Library Journal*, Cathy Chauvette deemed the book "a riveting and relentless fairy tale, told in ravishing prose." Another novel with adult themes, McKinley's vampire novel *Sunshine* was awarded the Mythopoeic Fantasy Award for Adult Literature in 2003.

With *Spindle's End,* McKinley once again revamps a fairy tale for modern readers. Using "Sleeping Beauty" as a template, she creates a "novel of complex imagery and characters," according to a critic for *Family Life*. In this tale the infant princess Briar Rose is cursed on her name day by the evil fairy, Pernicia. Then—as in the original—she is taken away to a remote and magical land to be raised, her real identity concealed, in an attempt to escape the fairy's wrath. In McKinley's take, the good fairy Katriona takes the young princess away to her village of Foggy Bottom, renames her Rosie, and raises the girl while awaiting the ill-fated twenty-first birthday, when Briar Rose will supposedly prick her finger on a spinning-wheel spindle and fall into an eternal sleep. In order to confound Pernicia, Rosie and her friend Peony trade places at on the prophesied birthday. Rosie's kiss awakens the sleeping Peony, who in turn marries the prince, leaving Rosie free to continue the simple life she loves and to marry the village blacksmith.

Writing in *School Library Journal*, Connie Tyrrell Burns felt that in *Spindle's End* "McKinley once again lends a fresh perspective to a classic fairy tale, developing the story of 'Sleeping Beauty' into a richly imagined, vividly depicted novel." In *Booklist* Estes noted that McKinley's reinterpretation of the old fairy tale "takes readers into a credibly developed world." "Full of humor and romance as well as magic and adventure, and with an ending that has a decided twist," Estes concluded, the "spellbinding novel is bound to attract McKinley's fans and those who relish the genre." A critic for *Publishers Weekly* called *Spindle's End* a "luscious, lengthy novel" that is "dense with magical detail and all-too-human feeling."

"Elegant prose and lyrical descriptions capture reader interest while an increasingly tense plot maintains it," wrote a *Kirkus Reviews* contributor in a review of McKinley's novel *Chalice*. In this original fantasy, the author spins a story that focuses on a young woman named

Mirasol. Serving the Master of Willowlands as a Chalice, or servant, Mirasol is also a beekeeper. However, her task now is a pressing one: to mend her damaged world by finding a way to bind her master—a Prince of Fire who causes everything he touches to burn—to the fragile land that is now wracked by earthquakes and other destruction. Noting that Mirasol is a characteristic McKinley heroine "who discovers her impressive powers as she finds her way," *Booklist* critic Lynn Rutan praised the novel's evocative narration as "a sensory delight." In *Publishers Weekly* an equally impressed reviewer characterized *Chalice* as a "high fantasy as perfectly shaped and eloquently told" as McKinley's best-known novels, the critic concluding that the romantic tale will be greeted as "a lavish and lasting treat" by the author's many fans. "Teens who long for beautiful phrases and descriptive writing will find themselves drinking in this rich fairy tale as if it were honey," predicted Heather M. Campbell in her review of *Chalice* for *School Library Journal.*

Booklist contributor Jennifer Mattson characterized McKinley's novel *Dragonhaven* as something of "a curveball" for the author's fans due to its modern-day setting. However, readers soon discover what Mattson dubbed "a distinctly fantastical aspect" to the Wyoming nature preserve where fifteen-year-old protagonist Jake lives with his naturalist father. Jake is studying *Draca Australiensis*, the last remaining species of dragon on Earth. When he secretly raises a young dragon whose mother has been killed by poachers, Jake challenges prevailing theories about how humans and dragons have coevolved and also gains an intimate knowledge of the gigantic fire-breathing creatures. In *Dragonhaven* "McKinley renders her imagined universe . . . potently," wrote a *Publishers Weekly* reviewer, the critic adding that the "tightly wound and solitary Jake" is a "classic McKinley" protagonist. According to a *Kirkus Reviews* writer, the novel treats readers to a "sharply incisive, wildly intelligent dragon fantasy involving profound layers of science and society, love and loss and nature and nurture." In *Kliatt* Paula Rohrlick wrote that McKinley's "engrossing fantasy is suspenseful and highly detailed," and Jake's "self-deprecating sense of humor helps make [*Dragonhaven*] . . . a truly wonderful read."

In addition to novel-length fiction, McKinley has also written original picture books for children. *Rowan* is a story about a girl selecting and loving a pet dog, while *My Father Is in the Navy* portrays a young girl whose father has been away for some time: as he is about to return, she tries to remember what her father looks like. Reviewing *Rowan*, a contributor for *Publishers Weekly* deemed it an "affable tale of a girl and her pet," while in *School Library Journal* JoAnn Rees called *My Father Is in the Navy* a "warm, loving look at a family group." Other books by McKinley that are geared for younger readers include short retellings of childhood classics like Anna Sewell's *Black Beauty*, George Mac-

Donald's *The Light Princess*, and Rudyard Kipling's *The Jungle Book.*

"As a compulsive reader myself, I believe that you are what you read . . . ," McKinley once told *SATA*. "My books are also about hope—I hope. Much of modern literature has given up hope and deals with anti-heroes and despair. It seems to me that human beings by their very natures need heroes, real heroes, and are happier with them. I see no point in talking about how life is over and it never mattered anyway. I don't believe it."

Biographical and Critical Sources

BOOKS

Authors and Artists for Young Adults, Gale (Detroit, MI), Volume 4, 1990, Volume 33, 2000.

Children's Literature Review, Volume 10, Gale (Detroit, MI), 1986.

Dictionary of Literary Biography, Volume 52: *American Writers for Children since 1960: Fiction,* Gale (Detroit, MI), 1986, pp. 262-266.

St. James Guide to Fantasy Writers, St. James Press (Detroit, MI), 1996.

St. James Guide to Young-Adult Writers, 2nd edition, St. James Press (Detroit, MI), 1999.

PERIODICALS

Booklist, October 1, 1982, Sally Estes, review of *The Blue Sword,* p. 198; August, 1994, Frances Bradburn, review of *A Knot in the Grain and Other Stories,* p. 2039; August, 1997, Sally Estes, review of *Rose Daughter,* p. 1898; November 1, 1998, Carolyn Phelan, review of *The Stone Fey,* p. 484; April, 15, 2000, Sally Estes, review of *Spindle's End,* p. 1543; April 15, 2002, Sally Estes, review of *Water: Tales of Elemental Spirits,* p. 1416; October 15, 2003, Kristine Huntley, review of *Sunshine,* p. 399; October 1, 2007, Jennifer Mattson, review of *Dragonhaven,* p. 44.

Bulletin of the Center for Children's Books, September, 1993, Betsy Hearne, review of *Deerskin,* p. 16; June, 1994, Betsy Hearne, review of *A Knot in the Grain and Other Stories,* p. 327.

Choice, July and August, 1979, review of *Beauty: A Retelling of the Story of Beauty and the Beast,* p. 668.

Family Life, December 1, 2000, review of *Spindle's End,* p. 127.

Horn Book, January-February, 1985, Mary M. Burns, review of *The Hero and the Crown,* pp. 59-60; July-August, 1985, Robin McKinley, "Newbery Medal Acceptance," pp. 395-405; July-August, 1985, Terri Windling, and Mark Alan Arnold, "Robin McKinley," pp. 406-409; July-August, 1994, Ann A. Flowers, review of *A Knot in the Grain and Other Stories,* pp.

458-459; September-October, 1997, Lauren Adams, review of *Rose Daughter,* pp. 574-575; May-June, 2000, Anita L. Burkam, review of *Spindle's End,* p. 317; July-August, 2002, Anita L. Burkham, review of *Water,* p. 466; September-October, 2007, Deirdre F. Baker, review of *Dragonhaven,* p. 581.

Kirkus Reviews, December 1, 1978, review of *Beauty,* p. 1307; June 1, 2002, review of *Water,* p. 808; August 15, 2003, review of *Sunshine,* p. 1039; August 1, 2007, review of *Dragonhaven;* August 15, 2008, review of *Chalice.*

Kliatt, May, 2005, Donna Scanlon, review of *Sunshine,* p. 34; September, 2007, Paula Rohrlick, review of *Dragonhaven,* p. 15.

New Statesman, November 8, 1985, Gillian Wilce, review of *The Hero and the Crown,* p. 28.

New York Times Book Review, January 27, 1985, Merri Rosenberg, review of *The Hero and the Crown,* p. 29; November 13, 1988, Michael Malone, review of *The Outlaws of Sherwood,* p. 54; January 18, 1998, Kathryn Harrison, review of *Rose Daughter,* p. 18; May 14, 2000, Elizabeth Devereaux, review of *Spindle's End,* p. 27.

Publishers Weekly, April 25, 1994, review of *A Knot in the Grain and Other Stories,* p. 80; June 16, 1997, review of *Rose Daughter,* p. 60; August 31, 1998, review of *The Stone Fey,* p. 77; March 27, 2000, review of *Spindle's End,* p. 82; September 2, 2002, review of *Water,* p. 77; September 29, 2003, review of *Sunshine,* p. 47, and Mitzi Brunsdale, interview with McKinley, p. 48; August 20, 2007, review of *Dragonhaven,* p. 69; July 21, 2008, review of *Chalice.*

School Library Journal, January, 1983, Karen Stang Hanley, review of *The Blue Sword,* p. 86; December, 1986, p. 108; May, 1992, JoAnn Rees, review of *My Father Is in the Navy,* p. 91; September, 1993, Cathy Chauvette, review of *Deerskin,* p. 261; September, 1997, Julie Cummins, review of *Rose Daughter,* pp. 219-220; January, 1999, Virginia Golodetz, review of *The Stone Fey,* p. 130; June, 2000, Connie Tyrrell Burns, review of *Spindle's End,* p. 150; June, 2002, John Peters, review of *Water,* p. 142; December, 2004, Beth Wright, "Once upon a Time: A Librarian Looks at Recent Young-Adult Novels Based on Fairy Tales," p. 40; September, 2007, Beth Wright, review of *Dragonhaven,* p. 203; October, 2008, Heather M. Campbell, review of *Chalice,* p. 154.

Science Fiction Review, August, 1983, Darrell Schweitzer, review of *The Blue Sword,* p. 46.

Voice of Youth Advocates, April, 1989, Shirley Wilton, review of *The Outlaws of Sherwood,* p. 44; August, 1993, Christy Tyson, review of *Deerskin,* p. 168.

Washington Post Book World, November 6, 1988, Michele Landsberg, review of *The Outlaws of Sherwood,* p. 15.

Wilson Library Bulletin, January, 1987, Frances Bradburn, review of *The Hero and the Crown,* p. 60.

ONLINE

Robin McKinley Home Page, http://www.robinmckinley. com (December 15, 2008).*

McKISSACK, Patricia C. 1944-
(L'Ann Carwell)

Personal

Born August 9, 1944, in Nashville, TN; daughter of Robert (a civil servant) and Erma (a civil servant) Carwell; married Fredrick L. McKissack (a writer and editor), December 12, 1964; children: Fredrick Lemuel Jr., Robert and John (twins). *Education:* Tennessee Agricultural and Industrial State University (now Tennessee State University), B.A., 1964; Webster University, M.A., 1975. *Politics:* "Independent." *Religion:* Methodist. *Hobbies and other interests:* Gardening.

Addresses

Home—Chesterfield, MO. *Office*—All-Writing Services, 225 S. Meramec, No. 206, Clayton, MO 63115.

Career

Junior high school English teacher in Kirkwood, MO, 1968-75; Forest Park College, St. Louis, MO, part-time instructor in English, beginning 1975. Children's book editor at Concordia Publishing House, 1976-81, and Institute of Children's Literature, beginning 1984; University of Missouri—St. Louis, instructor, beginning 1978; co-owner with Fredrick L. McKissack of All-Writing Services, 1981—. Educational consultant on minority literature.

Member

Society of Children's Book Writers and Illustrators, Children's Book and Literacy Alliance (member of board of directors).

Awards, Honors

Helen Keating Ott Award, National Church and Synagogue Librarians Association, 1980, for editorial work at Concordia Publishing House; C.S. Lewis Silver Medal awards, Christian Educators Association, 1984, for *It's the Truth, Christopher* and 1985, for *Abram, Abram, Where Are We Going?;* Caldecott Honor Award, 1989, for illustrations by Jerry Pinkney for *Mirandy and Brother Wind;* Parents' Choice Award, 1989, for *Nettie Jo's Friends;* Jane Addams Children's Book Award, Women's International League for Peace and Freedom, and Coretta Scott King Award, both 1990, both for *A Long Hard Journey;* Woodson Merit award, 1991, for *W.E.B. DuBois;* Hungry Mind Award, 1993, for *The World in 1492;* Newbery Honor Award and Coretta Scott King Author Award, both 1993, both for *The Dark-Thirty;* Coretta Scott King Honor Award and *Boston Globe/Horn Book* Award, both 1993, both for *Sojourner Truth;* Coretta Scott King Award, 1995, for *Christmas in the Big House, Christmas in the Quarters;* Coretta Scott King Honor Book designation, 1995, for *Black Diamond,* 1997, for *Rebels against Slavery,* 2000, for *Black Hands, White Sails,* 2004, for *Days of Jubi-*

lee; Image Award for Outstanding Literary Work for Children, National Association for the Advancement of Colored People, 1999, for *Let My People Go;* Virginia Hamilton Literary Award established at Kent State University's Virginia Hamilton Conference, 2001; Notable Children's Book selection, ALA, 2007, both for *Porch Lies* and *The All-I'll-Ever-Want Christmas Doll.*

Writings

FOR CHILDREN

(Under name L'Ann Carwell) *Good Shepherd Prayer,* Concordia (St. Louis, MO), 1978.

(Under name L'Ann Carwell) *God Gives New Life,* Concordia (St. Louis, MO), 1979.

Ask the Kids, Concordia (St. Louis, MO), 1979.

Who Is Who?, Children's Press (Chicago, IL), 1983.

Martin Luther King, Jr.: A Man to Remember, Children's Press (Chicago, IL), 1984.

Paul Laurence Dunbar: A Poet to Remember, Children's Press (Chicago, IL), 1984.

Michael Jackson, Superstar, Children's Press (Chicago, IL), 1984.

Lights out, Christopher, illustrated by Bartholomew, Augsburg (Minneapolis, MN), 1984.

It's the Truth, Christopher, illustrated by Bartholomew, Augsburg (Minneapolis, MN), 1984.

The Apache, Children's Press (Chicago, IL), 1984.

Mary McLeod Bethune: A Great American Educator, Children's Press (Chicago, IL), 1985.

Aztec Indians, Children's Press (Chicago, IL), 1985.

The Inca, Children's Press (Chicago, IL), 1985.

The Maya, Children's Press (Chicago, IL), 1985.

Flossie and the Fox, illustrated by Rachel Isadora, Dial (New York, NY), 1986.

Our Martin Luther King Book, illustrated by Rachel Isadora, Child's World (Elgin, IL), 1986.

Who Is Coming?, illustrated by Clovis Martin, Children's Press (Chicago, IL), 1986.

Give It with Love, Christopher: Christopher Learns about Gifts and Giving, illustrated by Bartholomew, Augsburg (Minneapolis, MN), 1988.

Speak up, Christopher: Christopher Learns the Difference between Right and Wrong, illustrated by Bartholomew, Augsburg (Minneapolis, MN), 1988.

A Troll in a Hole, Millikin (St. Louis, MO), 1988.

Nettie Jo's Friends, illustrated by Scott Cook, Knopf (New York, NY), 1988.

Mirandy and Brother Wind, illustrated by Jerry Pinkney, Knopf (New York, NY), 1988.

Monkey-Monkey's Trick: Based on an African Folk-Tale, illustrated by Paul Meisel, Random House (New York, NY), 1989.

Jesse Jackson: A Biography, Scholastic (New York, NY), 1989.

(With Ruthilde Kronberg) *A Piece of the Wind and Other Stories to Tell,* Harper (New York, NY), 1990.

No Need for Alarm, Millikin (St. Louis, MO), 1990.

A Million Fish—More or Less, illustrated by Dena Schutzer, Knopf (New York, NY), 1992.

The Dark-Thirty: Southern Tales of the Supernatural, illustrated by Brian Pinkney, Knopf (New York, NY), 1992.

History of Haiti, Holt (New York, NY), 1996.

(With Robert L. Duyff) *All Our Fruits and Vegetables,* Many Hands Media (New York, NY), 1996.

(With Robert L. Duyff) *It's a Sandwich!,* Many Hands Media (New York, NY), 1996.

A Picture of Freedom: The Diary of Clotee, a Slave Girl, Scholastic (New York, NY), 1997.

Ma Dear's Aprons, illustrated by Floyd Cooper, Atheneum (New York, NY), 1997.

Run away Home, Scholastic (New York, NY), 1997.

Color Me Dark: The Diary of Nellie Lee Love, the Great Migration North, Scholastic (New York, NY), 2000.

Goin' Someplace Special, illustrated by Jerry Pinkney, Atheneum (New York, NY), 2000.

The Honest-to-Goodness Truth, illustrated by Giselle Potter, Atheneum (New York, NY), 2000.

Tippy Lemmey, illustrated by Susan Keeter, Aladdin (New York, NY), 2003.

(With Onawumi Jean Moss) *Precious and the Boo Hag,* illustrated by Kyrsten Brooker, Atheneum (New York, NY), 2004.

Look to the Hills: The Diary of Lozette Moreau, a French Slave Girl, Scholastic (New York, NY), 2004.

(With James Carville) *Lu and the Swamp Ghost,* illustrated by David Catrow, Atheneum (New York, NY), 2004.

(With Arlene Zarembka) *To Establish Justice,* Knopf (New York, NY), 2004.

Where Crocodiles Have Wings, illustrated by Bob Barner, Holiday House (New York, NY), 2005.

Amistad: The Story of a Slave Ship, illustrated by Sanna Stanley, Grosset & Dunlap (New York, NY), 2005.

Abby Takes a Stand ("Scraps of Time" series), illustrated by Gordon C. James, Viking (New York, NY), 2005.

Loved Best, illustrated by Felicia Marshall, Aladdin (New York, NY), 2005.

Porch Lies: Tales of Slicksters, Tricksters, and Other Wily Characters, illustrated by André Carrilho, Schwartz & Wade (New York, NY), 2006.

Away West ("Scraps of Time" series), illustrated by Gordon C. James, Viking (New York, NY), 2006.

Stitchin' and Pullin': A Gee's Bend Quilt, illustrated by Cozbi Cabrera, Random House (New York, NY), 2007.

A Song for Harlem ("Scraps of Time" series), illustrated by Gordon C. James, Viking (New York, NY), 2007.

A Friendship for Today, Scholastic (New York, NY), 2007.

The All-I'll-Ever-Want Christmas Doll, illustrated by Jerry Pinkney, Schwartz & Wade (New York, NY), 2007.

The Homerun King ("Scraps of Time" series), illustrated by Gordon C. James, Viking (New York, NY), 2008.

The Adventures of Deadwood Dick, illustrated by Randy DuBurke, Chronicle Books (San Francisco, CA), 2009.

FOR CHILDREN; WITH HUSBAND, FREDRICK L. MCKISSACK

Look What You've Done Now, Moses, illustrated by Joe Boddy, David Cook, 1984.

Abram, Abram, Where Are We Going?, illustrated by Joe Boddy, David Cook, 1984.

Cinderella, illustrated by Tom Dunnington, Children's Press (Chicago, IL), 1985.

Country Mouse and City Mouse, illustrated by Anne Sikorski, Children's Press (Chicago, IL), 1985.

The Little Red Hen, illustrated by Dennis Hockerman, Children's Press (Chicago, IL), 1985.

The Three Bears, illustrated by Virginia Bala, Children's Press (Chicago, IL), 1985.

The Ugly Little Duck, illustrated by Peggy Perry Anderson, Children's Press (Chicago, IL), 1986.

When Do You Talk to God? Prayers for Small Children, illustrated by Gary Gumble, Augsburg (Minneapolis, MN), 1986.

King Midas and His Gold, illustrated by Tom Dunnington, Children's Press (Chicago, IL), 1986.

Frederick Douglass: The Black Lion, Children's Press (Chicago, IL), 1987.

A Real Winner, illustrated by Quentin Thompson and Ken Jones, Millikin (St. Louis, MO), 1987.

The King's New Clothes, illustrated by Gwen Connelly, Children's Press (Chicago, IL), 1987.

Tall Phil and Small Bill, illustrated by Kathy Mitter, Millikin (St. Louis, MO), 1987.

Three Billy Goats Gruff, illustrated by Tom Dunnington, Children's Press (Chicago, IL), 1987.

My Bible ABC Book, illustrated by Reed Merrill, Augsburg (Minneapolis, MN), 1987.

The Civil Rights Movement in America from 1865 to the Present, Children's Press (Chicago, IL), 1987, second edition, 1991.

All Paths Lead to Bethlehem, illustrated by Kathryn E. Shoemaker, Augsburg (Minneapolis, MN), 1987.

Messy Bessey, illustrated by Richard Hackney, Children's Press (Chicago, IL), 1987.

The Big Bug Book of Counting, illustrated by Bartholomew, Millikin (St. Louis, MO), 1987.

The Big Bug Book of Opposites, illustrated by Bartholomew, Millikin (St. Louis, MO), 1987.

The Big Bug Book of Places to Go, illustrated by Bartholomew, Millikin (St. Louis, MO), 1987.

The Big Bug Book of the Alphabet, illustrated by Bartholomew, Millikin (St. Louis, MO), 1987.

The Big Bug Book of Things to Do, illustrated by Bartholomew, Millikin (St. Louis, MO), 1987.

Bugs!, illustrated by Clovis Martin, Children's Press (Chicago, IL), 1988.

The Children's ABC Christmas, illustrated by Kathy Rogers, Augsburg (Minneapolis, MN), 1988.

Constance Stumbles, illustrated by Tom Dunnington, Children's Press (Chicago, IL), 1988.

Oh, Happy, Happy Day! A Child's Easter in Story, Song, and Prayer, illustrated by Elizabeth Swisher, Augsburg (Minneapolis, MN), 1989.

God Made Something Wonderful, illustrated by Ching, Augsburg (Minneapolis, MN), 1989.

Messy Bessey's Closet, illustrated by Richard Hackney, Children's Press (Chicago, IL), 1989, new edition illustrated by Dana Regan, Children's Press (New York, NY), 2001.

James Weldon Johnson: "Lift Every Voice and Sing," Children's Press (Chicago, IL), 1990.

A Long Hard Journey: The Story of the Pullman Porter, Walker (New York, NY), 1990.

Taking a Stand against Racism and Racial Discrimination, F. Watts (New York, NY), 1990.

W.E.B. DuBois, F. Watts (New York, NY), 1990.

The Story of Booker T. Washington, Children's Press (Chicago, IL), 1991.

Messy Bessey's Garden, illustrated by Clovis Martin, Children's Press (Chicago, IL), 1991, new edition illustrated by Dana Regan, Children's Press (New York, NY), 2002.

From Heaven Above, Augsburg (Minneapolis, MN), 1992.

Sojourner Truth: Ain't I a Woman?, Scholastic (New York, NY), 1992.

God Makes All Things New, illustrated by Ching, Augsburg (Minneapolis, MN), 1993.

African-American Inventors, Millbrook (Brookfield, CT), 1994.

African-American Scientists, Millbrook (Brookfield, CT), 1994.

African Americans, illustrated by Michael McBride, Millikin (St. Louis, MO), 1994.

Sports, Millikin (St. Louis, MO), 1994.

Black Diamond: The Story of the Negro Baseball Leagues, Scholastic (New York, NY), 1994.

The Royal Kingdoms of Ghana, Mali, and Songhay: Life in Medieval Africa, Holt (New York, NY), 1994.

Christmas in the Big House, Christmas in the Quarters, illustrated by John Thompson, Scholastic (New York, NY), 1994.

Red-tail Angels: The Story of the Tuskegee Airmen of World War II, Walker (New York, NY), 1995.

Rebels against Slavery: American Slave Revolts, Scholastic (New York, NY), 1996.

Let My People Go: Bible Stories of Faith, Hope, and Love, as Told by Price Jefferies, a Free Man of Color, to His Daughter, Charlotte, in Charleston, South Carolina, 1806-1816, illustrated by James Ransome, Atheneum (New York, NY), 1998.

Young, Black, and Determined: A Biography of Lorraine Hansberry, Holiday House (New York, NY), 1998.

Messy Bessey and the Birthday Overnight, illustrated by Dana Regan, Children's Press (Chicago, IL), 1998.

Messy Bessey's School Desk, illustrated by Dana Regan, Children's Press (Chicago, IL), 1998.

Black Hands, White Sails: The Story of African-American Whalers, Scholastic (New York, NY), 1999.

Messy Bessey's Holidays, illustrated by Dana Regan, Children's Press (Chicago, IL), 1999.

Messy Bessey's Family Reunion, illustrated by Dana Regan, Children's Press (Chicago, IL), 2000.

Miami Gets It Straight, illustrated by Michael Chesworth, Golden Books (New York, NY), 2000.

Bugs!, illustrated by Michael Cressy, Children's Press (New York, NY), 2000.

Miami Makes the Play, illustrated by Michael Chesworth, Golden Books (New York, NY), 2001.

Miami Sees It Through, illustrated by Michael Chesworth, Golden Books (New York, NY), 2002.

Days of Jubilee: The End of Slavery in the United States, Scholastic (New York, NY), 2003.

(Adaptors) *Itching and Twitching: A Nigerian Folktale,* illustrated by Laura Freeman, Scholastic (New York, NY), 2003.

Hard Labor: The First African Americans, 1619, illustrated by Joseph Daniel Fiedler, Aladdin (New York, NY), 2004.

FOR CHILDREN; "GREAT AFRICAN AMERICANS" SERIES; WITH HUSBAND, FREDRICK L. MCKISSACK

Carter G. Woodson: The Father of Black History, illustrated by Ned Ostendorf, Enslow (Berkeley Heights, NJ), 1991, revised edition, 2002.

Frederick Douglass: Leader against Slavery, illustrated by Ned Ostendorf, Enslow (Berkeley Heights, NJ), 1991, revised edition, 2002.

George Washington Carver: The Peanut Scientist, illustrated by Ned Ostendorf, Enslow (Berkeley Heights, NJ), 1991, revised edition, 2002.

Ida B. Wells-Barnett: A Voice against Violence, illustrated by Ned Ostendorf, Enslow (Berkeley Heights, NJ), 1991, revised edition, 2001.

Louis Armstrong: Jazz Musician, illustrated by Ned Ostendorf, Enslow (Berkeley Heights, NJ), 1991, revised edition, 2001.

Marian Anderson: A Great Singer, illustrated by Ned Ostendorf, Enslow (Berkeley Heights, NJ), 1991, revised edition, 2001.

Martin Luther King, Jr.: Man of Peace, illustrated by Ned Ostendorf, Enslow (Berkeley Heights, NJ), 1991, revised edition, 2001.

Mary Church Terrell: Leader for Equality, illustrated by Ned Ostendorf, Enslow (Berkeley Heights, NJ), 1991, revised edition, 2002.

Mary McLeod Bethune: A Great Teacher, illustrated by Ned Ostendorf, Enslow (Berkeley Heights, NJ), 1991, revised edition, 2001.

Ralph J. Bunche: Peacemaker, illustrated by Ned Ostendorf, Enslow (Berkeley Heights, NJ), 1991, revised edition, 2002.

Jesse Owens: Olympic Star, illustrated by Michael David Biegel, Enslow (Berkeley Heights, NJ), 1992, revised edition, 2001.

Langston Hughes: Great American Poet, illustrated by Michael David Biegel, Enslow (Berkeley Heights, NJ), 1992, revised edition, 2002.

Zora Neale Hurston: Writer and Storyteller, illustrated by Michael Bryant, Enslow (Berkeley Heights, NJ), 1992, revised edition, 2002.

Satchel Paige: The Best Arm in Baseball, illustrated by Michael David Biegel, Enslow (Berkeley Heights, NJ), 1992, revised edition, 2002.

Sojourner Truth: Voice for Freedom, illustrated by Michael Bryant, Enslow (Berkeley Heights, NJ), 1992, revised edition, 2002.

Madam C.J. Walker: Self-made Millionaire, illustrated by Michael Bryant, Enslow (Berkeley Heights, NJ), 1992, revised edition, 2001.

Paul Robeson: A Voice to Remember, illustrated by Michael David Biegel, Enslow (Berkeley Heights, NJ), 1992, revised edition, 2001.

Booker T. Washington: Leader and Educator, illustrated by Michael Bryant, Enslow (Berkeley Heights, NJ), 1992, revised edition, 2001.

OTHER

Also contributor, with Fredrick L. McKissack, to *The World of 1492,* edited by Jean Fritz, Holt (New York, NY), 1992; coauthor, with F.L. McKissack, of "Start Up" series for beginning readers, four volumes, Children's Press (Chicago, IL), 1985; co-editor, with F.L. McKissack, of "Reading Well" series and "Big Bug Books" series, both for Milliken. Writer for preschool series "L Is for Listening," broadcast by KWMU-Radio, 1975-77. Author of radio and television scripts. Contributor of articles and short stories to magazines, including *Friend, Happy Times,* and *Evangelizing Today's Child.* Coauthor, with Mavis Jukes, of short-subject film script *Who Owns the Sun?,* Disney Educational Productions, 1991.

Sidelights

Patricia C. McKissack has written well over one hundred titles under her own name, as well as working in collaboration with her husband, Fredrick L. McKissack. The author of historical fiction and biographies for children, McKissack focuses on religious as well as African-American themes, and she has also worked for many years an English instructor at both the middle-school and college levels. "I write because there's a clear *need* for books written about the minority experience in America—fiction and nonfiction," she remarked on the *Random House* Web site. "I also write for the love of it!"

The recipient of a 1993 Newbery Honor award for the short stories she gathers in *The Dark-Thirty: Southern Tales of the Supernatural,* McKissack has also won several Coretta Scott King awards. Teaming up with her husband, she has also contributed numerous titles to Enslow's "Great African Americans" series, as well as to non-series books on little-known aspects of African-American history that include *Red-Tail Angels: The Story of the Tuskegee Airmen of World War II* and *Black Diamonds: The Story of the Negro Baseball Leagues.* McKissack has also written numerous solo works, including *The All-I'll-Ever-Want Christmas Doll* and *Stitchin' and Pullin': A Gee's Bend Quilt.*

The McKissacks' lives were shaped by one of the most optimistic eras in American history: the 1960s. "We're Kennedy products, and we were very idealistic," McKissack once told *SATA.* "That was the period in which African Americans were really looking up, coming out of darkness, segregation, and discrimination, and doors were beginning to open—ever so slightly, but still opening." The optimism of those days can be seen in the McKissacks' books *Civil Rights Movement in America from 1865 to the Present* and *Martin Luther King, Jr.: Man of Peace.*

Born in 1944 in Nashville, Tennessee, McKissack experienced first hand many of the injustices about which she and her husband write. These were the days of segregation, in which a black person was not allowed to drink from the same public water fountain as a white, nor allowed into the same restaurants as whites. At home, however, McKissack's life was rich and filled with the tales that her storytelling grandfather shared. She grew up with a love of narrative and a love of reading.

She also grew up with her future husband, Fred McKissack, "in the same town, where every family knew every other family," as McKissack once told *SATA,* "but he was five years older and you just didn't date boys who were five years older than you. When I was fifteen and he was twenty that just would have been forbidden." But then Fred went away to the Marines for several years; later, they both attended college together, graduating in 1964 from Tennessee State University in Nashville, and suddenly the two seemed not so far removed in age. They were married after graduation. "All of our friends said it wouldn't last six months. They said it was ridiculous, and our families were a bit concerned," McKissack recalled for *SATA.* "But we just knew. We talked all the time and we still do. We have always had a very, very close relationship from the first date we had. We just had so much fun together that we knew."

One thing the McKissacks discovered they had in common was a love of literature, including the works of Ayn Rand and Aldous Huxley. Other influences included Julius Lester, an author known for his historically accurate, heroic depictions of black characters. Lester had graduated in 1960 from Fisk University, also in Nashville. While the era was filled with hope and opportunities, it was also a time of violent change. Sit-ins and demonstrations by Southern blacks were finally shaking the segregationist foundations of the region. Schools became desegregated; integration was in the works. "Our generation was the first to do it," McKissack once recalled to *SATA.* "I remember when Fred took me to dinner at Morrison's [a local restaurant]. I was nervous as a flea because a sit-in had occurred [there] only a few years earlier, and there had been people putting shotguns at young people's heads and saying, 'If you sit here we will blow you away.' And that happened to Fred" when he joined a sit-in at a Woolworth department store. The visit to Morrison's was among many firsts for the McKissacks; after years of seeing them only from the outside, the two finally entered a Kentucky Fried Chicken restaurant, a Shoney's, a McDonald's, and a Hardee's. When her younger brother

got a job at Shoney's, McKissack realized that "things were opening up. And we were very proud that we were the first generation to come through that."

Then came the Vietnam War and the "white backlash" to the civil rights movement. McKissack found the television footage at that time, the first ever shown of American soldiers in combat, profoundly disturbing. "That was horrible for us to watch—the body bags coming back in," she related. "I was a young mother—I had three little boys—and I said, 'My God, I hope we never have to go through anything this nonsensical again.'" The assassinations of U.S. President John F. Kennedy as well as of Kennedy's brother Robert Kennedy, Dr. Martin Luther King, Jr., Medgar Evers, and Malcolm X, along with church bombings and innumerable other violent incidents, all served to temper the McKissacks' positive attitude. "Just as blacks experienced white resistance to equality during Reconstruction, there was another backlash to the civil rights movement of the 1960s," McKissack commented. "By 1980 blacks were once again on the defense, trying to safeguard their and their children's rights."

These experiences have all combined to produce the variety and depth of writing McKissack has produced. One of her goals is to write in such a way that the past comes alive for her young readers. One of her first writing projects was a biography of Paul Laurence Dunbar, written while teaching eighth-grade English in Kirkwood, Missouri. "The school was twenty-five-percent black and I wanted to teach about an African-American writer who I had come to know and appreciate when I was growing up," McKissack recalled. When she began researching Dunbar, "I couldn't find a biography, so I wrote his biography myself for my students." She also sought information on Langston Hughes and James Weldon Johnson, both of whom she and her husband have since written. Many more biographies have followed.

James Weldon Johnson: "Lift Every Voice and Sing," coauthored with her husband, "makes Johnson come alive for young readers," Jeanette Lambert commented in *School Library Journal.* Readers learn that Johnson was the author of "Lift Every Voice and Sing," the song recognized as the African-American national anthem, and also was the first black to pass the Florida state bar exam, serve as principal of the first black high school in Jacksonville, Florida, and become executive secretary of the National Association for the Advancement of Colored People.

Together, the McKissacks have penned several biographies in Enslow's "Great African Americans" series, brief nonfiction titles intended for the primary grades. These books describe the lives of important black leaders, both cultural and political, in brief chapters using a basic, concise style accompanied by photographs and other illustrations. In a review of the McKissacks' *Ida B. Wells-Barnett: A Voice against Violence, Marian Anderson: A Great Singer, Martin Luther King, Jr.:*

Cover of Patricia C. McKissack's inspiring biography **Sojourner Truth: Ain't I a Woman?** (Scholastic, Inc., 1992. Image courtesy of Sophia Smith Collection, Smith College.)

Man of Peace, and *Ralph J. Bunche: Peacemaker,* Phyllis Stephens noted that the authors present each of their subjects as people with convictions so strong that "not even a racially biased society could provide effective obstacles to deter them" from achieving their dreams. Writing about *Paul Robeson: A Voice to Remember* and *Booker T. Washington: Leader and Educator,* Laura Culberg noted in *School Library Journal* that these brief biographies "fill a need for materials on noted African-Americans for primary-grade readers." Culberg went on to conclude that "the books will find an eager audience among beginning readers." Reviewing the biographies on notables including black historian Carter G. Woodson, anti-slavery leader Frederick Douglass, scientist George Washington Carver, jazz musician Louis Armstrong, and equal-rights proponent Mary Church Terrell, Anna DeWind noted in *School Library Journal* that all five books "have simplified vocabularies, large print, and plenty of black-and-white photographs and illustrations." DeWind further commented that in spite some "flaws," the couple's biographies "are a step in the right direction."

Many books in the "Great African Americans" series have been revised for 2001 and 2002 editions that fea-

ture original black-and-white photographs. In a review of the revision of *Marian Anderson,* Kristen Oravec concluded in *School Library Journal* that the volume ranks as a "fresh and appealing new edition." *Booklist* contributor Gillian Engberg noted in a review of *Booker T. Washington* that "the visuals and formats have been much improved." Commenting on the revised series, *School Library Journal* critic Dorothy N. Bowen considered the books to be "attractive replacements" for the old series.

The McKissacks also have several non-series biographies to their credit. "A revealing book," *W.E.B. DuBois* "should entice readers to seek more information about this complex man," Lydia Champlin remarked in *School Library Journal. Voice of Youth Advocates* reviewer Bruce Lee Siebers recommended *W.E.B. DuBois* as "a good addition to African American history and biography collections." With *Sojourner Truth: Ain't I a Woman,* a Coretta Scott King honor book, they tell the story of the nineteenth-century preacher, abolitionist, and activist for the rights of both African Americans and women. Born Isabella van Wagener, a slave, she was later freed and at age forty-six felt the calling to "walk in the light of His truth." Thereafter, she adopted the name of Sojourner Truth and fought for the rights of slaves and women. "With compassion and historical detail, the McKissacks offer a rich profile" of the woman, remarked Gerry Larson in a *School Library Journal* review. "Middle grade readers and researchers will enjoy the readability, quotes, and documentary photos, all of which breathe life into the personality and times of Sojourner Truth."

The McKissacks tell the story of brilliant black writer Lorraine Hansberry in *Young, Black, and Determined.* The author of the acclaimed play, *A Raisin in the Sun,* Hansberry fought prejudice throughout her brief career. "The McKissacks' biography sparkles with the energy and passion that characterize [their] . . . subject," observed *Booklist* contributor Anne O'Malley. Marilyn Heath, reviewing the same book in *School Library Journal,* called *Young, Black, and Determined* a "well-written biography" that is "lively and engaging" and that "brings its subject to life by successfully capturing that unique spark that makes Hansberry noteworthy and interesting."

Other history books of note include *Black Diamond, Red-Tail Angels,* and *Black Hands, White Sails,* all collaborative efforts. Racism in sports is brought into focus in the first of these, "a lucid, comprehensive study of a vital chapter of baseball history," according to Randy M. Brough in a review of *Black Diamond* for *Kliatt.* In *Red-Tail Angels,* the authors tell the little-known story of the black pilots who fought in World War II in a special squadron because the regular Air Force was still segregated. Mary M. Burns enthusiastically praised this history in a *Horn Book* review: "Impeccably documented, handsomely designed, thoughtfully executed," she wrote, "this book by two of our most committed and talented writers gives these pioneers' accomplishments meaning for a new generation." David A. Lindsey, reviewing *Red-Tail Angels* in *School Library Journal,* commented: "The prolific McKissacks have collaborated once again to produce yet another well-crafted, thoroughly researched account of a little-known facet of African American history." Of *Black Hands, White Sails,* a reviewer for *Booklist* called it a "fascinating look at the convergent histories of whaling and the abolitionist movement" that "weaves seemingly disparate threads into a detailed tapestry."

Patricia McKissack also has numerous solo books in history and fiction to her credit. Her books for very young readers, such as *Flossie and the Fox* and the Caldecott honor book *Mirandy and Brother Wind,* have won critical praise and a wide readership. A contributor for *Kirkus Reviews* called *Flossie and the Fox,* based on a tale McKissack's grandfather once told her, "a perfect picture book." *Mirandy and Brother Wind* was also inspired by McKissack's grandfather, more specifically from a photograph of both her grandfather and grandmother as teenagers after they had won a cakewalk contest in 1906. In the book, Mirandy enlists Brother Wind

Cover of McKissack's award-winning story collection **The Dark-Thirty,** *featuring artwork by Brian Pinkney.* (Illustration copyright © 1992 by Brian Pinkney. Used by permission of Alfred A. Knopf, an imprint of Random House Children's Books, a division of Random House, Inc.)

as her partner in a cakewalk contest in a "delightful book," according to Valerie Wilson Wesley, writing in the *New York Times Book Review.* Wesley concluded, "each page of *Mirandy and Brother Wind* sparkles with life," while *Booklist* contributor Ilene Cooper called the book "a graceful fantasy." Remembrances of her great-grandmother and her eternal apron inspired *Ma Dear's Aprons,* a book that a contributor to the *New York Times Book Review* called "affectionate, appealing and full of information about the routines of domestic life."

McKissack became the recipient of a Newbery honor award for the stories collected in *The Dark-Thirty.* The title comes from that half-hour before dark in which kids were still allowed to play outside when McKissack herself was growing up. The ten original stories in the collection reflect African-American history and culture. "Some are straight ghost stories," commented Kay McPherson in a *School Library Journal* review, "many of which are wonderfully spooky and all of which have well-woven narratives." McPherson concluded, "This is a stellar collection."

McKissack's story of a vicious dog who becomes a valuable friend is the focus of *Tippy Lemmey,* a chapter book for middle readers. "The book's short chapters, straightforward prose, and suspense will keep the pages turning," wrote Shelle Rosenfeld in her *Booklist* review. B. Allison Gray, in *School Library Journal,* considered the title "perfect for readers just venturing into chapter-book territory," while Roger Sutton, writing for *Horn Book,* noted that "McKissack's storytelling chops go on display right from the beginning."

McKissack teamed up with Southern-born political commentator James Carville to retell a folktale from Carville's childhood with *Lu and the Swamp Ghost.* Lu finds a mud-covered monster in the swamps near her Louisiana home; after escaping from it, she decides maybe the monster just needs a friend. When she attempts to tame the ghost, she discovers it isn't a monster after all, but someone who needs her help. "Lu's innocent selflessness and genuine, sweet nature set this story apart," commended a reviewer for *Publishers Weekly.* Judith Constantinides considered *Lu and the Swamp Ghost* "a fun selection for home and storytime enjoyment."

In another collaboration, McKissack joined Onawumi Jean Moss in the retelling of another folk story in *Precious and the Boo Hag.* Precious is left home alone, and warned not to let the Boo Hag in. Her brother warns her that the Boo Hag can change her appearance, so when the Boo Hag tries to come in by disguising herself as a shiny penny, Precious knows better than to bring her inside. A critic for *Kirkus Reviews* considered the tale to be "fine fare for Halloween, or general under-the-covers reading." Susan Dove Lempke, writing in *Horn Book,* praised *Precious and the Boo Hag* as "lively, funny, and . . . a great choice for storytelling," while a *Publishers Weekly* reviewer commented on the "lively language, pleasing cadence, and effective repetition" that would make this book "a buoyant read-aloud."

In *Porch Lies: Tales of Slicksters, Tricksters, and Other Wily Characters,* McKissack presents ten of her favorite childhood stories, told to her by her grandparents. The tales "blend history and legend with sly humor, creepy horror, villainous characters, and wild farce," noted *Booklist* critic Hazel Rochman. *Stitchin' and Pullin',* a work told in verse, casts light on the women of Gee's Bend, Alabama, a group of former slaves who depict their heritage through their vibrant quilts. Writing in *Horn Book,* Robin L. Smith noted that "it's marvelously clear that McKissack understands the creative pulse of the quilter and artist," and a contributor in *Kirkus Reviews* described the work as "an outstanding way to introduce aspects of African-American history and explore the power of community."

McKissack again mines history for the works in her "Scraps of Time" series. Set in Tennessee during the 1960s, *Abby Takes a Stand* concerns a young African-American girl's efforts to fight discrimination through nonviolent protest. "This accessible, lively, and heartfelt chapter book reads like a memoir," Smith commented. In *Away West,* a family learns about the experiences of their ancestor who settled in Nicodemus, Kansas, a town founded by emancipated slaves. A critic in *Kirkus Reviews* deemed the work "a must for young history buffs." McKissack examines the creative era known as the Harlem Renaissance in *A Song for Harlem,* the third work in the series. According to *School Library Journal* reviewer Donna Atmur, the prose for this book "convey[s] a feel for the characters and the time, and a vivid sense of place."

Other works for older readers include several fictionalized diaries of African-American girls for Scholastic: *A Picture of Freedom: The Diary of Clotee, a Slave Girl* and *Color Me Dark: The Diary of Nellie Lee Love, the Great Migration North. A Picture of Freedom* is set on a Virginia plantation in 1859, and *Color Me Dark* follows the fortunes of a young girl who migrates to Chicago after World War I. Reviewing *A Picture of Freedom* for *School Library Journal,* Melissa Hudek called the book "an inspiring look at a young girl coming of age in terrible circumstances who manages to live life to the fullest." *Booklist* critic Carolyn Phelan, reviewing *Color Me Dark,* felt that "the strong narrative will keep children involved and give them a great deal of social history to absorb along the way." Jennifer Ralston in *School Library Journal* noted that in *Color Me Dark,* "the time period is well developed, and serves as a compelling backdrop to the Love family's struggle."

In *Run away Home* McKissack tells the story of a young Apache who escapes federal custody and is aided by an African-American family. Reviewing this historical novel in *Horn Book,* Burns noted that "McKissack knows how to pace a story, create suspense, and interweave period details of the late nineteenth century into a coherent narrative." According to Burns, *Run away Home* is "sophisticated in content yet tuned to the understanding of a middle-school audience—no small accomplishment."

With *Goin' Somewhere Special,* McKissack revisits scenes from her childhood in a segregated Nashville. Young 'Tricia Ann goes off on a journey by herself to a special place, but on the way, she is faced with cruelty and people who want to bring her down and make her less of a person. Gathering strength from the words of her grandmother, 'Tricia Ann makes it to her special place: the local library, which is not segregated and where knowledge is available to everyone equally. Denise Wilms noted in *Booklist* that *Goin' Somewhere Special* "carries a strong message of pride and self-confidence," while *School Library Journal* reviewer Mary Elam considered it "a thought-provoking story." Noting how the topics lead easily into discussion, a *Kirkus Reviews* contributor called *Goin' Someplace Special* "a natural for group sharing," while *Horn Book* contributor Robin Smith praised the title for being "informative without being preachy; hopeful without being sentimental."

McKissack is also the coauthor, with Arlene Zarembka, of a reference book on citizenship titled *To Establish Justice: Citizenship and the Constitution.* Here the authors cover U.S. Supreme Court decisions that have affected civil and human rights from the early 1800s through to the present, and "present a compelling mix of analyses and quoted passages from judicial opinions," noted a contributor to *Kirkus Reviews.* Jane G. Connor, in her *School Library Journal* review, noted that McKissack and Zarembka "do a fine job of providing the history, background, and events surrounding each Supreme Court decision." Carolyn Phelan, in *Booklist,* called *To Establish Justice* an "excellent resource [that] pulls together a great deal of information," while a reviewer for *Children's Bookwatch* considered it useful to voters and "a fine guide in any year."

McKissack sees her work as something that can possibly unite disparate communities in this country. "It's a kind of freedom," she once told *SATA.* "Writing has allowed us to do something positive with our experiences, although some of our experiences have been very negative. We try to enlighten, to change attitudes, to form new attitudes—to build bridges with books." And for her, reaching children with her books is vital. "I am a *wordsmith,* one who crafts words into books for young readers," McKissack wrote in *Sitting at the Feet of the Past: Retelling the North American Folk Tale for Children.* "According to the late child psychologist Bruno Bettelheim, the stories children hear and read early in life help shape their adult decision-making and problem-solving skills. And I believe it, too."

Biographical and Critical Sources

BOOKS

Children's Literature Review, Gale (Detroit, MI), Volume 23, 1991, Volume 55, 1999, Volume 129, 2008.

Schmidt, Gary D., and Donald R. Hettinga, editors, *Sitting at the Feet of the Past: Retelling the North American Folk Tale for Children,* Greenwood Press (Westport, CT), 1992.

PERIODICALS

Book, November-December, 2001, review of *Goin' Someplace Special,* p. 75.

Booklist, January 1, 1992, Hazel Rochman, review of *Frederick Douglass: Leader against Slavery,* p. 832; February 1, 1992, Ilene Cooper, review of *Mirandy and Brother Wind,* p. 1037; February 15, 1996, Ilene Cooper, review of *Rebels against Slavery;* February 15, 1998, Anne O'Malley, review of *Young, Black, and Determined: A Biography of Lorraine Hansberry,* p. 995; October 1, 1998, Hazel Rochman, review of *Let My People Go,* p. 339; September 1, 1999, review of *Black Hands, White Sails,* p. 77; December 15, 1999, Hazel Rochman, review of *The Honest-to-Goodness Truth,* p. 791; February 15, 2000, Carolyn Phelan, review of *Color Me Dark: The Diary of Nellie Lee Love, the Great Migration North,* p. 1113; December 1, 2000, Hazel Rochman, review of *Messy Bessey's Family Reunion,* p. 726; February 15, 2001, Hazel Rochman, review of *Color Me Dark,* p. 1149; Henrietta M. Smith, review of *Ma Dear's Aprons,* p. 1161; May 1, 2001, Gillian Engberg, review of *Miami Makes the Play,* p. 1683; August, 2001, Denise Wilms, review of *Goin' Someplace Special,* p. 2117; January 1, 2002, Gillian Engberg, reviews of *Booker T. Washington: Leader and Educator* and *Marian Anderson: A Great Singer,* p. 853; January 1, 2003, Shelle Rosenfeld, review of *Tippy Lemmey,* p. 892; February 15, 2003, Carolyn Phelan, review of *Days of Jubilee: The End of Slavery in the United States,* p. 1082; March 1, 2004, Hazel Rochman, review of *Look to the Hills: The Diary of Lozette Moreau, a French Slave Girl,* pp. 1201-1202; October 15, 2004, Carolyn Phelan, review of *To Establish Justice: Citizenship and the Constitution,* p. 397; April 15, 2006, Kay Weisman, review of *Away West,* p. 59; May 15, 2006, Hazel Rochman, review of *Porch Lies: Tales of Slicksters, Tricksters, and Other Wily Characters,* p. 46; August, 2007, Carolyn Phelan, review of *A Song for Harlem,* p. 62.

Bulletin of the Center for Children's Books, June, 1991, Elizabeth Bush, review of *Rebels against Slavery,* pp. 345-346; February, 1994, Betsy Hearne, review of *The Royal Kingdoms of Ghana, Mali, and Songhay,* p. 194; December, 1998, Janice M. DelNegro, review of *Let My People Go,* p. 137.

Childhood Education, spring, 2000, Nicole Donovan, review of *Black Hands, White Sails,* p. 172; winter, 2000, Terry Stahler, review of *Color Me Dark,* p. 108.

Children's Bookwatch, November, 2004, review of *To Establish Justice.*

Horn Book, January-February, 1995, Lois F. Anderson, review of *Christmas in the Big House,* p. 68; March-April, 1996, Mary M. Burns, review of *Red-Tail Angels,* p. 226; November-December, 1997, Mary M. Burns, review of *Run Away Home,* p. 681; November, 1999, Mary M. Burns, review of *Black Hands, White Sails,* p. 758; November-December, 2001, Robin Smith, review of *Goin' Someplace Special,* pp. 736-737; March-April, 2003, Roger Sutton, review of *Tippy Lemmey,* pp. 213-216; January-February, 2005, Susan Dove Lempke, review of *Precious and the Boo Hag,* p. 77; September-October, 2005, Robin Smith, review of *Abby Takes a Stand,* p. 585; September-October, 2006, Barbara Bader, review of *Porch Lies,* p. 592; March-April, 2007, Barbara Bader, "For the McKissacks, Black Is Boundless," p. 149, and Robin Smith, review of *A Friendship for Today,* p. 198; November-December, 2007, Kitty Flynn, review of *The All-I'll-Ever-Want Christmas Doll,* p. 633; November-December, 2008, Robin L. Smith, review of *Stitchin' and Pullin': A Gee's Bend Quilt,* p. 693.

Kirkus Reviews, November 1, 1988, review of *Flossie and the Fox,* p. 1067; December 15, 1991; September 15, 2001, review of *Goin' Someplace Special,* p. 1362; December 15, 2003, review of *Hard Labor: The First African Americans,* p. 239; August 15, 2004, review of *Lu and the Swamp Ghost,* p. 803, review of *To Establish Justice,* p. 810; December 15, 2004, review of *Precious and the Boo Hag,* p. 1205; February 15, 2006, review of *Away West,* p. 187; September 15, 2008, review of *Stitchin' and Pullin'.*

Kliatt, November, 1998, Randy M. Brough, review of *Black Diamonds,* p. 40.

New York Times Book Review, November 20, 1988, Valerie Wilson Wesley, review of *Mirandy and Brother Wind,* p. 48; August 3, 1997, review of *Ma Dear's Aprons,* p. 14.

Publishers Weekly, October 26, 1998, review of *Let My People Go,* p. 62; August 6, 2001, review of *Goin' Someplace Special,* p. 89, interview with McKissack, p. 90; January 20, 2003, review of *Days of Jubilee: The End of Slavery in the United States,* p. 83; August 23, 2004, review of *Lu and the Swamp Ghost,* p. 53; January 3, 2005, review of *Precious and the Boo Hag,* p. 54; July 25, 2005, review of *Abby Takes a Stand,* p. 77; July 10, 2006, review of *Porch Lies,* p. 82; January 8, 2007, review of *A Friendship for Today,* p. 52; October 22, 2007, review of *The All-I'll-Ever-Want Christmas Doll,* p. 56.

School Library Journal, January, 1991, Lydia Champlin, review of *W.E.B. DuBois,* p. 103; February, 1991, Jeanette Lambert, review of *James Weldon Johnson: "Lift Every Voice and Sing,"* p. 79; November, 1991, Phyllis Stephens, reviews of *Ida B. Wells-Barnett: A Voice against Violence, Marian Anderson, Martin Luther King, Jr.: Man of Peace,* and *Ralph J. Bunche: Peacemaker,* all p. 111; February, 1992, Anna DeWind, review of *Carter G. Woodson: The Father of Black History,* p. 83; October, 1992, Laura Culberg, review of *Paul Robeson: A Voice to Remember,* pp. 105-106; December, 1992, Kay McPherson, review of *The Dark-Thirty: Southern Tales of the Supernatural,* p. 113, Ann Welton, review of *Madam C.J. Walker: Self-made Millionaire,* p. 124; January, 1993, Susan

Knorr, review of *Langston Hughes: Great American Poet,* pp. 116, 118; February, 1993, Gerry Larson, review of *Sojourner Truth: Ain't I a Woman?* p. 100; June, 1994, Susan Gifford, review of *The Royal Kingdoms of Ghana, Mali, and Songhay,* pp. 140-141; September, 1994, pp. 251-252; November, 1994, Margaret M. Hagel, review of *African-American Inventors,* p. 115; February, 1996, David A. Lindsey, review of *Red-Tail Angels,* p. 119; September, 1997, Melissa Hudek, review of *A Picture of Freedom,* pp. 199, 220; August, 1998, Sharon R. Pearce, review of *Messy Bessey's School Desk,* p. 144, and Marilyn Heath, review of *Young, Black, and Determined,* pp. 148-149; July, 2000, Jennifer Ralston, review of *Color Me Dark* p. 107; August, 2001, Eunice Weech, review of *Jesse Owens: Olympic Star,* p. 170; September, 2001, Mary Elam, review of *Goin' Someplace Special,* p. 199; January, 2002, Kristen Oravec, review of *Marion Anderson,* p. 121; May, 2002, Pamela K. Bomboy, review of *Martin Luther King, Jr.,* Dorothy N. Bowen, review of *Frederick Douglas* and *Mary Church Terrell: Leader for Equality,* p. 140; January, 2003, B. Allison Gray, review of *Tippy Lemmey,* p. 106; March, 2004, Tracy Bell, review of *Hard Labor: The First African Americans,* p. 329; May, 2004, Nancy P. Reeder, review of *Look to the Hills,* p. 152; October, 2004, Mary N. Oluonye, review of *Goin' Someplace Special,* p. 65, Mary N. Oluonye, review of *Color Me Dark,* p. 66, Mary N. Oluonye, review of *The Civil Rights Movement in America from 1865 to the Present,* p. 68, Judith Constantinides, review of *Lu and the Swamp Ghost,* p. 110, Jane G. Connor, review of *To Establish Justice,* p. 192; May, 2006, Pat Leach, review of *Away West,* p. 94; September, 2006, Susan Hepler, review of *Porch Lies,* p. 212; September, 2007, Donna Atmur, review of *A Song for Harlem,* p. 171; November, 2008, Lisa Glasscock, review of *Stitchin' and Pullin',* p. 94.

Tribune Books (Chicago, IL), December 4, 1994, Mary Harris Veeder, "Up Pops Christmas," p. 9.

Voice of Youth Advocates, October, 1990, Bruce Lee Siebers, review of *W.E.B. DuBois,* p. 248.

ONLINE

Random House Web site, http://www.randomhouse.com/ (December 1, 2008), "Author Spotlight: Patricia C. McKissack."

Scholastic Web site, http://www2.scholastic.com/ (December 1, 2008), "Patricia C. McKissack."*

*   *   *

MEUNIER, Brian 1954-

Personal

Born 1954, in Gardner, MA; married Perky Edgerton (an artist); children: two daughters. *Education:* University of Massachusetts, B.F.A., 1976; Tyler School of Art, M.F.A., 1978.

Addresses

Office—Swarthmore College, Department of Art, Beardsley 214, Swarthmore, PA 19081. *E-mail*—bmeunie1@ swarthmore.edu.

Career

Sculptor, educator, and author. Swarthmore College, Swarthmore, PA, 1979—, currently professor of studio arts and department chair. *Exhibitions:* Work exhibited at Herter Gallery, University of Massachusetts, 1975; Fleisher Art Memorial, Philadelphia, PA, 1982; Noyes Museum of Art, Oceanville, NJ, 1992; and List Gallery, Swarthmore College, 2008. Work included in group exhibitions at Barbara Okun Gallery, St. Louis, MO, 1978; Karen Lenox Gallery, Chicago, IL, 1983; Carnegie-Mellon University Art Gallery, Pittsburgh, PA, 1987; Philadelphia Museum of Art, 1990; Freeman Gallery, Philadelphia, 2002; and Noyes Museum of Art, 2006.

Awards, Honors

Ford Foundation grant, 1975; Provincetown Art Workshop fellowship, 1982; Mellon grant, Swarthmore College, 1982; Pennsylvania Council on the Arts fellowship, 1983; Franklin Town Corporation grant, 1983; National Endowment for the Arts fellowship, 1984; Blanchard fellowship, Swarthmore College, 1986; Pennsylvania Council on the Arts fellowship, 1989; Eugene M. Lang faculty fellowship, Swarthmore College, 1998; James Michener faculty fellowship, Swarthmore College, 2002.

Writings

Pipiolo and the Roof Dogs, illustrated by wife, Perky Edgerton, Dutton (New York, NY), 2003.

Bravo, Tavo!, illustrated by Perky Edgerton, Dutton (New York, NY), 2007.

Sidelights

Brian Meunier is the author of a pair of well-received books for young readers that are illustrated by his wife, artist Perky Edgerton. In addition, Meunier is a professor of studio art at Swarthmore College as well as an award-winning sculptor. "I am drawn to objects that activate my sense of wonder," he told Andrea Packard in an interview posted on his home page. "In the beginning, middle, and end of making the work, I require an intuitive and transcendent experience—for myself and, I hope, for the viewer."

Set in the small Mexican village of San Pablo Etla, Meunier's debut picture book, *Pipiolo and the Roof Dogs,* centers on young Lupe and her amazingly heroic pet, Pipiolo. Inspired by old Western movies, Pipiolo concocts an ingenious escape plan for the other canines in town that are confined to their owner's hot, flat roofs as watchdogs. According to *Booklist* reviewer Gillian Engberg, readers "will respond to the unusual, dreamlike story," and Nina Lindsay noted in *School Library Journal* that "children will love the idea of the dogs' liberation, and will remember Lupe and Pipiolo as likable characters well developed through text and picture."

Brian Meunier's picture book Bravo, Tavo! *features artwork by Meunier's wife, Perky Edgerton.* (Illustration copyright © 2007 by Perky Edgerton. Reproduced by permission of Dutton Children's Books, a division of Penguin Putnam Books for Young Readers.)

A basketball-loving youngster helps save his family farm in *Bravo, Tavo!,* a "charming story set in Mexico," according to a critic in *Kirkus Reviews.* Although Tavo dreams of hoops stardom, he cannot afford to replace his decrepit sneakers, which are patched with duct tape. After clearing a series of irrigation ditches that bring water to the family's parched croplands, the boy is rewarded by an elderly neighbor with a new pair of shoes that may have magical powers. According to *Booklist* contributor Randall Enos, Meunier's "unusual" story "bring[s] . . . issues like wealth and poverty to younger children."

Biographical and Critical Sources

PERIODICALS

Booklist, October 1, 2003, Gillian Engberg, review of *Pipiolo and the Roof Dogs,* p. 328; May 15, 2007, Randall Enos, review of *Bravo, Tavo!,* p. 49.
Kirkus Reviews, July 1, 2003, review of *Pipiolo and the Roof Dogs,* p. 912; July 1, 2007, review of *Bravo, Tavo!*
Publishers Weekly, August 25, 2003, review of *Pipiolo and the Roof Dogs,* p. 64.

School Library Journal, October, 2003, Nina Lindsay, review of *Pipiolo and the Roof Dogs,* p. 131; August, 2007, Mary Jean Smith, review of *Bravo, Tavo!,* p. 86.

ONLINE

Brian Meunier Home Page, http://www.brianmeunier.com (November 10, 2008).
Swarthmore College Web site, http://www.swarthmore.edu/ (November 10, 2008), "Brian Meunier."

* * *

MICHAELS, Jamie

Personal
Born in New York, NY.

Addresses
Home—New York, NY. *Agent*—Michael Bourret, Dystel & Goderich Literary Management, One Union Sq. W., Ste. 904, New York, NY 10003.

Career
Novelist.

Writings

Kiss My Book, Delacorte Press (New York, NY), 2007.

Sidelights

Jamie Michaels is a writer based in New York City whose first novel, *Kiss My Book,* also focuses on a home-grown Manhattan writer. Fifteen-year-old Ruby Crane, Michaels' protagonist, seems to be on the fast track: not only has she got a publishing contract, but her first novel is also slated to be made into a feature film. Ruby's rise in popularity is on par with her literary success, and she has even gained the attention of the cutest boy in her high school, until her world comes crashing down when the charge of plagiarism is levelled against her on national television. Shame and loneliness prompt Ruby to flee to Aunt Fin's home in upstate New York where, under the name Georgia, she determines to create a new life. As she begins to learn about her new home town of Whispering Oaks, the young teen realizes that personal missteps affect many lives and that it is possible to transcend secrets that are worse than her own.

While *Booklist* critic Debbie Carton wrote that *Kiss My Book* is made confusing due to its multiple subplots, she nonetheless praised "Ruby's contagious passion for words and truth." In contrast, *Kliatt* reviewer Amanda MacGregor paired praise for Ruby with praise for Michaels' novel, writing that the book's "unpredictable plot, wild cast of townsfolk, and multiple plotlines make for a winning combination." Calling *Kiss My Book* a story of "growth, love, acceptance, friendship, and ghosts," *School Library Journal* critic Jill Heritage Maza predicted that teens "will end up rooting for [the] . . . redemption" of the book-loving young heroine. In her novel Michaels references "many superb books and sonnets, making [*Kiss My Book*] . . . a veritable primer of must-reads," observed a *Kirkus Reviews* writer.

Biographical and Critical Sources

PERIODICALS

Booklist, October 1, 2007, Debbie Carton, review of *Kiss My Book,* p. 46.

Kirkus Reviews, July 15, 2007, review of *Kiss My Book.*

Kliatt, September, 2007, Amanda MacGregor, review of *Kiss My Book,* p. 25.

School Library Journal, February, 2008, Jill Heritage Maza, review of *Kiss My Book,* p. 122.*

N-P

NIELSEN, Susin 1964-
(Susin Nielsen-Fernlund)

Personal
Born 1964; married Goran Fernlund; children: Oskar.

Addresses
Home—Vancouver, British Columbia, Canada.

Career
Producer, screenwriter and author. Creator, with Cathy Moss, of television series *Franny's Feet* and *Robeson Arms.* Presenter at conference.

Awards, Honors
Gemini Award; two Canadian Screenwriter awards; Mr. Christie's Silver Medal, 2003, for *Hank and Fergus.*

Writings

FOR CHILDREN

Hank and Fergus, illustrated by Louise Andrée Laliberté, Orca Book Publishers (Victoria, British Columbia, Canada), 2003.
Mormor Moves In, illustrated by Louise Andrée Laliberté, Orca Book Publishers (Victoria, British Columbia, Canada), 2004.
The Magic Beads, illustrated by Genevieve Côte, Simply Read Books, 2007.
Word Nerd, Tundra Books (Toronto, Ontario, Canada), 2008.

"DEGRASSI JUNIOR HIGH" SERIES; BASED ON THE TELEVISION SERIES

Shane, J. Lorimer (Toronto, Ontario, Canada), 1988, reprinted, 2006.

Melanie, J. Lorimer (Toronto, Ontario, Canada), 1989, reprinted, 2006.
Wheels, J. Lorimer (Toronto, Ontario, Canada), 1990, reprinted, 2006.
Snake, J. Lorimer (Toronto, Ontario, Canada), 1991, reprinted, 2006.

OTHER

Also author of television scripts, including for series *Ready or Not, The Adventures of Shirley Holmes, Madison,* and *Edgement.* Author of videorecording *Monet: Shadow and Light,* directed by David Devine, 1999. Adaptor of television film *Alice, I Think* (based on a book by Susan Juby).

Biographical and Critical Sources

PERIODICALS

Kirkus Reviews, July 1, 2007, review of *The Magic Beads.*
Resource Links, October, 2007, Rachelle Gooden, review of *The Magic Beads,* p. 9.

ONLINE

Open Book Toronto Web site, http://www.openbooktoronto.com/ (November 1, 2008), "Ten Questions with Susin Nielsen."
Tundra Books Web site, http://www.tundrabooks.com/ (November 1, 2008), "Susin Nielsen."*

*   *   *

NIELSEN-FERNLUND, Susin
See NIELSEN, Susin

NUZUM, K.A.

Personal

Born in CO; married; children: two sons. *Education:* Vermont College, M.F.A. (writing for children and young adults).

Addresses

Home—Eastern CO.

Career

Writer, 2006—. Also worked as a ballroom dancer, master gardener, and radio-show host.

Writings

A Small White Scar (novel), Joanna Cotler Books (New York, NY), 2006.

Sidelights

K.A. Nuzum's debut novel, *A Small White Scar,* is set in 1940s Colorado and tells the coming-of-age story of Will, a young Colorado cowboy who dreams of competing in the professional rodeo circuit. For Will, this dream is kept out of reach due to his responsibility to care for little brother Denny. Denny is afflicted with Down syndrome and Will is deeply connected to and intensely protective of the boy. When Will flees from home and its responsibilities in an attempt to break from his family and become independent, Denny follows him into the wilderness and, eventually, to the rodeo circuit.

"Although Will is the narrator," Wendy Smith-D'Arezzo explained in her *School Library Journal* review of *A Small White Scar* that "readers also hear the voice of Denny through dialogue and through Will's projections of his brother's thoughts." In the end, stated *Kliatt* contributor Paula Rohrlick, "Will comes to understand how his caring for Denny has helped to make him a better person." "Part family tale, part adventure, part journey narrative," according to Carolyn Phelan in *Booklist,* Nuzum's *A Small White Scar* is a "coming-of-age story [that] has an emotional core that will [even] touch . . . readers" who have never experienced a rodeo.

Biographical and Critical Sources

PERIODICALS

Booklist, August 1, 2006, Carolyn Phelan, review of *A Small White Scar,* p. 75.
Kirkus Reviews, June 15, 2006, review of *A Small White Scar,* p. 636.
Kliatt, July, 2006, Paula Rohrlick, review of *A Small White Scar,* p. 12.
School Library Journal, August, 2006, Wendy Smith-D'Arezzo, review of *A Small White Scar,* p. 126.*

*   *   *

PALEN, Debbie 1964-

Personal

Born December 19, 1964. *Hobbies and other interests:* Yoga, writing, reading comics.

Addresses

Home—Cleveland, OH. *E-mail*—dpalen@fmgirl.com.

Career

Illustrator.

Illustrator

Kathlyn Gay, *Keep the Buttered Side Up: Food Superstitions from around the World,* Walker & Company (New York, NY), 1995.
Karen Gravelle and Jennifer Gravelle, *The Period Book: Everything You Don't Want to Ask (but Need to Know),* Walker & Company (New York, NY), 1996, updated edition, 2006.
Judith Harlan, *Girl Talk: Staying Strong, Feeling Good, Sticking Together,* Walker & Company (New York, NY), 1997.
Amy Nathan, *The Kids' Allowance Book,* Walker & Company (New York, NY), 1998.
Bennett Cerf, *Riddles and More Riddles,* Random House (New York, NY), 1999.
William Boniface, *Trim the Tree for Christmas!,* Price Stern Sloan (New York, NY), 2000.
Karen Bokram and Alexis Sinex, editors, *The Girls' Life Guide to Growing Up,* Beyond Words (Hillsboro, OR), 2000.
William Boniface, *What Do You Want on Your Sundae?,* Price Stern Sloan (New York, NY), 2001.
J.C. Greenburg, *On the Dog* ("Andrew Lost" series), Random House (New York, NY), 2002.
J.C. Greenburg, *In the Bathroom* ("Andrew Lost" series), Random House (New York, NY), 2002.
J.C. Greenburg, *In the Kitchen* ("Andrew Lost" series), Random House (New York, NY), 2002.
Joan Holub, *The Gingerbread Kid Goes to School,* Grosset & Dunlap (New York, NY), 2002.
J.C. Greenburg, *In the Garden* ("Andrew Lost" series), Random House (New York, NY), 2003.
Cathy Hapka and Ellen Titlebaum, *How Not to Babysit Your Brother,* Random House (New York, NY), 2005.
Cathy Hapka and Ellen Titlebaum, *How Not to Start Third Grade,* Random House (New York, NY), 2007.

Contributor of illustrations to periodicals, including *Chicago Tribune, Yoga Journal, Natural Health, Utne Reader, Ranger Rick, Los Angeles Times Magazine, Girls' Life,* and *Travel & Leisure.*

Sidelights

Debbie Palen, an illustrator based in Cleveland, Ohio, is best known for her humorous drawings done in pastel or pen and ink. In addition to her work for such corporate clients as Proctor & Gamble and Zany Brainy, Palen has provided the art for more than a dozen children's books, including the humorous _How Not to Babysit Your Brother_ by Cathy Hapka and Ellen Titlebaum. Her illustrations have also appeared in such publications as the _Chicago Tribune, Yoga Journal,_ and _Utne Reader._

One of Palen's early illustration projects, _The Period Book: Everything You Don't Want to Ask (but Need to Know)_ by Karen Gravelle and Gravelle's fifteen-year-old niece Jennifer Gravelle, is aimed at adolescent readers and explores the physical and emotional changes that come with puberty. According to a contributor in _Publishers Weekly,_ "Palen's cartoon illustrations echo the candor of the text and reinforce its kid-friendly approach."

Girl Talk: Staying Strong, Feeling Good, Sticking Together, a nonfiction work by Judith Harlan, focuses on building self-esteem by examining such topics as friend-ship and career planning. "Palen's comical artwork is a major part of the book," noted Stephanie Zvirin in a review of the work for _Booklist. The Girls' Life Guide to Growing Up,_ edited by Karen Bokram and Alexis Sinex, is another title for teen readers that addresses typical teen topics, in this case dating, eating disorders, and education. Palen's artwork for this volume again drew praise; her "quirky cartoons add humor and punctuate important points," according to _School Library Journal_ contributor Elaine Baran Black.

Palen has also served as the illustrator for several titles in J.C. Greenburg's "Andrew Lost" series of humorous science-based books. In _On the Dog,_ budding inventor Andrew Lost creates the Atom Sucker, a device that shrinks its designer, Andrew's cousin Judy, and his robot companion Thudd to microscopic proportions. The trio soon becomes tangled in the fur of a neighbor's dog and encounters a host of crawling creatures while trying to escape. In Greenburg's follow-up, _In the Bathroom,_ the still-miniaturized Andrew, Judy, and Thudd combat mold, mildew, and spiders after their neighbor decides to give the dog a bath. After they are flushed down the toilet, the intrepid threesome maneuver through a labyrinth of plumbing pipes to safety, and their adventures there are told in _In the Kitchen._ Rounding out the quartet, _In the Garden_ finds Andrew, Judy, and Thudd hitching a ride on a fly's back as they try to reach home and reverse the effects of the Atom Sucker. Palen contributed black-and-white drawings to each work; reviewing _In the Bathroom_ for _School Library Journal,_ Pat Leach stated that the book's illustrations "underscore the exaggerated sense of alarm" in Greenburg's humorous text.

Palen has also collaborated with Cathy Hapka and Ellen Titlebaum on a pair of chapter books for young readers. In _How Not to Babysit Your Brother_ young Will takes charge of the household after his grandmother falls asleep. Will's little brother has other ideas, however, and he begins wreaking havoc as Grandma snores away. In _School Library Journal_ Lisa S. Schindler complimented Palen's full-color artwork for _How Not to Babysit Your Brother,_ remarking that the characters' "wonderful facial expressions will make readers laugh even without reading the text." In a sequel, _How Not to Start Third Grade,_ Will once again tries to corral his brother, who has just entered kindergarten, as well as the family dog, which has invaded the halls of Will's school. Palen's drawings "extend the mayhem with cartoonish characters, exaggerated expressions, and lots of activity," observed Gillian Engberg in a _Booklist_ review.

Biographical and Critical Sources

PERIODICALS

Booklist, March 15, 1996, Stephanie Zvirin, review of _The Period Book: Everything You Don't Want to Ask (but_

Readers enjoy an unusual perspective in Debbie Palen's illustrations for J.C. Greenburg's picture book **On the Dog.** (Illustration copyright © 2002 by Debbie Palen. All rights reserved. Used by permission Random House Children's Books, a division of Random House, Inc.)

Palen's quirky art focuses on some anxious students in Cathy Hapka and Ellen Titlebaum's amusing chapter book **How Not to Start Third Grade.** (Illustration copyright © 2007 by Debbie Palen. All rights reserved. Used by permission of Random House Children's Books, a division of Random House, Inc.)

Need to Know), p. 1258; July, 1998, Karen Hutt, review of *The Kids' Allowance Book,* p. 1876; December 1, 1997, Stephanie Zvirin, review of *Girl Talk: Staying Strong, Feeling Good, Sticking Together,* p. 620; September 1, 2007, Gillian Engberg, review of *How Not to Start Third Grade,* p. 126.

Booklist, February 19, 1996, review of *The Period Book,* p. 217; June 5, 2000, review of *The Girls' Life Guide to Growing Up,* p. 95; February 5, 2001, review of *What Do You Want on Your Sundae?,* p. 90.

School Library Journal, October, 2000, Elaine Baran Black, review of *The Girls' Life Guide to Growing Up,* p. 178; December, 2002, Pat Leach, review of *In the Bathroom,* p. 96; August, 2005, Lisa S. Schindler, review of *How Not to Babysit Your Brother,* p. 96; July, 2007, Susan Lissim, review of *How Not to Start Third Grade,* p. 76.

ONLINE

Debbie Palen Home Page, http://debbiepalen.com (November 10, 2008).*

PELLETIER, Andrew T. (Andrew Thomas Pelletier)

Personal

Male.

Addresses

Home—Altamont, NY.

Career

Author of children's picture books.

Writings

Sixteen Miles to Spring, illustrated by Katya Krenina, Albert Whitman (Morton Grove, IL), 2002.
The Amazing Adventures of Bathman!, illustrated by Peter Elwell, Dutton (New York, NY), 2005.
The Toy Farmer, illustrated by Scott Nash, Dutton (New York, NY), 2007.

Sidelights

Since publishing his first children's book in 2002, Andrew T. Pelletier has contributed several stories to the picture-book pantheon available to young readers and listeners. In *Sixteen Miles to Spring,* he focuses on the changing season in a story about two teens—Wilbur and Wiley—whose slow, leisurely motor trip north in the early months of the year spreads warmth and the start of the growing season due to the magical mixture of seed, soil, and straw that they carry with them and cast from their pickup truck along the way. While noting that Pelletier's storytelling borders on the sentimental, Wendy S. Carroll added in her review for *School Library Journal* that the "idea of the story is cleverly brought forward." "Pelletier's fanciful imaginings are given colorful substance and texture through . . . spirited paintings" by artist Katya Krenina, concluded *Booklist* critic Ellen Mandel in her appraisal of *Sixteen Miles to Spring.* Calling the tale "lovely and carefree," a *Kirkus Reviews* writer added that Pelletier's porquois tale is "richly imaginative, with the harbingers of spring quirky enough . . . to impart a sense of the magic in store for all of us."

Pelletier tells a more rambunctious story in *The Amazing Adventures of Bathman!,* which finds an imaginative young bather determined to right the wrongs of Cap'n Squeegee, terrorizer of tubby time. When the ornery Squeegee kidnaps Rubber Ducky, the young boy transforms into the brave and squeaky-clean Bathman and endeavors to save Rubber Ducky before Mom calls him for dinner and pulls the plug on bathtub fun. Nostalgic, 'fifties-style artwork by Peter Elwell "complement[s] the clever text well, reinforcing the humor" of Pelletier's story, wrote *School Library Journal* contributor Lisa S. Schindler. As Schindler added, *The Amazing Adventures of Bathman!* will encourage children to engage in creative play and even "make them eager to hop into the tub," while another critic concluded in *Kirkus Reviews* that "Pelletier's first effort deftly mixes bath-time antics with superhero bravado and a touch of hard-boiled detecting."

Brought to life in pastel-toned illustrations by Scott Nash, Pelletier's *The Toy Farmer* recounts a story about a boy who is carried on a dreamlike adventure by a cast-off toy. Searching around his home's attic, young Jed discovers his father's old toy tractor and a miniature farmer that fits in the tractor's driver's seat. The morning after playing with the toy in his room, Jed awakes to find that his bedroom carpet has transformed into sprouting vegetation, and a pumpkin vine now sprouts huge pumpkins that cover his bedroom furniture. The pumpkin continues to grow until it so large that Jed submits it to the judging at a local fair, but when he returns home with his first-place prize, the magic is gone and the tin toy farmer is just a toy. In *Kirkus Reviews* a contributor dubbed *The Toy Farmer*

"a gentle homage to the power of a child's imagination," and a *Publishers Weekly* critic praised Nash's "irresistible retro-inspired illustrations" for "light[ing] up" Pelletier's magical tale.

Biographical and Critical Sources

PERIODICALS

Booklist, May 1, 2002, Ellen Mandel, review of *Sixteen Miles to Spring,* p. 1535; August, 2007, Carolyn Phelan, review of *The Toy Farmer,* p. 89.

Kirkus Reviews, February 15, 2002, review of *Sixteen Miles to Spring,* p. 262; April 15, 2005, review of *The Amazing Adventures of Bathman!,* p. 479; July 1, 2007, review of *The Toy Farmer.*

New York Times, December 2, 2007, Krystyna Poray Goddu, review of *The Toy Farmer.*

Publishers Weekly, August 13, 2007, review of *The Toy Farmer,* p. 67.

School Library Journal, June, 2002, Wendy S. Carroll, review of *Sixteen Miles to Spring,* p. 107; July, 2005, Lisa S. Schindler, review of *The Amazing Adventures of Bathman!,* p. 81.*

Andrew T. Pelletier teams up with artist Peter Elwell to follow a young superhero in **The Amazing Adventures of Bathman!** (Illustration copyright © by Peter Elwell, 2005. Reproduced by permission of Puffin Books, a division of Penguin Putnam Books for Young Readers.)

PELLETIER, Andrew Thomas
See PELLETIER, Andrew T.

*　　*　　*

PICKERING, Jimmy

Personal

Born in Talent, OR. *Education:* California Institute of the Arts, degree.

Addresses

Home—OR. *Agent*—Shannon Associates, 630 9th Ave., Ste. 707, New York, NY 10036. *E-mail*—jimmy@jimmypickering.com.

Career

Artist, designer, and author. Has worked for Walt Disney Imagineering, Hallmark Cards, and Universal Studios. *Exhibitions:* Solo exhibitions include DvA Gallery, Chicago, IL, 2007, and Copro Nason Gallery, Santa Monica, CA, 2008. Group exhibitions include Art Institute of Portland, Portland, OR, 2007; Disney Gallery, Anaheim, CA, 2007; and Society of Illustrators, New York, NY, 2007.

Writings

SELF-ILLUSTRATED

It's Fall, Smallfellow Press (Los Angeles, CA), 2002.
It's Winter, Smallfellow Press (Los Angeles, CA), 2002.
It's Spring, Smallfellow Press (Los Angeles, CA), 2003.
It's Summer, Smallfellow Press (Los Angeles, CA), 2003.
Skelly the Skeleton Girl, Simon & Schuster (New York, NY), 2007.
Skelly and Femur, Simon & Schuster (New York, NY), 2009.

ILLUSTRATOR

Scott Allen, *Somethin' Pumpkin,* Smallfellow Press (Los Angeles, CA), 2001.
Stephen Krensky, *Bubble Trouble,* Aladdin Paperbacks (New York, NY), 2004.
Jeffrey Fulmer, *My Imagination Kit,* Mondo (New York, NY), 2004.
Robyn Parnell, *My Closet Threw a Party,* Sterling Publishing (New York, NY), 2005.
Alan Jardine, *Sloop John B: A Pirate's Tale* (with CD), Milk & Cookies Press (New York, NY), 2005.
Elizabeth Hatch, *Halloween Night,* Random House (New York, NY), 2005.
Angie Sage, *The Sword in the Grotto,* Katherine Tegen Books (New York, NY), 2006.

Angie Sage, *My Haunted House,* Katherine Tegen Books (New York, NY), 2006.
Angie Sage, *Vampire Brat,* Katherine Tegen Books (New York, NY), 2007.
Angie Sage, *Frognapped,* Katherine Tegen Books (New York, NY), 2007.
Angie Sage, *Ghostsitters,* Katherine Tegen Books (New York, NY), 2008.
Jack Prelutsky, *The Swamps of Sleethe: Poems from beyond the Solar System,* Knopf (New York, NY), 2009.

Sidelights

Jimmy Pickering, a painter and designer who has worked at such companies as Walt Disney Imagineering and Universal Studios, also provides artwork for picture books such as *Vampire Brat* by Angie Sage and *Halloween Night* by Elizabeth Hatch. Pickering is an author as well as illustrator, however, and he counts *Skelly the Skeleton Girl* among his original self-illustrated stories. Noting that his own artistic style blends elements of Dr. Seuss, Edward Gorey, the movie *Pirates of the Caribbean,* and "crazy foam," Pickering stated on his home page that "the results are something odd, strange a little scary, but somehow funny and harmless."

Written by Alan Jardine, cofounder of the popular surf band the Beach Boys, *Sloop John B: A Pirate's Tale* concerns the adventures of a youngster and his grandfather after they run afoul of some buccaneers. "The vibrant illustrations add humor to the story with many amusing details and characterizations," Linda L. Walkins noted in *School Library Journal,* and a *Publishers Weekly* contributor observed that "Pickering's often-dazzling mixed-media compositions" for Jardine's tale "bring the watery setting to life." In *Halloween Night,* Hatch's cumulative story based on "The House That Jack Built," a tiny mouse hiding inside a jack-o'-lantern unleashes a wild chain of events. A *Kirkus Reviews* critic praised Pickering's art for the book, stating that "wacky perspectives and silly details keep the pictures on the playful side of thrilling."

An eerie little girl searches for the owner of a misplaced bone in *Skelly the Skeleton Girl,* a "charmingly simple tale," according to Amelia Jenkins in *School Library Journal.* After questioning a host of spooky creatures, including her spidery neighbor, several ghostly visitors, and some man-eating plants, Skelly solves the mystery. "Despite the ghoulish subtext, midnight palette and inky backdrops, Pickering keeps the mood breezy," a *Publishers Weekly* critic remarked, and a contributor in *Kirkus Reviews* recommended *Skelly the Skeleton Girl* as a "gothic treat [that] is perfect for those who like to be scared—just a tiny bit."

Biographical and Critical Sources

PERIODICALS

Kirkus Reviews, May 1, 2005, review of *Sloop John B: A Pirate's Tale,* p. 540; August 1, 2005, review of *Hal-*

***Jimmy Pickering's humorously macabre art is the star of his self-illustrated* Skelly the Skeleton Girl.** (Copyright © 2007 by Jimmy Pickering. Reprinted with the permission of Simon & Schuster Books for Young Readers, an imprint of Simon & Schuster Children's Publishing Division.)

loween Night, p. 849; July 1, 2007, review of *Skelly the Skeleton Girl.*

Publishers Weekly, May 9, 2005, review of *Sloop John B,* p. 69; August 1, 2005, review of *Halloween Night,* p. 63; August 14, 2006, review of *My Haunted House,* p. 205; September 24, 2007, review of *Skelly the Skeleton Girl,* p. 72.

School Library Journal, July, 2003, Doris Losey, review of *It's Spring* and *It's Summer,* p. 104; June, 2005, Wendy Woodfill, review of *My Closet Threw a Party,* p. 124; July, 2005, Linda L. Walkins, review of *Sloop John B,* p. 75; August, 2005, Marge Loch-Wouters, review of *Halloween Night,* p. 113; August, 2007, Amelia Jenkins, review of *Skelly the Skeleton Girl,* p. 88; September, 2007, Walter Minkel, review of *Frognapped,* p. 175.

ONLINE

Jimmy Pickering Home Page, http://www.jimmypickering. com (November 10, 2008).

Jimmy Pickering Web log, http://jimmypickering.blogspot. com/ (November 10, 2008).

Shannon Associates Web site, http://www.shannon associates.com/ (November 10, 2008), "Jimmy Pickering."*

*   *   *

POHRT, Tom 1953-

Personal

Born 1953, in Flint, MI; married; children: one daughter. *Education:* Attended University of Michigan, Flint.

Addresses

Home—Ann Arbor, MI.

Career

Illustrator and author of children's books. Formerly worked in automobile factories and in small-press publishing.

Awards, Honors

Lee Bennett Hopkins Award for Children's Poetry, 2004, for *The Wishing Bone and Other Poems* by Stephen Mitchell; American Library Association Notable Children's Book designation, 2004, for *The Little Gentleman* by Philippa Pearce.

Writings

SELF-ILLUSTRATED

(Reteller) *Coyote Goes Walking,* Farrar, Straus (New York, NY), 1995.

Having a Wonderful Time, Farrar, Straus (New York, NY), 1999.

ILLUSTRATOR

Howard Norman, *Who Met the Ice Lynx?,* Grey Wolf Press, 1978.

Jim Henen, *The Man Who Kept Cigars in His Cap,* Grey Wolf Press, 1978.

Ted Kooser, *The Blizzard Voices* (poetry), Bieler Press (Minneapolis, MN), 1986.

Barry Lopez, *Crow and Weasel,* North Point Press, 1992.

Bruce Donehower, *Miko, Little Hunter of the North,* Farrar, Straus (New York, NY), 1990.

Elizabeth Hauge and Victoria Glournoy McCarthy, editors, *A Child's Anthology of Poetry,* Ecco Press (Hopewell, NJ), 1995.

Tony Johnston, *An Old Shell: Poems of the Galapagos,* Farrar, Straus (New York, NY), 1999.

Howard Norman, *Trickster and the Fainting Birds,* Harcourt Brace (San Diego, CA), 1999.

John Frank, *The Tomb of the Boy King: A True Story in Verse,* Farrar, Straus (New York, NY), 2000.

Jim Harrison, *The Boy Who Ran to the Woods,* Atlantic Monthly Press (New York, NY), 2000.

Stephen Mitchell, *The Wishing Bone and Other Poems,* Candlewick Press (Cambridge, MA), 2003.

Philippa Pearce, *The Little Gentleman,* Greenwillow Books (New York, NY), 2004.

Stephen Mitchell, reteller, *Genies, Meanies, and Magic Rings: Three Tales from the Arabian Nights,* Walker & Co. (New York, NY), 2007.

Julia Durango, *The Walls of Cartagena,* Simon & Schuster (New York, NY), 2008.

Sidelights

Illustrator and children's author Tom Pohrt grew up in the automobile-manufacturing town of Flint, Michigan. A self-taught artist whose love of animals is evident in his artwork, Pohrt has been interested in writing and drawing ever since he was a little boy. Despite his lack of guidance as a youngster, Pohrt has become a well-established illustrator, working with texts by authors such as Philippa Pierce, Julia Durango, and Jim Harrison as well as penning the text for two self-illustrated books featuring his original stories. "The precise, delicate lines of his drawings, coupled with his slightly moody, sepia-toned palette, suggest antique etchings," wrote a *Publishers Weekly* contributor in reviewing Pohrt's work for Howard Norman's *Trickster and the Fainting Birds,* the critic dubbing the picture book "beautifully designed and presented."

In *Coyote Goes Walking* Pohrt retells four Native-American trickster tales, bringing his animal characters to life in what a *Publishers Weekly* contributor described as "warm, earth-toned watercolors" that contain a "subtle humor." Described by a *Publishers Weekly* contributor as "one off-beat destination that's definitely worth a visit," Pohrt's quirky picture book *Having a Wonderful Time* finds a girl and a talking cat on a vacation where unexpected animal-sightings abound. The reviewer had special praise for the author/illustrator's "confidently deadpan" text with its "dry, understated humor," but also commended the author's characteristic detailed pen-and-ink drawings.

Praising Pohrt's contribution to John Frank's *The Tomb of the Boy King: A True Story in Verse,* *School Library Journal* contributor Barbara Buckley noted that the artist's "informative pen-and-watercolor paintings . . . will be a real draw" for young readers, and Ilene Cooper called them "expertly executed" in her *Booklist* review. Additional praise was accorded Pohrt's illustrations for Howard Norman's *Trickster and the Fainting Birds,* a *Publishers Weekly* reviewer praising the renderings of the story's animal characters as "meticulously executed" and "precise, delicate" pen drawings.

The award-winning anthology *The Wishing Bone and Other Poems,* one of several collaborations between Pohrt and author Stephen Mitchell, exemplifies Pohrt's skill as an illustrator. This collection of nine poems delves into the mysteries of life as seen through the eyes of a child, describing what might happen if you make a wish on a wishing bone, among other fanciful themes. Pohrt's illustrations allow readers to visualize childhood imaginings through his ability to balance attention to detail with the playfulness of Mitchell's verse. A second collaboration, *Genies, Meanies, and Magic Rings: Three Tales from the Arabian Nights,* also delves into the world of fantasy, pairing Mitchell's retelling of the famous 1,001 tales with "lively informal black-and-white drawings that add to the fun," according to *Booklist* critic Hazel Rochman. Cooper, reviewing *The Wishing Bone and Other Poems* for the same periodical, called that volume "a lovely piece of bookmaking that combines poems that are both whimsical and thought-provoking with delightful ink-and-watercolor pictures that spill across the pages." A *Kirkus Reviews* contributor agreed, deeming Mitchell's poetry collection "a handsomely packaged, nicely diverse gathering of words and art."

Tom Pohrt creates whimsical illustrations to grace the pages of Stephen Mitchell's **The Wishing Bone and Other Poems.** (Illustration copyright © 2003 by Tom Pohrt. Reproduced by permission of the publisher Candlewick Press, Inc., Cambridge, MA.)

Other books featuring Pohrt's illustrations include the elementary-grade novels *The Little Gentleman* by Philippa Pearce and Julia Durango's *The Walls of Cartagena,* the latter an historical novel about a young teen's work to fight slavery in eighteenth-century Spain. *The Little Gentleman* relates a sophisticated story about the friendship between a young housekeeper and a talking mole that Cooper described as "walk[ing] . . . the line between pure fantasy and magic realism." Pohrt's illustrations for Pearce's text "contribute to the tale's feeling of a good old-fashioned storybook," wrote a *Publishers Weekly* contributor, and a *Kirkus Reviews* critic dubbed *The Little Gentleman* "perfectly unusual, [and] perfectly lovely."

Biographical and Critical Sources

PERIODICALS

Booklist, December 15, 1995, Karen Hutt, review of *Coyote Goes Walking,* p. 706; December 1, 1999,

GraceAnne A. DeCandido, review of *An Old Shell: Poems of the Galapagos,* p. 700; January 1, 2000, Karen Hutt, review of *Trickster and the Fainting Birds,* p. 916; March 1, 2001, Ilene Cooper, review of *The Tomb of the Boy King,* p. 1284; April 1, 2003, Ilene Cooper, review of *The Wishing Bone and Other Poems,* p. 1407; August, 2004, Ilene Cooper, review of *The Little Gentleman,* p. 1937; October 1, 2007, Hazel Rochman, review of *Genies, Meanies, and Magic Rings: Three Tales from the Arabian Nights,* p. 50.

Horn Book, November, 1999, Nancy Vasilakis, review of *Trickster and the Fainting Birds,* p. 749; March, 2001, review of *The Tomb of the Boy King,* p. 228; July-August, 2003, Susan P. Bloom, review of *The Wishing Bone and Other Poems,* p. 474; September-October, 2004, Sarah Ellis, review of *The Little Gentleman,* p. 594; September-October, 2007, Susan P. Bloom, review of *Genies, Meanies, and Magic Rings,* p. 83.

Kirkus Reviews, March 1, 2003, review of *The Wishing Bone and Other Poems,* p. 393; July 15, 2004, Philippa Pearce, review of *The Little Gentleman,* p. 692; July 1, 2007, review of *Genies, Meanies, and Magic Rings.*

New York Times Book Review, November 25, 1990, review of *Crow and Weasel,* p. 17.

Publishers Weekly, November 20, 1995, review of *Coyote Goes Walking,* p. 76; September 7, 1998, review of *Crow and Weasel,* p. 97; April 19, 1999, review of *Having a Wonderful Time,* p. 72; October 25, 1999, review of *Trickster and the Fainting Birds,* p. 81; November 8, 1999, review of *An Old Shell,* p. 67; October 2, 2000, review of *The Boy Who Ran to the Woods,* p. 82; March 12, 2001, review of *The Tomb of the Boy King,* p. 90; February 17, 2003, review of *The Wishing Bone and Other Poems,* p. 76; November 8, 2004, review of *The Little Gentleman,* p. 56.

School Library Journal, August, 1990, Denise Anton Wright, review of *Miko, Little Hunter of the North,* p. 146; December, 1995, Patricia Lothrop Green, review of *Coyote Goes Walking,* p. 89; April, 1999, Marianne Saccardi, review of *Having a Wonderful Time,* p. 107; May, 2001, Barbara Buckley, review of *The Tomb of the Boy King,* p. 164; May, 2003, Sally R. Dow, review of *The Wishing Bone and Other Poems,* p. 140; September, 2004, Eva Mitnick, review of *The Little Gentleman,* p. 177.*

*   *   *

POWERS, Jessica
See POWERS, J.L.

*   *   *

POWERS, Jessica Lynn
See POWERS, J.L.

POWERS, J.L. 1974-
(Jessica Powers, Jessica Lynn Powers)

Personal

Born June 23, 1974, in El Paso, TX; daughter of a geologist and a journalist. *Education:* New Mexico State University, B.A. (literature and writing); University of Texas at El Paso, M.F.A. (writing), 1999; University at Albany, State University of New York, M.A. (African history), 2001; Stanford University, M.A. (African history), 2008. *Hobbies and other interests:* Travel, reading, Africa, photography, literature, Latino culture in the United States.

Addresses

Home—CA. *E-mail*—jlpowers@evaporites.com.

Career

Writer and educator. Performer in street theater in India, Uzbekistan, Kenya, Nicaragua, and Mexico; Cinco Puntos Press, El Paso, TX, former senior editor; has taught African history and composition, research, and argument at universities and community colleges, including University of Texas at El Paso, El Paso Community College, and Dona Ana Branch Community College.

Writings

The Confessional (young-adult novel), Knopf (New York, NY), 2007.

UNDER NAME JESSICA POWERS

A Bark in the Park: The Forty-five Best Places to Hike with Your Dog in the El Paso/Las Cruces Region, Cruden Bay Books (Montchanin, DE), 2003.
(Editor) *Labor Pains and Birth Stories: Essays on Pregnancy, Childbirth, and Becoming a Parent,* Datalyst Book Press (CA), 2009.

Also contributor to *Frontera Dreams: A Hector Belascoaran Shayne Mystery,* by Paco Ignacio Taibo II and translated by Bill Vernon. Contributor of articles to periodicals, including *Colorlines, Revista Maryknoll, Revista Tradicion,* and *Suite101.com.* Contributor of book reviews and articles to *NewPages.com.*

Sidelights

J.L. Powers, a writer, editor, and educator who grew up near the border between the United States and Mexico, is the author of the young-adult novel *The Confessional,* a work that "powerfully combines timely storylines regarding illegal immigration, school violence and racial tension," observed a critic in *Publishers Weekly.* "The *Confessional* is a kind of love letter for the border re-

gion and for young people," Powers remarked on her home page. "It represents my hope that the young people of the U.S. and the young people of Mexico can achieve true healing from wounds caused by prejudice and institutional violence."

Set in El Paso, Texas, *The Confessional* examines the aftereffects of a teenager's brutal murder. After a confrontation with a Mexican student from his Jesuit high school, MacKenzie "Mac" Malone is found stabbed to death in his family's yard. In alternating chapters, Mac's classmates try to make sense of the episode, in the process revealing their own internal struggles and confronting their own prejudices. "The six distinct voices used to examine the tension between adopted country and ethnic pride rarely falter," a critic in *Kirkus Reviews* stated. Writing in *School Library Journal,* Shelley Huntington observed that Powers' "characters will reach mature teens eager to hear their own preoccupations echoed and, perhaps, clarified."

Biographical and Critical Sources

PERIODICALS

Kirkus Reviews, July 15, 2007, review of *The Confessional.*
Publishers Weekly, July 30, 2007, review of *The Confessional,* p. 85.
School Library Journal, December, 2007, Shelley Huntington, review of *The Confessional,* p. 142.

ONLINE

California Readers Web site, http://www.californiareaders. org/ (November 10, 2008), Bonnie O'Brian, "Meet J.L. Powers."
J.L. Powers Home Page, http://www.jlpowers.net (November 10, 2008).

*   *   *

PUYBARET, Eric 1976-

Personal

Born 1976, in France. *Education:* Attended École National Supérrieure des Arts Décoratifs.

Addresses

Home—France.

Career

Illustrator. *Exhibitions:* Work exhibited at Bologna Children's Book Fair, 1999.

Writings

SELF-ILLUSTRATED

Les échasses rouges, Gautier-Languereau (Paris, France), 2006.

ILLUSTRATOR

Laurence Tichit, *Gaspard le renard et gaston le héron,* Gautier-Languereau (Paris, France), 2000.

Florence Grazia, *Barnabé le chat beauté,* Gautier-Languereau (Paris, France), 2000.

Christine Frasseto, *Moitié de poulet,* Flammarion (Paris, France), 2001.

Christine Frasseto, *Un cadeau en hiver,* Flammarion (Paris, France), 2002.

Claire Mazard, *L'été de mes dix ans,* Flammarion (Paris, France), 2002.

Christian Jolibois, *Le grand voyage de mimolette,* Flammarion (Paris, France), 2002.

Philippe Barbeau, *Gare au Dragon!,* Flammarion (Paris, France), 2002.

Anne-Sophie Baumann, *Au Zoo!,* Mondo Mino, 2003.

Catherine Lamon-Mignot, *Une sorcière dans le coffre à jouets,* Hachette (Paris, France), 2004.

Mathilde Barat, *Le grand orchestre von Bémol,* Gautier-Languereau (Paris, France), 2005.

Philippe Lechermeier, *Graines de cabanes,* Gautier-Languereau (Paris, France), 2005.

Didier Sustrac, *Chut, le roi pourrait t'entendre!,* Gautier-Languereau (Paris, France), 2007.

Pol-Serge Kakon, *L'opéra plouf* (with CD), Père Castor Flammarion (Paris, France), 2007.

Peter Yarrow and Peggy Lipton, *Puff, the Magic Dragon* (with CD), Sterling Publishers (New York, NY), 2007.

Jennifer Berne, *Manfish: The Story of Jacques Cousteau,* Chronicle Books (New York, NY), 2008.

Biographical and Critical Sources

PERIODICALS

Booklist, September 15, 2007, Janice Del Negro, review of *Puff, the Magic Dragon,* p. 70.

Kirkus Reviews, July 15, 2007, review of *Puff, the Magic Dragon.*

Publishers Weekly, June 11, 2007, review of *Puff, the Magic Dragon,* p. 58.

School Library Journal, August, 2007, Marge Loch-Wouters, review of *Puff, the Magic Dragon,* p. 108.

ONLINE

Ricochet-Jeunes Web site, http://www.ricochet-jeunes.org/ (December 15, 2008), "Eric Puybaret."*

R-S

RATNER, Sue Lynn
See ALEXANDER, Sue

* * *

REILLY, Joan

Personal
Female.

Addresses
Home—New York, NY. *E-mail*—illustration@joanreilly. com.

Career
Illustrator and cartoonist, 1996—.

Awards, Honors
Pcom Creative Award, 2008.

Illustrator
Bert Metter, *Bar Mitzvah, Bat Mitzvah: The Ceremony, the Party, and How the Day Came to Be,* Clarion Books (New York, NY), 2007.

Contributing editor to Hi-Horse Comics. Creator of "Hank and Barbara" (Web comic), posted at *Next-Door Neighbor,* http://www.smithmag.net. Contributor to *Hi-Horse Omnibus,* Alternative Comics; *Studs Terkel's Working: A Graphic Adaptation,* by Harvey Pekar, New Press; and *I Saw You . . .,* edited by Julia Wertz, Three Rivers Press, 2009. Contributor of illustrations to "Goodwords" (puzzle feature of "Ask Marilyn" weekly column), *Parade* magazine.

Biographical and Critical Sources

PERIODICALS

Booklist, July 1, 2007, Kay Weisman, review of *Bar Mitzvah, Bat Mitzvah: The Ceremony, the Party, and How the Day Came to Be,* p. 52.

Kirkus Reviews, July 15, 2007, review of *Bar Mitzvah, Bat Mitzvah.*
School Library Journal, November, 2007, Rachel Kamin, review of *Bar Mitzvah, Bat Mitzvah,* p. 110.

ONLINE

Creativeshake.com, http://www.creativeshake.com/ (November 1, 2008), "Joan Reilly."
Ispot.com, http://www.theispot.com/ (November 1, 2008), "Joan Reilly."
Joan Reilly Home Page, http://www.joanreilly.com (November 1, 2008).*

* * *

RYLANT, Cynthia 1954-

Personal
Surname pronounced "Rye-*lunt*"; born June 6, 1954, in Hopewell, VA; daughter of John Tune (an army sergeant) and Leatrel (a nurse) Smith; twice married (divorced); children (first marriage): Nathaniel. *Education:* Morris Harvey College (now University of Charleston), B.A., 1975; Marshall University (Huntington, WV), M.A., 1976; Kent State University, M.L.S., 1982. *Politics:* Democrat. *Religion:* "Christian, no denomination." *Hobbies and other interests:* Pets, reading, going to movies, going to the seashore.

Addresses
Home—Eugene, OR. *Agent*—Steven Malk, Writers House, 3368 Governor Dr., Ste. 224-F, San Diego, CA 92122.

Career
Writer, educator, and librarian. Marshall University, Huntington, WV, part-time English instructor, 1979-80; Akron Public Library, Akron, OH, children's librarian,

1983; University of Akron, Akron, part-time English lecturer, 1983-84; Northeast Ohio Universities College of Medicine, Rootstown, part-time lecturer, 1991—.

Awards, Honors

American Book Award nomination, and American Library Association (ALA) Notable Book designation, both 1983, and English-speaking Union Book-across-the-Sea Ambassador of Honor Award, 1984, all for *When I Was Young in the Mountains;* National Council for Social Studies Best Book designation, and ALA Notable Book designation, both 1984, and Society of Midland Authors Best Children's Book designation, 1985, all for *Waiting to Waltz . . . a Childhood;* Children's Book of the Year designation, Child Study Association of America (CSA), 1985, for *The Relatives Came;* Children's Book of the Year designation, CSA, 1985, for *A Blue-eyed Daisy;* Parents' Choice Award, 1986, and Newbery Medal Honor Book designation, 1987, both for *A Fine White Dust;* ALA Best Book for Young Adults citation, 1988, for *A Kindness;* Ohioana Award, 1990, for *But I'll Be Back Again;* ALA Best Book for Young Adults citation, 1990, for *A Couple of Kooks and Other Stories about Love;* Parents' Choice Award (picture book) and *Boston Globe/Horn Book* Honor Book for Nonfiction designation, both 1991, and Ohioana Award, 1992, all for *Appalachia; Boston Globe/Horn Book* Award for Children's Fiction, Reading Magic Award, and Parents' Choice Award, all 1992, and John Newbery Medal and *Hungry Mind Review* Award, both 1993, all for *Missing May; Boston Globe/Horn Book* Honor Book designation, 2004, for *God Went to Beauty School.* Several of Rylant's "Henry and Mudge" books received child-selected awards, including Garden State Children's Book Award, Children's Services Section of the New Jersey Library Association, and Children's Choice Award, Association of Booksellers for Children. In 1983, *When I Was Young in the Mountains* was named a Caldecott Honor Book for its illustrations by Diane Goode. *The Relatives Came* was named a *New York Times* best illustrated book, 1985, and a Caldecott Medal honor book, 1986, for illustrations by Stephen Gammell.

Writings

FOR CHILDREN; PICTURE BOOKS AND EARLY FICTION, EXCEPT AS NOTED

When I Was Young in the Mountains, illustrated by Diane Goode, Dutton (New York, NY), 1982.

Miss Maggie, illustrated by Thomas DiGrazia, Dutton (New York, NY), 1983.

This Year's Garden, illustrated by Mary Szilagyi, Bradbury (New York, NY), 1984.

The Relatives Came, illustrated by Stephen Gammell, Bradbury (New York, NY), 1985.

Night in the Country, illustrated by Mary Szilagyi, Bradbury (New York, NY), 1986.

Birthday Presents, illustrated by Suçie Stevenson, Orchard Books (New York, NY), 1987.

All I See, illustrated by Peter Catalanotto, Orchard Books (New York, NY), 1988.

Mr. Griggs' Work, illustrated by Julie Downing, Orchard Books (New York, NY), 1989.

An Angel for Solomon Singer, illustrated by Peter Catalanotto, Orchard Books (New York, NY), 1992.

Best Wishes (autobiographical picture book), photographs by Carlo Ontal, Richard C. Owen (Katonah, NY), 1992.

The Dreamer, illustrated by Barry Moser, Blue Sky Press (New York, NY), 1993.

(Self-illustrated) *Dog Heaven,* Blue Sky Press (New York, NY), 1995.

Gooseberry Park, illustrated by Arthur Howard, Harcourt (San Diego, CA), 1995.

The Van Gogh Cafe (middle-grade fiction), Harcourt (San Diego, CA), 1995.

The Bookshop Dog, Blue Sky Press (New York, NY), 1996.

The Whales, Blue Sky Press (New York, NY), 1996.

The Old Woman Who Named Things, illustrated by Kathryn Brown, Harcourt (San Diego, CA), 1996.

(Self-illustrated) *Cat Heaven,* Blue Sky Press (New York, NY), 1997.

An Everyday Book, Simon & Schuster (New York, NY), 1997.

Bear Day, illustrated by Jennifer Selby, Harcourt (San Diego, CA), 1998.

Tulip Sees America, illustrated by Lisa Desimini, Blue Sky Press (New York, NY), 1998.

The Bird House, illustrated by Barry Moser, Blue Sky Press (New York, NY), 1998.

Scarecrow, illustrated by Lauren Stringer, Harcourt (San Diego, CA), 1998.

The Heavenly Village, Blue Sky Press (New York, NY), 1999.

The Cookie-Store Cat, Blue Sky Press (New York, NY), 1999.

Bunny Bungalow, illustrated by Nancy Hayashi, Harcourt (San Diego, CA), 1999.

The Troublesome Turtle, Greenwillow (New York, NY), 1999.

Puzzling Possum, Greenwillow (New York, NY), 1999.

Let's Go Home: The Wonderful Things about a House, illustrated by Wendy Anderson Halperin, Simon & Schuster (New York, NY), 2000.

In November, illustrated by Jill Kastner, Harcourt (San Diego, CA), 2000.

Thimbleberry Stories, illustrated by Maggie Kneen, Harcourt (San Diego, CA), 2000.

The Ticky-Tacky Doll, illustrated by Harvey Stevenson, Harcourt (San Diego, CA), 2000.

The Great Gracie Chase, illustrated by Mark Teague, Blue Sky Press (New York, NY), 2001.

Good Morning Sweetie Pie, and Other Poems for Little Children, illustrated by Jane Dyer, Simon & Schuster (New York, NY), 2001.

Old Town in the Green Groves: The Lost Little-House Years, illustrated by Jim LaMarche, HarperCollins (New York, NY), 2002.

Christmas in the Country, illustrated by Diane Goode, Blue Sky Press (New York, NY), 2002.

Moonlight, the Halloween Cat, illustrated by Melissa Sweet, HarperCollins (New York, NY), 2003.

Long Night Moon, illustrated by Mark Siegel, Simon & Schuster (New York, NY), 2004.

The Stars Will Still Shine, illustrated by Tiphanie Beeke, HarperCollins (New York, NY), 2005.

Puppies and Piggies, illustrated by Ivan Bates, Harcourt (San Diego, CA), 2005.

Miracles in Motion, illustrated by Lambert Davis, Blue Sky Press (New York, NY), 2005.

If You'll Be My Valentine, illustrated by Fumi Kosaka, HarperCollins (New York, NY), 2005.

The Case of the Desperate Duck, illustrated by G. Brian Karas, Greenwillow Books (New York, NY), 2005.

The Journey: Stories of Migration, illustrated by Lambert Davis, Blue Sky Press (New York, NY), 2006.

(Adaptor) *Walt Disney's Cinderella,* Disney Press (New York, NY), 2007.

Alligator Boy, illustrated by Diane Goode, Harcourt (Orlando, FL), 2007.

Snow, illustrated by Lauren Stringer, Harcourt (Orlando, FL), 2008.

Puppies and Piggies, illustrated by Ivan Bates, Harcourt (Orlando, FL), 2008.

(Reteller) *Hansel and Gretel,* illustrated by Jen Corace, Hyperion (New York, NY), 2008.

The Beautiful Stories of Life: Six Greek Myths, Retold, illustrated by Carson Ellis, Harcourt (Orlando, FL), 2008.

Baby Face: A Book of Love for Baby, illustrated by Diane Goode, Simon & Schuster (New York, NY), 2008.

Brownie and Pearl Step Out, illustrated by Brian Biggs, Harcourt (Orlando, FL), 2009.

Rylant's papers are housed in Special Collections at Kent State University, Kent, OH.

"HENRY AND MUDGE" SERIES; BEGINNING READERS

Henry and Mudge: The First Book of Their Adventures, illustrated by James Stevenson, Macmillan (New York, NY), 1987.

Henry and Mudge in Puddle Trouble: The Second Book of Their Adventures, illustrated by James Stevenson, Macmillan (New York, NY), 1987.

Henry and Mudge in the Green Time: The Third Book of Their Adventures, illustrated by Suçie Stevenson, Macmillan (New York, NY), 1987.

Henry and Mudge under the Yellow Moon: The Fourth Book of Their Adventures, illustrated by Suçie Stevenson, Macmillan (New York, NY), 1987.

Henry and Mudge in the Sparkle Days: The Fifth Book of Their Adventures, illustrated by Suçie Stevenson, Macmillan (New York, NY), 1988.

Henry and Mudge and the Forever Sea: The Sixth Book of Their Adventures, illustrated by Suçie Stevenson, Macmillan (New York, NY), 1989.

Henry and Mudge Get the Cold Shivers: The Seventh Book of Their Adventures, illustrated by Suçie Stevenson, Macmillan (New York, NY), 1989.

Henry and Mudge and the Happy Cat: The Eighth Book of Their Adventures, illustrated by Suçie Stevenson, Macmillan (New York, NY), 1990.

Henry and Mudge and the Bedtime Thumps: The Ninth Book of Their Adventures, illustrated by Suçie Stevenson, Macmillan (New York, NY), 1991.

Henry and Mudge Take the Big Test: The Tenth Book of Their Adventures, illustrated by Suçie Stevenson, Macmillan (New York, NY), 1991.

Henry and Mudge and the Long Weekend: The Eleventh Book of Their Adventures, illustrated by Suçie Stevenson, Macmillan (New York, NY), 1992.

Henry and Mudge and the Wild Wind: The Twelfth Book of Their Adventures, illustrated by Suçie Stevenson, Macmillan (New York, NY), 1992.

Henry and Mudge and the Careful Cousin: The Thirteenth Book of Their Adventures, illustrated by Suçie Stevenson, Macmillan (New York, NY), 1994.

Henry and Mudge and the Best Day of All: The Fourteenth Book of Their Adventures, illustrated by Suçie Stevenson, Bradbury Press (New York, NY), 1995.

Henry and Mudge in the Family Trees: The Fifteenth Book of Their Adventures, illustrated by Suçie Stevenson, Simon & Schuster (New York, NY), 1997.

Henry and Mudge and the Sneaky Crackers: The Sixteenth Book of Their Adventures, illustrated by Suçie Stevenson, Simon & Schuster (New York, NY), 1998.

Henry and Mudge and the Starry Night: The Seventeenth Book of Their Adventures, illustrated by Suçie Stevenson, Simon & Schuster (New York, NY), 1998.

Henry and Mudge and Annie's Good Move: The Eighteenth Book of Their Adventures, illustrated by Suçie Stevenson, Simon & Schuster (New York, NY), 1998.

Henry and Mudge and the Snowman Plan: The Nineteenth Book of Their Adventures, illustrated by Suçie Stevenson, Simon & Schuster (New York, NY), 1999.

Henry and Mudge and Annie's Perfect Pet: The Twentieth Book of Their Adventures, illustrated by Suçie Stevenson, Simon & Schuster (New York, NY), 2000.

Henry and Mudge and the Tall Tree House: The Twenty-first Book of Their Adventures, illustrated by Carolyn Bracken, Simon & Schuster (New York, NY), 2002.

Henry and Mudge and Mrs. Hopper's House: The Twenty-second Book of Their Adventures, illustrated by Carolyn Bracken, 2003.

Henry and Mudge and the Wild Goose Chase: The Twenty-third Book of Their Adventures, illustrated by Carolyn Bracken, Simon & Schuster (New York, NY), 2003.

Henry and Mudge and the Funny Lunch: The Twenty-fourth Book of Their Adventures, illustrated by Carolyn Bracken, Simon & Schuster (New York, NY), 2004.

Henry and Mudge and a Very Special Merry Christmas: The Twenty-fifth Book of Their Adventures, illustrated by Suçie Stevenson, Simon & Schuster (New York, NY), 2005.

Henry and Mudge and the Great Grandpas: The Twenty-sixth Book of Their Adventures, illustrated by Suçie Stevenson, Simon & Schuster (New York, NY), 2005.

Henry and Mudge and the Tumbling Trip: The Twenty-seventh Book of Their Adventures, illustrated by Carolyn Bracken, Simon & Schuster (New York, NY), 2005.

Henry and Mudge and the Big Sleepover: The Twenty-eighth Book of Their Adventures, illustrated by Suçie Stevenson, Simon & Schuster (New York, NY), 2006.

Some of Rylant's "Henry and Mudge" books have been translated into Spanish and published in Braille.

ILLUSTRATOR; "ANNIE AND SNOWBALL" CHILDREN'S BOOKS

Annie and Snowball and the Dress-up Birthday: The First Book of Their Adventures, illustrated by Suçie Stevenson, Simon & Schuster (New York, NY), 2007.
Annie and Snowball and the Prettiest House: The Second Book of Their Adventures, illustrated by Suçie Stevenson, Simon & Schuster (New York, NY), 2007.
Annie and Snowball and the Teacup Club: The Third Book of Their Adventures, illustrated by Suçie Stevenson, Simon & Schuster (New York, NY), 2008.
Annie and Snowball and the Pink Surprise: The Fourth Book of Their Adventures, illustrated by Suçie Stevenson, Simon & Schuster (New York, NY), 2008.
Annie and Snowball and the Cozy Nest: The Fifth Book of Their Adventures, illustrated by Suçie Stevenson, Simon & Schuster (New York, NY), 2009.

"PUPPY MUDGE" SERIES; BEGINNING READERS

Puppy Mudge Takes a Bath, illustrated by Isidre Mones, Simon & Schuster (New York, NY), 2002.
Puppy Mudge Has a Snack, illustrated by Isidre Mones, Simon & Schuster (New York, NY), 2003.
Puppy Mudge Loves His Blanket, illustrated by Isidre Mones, Simon & Schuster (New York, NY), 2005.
Puppy Mudge Wants to Play, illustrated by Isidre Mones, Simon & Schuster (New York, NY), 2005.
Puppy Mudge Finds a Friend, illustrated by Isidre Mones, Simon & Schuster (New York, NY), 2005.

"EVERYDAY BOOKS" SERIES; SELF-ILLUSTRATED BOARD BOOKS

The Everyday Pets, Macmillan (New York, NY), 1993.
The Everyday Children, Macmillan (New York, NY), 1993.
The Everyday Garden, Macmillan (New York, NY), 1993.
The Everyday House, Macmillan (New York, NY), 1993.
The Everyday School, Macmillan (New York, NY), 1993.
The Everyday Town, Macmillan (New York, NY), 1993.

"MR. PUTTER AND TABBY" SERIES; BEGINNING READERS

Mr. Putter and Tabby Walk the Dog, illustrated by Arthur Howard, Harcourt (San Diego, CA), 1994.
Mr. Putter and Tabby Pour the Tea, illustrated by Arthur Howard, Harcourt (San Diego, CA), 1994.
Mr. Putter and Tabby Bake the Cake, illustrated by Arthur Howard, Harcourt (San Diego, CA), 1994.
Mr. Putter and Tabby Pick the Pears, illustrated by Arthur Howard, Harcourt (San Diego, CA), 1995.

Mr. Putter and Tabby Fly the Plane, illustrated by Arthur Howard, Harcourt (San Diego, CA), 1997.
Mr. Putter and Tabby Row the Boat, illustrated by Arthur Howard, Harcourt (San Diego, CA), 1997.
Mr. Putter and Tabby Toot the Horn, illustrated by Arthur Howard, Harcourt (San Diego, CA), 1998.
Mr. Putter and Tabby Take the Train, illustrated by Arthur Howard, Harcourt (San Diego, CA), 1998.
Mr. Putter and Tabby Paint the Porch, illustrated by Arthur Howard, Harcourt (San Diego, CA), 2000.
Mr. Putter and Tabby Feed the Fish, illustrated by Arthur Howard, Harcourt (San Diego, CA), 2001.
Mr. Putter and Tabby Catch the Cold, illustrated by Arthur Howard, Harcourt (San Diego, CA), 2002.
Mr. Putter and Tabby Stir the Soup, illustrated by Arthur Howard, Harcourt (San Diego, CA), 2003.
Mr. Putter and Tabby Write the Book, illustrated by Arthur Howard, Harcourt (San Diego, CA), 2004.
Mr. Putter and Tabby Make a Wish, illustrated by Arthur Howard, Harcourt (San Diego, CA), 2005.
Mr. Putter and Tabby Spin the Yarn, illustrated by Arthur Howard, Harcourt (San Diego, CA), 2006.
Mr. Putter and Tabby See the Stars, illustrated by Arthur Howard, Harcourt (San Diego, CA), 2007.
Mr. Putter and Tabby Run the Race, illustrated by Arthur Howard, Harcourt (San Diego, CA), 2008.
Mr. Putter and Tabby Spill the Beans, illustrated by Arthur Howard, Harcourt (San Diego, CA), 2009.

"BLUE HILL MEADOWS" SERIES; MIDDLE-GRADE FICTION

The Blue Hill Meadows, illustrated by Ellen Beier, Harcourt (San Diego, CA), 1997.
The Blue Hill Meadows and the Much-loved Dog, illustrated by Ellen Beier, Harcourt (San Diego, CA), 1997.

"POPPLETON" SERIES; BEGINNING READERS

Poppleton, illustrated by Mark Teague, Blue Sky Press (New York, NY), 1997.
Poppleton and Friends, illustrated by Mark Teague, Blue Sky Press (New York, NY), 1997.
Poppleton Everyday, illustrated by Mark Teague, Blue Sky Press (New York, NY), 1998.
Poppleton Forever, illustrated by Mark Teague, Blue Sky Press (New York, NY), 1998.
Poppleton in Fall, illustrated by Mark Teague, Blue Sky Press (New York, NY), 1999.
Poppleton in Spring, illustrated by Mark Teague, Blue Sky Press (New York, NY), 1999.
Poppleton in Winter, illustrated by Mark Teague, Blue Sky Press (New York, NY), 2001.

"COBBLE STREET COUSINS" SERIES; MIDDLE-GRADE FICTION

In Aunt Lucy's Kitchen, illustrated by Wendy Anderson Halperin, Simon & Schuster (New York, NY), 1998.
A Little Shopping, illustrated by Wendy Anderson Halperin, Simon & Schuster (New York, NY), 1998.

Some Good News, illustrated by Wendy Anderson Halperin, Simon & Schuster (New York, NY), 1999.

Special Gifts, (also published as *Winter Gifts*), illustrated by Wendy Anderson Halperin, Simon & Schuster (New York, NY), 1999.

Spring Deliveries, illustrated by Wendy Anderson Halperin, Simon & Schuster (New York, NY), 1999.

Summer Party, illustrated by Wendy Anderson Halperin, Simon & Schuster (New York, NY), 2001.

Wedding Flowers, illustrated by Wendy Anderson Halperin, Simon & Schuster (New York, NY), 2002.

"HIGH-RISE PRIVATE EYES" SERIES

The Case of the Missing Monkey, illustrated by G. Brian Karas, Greenwillow (New York, NY), 2000.

The Case of the Climbing Cat, illustrated by G. Brian Karas, Greenwillow (New York, NY), 2000.

The Case of the Puzzling Possum, illustrated by G. Brian Karas, Greenwillow (New York, NY), 2001.

The Case of the Troublesome Turtle, illustrated by G. Brian Karas, Greenwillow (New York, NY), 2001.

The Case of the Sleepy Sloth, illustrated by G. Brian Karas, Greenwillow (New York, NY), 2002.

The Case of the Fidgety Fox, illustrated by G. Brian Karas, Greenwillow (New York, NY), 2003.

The Case of the Baffled Bear, illustrated by G. Brian Karas, Greenwillow (New York, NY), 2004.

The Case of the Desperate Duck, illustrated by G. Brian Karas, Greenwillow (New York, NY), 2005.

"LITTLE WHISTLE" SERIES

Little Whistle, illustrated by Tim Bowers, Harcourt (San Diego, CA), 2000.

Little Whistle's Dinner Party, illustrated by Tim Bowers, Harcourt (San Diego, CA), 2001.

Little Whistle's Medicine, illustrated by Tim Bowers, Harcourt (San Diego, CA), 2002.

Little Whistle's Christmas, illustrated by Tim Bowers, Harcourt (San Diego, CA), 2003.

"LIGHTHOUSE FAMILY" SERIES

The Storm, illustrated by Preston McDaniels, Simon & Schuster (New York, NY), 2002.

The Whale, illustrated by Preston McDaniels, Simon & Schuster (New York, NY), 2003.

The Eagle, illustrated by Preston McDaniels, Simon & Schuster (New York, NY), 2004.

The Turtle, illustrated by Preston McDaniels, Simon & Schuster (New York, NY), 2005.

The Octopus, illustrated by Preston McDaniels, Simon & Schuster (New York, NY), 2005.

YOUNG-ADULT FICTION

A Blue-eyed Daisy (novel), Bradbury (New York, NY), 1985, published as *Some Year for Ellie,* illustrated by Kate Rogers, Viking Kestrel (London, England), 1986.

Every Living Thing (short stories), illustrated by S.D. Schindler, Bradbury (New York, NY), 1985.

A Fine White Dust (novel), Bradbury (New York, NY), 1986, reprinted, Aladdin (New York, NY), 2007.

Children of Christmas: Stories for the Season, illustrated by S.D. Schindler, Orchard Books (New York, NY), 1987, published as *Silver Packages and Other Stories,* [London, England], 1987, selection published as *Silver Packages: An Appalachian Christmas Story,* illustrated by Chris K. Soentpiet, Orchard Books, 1997.

A Kindness (novel), Orchard Books (New York, NY), 1988.

A Couple of Kooks, and Other Stories about Love, Orchard Books (New York, NY), 1990.

Missing May (novel), Orchard Books (New York, NY), 1992.

I Had Seen Castles (novel), Harcourt Brace (San Diego, CA), 1993.

The Islander (novel), DK Ink (New York, NY), 1998.

Ludie's Life, Harcourt (Orlando, FL), 2006.

FOR YOUNG ADULTS; POETRY

Waiting to Waltz . . . a Childhood, illustrated by Stephen Gammell, Bradbury (New York, NY), 1984.

Soda Jerk, illustrated by Peter Catalanotto, Orchard Books (New York, NY), 1990.

Something Permanent, photographs by Walker Evans, Harcourt (San Diego, CA), 1994.

God Went to Beauty School, HarperCollins (New York, NY), 2003.

Boris, Harcourt (Orlando, FL), 2005.

FOR YOUNG ADULTS; NONFICTION

But I'll Be Back Again: An Album (autobiography), Orchard Books (New York, NY), 1989.

Appalachia: The Voices of Sleeping Birds, illustrated by Barry Moser, Harcourt (San Diego, CA), 1991.

Margaret, Frank, and Andy: Three Writers' Stories (biography) Harcourt (San Diego, CA), 1996, published in three volumes as *A Story of Margaret Wise Brown, A Story of L. Frank Baum,* and *A Story of E.B. White.*

Bless Us All: A Child's Yearbook of Blessings, Simon & Schuster (New York, NY), 1998.

Give Me Grace: A Child's Daybook of Prayers, Simon & Schuster (New York, NY), 1999.

Adaptations

When I Was Young in the Mountains, 1983, *This Year's Garden,* 1983, and *The Relatives Came,* 1986, were adapted as filmstrips by Random House. Several books were adapted as audiobooks by SRA McGraw-Hill, including *When I Was Young in the Mountains* and *The Relatives Came,* both 1985; *This Year's Garden,* 1987; and *Henry and Mudge in the Green Time,* 1988. *Children of Christmas* and *Every Living Thing* were released as book-and-audio versions in 1993, and as audiobooks by Chivers North America, 1997. *Missing May* was released as an audiobook by BDD Audio,

1996, and Recorded Books, 1997. *A Fine White Dust* was released on audio cassette by Recorded Books, 1997. Many of Rylant's "Henry and Mudge" books have been adapted as audiobooks by Recorded Books and Live Oak Media, 1997-98. The stage play *Henry and Mudge,* produce in New York, NY, 2007, is based on Rylant's books.

Sidelights

A prolific author and illustrator, Cynthia Rylant often bases her works on her own background, especially on her childhood in the Appalachian region of West Virginia. Among her award-winning books for children and young adults are contemporary novels and historical fiction for young adults, middle-grade novels, lyrical prose poems, beginning readers, short stories, poetry, books of prayers, autobiographies, and nonfiction. Many of Rylant's books for beginning readers are published in series, such as her beloved "Henry and Mudge" books about a small boy and his very large dog. Other easy-to-read volumes by Rylant include rhyming picture-books such as *If You'll Be My Valentine, Long Night Moon, Baby Face: A Book of Love for Baby,* and *Alligator Boy.* In *Kirkus Reviews* a critic praised *Alligator Boy* for its "witty language . . . as well as the warmly nostalgic atmosphere" created by Rylant, while *School Library Journal* contributor Kathleen Whalin wrote of *Long Night Moon* that "books this good come along once in a blue moon."

While her elementary-school-aged fans are legion, Rylant is perhaps best known as a novelist. Characteristically, she portrays introspective, compassionate young people who live in rural settings or in small towns and who tend to be set apart from their peers. Her young male and female protagonists meet challenges with the help of their families and friends as well as from within their strong, supportive communities. Praised for her sensitive depiction of young people and their emotions, Rylant is also acknowledged for her rounded characterizations of adults, especially the elderly, and for exploring topics such as religion and death that are not often addressed in children's literature. She often focuses on relationships between the old and the young and between people and animals. In addition, she underscores her works with such themes as the act of creation, both by God and by human artists; the transforming power of love; the importance of all living things; and the need to let go.

Writing in *Children's Books and Their Creators,* Eden K. Edwards noted that Rylant "demonstrates an inimitable ability to evoke the strongest of emotions from the simplest of words. . . . In her work, Rylant gives depth and dignity to a litany of quiet characters and sagaciously reflects on some of life's most confusing mysteries." Miriam Lang Budin noted in *School Library Journal* that readers "have come to expect resonant, deeply felt work from Rylant," while Hollis Lowery-Moore, a contributor to the *St. James Guide to Young-*

Cover of Cynthia Rylant's award-winning novel Missing May, *featuring artwork by Rene Ade.* (Cover illustration copyright © 1992 by Rene Ade. Reproduced by permission of Orchard Books, an imprint of Scholastic, Inc.)

Adult Writers concluded: "All of Rylant's stories, including her picture story books marketed for younger readers, create memorable characters and places and provide teens with a window on the world."

In addition to writing, Rylant also contributes illustrations to her own books on occasion. She began illustrating some of her picture-book texts in the early 1990s and the folk-art style she has developed complements her stories. She has also worked with several outstanding illustrators, including Peter Catalanotto, Barry Moser, G. Brian Karas, James and Suçie Stevenson, and Walker Evans. Two of her books, *When I was Young in the Mountains* and *The Relatives Came,* were honored by the Caldecott Medal committee for their illustrations by Diane Goode and Stephen Gammell, respectively.

Many of Rylant's works are rooted in the memories and images of her childhood. Born in Hopewell, West Virginia, she spent her first four years in Illinois, where she lived with her father, John Tune Smith, a sergeant in the U.S. Army who had fought in the Korean War, and her mother, Leatrel Rylant Smith. When she was four, Rylant's parents separated, and she went to live with her mother's parents in the Appalachian mining town of Coal Ridge, West Virginia. Rylant never saw her father again; he died in a veteran's hospital in Florida when she was thirteen years old. As the author later recalled in her autobiography *But I'll Be Back Again: An Album,* "I did not have a chance to know him or to say goodbye to him, and that is all the loss I needed to become a writer."

Rylant's mother soon left the family to attend nursing school, and she was gone for nearly four years. Although Leatrel Smith wrote regularly and visited a few times a year, "it was," Rylant recalled in her autobiography, "not enough for a little girl." Happily, though, Rylant's grandparents and extended family provided a positive, nurturing environment, and it was in her grandmother's "love and safety, and the kind presence of my grandfather, that I managed to survive the loss of my dear parents." Quiet, gentle people, Rylant's grandparents raised six children without much income. After her grandfather, a coal miner, became disabled during a slate fall in a mine, the family lived by the couple's wits and on food supplied by the U.S. government. Living in a four-room house without running water or indoor plumbing, Rylant learned about the joys of country life and the kindness of local townspeople. She summarized her years in Coal Ridge in *But I'll Be Back Again:* "My years with my grandparents were good ones, and while I waited for both my father and my mother to come back, I had big stacks of pancakes and hot cocoa, hot dogs and chickens, teaberry leaves and honeysuckle, and aunts and cousins to sleep with at night and hug until someone could return for me." When Rylant was eight years old, her mother returned for her and the two moved to Beaver, a town near Coal Ridge. There they settled in a three-room apartment with running water, an indoor bathroom, and a television set.

During her early years, Rylant was not much of a reader. In fact, as she wrote in *Something about the Author Autobiography Series* (*SAAS*), "I did not *see* many books." There were no libraries or bookstores in Beaver, so adults got paperbacks from the drug stores and children read comic books. "I guess most people assume that future famous authors are supposed to be reading fat hardbound books and writing poetry by age ten," she mused. "But all I wanted to do was read *Archie* and play the Beatles."

Enrolling at Morris Harvey College (now the University of Charleston), Rylant initially planned to go into nursing like her mother, but she switched her major after taking her first college English class. As she recalled in *SAAS,* "I heard and read stories I had never heard or read before, and I was in love with words." While she did well academically, for her "the real achievement . . . was more personal. I began to think for myself, to throw off some of the RULES OF LIFE that had been drummed into me in my small town, and my mind began to grow and blossom." She became editor of the

campus newspaper and was active in a variety of other campus activities. "I liked college so much that when I finished I didn't want to stop being a student," Rylant later admitted in *SAAS.*

Rylant's first year of graduate school at Marshall University in Huntington, West Virginia, was "without a doubt the happiest year of my life. . . . I loved literature so much and every day all I had to do was attend class and listen to it and talk about it and write about it. Like a chocolate lover at a Hershey's factory, I was completely content." After receiving her master's degree in 1976, she married a young man who taught classical guitar and was learning to be a carpenter. She also got a job at the public library in Huntington, working in the children's room. Reading the books she was supposed to be shelving, she discovered a brand new world. She bought a copy of *The Writer's Market,* a book containing publisher information, and started writing.

Shortly after she started writing, Rylant and her husband had a son, whom they named after Nathaniel Hawthorne, one of Rylant's favorite authors. Even while keeping up with the many tasks of motherhood, Rylant managed to keep writing; six months after the birth of Nathaniel she wrote the words "when I was young in the mountains." Within an hour, Rylant had finished her first book. Without revising it, she sent the manuscript

Rylant's text for **Appalachia: The Voices of Sleeping Birds** *is brought to life in Barry Moser's sun-filled paintings.* (Voyager, 1998. Illustration copyright © 1991 by Pennyroyal Press, reprinted by permission of Houghton Mifflin Harcourt Publishing Company.)

to E.P. Dutton publishers, and *When I Was Young in the Mountains* was published in 1982.

A picture book describing Rylant's childhood spent with her grandparents in Appalachia, *When I Was Young in the Mountains* is a collection of vignettes about the busy, joyous life of a small community. The book was favorably received by critics such as a *Publishers Weekly* reviewer who stated that the author's debut "proves she knows precisely how to tell a story that brings the reader into the special world of her recollecting. . . . These are memories of a way of living that will entrance readers and broaden their outlook." Writing in the *Bulletin of the Center for Children's Books,* Zena Sutherland noted that *When I Was Young in the Mountains* "is given appeal by the warmth and contentment that emerge from an account of daily satisfaction and small, occasional joys, described with appropriate simplicity."

After the success of her first book, Rylant began to mine what she later referred to in *SAAS* as the "gold mine of stories stored up in my head. Memories I could use to make books. I wrote and wrote, sold book after book, most of them true or partly true. All of them realistic. And most coming as quick and pure as that first book came." Published in 1984, Rylant's *Waiting to Waltz: A Childhood* includes thirty autobiographical free-verse poems that outline the author's memories of growing up in Beaver, West Virginia. In this work, Rylant shares the happy and sad times while also offering incisive portraits of local townspeople. A reviewer in *Publishers Weekly* wrote of *Waiting to Waltz* that everyone in Beaver "becomes as real to the reader as they are to Rylant," while Ethel R. Twichell predicted in *Horn Book* that the poems "will gently pluck a long-forgotten memory or awaken a shared experience."

Rylant's marriage to her first husband ended after a few years, and she then was married briefly to a college professor. Meanwhile, she worked as a part-time English teacher at Marshall University for a year, then relocated to Kent, Ohio. Rylant received her library science degree from Kent State University in 1982 and got a job at the Akron Public Library as a children's librarian and at the University of Akron as a part-time English teacher. In 1985 she published her first novel, *A Blue-eyed Daisy.*

A Blue-eyed Daisy describes a year in the life of Ellie Farley, an eleven year old living in the hills of West Virginia. Ellie recounts several memorable moments that occur over the course of her eleventh year, such as getting kissed at her first co-ed party and attending the funeral of a classmate. Throughout the narrative, Ellie deepens her relationship with her father, Okey, a former miner who lost his job in an accident. A reviewer in *Publishers Weekly* wrote of *A Blue-eyed Daisy:* "No reader will be able to resist Ellie or her kith and kin. Their ability to live life and endure ills is the core of an exquisite novel, written with love." Katherine Bruner,

writing in *School Library Journal,* added that Rylant's "low-key, evocative style . . . is the shining quality which sets this book apart."

In her autobiographical *But I'll Be Back Again,* Rylant also reflects on the region where she was raised, and her picture book *Appalachia: The Voices of Sleeping Birds* poetically evokes the spirit of Appalachia in a tribute to that region and its people. *Appalachia* describes the living conditions, hard work, customs, activities, and personalities of the Appalachian people. The book's lyrical prose is paired with realistic paintings by artist Barry Moser who, like Rylant, has roots in Appalachia. Praising the book as an excellent marriage of text and picture, Barbara Chatton noted in *School Library Journal* that *Appalachia* should "encourage original writing or art as it reveals how illustrations and words can interact, how prose can illuminate a painting, and how simple paintings can bring power to prose." A critic in *Kirkus Reviews,* citing Rylant's "carefully pitched, melodious voice," called *Appalachia* "a special book for creative sharing." In *Publishers Weekly* a critic wrote that Rylant's "text offers pure nostalgia—a skillfully structured essay that appears, deceptively, to meander like a dusty country lane and underscores the warmth, generosity of spirit and steadfastness" of the Appalachian people.

In 1986 Rylant published one of her most well-received books, the young-adult novel *A Fine White Dust.* In this work, Pete, a seventh grader who lives in the rural South, becomes a born-again Christian after being converted by charismatic preacher James W. Carson. When Carson offers Pete the chance to go with him as his disciple, the boy decides, after much soul-searching, to leave his parents and his best friend, Rufus. Carson, who is viewed by Pete as God in the flesh, eventually runs off with Darlene, a young woman who works at the town soda fountain. Although Pete feels betrayed, he comes through his experience with an unshaken faith in God and a more realistic view of human nature. A critic in *Kirkus Reviews* stated that "Rylant has explored a theme vital to many young people but rare in children's books." Writing in *School Library Journal,* Julie Cummins noted: "Few books have explored young people's fascination with God and their soul. . . . Like Peter, this story has soul." Calling the novel "an achingly resonant portrayal of a naive youth," Denise M. Wilms added in her *Booklist* review that *A Fine White Dust* is "poignant and perceptive, with almost all of the characters subtly drawn." *A Fine White Dust* was designated as a Newbery Medal honor book in 1987.

With *Missing May,* a novel for teens that was published in 1992, Rylant creates what is perhaps her most highly acclaimed book. The story outlines how twelve-year-old Summer, who came to stay with her Aunt May and Uncle Ob in West Virginia after the death of her mother six years before, attempts to save her uncle from despair after the death of his beloved wife. In the midst of his mourning, Ob senses May's presence. Looking for an interpreter, Ob and Summer settle on Cletus, an unusual boy from Summer's class who once had a near-death experience and is, according to *Voice of Youth Advocates* reviewer Caroline S. McKinney, "as full of the energy for living as Ob is with the numbness of grieving." Through the boy's suggestion, the trio goes to Charleston to find a medium at the Spiritualist Church, and the trip begins a personal quest for each of them. McKinney concluded that "*Missing May* will be passed around by many of us who love beautiful words. It will speak in that warm, flowing West Virginia tongue to young people and old." Betsy Hearne wrote in a *Bulletin of the Center for Children's Books* review that "strong nuances of despair and hope create a suspense that forcefully replaces action and that will touch readers to tears," while *Booklist* contributor Ilene Cooper noted that "Rylant makes us aware of the possibilities of life, even in the midst of tragedy. There is a freshness here that feels like a cool breeze." *Missing May* earned Rylant a Newbery medal in 1993.

Another novel that draws from Appalachia and Rylant's family history, *Ludie's Life,* evokes the life of a young girl facing struggles as she attempts to survive the challenges of rural West Virginia in a life spanning most of the twentieth century. Married to a coal miner in 1925 at age fifteen, Ludie raises six children and watches as their lives stretch beyond her beloved Appalachia. With an introspective nature, Ludie grows in her understanding of life while never regretting the limitations that have tied her to her rural home. In *Booklist* Cooper described *Ludie's Life* as "infused with poetry, pathos, and an everyday heroism," and Pat Leach, while asserting that Rylant's novel is more appropriate for an adult readership, wrote that the work is enriched by "luminous moments told in lovely language."

Henry and Mudge: The First Book of Their Adventures made its appearance in 1987. Based on her own son and a dog Rylant once knew, the book introduces Henry, an only child. When Henry receives a pet, Mudge, a three-foot-tall dog that appears to be a cross between a Saint Bernard and a Great Dane, the two form a deep attachment. Tension comes when Mudge is lost, but happiness is restored when he is found again. Rylant presents lots of humorous details, such as Mudge's drooling and love of dirty socks, in prose that is designed for beginning readers. Reviewing *Henry and Mudge* and the second volume of the series, *Henry and Mudge in Puddle Trouble,* a critic for *Kirkus Reviews* called the author's language "easy to read but vividly evocative" and concluded: "Warm, loving, and gently philosophical, these stories about an only child and his closest companion deserve a place in every library collection."

Rylant has written dozens of other volumes in the "Henry and Mudge" series, easy-reading books that feature illustrations by noted cartoonist James Stevenson as well as by his artist daughter, Suçie Stevenson. In *Henry and Mudge and the Happy Cat: The Eighth Book*

of Their Adventures, Rylant describes the arrival of a scraggly lost kitty to Henry's home. Mudge and the cat form an immediate bond, and the dog is heartbroken when the cat's owner finally claims the kitty; however, Mudge is pleased with the owner's gift of thirty huge bones. Writing in *School Library Journal,* Trev Jones concluded that *Henry and Mudge and the Happy Cat* "sparkles with good humor and affection," while Hearne stated in the *Bulletin of the Center for Children's Books* that while "it's hard to keep a series fresh, especially at the easy-to-read level, . . . this may be the best Henry and Mudge book since the first two."

In *Henry and Mudge and the Bedtime Thumps: The Ninth Book of Their Adventures* the pair take a trip to Grandmother's house in the country. When Mudge is deemed too large for the small home and is made to sleep outside, Henry is afraid both for Mudge and for himself. However, the large hound finds a spot under a large table on the porch, and both he and Henry curl up happily and fall sleep. *Henry and Mudge and the Wild Goose Chase: The Twenty-third Book of Their Adventures* find the pair find adventure on an egg-buying trip to a local farm, while in *Henry and Mudge and the Funny Lunch: The Twenty-fourth Book of Their Adventures* Henry and his dad cook up something incredible for Mother's Day. Writing in *Horn Book,* Elizabeth S. Watson noted that in *Henry and Mudge and the Bedtime Thumps* Rylant "has developed a fresh, warm, imaginative, and yet absolutely realistic tale for the beginning reader." Hazel Rochman praised the more recent *Henry and Mudge and the Funny Lunch,* noting that the 2004 book is "bound to get kids laughing, reading, and maybe cooking, too."

Since the early 1990s, with the success of the "Henry and Mudge" books, Rylant has increasingly concentrated on developing series titles for younger readers, such as the "Lighthouse Family," High-rise Private Eyes," and self-illustrated "Everyday Books" series. "Short sentences, peppy dialogue, and well developed characters" are the hallmarks of the "High-rise Private Eyes" series, according to *Horn Book* reviewer Kitty Flynn. In books such as *The Case of the Baffled Bear* and *The Case of the Troublesome Turtle,* a pair of animal detectives solves a series of simple quandaries that find their friends in a pickle. Board books for very young children, the "Everyday Books" introduce toddlers to literature by centering on subjects familiar to them, such as their homes and pets. The first of Rylant's works to include her own illustrations, the "Everyday Books" feature child-friendly collages.

Rylant's other self-illustrated titles include *The Whales, The Cookie-Store Cat,* and *Dog Heaven.* A playful book, *Dog Heaven* depicts the author/illustrator's idea of what dogs experience in the afterlife, such as fields to run in, plenty of angel children to pet them, and appetizing cat-shaped biscuits to eat. The book is illustrated in bright acrylics that blend naïve forms with unusual colors. According to a critic in *Kirkus Reviews,* the author's illus-

Suçie Stevenson collaborates with Rylant in illustrating such series books as **Annie and Snowball and the Dress-Up Birthday.** (Annie and Snowball and the Dress-up Birthday, by Cynthia Rylant. Aladdin Paperbacks, 2007. Illustration copyright © 2007 by Suçie Stevenson. Reprinted with the permission of Simon & Schuster Books for Young Readers, an imprint of Simon & Schuster Children's Publishing Division.)

trations are "infused with simple doggy joy," while in the *Bulletin of the Center for Children's Books* Roger Sutton concluded that Rylant maintains "a plain, conversational tone that resists gooeyness" while her "paintings allow viewers to imagine their own pets at play in the fields of the Lord." Another self-illustrated work, *Cat Heaven,* describes a kitty afterlife that is full of trees and clouds to perch on, soft angel laps to sit on, lots of toys to play with, and full dishes of food to eat. A critic in *Kirkus Reviews* called the book "every bit as rich in eye-dimming sentiment as *Dog Heaven*" and a work sure to "kindle sighs even from the feline-indifferent."

A love of cats figures prominently in several of Rylant's works, including her multi-book series "Mr. Putter and Tabby," and the poetry collection *Boris.* The "Mr. Putter and Tabby" series features the domestic duo engaged in riveting adventures that are set forth in titles such as *Mr. Putter and Tabby Stir the Soup, Mr. Putter*

and Tabby Catch the Cold, and *Mr. Putter and Tabby Spin the Yarn.* Each of these easy-to read volumes features the man and his pet attending to simple activities only to be thwarted by unruly appliances or other silly obstructions. In *Mr. Putter and Tabby Stir the Soup* plans for a favorite dinner are put on the back burner when the stove refuses to light, forcing the cooks to bring their recipe to neighbor Mrs. Teaberry's kitchen. Mrs. Teaberry again becomes their rescuer in *Mr. Putter and Tabby Catch the Cold,* when man and cat are laid low by the sniffles, while in *Mr. Putter and Tabby Make a Wish,* Mr. Putter realizes that one is never too old to celebrate a birthday. Helping Mrs. Teaberry complete a senior marathon race puts Rylant's characters on an unusual exercise regimen in *Mr. Putter and Tabby Run the Race,* which features what Carolyn Phelan described in *Booklist* as an "amusing but affectionate portrayal of Mr. Putter's foibles." A *School Library Journal* writer dubbed *Mr. Putter and Tabby Stir the Soup* a "satisfyingly silly romp."

Boris joins works such as Rylant's award-winning *God Went to Beauty School* as an acclaimed collection of poetry that presents the author's more reflective side. Containing nineteen poems, *Boris* comprises what *Horn Book* reviewer Jennifer M. Brabander praised as an "accessible, compelling story" describing a beloved gray cat and its many adventures after arriving at Rylant's door. While Brabander predicted that *Boris* will satisfy pet-loving readers who "will easily relate to the poems and their theme of companionship," Cooper noted in *Booklist* that the volume also speaks to deeper issues through its "subtext" about "the inevitability of change."

In an interview with Anita Silvey for *Horn Book,* Rylant once commented that writing "has given me a sense of self-worth that I didn't have my whole childhood. I am really proud of that. The [books] have carried me through some troubled times and have made me feel that I am worthy of having a place on this earth." In *SAAS,* the author concluded: "I will write, because I have to earn my way and because it seems to be what God put me here to do. I hope one day to write a great book, a magnificent book, which people will buy for those they love best, which they will place in someone else's hands and say: 'Before you do anything else, *you must read this.*'"

Biographical and Critical Sources

BOOKS

Authors & Artists for Young Adults, Volume 10, Gale (Detroit, MI), 1993, pp. 163-168.

Children's Books and Their Creators, edited by Anita Silvey, Houghton Mifflin (Boston, MA), 1995, p. 567.

Children's Literature Review, Volume 15, Gale (Detroit, MI), 1988, pp. 167-174.

Rylant, Cynthia, *Best Wishes,* Richard C. Owen, 1992, pp. 5-7.

Rylant, Cynthia, *But I'll Be Back Again: An Album,* Beech Tree Books/Orchard Books (New York, NY), 1993.

St. James Guide to Children's Writers, 5th edition, St. James Press (Detroit, MI), 1999.

St. James Guide to Young-Adult Writers, edited by Tom and Sara Pendergast, St. James Press (Detroit, MI), 1999, pp. 731-733.

Something about the Author Autobiography Series, Volume 13, Gale (Detroit, MI), 1991, pp. 155-163.

PERIODICALS

Booklist, September 1, 1986, Denise M. Wilms, review of *A Fine White Dust,* p. 67; May 15, 1989, Denise M. Wilms, review of *But I'll Be Back Again: An Album,* p. 1655; February 15, 1992, Ilene Cooper, "The Other Side of Good-bye," p. 1105; May 15, 2001, Gillian Engberg, review of *The Case of the Troublesome Turtle,* p. 1753; June 1, 2001, Ilene Cooper, review of *Summer Party,* p. 1884; September 15, 2001, Ilene Cooper, review of *Good Morning, Sweetie Pie, and Other Poems for Children,* p. 229; February, 15, 2002, Lauren Peterson, review of *Wedding Flowers,* p. 1015; March 1, 2002, Gillian Engberg, review of *Little Whistle's Medicine,* p. 1144; April 15, 2002, Ilene Cooper, review of *Let's Go Home: The Wonderful Things about a House,* p. 68; May 1, 2002, Kay Weisman, review of *Old Town in the Green Groves,* p. 1527; September 1, 2002, Ilene Cooper, review of *The Ticky-Tacky Doll,* p. 137; September 15, 2002, Diane Foote, review of *Christmas in the Country,* p. 247; November 1, 2002, Ilene Cooper, review of *Mr. Putter and Tabby Catch the Cold,* p. 509; January 1, 2003, Hazel Rochman, review of *Henry and Mudge and the Tall Tree House: The Twenty-first Book of Their Adventures,* p. 910; January 1, 2003, Connie Fletcher, review of *The Case of the Sleepy Sloth,* p. 893; March 15, 2003, Gillian Engberg, review of *Henry and Mudge and Mrs. Hopper's House: The Twenty-second Book of Their Adventures,* p. 1333; September 1, 2003, Kay Weisman, review of *The Whale,* p. 121; October 1, 2003, Carolyn Phelan, review of *Henry and Mudge and the Wild Goose Chase: The Twenty-third Book of Their Adventures,* p. 329; March 15, 2004, Hazel Rochman, review of *Henry and Mudge and the Funny Lunch: The Twenty-fourth Book of Their Adventures,* p. 1310; July, 2004, Carolyn Phelan, review of *The Case of the Baffled Bear,* p. 1852; November 15, 2004, Ilene Cooper, review of *Long Night Moon,* p. 591; February 15, 2005, Ilene Cooper, review of *Boris,* p. 1074; May 15, 2005, Hazel Rochman, review of *Puppy Mudge Wants to Play,* p. 1667; October 15, 2006, Ilene Cooper, review of *Ludie's Life,* p. 41; May 15, 2007, Randall Enos, review of *Alligator Boy,* p. 48; April 1, 2008, Carolyn Phelan, review of *Mr. Putter and Tabby Run the Race,* p. 58; April 1, 2008, Julie Cummins, review of *Puppies and Piggies,* p. 57; October 15, 2008, Ilene Cooper, review of *Snow,* p. 41.

Bulletin of the Center for Children's Books, April, 1982, Zena Sutherland, review of *When I Was Young in the Mountains,* p. 157; July-August, 1989, Betsy Hearne, review of *But I'll Be Back Again,* p. 283; October, 1990, Betsy Hearne, review of *Henry and Mudge and the Happy Cat: The Eighth Book of Their Adventures,* pp. 43-44; March, 1992, Betsy Hearne, review of *Missing May,* p. 192; October, 1995, Roger Sutton, review of *Dog Heaven,* pp. 66-67; November, 1997, Pat Mathews, review of *Cat Heaven,* p. 100; December, 2001, review of *Poppleton in Winter,* p. 152; July, 2003, review of *God Went to Beauty School,* p. 461.

Children's Book Review Service, November, 1984, Leigh Dean, review of *Waiting to Waltz . . . : A Childhood,* p. 32.

Horn Book, January-February, 1985, Ethel R. Twichell, review of *Waiting to Waltz,* p. 64; November-December, 1987, Anita Silvey, interview with Rylant, pp. 695-703; May-June, 1991, Elizabeth S. Watson, review of *Henry and Mudge and the Bedtime Thumps,* pp. 328-329; March-April, 1992, p. 206; May, 2001, review of *The Case of the Troublesome Turtle,* p. 337; November-December, 2002, Mary M. Burns, review of *Christmas in the Country,* p. 738; September-

October, 2004, Kitty Flynn, review of *The Case of the Baffled Bear,* p. 599; January-February, 2005, review of *God Went to Beauty School,* p. 30; May-June, 2005, Jennifer M. Brabander, review of *Boris,* p. 341; November-December, 2005, Jeannine M. Chapman, review of *The Stars Will Still Shine,* p. 696; January-February, 2008, Christine M. Heppermann, review of *Walt Disney's Cinderella,* p. 100; November-December, 2008, Joanna Rudge Long, review of *Hansel and Gretel,* p. 720.

Kirkus Reviews, July 1, 1986, review of *A Fine White Dust,* pp. 1023-1024; February 15, 1987, review of *Henry and Mudge* and *Henry and Mudge in Puddle Trouble,* p. 300; February 1, 1991, review of *Henry and Mudge and the Bedtime Thumps,* p. 184; March 1, 1991, review of *Appalachia: The Voices of Sleeping Birds,* p. 322; July 1, 1995, review of *Dog Heaven,* p. 951; July 1, 1997, review of *Cat Heaven,* p. 1035; September 1, 2001, p. 1300; January 15, 2002, review of *Little Whistle's Medicine,* p. 108; April 15, 2002, review of *Let's Go Home,* p. 577; June 15, 2002, review of *The Case of the Sleepy Sloth,* p. 888; August 1, 2002, review of *The Ticky-Tacky Doll,* p. 141; October 15, 2002, review of *Mr. Putter and Tabby Catch the Cold,* p. 1538; November 1, 2002, review of *Christmas in the Country,* p. 135; March 1, 2003, review of *The Case of the Fidgety Fox,* p. 397; June 15, 2003, review of *God Went to Beauty School,* p. 864; December 15, 2004, review of *If You'll Be My Valentine,* p. 1207; March 1, 2005, review of *The Turtle,* p. 294; March 15, 2005, review of *Boris,* p. 357; February 1, 2006, review of *The Journey: Stories of Migration,* p. 36; November 1, 2006, review of *Ludie's Life,* p. 1124; May 15, 2007, review of *Alligator Boy;* January 1, 2008, review of *Puppies and Piggies;* September 15, 2008, review of *Snow.*

Kliatt, May, 2002, Paula Rohrlick, "The Heavenly Village," p. 29.

New York Times Book Review, June 3, 1990, Valerie Sayers, review of *Soda Jerk,* p. 24; May 30, 1993, review of *Henry and Mudge and the Wild Wind,* p. 19; December 7, 2008, review of *Snow,* p. 52.

Publishers Weekly, March 19, 1982, review of *When I Was Young in the Mountains,* pp. 70-71; August 17, 1984, review of *Waiting to Waltz: A Childhood,* p. 60; March 8, 1985, review of *A Blue-eyed Daisy,* p. 91; March 1, 1991, review of *Appalachia,* p. 74; April 2, 2001, review of *Little Whistle,* p. 63; September, 3, 2001, review of *Good Morning, Sweetie Pie,* p. 86; April 22, 2002, review of *Let's Go Home,* p. 68; August 5, 2002, review of *The Ticky-Tacky Doll,* p. 71; August 26, 2002, review of *The Storm,* p. 69; June 89, 2003, review of *God Went to Beauty School,* p. 53; October 6, 2003, review of *The Whale,* p. 86; January 17, 2005, review of *Long Night Moon,* p. 54; February 20, 2006, review of *The Journey,* p. 156; February 18, 2006, review of *Baby Face: A Book of Love for Baby,* p. 152; October 6, 2008, review of *Snow,* p. 53.

Quill & Quire, December, 1990, Susan Perren, review of *Henry and Mudge and the Happy Cat,* p. 19.

School Library Journal, November, 1984, Margaret C. Howell, review of *Waiting to Waltz,* p. 138; April, 1985, Katherine Bruner, review of *A Blue-eyed Daisy,* p. 92; September, 1986, Julie Cummins, review of *A Fine White Dust,* p. 138; July, 1989, Amy Kellman, review of *But I'll Be Back Again,* p. 97; August, 1990, Trev Jones, review of *Henry and Mudge and the Happy Cat,* p. 134; April, 1991, Nancy Seiner, review of *Henry and Mudge and the Bedtime Thumps,* p. 101; April, 1991, Barbara Chatton, review of *Appalachia,* p. 137; October, 1995, Joy Fleishhacker, review of *Dog Heaven,* p. 115; January, 1999, Miriam Lang Budin, review of *Bear Day,* pp. 101-102; October, 2001, Patricia Manning, review of *Poppleton in Winter,* p. 130; December, 2001, p. 128; April, 2002, Carol A. Edwards, review of *Old Town in the Green Groves,* p. 156; June, 2002, Blair Christolon, review of *Let's Go Home,* p. 124; August, 2002, pat Leach, review of *Wedding Flowers,* p. 166; October, 2002, Susan Patron, review of *Christmas in the Country,* p. 63, and Lynda S. Poling, review of *Mr. Putter and Tabby Catch the Cold,* p. 130; November, 2002, Sheilah Kosco, review of *The Ticky-Tacky Doll,* p. 134; December, 2002, Laura Scott, review of *The Case of the Sleepy Sloth,* p. 108; February, 2003, Lee Bock, review of *The Old Woman Who Named Things,* p. 97; April, 2003, Marilyn Taniguchi, review of *Puppy Mudge Takes a Bath,* p. 137; May, 2003, Doris Losey, review of *The Case of the Fidgety Fox,* p. 129; July, 2003, Maura Smith, review of *Henry and Mudge and the Snowman Plan,* p. 59; October, 2003, Maureen Wade, review of *Little Whistle's Christmas,* p. 67, Maren Ostergard, review of *The Case of the Troublesome Turtle,* p. 87, and Laura Scott, review of *Henry and Mudge and the Wild Goose Chase,* p. 137; November, 2003, Barbara Buckley, review of *The Whale,* p. 115; January, 2004, Laura Scott, review of *Puppy Mudge Has a Snack,* p. 104; September, 2004, Susan Lissim, review of *Mr. Putter and Tabby Write the Book,* and Bethany L.W. Hankinson, review of *The Case of the Baffled Bear,* p. 178; November, 2004, Debbie Steward Hoskins, review of *The Eagle,* p. 117; December, 2004, Rhona Campbell, review of *Long Night Moon,* p. 120; April, 2005, Cris Riedel, review of *Boris,* p. 156; April, 2007, Kathleen Pavin, review of *Mr. Putter and Tabby Spin the Yarn,* p. 126; April, 2007, Pat Leach, review of *Ludie's Life,* p. 148; June, 2007, Marianne Saccardi, review of *Alligator Boy,* p. 123; September, 2007, Erika Qualls, review of *Mr. Putter and Tabby See the Stars,* p. 175; February, 2008, Kelly Roth, review of *Mr. Putter and Tabby Run the Race,* p. 96; August, 2008, Amelia Jenkins, review of *Baby Face,* p. 101.

Voice of Youth Advocates, April, 1992, Caroline S. McKinney, review of *Missing May,* pp. 35-36; April, 2005, Jan Chapman, review of *Boris,* p. 48; February, 2007, Debbie Clifford, review of *Ludie's Life,* p. 531.

ONLINE

KidsReads.com, http://www.kidsreads.com/ (December 15, 2008), "Cynthia Rylant."*

SALISBURY, Graham 1944-

Personal

Born April 11, 1944, in Philadelphia, PA; son of Henry Forester Graham (an officer in the U.S. Navy) and Barbara Twigg-Smith; married second wife, Robyn Kay Cowan, October 26, 1988; children: Sandi Weston, Miles, Ashley, Melanie, Alex, Keenan, Zachary, Annie Rose (adopted). *Education:* California State University at Northridge, B.A. (magna cum laude), 1974; Vermont College of Norwich University, M.F.A., 1990. *Politics:* "Middle of the road." *Hobbies and other interests:* Boating and fishing, biking, running.

Addresses

Office—Lake Oswego, OR. *Agent*—Barry Goldblatt, Barry Goldblatt Literary, 320 7th Ave., No. 266, Brooklyn, NY 11215.

Career

Writer. Worked variously as a deckhand, glass-bottom-boat skipper, singer/songwriter, graphic artist, and teacher; manager of historic office-buildings in downtown Portland, OR.

Member

Society of Children's Book Writers and Illustrators, American Library Association, Hawaiian Mission Children's Society, National Council of Teachers of English.

Awards, Honors

Parents' Choice Award, Bank Street College Child Study Children's Book Award, Judy Lopez Memorial Award for Children's Literature, Women's National Book Association, Best Books for Young Adults designation, American Library Association (ALA), and Best Books designation, *School Library Journal,* all 1992, Notable Trade Book in the Language Arts, National Council of Teachers of English (NCTE), and Oregon Book Award, both 1993, all for *Blue Skin of the Sea;* PEN/Norma Klein Award for emerging voice among American writers of children's fiction, 1992; Parents' Choice Honor Award, Editors' Choice, *Booklist,* Scott O'Dell Award, ALA Best Books for Young Adults and Notable Children's Books designations, and Books in the Middle designation, *Voice of Youth Advocates,* all 1994, Teacher's Choice, International Reading Association, Notable Children's Trade Book in the Field of Social Studies, National Council for the Social Studies/Children's Book Council (NCSS/CBC), Notable Children's Books selection, Library of Congress, New York Public Library Books for the Teen Age selection, Hawaii Nene Award, California Young Reader Medal, and Oregon Book Award, all 1995, all for *Under the Blood-Red Sun;* Oregon Book Award, 1998, and Parents' Choice Honor Award, both for *Shark Bait;* New

Graham Salisbury (Reproduced by permission.)

York Public Library Books for the Teen Age selection, and ALA Best Books for Young Adults designation, both 1999, both for *Jungle Dogs;* Parents' Choice Gold Award, Capitol Choices selection, New York Public Library Title for Reading and Sharing, and *Booklist* Editor's Choice, all 2001, *Riverbank Review* Children's Book of Distinction finalist, *Boston Globe/Horn Book* award, and ALA Best Book for Young Adults, all 2002, and Cooperative Children's Book Center Best of the Year selection, all for *Lord of the Deep; Booklist* Editor's Choice, 2002, and New York Public Library Books for the Teen Age selection and Chicago Public Library Best of the Best designation, both 2003, all for *Island Boyz;* John Unterecker Award for Fiction, Chaminade University/Hawaii Literary Arts Council, for body of work; Notable Children's Trade Book in the Field of Social Studies, NCSS/CBC, New York Public Library Books for the Teen Age selection, ALA Best Books for Young Adults designation, and PEN USA Literary Award finalist, all 2006, all for *Eyes of the Emperor;* New York Public Library Books for the Teen Age selection, ALA Notable Book selection, and Outstanding Merit citation, Bank Street College of Education, all 2007, all for *House of the Red Fish;* New York Public Library's 100 Titles for Reading and Sharing, 2007, Best Children's Book of the Year, Bank Street College of Education, Notable Children's Trade Book in the Field of Social Studies, NCSS/CBC, and New York Public Library Books for the Teen Age, all 2008, all for *Night of the Howling Dogs.*

Writings

Blue Skin of the Sea, Delacorte (New York, NY), 1992.

Under the Blood-Red Sun, Delacorte (New York, NY), 1994.

Shark Bait, Delacorte (New York, NY), 1997.

Jungle Dogs, Delacorte (New York, NY), 1998.

Lord of the Deep, Delacorte (New York, NY), 2001.

Island Boyz: Short Stories, Wendy Lamb Books (New York, NY), 2002.

Eyes of the Emperor, Wendy Lamb Books (New York, NY), 2005.

House of the Red Fish, Wendy Lamb Books (New York, NY), 2006.

Night of the Howling Dogs, Wendy Lamb Books (New York, NY), 2007.

Contributor to anthologies, including *Ultimate Sports: Short Stories by Outstanding Writers for Young Adults,* edited by Donald R. Gallo, Delacorte (New York, NY), 1995; *Going Where I'm Coming From: Memoirs of American Youth,* edited by Anne Mazer, Persea, 1995; *No Easy Answers: Short Stories about Teenagers Making Tough Decisions,* edited by Gallo, Delacorte (New York, NY), 1997; *Working Days: Short Stories about Teenagers at Work,* edited by Anne Mazer, Persea, 1997; *Dirty Laundry: Stories about Family Secrets,* edited by Lisa Rowe Fraustino, Viking (New York, NY), 1998; *Time Capsule: Short Stories about Teenagers throughout the Twentieth Century,* edited by Gallo, Delacorte (New York, NY), 1999, and *Shattered: Stories of Children and War,* edited by Jennifer Armstrong, Knopf (New York, NY), 2002. Contributor to periodicals, including *Bamboo Ridge, Chaminade Literary Review, Hawaii Pacific Review, Journal of Youth Services in Libraries, Manoa: A Journal of Pacific and International Writing, Northwest, Booklist, ALAN Review, SIGNAL Journal,* and *Hawaii Library Association Journal.*

Adaptations

A number of Salisbury's works have been recorded as audio books.

Sidelights

Characterizing himself as an author who writes for and about teenage boys, Graham Salisbury has published several well-received novels, among them *Blue Skin of the Sea, Jungle Dogs,* and *House of the Red Fish,* as well as the collection *Island Boyz: Short Stories.* All of his books are set on the Hawaiian islands, where Salisbury was raised. In addition to their exotic island setting, these fictional coming-of-age tales feature intricate interpersonal relationships that force young protagonists to take distinct, conscious steps toward maturity. Echoing the qualities many reviewers have cited in Salisbury's works, *School Library Journal* contributor Alison Follos noted of the short stories in *Island Boyz* that, using "creative and credible narrative voices" and "difficult situations," the author weaves together tales in which readers will discern "recognizable facts of life."

Although Salisbury was born in Pennsylvania, his family has its roots on the islands of Hawaii, where Salisbury's ancestors served as missionaries in the early nineteenth century. His father, an ensign in the U.S. Navy, was at Pearl Harbor during the Japanese attack on December 7, 1941; although he survived that ordeal, the man died a few years later, shot down in his fighter plane on April 11, 1945, his son's first birthday. Young Salisbury and his widowed mother continued to make their home on the islands, and the author's love for this tropical region is reflected in his books.

Unlike many writers, Salisbury was not interested in reading as a child. Because of his father's untimely death, he was raised without a solid male role-model to provide guidance, and he was left with a lot of time on his hands in which to wander the islands with his friends. Salisbury's mother, immersed in her own problems, was distant both emotionally and physically, leaving her son to seek guidance and approval from other adults in his life, such as friends, relatives, and teachers.

When Salisbury enrolled in boarding school in grade seven, he finally gained the structure and guidance he had missed earlier in life. However, until his college days at California State University at Northridge, where he graduated with a bachelor's degree in 1974, the idea of being a writer never occurred to him. "I didn't read until I was a little past thirty," Salisbury once confided to *SATA*. "Sure, I . . . read the required *Iliad* and *Odyssey* in high school, but I didn't read of my own choice until my first son was born. Then I read Alex Haley's *Roots,* which changed my life forever." It was *Roots* that inspired Salisbury to become a voracious reader and then to write books of his own. He also earned a master's degree in fine arts at Vermont College of Norwich University in 1990.

Published in 1992, Salisbury's first novel, *Blue Skin of the Sea,* is composed of a series of eleven interlinking short stories that center on Sonny Mendoza and his cousin Keo. The boys are growing up in Hawaii during the 1950s and 1960s, at a time when the old island ways are fading due to the increasing influx of tourists and other newcomers. Keo is fearless, while Sonny, whose mother died when he was very young, is more thoughtful and introspective. Still, as friends, the two cousins balance one another. Throughout the novel, the boys learn to deal with the school bully, try to cope with their growing attraction to girls, figure out ways to earn spending money, and jump other hurdles of everyday teen life. Along the way they meet up with a Hollywood film crew that is filming actor Spencer Tracy in *The Old Man and the Sea.* The boys, thinking that the props make the action look unrealistic, decide to educate the veteran actor in how to deal with real, rather than fake sharks.

A *New York Times Book Review* critic termed *Blue Skin of the Sea* an "impressive debut," while *Five Owls* contributor Gary D. Schmidt deemed the novel "entertaining, moving, and poignant," adding praise for Salisbury's realistic depiction of island life, with all its "pressures and tensions and loves and fears." *Blue Skin of the Sea* won several awards, and was chosen one of the American Library Association's Best Books for Young Adults.

Reflecting upon his father's experiences during and after the bombing raid at Pearl Harbor, Salisbury began a new novel when he imagined what it would be like to be there, as a boy, during the bombing and its aftermath. *Under the Blood-Red Sun,* published in 1994, is the story of Japanese-American eighth-grader Tomikazu "Tomi" Nakaji, whose parents had left Japan to find a better life in the United States and now live on the island of Oahu. Tomi's life is suddenly, radically altered after the Japanese attack on Pearl Harbor, an action that prompted the U.S. government to enter World War II. Where baseball, school assignments, and a local bully once occupied his thoughts, young Tomi now must worry about battling the increased tensions between Japanese immigrants and native islanders. Of real difficulty is toning down his elderly grandfather's proud display of his Japanese heritage, a heritage that is now viewed with suspicion by the Nakajis' American neighbors. Praising Salisbury for "subtly reveal[ing] the natural suspicions of the Americans and the equally natural

Cover of Salisbury's adventure novel Under the Blood-Red Sun, *featuring artwork by Kazu Sano.* (Dell Books, 1995. Used by permission of Random House Children's Books, a division of Random House, Inc.)

bewilderment of the Japanese immigrants," *Booklist* contributor Frances Bradburn wrote of *Under the Blood-Red Sun* that it is "a tribute to the writer's craft that, though there are no easy answers in the story, there is empathy for both cultures." *Voice of Youth Advocates* reviewer John R. Lord also praised *Under the Blood-Red Sun,* noting that, "in a time when positive co-existence is being touted in our schools, this novel is an outstanding example of thought-provoking—and at the same time eerily entertaining—prose for the YA reader."

House of the Red Fish, a sequel to *Under the Blood-Red Sun,* "conveys a sense of community that cuts across race and generations," noted *Booklist* contributor Hazel Rochman. Set in 1943, the work concerns Tomi's efforts to raise and restore his father's fishing boat, which has been sunk by the U.S. Army. With his father and grandfather imprisoned in internment camps, Tomi relies on his friends and neighbors to help with the rescue effort, despite threats from a vigilante gang. Connie Tyrrell Burns praised the novel in *School Library Journal,* stating that Salisbury "writes with balance of the ways in which war touches people, creating characters with fully realized motivations."

The world of boyhood is central to Salisbury's writing, and it contains elements that he well remembers, particularly what he calls the "Silent Code of Conduct." In his *ALAN Review* interview, he recalled a scene from his youth, when he and friends were surfing. While sitting on their surfboards, legs dangling knee-deep in the salt water, one of the boys pointed out to a nearby reef and stated, simply: "'Got one shark surfing with us,' as if it were a mullet, or one of those fat hotel-pond carps," Salisbury remembered. "The strength in my arms suddenly felt like jelly," he continued, adding that stories of the infrequent shark attacks around the island of Oahu quickly reeled through his mind. "None of us moved. None of us started paddling in to shore. We just kept sitting there with our legs, from the knee down, dangling underwater," Salisbury recalled. "I sat there with the rest of them, keeping an eye on the shark . . . trying not to look nervous, which I was." Salisbury attributes the young boys' desires to be accepted to "that unspoken 'code' lurking in the corner of [our] mind."

In Salisbury's novel *Shark Bait,* that silent code of male conduct weighs heavily on fourteen-year-old protagonist Eric Chock, nicknamed "Mokes" or "tough guy." Mokes is unsure where his loyalties lie when he and his school friends hear through the grapevine that tensions between native kids and Navy sailors from a destroyer docked nearby are about to spark a showdown. Mokes's father, the police chief in their small Hawaiian town, working to uphold the law and keep the peace, imposes a six o'clock evening curfew, but Mokes's best friend, seventeen-year-old Booley, plans to go to the fight and vows to kill one of the white sailors if he has the chance during the brawl. Mokes wants to obey his father, but also feels he should stand by his friend in battle. Things

Cover of Salisbury's novel **House of the Red Fish,** *featuring artwork by* **Phil Heffernan.** (Laurel-Leaf, 2006. Cover illustration copyright © 2006 by Phil Heffernan. All rights reserved. Used by permission of Random House Children's Books, a division of Random House, Inc.)

take a sharp turn for the worse when it is discovered that one of the island kids is going to the fight with a loaded gun.

Praising Salisbury's "surefooted" portrayal of "the teen milieu of fast cars, faster girls, rivalries, and swagger," *Bulletin of the Center for Children's Books* critic Elizabeth Bush commended *Shark Bait* as "a lot more diverting than luaus and ukuleles." While somewhat concerned about Salisbury's casual treatment of alcohol and drug use among the novel's teen protagonists, *School Library Journal* contributor Coop Renner deemed *Shark Bait* "a consistently engaging, well-written problem novel in a well-realized setting."

In *Shark Bait,* Salisbury's characters speak Pidgin English, a dialect used by many people native to the islands. *Booklist* contributor Helen Rosenberg praised the author's use of dialect, writing that it adds to his "col-

orful picture of island life, complete with love interests and local superstitions. Along with the local color, there's some riveting action and a [powerful] climax."

Again featuring a Hawaiian setting, *Jungle Dogs* centers on twelve-year-old Boy Regis, who is growing up in a tough neighborhood in which he must learn to conquer his fears and stand up for his convictions. Boy's older brother, who belongs to a gang, believes he must fight all his younger sibling's battles for him, often making things more difficult for Boy. At the same time, Boy's family relies on income he earns from his paper route—a route requiring that he daily pass a pack of wild jungle dogs on one of the paths to his deliveries. A *Publishers Weekly* reviewer praised the novel as a "tightly drawn drama," noting that Salisbury's "somewhat exotic scenery and dialect are backdrop for sharp characterizations and inventive, subtle plot twists." Janice M. Del Negro noted in the *Bulletin of the Center for Children's Books* that "The lush Hawaii setting adds a physical dimension that strongly colors the action as Boy faces both canine and human packs with tenacity and nerve that will hearten young readers confronting their own demons."

Winner of the *Boston Globe/Horn Book* award, *Lord of the Deep* introduces readers to thirteen-year-old Mickey Donovan, who works alongside his stepfather, Bill, as a deck hand Bill's charter boat, the *Crystal C.* To Mickey, Bill is not only the boy's mentor and the man who gave his family emotional and financial stability; Bill is the best skipper on the islands. Bill is also patient with his stepson as Mickey tries hard to learn the ropes, from piloting the boat to swimming under the *Crystal C.* to detangle fishing lines. However, the boy watches his idol tarnish when the older man tolerates the mistreatment of two fishing clients, loutish brothers Ernie and Cal, during a three-day fishing charter. When Ernie strong-arms Bill to let him take credit for a huge, world-record shattering mahi-mahi that Bill actually brought in by offering the captain money, Mickey is crushed to see that his stepfather agrees to go along with the lie. While his reaction is at first raw anger, the boy eventually realizes that, all along, his stepfather has been exhibiting the most important attributes of adulthood: patience and the strength to forgive.

In *Horn Book* a contributor deemed *Lord of the Deep* a "masterpiece of subtlety," while *School Library Journal* reviewer Caroline Ward praised it as "a winning combination of riveting deep-sea fishing action, a sensitive depiction of family relationships, and an intriguing exploration of the fine line between lying and telling the truth." While the novel "vividly conveys the pace and dangers of sport fishing," according to *Booklist* contributor John Peters, the critic added that the overlying plot hinges on the "ethical conundrum" of Salisbury's young protagonist, revealing, as the *Horn Book* contributor noted, "the perilous undercurrents that can lie beneath even the best of human relationships."

Based on actual events, *Eyes of the Emperor* centers on Eddy Okubo, a sixteen-year-old Japanese American who doctors his birth certificate so he can serve in the U.S. Army with his friends. Just weeks after Eddy enlists, Pearl Harbor is attacked and America enters World War II; Eddy and his comrades soon find themselves segregated from their unit because of their ancestry. Dispatched to Cat Island, Mississippi, Eddy and twenty-five other Japanese-American soldiers are used as "bait" to train attack dogs that will hunt the enemy in the Pacific. "The shameful way Japanese American soldiers were treated will be eye-opening to most readers," noted *Kliatt* reviewer Paula Rohrlick, "and the scenes on Cat Island are dramatic and horrifying." According to a *Publishers Weekly* reviewer, *Eyes of the Emperor* "is a valuable and gripping addition to the canon of WW II historical fiction from a perspective young readers rarely see."

In *Night of the Howling Dogs,* Salisbury offers a fictional account of a natural disaster that occurred in Hawaii in 1975. Narrated by Dylan, a Boy Scout patrol leader, the work describes a camping trip that threatens to end in disaster when an earthquake hits the area, followed by a violent tsunami. Along with Louie, a troubled member of the scout troop, Dylan mounts a rescue effort that involves an arduous trek along the coastline. "A strong sense of place informs the plot as well as the setting of this convincing story," Carolyn Phelan remarked in *Booklist,* and *School Library Journal* critic Joel Shoemaker observed that "Salisbury's tale of courage, strength, and survival is appealing, exciting, and insightful."

Island Boyz contains ten stories, including five previously unpublished works, that examine the lives of young men in Hawaii. "Mrs. Noonan" centers on a boarding student's obsession with a faculty member's wife, and "Angel-Baby" tells a story of first love. Critics especially praised "Waiting for the War," which describes a soldier's gesture of kindness before he is shipped off to battle, and "Hat of Clouds," a tale of two brothers whose relationship changes after one is wounded in Vietnam. Calling the collection "memorable," Gillian Engberg added in *Booklist* that each story pairs the island's "tropical setting with vivid, tangible details that electrify each boy's drama."

Understanding that his books are read by impressionable youngsters, Salisbury takes his writing seriously. "I was told by a young reader that a scene in *Under the Blood-Red Sun* was so powerful to him, so moving, that it became, for him, a seminal life moment," the author remarked in an interview on the *Ya Ya Yas* Web log. "In a realistic, human way, that one scene (in the context of the novel) turned him into a Lifetime Reader. That is what it's all about. I call that a home run."

Salisbury once told *SATA:* "The important thing for me to understand as a writer for young readers is that though the world has changed, the basic needs of young people haven't. There are many, many kids out there with holes in their lives that they desperately want to fill. I can write about those holes. I can do this because I am human and have suffered and soared myself. Strange as it sounds to say, I—as a writer—consider myself lucky, indeed, to have all the holes I have in my own life. Because when I write, I remember, I understand, I empathize, and I feel a need to explore those holes and maybe even fill a couple of them—for myself and for any reader with a similar need who happens to stumble onto my work."

Salisbury is certainly appreciative of his talents, as he noted in an essay on the *Random House* Web site: "I have been honored by the universe. Writing is often as mysterious as the concept of eternity. How a twerp like me ever got this lucky, I'll never know." He concluded, "The magic comes, really, in the writing. Something happens between my fingertips and the keyboard. I don't understand it, but it's absolutely the most fabulous and surely the most mysterious part of the writing process: write, and things happen."

Biographical and Critical Sources

BOOKS

Gill, David Macinnis, *Graham Salisbury: Island Boy,* Scarecrow Press (Lanham, MD), 2005.

PERIODICALS

ALAN Review, fall, 1994, Graham Salisbury, "A Leaf on the Sea," pp. 11-14; winter, 1997, Janet Benton, "'Writing My Way Home': An Interview with Salisbury."

Booklist, October 15, 1994, Frances Bradburn, review of *Under the Blood-Red Sun,* p. 425; September 1, 1997, Helen Rosenberg, review of *Shark Bait,* p. 107; September 15, 1998, Hazel Rochman, review of *Jungle Dogs,* p. 110; March 1, 2001, Anna Rich, review of *Jungle Dogs,* p. 1295; August, 2001, John Peters, review of *Lord of the Deep,* p. 2108; April 15, 2002, Gillian Engberg, review of *Island Boyz,* p. 1399; May 15, 2005, Hazel Rochman, review of *Eyes of the Emperor,* p. 1669; April 15, 2006, Hazel Rochman, review of *House of the Red Fish,* p. 64; August, 2007, Carolyn Phelan, review of *Night of the Howling Dogs,* p. 70.

Bulletin of the Center for Children's Books, December, 1997, Elizabeth Bush, review of *Shark Bait,* pp. 138-139; February, 1999, Janice M. Del Negro, review of *Jungle Dogs,* p. 216.

Five Owls, May-June, 1992, Gary D. Schmidt, review of *Blue Skin of the Sea,* p. 66.

Horn Book, September-October, 1998, Susan P. Bloom, review of *Jungle Dogs,* p. 614; September, 2001, Peter D. Sieruta, review of *Lord of the Deep,* p. 595; March-

April, 2002, Peter D. Sieruta, review of *Island Boyz,* p. 219; January-February, 2003, Graham Salisbury, "E Komo Mai" (award acceptance speech), p. 39; July-August, 2005, Peter D. Sieruta, review of *Eyes of the Emperor,* p. 480; September-October, 2007, Betty Carter, review of *Night of the Howling Dogs,* p. 589.

Journal of Adolescence and Adult Literacy, November, 2002, James Blasingame, review of *Lord of the Deep,* p. 267.

Kirkus Reviews, March 15, 2002, review of *Island Boyz,* p. 425.

Kliatt, July, 2002, Jean Palmer, review of *Lord of the Deep,* p. 53; May, 2003, Paula Rohrlick, review of *Lord of the Deep,* p. 20; March, 2004, Olivia Durant, review of *Island Boyz,* p. 28; July, 2005, Paula Rohrlick, review of *Eyes of the Emperor,* p. 16; July, 2006, Paula Rohrlick, review of *House of the Red Fish,* p. 14.

New York Times Book Review, May 2, 1993, review of *Blue Skin of the Sea,* p. 24.

Publishers Weekly, July 13, 1998, review of *Jungle Dogs,* p. 78; July 30, 2001, review of *Lord of the Deep,* p. 86; September 5, 2005, review of *Eyes of the Emperor,* p. 64.

School Library Journal, September, 1997, Coop Renner, review of *Shark Bait,* p. 225; October, 2000, Todd Dunkelberg, review of *Jungle Dogs,* p. 94; August, 2001, Caroline Ward, review of *Lord of the Deep,* p. 188; March, 2002, Alison Follos, review of *Island Boyz,* p. 238; August, 2001, Caroline Ward, review of *Lord of the Deep,* p. 188; September, 2005, Carol A. Edwards, review of *Eyes of the Emperor,* p. 213; August, 2006, Connie Tyrell Burns, review of *House of the Red Fish,* p. 128; August, 2007, Joel Shoemaker, review of *Night of the Howling Dogs,* p. 125.

Voice of Youth Advocates, October, 1994, John R. Lord, review of *Under the Blood-Red Sun,* p. 216.

ONLINE

Graham Salisbury Home Page, http://www.grahamsalisbury.com (November 10, 2008).

Random House Web site, http://www.randomhouse.com/ (November 10, 2008), biographical essay by Salisbury.

Ya Ya Yas Web log, http://theyayayas.wordpress.com/ (May 17, 2007), interview with Salisbury.*

* * *

SCHEMBRI, Pamela 1969-

Personal

Born 1969. *Education:* College degree.

Addresses

Home—Montgomery, NY.

Career

Librarian and author. Highview Elementary School, Nanuet, NY, media specialist.

Writings

FOR CHILDREN

(With Peter Catalanotto) *The Secret Lunch Special,* illustrated by Catalanotto, Henry Holt (New York, NY), 2006.

(With Peter Catalanotto) *No More Pumpkins,* illustrated by Catalanotto, Henry Holt (New York, NY), 2007.

(With Peter Catalanotto) *The Veteran's Day Visitor,* illustrated by Catalanotto, Henry Holt (New York, NY), 2008.

OTHER

Scary Stories You Won't Be Afraid to Use: Resources and Activities for a K-6 Audience, Linworth Publishing (Worthington, OH), 2001.

Using Scary Stories in the Classroom: Lesson Plans, Activities, and Curriculum Connections, Linworth Publishing (Worthington, OH), 2002.

Contributor of reviews to *Book Report.*

Sidelights

Pamela Schembri, a librarian and working in New York state, has also established authorial credits through her work with author/illustrator Peter Catalanotto. Their

Pamela Schembri's text for **The Secret Lunch Special** *features artwork by Peter Catalanotto.* (Illustration copyright © 2006 by Peter Catalanotto. All rights reserved. Reprinted by permission of Henry Holt and Company, LLC.)

"Second Grade Friends" series, which includes the books *No More Pumpkins, The Secret Lunch Special,* and *The Veterans Day Visitor,* provide budding book-worms with a painless and entertaining introduction to chapter books.

In *The Secret Lunch Special* readers meet Emily as she embarks on her first day of second grade. When Emily leaves her new lunch bag on the seat of her school bus, worries over what she will have for lunch soon take center stage in a book that *Booklist* critic Carolyn Phelan deemed "a good choice" for young readers. Emily returns in *No More Pumpkins,* as she and her class study pumpkins, make pumpkin art, and write pumpkin stories. After her carved Jack o' lantern is in-tentionally damaged by bossy classmate Vincetta Lou-ise, the second grader feels hurt, until Emily under-stands the feelings that prompted Vinni's act. *The Veterans Day Visitor,* described by *Horn Book* critic Robin L. Smith as a "welcome addition" to classroom discussions of the contributions of U.S. servicemen and women, also features line art by Schembri's coauthor, Catalanotto. Phelan, in a review of *No More Pumpkins,* praised the book for its realistic elementary-school set-ting and "wide range of true-to-life emotions." Compar-ing the "Second Grade Friends" books to popular be-ginning readers by Barbara Park and Patricia Reilly Giff, *School Library Journal* critic Kelly Roth added that *No More Pumpkins* is an enjoyable contribution to Schembri and Catalanotto's series.

Biographical and Critical Sources

PERIODICALS

Booklist, September 1, 2006, Carolyn Phelan, review of *The Secret Lunch Special,* p. 134; August, 2007, Caro-lyn Phelan, review of *No More Pumpkins,* p. 62.
Horn Book, September-October, 2006, Robin Smith, re-view of *The Secret Lunch Special,* p. 575.
School Library Journal, May, 2002, Mary Lankford, re-view of *Scary Stories You Won't Be Afraid to Use: Re-sources and Activities for a K-6 Audience,* p. 183; September, 2006, Adrienne Furness, review of *The Se-cret Lunch Special,* p. 161; September, 2007, Kelly Roth, review of *No More Pumpkins,* p. 160.*

*   *   *

SHEPPARD, Kate

Personal
Female.

Addresses
E-mail—kate.sheppard@ukonline.co.uk.

Career
Illustrator.

Illustrator

Leon Rosselson, *Bernie Works a Miracle,* A. & C. Black (London, England), 1992.

Terry Deary, *The Blitzed Brits,* Hippo (London, England), 1994, new edition, illustrated with Martin Brown, Scholastic (London, England), 2007.

Terry Deary, *Cruel Kings and Mean Queens,* André Deut-sch (London, England), 1995.

Rebecca Lisle, *Petrified,* Corgi (London, England), 1996.

Marjorie Newman, *Yo Ho Ho!* Corgi (London, England), 1996.

Annie Dalton, *Tilly Beany Saves the World,* Mammoth (London, England), 1997.

Pat Thomson, compiler, *A Crate of Stories for Eight Year Olds,* Corgi (London, England), 1997.

Ana Sanderson, compiler, *Me: Songs for Four to Seven Year Olds,* A. & C. Black (London, England), 1997.

Sheila Lavelle, *Tiger,* Orchard (London, England), 1998.

Helen Paiba, compilers, *Funny Stories for Six Year Olds,* Macmillan (London, England), 1999.

Natalie Grice, *Boudicca Strikes Back,* Franklin Watts (Lon-don, England), 1999.

Jon Blake, *The Canal Diggers,* Franklin Watts (London, England), 1999.

Jennifer Curry, compiler, *School Poems,* Hippo (London, England), 1999.

Natalie Grice, *A School for Girls!,* Franklin Watts (Lon-don, England), 2000.

Fiona Cummings, *The Little Book of Chat,* Red Fox (Lon-don, England), 2001.

Olivia Warbuton, *The Thing about Mums,* Lion (Oxford, England), 2001.

Mike Yaconelli, *A Gift for Life's Ups and Downs,* Lion (Oxford, England), 2002.

Mike Yaconelli, *A Gift for My Daughter,* Lion (Oxford, England), 2002.

Mike Yaconelli, *A Gift for My Grandchild,* Lion (Oxford, England), 2002.

Mike Yaconelli, *A Gift for New Parents,* Lion (Oxford, England), 2002.

Deri Robins, *A Smart Girl's Guide to Boys,* 2002.

Alison Prince, *Boojer,* Corgi (London, England), 2002.

Alison Prince, *Spud,* Corgi (London, England), 2003.

Lizz Babbs, *The Thing about Calories,* Lion (Oxford, England), 2003.

Mike Yaconelli, *The Thing about Kids,* Lion (Oxford, England), 2003.

Margaret Nash, reteller, *The North Wind and the Sun,* Franklin Watts (London, England), 2004.

Tracey Turner, *The A-Z of Crackers, Mistletoe, and Other Christmas Turkeys,* Scholastic (London, England), 2004.

Tracey Turner, *The A-Z of Ghosts, Skeletons, and Other Haunting Horrors,* Scholastic (London, England), 2004.

Kate Sheppard creates the illustrations for Claire Llewellyn's informative picture book Ask Dr. K. Fisher about Dinosaurs. (Copyright © 2007 by Kingfisher Publications Plc. Reproduced by permission of Houghton Mifflin Company.)

Tracey Turner, *The A-Z of Lovehearts, Friendships, and Other Slushy Stuff,* Scholastic (London, England), 2005, Scholastic Canada (Toronto, Ontario, Canada), 2006.

Jillian Powell, *Blushing Becky,* Franklin Watts (London, England), 2005.

Rob Childs, *Keeper's Ball,* Corgi (London, England), 2005.

Ann Bryant, *But, Mum!,* Franklin Watts (London, England), 2006.

Kaye Umansky, *I Am a Tree,* A. & C. Black (London, England), 2006.

Claire Llewellyn, *Ask Dr. K. Fisher about Animals,* Kingfisher (Boston, MA), 2007.

Claire Llewellyn, *Ask Dr. K. Fisher about Dinosaurs,* Kingfisher (Boston, MA), 2007.

Russell Punter, *Percy and the Pirates,* Usborne (London, England), 2007.

Josephine Feeney, *Robin Hood's Day,* Walker (London, England), 2007.

Claire Llewellyn, *Ask Dr. K. Fisher about Reptiles,* Kingfisher (Boston, MA), 2008.

Claire Llewellyn, *Ask Dr. K. Fisher about Creepy-crawlies,* Kingfisher (Boston, MA), 2008.

Also illustrator of numerous other fiction and nonfiction books.

Sidelights

British illustrator Kate Sheppard has provided the artwork for more than one hundred works of fiction and nonfiction for young readers. She has enjoyed successful collaborations with authors such as Terry Deary, Tracey Turner, Mike Yaconelli, Natalie Grice, and Alison Prince. Sheppard has also teamed with writer Claire Llewellyn to produce a critically acclaimed series of books that look at the everyday concerns of nature's creatures.

In Llewellyn's *Ask Dr. K. Fisher about Animals,* which is formatted as an advice column, the kindly doctor offers helpful advice to a tadpole that is concerned about its rapidly changing body, an orb spider that seeks help with relationships, a giraffe that is embarrassed by the length of its neck, and a dung beetle that wants to change its diet. "Sheppard's brightly colored cartoon illustrations are fabulously quirky," observed a critic in *Kirkus Reviews.* A *Publishers Weekly* contributor also offered praise for the work, stating that "Sheppard's illustrations feature an expressive cast of creatures in a collage-like assemblage of Polaroid-style photos, dog-eared letters, envelopes and more." In *Ask Dr. K. Fisher about Dinosaurs,* a companion volume that also features Llewellyn's text, the helpful columnist answers queries from, among others, a Diplodocus concerned about its weight. According to *School Library Journal* reviewer Donna Atmur, *Ask Dr. K. Fisher about Dinosaurs* benefits from Sheppard's "humorous watercolor cartoons."

Biographical and Critical Sources

PERIODICALS

Kirkus Reviews, July 15, 2007, review of *Ask Dr. K. Fisher about Animals.*
Publishers Weekly, July 30, 2007, review of *Ask Dr. K. Fisher about Animals,* p. 86.
Resource Links, December, 2006, Mavis Holder, review of *The A-Z of Crackers, Mistletoe, and Other Christmas Turkeys,* p. 28; April, 2007, Carolyn Cutt, review of *The A-Z of Lovehearts, Friendship, and Other Slushy Stuff,* p. 92.

ONLINE

AOI Portfolios Web site, http://www.aoiportfolios.com/ (December 15, 2008), "Kate Sheppard."*

*   *   *

SIERRA, Judy 1945-

Personal

Born Judy Strup, June 8, 1945, in Washington, DC; name legally changed, 1985; daughter of Joseph L. (a photographer) and Jean (a librarian) Strup; married Robert Walter Kaminski (a puppeteer and elementary schoolteacher); children: Christopher Robin Strup. *Education:* American University, B.A., 1968; California State University—San Jose (now San Jose State University), M.A., 1973; University of California—Los Angeles, Ph.D.

Addresses

Home—Castro Valley, CA.

Career

Writer. Puppeteer and storyteller, beginning 1976. Part-time librarian at Los Angeles Public Library, beginning 1986; teacher of children's literature and storytelling at Extension of University of California—Los Angeles. Artist-in-residence at Smithsonian Institution, 1984.

Member

National Association for the Preservation and Perpetuation of Storytelling, American Folklore Society, California Folklore Society.

Awards, Honors

Best Books designation, *Publishers Weekly,* 1996, Fanfare List includee, *Horn Book,* 1997, and Notable Books for Children designation, American Library Association (ALA), 1997, all for *Nursery Tales around the World;* Notable Book citation, ALA, 2005, Irma Simonton Black Honor Book, Bank Street College of Education, and E.B. White Read-Aloud Award, Association of Booksellers for Children, all for *Wild about Books.*

Writings

FOR YOUNG READERS

The Elephant's Wrestling Match, illustrated by Brian Pinkney, Lodestar (New York, NY), 1992.
The House That Drac Built, illustrated by Will Hillenbrand, Harcourt Brace (San Diego, CA), 1995.
Good Night, Dinosaurs, illustrated by Victoria Chess, Clarion (New York, NY), 1996.
(Reteller) *Wiley and the Hairy Man,* illustrated by Brian Pinkney, Lodestar (New York, NY), 1996.
(Reteller) *The Mean Hyena: A Folktale from Malawi,* illustrated by Michael Bryant, Lodestar (New York, NY), 1997.
Counting Crocodiles, illustrated by Will Hillenbrand, Harcourt Brace (San Diego, CA), 1997.
Antarctic Antics: A Book of Penguin Poems, illustrated by Jose Aruego and Ariane Dewey, Harcourt Brace (San Diego, CA), 1998.
Tasty Baby Belly Buttons: A Japanese Folktale, illustrated by Meilo So, Alfred A. Knopf (New York, NY), 1998.

The Dancing Pig, illustrated by Jesse Sweetwater, Harcourt Brace (San Diego, CA), 1999.

(Reteller) *The Beautiful Butterfly: A Folktale from Spain,* illustrated by Victoria Chess, Clarion (New York, NY), 2000.

The Gift of the Crocodile: A Cinderella Story, illustrated by Reynold Ruffins, Simon & Schuster (New York, NY), 2000.

There's a Zoo in Room Twenty-two, illustrated by Barney Saltzberg, Harcourt Brace (San Diego, CA), 2000.

Preschool to the Rescue, illustrated by Will Hillenbrand, Harcourt Brace (San Diego, CA), 2001.

Monster Goose, illustrated by Jack E. Davis, Harcourt Brace (San Diego, CA), 2001.

'Twas the Fright before Christmas, illustrated by Will Hillenbrand, Harcourt Brace (San Diego, CA), 2002.

Coco and Cavendish: Circus Dogs, illustrated by Paul Meisel, Random House (New York, NY), 2003.

Coco and Cavendish: Fire Dogs, illustrated by Paul Meisel, Random House (New York, NY), 2004.

What Time Is It, Mr. Crocodile?, illustrated by Doug Cushman, Gulliver (Orlando, FL), 2004.

Wild about Books, illustrated by Marc Brown, Knopf (New York, NY), 2004.

(Selector) *Schoolyard Rhymes: Kids' Own Rhymes for Rope Skipping, Hand Clapping, Ball Bouncing, and Just Plain Fun,* illustrated by Melissa Sweet, Knopf (New York, NY), 2005.

The Gruesome Guide to World Monsters, illustrated by Henrik Drescher, Candlewick Press (Cambridge, MA), 2005.

The Secret Science Project That Almost Ate the School, illustrated by Stephen Gammell, Simon & Schuster (New York, NY), 2006.

Thelonius Monster's Sky-high Fly Pie: A Revolting Rhyme, illustrated by Edward Koren, Knopf (New York, NY), 2006.

Mind Your Manners, B.B. Wolf, illustrated by J. Otto Seibold, Knopf (New York, NY), 2007.

Born to Read, illustrated by Marc Brown, Knopf (New York, NY), 2008.

Beastly Rhymes to Read after Dark, illustrated by Brian Biggs, Knopf (New York, NY), 2008.

Saving Ballyhoo Bay, illustrated by Derek Anderson, Simon & Schuster (New York, NY), 2009.

Sleepy Little Alphabet: A Bedtime Story from Alphabet Town, illustrated by Melissa Sweet, Knopf (New York, NY), 2009.

STORY COLLECTIONS

(With Robert Kaminski) *Twice upon a Time: Stories to Tell, Retell, Act Out, and Write About,* H.W. Wilson (Bronx, NY), 1989.

(With Robert Kaminski) *Multicultural Folktales: Stories to Tell Young Children,* Oryx Press (Phoenix, AZ), 1991.

(Compiler) *Cinderella,* illustrated by Joanne Caroselli, Oryx Press (Phoenix, AZ), 1992.

(Editor and annotator) *Quests and Spells: Fairy Tales from the European Oral Tradition,* Bob Kaminski Media Arts (Ashland, OR), 1994.

Mother Goose's Playhouse: Toddler Tales and Nursery Rhymes, with Patterns for Puppets and Feltboards, Bob Kaminski Media Arts (Ashland, OR), 1994.

(Selector and reteller) *Nursery Tales around the World,* illustrated by Stefano Vitale, Clarion (New York, NY), 1996.

Multicultural Folktales for the Feltboard and Readers' Theater, Oryx Press (Phoenix, AZ), 1996.

Can You Guess My Name?: Traditional Tales around the World, illustrated by Stefano Vitale, Clarion (New York, NY), 2002.

Silly and Sillier: Read-Aloud Tales from around the World, illustrated by Valeri Gorbachev, Knopf (New York, NY), 2002.

NONFICTION

The Flannel Board Storytelling Book, H.W. Wilson (Bronx, NY), 1987.

Storytelling and Creative Dramatics, H.W. Wilson (Bronx, NY), 1989.

Fantastic Theater: Puppets and Plays for Young Performers and Young Audiences, H.W. Wilson (Bronx, NY), 1991.

(With Robert Kaminski) *Children's Traditional Games: Games from 137 Countries and Cultures,* Oryx Press (Phoenix, AZ), 1995.

Storytellers' Research Guide: Folktales, Myths, and Legends, Folkprint (Eugene, OR), 1996.

Celtic Baby Names: Traditional Names from Ireland, Scotland, Wales, Brittany, Cornwall, and the Isle of Man, Folkprint (Eugene, OR), 1997.

Spanish Baby Names: Traditional and Modern First Names of Spain and the Americas, Folkprint (Eugene, OR), 2002.

Editor of *Folklore and Mythology Journal,* 1988—.

Adaptations

Antarctic Antics was adapted as an animated film and as a sound recording.

Sidelights

Interested in storytelling and puppetry arts from childhood, Judy Sierra has built a career as a writer of imaginative stories for young readers, including *Good Night, Dinosaurs, The Gift of the Crocodile,* and *Mind Your Manners, B.B. Wolf.* "In my books," Sierra remarked in an interview on the *Powell's Books* Web site, "I try to create small, exciting worlds that take children away from the everyday."

Many of Sierra's popular works are adaptations of folk tales from other countries. The original story inspiring *The Elephant's Wrestling Match,* for instance, comes from the African nation of Cameroon. In Sierra's retelling, the mighty elephant challenges all the other animals to a test of strength, and each fails: "The leopard, crocodile, and rhinoceros all respond," Linda Greengrass reported in *School Library Journal,* "only to be easily thwarted by the mighty beast. Each time, Monkey beats out the results on the drum." In a surprising twist, a small but clever bat turns out to be the winner, although that is not the resolution of the story. The tale concludes by explaining that, because of his anger at Monkey for spreading the news of his defeat, Elephant smashes Monkey's drum; for this reason, "you don't see monkeys playing the talking drum." A reviewer in *Publishers Weekly* noted that "Sierra's staccato retelling of this lively African tale crackles with energy," and Greengrass added that "listeners can almost hear the beating of the drum." As Betsy Hearne, reviewing *The Elephant's Wrestling Match* for the *Bulletin of the Center for Children's Books,* maintained that "the drama is simple enough for toddlers to follow but sturdy enough to hold other kids' attention as well."

In *The House That Drac Built* Sierra and artist Will Hillenbrand take on literary and folk symbols more familiar to American children, inserting the character of Dracula into the nursery rhyme "The House That Jack Built." Thus as Nancy Vasilakas recounted in *Horn Book,* "Young audiences are introduced to the bat that lived in the house that Drac built, then to the cat that bit the bat, the werewolf that chased the cat that bit the bat, and so on through 'fearsome' manticore, coffin, mummy, zombie, and fiend of Bloodygore." Ghoulish as all this sounds, the story has a humorous twist, as a group of trick-or-treaters enters the house and puts everything right, re-wrapping the mummy and tending to the bitten bat. Noting its appeal at Halloween, *School Library Journal* contributor Beth Irish called *The House That Drac Built* "a definite hit for holiday story programs."

Sierra and Hillenbrand make reference to their *The House That Drac Built* collaboration in *'Twas the Fright before Christmas.* Here trouble starts when Santa Mouse, who delivers presents in a sleigh pulled by eight bats, tickles a dragon's nose. A werewolf finds himself at the end of the chain of events with a pinched and sore tail, and he tries to figure out just what started the mess. Once the mystery is solved, Santa Mouse apologizes and suggests that they all read a story, which, in Hillenbrand's illustration, is *The House That Drac Built.* Mummies and other monsters fill the pages of the book, which a *Kirkus Reviews* contributor considered "another innovation on a well-known text."

Sierra joins forces with cartoonist Edward Koren for another monstrous tale, *Thelonius Monster's Sky-high Fly Pie: A Revolting Rhyme.* Spoofing the classic rhyme "I Know an Old Lady Who Swallowed a Fly," Sierra offers a story about a shaggy and repulsive—but well-meaning—chef who decides to create a tasty treat for his hungry friends. Just before the guests can dig in, however, the main ingredients in Thelonius's grand dessert plan their escape. "Children will love the illustrated jokes," noted *School Library Journal* contributor Susan Weitz of the book.

Whereas *Thelonius Monster's Sky-high Fly Pie* may not exactly be bedtime reading, *Good Night, Dinosaurs* certainly is. Here Sierra's book describes a family of dinosaurs getting ready for bed, brushing their teeth and then listening to lullabies and stories from their parents. "Young dinosaur fanciers will be charmed and undoubtedly claim this as their favorite go-to-sleep book," concluded Ann A. Flowers in *Horn Book.* Beth Tegart, writing in *School Library Journal,* dubbed *Good Night, Dinosaurs* "a pleasant read at bedtime for dinosaur fans as well as those who need a chuckle at the end of the day."

With *Wiley and the Hairy Man,* Sierra retells another folk tale, this one with roots in the American South. Frightened by the Hairy Man, Wiley enlists the help of his mother to trick the monster three times, and thus forces the Hairy Man to leave them alone. "Through the use of dialogue without dialect and a lissome narration," commented Maria B. Salvadore in *Horn Book,* "Sierra captures the cadence of the oral language of Alabama."

Like *The Elephant's Wrestling Match,* Sierra's folk-tale adaptation *The Mean Hyena* comes originally from Africa, in this case the country of Malawi. There the Nyanja people tell how the turtle gets his revenge on the title character after the hyena plays a cruel trick on him. *School Library Journal* contributor Marilyn Iarusso called *The Mean Hyena* "a must for all folk-tale collections."

Counting Crocodiles takes place in a tropical location, although its setting is perhaps even more fanciful than that of Sierra's earlier tales. An unfortunate monkey finds herself on an island with nothing to eat but lemons, and longs to make her way to a nearby island with banana trees. There is only one problem: the Sillabobble Sea, which separates the two pieces of land, is filled with crocodiles. However, the monkey, like many another small but clever creature in Sierra's stories, devises an ingenious plan to trick the crocodiles and obtain not only a bunch of bananas, but a sapling from which she can acquire fruit in the future. "The whimsical rhyme . . . and the lively alliteration . . . add to the appeal," wrote Kathleen Squires in *Booklist.* A reviewer in *Publishers Weekly* also praised Sierra's collaboration with illustrator Will Hillenbrand: "Working with traditional materials, author and artist arrive at an altogether fresh presentation."

After retelling a tale from Japan in *Tasty Baby Belly Buttons,* and spinning a story about two girls who are able to evade a witch due to their kindness to animals in *The Dancing Pig,* Sierra returned to crocodiles with a Cinderella story set in Indonesia. In *The Gift of the Crocodile* no fairy godmother comes to Damara's rescue when her stepmother shows her cruelty; instead, Grandmother Crocodile rewards the girl for her honesty and good heart. When the prince announces plans to host a lavish ball, Damara goes to the generous Grand-

***Will Hillenbrand creates the whimsical characters that star in Judy Sierra's picture book* Counting Crocodiles.** (Illustration copyright © 1997 by Will Hillenbrand. All rights reserved. Reprinted by permission of Houghton Mifflin Harcourt Publishing Company.)

mother Crocodile for Fairy Godmother-type assistance. "Sierra's unadorned retelling is straightforward" wrote a *Horn Book* reviewer, the critic concluding that the author's "Southeast Asian variation adds some tropical zest to the oft-told tale." Hazel Rochman, writing for *Booklist,* called *The Gift of the Crocodile* "a storytelling treat."

Leaving fairy tales behind and heading for the playground, Sierra shows how a giant mud puddle is thwarted in *Preschool to the Rescue.* The mud puddle lurks, waiting until it can capture anything that passes through it—which, over the course of the story, includes a pizza van and four other vehicles. Only the preschoolers know how to deal with the mud, by making it into mud pies until the sun comes out and dries it away. "In a feast of unbridled mud-food making, the heroic preschoolers completely consume the rogue puddle," explained a *Publishers Weekly* reviewer. Marlene Gawron commented in *School Library Journal* on the onomatopoeia Sierra uses in her text: "What a wonderful noisy book this is." Gawron concluded, "The fun doesn't stop until the book is closed." As a *Horn Book*

contributor recommended, "This uncomplicated story . . . has rainy-day read-aloud written all over it."

Twisted versions of Mother Goose rhymes fill the pages of *Monster Goose.* Featuring such characters as Little Miss Mummy, Cannibal Horner, and the Zombie who lives in a shoe. Sierra's revisions of familiar Mother Goose rhymes might be too much for particularly young readers, warned a reviewer for *Kirkus Reviews.* "but it's a fiendishly good time for everyone else." A critic for *Publishers Weekly* noted that "the Goose has been spoofed before, but this volume strikes a nice balance between goofy and ghastly," while *School Library Journal* reviewer Gay Lynn Van Vleck advised school librarians to keep extra copies of *Monster Goose* for students, "since teachers may hoard it for themselves." Gillian Engberg, writing in *Booklist,* recommended the book as "perfect for rowdy Halloween read-alouds."

In *The Gruesome Guide to World Monsters,* illustrated by Henrik Drescher, Sierra offers an introduction to more than sixty ghoulish creatures of legend. Among those profiled are the Mansusopsop, a blood-sucking bat from the Philippines; the Dziwozony, a race of wild women found in Polish forests; and the Chiruwi, a human-bird hybrid located in Malawi. A contributor in *Publishers Weekly* noted that "every page provides imaginative fodder for chilling tales," and Jennifer Mattson, writing in *Booklist,* praised the combination of Sierra's prose and Drescher's artwork, noting that the "controlled text provides a counterweight to artwork that's like graffiti scribbled on the walls of Bedlam."

A youngster inadvertently creates her own terrifying beast in *The Secret Science Project That Almost Ate the School,* a humorous work illustrated by Stephen Gammell. When a third grader needs a project for her upcoming science fair, she orders Professor Swami's Super Slime over the Internet. Disregarding the product warnings about releasing the mutant yeast too early, the student unleashes a gooey glob that threatens to swallow everything in its path. Engberg described the work as "an energetic, darkly comic spin on the common story of a science project gone wrong," and a contributor in *Publishers Weekly* remarked, "Gammell's illustrations amplify the energy and fun of Sierra's bouncy verse."

Wild about Books is a celebration of zoos, libraries, and Dr. Seuss. Here Sierra teams up with award-winning illustrator Marc Brown to tell the story of a librarian who accidentally takes the bookmobile into the zoo, only to find that all of the animals want to learn to read. She begins to read to them, picking out the perfect books for each species (tall books for the giraffes, featuring basketball and skyscrapers, books written in Chinese for the pandas, and dramas for the llamas). However, for many of the animals, reading is not enough: the dung beetles write haiku and a hippo wins the "Zoolitzer" prize. *Wild about Books* is "both homage to and reminiscent of Dr. Seuss's epic rhyming sagas," praised *School Library Journal* reviewer Marge Loch-Wouters. A *Publishers Weekly* contributor called Sierra's tale a "winning paean to reading and writing," while a *Kirkus Reviews* critic considered it "a storytime spectacular."

Born to Read, a follow-up to *Wild about Books,* centers on a youngster with an insatiable appetite for literature. After Sam learns about an upcoming bicycle race, he pores over every book he can find about the subject and ends up defeating his adult competition. Sam later saves his city from a giant baby by soothing the towering infant with a basketful of stories and snacks. Sierra's "rich vocabulary gives the story a jaunty tempo, as do the appealing full-color gouache cartoon illustrations," a contributor in *Publishers Weekly* observed.

Crocodiles and mischievous monkeys again live large in *What Time Is It, Mr. Crocodile?* Mr. Crocodile has a list of things to accomplish during his day, one of which is to capture and dine on the pesky monkeys who constantly pester him for the time of day. However, due to monkey meddling, things don't quite go as Mr. Croco-

dile planned, and he decides to make peace with the monkeys instead. A *Kirkus Reviews* contributor complimented, "any time [is] the right time for this irresistible rhyme." A *School Library Journal* reviewer warned readers to be ready for "some memorable monkey business in this entertaining tale," while Ilene Cooper noted in *Booklist* that "the best part of the book is Sierra's handy way with a rhyming text." Lauren Peterson, also writing for *Booklist,* praised *What Time Is It, Mr. Crocodile?,* adding that "Sierra's bouncy rhyming text will make this a fun read-aloud."

Sierra presents an unusual take on a familiar literary character in *Mind Your Manners, B.B. Wolf,* illustrated by J. Otto Seibold. When the now-elderly Big Bad Wolf is invited to a storybook tea at his local library, he consults with a friendly crocodile who teaches him the finer points of etiquette. Though the other guests, including Little Red Riding Hood and the Gingerbread Boy, are initially put off by the wolf's appearance, B.B. manages to score points with the librarian due to his exceedingly polite ways. A *Publishers Weekly* critic noted of *Mind Your Manners, B.B. Wolf* that "Sierra and Seibold expertly tweak the tension and the levity in this story of a trickster's golden years."

Sierra collects silly tales, traditional tales, and bedtime stories in such titles as *Can You Guess My Name?* and *Silly and Sillier: Read-Aloud Tales from around the World.* With *Can You Guess My Name?* she assembles similar tales from different cultures around the world, among them contrasting versions of the "Three Little Pigs," "The Brementown Musicians," and "Rumplestiltskin." A *Kirkus Reviews* contributor noted that "this beautifully illustrated volume presents readable examples that just might send readers to the shelves to search for single editions" of the stories included. Lee Bock, writing in *School Library Journal,* noted that "each section is fascinating for both the similarities among the tales, and the differences," and added that the book "can open doors to other cultures" for its readers. John Peters, writing in *Booklist,* considered the book to be a "handsome, horizon-expanding collection," while *Horn Book* contributor Mary M. Burns called *Can You Guess My Name?* "an outstanding example of what folklore collections for children can and should be."

Silly and Sillier brings together funny tales from around the world, including a trickster tale from Argentina, a story of an exploding mitten from Russia, and tales from countries including Bangladesh, Ireland, and Mexico. "Balancing nonsense capers and trickster tales, Sierra occasionally integrates words from the language of the country of origin," a *Publishers Weekly* reviewer pointed out, while Rochman noted that "it's fun to see trickster tales from around the world." Carol L. MacKay, in her *School Library Journal* review of *Silly and Sillier,* commented on the lessons given in many of the tales: "Children will discover that these themes of justice are as universal as laughter."

Sierra has also compiled a number of verse collections, including *Antarctic Antics: A Book of Penguin Poems* and *Beastly Rhymes to Read after Dark.* In *Schoolyard Rhymes: Kids' Own Rhymes for Rope Skipping, Hand Clapping, Ball Bouncing, and Just Plain Fun,* a volume illustrated by Melissa Sweet, Sierra presents such memorable rhymes as "Liar, Liar, Pants on Fire" and "Miss Mary Mack, Mack, Mack." According to *Horn Book* critic Susan Dove Lempke, "kids will enjoy this celebration of naughtiness and childhood fun." "The rhythms and nonsense rhymes are irresistible," wrote Bock, "compelling memorization and participation in the fun."

With more than forty works of fiction and nonfiction to her credit, Sierra shows no signs of slowing down. When asked if she enjoyed being a writer, she responded on her home page: "Yes, but writing is a job, and there are many difficult and frustrating times. The most enjoyable part of being a writer is spending time with children and adults who love to read."

Biographical and Critical Sources

PERIODICALS

Booklist, September 1, 1997, Kathleen Squires, review of *Counting Crocodiles,* p. 135; April 15, 2001, Amy Brandt, review of *Preschool to the Rescue,* p. 1566; July, 2001, Stephanie Zvirin, review of *The Gift of the Crocodile,* p. 2011; September 15, 2001, Gillian Engberg, review of *Monster Goose,* p. 237; January 1, 2002, Hazel Rochman, review of *The Gift of the Crocodile: A Cinderella Story,* p. 962; November 15, 2002, John Peters, review of *Can You Guess My Name?: Traditional Tales around the World,* p. 599; December 15, 2002, Hazel Rochman, review of *Silly and Sillier: Read-Aloud Tales from around the World,* p. 765; January 1, 2004, Ilene Cooper, review of *Coco and Cavendish: Circus Dogs,* p. 882; September 1, 2004, Ilene Cooper, review of *What Time Is It, Mr. Crocodile?,* p. 123; September 15, 2004, Lauren Peterson, review of *What Time Is It, Mr. Crocodile?,* p. 254; September 1, 2004, Ilene Cooper, review of *Wild about Books,* p. 123; September 15, 2005, Jennifer Mattson, review of *The Gruesome Guide to World Monsters,* p. 63; May 1, 2006, Jennifer Mattson, review of *Thelonius Monster's Sky-high Fly Pie,* p. 94; August 1, 2006, Gillian Engberg, review of *The Secret Science Project That Almost Ate the School,* p. 94; September 1, 2007, Gillian Engberg, review of *Mind Your Manners, B.B. Wolf,* p. 128; August 1, 2008, Randall Enos, review of *Born to Read,* p. 75.

Bulletin of the Center for Children's Books, February, 1993, Betsy Hearne, review of *The Elephant's Wrestling Match,* pp. 190-191.

Horn Book, November-December, 1995, Nancy Vasilakas, review of *The House That Drac Built,* pp. 730-731; May-June, 1996, Maria B. Salvadore, review of *Wiley and the Hairy Man,* pp. 343-344; July-August, 1996, Ann A. Flowers, review of *Good Night, Dinosaurs,* pp. 474-475; January, 2001, review of *The Gift of the Crocodile,* p. 104; May, 2001, review of *Preschool to the Rescue,* p. 317; January-February, 2003, Mary M. Burns, review of *Can You Guess My Name?,* p. 87; September-October, 2005, Susan Dove Lempke, review of *Schoolyard Rhymes: Kids' Own Rhymes for Rope Skipping, Hand Clapping, Ball Bouncing, and Just Plain Fun,* p. 597; July-August, 2007, Susan Dove Lempke, review of *Mind Your Manners, B.B. Wolf,* p. 385.

Instructor, September, 2001, Judy Freeman, review of *The Gift of the Crocodile,* p. 28; April, 2003, Judy Freeman, review of *Can You Guess My Name?,* p. 55.

Kirkus Reviews, August 1, 2001, review of *Monster Goose,* p. 1131; September 15, 2002, review of *Silly and Sillier,* p. 1400; October 15, 2002, review of *Can You Guess My Name?,* p. 1538; November 1, 2002, review of *'Twas the Night before Christmas,* p. 1625; July 1, 2004, review of *Wild about Books* and *What Time Is It, Mr. Crocodile?,* p. 636.

Library Talk, May-June, 2002, Sharron L. McElmeel, "Author Profile: Judy Sierra."

Publishers Weekly, July 13, 1992, review of *The Elephant's Wrestling Match,* p. 55; June 30, 1997, review of *Counting Crocodiles,* p. 75; March 19, 2001, review of *Preschool to the Rescue,* p. 98; August 13, 2001, review of *Monster Goose,* p. 312; September 30, 2002, review of *Silly and Sillier,* p. 71; June 14, 2004, review of *Wild about Books,* p. 62; August 1, 2005, review of *The Gruesome Guide to World Monsters,* p. 65; May 15, 2006, review of *Thelonius Monster's Sky-high Fly Pie,* p. 71; October 16, 2006, review of *The Secret Science Project That Almost Ate the School,* p. 53; July 16, 2007, review of *Mind Your Manners, B.B. Wolf,* p. 164; June 23, 2008, review of *Born to Read,* p. 53.

School Library Journal, September, 1992, Linda Greengrass, review of *The Elephant's Wrestling Match,* p. 211; September, 1995, Beth Irish, review of *The House That Drac Built,* p. 186; April, 1996, Beth Tegart, review of *Good Night, Dinosaurs,* p. 118; April, 1997, p. 51; October, 1997, Marilyn Iarusso, review of *The Mean Hyena,* pp. 123-124; December, 2000, review of *The Gift of the Crocodile,* p. 55; May, 2001, Marlene Gawron, review of *Preschool to the Rescue,* p. 135; September, 2001, Gay Lynn Van Vleck, review of *Monster Goose,* p. 254; October, 2002, Eva Mitnick, review of *'Twas the Fright before Christmas,* p. 63; November, 2002, Lee Bock, review of *Can You Guess My Name?,* p. 148, Carol L. MacKay, review of *Silly and Sillier,* p. 150; August, 2004, Marge Loch-Wouters, review of *Wild about Books,* p. 94; September, 2004, review of *What Time Is It, Mr. Crocodile?,* p. 180; September, 2005, John Peters, review of *The Gruesome Guide to World Monsters,* p. 234; October, 2005, Lee Bock, review of *Schoolyard Rhymes,* p. 146; May, 2006, Susan Weitz, review of *Thelonius Monster's Sky-high Fly Pie,* p. 104; November, 2006, Susan Lissim, review of *The Secret Science Project That Almost Ate the School,* p. 113; August, 2007, Mary Hazelton, review of *Mind Your Manners, B.B. Wolf,* p. 92.

ONLINE

Judy Sierra Home Page, http://www.judysierra.net (November 10, 2008).
Powell's Books Web site, http://www.powells.com/ (November 10, 2008), "Kids' Q&A: Judy Sierra and Marc Brown."
Random House Web site, http://www.randomhouse.com/ (November 10, 2008), "Author Spotlight: Judy Sierra."*

*　　*　　*

SNIEGOSKI, Thomas E.
(Tom Sniegoski)

Personal

Born in MA; married; wife's name LeeAnne.

Addresses

Home—Stoughton, MA. *E-mail*—tsniegoski@comcast.net.

Career

Novelist, comic-book writer, and journalist.

Writings

NOVELS

Angel: Soul Trade, Pocket Books (New York, NY), 2001.
(With Christopher Golden) *Force Majeure,* Simon Pulse (New York, NY), 2002.
(With Christopher Golden) *Monster Island,* Simon Pulse (New York, NY), 2003.
Hellboy: The God Machine, Pocket Star (New York, NY), 2006.
A Kiss before the Apocalypse, ROC (New York, NY), 2008.
Dancing on the Head of a Pin, ROC (New York, NY), 2009.
Mean Streets (novella), Noah's Orphans (New York, NY), 2009.
Lobster Johnson: The Satan Factory, Dark Horse Books (Milwaukie, OR), 2009.

"THE FALLEN" NOVEL SERIES

The Fallen, Simon Pulse (New York, NY), 2003.
Leviathan, Simon Pulse (New York, NY), 2003.
Aerie, Simon Pulse (New York, NY), 2003.
Reckoning, Simon Pulse (New York, NY), 2004.

"OUTCAST" NOVEL SERIES

(With Christopher Golden) *The Un-Magician,* Aladdin (New York, NY), 2004.

(With Christopher Golden) *Dragon Secrets,* Aladdin (New York, NY), 2004.
(With Christopher Golden) *Ghostfire,* Aladdin (New York, NY), 2005.
(With Christopher Golden) *Wurm War,* Aladdin (New York, NY), 2005.

"MENAGERIE" NOVEL SERIES

(With Christopher Golden) *The Nimble Man,* Berkley (New York, NY), 2004.
(With Christopher Golden) *Tears of the Furies,* Berkley (New York, NY), 2005.
(With Christopher Golden) *Stones Unturned,* Berkley (New York, NY), 2006.
(With Christopher Golden) *Crashing Paradise,* Berkley (New York, NY), 2007.

"SLEEPER CONSPIRACY" NOVEL SERIES

Sleeper Code, Razorbill (New York, NY), 2006.
Sleeper Agenda, Razorbill (New York, NY), 2006.

"BILLY HOOTEN" NOVEL SERIES

Billy Hooten, Owlboy, illustrated by Eric Powell, Yearling (New York, NY), 2007.
The Girl with the Destructo Touch, illustrated by Eric Powell, Yearling (New York, NY), 2007.
Tremble at the Terror of Zis-Boom-Bah, illustrated by Eric Powell, Yearling (New York, NY), 2008.
The Flock of Fury, illustrated by Eric Powell, Yearling (New York, NY), 2008.

"BRIMSTONE NETWORK" NOVEL SERIES; UNDER NAME TOM SNIEGOSKI

The Brimstone Network, Aladdin (New York, NY), 2008.
The Shroud of A'ranka, Aladdin (New York, NY), 2008.
Specter Rising, Aladdin (New York, NY), 2009.

OTHER

(With Christopher Golden and Stephen R. Bissette) *Buffy the Vampire Slayer: The Monster Guide* (nonfiction), Pocket (New York, NY), 2000.

Author of comic books, including: (with Mark Masztal) *Swords of Shar Pei,* Caliber Comics (Westland, MI), 1991, *Guns of Shar Pei,* Caliber Comics, 1992, and *Gutter Rat,* Caliber Comics, 1993; *Chains of Chaos,* Harris Comics (New York, NY), 1994; (with Jim Valentino) *Shadowhawk/Vampirella: Creatures of the Night,* Harris Comics, 1995; *The Rook,* illustrated by Kirk Van Wormer, Harris Comics, 1995; *Vampirella Strikes,* Harris Comics, 1995; (with Valentino) *The Others,* Image Comics, 1995; (with Christopher Golden) *Vampirella: Death and Destruction,* illustrated by Amanda Conner,

Harris Comics, 1996; (with Masztal) *Dogs o' War,* Crusade Comics, 1996; *Temptress,* illustrated by Eric Powell, Caliber Comics, 1997; (with Golden) *Shi: Masquerade,* Crusade Comics, 1997; *Shi: Black, White, and Red,* illustrated by Jay G. Jones, Crusade Comics, 1997; *King Zombie,* illustrated by Jacen Burrows, Caliber Comics, 1997; (with Golden) *Waterworld,* Acclaim Comics, 1997; *Blast Corps,* Dark Horse Comics (Milwaukie, OR), 1998; *Stupid, Stupid Rat-Tails: The Adventures of Big Johnson Bone,* illustrated by Jeff Smith, Cartoon Books (Columbus, OH), 1999; (with Golden) *Night Tribes,* illustrated by Joyce Chin, Wildstorm (La Jolla, CA), 1999; (with Golden) *Wolverine/Punisher: Revelation,* Marvel (New York, NY), 1999; (with Golden) *Star Trek: The Next Generation: Embrace the Wolf,* Wildstorm, 1999; (with Golden) *Buffy the Vampire Slayer: Giles* and *Buffy/Angel: Past Lives,* Dark Horse Comics, both 2000; (with Golden) *Batman: Real World,* DC Comics (New York, NY), 2000; (with Randy Green) *Dollz,* Image Comics, 2001; (with Golden and Mike Mignola) *B.P.R.D: The Hollow Earth,* Dark Horse Comics, 2002; *Chastity: Heartbreaker,* Chaos Comics, 2002; *Daredevil/Shi; Riblet; Hellboy: Weird Tales; Devil Dinosaur,* Marvel, 2005; (with Golden) *Monster War,* Dynamite Entertainment; (with Golden) *Talent,* Boom! Studios, 2007; and (with Golden) *The Sisterhood,* Archaia Studios Press, 2007. Author of comic mini-series, including *Jade: Turn Loose the Dragon* and *Jade: Redemption,* Chaos Comics. Contributor to comic anthologies, including *Taboo No. 1,* Aardvark-Vanaheim, 1989.

Contributor to literary journals, including *Haunts* and *Northeastern Literary Magazine.* Also author, with Golden, of scripts for "Buffy the Vampire Slayer" video games for Electronic Arts and Microsoft X-Box game system.

Adaptations

The Fallen was adapted as a television mini-series, ABC Family, 2007-08.

Sidelights

Thomas E. Sniegoski is a popular and prolific novelist, comic-book writer, and journalist. Working in the comics industry for more than two decades, Sniegoski has contributed to several series, including "Batman" and "Star Trek: The Next Generation," as well as writing numerous original titles. He also works with collaborators such as Christopher Golden, with whom he created the popular "Outcast" fantasy-novel series for young adults. In an interview on the *Bildungsroman* Web site, Sniegoski commented: "People want something good—something entertaining, thought-provoking, exciting, and funny—for their hard-earned cash, and I don't blame them one bit. When I buy a book, that's exactly what I'm looking for. I want the writer to have done his job. It's what I bring to every book I write, whatever the age group."

One of Sniegoski's best-known novel series, the "Fallen" quartet, focuses on the Nephilim, the offspring of fallen angels and mortal women. In the opening work, *The Fallen,* eighteen-year-old Aaron Corbet suddenly develops strange and unusual powers. Contacted by a pair of mysterious strangers, Aaron learns that he is at the heart of a battle between the fallen angels and The Powers, a race of angels that seek to destroy the Nephilim. In *Leviathan,* Aaron must use his angelic powers to help the people in a small Maine town conquer a diabolical beast. Two other novels, *Aerie* and *Reckoning,* conclude the series, which was adapted for television and earned critical praise. In *School Library Journal,* Kim Carlson described *The Fallen* as a "fast-paced fantasy."

The Un-Magician, the first work in Sniegoski's "Outcast" series, introduces Timothy Cade, the only resident of Arcanum who cannot perform magic. Timothy does possess some incredible mechanical skills, however, and he also proves to be immune to enchantments. Those abilities make the youngster a worthy adversary to the evil Nicodemus, who plans to overthrow the Parliament of Mages. Tasha Saecker, writing in *School Library Journal,* stated that "the premise is clever," adding that Sniegoski and Golden "have created a unique story filled with adventure." In *Dragon Secrets,* Timothy comes to the rescue of his friend, Verlis, an imprisoned member of the Wurm clan of magicians who are descended from dragons. Farida S. Dowler, writing in *School Library Journal,* complimented the "ornate, suspense-filled installment in the series." The battle for control of Arcanum continues in *Ghostfire* and *Wurm War.*

Originally planned as a comic book, Sniegoski's middle-grade fantasy *Billy Hooten, Owlboy* centers on the title character, an intelligent but nerdy youngster who is often bullied at school. When Billy responds to a cry for help emanating from a cemetery near his home, he meets Archebold. A goblin, Archebold resides in Monstros City, an underground world that is being overrun by a host of hideous creature now that its protector, Owlboy, has disappeared. Donning the special goggles and elaborate costume of the missing superhero, Billy ventures into Monstros City, where he does battle with a gang of Slovakian, rot-toothed, hopping, monkey demons. According to Tim Wadham in *School Library Journal,* "Sniegoski clearly knows his superhero stories and fills this book with tropes that hark back to Batman, Superman, and Spider-Man."

Biographical and Critical Sources

PERIODICALS

Booklist, October 15, 2004, Kristine Huntley, review of *The Nimble Man,* p. 395.

Kirkus Reviews, July 15, 2004, review of *The Un-Magician,* p. 685; July 1, 2007, review of *Billy Hooten, Owlboy.*

Publishers Weekly, February 3, 2003, review of *The Fallen,* p. 77; March 31, 2008, review of *A Kiss before the Apocalypse,* p. 43.

School Library Journal, December, 2002, Julie Webb, review of *Force Majeure,* p. 138; May, 2003, Kim Carlson, review of *The Fallen,* p. 160; October, 2003, Susan L. Rogers, review of *Leviathan,* p. 178; October, 2004, Tasha Saecker, review of *The Un-Magician,* p. 165; April, 2005, Farida S. Dowler, review of *Dragon Secrets,* p. 130; September, 2007, Tim Wadham, review of *Billy Hooten, Owlboy,* p. 208.

ONLINE

Thomas E. Sniegoski Home Page, http://www.sniegoski. com (November 10, 2008).

Bildungsroman Web site, http://slayground.livejournal. com/ (July 2-23, 2006), interview with Sniegoski; (November 5, 2008) interview with Sniegoski; (July 16, 2007), interview with Sniegoski.

*   *   *

SNIEGOSKI, Tom
See SNIEGOSKI, Thomas E.

*   *   *

SPINELLI, Jerry 1941-

Personal

Born February 1, 1941, in Norristown, PA; son of Louis A. (a printer) and Lorna Mae Spinelli; married Eileen Mesi (a writer), May 21, 1977; children: Kevin, Barbara, Jeffrey, Molly, Sean, Ben. *Education:* Gettysburg College, A.B., 1963; Johns Hopkins University, M.A., 1964; attended Temple University, 1964. *Hobbies and other interests:* Tennis, country music, travel, pet rats.

Addresses

Home—PA.

Career

Writer. Chilton Company (magazine publishers), Radnor, PA, editor, 1966-89. *Military service:* U.S. Naval Reserve, 1966-72.

Awards, Honors

Boston Globe/Horn Book Award, 1990, Newbery Medal, American Library Association (ALA), and Carolyn Field Award, both 1991, Dorothy Canfield Fisher Award, Indian Paintbrush Award, Rhode Island Children's Book Award, Flicker Tale Award, Charlotte Award, Mark

Jerry Spinelli (Reproduced by permission.)

Twain Award, and Nevada Young Readers' Award, all 1992, and William Allen White Award, Pacific Northwest Award, Massachusetts Children's Book Award, Rebecca Caudhill Award, West Virginia Children's Book Award, Buckeye Children's Book Award, Land of Enchantment Award, all 1993, all for *Maniac Magee;* South Carolina Children's Book Award, 1993, for *Fourth Grade Rats;* California Young Readers' Medal, 1993, for *There's a Girl in My Hammerlock;* Best Book for Young Adults designation, ALA, 1996, for *Crash;* Newbery Honor Book designation, 1998, Carolyn Field Award, and Josette Frank Award, all for *Wringer;* Golden Kite Award for fiction, Society of Children's Book Writers and Illustrators, and Carolyn Field Award (co-winner), both 2003, and Best Book for Young Adults designation, ALA, 2004, all for *Milkweed;* Dorothy Canfield Fisher Award, 2004, for *Loser;* Children's Literature citation, Drexel University, and Milner Award (Atlanta, GA), both for body of work. Spinelli's works have garnered Readers' Choice Awards from more than twenty U.S. and Canadian states and provinces.

Writings

Space Station Seventh Grade, Little, Brown (Boston, MA), 1982.

Who Put That Hair in My Toothbrush?, Little, Brown (Boston, MA), 1984.

Night of the Whale, Little, Brown (Boston, MA), 1985.

Jason and Marceline, Little, Brown (Boston, MA), 1986.

Dump Days, Little, Brown (Boston, MA), 1988.

Maniac Magee, Little, Brown (Boston, MA), 1990.

The Bathwater Gang, illustrated by Meredith Johnson, Little, Brown (Boston, MA), 1990.

There's a Girl in My Hammerlock, Simon & Schuster (New York, NY), 1991.

Fourth Grade Rats, Scholastic (New York, NY), 1991.

School Daze: Report to the Principal's Office, Scholastic (New York, NY), 1991.

Who Ran My Underwear up the Flagpole?, Scholastic (New York, NY), 1992.

Do the Funky Pickle, Scholastic (New York, NY), 1992.

The Bathwater Gang Gets down to Business, illustrated by Meredith Johnson, Little, Brown (Boston, MA), 1992.

Picklemania, Scholastic (New York, NY), 1993.

Tooter Pepperday: A Tooter Tale, illustrated by Donna Nelson, Random House (New York, NY), 1995.

Crash, Knopf (New York, NY), 1996.

The Library Card, Scholastic (New York, NY), 1997.

Wringer, HarperCollins (New York, NY), 1997.

Blue Ribbon Blues: A Tooter Tale, illustrated by Donna Nelson, Random House (New York, NY), 1998.

Knots in My Yo-Yo String: The Autobiography of a Kid, Knopf (New York, NY), 1998.

Stargirl, Knopf (New York, NY), 2000.

Loser, Joanna Cotler Books (New York, NY), 2002.

Milkweed, Knopf (New York, NY), 2003.

My Daddy and Me, illustrated by Seymour Chwast, Random House (New York, NY), 2003.

Eggs, Little, Brown (New York, NY), 2007.

Love, Stargirl (sequel to *Stargirl*), Knopf (New York, NY), 2007.

Smiles to Go, Joanna Cotler Books (New York, NY), 2008.

Contributor to books, including *Our Roots Grow Deeper than We Know: Pennsylvania Writers—Pennsylvania Life*, edited by Lee Gutkind, University of Pittsburgh Press (Pittsburgh, PA), 1985, *Noble Pursuits*, edited by Virginia A. Arnold and Carl B. Smith, Macmillan (New York, NY), 1988, and *Baseball Crazy: Ten Short Stories That Cover All the Bases*, edited by Nancy E. Mercado, Dial (New York, NY), 2008. Work represented in anthologies, including *Best Sports Stories of 1982*, Dutton, 1982, and *Connections: Short Stories by Outstanding Writers for Young Adults*, edited by Donald R. Gallo, Delacorte (New York, NY), 1989. *Maniac Magee* was included in the anthology *Newbery Award IV*, Harper Trophy (New York, NY), 1998.

Adaptations

Crash, Space Station Seventh Grade, Who Put That Hair in My Toothbrush?, and *Wringer* were all adapted as audiobooks by Recorded Books; *Maniac Magee* was adapted as an audiobook by Pharaoh Audiobooks and as a filmstrip by AIMS Media; *Stargirl* and *Milkweed* were adapted as audiobooks by Listening Library, 2004;

Love, Stargirl was adapted as an audiobook by Listening Library, 2007; *Eggs* was adapted as an audiobook by Hatchette Audio, 2007.

Sidelights

Best known for his Newbery Award-winning book *Maniac Magee*, as well as for the novels *Stargirl, There's a Girl in My Hammerlock,* and *Eggs*, Jerry Spinelli's written work is distinguished by his accurate and humorous depiction of adolescent life. *Washington Post Book World* contributor Deborah Churchman deemed Spinelli "a master of those embarrassing, gloppy, painful and suddenly wonderful things that happen on the razor's edge between childhood and full-fledged adolescence."

Spinelli is additionally recognized for creating novels in which he balances substantial moral issues with a simple, light-hearted prose style. According to a contributor in the *St. James Guide to Young-Adult Writers*, Spinelli "creates realistic fiction with humorous dialogue and situations, but his stories go beyond humor: Spinelli's characters stumble and blunder through their lives until they emerge from the fog of adolescence guided by an optimistic light that readies them for their next challenge."

Spinelli's first claim to literary fame came about when a local paper published a poem he wrote about a hometown team's football victory. Although an early dream had been to become a cowboy, this experience prompted Spinelli to reconsider his career plans, and began to seriously consider writing as an option. However, he did not discover his narrative voice until he was married and a parent: One of his children's feats—pilfering food Spinelli was saving for his own snack—became the inspiration for his first novel, *Space Station Seventh Grade*. Spinelli remarked on the Scholastic Web site that when he started writing about youngsters he began to see "the first fifteen years of my life turned out to be one big research project. I thought I was simply growing up in Norristown, Pennsylvania; looking back now I can see that I was also gathering material that would one day find its way into my books."

Space Station Seventh Grade recounts the everyday adventures of middle-schooler Jason Herkimer. With seemingly mundane events—such as masterminding classroom pranks and chasing after girls—the author traces Jason's awkward entrance into adolescence. Although Jason seems impulsive and has a penchant for getting into trouble because he speaks before he thinks, he must also contend with more serious issues, including coping with divorced parents and accepting a stepfather. Some critics disapproved of the crude humor in the novel, but judged that Spinelli accurately represents the adolescent milieu. *Voice of Youth Advocates* contributor James J. McPeak called the story "first-rate," and Twichell, writing in *Horn Book*, deemed *Space Station Seventh Grade* a "truly funny book."

Jason and Marceline is a sequel to *Space Station Seventh Grade.* Now a ninth grader, Jason continues to cope with the daily trials of adolescence, such as his attempt at sparking a romance with Marceline, a trombone-playing classmate who once beat him up. Marceline initially rejects Jason's advances because he exhibits the same bravado and macho behavior his friends employ in their romantic conquests. When he shows his caring side in a heroic lunchroom incident, however, she forgives Jason's antics and their relationship progresses. With *Jason and Marceline* Spinelli earned praise for pointing out that respect and friendship are necessary in a loving relationship between people of any age. Writing again in *Horn Book,* Twichell noted that Jason "truly sounds like a teenager."

In *Who Put That Hair in My Toothbrush?* chapters alternate between the first-person narration of Megin and Greg, siblings who are two years apart and who have vastly different personalities. Greg is preoccupied with a possible romance, while sports-crazy Megin secretly befriends an elderly woman confined to a nursing home. The pair fights constantly, but when a crisis nearly erupts they join forces. Critics appreciated Spinelli's humorous depiction of sibling rivalry mixed with his inclusion of weighty themes. In a review for *Horn Book,* Karen Jameyson credited the author with a "sure ear for adolescent dialogue" and called the novel "hilarious."

Maniac Magee, Spinelli's Newbery Medal winner, is about an athletically gifted boy whose accomplishments ignite legends about him. Jeffrey "Manic" Magee is a Caucasian orphan who has run away from his foster home. His search for a loving household is problematic in the racially divided town of Two Mills. Maniac's first stay is with a black family, but after racist graffiti is spray-painted on their house, he leaves. He spends several happy months with an old man in a park equipment room, but the man eventually dies. Maniac then moves in with a white family, but finds the house filled with roaches, alcohol, and cursing. Maniac then attempts his greatest feat: initiating better relations between blacks and whites in Two Mills.

Although some critics felt that Spinelli dilutes his message about the absurdity of racism by presenting *Maniac Magee* as a fable, others cited the author's focus on such an incident as noteworthy. Alison Teal, in her *New York Times Book Review* appraisal, judged that "Spinelli grapples . . . with a racial tension rarely addressed in fiction for children in the middle grades," and *Washington Post Book World* contributor Claudia Logan lauded Spinelli's "colorful writing and originality."

In *Crash* a smug jock is transformed into a more empathetic young person. Seventh-grader Crash Coogan has the athletic ability of Maniac Magee but nowhere near the same sensitivity to others. He bullies kids smaller than he, including Penn Webb, a target since first grade; he even threatens a girl who rejects his romantic ad-

Cover of Spinelli's award-winning novel **Maniac Magee,** *featuring photography by Carol Palmer.* (Little, Brown Books for Young Readers, 1990. Reproduced by permission.)

vances. Crash is competitive about everything, and it is not until his beloved grandfather suffers a life-threatening stroke that the teen begins to show some humanity. A *Publishers Weekly* contributor wrote that, "without being preachy, Spinelli packs a powerful moral wallop, leaving it to the pitch-perfect narration to drive home his point." Reviewing the novel in *School Library Journal,* Connie Tyrrell Burns concluded that "readers will devour this humorous glimpse at what jocks are made of while learning that life does not require crashing helmet-headed through it."

Stargirl focuses on nonconformity and popularity. When the eponymous protagonist enters all-white middle-class Mica High School in Arizona, she attracts considerable notice for her off-beat behavior, odd clothing, and her habit of cheering for both sides after making the cheerleading squad. Though Stargirl is initially admired, when she does not conform to the culture of her new school she finds herself "dropped" by her supposed friends. Some reviewers found the novel one-dimensional and heavy-handed; as Ilene Cooper noted in *Booklist,* Spinelli's protagonist is so unbelievable that "readers may feel more sympathy for the bourgeois teens than the earnest, kind, magic Stargirl." Others, however, praised the author's handling of a complex and relevant theme. "As always respectful of his audience," wrote a reviewer for *Publishers Weekly*, "Spinelli poses searching questions about loyalty to one's friends and oneself and leaves readers to form their own answers."

In a sequel, *Love, Stargirl*, the title character has moved to Pennsylvania with her family, where she attempts to construct a new life with the help of an eclectic group of friends: Dootsie, a talkative five year old; Bettie, an agoraphobic divorcee; Charlie, a lonely widower, and Alvina, an angry tomboy. Stargirl also enters a relationship with Perry, a petty thief who helps heal the wounds left by her old boyfriend. Though some reviewers found the work overly sentimental, a *Publishers Weekly* contributor stated that "readers should embrace Stargirl's originality and bigheartedness," and Terri Clark, writing in *School Library Journal*, called the novel "both profound and funny."

Other novels that chronicle the perils of the middle grades include *There's a Girl in My Hammerlock*, which finds eighth-grader Maisie Potter trying out for the school wrestling team. The school allows her to participate, but Maisie encounters various roadblocks, including her teammates' jealousy about the media attention she receives. Also for younger teens is Spinelli's "School Daze" series, which includes *Report to the Principal's Office, Do the Funky Pickle, Who Ran My Underwear up the Flagpole?*, and *Picklemania*. Featuring Eddie, Salem, Sunny, and Pickles, these books chronicle the antics ongoing at Plumstead Middle School. Sunny is a grump, Eddie is something of a wimp who is in love with Sunny, Salem is an aspiring writer, and Pickles is . . ., well, uniquely Pickles.

Spinelli's award winning novel *Loser* finds goofy, awkward Donald Zinkoff slowly transform from class clown to class loser as he moves from elementary school into middle school. Despite the taunts and barbs of his critical classmates, Donald maintains a "what, me worry?" attitude due to a healthy optimism and a lack of concern for what others think. Peter D. Sieruta noted in a *Horn Book* review that through the novel's "present-tense, omniscient narrative," readers are introduced to another one of "Spinelli's larger-than-life protagonists," and praised the novel as "a wonderful character study." In *School Library Journal* Edward Sullivan called Donald "a flawed but tough kid with an unshakable optimism that readers will find endearing," while a *Kirkus* reviewer dubbed *Loser* "a masterful character portrait; here's one loser who will win plenty of hearts."

A library card becomes the ticket out of mundane and often impoverished lives for four youngsters in a group of interlinking stories published as *The Library Card*. Shoplifting Mongoose leaves his thieving ways behind when he enters a library for the first time and discovers

a world of facts; Brenda is a TV addict who discovers a new world of invention in books; Sonseray recaptures memories of his mother in an adult romance title; a hijacker even falls under the spell of books in a bookmobile. A *Publishers Weekly* critic felt that "while the premise (the card) behind the stories may seem contrived, the author uses it effectively" to create "four vaguely unsettling tales." Joan Hamilton asserted in *Horn Book* that "Spinelli's characters are unusual and memorable; his writing both humorous and convincing."

Fourth Grade Rats focuses on peer pressure and growing up too fast. The main characters are Suds and Joey, friends who decide they have to become tough and mean now that they are entering fourth grade. Nice-guy Suds initially balks at the plan, but Joey's relentless needling persuades him to reconsider. The experiment is short-lived, however, as both boys are forced to resume their normal behavior—and relieved when this happens. *Tooter Pepperday* and its sequel, *Blue Ribbon Tales*, feature a reluctant young transplant to suburbia and her adventures adapting to her new environment.

With his 1998 Newbery Honor book *Wringer*, Spinelli returns to the weightier themes that made *Maniac Magee* so popular. A tenth birthday is something to be dreaded for nine-year-old Palmer LaRue. At that time he will qualify as a wringer, one of the boys who wring the necks of wounded birds in the annual pigeon shoot in Palmer's rural hometown. While other kids cannot wait to perform this role, Palmer is different. He secretly harbors a pet in his room, a stray pigeon he calls Nipper. Palmer leads a double life, trying to fit in on the outside, until the pigeon shoot forces him to act on his true beliefs when Nipper is endangered.

In a *School Library Journal* review of *Wringer*, Tim Rausch cited the novel for "Humor, suspense, a bird with a personality, and a moral dilemma familiar to everyone," characters who are "memorable, convincing, and both endearing and villainous," and a "riveting plot." Suzanne Manczuk, writing in *Voice of Youth Advocates*, commented that "Spinelli has given us mythic heroes before, but none more human or vulnerable than Palmer." *New York Times Book Review* critic Benjamin Cheever also had high praise for *Wringer*, describing the novel as "both less antic and more deeply felt" than *Maniac Magee*, and adding that Spinelli presents Palmer's moral dilemma "with great care and sensitivity."

In 2003 Spinelli produced two works that marked a change of pace for the longtime novelist. For one, he made his debut as a picture-book writer with *My Daddy and Me*, which chronicles the close relationship between a puppy and his dog-father in illustrations by Seymore Chwast. Spinelli's novel *Milkweed* also found the author charting new territory due to its setting in Poland during World War II. The novel focuses on orphaned Misha Pilsudski, who is trying to survive by his wits in the Warsaw ghetto. A capable thief and liar,

Misha manages to escape the violence meted out to others in the ghetto and eventually finds a home with a Jewish family. Despite his miserable circumstances, the character of Misha "is another of Spinelli's exuberant, goodhearted protagonists," wrote Sieruta, while in *School Library Journal* Ginny Gustin noted that *Milkweed* would be "appreciated . . . by those who share Misha's innocence and will discover the horrors of this period in history along with him." Praising the author's choice of narrator as a "masterstroke" in terms of illustrating the horrors of the war for a younger readership, a *Kirkus Reviews* writer explained that Misha "simply reports graphically, almost clinically, on the slow devastation" suffered by Warsaw's Jewish population during the Holocaust.

A pair of vulnerable, quirky children forms an unlikely friendship in *Eggs,* a middle-grade novel. Since the death of his mother, nine-year-old David lives at his grandma's Pennsylvania home while his workaholic father travels during the week. At an Easter egg hunt, David meets Primrose, a sarcastic thirteen year old being raised by an indifferent single mother. The duo begins to meet after dark, searching through trash, hunting for worms, and spending time with an eccentric neighbor. "Spinelli skillfully portrays David and Primrose's fragile psyches, leading them to simultaneously cling to and lash out at one another," noted *Horn Book* contributor Christine M. Heppermann.

Smiles to Go centers on Will Tuppence, an intelligent but obsessive high school freshman who loves science, tolerates his precocious little sister, Tabby, and longs for Mi-Su, his good friend and Monopoly partner. Will's carefully structured life is turned inside-out when he learns that physicists have found evidence of proton decay in the universe, and worse still, he spies Mi-Su kissing his best friend, BT. "Will's teenage insecurities, overanalyzing, and mood swings are entirely believable," observed *School Library Journal* reviewer Emma Runyan, and a *Publishers Weekly* critic stated that "the Spinelli touch remains true in this funny and thoroughly enjoyable read."

Spinelli, while often irreverent and sometimes crude to the adult ear, has gained a reputation for speaking to young readers in terms they can understand. As *Booklist* reviewer Hazel Rochman maintained, whether it is gender roles he is writing about, as in *There's a Girl in My Hammerlock,* or the power of myth, as in *Maniac Magee,* or a bevy of kids learning the joys of the library, as in *The Library Card,* Spinelli "is able to convey the message with humor and tenderness and with a fast-talking immediacy about the preteen scene." For fans interested in the inspiration for much of Spinelli's work as well as an introduction to the early life of the writer, Spinelli's partial autobiography, *Knots in My Yo-Yo,* is an indispensable guide. A reviewer for *Publishers Weekly* called this 1998 memoir a "montage of sharply focused memories," and concluded that as "Spinelli ef-

fortlessly spins the story of an ordinary Pennsylvania boy, he also documents the evolution of an exceptional author."

With his casual yet introspective novels, Spinelli is often cited as one of the most gifted children's authors of his generation. Discussing his career with interviewer Beth Bakkum in the *Writer,* he remarked, "I think, in part, writing is a way to complete my experience. It's as if something—an episode, thought, emotion—hasn't fully happened until I put it into words. It's somehow not enough just to receive experience, to catch it like a baseball in a glove, so to speak, as I used to when I played catch with my father in the backyard. I need to throw it back."

Biographical and Critical Sources

BOOKS

Authors and Artists for Young Adults, Gale (Detroit, MI), Volume 41, 2001, Volume 82, 2003.

Beacham's Guide to Literature for Young Adults, Volume 7, Beacham Publishing (Osprey, FL), 1994, Volume 10, Gale (Detroit, MI), 2000.

Children's Literature Review, Volume 26, Gale (Detroit, MI), 1992.

Micklos, John, Jr., *Jerry Spinelli: Master Teller of Teen Takes,* Enslow (Berkeley Heights, NJ), 2007.

St. James Guide to Young-Adult Writers, second edition, St. James Press (Detroit, MI), 1999, pp. 783-785.

Seidman, David, *Jerry Spinelli,* Rosen (New York, NY), 2004.

Silvey, Anita, editor, *Children's Books and Their Creators,* Houghton Mifflin (Boston, MA), 1995.

PERIODICALS

Book, September-October, 2002, review of *Loser,* p. 40.

Booklist, June 1, 1990, Deborah Abbott, review of *Maniac Magee,* p. 1902; February 1, 1997, Hazel Rochman, review of *The Library Card,* p. 942; May 1, 1998, GraceAnne A. DeCandido, review of *Knots in My Yo-Yo String: The Autobiography of a Kid,* p. 1514; June 1, 2000, Ilene Cooper, review of *Stargirl,* p. 1883; May 15, 2002, Michael Cart, review of *Loser,* p. 1597; March 1, 2003, Julie Cummins, review of *My Daddy and Me,* p. 1204; April 1, 2007, Carolyn Phelan, review of *Eggs,* p. 52; August, 2007, Michael Cart, review of *Love, Stargirl,* p. 64; February 15, 2008, Thom Barthelmess, review of *Smiles to Go,* p. 76.

Horn Book, June, 1984, Karen Jameyson, review of *Who Put That Hair in My Toothbrush?,* pp. 343-344; March, 1987, Ethel R. Twichell, review of *Jason and Marceline,* p. 217; May, 1988, Ethel R. Twichell, review of *Dump Days,* p. 355; May-June, 1990, Ethel R. Twichell, review of *Maniac Magee,* p. 340; July-

August, 1991, Jerry Spinelli, "Newbery Medal Acceptance," pp. 426-432; September-October, 1995, Elizabeth S. Watson, review of *Tooter Pepperday,* p. 595; September-October, 1996, p. 600; March-April, 1997, Joan Hamilton, review of *The Library Card,* pp. 204-205; January, 1999, Peter D. Sieruta, review of *Knots in My Yo-Yo String,* p. 87; July 2000, review of *Stargirl,* p. 465; July-August, 2002, Peter D. Sieruta, review of *Loser,* p. 472; November-December, 2003, Peter D. Sieruta, review of *Milkweed,* p. 756; July-August, 2007, Christine M. Heppermann, review of *Eggs,* p. 404; September-October, 2007, Martha V. Parravano, review of *Love, Stargirl,* p. 589; May-June, 2008, Betty Carter, review of *Smiles to Go,* p. 327.

Journal of Adolescent & Adult Literacy, October, 2001, "Social Worlds of Adolescents Living on the Fringe," p. 170; October, 2001, Kelly Emminger and Brooks Palermo, review of *Stargirl,* p. 170.

Kirkus Reviews, November 1, 1982, review of *Space Station Seventh Grade,* pp. 1196-1197; April 1, 2002, review of *Loser,* p. 499; March 15, 2003, review of *My Daddy and Me,* p. 479; August 1, 2003, review of *Milkweed,* p. 1024.

New York Times Book Review, April 21, 1991, Alison Teal, review of *Maniac Magee,* p. 33; November 16, 1997, Benjamin Cheever, "Pigeon English," p. 52; September 17, 2000, Betsy Groban, review of *Stargirl,* p. 33.

Publishers Weekly, March 25, 1996, review of *Crash,* p. 84; February 10, 1997, review of *The Library Card,* p. 84; April 6, 1998, review of *Knots in My Yo-Yo String: The Autobiography of a Kid,* p. 79; July 17, 2000, Jennifer M. Brown, "Homer on George Street" (interview), p. 168; June 26, 2000, review of *Stargirl,* p. 76; February, 11, 2002, review of *Loser,* p. 188; February 17, 2003, review of *My Daddy and Me,* p. 73; September 1, 2003, review of *Milkweed,* p. 90; May 21, 2007, review of *Eggs,* p. 55; July 16, 2007, review of *Love, Stargirl,* p. 167; March 3, 2008, Gennifer Choldenko, review of *Smiles to Go,* p. 48.

School Library Journal, July, 1995, Eldon Younce, review of *Tooter Pepperday,* p. 82; June, 1996, Connie Tyrrell Burns, review of *Crash,* pp. 125-126; March, 1997, Steven Engelfried, review of *The Library Card,* p. 192; September, 1997, Tim Rausch, review of *Wringer,* p. 226; June, 1998, Kate Kohlbeck, review of *Knots in My Yo-Yo String,* p. 170; August, 2000, Sharon Grover, review of *Stargirl,* p. 190; May, 2002, Edward Sullivan, review of *Loser,* p. 160; November, 2003, Ginny Gustin, review of *Milkweed,* p. 149; July, 2007, D. Maria LaRocco, review of *Eggs,* p. 111; September, 2007, Terri Clark, review of *Love, Stargirl,* p. 208; May, 2008, Emma Runyan, review of *Smiles to Go,* p. 138.

Voice of Youth Advocates, April, 1983, James J. McPeak, review of *Space Station Seventh Grade,* p. 42; February, 1998, Suzanne Manczuk, review of *Wringer,* pp. 366-367.

Washington Post Book World, January 13, 1985, Deborah Churchman, "Tales of the Awkward Age," p. 8; August 11, 1991, Claudia Logan, review of *Fourth Grade Rats,* p. 11.

Writer, July, 2008, Beth Bakkum, "Jerry Spinelli" (interview), p. 58.

ONLINE

Jerry Spinelli Home Page, http://www.jerryspinelli.com (December 1, 2008).

Scholastic Web site, http://www2.scholastic.com/ (December 1, 2008), "Jerry Spinelli."*

* * *

STEFFENSMEIER, Alexander 1977-

Personal

Born 1977, in Lippstadt, Germany. *Education:* University of Münster, degree, 2004.

Addresses

Office—Goebenstraße 51, 48151 Münster, Germany. *E-mail*—mail@alexandersteffensmeier.de.

Career

Illustrator, 2003—.

Writings

SELF-ILLUSTRATED

Wenn der Dachs Geburtstag hat, Friedrich Oetinger (Münster, Germany), 2004.

Was machen die Handwerker?, Friedrich Oetinger (Münster, Germany), 2005.

Lieselotte Lauert, Patmos Verlagshaus (Düsseldorf, Germany), 2006, translated as *Millie Waits for the Mail,* Walker (New York, NY), 2007.

Gute Idee!: Erfinder verändern die Welt, Patmos Verlagshaus (Düsseldorf, Germany), 2007.

Lieselotte im Schnee, Patmos Verlagshaus (Düsseldorf, Germany), 2007, translated as *Millie in the Snow,* Walker (New York, NY), 2008.

ILLUSTRATOR

Norbert Landa, *Wo ist meine kleine Maus?,* Friedrich Oetinger (Hamburg, Germany), 2003.

Christa Wißkirchen, *Urlaubsfieber auf dem Bauernhof,* Friedrich Oetinger (Münster, Germany), 2004.

Andreas Korn-Müller, *Das verrückte Chemie-Labor,* Patmos Verlagshaus (Düsseldorf, Germany), 2004.

Werner Fäber, *Bildermaus: Geschichten von der Piratenin-sel,* Loewe (Bindlach, Germany), 2004.

Karl Rühmann, *Olli und sein Schlitten,* Carlsen (Hamburg, Germany), 2005.

Fabian Lenk, *Detektivgeschichten zum Mitraten,* Ravensburger (Ravensburg, Germany), 2005.

Manuela Mechtel, *Fritzi kocht Nudeln,* Carlsen (Hamburg, Germany), 2006.

Monika Wittmann, *Große Fahrzeuge auf dem Bauernhof,* Carlsen (Hamburg, Germany), 2006.

Monika Wittmann, *Große Fahrzeuge auf der Baustelle,* Carlsen (Hamburg, Germany), 2007.

Anja Kemmerzell, *Ben und Finn in einem Boot,* Carlsen (Hamburg, Germany), 2007.

Biographical and Critical Sources

PERIODICALS

Kirkus Reviews, July 15, 2007, review of *Millie Waits for the Mail;* November 1, 2008, review of *Millie in the Snow.*

Publishers Weekly, August 6, 2007, review of *Millie Waits for the Mail,* p. 187.

School Library Journal, August, 2007, Ieva Bates, review of *Millie Waits for the Mail,* p. 93; October, 2008, Eva Mitnick, review of *Millie in the Snow,* p. 99.

ONLINE

Alexander Steffensmeier Home Page, http://www.alexandersteffensmeier.de (November 1, 2008).*

*　　*　　*

STEIN, Mathilde 1969-

Personal

Born 1969, in Netherlands. *Education:* Attended Académie des Beaux-Arts.

Addresses

Home—Netherlands.

Career

Writer. Also works as a communication and organization adviser.

Awards, Honors

Kinderboekwinkelprijs (Children's Bookshop Prize), Association of Co-operating Children's Bookshops, for *Bang Mannetje.*

Writings

(With Maaike Lahaise) *Gutten Som Ikke Ville Være Redd,* illustrated by Mies van Hout, Lemniscaat (Rotterdam, Netherlands), 2005.

(With Aino Roscher) *Bange Bent,* illustrated by Mies van Hout, Lemniscaat (Rotterdam, Netherlands), 2005.

Bang Mannetje, illustrated by Mies van Hout, Lemniscaat (Rotterdam, Netherlands), 2005, translation published as *Brave Ben,* Front Street (Asheville, NC), 2005.

Monsterlied, illustrated by Gerdien van der Linden, Lemniscaat (Rotterdam, Netherlands), 2006, translation published as *Monstersong,* Front Street (Asheville, NC), 2007.

Van Mij!, illustrated by Mies van Hout, Lemniscaat (Rotterdam, Netherlands), 2006, translation published as *Mine!,* Lemniscaat (Asheville, NC), 2007.

De Kindereter, illustrated by Mies van Hout, Lemniscaat (Rotterdam, Netherlands), 2007, translation published as *The Child Cruncher,* Lemniscaat (Asheville, NC), 2008.

Sidelights

Mathilde Stein, a Dutch author, has written a number of books for children that offer fresh twists on familiar premises. In *Brave Ben,* one of Stein's books to be translated into English, a youngster who is fearful of just about everything, from speaking his mind to the monsters under his bed, decides to take control of his life. Ben searches through the phonebook for help, and he discovers an advertisement for a magic tree that promises results. To meet the consultant, the boy must venture through an enchanted forest where he bravely encounters an assortment of spooky creatures, including a dragon, a witch, and huge spiders. Reviewing *Brave*

A European import, Mathilde Stein's gentle story in Mine! *is paired with engaging art by Mies van Hout.* (Illustration copyright © 2006 by Mies van Hout. All rights reserved. Reproduced by permission of Boyds Mills Press.)

Ben in *School Library Journal,* Julie Roach commented that Stein's "fun and quirky text will keep readers and listeners engaged," and a critic in *Kirkus Reviews* observed that the work offers "a nice lesson."

Like Ben, the protagonist of *Monstersong* is frightened by the five ghouls that live under his bed. Though the piglet frequently complains to his mother about his difficulty sleeping, Mother Pig fails to resolve the situation to his satisfaction; in fact, she invites the goblins to share the bed! When the frustrated piglet grows tired of his unruly new bedmates, he devises a clever solution to his problem. A *Kirkus Reviews* contributor praised the "crowd-pleasing kicker" that closes Stein's tale.

A possessive ghost learns to share with others in *Mine!,* also illustrated by van Hout. In this story, Charlotte awakens one night to spy a tiny ghost clutching her blanket and shouting "Mine!" Though mild mannered, Charlotte politely accepts the intruder's presence, as the days pass, the spirit continues its selfish ways, hogging Charlotte's bath toys, her breakfast toast, and her backyard swing set. When Charlotte finally refuses to tolerate the ghost's bad behavior and goes off to play by herself, the spirit has a change of heart. "Stein tells the tale without explicit lessons," noted a critic in *Kirkus Reviews,* and Martha Simpson, writing in *School Library Journal,* described *Mine!* as "simple and sweet."

Biographical and Critical Sources

PERIODICALS

Booklist, March 1, 2006, Jennifer Mattson, review of *Brave Ben,* p. 101.
Kirkus Reviews, March 1, 2006, review of *Brave Ben,* p. 240; February 1, 2007, review of *Monstersong,* p. 129; July 1, 2007, review of *Mine!*
School Library Journal, April, 2006, Julie Roach, review of *Brave Ben,* p. 119; May, 2007, Linda Ludke, review of *Monstersong,* p. 108; August, 2007, Martha Simpson, review of *Mine!,* p. 94.*

*   *   *

STEVENSON, James 1929-

Personal

Born 1929, in New York, NY; son of Harvey (an architect) and Winifred Stevenson; married Jane Walker, 1953 (deceased); married Josephine Merck (a painter), 1993; children: five sons, four daughters, including author/illustrator Suçie Stevenson. *Education:* Yale University, B.A., 1951.

Addresses

Home—CT.

James Stevenson (Photo © by Edwina Stevenson. Reproduced by permission.)

Career

Cartoonist and writer. *Life,* New York, NY, reporter, 1954-56; *New Yorker,* New York, NY, cartoonist, cover artist, and writer for "Talk of the Town," 1956-63. Creator of *Capitol Games* (syndicated political comic strip). Writer and illustrator, 1962—. *Military service:* U.S. Marine Corps, 1951-53.

Awards, Honors

New York Times Outstanding Children's Book of the Year designation, 1977, for *"Could Be Worse!";* American Library Association (ALA) Notable Book designation, 1978, for *The Sea View Hotel,* 1979, for *Fast Friends,* 1980, for *That Terrible Halloween Night;* Children's Choice Award, International Reading Association, 1979, for *The Worst Person in the World,* 1980, for *That Terrible Halloween Night,* 1982, for *The Night after Christmas,* 1989, for *The Supreme Souvenir Factory,* and 1990, for *Oh No, It's Waylon's Birthday!;* Best Illustrated Book and Outstanding Book honors, both *New York Times,* both 1980, both for *Howard;* Boston Globe/Horn Book Honor Book designation, 1981, for *The Night after Christmas,* and 1987, for *Georgia Music;* Christopher Award, 1982, for *We Can't Sleep;* Parents Choice Award, 1982, for *Oliver, Clarence, and Violet;* Boston Globe/Horn Book Honor Book designation, ALA Notable Book designation, and *School Library Journal* Best Books designation, all 1983, all for *What's under My Bed?;* Garden State Children's Book Award, New Jersey Library Association, 1983, for *Clams Can't Sing;* ALA Notable Book designation, 1986, for *When I Was Nine;* Parents' Choice designation, and *Redbook* award, both 1987, both for *Higher on the Door;* Parents' Choice Picture Book Award, 1987, for *Granddaddy's Place,* and 1992, for *Don't You Know There's a War On?;* Garden State Children's Book Award, 1990, for *Henry and Mudge in Puddle Trouble;* Kentucky Bluegrass Award, 1992, for *Something Big Has Been Here*; International Reading Association/Children's Book Council Children's Choice designation, and Parent's Choice Award, both 2004, both for *No Laughing, No Smiling, No Giggling.*

Writings

Do Yourself a Favor, Kid (novel), Macmillan (New York, NY), 1962.

The Summer Houses, Macmillan (New York, NY), 1963.

Sorry, Lady, This Beach Is Private! (cartoons), Macmillan (New York, NY), 1963.

Sometimes, But Not Always (autobiographical novel), Little, Brown (Boston, MA), 1967.

Something Marvelous Is About to Happen (humor), Harper (New York, NY), 1971.

Cool Jack and the Beanstalk, Penguin (New York, NY), 1976.

Let's Boogie! (cartoons), Dodd (New York, NY), 1978.

Uptown Local, Downtown Express, Viking (New York, NY), 1983.

Rolling in Dough, (a musical), music by Dick Robert, performed at the Granbury Opera House, Granbury, TX, 1997.

Lost and Found New York: Oddballs, Heroes, Heartbreakers, Scoundrels, Thugs, Mayors, and Mysteries (collected columns), HarperCollins (New York, NY), 2007.

Also author of plays and television sketches. Contributor of articles to *New Yorker, Preservation, Country Journal,* and *American Film.* Author of column "Lost and Found New York," for *New York Times,* beginning 2003.

FOR CHILDREN; SELF-ILLUSTRATED, EXCEPT AS INDICATED

Walker, the Witch, and the Striped Flying Saucer, Little, Brown (Boston, MA), 1969.

The Bear Who Had No Place to Go, Harper (New York, NY), 1972.

Here Comes Herb's Hurricane!, Harper (New York, NY), 1973.

"Could Be Worse!," Greenwillow (New York, NY), 1977.

Wilfred the Rat, Greenwillow (New York, NY), 1977.

(With daughter, Edwina Stevenson) *"Help!" Yelled Maxwell,* Greenwillow (New York, NY), 1978.

The Sea View Hotel, Greenwillow, 1978.

Winston, Newton, Elton, and Ed, Greenwillow (New York, NY), 1978.

The Worst Person in the World, Greenwillow (New York, NY), 1978.

Fast Friends: Two Stories, Greenwillow (New York, NY), 1979.

Monty, Greenwillow (New York, NY), 1979.

Howard, Greenwillow (New York, NY), 1980.

That Terrible Halloween Night, Greenwillow (New York, NY), 1980.

Clams Can't Sing, Greenwillow (New York, NY), 1980.

The Night after Christmas, Greenwillow (New York, NY), 1981.

The Wish Card Ran Out!, Greenwillow (New York, NY), 1981.

The Whale Tale, Random House (New York, NY), 1981.

Oliver, Clarence, and Violet, Greenwillow (New York, NY), 1982.

We Can't Sleep, Greenwillow (New York, NY), 1982.

What's under My Bed?, Greenwillow (New York, NY), 1983.

The Great Big Especially Beautiful Easter Egg, Greenwillow (New York, NY), 1983.

Barbara's Birthday, Greenwillow (New York, NY), 1983.

Grandpa's Great City Tour: An Alphabet Book, Greenwillow (New York, NY), 1983.

Worse than Willy!, Greenwillow (New York, NY), 1984.

Yuck!, Greenwillow (New York, NY), 1984.

Emma, Greenwillow (New York, NY), 1985.

Are We Almost There?, Greenwillow (New York, NY), 1985.

That Dreadful Day, Greenwillow (New York, NY), 1985.

Fried Feathers for Thanksgiving, Greenwillow (New York, NY), 1986.

No Friends, Greenwillow (New York, NY), 1986.

There's Nothing to Do!, Greenwillow (New York, NY), 1986.

When I Was Nine (autobiographical), Greenwillow (New York, NY), 1986.

Happy Valentine's Day, Emma!, Greenwillow (New York, NY), 1987.

Higher on the Door (sequel to *When I Was Nine*), Greenwillow (New York, NY), 1987.

No Need for Monty, Greenwillow (New York, NY), 1987.

Will You Please Feed Our Cat?, Greenwillow (New York, NY), 1987.

The Supreme Souvenir Factory, Greenwillow (New York, NY), 1988.

We Hate Rain!, Greenwillow (New York, NY), 1988.

The Worst Person in the World at Crab Beach, Greenwillow (New York, NY), 1988.

Grandpa's Too-Good Garden, Greenwillow (New York, NY), 1989.

Oh No, It's Waylon's Birthday!, Greenwillow (New York, NY), 1989.

Un-Happy New Year, Emma!, Greenwillow (New York, NY), 1989.

Emma at the Beach, Greenwillow (New York, NY), 1990.

July, Greenwillow (New York, NY), 1990.

National Worm Day, Greenwillow (New York, NY), 1990.

Quick! Turn the Page!, Greenwillow (New York, NY), 1990.

The Stowaway, Greenwillow (New York, NY), 1990.

Which One Is Whitney?, Greenwillow (New York, NY), 1990.

Mr. Hacker, illustrated by Frank Modell, Greenwillow (New York, NY), 1990.

Brrr!, Greenwillow (New York, NY), 1991.

That's Exactly the Way It Wasn't, Greenwillow (New York, NY), 1991.

The Worst Person's Christmas, Greenwillow (New York, NY), 1991.

Rolling Rose, Greenwillow (New York, NY), 1991.

Don't You Know There's a War On?, Greenwillow (New York, NY), 1992.

And Then What?, Greenwillow (New York, NY), 1992.

The Flying Acorns, Greenwillow (New York, NY), 1993.

The Pattaconk Brook, Greenwillow (New York, NY), 1993.

Worse than Worst, Greenwillow (New York, NY), 1994.

Fun—No Fun, Greenwillow (New York, NY), 1994.

The Mud Flat Olympics, Greenwillow (New York, NY), 1994.

A Village Full of Valentines, Greenwillow (New York, NY), 1995.

All Aboard!, Greenwillow (New York, NY), 1995.

Sweet Corn, Greenwillow (New York, NY), 1995.

The Bones in the Cliff (juvenile novel), Greenwillow (New York, NY), 1995.

The Worst Goes South, Greenwillow (New York, NY), 1995.

I Had a Lot of Wishes, Greenwillow (New York, NY), 1995.

Yard Sale, Greenwillow (New York, NY), 1996.

I Meant to Tell You, Greenwillow (New York, NY), 1996.

The Oldest Elf, Greenwillow (New York, NY), 1996.

Heat Wave at Mud Flat, Greenwillow (New York, NY), 1997.

The Mud Flat Mystery, Greenwillow (New York, NY), 1997.

The Unprotected Witness (novel; sequel to *The Bones in the Cliff*), Greenwillow (New York, NY), 1997.

Sam the Zamboni Man, illustrated by son, Harvey Stevenson, Greenwillow (New York, NY), 1998.

Mud Flat April Fool, Greenwillow (New York, NY), 1998.

Popcorn, Greenwillow (New York, NY), 1998.

Candy Corn, Greenwillow (New York, NY), 1999.

Mud Flat Spring, Greenwillow (New York, NY), 1999.

Don't Make Me Laugh, Farrar, Straus & Giroux (New York, NY), 1999.

Cornflakes, Greenwillow (New York, NY), 2000.

The Most Amazing Dinosaur, Greenwillow (New York, NY), 2000.

Christmas at Mud Flat, Greenwillow (New York, NY), 2000.

Just around the Corner: Poems, Greenwillow (New York, NY), 2001.

Corn-Fed: Poems, Greenwillow (New York, NY), 2002.

The Castaway, Greenwillow (New York, NY), 2002.

Runaway Horse!, Greenwillow (New York, NY), 2003.

Corn Chowder, Greenwillow (New York, NY), 2003.

No Laughing, No Smiling, No Giggling: Is That Understood?, Farrar, Straus (New York, NY), 2004.

Flying Feet: A Mud Flat Story, Greenwillow (New York, NY), 2004.

ILLUSTRATOR

William K. Zinsser, *Weekend Guests: From "We're So Glad You Could Come" to "We're So Sorry You Have to Go," and Vice-Versa* (adult), Harper (New York, NY), 1963.

James Walker Stevenson, *If I Owned a Candy Factory,* Little, Brown (Boston, MA), 1968.

Eric Stevenson, *Tony and the Toll Collector,* Little, Brown (Boston, MA), 1969.

Lavinia Ross, *Alec's Sand Castle,* Harper (New York, NY), 1972.

Alan Arkin, *Tony's Hard Work Day,* Harper (New York, NY), 1972.

Sara D. Gilbert, *What's a Father For?: A Father's Guide to the Pleasures and Problems of Parenthood with Advice from the Experts,* Parents Magazine Press (New York, NY), 1975.

John Donovan, *Good Old James,* Harper (New York, NY), 1975.

Janet Schulman, *Jack the Bum and the Halloween Handout,* Greenwillow (New York, NY), 1977.

Schulman, *Jack the Bum and the Haunted House,* Greenwillow (New York, NY), 1977.

Schulman, *Jack the Bum and the UFO,* Greenwillow (New York, NY), 1978.

Charlotte Zolotow, *Say It!,* Greenwillow (New York, NY), 1980.

Jack Prelutsky, *The Baby Uggs Are Hatching* (poetry), Greenwillow (New York, NY), 1982.

Louis Phillips, *How Do You Get a Horse out of the Bathtub?: Profound Answers to Preposterous Questions,* Viking (New York, NY), 1983.

Wilson Gage (pseudonym of Mary Q. Steele), *Cully Cully and the Bear,* Greenwillow (New York, NY), 1983.

Charlotte Zolotow, *I Know a Lady,* Greenwillow (New York, NY), 1984.

Jack Prelutsky, *The New Kid on the Block* (poems), Greenwillow (New York, NY), 1984.

John Thorn, editor, *The Armchair Book of Baseball,* Macmillan (New York, NY), 1985.

Franz Brandenberg, *Otto Is Different,* Greenwillow (New York, NY), 1985.

Louis Phillips, *Brain Busters: Just How Smart Are You, Anyway?,* Viking, 1985.

Helen V. Griffith, *Georgia Music,* Greenwillow (New York, NY), 1986.

Cynthia Rylant, *Henry and Mudge,* Bradbury (New York, NY), 1987.

Cynthia Rylant, *Henry and Mudge in Puddle Trouble,* Bradbury (New York, NY), 1987.

Helen V. Griffith, *Grandaddy's Place,* Greenwillow (New York, NY), 1987.

Dr. Seuss (pseudonym of Theodor Seuss Geisel), *I Am Not Going to Get up Today!,* Random House (New York, NY), 1987.

Louis Phillips, *How Do You Lift a Walrus with One Hand?: More Profound Answers to Preposterous Questions,* Viking (New York, NY), 1988.

Else Holmelund Minarik, *Percy and the Five Houses,* Greenwillow (New York, NY), 1989.

Jack Prelutsky, *Something Big Has Been Here* (poetry), Greenwillow (New York, NY), 1990.

Barbara Dugan, *Loop the Loop,* Greenwillow (New York, NY), 1992.

Susanna Van Rose, *Volcano and Earth,* Knopf (New York, NY), 1992.

Helen V. Griffith, *Grandaddy and Janetta*, Greenwillow (New York, NY), 1993.

Charles C. Black, *The Royal Nap*, Viking (New York, NY), 1995.

Helen V. Griffith, *Grandaddy's Stars*, Greenwillow (New York, NY), 1995.

William Maxwell, *Mrs. Donald's Dog Bun and His Home away from Home*, Knopf (New York, NY), 1995.

Jack Prelutsky, *A Pizza the Size of the Sun*, Greenwillow (New York, NY), 1996.

Anna Quindlen, *Happily Ever After*, Viking Penguin (New York, NY), 1997.

Jack Prelutsky, *It's Raining Pigs and Noodles: Poems*, Greenwillow (New York, NY), 2000.

Carol Otis Hurst, *Rocks in His Head*, Greenwillow (New York, NY), 2001.

Helen V. Griffith, *Grandaddy and Janetta Together: The Three Stories in One Book*, Greenwillow (New York, NY), 2001.

Judy Blume, *Soupy Saturdays with The Pain and the Great One*, Delacorte (New York, NY), 2007.

Judy Blume, *Going, Going, Gone! with The Pain and the Great One*, Delacorte (New York, NY), 2008.

Judy Blume, *Cool Zone with The Pain and the Great One*, Delacorte (New York, NY), 2008.

Jack Prelutsky, *My Dog May Be a Genius: Poems*, Greenwillow (New York, NY), 2008.

Judy Blume, *Friend or Fiend? with The Pain and the Great One*, Delacorte (New York, NY), 2009.

Adaptations

Many of Stevenson's books were adapted for filmstrip or audiocassette, including *Fast Friends*, Educational Enrichment Materials, 1981; *"Could Be Worse!"* and *That Terrible Halloween Night*, both Educational Enrichment Materials, 1982; *What's under My Bed?*, Weston Woods, 1984; and *We Can't Sleep*, Random House, 1984, re-released on videocassette, 1988. *Howard* was adapted for film as *New Friends*, Made-to-Order Library Products. *Could Be Worse!* and *What's under My Bed?* were highlighted on *Reading Rainbow*, PBS-TV.

Sidelights

Known for his antic touch and light humor, cartoonist and writer James Stevenson is the creator of such beloved characters as the irascible Worst—a grandfather who is anything but lovable—and the more endearing Grandpa, who enjoys telling tall tales and whoppers to his gullible grandchildren. Sharing his upbeat view of life with readers, Stevenson's droll and animated stories include *Clams Can't Sing*, *Wilfred the Rat*, *Higher on the Door*, and his humorous "Corn" and "Mud Flat" book series. The sketchy, high-spirited drawing style he uses in his cartooning for his books and *New York Times* column has also enriched books featuring texts by such notable children's authors as Dr. Seuss, Else Holmelund Minarik, Judy Blume, Charlotte Zolotow, and Jack Prelutsky. As Karla Kuskin wrote in the *New York Times*

Book Review: "Whether writing or drawing, Mr. Stevenson understands perfectly the strength of a simple understated line and a quiet laugh."

Stevenson was born in New York City, and was raised in the nearby town of Croton-on-Hudson. He credits his early education with having a great impact on his life: "Hessian Hills School had a policy of telling you that everybody could do everything. Everybody could sing, dance, act, play musical instruments, write stories, make pictures and change the world," he recalled to Kimberly Olson Fakih in *Publishers Weekly*. Stevenson began writing and drawing as a boy and was encouraged by his father who was a watercolorist. His eventual artistic style was influenced by movies and comics rather than any of the children's books he read as a child.

At Yale University, Stevenson majored in English with the intention of becoming a writer. His first success was with art rather than writing, however; he was selling ideas for cartoons to the *New Yorker* magazine while still a college student. After graduating in 1951, Stevenson spent two years in the U.S. Marine Corps, followed by another two years as a *Life* reporter. In 1956, he moved to the *New Yorker* art department full-time, developing cartoon ideas for staff artists. Four years later, in 1960, Stevenson began work as a *New Yorker* reporter; in addition he wrote three adult novels and compiled a volume of original cartoons. These novels, as well as the many cartoons he contributed to the *New Yorker*, are full of social and political satire, poking fun at suburban living, the media, and other aspects of modern American life.

Gradually Stevenson's focus shifted away from current issues, and as a father he became interested in subjects of concern to a younger audience. His first involvement with picture books was a collaboration with his then-eight-year-old son James, and he recalled to Fakih how it came about. "[I said to James,] 'Tell me a story and we'll make a book.' He stood at my desk and narrated a story; I wrote it down and then did the pictures." The book that resulted was *If I Owned a Candy Factory*, and it was published in 1968.

Stevenson's books are often illustrated in comic-book or cartoon style. The intermix of story line with dialogue "balloons" and graffiti adds energy and dimension to his humorously-drawn tales. The use of pencil as an artistic medium in drawing his appealing, scruffy characters brings an air of informality and spontaneity to his stories. He adds a wash of soft color to his drawings, avoiding the vivid contrasts of the traditional comic book in favor of a more subtle effect.

Stevenson's first original self-illustrated children's book, *Walker, the Witch, and the Striped Flying Saucer*, was published the following year; *"Could Be Worse!"* firmly established him as a writer of children's books, as well as introducing his picture-book alter ego, the character "Grandpa." "A more engaging character than Grandpa has not emerged in recent picture books," commented Gertrude Herman in *Horn Book*. A master of the incredibly tall tale, Grandpa always responds to grandchildren Mary Ann and Louie's concern that his life is boring by recounting a recent—and totally unbelievable—adventure. Stevenson combines verbal nonsense with humorous drawings of Grandpa and his younger brother, Uncle Wainwright, as mustachioed children to appeal directly to children's love of the silly and absurd. Louie and Mary Ann—together with Stevenson's young readers—can count on the fact that, whatever their problem, Grandpa has experienced one like it, but so much worse that their own worry diminishes upon comparison.

Throughout Stevenson's "Grandpa" books, Grandpa helps his grandchildren deal with various problems, concocting whoppers that console Mary Ann and Louie when they come home from a terrible first day of school in *That Dreadful Day*; adjust to a move to a new neighborhood in *No Friends*; and combat a fear of the dark in *What's under My Bed?* In *That Terrible Halloween Night*, Mary Ann and Louie are busy attempting to frighten Grandpa, but no matter what they try, the old man remains unruffled behind his newspaper. When prodded, he tells his grandchildren about what happened to him on a Halloween long ago, complete with pumpkins, a haunted house, spiders, and lots of yucky green stuff. Grandpa's story ends on a typically Stevensonian note: with a quiet chuckle and a warm smile.

Stevenson's cast of characters has expanded throughout his career as a children's author. *Emma, Happy Valentine's Day, Emma!, Un-happy New Year, Emma!*, and *Emma at the Beach* all focus on a good-natured young witch/apprentice who triumphs over the efforts of older sorceresses Dolores and Lavinia to undermine her attempts at magic. While Emma remains popular with readers, Stevenson's "Worst" books have gained an even larger following among his fans. The Worst is a lonely, crotchety old gentleman who disguises his need for companionship by grumbling and complaining where the most people will hear him. In *The Worst Person's Christmas*, for example, the curmudgeon celebrates the holiday season by doing such things as scolding carol-singers off his property. *The Worst Person in the World* and *The Worst Person in the World at Crab Beach*, like other "Worst" titles, follow the old grouch through a series of mishaps that do not make him any nicer.

The misadventures of the Worst continue in *Worse than Worst*, as the Worst almost meets his match in great-nephew Warren. The two trade insults, with Warren often on the winning end, even taking over his uncle's bedroom while his dog disrupts things in the Worst's home. Writing in the *Bulletin of the Center for Children's Books* Deborah Stevenson cited the "snappy patter, outrageous sass, and loony high-action art" in Stevenson's book and applauded the fact that the author/illustrator does not make the Worst too nice. "May the Worst continue to plummet to ever deeper lengths," the critic concluded.

In *The Worst Goes South*, "Worst is back again in all his grumpy glory," announced Beth Irish in her review of the book for *School Library Journal*. To avoid his town's harvest festival, the old codger decides to head off to Florida. Stopping a motel along the way, the Worst is nearly bested in grumpiness by the owner while he arranges for a room for the night. The next morning the Worst discovers that the grouchy motel owner is in fact his brother. "Once again, Stevenson's dry wit and watercolor-and-pen cartoon sketches pair up to make a winner," commented Irish, and Leone McDermott noted in a review of *The Worst Goes South* for *Booklist* that "Stevenson fans will cheer the return of that comic curmudgeon at his worst."

Also featuring the author/illustrator's wry humor, Stevenson's "Mud Flat" books feature a zany cast of animal characters. In *The Mud Flat Olympics*, for example, a group of animal athletes test their metal in contests of prowess. Laugh-producing competitions include snails on the high hurdles and the smelliest skunk contest, all of which allow young readers to "have a chance to see friendship, fair play, and fun in action," according to *Booklist* critic Stephanie Zvirin. A critic in *Kirkus Reviews* dubbed *The Mud Flat Olympics* a "lovely early chapter book that adults will find difficult to resist sharing aloud." The animals of Mud Flat get their unwanted junk together to sell in *Yard Sale*, a "dear, funny book for children who appreciate a more subtle sort of humor," according to Zvirin. Louise L. Sherman noted of the same book in *School Library Journal* that Stevenson's animal characters "are filled with personality and expression."

In *Heat Wave at Mud Flat*, the residents are suffering from a hot spell until they dream of an ingenious way to deal with the temperature: Marty the elephant gains sudden popularity as a provider of shade. Hanna B. Zeigler commented in *Horn Book* that with this "Mud Flat" installment "Stevenson has once again created a humorous and affectionate peek at this world in microcosm." Zeigler went on to conclude in her review of *Heat Wave at Mud Flat* that the book is a "treat for anyone, young or old, who has ever experienced the dog days of summer." Jokes and tricks aplenty can be found in *Mud Flat April Fool*, in which Stevenson "cleverly introduces the calendar event through a series of vignettes starring his familiar woodland creatures," according to Marty Abbott Goodman in *School Library Journal*.

Christmas at Mud Flat describes the hectic preparations required to ready the Mud Flat community for the holiday season. Freddie, the owner of the fix-it shop, has more repair work than he can handle, and it is all due by Christmas day, and Sherwood cannot possibly wrap all his presents in time. Despite such challenges, the town's big party comes off, with Priscilla the snail dressing as Santa Claus. *Flying Feet: A Mud Flat Story* finds everyone in the community signing up for tap-dance lessons when Tonya and Ted arrive in town with their dance school. However, the dance the couple has promised to host is in danger of being canceled when Tonya and Ted skedaddle in the middle of the night, along with the money from the lessons. Martha V. Parravano, reviewing *Christmas at Mud Flat* in *Horn Book,* called it "a solid entry in an often sublime series," while Linda Perkins wrote in *Booklist* that in *Flying Feet* the author/illustrator's characteristic "watercolor illustrations provide their customary wit and humor." Laura Scott, writing in *School Library Journal,* concluded of the same book that "children will enjoy this zany story."

Stevenson turns from prose to poetry in his "Corn" books, juxtaposing original verses presented in various typefaces and colors with watercolors images in *Sweet Corn, Popcorn, Candy Corn, Corn-Fed,* and *Corn Chowder.* Reviewing *Corn Chowder,* Parravano explained that the book's "words, typeface, and illustrations combine to create a distinctive space for each poem." "Often the full meaning of the poem depends upon the illustration," explained Lee Bock in a review of the same book for *School Library Journal.* The poems are "delectable tidbits that tickle the taste buds," wrote Beth Tegart in a *School Library Journal* of *Corn Chowder.* Reviewing *Corn-Fed,* Hazel Rochman concluded in *Booklist* that "Stevenson's gift is to reveal wonder in the ordinary."

Several books by Stevenson focus on Hubie, a mouse who loves to take photographs during his many travels. In *The Castaway,* Hubie and his family are traveling by dirigible to Barabooda Island in the South Pacific. While snapping some pictures of the scenery, the little mouse falls out of the aircraft and down onto a deserted island. There he befriends Leo, an inventor who has been living alone on the island for ten years. Leo has used his ingenuity to construct a baseball diamond, speedboat, and giant treehouse, and now the new island-mates have a great time. Then, during a trip over a waterfall, Hubie is thrown upward, landing in the dirigible and reuniting with his family (who did not notice that he was missing). Later, Hubie's family is puzzled by his photos from the trip, which show places and things they never saw. Stevenson's illustrations, as Carol Ann Wilson wrote in *School Library Journal,* "give marvelous personality to every character," and Mary M. Burns concluded in *Horn Book* that there are "several thrills, a couple of chills, some spills, and plenty of fun" in *The Castaway.*

Marking a departure for Stevenson, *The Bones in the Cliff* and *The Unprotected Witness* are middle-grade novels that feature a boy whose father is on the run from the mob. In the first novel, Pete's mother is in a mental institution and his father drinks too much. Pete's job is to watch the arrival of ferries at the tiny island where his family now lives; his father fears that a hit man is looking for him and he trusts Pete to warn him in that event. Meanwhile, Pete meets Rootie, a girl who quickly becomes his confidant friend. While he is with Rootie, Pete misses the one ferry that is important, and when the gunman goes for his father Pete must over-

come his own fear to intervene. A reviewer in *Kirkus Reviews* remarked of *The Bones in the Cliff* that the author "has written a surprisingly gritty novel that, with its economy of language, can easily be enjoyed by readers younger than its intended audience. . . . It should be a hit with reluctant readers and middle graders who are ready for a bit of realism and tension." Susan Patron, reviewing the same title in *Five Owls,* concluded that the "exciting and fast-paced story, with its dabs of humor shining through like sunlight in a painting, highlights . . . Stevenson's well-proven talent in writing simple stories that are rich in characterization and meaning."

Stevenson continues Pete's story in *The Unprotected Witness.* Here Pete is living in Manhattan with Rootie and Rootie's rich grandmother while his father is in Missouri in a witness protection program. When the program fails and his dad is murdered, Pete soon discovers the location of stolen money that the Mafia wants. "The suspense mounts to an almost unbearable level as Pete and his friends attempt to get to the treasure before the bad guys get them," noted Eva Mitnick in a *School Library Journal* review of *The Unprotected Witness.* "Hand [this book] to any kid who craves suspense," Mitnick concluded.

Stevenson explores the world of his own youth in books such as *When I Was Nine, Higher on the Door, July* and *Don't You Know There's a War On?,* the last which details life in small-town America during World War II. Victory gardens and rations figure largely in the boy's life in *Don't You Know There's a War On?,* but most significant is the family's sadness at the departure of Stevenson's father, who is an enlisted man in the military. "With all that's not said and shown, this memoir leaves space for us to imagine," remarked *Booklist* critic Hazel Rochman, while Anna Biagioni Hart wrote in *School Library Journal* that the "small watercolor pictures float on white pages, making this a scrapbook of memories." Joan Weller and Susan Stan, writing in *Five Owls,* commented that "Stevenson's ability to capture the feelings and complexities surrounding an event makes his picture-book biographies meaningful on many levels."

Further reminiscences inspired *Fun—No Fun,* and here, "once again, Stevenson finds an imaginative and appealing perspective from which to present America as it was when he was growing up a couple of generations ago," according to a *Kirkus Reviews* contributor. In both words and pictures, Stevenson waxes nostalgic about the anticipated arrival of the ice-cream truck and time spent listening to radio shows, matching each memory with small, intentionally soft-focus watercolor pictures. He gives a similar treatment to sometimes unfulfilled childhood hopes and dreams in *I Had a Lot of Wishes.* This book provides a "pleasant journey for children," according to Pamela K. Bomboy in *School Library Journal,* "especially when shared with a sympathetic adult." Stevenson gives a nod to times enjoyed with his own children in *I Meant to Tell You,* which *School Library Journal* critic Judith Constantinides called "a wonderful read-aloud for story times on families." Rochman noted in *Booklist* that, with this picture-book autobiography, "Love is in the direct, affectionate voice, in the images [Stevenson] remembers, in the sharing of those memories."

In addition to his original books for children, Stevenson has been much-sought-after as an illustrator. Illustration projects include *Rocks in His Head,* a remembrance by Carol Otis Hurst about her rock-collecting father, as well as Cynthia Rylant's *Henry and Mudge,* Judy Blume's *Cool Zone with The Pain and the Great One* and *Soupy Saturdays with The Pain and the Great One,* and Jack Prelutsky's *It's Raining Pigs and Noodles.* Reviewing *Rocks in His Head,* Kathleen Kelly MacMillan wrote in *School Library Journal* that Stevenson's images "capture the mild-mannered hero perfectly," and a critic for *Publishers Weekly* concluded that the book's "artwork convincingly evokes both the personality of this endearing protagonist and the period in which he lived." "Stevenson's small, scribbly, casual ink drawings extend the humor [of *It's Raining Pigs and Noodles*] with character and mischief," according to Rochman, and Cooper concluded of Stevenson's collaboration with Blume that the "signature ink artwork" he contributes to *Soupy Saturdays with The Pain and the Great One* "boosts the tale with amusing pictures that pull the reader along."

Biographical and Critical Sources

BOOKS

Children's Literature Review, Volume 17, Gale (Detroit, MI), 1989.

Kingman, Lee, and others, compilers, *Illustrators of Children's Books: 1967-1976,* Horn Book (Boston, MA), 1978.

St. James Guide to Children's Writers, fifth edition, edited by Sara Pendergast and Tom Pendergast, St. James Press (Detroit, MI), 1999.

PERIODICALS

Booklist, November 1, 1992, Hazel Rochman, review of *Don't You Know There's a War On?* p. 511; September 1, 1994, Stephanie Zvirin, review of *The Mud Flat Olympics,* p. 43; September 1, 1995, Leone McDermott, review of *The Worst Goes South,* p. 89; March 15, 1996, Stephanie Zvirin, review of *Yard Sale,* p. 1264; April 1, 1996, Hazel Rochman, review of *I Meant to Tell You,* p. 1369; January 1, 2001, Hazel Rochman, review of *Just around the Corner,* p. 954; June 1, 2001, Shelle Rosenfeld, review of *Rocks in His Head,* p. 1890; March 1, 2002, Hazel Rochman, review of *Corn-Fed,* p. 1138; June 1, 2002,

Michael Cart, review of *The Castaway,* p. 1726; June 1, 2003, Hazel Rochman, review of *Corn Chowder,* p. 1768; February 1, 2004, Linda Perkins, review of *Flying Feet: A Mud Flat Tale,* p. 982; August, 2004, Jennifer Mattson, review of *No Laughing, No Smiling, No Giggling: Is That Understood?,* p. 1946; August, 2007, Ilene Cooper, review of *Soupy Saturdays with The Pain and The Great One,* p. 78; March 1, 2008, Gillian Engberg, review of *My Dog May Be a Genius,* p. 64.

Bulletin of the Center for Children's Books, July-August, 1994, Deborah Stevenson, review of *Worse than the Worst,* pp. 374-375; November, 2000, review of *Christmas at Mud Flat,* p. 121; April, 2002, review of *Corn-Fed,* p. 297; September, 2003, review of *Corn Chowder,* p. 45.

Five Owls, November-December, 1992, Joan Weller and Susan Stan, review of *Don't You Know There's a War On?,* p. 27; May-June, 1995, Susan Patron, review of *The Bones in the Cliff,* pp. 203-204.

Horn Book, September-October, 1985, Gertrude Herman, "A Picture Is Worth Several Hundred Words," p. 605; July-August, 1997, Hanna B. Zeigler, review of *Heat Wave at Mud Flat,* pp. 463-464; November, 2000, Martha V. Parravano, review of *Christmas at Mud Flat,* p. 750, and Margaret A. Bush, review of *It's Raining Pigs and Noodles,* p. 766; July, 2001, review of *Rocks in His Head,* p. 440; July-August, 2002, Mary M. Burns, review of *The Castaway,* p. 452; May-June, 2003, Martha V. Parravano, review of *Corn Chowder,* p. 365; November-December, 2004, Susan Dove Lempke, review of *No Laughing, No Smiling, No Giggling,* p. 701; March-April, 2008, Susan Dove Lempke, review of *My Dog May Be a Genius,* p. 224.

Kirkus Reviews, May 1, 1994, review of *Fun—No Fun,* p. 637; October 15, 1994, review of *Mud Flat Olympics,* p. 1416; May 1, 1995, review of *The Bones in the Cliff,* p. 640; January 1, 2002, review of *Corn-Fed,* p. 52; March 1, 2002, review of *The Castaway,* p. 345; March 1, 2003, review of *Corn Chowder,* p. 399; January 1, 2004, review of *Flying Feet,* p. 41; July 15, 2004, review of *No Laughing, No Smiling, No Giggling,* p. 694; April 1, 2008, review of *Cool Zone with The Pain and The Great One;* July 1, 2008, review of *Going, Going, Gone! With The Pain and The Great One.*

New York Times Book Review, November 15, 1981, Karla Kuskin, "The Art of Picture Books," p. 57.

Publishers Weekly, February 27, 1987, Kimberly Olsen Fakih, "James Stevenson," pp. 148-149; April 30, 2001, review of *Rocks in His Head,* p. 78; January 27, 2003, review of *The Mudflat Mystery,* p. 262; June 18, 2007, review of *Soupy Saturdays with The Pain and The Great One,* p. 53; March 3, 2008, review of *My Dog May Be a Genius,* p. 46.

School Library Journal, October, 1992, Anna Biagioni Hart, review of *Don't You Know There's a War On?,* p. 96; October, 1995, Beth Irish, review of *The Worst Goes South,* p. 120; February, 1996, Pamela K. Bomboy, review of *I Had a Lot of Wishes,* p. 90; July, 1996, Louise L. Sherman, review of *Yard Sale,* p. 74; August, 1996, Judith Constantinides, review of *I*

Meant to Tell You, p. 141; September, 1997, Eva Mitnick, review of *The Unprotected Witness,* p. 226; March, 1998, Marty Abbott Goodman, review of *Mud Flat April Fool,* p. 188; May, 1999, Beth Tegart, review of *Candy Corn,* p. 113; March, 2001, Wendy S. Carroll, review of *Just around the Corner,* p. 243; June, 2001, Kathleen Kelly MacMillan, review of *Rocks in His Head,* p. 118; March, 2002, Nina Lindsay, review of *Corn-Fed,* p. 221; May, 2002, Carol Ann Wilson, review of *The Castaway,* p. 128; May, 2003, Lee Bock, review of *Corn Chowder,* p. 142; March, 2004, Laura Scott, review of *Flying Feet,* p. 182; August, 2004, Sheilah Kosco, review of *No Laughing, No Smiling, No Giggling,* p. 94; August, 2007, Laura Lutz, review of *Soupy Saturdays with The Pain and The Great One,* p. 77; February, 2008, Lee Bock, review of *My Dog May Be a Genius,* p. 108; September, 2008, Kathleen Meulen, review of *Going, Going, Gone! with The Pain and The Great One,* p. 138.

ONLINE

Carol Hurst's Children's Literature Web Site, http://www.carolhurst.com/ (May 8, 2005), Carol Otis Hurst, "Featured Author and Illustrator: James Stevenson" and review of *Rocks in His Head.**

*   *   *

STOWER, Adam

Personal

Male. *Education:* Norwich School of Art, B.A. (with honors); University of Brighton, M.A.

Addresses

Home—Brighton, England. *Agent*—Arena Agency, 31 Eleanor Rd., London E15 4AB, England. *E-mail*—adam@worldofadam.com.

Career

Illustrator and author.

Awards, Honors

Norfolk Library Silver Award for Children's Books, 2005, for *Slam!: A Tale of Consequences.*

Writings

SELF-ILLUSTRATED

Two Left Feet, Bloomsbury (New York, NY), 2004.
The Den, Bloomsbury (London, England), 2005.
Slam!: A Tale of Consequences, Templar (Dorking, England), 2005.

(With Nick Denchfield) *The Diary of a Monster Catcher* (pop-up book), Alison Green/Scholastic (London, England), 2008.

ILLUSTRATOR

(With Jonathon Heap) Robert Hull, reteller, *Norse Stories,* Thomson Learning (New York, NY), 1993.
(With Claire Robinson) Robert Hull, reteller, *Greek Stories,* Thomson Learning (New York, NY), 1994.
Chris Culshaw, *A Bit of a Drip, and The Letter,* Oxford University Press (Oxford, England), 1995.
Roger Norman, *Treetime,* Faber (London, England), 1997.
Honor Head, *Ed Mouse Finds out about Size and Shape,* Belitha (London, England), 1997, Raintree Steck-Vaughn (Austin, TX), 1999.
Honor Head, *Ed Mouse Finds out about Direction,* Belitha (London, England), 1997, Raintree Steck-Vaughn (Austin, TX), 1999.
Honor Head, *Ed Mouse Finds out about Opposites,* Belitha (London, England), 1998, Raintree Steck-Vaughn (Austin, TX), 1999.
Honor Head, *Ed Mouse Finds out about Times of Day,* Belitha (London, England), 1998, Raintree Steck-Vaughn (Austin, TX), 1999.
(With Tim Hayward and Robin Carter) Steve Parker, *It's an Ant's Life,* Reader's Digest Children's Books (Pleasantville, NY), 1999.
Emily Moore, *The Monarchy,* Hodder (London, England), 2000.
Sue Arengo, reteller, *The Shoemaker and the Elves,* Oxford University Press (Oxford, England), 2000.
Gillian Clements, *Romans Go Home!,* Pearson Education (Harlow, England), 2001.
Diane Mowat, reteller, *A Pair of Ghostly Hands and Other Stories,* Oxford University Press (Oxford, England), 2002.
John Escott, reteller, *William Tell and Other Stories,* Oxford University Press (Oxford, England), 2002.
Terence Blacker, *You Have Ghost Mail,* Macmillan (London, England), 2002.
Kate Saunders, *Cat and the Stinkwater War,* Macmillan (London, England), 2003.
Roger McGough, compiler, *Favourite Funny Stories,* Kingfisher (London, England), 2003, published as *More Funny Stories,* Kingfisher (Boston, MA), 2003.
Alan Temperley, *The Magician of Samarkand,* Macmillan (London, England), 2003.
Jane Bingham, adapter, *Around the World in Eighty Days,* Usborne (London, England), 2004.
Jimmy Fallon, *Snowball Fight!,* Dutton (New York, NY), 2005.
Roger McGough, compiler, *Comic Stories,* Kingfisher (London, England), 2005.
Timothy Knapman, *Mungo and the Picture Book Pirates,* Puffin (London, England), 2005.
Heather Vogel Frederick, *For Your Paws Only* ("Spy Mice" series), Puffin (London, England), 2006.
Heather Vogel Frederick, *The Black Paw* ("Spy Mice" series), Puffin (London, England), 2006.
Jane Johnson, *The Secret Country* ("Eidolon Chronicles"), Simon & Schuster (New York, NY), 2006.

Jane Johnson, *The Shadow World* ("Eidolon Chronicles"), Simon & Schuster (New York, NY), 2007.

Lucy Bowman, *Antarctica,* Usborne (London, England), 2007.

Heather Vogel Frederick, *Goldwhiskers* ("Spy Mice" series), Puffin (London, England), 2007.

Timothy Knapman, *Mungo and the Spiders from Space,* Puffin (London, England), 2007.

Timothy Knapman, *Mungo and the Dinosaur Island!,* Puffin (London, England), 2008.

Sidelights

Adam Stower is a British illustrator whose work has been influenced by such well-known picture-book artists as Heath Robinson, Edmund Dulac, and Arthur Rackham. A graduate of the Norwich School of Art and the University of Brighton, Stower has provided artwork for texts by Honor Head, Roger McGough, Timothy Knapman, Heather Vogel Frederick, and other authors. He has also written and illustrated his own titles, among them *Two Left Feet.*

Stower introduces Rufus, a cheerful, blue-skinned monster, in *Two Left Feet,* his debut self-illustrated work. Although Rufus loves to dance with his friends, he inevitably winds up on the floor after tripping over his own feet, both of which are, quite literally, left ones. When a messenger from the Glittering Palace invites the monsters to attend a ballroom dancing competition, Rufus cannot find a partner who wants to pair off with him. A dejected Rufus prepares to sit out the contest, until he is approached by Maddie, a boggart with her own anatomical quirk: she has two right feet. "The subtle humor of Rufus's predicament leads to a predictable conclusion," Bethany L.W. Hankinson stated in *School Library Journal.* Other reviewers also complimented Stower's book, a critic in *Publishers Weekly* remarking that "the delicate ink lines and golden, shimmery colors at times give the artwork the appearance of classic hand-tinted etchings." A *Kirkus Reviews* contributor dubbed *Two Left Feet* "a terpsichorean triumph that will send even younger readers into a twirl."

Stower has also illustrated *Snowball Fight!,* a story by Jimmy Fallon, an actor best known for his work on *Saturday Night Live.* Inspired by a track from *The Bathroom Wall,* Fallon's comedy album, *Snowball Fight!* follows a young boy as he dashes outside on a wintry day to construct a fort that will withstand a snowy onslaught from his playful neighbors. Just when he runs out of ammunition and appears to be overrun, the protagonist receives such much-needed assistance from his younger sister. "Stower's watercolors, featuring pugnosed, wide-eyed kids, exude an old-fashioned winter friskiness," remarked a contributor in *Publishers Weekly,* and Sally R. Dow similarly noted in *School Library Journal* that Stower's "energetic cartoon-style illustrations capture the action and humor."

Stower collaborates with Jane Johnson on *The Secret Country* and *The Shadow World,* a pair of adventure tales from Johnson's "Eidolon Chronicles." After purchasing a talking cat named Iggy from Mr. Dodds' Pet Emporium, young Ben Arnold learns that his ailing mother is the rightful queen of Eidolon, a mythic world, in *The Secret Country.* Ben and his sisters must now prevent Dodd, who has joined forces with their evil Uncle Aleister, from kidnapping the magical animals that inhabit Eidolon and restore order to that realm. In *The Shadow World,* Ben encounters a host of creatures, including a centaur, a mermaid, and selkies, when he crosses into Eidolon to rescue his older sister who has been captured by the nefarious Dodman. Praising Stower's contributions to *The Shadow World,* *School Library Journal* reviewer Sharon Grover remarked that "a whimsical black-and-white drawing opens each chapter."

Biographical and Critical Sources

PERIODICALS

Booklist, June 1, 2006, Sally Estes, review of *The Secret Country,* p. 71; December 1, 2007, Sally Estes, review of *The Shadow World,* p. 42.

Kirkus Reviews, July 1, 2004, review of *Two Left Feet,* p. 638; April 15, 2006, review of *The Secret Country,* p. 408.

Publishers Weekly, August 9, 2004, review of *Two Left Feet,* p. 250; April 15, 2005, review of *Snowball Fight!,* p. 58.

School Library Journal, October, 2004, Bethany L.W. Hankinson, review of *Two Left Feet,* p. 135; November, 2005, Sally R. Dow, review of *Snowball Fight!,* p. 90; April, 2006, Margaret A. Chang, review of *The Secret Country,* p. 141; November, 2007, Sharon Grover, review of *The Shadow World,* p. 126.

ONLINE

Adam Stower Home Page, http://www.worldofadam.com (November 10, 2008).

T

THACH, James Otis 1969-

Personal

Born November 1, 1969. *Education:* Attended Pomona College and California State University, Northridge.

Addresses

Home—Los Angeles, CA. *E-mail*—james@jamesthach. com.

Career

Author. Co-owner of tutoring company; has also worked in the entertainment industry.

Writings

A Child's Guide to Common Household Monsters, illustrated by David Udovic, Front Street (Asheville, NC), 2007.
The Tickle Monster Is Coming!, illustrated by David Barneda, Bloomsbury (New York, NY), 2008.
The Seal Pup, 2010.

Sidelights

A Child's Guide to Common Household Monsters is the debut picture book of James Otis Thach, a writer and owner of a tutoring company based in Los Angeles, California. A work told in verse, *A Child's Guide to Common Household Monsters* examines a common childhood fear: the creepy creatures that lurk in the shadows of one's home. As a young girl and her pet cat investigate a series of strange noises at night, they find a host of odd-looking beings living under the bed, inside the closet, and behind the washing machine. To her great surprise, however, the girl learns that the monsters are quite harmless; in fact, they are actually a bit comical and have fears of their own. "The reversal is both reassuring and deliciously creepy," noted Hazel Roch-

man in a *Booklist* review of Thach's picture-book debut. The story's "rhyming text flows smoothly as it follows the girl and her cat from room to room," wrote a contributor in *Kirkus Reviews,* while in *School Library Journal* Mary Hazelton dubbed *A Child's Guide to Common Household Monsters* "a terrific way to begin talking about nighttime fears with children."

Thach writes about another not-so-ominous creature in *The Tickle Monster Is Coming!* This time his story cen-

James Otis Thach takes a fun slant on childhood fears in **A Child's Guide to Common Household Monsters,** *featuring artwork by David Udovic.* (Illustration copyright © 2007 by David Udovic. Reproduced by permission of Boyds Mills Press.)

ters on a youngster who awaits an attack from the nocturnal Tickle Monster. According to a *Kirkus Reviews* critic, "there's just enough tame scariness here to thrill very little ones" who enjoy a bedtime tale.

Biographical and Critical Sources

PERIODICALS

Booklist, August, 2007, review of *A Child's Guide to Common Household Monsters,* p. 81.
Kirkus Reviews, July 15, 2007, review of *A Child's Guide to Common Household Monsters;* August 1, 2008, review of *The Tickle Monster Is Coming!*
School Library Journal, August, 2007, Mary Hazelton, review of *A Child's Guide to Common Household Monsters,* p. 94; October, 2008, Linda Ludke, review of *The Tickle Monster Is Coming!,* p. 126.

ONLINE

James Otis Thach Home Page, http://www.jamesthach.com (November 10, 2008).
Tickle Monster Web site, http://theticklemonster.com/ (November 10, 2008), "James Otis Thach."

* * *

TITLEBAUM, Ellen

Personal
Female.

Addresses
Home—New York, NY.

Career
Writer.

Writings

I Love You, Winnie the Pooh, illustrated by Robbin Cuddy, Disney Press (New York, NY), 1999.
(Adaptor) *Beauty and the Beast: A Read-aloud Storybook,* Disney Press (New York, NY), 1999.
Sabrina Down Under (based on television movie written by Daniel Berendsen), Pocket Books (New York, NY), 1999.
(Adaptor) *The Tigger Movie: A Read-aloud Storybook,* Mouse Works (New York, NY), 2000.

"STEP INTO READING" SERIES

(With Cathy Hapka) *How Not to Babysit Your Brother,* illustrated by Debbie Palen, Random House (New York, NY), 2005.

(With Cathy Hapka) *How Not to Start Third Grade,* illustrated by Debbie Palen, Random House (New York, NY), 2007.

Sidelights
Ellen Titlebaum has written a number of works based on Disney favorites, including *I Love You, Winnie the Pooh* and *Beauty and the Beast: A Read-aloud Storybook.* She is also the coauthor, with Cathy Hapka, of *How Not to Babysit Your Brother* and *How Not to Start Third Grade,* two works in the "Step into Reading" series. In the former, a youngster decides to take charge of his rambunctious little brother when their grandmother falls asleep while babysitting. After Will loses sight of unruly Steve, however, the preschooler wreaks havoc on their home. According to Lisa S. Schindler, writing in *School Library Journal,* the tale "is all in good fun and not to be taken too seriously."

Will and Steve return in *How Not to Start Third Grade.* Although Will looks forward to his first day as a third-grader, he is also wary of his brother's arrival in the kindergarten classroom. Sure enough, Steve romps through the hallways and starts a food fight in the cafeteria, and the family dog makes an equally wild appearance. "Simply constructed sentences and brisk dialogue make use of lively vocabulary," Gillian Engberg remarked in *Booklist.*

Biographical and Critical Sources

PERIODICALS

Booklist, September 1, 2007, Gillian Engberg, review of *How Not to Start Third Grade,* p. 126.
School Library Journal, August, 2005, Lisa S. Schindler, review of *How Not to Babysit Your Brother,* p. 96; July, 2007, Susan Lissim, review of *How Not to Start Third Grade,* p. 76.*

* * *

TODD, Chuck

Personal
Married; children: two daughters. *Education:* Southwest Missouri State University, B.F.A., 1989; Academy of Art College, M.F.A., 1999.

Addresses
Home—CA. *E-mail*—chuck@chucktodd.net.

Career
Sequential artist, illustrator, and educator. Southwest Missouri State University Publications, Springfield, MO, designer, 1989; *News-Leader,* Springfield, graphic artist

and illustrator, 1989-96; Academy of Art College, San Francisco, CA, instructor, 1999-2003; *Contra Costa Times,* Walnut Creek, CA, news artist, 1999-2003, graphics chief, 2003-05, presentation editor, 2005—. *Exhibitions:* Springfield Art Museum, Springfield, MO, 1989; "Private Apparitions," Springfield, 1990; The Annual Show, San Francisco Society of Illustrators, San Francisco, CA, 1997; and Spring Show, Academy of Art College, San Francisco, 1997, 1998, 1999.

Awards, Honors

First place for informational graphic, Missouri Press Association, 1993; third place and two honorable mentions for informational graphics, Kansas and Missouri Associated Press Graphics Contest, 1994; first place for informational graphics, Kansas and Missouri Associated Press Graphics Contest, 1996; awards from East Bay Press Club, 1999, 2001; awards from California Newspaper Publishers Association, 2001, 2002, 2003, 2004; awards from Society of Newspaper Design, 2002, 2006.

Illustrator

Gary Bogue, *The Raccoon Next Door: Getting Along with Urban Wildlife,* Heyday Books (Berkeley, CA), 2003.
Gary Bogue, *There's an Opossum in My Backyard,* Heyday Books (Berkeley, CA), 2007.

Also creator of *The Heart of Stone,* a graphic novel based on "A Fratricide" by Franz Kafka.

Biographical and Critical Sources

PERIODICALS

Booklist, August, 2007, Ilene Cooper, review of *There's an Opossum in My Backyard,* p. 86.
School Library Journal, February, 2008, Susan E. Murray, review of *There's an Opossum in My Backyard,* p. 83.

ONLINE

Chuck Todd Home Page, http://www.chucktodd.net (November 1, 2008).*

*   *   *

TREWELLARD, J.M.
(Juliet Trewellard)

Personal

Born in England; children: two. *Education:* Attended Sussex University and Central School of Speech and Drama.

Addresses

Home—Cornwall, England, and London, England.

Career

Writer. Has worked as an actor; founder and artistic director of a touring theatre company in Cornwall, England. Has also taught literature and theatre studies.

Writings

Butterfingers, illustrated by Ian Beck, David Fickling Books (New York, NY), 2007.

Also author of stage plays, radio plays, poems, and short stories.

Sidelights

J.M. Trewellard, an actor, theater director, and educator, is the author of the fairy tale *Butterfingers,* her first work for children. Trewellard, who attended the Central School of Speech and Drama in London and founded a touring theatre company, also pens short stories, plays, and poetry.

Butterfingers centers on Ned, a clumsy, good-hearted stable boy who pines for the lovely Princess Bella. When the princess is snatched up by a fire-breathing dragon, Ned decides to mount a rescue attempt after the palace knights fail to save Bella. Taking possession of Bella's golden ball, Ned sets out on his dangerous mission, accompanied by Dilly the pony and Tuff the dog. Along the way, they encounter a host of talking animals, including an otter, a lark, and a fox, who join them on their quest.

Butterfingers earned generally strong reviews. Writing in *School Library Journal,* Kelly Roth recommended Trewellard's "well-told story [as] . . . a simple fantasy for beginning chapter-book readers." Other reviewers praised the fantasy elements in the story. Debbie Carton, writing in *Booklist,* noted that "readers will appreciate the lovable and distinct characteristics each animal brings to the rescue team." A critic in *Kirkus Reviews* observed that Trewellard "kicks up her debut with tried-and-true folktale motifs."

Biographical and Critical Sources

PERIODICALS

Booklist, December 1, 2007, Debbie Carton, review of *Butterfingers,* p. 38.
Kirkus Reviews, July 15, 2007, review of *Butterfingers.*
School Library Journal, September, 2007, Kelly Roth, review of *Butterfingers,* p. 1778.

ONLINE

Random House Web site, http://www.randomhouse.co.uk/ (December 15, 2008), "J.M. Trewellard."*

TREWELLARD, Juliet
  See **TREWELLARD, J.M.**

U-V

UHLIG, Richard 1970-

Personal

Born February 19, 1970, in Herington, KS; son of a doctor and an office manager; married. *Education:* Attended New York University.

Addresses

Home—New York, NY. *E-mail*—author@richarduhlig. com.

Career

Novelist and screenwriter. Has taught at Gotham Writer's Workshop and Wilkes University.

Writings

NOVELS

Last Dance at the Frosty Queen, Knopf (New York, NY), 2007.
Boy minus Girl, Knopf (New York, NY), 2008.

SCREENPLAYS

(With Steve Seitz) *Viva Las Nowhere,* (released on video as *Dead Simple*), Franchise Pictures, 2001.
Kept, Phoenician Entertainment, 2001.

Sidelights

A native of Kansas, Richard Uhlig has set his two well-received young-adult novels, *Last Dance at the Frosty Queen* and *Boy minus Girl,* in his home state. Uhlig, who originally pursued a career as a film director, wrote a number of screenplays before turning his attention to novels. "Reading and writing books is wonderful because it's so personal—it's you, alone, taking in what the author has written," he stated in an essay on the *Random House* Web site. "There's no laugh track to tell you something is funny, no composer writing songs to tell you when to cry. It's you and the written word. The author provides you images, dialogue, and plot, but it's up to you, the reader, to fill in the details based on your own experiences."

Last Dance at the Frosty Queen centers on Arty Flood, a high-school senior who desperately wants to escape the stifling, small-town atmosphere of Harker City, Kansas. Arty's life is full of complications, however; his father's funeral business is failing, the sheriff has blackmailed Arty into dating his daughter, and the teen is having an affair with one of his teachers. After he meets Vanessa, a California beauty who comes to Harker for a short stay, he begins to see his hometown in a new light. A critic in *Publishers Weekly* credited Uhlig with creating a likable protagonist, noting that Arty's "ambitions to make a future for himself and his desires loom at least as large as the outrageous situations that bedevil him." Writing in *School Library Journal,* Amy S. Pattee remarked that the author's "evocation of small-town life is perfect: everybody is in everybody else's business, and the townspeople's odd enterprises are well described."

In *Boy minus Girl,* eighth-grader Les Ekhardt dreads the thought of spending another dull summer with his parents until Uncle Ray, a free-wheeling bachelor who loves booze and women, arrives in town. Though Les clearly idolizes his uncle, the youngster has a change of heart after he learns that Ray has run from trouble. Reviewing Uhlig's middle-grade novel for *Booklist,* contributor Frances Bradburn called *Boy minus Girl* "a substantive young-adult novel" and described the characters as "vivid and authentic."

Biographical and Critical Sources

PERIODICALS

Booklist, July 1, 2007, Lynn Rutan, review of *Last Dance at the Frosty Queen,* p. 49; September 15, 2008, Frances Bradburn, review of *Boy minus Girl,* p. 59.

Kirkus Reviews, July 15, 2007, review of *Last Dance at the Frosty Queen;* November 15, 2008, review of *Boy minus Girl.*

Kliatt, July, 2007, Myrna Marler, review of *Last Dance at the Frosty Queen,* p. 21.

Publishers Weekly, August 13, 2007, review of *Last Dance at the Frosty Queen,* p. 68.

School Library Journal, July 1, 2007, Amy S. Pattee, review of *Last Dance at the Frosty Queen,* p. 138.

ONLINE

Random House Web site, http://www.randomhouse.com/ (November 10, 2008, "Author Spotlight: Richard Uhlig."

Richard Uhlig Home Page, http://www.richarduhlig.com (November 10, 2008).

* * *

van STRAATEN, Harmen 1961-

Personal

Born 1961, in Arnheim, Netherlands. *Education:* Attended Leiden University.

Addresses

Office—Uitgeverij Pimento, Postbus, 1001 AK Amsterdam, Netherlands. *E-mail*—info@harmenvanstraaten.nl.

Career

Author and illustrator. Also worked as a lawyer and a teacher.

Awards, Honors

Grand Prix for Best Book, 2002; Golden Apple, Biennial of Illustrations Bratislava, 2003; Sankei Children's Book Award, 2003.

Writings

SELF-ILLUSTRATED

Betoverd door jou, Uitgeverij Pimento (Amsterdam, Netherlands), 2005.

Luchtacrobaten, Uitgeverij Pimento (Amsterdam, Netherlands), 2006.

Duck's Tale, translated by Marianne Martens, North-South Books (New York, NY), 2007.

For Me?, translated by MaryChris Bradley, North-South Books (New York, NY), 2007.

Also author of numerous works published in the Netherlands, including *Fien telt voor tien, De liefste kusjes zijn voor jou, Spuit Elf en de brandweerolifanten, Het verhaal van eend, De wedstrijd van eend, Eend tovert een taart, Eend ziet wat jij niet ziet, Kees en Ko detectivebureau, Kees en Ko en de scooterbende, Tim en de boot naar Timboektoe, Tim en de tsjoek tsjoek tovertrein, Tim en de toet toet toeringbus, Tim en de sneeuwman, Timsalabim, Tim gaat naar Verweggistan, Tim en de berg van goud, Tim is een bink, Tim in Robotland,* and *Tim en de vliegmachine.*

Sidelights

Harmen van Straaten is a prolific Dutch author and illustrator who has produced more than 200 works for young readers. *Duck's Tale,* the first of van Straaten's book to be translated into English, introduced him to U.S. audiences in 2007. After seeing that his friend, Toad, can read after getting a new pair of glasses, Duck assumes that he should be able to write a story when he discovers a pen. A serious-minded fellow, Duck scribbles on a sheet of paper and proudly hands his composition to Toad, who liberally interprets the "story" during a read-aloud session with Duck, Otter, and Hedgehog. According to *School Library Journal* contributor Kristen M. Todd, "the warm, softly colored illustrations suit the calm atmosphere of the story." In *Duck's Tale,* "respect for each other and friendship are key words," van Straaten told an interviewer on the *North-South Books* Web site. The author continued, "In this story, both Duck and Toad realize that they need each other. Duck can't read the story himself and from Toad, we are not sure if he can read at all. However, they are very respectful towards each other."

In a follow-up, *For Me?,* Duck, Toad, Otter, and Hedgehog attempt to learn the identity of the anonymous individual who has left a red rose and a drawing of a heart at each of their doorsteps. A *Kirkus Reviews* critic noted that van Straaten's "illustrations executed in bold lines and primary color washes capture the confusion and eventual camaraderie of these puzzled pals." A contributor in *Publishers Weekly* described the characters as "vividly imagined and drawn," and Shelley B. Sutherland, writing in *School Library Journal,* complimented *For Me?* for its "sweet simplicity."

Biographical and Critical Sources

PERIODICALS

Kirkus Reviews, March 15, 2007, review of *Duck's Tale;* July 15, 2007, review of *For Me?*

Publishers Weekly, January 21, 2008, review of *For Me?,* p. 169.

School Library Journal, May, 2007, Kristen M. Todd, review of *Duck's Tale,* p. 110; January, 2008 Shelley B. Sutherland, review of *For Me?,* p. 100.

ONLINE

Harmen van Straaten Home Page, http://www.harmenvan straaten.nl (April 1, 2008).

North-South Books Web site, http://www.northsouth.com/ (April 1, 2008), interview with van Straaten.*

* * *

VARON, Sara

Personal

Born in Chicago, IL. *Education:* School of Visual Arts (New York, NY), M.F.A. *Hobbies and other interests:* Movies, bike riding, dogs.

Addresses

Home—Brooklyn, NY. *E-mail*—sara.varon@gmail.com.

Career

Comics artist, printmaker, and illustrator

Awards, Honors

Runner-up for best animation, South by Southwest, and director's citation, Black Maria Film Festival, both 1998, both for *The Tongue;* Harvey Award nomination for Best New Talent, 2004; Parents' Choice Silver Honor, 2006, and *Kirkus Reviews* Best Children's Books designation, and *Publishers Weekly* Best Books designation, both 2007, all for *Chicken and Cat.*

Writings

SELF-ILLUSTRATED PICTURE BOOKS

Chicken and Cat, Scholastic (New York, NY), 2006.
Robot Dreams, First Second Books (New York, NY), 2007.
Chicken and Cat Clean Up, Scholastic (New York, NY), 2009.

OTHER

Creator of animated film *The Tongue,* 1997. Creator of graphic novels *Sweaterweather,* Alternative Comics, and *The Present.* Contributor to numerous periodicals, including *New York Times* and *National Post,* and to anthologies, including *Declare Yourself,* HarperTeen.

Sidelights

Sara Varon, a comic-book artist, printmaker, and illustrator based in Brooklyn, New York, is the creator of a number of graphic novels, including *Robot Dreams,* as well as the wordless picture book *Chicken and Cat.* "I just really like stories and storytelling," Varon remarked to *Comicreaders.com* interviewer Dana Tillusz. "I am kind of quiet and not particularly articulate, so it's nice to have an alternative to telling stories with words."

In *Chicken and Cat,* her first self-illustrated work for young readers, Varon depicts the friendship between a city-dwelling chicken and her feline visitor from the country. Upon arriving in New York City, Cat is taken aback by the drab sights, loud noises, and overpowering smells of the urban environment. Despite trips to Central Park, where the pair ride bikes rides and eat ice cream, and Coney Island, where they frolic on the beach, Chicken is unable to lift her friend's troubled spirits. When Chicken notices that a daffodil brightens Cat's mood, however, the duo concoct a plan to spruce up the view from Cat's apartment window.

Noting the autobiographical elements in *Chicken and Cat,* Varon told *Publishers Weekly* interviewer Rick Margolis, "I thought it was a story about me and my friend Sheila, who comes to visit a lot from Chicago, which is where I'm from. I thought she was the chicken, and I was the cat. She's a really good friend of mine, and our friendship was the basis for the two characters." Critics praised the work; *Horn Book* reviewer Kitty Flynn noted that Varon "brings a hip, droll sensibility" to her tale, and a *Publishers Weekly* contributor stated that her "quiet characters look equally kitschy and good-natured, and her earthy palette suits the city environment." According to Susan Weitz, writing in *School Library Journal, Chicken and Cat* "is packed with details that kids will relish discovering in successive readings."

In her interview with Tillusz, Varon noted that many of her stories feature animal characters. She remarked that "one thing that's nice about using animals is that they have qualities that people automatically associate with them. Like a goat or a raccoon really likes to eat garbage. Or that a bear spends the winter sleeping. Or that a snowman can only stick around until the seasons change. Since my stories are really simple, using a specific animal can be a device for providing background info on a character."

In *Robot Dreams,* a nearly wordless graphic novel, Varon examines friendship, change, and loss. Dog orders a build-your-own-robot kit through the mail and, after completing the assembly, begins a series of adventures with his metallic companion. During an ill-fated trip to the beach, the saltwater corrodes Robot's body, rendering him immobile, and Dog must abandon him on the sand. Over the next year, Dog attempts to fill the void in his heart by starting friendships with a variety of other creatures, while Robot, his body battered by the elements, dreams of being rescued. According to a critic in *Kirkus Reviews,* Varon denies readers a stereotypically happy ending, instead "offering them the harder-edged truth that friendships change and die—but

Sara Varon enlivens her self-illustrated picture book Chicken and Cat *with her unique cartoon art.* (Copyright © 2006 by Sara Varon. Reproduced by permission of Scholastic, Inc.)

others can rise in their place." Writing in *School Library Journal*, Andrea Lipinski called the work "by turns funny and poignant," and *Booklist* contributor Kevin King remarked that although Varon's "story line seems equally simple, it is invested with true emotion."

Biographical and Critical Sources

PERIODICALS

Booklist, February 1, 2006, Jennifer Mattson, review of *Chicken and Cat*, p. 59; August, 2007, Kevin King, review of *Robot Dreams*, p. 71.

Horn Book, March-April, 2006, Kitty Flynn, review of *Chicken and Cat*, p. 177.

Kirkus Reviews, January 1, 2006, review of *Chicken and Cat*, p. 46; July 1, 2007, review of *Robot Dreams*.

Publishers Weekly, January 30, 2006, review of *Chicken and Cat*, p. 69; August 13, 2007, review of *Robot Dreams*, p. 67.

School Library Journal, May, 2006, Rick Margolis, "Hip Chick, Cool Cat: Artist Sara Varon Talks about Her First Children's Book—A Sweet Wordless Wonder," p. 43, and Susan Weitz, review of *Chicken and Cat*, p. 106; September, 2007, Andrea Lipinski, review of *Robot Dreams*, p. 225.

ONLINE

Comicreaders.com, http://www.comicreaders.com/ (November 10, 2008), Dana Tillusz, "Sara Varon."

Sara Varon Home Page, http://www.chickenopolis.com (November 10, 2008).

Walker Art Center Web log, http://blogs.walkerart.org/ (July 18, 2006), Paul Schmelzer, "Profile: Comic-book Artist Sara Varon."

VAUGHT, Susan 1965-

Personal

Born October 22, 1965. *Education:* University of Mississippi, B.A.; Vanderbilt University, M.S., Ph.D. *Hobbies and other interests:* Books, cats, dogs, birds, and history.

Addresses

E-mail—susan@susanvaught.com.

Career

Neuropsychologist and author. Staff neuropsychologist, director of neuropsychology, and clinical director for a post-acute head injury hospital in Tennessee.

Awards, Honors

Temple University Health Sciences Center, PA, fellowship; Carl Brandon Kindred Award for best novel, Carl Brandon Society, 2006, for *Stormwitch.*

Writings

YOUNG ADULT NOVELS

Fat Tuesday, OnStage Publishing (Decatur, AL), 2004.
(With Debbie Tanner Federici) *L.O.S.T.,* Llewellyn Publications (St. Paul, MN), 2004.
(With Debbie Tanner Federici) *Shadowqueen: The L.O.S.T. Story Continues,* Llewellyn Publications (Woodbury, MN), 2005.
Stormwitch, Bloomsbury Children's Books (New York, NY), 2005.
(With Debbie Tanner Federici) *Witch Circle,* Llewellyn Worldwide (Woodbury, MN), 2006.
Trigger, Bloomsbury Children's Books (New York, NY), 2006.
Big Fat Manifesto, Bloomsbury Children's Books (New York, NY), 2007.
Exposed, Bloomsbury Children's Books (New York, NY), 2008.
(With J.B. Redmond) *Assassin's Apprentice,* Bloomsbury Children's Books (New York, NY), 2009.

Sidelights

A practicing neuropsychologist, Susan Vaught is also the author of young-adult novels that include *Stormwitch, Trigger, Big Fat Manifesto,* and *Exposed.* As a neuropsychologist, Vaught has found working with teens to be a significant source of inspiration; on the *Stay Alive* Web site the author stated: "No matter how busy I get, the voices of my teen patients live in my mind and heart." Vaught went on to say that these voices unite in Jersey Hatch, protagonist and narrator of *Trigger.*

In *Trigger,* a failed suicide attempt renders Jersey physically deformed, brain damaged, and unable to remember the preceding year. The book chronicles his effort to make sense of the past and present and to discover what led him to pull the trigger in the first place, all while navigating multiple handicaps and prejudices. Claire E. Gross, a reviewer for *Horn Book,* remarked that Vaught's "portrayal of brain damage is precise, comprehensible (but never condescending), and seamlessly woven into Jersey's narrative voice." However, *School Library Journal* contributor Hillias J. Martin felt that the narrator's "abstract patterns of thought and mutterings are perhaps too realistic for less-determined readers." A *Kirkus* review further noted a "tendency to essentialize good and evil characters." Nevertheless, *Curled up with a Good Kid's Book* reviewer Jocelyn Pearce called the book "powerful, moving, and emotional," and stated that Vaught "manages to get readers inside of Jersey's (damaged) mind in a way that makes them sympathize completely with him."

While dark realism characterized *Trigger,* mysticism plays a significant role in many of Vaught's other books for teens, including *L.O.S.T., Shadowqueen: The L.O.S.T. Story Continues,* and *Witch Circle,* all written with Debbie Tanner Federici. Vaught's award-winning *Stormwitch* is also a mystical novel for young adults. The story features Ruba, a Haitian girl raised by her grandmother Ba, an African warrior who uses magic to fight storms. After Ba dies battling a tempest, Ruba moves to segregated Mississippi, where, despite pressure to relinquish her beliefs and native customs, she must use the magic Ba taught her to combat Hurricane Camille. Gerry Larson, writing in the *School Library Journal,* thought some of the plot elements were "far-fetched," but felt that Ruba is "an intriguing adolescent mix of cultural pride, emotional insecurity, and stubborn determination." On the other hand, a critic for the *Endicott Studio for Mythic Arts* Web site found the plot "gripping" and observed that "the novel manages to succinctly touch [on] many themes: the search for identity, the brutality of racism, and the powerful force of love and compassion when mixed with courage and conviction."

Biographical and Critical Sources

PERIODICALS

Booklist, February 15, 2005, Gillian Engberg, review of *Stormwitch,* p. 1074; December 1, 2006, Holly Koelling, review of *Trigger,* p. 45; December 15, 2007, Ilene Cooper, review of review of *Big Fat Manifesto,* p. 42; November 15, 2008, Michael Cart, review of *Exposed,* p. 37.
Horn Book, September-October, 2006, Claire E. Gross, review of *Trigger,* p. 598.
Kirkus, December 15, 2004, review of *Stormwitch,* p. 1210; September 1, 2006, review of *Trigger;* Novem-

ber 15, 2007, review of *Big Fat Manifesto;* November 1, 2008, review of *Exposed.*

Publishers Weekly, November 20, 2006, review of *Trigger,* p. 61; January 7, 2008, review of *Big Fat Manifesto,* p. 56; November 10, 2008, review of *Exposed,* p. 51.

School Library Journal, January, 2005, Saleena L. Davidson, review of *L.O.S.T.,* p. 128; May, 2005, Gerry Larson, review of *Stormwitch,* p. 140; October, 2005, Michele Capozzella, review of *Shadowqueen: The L.O.S.T. Story Continues,* p. 160; November, 2006, Hillias J. Martin, review of *Trigger,* p. 156; January, 2008, Miranda Doyle, review of *Big Fat Manifesto,* p. 128.

ONLINE

Curled up with a Good Kid's Book Web site, http://www.curledupkids.com/ (February 28, 2007), Jocelyn Pearce, review of *Trigger.*

Endicott Studio for Mythic Arts Web site, http://endicottstudio.typepad.com/ (March 7, 2007), review of *Stormwitch.*

Stay Alive Web site, http://www.susanvaught.moonfruit.com/ (February 28, 2007), "Susan Vaught."

Suite101.com, http://teenfiction.suite101.com/ (February 16, 2007), Mechele R. Dillard, interview with Vaught.

Susan Vaught Home Page, http://www.susanvaught.com (February 28, 2007).*

W-Y

WALLACE, Daisy
See CUYLER, Margery

*   *   *

WALSH, Marissa 1972-
(Marissa "Mitzy" Walsh)

Personal

Born June 8, 1972. *Education:* Smith College, B.A., 1994.

Addresses

Home—New York, NY.

Career

Author and editor. Former children's book editor, New York, NY; instructor at Gotham Writers' Workshop.

Writings

American Idol: The Search for a Superstar—The Official Book, Bantam (New York, NY), 2002.

(As Marissa "Mitzy" Walsh; with Matt "Johnnie" Walker) *Tipsy in Madras: A Complete Guide to '80s Preppy Drinking, Including Proper Attire, Cocktails for Every Occasion, the Best Beer, the Right Mixers, and More!,* Perigee (New York, NY), 2004.

(Editor) *Not like I'm Jealous or Anything: The Jealousy Book,* Delacorte (New York, NY), 2006.

Girl with Glasses: My Optic History (memoir), Simon Spotlight Entertainment (New York, NY), 2006.

A Field Guide to High School (novel), Delacorte (New York, NY), 2007.

(Editor) *Does This Book Make Me Look Fat?,* Clarion (New York, NY), 2008.

Sidelights

Marissa Walsh is the author and editor of a number of books for young adults, including *A Field Guide to High School,* her debut novel. In *Not like I'm Jealous or Anything: The Jealousy Book,* a collection of essays, short stories, and poems concerning the "green-eyed monster," Walsh includes works by such authors as Jaclyn Moriarty, E. Lockhart, and Susan Juby. "I Think They Got Your Numbah," a tale by Siobhan Adcock, centers on a girl who longs to throw a huge birthday party to impress her friends, and "A Genius for Sauntering" is a short story by Thatcher Heldring that depicts a friendship which dissolves after the purchase of a car. Reviewing *Not like I'm Jealous or Anything* in *Booklist,* Frances Bradburn stated that Walsh's selections provide "the right mix of situations and characters to make readers slightly uncomfortable." *School Library Journal* contributor Rhona Campbell described the volume as "an entertaining read and a good invitation to introspection," and a critic in *Kirkus Reviews* remarked that "the pieces are well-written and entertaining, and the collection is cohesively crafted."

In *Girl with Glasses: My Optic History* Walsh presents a series of essays that chronicle her experiences with a variety of eyeglasses, from clunky monstrosities to chic designer specs. According to *Memoirville* online contributor Rachel Kramer Bussel, Walsh "names each pair ('The Too Cool for School Pair,' 'The If You Can Make It There Pair') and guides us through various schools, jobs, apartments, and relationships, where how she was seen was just as important as her own vision." Originally planned as a work of nonfiction, *Girl with Glasses* evolved into something much more personal, Walsh remarked to Bussel. "It became this timeline, the chronology of my eyewear." "It became clear that each pair did represent that time in my life so there could be a larger discussion of what was going on for me, that could be universal." Wearing eyeglasses, Walsh continued, is "a form of self-expression, because there is this stereotype about women who wear glasses as being either prudish or uptight or smart and certainly, as with every stereotype, it comes out of some truth." She added, "Women who choose to wear glasses are working against that stereotype. 'It's okay if you think I'm smart because I am,' and I think that's interesting that people are just embracing it now and trying to own it more."

A Field Guide to High School, a work of young-adult fiction, centers on the bond between two vastly different siblings. Andie, a high-school-freshman-to-be, discovers a handwritten guidebook left behind by Yale-bound older sister, Claire, that is intended to help Andie navigate the treacherous waters at prestigious Plumstead Country Day School. With her best friend, Bess, Andie pours through the manual, noting what to wear, who to meet, and how to be successful. The "book-within-the-book idea is an interesting one," a contributor in *Kirkus Reviews* stated, and *School Library Journal* reviewer Emily Garrett commented that "Claire's voice is witty and wry and easy to read." Filled with pop-culture references, *A Field Guide to High School* "is cute and trendy," as Janis Flint-Ferguson remarked in *Kliatt.*

Biographical and Critical Sources

BOOKS

Walsh, Marissa, *Girl with Glasses: My Optic History,* Simon Spotlight Entertainment (New York, NY), 2006.

PERIODICALS

Booklist, February 1, 2006, Frances Bradburn, review of *Not like I'm Jealous or Anything: The Jealousy Book,* p. 45; June 1, 2007, Heather Booth, review of *A Field Guide to High School,* p. 57.

Kirkus Reviews, January 15, 2006, review of *Not like I'm Jealous or Anything,* p. 90; July 15, 2007, review of *A Field Guide to High School.*

Kliatt, July, 2006, Olivia Durant, review of *Not like I'm Jealous or Anything,* p. 31; July, 2007, Janis Flint-Ferguson, review of *A Field Guide to High School,* p. 21.

Publishers Weekly, March 20, 2006, review of *Not like I'm Jealous or Anything,* p. 58; August 6, 2007, review of *A Field Guide to High School,* p. 190.

School Library Journal, April, 2006, Rhona Campbell, review of *Not like I'm Jealous or Anything,* p. 164; September, 2007, Emily Garrett, review of *A Field Guide to High School,* p. 209.

ONLINE

Memoirville Web site, http://www.smithmag.net/memoirville/ (March 5, 2007), Rachel Kramer Bussel, interview with Walsh.*

* * *

WALSH, Marissa "Mitzy"
See WALSH, Marissa

WILLIS, Jeanne 1959-

Personal

Born November 5, 1959, in St. Albans, Hertfordshire, England; daughter of David Alfred (a language teacher) and Dorothy Hilda Celia (a teacher of domestic science) Willis; married Ian James Wilcock (an animator), May 26, 1989; children: one son, one daughter. *Education:* Watford College of Art, diploma in advertising writing, 1979.

Addresses

Home—London, England. *Agent*—Rod Hall Agency Ltd., Fairgate House, 78 Oxford St., 6th Fl., London WC1A 1HB, England.

Career

Children's book author. Doyle, Dane, Berenbach, London, England, advertising copywriter, 1979–81; Young & Rubicam Ltd., London, senior writer, group head, and member of board of directors, c. 1980s.

Member

British Herpetological Association.

Awards, Honors

Top Ten Picture Books designation, *Redbook,* 1987, for *The Monster Bed;* Whitbread Award nomination, 2003, for *Naked without a Hat;* Smarties Silver Medal, 2004, for *Tadpole's Promise;* recipient of several advertising industry awards.

Writings

The Tale of Georgie Grub, Andersen (London, England), 1981, Holt (New York, NY), 1982.

The Tale of Fearsome Fritz, Andersen (London, England), 1982, Holt (New York, NY), 1983.

The Tale of Mucky Mabel, Andersen (London, England), 1984.

The Monster Bed, illustrated by Susan Varley, Andersen (London, England), 1986, Lothrop, (New York, NY), 1987.

The Long Blue Blazer, illustrated by Susan Varley, Andersen (London, England), 1987, Dutton (New York, NY), 1988.

Toffee Pockets (poems), illustrated by George Buchanan, Bodley Head (London, England), 1992.

In Search of the Hidden Giant, illustrated by Ruth Brown, Andersen (London, England), 1993, published as *In Search of the Giant,* Dutton (New York, NY), 1994.

The Lion's Roar, illustrated by Derek Collin, Ginn (London, England), 1994.

The Rascally Cake, illustrated by Paul Korky, Andersen (London, England), 1994.

Two Sea Songs, Ginn (London, England), 1994.

The Monster Storm, illustrated by Susan Varley, Andersen (London, England), Lothrop (New York, NY), 1995.

Dolly Dot, Ginn (London, England), 1995.

Flower Pots and Forget–Me–Nots, Ginn (London, England), 1995.

Wilbur and Orville Take Off, illustrated by Roger Wade Walker, Macdonald Young (Hemel Hempstead, England), 1995.

The Princess and the Parlour Maid, illustrated by Pauline Hazelwood, Macdonald Young (Hemel Hempstead, England), 1995.

Tom's Lady of the Lamp, illustrated by Amy Burch, Macdonald Young (Hemel Hempstead, England), 1995.

The Pet Person, illustrated by Tony Ross, Dial (New York, NY), 1996.

The Pink Hare, illustrated by Ken Brown, Andersen (London, England), 1996.

What Do You Want to Be, Brian?, illustrated by Mary Rees, Andersen (London, England), 1996.

Sloth's Shoes, illustrated by Tony Ross, Andersen (London, England), 1997, Kane/Miller (Brooklyn, NY), 1998.

The Wind in the Wallows (poetry), illustrated by Tony Ross, Andersen (London, England), 1998.

The Boy Who Lost His Belly Button, illustrated by Tony Ross, Andersen (London, England), 1999, Dorling Kindersley (New York, NY), 2000.

Tinkerbill, illustrated by Paul Cox, Collins (London, England), 1999.

Susan Laughs, illustrated by Tony Ross, Andersen (London, England), 1999, Holt (New York, NY), 2000.

Take Turns, Penguin!, illustrated by Mark Birchall, Carolrhoda (Minneapolis, MN), 2000.

Parrot Goes to Playschool, illustrated by Mark Birchall, Andersen (London, England), 2000, published as *Be Quiet, Parrot!,* Carolrhoda (Minneapolis, MN), 2000.

What Did I Look like When I Was a Baby?, illustrated by Tony Ross, Putnam (New York, NY), 2000.

Do Little Mermaids Wet Their Beds?, illustrated by Penelope Jossen, Albert Whitman (Morton Grove, IL), 2001.

No Biting, Panther!, illustrated by Mark Birchall, Carolrhoda (Minneapolis, MN), 2001.

Be Gentle, Python!, illustrated by Mark Birchall, Carolrhoda (Minneapolis, MN), 2001.

No Biting, Puma!, Carolrhoda Books (Minneapolis, MN), 2001.

The Boy Who Thought He Was a Teddy Bear: A Fairy Tale, illustrated by Susan Varley, Peachtree (Atlanta, GA), 2002.

Don't Let Go!, illustrated by Tony Ross, Andersen (London, England), 2002, G.P. Putnam's Sons (New York, NY), 2003.

The Hard Man of the Swings (young-adult novel), Faber & Faber (London, England), 2000, published as *The Truth or Something,* Henry Holt (New York, NY), 2002.

Rocket Science, Faber Children's Books (London, England), 2002.

Sleepover!: The Best Ever Party Kit, illustrated by Lydia Monks, Candlewick Press (Cambridge, MA), 2002.

I Want to Be a Cowgirl, illustrated by Tony Ross, Henry Holt (New York, NY), 2002.

The Beast of Crowsfoot Cottage ("Shock Shop" series), Macmillan Children's Books (London, England), 2003.

Naked without a Hat (young-adult novel), Faber & Faber (London, England), 2003, Delacorte (New York, NY), 2004.

Adventures of Jimmy Scar, Andersen (London, England), 2003.

New Shoes, Andersen (London, England), 2003.

When Stephanie Smiled, illustrated by Penelope Jossen, Andersen (London, England), 2003.

Zitz, Glitz, and Body Blitz, illustrated by Lydia Monks, Walker Books (London, England), 2004.

Shhh!, illustrated by Tony Ross, Hyperion Books for Children (New York, NY), 2004.

I Hate School, illustrated by Tony Ross, Atheneum Books for Young Readers (New York, NY), 2004.

Bits, Boobs, and Blobs, illustrated by Lydia Monks, Walker Books (London, England), 2004.

Snogs, Sex, and Soulmates, illustrated by Lydia Monks, Walker Books (London, England), 2004.

Manky Monkey illustrated by Tony Ross, Andersen (London, England), 2004.

The Magic Potty Show with Trubble and Trixie, illustrated by Edward Eaves, Pan MacMillan (London, England), 2004.

Misery Moo, illustrated by Tony Ross, Henry Holt (New York, NY), 2005.

Tadpole's Promise, illustrated by Tony Ross, Atheneum Books for Young Readers (New York, NY), 2005.

Operation Itchy, illustrated by Penny Dann, Candlewick Press (Cambridge, MA), 2005.

Never Too Little to Love, illustrated by Jan Fearnley, Candlewick Press (Cambridge, MA), 2005.

Secret Fairy Talent Show ("Secret Fairy" series), illustrated by Penny Dann, Orchard Books (London, England), 2005.

Dumb Creatures, illustrated by Nicola Slater, Macmillan Children's Books (London, England), 2005.

Daft Bat, illustrated by Tony Ross, Andersen (London, England), 2006, Sterling Publishing (New York, NY), 2008.

Really Rude Rhino, illustrated by Tony Ross, Andersen (London, England), 2006.

Dozy Mare, Andersen (London, England), 2006.

Mayfly Day, Andersen (London, England), 2006.

Gorilla! Gorilla!, illustrated by Tony Ross, Atheneum Books for Young Readers (New York, NY), 2006.

Rat Heaven, Macmillan Children's Books (London, England), 2006.

Deliah Darling Is in the Library, illustrated by Rosie Reeve, Puffin (London, England), 2006, published as *Delilah D. at the Library,* Clarion Books (New York, NY), 2007.

Who's in the Bathroom?, illustrated by Adrian Reynolds, Simon & Schuster Books for Young Readers (New York, NY), 2007.

Grill Pan Eddy, illustrated by Tony Ross, Andersen (London, England), 2007.

Killer Gorilla, Andersen (London, England), 2007.

Deliah Darling Is in the Classroom, illustrated by Rosie Reeve, Puffin (London, England), 2007.

The Monster Bed, illustrated by Susan Varley, Andersen (London, England), 2007.

Grandad and John, illustrated by Jessica Meserve, Walker Books (London, England), 2007.

Cottonwool Colin, illustrated by Tony Ross, Andersen (London, England), 2007, published as *Cottonball Colin,* Eerdmans (Grand Rapids, MI), 2008.

Shamanka, Walker Books (London, England), 2007, Candlewick Press (Somerville, MA), 2009.

Princess Candytuft, illustrated by Penny Dann, Orchard (London, England), 2007.

Mommy, Do You Love Me?, illustrated by Jan Feanley, Candlewick Press (Cambridge, MA), 2008.

Flabby Cat and Slobby Dog, illustrated by Tony Ross, Carolrhoda Books (Minneapolis, MN), 2009.

The Bog Baby, illustrated by Gwen Millward, Schwartz & Wade (New York, NY), 2009.

Writer of educational CD-ROM scripts for Dorling Kindersley; writer for television series, including *Marvelous Millie,* 1999; *The Ark,* 2002; *Dr. Xargle,* HTV/Cinar; *Maisy,* Polygram; *Dog and Duck,* United Films; and *The Slow Norris,* HTV/United.

"DR. XARGLE" SERIES; FOR YOUNG READERS

Dr. Xargle's Book of Earthlets, illustrated by Tony Ross, Andersen (London, England), 1988, published as *Earthlets, as Explained by Professor Xargle,* Dutton (New York, NY), 1989.

Dr. Xargle's Book of Earth Hounds, illustrated by Tony Ross, Anderson (London, England), 1989, published as *Earth Hounds, as Explained by Professor Xargle,* Dutton (New York, NY), 1990.

Dr. Xargle's Book of Earth Tiggers, illustrated by Tony Ross, Anderson (London, England), 1990, published as *Earth Tigerlets, as Explained by Professor Xargle,* Dutton (New York, NY), 1991.

Dr. Xargle's Book of Earth Mobiles, illustrated by Tony Ross, Andersen (London, England), 1991, published as *Earth Mobiles, as Explained by Professor Xargle,* Dutton (New York, NY), 1992.

Dr. Xargle's Book of Earth Weather, illustrated by Tony Ross, Anderson (London, England), 1992, published as *Earth Weather, as Explained by Professor Xargle,* Dutton (New York, NY), 1993.

Dr. Xargle's Book of Earth Relations, illustrated by Tony Ross, Andersen (London, England), 1993, published as *Relativity, as Explained by Professor Xargle,* Dutton (New York, NY), 1994.

"CRAZY JOBS" SERIES; FOR YOUNG READERS

Annie the Gorilla Nanny, illustrated by Paul Korky, Orchard Books (London, England), 2005.

Gabby the Vampire Cabby, illustrated by Paul Korky, Orchard Books (London, England), 2005.

Jeff, the Witch's Chef, illustrated by Paul Korky, Orchard Books (London, England), 2005.

Lillibet, the Monster Vet, illustrated by Paul Korky, Orchard Books (London, England), 2005.

Norman the Demon Doorman, illustrated by Paul Korky, Orchard Books (London, England), 2005.

Vanessa, the Werewolf Hairdresser, illustrated by Paul Korky, Orchard Books (London, England), 2005.

Bert the Fairies' Fashion Expert, illustrated by Paul Korky, Orchard Books (London, England), 2005.

Iddy Bogey the Ogre Yogi, illustrated by Paul Korky, Orchard Books (London, England), 2005.

Sidelights

British children's writer Jeanne Willis has penned a number of critically acclaimed books that instruct as well as amuse. A former advertising executive, Willis once said: "I had a very vivid imagination as a child. I think I felt everything deeply, and in many respects that was good. My happiness, my excitements, seemed to be bigger emotions than other children felt. The bad side of the coin is obvious: deep hurt, dreadful fears. Fear is the downside of having an active imagination. Because I was not confidently articulate, I exorcised these intense feelings on paper. I still do. One day somebody pointed out that such things were commercially viable, so they found their way into stories. One day I shall publish my poetry—my adult poetry. In the meantime, I have to go and feed my toads. Reptiles and amphibians are dear to my heart."

Born in 1959, in Hertfordshire, England, Willis is the daughter of two teachers. As she once recalled: "I grew up in a very safe, suburban environment. I went to a wonderful school which had a huge wheatfield growing next to our playground. I was a useless mathematician, but was one of the first to read and write creatively. I belonged to the World Wildlife Guard (now the Worldwide Guard for Wildlife) and had a bedroom full of strange creatures—locusts, stick insects, newts, caterpillars, etc. The fascination with these beasts has remained with me all my life. Indeed when I got married our blessing was held in the Aquarium at the London Zoo in front of the shark tank."

Willis first won acclaim for her "Professor Xargle" series of science books for early elementary grades. Initially published in England, each has been published under a revised title for U.S. audiences. The premise is the same throughout the series: the misinformed alien professor of the title tries to explain the odd life forms on Earth. He takes a scientific tone, but his lectures are full of comical errors. In *Dr. Xargle's Book of Earthlets,* for example, he strains to enlighten his class of fellow aliens about infant humans. He moves on to *Dr. Xargle's Book of Earth Hounds,* discussing dogs on the planet and how humans spread newspapers on the floor for their young "houndlets" to read. The professor tackles the subject of cats in *Dr. Xargle's Book of Earth Tiggers,* telling the class that felines' bizarre behavior includes planting "brown stinkseeds" that never grow and leaving "squishy puddings" on the stairs, through which humans then trod. Willis's "writing is fresh and fun, the scope of her imagination limitless," enthused a *Publishers Weekly* critic reviewing the American edition, titled *Earth Tigerlets, as Explained by Professor Xargle.*

Willis noted that her "Dr. Xargle" series is simply the result of realizing how absurd human and animal behavior is, and also a desire to believe in "the alien." "I'm sure they exist. In fact, I'm sure they're here already. I often get the feeling I'm on the wrong planet, so perhaps I'm one." In *Dr. Xargle's Book of Earth Mobiles* Xargle enlightens the class on the various modes of transportation on Earth, such as the very popular "stinkfumer," his term for the automobile. *Dr. Xargle's Book of Earth Weather* tackles meteorology. Humans, the professor explains, cope with wet weather by growing large rubber feet that they then have difficulty removing. During hot weather, they enjoy lying in what appears to be nests of brown sugar. "Subtle as well as slapstick humor will appeal to a wide variety of ages," noted Claudia Cooper in her assessment of *Earth Weather, as Explained by Professor Xargle* for *School Library Journal. Dr. Xargle's Book of Earth Relations,* the last title in the series, was published in the United States as *Relativity, as Explained by Professor Xargle.* Here the alien academic talks about human families and how they "belong to each other whether they like it or not."

Willis has also written poetry, including the volume *Toffee Pockets.* Featuring a number of poems about grandparents and grandchildren, the collection was described by *Books for Keeps* contributor Judith Sharman as "easy to read and comforting to hear." Other titles from Willis have used rhyme to tell a story for young readers, such as *In Search of the Hidden Giant.* In this story, a narrator and his sister trek through a forest determined to find the giant they believe lives there. They find many clues: tree roots, they assume, are strands of his hair, while the crackling of tree branches overhead seem to signify his presence to them. In a review of the U.S. edition, a *Publishers Weekly* critic noted that *In Search of the Giant* is deliberately vague, but "it often exemplifies a way of seeing that naturally delights children."

In *The Rascally Cake* Willis presents the rhyming tale of Rufus and his attempt to bake a Christmas cake. He uses so many dreadful ingredients that it turns into a monster and chases him. Wendy Timothy, in her review for *School Librarian,* called it "wonderfully horrid." Willis also uses humor in *The Pet Person,* a book about a dog's birthday wish for a "person" of his own. His dog parents try to dissuade him, reminding him that such creatures often develop revolting habits, such as eating at the table. In *Sloth's Shoes,* Willis describes a birthday party in the jungle for Sloth, who is so slow in getting there that he misses it entirely. In *Tinkerbill,* Willis's heroine, Sally, learns her parents are expecting a brother or sister for her. Unhappy about this coming

change, she makes a wish and believes it comes true when she begins to suspect that her new infant brother is a fairy. Andrea Rayner, writing in *School Librarian,* called *Tinkerbill* "a funny story about sibling rivalry," and one that "is not censorious about the child's jealousy."

Willis also created an amusing storyline for *What Did I Look like When I Was a Baby?* After a little boy asks his mother the title question, she replies that he looked bald and wrinkled like his grandfather. Across the subsequent pages, young animals in the jungle posit the same question to their mothers. Only the bullfrog is traumatized by the photograph of himself as a tadpole, and his friends must sing a song to get him to come out of hiding. "Ross's cartoonlike illustrations complement the puns and double entendres in the text," noted a *Publishers Weekly* reviewer.

The Boy Who Lost His Belly Button was described as "another whimsical offering from Willis," by *School Library Journal* reviewer Carolyn Janssen. The youngster wakes up one day, realizes that his navel has disappeared, and ventures into the jungle to look for it. He asks various animals, including a gorilla, lion, elephant, and even mouse, each of whom display their own belly buttons. He finally learns that a crocodile has stolen his navel and bravely enters a swamp to retrieve it—a scene that possesses "a cinematic–like tension," according to a *Publishers Weekly* critic. Another Willis title, *Susan Laughs,* is a rhyming tale about a little girl and her everyday activities and various moods. Only on the last page is she shown in her wheelchair, but the text reminds readers that she is "just like me, just like you." Hazel Rochman, writing in *Booklist,* praised a message that is conveyed "without being condescending or preachy."

Willis has also penned a series of picture books for very young readers about to embark on the preschool adventure to help them learn the rules of the classroom. *Parrot Goes to Playschool* features a parrot who talks incessantly, but finally gets his beak shut temporarily when he eats his elephant classmate's caramels. In *Take Turns, Penguin!* an ostrich teacher does not seem to notice Penguin's self–centeredness, but the other animal classmates step in to solve the problem themselves. Other titles in the series include *No Biting, Panther!, No Biting, Puma!,* and *Be Gentle, Python!*

Don't Let Go! is the story of a girl who asks her father to teach her to ride her two-wheel bike so that she can ride from her house, where she lives with her mother, to his, thus imparting a separate message about letting go and returning to those whom we love and who love us. The little boy of *The Boy Who Thought He Was a Teddy Bear: A Fairy Tale* spends his years with a group of bears after being deposited with them by fairies. When the bears return him to his human mother, the boy discovers that being a human is just as much fun.

The child in *I Want to Be a Cowgirl* tells her father that she wants to trade in her girly girl city lifestyle for a Western image and goes so far as to cut a pair of chaps out of their rug, acquire a cowgirl hat, and play guitar under make-believe Texas skies before her fantasy runs its course. Willis wrote a guide to help girls planning an overnight with their friends titled *Sleepover!: The Best Ever Party Kit.* The book contains ideas, recipes, games, invitations, beauty tips, and even ghost stories.

Mick Stokes is the narrator of Willis's young-adult novel set in postwar London, titled *The Truth or Something.* Mick grew up not knowing what happened to his baby sister. He is also ignorant of the truth about his father, a man who eventually sexually molests him, and his unstable mother, who serves time in jail. Eventually, Mick learns about his life and his large family, then moves on to find his place in the world. *School Library Journal* reviewer Todd Morning wrote that *The Truth or Something* "brilliantly captures a child's voice and point of view, subtly changing as the boy matures into an adolescent." In *Booklist* Anne O'Malley wrote that this is "a powerful novel with an appealing protagonist who struggles with the cruel hand dealt to him."

Naked without a Hat is the story of Will Avery, a developmentally slow nineteen-year-old man who leaves home and his mother to live with roommates Rocko, James, and landlady Chrissy. He also makes another friend in Zara, an Irish gypsy with whom he has a sexual relationship. *The Adventures of Jimmy Scar* follows Jimmy as he is taken by Gemma Diamond, a young girl who avoids being placed in foster care, and learns self-sufficiency from a female hermit named Monti, who lives in the forest. In *When Stephanie Smiled* Willis demonstrates how the smile of a girl can brighten the mood and academic performance of a young boy.

Willis pushes the envelope with her rhyming *I Hate School.* Here protagonist Honor Brown proclaims the mistreatment of her teachers. A *Publishers Weekly* reviewer wrote that children will "identify with and chuckle at her sense of drama." In *Never Too Little to Love* a tiny mouse stacks one thing on top of another to reach the object of its affection, and the award-winning *Tadpole's Promise* relates another love story, this one about a caterpillar and a polliwog who vow to love each other and promise never to change. The mother mouse in *Gorilla! Gorilla!* misinterprets the intent of the gorilla who follows her across the world in an attempt to return her lost baby. *School Library Journal* contributor Kathleen Kelly MacMillan noted that in addition to being a fine story, *Gorilla! Gorilla!* "subtly conveys a great message about prejudices."

Willis once remarked that her books "arrive in my head when they're ready, sometimes they write themselves. I did start a novel, but suddenly the characters started to misbehave and I lost control of them. It was quite frightening, it was a little like dabbling with the occult. If they were alter–egos, then they were better destroyed. I didn't want to be a part of their world."

"I have been interested in writing for as long as I can remember," the author more-recently commented. "I'm not sure what started it, but I have been doing it since I was five without a break. I have preserved copies of my first ever work of fiction written in 1965 in pencil and stitched together with a needle and green cotton.

"What influences my work? Pretty much everything— everywhere I go, everything I see, everyone I talk to can be turned into a story. I have too much material. It is exhausting. I pray for Writers Block (and I bet my editors do too). I usually write from nine in the morning til three in the afternoon. If I'm writing a novel, I may do nights and forget to go to bed. I usually have several books on the go at any time—a mixture of novels, picture books and novelty books.

"The most surprising thing I've learnt as a writer is that the books I work at the least are the best loved. Also that sometimes, when I re-read my own material, I can't remember having written some of it—which is rather nice because it's like reading someone else's book. My favourite picture book is probably *Tadpole's Promise* because it has all the elements I would hope to find in a picture book-great illustrations, an interesting format and a surprise ending."

Biographical and Critical Sources

PERIODICALS

Booklist, July, 1994, Julie Corsaro, review of *In Search of the Giant,* p. 1956; June 1, 1998, Annie Ayres, review of *Sloth's Shoes,* p. 1785; August, 2000, Hazel Rochman, review of *Susan Laughs,* p. 2151; December 1, 2000, Gillian Engberg, review of *Be Quiet, Parrot!,* and *Take Turns, Penguin!,* p. 727; December 15, 2000, Connie Fletcher, review of *What Did I Look like When I Was a Baby?,* p. 829; March 15, 2002, Kay Weisman, review of *I Want to Be a Cowgirl,* p. 1265; June 1, 2002, Anne O'Malley, review of *The Truth or Something,* p. 1710; July, 2004, Michael Cart, review of *Naked without a Hat,* p. 1835; February 1, 2005, Ilene Cooper, review of *Never Too Little to Love,* p. 966.

Books, April–May, 1996, review of *The Pet Person,* p. 26; summer, 1998, review of *The Wind in the Wallows,* p. 19.

Books for Keeps, March, 1993, Gill Roberts, review of *Dr. Xargle's Book of Earth Tiggers,* p. 11; May, 1993, Jeff Hynds, review of *In Search of the Hidden Giant,* p. 36; November, 1993, Judith Sharman, review of *Toffee Pockets,* p. 11, and Jessica Yates, review of *The Long Blue Blazer,* p. 26; May, 1994, Jill Bennett, review of *Dr. Xargle's Book of Earth Weather,* p. 12; July, 1995, Jill Bennett, review of *Dr. Xargle's Book of Earth Relations,* p. 11; July, 1999, Margaret Mallett, review of *Tom's Lady of the Lamp,* p. 3.

Books for Young Children, summer, 1991, Leonie Bennett, review of *The Tale of Mucky Mabel,* p. 5.

Guardian (London, England), January 7, 2004, Dina Rabinovitch, "Author of the Month: Jeanne Willis."

Horn Book, September, 1994, Hanna B. Zeiger, review of *In Search of the Giant,* p. 582; July-August, 2002, Susan P. Bloom, review of *The Truth or Something,* p. 474.

Junior Bookshelf, December, 1994, review of *The Rascally Cake,* p. 209; April, 1995, review of *In Search of the Hidden Giant,* p. 69.

Kirkus Reviews, June 1, 1991, review of *Earth Tigerlets, as Explained by Professor Xargle,* p. 738; December 1, 1991, review of *Earth Mobiles, as Explained by Professor Xargle,* p. 1541; May 1, 2002, review of *The Truth or Something,* p. 670; August 15, 2002, review of *The Boy Who Thought He Was a Teddy Bear: A Fairy Tale,* p. 1239; April 15, 2003, review of *Don't Let Go!,* p. 613; April, 2004, review of *Naked without a Hat,* p. 403; June 15, 2004, review of *I Hate School,* p. 583; May 15, 2005, review of *Tadpole's Promise,* p. 597; May 1, 2006, review of *Gorilla! Gorilla!,* p. 470.

Publishers Weekly, June 7, 1991, review of *Earth Tigerlets, as Explained by Professor Xargle,* p. 64; May 30, 1994, review of *In Search of the Giant,* p. 56; February 23, 1998, review of *Sloth's Shoes,* p. 76; May 22, 2000, review of *The Boy Who Lost His Belly Button,* p. 91; October 2, 2000, review of *What Did I Look like When I Was a Baby?,* p. 81; February 4, 2002, review of *I Want to Be a Cowgirl,* p. 76; May 20, 2002, review of *The Truth or Something,* p. 68; August 12, 2002, review of *The Boy Who Thought He Was a Teddy Bear,* p. 299; September 9, 2002, review of *Sleepover!: The Best Ever Party Kit,* p. 71; April 7, 2003, review of *Don't Let Go!,* p. 66; May 31, 2004, review of *Naked without a Hat,* p. 75; June 28, 2004, review of *I Hate School,* p. 49; December 6, 2004, review of *Never Too Little to Love,* p. 59; May 9, 2005, review of *Misery Moo,* p. 70; May 15, 2005, review of *Tadpole's Promise,* p. 597.

Reading Today, August, 2000, Lynne T. Burke, review of *Susan Laughs,* p. 32; April-May, 2006, David L. Richardson, review of *Tadpole's Promise,* p. 32.

School Librarian, August, 1992, Margaret Banerjee, review of *Toffee Pockets,* p. 111; April, 1994, Wendy Timothy, review of *The Rascally Cake,* p. 154; February, 1996, Teresa Scragg, review of *The Monster Storm,* p. 17; February, 1997, Trevor Dickinson, review of *The Pink Hare,* p. 22; April, 1999, Andrea Rayner, review of *Tinkerbill,* p. 201.

School Library Journal, April, 1991, John Peters, review of *Earth Hounds, as Explained by Professor Xargle,* p. 106; August, 1991, Rachel S. Fox, review of *Earth Tigerlets, as Explained by Professor Xargle,* p. 157; March, 1992, Joan McGrath, review of *Earth Mobiles, as Explained by Professor Xargle,* p. 226; April, 1993, Claudia Cooper, review of *Earth Weather, as Explained by Professor Xargle,* p. 104; March, 1995, Ronald Jobe, review of *Relativity, as Explained by Professor Xargle,* p. 195; August, 1998, Christy Norris Blanchette, review of *Sloth's Shoes,* p. 147; April, 1999, Carol Schene, review of *What Do You Want to Be, Brian?,* p. 110; May, 2000, Carolyn Janssen, review of *The Boy Who Lost His Belly Button,* p. 158; November, 2000, Linda M. Kenton, review of *Susan Laughs,* p. 137; January, 2001, Kathy M. Newby, reviews of *Be Quiet, Parrot!* and *Take Turns, Penguin!,* p. 112; September, 2001, Melinda Piehler, review of *Be Gentle, Python!,* p. 209; May, 2002, Todd Morning, review of *The Truth or Something,* p. 163; July, 2002, Ruth Semrau, review of *I Want to Be a Cowgirl,* p. 102; December, 2002, Barbara Buckley, review of *The Boy Who Thought He Was a Teddy Bear,* p. 112; June, 2004, Johanna Lewis, review of *Naked without a Hat,* p. 152; August, 2004, Marian Creamer, review of *I Hate School,* p. 104; September, 2004, Sally R. Dow, review of *When Stephanie Smiled,* p. 182; October, 2004, Beth Jones, review of *The Adventures of Jimmy Scar,* p. 182; May, 2005, Joy Fleishhacker, review of *Tadpole's Promise,* p. 104; June, 2005, Rachel G. Payne, review of *Misery Moo,* p. 131; July, 2006, Kathleen Kelly MacMillan, review of *Gorilla! Gorilla!,* p. 90.

ONLINE

Rod Hall Agency, Ltd. Web site, http://www.rodhallagency.com/ (August 22, 2006), "Jeanne Willis."
Teen Reads, http:// www.teenreads.com/ (August 22, 2006), Renee Kirchner, review of *Naked without a Hat.*
Walker Books Web site, http:// www.walkerbooks.co.uk/ (August 22, 2006), "Jeanne Willis."*

*   *   *

WOHNOUTKA, Mike

Personal

Born in Spicer, MN; married; children: Franklin, Olivia. *Education:* Savannah College of Art and Design, B.F.A., 1993.

Addresses

Home—Minneapolis, MN. *E-mail*—mwtka@yahoo.com.

Career

Illustrator and fine-art painter. Formerly worked as a designer for a gift company. *Exhibitions:* Work included in Original Art Show, Society of Illustrators, New York, NY, 2008.

Illustrator

Julie Glass, *Counting Sheep,* Random House (New York, NY), 2000.

David L. Harrison, *Johnny Appleseed: My Story,* Random House (New York, NY), 2001.

Kitty Griffin and Kathy Combs, *Cowboy Sam and Those Confounded Secrets,* Clarion (New York, NY), 2001.

Patricia Harrison Easton, *Davey's Blue-eyed Frog,* Clarion (New York, NY), 2003.

A loving relationship is captured in Mike Wohnoutka's humorous paintings for Marjorie Blain Parker's **Mama's Little Duckling.** (Illustration copyright 2008 by Mike Wohnoutka. All rights reserved. Reproduced by permission of Dutton Children's Books, a division of Penguin Putnam Books for Young Readers.)

Kitty Griffin and Kathy Combs, *The Foot-stomping Adventures of Clementine Sweet,* Clarion (New York, NY), 2004.

Stephen Krensky, *My Dad Can Do Anything,* Random House (New York, NY), 2004.

This Little Piggy, Kindermusik International (Greensboro, NC), 2005.

Gary Hogg, *Look What the Cat Dragged In!,* Dutton (New York, NY), 2005.

Roni Schotter, *When the Wizzy Foot Goes Walking,* Dutton (New York, NY), 2007.

Karen Magnuson Beil, *Jack's House,* Holiday House (New York, NY), 2008.

Marjorie Blain Parker, *Mama's Little Duckling,* Dutton (New York, NY), 2008.

Contributor to periodicals, including *Spider.*

Sidelights

A graduate of the Savannah College of Art and Design, Mike Wohnoutka works in advertising and editorial illustration, and he has provided the artwork for numerous children's books, including *Cowboy Sam and Those Confounded Secrets* by coauthors Kitty Griffin and Kathy Combs and *When the Wizzy Foot Goes Walking* by Roni Schotter.

Wohnoutka made his children's book debut by illustrating *Counting Sheep,* a story by Julie Glass. When a youngster struggles to fall asleep one night, he begins counting off a series of creatures, including sheep, kangaroos, monkeys, and bees, that enter his room. Wohnoutka creates "pleasing paintings that ably balance fantasy and humor," *Booklist* reviewer Carolyn Phelan stated of the picture book. Wohnoutka has also contributed the pictures for David L. Harrison's easy reader, *Johnny Appleseed: My Story.* In the tale, the legendary American figure offers his help to a pioneer family and then recounts his life for the children's amusement. Wohnoutka offers "buoyant paintings that capture the beauty of the landscape," Phelan noted.

Set in Dry Gulch, Texas, *Cowboy Sam and Those Confounded Secrets* is a tall tale by Griffin and Combs. The dedicated keeper of the residents' private thoughts, Cowboy Sam keeps every secret stashed under his ten-gallon hat. When the hat fills up, however, it begins popping off Sam's head, threatening to spill its contents. Sam tries to weigh down the hat with horseshoes and bags of oats, to no avail, until he concocts the perfect solution to the problem. A *Publishers Weekly* reviewer compared Wohnoutka's illustrations to those of Mark Teague, "particularly in their large-as-life perspectives and round, stylized faces, but the palette here is milder, brushed with the soft colors of the Southwest."

Wohnoutka also collaborated with Griffin and Combs on *The Foot-stomping Adventures of Clementine Sweet,* another humorous tale. Angered that her sixth birthday has been forgotten, Clementine disrupts a family re-union by stomping on the feet of her relatives, which soon becomes her trademark manner of expressing frustration. When a twister threatens her town, the youngster puts her strong legs to work for a good cause. According to *School Library Journal* critic Grace Oliff, the "acrylic cartoon illustrations provide a sunny landscape and a pugnacious heroine seen from a variety of amusing perspectives."

Writer Patricia Harrison Easton is helped by Wohnoutka in putting a visual twist on a familiar tale in her picture-book text for *Davey's Blue-eyed Frog.* After a spell transforms Princess Amelia into a frog, she is discovered by Davey, a youngster who despises the thought of kissing an amphibian and hates Amelia's bossy manner. "Wohnoutka's light, cartoony pencil illustrations keep the story hopping along," remarked a critic in *Kirkus Reviews,* and Phelan observed that in "sympathetic and often amusing depictions of the characters," Wohnoutka's illustrations "enhance the story's child appeal." In Gary Hogg's *Look What the Cat Dragged In!,* the members of the Lazybone family bully their frantic feline into completing numerous household chores. When the Lazybones contemplate getting a dog, however, the cat decides to even the score. Wohnoutka's "animated scenes put the right spin on the absurdity," wrote Julie Cummins in *Booklist.*

A work told in verse, Schotter's *When the Wizzy Foot Goes Walking* follows an energetic toddler throughout his day. Writing in *School Library Journal,* Amy Lilien-Harper commented that "Wohnoutka's boldly painted cartoons are full of motion and fit the story well." In *Mama's Little Duckling,* a read-aloud by Marjorie Blain Parker, Mama Quack cautiously watches over her inquisitive youngster, Dandelion Duckling, who loves exploring. When Dandelion alerts his mother to danger, though, she gains confidence in his abilities. Wohnoutka's illustrations for Parker's text again garnered praise. "Glowing with bold shades of turquoise, orange, gold, and green, the oversize illustrations vibrantly depict" the setting and action of the story, Judith Constantinides remarked in *School Library Journal.*

Wohnoutka told *SATA:* "Ever since I can remember I knew I wanted to be an artist. My dad, who was an engineer at the Highway Department, would bring home reams of paper that had highway plans on one side and were blank on the other. I would be so excited to have all that paper to draw on and would fill each sheet with race cars, snowmobiles, baseball players, super heroes, everything I was interested in. In high school my art teacher, Mr. Chase, encouraged me to pursue art as a career. This, along with a scholarship, led me to the Savannah College of Art and Design in Savannah, Georgia. Since graduating with a B.F.A. in illustration, I have worked with various clients. Even though I was a trouble maker in grade school (principals still make me nervous), I enjoy visiting schools and talking to students about illustrating children's books.

Biographical and Critical Sources

PERIODICALS

Booklist, December 1, 2000, Carolyn Phelan, review of *Counting Sheep,* p. 725; February 1, 2002, Carolyn Phelan, review of *Johnny Appleseed: My Story,* p. 949; March 1, 2003, Carolyn Phelan, review of *Davey's Blue-eyed Frog,* p. 1197; March 1, 2004, Ilene Cooper, review of *The Foot-stomping Adventures of Clementine Sweet,* p. 1204; November 1, 2005, Julie Cummins, review of *Look What the Cat Dragged In!,* p. 52.

Kirkus Reviews, April 15, 2003, review of *Davey's Blue-eyed Frog,* p. 606; November 1, 2005, review of *Look What the Cat Dragged In!,* p. 1184; July 15, 2007, review of *When the Wizzy Foot Goes Walking;* January 15, 2008, review of *Mama's Little Duckling.*

Publishers Weekly, July 16, 2001, review of *Cowboy Sam and Those Confounded Secrets,* p. 180; January 14, 2008, review of *Mama's Little Duckling,* p. 56.

School Library Journal, December, 2001, Shara Alpern, review of *Cowboy Sam and Those Confounded Secrets,* p. 103; July, 2003, Linda B. Zeilstra, review of *Davey's Blue-eyed Frog,* p. 95; March, 2004, Grace Oliff, review of *The Foot-stomping Adventures of Clementine Sweet,* p. 169; February, 2006, Julie Roach, review of *Look What the Cat Dragged In!,* p. 104; August, 2007, Amy Lilien-Harper, review of *When the Wizzy Foot Goes Walking,* p. 90; February, 2008, Judith Constantinides, review of *Mama's Little Duckling,* p. 94.

ONLINE

Mike Wohnoutka Home Page, http://mikewohnoutka.com (November 10, 2008).

* * *

YARROW, Peter 1938-

Personal

Born May 31, 1938, in New York, NY; children: Bethany.

Addresses

Agent—Folklore Productions, 1671 Appian Way, Santa Monica, CA 90401-3293.

Career

Musician, activist, producer, and author. Performer as solo folk musician, then with singing group Peter, Paul, and Mary, 1962-70, 1978—, including at Carnegie Hall, 2005. Performer on solo recordings, including *That's Enough for Me,* 1973; performer (with Peter, Paul, and Mary) on *Peter, Paul, and Mary,* 1962, *Moving,* 1963,

In the Wind, 1963, _Peter, Paul, and Mary in Concert,_ 1964, _A Song Will Rise,_ 1995, _See What Tomorrow Brings,_ 1965, _Album,_ 1966, _Album 1700,_ 1967, _Late Again,_ 1968, _Peter, Paul, and Mommy,_ 1969, _Reunion,_ 1978, _A Holiday Celebration,_ 1988, _Lifelines,_ 1995, (and coproducer) _In These Times_ and _Carry It On,_ both 2004, and _The Very Best of Peter, Paul, and Mary,_ 2005; performer on solo albums _Love Songs,_ 1975, and on _Joan Baez: Live at Newport,_ 1996, _Inscriptions of Hope,_ 1997, and _Puff, and Other Family Favorites,_ 2008. Organizer of March on Washington, 1969, and anti-nuclear benefit, 1978. Cofounder of Newport Folk Festival, 1962; creator of "Operation: Respect" (anti-bullying curriculum program), introduced in New York City public schools, 2006.

Awards, Honors

Allard K. Lowenstein Award, 1982, for work advancing human rights, peace, and freedom; Tikkun Olam Award, Miami Jewish Federation, 1995. (With Mary Travers and Noel Paul Stookey) five Grammy Awards, including 1963; eight gold albums, five platinum albums; Lifetime Achievement Award, Songwriters Hall of Fame, 2006.

Writings

(Author of afterword) Steve Seskin and Allen Shamblin, _Don't Laugh at Me_ (includes CD), illustrated by Gun Dibley, Tricycle Press, 2002.
(With Leonard Lipton), _Puff, the Magic Dragon_ (song lyrics; with CD), illustrated by Eric Puybaret, Sterling Publishers (New York, NY), 2007.
Peter Yarrow Songbook: Sleepytime Songs, illustrated by Terry Widener, Sterling Publishers (New York, NY), 2008.

Lyricist, with Mary Travers and Noel Paul Stookey, on recordings by Peter, Paul, and Mary, including _No Easy Walk to Freedom,_ 1987.

Sidelights

A singer and songwriter, Peter Yarrow gained fame in the mid-twentieth century as the founder of the iconic folk-music trio Peter, Paul, and Mary. In the years since, Yarrow has combined his musical career with his work as an activist, sponsoring marches and benefit concerts and founding Operation Respect, an anti-bullying curriculum that was adopted by New York City in 2006. In 2008 Yarrow revisited a song that Peter, Paul, and Mary made famous over four decades before, adapting "Puff, the Magic Dragon" as a picture book.

Formed by Noel Paul Stookey, Mary Travers, and Yarrow, Peter, Paul, and Mary began performing in New York City's Greenwich Village in 1961. Yarrow, the last member to join the trio, had already begun a solo career

and performed at the Newport Folk Festival the year before. The trio's tight harmonies and intricate guitar melodies captivated audiences and their rise to national fame and airplay was meteoric. Although their style was grounded in the folk-music movement, they also performed original tunes, including political songs, humorous ditties, children's songs such as "Puff, the Magic Dragon," and other contemporary-themed songs. They have also been credited for helping to popularize younger performers such as Bob Dylan and Gordon Lightfoot among national audiences, as well as introducing the traditional American music of Woody Guthrie and Pete Seeger to younger, college-aged listeners.

Featuring stylized acrylic paintings by French illustrator Eric Puybaret, _Puff, the Magic Dragon_ transforms the song originally written by Yarrow and Leonard Lipton into what a _Kirkus Reviews_ writer described as "a satisfying read-aloud" with equal appeal to listeners of all ages. In the story, Puff lives in a magical place called Honalee Bay, sharing his cozy lava cave with Jackie Paper until the boy grows up. Although the dragon becomes lonely, Jackie eventually returns, bringing his young daughter to play with the friendly dragon. While Marge Loch-Wouters predicted that "fans of the song will be the book's primary audience," the critic added in her _School Library Journal_ review that Puybaret's "lush" and detailed paintings in tones of green and blue "feature sweeping panoramas" that echo the magic in Yarrow and Lipton's lyrics. In _Publishers Weekly_ a reviewer dubbed _Puff, the Magic Dragon_ "an impressive performance all around," citing the book's quality art and text as well as the accompanying CD recording featuring three child-friendly songs performed by Yarrow and his daughter, Bethany Yarrow. Although _Booklist_ critic Janice Del Negro ranked the song's picture-book adaptation as "slick but appealing," in _Kirkus Reviews_ a reviewer called the book-and-CD offering "a very nice package indeed."

In addition to performing as an accompaniment to the picture-book version of his famous song, Yarrow has also joined daughter Bethany and cellist Rufus Cappadocia to perform a new rendition of "Puff, the Magic Dragon" as part of a 2007 recording geared for children titled _Puff, and Other Family Classics._

Biographical and Critical Sources

BOOKS

St. James Encyclopedia of Popular Culture, St. James Press (Detroit, MI), 2000.

PERIODICALS

Booklist, September 15, 2007, Janice Del Negro, review of _Puff, the Magic Dragon,_ p. 70.

Goldmine, April 12, 1996, William Ruhlmann, "Peter, Paul, and Mary: A Song to Sing all over This Land," pp. 20-50.

Kirkus Reviews, July 15, 2007, review of *Puff, the Magic Dragon.*

Publishers Weekly, December 4, 2006, Diane Roback, "Puff Comes to Life," p. 16; June 11, 2007, review of *Puff, the Magic Dragon,* p. 58.

School Library Journal, August, 2007, Marge Loch-Wouters, review of *Puff, the Magic Dragon,* p. 108.

ONLINE

Peter, Paul, and Mary Web site, http://www.peterpaul andmary.com/ (December 15, 2008), "Peter Yarrow."*

Illustrations Index

(In the following index, the number of the *volume* in which an illustrator's work appears is given *before* the colon, and the *page number* on which it appears is given *after* the colon. For example, a drawing by Adams, Adrienne appears in Volume 2 on page 6, another drawing by her appears in Volume 3 on page 80, another drawing in Volume 8 on page 1, and so on and so on. . . .)

YABC

Index references to *YABC* refer to listings appearing in the two-volume *Yesterday's Authors of Books for Children,* also published by Gale, Cengage Learning. *YABC* covers prominent authors and illustrators who died prior to 1960.

A

Aas, Ulf *5:* 174
Abbe, S. van
  See van Abbe, S.
Abel, Raymond *6:* 122; *7:* 195; *12:* 3; *21:* 86; *25:* 119
Abelliera, Aldo *71:* 120
Abolafia, Yossi *60:* 2; *93:* 163; *152:* 202
Abrahams, Hilary *26:* 205; *29:* 24, 25; *53:* 61
Abrams, Kathie *36:* 170
Abrams, Lester *49:* 26
Abulafia, Yossi *154:* 67; *177:* 3
Accardo, Anthony *191:* 3, 8
Accornero, Franco *184:* 8
Accorsi, William *11:* 198
Acs, Laszlo *14:* 156; *42:* 22
Adams, Adrienne *2:* 6; *3:* 80; *8:* 1; *15:* 107; *16:* 180; *20:* 65; *22:* 134, 135; *33:* 75; *36:* 103, 112; *39:* 74; *86:* 54; *90:* 2, 3
Adams, Connie J. *129:* 68
Adams, John Wolcott *17:* 162
Adams, Lynn *96:* 44
Adams, Norman *55:* 82
Adams, Pam *112:* 1, 2
Adams, Sarah *98:* 126; *164:* 180
Adamson, George *30:* 23, 24; *69:* 64
Addams, Charles *55:* 5
Addison, Kenneth *192:* 173
Addy, Sean *180:* 8
Ade, Rene *76:* 198; *195:* 162
Adinolfi, JoAnn *115:* 42; *176:* 2
Adkins, Alta *22:* 250
Adkins, Jan *8:* 3; *69:* 4; *144:* 2, 3, 4
Adler, Kelynn *195:* 47
Adler, Peggy *22:* 6; *29:* 31
Adler, Ruth *29:* 29
Adlerman, Daniel *163:* 2
Adragna, Robert *47:* 145
Agard, Nadema *18:* 1
Agee, Jon *116:* 8, 9, 10; *157:* 4
Agre, Patricia *47:* 195
Aguirre, Alfredo *152:* 218
Ahl, Anna Maria *32:* 24
Ahlberg, Allan *68:* 6, 7, 9; *165:* 5
Ahlberg, Janet *68:* 6, 7, 9
Aicher-Scholl, Inge *63:* 127
Aichinger, Helga *4:* 5, 45
Aitken, Amy *31:* 34
Akaba, Suekichi *46:* 23; *53:* 127

Akasaka, Miyoshi *YABC 2:* 261
Akib, Jamel *181:* 13; *182:* 99
Akino, Fuku *6:* 144
Alain *40:* 41
Alajalov *2:* 226
Alborough, Jez *86:* 1, 2, 3; *149:* 3
Albrecht, Jan *37:* 176
Albright, Donn *1:* 91
Alcala, Alfredo *91:* 128
Alcantará, Felipe Ugalde *171:* 186
Alcorn, John *3:* 159; *7:* 165; *31:* 22; *44:* 127; *46:* 23, 170
Alcorn, Stephen *110:* 4; *125:* 106; *128:* 172; *150:* 97; *160:* 188; *165:* 48
Alcott, May *100:* 3
Alda, Arlene *44:* 24; *158:* 2
Alden, Albert *11:* 103
Aldridge, Andy *27:* 131
Aldridge, George *105:* 125
Aldridge, Sheila *192:* 4
Alejandro, Cliff *176:* 75
Alex, Ben *45:* 25, 26
Alexander, Ellen *91:* 3
Alexander, Lloyd *49:* 34
Alexander, Martha *3:* 206; *11:* 103; *13:* 109; *25:* 100; *36:* 131; *70:* 6, 7; *136:* 3, 4, 5; *169:* 120
Alexander, Paul *85:* 57; *90:* 9
Alexeieff, Alexander *14:* 6; *26:* 199
Alfano, Wayne *80:* 69
Aliki
  See Brandenberg, Aliki
Allamand, Pascale *12:* 9
Allan, Judith *38:* 166
Alland, Alexandra *16:* 255
Allen, Gertrude *9:* 6
Allen, Graham *31:* 145
Allen, Jonathan *131:* 3, 4; *177:* 8, 9, 10
Allen, Joy *168:* 185
Allen, Pamela *50:* 25, 26, 27, 28; *81:* 9, 10; *123:* 4, 5
Allen, Rowena *47:* 75
Allen, Thomas B. *81:* 101; *82:* 248; *89:* 37; *104:* 9
Allen, Tom *85:* 176
Allender, David *73:* 223
Alley, R.W. *80:* 183; *95:* 187; *156:* 100, 153; *169:* 4, 5; *179:* 17
Allison, Linda *43:* 27
Allon, Jeffrey *119:* 174
Allport, Mike *71:* 55

Almquist, Don *11:* 8; *12:* 128; *17:* 46; *22:* 110
Aloise, Frank *5:* 38; *10:* 133; *30:* 92
Alsenas, Linas *186:* 2
Althea
  See Braithwaite, Althea
Altschuler, Franz *11:* 185; *23:* 141; *40:* 48; *45:* 29; *57:* 181
Alvin, John *117:* 5
Ambrus, Victor G. *1:* 6, 7, 194; *3:* 69; *5:* 15; *6:* 44; *7:* 36; *8:* 210; *12:* 227; *14:* 213; *15:* 213; *22:* 209; *24:* 36; *28:* 179; *30:* 178; *32:* 44, 46; *38:* 143; *41:* 25, 26, 27, 28, 29, 30, 31, 32; *42:* 87; *44:* 190; *55:* 172; *62:* 30, 144, 145, 148; *86:* 99, 100, 101; *87:* 66, 137; *89:* 162; *134:* 160
Ames, Lee J. *3:* 12; *9:* 130; *10:* 69; *17:* 214; *22:* 124; *151:* 13
Amon, Aline *9:* 9
Amoss, Berthe *5:* 5
Amstutz, Andre *152:* 102
Amundsen, Dick *7:* 77
Amundsen, Richard E. *5:* 10; *24:* 122
Ancona, George *12:* 11; *55:* 144; *145:* 7
Anderson, Alasdair *18:* 122
Andersen, Bethanne *116:* 167; *162:* 189; *175:* 17; *191:* 4, 5
Anderson, Bob *139:* 16
Anderson, Brad *33:* 28
Anderson, C.W. *11:* 10
Anderson, Carl *7:* 4
Anderson, Catherine Corley *72:* 2
Anderson, Cecil *127:* 152
Anderson, David Lee *118:* 176
Anderson, Derek *169:* 9; *174:* 180
Anderson, Doug *40:* 111
Anderson, Erica *23:* 65
Anderson, Laurie *12:* 153, 155
Anderson, Lena *99:* 26
Anderson, Peggy Perry *179:* 2
Anderson, Sara *173:* 3
Anderson, Scoular *138:* 13
Anderson, Susan *90:* 12
Anderson, Tara *188:* 132
Anderson, Wayne *23:* 119; *41:* 239; *56:* 7; *62:* 26; *147:* 6
Andreasen, Daniel *86:* 157; *87:* 104; *103:* 201, 202; *159:* 75; *167:* 106, 107; *168:* 184; *180:* 247; *186:* 9
Andrew, Ian *111:* 37; *116:* 12; *166:* 2
Andrew, John *22:* 4

223

Andrews, Benny *14:* 251; *31:* 24; *57:* 6, 7; *183:* 8
Andrews, Vaughn *166:* 28
Anelay, Henry *57:* 173
Angel, Marie *47:* 22
Angelo, Valenti *14:* 8; *18:* 100; *20:* 232; *32:* 70
Anglund, Joan Walsh *2:* 7, 250, 251; *37:* 198, 199, 200
Anholt, Catherine *74:* 8; *131:* 7; *141:* 5
Anholt, Laurence *141:* 4
Anno, Mitsumasa *5:* 7; *38:* 25, 26, 27, 28, 29, 30, 31, 32; *77:* 3, 4; *157:* 10, 11
Antal, Andrew *1:* 124; *30:* 145
Antram, David *152:* 133
Apostolou, Christy Hale
   See Hale, Christy
Apple, Margot *33:* 25; *35:* 206; *46:* 81; *53:* 8; *61:* 109; *64:* 21, 22, 24, 25, 27; *71:* 176; *77:* 53; *82:* 245; *92:* 39; *94:* 180; *96:* 107; *152:* 4, 5; *162:* 192, 194; *173:* 44
Appleyard, Dev *2:* 192
Aragones, Sergio *48:* 23, 24, 25, 26, 27
Araneus *40:* 29
Arbo, Cris *103:* 4
Archambault, Matt *85:* 173; *138:* 19, 20; *143:* 33; *145:* 144; *179:* 103; *187:* 7
Archer, Janet *16:* 69; *178:* 156
Ardizzone, Edward *1:* 11, 12; *2:* 105; *3:* 258; *4:* 78; *7:* 79; *10:* 100; *15:* 232; *20:* 69,178; *23:* 223; *24:* 125; *28:* 25, 26, 27, 28, 29, 30, 31,33, 34, 35, 36, 37; *31:* 192, 193; *34:* 215, 217; *60:* 173; *64:* 145; *87:* 176; *YABC 2:* 25
Arena, Jill *176:* 49
Arenella, Roy *14:* 9
Argent, Kerry *103:* 56; *138:* 17; *158:* 134
Arisman, Marshall *162:* 50
Armer, Austin *13:* 3
Armer, Laura Adams *13:* 3
Armer, Sidney *13:* 3
Armitage, David *47:* 23; *99:* 5; *155:* 4
Armitage, Eileen *4:* 16
Armstrong, George *10:* 6; *21:* 72
Armstrong, Shelagh *102:* 114
Armstrong-Ellis, Carey *185:* 196
Arno, Enrico *1:* 217; *2:* 22, 210; *4:* 9; *5:* 43; *6:* 52; *29:* 217, 219; *33:* 152; *35:* 99; *43:* 31, 32, 33; *45:* 212, 213, 214; *72:* 72; *74:* 166; *100:* 169
Arnold, Alli *187:* 40, 41
Arnold, Caroline *174:* 5
Arnold, Emily *76:* 7, 9, 10
Arnold, Katya *115:* 11; *168:* 2, 3
Arnold, Tedd *116:* 14; *133:* 152; *160:* 5
Arnosky, Jim *22:* 20; *70:* 9, 10, 11; *118:* 3, 5; *160:* 8, 10; *189:* 5, 7, 8, 9, 10
Arnsteen, Katy Keck *105:* 97; *116:* 145
Arrowood, Clinton *12:* 193; *19:* 11; *65:* 210
Artell, Mike *89:* 8
Arting, Fred J. *41:* 63
Artzybasheff, Boris *13:* 143; *14:* 15; *40:* 152, 155
Aruego, Ariane *6:* 4
Aruego, José *4:* 140; *6:* 4; *7:* 64; *33:* 195; *35:* 208; *68:* 16, 17; *75:* 46; *93:* 91, 92; *94:* 197; *109:* 65, 67; *125:* 2, 3, 4, 5; *127:* 188; *143:* 25; *178:* 17, 19, 74; *188:* 166
Arzoumanian, Alik *177:* 12; *194:* 115
Asare, Meshack *86:* 9; *139:* 19
Ascensios, Natalie *105:* 139
Asch, Frank *5:* 9; *66:* 2, 4, 6, 7, 9, 10; *102:* 18, 19,21; *154:* 12
Ashby, Gail *11:* 135
Ashby, Gil *146:* 4
Ashby, Gwynneth *44:* 26
Ashley, C.W. *19:* 197
Ashmead, Hal *8:* 70
Aska, Warabe *56:* 10
Assel, Steven *44:* 153; *77:* 22, 97
Astrop, John *32:* 56
Atene, Ann *12:* 18

Atherton, Lisa *38:* 198
Atkinson, Allen *60:* 5
Atkinson, J. Priestman *17:* 275
Atkinson, Janet *86:* 147; *103:* 138
Atkinson, Mike *127:* 74
Atkinson, Wayne *40:* 46
Attebery, Charles *38:* 170
Atwell, Debby *150:* 6
Atwood, Ann *7:* 9
Aubrey, Meg Kelleher *77:* 159
Auch, Herm *173:* 7, 8
Auch, Mary Jane *173:* 7
Augarde, Steve *25:* 22; *159:* 7
Austerman, Miriam *23:* 107
Austin, Margot *11:* 16
Austin, Robert *3:* 44
Austin, Virginia *81:* 205; *127:* 221
Auth, Tony *51:* 5; *192:* 18
Avendano, Dolores *158:* 74
Avedon, Richard *57:* 140
Averill, Esther *1:* 17; *28:* 39, 40, 41
Axeman, Lois *2:* 32; *11:* 84; *13:* 165; *22:* 8; *23:* 49; *61:* 116; *101:* 124
Axtel, David *155:* 110
Ayer, Jacqueline *13:* 7
Ayer, Margaret *15:* 12; *50:* 120
Ayers, Alan *91:* 58; *107:* 169
Ayliffe, Alex *95:* 164
Ayto, Russell *111:* 5; *112:* 54
Azarian, Mary *112:* 9, 10; *114:* 129; *117:* 171; *137:* 163; *171:* 4, 5; *181:* 161; *188:* 128

B

B.T.B.
   See Blackwell, Basil T.
Babbitt, Bradford *33:* 158
Babbitt, Natalie *6:* 6; *8:* 220; *68:* 20; *70:* 242, 243; *194:* 8, 9
Baca, Maria *104:* 5
Bacchus, Andy *94:* 87
Bacha, Andy *109:* 169
Bachem, Paul *48:* 180; *67:* 65; *144:* 206
Back, Adam *63:* 125
Back, George *31:* 161
Backes, Nick *190:* 72
Backhouse, Colin *78:* 142
Bacon, Bruce *4:* 74
Bacon, Paul *7:* 155; *8:* 121; *31:* 55; *50:* 42; *56:* 175; *62:* 82, 84
Bacon, Peggy *2:* 11, 228; *46:* 44
Baek, Matthew J. *169:* 95
Baer, Julie *161:* 2
Baicker-McKee, Carol *177:* 15; *180:* 215
Bailey, Peter *58:* 174; *87:* 221; *194:* 12
Bailey, Sheila *155:* 11
Baker, Alan *22:* 22; *61:* 134; *93:* 11, 12; *146:* 6, 7, 10
Baker, Charlotte *2:* 12
Baker, Garin *89:* 65
Baker, Jeannie *23:* 4; *88:* 18, 19, 20
Baker, Jim *22:* 24
Baker, Joe *82:* 188; *111:* 55; *124:* 70
Baker, Keith *179:* 6, 7
Baker, Leslie *112:* 214; *132:* 103, 246; *180:* 74, 246
Baldacci, Rudy *184:* 9
Baldridge, Cyrus LeRoy *19:* 69; *44:* 50
Baldus, Zachary *152:* 231; *187:* 60
Balet, Jan *11:* 22
Balian, Lorna *9:* 16; *91:* 16
Balit, Christina *102:* 24; *159:* 9; *162:* 118, 119
Ballantyne, R.M. *24:* 34
Ballis, George *14:* 199
Balouch, Kristen *176:* 11
Baltzer, Hans *40:* 30
Banbery, Fred *58:* 15
Banfill, A. Scott *98:* 7; *112:* 59

Bang, Molly Garrett *24:* 37, 38; *69:* 8, 9, 10; *111:* 7,9, 10, 11; *140:* 11; *158:* 37, 38, 39; *195:* 3
Banik, Yvette Santiago *21:* 136
Banner, Angela
   See Maddison, Angela Mary
Bannerman, Helen *19:* 13, 14
Bannon, Laura *6:* 10; *23:* 8
Bantock, Nick *74:* 229; *95:* 6
Banyai, Istvan *185:* 209; *193:* 14, 16
Baptist, Michael *37:* 208
Baracca, Sal *135:* 206
Baranaski, Marcin *182:* 113
Barasch, Lynne *126:* 16; *186:* 15
Barbarin, Lucien C., Jr. *89:* 88
Barbour, Karen *96:* 5; *74:* 209; *170:* 16
Bare, Arnold Edwin *16:* 31
Bare, Colleen Stanley *32:* 33
Barger, Jan *147:* 11
Bargery, Geoffrey *14:* 258
Barkat, Jonathan *149:* 177; *164:* 254; *181:* 106; *184:* 186
Barker, Carol *31:* 27
Barker, Cicely Mary *49:* 50, 51
Barkley, James *4:* 13; *6:* 11; *13:* 112
Barks, Carl *37:* 27, 28, 29, 30, 31, 32, 33, 34
Barling, Joy *62:* 148
Barling, Tom *9:* 23
Barlow, Gillian *62:* 20
Barlow, Perry *35:* 28
Barlowe, Dot *30:* 223
Barlowe, Wayne *37:* 72; *84:* 43; *105:* 5
Barnard, Bryn *88:* 53; *13:* 55; *169:* 13; *193:* 194
Barner, Bob *29:* 37; *128:* 33; *136:* 19, 20; *177:* 27
Barnes, Hiram P. *20:* 28
Barnes, Tim *137:* 28
Barnes-Murphy, Rowan *88:* 22
Barnett, Charles II *175:* 150
Barnett, Ivan *70:* 14
Barnett, Moneta *16:* 89; *19:* 142; *31:* 102; *33:* 30, 31, 32; *41:* 153; *61:* 94, 97
Barney, Maginel Wright *39:* 32, 33, 34; *YABC 2:* 306
Barnum, Jay Hyde *11:* 224; *20:* 5; *37:* 189, 190
Baron, Alan *80:* 3; *89:* 123
Barr, George *60:* 74; *69:* 64
Barragan, Paula S. *134:* 116; *186:* 158
Barrall, Tim *115:* 152
Barraud, Martin *189:* 38
Barrauds *33:* 114
Barrer-Russell, Gertrude *9:* 65; *27:* 31
Barret, Robert *85:* 134
Barrett, Angela *40:* 136, 137; *62:* 74; *75:* 10; *76:* 142; *144:* 137; *145:* 14
Barrett, Jennifer *58:* 149
Barrett, John E. *43:* 119
Barrett, Moneta *74:* 10
Barrett, Peter *55:* 169; *86:* 111
Barrett, Robert *62:* 145; *77:* 146; *82:* 35
Barrett, Ron *14:* 24; *26:* 35
Barron, John N. *3:* 261; *5:* 101; *14:* 220
Barrow, Ann *136:* 27
Barrows, Walter *14:* 268
Barry, Ethelred B. *37:* 79; *YABC 1:* 229
Barry, James *14:* 25
Barry, Katharina *2:* 159; *4:* 22
Barry, Robert E. *6:* 12
Barry, Scott *32:* 35
Bartenbach, Jean *40:* 31
Barth, Ernest Kurt *2:* 172; *3:* 160; *8:* 26; *10:* 31
Bartlett, Alison *101:* 88; *165:* 93
Barton, Byron *8:* 207; *9:* 18; *23:* 66; *80:* 181; *90:* 18, 19, 20, 21; *126:* 29, 30
Barton, Harriett *30:* 71
Barton, Jill *129:* 108; *135:* 120; *145:* 185, 189; *184:* 177
Bartram, Robert *10:* 42

Bartsch, Jochen 8: 105; 39: 38
Bascove, Barbara 45: 73
Base, Graeme 101: 15, 16, 17, 18; 162: 8, 10, 12
Baseman, Gary 174: 12
Bash, Barbara 132: 9
Baskin, Leonard 30: 42, 43, 46, 47; 49: 125, 126, 128, 129,133; 173: 120
Bass, Saul 49: 192
Bassett, Jeni 40: 99; 64: 30
Basso, Bill 99: 139; 189: 134
Batchelor, Joy 29: 41, 47, 48
Bate, Norman 5: 16
Bates, Amy June 188: 170; 189: 27, 28
Bates, Leo 24: 35
Batet, Carmen 39: 134
Batherman, Muriel 31: 79; 45: 185
Battaglia, Aurelius 50: 44
Batten, John D. 25: 161, 162
Batten, Mary 162: 14, 15
Battles, Asa 32: 94, 95
Bauer, Carla 193: 6
Bauer, Jutta 150: 32
Bauernschmidt, Marjorie 15: 15
Baum, Allyn 20: 10
Baum, Willi 4: 24, 25; 7: 173
Bauman, Leslie 61: 121
Baumann, Jill 34: 170
Baumhauer, Hans 11: 218; 15: 163, 165, 167
Baxter, Glen 57: 100
Baxter, Leon 59: 102
Baxter, Robert 87: 129
Bayer, Herbert 181: 16
Bayley, Dorothy 37: 195
Bayley, Nicola 40: 104; 41: 34, 35; 69: 15; 129: 33, 34, 35
Baylin, Mark 158: 233
Baynes, Pauline 2: 244; 3: 149; 13: 133, 135,137, 141; 19: 18, 19, 20; 32: 208, 213, 214; 36: 105, 108; 59: 12, 13, 14, 16, 17, 18, 20; 100: 158, 159, 243; 133: 3, 4
Beach, Lou 150: 150
Beame, Rona 12: 40
Bear's Heart 73: 215
Beard, Dan 22: 31, 32
Beard, J.H. YABC 1: 158
Bearden, Romare 9: 7; 22: 35
Beardshaw, Rosalind 169: 22; 190: 22
Beardsley, Aubrey 17: 14; 23: 181; 59: 130, 131
Bearman, Jane 29: 38
Beaton, Cecil 24: 208
Beaton, Clare 125: 28
Beauce, J.A. 18: 103
Beaujard, Sophie 81: 54
Beccia, Carlyn 189: 29
Beck, Charles 11: 169; 51: 173
Beck, Ian 138: 27; 182: 150; 190: 25
Beck, Ruth 13: 11
Becker, Harriet 12: 211
Beckett, Sheilah 25: 5; 33: 37, 38
Beckhoff, Harry 1: 78; 5: 163
Beckhorn, Susan Williams 189: 32
Beckman, Kaj 45: 38, 39, 40, 41
Beckman, Per 45: 42, 43
Beddows, Eric 72: 70
Bedford, F.D. 20: 118, 122; 33: 170; 41: 220, 221,230, 233
Bee, Joyce 19: 62
Bee, William 188: 6
Beeby, Betty 25: 36
Beech, Carol 9: 149
Beech, Mark 192: 122
Beek 25: 51, 55, 59
Beeke, Tiphanie 177: 127
Beekman, Doug 125: 146, 148
Beerbohm, Max 24: 208
Beeson, Bob 108: 57
Begin, Maryjane 82: 13
Beha, Philippe 172: 85
Behr, Joyce 15: 15; 21: 132; 23: 161

Behrens, Hans 5: 97
Beier, Ellen 135: 170; 139: 47; 183: 164
Beinicke, Steve 69: 18
Beisner, Monika 46: 128, 131; 112: 127
Belden, Charles J. 12: 182
Belina, Renate 39: 132
Bell, Corydon 3: 20
Bell, Graham 54: 48
Bell, Julia 151: 214
Bell, Julie 159: 172; 165: 18
Bell, Thomas P. 76: 182
Bellamy, Glen 127: 15
Beltran, Alberto 43: 37
Bemelmans, Ludwig 15: 19, 21; 100: 27
Ben-Ami, Doron 75: 96; 84: 107; 108: 132; 110: 63; 159: 157
Bendall-Brunello, John 150: 4; 157: 163; 185: 3, 4
Benda, Wladyslaw T. 15: 256; 30: 76, 77; 44: 182
Bender, Robert 77: 162; 79: 13; 160: 23
Bendick, Jeanne 2: 24; 68: 27, 28
Benioff, Carol 121: 42; 175: 23
Benner, Cheryl 80: 11
Bennett, Charles H. 64: 6
Bennett, Erin Susanne 165: 216
Bennett, F.I. YABC 1: 134
Bennett, James 146: 240
Bennett, Jill 26: 61; 41: 38, 39; 45: 54
Bennett, Rainey 15: 26; 23: 53
Bennett, Richard 15: 45; 21: 11, 12, 13; 25: 175
Bennett, Susan 5: 55
Benny, Mike 142: 78
Benoit, Elise 77: 74
Benson, Linda 60: 130; 62: 91; 75: 101; 79: 156; 134: 129
Benson, Patrick 68: 162; 147: 17, 18, 19, 20
Bentley, Carolyn 46: 153
Bentley, James 149: 30
Bentley, Roy 30: 162
Benton, Jim 172: 22
Benton, Thomas Hart 2: 99
Berelson, Howard 5: 20; 16: 58; 31: 50
Berenstain, Jan 12: 47; 64: 33, 34, 36, 37, 38, 40, 42, 44; 135: 25, 28, 31, 35
Berenstain, Stan 12: 47; 64: 33, 34, 36, 37, 38, 40, 42, 44; 135: 25, 28, 31, 35
Berenzy, Alix 65: 13; 73: 6; 78: 115
Berg, Joan 1: 115; 3: 156; 6: 26, 58
Berg, Ron 36: 48, 49; 48: 37, 38; 67: 72
Bergen, David 115: 44
Berger, Barbara 77: 14
Berger, Carin 185: 6
Berger, William M. 14: 143; YABC 1: 204
Bergherr, Mary 74: 170; 151: 123
Bergin, Mark 114: 8, 9; 143: 95; 160: 26, 27
Bergstreser, Douglas 69: 76
Bergum, Constance R. 121: 14, 15
Bering, Claus 13: 14
Berkeley, Jon 139: 218
Berkowitz, Jeanette 3: 249
Berman, Paul 66: 14
Bernal, Richard 154: 176
Bernadette
  See Watts, Bernadette
Bernardin, James 112: 24; 167: 94
Bernasconi, Pablo 183: 10, 11
Bernath, Stefen 32: 76
Bernhard, Durga 80: 13
Bernstein, Michel J. 51: 71
Bernstein, Ted 38: 183; 50: 131
Bernstein, Zena 23: 46
Berridge, Celia 86: 63
Berrill, Jacquelyn 12: 50
Berry, Erick
  See Best, Allena
Berry, William D. 14: 29; 19: 48
Berry, William A. 6: 219

Berson, Harold 2: 17, 18; 4: 28, 29, 220; 9: 10; 12: 19; 17: 45; 18: 193; 22: 85; 34: 172; 44: 120; 46: 42; 80: 240
Berton, Patsy 99: 16
Bertholf, Bret 187: 9; 189: 32, 33
Bertschmann, Harry 16: 1
Besco, Don 70: 99
Beskow, Elsa 20: 13, 14, 15
Bess, Clayton 63: 94
Best, Allena 2: 26; 34: 76
Betera, Carol 74: 68
Bethell, Thomas N. 61: 169
Bethers, Ray 6: 22
Bettina
  See Ehrlich, Bettina
Betts, Ethel Franklin 17: 161, 164, 165; YABC 2: 47
Betz, Rudolf 59: 161
Bewick, Thomas 16: 40, 41, 43, 44, 45, 47; 54: 150; YABC 1: 107
Beyer, Paul J. III 74: 24
Bezencon, Jacqueline 48: 40
Biamonte, Daniel 40: 90
Bianchi, John 91: 19
Bianco, Pamela 15: 31; 28: 44, 45, 46
Bible, Charles 13: 15
Bice, Clare 22: 40
Biedrzycki, David 186: 170
Bierman, Don 57: 184
Biggers, John 2: 123
Biggs, Brian 192: 38
Bileck, Marvin 3: 102; 40: 36, 37
Bilibin, Ivan 61: 8, 9, 12, 13, 14, 15, 151, 152, 154, 162
Billington, Patrick 98: 71
Billout, Guy 144: 38, 39
Bimen, Levent 5: 179
Binch, Caroline 81: 18; 140: 15, 16; 144: 115
Binder, Hannes 169: 163
Bing, Christopher 126: 34
Binger, Bill 121: 46
Binks, Robert 25: 150
Binzen, Bill 24: 47
Birch, Reginald 15: 150; 19: 33, 34, 35, 36; 37: 196,197; 44: 182; 46: 176; YABC 1: 84; 2: 34, 39
Birchall, Mark 123: 188
Bird, Esther Brock 1: 36; 25: 66
Birdsong, Keith 167: 85
Birkett, Rachel 78: 206
Birling, Paul 109: 30
Birmingham, Christian 132: 243; 143: 114
Birmingham, Lloyd P. 12: 51; 83: 13
Biro, Val 1: 26; 41: 42; 60: 178; 67: 23, 24; 84: 242, 243
Bischoff, Ilse 44: 51
Bishop, Gavin 97: 17, 18; 144: 42, 44
Bishop, Kathleen Wong 115: 67
Bishop, Rich 56: 43
Bite, I. 60: 14
Bittinger, Ned 93: 117
Bjorklund, Lorence 3: 188, 252; 7: 100; 9: 113; 10: 66; 19: 178; 33: 122, 123; 35: 36, 37, 38, 39,41, 42, 43; 36: 185; 38: 93; 47: 106; 66: 194; YABC 1: 242
Bjorkman, Steve 91: 199; 160: 110
Black Sheep 164: 100
Blackburn, Loren H. 63: 10
Blackall, Sophie 194: 140
Blackford, John 137: 105; 180: 36
Blackwell, Basil T. YABC 1: 68, 69
Blackwood, Gary L. 118: 17
Blades, Ann 16: 52; 37: 213; 50: 41; 69: 21; 99: 215
Blair, Jay 45: 46; 46: 155
Blaisdell, Elinore 1: 121; 3: 134; 35: 63
Blake, Anne Catharine 189: 71
Blake, Quentin 3: 170; 10: 48; 13: 38; 21: 180; 26: 60; 28: 228; 30: 29, 31; 40: 108; 45: 219; 46: 165, 168; 48: 196; 52: 10, 11,

12,13, 14, 15, 16, 17; *73:* 41, 43; *78:* 84, 86;
80: 250, 251; *84:* 210, 211, 212; *87:* 177;
96: 24, 26, 28; *124:* 79; *125:* 32, 34; *181:*
139
Blake, Robert J. *37:* 90; *53:* 67; *54:* 23; *160:*
28, 29
Blake, William *30:* 54, 56, 57, 58, 59, 60
Blanchard, N. Taylor *82:* 140
Blass, Jacqueline *8:* 215
Blazek, Scott R. *91:* 71
Bleck, Cathie *118:* 116
Blegvad, Erik *2:* 59; *3:* 98; *5:* 117; *7:* 131; *11:*
149; *14:* 34, 35; *18:* 237; *32:* 219; *60:* 106;
66: 16, 17, 18, 19; *70:* 233; *76:* 18; *82:* 106;
87: 45; *100:* 188; *129:* 125; *132:* 17, 18, 19,
20; *176:* 14; *YABC 1:* 201
Blessen, Karen *93:* 126
Bliss, Corinne Demas *37:* 38
Blitt, Barry *179:* 199; *187:* 13
Bloch, Lucienne *10:* 12
Blondon, Herve *129:* 48; *183:* 22
Bloom, Lloyd *35:* 180; *36:* 149; *47:* 99; *62:*
117; *68:* 231; *72:* 136; *75:* 185; *83:* 99; *108:*
19
Bloom, Suzanne *172:* 23, 24
Blossom, Dave *34:* 29
Blumenschein, E.L. *YABC 1:* 113, 115
Blumer, Patt *29:* 214
Blundell, Kim *29:* 36
Bluthenthal, Diana Cain *93:* 32; *104:* 106;
177: 26
Blythe, Benjamin *128:* 7
Blythe, Gary *112:* 52; *181:* 166; *182:* 64; *185:*
7; *186:* 116, 117
Boake, Kathy *176:* 185
Board, Perry *171:* 99
Boardman, Gwenn *12:* 60
Bober, Richard *125:* 145; *132:* 40
Bobri *30:* 138; *47:* 27
Bock, Vera *1:* 187; *21:* 41
Bock, William Sauts *8:* 7; *14:* 37; *16:* 120; *21:*
141; *36:* 177; *62:* 203
Bodecker, N(iels) M(ogens) *8:* 13; *14:* 2; *17:*
55, 56, 57; *73:* 22, 23, 24
Boehm, Linda *40:* 31
Bogacki, Tomek *138:* 31, 32; *144:* 123
Bogdan, Florentina *107:* 43
Bohdal, Susi *22:* 44; *101:* 20
Bohlen, Nina *58:* 13
Boies, Alex *96:* 53
Bolam, Emily *101:* 216; *159:* 12
Bolian, Polly *3:* 270; *4:* 30; *13:* 77; *29:* 197
Bolle, Frank *87:* 100
Bollen, Roger *79:* 186; *83:* 16
Bolling, Vickey *114:* 44
Bollinger, Peter *101:* 7; *128:* 198; *172:* 26
Bolognese, Don *2:* 147, 231; *4:* 176; *7:* 146;
17: 43; *23:* 192; *24:* 50; *34:* 108; *36:* 133;
71: 24, 25; *103:* 131; *129:* 39, 40
Bolster, Rob *186:* 169
Bolton, A.T. *57:* 158
Bond, Arnold *18:* 116
Bond, Barbara Higgins *21:* 102
Bond, Bruce *52:* 97
Bond, Felicia *38:* 197; *49:* 55, 56; *89:* 170;
90: 171; *126:* 37
Bond, Higgins *177:* 22, 23
Bonn, Pat *43:* 40
Bonners, Susan *41:* 40; *85:* 36; *94:* 99, 100;
151: 105, 106
Bono, Mary *184:* 73
Bonsall, Crosby *23:* 6
Boon, Debbie *103:* 6; *144:* 188
Boon, Emilie *86:* 23, 24
Boone, Debbie *165:* 77
Boore, Sara *60:* 73
Bootman, Colin *155:* 13; *159:* 35; *174:* 192
Booth, Franklin *YABC 2:* 76
Booth, George *191:* 13
Booth, Graham *32:* 193; *37:* 41, 42
Borda, Juliette *102:* 188

Bordier, Georgette *16:* 54
Boren, Tinka *27:* 128
Borges, Jose Francisco *119:* 62
Borja, Robert *22:* 48
Born, Adolf *49:* 63
Bornstein, Ruth *14:* 44; *88:* 45, 46; *107:* 30
Borten, Helen *3:* 54; *5:* 24
Bosin, Blackbear *69:* 104
Bossom, Naomi *35:* 48
Bostock, Mike *83:* 221; *114:* 14; *188:* 205
Boston, Peter *19:* 42
Bosustow, Stephen *34:* 202
Boszko, Ron *75:* 47
Bottner, Barbara *14:* 46
Boucher, Joelle *41:* 138
Boulat, Pierre *44:* 40
Boulet, Susan Seddon *50:* 47
Bouma, Paddy *118:* 25; *128:* 16
Bour, Daniele *66:* 145
Bourke-White, Margaret *15:* 286, 287; *57:* 102
Boutet de Monvel, M. *30:* 61, 62, 63, 65
Bowen, Betsy *105:* 222
Bowen, Richard *42:* 134
Bowen, Ruth *31:* 188
Bower, Ron *29:* 33
Bowers, David *95:* 38; *115:* 20; *127:* 169, 170;
165: 57
Bowers, Tim *185:* 35
Bowman, Claire *174:* 177
Bowman, Eric *151:* 23
Bowman, Leslie *85:* 203; *105:* 108; *116:* 76;
128: 234; *182:* 24, 25
Bowman, Peter *146:* 214, 215; *150:* 115
Bowser, Carolyn Ewing *22:* 253
Boxall, Ed *178:* 28
Boyd, Aaron *158:* 242
Boyd, Patti *45:* 31
Boyle, Eleanor Vere *28:* 50, 51
Boynton, Sandra *57:* 13, 14, 15; *107:* 36, 37;
152: 12, 13, 14
Bozzo, Frank *4:* 154
Brabbs, Derry *55:* 170
Brace, Eric *132:* 193, 194; *152:* 71; *184:* 195
Brackers de Hugo, Pierre *115:* 21
Bradford, June *158:* 138
Bradford, Ron *7:* 157
Bradley, David P. *69:* 105
Bradley, Richard D. *26:* 182
Bradley, William *5:* 164
Brady, Irene *4:* 31; *42:* 37; *68:* 191
Bragg, Michael *32:* 78; *46:* 31
Bragg, Ruth Gembicki *77:* 18
Brainerd, John W. *65:* 19
Braithwaite, Althea *23:* 12, 13; *119:* 16
Brak, Syd *146:* 187
Bralds, Braldt *90:* 28; *91:* 151
Bram, Elizabeth *30:* 67
Bramley, Peter *4:* 3
Brandenberg, Aliki *2:* 36, 37; *24:* 222; *35:* 49,
50, 51,52, 53, 54, 56, 57; *75:* 15, 17; *92:*
205; *113:* 18, 19, 20; *157:* 28; *156:* 111
Brandenburg, Alexa *75:* 19
Brandenburg, Jim *47:* 58; *150:* 212
Brandi, Lillian *31:* 158
Brandon, Brumsic, Jr. *9:* 25
Bransom, Paul *17:* 121; *43:* 44
Braren, Loretta Trezzo *87:* 193
Brassard, France *186:* 22
Braun, Wendy *80:* 17, 18
Brautigam, Don *115:* 175, 176
Brazell, Derek *75:* 105; *79:* 9
Breathed, Berkeley *86:* 27, 28, 29; *161:* 13, 14
Breckenreid, Julia *192:* 209
Breen, Steve *186:* 23
Brennan, Steve *83:* 230; *101:* 184
Brenner, Fred *22:* 85; *36:* 34; *42:* 34
Brett, Bernard *22:* 54
Brett, Harold M. *26:* 98, 99, 100
Brett, Jan *30:* 135; *42:* 39; *71:* 31, 32; *130:*
23, 24, 25, 26, 27; *171:* 15, 16
Brewer, Paul *106:* 115; *145:* 202

Brewer, Sally King *33:* 44
Brewster, Patience *40:* 68; *45:* 22, 183; *51:* 20;
66: 144; *89:* 4; *97:* 30, 31
Brick, John *10:* 15
Brickman, Robin D. *131:* 88; *142:* 150; *155:*
18; *178:* 109; *184:* 32
Bridge, David R. *45:* 28
Bridgman, L.J. *37:* 77
Bridwell, Norman *4:* 37; *138:* 36, 37, 40
Brierley, Louise *91:* 22; *96:* 165; *183:* 51
Briggs, Harry *172:* 187
Briggs, Raymond *10:* 168; *23:* 20, 21; *66:* 29,
31, 32; *131:* 28, 29; *184:* 15, 16
Brigham, Grace A. *37:* 148
Bright, Robert *24:* 55
Brighton, Catherine *107:* 39
Brinckloe, Julie *13:* 18; *24:* 79, 115; *29:* 35;
63: 140; *81:* 131
Brion *47:* 116
Brisley, Joyce L. *22:* 57
Brisson, James F. *110:* 60
Brittingham, Geoffrey *88:* 37
Brix-Henker, Silke *81:* 194
Brock, Charles E. *15:* 97; *19:* 247, 249; *23:*
224, 225; *36:* 88; *42:* 41, 42, 43, 44, 45;
100: 189; *YABC 1:* 194, 196, 203
Brock, Emma *7:* 21
Brock, Henry Matthew *15:* 81; *16:* 141; *19:*
71; *34:* 115; *40:* 164; *42:* 47, 48, 49; *49:* 66
Brocksopp, Arthur *57:* 157
Broda, Ron *136:* 180; *174:* 123
Brodkin, Gwen *34:* 135
Brodovitch, Alexi *52:* 22
Bromhall, Winifred *5:* 11; *26:* 38
Bromley, Lizzy *159:* 179
Bronson, Linda *150:* 210; *174:* 133
Brooke, L. Leslie *16:* 181, 182, 183, 186; *17:*
15, 16, 17; *18:* 194
Brooker, Christopher *15:* 251
Brooker, Krysten *111:* 94; *140:* 28; *162:* 111;
175: 108; *186:* 42, 225
Brooks, Erik *166:* 52; *182:* 30
Brooks, Karen Stormer *186:* 110
Brooks, Maya Itzna *92:* 153
Brooks, Ron *94:* 15
Brooks, S.G. *178:* 127
Broomfield, Maurice *40:* 141
Brotman, Adolph E. *5:* 21
Brown, Buck *45:* 48
Brown, Calef *179:* 18
Brown, Christopher *62:* 124, 125, 127, 128
Brown, Craig McFarland *73:* 28; *84:* 65
Brown, Dan *61:* 167; *115:* 183, 184; *116:* 28,
29; *193:* 190
Brown, David *7:* 47; *48:* 52
Brown, Denise *11:* 213
Brown, Don *172:* 29
Brown, Elbrite *195:* 39
Brown, Ford Madox *48:* 74
Brown, Hunter *191:* 111, 112
Brown, Judith Gwyn *1:* 45; *7:* 5; *8:* 167; *9:*
182, 190; *20:* 16, 17, 18; *23:* 142; *29:* 117;
33: 97; *36:* 23, 26; *43:* 184; *48:* 201, 223;
49: 69; *86:* 227; *110:* 188; *153:* 7
Brown, Kathryn *98:* 26
Brown, Lisa *187:* 175
Brown, Laurie Krasny *99:* 30
Brown, Marc (Tolon) *10:* 17, 197; *14:* 263;
51: 18; *53:* 11, 12, 13, 15, 16, 17; *75:* 58;
80: 24, 25, 26; *82:* 261; *99:* 29; *145:* 22, 23,
25, 27; *162:* 198
Brown, Marcia *7:* 30; *25:* 203; *47:* 31, 32, 33,
34, 35,36, 37, 38, 39, 40, 42, 43, 44; *YABC
1:* 27
Brown, Margery W. *5:* 32, 33; *10:* 3
Brown, Martin *101:* 43
Brown, Mary Barrett *97:* 74
Brown, Palmer *36:* 40
Brown, Paul *25:* 26; *26:* 107
Brown, Richard *61:* 18; *67:* 30
Brown, Rick *78:* 71; *150:* 154

Brown, Robert S. *85:* 33
Brown, Rod *157:* 142
Brown, Ruth *55:* 165; *86:* 112, 113; *105:* 16, 17, 18; *171:* 178
Brown, Trevor *99:* 160; *139:* 247; *189:* 206
Browne, Anthony *45:* 50, 51, 52; *61:* 21, 22, 23, 24, 25; *105:* 21, 22, 23, 25
Browne, Dik *8:* 212; *67:* 32, 33, 35, 37, 39
Browne, Gordon *16:* 97; *64:* 114, 116, 117, 119, 121
Browne, Hablot K. *15:* 65, 80; *21:* 14, 15, 16, 17, 18, 19,20; *24:* 25
Browne, Jane *165:* 222
Browning, Coleen *4:* 132
Browning, Mary Eleanor *24:* 84
Bruce, Robert *23:* 23
Brude, Dick *48:* 215
Bruel, Nick *166:* 41
Brule, Al *3:* 135
Brumbeau, Jeff *157:* 29
Bruna, Dick *43:* 48, 49, 50; *76:* 27, 28
Brundage, Frances *19:* 244
Brunhoff, Jean de *24:* 57, 58
Brunhoff, Laurent de *24:* 60; *71:* 35, 36, 37
Brunkus, Denise *84:* 50; *123:* 117; *178:* 209; *193:* 99
Brunson, Bob *43:* 135
Bryan, Ashley *31:* 44; *72:* 27, 28, 29; *107:* 92; *116:* 192; *132:* 24; *178:* 33, 34, 35
Bryant, Laura J. *176:* 36; *183:* 168
Bryant, Michael *93:* 74
Brychta, Alex *21:* 21
Bryer, Diana *107:* 121
Bryson, Bernarda *3:* 88, 146; *39:* 26; *44:* 185; *131:* 40
Buba, Joy *12:* 83; *30:* 226; *44:* 56
Buchanan, George *166:* 198
Buchanan, Lilian *13:* 16
Buchanan, Rachel *171:* 71
Bucholtz-Ross, Linda *44:* 137
Buchs, Thomas *40:* 38
Buck, Margaret Waring *3:* 30
Buckhardt, Marc *172:* 59
Buckley, Mike *166:* 180
Budwine, Greg *175:* 172
Buehner, Mark *104:* 12, 15; *105:* 160; *119:* 98; *157:* 188; *159:* 39, 40, 43; *192:* 111
Buehr, Walter *3:* 31
Buff, Conrad *19:* 52, 53, 54
Buff, Mary *19:* 52, 53
Bull, Charles Livingston *18:* 207; *88:* 175, 176
Bullen, Anne *3:* 166, 167
Bullock, Kathleen *77:* 24
Bumgarner-Kirby, Claudia *77:* 194
Burbank, Addison *37:* 43
Burchard, Peter Duncan *3:* 197; *5:* 35; *6:* 158, 218; *143:* 17
Burckhardt, Marc *94:* 48; *110:* 89
Burger, Carl *3:* 33; *45:* 160, 162
Burgeson, Marjorie *19:* 31
Burgess, Anne *76:* 252
Burgess, Gelett *32:* 39, 42
Burgess, Mark *157:* 31
Burke, Jim *179:* 19; *185:* 63
Burke, Phillip *95:* 117
Burkert, Nancy Ekholm *18:* 186; *22:* 140; *24:* 62, 63,64, 65; *26:* 53; *29:* 60, 61; *46:* 171; *YABC 1:* 46
Burkhardt, Bruce *142:* 86
Burkhardt, Melissa A. *142:* 86
Burleson, Joe *104:* 35; *172:* 139
Burn, Doris *6:* 172
Burn, Jeffrey *89:* 125; *152:* 132
Burn, Ted
    See Burn, Thomas E.
Burn, Thomas E. *151:* 41
Burnard, Damon *115:* 23
Burnett, Virgil *44:* 42
Burningham, John *9:* 68; *16:* 60, 61; *59:* 28, 29, 30,31, 32, 33, 35; *111:* 18, 19, 21; *160:* 37

Burns, Howard M. *12:* 173
Burns, Jim *47:* 70; *86:* 32; *91:* 197; *123:* 16
Burns, M.F. *26:* 69
Burns, Raymond *9:* 29
Burns, Robert *24:* 106
Burr, Dan *65:* 28; *108:* 134; *164:* 203; *182:* 68
Burr, Dane *12:* 2
Burra, Edward *YABC 2:* 68
Burrell, Galen *56:* 76
Burri, Rene *41:* 143; *54:* 166
Burridge, Marge Opitz *14:* 42
Burris, Burmah *4:* 81
Burroughs, John Coleman *41:* 64
Burroughs, Studley O. *41:* 65
Burton, Marilee Robin *46:* 33
Burton, Virginia Lee *2:* 43; *44:* 49, 51; *100:* 46, 47; *YABC 1:* 24; *147:* 56
Busoni, Rafaello *1:* 186; *3:* 224; *6:* 126; *14:* 5; *16:* 62, 63
Butchkes, Sidney *50:* 58
Butler, Geoff *94:* 20
Butler, Ralph *116:* 212
Butterfield, Ned *1:* 153; *27:* 128; *79:* 63
Butterworth, Ian *184:* 48, 49
Butterworth, Nick *106:* 43, 44; *149:* 34
Buxton, John *123:* 12
Buzelli, Christopher *105:* 149
Buzonas, Gail *29:* 88
Buzzell, Russ W. *12:* 177
Byard, Carole *39:* 44; *57:* 18, 19, 20; *60:* 60; *61:* 93, 96; *69:* 210; *78:* 246; *79:* 227
Byars, Betsy *46:* 35
Byfield, Barbara Ninde *8:* 18
Byfield, Graham *32:* 29
Bynum, Janie *176:* 50
Byrd, Robert *13:* 218; *33:* 46; *158:* 70
Byrd, Samuel *123:* 104

C

Cabat, Erni *74:* 38
Cabban, Vanessa *138:* 73; *176:* 39; *185:* 65
Cabrera, Jane *103:* 24; *152:* 27; *182:* 33, 34
Caddy, Alice *6:* 41
Cady, Harrison *17:* 21, 23; *19:* 57, 58
Caffrey, Aileen *72:* 223; *141:* 154
Cairns, Julia *177:* 37
Caldecott, Randolph *16:* 98, 103; *17:* 32, 33, 36, 38, 39; *26:* 90; *100:* 49, 50; *YABC 2:* 172
Calder, Alexander *18:* 168
Calderón, Gloria *179:* 5
Calderon, W. Frank *25:* 160
Caldwell, Ben *105:* 75; *149:* 60; *195:* 61
Caldwell, Clyde *98:* 100; *116:* 39
Caldwell, Doreen *23:* 77; *71:* 41
Caldwell, John *46:* 225
Call, Greg *126:* 135; *165:* 49; *182:* 105, 163
Callahan, Kevin *22:* 42
Callahan, Philip S. *25:* 77
Callan, Jamie *59:* 37
Calvin, James *61:* 92
Camburn-Bracalente, Carol A. *118:* 22
Cameron, Chad *190:* 144
Cameron, Julia Margaret *19:* 203
Cameron, Scott *99:* 18
Camm, Martin *140:* 208, 209, 210
Campbell, Ann *11:* 43; *123:* 182; *183:* 68
Campbell, Bill *89:* 39
Campbell, Ken *126:* 143
Campbell, Robert *55:* 120
Campbell, Rod *51:* 27; *98:* 34
Campbell, Walter M. *YABC 2:* 158
Camps, Luis *28:* 120, 121; *66:* 35
Canga, C.B. *187:* 165
Cann, Helen *124:* 50; *141:* 78; *170:* 138; *179:* 22, 23
Cannon, Janell *78:* 25; *128:* 40
Canright, David *36:* 162

Cantone, AnnaLaura *182:* 146
Canty, Thomas *85:* 161; *92:* 47; *113:* 192; *134:* 60; *185:* 117
Canyon, Christopher *150:* 44; *151:* 112
Caporale, Wende *70:* 42
Capp, Al *61:* 28, 30, 31, 40, 41, 43, 44
Cappon, Manuela *154:* 64
Caras, Peter *36:* 64
Caraway, Caren *57:* 22
Caraway, James *3:* 200, 201
Carbe, Nino *29:* 183
Cares, Linda *67:* 176
Carigiet, Alois *24:* 67
Carle, Eric *4:* 42; *11:* 121; *12:* 29; *65:* 32,33, 34, 36; *73:* 63, 65; *163:* 55, 56
Carling, Amelia Lau *164:* 46
Carlino, Angela *168:* 43; *188:* 20
Carlson, Nancy L. *41:* 116; *56:* 25; *90:* 45; *144:* 48, 50
Carlluccio, Maria *175:* 129
Carmi, Giora *79:* 35; *149:* 40
Carpenter, Nancy *76:* 128; *86:* 173; *89:* 171; *131:* 186; *134:* 8; *138:* 215; *153:* 204; *159:* 93; *165:* 232
Carr, Archie *37:* 225
Carrick, Donald *5:* 194; *39:* 97; *49:* 70; *53:* 156; *63:* 15, 16, 17, 18, 19, 21; *80:* 131; *86:* 151; *118:* 24
Carrick, Malcolm *28:* 59, 60
Carrick, Paul *118:* 26; *194:* 28
Carrick, Valery *21:* 47
Carrier, Lark *71:* 43
Carroll, Jim *88:* 211; *140:* 177; *153:* 99; *195:* 75
Carroll, Lewis
    See Dodgson, Charles L.
Carroll, Michael *72:* 5
Carroll, Pamela *84:* 68; *128:* 214
Carroll, Ruth *7:* 41; *10:* 68
Carter, Abby *81:* 32; *97:* 121; *102:* 61; *163:* 139; *164:* 125; *184:* 22, 23; *191:* 85
Carter, Barbara *47:* 167, 169
Carter, David A. *114:* 24, 25; *170:* 42, 43
Carter, Don *124:* 54; *184:* 100; *192:* 43, 44, 45
Carter, Harry *22:* 179
Carter, Helene *15:* 38; *22:* 202, 203; *YABC 2:* 220, 221
Carter, Penny *173:* 91
Cartlidge, Michelle *49:* 65; *96:* 50, 51
Cartwright, Reg *63:* 61, 62; *78:* 26; *143:* 4
Cartwright, Shannon *78:* 81
Carty, Leo *4:* 196; *7:* 163; *58:* 131
Cary *4:* 133; *9:* 32; *20:* 2; *21:* 143
Cary, Page *12:* 41
Casale, Paul *71:* 63; *109:* 122; *136:* 28
Case, Sandra E. *16:* 2
Caseley, Judith *87:* 36; *159:* 47, 48, 49
Casilla, Robert *78:* 7; *167:* 124
Casino, Steve *85:* 193
Cassel, Lili
    See Wronker, Lili Cassel
Cassel-Wronker, Lili
    See Wronker, Lili Cassel
Cassels, Jean *8:* 50; *150:* 119; *173:* 37; *186:* 182
Cassen, Melody *140:* 51
Cassity, Don *104:* 24
Cassler, Carl *75:* 137, 138; *82:* 162
Casson, Hugh *65:* 38, 40, 42, 43
Castellon, Federico *48:* 45, 46, 47, 48
Castle, Jane *4:* 80
Castro, Antonio *84:* 71
Catalano, Dominic *94:* 79; *163:* 60, 61; *162:* 54
Catalanotto, Peter *63:* 170; *70:* 23; *71:* 182; *72:* 96; *74:* 114; *76:* 194, 195; *77:* 7; *79:* 157; *80:* 28, 67; *83:* 157; *85:* 27; *108:* 11; *113:* 30, 31, 33, 34, 36; *114:* 27, 28, 29; *117:* 53; *124:* 168; *159:* 54, 55; *195:* 19, 20, 21, 22, 24, 174
Catania, Tom *68:* 82

Cather, Carolyn *3:* 83; *15:* 203; *34:* 216
Catrow, David *117:* 179; *152:* 31, 33; *173:* 24
Cauley, Lorinda Bryan *44:* 135; *46:* 49
Cayard, Bruce *38:* 67
Cazet, Denys *52:* 27; *99:* 39, 40; *163:* 65, 66; *191:* 25, 27, 28
Ceccoli, Nicoletta *181:* 39; *188:* 99
Cecil, Randy *127:* 132, 133; *187:* 16, 17; *191:* 168
Cellini, Joseph *2:* 73; *3:* 35; *16:* 116; *47:* 103
Cepeda, Joe *90:* 62; *109:* 91; *134:* 172; *159:* 57, 58, 164
Chabrian, Debbi *45:* 55
Chabrian, Deborah *51:* 182; *53:* 124; *63:* 107; *75:* 84; *79:* 85; *82:* 247; *89:* 93; *101:* 197
Chagnon, Mary *37:* 158
Chalmers, Mary *3:* 145; *13:* 148; *33:* 125; *66:* 214
Chamberlain, Christopher *45:* 57
Chamberlain, Margaret *46:* 51; *106:* 89; *188:* 193
Chamberlain, Nigel *78:* 140
Chambers, C.E. *17:* 230
Chambers, Dave *12:* 151
Chambers, Jill *134:* 110
Chambers, Mary *4:* 188
Chambliss, Maxie *42:* 186; *56:* 159; *93:* 163, 164; *103:* 178; *186:* 33, 34
Champlin, Dale *136:* 124
Chan, Harvey *96:* 236; *99:* 153; *143:* 218; *179:* 144
Chandler, David P. *28:* 62
Chaney, Howard *139:* 27
Chang, Warren *101:* 209
Chapel, Jody *68:* 20
Chapman, C.H. *13:* 83, 85, 87
Chapman, Frederick T. *6:* 27; *44:* 28
Chapman, Gaynor *32:* 52, 53
Chapman, Jane *145:* 186; *150:* 56; *166:* 220; *174:* 202; *176:* 43, 44; *179:* 131
Chapman, Lynne *175:* 31
Chappell, Warren *3:* 172; *21:* 56; *27:* 125
Charles, Donald *30:* 154, 155
Charlip, Remy *4:* 48; *34:* 138; *68:* 53, 54; *119:* 29, 30
Charlot, Jean *1:* 137, 138; *8:* 23; *14:* 31; *48:* 151; *56:* 21
Charlot, Martin *64:* 72
Charlton, Michael *34:* 50; *37:* 39
Charmatz, Bill *7:* 45
Chartier, Normand *9:* 36; *52:* 49; *66:* 40; *74:* 220; *145:* 169; *168:* 91; *177:* 108
Chase, Lynwood M. *14:* 4
Chast, Roz *97:* 39, 40
Chastain, Madye Lee *4:* 50
Chateron, Ann *152:* 19
Chatterton, Martin *68:* 102; *152:* 19
Chau, Tungwai *140:* 35
Chauncy, Francis *24:* 158
Chayka, Doug *145:* 97; *177:* 150
Chee, Cheng-Khee *79:* 42; *81:* 224; *180:* 245
Chen, Chih-sien *90:* 226
Chen, Tony *6:* 45; *19:* 131; *29:* 126; *34:* 160
Chen, Yong *183:* 34
Cheney, T.A. *11:* 47
Cheng, Judith *36:* 45; *51:* 16
Chermayeff, Ivan *47:* 53
Cherry, David *93:* 40
Cherry, Lynne *34:* 52; *65:* 184; *87:* 111; *99:* 46, 47
Chesak, Lina *135:* 118
Chess, Victoria *12:* 6; *33:* 42, 48, 49; *40:* 194; *41:* 145; *69:* 80; *72:* 100; *92:* 33, 34; *104:* 167
Chessare, Michele *41:* 50; *56:* 48; *69:* 145
Chesterton, G.K. *27:* 43, 44, 45, 47
Chestnutt, David *47:* 217
Chesworth, Michael *75:* 24, 152; *88:* 136; *94:* 25; *98:* 155; *160:* 42
Chetham, Celia *134:* 34
Chetwin, Grace *86:* 40

Cheung, Irving *158:* 96
Chevalier, Christa *35:* 66
Chew, Ruth *7:* 46; *132:* 147
Chewning, Randy *92:* 206
Chichester Clark, Emma *72:* 121; *77:* 212; *78:* 209; *87:* 143; *117:* 37, 39, 40; *144:* 138; *156:* 24, 25
Chifflart *47:* 113, 127
Child, Lauren *119:* 32; *183:* 30, 31
Chin, Alex *28:* 54
Chitwood, Susan Tanner *163:* 16
Cho, Shinta *8:* 126
Chodos-Irvine, Margaret *52:* 102, 103, 107; *152:* 44
Choi, Yangsook *171:* 134; *173:* 135; *178:* 38, 39, 40
Chollat, Emilie *170:* 203
Chollick, Jay *25:* 175
Choma, Christina *99:* 169
Chomey, Steve *188:* 53
Chorao, Kay *7:* 200, 201; *8:* 25; *11:* 234; *33:* 187; *35:* 239; *69:* 35; *70:* 235; *123:* 174; *193:* 179
Chowdhury, Subrata *62:* 130; *162:* 22, 23
Christelow, Eileen *38:* 44; *83:* 198, 199; *90:* 57, 58; *184:* 26
Christensen, Bonnie *93:* 100; *153:* 67
Christensen, Gardell Dano *1:* 57
Christensen, James C. *140:* 226
Christiana, David *90:* 64; *135:* 13; *171:* 7; *195:* 26, 27
Christiansen, Per *40:* 24
Christie, R. Gregory *116:* 107; *127:* 20, 21; *162:* 179; *164:* 114; *165:* 137; *174:* 157; *179:* 172; *185:* 17, 18, 19
Christy, Howard Chandler *17:* 163, 164, 165, 168, 169; *19:* 186, 187; *21:* 22, 23, 24, 25
Christy, Jana *194:* 21
Chronister, Robert *23:* 138; *63:* 27; *69:* 167
Church, Caroline Jayne *179:* 27
Church, Frederick *YABC 1:* 155
Chute, Marchette *1:* 59
Chwast, Jacqueline *1:* 63; *2:* 275; *6:* 46, 47; *11:* 125; *12:* 202; *14:* 235
Chwast, Seymour *3:* 128, 129; *18:* 43; *27:* 152; *92:* 79; *96:* 56, 57, 58; *146:* 32, 33
Cieslawksi, Steve *101:* 142; *127:* 116; *158:* 169, 171; *190:* 174
Cinelli, Lisa *146:* 253
Cirlin, Edgard *2:* 168
Clairin, Georges *53:* 109
Clapp, John *105:* 66; *109:* 58; *126:* 7; *129:* 148; *130:* 165; *195:* 48
Clark, Brenda *119:* 85; *153:* 55
Clark, David *77:* 164; *134:* 144, 145
Clark, Emma Chichester
   See Chichester Clark, Emma
Clark, Victoria *35:* 159
Clarke, Greg *169:* 134
Clarke, Gus *72:* 226; *134:* 31
Clarke, Harry *23:* 172, 173
Clarke, Peter *75:* 102
Claverie, Jean *38:* 46; *88:* 29
Clavis, Philippe Goossens *182:* 167
Clayton, Elaine *159:* 60
Clayton, Robert *9:* 181
Cleary, Brian P. *186:* 37
Cleaver, Elizabeth *8:* 204; *23:* 36
Cleland, T.M. *26:* 92
Clemens, Peter *61:* 125
Clement, Charles *20:* 38
Clement, Gary *186:* 79; *191:* 32
Clement, Janet *182:* 50
Clement, Rod *97:* 42
Clement, Stephen *88:* 3
Clementson, John *84:* 213
Clemesha, David *192:* 49, 50
Clevin, Jorgen *7:* 50
Clifford, Judy *34:* 163; *45:* 198
Clokey, Art *59:* 44
Clouse, Dennis *187:* 158

Clouse, James *84:* 15
Clouse, Nancy L. *78:* 31; *114:* 90
Clover, Peter *152:* 45
Cneut, Carll *156:* 166; *165:* 67
Coalson, Glo *9:* 72, 85; *25:* 155; *26:* 42; *35:* 212; *53:* 31; *56:* 154; *94:* 37, 38, 193
Cober, Alan E. *17:* 158; *32:* 77; *49:* 127
Cober-Gentry, Leslie *92:* 111
Cocca-Leffler, Maryann *80:* 46; *136:* 60; *139:* 193; *194:* 31, 33, 34
Cochran, Bobbye *11:* 52
CoConis, Ted *4:* 41; *46:* 41; *51:* 104
Cocozza, Chris *87:* 18; *110:* 173; *111:* 149
Cockroft, Jason *152:* 20
Coerr, Eleanor *1:* 64; *67:* 52
Coes, Peter *35:* 172
Cogancherry, Helen *52:* 143; *69:* 131; *77:* 93; *78:* 220; *109:* 204; *110:* 129
Coggins, Jack *2:* 69
Cohen, Alix *7:* 53
Cohen, Miriam *155:* 23, 24
Cohen, Nancy R. *165:* 35
Cohen, Santiago *164:* 26
Cohen, Sheldon *105:* 33, 34; *166:* 46, 47
Cohen, Vincent O. *19:* 243
Cohen, Vivien *11:* 112
Coker, Paul *51:* 172
Colbert, Anthony *15:* 41; *20:* 193
Colby, C.B. *3:* 47
Cole, Babette *58:* 172; *96:* 63, 64; *155:* 29
Cole, Brock *68:* 223; *72:* 36, 37, 38, 192; *127:* 23; *136:* 64, 65
Cole, Gwen *87:* 185
Cole, Henry *178:* 120; *181:* 42, 43; *189:* 60
Cole, Herbert *28:* 104
Cole, Michael *59:* 46
Cole, Olivia H.H. *1:* 134; *3:* 223; *9:* 111; *38:* 104
Colin, Paul *102:* 59; *123:* 118; *126:* 152; *192:* 129
Collicott, Sharleen *98:* 39; *143:* 29, 30
Collier, Bryan *126:* 54; *151:* 166; *174:* 16, 17, 18
Collier, David *13:* 127
Collier, John *27:* 179
Collier, Steven *50:* 52
Collier-Morales, Roberta *168:* 61
Collins, Heather *66:* 84; *67:* 68; *81:* 40; *98:* 192, 193; *129:* 95, 96, 98
Collins, Matt *167:* 90
Collins, Ross *140:* 23, 24
Colman, Audrey *146:* 161
Colón, Raul *108:* 112; *113:* 5; *117:* 167; *134:* 112; *146:* 23; *159:* 92; *166:* 73; *180:* 107; *186:* 156; *190:* 6; *193:* 24, 205
Colonna, Bernard *21:* 50; *28:* 103; *34:* 140; *43:* 180; *78:* 150
Comport, Sally Wern *117:* 169; *169:* 104; *190:* 42
Conde, J.M. *100:* 120
Condon, Grattan *54:* 85 Condon, Ken *161:* 44; *195:* 28, 29
Cone, Ferne Geller *39:* 49
Cone, J. Morton *39:* 49
Conklin, Paul *43:* 62
Connolly, Howard *67:* 88
Connolly, Jerome P. *4:* 128; *28:* 52
Connolly, Peter *47:* 60
Conoly, Walle *110:* 224
Conover, Chris *31:* 52; *40:* 184; *41:* 51; *44:* 79
Contreras, Gerry *72:* 9
Converse, James *38:* 70
Conway *62:* 62
Conway, Michael *69:* 12; *81:* 3; *92:* 108
Cook, Ande *188:* 135
Cook, G.R. *29:* 165
Cook, Joel *108:* 160
Cookburn, W.V. *29:* 204
Cooke, Donald E. *2:* 77
Cooke, Tom *52:* 118
Coomaraswamy, A.K. *50:* 100

Coombs, Charles *43:* 65
Coombs, Deborah *139:* 175
Coombs, Patricia *2:* 82; *3:* 52; *22:* 119; *51:* 32, 33, 34, 35, 36, 37, 38, 39, 40, 42, 43
Cooney, Barbara *6:* 16, 17, 50; *12:* 42; *13:* 92; *15:* 145; *16:* 74, 111; *18:* 189; *23:* 38, 89, 93; *32:* 138; *38:* 105; *59:* 48, 49, 51, 52, 53; *74:* 222; *81:* 100; *91:* 25; *96:* 71, 72, 74; *100:* 149; *YABC2:* 10
Cooper, Elisha *157:* 38, 39
Cooper, Floyd *79:* 95; *81:* 45; *84:* 82; *85:* 74; *91:* 118; *96:* 77, 78; *103:* 149; *144:* 54; *145:* 151; *159:* 198; *176:* 133, 134; *187:* 26, 27, 28, 29; *188:* 22
Cooper, Heather *50:* 39
Cooper, Helen *102:* 42, 43, 44
Cooper, Mario *24:* 107
Cooper, Marjorie *7:* 112
Cope, Jane *61:* 201; *108* 52
Copeland, Mark *180:* 12
Copelman, Evelyn *8:* 61; *18:* 25
Copley, Heather *30:* 86; *45:* 57
Corbett, Grahame *30:* 114; *43:* 67
Corbino, John *19:* 248
Corcos, Lucille *2:* 223; *10:* 27; *34:* 66
Corey, Robert *9:* 34
Corlass, Heather *10:* 7
Cornell, James *27:* 60
Cornell, Jeff *11:* 58
Cornell, Laura *94:* 179; *95:* 25
Corrigan, Barbara *8:* 37
Corrigan, Patrick *145:* 149
Corwin, Judith Hoffman *10:* 28
Corwin, Oliver *191:* 119
Cory, Fanny Y. *20:* 113; *48:* 29
Cosentino, Ralph *169:* 32
Cosgrove, Margaret *3:* 100; *47:* 63; *82:* 133
Costabel, Eva Deutsch *45:* 66, 67
Costanza, John *58:* 7, 8, 9
Costello, Chris *86:* 78
Costello, David F. *23:* 55
Côté, Geneviéve *184:* 37, 39
Cote, Nancy *126:* 139; *156:* 101; *174:* 101; *182:* 53, 54, 55
Cottenden, Jeff *190:* 45
Couch, Greg *94:* 124; *110:* 13; *162:* 31; *168:* 149
Councell, Ruth Tietjen *79:* 29
Courtney, Cathy *58:* 69, 144; *59:* 15; *61:* 20, 87
Courtney, R. *35:* 110
Counihan, Claire *133:* 106
Cousineau, Normand *89:* 180; *112:* 76
Cousins, Lucy *172:* 53, 54
Couture, Christin *41:* 209
Covarrubias, Miguel *35:* 118, 119, 123, 124, 125
Coville, Katherine *32:* 57; *36:* 167; *92:* 38
Covington, Neverne *113:* 87
Cowdrey, Richard *169:* 170; *178:* 205
Cowell, Cressida *140:* 39
Cowell, Lucinda *77:* 54
Cox *43:* 93
Cox, Charles *8:* 20
Cox, David *56:* 37; *90:* 63; *119:* 38
Cox, Palmer *24:* 76, 77
Cox, Steve *140:* 96
Coxe, Molly *69:* 44
Coxon, Michele *158:* 80
Crabb, Gordon *70:* 39
Crabtree, Judith *98:* 42
Craft, Kinuko *22:* 182; *36:* 220; *53:* 122, 123, 148,149; *74:* 12; *81:* 129; *86:* 31; *89:* 139; *127:* 27, 28, 29; *132:* 142; *139:* 38
Craig, Daniel *177:* 67; *180:* 11; *185:* 203
Craig, David *136:* 198
Craig, Helen *49:* 76; *62:* 70, 71, 72; *69:* 141; *94:* 42, 43, 44; *112:* 53; *135:* 101, 102
Crane, Alan H. *1:* 217
Crane, H.M. *13:* 111
Crane, Jack *43:* 183

Crane, Jordan *174:* 21
Crane, Walter *18:* 46, 47, 48, 49, 53, 54, 56, 57, 59, 60, 61; *22:* 128; *24:* 210, 217; *100:* 70, 71
Cravath, Lynne W. *98:* 45; *182:* 58, 59
Crawford, Denise *137:* 213
Crawford, Will *43:* 77
Credle, Ellis *1:* 69
Czernecki, Stefan *154:* 104; *178:* 68, 69
Crespi, Francesca *87:* 90
Cressy, Michael *124:* 55
Crews, Donald *32:* 59, 60; *76:* 42, 43, 44
Crews, Nina *97:* 49
Crichlow, Ernest *74:* 88; *83:* 203
Croft, James *150:* 57
Crofut, Bob *80:* 87; *81:* 47
Crofut, Susan *23:* 61
Croll, Carolyn *80:* 137; *102:* 52
Cross, Peter *56:* 78; *63:* 60, 65
Crowe, Elizabeth *88:* 144
Crowell, Pers *3:* 125
Cruikshank, George *15:* 76, 83; *22:* 74, 75, 76, 77, 78, 79,80, 81, 82, 84, 137; *24:* 22, 23
Crump, Fred H. *11:* 62
Cruz, Ray *6:* 55; *70:* 234; *123:* 173; *172:* 192
Csatari, Joe *44:* 82; *55:* 152; *63:* 25, 28; *102:* 58
Cuetara, Mittie *158:* 85
Cuffari, Richard *4:* 75; *5:* 98; *6:* 56; *7:* 13,84, 153; *8:* 148, 155; *9:* 89; *11:* 19; *12:* 55, 96,114; *15:* 51, 202; *18:* 5; *20:* 139; *21:* 197; *22:* 14, 192; *23:* 15, 106; *25:* 97; *27:* 133; *28:* 196; *29:* 54; *30:* 85; *31:* 35; *36:* 101; *38:* 171; *42:* 97; *44:* 92, 192; *45:* 212, 213; *46:* 36, 198; *50:* 164; *54:* 80, 136, 137, 145; *56:* 17; *60:* 63; *66:* 49, 50; *70:* 41; *71:* 132; *77:* 157; *78:* 58, 149; *79:* 120; *85:* 2, 152
Cugat, Xavier *19:* 120
Cumings, Art *35:* 160
Cummings, Chris *29:* 167
Cummings, Michael *159:* 142
Cummings, Pat *42:* 61; *61:* 99; *69:* 205; *71:* 57,58; *78:* 24, 25; *93:* 75; *107:* 49, 50; *164:* 259
Cummings, Richard *24:* 119
Cunette, Lou *20:* 93; *22:* 125
Cunningham, Aline *25:* 180
Cunningham, David *11:* 13
Cunningham, Imogene *16:* 122, 127
Cunningham, Kelley *176:* 159
Cupples, Pat *107:* 12; *126:* 109; *182:* 13
Curlee, Lynn *98:* 48; *141:* 39; *190:* 48
Currey, Anna *190:* 145
Curry, John Steuart *2:* 5; *19:* 84; *34:* 36; *144:* 126
Curry, Tom *127:* 131; *185:* 25, 26
Curtis, Bruce *23:* 96; *30:* 88; *36:* 22
Curtis, Neil *167:* 30
Cusack, Margaret *58:* 49, 50, 51
Cushman, Doug *65:* 57; *101:* 39, 40; *133:* 179; *157:* 45; *186:* 157
Cyrus, Kurt *132:* 39; *179:* 36, 37
Czechowski, Alicia *95:* 21; *171:* 37
Czernecki, Stefan *117:* 173

D

Dabcovich, Lydia *25:* 105; *40:* 114; *99:* 75, 76
Dacey, Bob *82:* 175; *152:* 65
d'Achille, Gino *127:* 175, 176
Dailey, Don *78:* 197
Dain, Martin J. *35:* 75
Dale, Penny *127:* 224; *151:* 57; *160:* 89
Dale, Rae *72:* 197
Daley, Joann *50:* 22
Dalton, Anne *40:* 62; *63:* 119
Daly, Deborah M. *74:* 213
Daly, Jim *103:* 60; *150:* 48
Daly, Jude *138:* 118, 119

Daly, Nicholas *37:* 53; *76:* 48, 49
Daly, Niki *107:* 15; *114:* 38, 39, 40; *164:* 86; *192:* 53
Daly, Paul *97:* 205
Dalziel, Brothers *33:* 113
D'Amato, Alex *9:* 48; *20:* 25
D'Amato, Janet *9:* 48; *20:* 25; *26:* 118
D'Amico, Steve *170:* 52
Danalis, Johnny *167:* 27
D'Andrea, Domenick *183:* 108
Daniel, Alan *23:* 59; *29:* 110; *76:* 50, 53, 55, 56; *153:* 76 *115:* 74; *134:* 70
Daniel, Lea *76:* 53, 55; *153:* 76
Daniel, Lewis C. *20:* 216
Daniels, Beau *73:* 4
Daniels, Steve *22:* 16
Daniels, Stewart *56:* 12
Dann, Bonnie *31:* 83
Dann, Penny *82:* 128
Danska, Herbert *24:* 219
Danyell, Alice *20:* 27
Darley, F.O.C. *16:* 145; *19:* 79, 86, 88, 185; *21:* 28,36; *35:* 76, 77, 78, 79, 80, 81; *YABC 2:* 175
Darling, Lois *3:* 59; *23:* 30, 31
Darling, Louis *1:* 40, 41; *2:* 63; *3:* 59; *23:* 30,31; *43:* 54, 57, 59; *121:* 53
Darrow, David R. *84:* 101
Darrow, Whitney, Jr. *13:* 25; *38:* 220, 221
Darwin, Beatrice *43:* 54
Darwin, Len *24:* 82
Dastolfo, Frank *33:* 179
Dauber, Liz *1:* 22; *3:* 266; *30:* 49
Daugherty, James *3:* 66; *8:* 178; *13:* 27, 28, 161; *18:* 101; *19:* 72; *29:* 108; *32:* 156; *42:* 84; *YABC 1:* 256; *2:* 174
d'Aulaire, Edgar Parin *5:* 51; *66:* 53
d'Aulaire, Ingri Parin *5:* 51; *66:* 53
Davalos, Felipe *99:* 197; *159:* 66; *174:* 163
Davenier, Christine *125:* 88; *127:* 32; *128:* 152; *179:* 39, 40
Davick, Linda *151:* 124
David, Jacques-Louis *193:* 22
David, Jonathan *19:* 37
Davidson, Kevin *28:* 154
Davidson, Raymond *32:* 61
Davie, Helen K. *77:* 48, 49
Davis, Allen *20:* 11; *22:* 45; *27:* 222; *29:* 157; *41:* 99; *47:* 99; *50:* 84; *52:* 105
Davis, Bette J. *15:* 53; *23:* 95
Davis, Dimitris *45:* 95
Davis, Hendon *151:* 122
Davis, Jack E. *145:* 139; *175:* 84, 85
Davis, Jim *32:* 63, 64
Davis, Katie *152:* 52, 53, 54
Davis, Lambert *110:* 23, 24; *176:* 58
Davis, Marguerite *31:* 38; *34:* 69, 70; *100:* 34; *YABC 1:* 126, 230
Davis, Nelle *69:* 191
Davis, Paul *78:* 214
Davis, Yvonne LeBrun *94:* 144
Davisson, Virginia H. *44:* 178
DaVolls, Andy *85:* 53
Dawson, Diane *24:* 127; *42:* 126; *52:* 130; *68:* 104
Day, Alexandra *67:* 59; *97:* 54; *166:* 65; *169:* 40
Day, Larry *169:* 88; *185:* 59
Day, Rob *94:* 110; *127:* 24
Dean, Bob *19:* 211
Dean, David *192:* 55
de Angeli, Marguerite *1:* 77; *27:* 62, 65, 66, 67, 69, 70, 72; *100:* 75, 76; *YABC 1:* 166
DeArmond, Dale *70:* 47
Deas, Michael *27:* 219, 221; *30:* 156; *67:* 134; *72:* 24; *75:* 155; *84:* 206; *88:* 124
Deas, Rich *191:* 87; *193:* 10
Debon, Nicolas *151:* 160; *177:* 46
de Bosschere, Jean *19:* 252; *21:* 4; *186:* 44, 45
De Bruyn, M(onica) G. *13:* 30, 31
Decker, C.B. *172:* 120

De Cuir, John F. *1:* 28, 29
Deeter, Catherine *74:* 110; *103:* 150; *137:* 50
Degen, Bruce *40:* 227, 229; *57:* 28, 29; *56:*
    156; *75:* 229; *76:* 19; *81:* 36, 37; *92:* 26; *93:*
    199; *97:* 56, 58, 59; *124:* 40; *147:* 39, 40,
    41; *168:* 23
De Grazia *14:* 59; *39:* 56, 57
DeGrazio, George *88:* 40
deGroot, Diane *9:* 39; *18:* 7; *23:* 123; *28:* 200,
    201; *31:* 58, 59; *34:* 151; *41:* 155; *43:* 88;
    46: 40, 200; *49:* 163; *50:* 89; *52:* 30, 34; *54:*
    43; *63:* 5; *70:* 136; *71:* 99; *73:* 117,156; *77:*
    34; *85:* 48; *86:* 201; *87:* 142; *90:* 72, 73,
    143; *95:* 182; *111:* 123; *118:* 160; *126:* 8;
    130: 130; *138:* 93, 94; *169:* 46, 47
de Groot, Lee *6:* 21
Deines, Brian *110:* 139
DeJohn, Marie *89:* 78
Dekhteryov, B. *61:* 158
de Kiefte, Kees *94:* 107
Delacre, Lulu *36:* 66; *156:* 35
Delaney, A. *21:* 78
Delaney, Michael *180:* 16
Delaney, Molly *80:* 43
Delaney, Ned *28:* 68; *56:* 80; *102:* 11
DeLange, Alex Pardo *179:* 128
DeLapine, Jim *79:* 21
De La Roche Saint Andre, Anne *75:* 37
de Larrea, Victoria *6:* 119, 204; *29:* 103; *72:*
    203; *87:* 199
Delessert, Étienne *7:* 140; *46:* 61, 62, 63, 65,
    67, 68; *130:* 38, 39, 40, 41, 42; *179:* 46, 47,
    48, 49; *YABC 2:* 209
Delezenne, Christine *186:* 126
DeLorenzo, Christopher *154:* 149
Delulio, John *15:* 54
DeLuna, Tony *88:* 95
Demarest, Chris L. *45:* 68, 69, 70; *73:* 172,
    173, 176; *78:* 106; *82:* 48, 49; *89:* 212; *92:*
    86; *128:* 57, 58; *175:* 46, 48
De Mejo, Oscar *40:* 67
Demi *11:* 135; *15:* 245; *66:* 129, 130; *89:* 216;
    102: 66, 67, 68
Denetsosie, Hoke *13:* 126; *82:* 34
Denise, Christopher *147:* 43, 44; *176:* 101;
    193: 35, 36, 37
Dennis, Morgan *18:* 68, 69; *64:* 89
Dennis, Wesley *2:* 87; *3:* 111; *11:* 132; *18:* 71,
    72, 73, 74; *22:* 9; *24:* 196, 200; *46:* 178; *69:*
    94, 96; *129:* 62
Denslow, W.W. *16:* 84, 85, 86, 87; *18:* 19, 20,
    24; *29:* 211; *100:* 21
Denton, Kady MacDonald *110:* 82; *130:* 70;
    181: 54, 55, 56; *192:* 75
Denton, Terry *72:* 163; *174:* 26; *186:* 52
DePalma, Mary Newell *132:* 114; *139:* 75;
    185: 30, 31; *186:* 121
de Paola, Tomie *8:* 95; *9:* 93; *11:* 69; 25; 103;
    28: 157; *29:* 80; *39:* 52, 53; *40:* 226; *46:*
    187; *59:* 61, 62, 63, 64, 65, 66, 67, 68, 69,
    71, 72, 74; *62:* 19; *108:* 63, 67, 68, 70; *155:*
    62, 64, 66; *180:* 105
Deraney, Michael J. *77:* 35; *78:* 148
deRosa, Dee *70:* 48; *71:* 210; *91:* 78
Dervaux, Isabelle *111:* 117
DeSaix, Deborah Durland *180:* 15; *188:* 24
De Saulles, Tony *119:* 39
de Seve, Peter *146:* 261
Deshaprabhu, Meera Dayal *86:* 192
Desimini, Lisa *86:* 68; *94:* 47; *96:* 7; *104:*
    107; *125:* 194; *131:* 180; *172:* 56
de St. Menin, Charles *70:* 17
Detmold, Edward J. *22:* 104, 105, 106, 107;
    35: 120; *64:* 5; *YABC 2:* 203
Detrich, Susan *20:* 133
Deutermann, Diana *77:* 175
DeVelasco, Joseph E. *21:* 51
de Veyrac, Robert *YABC 2:* 19
DeVille, Edward A. *4:* 235
de Visser, John *55:* 119
Devito, Bert *12:* 164

Devlin, Harry *11:* 74; *74:* 63, 65; *136:* 77, 78
Dewan, Ted *108:* 73; *157:* 55; *165:* 129
Dewar, Nick *133:* 122
Dewdney, Anna *184:* 43, 44
Dewey, Ariane *7:* 64; *33:* 195; *35:* 208; *68:*
    16,17; *75:* 46; *93:* 91; *94:* 197; *109:* 65, 66,
    67; *125:* 2, 3, 4, 5; *127:* 188; *143:* 25; *178:*
    17, 19, 74; *188:* 166
Dewey, Jennifer (Owings) *58:* 54; *64:* 214; *65:*
    207; *88:* 169; *103:* 45
Dewey, Kenneth *39:* 62; *51:* 23; *56:* 163
de Zanger, Arie *30:* 40
Diakité, Baba Wagué *174:* 28
Diamond, Donna *21:* 200; *23:* 63; *26:* 142; *35:*
    83, 84, 85, 86, 87, 88, 89; *38:* 78; *40:* 147;
    44: 152; *50:* 144; *53:* 126; *69:* 46, 47, 48,
    201; *71:* 133; *123:* 19
Dias, Ron *71:* 67
Diaz, David *80:* 213; *96:* 83, 84; *108:* 228;
    110: 29; *149:* 106; *150:* 63; *179:* 160; *184:*
    95, 97; *189:* 51, 52, 53
Dibley, Glin *138:* 83; *141:* 128
DiCesare, Joe *70:* 38; *71:* 63, 106; *79:* 214;
    93: 147; *116:* 217; *143:* 111; *166:* 57
Dick, John Henry *8:* 181
Dickens, Frank *34:* 131
Dickey, Robert L. *15:* 279
Dickson, Mora *84:* 21
Didier, Sam *166:* 114
Dietz, James *128:* 223; *193:* 136
di Fate, Vincent *37:* 70; *90:* 11; *93:* 60; *109:*
    219, 220
Di Fiori, Lawrence *10:* 51; *12:* 190; *27:* 97;
    40: 219; *93:* 57; *130:* 45
Digby, Desmond *97:* 180
Di Grazia, Thomas *32:* 66; *35:* 241
Dillard, Annie *10:* 32
Dillard, Sarah *136:* 186
Dillon, Corinne B. *1:* 139
Dillon, Diane *4:* 104, 167; *6:* 23; *13:* 29; *15:*
    99; *26:* 148; *27:* 136, 201; *51:* 29, 48, 51,
    52, 53, 54,55, 56, 57, 58, 59, 60, 61, 62; *54:*
    155; *56:* 69; *58:* 127,128; *61:* 95; *62:* 27;
    64: 46; *68:* 3; *69:* 209; *74:* 89; *79:* 92; *86:*
    89; *92:* 28, 177; *93:* 7, 210; *94:* 239, 240;
    97: 167; *106:* 58, 59,61, 64; *107:* 3; *139:*
    246; *167:* 77; *189:* 202; *191:* 191; *194:* 45,
    46, 48, 49
Dillon, Leo *4:* 104, 167; *6:* 23; *13:* 29; *15:* 99;
    26: 148; *27:* 136, 201; *51:* 29, 48, 51, 52,
    53, 54,55, 56, 57, 58, 59, 60, 61, 62; *54:*
    155; *56:* 69; *58:* 127,128; *61:* 95; *62:* 27;
    64: 46; *68:* 3; *69:* 209; *74:* 89; *79:* 92; *86:*
    89; *92:* 28, 177; *93:* 7, 210; *94:* 239, 240;
    97: 167; *106:* 58, 59,61, 64; *107:* 3; *139:*
    246; *167:* 77; *189:* 202; *191:* 191; *194:* 45,
    46, 48, 49
Dillon, Sharon Saseen *59:* 179, 188
DiMaccio, Gerald *121:* 80
DiMaggio, Joe *36:* 22
DiMassi, Gina *169:* 17
Dinan, Carol *25:* 169; *59:* 75
Dines, Glen *7:* 66, 67
Dinesen, Thomas *44:* 37
Dinh, Pham Viet *167:* 184
Dinnerstein, Harvey *42:* 63, 64, 65, 66, 67, 68;
    50: 146
Dinsdale, Mary *10:* 65; *11:* 171
Dinyer, Eric *86:* 148; *109:* 163; *110:* 239; *124:*
    11; *150:* 69; *170:* 4; *171:* 30
Dion, Nathalie *170:* 124
DiRocco, Carl *181:* 23
DiSalvo-Ryan, DyAnne *59:* 77; *62:* 185; *117:*
    46; *144:* 64; *150:* 153; *186:* 162
Disney, Walt *28:* 71, 72, 73, 76, 77, 78, 79,
    80, 81, 87, 88, 89,90, 91, 94
DiTerlizzi, Tony *105:* 7; *147:* 22; *154:* 31, 32,
    33
Divito, Anna *83:* 159
Dixon, Don *74:* 17; *109:* 196
Dixon, Larry *127:* 125

Dixon, Maynard *20:* 165
Doares, Robert G. *20:* 39
Dobias, Frank *22:* 162
Dobrin, Arnold *4:* 68
Dobson, Steven Gaston *102:* 103
Dockray, Tracy *139:* 77
Docktor, Irv *43:* 70
Dodd, Ed *4:* 69
Dodd, Julie *74:* 73
Dodd, Lynley *35:* 92; *86:* 71; *132:* 45, 46, 47
Dodge, Bill *96:* 36; *118:* 7, 8, 9; *133:* 135
Dodgson, Charles L. *20:* 148; *33:* 146; *YABC
    2:* 98
Dodson, Bert *9:* 138; *14:* 195; *42:* 55; *54:* 8;
    60: 49; *101:* 125
Dodson, Liz Brenner *105:* 117; *111:* 15
Dohanos, Stevan *16:* 10
Dolce, J. Ellen *74:* 147; *75:* 41
Dolch, Marguerite P. *50:* 64
Dolesch, Susanne *34:* 49
Dollar, Diane *57:* 32
Dolobowsky, Mena *81:* 54
Dolson, Hildegarde *5:* 57
Domanska, Janina *6:* 66, 67; *YABC 1:* 166
Domi *134:* 113
Dominguez, El *53:* 94
Domjan, Joseph *25:* 93
Domm, Jeffrey C. *84:* 69; *135:* 70
Donahey, William *68:* 209
Donahue, Dorothy *76:* 170
Donahue, Vic *2:* 93; *3:* 190; *9:* 44
Donald, Elizabeth *4:* 18
Donalty, Alison *149:* 195, 196, 197
Donato *85:* 59; *149:* 204; *191:* 19
Doney, Todd L.W. *87:* 12; *93:* 112; *98:* 135;
    101: 57; *104:* 40; *118:* 163; *135:* 162, 163;
    151: 18
Donna, Natalie *9:* 52
Donohue, Dorothy *95:* 2; *132:* 30; *176:* 54, 55;
    178: 77, 78, 79
Dooling, Michael *82:* 19; *105:* 55; *106:* 224;
    125: 135; *171:* 46; *172:* 12; *176:* 120
Doran, Ben-Ami *128:* 189
Dore, Gustave *18:* 169, 172, 175; *19:* 93, 94,
    95, 96, 97, 98,99, 100, 101, 102, 103, 104,
    105; *23:* 188; *25:* 197, 199
Doremus, Robert *6:* 62; *13:* 90; *30:* 95, 96, 97;
    38: 97
Dorfman, Ronald *11:* 128
Doriau *86:* 59; *91:* 152
Dorros, Arthur *78:* 42, 43; *91:* 28
Doruyter, Karel *165:* 105
dos Santos, Joyce Audy *57:* 187, 189
Doty, Roy *28:* 98; *31:* 32; *32:* 224; *46:* 157;
    82: 71; *142:* 7
Doucet, Bob *132:* 238; *169:* 159
Dougherty, Charles *16:* 204; *18:* 74
Doughty, Rebecca *177:* 174
Doughty, Thomas *118:* 31; *140:* 60
Douglas, Aaron *31:* 103
Douglas, Carole Nelson *73:* 48
Douglas, Goray *13:* 151
Dow, Brian *150:* 92
Dowd, Jason *132:* 51, 52; *164:* 244
Dowd, Vic *3:* 244; *10:* 97
Dowden, Anne Ophelia *7:* 70, 71; *13:* 120
Dowdy, Mrs. Regera *29:* 100
Downes, Belinda *180:* 29
Downing, Julie *60:* 140; *81:* 50; *86:* 200; *99:*
    129
Doyle, Janet *56:* 31
Doyle, Richard *21:* 31, 32, 33; *23:* 231; *24:*
    177; *31:* 87
Draper, Angie *43:* 84
Drath, Bill *26:* 34
Drawson, Blair *17:* 53; *126:* 65
Dray, Matt *177:* 47
Drescher, Henrik *105:* 60, 62, 63; *172:* 72
Drescher, Joan *30:* 100, 101; *35:* 245; *52:* 168;
    137: 52
Dressell, Peggy *186:* 41

Drew, Patricia *15:* 100
Drummond, V.H. *6:* 70
Drury, Christian Potter *105:* 97; *186:* 224
Dubanevich, Arlene *56:* 44
Dubois, Gerard *182:* 9
DuBurke, Randy *187:* 89
Ducak, Danilo *99:* 130; *108:* 214
Duchesne, Janet *6:* 162; *79:* 8
Duda, Jana *102:* 155
Dudash, Michael *32:* 122; *77:* 134; *82:* 149
Duer, Douglas *34:* 177
Duewell, Kristina *195:* 76
Duffy, Daniel Mark *76:* 37; *101:* 196; *108:* 147, 148
Duffy, Joseph *38:* 203
Duffy, Pat *28:* 153
Dugan, Karen *181:* 26
Dugin, Andrej *77:* 60
Dugina, Olga *77:* 60
Duke, Chris *8:* 195; *139:* 164
Duke, Kate *87:* 186; *90:* 78, 79, 80, 81; *192:* 21, 59, 60, 61, 63
Duke, Marion *165:* 87
Dulac, Edmund *19:* 108, 109, 110, 111, 112, 113, 114, 115, 117; *23:* 187; *25:* 152; *YABC 1:* 37; *2:* 147
Dulac, Jean *13:* 64
Dumas, Philippe *52:* 36, 37, 38, 39, 40, 41, 42, 43, 45; *119:* 40, 41, 42
Dunaway, Nancy *108:* 161
Dunbar, James *76:* 63
Dunbar, Polly *181:* 60, 61
Duncan, Beverly *72:* 92
Duncan, John *116:* 94
Dunn, H.T. *62:* 196
Dunn, Harvey *34:* 78, 79, 80, 81
Dunn, Iris *5:* 175
Dunn, Phoebe *5:* 175
Dunne, Jeanette *72:* 57, 173, 222
Dunnick, Regan *176:* 51; *178:* 83, 84
Dunnington, Tom *3:* 36; *18:* 281; *25:* 61; *31:* 159; *35:* 168; *48:* 195; *79:* 144; *82:* 230
Dunn-Ramsey, Marcy *117:* 131
Dunrea, Olivier *59:* 81; *118:* 53, 54; *124:* 43
Duntze, Dorothee *88:* 28; *160:* 76
Dupasquier, Philippe *86:* 75; *104:* 76; *151:* 63
DuQuette, Keith *90:* 83; *155:* 73, 74
Durham, Sarah *192:* 248
Duroussy, Nathalie *146:* 150
Durrell, Julie *82:* 62; *94:* 62
Dutz *6:* 59
Duvoisin, Roger *2:* 95; *6:* 76, 77; *7:* 197; *28:* 125; *30:* 101, 102, 103, 104, 105, 107; *47:* 205; *84:* 254
Dyer, Dale *141:* 71
Dyer, Jane *75:* 219; *129:* 28; *147:* 49, 50, 51; *168:* 121; *190:* 4; *191:* 57, 59, 60
Dypold, Pat *15:* 37

E

E.V.B.
See Boyle, Eleanor Vere (Gordon)
Eachus, Jennifer *29:* 74; *82:* 201; *164:* 153
Eadie, Bob *63:* 36
Eagle, Bruce *95:* 119
Eagle, Ellen *82:* 121; *89:* 3
Eagle, Jeremy *141:* 71
Eagle, Michael *11:* 86; *20:* 9; *23:* 18; *27:* 122; *28:* 57; *34:* 201; *44:* 189; *73:* 9; *78:* 235; *85:* 43
Earl-Bridges, Michele *159:* 128
Earle, Edwin *56:* 27
Earle, Olive L. *7:* 75
Earle, Vana *27:* 99
Earley, Lori *132:* 2; *186:* 4; *195:* 8
Early, Margaret *72:* 59
East, Stella *131:* 223
Eastman, P.D. *33:* 57

Easton, Reginald *29:* 181
Eaton, Tom *4:* 62; *6:* 64; *22:* 99; *24:* 124
Ebbeler, Jeffrey *193:* 62
Ebel, Alex *11:* 89
Eberbach, Andrea *192:* 115
Ebert, Len *9:* 191; *44:* 47
Echevarria, Abe *37:* 69
Echo Hawk, Bunky *187:* 192
Eckersley, Maureen *48:* 62
Eckert, Horst *72:* 62
Ede, Janina *33:* 59
Edens, Cooper *49:* 81, 82, 83, 84, 85; *112:* 58
Edens, John *109:* 115
Edgar, Sarah E. *41:* 97
Edgerton, Perky *195:* 144
Edliq, Emily S. *131:* 107
Edrien *11:* 53
Edwards, Freya *45:* 102
Edwards, George Wharton *31:* 155
Edwards, Gunvor *2:* 71; *25:* 47; *32:* 71; *54:* 106
Edwards, Jeanne *29:* 257
Edwards, Linda Strauss *21:* 134; *39:* 123; *49:* 88, 89
Edwards, Michelle *152:* 62, 63
Edwards, Wallace *170:* 55
Egan, Tim *155:* 76, 77, 78
Egge, David *102:* 71
Eggenhofer, Nicholas *2:* 81
Eggleton, Bob *74:* 40; *81:* 190, 191; *105:* 6; *121:* 183; *149:* 203; *166:* 215
Egielski, Richard *11:* 90; *16:* 208; *33:* 236; *38:* 35; *49:* 91, 92, 93, 95, 212, 213, 214, 216; *79:* 122; *106:* 67, 68, 69; *134:* 135; *144:* 244; *163:* 82, 84
Ehlert, Lois *35:* 97; *69:* 51; *112:* 7; *113:* 208; *128:* 63, 64, 65; *172:* 77, 79, 80
Ehrlich, Bettina *1:* 83
Eitan, Ora *160:* 165
Eichenberg, Fritz *1:* 79; *9:* 54; *19:* 248; *23:* 170; *24:* 200; *26:* 208; *50:* 67, 68, 69, 70, 71, 72, 73,74, 75, 77, 79, 80, 81; *60:* 165; *100:* 137; *YABC 1:* 104, 105; *2:* 213
Einsel, Naiad *10:* 35; *29:* 136
Einsel, Walter *10:* 37
Einzig, Susan *3:* 77; *43:* 78; *67:* 155; *129:* 154
Eisner, Will *165:* 82, 83
Eitzen, Allan *9:* 56; *12:* 212; *14:* 226; *21:* 194; *38:* 162; *76:* 218
Eldridge, H. *54:* 109
Eldridge, Harold *43:* 83
Elgaard, Greta *19:* 241
Elgin, Kathleen *9:* 188; *39:* 69
Ellacott, S.E. *19:* 118
Elliot, David *192:* 26
Elliott, Mark *93:* 69; *105:* 108; *107:* 123; *140:* 53; *165:* 189; *173:* 67; *195:* 95
Elliott, Sarah M. *14:* 58
Ellis, Dianne *130:* 208
Ellis, Jan Davey *88:* 50; *115:* 80
Ellis, Richard *130:* 47, 48
Ellison, Pauline *55:* 21
Elmer, Richard *78:* 5
Elmore, Larry *90:* 8
Elschner, Géraldine *183:* 38
Elwell, Peter *195:* 150
Elwell, Tristan *110:* 39; *121:* 182; *127:* 46; *137:* 144; *141:* 173; *151:* 236; *158:* 264; *167:* 119, 120, 121; *169:* 20; *190:* 12
Elzbieta *88:* 80, 81
Emberley, Ed *8:* 53; *70:* 53, 54; *146:* 65, 69, 70
Emberley, Michael *34:* 83; *80:* 72; *119:* 47, 48; *147:* 100; *158:* 115; *189:* 62, 64
Emerling, Dorothy *104:* 27
Emery, Leslie *49:* 187
Emmett, Bruce *49:* 147; *80:* 175; *101:* 206
Emry-Perrott, Jennifer *61:* 57
Emshwiller, Ed *174:* 45
Endle, Kate *191:* 167
Engel, Diana *70:* 57

Engle, Mort *38:* 64
Englebert, Victor *8:* 54
English, Mark *101:* 207
Enik, Ted *142:* 39
Enos, Randall *20:* 183
Enright, Maginel Wright *19:* 240, 243; *39:* 31, 35, 36
Enrique, Romeo *34:* 135
Ensor, Barbara *180:* 30
Epstein, Stephen *50:* 142, 148
Erdogan, Buket *174:* 179
Erdrich, Louise *141:* 62
Erhard, Walter *1:* 152
Erickson, Phoebe *11:* 83; *59:* 85
Erikson, Mel *31:* 69
Eriksson, Eva *63:* 88, 90, 92, 93
Ering, Timothy Basil *131:* 100; *176:* 63, 64
Erlbruch, Wolf *181:* 66
Ernst, Lisa Campbell *47:* 147; *95:* 47; *154:* 46, 47, 48; *164:* 88
Esco, Jo *61:* 103
Escourido, Joseph *4:* 81
Escrivá, Viví *119:* 51; *181:* 36
Este, Kirk *33:* 111
Estep, David *73:* 57
Estes, Eleanor *91:* 66
Estoril, Jean *32:* 27
Estrada, Pau *74:* 76
Estrada, Ric *5:* 52, 146; *13:* 174
Etchemendy, Teje *38:* 68
Etheredges, the *73:* 12
Etienne, Kirk-Albert *145:* 184
Ets, Marie Hall *2:* 102
Ettlinger, Doris *171:* 98; *186:* 106
Eulalie *YABC 2:* 315
Evans, Greg *73:* 54, 55, 56; *143:* 40, 41
Evans, Katherine *5:* 64
Evans, Leslie *144:* 227
Evans, Shane W. *159:* 142; *160:* 190; *168:* 39; *188:* 88; *189:* 66, 67, 68
Everitt, Betsy *151:* 110
Ewart, Claire *76:* 69; *145:* 59, 60
Ewing, Carolyn *66:* 143; *79:* 52
Ewing, Juliana Horatia *16:* 92
Eyolfson, Norman *98:* 154

F

Fabian, Limbert *136:* 114
Facklam, Paul *132:* 62
Falconer, Ian *125:* 66; *179:* 59
Falconer, Pearl *34:* 23
Falkenstern, Lisa *70:* 34; *76:* 133; *78:* 171; *127:* 16; *191:* 151
Falls, C.B. *1:* 19; *38:* 71, 72, 73, 74
Falter, John *40:* 169, 170
Falwell, Cathryn *118:* 77; *137:* 185
Fancher, Lou *138:* 219; *141:* 64; *144:* 199; *177:* 51
Fanelli, Sara *89:* 63; *126:* 69
Faria, Rosana *150:* 143
Faricy, Patrick *185:* 182
Farmer, Andrew *49:* 102
Farmer, Peter *24:* 108; *38:* 75
Farnsworth, Bill *93:* 189; *116:* 147; *124:* 8; *135:* 52; *146:* 242, 243, 244; *182:* 176; *186:* 31, 83, 84, 85; *191:* 197
Farquharson, Alexander *46:* 75
Farrell, David *40:* 135
Farris, David *74:* 42
Fasolino, Teresa *118:* 145
Fatigati, Evelyn *24:* 112
Fatus, Sophie *182:* 74; *190:* 218
Faul-Jansen, Regina *22:* 117
Faulkner, Jack *6:* 169
Faulkner, Matt *161:* 174; *167:* 75
Fava, Rita *2:* 29
Fax, Elton C. *1:* 101; *4:* 2; *12:* 77; *25:* 107
Fay *43:* 93

Fearnley, Jan *153:* 82, 83
Fearrington, Ann *146:* 80
Federspiel, Marian *33:* 51
Fedorov, Nickolai Ivanovich *110:* 102
Feelings, Tom *5:* 22; *8:* 56; *12:* 153; *16:* 105; *30:* 196; *49:* 37; *61:* 101; *69:* 56, 57; *93:* 74; *105:* 88
Fehr, Terrence *21:* 87
Feiffer, Jules *3:* 91; *8:* 58; *61:* 66, 67, 70, 74, 76,77, 78; *111:* 47, 48, 49, 50; *132:* 122; *157:* 62
Feigeles, Neil *41:* 242
Feldman, Elyse *86:* 7
Feller, Gene *33:* 130
Fellows, Muriel H. *10:* 42
Felstead, Cathie *116:* 85
Felts, Shirley *33:* 71; *48:* 59
Fennell, Tracy *171:* 69
Fennelli, Maureen *38:* 181
Fenton, Carroll Lane *5:* 66; *21:* 39
Fenton, Mildred Adams *5:* 66; *21:* 39
Ferguson, Peter *177:* 30, 31; *181:* 154
Ferguson, Walter W. *34:* 86
Fernandes, Eugenie *77:* 67
Fernandes, Stanislaw *70:* 28
Fernandez, Fernando *77:* 57
Fernandez, Laura *77:* 153; *101:* 117; *131:* 222; *170:* 119; *175:* 182
Ferrari, Alex *188:* 121
Ferrington, Susan *172:* 22
Fetz, Ingrid *11:* 67; *12:* 52; *16:* 205; *17:* 59; *29:* 105; *30:* 108, 109; *32:* 149; *43:* 142; *56:* 29; *60:* 34; *85:* 48; *87:* 146
Fiammenghi, Gioia *9:* 66; *11:* 44; *12:* 206; *13:* 57, 59; *52:* 126, 129; *66:* 64; *85:* 83; *91:* 161; *166:* 169
Fiedler, Joseph Daniel *96:* 42; *113:* 173; *129:* 164; *146:* 17; *159:* 68; *162:* 104
Field, Rachel *15:* 113
Fielding, David *70:* 124
Fieser, Stephen *152:* 36
Fine, Howard *145:* 159; *159:* 64; *165:* 134; *174:* 129; *181:* 68
Fine, Peter K. *43:* 210
Finger, Helen *42:* 81
Fink, Sam *18:* 119
Finlay, Winifred *23:* 72
Finney, Pat *79:* 215
Fiore, Peter *99:* 196; *125:* 139; *144:* 225; *160:* 169; *180:* 72
Fiorentino, Al *3:* 240
Firehammer, Karla *174:* 202
Firmin, Charlotte *29:* 75; *48:* 70
Firmin, Peter *58:* 63, 64, 65, 67, 68, 70, 71
Firth, Barbara *81:* 208; *127:* 218; *179:* 62
Fischel, Lillian *40:* 204
Fischer, Hans *25:* 202
Fischer-Nagel, Andreas *56:* 50
Fischer-Nagel, Heiderose *56:* 50
Fisher, Carolyn *154:* 50
Fisher, Chris *79:* 62; *158:* 248; *188:* 195
Fisher, Cynthia *117:* 45; *137:* 118; *195:* 40
Fisher, Jeffrey *142:* 80
Fisher, Leonard Everett *3:* 6; *4:* 72, 86; *6:* 197; *9:* 59; *16:* 151, 153; *23:* 44; *27:* 134; *29:* 26; *34:* 87, 89, 90, 91, 93, 94, 95, 96; *40:* 206; *50:* 150; *60:* 158; *73:* 68, 70, 71, 72, 73; *176:* 71, 72, 73; *YABC 2:* 169
Fisher, Lois *20:* 62; *21:* 7
Fisher, Valorie *177:* 55
Fisk, Nicholas *25:* 112
Fitschen, Marilyn *2:* 20, 21; *20:* 48
Fitz-Maurice, Jeff *175:* 2
Fitzgerald, F.A. *15:* 116; *25:* 86, 87
Fitzhugh, Louise *1:* 94; *9:* 163; *45:* 75, 78
Fitzgerald, Joanne *157:* 153, 154
Fitzhugh, Susie *11:* 117
Fitzpatrick, Jim *109:* 130
Fitzpatrick, Marie-Louise *125:* 69, 70; *189:* 72, 73
Fitzsimmons, Arthur *14:* 128

Fix, Philippe *26:* 102
Flack, Marjorie *21:* 67; *100:* 93; *YABC 2:* 122
Flagg, James Montgomery *17:* 227
Flavin, Teresa *132:* 115; *186:* 119
Flax, Zeona *2:* 245
Fleetwood, Tony *171:* 51
Fleishman, Seymour *14:* 232; *24:* 87
Fleming, Denise *71:* 179; *81:* 58; *126:* 71, 72, 73; *173:* 52, 53
Fleming, Guy *18:* 41
Flesher, Vivienne *85:* 55
Fletcher, Claire *80:* 106; *157:* 159
Flint, Russ *74:* 80
Floate, Helen *111:* 163
Floca, Brian *155:* 88, 89; *190:* 10, 66, 67
Floethe, Richard *3:* 131; *4:* 90
Floherty, John J., Jr. *5:* 68
Flook, Helen *160:* 81
Flora, James *1:* 96; *30:* 111, 112
Florczak, Robert *166:* 51
Florian, Douglas *19:* 122; *83:* 64, 65; *125:* 71, 72, 74, 76; *128:* 130; *177:* 58, 60
Flory, Jane *22:* 111
Flower, Renee *125:* 109
Floyd, Gareth *1:* 74; *17:* 245; *48:* 63; *62:* 35,36, 37, 39, 40, 41; *74:* 245; *79:* 56
Fluchere, Henri A. *40:* 79
Flynn, Alice *183:* 2
Flynn, Barbara *7:* 31; *9:* 70
Fogarty, Thomas *15:* 89
Foley, Greg *190:* 69
Folger, Joseph *9:* 100
Folkard, Charles *22:* 132; *29:* 128, 257, 258
Foott, Jeff *42:* 202
Forberg, Ati *12:* 71, 205; *14:* 1; *22:* 113; *26:* 22; *48:* 64, 65
Ford, George *24:* 120; *31:* 70, 177; *58:* 126; *81:* 103; *107:* 91; *136:* 100; *194:* 47
Ford, H.J. *16:* 185, 186
Ford, Jason *174:* 119
Ford, Pamela Baldwin *27:* 104
Fordham, John *168:* 160, 161
Foreman, Michael *2:* 110, 111; *67:* 99; *73:* 78, 79, 80,81, 82; *93:* 146; *135:* 55, 56, 57; *184:* 58, 59
Forrester, Victoria *40:* 83
Forsey, Chris *140:* 210
Fortnum, Peggy *6:* 29; *20:* 179; *24:* 211; *26:* 76, 77, 78; *39:* 78; *58:* 19, 21, 23, 27; *YABC 1:* 148
Fortune, Eric *191:* 52
Foster, Brad W. *34:* 99
Foster, Genevieve *2:* 112
Foster, Gerald *7:* 78
Foster, Jon *146:* 18
Foster, Laura Louise *6:* 79
Foster, Marian Curtis *23:* 74; *40:* 42
Foster, Sally *58:* 73, 74
Foucher, Adele *47:* 118
Foust, Mitch *168:* 50
Fowler, Jim *184:* 190
Fowler, Mel *36:* 127
Fowler, Richard *87:* 219
Fowles, Selley *165:* 127
Fox, Charles Phillip *12:* 84
Fox, Christyan *188:* 36
Fox, Jim *6:* 187
Fox-Davies, Sarah *76:* 150; *182:* 63
Frace, Charles *15:* 118
Frailey, Joy *72:* 108
Frame, Paul *2:* 45, 145; *9:* 153; *10:* 124; *21:* 71; *23:* 62; *24:* 123; *27:* 106; *31:* 48; *32:* 159; *34:* 195; *38:* 136; *42:* 55; *44:* 139; *60:* 39, 40, 41, 42, 43, 44, 46; *73:* 183
Frampton, David *85:* 72; *102:* 33; *139:* 182; *152:* 37; *189:* 171
Francois, Andre *25:* 117
Francoise
  See Seignobosc, Francoise
Frank, Lola Edick *2:* 199
Frank, Mary *4:* 54; *34:* 100

Franke, Phil *45:* 91
Frankel, Alona *66:* 70
Frankel, Julie *40:* 84, 85, 202
Frankenberg, Robert *22:* 116; *30:* 50; *38:* 92, 94, 95; *68:* 111
Frankfeldt, Gwen *84:* 223; *110:* 92
Frankland, David *169:* 137; *182:* 164
Franklin, Ashton *165:* 144
Franklin, John *24:* 22
Franson, Leanne R. *111:* 57, 58; *151:* 7
Frascino, Edward *9:* 133; *29:* 229; *33:* 190; *48:* 80, 81, 82, 83, 84, 85, 86
Frasconi, Antonio *6:* 80; *27:* 208; *53:* 41, 43, 45, 47,48; *68:* 145; *73:* 226; *131:* 68
Fraser, Betty *2:* 212; *6:* 185; *8:* 103; *31:* 72,73; *43:* 136; *111:* 76
Fraser, Eric *38:* 78; *41:* 149, 151
Fraser, F.A. *22:* 234
Fraser, James *171:* 68
Fraser, Mary Ann *137:* 63
Frasier, Debra *69:* 60; *112:* 67; *182:* 81, 82, 83
Fraustino, Lisa Rowe *146:* 87
Frazee, Marla *72:* 98; *105:* 79, 80; *151:* 67, 68; *164:* 165; *171:* 190, 191; *187:* 53, 54,55, 56, 143
Frazetta, Frank *41:* 72; *58:* 77, 78, 79, 80, 81, 82, 83
Frazier, Craig *177:* 63
Freas, John *25:* 207
Fredrickson, Mark *103:* 33
Freeland, Michael J. *118:* 115
Freeman, Don *2:* 15; *13:* 249; *17:* 62, 63, 65, 67, 68; *18:* 243; *20:* 195; *23:* 213, 217; *32:* 155; *55:* 129
Freeman, Irving *67:* 150
Freeman, Laura *144:* 111
Freeman, Pietri *140:* 223
Freeman, Tom *167:* 118
Freeman, Tor *164:* 93
Fregosi, Claudia *24:* 117
Fremaux, Charlotte Murray *138:* 29; *141:* 95
French, Fiona *6:* 82, 83; *75:* 61; *109:* 170; *132:* 79, 80, 81, 82
French, Martin *163:* 4
Frendak, Rodney *126:* 97, 98
Freschet, Gina *175:* 73
Freynet, Gilbert *72:* 221
Friedman, Judith *43:* 197; *131:* 221
Friedman, Marvin *19:* 59; *42:* 86
Frinta, Dagmar *36:* 42
Frith, Michael K. *15:* 138; *18:* 120
Fritz, Ronald *46:* 73; *82:* 124
Fromm, Lilo *29:* 85; *40:* 197
Frost, A.B. *17:* 6, 7; *19:* 123, 124, 125, 126, 127, 128, 129,130; *100:* 119; *YABC 1:* 156, 157, 160; *2:* 107
Frost, Helen *183:* 51
Frost, Kristi *118:* 113
Frost, Michael *151:* 209
Froud, Brian *150:* 82, 83
Froud, Wendy *151:* 237
Fry, Guy *2:* 224
Fry, Rosalie *3:* 72; *YABC 2:* 180, 181
Fry, Rosalind *21:* 153, 168
Fryer, Elmer *34:* 115
Fuchs, Bernie *110:* 10; *162:* 46
Fuchs, Erich *6:* 84
Fuchshuber, Annegert *43:* 96
Fufuka, Mahiri *32:* 146
Fuge, Charles *144:* 91, 93
Fujikawa, Gyo *39:* 75, 76; *76:* 72, 73, 74
Fulford, Deborah *23:* 159
Fuller, Margaret *25:* 189
Fulweiler, John *93:* 99
Funai, Mamoru *38:* 105
Funk, Tom *7:* 17, 99
Furchgott, Terry *29:* 86
Furness, William Henry, Jr. *94:* 18
Furukawa, Mel *25:* 42
Fusari, Erika *164:* 227

G

Gaadt, David *78:* 212; *121:* 166
Gaadt, George *71:* 9
Gaber, Susan *99:* 33; *115:* 57, 58; *164:* 195;
   169: 61, 62, 63; *185:* 50, 51; *188:* 124
Gaberell, J. *19:* 236
Gable, Brian *195:* 68, 69
Gabler, Mirko *99:* 71; *195:* 32
Gackenbach, Dick *19:* 168; *41:* 81; *48:* 89, 90,
   91, 92,93, 94; *54:* 105; *79:* 75, 76, 77
Gad, Victor *87:* 161
Gaetano, Nicholas *23:* 209
Gaffney-Kessell, Walter *94:* 219; *174:* 188
Gag, Flavia *17:* 49, 52
Gag, Wanda *100:* 101, 102; *YABC 1:* 135, 137,
   138, 141, 143
Gagnon, Cecile *11:* 77; *58:* 87
Gal, Laszlo *14:* 127; *52:* 54, 55, 56; *65:* 142;
   68: 150; *81:* 185; *96:* 104, 105
Galazinski, Tom *55:* 13
Galdone, Paul *1:* 156, 181, 206; *2:* 40, 241; *3:*
   42,144; *4:* 141; *10:* 109, 158; *11:* 21; *12:*
   118, 210; *14:* 12; *16:* 36, 37; *17:* 70, 71, 72,
   73, 74; *18:* 111, 230; *19:* 183; *21:* 154; *22:*
   150, 245; *33:* 126; *39:* 136, 137; *42:* 57; *51:*
   169; *55:* 110; *66:* 80, 82, 139; *72:* 73; *100:*
   84
Gale, Cathy *140:* 22; *143:* 52
Gall, Chris *176:* 79, 80
Gallagher, Jack *187:* 100
Gallagher, S. Saelig *105:* 154
Gallagher, Sears *20:* 112
Galloway, Ewing *51:* 154
Galouchka, Annouchka Gravel *95:* 55; *182:* 40
Galster, Robert *1:* 66
Galsworthy, Gay John *35:* 232
Galvez, Daniel *125:* 182
Gamble, Kim *112:* 64, 65; *124:* 77; *183:* 40,
   42, 43, 56, 57; *187:* 170
Gammell, Stephen *7:* 48; *13:* 149; *29:* 82; *33:*
   209; *41:* 88; *50:* 185, 186, 187; *53:* 51, 52,
   53, 54, 55, 56,57, 58; *54:* 24, 25; *56:* 147,
   148, 150; *57:* 27, 66; *81:* 62, 63; *87:* 88; *89:*
   10; *106:* 223; *126:* 2; *128:* 71, 73, 74, 77;
   154: 34
Gamper, Ruth *84:* 198
Gampert, John *58:* 94
Ganly, Helen *56:* 56
Gannett, Ruth Chrisman *3:* 74; *18:* 254; *33:*
   77, 78
Gantschev, Ivan *45:* 32
Garafano, Marie *73:* 33
Garbot, Dave *131:* 106
Garbutt, Bernard *23:* 68
Garcia *37:* 71
Garcia, Manuel *74:* 145
Garcia-Franco, Rebecca *173:* 46
Gardiner, Lindsey *178:* 128; *186:* 137
Gardner, Earle *45:* 167
Gardner, Joan *40:* 87
Gardner, Joel *40:* 87, 92
Gardner, John *40:* 87
Gardner, Lucy *40:* 87
Gardner, Richard
   See Cummings, Richard
Gardner, Sally *171:* 177; *177:* 66, 68
Gargiulo, Frank *84:* 158
Garland, Michael *36:* 29; *38:* 83; *44:* 168; *48:*
   78, 221, 222; *49:* 161; *60:* 139; *71:* 6, 11;
   72: 229; *74:* 142; *89:* 187; *93:* 183; *104:*
   110; *131:* 55; *139:* 209; *168:* 56
Garland, Peggy *60:* 139
Garland, Sarah *62:* 45; *135:* 67, 68; *171:* 118
Garn, Aimee *75:* 47
Garner, Joan *128:* 170
Garneray, Ambroise Louis *59:* 140
Garnett, Eve *3:* 75
Garnett, Gary *39:* 184
Garns, Allen *80:* 125; *84:* 39; *165:* 231

Garófoli, Viviana *186:* 123
Garraty, Gail *4:* 142; *52:* 106
Garrett, Agnes *46:* 110; *47:* 157
Garrett, Edmund H. *20:* 29
Garrett, Tom *107:* 194
Garrick, Jacqueline *67:* 42, 43; *77:* 94
Garrison, Barbara *19:* 133; *104:* 146; *109:* 87
Garro, Mark *108:* 131; *128:* 210
Garvey, Robert *98:* 222
Garza, Carmen Lomas *80:* 211; *182:* 86
Garza, Xavier *184:* 64
Gates, Frieda *26:* 80
Gaughan, Jack *26:* 79; *43:* 185
Gaver, Becky *20:* 61
Gawing, Toby *72:* 52
Gay, Marie-Louise *68:* 76, 77, 78; *102:* 136;
   126: 76, 78, 81, 83; *127:* 55, 56; *179:* 70,
   72, 73, 74
Gay, Zhenya *19:* 135, 136
Gaydos, Tim *62:* 201
Gazsi, Ed *80:* 48
Gazso, Gabriel *73:* 85
Geary, Clifford N. *1:* 122; *9:* 104; *51:* 74
Geary, Rick *142:* 44, 46
Gee, Frank *33:* 26
Geehan, Wayne *157:* 181
Geer, Charles *1:* 91; *3:* 179; *4:* 201; *6:* 168; *7:*
   96; *9:* 58; *10:* 72; *12:* 127; *39:* 156,157, 158,
   159, 160; *42:* 88, 89, 90, 91; *55:* 111, 116
Geerinck, Manuel *173:* 128
Gehm, Charlie *36:* 65; *57:* 117; *62:* 60, 138
Geis, Alissa Imre *189:* 77
Geisel, Theodor Seuss *1:* 104, 105, 106; *28:*
   108, 109, 110,111, 112, 113; *75:* 67, 68, 69,
   70, 71; *89:* 127, 128; *100:* 106, 107, 108
Geisert, Arthur *92:* 67, 68; *133:* 72, 73, 74;
   165: 97, 98; *171:* 64, 65
Geldart, William *15:* 121; *21:* 202
Genia *4:* 84
Gentry, Cyrille R. *12:* 66
Genzo, John Paul *136:* 74
George, Jean *2:* 113
George, Lindsay Barrett *95:* 57; *155:* 97, 98
Geraghty, Paul *130:* 60, 61
Gerard, Jean Ignace *45:* 80
Gerard, Rolf *27:* 147, 150
Gerber, Mark *61:* 105
Gerber, Mary Jane *112:* 124; *171:* 56
Gerber, Stephanie *71:* 195
Gerdstein, Mordecai *169:* 105
Gergely, Tibor *54:* 15, 16
Geritz, Franz *17:* 135
Gerlach, Geff *42:* 58
Gerrard, Roy *47:* 78; *90:* 96, 97, 98, 99
Gerritsen, Paula *177:* 69
Gershinowitz, George *36:* 27
Gerstein, Mordicai *31:* 117; *47:* 80, 81, 82, 83,
   84, 85, 86; *51:* 173; *69:* 134; *107:* 122; *142:*
   49, 52; *165:* 209; *176:* 119; *178:* 95, 97, 99
Gervase *12:* 27
Geter, Tyrone *146:* 249; *150:* 86
Getz, Arthur *32:* 148
Gévry, Claudine *188:* 47
Gewirtz, Bina *61:* 81
Giancola, Donato *95:* 146; *164:* 226
Gibbons, Gail *23:* 78; *72:* 77, 78, 79; *82:* 182;
   104: 65; *160:* 99, 100
Gibbs, Tony *40:* 95
Gibran, Kahlil *32:* 116
Gider, Iskender *81:* 193
Giebfried, Rosemary *170:* 135
Giesen, Rosemary *34:* 192, 193
Giffard, Hannah *83:* 70
Giguere, George *20:* 111
Gilbert, John *19:* 184; *54:* 115; *YABC 2:* 287
Gilbert, W.S. *36:* 83, 85, 96
Gilbert, Yvonne *116:* 70; *128:* 84; *149:* 119;
   185: 69; *192:* 25; *195:* 81
Gilchrist, Jan Spivey *72:* 82, 83, 84, 85, 87;
   77: 90; *105:* 89, 91; *130:* 63, 64; *155:* 105,
   107; *182:* 67

Giles, Will *41:* 218
Gili, Phillida *70:* 73
Gill, Margery *4:* 57; *7:* 7; *22:* 122; *25:* 166;
   26: 146, 147
Gillen, Denver *28:* 216
Gillette, Henry J. *23:* 237
Gilliam, Stan *39:* 64, 81
Gillies, Chuck *62:* 31
Gilliland, Jillian *87:* 58
Gillman, Alec *98:* 105
Gilman, Esther *15:* 124
Gilman, Phoebe *104:* 70, 71
Ginsberg, Sari *111:* 184
Ginsburg, Max *62:* 59; *68:* 194 *Girard, Roge*
   161: 30
Girouard, Patrick *155:* 100
Giovanopoulos, Paul *7:* 104; *60:* 36
Giovine, Sergio *79:* 12; *93:* 118; *139:* 118
Githens, Elizabeth M. *5:* 47
Gladden, Scott *99:* 108; *103:* 160; *193:* 46, 47
Gladstone, Gary *12:* 89; *13:* 190
Gladstone, Lise *15:* 273
Glanzman, Louis S. *2:* 177; *3:* 182; *36:* 97,
   98; *38:* 120, 122; *52:* 141, 144; *71:* 191; *91:*
   54, 56
Glaser, Byron *154:* 59, 60
Glaser, Milton *3:* 5; *5:* 156; *11:* 107; *30:* 26;
   36: 112; *54:* 141; *151:* 70
Glass, Andrew *36:* 38; *44:* 133; *48:* 205; *65:*
   3; *68:* 43, 45; *90:* 104, 105; *150:* 89
Glass, Marvin *9:* 174
Glasser, Judy *41:* 156; *56:* 140; *69:* 79; *72:*
   101
Glattauer, Ned *5:* 84; *13:* 224; *14:* 26
Glauber, Uta *17:* 76
Gleeson, J.M. *YABC 2:* 207
Glegg, Creina *36:* 100
Glienke, Amelie *63:* 150
Gliewe, Unada *3:* 78, 79; *21:* 73; *30:* 220
Gliori, Debi *72:* 91; *138:* 82; *162:* 37; *189:* 79,
   81, 82
Glovach, Linda *7:* 105
Gobbato, Imero *3:* 180, 181; *6:* 213; *7:* 58; *9:*
   150; *18:* 39; *21:* 167; *39:* 82, 83; *41:* 137,
   251; *59:* 177
Goble, Paul *25:* 121; *26:* 86; *33:* 65; *69:* 68,
   69; *131:* 79, 80
Goble, Warwick *46:* 78, 79; *194:* 143
Godal, Eric *36:* 93
Godkin, Celia *145:* 84, 86
Godfrey, Michael *17:* 279
Godon, Ingrid *166:* 163; *186:* 99
Goembel, Ponder *42:* 124
Goffe, Toni *61:* 83, 84, 85; *89:* 11; *90:* 124;
   178: 118
Goffstein, M.B. *8:* 71; *70:* 75, 76, 77
Golbin, Andre *15:* 125
Gold, Robert *166:* 151, 152
Goldfeder, Cheryl *11:* 191
Goldfinger, Jennifer P. *185:* 71
Goldsborough, June *5:* 154, 155; *8:* 92; *14:*
   226; *19:* 139; *54:* 165
Goldsmith, Robert *110:* 77
Goldstein, Leslie *5:* 8; *6:* 60; *10:* 106
Goldstein, Nathan *1:* 175; *2:* 79; *11:* 41, 232;
   16: 55
Goldstrom, Robert *98:* 36; *145:* 51, 52
Golembe, Carla *79:* 80, 81; *136:* 91; *144:* 113;
   193: 53
Golin, Carlo *74:* 112
Gomez, Elena *188:* 122; *191:* 72
Gomez, Elizabeth *127:* 70; *133:* 76
Gomi, Taro *64:* 102; *103:* 74, 76
Gon, Adriano *101:* 112
Gonsalve, Ron *178:* 213
Gonzalez, Maya Christina *104:* 3; *136:* 92
Goodall, John S. *4:* 92, 93; *10:* 132; *66:* 92,
   93; *YABC 1:* 198
Goode, Diane *15:* 126; *50:* 183; *52:* 114, 115;
   76: 195; *84:* 94; *99:* 141; *114:* 76, 77, 78;
   170: 99, 101

Goodelman, Aaron *40:* 203
Goodenow, Earle *40:* 97
Goodfellow, Peter *62:* 95; *94:* 202
Goodman, Joan Elizabeth *50:* 86
Goodman, Vivienne *82:* 251; *146:* 181, 182
Goodnow, Patti *117:* 33
Goodwin, Harold *13:* 74
Goodwin, Philip R. *18:* 206
Goor, Nancy *39:* 85, 86
Goor, Ron *39:* 85, 86
Goossens, Philippe *195:* 71
Gorbachev, Valeri *89:* 96; *112:* 97; *143:* 63, 64; *184:* 66, 67, 68, 101
Gordon, Gwen *12:* 151
Gordon, Margaret *4:* 147; *5:* 48, 49; *9:* 79
Gordon, Mike *101:* 62, 63, 64
Gordon, Russell *136:* 204; *137:* 214
Gordon, Walter *138:* 9
Gore, Leonid *89:* 51; *94:* 74; *136:* 8; *158:* 117; *166:* 136; *168:* 36; *170:* 107; *181:* 94; *185:* 73
Gorecka-Egan, Erica *18:* 35
Gorey, Edward *1:* 60, 61; *13:* 169; *18:* 192; *20:* 201; *29:* 90, 91, 92, 93, 94, 95, 96, 97, 98, 99, 100; *30:* 129; *32:* 90; *34:* 200, *65:* 48; *68:* 24, 25; *69:* 79; *70:* 80, 82, 83, 84; *85:* 136; *127:* 62
Gorsline, Douglas *1:* 98; *6:* 13; *11:* 113; *13:* 104; *15:* 14; *28:* 117, 118; *YABC 1:* 15
Gorton, Julia *108:* 94; *178:* 81, 82
Gosfield, Josh *118:* 165, 166; *149:* 67
Gosner, Kenneth *5:* 135
Gosney, Joy *167:* 142
Gotlieb, Jules *6:* 127
Goto, Scott *115:* 86; *136:* 69
Gottlieb, Dale *67:* 162; *107:* 16; *149:* 6
Goudey, Ray *97:* 86
Gough, Alan *91:* 57
Gough, Philip *23:* 47; *45:* 90
Gould, Chester *49:* 112, 113, 114, 116, 117, 118
Gould, Jason *151:* 232
Gourbault, Martine *177:* 159
Govern, Elaine R. *26:* 94
Gower, Teri *102:* 184
Gowing, Toby *60:* 25; *63:* 33; *78:* 70, 252; *83:* 228; *86:* 187; *93:* 145; *108:* 133; *110:* 217; *184:* 125
Grabianski *20:* 144
Grabianski, Janusz *39:* 92, 93, 94, 95
Graboff, Abner *35:* 103, 104
Graef, Renee *61:* 188; *72:* 207
Grafe, Max *156:* 173; *178:* 237; *192:* 240
Graham, A.B. *11:* 61
Graham, Bob *101:* 66, 67, 68; *151:* 74, 75; *187:* 65, 67, 68, 70
Graham, Georgia *188:* 3; *190:* 75
Graham, L. *7:* 108
Graham, Margaret Bloy *11:* 120; *18:* 305, 307
Graham, Mark *88:* 208; *159:* 153; *182:* 3
Grahame-Johnstone, Janet *13:* 61
Grahame-Johnstone, Anne *13:* 61
Grainger, Sam *42:* 95
Gralley, Jean *166:* 86
Gramatky, Hardie *1:* 107; *30:* 116, 119, 120, 122, 123
Gran, Julie *168:* 118
Granahan, Julie *84:* 84
GrandPré, Mary *84:* 131; *109:* 199; *118:* 76; *180:* 65; *184:* 70, 71, 180; *192:* 87
Grandström, Brita *176:* 139
Grandville, J.J. *45:* 81, 82, 83, 84, 85, 86, 87, 88; *47:* 125; *64:* 10
Granger, Paul *39:* 153
Granström, Brita *162:* 35; *167:* 46
Grant, (Alice) Leigh *10:* 52; *15:* 131; *20:* 20; *26:* 119; *48:* 202
Grant, Gordon *17:* 230, 234; *25:* 123, 124, 125, 126; *52:* 69; *YABC 1:* 164
Grant, Melvyn *159:* 186, 187; *170:* 48, 49
Grant, Renee *77:* 40

Grant, Shirley *109:* 45
Graves, Elizabeth *45:* 101
Graves, Keith *167:* 89; *191:* 74
Gray, Harold *33:* 87, 88
Gray, Les *82:* 76; *83:* 232
Gray, Reginald *6:* 69
Greco, Tony *184:* 6
Greder, Armin *76:* 235
Green, Ann Canevari *62:* 48
Green, Eileen *6:* 97
Green, Elizabeth Shippen *139:* 109
Green, Jonathan *86:* 135; *105:* 109
Green, Ken *111:* 68
Green, Michael *32:* 216
Green, Robina *87:* 138
Green, Jonathan *157:* 105
Greene, Jeffrey *117:* 93
Greenaway, Kate *17:* 275; *24:* 180; *26:* 107; *41:* 222, 232; *100:* 115, 116; *YABC 1:* 88, 89; *2:* 131, 133, 136,138, 139, 141
Greenberg, Melanie Hope *72:* 93; *80:* 125; *101:* 174; *133:* 180; *186:* 189
Greenseid, Diane *178:* 106, 107
Greenstein, Elaine *150:* 100
Greenwald, Sheila *1:* 34; *3:* 99; *8:* 72
Greger, Carol *76:* 86
Gregorian, Joyce Ballou *30:* 125
Gregory, Emilian *177:* 146; *187:* 10
Gregory, Fran *130:* 4; *140:* 93
Gregory, Frank M. *29:* 107
Greiffenhagen, Maurice *16:* 137; *27:* 57; *YABC 2:* 288
Greiner, Robert *6:* 86
Gretter, J. Clemens *31:* 134
Gretz, Susanna *7:* 114
Gretzer, John *1:* 54; *3:* 26; *4:* 162; *7:* 125; *16:* 247; *18:* 117; *28:* 66; *30:* 85, 211; *33:* 235; *56:* 16
Grey, Mini *166:* 90; *192:* 71
Grey Owl *24:* 41
Gri *25:* 90
Grieder, Walter *9:* 84
Griesbach/Martucci *59:* 3
Grifalconi, Ann *2:* 126; *3:* 248; *11:* 18; *13:* 182; *46:* 38; *50:* 145; *66:* 99, 100, 101, 104, 106; *69:* 38; *70:* 64; *87:* 128; *90:* 53; *93:* 49; *128:* 48; *133:* 79, 81
Griffin, Gillett Good *26:* 96
Griffin, James *30:* 166
Griffin, John Howard *59:* 186
Griffin, Rachel *131:* 23
Griffith, Gershom *94:* 214
Griffiths, Dave *29:* 76
Griffiths, Dean *168:* 180; *169:* 182
Grimly, Gris *186:* 102; *192:* 112
Grimsdell, Jeremy *83:* 75
Grimwood, Brian *82:* 89
Gringhuis, Dirk *6:* 98; *9:* 196
Gripe, Harald *2:* 127; *74:* 98
Grisha *3:* 71
Grohmann, Susan *84:* 97
Gropper, William *27:* 93; *37:* 193
Gros *60:* 199
Grose, Helen Mason *YABC 1:* 260; *2:* 150
Grossman, Nancy *24:* 130; *29:* 101
Grossman, Robert *11:* 124; *46:* 39
Groth, John *15:* 79; *21:* 53, 54; *83:* 230
Grover, Lorie Ann *168:* 59
Grubb, Lisa *160:* 116
Grue, Lisa *187:* 193
Gruelle, Johnny *35:* 107
Gschwind, William *11:* 72
Guay-Mitchell, Rebecca *110:* 95, 96; *135:* 240; *180:* 76; *181:* 71, 73
Guback, Georgia *88:* 102
Guerguerion, Claudine *105:* 73
Guevara, Susan *97:* 87; *167:* 49; *194:* 54
Guggenheim, Hans *2:* 10; *3:* 37; *8:* 136
Guhathaakurta, Ajanta *183:* 199
Guida, Lisa Chauncy *172:* 188
Guilbeau, Honore *22:* 69

Guillette, Joseph *137:* 37
Guisewite, Cathy *57:* 52, 53, 54, 56, 57
Gukova, Julia *95:* 104; *154:* 103; *168:* 195
Gundersheimer, Karen *35:* 240; *82:* 100
Gunderson, Nick *57:* 120
Gunnella *192:* 144
Gurney, James *76:* 97; *86:* 32
Gurney, John Steven *75:* 39, 82; *110:* 175; *143:* 67, 68; *169:* 172
Gusman, Annie *38:* 62
Gustafson, Scott *34:* 111; *43:* 40
Gustavson, Adam *104:* 10; *171:* 183; *176:* 87
Guthridge, Bettina *108:* 79; *186:* 92
Guthrie, R. Dale *64:* 143
Guthrie, Robin *20:* 122
Gutierrez, Akemi *172:* 87
Gutierrez, Alan *136:* 31, 32
Gutierrez, Rudy *97:* 162
Gutmann, Bessie Pease *73:* 93, 94
Gwynne, Fred *41:* 94, 95
Gyberg, Bo-Erik *38:* 131

H

Haas, Irene *17:* 77; *87:* 46; *96:* 117
Hack, Konrad *51:* 127
Hader, Berta H. *16:* 126
Hader, Elmer S. *16:* 126
Haeffele, Deborah *76:* 99
Haemer, Alan *62:* 109
Hafner, Marylin *22:* 196, 216; *24:* 44; *30:* 51; *35:* 95; *51:* 25, 160, 164; *86:* 16; *105:* 196; *121:* 93, 94; *149:* 208, 209; *179:* 82, 83, 84, 115; *190:* 200
Hagerty, Sean *62:* 181
Hague, Michael *32:* 128; *48:* 98, 99, 100, 101, 103, 105,106, 107, 108, 109, 110; *49:* 121; *51:* 105; *64:* 14, 15; *79:* 134; *80:* 91, 92; *83:* 135; *100:* 241; *102:* 29; *129:* 101, 103, 104; *185:* 80, 81, 82
Hair, Jonathan *115:* 135
Halas, John *29:* 41, 47, 48
Haldane, Roger *13:* 76; *14:* 202
Hale, Christy *79:* 124; *84:* 200; *114:* 201; *128:* 2, 3; *146:* 203; *158:* 243; *167:* 99; *179:* 87
Hale, Irina *26:* 97
Hale, James Graham *88:* 207
Hale, Kathleen *17:* 79; *66:* 114, 116, 118
Haley, Gail E. *43:* 102, 103, 104, 105; *78:* 65, 67; *136:* 106, 107
Hall, Amanda *96:* 110
Hall, Chuck *30:* 189
Hall, Douglas *15:* 184; *43:* 106, 107; *86:* 100; *87:* 82; *129:* 72
Hall, H. Tom *1:* 227; *30:* 210
Hall, Melanie *116:* 48, 49; *169:* 77, 78
Hall, Sydney P. *31:* 89
Hall, Tim *164:* 196
Hall, Vicki *20:* 24
Hallinan, P.K. *39:* 98
Hallman, Tom *98:* 166
Hally, Greg *101:* 200; *151:* 224
Halperin, Wendy Anderson *96:* 151; *125:* 96, 97, 98, 99; *139:* 22; *140:* 84
Halpern, Joan *10:* 25
Halpern, Shari *174:* 172
Halsey, Megan *96:* 172; *114:* 185; *180:* 8; *185:* 85
Halstead, Virginia *125:* 105
Halverson, Janet *49:* 38, 42, 44
Hallensleben, Georg *134:* 5, 6; *172:* 17
Hamanaka, Sheila *71:* 100
Hamann, Brad *78:* 151
Hamann, Sigune *104:* 115
Hamberger, John *6:* 8; *8:* 32; *14:* 79; *34:* 136; *88:* 78
Hamil, Tom *14:* 80; *43:* 163
Hamilton, Bill and Associates *26:* 215
Hamilton, Helen S. *2:* 238

Hamilton, J. *19:* 83, 85, 87
Hamilton, Laurie *116:* 210
Hamilton, Todd Cameron *84:* 15
Hamlin, Janet *97:* 136; *124:* 90; *137:* 157; *182:* 117
Hamlin, Louise *71:* 135
Hammond, Chris *21:* 37
Hammond, Elizabeth *5:* 36, 203
Hampshire, Michael *5:* 187; *7:* 110, 111; *48:* 150; *51:* 129
Hampson, Denman *10:* 155; *15:* 130
Hampton, Blake *41:* 244
Handford, Martin *64:* 105, 106, 107, 109
Handforth, Thomas *42:* 100, 101, 102, 103, 104, 105, 107
Handville, Robert *1:* 89; *38:* 76; *45:* 108, 109
Hane, Roger *17:* 239; *44:* 54
Haney, Elizabeth Mathieu *34:* 84
Hanke, Ted *71:* 10
Hankinson, Phil *181:* 164
Hanley, Catherine *8:* 161
Hann, Jacquie *19:* 144
Hanna, Cheryl *91:* 133
Hanna, Wayne A. *67:* 145
Hannon, Mark *38:* 37
Hansen, Gaby *159:* 11; *186:* 25
Hansen, Mia *149:* 76
Hanson, Joan *8:* 76; *11:* 139
Hanson, Peter E. *52:* 47; *54:* 99, 100; *73:* 21; *84:* 79; *116:* 144
Hansson, Gunilla *64:* 111, 112
Hardcastle, Nick *121:* 82; *175:* 185
Hardy, David A. *9:* 96; *119:* 74
Hardy, Paul *YABC 2:* 245 *Haring, Keith 145:* 65
Harlan, Jerry *3:* 96
Harlin, Greg *89:* 194; *103:* 82; *118:* 161; *121:* 167; *182:* 76
Harness, Cheryl *106:* 80; *131:* 87; *178:* 111
Harnischfeger *18:* 121
Harper, Arthur *YABC 2:* 121
Harper, Betty *126:* 90
Harper, Jamie *174:* 71
Harper, Piers *79:* 27; *105:* 102; *161:* 67
Harrington, Glenn *82:* 18; *94:* 66, 68; *185:* 118
Harrington, Jack *83:* 162
Harrington, Richard *5:* 81
Harris, Andrew N. *191:* 78
Harris, Jim *127:* 130; *183:* 4
Harris, John *83:* 25
Harris, Nick *86:* 177
Harris, Susan Yard *42:* 121
Harrison, Florence *20:* 150, 152
Harrison, Harry *4:* 103
Harrison, Jack *28:* 149
Harrison, Mark *105:* 157; *165:* 190
Harrison, Ted *56:* 73
Harsh, Fred *72:* 107
Harston, Jerry *105:* 143
Hart, Lewis *98:* 115
Hart, Thomas *181:* 165
Hart, William *13:* 72
Hartland, Jessie *171:* 80, 81; *186:* 165
Hartung, Susan Kathleen *150:* 107, 108; *173:* 106; *175:* 106; *192:* 78
Hartelius, Margaret *10:* 24
Hartshorn, Ruth *5:* 115; *11:* 129
Harvey, Amanda *145:* 44
Harvey, Bob *48:* 219
Harvey, Gerry *7:* 180
Harvey, Lisa *97:* 21
Harvey, Paul *88:* 74
Harvey, Roland *71:* 88; *123:* 63; *179:* 94
Haskamp, Steve *195:* 36
Hassall, Joan *43:* 108, 109
Hassell, Hilton *YABC 1:* 187
Hassett, John *162:* 59
Hasselriis, Else *18:* 87; *YABC 1:* 96
Hastings, Glenn *89:* 183
Hastings, Ian *62:* 67

Hauman, Doris *2:* 184; *29:* 58, 59; *32:* 85, 86, 87
Hauman, George *2:* 184; *29:* 58, 59; *32:* 85, 86, 87
Hausherr, Rosmarie *15:* 29
Hawkes, Kevin *78:* 72; *104:* 198; *105:* 197; *112:* 109; *126:* 87; *144:* 88; *149:* 210; *150:* 110, 135; *156:* 94; *164:* 35; *186:* 18; *190:* 197
Hawkins, Jacqui *112:* 86; *162:* 64
Hawkinson, John *4:* 109; *7:* 83; *21:* 64
Hawkinson, Lucy *21:* 64
Hawthorne, Mike *140:* 228
Haxton, Elaine *28:* 131
Haydock, Robert *4:* 95
Hayes, Geoffrey *26:* 111; *44:* 133; *91:* 85
Haynes, Max *72:* 107
Hays, Michael *73:* 207; *83:* 93; *139:* 197; *146:* 202, 250
Haywood, Carolyn *1:* 112; *29:* 104
Heale, Jonathan *104:* 117
Healy, Daty *12:* 143
Healy, Deborah *58:* 181, 182; *101:* 111
Heap, Sue *102:* 207; *150:* 113, 114; *187:* 84, 85, 87
Hearn, Diane Dawson *79:* 99; *113:* 13
Hearon, Dorothy *34:* 69
Heaslip, William *57:* 24, 25
Hechtkopf, H. *11:* 110
Heck, Ed *173:* 81
Hedderwick, Mairi *30:* 127; *32:* 47; *36:* 104; *77:* 86; *145:* 91, 93, 95
Heffernan, Phil *146:* 197; *195:* 172
Hefter, Richard *28:* 170; *31:* 81, 82; *33:* 183
Hehenberger, Shelly *126:* 91
Heigh, James *22:* 98
Heighway, Richard *25:* 160; *64:* 4
Heighway-Bury, Robin *159:* 89
Heine, Helme *67:* 86; *135:* 91, 92
Heinly, John *45:* 113
Hellard, Susan *81:* 21
Hellebrand, Nancy *26:* 57
Heller, Linda *46:* 86
Heller, Ruth M. *66:* 125; *77:* 30, 32
Hellmuth, Jim *38:* 164
Helms, Georgeann *33:* 62
Helquist, Brett *142:* 203; *146:* 133, 134; *156:* 10; *173:* 25; *180:* 106; *187:* 90, 91; *193:* 12
Helweg, Hans *41:* 118; *50:* 93; *58:* 22, 26
Hemphill, Helen *179:* 95
Henba, Bobbie *90:* 195
Henderson, Dave *73:* 76; *75:* 191, 192, 193, 194; *82:* 4
Henderson, Douglas *103:* 68
Henderson, Kathy *55:* 32; *155:* 118
Henderson, Keith *35:* 122
Henderson, Meryl *127:* 58, 60; *169:* 81
Hendrix, John *187:* 133
Hendry, Linda *80:* 104; *83:* 83; *164:* 216
Hengeveld, Dennis *142:* 86
Henkes, Kevin *43:* 111; *108:* 106, 107, 108
Henneberger, Robert *1:* 42; *2:* 237; *25:* 83
Henriksen, Harold *35:* 26; *48:* 68
Henriquez, Celeste *103:* 137
Henriquez, Elsa *82:* 260
Henriquez, Emile F. *89:* 88
Henry, Everett *29:* 191
Henry, Matthew *117:* 58
Henry, Paul *93:* 121; *194:* 125
Henry, Thomas *5:* 102
Hensel *27:* 119
Henshaw, Jacqui *141:* 127
Henstra, Friso *8:* 80; *36:* 70; *40:* 222; *41:* 250; *73:* 100, 101
Henterly, Jamichael *93:* 4
Heo, Yumi *89:* 85, 86; *94:* 89, 90; *146:* 40, 137, 138; *163:* 227
Hepple, Norman *28:* 198
Herbert, Helen *57:* 70
Herbert, Jennifer *189:* 47
Herbert, Wally *23:* 101

Herbster, Mary Lee *9:* 33
Herder, Edwin *182:* 104
Herge
   See Remi, Georges
Hermansen, Pal *133:* 113
Hermanson, Dennis *10:* 55
Hermes, Gertrude *54:* 161
Herr, Margo *57:* 191
Herr, Susan *83:* 163
Herriman, George *140:* 74, 75, 76, 77, 78
Herriman, Lisa *87:* 190
Herring, Michael *121:* 76; *182:* 103
Herrington, Roger *3:* 161
Herscovici, C. *165:* 240
Hescox, Richard *85:* 86; *90:* 30; *139:* 35
Heslop, Mike *38:* 60; *40:* 130
Hess, Lydia J. *85:* 17
Hess, Mark *111:* 146; *113:* 207
Hess, Paul *134:* 47; *166:* 133; *193:* 13
Hess, Richard *42:* 31
Hester, Ronnie *37:* 85
Heuser, Olga J. *121:* 116
Heusser, Sibylle *168:* 195
Heustis, Louise L. *20:* 28
Hewitson, Jennifer *74:* 119; *124:* 167
Hewitt, Kathryn *80:* 126; *149:* 105; *184:* 93
Hewitt, Margaret *84:* 112
Heyduck-Huth, Hilde *8:* 82
Heyer, Carol *74:* 122; *130:* 72, 73; *192:* 35
Heyer, Hermann *20:* 114, 115
Heyer, Marilee *102:* 108
Heyman, Ken *8:* 93; *34:* 113
Heyne, Ulrike *146:* 151
Heywood, Karen *48:* 114
Hickling, P.B. *40:* 165
Hickman, Stephen *85:* 58; *136:* 33; *171:* 128
Hierstein, Judy *56:* 40; *162:* 168
Higashi, Sandra *154:* 59, 60
Higginbottom, J. Winslow *8:* 170; *29:* 105, 106
Higgins, Chester *101:* 79
Higham, David *50:* 104
Hilb, Nora *176:* 8
Hildebrandt, Greg *8:* 191; *55:* 35, 36, 38, 39, 40, 42, 46; *172:* 110
Hildebrandt, Tim *8:* 191; *55:* 44, 45, 46
Hilder, Rowland *19:* 207
Hill, Eric *66:* 127, 128; *133:* 91
Hill, Gregory *35:* 190
Hill, Pat *49:* 120
Hillenbrand, Will *84:* 115; *92:* 76, 80; *93:* 131; *104:* 168; *128:* 137; *145:* 187; *146:* 184; *147:* 105, 106, 107; *152:* 59; *184:* 179; *195:* 34, 180
Hilliard, Richard *183:* 74
Hillier, Matthew *45:* 205
Hillman, Priscilla *48:* 115
Hills, Tad *113:* 4; *137:* 147; *173:* 83
Himler, Ronald *6:* 114; *7:* 162; *8:* 17, 84, 125; *14:* 76; *19:* 145; *26:* 160; *31:* 43; *38:* 116; *41:* 44, 79; *43:* 52; *45:* 120; *46:* 43; *54:* 44, 83; *58:* 180; *59:* 38; *68:* 146; *69:* 231; *70:* 98; *71:* 177, 178; *77:* 219; *79:* 212; *83:* 62; *89:* 5; *91:* 160; *92:* 91, 92, 93; *94:* 93; *95:* 69, 174, 194; *99:* 99, 112; *113:* 92; *118:* 114; *137:* 73, 74, 77, 167; *163:* 99; *165:* 138; *178:* 9, 220; *183:* 77, 79, 80, 81; *184:* 80, 83
Himmelman, John *47:* 109; *65:* 87; *94:* 96, 97; *159:* 85
Hinds, Bill *37:* 127, 130
Hines, Anna Grossnickle *51:* 90; *74:* 124; *95:* 78, 79, 80, 81
Hines, Bob *135:* 149, 150
Hiroko *99:* 61
Hiroshige *25:* 71
Hirsh, Marilyn *7:* 126
Hiscock, Bruce *137:* 80, 81
Hissey, Jane *103:* 90; *130:* 81
Hitch, Jeff *99:* 206; *128:* 86
Hitz, Demi *11:* 135; *15:* 245; *66:* 129, 130; *152:* 94, 95

Hnizdovsky, Jacques *32:* 96; *76:* 187
Ho, Kwoncjan *15:* 132
Hoban, Lillian *1:* 114; *22:* 157; *26:* 72; *29:* 53; *40:* 105, 107, 195; *41:* 80; *69:* 107, 108; *71:* 98; *77:* 168; *106:* 50; *113:* 86; *136:* 118
Hoban, Tana *22:* 159; *104:* 82, 83, 85
Hobbie, Jocelyn *190:* 78
Hobbs, Leigh *166:* 95
Hoberman, Norman *5:* 82
Hobson, Sally *77:* 185
Hockerman, Dennis *39:* 22; *56:* 23
Hodgell, P.C. *42:* 114
Hodges, C. Walter *2:* 139; *11:* 15; *12:* 25; *23:* 34; *25:* 96; *38:* 165; *44:* 197; *45:* 95; *100:* 57; *YABC 2:* 62, 63
Hodges, David *9:* 98
Hodgetts, Victoria *43:* 132
Hofbauer, Imre *2:* 162
Hoff, Syd *9:* 107; *10:* 128; *33:* 94; *72:* 115,116, 117, 118; *138:* 114, 115
Hoffman, Rosekrans *15:* 133; *50:* 219; *63:* 97
Hoffman, Sanford *38:* 208; *76:* 174; *88:* 160, 161; *151:* 156
Hoffmann, Felix *9:* 109
Hoffnung, Gerard *66:* 76, 77
Hofsinde, Robert *21:* 70
Hogan, Inez *2:* 141
Hogan, Jamie *192:* 94
Hogarth, Burne *41:* 58; *63:* 46, 48, 49, 50, 52, 53, 54, 55,56
Hogarth, Paul *41:* 102, 103, 104; *YABC 1:* 16
Hogarth, William *42:* 33
Hogenbyl, Jan *1:* 35
Hogner, Nils *4:* 122; *25:* 144
Hogrogian, Nonny *3:* 221; *4:* 106, 107; *5:* 166; *7:* 129; *15:* 2; *16:* 176; *20:* 154; *22:* 146; *25:* 217; *27:* 206; *74:* 127, 128, 129, 149, 152; *127:* 99; *YABC 2:* 84, 94
Hokanson, Lars *93:* 111; *172:* 137
Hokusai *25:* 71
Hol, Colby *126:* 96
Holberg, Richard *2:* 51
Holbrook, Kathy *107:* 114
Holcroft, Tina *38:* 109
Holden, Caroline *55:* 159
Holder, Heidi *36:* 99; *64:* 9
Holder, Jimmy *151:* 224
Holiday, Henry *YABC 2:* 107
Holl, F. *36:* 91
Holland, Brad *45:* 59, 159
Holland, Gay W. *128:* 105
Holland, Janice *18:* 118
Holland, Marion *6:* 116
Holldobler, Turid *26:* 120
Holliday, Keaf *144:* 236
Holling, Holling C. *15:* 136, 137
Hollinger, Deanne *12:* 116
Holm, Sharon Lane *114:* 84; *115:* 52
Holmes, B. *3:* 82
Holmes, Bea *7:* 74; *24:* 156; *31:* 93
Holmes, Dave *54:* 22
Holmes, Lesley *135:* 96
Holmgren, George Ellen *45:* 112
Holmlund, Heather D. *150:* 140
Holt, Norma *44:* 106
Holt, Pater *151:* 188
Holtan, Gene *32:* 192
Holub, Joan *149:* 2
Holyfield, John *149:* 231
Holz, Loretta *17:* 81
Hom, Nancy *79:* 195
Homar, Lorenzo *6:* 2
Homer, Winslow *128:* 8; *YABC 2:* 87
Honey, Elizabeth *112:* 95, 96; *137:* 93, 94
Honeywood, Varnette P. *110:* 68, 70
Hong, Lily Toy *76:* 104
Honigman, Marian *3:* 2
Honore, Paul *42:* 77, 79, 81, 82
Hood, Alun *69:* 145, 218; *72:* 41; *80:* 226; *87:* 4; *95:* 139
Hood, Susan *12:* 43

Hook, Christian *104:* 103
Hook, Frances *26:* 188; *27:* 127
Hook, Jeff *14:* 137; *103:* 105
Hook, Richard *26:* 188
Hooks *63:* 30
Hooper, Hadley *177:* 145
Hoover, Carol A. *21:* 77
Hoover, Russell *12:* 95; *17:* 2; *34:* 156
Hope, James *141:* 116
Hopkins, Chris *99:* 127
Hopman, Philip *178:* 184
Hoppin, Augustus *34:* 66
Horacek, Petr *163:* 117
Horder, Margaret *2:* 108; *73:* 75
Horen, Michael *45:* 121
Horne, Daniel *73:* 106; *91:* 153; *109:* 127; *110:* 232; *164:* 176
Horne, Richard *111:* 80
Horse, Harry *128:* 195; *169:* 86
Horvat, Laurel *12:* 201
Horvath, David *192:* 95
Horvath, Ferdinand Kusati *24:* 176
Horvath, Maria *57:* 171
Horwitz, Richard *57:* 174
Hotchkiss, De Wolfe *20:* 49
Hough, Charlotte *9:* 112; *13:* 98; *17:* 83; *24:* 195
Houlihan, Ray *11:* 214
House, Caroline *183:* 121
Housman, Laurence *25:* 146, 147
Houston, James *13:* 107; *74:* 132, 134, 135
Hovland, Gary *88:* 172; *171:* 148
Hoyt, Eleanor *158:* 231
How, W.E. *20:* 47
Howard, Alan *16:* 80; *34:* 58; *45:* 114
Howard, Arthur *165:* 111, 112; *190:* 5
Howard, J.N. *15:* 234
Howard, John *33:* 179
Howard, Kim *116:* 71
Howard, Paul *142:* 126, 129; *144:* 187
Howard, Rob *40:* 161
Howarth, Daniel *170:* 34
Howe, John *115:* 47; *176:* 106
Howe, John F. *79:* 101; *80:* 150
Howe, Phillip *79:* 117; *175:* 115
Howe, Stephen *1:* 232
Howell, Karen *119:* 123
Howell, Pat *15:* 139
Howell, Troy *23:* 24; *31:* 61; *36:* 158; *37:* 184; *41:* 76, 235; *48:* 112; *56:* 13; *57:* 3; *59:* 174; *63:* 5; *74:* 46; *89:* 188; *90:* 231; *95:* 97; *98:* 130; *99:* 189; *153:* 156, 157, 158; *176:* 104
Howes, Charles *22:* 17
Hoyt, Ard *145:* 141; *190:* 82
Hranilovich, Barbara *127:* 51
Hu, Ying-Hwa *116:* 107; *152:* 236; *173:* 171
Huang, Benrei *137:* 55
Huang, Zhong-Yang *117:* 30, 32
Hubbard, Woodleigh Marx *98:* 67; *115:* 79; *160:* 138
Hubley, Faith *48:* 120, 121, 125, 130, 131, 132, 134
Hubley, John *48:* 125, 130, 131, 132, 134
Hudak, Michal *143:* 74
Hudnut, Robin *14:* 62
Huerta, Catherine *76:* 178; *77:* 44, 45; *90:* 182
Huffaker, Sandy *10:* 56
Huffman, Joan *13:* 33
Huffman, Tom *13:* 180; *17:* 212; *21:* 116; *24:* 132; *33:* 154; *38:* 59; *42:* 147
Hughes, Arthur *20:* 148, 149, 150; *33:* 114, 148, 149
Hughes, Darren *95:* 44
Hughes, David *36:* 197
Hughes, Shirley *1:* 20, 21; *7:* 3; *12:* 217; *16:* 163; *29:* 154; *63:* 118; *70:* 102, 103, 104; *73:* 169; *88:* 70; *110:* 118, 119; *159:* 103
Hugo, Victor *47:* 112
Hull, Cathy *78:* 29
Hull, Richard *95:* 120; *123:* 175; *172:* 195

Hulsmann, Eva *16:* 166
Hume, Lachie *189:* 93
Hummel, Berta *43:* 137, 138, 139
Hummel, Lisl *29:* 109; *YABC 2:* 333, 334
Humphrey, Henry *16:* 167
Humphreys, Graham *25:* 168
Humphries, Tudor *76:* 66; *80:* 4; *124:* 4, 5
Huneck, Stephen *183:* 88, 89
Hunt, James *2:* 143
Hunt, Jonathan *84:* 120
Hunt, Paul *119:* 104; *129:* 135; *139:* 160; *173:* 112
Hunt, Robert *110:* 206, 235; *147:* 136, 137; *170:* 3
Hunt, Scott *190:* 143
Hunter, Anne *133:* 190; *178:* 150
Huntington, Amy *180:* 99
Hurd, Clement *2:* 148, 149; *64:* 127, 128, 129, 131, 133, 134,135, 136; *100:* 37, 38
Hurd, Peter *24:* 30, 31,; *YABC 2:* 56
Hurd, Thacher *46:* 88, 89; *94:* 114, 115, 116; *123:* 81, 82, 84
Hurlimann, Ruth *32:* 99
Hurst, Carol Otis *185:* 92
Hurst, Tracey *192:* 238
Hussar, Michael *114:* 113; *117:* 159
Hustler, Tom *6:* 105
Hutchins, Laurence *55:* 22
Hutchins, Pat *15:* 142; *70:* 106, 107, 108; *178:* 131, 132
Hutchinson, Sascha *95:* 211
Hutchinson, William M. *6:* 3, 138; *46:* 70
Hutchison, Paula *23:* 10
Hutton, Clarke *YABC 2:* 335
Hutton, Kathryn *35:* 155; *89:* 91
Hutton, Warwick *20:* 91
Huyette, Marcia *29:* 188
Hyatt, John *54:* 7
Hyatt, Mitch *178:* 162
Hyde, Maureen *82:* 17; *121:* 145, 146
Hyman, David *117:* 64
Hyman, Trina Schart *1:* 204; *2:* 194; *5:* 153; *6:* 106; *7:* 138, 145; *8:* 22; *10:* 196; *13:* 96; *14:* 114; *15:* 204; *16:* 234; *20:* 82; *22:* 133; *24:* 151; *25:* 79, 82; *26:* 82; *29:* 83; *31:* 37, 39; *34:* 104; *38:* 84, 100, 128; *41:* 49; *43:* 146; *46:* 91, 92, 93, 95, 96, 97, 98, 99, 100, 101, 102, 103, 104, 105,108, 109, 111, 197; *48:* 60, 61; *52:* 32; *60:* 168; *66:* 38; *67:* 214; *72:* 74; *75:* 92; *79:* 57; *82:* 95, 238; *89:* 46; *95:* 91, 92, 93; *100:* 33, 199; *132:* 12; *147:* 33, 35, 36; *167:* 58, 60; *177:* 189, 190

I

Ibarra, Rosa *147:* 91
Ibatoulline, Bagram *156:* 48; *174:* 33, 82
Ichikawa, Satomi *29:* 152; *41:* 52; *47:* 133, 134,135, 136; *78:* 93, 94; *80:* 81; *146:* 143, 145, 146
Ide, Jacqueline *YABC 1:* 39
Ilsley, Velma *3:* 1; *7:* 55; *12:* 109; *37:* 62; *38:* 184
Imai, Ayano *190:* 85, 86
in den Bosch, Nicole *150:* 204
Inga *1:* 142
Ingman, Bruce *134:* 50; *182:* 91, 92
Ingpen, Robert *109:* 103, 104; *132:* 138; *137:* 177; *166:* 103; *181:* 140
Ingraham, Erick *21:* 177; *84:* 256; *103:* 66
Inkpen, Mick *99:* 104, 105; *106:* 44
Innerst, Stacy *149:* 104
Innocenti, Roberto *21:* 123; *96:* 122; *159:* 111, 197
Inoue, Yosuke *24:* 118
Iofin, Michael *97:* 157
Iosa, Ann *63:* 189

Ipcar, Dahlov *1:* 124, 125; *49:* 137, 138, 139, 140, 141, 142,143, 144, 145; *147:* 122, 124, 126
Irvin, Fred *13:* 166; *15:* 143, 144; *27:* 175
Irving, Jay *45:* 72
Irving, Laurence *27:* 50
Isaac, Joanne *21:* 76
Isaacs, Gary *170:* 188
Isadora, Rachel *43:* 159, 160; *54:* 31; *79:* 106, 107,108; *121:* 100, 102; *165:* 116, 117
Ishmael, Woodi *24:* 111; *31:* 99
Ives, Ruth *15:* 257
Iwai, Melissa *149:* 233; *183:* 92

J

Jabar, Cynthia *101:* 201
Jackness, Andrew *94:* 237
Jackson, Julian *91:* 104, 106
Jackson, Michael *43:* 42
Jackson, Shelley *79:* 71; *99:* 109; *187:* 82
Jacob, Murv *89:* 30
Jacobi, Kathy *62:* 118
Jacobs, Barbara *9:* 136
Jacobs, Lou, Jr. *9:* 136; *15:* 128
Jacobsen, Laura *176:* 98; *177:* 85, 86
Jacobson, Rick *131:* 222; *170:* 119
Jacobus, Tim *79:* 140; *109:* 126; *129:* 180
Jacques, Robin *1:* 70; *2:* 1; *8:* 46; *9:* 20; *15:* 187; *19:* 253; *32:* 102, 103, 104; *43:* 184; *73:* 135; *YABC 1:* 42
Jaeggi, Yoshiko *186:* 184
Jaffee, Al *66:* 131, 132
Jagr, Miloslav *13:* 197
Jahn-Clough, Lisa *88:* 114; *152:* 104; *193:* 70, 71
Jahnke, Robert *84:* 24
Jainschigg, Nicholas *80:* 64; *91:* 138; *95:* 63; *99:* 25; *108:* 50; *171:* 41
Jakesavic, Nenad *85:* 102
Jakobsen, Kathy *116:* 83
Jakubowski, Charles *14:* 192
Jambor, Louis *YABC 1:* 11
James, Ann *73:* 50; *82:* 113; *158:* 61; *183:* 44
James, Brian *140:* 91
James, Curtis E. *182:* 93
James, Derek *35:* 187; *44:* 91; *61:* 133; *74:* 2; *80:* 57; *86:* 88; *130:* 30; *179:* 29
James, Gilbert *YABC 1:* 43
James, Gordon C. *195:* 89
James, Harold *2:* 151; *3:* 62; *8:* 79; *29:* 113; *51:* 195; *74:* 90
James, Kennon *126:* 211
James, Robin *50:* 106; *53:* 32, 34, 35
James, Will *19:* 150, 152, 153, 155, 163
Janosch
    See Eckert, Horst
Janovitch, Marilyn *68:* 168
Janovitz, Marilyn *87:* 187; *130:* 198; *194:* 91
Jansons, Inese *48:* 117
Jansson, Tove *3:* 90; *41:* 106, 108, 109, 110, 111, 113, 114
Jaques, Faith *7:* 11, 132, 133; *21:* 83, 84; *69:* 114,116; *73:* 170
Jaques, Frances Lee *29:* 224
Jauss, Anne Marie *1:* 139; *3:* 34; *10:* 57, 119; *11:* 205; *23:* 194
Jay, Alison *158:* 97, 98; *183:* 126, 127
Jeffers, Oliver *175:* 111
Jeffers, Susan *17:* 86, 87; *25:* 164, 165; *26:* 112; *50:* 132, 134, 135; *70:* 111, 112, 113; *137:* 107, 108, 109, 110, 111
Jefferson, Louise E. *4:* 160
Jenkin-Pearce, Susie *78:* 16
Jenkins, Debra Reid *85:* 202; *114:* 89; *173:* 134
Jenkins, Jean *98:* 79, 102
Jenkins, Leonard *157:* 169; *167:* 128; *189:* 96, 97; *190:* 89

Jenkins, Patrick *72:* 126
Jenkins, Steve *124:* 177; *154:* 90, 91, 92, 93; *185:* 194; *188:* 81, 82, 83, 84, 85, 86
Jenks, Aleta *73:* 117; *124:* 225
Jenkyns, Chris *51:* 97
Jensen, Bruce *95:* 39
Jensinius, Kirsten *56:* 58
Jeram, Anita *89:* 135; *102:* 122, 123; *129:* 112; *154:* 96, 97, 98; *164:* 154
Jernigan, E. Wesley *85:* 92
Jerome, Karen A. *72:* 194
Jeruchim, Simon *6:* 173; *15:* 250
Jeschke, Susan *20:* 89; *39:* 161; *41:* 84; *42:* 120
Jessel, Camilla *29:* 115
Jessell, Tim *159:* 3; *177:* 87; *181:* 95
Jeyaveeran, Ruth *182:* 100
Jiang, Cheng An *109:* 108
Jiang, Wei *109:* 108
Jimenez, Maria *77:* 158; *93:* 127
Jobling, Curtis *138:* 74
Jocelyn, Marthe *118:* 83; *137:* 219; *163:* 119, 120
Joerns, Consuelo *38:* 36; *44:* 94
John, Diana *12:* 209
John, Helen *1:* 215; *28:* 204
Johns, Elizabeth *127:* 33
Johns, Jasper *61:* 172
Johns, Jeanne *24:* 114
Johnson, Adrian *143:* 50
Johnson, Bruce *9:* 47
Johnson, Cathy *92:* 136
Johnson, Crockett
    See Leisk, David
Johnson, D. William *23:* 104
Johnson, D.B. *183:* 98, 139
Johnson, David *175:* 18; *191:* 91
Johnson, Gillian *119:* 175; *164:* 217
Johnson, Harper *1:* 27; *2:* 33; *18:* 302; *19:* 61; *31:* 181; *44:* 46, 50, 95
Johnson, Ingrid *37:* 118
Johnson, James Ralph *1:* 23, 127
Johnson, James David *12:* 195
Johnson, Jane *48:* 136
Johnson, Joel Peter *98:* 18; *128:* 111
Johnson, John E. *34:* 133
Johnson, Kevin *72:* 44
Johnson, Kevin Eugene *109:* 215
Johnson, Larry *47:* 56; *123:* 107; *159:* 203
Johnson, Layne *187:* 94
Johnson, Margaret S. *35:* 131
Johnson, Meredith Merrell *71:* 181; *83:* 158; *89:* 103; *104:* 88
Johnson, Milton *1:* 67; *2:* 71; *26:* 45; *31:* 107; *60:* 112; *68:* 96
Johnson, Pamela *16:* 174; *52:* 145; *62:* 140; *73:* 116; *85:* 64
Johnson, Paul Brett *83:* 95; *132:* 119
Johnson, Stephen T. *80:* 15; *131:* 35; *141:* 96; *145:* 40; *164:* 187; *175:* 32; *189:* 99, 100
Johnson, Steve *138:* 219; *141:* 64; *144:* 199; *177:* 51
Johnson, William R. *38:* 91
Johnson-Petrov, Arden *115:* 206
Johnston, David McCall *50:* 131, 133
Johnston, Lynne *118:* 85, 87, 89
Johnstone, Anne *8:* 120; *36:* 89
Johnstone, Janet Grahame *8:* 120; *36:* 89
Jonas, Ann *50:* 107, 108, 109; *135:* 113
Jones, Bob *71:* 5; *77:* 199
Jones, Carol *5:* 131; *72:* 185, 186; *153:* 111, 112
Jones, Chuck *53:* 70, 71
Jones, Davy *89:* 176
Jones, Douglas B. *185:* 192
Jones, Elizabeth Orton *18:* 124, 126, 128, 129
Jones, Harold *14:* 88; *52:* 50
Jones, Holly *127:* 3
Jones, Jeff *41:* 64
Jones, Laurian *25:* 24, 27
Jones, Margaret *74:* 57

Jones, Noah Z. *182:* 37
Jones, Randy *131:* 104
Jones, Richard *127:* 222
Jones, Robert *25:* 67
Jones, Wilfred *35:* 115; *YABC 1:* 163
Jordan, Charles *89:* 58
Jordan, Jess *158:* 136
Jordan, Martin George *84:* 127
Jordan, Richard *84:* 36
Jorgenson, Andrea *91:* 111
Jorisch, Stéphane *153:* 56, 193; *177:* 29; *178:* 138, 139; *187:* 23
Joseph, James *53:* 88
Joudrey, Ken *64:* 145; *78:* 6
Joyce, William *72:* 131, 132, 133, 134; *73:* 227; *145:* 37
Joyner, Jerry *34:* 138
Juan, Ana *175:* 38; *179:* 111, 112
Jucker, Sita *5:* 93
Judge, Lita *192:* 99
Judkis, Jim *37:* 38
Juhasz, Victor *31:* 67
Jullian, Philippe *24:* 206; *25:* 203
Jung, Tom *91:* 217
Junge, Alexandra *183:* 37
Junge, Walter *67:* 150
Jupo, Frank *7:* 148, 149
Jurisch, Stephane *154:* 105
Justice, Martin *34:* 72

K

Kabatova-Taborska, Zdenka *107:* 153
Kachik, John *165:* 230
Kaczman, James *156:* 98
Kadair, Deborah Ousley *184:* 45, 89
Kahl, David *74:* 95; *97:* 35; *109:* 174; *110:* 213
Kahl, M.P. *37:* 83
Kahl, Virginia *48:* 138
Kahn, Katherine Janus *90:* 135
Kakimoo, Kozo *11:* 148
Kalett, Jim *48:* 159, 160, 161
Kalin, Victor *39:* 186
Kalman, Maira *96:* 131, 132; *137:* 115
Kalmenoff, Matthew *22:* 191
Kalow, Gisela *32:* 105
Kamen, Gloria *1:* 41; *9:* 119; *10:* 178; *35:* 157; *78:* 236; *98:* 82
Kaminsky, Jef *102:* 153
Kandell, Alice *35:* 133
Kane, Henry B. *14:* 90; *18:* 219, 220
Kane, Robert *18:* 131
Kanfer, Larry *66:* 141
Kappes, Alfred *28:* 104
Karalus, Bob *41:* 157
Karas, G. Brian *80:* 60; *99:* 179; *115:* 41; *118:* 50; *136:* 168; *145:* 166; *149:* 245; *159:* 65; *171:* 192; *178:* 142, 143
Karasz, Ilonka *128:* 163
Karlin, Eugene *10:* 63; *20:* 131
Karlin, Nurit *63:* 78; *103:* 110
Karpinski, Tony *134:* 160
Kasamatsu, Shiro *139:* 155
Kasparavicius, Kestutis *139:* 210
Kassian, Olena *64:* 94
Kastner, Jill *79:* 135; *117:* 84, 85
Kasuya, Masahiro *41:* 206, 207; *51:* 100
Kasza, Keiko *191:* 99, 100, 101, 102, 103
Katona, Robert *21:* 85; *24:* 126
Katz, Karen *158:* 123
Kauffer, E. McKnight *33:* 103; *35:* 127; *63:* 67
Kaufman, Angelika *15:* 156
Kaufman, Joe *33:* 119
Kaufman, John *13:* 158
Kaufman, Stuart *62:* 64; *68:* 226; *137:* 44
Kaufmann, John *1:* 174; *4:* 159; *8:* 43, 1; *10:* 102; *18:* 133, 134; *22:* 251
Kaye, Graham *1:* 9; *67:* 7, 8

Kaye, M.M. *62:* 95
Kazalovski, Nata *40:* 205
Keane, Bil *4:* 135
Kearney, David *72:* 47; *121:* 83
Keating, Pamel T. *77:* 37
Keats, Ezra Jack *3:* 18, 105, 257; *14:* 101, 102; *33:* 129; *57:* 79, 80, 82, 83, 84, 87
Keegan, Charles *166:* 211
Keegan, Marcia *9:* 122; *32:* 93
Keeler, Patricia A. *81:* 56; *183:* 102, 103
Keely, Jack *119:* 95
Keely, John *26:* 104; *48:* 214
Keen, Eliot *25:* 213
Keep, Richard C. *170:* 122
Keeping, Charles *9:* 124, 185; *15:* 28, 134; *18:* 115; *44:* 194, 196; *47:* 25; *52:* 3; *54:* 156; *69:* 123, 124; *74:* 56; *155:* 9
Keeter, Susan *168:* 46; *183:* 192
Keith, Eros *4:* 98; *5:* 138; *31:* 29; *43:* 220; *52:* 91, 92, 93, 94; *56:* 64, 66; *60:* 37; *79:* 93
Keleinikov, Andrei *65:* 101, 102
Kelen, Emery *13:* 115
Keller, A.J. *62:* 198
Keller, Arthur I. *26:* 106
Keller, Dick *36:* 123, 125
Keller, Holly *45:* 79; *76:* 118, 119, 120, 121; *108:* 137, 138, 140; *157:* 117, 118, 119
Keller, Katie *79:* 222; *93:* 108
Keller, Ronald *45:* 208
Kelley, Gary *183:* 105
Kelley, True *41:* 114, 115; *42:* 137; *75:* 35; *92:* 104, 105; *124:* 62; *130:* 100, 101; *179:* 120, 121, 122; *192:* 251
Kellogg, Steven *8:* 96; *11:* 207; *14:* 130; *20:* 58; *29:* 140, 141; *30:* 35; *41:* 141; *57:* 89, 90, 92,93, 94, 96; *59:* 182; *73:* 141; *77:* 129; *130:* 105, 106; *177:* 94, 95, 96, 97; *YABC 1:* 65, 73
Kelly, Billy *158:* 143
Kelly, Geoff *97:* 196; *112:* 25
Kelly, Irene *147:* 134
Kelly, John *194:* 186
Kelly, Joseph *174:* 94
Kelly, Kathleen M. *71:* 109
Kelly, Laura *89:* 217
Kelly, True *163:* 87
Kelly, Walt *18:* 136, 137, 138, 139, 140, 141, 144, 145, 146, 148, 149
Kemble, E.W. *34:* 75; *44:* 178; *YABC 2:* 54, 59
Kemp-Welsh, Lucy *24:* 197; *100:* 214
Kendall, Jane *150:* 105; *186:* 109
Kendall, Peter *152:* 85
Kendrick, Dennis *79:* 213
Kennaway, Adrienne *60:* 55, 56; *171:* 88, 89
Kennedy, Doug *189:* 104
Kennedy, Paul Edward *6:* 190; *8:* 132; *33:* 120
Kennedy, Richard *3:* 93; *12:* 179; *44:* 193; *100:* 15; *YABC 1:* 57
Kent, Jack *24:* 136; *37:* 37; *40:* 81; *84:* 89; *86:* 150; *88:* 77
Kent, Rockwell *5:* 166; *6:* 129; *20:* 225, 226, 227,229; *59:* 144
Kenyon, Tony *81:* 201; *127:* 74
Kepes, Juliet *13:* 119
Kerins, Anthony *76:* 84
Kerr, Judity *24:* 137
Kerr, Phyllis Forbes *72:* 141
Kessler, Leonard *1:* 108; *7:* 139; *14:* 107, 227; *22:* 101; *44:* 96; *67:* 79; *82:* 123
Kest, Kristin *168:* 99; *173:* 23
Kesteven, Peter *35:* 189
Ketcham, Hank *28:* 140, 141, 142
Kettelkamp, Larry *2:* 164
Key, Alexander *8:* 99
Khalsa, Dayal Kaur *62:* 99
Kiakshuk *8:* 59
Kidd, Chip *94:* 23
Kidd, Richard *152:* 110
Kidd, Tom *64:* 199; *81:* 189; *185:* 173

Kiddell-Monroe, Joan *19:* 201; *55:* 59, 60; *87:* 174; *121:* 112
Kidder, Harvey *9:* 105; *80:* 41
Kidwell, Carl *43:* 145
Kieffer, Christa *41:* 89
Kiesler, Kate *110:* 105; *136:* 142
Kiff, Ken *40:* 45
Kilbride, Robert *37:* 100
Kilby, Don *141:* 144
Kim, Glenn *99:* 82
Kimball, Anton *78:* 114; *119:* 105
Kimball, Yeffe *23:* 116; *37:* 88
Kimber, Murray *171:* 91
Kimmel, Warren *176:* 112
Kincade, Orin *34:* 116
Kindersley, Barnabas *96:* 110
Kindred, Wendy *7:* 151
King, Colin *53:* 3
King, Robin *10:* 164, 165
King, Stephen Michael *141:* 31
King, Tara Calahan *139:* 172
King, Tony *39:* 52
Kingman, Dong *16:* 287; *44:* 100, 102, 104
Kingsley, Charles *YABC 2:* 182
Kingston, Julie *147:* 14
Kingston, Maxine Hong *53:* 92
Kinney, Jeff *187:* 97
Kipling, John Lockwood *YABC 2:* 198
Kipling, Rudyard *YABC 2:* 196
Kipniss, Robert *29:* 59
Kirchherr, Astrid *55:* 23
Kirchhoff, Art *28:* 136
Kirk, Daniel *153:* 115, 116, 117; *173:* 101
Kirk, David *117:* 88, 89; *161:* 97, 98
Kirk, Ruth *5:* 96
Kirk, Steve *170:* 37
Kirk, Tim *32:* 209, 211; *72:* 89; *83:* 49
Kirmse, Marguerite *15:* 283; *18:* 153
Kirsch, Vincent X. *124:* 207
Kirschner, Ruth *22:* 154
Kish, Ely *73:* 119; *79:* 2
Kitamura, Satoshi *62:* 102; *98:* 91; *101:* 147; *138:* 2; *143:* 83, 85, 86
Kiss, Andrew *168:* 115
Kitchel, JoAnn E. *133:* 32
Kitchen, Bert *70:* 126; *193:* 49
Kittelsen, Theodor *62:* 14
Kiuchi, Tatsuro *114:* 71
Kiwak, Barbara *172:* 135
Klahr, Susan *176:* 196
Klapholz, Mel *13:* 35
Klein, Bill *89:* 105
Klein, Robert *55:* 77
Klein, Suzanna *63:* 104
Kleinman, Zalman *28:* 143
Kleven, Elisa *173:* 96, 97
Kliban, B. *35:* 137, 138
Kline, Michael *127:* 66
Klise, M. Sarah *180:* 117, 118; *181:* 97
Knabel, Lonnie *73:* 103; *75:* 187, 228; *194:* 216
Kneen, Maggie *140:* 139
Knight, Ann *34:* 143
Knight, Christopher *13:* 125
Knight, Hilary *1:* 233; *3:* 21; *15:* 92, 158, 159; *16:* 258, 259, 260; *18:* 235; *19:* 169; *35:* 242; *46:* 167; *52:* 116; *69:* 126, 127; *132:* 129; *YABC 1:* 168, 169, 172
Knorr, Peter *126:* 92, 93
Knotts, Howard *20:* 4; *25:* 170; *36:* 163
Knutson, Barbara *112:* 134
Knutson, Kimberley *115:* 90
Kobayashi, Ann *39:* 58
Kocsis, J.C.
    See Paul, James
Koehler, Hanne Lore *176:* 203
Koehn, Ilse *34:* 198; *79:* 123
Koelsch, Michael *99:* 182; *107:* 164; *109:* 239; *138:* 142; *150:* 94; *176:* 105; *187:* 63
Koering, Ursula *3:* 28; *4:* 14; *44:* 5; *64:* 140,141; *85:* 46

Koerner, Henry
    See Koerner, W.H.D.
Koerner, W.H.D. *14:* 216; *21:* 88, 89, 90, 91; *23:* 211
Koetsch, Mike *166:* 68
Koffler, Camilla *36:* 113
Kogan, Deborah Ray *161:* 101, 102
Koide, Yasuko *50:* 114
Kolado, Karen *102:* 228
Komoda, Kiyo *9:* 128; *13:* 214
Kompaneyets, Marc *169:* 92
Konashevich, Vladimir *61:* 160
Konashevicha, V. *YABC 1:* 26
Konigsburg, E.L. *4:* 138; *48:* 141, 142, 144, 145; *94:* 129, 130; *126:* 129, 130, 131; *194:* 95, 98
Kono, Erin Eitter *177:* 99
Kooiker, Leonie *48:* 148
Koonook, Simon *65:* 157
Koontz, Robin Michal *136:* 155
Koopmans, Loek *101:* 121
Kopelke, Lisa *154:* 107
Kopper, Lisa *72:* 152, 153; *105:* 135, 136
Korach, Mimi *1:* 128, 129; *2:* 52; *4:* 39; *5:* 159; *9:* 129; *10:* 21; *24:* 69
Koren, Edward *5:* 100; *65:* 65, 67
Kosaka, Fumi *164:* 130
Koscielniak, Bruce *99:* 122; *153:* 120, 121, 122
Koshkin, Alexander *92:* 180
Kossin, Sandy *10:* 71; *23:* 105
Kostin, Andrej *26:* 204
Kosturko, Bob *164:* 56
Kotzky, Brian *68:* 184
Kovacevic, Zivojin *13:* 247
Kovalski, Maryann *58:* 120; *84:* 88; *97:* 124, 125, 126; *158:* 3; *186:* 80
Krahn, Fernando *2:* 257; *34:* 206; *49:* 152
Kramer, Anthony *33:* 81
Kramer, David *96:* 162; *109:* 132; *150:* 220
Kramer, Frank *6:* 121
Krantz, Kathy *35:* 83
Kratter, Paul *139:* 65
Kraus, Robert *13:* 217; *65:* 113; *93:* 93, 94
Krause, Jon *176:* 62
Krauss, Trisha *174:* 10
Kredel, Fritz *6:* 35; *17:* 93, 94, 95, 96; *22:* 147; *24:* 175; *29:* 130; *35:* 77; *YABC 2:* 166, 300
Kreloff, Eliot *189:* 107, 108
Krementz, Jill *17:* 98; *49:* 41
Krenina, Katya *117:* 106; *125:* 133; *176:* 117
Kresin, Robert *23:* 19
Krieger, Salem *54:* 164
Kriegler, Lyn *73:* 29
Krinitz, Esther Nisenthal *193:* 196
Krommes, Beth *128:* 141; *149:* 136; *181:* 100, 101; *184:* 105; *188:* 125
Krone, Mike *101:* 71
Kronheimer, Ann *135:* 119
Krosoczka, Jarrett J. *155:* 142
Kruck, Gerald *88:* 181
Krupinski, Loretta *67:* 104; *102:* 131; *161:* 105, 106
Krupp, Robin Rector *53:* 96, 98
Krush, Beth *1:* 51, 85; *2:* 233; *4:* 115; *9:* 61; *10:* 191; *11:* 196; *18:* 164, 165; *32:* 72; *37:* 203; *43:* 57; *60:* 102, 103, 107, 108, 109
Krush, Joe *2:* 233; *4:* 115; *9:* 61; *10:* 191; *11:* 196; *18:* 164, 165; *32:* 72, 91; *37:* 203; *43:* 57; *60:* 102, 103, 107, 108, 109
Krych, Duane *91:* 43
Krykorka, Vladyana *96:* 147; *143:* 90, 91; *168:* 14
Kubick, Dana *165:* 91
Kubinyi, Laszlo *4:* 116; *6:* 113; *16:* 118; *17:* 100; *28:* 227; *30:* 172; *49:* 24, 28; *54:* 23; *167:* 149
Kubricht, Mary *73:* 118
Kucharik, Elena *139:* 31
Kuchera, Kathleen *84:* 5

Kuhn, Bob *17:* 91; *35:* 235
Kulikov, Boris *163:* 185; *185:* 23
Kulka, Joe *188:* 110
Kukalis, Romas *90:* 27; *139:* 37
Kuklin, Susan *63:* 82, 83, 84
Kunhardt, Dorothy *53:* 101
Kunhardt, Edith *67:* 105, 106
Kunstler, Mort *10:* 73; *32:* 143
Kurchevsky, V. *34:* 61
Kurczok, Belinda *121:* 118
Kurelek, William *8:* 107
Kuriloff, Ron *13:* 19
Kurisu, Jane *160:* 120
Kuskin, Karla *2:* 170; *68:* 115, 116; *111:* 116
Kutzer, Ernst *19:* 249
Kuzma, Steve *57:* 8; *62:* 93
Kuznetsova, Berta *74:* 45
Kvasnosky, Laura McGee *93:* 103; *142:* 83; *182:* 108
Kwas, Susan Estelle *179:* 116
Kyong, Yunmee *165:* 139

L

LaBlanc, Andre *24:* 146
Laboccetta, Mario *27:* 120
LaBrose, Darcie *157:* 134
Labrosse, Darcia *58:* 88; *108:* 77; *178:* 89
LaCava, Vince *95:* 118
Laceky, Adam *32:* 121
Lacis, Astra *85:* 117
Lacome, Julie *174:* 96, 97
La Croix *YABC 2:* 4
Ladwig, Tim *98:* 212; *117:* 76
La Farge, Margaret *47:* 141
LaFave, Kim *64:* 177; *72:* 39; *97:* 146; *99:* 172; *106:* 123; *149:* 126
Lafontaine, Roger *167:* 158
Lagarrigue, Jerome *136:* 102; *187:* 81
Laimgruber, Monika *11:* 153
Laite, Gordon *1:* 130, 131; *8:* 209; *31:* 113; *40:* 63; *46:* 117
Laliberté, Louise-Andrée *169:* 98
LaMarche, Jim *46:* 204; *61:* 56; *94:* 69; *114:* 22; *129:* 163; *162:* 78, 80
Lamb, Jim *10:* 117
Lambase, Barbara *101:* 185; *150:* 221; *166:* 234
Lambert, J.K. *38:* 129; *39:* 24
Lambert, Sally Anne *133:* 191
Lambert, Saul *23:* 112; *33:* 107; *54:* 136
Lambert, Stephen *109:* 33; *174:* 99
Lambo, Don *6:* 156; *35:* 115; *36:* 146
Lamontagne, Jacques *166:* 227
Lamut, Sonja *57:* 193
Lamut, Sonya *85:* 102
Landa, Peter *11:* 95; *13:* 177; *53:* 119
Landau, Jacob *38:* 111
Landis, Joan *104:* 23
Landon, Lucinda *79:* 31
Landshoff, Ursula *13:* 124
Landström, Lena *146:* 165, 166
Landström, Olof *146:* 166, 168; *170:* 22
Lane, Daniel *112:* 60
Lane, John R. *8:* 145
Lane, John *15:* 176, 177; *30:* 146
Lane, Nancy *166:* 74
Lang, G.D. *48:* 56
Lang, Gary *73:* 75
Lang, Jerry *18:* 295
Langdo, Bryan *186:* 187; *191:* 113, 114, 115
Lange, Dorothea *50:* 141
Langley, Jonathan *162:* 128
Langner, Nola *8:* 110; *42:* 36
Lanino, Deborah *105:* 148
Lantz, Paul *1:* 82, 102; *27:* 88; *34:* 102; *45:* 123
Larkin, Bob *84:* 225
Laroche, Giles *126:* 140; *146:* 81

LaRochelle, David *171:* 97
Larrecq, John *44:* 108; *68:* 56
Larsen, Suzanne *1:* 13
Larson, Gary *57:* 121, 122, 123, 124, 125, 126, 127
Larsson, Carl *35:* 144, 145, 146, 147, 148, 149, 150, 152, 153, 154
Larsson, Karl *19:* 177
Lartitegui, Ana G. *105:* 167
LaRue, Jenna *167:* 20
La Rue, Michael D. *13:* 215
Lasker, Joe *7:* 186, 187; *14:* 55; *38:* 115; *39:* 47; *83:* 113, 114, 115
Latham, Barbara *16:* 188, 189; *43:* 71
Lathrop, Dorothy *14:* 117, 118, 119; *15:* 109; *16:* 78, 79, 81; *32:* 201, 203; *33:* 112; *YABC 2:* 301
Lattimore, Eleanor Frances *7:* 156
Lauden, Claire *16:* 173
Lauden, George, Jr. *16:* 173
Laune, Paul *2:* 235; *34:* 31
Laure, Jason *49:* 53; *50:* 122
Lauter, Richard *63:* 29; *67:* 111; *77:* 198
Lavallee, Barbara *74:* 157; *92:* 154; *96:* 126; *145:* 193; *166:* 125, 126; *186:* 155; *192:* 172
Lave, Fitz Hugh *59:* 139
Lavis, Stephen *43:* 143; *87:* 137, 164, 165
Layton, Neal *152:* 120, 121; *182:* 65; *187:* 103, 105, 106
Lawrason, June *168:* 30
Lawrence, John *25:* 131; *30:* 141; *44:* 198, 200
Lawrence, Stephen *20:* 195
Lawson, Carol *6:* 38; *42:* 93, 131; *174:* 56; *189:* 89
Lawson, George *17:* 280
Lawson, Robert *5:* 26; *6:* 94; *13:* 39; *16:* 11; *20:* 100, 102, 103; *54:* 3; *66:* 12; *100:* 144, 145; *YABC 2:* 222, 224, 225, 227, 228, 229, 230, 231, 232, 233, 234, 235, 237, 238, 239, 240, 241
Layfield, Kathie *60:* 194
Lazare, Jerry *44:* 109; *74:* 28
Lazarevich, Mila *17:* 118
Lazarus, Claire *103:* 30
Lazarus, Keo Felker *21:* 94
Lazzaro, Victor *11:* 126
Lea, Bob *166:* 208
Lea, Tom *43:* 72, 74
Leacroft, Richard *6:* 140
Leaf, Munro *20:* 99
Leake, Donald *70:* 41
Leander, Patricia *23:* 27
Lear, Edward *18:* 183, 184, 185
Lear, Rebecca *149:* 46
Lebenson, Richard *6:* 209; *7:* 76; *23:* 145; *44:* 191; *87:* 153
Le Cain, Errol *6:* 141; *9:* 3; *22:* 142; *25:* 198; *28:* 173; *68:* 128, 129; *86:* 49
Lechon, Daniel *113:* 211
Leder, Dora *129:* 172
Ledger, Bill *181:* 58
Leduc, Bernard *102:* 36
Lee, Alan *62:* 25, 28
Lee, Bryce *99:* 60; *101:* 195
Lee, Chinlun *181:* 138; *182:* 112
Lee, Declan *191:* 20
Lee, Dom *83:* 118, 120; *93:* 123; *121:* 121, 126; *146:* 174, 175, 206, 207; *174:* 204
Lee, Doris *13:* 246; *32:* 183; *44:* 111
Lee, Hector Viveros *115:* 96
Lee, Jeanne M. *158:* 56
Lee, Jared *93:* 200; *157:* 229
Lee, Jody *81:* 121; *82:* 225; *91:* 155; *100:* 182
Lee, Jody A. *127:* 124, 126, 127
　See also Lee, Jody
Lee, Manning de V. *2:* 200; *17:* 12; *27:* 87; *37:* 102, 103, 104; *YABC 2:* 304
Lee, Marie G. *138:* 157
Lee, Paul *97:* 100; *105:* 72, 209; *109:* 177; *128:* 113

Lee, Robert J. *3:* 97; *67:* 124
Lee, Victor *96:* 228; *105:* 182; *140:* 196
Leech, Dorothy *98:* 76
Leech, John *15:* 59
Leedy, Loreen *84:* 142; *128:* 144, 145, 146; *175:* 125, 126, 127
Leeman, Michael *44:* 157
Leeming, Catherine *87:* 39
Lees, Harry *6:* 112
LeFever, Bill *88:* 220, 221
Legenisel *47:* 111
Legrand, Edy *18:* 89, 93
Lehman, Barbara *73:* 123; *170:* 130
Lehrman, Rosalie *2:* 180
Leichman, Seymour *5:* 107
Leighton, Clare *25:* 130; *33:* 168; *37:* 105, 106, 108,109
Leisk, David *1:* 140, 141; *11:* 54; *30:* 137, 142, 143,144
Leister, Brian *89:* 45; *106:* 37; *114:* 67; *149:* 236
Leloir, Maurice *18:* 77, 80, 83, 99
Lemaître, Pascal *144:* 175; *176:* 130; *189:* 135
Lemieux, Michele *100:* 148; *139:* 153
Lemke, Horst *14:* 98; *38:* 117, 118, 119
Lemke, R.W. *42:* 162
Lemon, David Gwynne *9:* 1
LeMoult, Adolph *82:* 116
Lenn, Michael *136:* 89
Lennon, John *114:* 100
Lennox, Elsie *95:* 163; *143:* 160
Lenski, Lois *1:* 144; *26:* 135, 137, 139, 141; *100:* 153, 154
Lent, Blair *1:* 116, 117; *2:* 174; *3:* 206, 207; *7:* 168, 169; *34:* 62; *68:* 217; *133:* 101; *183:* 60
Leonard, Richard *91:* 128
Leone, Leonard *49:* 190
Lerner, Carol *86:* 140, 141, 142
Lerner, Judith *116:* 138
Lerner, Sharon *11:* 157; *22:* 56
Leroux-Hugon, Helene *132:* 139
Leslie, Cecil *19:* 244
Lessac, Frane *80:* 182, 207; *96:* 182
Lessing, Erich *167:* 52; *173:* 60
Lester, Alison *50:* 124; *90:* 147, 148; *129:* 130
Lethcoe, Jason *191:* 116, 117
Le Tord, Bijou *49:* 156; *95:* 112
Leutz, Emanuel *165:* 27
Levai, Blaise *39:* 130
Levin, Ted *12:* 148
Levine, David *43:* 147, 149, 150, 151, 152; *64:* 11
Levine, Joe *71:* 88
Levine, Marge *81:* 127
Levinson, David *178:* 232
Levit, Herschel *24:* 223
Levstek, Ljuba *131:* 192; *134:* 216; *149:* 65; *168:* 180
Levy, Jessica Ann *19:* 225; *39:* 191
Levy, Lina *117:* 126
Lewin, Betsy *32:* 114; *48:* 177; *90:* 151; *91:* 125; *92:* 85; *115:* 105; *169:* 110, 111; *178:* 47; *186:* 188; *194:* 201
Lewin, Ted *4:* 77; *8:* 168; *20:* 110; *21:* 99,100; *27:* 110; *28:* 96, 97; *31:* 49; *45:* 55; *48:* 223; *60:* 20, 119, 120; *62:* 139; *66:* 108; *71:* 12; *72:* 21, 74; *74:* 226; *76:* 139, 140; *77:* 82; *79:* 87; *85:* 49, 177; *86:* 55; *88:* 182; *93:* 28, 29; *94:* 34, 182, 194; *99:* 156; *104:* 8; *115:* 123; *118:* 74; *119:* 114, 116; *131:* 54; *145:* 99; *165:* 151; *177:* 75; *178:* 42; *190:* 30; *192:* 86; *195:* 101, 102
Lewis, Allen *15:* 112
Lewis, E.B. *88:* 143; *93:* 109; *119:* 79; *124:* 113; *128:* 49; *151:* 167; *168:* 110; *173:* 121; *174:* 66; *176:* 7; *184:* 150; *185:* 191
Lewis, H.B. *170:* 124
Lewis, J. Patrick *162:* 83
Lewis, Jan *81:* 22
Lewis, Kim *136:* 165

Lewis, Richard W. *52:* 25
Lewis, Robin Baird *98:* 193
Leydon, Rita Floden *21:* 101
Li, Xiojun *187:* 172
Lichtenheld, Tom *152:* 125, 126
Lieblich, Irene *22:* 173; *27:* 209, 214
Lieder, Rick *108:* 197
Lies, Brian *92:* 40; *141:* 101; *150:* 138; *190:* 97, 98, 99,
Liese, Charles *4:* 222
Life, Kay *79:* 49
Lifton, Robert Jay *66:* 154
Lightburn, Ron *86:* 153; *91:* 122
Lightfoot, Norman R. *45:* 47
Lignell, Lois *37:* 114
Lill, Debra *121:* 70
Lilly, Charles *8:* 73; *20:* 127; *48:* 53; *72:* 9,16; *77:* 98; *102:* 94
Lilly, Ken *37:* 224
Lim, John *43:* 153
Limona, Mercedes *51:* 183
Lin, Grace *143:* 217; *162:* 86, 87; *174:* 185
Lincoln, Patricia Henderson *27:* 27; *78:* 127
Lindahn, Ron *84:* 17
Lindahn, Val *84:* 17
Lindberg, Howard *10:* 123; *16:* 190
Lindberg, Jeffrey *64:* 77; *77:* 71; *79:* 54; *80:* 149; *174:* 109; *179:* 52
Linden, Seymour *18:* 200, 201; *43:* 140
Lindenbaum, Pija *144:* 143; *183:* 113
Linder, Richard *27:* 119
Lindman, Maj *43:* 154
Lindsay, Norman *67:* 114
Lindsay, Vachel *40:* 118
Lindstrom, Jack *145:* 118
Line, Les *27:* 143
Linell
    See Smith, Linell
Lionni, Leo *8:* 115; *72:* 159, 160, 161
Lipinsky, Lino *2:* 156; *22:* 175
Lippincott, Gary A. *70:* 35; *119:* 118
Lippman, Peter *8:* 31; *31:* 119, 120, 160
Lisi, Victoria *89:* 145
Lisker, Emily *169:* 114
Lisker, Sonia O. *16:* 274; *31:* 31; *44:* 113, 114
Lisowski, Gabriel *47:* 144; *49:* 157
Lissim, Simon *17:* 138
Little, Ed *89:* 145; *151:* 53
Little, Harold *16:* 72
Little, Mary E. *28:* 146
Littlewood, Karen *165:* 126
Litty, Julie *111:* 63
Litzinger, Rosanne *151:* 101; *176:* 118
Liu, Lesley *143:* 72
Livesly, Lorna *19:* 216
Livingston, Susan *95:* 22
Liwska, Renata *164:* 113
Ljungkvist, Laura *180:* 120
Llerena, Carlos Antonio *19:* 181
Lloyd, Errol *11:* 39; *22:* 178
Lloyd, Megan *77:* 118; *80:* 113; *97:* 75; *117:* 94, 95; *189:* 121, 122
Lloyd, Sam *183:* 116, 117
Lo, Beth *165:* 154
Lo, Koon-chiu *7:* 134
Loates, Glen *63:* 76
Lobel, Anita *6:* 87; *9:* 141; *18:* 248; *55:* 85,86, 87, 88, 93, 104; *60:* 67; *78:* 263; *82:* 110; *96:* 157, 159; *101:* 84; *132:* 35; *162:* 93, 94
Lobel, Arnold *1:* 188, 189; *5:* 12; *6:* 147; *7:* 167, 209; *18:* 190, 191; *25:* 39, 43; *27:* 40; *29:* 174; *52:* 127; *55:* 89, 91, 94, 95, 97, 98, 99, 100, 101, 102,103, 105, 106; *60:* 18, 31; *66:* 181, 183; *75:* 57; *82:* 246; *136:* 146
Lobel, Gillian *190:* 21
Locker, Thomas *109:* 134
Lodge, Bernard *107:* 125, 126; *153:* 93
Loeb, Jeph *153:* 177
Lodge, Jo *112:* 119
Loefgren, Ulf *3:* 108
Loescher, Ann *20:* 108

Loescher, Gil *20:* 108
Loew, David *93:* 184; *171:* 120
Lofting, Hugh *15:* 182, 183; *100:* 161, 162
Lofts, Pamela *60:* 188
Loh, George *38:* 88
Lomberg, Jon *58:* 160
Lonette, Reisie *11:* 211; *12:* 168; *13:* 56; *36:* 122; *43:* 155
Long, Ethan *168:* 146; *178:* 12; *182:* 120, 121
Long, Laurel *162:* 135; *190:* 11
Long, Loren *99:* 176; *172:* 65; *182:* 78; *188:* 114, 115
Long, Melinda *152:* 128
Long, Miles *115:* 174
Long, Sally *42:* 184
Long, Sylvia *74:* 168; *132:* 63; *179:* 134
Longoni, Eduardo *73:* 85
Longtemps, Ken *17:* 123; *29:* 221; *69:* 82
Looser, Heinz *YABC 2:* 208
Lopez, Loretta *190:* 100
Lopshire, Robert *6:* 149; *21:* 117; *34:* 166; *73:* 13
Lord, John Vernon *21:* 104; *23:* 25; *51:* 22
Lorenz, Albert *40:* 146; *115:* 127
Loretta, Sister Mary *33:* 73
Lorraine, Walter H. *3:* 110; *4:* 123; *16:* 192; *103:* 119
Los, Marek *146:* 22; *193:* 23
Loss, Joan *11:* 163
Louderback, Walt *YABC 1:* 164
Lousada, Sandra *40:* 138
Louth, Jack *149:* 252; *151:* 191, 192
Love, Judy *173:* 43
Low, Joseph *14:* 124, 125; *18:* 68; *19:* 194; *31:* 166; *80:* 239
Low, William *62:* 175; *80:* 147; *112:* 194; *150:* 202; *169:* 175; *177:* 110; *192:* 27
Lowe, Vicky *177:* 130
Lowenheim, Alfred *13:* 65, 66
Lowenstein, Sallie *116:* 90, 91
Lowitz, Anson *17:* 124; *18:* 215
Lowrey, Jo *8:* 133
Lubach, Vanessa *142:* 152
Lubell, Winifred *1:* 207; *3:* 15; *6:* 151
Lubin, Leonard B. *19:* 224; *36:* 79, 80; *45:* 128, 129,131, 132, 133, 134, 135, 136, 137, 139, 140, 141; *70:* 95; *YABC2:* 96
Lucht, Irmgard *82:* 145
Ludwig, Helen *33:* 144, 145
Lufkin, Raymond *38:* 138; *44:* 48
Luhrs, Henry *7:* 123; *11:* 120
Lujan, Tonita *82:* 33
Lupo, Dom *4:* 204
Lustig, Loretta *30:* 186; *46:* 134, 135, 136, 137
Luthardt, Kevin *172:* 125, 126
Luxbacher, Irene *153:* 145
Luzak, Dennis *52:* 121; *99:* 142
Lydbury, Jane *82:* 98
Lydecker, Laura *21:* 113; *42:* 53
Lynch, Charles *16:* 33
Lynch, Marietta *29:* 137; *30:* 171
Lynch, P.J. *126:* 228; *129:* 110; *132:* 247; *183:* 64
Lyne, Alison Davis *188:* 118, 198
Lyon, Carol *102:* 26
Lyon, Elinor *6:* 154
Lyon, Fred *14:* 16
Lyon, Tammie *175:* 170
Lyons, Oren *8:* 193
Lyster, Michael *26:* 41

M

Maas, Dorothy *6:* 175
Maas, Julie *47:* 61
Macaulay, David *46:* 139, 140, 141, 142, 143, 144, 145, 147, 149, 150; *72:* 167, 168, 169; *137:* 129, 130, 131, 132

MacCarthy, Patricia *69:* 141
Macdonald, Alister *21:* 55
Macdonald, Roberta *19:* 237; *52:* 164
MacDonald, Norman *13:* 99
MacDonald, Suse *54:* 41; *109* 138; *130:* 156; *193:* 106, 107, 109, 110
Mace, Varian *49:* 159
Macguire, Robert Reid *18:* 67
Machetanz, Fredrick *34:* 147, 148
MacInnes, Ian *35:* 59
MacIntyre, Elisabeth *17:* 127, 128
Mack, Jeff *161:* 128; *194:* 119, 120
Mack, Stan *17:* 129; *96:* 33
Mackay, Donald *17:* 60
MacKaye, Arvia *32:* 119
Mackenzie, Stuart *73:* 213
MacKenzie, Garry *33:* 159
Mackie, Clare *87:* 134
Mackinlay, Miguel *27:* 22
MacKinstry, Elizabeth *15:* 110; *42:* 139, 140, 141, 142, 143,144, 145
MacLeod, Lee *91:* 167
Maclise, Daniel *YABC 2:* 257
Macnaughton, Tina *182:* 145
MacRae, Tom *181:* 112
Madden, Don *3:* 112, 113; *4:* 33, 108, 155; *7:* 193; *78:* 12; *YABC 2:* 211
Maddison, Angela Mary *10:* 83
Madsen, Jim *146:* 259; *152:* 237; *184:* 106
Maestro, Giulio *8:* 124; *12:* 17; *13:* 108; *25:* 182; *54:* 147; *59:* 114, 115, 116, 117, 118, 121, 123, 124, 125,126, 127; *68:* 37, 38; *106:* 129, 130, 131, 136, 137, 138
Maffia, Daniel *60:* 200
Maggio, Viqui *58:* 136, 181; *74:* 150; *75:* 90; *85:* 159; *90:* 158; *109:* 184; *193:* 113
Magnus, Erica *77:* 123
Magnuson, Diana *28:* 102; *34:* 190; *41:* 175
Magoon, Scott *181:* 104
Magovern, Peg *103:* 123
Maguire, Sheila *41:* 100
Magurn, Susan *91:* 30
Mahony, Will *37:* 120
Mahony, Will *85:* 116
Mahood, Kenneth *24:* 141
Mahurin, Matt *164:* 225; *175:* 95; *189:* 37
Maik, Henri *9:* 102
Maione, Heather *106:* 5; *178:* 8; *189:* 126, 127; *193:* 58
Maisto, Carol *29:* 87
Maitland, Antony *1:* 100, 176; *8:* 41; *17:* 246; *24:* 46; *25:* 177, 178; *32:* 74; *60:* 65, 195; *67:* 156; *87:* 131; *101:* 110
Majewski, Dawn W. *169:* 95
Mak, Kam *72:* 25; *75:* 43; *87:* 186; *97:* 24; *102:* 154; *149:* 195; *186:* 28
Makie, Pam *37:* 117
Maktima, Joe *116:* 191
Maland, Nick *99:* 77
Male, Alan *132:* 64
Malone, James Hiram *84:* 161
Malone, Nola Langner *82:* 239
Malone, Peter *191:* 121, 122, 123
Malsberg, Edward *51:* 175
Malvern, Corinne *2:* 13; *34:* 148, 149
Manchess, Gregory *165:* 241
Mancusi, Stephen *63:* 198, 199
Mandelbaum, Ira *31:* 115
Manders, John *138:* 152, 155; *188:* 171; *190:* 92
Manet, Edouard *23:* 170
Mangiat, Jeff *173:* 127
Mangurian, David *14:* 133
Manham, Allan *42:* 109; *77:* 180; *80:* 227
Manley, Matt *103:* 167; *117:* 98; *172:* 49
Manna, Giovanni *178:* 44
Manniche, Lise *31:* 121
Manning, Jane *96:* 203
Manning, Jo *63:* 154
Manning, Lawrence *191:* 153
Manning, Mick *176:* 139

Manning, Samuel F. *5:* 75
Mantel, Richard *57:* 73; *63:* 106; *82:* 255
Maraja *15:* 86; *YABC 1:* 28; *2:* 115
Marcellino, Fred *20:* 125; *34:* 222; *53:* 125;
   58: 205; *61:* 64, 121, 122; *68:* 154, 156,
   157, 158, 159; *72:* 25; *86:* 184; *98:* 181;
   118: 129, 130, 131; *149:* 218; *194:* 7
Marchesi, Stephen *34:* 140; *46:* 72; *50:* 147;
   66: 239; *70:* 33; *73:* 18, 114, 163; *77:* 47,
   76,147; *78:* 79; *80:* 30; *81:* 6; *89:* 66; *93:*
   21,130; *94:* 94; *97:* 66; *98:* 96; *114:* 115,
   116
Marchiori, Carlos *14:* 60
Marciano, John Bemelmans *118:* 133; *167:*
   110, 111, 112
Marcus, Barry David *139:* 248; *145:* 18
Margules, Gabriele *21:* 120
Mariana
   See Foster, Marian Curtis
Mariano, Michael *52:* 108
Marino, Dorothy *6:* 37; *14:* 135
Mario, Heide Stetson *101:* 202
Maris, Ron *71:* 123
Maritz, Nicolaas *85:* 123
Mark, Mona *65:* 105; *68:* 205; *116:* 213
Markham, R.L. *17:* 240
Marks, Alan *104:* 104; *109:* 182; *164:* 92;
   185: 134; *187:* 120, 121, 122
Marks, Cara *54:* 9
Marokvia, Artur *31:* 122
Marquez, Susan *108:* 121
Marrella, Maria Pia *62:* 116
Marriott, Pat *30:* 30; *34:* 39; *35:* 164, 165,
   166; *44:* 170; *48:* 186, 187, 188, 189, 191,
   192, 193; *91:* 92
Mars, W.T. *1:* 161; *3:* 115; *4:* 208, 225; *5:* 92,
   105, 186; *8:* 214; *9:* 12; *13:* 121; *27:* 151;
   31: 180; *38:* 102; *48:* 66; *62:* 164, 165; *64:*
   62; *68:* 229; *79:* 55
Marschall, Ken *85:* 29
Marsh, Christine *3:* 164
Marsh, James *73:* 137
Marsh, Reginald *17:* 5; *19:* 89; *22:* 90, 96
Marshall, Anthony D. *18:* 216
Marshall, Felicia *170:* 190
Marshall, James *6:* 160; *40:* 221; *42:* 24, 25,
   29; *51:* 111, 112, 113, 114, 115, 116, 117,
   118, 119, 120, 121; *64:* 13; *75:* 126, 127,
   128, 129; *102:* 10, 12
Marshall, Janet *97:* 154
Marstall, Bob *55:* 145; *84:* 153, 170; *104:* 145;
   154: 166, 167, 168
Martchenko, Michael *50:* 129, 153, 155, 156,
   157; *83:* 144,145; *154:* 137, 138, 139
Marten, Ruth *129:* 52
Martin, Charles E. *70:* 144
Martin, David Stone *24:* 232; *62:* 4
Martin, Fletcher *18:* 213; *23:* 151
Martin, Rene *7:* 144; *42:* 148, 149, 150
Martin, Richard E. *51:* 157; *131:* 203
Martin, Ron *32:* 81
Martin, Stefan *8:* 68; *32:* 124, 126; *56:* 33
Martin, Whitney *166:* 137
Martinez, Ed *58:* 192; *72:* 231; *77:* 33; *80:*
   214; *167:* 123
Martinez, John *6:* 113; *118:* 13; *139:* 143
Martinez, Sergio *158:* 190
Martini, Angela *183:* 161
Martiniere, Stephan *171:* 130
Marton, Jirina *95:* 127, 128; *144:* 145
Martorell, Antonio *84:* 6; *97:* 161
Martucci, Griesbach *52:* 106
Marvin, Frederic *83:* 86
Marx, Robert F. *24:* 143
Marzollo, Jean *190:* 127
Masefield, Judith *19:* 208, 209
Masheris, Robert *78:* 51
Masiello, Ralph *186:* 171
Mason, George F. *14:* 139
Mason, Robert *84:* 96
Massey, Barbara *68:* 142

Massie, Diane Redfield *16:* 194
Massie, Kim *31:* 43
Mataya, David *121:* 66
Mathers, Petra *119:* 135; *163:* 104; *176:* 143,
   144; *187:* 142
Mathewuse, James *51:* 143
Mathieu, Joseph *14:* 33; *39:* 206; *43:* 167; *56:*
   180; *79:* 126; *94:* 147; *185:* 140
Matje, Martin *169:* 177, 178; *172:* 180
Matsubara, Naoko *12:* 121
Matsuda, Shizu *13:* 167
Matsuoka, Mei *192:* 135
Matte, L'Enc *22:* 183
Mattelson, Marvin *36:* 50, 51
Mattheson, Jenny *180:* 132
Matthews, Elizabeth *194:* 128
Matthews, F. Leslie *4:* 216
Matthews, Tina *190:* 130
Mattingly, David *71:* 76, 77; *82:* 64; *91:* 216,
   217; *109:* 25
Matulay, Laszlo *5:* 18; *43:* 168
Matus, Greta *12:* 142
Maughan, William *181:* 31
Mauldin, Bill *27:* 23
Mauterer, Erin Marie *119:* 5
Mawicke, Tran *9:* 137; *15:* 191; *47:* 100
Mawson, Matt *74:* 115
Max, Peter *45:* 146, 147, 148, 149, 150
Maxie, Betty *40:* 135
Maxwell, John Alan *1:* 148
Mayan, Earl *7:* 193
Mayer, Danuta *117:* 103
Mayer, Marianna *32:* 132
Mayer, Mercer *11:* 192; *16:* 195, 196; *20:* 55,
   57; *32:* 129, 130, 132, 133, 134; *41:* 144,
   248, 252; *58:* 186; *73:* 140, 142, 143; *137:*
   137, 138
Mayforth, Hal *166:* 77
Mayhew, James *85:* 121; *138:* 187; *149:* 140
Mayhew, Richard *3:* 106
Mayo, Gretchen Will *38:* 81; *84:* 166
Mays, Victor *5:* 127; *8:* 45, 153; *14:* 245; *23:*
   50; *34:* 155; *40:* 79; *45:* 158; *54:* 91; *66:*
   240
Mazal, Chanan *49:* 104
Maze, Deborah *71:* 83
Mazellan, Ron *75:* 97, 98
Mazetti, Alan *112:* 72
Mazille, Capucine *96:* 168
Mazza, Adriana Saviozzi *19:* 215
Mazzella, Mary Jo *82:* 165
Mazzetti, Alan *45:* 210
McAfee, Steve *135:* 146; *167:* 176; *191:* 84
McAlinden, Paul *112:* 128
McBride, Angus *28:* 49; *103:* 40
McBride, Will *30:* 110
McCaffery, Janet *38:* 145
McCallum, Graham *78:* 78
McCallum, Stephen *141:* 143; *156:* 5; *166:*
   228
McCann, Gerald *3:* 50; *4:* 94; *7:* 54; *41:* 121
McCarthy, Dan *174:* 74
McCarthy, Linda *177:* 128
McCarthy, Meghan *168:* 134
McCauley, Adam *157:* 36; *184:* 199; *193:* 100
McCay, Winsor *41:* 124, 126, 128, 129, 130,
   131; *134:* 77, 79
McClary, Nelson *1:* 111
McClintock, Barbara *57:* 135; *95:* 130; *146:*
   190
McClintock, Theodore *14:* 141
McCloskey, Robert *1:* 184, 185; *2:* 186, 187;
   17: 209; *39:* 139, 140, 141, 142, 143, 146,
   147, 148; *85:* 150, 151; *100:* 172, 173, 174
McClung, Robert *2:* 189; *68:* 166, 167
McClure, Gillian *31:* 132; *150:* 53
McConnel, Jerry *31:* 75, 187
McConnell, Mary *102:* 49
McCord, Kathleen Garry *78:* 236
McCormack, John *66:* 193
McCormick, A.D. *35:* 119

McCormick, Dell J. *19:* 216
McCrady, Lady *16:* 198; *39:* 127
McCrea, James *3:* 122; *33:* 216
McCrea, Ruth *3:* 122; *27:* 102; *33:* 216
McCue, Lisa *65:* 148, 149; *77:* 54; *80:* 132;
   175: 33; *177:* 133, 135
McCully, Emily Arnold *2:* 89; *4:* 120, 121,
   146, 197; *5:* 2, 129; *7:* 191; *11:* 122; *15:*
   210; *33:* 23; *35:* 244; *37:* 122; *39:* 88; *40:*
   103; *50:* 30,31, 32, 33, 34, 35, 36, 37; *52:*
   89, 90; *57:* 6; *62:* 3; *70:* 195; *86:* 82; *96:*
   192; *97:* 93; *110:* 143,144; *117:* 47; *167:* 96
McCurdy, Michael *13:* 153; *24:* 85; *81:* 160;
   82: 157, 158; *86:* 125; *97:* 92; *117:* 178;
   132: 6; *147:* 159, 160
McCusker, Paul *99:* 19
McDaniel, Jerry *132:* 135
McDaniel, Preston *160:* 206; *170:* 139
McDermott, Beverly Brodsky *11:* 180
McDermott, Gerald *16:* 201; *74:* 174, 175;
   163: 150, 151
McDermott, Mike *96:* 187
McDonald, Jill *13:* 155; *26:* 128
McDonald, Mercedes *169:* 118
McDonald, Ralph J. *5:* 123, 195
McDonnell, Flora *146:* 199, 200
McDonnell, Patrick *179:* 153, 154
McDonough, Don *10:* 163
McElmurry, Jill *137:* 148; *163:* 141
McElrath-Eslick, Lori *129:* 145; *142:* 21; *173:*
   123
McEntee, Dorothy *37:* 124
McEwan, Keith *88:* 116; *165:* 122, 123
McEwen, Katharine *169:* 34
McFall, Christie *12:* 144
McFeely, Daniel *160:* 213
McGaw, Laurie *109:* 243; *143:* 216
McGee, Barbara *6:* 165
McGee, Marni *163:* 153
McGillvray, Kim *158:* 171; *165:* 213; *186:*
   183; *190:* 175
McGinley-Nally, Sharon *131:* 19
McGinnis, Robert *110:* 113; *177:* 80
McGovern, Tara *98:* 171
McGraw, Sheila *83:* 146
McGregor, Malcolm *23:* 27
McGrory, Anik *193:* 120
McGuirk, Leslie *152:* 159
McHale, John *138:* 190
McHenry, E.B. *193:* 122
McHugh, Tom *23:* 64
McIntosh, Jon *42:* 56
McKay, Donald *2:* 118; *32:* 157; *45:* 151, 152
McKean, Dave *150:* 71; *174:* 156
McKeating, Eileen *44:* 58
McKee, David *10:* 48; *21:* 9; *70:* 154, 155;
   107: 139, 140, 141; *134:* 218; *158:* 148, 149,
   150, 151
McKee, Diana *109:* 185
McKelvey, Patrick *164:* 141
McKendry, Joe *170:* 136
McKeveny, Tom *164:* 60; *173:* 79
McKie, Roy *7:* 44
McKillip, Kathy *30:* 153
McKinney, Ena *26:* 39
McKinnon, James *136:* 75
McKowen, Scott *172:* 63
McLachlan, Edward *5:* 89
McLaren, Chesley *133:* 53
McLaren, Kirsty *123:* 99; *124:* 226
Mclean, Andrew *113:* 117, 118, 120, 121; *172:*
   130, 131
Mclean, Janet *172:* 130
McLean, Meg *94:* 196
McLean, Sammis *32:* 197
McLean, Wilson *90:* 29; *113:* 195
McLoughlin, John C. *47:* 149
McLoughlin, Wayne *102:* 230; *134:* 178
McMahon, Robert *36:* 155; *69:* 169
McManus, Shawn *85:* 71
McMenemy, Sarah *156:* 139

McMillan, Bruce *22:* 184
McMullan, James *40:* 33; *67:* 172; *87:* 142; *99:* 63, 64; *189:* 133
McMullen, Nigel *146:* 177
McNeely, Tom *162:* 55
McNaught, Harry *12:* 80; *32:* 136
McNaughton, Colin *39:* 149; *40:* 108; *92:* 144, 145, 146; *134:* 104, 106
McNicholas, Maureen *38:* 148
McNicholas, Shelagh *173:* 61; *191:* 125, 126
McPhail, David *14:* 105; *23:* 135; *37:* 217, 218, 220,221; *47:* 151, 152, 153, 154, 155, 156, 158, 159, 160, 162, 163, 164; *71:* 211; *81:* 139, 140, 142; *86:* 123; *132:* 150; *140:* 129, 131, 132; *183:* 134, 135, 137; *189:* 132
McPhee, Richard B. *41:* 133
McPheeters, Neal *78:* 132; *86:* 90; *99:* 162; *111:* 141; *142:* 162
McQuade, Jacqueline *124:* 223
McQueen, Lucinda *28:* 149; *41:* 249; *46:* 206; *53:* 103
McQuillan, Mary *153:* 97
McVay, Tracy *11:* 68
McVicker, Charles *39:* 150
Mead, Ben Carlton *43:* 75
Meade, Holly *90:* 102; *94:* 101; *149:* 8; *151:* 107
Mecray, John *33:* 62
Meddaugh, Susan *20:* 42; *29:* 143; *41:* 241; *77:* 50; *84:* 173, 174, 175, 176, 177, 178; *125:* 160, 161, 162; *176:* 148, 149, 150, 151
Meehan, Dennis B. *56:* 144
Meents, Len W. *73:* 147, 150
Meers, Tony *99:* 113
Meisel, Paul *98:* 137; *124:* 18; *162:* 180; *179:* 16; *181:* 62; *194:* 154
Melanson, Luc *149:* 229
Melendez, Francisco *72:* 180
Melnychuk, Monika *153:* 65
Melo, John *16:* 285; *58:* 203
Meloni, Maria Teresa *98:* 62
Meltzer, Ericka
  See O'Rourke, Ericka
Menasco, Milton *43:* 85
Menchin, Scott *188:* 129
Mendelson, Steven T. *86:* 154
Mendelssohn, Felix *19:* 170
Mendola, Christopher *88:* 223
Meng, Heinz *13:* 158
Merian, Maria Sibylla *140:* 88
Mero, Lee *34:* 68
Merrill, Frank T. *16:* 147; *19:* 71; *YABC 1:* 226, 229,273
Merriman, Rachel *98:* 108; *114:* 122; *149:* 142
Meryman, Hope *27:* 41
Meryweather, Jack *10:* 179
Meseldzija, Petar *168:* 97
Meserve, Jess *184:* 137
Messick, Dale *64:* 150, 151, 152
Meth, Harold *24:* 203
Meyer, Herbert *19:* 189
Meyer, Renate *6:* 170
Meyers, Bob *11:* 136
Meyers, Nancy *172:* 124
Meynell, Louis *37:* 76
Micale, Albert *2:* 65; *22:* 185
Miccuci, Charles *82:* 163; *144:* 150
Micich, Paul *163:* 163
Middleton, Jeffrey *177:* 173
Middleton-Sandford, Betty *2:* 125
Mieke, Anne *45:* 74
Mighell, Patricia *43:* 134
Miglio, Paige *101:* 203; *151:* 223
Mikolaycak, Charles *9:* 144; *12:* 101; *13:* 212; *21:* 121; *22:* 168; *30:* 187; *34:* 103, 150; *37:* 183; *43:* 179; *44:* 90; *46:* 115, 118, 119; *49:* 25; *78:* 121, 122, 205, 207; *81:* 4
Milelli, Pascal *129:* 66; *135:* 153; *187:* 45
Miles, Elizabeth *117:* 77
Miles, Jennifer *17:* 278
Milgrim, David *158:* 157; *187:* 125, 126, 128

Milhous, Katherine *15:* 193; *17:* 51
Millais, John E. *22:* 230, 231
Millar, H.R. *YABC 1:* 194, 195, 203
Millard, C.E. *28:* 186
Millard, Kerry *105:* 124
Miller, Don *15:* 195; *16:* 71; *20:* 106; *31:* 178
Miller, Edna *29:* 148
Miller, Edward *115:* 64; *183:* 140, 141
Miller, Frank J. *25:* 94
Miller, Grambs *18:* 38; *23:* 16
Miller, Ian *99:* 128
Miller, Jane *15:* 196
Miller, Marcia *13:* 233
Miller, Marilyn *1:* 87; *31:* 69; *33:* 157
Miller, Mitchell *28:* 183; *34:* 207
Miller, Phil *175:* 150
Miller, Shane *5:* 140
Miller, Virginia *81:* 206
Millman, Isaac *172:* 18
Mills, Elaine *72:* 181
Mills, Judith Christine *130:* 168, 169
Mills, Lauren *92:* 170
Mills, Yaroslava Surmach *35:* 169, 170; *46:* 114
Millsap, Darrel *51:* 102
Milone, Karen *89:* 169
Milord, Susan *147:* 163, 164
Milton, Debbie *162:* 161
Mims, Ashley *170:* 51
Miner, Julia *98:* 69
Minor, Wendell *39:* 188; *52:* 87; *56:* 171; *58:* 116; *62:* 56; *66:* 109; *74:* 93; *78:* 129; *94:* 67; *117:* 12, 13; *124:* 84, 86; *136:* 121; *164:* 168, 169; *170:* 71
Minter, Daniel *176:* 154; *179:* 177
Mirocha, Paul *81:* 133; *192:* 148; *194:* 36
Misako Rocks! *192:* 149, 150
Mitchell, Judith *109:* 117
Mitchell, Mark *91:* 208
Mitchell, Tracy *190:* 15
Mitgutsch, Ali *76:* 161
Mitsuhashi, Yoko *45:* 153
Miyake, Yoshi *38:* 141
Mizumura, Kazue *10:* 143; *18:* 223; *36:* 159
Mochi, Ugo *8:* 122; *38:* 150
Mock, Paul *55:* 83; *123:* 32
Modarressi, Mitra *90:* 236; *126:* 168; *173:* 165, 166
Modell, Frank *39:* 152
Mogenson, Jan *74:* 183
Mohn, Susan *89:* 224
Mohr, Mark *133:* 201
Mohr, Nicholasa *8:* 139; *113:* 127
Molan, Christine *60:* 177; *84:* 183
Moldon, Peter L. *49:* 168
Molk, Laurel *92:* 150
Momaday, N. Scott *48:* 159
Mombourquette, Paul *112:* 91; *126:* 142
Monk, Julie *165:* 231; *191:* 96
Monks, Lydia *189:* 136, 137
Montgomery, Lucy *150:* 126
Montgomery-Higham, Amanda *169:* 131
Montiel, David *69:* 106; *84:* 145
Montijo, Rhode *193:* 164
Montresor, Beni *2:* 91; *3:* 138; *38:* 152, 153, 154,155, 156, 157, 158, 159, 160; *68:* 63
Montserrat, Pep *128:* 135; *181:* 119; *184:* 53
Moon, Carl *25:* 183, 184, 185
Moon, Eliza *14:* 40
Moon, Ivan *22:* 39; *38:* 140
Moore, Adrienne *67:* 147
Moore, Agnes Kay Randall *43:* 187
Moore, Cyd *107:* 107, 108; *159:* 137, 138; *186:* 148, 149, 151
Moore, Gustav *127:* 181, 182; *170:* 162, 163
Moore, Jackie *128:* 79
Moore, Janet *63:* 153
Moore, Margie *176:* 156
Moore, Mary *29:* 160
Moore, Patrick *184:* 121
Moore, Yvette *101:* 11, 12; *154:* 141

Mora, Giovanni *179:* 127; *184:* 11
Mora, Raul Mina *20:* 41
Moraes, Odilon *102:* 144
Morales, Yuyi *154:* 144
Moran, Rosslyn *111:* 26
Moran, Tom *60:* 100
Mordan, C.B. *193:* 115
Mordvinoff, Nicolas *15:* 179
Moreno, René King *169:* 59; *190:* 133, 209
Morgan, Barbara *169:* 116
Morgan, Jacqui *58:* 57
Morgan, Mary *114:* 133, 134, 135; *123:* 11
Morgan, Tom *42:* 157
Morgan, Pierr *173:* 148
Morgenstern, Michael *158:* 7, 57; *171:* 103; *174:* 60
Morice, Dave *93:* 142
Morin, Paul *73:* 132; *79:* 130; *88:* 140; *137:* 143
Moriuchi, Mique *177:* 203
Morozumi, Atsuko *110:* 155
Morrill, Leslie *18:* 218; *29:* 177; *33:* 84; *38:* 147; *42:* 127; *44:* 93; *48:* 164, 165, 167, 168, 169, 170,171; *49:* 162; *63:* 136, 180; *70:* 72; *71:* 70, 91,92; *72:* 228; *80:* 163, 164, 165; *90:* 121; *121:* 88; *178:* 117
Morrill, Rowena A. *84:* 16; *98:* 163
Morris *47:* 91
Morris, Frank *55:* 133; *60:* 28; *76:* 2
Morris, Harry O. *119:* 138
Morris, Jackie *128:* 194; *144:* 119; *151:* 146
Morris, Jennifer E. *179:* 157
Morris, Oradel Nolen *128:* 180
Morris, Tony *62:* 146; *70:* 97
Morrison, Bill *42:* 116; *66:* 170; *69:* 40
Morrison, Gordon *87:* 150; *113:* 93; *128:* 181, 182; *183:* 144, 145, 146
Morrison, Frank *169:* 162
Morrison, Taylor *159:* 144, 145; *187:* 131
Morrow, Gray *2:* 64; *5:* 200; *10:* 103, 114; *14:* 175
Morton, Lee Jack *32:* 140
Morton, Marian *3:* 185
Mosberg, Hilary *117:* 195; *118:* 164; *149:* 55
Moser, Barry *56:* 68, 117, 118, 119, 120, 121, 122, 123, 124; *59:* 141; *60:* 160; *79:* 91, 147, 149, 151, 152; *82:* 81; *90:* 118; *91:* 35; *95:* 210; *97:* 91, 93; *102:* 152; *126:* 4; *128:* 175; *133:* 141; *138:* 167, 171, 174; *153:* 205; *174:* 130; *185:* 152, 154; *195:* 163
Moser, Cara *90:* 118; *138:* 167
Moses, Grandma *18:* 228
Moses, Will *178:* 170, 171
Moskof, Martin Stephen *27:* 152
Mosley, Francis *57:* 144
Moss, Donald *11:* 184
Moss, Geoffrey *32:* 198
Moss, Marissa *71:* 130; *104:* 127; *163:* 156
Most, Bernard *48:* 173; *91:* 142, 143; *134:* 120
Mowll, Joshua *188:* 133
Mowry, Carmen *50:* 62
Moxley, Sheila *96:* 174; *169:* 26
Moyers, William *21:* 65
Moyler, Alan *36:* 142
Mozley, Charles *9:* 87; *20:* 176, 192, 193; *22:* 228; *25:* 205; *33:* 150; *43:* 170, 171, 172, 173, 174; *YABC2:* 89
Mueller, Hans Alexander *26:* 64; *27:* 52, 53
Mugnaini, Joseph *11:* 35; *27:* 52, 53; *35:* 62
Mujica, Rick *72:* 67; *88:* 95; *111:* 53; *180:* 185
Mullen, Douglas *180:* 178
Muller, Robin *86:* 161
Muller, Steven *32:* 167
Muller, Jorg *35:* 215; *67:* 138, 139
Mulock, Julie *163:* 112
Mullins, Edward S. *10:* 101
Mullins, Patricia *51:* 68
Multer, Scott *80:* 108
Munari, Bruno *15:* 200
Munch, Edvard *140:* 143
Munowitz, Ken *14:* 148; *72:* 178, 179

Munro, Roxie *58:* 134; *136:* 177; *137:* 218; *184:* 133, 134
Munsinger, Lynn *33:* 161; *46:* 126; *71:* 92; *82:* 80; *89:* 218; *92:* 125; *94:* 157, 158, 159, 160; *98:* 196; *103:* 198; *142:* 143; *145:* 133, 134, 136; *153:* 203; *176:* 162; *177:* 140, 141, 142; *189:* 113, 114, 116, 117
Munson, Russell *13:* 9
Munster, Sebastian *166:* 107
Munoz, William *42:* 160
Munzar, Barbara *149:* 75
Murdocca, Salvatore *73:* 212; *98:* 132; *111:* 168; *157:* 228; *164:* 257
Murphy, Bill *5:* 138; *130:* 170
Murphy, Jill *37:* 142; *70:* 166; *142:* 132, 134
Murphy, Kelly *130:* 212; *143:* 119; *176:* 158; *190:* 135
Murphy, Tom *192:* 40
Murr, Karl *20:* 62
Murray, Joe *175:* 37
Murray, Ossie *43:* 176
Mussino, Attilio *29:* 131; *100:* 164
Mutchler, Dwight *1:* 25
Myers, Bernice *9:* 147; *36:* 75; *81:* 146, 147, 148
Myers, Jon J. *165:* 169; *167:* 109; *190:* 227; *193:* 59
Myers, Christopher *183:* 150; *193:* 139
Myers, Duane O. *99:* 145
Myers, Tim *147:* 168
Myers, V.G. *142:* 41
Myers, Lou *11:* 2

N

Nachreiner, Tom *29:* 182
Nacht, Merle *65:* 49
Nadler, Ellis *88:* 91
Nagle, Shane *180:* 223
Nagy, Ian *195:* 64
Najaka, Marlies *62:* 101
Nakai, Michael *30:* 217; *54:* 29
Nakata, Hiroe *157:* 156; *162:* 30
Nakatani, Chiyoko *12:* 124
Narahashi, Keiko *77:* 188; *82:* 213; *115:* 142, 143, 144
Nascimbene, Yan *133:* 128; *173:* 132, 133
Nash, Lesa *87:* 135
Nash, Linell *46:* 175
Nash, Scott *130:* 36; *188:* 196
Naso, John *33:* 183
Nason, Thomas W. *14:* 68
Nasser, Muriel *48:* 74
Nast, Thomas *21:* 29; *28:* 23; *51:* 132, 133, 134, 135,136, 137, 138, 139, 141
Nasta, Vincent *78:* 185
Natale, Vincent *76:* 3; *78:* 125; *112:* 47; *166:* 81; *174:* 189; *185:* 212
Natchev, Alexi *96:* 177
Nathan, Charlott *125:* 151
Nathan, Cheryl *150:* 104; *186:* 112
Natti, Susanna *20:* 146; *32:* 141, 142; *35:* 178; *37:* 143; *71:* 49; *93:* 98; *125:* 166, 168; *126:* 228; *151:* 6; *178:* 8; *188:* 106
Navarra, Celeste Scala *8:* 142
Naylor, Penelope *10:* 104
Nazz, James *72:* 8
Nebel, M. *45:* 154
Neebe, William *7:* 93
Needler, Jerry *12:* 93
Neel, Alice *31:* 23
Neely, Beth *119:* 184
Neely, Keith R. *46:* 124
Neff, Leland *78:* 74
Negri, Rocco *3:* 213; *5:* 67; *6:* 91, 108; *12:* 159
Negrin, Fabian *174:* 125; *175:* 15
Neidigh, Sherry *128:* 53
Neilan, Eujin Kim *180:* 241

Neill, John R. *18:* 8, 10, 11, 21, 30; *100:* 22
Neilsen, Cliff *158:* 131; *177:* 112, 121
Neilsen, Terese *116:* 74
Nelson, Craig *62:* 151; 153; *183:* 86
Nelson, Gail White *68:* 140
Nelson, Jennifer *129:* 152
Nelson, Kadir *151:* 185; *154:* 146, 147; *157:* 189, 222; *181:* 122, 124
Nelson, S.D. *131:* 34; *181:* 126, 127
Ness, Evaline *1:* 164, 165; *2:* 39; *3:* 8; *10:* 147; *12:* 53; *26:* 150, 151, 152, 153; *49:* 30, 31, 32; *56:* 30; *60:* 113
Neubecker, Robert *170:* 143
Neville, Vera *2:* 182
Nevins, Daniel *191:* 173
Nevwirth, Allan *79:* 168
Newberry, Clare Turlay *1:* 170
Newbold, Greg *108:* 125; *145:* 199; *151:* 23; *193:* 178
Newfeld, Frank *14:* 121; *26:* 154
Newman, Andy *149:* 61; *195:* 63
Newman, Ann *43:* 90
Newman, Barbara Johansen *191:* 137, 138
Newsham, Ian *143:* 162
Newsom, Carol *40:* 159; *44:* 60; *47:* 189; *65:* 29; *70:* 192; *80:* 36; *85:* 137, 138; *92:* 167; *191:* 82
Newsom, Tom *49:* 149; *71:* 13, 62; *75:* 156; *91:* 113
Newton, Jill *83:* 105
Ng, Michael *29:* 171
Ng, Simon *167:* 7
Nguyen, Vincent *189:* 49
Nicholson, William *15:* 33, 34; *16:* 48
Nickens, Bessie *104:* 153
Nicklaus, Carol *45:* 194; *62:* 132, 133
Nickle, John *181:* 128
Nickless, Will *16:* 139
Nicholas, Corasue *154:* 20
Nicolas *17:* 130, 132, 133; *YABC 2:* 215
Niebrugge, Jane *6:* 118
Nielsen, Jon *6:* 100; *24:* 202
Nielsen, Kay *15:* 7; *16:* 211, 212, 213, 215, 217; *22:* 143; *YABC 1:* 32, 33
Nielsen, Cliff *95:* 207, 208; *105:* 58; *114:* 112; *124:* 12; *125:* 91, 92; *132:* 224; *135:* 187; *136:* 40; *137:* 168; *145:* 54; *149:* 28; *158:* 129; *165:* 64, 158; *168:* 169; *170:* 6; *175:* 114, 116, 187; *194:* 107
Niemann, Christoph *191:* 141
Nikola-Lisa, W. *180:* 180
Niland, Deborah *25:* 191; *27:* 156; *135:* 50; *172:* 143
Niland, Kilmeny *25:* 191; *75:* 143
Nino, Alex *59:* 145
Ninon *1:* 5; *38:* 101, 103, 108
Nissen, Rie *44:* 35
Nithael, Mark *158:* 237
Nivola, Claire A. *78:* 126; *140:* 147
Nixon, K. *14:* 152
Nobati, Eugenia *194:* 118
Noble, Louise *61:* 170
Noble, Marty *97:* 168; *125:* 171
Noble, Trinka Hakes *39:* 162; *84:* 157
Noda, Takayo *168:* 143
Noguchi, Yoshie *30:* 99
Nolan, Dennis *42:* 163; *67:* 163; *78:* 189; *82:* 225; *83:* 26; *92:* 169, 170; *103:* 166; *111:* 35; *112:* 213; *127:* 171; *166:* 161; *194:* 218
Noll, Sally *82:* 171
Nolte, Larry *121:* 63, 65
Nones, Eric Jon *61:* 111; *76:* 38; *77:* 177
Noonan, Daniel *100:* 224
Noonan, Julia *4:* 163; *7:* 207; *25:* 151; *91:* 29; *95:* 149
Norcia, Ernie *108:* 155; *140:* 47
Nordenskjold, Birgitta *2:* 208
Noreika, Robert *173:* 20
Norling, Beth *149:* 153, 154
Norman, Elaine *77:* 72, 176; *94:* 35; *136:* 63; *178:* 42

Norman, Mary *36:* 138, 147
Norman, Michael *12:* 117; *27:* 168
Northway, Jennifer *85:* 96
Nostlinger, Christiana *162:* 131
Novak, Linda *166:* 205
Novak, Matt *104:* 132, 133; *165:* 173, 174
Novelli, Luca *61:* 137
Nugent, Cynthia *106:* 189
Numeroff, Laura Joffe *28:* 161; *30:* 177
Nurse, Chris *164:* 91
Nussbaumer, Paul *16:* 219; *39:* 117
Nutt, Ken *72:* 69; *97:* 170
Nyce, Helene *19:* 219
Nygren, Tord *30:* 148; *127:* 164

O

Oakley, Graham *8:* 112; *30:* 164, 165; *84:* 188,189, 190, 191, 192
Oakley, Thornton *YABC 2:* 189
Oberheide, Heide *118:* 37
Obligado, Lilian *2:* 28, 66, 67; *6:* 30; *14:* 179; *15:* 103; *25:* 84; *61:* 138, 139, 140, 141, 143
Oblinski, Rafael *190:* 139
Obrant, Susan *11:* 186
O'Brien, Anne Sibley *53:* 116, 117; *155:* 115
O'Brien, John *41:* 253; *72:* 12; *89:* 59, 60; *98:* 16; *161:* 185; *169:* 16; *180:* 196
O'Brien, Patrick *193:* 142, 143, 144
O'Brien, Teresa *87:* 89
O'Brien, Tim *93:* 25; *136:* 94; *164:* 57; *169:* 57; *173:* 55; *175:* 86; *184:* 192; *191:* 134; *193:* 137
O'Clair, Dennis *127:* 25
O'Connor, George *183:* 153
Odell, Carole *35:* 47
Odem, Mel *99:* 164; *167:* 84, 87
O'Donohue, Thomas *40:* 89
Oechsli, Kelly *5:* 144, 145; *7:* 115; *8:* 83, 183; *13:* 117; *20:* 94; *81:* 199
Offen, Hilda *42:* 207
Ogden, Bill *42:* 59; *47:* 55
Ogg, Oscar *33:* 34
Ogle, Nancy Gray *163:* 144
Ohi, Ruth *90:* 175, 177; *131:* 63; *135:* 106; *175:* 107; *179:* 55
Ohlsson, Ib *4:* 152; *7:* 57; *10:* 20; *11:* 90; *19:* 217; *41:* 246; *82:* 106; *92:* 213
Ohtomo, Yasuo *37:* 146; *39:* 212, 213
O'Keefe, Jennifer *136:* 184
O'Kelley, Mattie Lou *36:* 150
Olbinski, Rafal *149:* 27; *158:* 77
Oliver, Isaac *171:* 182
Oliver, Jenni *23:* 121; *35:* 112
Oliver, Narelle *152:* 192
Oller, Erika *128:* 186; *134:* 126
Olschewski, Alfred *7:* 172
Olsen, Ib Spang *6:* 178, 179; *81:* 164
Olson, Alan *77:* 229
Olson-Brown, Ellen *183:* 154
Olugebefola, Ademola *15:* 205
O'Malley, Kevin *94:* 180; *106:* 8; *113:* 108; *136:* 70; *157:* 193; *191:* 146
O'Neil, Dan IV *7:* 176
O'Neill, Catharine *72:* 113; *84:* 78; *134:* 153
O'Neill, Jean *22:* 146
O'Neill, Martin *187:* 39
O'Neill, Michael J. *54:* 172
O'Neill, Rose *48:* 30, 31
Ono, Chiyo *7:* 97
Orbaan, Albert *2:* 31; *5:* 65, 171; *9:* 8; *14:* 241; *20:* 109
Orbach, Ruth *21:* 112
Orfe, Joan *20:* 81
Org, Ed *119:* 93
Ormai, Stella *72:* 129
Ormerod, Jan *55:* 124; *70:* 170, 171; *90:* 39; *132:* 172, 173, 174; *147:* 98

Ormsby, Virginia H. *11:* 187
O'Rourke, Ericka *108:* 216; *117:* 194; *111:* 142; *119:* 194; *137:* 152; *150:* 134; *167:* 64; *172:* 164; *188:* 163; *191:* 172
O'Rourke, Ericka Meltzer
    See O'Rourke, Ericka
Orozco, Jose Clemente *9:* 177
Orr, Forrest W. *23:* 9
Orr, N. *19:* 70
Ortiz, Vilma *88:* 158
Osborn, Cathy *152:* 232
Osborn, Robert *65:* 49
Osborne, Billie Jean *35:* 209
Osmond, Edward *10:* 111
O'Sullivan, Tom *3:* 176; *4:* 55; *78:* 195
Otani, June *124:* 42; *156:* 53
Otis, Rebecca *185:* 92
Ottley, Matt *147:* 221; *171:* 133
Otto, Svend *22:* 130, 141; *67:* 188, 189
Oudry, J.B. *18:* 167
Oughton, Taylor *5:* 23; *104:* 136
Overeng, Johannes *44:* 36
Overlie, George *11:* 156
Owens, Carl *2:* 35; *23:* 521
Owens, Gail *10:* 170; *12:* 157; *19:* 16; *22:* 70; *25:* 81; *28:* 203, 205; *32:* 221, 222; *36:* 132; *46:* 40; *47:* 57; *54:* 66, 67, 68, 69, 70, 71, 72, 73; *71:* 100; *73:* 64; *77:* 157; *80:* 32; *82:* 3; *99:* 226
Owens, Mary Beth *113:* 202, 203; *191:* 148, 149
Owens, Nubia *84:* 74
Oxenbury, Helen *3:* 150, 151; *24:* 81; *68:* 174, 175,176; *81:* 209; *84:* 213, 245; *129:* 56; *149:* 159; *184:* 181
Oz, Robin *88:* 167; *185:* 181

P

Padgett, Jim *12:* 165
Page, Homer *14:* 145
Page, Mark *162:* 70
Paget, Sidney *24:* 90, 91, 93, 95, 97
Paget, Walter *64:* 122
Paillot, Jim *173:* 89
Pajouhesh, Noushin *160:* 121
Pak *12:* 76
Pak, Yu Cha *86:* 174
Paladino, Lance *134:* 30
Palazzo, Tony *3:* 152, 153
Palecek, Josef *56:* 136; *89:* 158
Palen, Debbie *135:* 88; *195:* 148, 149
Palencar, John Jude *84:* 12, 45; *85:* 87; *92:* 187; *99:* 128; *110:* 204; *150:* 122; *171:* 86
Palin, Nicki *81:* 201; *89:* 161
Palladini, David *4:* 113; *40:* 176, 177, 178, 179, 181,224, 225; *50:* 138; *78:* 186
Pallarito, Don *43:* 36
Palmer, Carol *158:* 230; *195:* 187
Palmer, Heidi *15:* 207; *29:* 102
Palmer, Jan *42:* 153; *82:* 161
Palmer, Judd *153:* 160, 161
Palmer, Juliette *6:* 89; *15:* 208
Palmer, Kate Salley *104:* 143; *154:* 169
Palmer, Lemuel *17:* 25, 29
Palmisciano, Diane *110:* 62; *162:* 26
Palmquist, Eric *38:* 133
Panesis, Nicholas *3:* 127
Panter, Gary *182:* 191
Panton, Doug *52:* 99
Paparone, Pamela *129:* 174
Papas, William *11:* 223; *50:* 160
Papin, Joseph *26:* 113
Papish, Robin Lloyd *10:* 80
Paradis, Susan *40:* 216
Paraquin, Charles H. *18:* 166
Paris, Peter *31:* 127
Parisi, Elizabeth B. *141:* 82; *164:* 57
Park, Nick *113:* 143

Park, Seho *39:* 110
Park, W.B. *22:* 189
Parker, Ant *82:* 87, 88; *104:* 121
Parker, Lewis *2:* 179
Parker, Nancy Winslow *10:* 113; *22:* 164; *28:* 47, 144; *52:* 7; *69:* 153; *91:* 171, 174; *132:* 175
Parker, Robert *4:* 161; *5:* 74; *9:* 136; *29:* 39
Parker, Robert Andrew *11:* 81; *29:* 186; *39:* 165; *40:* 25; *41:* 78; *42:* 123; *43:* 144; *48:* 182; *54:* 140; *74:* 141; *91:* 24; *111:* 115; *151:* 201; *154:* 156
Parker-Rees, Guy *149:* 145; *193:* 149, 150
Parkin, Trevor *140:* 151
Parkins, David *114:* 123; *146:* 176; *176:* 168; *192:* 107
Parkinson, Kathy *71:* 143; *144:* 234
Parkinson, Keith *70:* 66
Parks, Gordon, Jr. *33:* 228
Parnall, Peter *5:* 137; *16:* 221; *24:* 70; *40:* 78; *51:* 130; *69:* 17, 155; *136:* 22, 23, 24
Parnall, Virginia *40:* 78
Parow, Lorraine *158:* 127
Parr, Todd *134:* 139, 140; *179:* 163, 164, 165
Parrish, Anne *27:* 159, 160
Parrish, Dillwyn *27:* 159
Parrish, Maxfield *14:* 160, 161, 164, 165; *16:* 109; *18:* 12, 13; *YABC 1:* 149, 152, 267; *2:* 146, 149
Parry, David *26:* 156
Parry, Marian *13:* 176; *19:* 179
Partch, Virgil *45:* 163, 165
Pascal, David *14:* 174
Paschkis, Julie *177:* 153, 154
Pasquier, J.A. *16:* 91
Pasternak, Robert *119:* 53
Paterson, Diane *13:* 116; *39:* 163; *59:* 164, 165, 166,167; *72:* 51, 53; *129:* 175; *177:* 156, 157
Paterson, Helen *16:* 93
Patkau, Karen *112:* 123
Paton, Jane *15:* 271; *35:* 176
Patrick, John *139:* 190
Patrick, Pamela *90:* 160; *93:* 211; *105:* 12
Patrick, Tom *190:* 103
Patterson, Geoffrey *54:* 75
Patterson, Robert *25:* 118
Patti, Joyce *187:* 145, 146
Patz, Nancy *111:* 40; *154:* 161
Paul, James *4:* 130; *23:* 161
Paul, Korky *102:* 85
Paull, Grace *24:* 157; *87:* 127
Paulsen, Ruth Wright *79:* 160, 164; *189:* 146
Pavlov, Elena *80:* 49
Payne, Adam S. *135:* 166
Payne, C.F. *145:* 138, 140; *179:* 168
Payne, Joan Balfour *1:* 118
Payne, Tom *170:* 27
Payson, Dale *7:* 34; *9:* 151; *20:* 140; *37:* 22
Payzant, Charles *21:* 147
Peacock, Ralph *64:* 118
Peake, Mervyn *22:* 136, 149; *23:* 162, 163, 164; *YABC2:* 307
Pearson, Larry *38:* 225
Pearson, Tracey Campbell *64:* 163, 164, 167, 168, 169; *118:* 51; *156:* 169, 171, 172; *163:* 140
Peat, Fern B. *16:* 115
Peck, Anne Merriman *18:* 241; *24:* 155
Peck, Beth *66:* 242; *79:* 166; *80:* 136; *91:* 34; *95:* 9; *101:* 77; *164:* 197; *190:* 170
Pedersen, Janet *193:* 152
Pedersen, Judy *66:* 217; *121:* 36; *172:* 67
Pedersen, Vilhelm *YABC 1:* 40
Pederson, Sharleen *12:* 92
Pedlar, Elaine *161:* 45
Peek, Merle *39:* 168
Peet, Bill *2:* 203; *41:* 159, 160, 161, 162, 163; *78:* 158, 159, 160, 161
Peguero, Adrian *116:* 133
Peguero, Gerard *116:* 133

Pels, Winslow Pinney *55:* 126
Peltier, Leslie C. *13:* 178
Penberthy, Mark *171:* 78
Pendle, Alexy *7:* 159; *13:* 34; *29:* 161; *33:* 215; *86:* 62
Pendola, Joanne *76:* 203; *81:* 125; *105:* 181; *178:* 152, 153
Pene du Bois, William *4:* 70; *10:* 122; *26:* 61; *27:* 145, 211; *35:* 243; *41:* 216; *68:* 180, 181; *73:* 45
Penfound, David *102:* 185
Pennington, Eunice *27:* 162
Peppe, Mark *28:* 142
Peppe, Rodney *4:* 164, 165; *74:* 187, 188, 189
Pepper, Hubert *64:* 143
Percy, Graham *63:* 2
Pericoli, Matteo *178:* 177
Perini, Ben *173:* 77
Perkins, David *60:* 68
Perkins, Lucy Fitch *72:* 199
Perkins, Lynne Rae *172:* 146
Perl, Susan *2:* 98; *4:* 231; *5:* 44, 45, 118; *6:* 199; *8:* 137; *12:* 88; *22:* 193; *34:* 54, 55; *52:* 128; *YABC 1:* 176
Perrone, Donna *78:* 166
Perry, Marie Fritz *165:* 180
Perry, Patricia *29:* 137; *30:* 171
Perry, Roger *27:* 163
Perske, Martha *46:* 83; *51:* 108, 147
Persson, Stina *175:* 166
Pesek, Ludek *15:* 237
Petach, Heidi *149:* 166
Peters, David *72:* 205; *182:* 116
Petersen, Jeff *181:* 95
Petersham, Maud *17:* 108, 147, 148, 149, 150, 151, 152, 153
Petersham, Miska *17:* 108, 147, 148, 149, 150, 151, 152, 153
Peterson, Eric *109:* 125
Peterson, Nisse *99:* 27
Peterson, R.F. *7:* 101
Peterson, Russell *7:* 130
Petie, Haris *2:* 3; *10:* 41, 118; *11:* 227; *12:* 70
Petricic, Dusan *153:* 75, 76, 77; *170:* 12; *172:* 13; *176:* 170; *179:* 56
Petrides, Heidrun *19:* 223
Petrone, Valeria *159:* 160; *171:* 92; *186:* 173
Petrosino, Tamara *177:* 40; *193:* 154, 155
Petruccio, Steven James *67:* 159; *127:* 5
Pettingill, Ondre *64:* 181; *70:* 64
Peyo *40:* 56, 57
Peyton, K.M. *15:* 212
Pfeifer, Herman *15:* 262
Pfister, Marcus *83:* 165, 166, 167; *146:* 152; *150:* 160
Pfloog, Jan *124:* 60
Pham, LeUyen *160:* 48; *175:* 154, 156; *179:* 149
Phelan, Matt *182:* 160; *184:* 222
Phillips, Craig *70:* 151
Phillips, Douglas *1:* 19
Phillips, F.D. *6:* 202
Phillips, Louise *133:* 67
Phillips, Matt *184:* 173
Phillips, Thomas *30:* 55
Philpot, Glyn *54:* 46
Phiz
    See Browne, Hablot K.
Piatti, Celestino *16:* 223
Pica, Steve *115:* 181
Picarella, Joseph *13:* 147
Picart, Gabriel *121:* 165
Pichon, Liz *174:* 139
Pickard, Charles *12:* 38; *18:* 203; *36:* 152
Picken, George A. *23:* 150
Pickens, David *22:* 156
Pickering, Jimmy *195:* 152
Pienkowski, Jan *6:* 183; *30:* 32; *58:* 140, 141, 142,143, 146, 147; *73:* 3; *87:* 156, 157; *131:* 189

Pignataro, Anna *163:* 220 *Pileggi, Steve 145:* 122

Pilkey, Dav *68:* 186; *115:* 164, 166; *166:* 173, 174, 175

Pimlott, John *10:* 205

Pincus, Harriet *4:* 186; *8:* 179; *22:* 148; *27:* 164, 165; *66:* 202

Pini, Wendy *89:* 166

Pinkett, Neil *60:* 8

Pinkney, Brian *81:* 184, 185; *94:* 107; *113:* 146, 147; *117:* 121, 166; *132:* 145; *158:* 108, 191; *160:* 189

Pinkney, Jerry *8:* 218; *10:* 40; *15:* 276; *20:* 66; *24:* 121; *33:* 109; *36:* 222; *38:* 200; *41:* 165, 166, 167, 168, 169, 170, 171, 173, 174; *44:* 198; *48:* 51; *53:* 20; *56:* 61, 68; *58:* 184; *60:* 59; *61:* 91; *71:* 146, 148, 149; *72:* 17; *73:* 149; *74:* 159,192; *75:* 45; *80:* 206; *81:* 44; *85:* 144; *95:* 50; *107:* 158, 159, 160; *108:* 164; *112:* 114, 115; *133:* 58; *195:* 140

Pinkwater, Daniel Manus *46:* 180, 181, 182, 185, 188, 189, 190; *151:* 161 *76:* 178, 179, 180

Pinkwater, Manus *8:* 156; *46:* 180
See also Pinkwater, Daniel Manus

Pinkwater, Jill *114:* 160, 161; *158:* 179; *188:* 143, 145, 146

Pinto, Ralph *10:* 131; *45:* 93

Pinon, Mark *74:* 22

Piven, Hanoch *173:* 142

Pistolesi *73:* 211

Pitcairn, Ansel *188:* 10

Pittman, Helena Clare *71:* 151

Pitz, Henry C. *4:* 168; *19:* 165; *35:* 128; *42:* 80; *YABC 2:* 95, 176

Pitzenberger, Lawrence J. *26:* 94

Pitzer, Susanna *181:* 131

Player, Stephen *82:* 190

Plecas, Jennifer *84:* 201; *106:* 124; *149:* 168

Ploog, Mike *180:* 19

Plowden, David *52:* 135, 136

Plume, Ilse *170:* 149

Plummer, William *32:* 31

Podevin, Jean François *184:* 185

Podwal, Mark *56:* 170, 173; *101:* 154, 155, 157; *149:* 176; *166:* 194

Pogany, Willy *15:* 46, 49; *19:* 222, 256; *25:* 214; *44:* 142, 143, 144, 145, 146, 147, 148

Pohrt, Tom *67:* 116; *104:* 80; *152:* 199; *195:* 154

Poirson, V.A. *26:* 89

Polacco, Patricia *74:* 195, 196, 197, 198; *123:* 121, 122, 123; *180:* 189, 190, 191, 193, 194

Polgreen, John *21:* 44

Politi, Leo *1:* 178; *4:* 53; *21:* 48; *47:* 173,174, 176, 178, 179, 180, 181

Pollema-Cahill, Phyllis *123:* 126

Pollen, Samson *64:* 80

Polonsky, Arthur *34:* 168

Polseno, Jo *1:* 53; *3:* 117; *5:* 114; *17:* 154; *20:* 87; *32:* 49; *41:* 245

Pomaska, Anna *117:* 148

Pons, Bernadette *184:* 100

Ponter, James *5:* 204

Poole, Colin *111:* 27

Poortvliet, Rien *6:* 212; *65:* 165, 166, 167

Pope, Kevin *183:* 158

Popp, Wendy *72:* 122; *158:* 68

Poppel, Hans *71:* 154, 155

Porfirio, Guy *76:* 134

Portal, Colette *6:* 186; *11:* 203

Porter, George *7:* 181

Porter, Janice Lee *136:* 175; *164:* 37

Porter, John *113:* 47

Porter, Pat Grant *84:* 112; *125:* 101

Porter, Sue *146:* 246, 247

Porter, Walter *124:* 175

Posada, Mia *187:* 151

Posen, Michael *175:* 82

Posthuma, Sieb *150:* 163

Postma, Lidia *79:* 17

Potter, Beatrix *100:* 194, 195; *132:* 179, 180, 181, 182; *YABC 1:* 208, 209, 210, 212, 213

Potter, Giselle *117:* 123; *143:* 44; *144:* 170, 197; *149:* 7; *150:* 165; *187:* 152, 153; *190:* 198

Potter, Katherine *104:* 147; *171:* 135; *173:* 136

Potter, Miriam Clark *3:* 162

Poulin, Stephane *98:* 140, 141

Poullis, Nick *146:* 210

Powell, Constance Buffington *174:* 141

Powell, Gary *151:* 208

Powell, Ivan *67:* 219

Power, Margaret *105:* 122

Powers, Daniel *161:* 173

Powers, Richard M. *1:* 230; *3:* 218; *7:* 194; *26:* 186

Powledge, Fred *37:* 154

Powzyk, Joyce *74:* 214

Poydar, Nancy *96:* 149; *190:* 180, 181, 182

Pracher, Richard *91:* 166

Prachaticka, Marketa *126:* 126

Prange, Beckie *181:* 169

Prap, Lila *177:* 165

Prater, John *103:* 142, 143, 144; *149:* 172

Pratt, Charles *23:* 29

Pratt, George *116:* 208

Pratt, Pierre *150:* 73; *166:* 183; *168:* 172

Prebenna, David *73:* 174

Preiss-Glasser, Robin *123:* 176; *152* 40; *172:* 194

Press, Jenny *116:* 95

Preston, Mark *152:* 162

Pretro, Korinna *91:* 126

Price, Christine *2:* 247; *3:* 163, 253; *8:* 166

Price, Cynthia *118:* 156

Price, Edward *33:* 34

Price, Garrett *1:* 76; *2:* 42

Price, Hattie Longstreet *17:* 13

Price, Norman *YABC 1:* 129

Price, Willard *48:* 184

Priceman, Marjorie *81:* 171; *136:* 169; *156:* 200; *168:* 153, 154; *188:* 45

Priestley, Alice *168:* 33

Primavera, Elise *26:* 95; *58:* 151; *73:* 37; *80:* 79; *86:* 156; *105:* 161

Primrose, Jean *36:* 109

Prince, Alison *86:* 188, 189

Prince, Leonora E. *7:* 170

Pritchett, Shelley *116:* 148

Prittie, Edwin J. *YABC 1:* 120

Proimos, James *176:* 4

Proimos, John *173:* 144

Prosmitsky, Jenya *132:* 33

Provensen, Alice *37:* 204, 215, 222; *70:* 176, 177, 178, 180, *71:* 213; *147:* 184; *191:* 190

Provensen, Martin *37:* 204, 215, 222; *70:* 176, 177, 178, 180; *71:* 213; *191:* 190

Pucci, Albert John *44:* 154

Pudlo *8:* 59

Pulver, Harry, Jr. *129:* 159

Pulver, Robin *160:* 4

Punchatz, Don *99:* 57

Purdy, Susan *8:* 162

Pursell, Weimer *55:* 18

Purtscher, Alfons *97:* 6

Puskas, James *5:* 141

Pyk, Jan *7:* 26; *38:* 123

Pyle, Chuck *99:* 149; *191:* 83

Pyle, Howard *16:* 225, 226, 227, 228, 230, 231, 232, 235; *24:* 27; *34:* 124, 125, 127, 128; *59:* 132; *100:* 198

Q

Quackenbush, Robert *4:* 190; *6:* 166; *7:* 175, 178; *9:* 86; *11:* 65, 221; *41:* 154; *43:* 157; *70:* 185, 186; *71:* 137; *85:* 47; *92:* 148; *133:* 154, 164, 169

Qualls, Sean *177:* 167, 168; *193:* 43

Quennell, Marjorie (Courtney) *29:* 163, 164

Quidor, John *19:* 82

Quirk, John *62:* 170

Quirk, Thomas *12:* 81

R

Rackham, Arthur *15:* 32, 78, 214-227; *17:* 105, 115; *18:* 233; *19:* 254; *20:* 151; *22:* 129, 131, 132, 133; *23:* 175; *24:* 161, 181; *26:* 91; *32:* 118; *64:* 18; *100:* 9, 16, 203, 204; *YABC 1:* 25, 45, 55, 147; *2:* 103, 142, 173, 210

Racz, Michael *56:* 134

Raczka, Bob *191:* 155, 156

Radcliffe, Andrew *82:* 215

Rader, Laura *101:* 219

Radunsky, Vladimir *177:* 170; *192:* 30

Rafilson, Sidney *11:* 172

Raglin, Tim *125:* 24

Raible, Alton *1:* 202, 203; *28:* 193; *35:* 181; *110:* 207

Raine, Patricia *82:* 74; *88:* 154

Ramá, Sue *173:* 45; *185:* 186; *190:* 184

Ramhorst, John *117:* 11

Ramirez, Gladys *177:* 19

Ramsey, James *16:* 41

Ramsey, Marcy Dunn *82:* 11; *180:* 186

Ramus, Michael *51:* 171

Rand, Paul *6:* 188

Rand, Ted *67:* 9, 10, 121, 123; *74:* 190; *84:* 170; *103:* 170; *112:* 6; *114:* 73; *139:* 168; *143:* 194; *156:* 154; *161:* 9, 10

Randazzo, Tony *81:* 98

Randell, William *55:* 54

Rane, Walter *93:* 144; *143:* 109; *184:* 126

Rankin, Joan *163:* 40

Rankin, Laura *176:* 173, 174; *179:* 150

Ransome, Arthur *22:* 201

Ransome, James E. *74:* 137; *75:* 80; *84:* 181; *94:* 108; *117:* 115; *123:* 128, 129, 130; *158:* 101, 102; *159:* 205; *178:* 188, 189, 190

Rantz, Don *119:* 184

Rao, Anthony *28:* 126

Raphael, Elaine *23:* 192; *71:* 24, 25

Rappaport, Eva *6:* 190

Raschka, Chris *80:* 187, 189, 190; *97:* 211; *115:* 210; *117:* 151, 152, 153, 154; *143:* 195; *145:* 153; *166:* 190, 191; *170:* 114

Rash, Andy *158:* 178; *162:* 172

Raskin, Ellen *2:* 208, 209; *4:* 142; *13:* 183; *22:* 68; *29:* 139; *36:* 134; *38:* 173, 174, 175, 176, 177, 178,179, 180, 181; *60:* 163; *86:* 81

Rathmann, Peggy *93:* 32; *94:* 168; *157:* 212, 214

Ratkus, Tony *77:* 133

Ratzkin, Lawrence *40:* 143

Rau, Margaret *9:* 157

Raverat, Gwen *YABC 1:* 152

Ravid, Joyce *61:* 73

Ravielli, Anthony *1:* 198; *3:* 168; *11:* 143

Ravilious, Robin *77:* 169

Rawlins, Donna *72:* 198; *73:* 15, 129

Rawlins, Janet *76:* 79

Rawlings, Steve *143:* 139; *151:* 54

Rawlinson, Debbie *75:* 132

Ray, Deborah Kogan *8:* 164; *29:* 238; *50:* 112, 113; *62:* 119; *78:* 191

Ray, Jane *96:* 166; *97:* 104; *152:* 208; *190:* 221

Ray, Ralph *2:* 239; *5:* 73

Rayann, Omar *162:* 205; *186:* 29, 30

Rayevsky, Robert *64:* 17; *70:* 173; *80:* 204; *117:* 79; *190:* 187, 188

Raymond, Larry *31:* 108; *97:* 109

Rayner, Hugh *151:* 170

Rayner, Mary *22:* 207; *47:* 140; *72:* 191; *87:* 171, 172; *192:* 104

Rayner, Shoo
   See Rayner, Hugh
Raynes, John *71:* 19
Raynor, Dorka *28:* 168
Raynor, Paul *24:* 73
Rayyan, Omar *110:* 222; *112:* 17; *125:* 131
Razzi, James *10:* 127
Read, Alexander D. *20:* 45
Reader, Dennis *71:* 157
Reasoner, Charles *53:* 33, 36, 37
Reczuch, Karen *115:* 132; *145:* 131
Redlich, Ben *163:* 221
Reed, Joseph *116:* 139
Reed, Lynn Rowe *115:* 173; *171:* 146
Reed, Tom *34:* 171
Reeder, Colin *74:* 202; *77:* 113
Rees, Mary *134:* 219
Reese, Bob *60:* 135
Reeve, Philip *171:* 50
Reeves, Eira B. *130:* 173, 174; *141:* 151
Reeves, Rick *181:* 179
Regan, Dana *117:* 116
Regan, Laura *103:* 198; *153:* 206
Reichert, Renée *169:* 127
Reid, Barbara *82:* 178; *92:* 17; *93:* 169, 170
Reid, Stephen *19:* 213; *22:* 89
Reim, Melanie *104:* 151; *150:* 98
Reinert, Kirk *89:* 138; *195:* 129
Reinertson, Barbara *44:* 150; *62:* 103
Reiniger, Lotte *40:* 185
Reisberg, Mira *119:* 2
Reisch, Jesse *158:* 130
Reiser, Lynn *81:* 175; *138:* 184; *180:* 200
Reiss, John J. *23:* 193
Relf, Douglas *3:* 63
Relyea, C.M. *16:* 29; *31:* 153
Remi, Georges *13:* 184
Remington, Frederic *19:* 188; *41:* 178, 179, 180, 181, 183,184, 185, 186, 187, 188; *62:* 197
Remkiewicz, Frank *67:* 102; *77:* 171; *80:* 130; *113:* 107; *152:* 116; *152:* 211, 212; *157:* 148
Rendon, Maria *116:* 141; *192:* 134: 152
Renfro, Ed *79:* 176
Renlie, Frank *11:* 200
Reschofsky, Jean *7:* 118
Rethi *60:* 181
Rethi, Lili *2:* 153; *36:* 156
Reusswig, William *3:* 267
Revell, Cindy *195:* 93
Rex, Adam *156:* 172; *169:* 91; *186:* 178, 179
Rex, Michael *157:* 147; *191:* 159, 160
Rey, H.A. *1:* 182; *26:* 163, 164, 166, 167, 169; *69:* 172, 173, 174, 175; *86:* 195, 196, 197; *100:* 211; *YABC 2:* 17
Reynolds, Adrian *192:* 159, 160
Reynolds, Doris *5:* 71; *31:* 77
Reynolds, Peter H. *142:* 12; *179:* 175, 176
Rhead, Louis *31:* 91; *100:* 228
Rhodes, Andrew *38:* 204; *50:* 163; *54:* 76; *61:* 123, 124; *87:* 200
Ribbons, Ian *3:* 10; *37:* 161; *40:* 76
Ricci, Regolo *93:* 22; *164:* 148
Rice, Elizabeth *2:* 53, 214
Rice, Eve *34:* 174, 175; *91:* 172
Rice, James *22:* 210; *93:* 173
Rich, Martha *195:* 16
Richards, Chuck *170:* 154
Richards, George *40:* 116, 119, 121; *44:* 179
Richards, Henry *YABC 1:* 228, 231
Richardson, Ernest *2:* 144
Richardson, Frederick *18:* 27, 31
Richardson, John *110:* 88
Richman, Hilda *26:* 132
Richmond, George *24:* 179
Riddell, Chris *114:* 170, 195; *166:* 179
Riddle, Tohby *74:* 204; *151:* 179
Riding, Peter *63:* 195
Rieniets, Judy King *14:* 28
Riger, Bob *2:* 166

Riggio, Anita *73:* 191; *85:* 63; *137:* 184; *172:* 165
Riley, Jon *74:* 70
Riley, Kenneth *22:* 230
Riley-Webb, Charlotte *153:* 143
Rinaldi, Angelo *165:* 60, 69
Ringgold, Faith *71:* 162; *114:* 173, 174, 176; *187:* 160, 161, 163
Ringi, Kjell *12:* 171
Rios, Tere
   See Versace, Marie
Ripper, Charles L. *3:* 175
Ripplinger, Henry *117:* 31
Ritchie, William *74:* 183
Ritter, John *175:* 14
Ritz, Karen *41:* 117; *72:* 239; *87:* 125; *102:* 7; *106:* 6
Rivers, Ruth *178:* 193
Rivkin, Jay *15:* 230
Rivoche, Paul *45:* 125
Roach, Marilynne *9:* 158
Robbin, Jodi *44:* 156, 159
Robbins, Frank *42:* 167
Robbins, Ken *147:* 191, 192
Robbins, Ruth *52:* 102
Roberts, Cliff *4:* 126
Roberts, David *154:* 4, 6; *191:* 162
Roberts, Doreen *4:* 230; *28:* 105
Roberts, Jim *22:* 166; *23:* 69; *31:* 110
Roberts, Tony *109:* 195, 214
Roberts, W. *22:* 2, 3
Robins, Arthur *137:* 172; *151:* 225
Robinson, Aminah Brenda Lynn *86:* 205; *103:* 55; *159:* 175
Robinson, Charles [1870-1937] *17:* 157, 171, 172, 173, 175, 176; *24:* 207; *25:* 204; *YABC 2:* 308, 309, 310, 331
Robinson, Charles *3:* 53; *5:* 14; *6:* 193; *7:* 150; *7:* 183; *8:* 38; *9:* 81; *13:* 188; *14:* 248, 249; *23:* 149; *26:* 115; *27:* 48; *28:* 191; *32:* 28; *35:* 210; *36:* 37; *48:* 96; *52:* 33; *53:* 157; *56:* 15; *62:* 142; *77:* 41; *111:* 148
Robinson, Jerry *3:* 262
Robinson, Joan G. *7:* 184
Robinson, Lolly *90:* 227
Robinson, T.H. *17:* 179, 181, 182, 183; *29:* 254
Robinson, W. Heath *17:* 185, 187, 189, 191, 193, 195, 197, 199, 202; *23:* 167; *25:* 194; *29:* 150; *YABC 1:* 44; *2:* 183
Rocco, John *187:* 4; *188:* 151
Roche, Christine *41:* 98
Roche, Denis *99:* 184; *180:* 32
Roche, P.K. *57:* 151, 152
Rocker, Fermin *7:* 34; *13:* 21; *31:* 40; *40:* 190,191
Rocklen, Margot *101:* 181
Rockwell, Anne *5:* 147; *33:* 171, 173; *71:* 166, 167,168; *114:* 183, 184; *194:* 152, 155
Rockwell, Gail *7:* 186
Rockwell, Harlow *33:* 171, 173, 175
Rockwell, Lizzy *114:* 182; *162:* 182; *185:* 189
Rockwell, Norman *23:* 39, 196, 197, 199, 200, 203, 204, 207; *41:* 140, 143; *123:* 47; *YABC 2:* 60
Rockwood, Richard *119:* 75
Rodanas, Kristina *156:* 183, 184
Rodegast, Roland *43:* 100
Rodgers, Frank *69:* 177
Rodriguez, Albert G. *182:* 50
Rodriguez, Christina *184:* 12
Rodriguez, Joel *16:* 65
Rodriguez, Robert *145:* 145
Rodriguez-Howard, Pauline *177:* 18
Roeckelein, Katrina *134:* 223
Roennfeldt, Robert *66:* 243
Roever, J.M. *4:* 119; *26:* 170
Roffey, Maureen *33:* 142, 176, 177
Rogasky, Barbara *46:* 90
Rogé *173:* 160
Rogers, Carol *2:* 262; *6:* 164; *26:* 129

Rogers, Chris M. *150:* 59
Rogers, Forest *87:* 160; *101:* 76
Rogers, Frances *10:* 130
Rogers, Gregory *104:* 76; *126:* 57; *171:* 26
Rogers, Jacqueline *78:* 249; *80:* 34; *86:* 54 *103:* 70; *115:* 72; *129:* 173; *131:* 57, 225; *143:* 211; *153:* 100; *193:* 186
Rogers, Sherry *191:* 66
Rogers, Walter S. *31:* 135, 138; *67:* 65, 168; *100:* 81
Rogers, William A. *15:* 151, 153, 154; *33:* 35
Rogoff, Barbara *95:* 20
Rohmann, Eric *103:* 152
Rojankovsky, Feodor *6:* 134, 136; *10:* 183; *21:* 128,129, 130; *25:* 110; *28:* 42; *68:* 120
Rolfsen, Alf *62:* 15
Romain, Trevor *134:* 157
Roman, Barbara J. *103:* 171
Romas *114:* 111; *165:* 63
Romano, Robert *64:* 68
Romero, Alejandro *187:* 185
Roos, Maryn *168:* 198
Root, Barry *80:* 212; *90:* 196; *146:* 78; *156:* 165; *159:* 161; *182:* 18, 172
Root, Kimberly Bulcken *86:* 72; *98:* 21; *108:* 111; *127:* 114; *159:* 162; *176:* 134; *192:* 163
Roper, Bob *65:* 153
Roraback, Robin *111:* 156
Rorer, Abigail *43:* 222; *85:* 155
Rosales, Melodye *80:* 35
Rosamilia, Patricia *36:* 120
Rose, Carl *5:* 62
Rose, David S. *29:* 109; *70:* 120
Rose, Gerald *68:* 200, 201; *86:* 48
Rose, Ted *93:* 178
Rosenbaum, Jonathan *50:* 46
Rosenberg, Amye *74:* 207, 208
Rosenberry, Vera *87:* 22, 26; *144:* 212, 213; *158:* 120
Rosenblum, Richard *11:* 202; *18:* 18
Rosier, Lydia *16:* 236; *20:* 104; *21:* 109; *22:* 125; *30:* 151, 158; *42:* 128; *45:* 214; *77:* 227, 228
Rosing, Jens *85:* 142
Ross
   See Thomson, Ross
Ross, Christine *83:* 172, 173
Ross, Clare Romano *3:* 123; *21:* 45; *48:* 199
Ross, Dave *32:* 152; *57:* 108
Ross, Herbert *37:* 78
Ross, John *3:* 123; *21:* 45
Ross, Johnny *32:* 190
Ross, Larry *47:* 168; *60:* 62
Ross, Ruth *109:* 233
Ross, Tony *17:* 204; *56:* 132; *65:* 176, 177, 179; *90:* 123; *123:* 186, 187, 190; *130:* 188, 190, 191, 192; *132:* 242; *174:* 159; *176:* 181, 182, 183
Rossetti, Dante Gabriel *20:* 151, 153
Rostant, Larry *180:* 221; *194:* 108; *195:* 96
Roth, Arnold *4:* 238; *21:* 133
Roth, Julie Jersild *180:* 206
Roth, Marci *135:* 223
Roth, R.G. *184:* 50
Roth, Rob *105:* 98; *146:* 41
Roth, Robert *176:* 159
Roth, Roger *61:* 128; *190:* 192
Roth, Stephanie *136:* 171, 172
Roth, Susan L. *80:* 38; *93:* 78; *134:* 165, 166; *181:* 145, 146
Rothenberg, Joani Keller *162:* 190, 191
Rothman, Michael *139:* 62; *184:* 34 *Rotman, Jeffrey L. 145:* 30
Rotondo, Pat *32:* 158
Roughsey, Dick *35:* 186
Rouille, M. *11:* 96
Rounds, Glen *8:* 173; *9:* 171; *12:* 56; *32:* 194; *40:* 230; *51:* 161, 162, 166; *56:* 149; *70:* 198, 199; *YABC 1:* 1, 2, 3; *112:* 163
Roundtree, Katherine *114:* 88; *168:* 102
Rowan, Evadne *52:* 51

Rowe, Eric *111:* 161
Rowe, Gavin *27:* 144; *72:* 47; *88:* 201
Rowe, John *132:* 70, 71; *180:* 126
Rowell, Kenneth *40:* 72
Rowen, Amy *52:* 143
Rowena *116:* 101
Rowland, Andrew *164:* 136
Rowland, Jada *83:* 73
Rowles, Daphne *58:* 24
Roy, Jeroo *27:* 229; *36:* 110
Royo *118:* 32; *144:* 105, 106, 108; *165:* 19; *166:* 166
Rubel, Nicole *18:* 255; *20:* 59; *81:* 66, 67; *95:* 169, 170; *119:* 60; *135:* 177, 179, 180; *169:* 68; *181:* 150
Rubel, Reina *33:* 217
Rud, Borghild *6:* 15
Ruddell, Gary *110:* 238; *116:* 207
Rudolph, Norman Guthrie *17:* 13
Rue, Leonard Lee III *37:* 164
Rueda, Claudia *183:* 170, 171
Ruelle, Karen Gray *126:* 193
Ruff, Donna *50:* 173; *72:* 203; *78:* 49; *80:* 120,121; *93:* 162; *164:* 121
Ruffins, Reynold *10:* 134, 135; *41:* 191, 192, 193, 194, 195, 196; *125:* 187, 188, 189; *162:* 197
Ruhlin, Roger *34:* 44
Ruiz, Art *95:* 154; *110:* 91
Rumford, James *193:* 167
Runnerstroem, Bengt Arne *75:* 161
Ruse, Margaret *24:* 155
Rush, Ken *98:* 74
Rush, Peter *42:* 75
Russell, Charles M. *167:* 171
Russell, E.B. *18:* 177, 182
Russell, Jim *53:* 134
Russell, P. Craig *80:* 196; *146:* 102; *162:* 186
Russo, Marisabina *84:* 51; *106:* 164; *151:* 183; *188:* 153, 154, 155, 156
Russo, Susan *30:* 182; *36:* 144
Russon, Mary *87:* 145
Ruth, Greg *183:* 125
Ruth, Rod *9:* 161
Rutherford, Alexa *110:* 108
Rutherford, Jenny *78:* 5
Rutherford, Meg *25:* 174; *34:* 178, 179; *69:* 73; *72:* 31
Rutland, Jonathan *31:* 126
Ruurs, Margriet *147:* 195
Ruzzier, Sergio *159:* 176, 177; *163:* 184
Ryan, Amy *188:* 50
Ryan, Will *86:* 134
Ryden, Hope *8:* 176
Rylant, Cynthia *112:* 170, 172
Rymer, Alta M. *34:* 181
Ryniak, Christopher *178:* 11
Rystedt, Rex *49:* 80

S

Saaf, Chuck *49:* 179
Saaf, Donald *101:* 220; *124:* 180
Sabaka, Donna R. *21:* 172
Sabin, Robert *45:* 35; *60:* 30; *99:* 161
Sabuda, Robert *170:* 166, 167, 168
Sacker, Amy *16:* 100
Saelig, S.M. *129:* 73; *173:* 59
Saffioti, Lino *36:* 176; *48:* 60
Saflund, Birgitta *94:* 2
Sagsoorian, Paul *12:* 183; *22:* 154; *33:* 106; *87:* 152
Sahara, Tony *168:* 106; *177:* 181; *178:* 228; *186:* 132
Sahlberg, Myron *57:* 165
Saidens, Amy *145:* 162; *191:* 131
Saint Exupery, Antoine de *20:* 157
Saint James, Synthia *152:* 220; *188:* 90
Saldutti, Denise *39:* 186; *57:* 178

Sale, Morton *YABC 2:* 31
Sale, Tim *153:* 177
Salerno, Steven *150:* 79; *176:* 188
Salter, George *72:* 128, 130
Saltzberg, Barney *135:* 184, 185; *194:* 160
Saltzman, David *86:* 209
Salwowski, Mark *71:* 54
Salzman, Yuri *86:* 12
Sambourne, Linley *YABC 2:* 181
Sampson, Katherine *9:* 197
Samson, Anne S. *2:* 216
San Souci, Daniel *40:* 200; *96:* 199, 200; *113:* 171; *157:* 149; *170:* 69; *192:* 167, 168
Sancha, Sheila *38:* 185
Sanchez, Enrique O. *155:* 84
Sand, George X. *45:* 182
Sandberg, Lasse *15:* 239, 241
Sanders, Beryl *39:* 173
Sanderson, Ruth *21:* 126; *24:* 53; *28:* 63; *33:* 67; *41:* 48, 198, 199, 200, 201, 202, 203; *43:* 79; *46:* 36,44; *47:* 102; *49:* 58; *62:* 121, 122; *85:* 3; *109:* 207, 208, 209, 210; *172:* 157, 158
Sandia *119:* 74
Sandin, Joan *4:* 36; *6:* 194; *7:* 177; *12:* 145,185; *20:* 43; *21:* 74; *26:* 144; *27:* 142; *28:* 224, 225; *38:* 86; *41:* 46; *42:* 35; *59:* 6; *80:* 136; *94:* 188; *140:* 116; *153:* 179, 180
Sandland, Reg *39:* 215
Sandoz, Edouard *26:* 45, 47
Sanford, John *66:* 96, 97
Sankey, Tom *72:* 103
Sano, Kazuhiko *153:* 208; *195:* 171
Santat, Dan *188:* 160
Santore, Charles *54:* 139
Santoro, Christopher *74:* 215
Santos, Jesse J. *99:* 24
Sapieha, Christine *1:* 180
Saport, Linda *123:* 137, 138
Sara
    See De La Roche Saint Andre, Anne
Sardinha, Rick *175:* 151
Sarg, Tony *YABC 2:* 236
Sargent, Claudia *64:* 181
Sargent, Robert *2:* 217
Saris *1:* 33
Sarony *YABC 2:* 170
Sasaki, Goro *170:* 46
Sasek, Miroslav *16:* 239, 240, 241, 242
Sassman, David *9:* 79
Satty *29:* 203, 205
Sauber, Robert *40:* 183; *76:* 256; *78:* 154; *87:* 92
Saunders, Dave *85:* 163, 164, 165
Savadier, Elivia *84:* 50; *145:* 45; *164:* 206
Savage, Naomi *56:* 172
Savage, Steele *10:* 203; *20:* 77; *35:* 28
Savage, Stephen *174:* 182
Savio *76:* 4
Savitt, Sam *8:* 66, 182; *15:* 278; *20:* 96; *24:* 192; *28:* 98
Sawyer, Kem Knapp *84:* 228, 229
Say, Allen *28:* 178; *69:* 182, 183, 232; *110:* 194, 195,196; *161:* 154, 155
Sayles, Elizabeth *82:* 93; *105:* 155; *109:* 116; *180:* 64
Scabrini, Janet *13:* 191; *44:* 128
Scanlan, Peter *83:* 27; *153:* 165; *187:* 149
Scanlon, Paul *83:* 87
Scannell, Reece *105:* 105
Scarry, Huck *35:* 204, 205
Scarry, Richard *2:* 220, 221; *18:* 20; *35:* 193, 194, 195,196, 197, 198, 199, 200, 201, 202; *75:* 165, 167, 168
Schachner, Judith Byron *88:* 180; *92:* 163; *93:* 102; *142:* 82; *178:* 199, 200; *190:* 140
Schaeffer, Mead *18:* 81, 94; *21:* 137, 138, 139; *47:* 128
Schaffer, Amanda *90:* 206
Schanzer, Rosalyn *138:* 192, 193
Scharl, Josef *20:* 132; *22:* 128

Scheel, Lita *11:* 230
Scheffler, Axel *180:* 23, 24
Scheib, Ida *29:* 28
Schermer, Judith *30:* 184
Schick, Eleanor *82:* 210, 211; *144:* 222
Schick, Joel *16:* 160; *17:* 167; *22:* 12; *27:* 176; *31:* 147, 148; *36:* 23; *38:* 64; *45:* 116, 117; *52:* 5, 85; *104:* 159
Shields, Gretchen *75:* 171, 203
Schindelman, Joseph *1:* 74; *4:* 101; *12:* 49; *26:* 51; *40:* 146; *56:* 158; *73:* 40
Schindler, Edith *7:* 22
Schindler, S.D. *38:* 107; *46:* 196; *74:* 162; *75:* 172, 173; *99:* 133; *112:* 177; *118:* 185, 186; *121:* 71; *136:* 159; *143:* 45; *149:* 120; *156:* 30; *169:* 135; *171:* 161, 162, 163; *172:* 9; *186:* 163; *194:* 109; *195:* 35
Schlesinger, Bret *7:* 77
Schmid, Eleanore *12:* 188; *126:* 196, 197
Schmiderer, Dorothy *19:* 224
Schmidt, Bill *73:* 34; *76:* 220, 222, 224
Schmidt, Elizabeth *15:* 242
Schmidt, George Paul *132:* 122
Schmidt, Karen Lee *54:* 12; *71:* 174; *92:* 56; *94:* 190, 191; *127:* 103
Schmidt, Lynette *76:* 205
Schneider, Christine M. *171:* 165
Schneider, Howie *181:* 159
Schneider, Rex *29:* 64; *44:* 171
Schnurr, Edward *170:* 62
Schoberle, Cecile *80:* 200; *92:* 134
Schoenherr, Ian *32:* 83; *173:* 41
Schoenherr, John *1:* 146, 147, 173; *3:* 39, 139; *17:* 75; *29:* 72; *32:* 83; *37:* 168, 169, 170; *43:* 164, 165; *45:* 160, 162; *51:* 127; *66:* 196, 197, 198; *68:* 83; *72:* 240; *75:* 225; *88:* 176
Scholder, Fritz *69:* 103
Schomburg, Alex *13:* 23
Schongut, Emanuel *4:* 102; *15:* 186; *47:* 218, 219; *52:* 147, 148, 149, 150; *185:* 27
Schoonover, Frank *17:* 107; *19:* 81, 190, 233; *22:* 88,129; *24:* 189; *31:* 88; *41:* 69; *YABC 2:* 282, 316
Schories, Pat *164:* 210
Schottland, Miriam *22:* 172
Schramm, Ulrik *2:* 16; *14:* 112
Schreiber, Elizabeth Anne *13:* 193
Schreiber, Ralph W. *13:* 193
Schreiter, Rick *14:* 97; *23:* 171; *41:* 247; *49:* 131
Schroeder, Binette *56:* 128, 129
Schroeder, E. Peter *12:* 112
Schroeder, Ted *11:* 160; *15:* 189; *30:* 91; *34:* 43
Schrotter, Gustav *22:* 212; *30:* 225
Schubert, Dieter *101:* 167, 168
Schubert-Gabrys, Ingrid *101:* 167, 168
Schucker, James *31:* 163
Schuett, Stacey *72:* 137
Schulder, Lili *146:* 29
Schulke, Debra *57:* 167
Schulke, Flip *57:* 167
Schulz, Barbara *167:* 24
Schulz, Charles M. *10:* 137, 138, 139, 140, 141, 142; *118:* 192, 193, 194, 196, 199
Schutzer, Dena *109:* 32
Schwark, Mary Beth *51:* 155; *72:* 175
Schwartz, Amy *47:* 191; *82:* 100; *83:* 178, 179, 180,181; *129:* 107; *131:* 197, 198; *189:* 166, 168
Schwartz, Carol *124:* 41; *130:* 199
Schwartz, Charles *8:* 184
Schwartz, Daniel *46:* 37
Schwartz, Joanie *124:* 170
Schwartzberg, Joan *3:* 208
Schweitzer, Iris *2:* 137; *6:* 207
Schweninger, Ann *29:* 172; *82:* 246; *159:* 202; *168:* 166
Schwinger, Laurence *84:* 44; *91:* 61
Scofield, Penrod *61:* 107; *62:* 160

Scott, Anita Walker 7: 38
Scott, Art 39: 41
Scott, Frances Gruse 38: 43
Scott, Julian 34: 126
Scott, Roszel 33: 238
Scott, Sally 87: 27
Scott, Steve 166: 230, 231; 171: 93
Scott, Trudy 27: 172
Scrace, Carolyn 143: 95, 96
Scribner, Joanne 14: 236; 29: 78; 33: 185; 34: 208; 78: 75; 164: 237
Scrofani, Joseph 31: 65; 74: 225
Scroggs, Kirk 187: 169
Seaman, Mary Lott 34: 64
Searle, Ronald 24: 98; 42: 172, 173, 174, 176, 177, 179; 66: 73, 74; 70: 205, 206, 207
Searle, Townley 36: 85
Sebree, Charles 18: 65
Sedacca, Joseph M. 11: 25; 22: 36
Seder, Jason 108: 102
Seeger, Laura Vaccaro 172: 162
Seegmiller, Don 174: 57
Seely, David 164: 173
Seeley, Laura L. 97: 105
Segal, John 178: 202
Segar, E.C. 61: 179, 181
Segur, Adrienne 27: 121
Seibold, J. Otto 83: 188, 190, 191; 149: 212, 214, 215, 216
Seignobosc, Francoise 21: 145, 146
Sejima, Yoshimasa 8: 187
Selig, Sylvie 13: 199
Seltzer, Isadore 6: 18; 133: 59
Seltzer, Meyer 17: 214
Selven, Maniam 144: 133
Selway, Martina 169: 157
Selznick, Brian 79: 192; 104: 25; 117: 175; 126: 156; 134: 171; 158: 76, 78; 169: 70; 171: 172, 173; 191: 106; 192: 130
Sempe, Jean-Jacques 47: 92; YABC 2: 109
Sendak, Maurice 1: 135, 190; 3: 204; 7: 142; 15: 199; 17: 210; 27: 181, 182, 183, 185, 186, 187, 189,190, 191, 192, 193, 194, 195, 197, 198, 199, 203; 28: 181, 182; 32: 108; 33: 148, 149; 35: 238; 44: 180, 181; 45: 97, 99; 46: 174; 73: 225; 91: 10, 11 YABC1: 167; 113: 163, 165, 167, 168; 118: 153; 127: 161
Senders, Marci 180: 79
Sengler, Johanna 18: 256
Senn, Steve 60: 145
Seredy, Kate 1: 192; 14: 20, 21; 17: 210
Sergeant, John 6: 74
Servello, Joe 10: 144; 24: 139; 40: 91; 70: 130, 131; 146: 159
Seton, Ernest Thompson 18: 260-269, 271
Seuss, Dr.
   See Geisel, Theodor
Severin, John Powers 7: 62
Sewall, Marcia 15: 8; 22: 170; 37: 171, 172, 173; 39: 73; 45: 209; 62: 117; 69: 185, 186; 71: 212; 90: 232; 96: 127; 102: 101; 107: 129; 119: 176, 177, 178, 180
Seward, James 70: 35
Seward, Prudence 16: 243
Sewell, Helen 3: 186; 15: 308; 33: 102; 38: 189, 190, 191, 192
Seymour, Stephen 54: 21
Sfar, Joann 182: 183
Shachat, Andrew 82: 179
Shahn, Ben 39: 178; 46: 193
Shalansky, Len 38: 167
Shanks, Anne Zane 10: 149
Shannon, David 57: 137; 107: 184; 112: 216; 135: 12; 152: 223, 224, 225; 158: 192
Sharp, Paul 52: 60
Sharp, William 6: 131; 19: 241; 20: 112; 25: 141
Sharratt, Nick 102: 207, 208; 104: 163; 153: 198; 175: 176; 192: 208
Shaw, Barclay 74: 14, 16; 118: 138

Shaw, Charles 21: 135; 38: 187; 47: 124; 126: 219
Shaw, Charles G. 13: 200
Shaw-Smith, Emma 144: 117
Shea, Edmund 56: 19
Shearer, Ted 43: 193, 194, 195, 196
Sheban, Chris 182: 185; 190: 102, 104
Shecter, Ben 16: 244; 25: 109; 33: 188, 191; 41: 77
Shed, Greg 74: 94; 84: 204; 129: 149, 167: 91; 179: 192
Sheeban, Chris 144: 190; 158: 163
Shefcik, James 48: 221, 222; 60: 141
Shefelman, Karl 58: 168
Shefts, Joelle 48: 210
Shein, Bob 139: 189
Shekerjian, Haig 16: 245
Shekerjian, Regina 16: 245; 25: 73
Sheldon, David 184: 174; 185: 204
Shelley, John 186: 223
Shemie, Bonnie 96: 207
Shenton, Edward 45: 187, 188, 189; YABC 1: 218, 219, 221
Shepard, Ernest H. 3: 193; 4: 74; 16: 101; 17: 109; 25: 148; 33: 152, 199, 200, 201, 202, 203, 204, 205, 206,207; 46: 194; 98: 114; 100: 111, 178, 179, 217, 219, 220,221; YABC 1: 148, 153, 174, 176, 180, 181
Shepard, Mary 4: 210; 22: 205; 30: 132, 133; 54: 150, 152, 153, 157, 158; 59: 108, 109, 111; 100: 246
Shepherd, Irana 171: 112
Sheppard, Kate 195: 176
Shepperson, Rob 96: 153; 177: 163; 178: 204
Sherman, Theresa 27: 167
Sherwan, Earl 3: 196
Shields, Charles 10: 150; 36: 63
Shields, Leonard 13: 83, 85, 87
Shiffman, Lena 139: 167; 168: 136
Shigley, Neil K. 66: 219
Shillabeer, Mary 35: 74
Shilston, Arthur 49: 61; 62: 58
Shimin, Symeon 1: 93; 2: 128, 129; 3: 202; 7: 85; 11: 177; 12: 139; 13: 202, 203; 27: 138; 28: 65; 35: 129; 36: 130; 48: 151; 49: 59; 56: 63, 65, 153
Shine, Andrea 104: 165; 128: 34
Shinn, Everett 16: 148; 18: 229; 21: 149, 150, 151; 24: 218
Shinn, Florence Scovel 63: 133, 135
Shore, Robert 27: 54; 39: 192, 193; YABC 2: 200
Shortall, Leonard 4: 144; 8: 196; 10: 166; 19: 227, 228, 229, 230; 25: 78; 28: 66, 167; 33: 127; 52: 125; 73: 12, 212
Shortt, T.M. 27: 36
Shpitalnik, Vladimir 83: 194
Shropshire, Sandy 170: 191
Shtainments, Leon 32: 161
Shulevitz, Uri 3: 198, 199; 17: 85; 22: 204; 27: 212; 28: 184; 50: 190, 191, 192, 193, 194, 195, 196,197, 198, 199, 201; 106: 181, 182, 183; 165: 203, 205; 166: 138
Shulman, Dee 180: 140
Shupe, Bobbi 139: 80, 81
Shute, A.B. 67: 196
Shute, Linda 46: 59; 74: 118
Siberell, Anne 29: 193
Sibley, Don 1: 39; 12: 196; 31: 47
Sibthorp, Fletcher 94: 111, 112
Sidjakov, Nicolas 18: 274
Siebel, Fritz 3: 120; 17: 145
Siebold, J. Otto 158: 227
Siegel, Hal 74: 246
Sieger, Ted 189: 172
Siegl, Helen 12: 166; 23: 216; 34: 185, 186
Silin-Palmer, Pamela 184: 102
Sill, John 140: 194; 141: 157
Sills, Joyce 5: 199
Silva, Simon 108: 122
Silver, Maggie 85: 210

Silveria, Gordon 96: 44
Silverstein, Alvin 8: 189
Silverstein, Shel 33: 211; 92: 209, 210
Silverstein, Virginia 8: 189
Silvey, Joe 135: 203
Simard, Remy 95: 156
Simmons, Elly 110: 2; 127: 69; 134: 181
Simon, Eric M. 7: 82
Simon, Hilda 28: 189
Simon, Howard 2: 175; 5: 132; 19: 199; 32: 163, 164, 165
Simont, Marc 2: 119; 4: 213; 9: 168; 13: 238,240; 14: 262; 16: 179; 18: 221; 26: 210; 33: 189, 194; 44: 132; 58: 122; 68: 117; 73: 204, 205, 206; 74: 221; 126: 199, 200; 133: 195; 164: 128
Sims, Agnes 54: 152
Sims, Blanche 44: 116; 57: 129; 75: 179, 180; 77: 92; 104: 192; 152: 117; 156: 160; 160: 70; 168: 174, 175
Singer, Edith G. 2: 30
Singer, Gloria 34: 56; 36: 43
Singer, Julia 28: 190
Singh, Jen 178: 146
Siomades, Lorianne 134: 45
Simont, Marc 163: 40
Siracusa, Catherine 68: 135; 82: 218
Sís, Peter 67: 179, 181, 183, 184, 185; 96: 96, 98; 106: 193, 194, 195; 149: 224, 226; 180: 177; 192: 180, 182
Sivard, Robert 26: 124
Sivertson, Liz 116: 84
Skardinski, Stanley 23: 144; 32: 84; 66: 122; 84: 108
Slack, Michael 185: 108; 189: 173, 174
Slackman, Charles B. 12: 201
Slade, Christian 193: 187
Slade, Paul 61: 170
Slark, Albert 99: 212
Slater, Rod 25: 167
Slavin, Bill 182: 14, 15
Sloan, Joseph 16: 68
Sloane, Eric 21: 3; 52: 153, 154, 155, 156, 157, 158, 160
Sloat, Teri 164: 231
Slobodkin, Louis 1: 200; 3: 232; 5: 168; 13: 251; 15: 13, 88; 26: 173, 174, 175, 176, 178, 179; 60: 180
Slobodkina, Esphyr 1: 201
Slonim, David 166: 167, 168
Small, David 50: 204, 205; 79: 44; 95: 189, 190, 191; 126: 203, 204; 136: 119; 143: 201, 202, 203; 144: 246; 150: 5; 161: 176; 183: 181, 182, 183, 184
Small, W. 33: 113
Smalley, Janet 1: 154
Smedley, William T. 34: 129
Smee, David 14: 78; 62: 30
Smee, Nicola 167: 156
Smith, A.G., Jr. 35: 182
Smith, Alvin 1: 31, 229; 13: 187; 27: 216; 28: 226; 48: 149; 49: 60
Smith, Andy 188: 20
Smith, Anne 194: 147
Smith, Anne Warren 41: 212
Smith, Barry 75: 183
Smith, Carl 36: 41
Smith, Cat Bowman 146: 39; 164: 219
Smith, Craig 97: 197; 172: 175
Smith, Donald A. 178: 7
Smith, Doris Susan 41: 139
Smith, Douglas 189: 159
Smith, Duane 171: 152
Smith, E. Boyd 19: 70; 22: 89; 26: 63; YABC 1: 4, 5, 240, 248, 249
Smith, Edward J. 4: 224
Smith, Elwood H. 157: 231; 181: 79
Smith, Eunice Young 5: 170
Smith, Gary 113: 216
Smith, George 102: 169
Smith, Howard 19: 196

Smith, J. Gerard *95:* 42
Smith, Jacqueline Bardner *27:* 108; *39:* 197
Smith, Jay J. *61:* 119
Smith, Jeff *93:* 191
Smith, Jessie Willcox *15:* 91; *16:* 95; *18:* 231; *19:* 57, 242; *21:* 29, 156, 157, 158, 159, 160, 161; *34:* 65; *100:* 223; *YABC 1:* 6; *2:* 180, 185, 191, 311, 325
Smith, Jos. A. *52:* 131; *72:* 120; *74:* 151; *84:* 147, 148; *85:* 146; *87:* 96; *94:* 219; *96:* 97; *104:* 33; *108:* 126, 127, 128; *111:* 140; *136:* 145; *181:* 173
Smith, Kenneth R. *47:* 182
Smith, Kevin Warren *89:* 112
Smith, L.H. *35:* 174
Smith, Lane *76:* 211, 213; *88:* 115; *105:* 202, 203,204, 205; *131:* 207; *160:* 217, 221; *179:* 183, 184, 185, 186
Smith, Lee *29:* 32
Smith, Linell Nash *2:* 195
Smith, Maggie Kaufman *13:* 205; *35:* 191; *110:* 158; *178:* 226; *190:* 204
Smith, Mavis *101:* 219
Smith, Moishe *33:* 155
Smith, Philip *44:* 134; *46:* 203
Smith, Ralph Crosby *2:* 267; *49:* 203
Smith, Robert D. *5:* 63
Smith, Sally J. *84:* 55
Smith, Susan Carlton *12:* 208
Smith, Terry *12:* 106; *33:* 158
Smith, Virginia *3:* 157; *33:* 72
Smith, William A. *1:* 36; *10:* 154; *25:* 65
Smith-Moore, J.J. *98:* 147
Smolinski, Dick *84:* 217
Smoljan, Joe *112:* 201
Smollin, Mike *39:* 203
Smyth, Iain *105:* 207
Smyth, M. Jane *12:* 15
Smythe, Fiona *151:* 213
Smythe, Theresa *141:* 37
Snair, Andy *176:* 4
Sneed, Brad *125:* 25; *191:* 175, 176
Snyder, Andrew A. *30:* 212
Snyder, Jerome *13:* 207; *30:* 173
Snyder, Joel *28:* 163
So, Meilo *162:* 201
Soentpiet, Chris K. *97:* 208; *110:* 33; *159:* 184; *161:* 10; *163:* 130
Sofia *1:* 62; *5:* 90; *32:* 166; *86:* 43
Sofilas, Mark *93:* 157
Sohn, Jiho *182:* 78
Sokol, Bill *37:* 178; *49:* 23
Sokolov, Kirill *34:* 188
Solbert, Ronni *1:* 159; *2:* 232; *5:* 121; *6:* 34; *17:* 249
Solomon, Michael *174:* 115
Solonevich, George *15:* 246; *17:* 47
Soma, Liana *81:* 118
Soman, David *90:* 122; *102:* 126; *140:* 120; *93:* 188; *188:* 43, 89
Sommer, Robert *12:* 211
Sorel, Edward *4:* 61; *36:* 82; *65:* 191, 193; *126:* 214
Sorensen, Henrik *62:* 16
Sorensen, Svend Otto *22:* 130, 141; *67:* 188, 189
Sorra, Kristin *155:* 80
Sostre, Maria *187:* 36
Sotomayor, Antonio *11:* 215
Souhami, Jessica *112:* 128; *176:* 193
Souza, Diana *71:* 139
Sovak, Jan *115:* 190
Soyer, Moses *20:* 177
Spaenkuch, August *16:* 28
Spafford, Suzy *160:* 228
Spain, Valerie *105:* 76
Spain, Sunday Sahara *133:* 204
Spalenka, Greg *149:* 69; *151:* 228; *184:* 195; *191:* 21

Spanfeller, James *1:* 72, 149; *2:* 183; *19:* 230, 231,232; *22:* 66; *36:* 160, 161; *40:* 75; *52:* 166; *76:* 37
Sparks, Mary Walker *15:* 247
Spears, Rick *182:* 187
Speidel, Sandra *78:* 233; *94:* 178; *134:* 180
Speirs, John *67:* 178
Spence, Geraldine *21:* 163; *47:* 196
Spence, Jim *38:* 89; *50:* 102
Spencer, Laurie *113:* 12
Spencer, Mark *57:* 170
Spengler, Kenneth J. *146:* 256
Sperling, Andrea *133:* 182
Spiegel, Beth *184:* 203
Spiegel, Doris *29:* 111
Spiegelman, Art *109:* 227
Spier, Jo *10:* 30
Spier, Peter *3:* 155; *4:* 200; *7:* 61; *11:* 78; *38:* 106; *54:* 120, 121, 122, 123, 124, 125, 126, 127, 128, 129, 130,131, 132, 133, 134
Spilka, Arnold *5:* 120; *6:* 204; *8:* 131
Spirin, Gennady *95:* 196, 197; *113:* 172; *128:* 9; *129:* 49; *134:* 210; *153:* 9
Spivak, I. Howard *8:* 10; *13:* 172
Spohn, David *72:* 233
Spohn, Kate *87:* 195; *147:* 201, 202
Spollen, Christopher J. *12:* 214
Spooner, Malcolm *40:* 142
Spowart, Robin *82:* 228; *92:* 149; *133:* 131; *176:* 163; *177:* 183, 184
Sprague, Kevin *150:* 60
Sprattler, Rob *12:* 176
Spring, Bob *5:* 60
Spring, Ira *5:* 60
Springer, Harriet *31:* 92
Spudvilas, Anne *110:* 74
Spurll, Barbara *78:* 199; *88:* 141, 142; *99:* 215
Spurrier, Steven *28:* 198
Spuvilas, Anne *85:* 114
Spy
See Ward, Leslie
Squires, Stuart *127:* 74
St. Aubin, Bruno *179:* 54
St. John, J. Allen *41:* 62
Stabin, Victor *101:* 131; *164:* 158
Stadler, John *62:* 33
Staffan, Alvin E. *11:* 56; *12:* 187
Stahl, Ben *5:* 181; *12:* 91; *49:* 122; *71:* 128; *87:* 206; *112:* 107
Stair, Gobin *35:* 214
Stallwood, Karen *73:* 126
Stamaty, Mark Alan *12:* 215
Stammen, JoEllen McAllister *113:* 14
Stampnick, Ken *51:* 142
Stanbridge, Joanne *150:* 91
Stanley, Diane *3:* 45; *37:* 180; *80:* 217, 219
Stanley, Sanna *145:* 228
Starcke, Helmut *86:* 217
Starr, Branka *73:* 25
Stasiak, Krystyna *49:* 181; *64:* 194
Staub, Leslie *103:* 54
Staunton, Ted *112:* 192
Stawicki, Matt *164:* 250
Stead, L. *55:* 51, 56
Steadman, Broeck *97:* 185, 186; *99:* 56; *121:* 48
Steadman, Ralph *32:* 180; *123:* 143, 145
Stearn, Nick *183:* 26
Steckler, June *90:* 178
Steele, Robert Gantt *169:* 174
Steichen, Edward *30:* 79
Steig, William *18:* 275, 276; *70:* 215, 216, 217, 218; *111:* 173, 174, 175, 176, 177
Stein, Harve *1:* 109
Steinberg, Saul *47:* 193
Steinel, William *23:* 146
Steiner, Charlotte *45:* 196
Steiner, Joan *110:* 219
Steirnagel, Michael *80:* 56
Stemp, Eric *60:* 184
Stephens, Alice Barber *66:* 208, 209

Stephens, Charles H. *YABC 2:* 279
Stephens, Pat *126:* 110; *128:* 101
Stephens, William M. *21:* 165
Steptoe, Javaka *151:* 203, 204; *190:* 169
Steptoe, John *8:* 197; *57:* 9; *63:* 158, 159, 160, 161,163, 164, 165, 166, 167; *96:* 4; *105:* 87
Stern, Simon *15:* 249, 250; *17:* 58; *34:* 192, 193
Sterret, Jane *53:* 27
Stetsios, Debbie *165:* 108, 109
Steven, Kat *158:* 237
Stevens, David *62:* 44
Stevens, Helen *189:* 31
Stevens, Janet *40:* 126; *57:* 10, 11; *80:* 112; *90:* 221, 222; *109:* 156; *130:* 34; *166:* 202; *176:* 53, 116; *193:* 199, 200, 202
Stevens, Mary *11:* 193; *13:* 129; *43:* 95
Stevenson, Harvey *66:* 143; *80:* 201, 221; *153:* 60; *191:* 166
Stevenson, James *42:* 182, 183; *51:* 163; *66:* 184; *71:* 185, 187, 188; *78:* 262; *87:* 97; *113:* 182, 183,184, 185; *161:* 182, 183
Stevenson, Sucie *92:* 27; *104:* 194, 195; *112:* 168; *160:* 202; *194:* 172, 173; *195:* 166
Stewart, April Blair *75:* 210
Stewart, Arvis *33:* 98; *36:* 69; *60:* 118; *75:* 91; *127:* 4
Stewart, Charles *2:* 205
Stewart, Joel *151:* 205
Stieg, William *172:* 58
Stiles, Fran *26:* 85; *78:* 56; *82:* 150
Stillman, Susan *44:* 130; *76:* 83
Stimpson, Tom *49:* 171
Stinemetz, Morgan *40:* 151
Stinson, Paul *110:* 86
Stirnweis, Shannon *10:* 164
Stites, Joe *86:* 96
Stobbs, William *1:* 48, 49; *3:* 68; *6:* 20; *17:* 117, 217; *24:* 150; *29:* 250; *60:* 179; *87:* 204, 205,206
Stock, Catherine *37:* 55; *65:* 198; *72:* 7; *99:* 225; *114:* 197, 198, 199; *126:* 3; *145:* 161; *161:* 82; *173:* 149
Stockman, Jack *113:* 24
Stoeke, Janet Morgan *90:* 225; *136:* 196
Stoerrle, Tom *55:* 147
Stolp, Jaap *49:* 98
Stolp, Todd *89:* 195
Stone, David L. *87:* 154
Stone, David *9:* 173
Stone, David K. *4:* 38; *6:* 124; *9:* 180; *43:* 182; *60:* 70
Stone, Helen V. *6:* 209
Stone, Helen *44:* 121, 122, 126
Stone, Kazuko G. *134:* 43
Stone, Phoebe *86:* 212; *134:* 213; *162:* 188
Stone, Steve *166:* 213
Stone, Tony *150:* 34, 35
Storrings, Michael *191:* 108
Stoud, Virginia A. *89:* 31
Stover, Jill *82:* 234
Stratton, Helen *33:* 151
Stratton-Porter, Gene *15:* 254, 259, 263, 264, 268, 269
Straub, Matt *192:* 176
Streano, Vince *20:* 173
Street, Janet Travell *84:* 235
Streeter, Clive *121:* 2
Stringer, Lauren *129:* 187; *154:* 172, 173; *161:* 127; *183:* 187, 188
Strodl, Daniel *47:* 95
Strogart, Alexander *63:* 139
Stromoski, Rick *111:* 179; *124:* 161, 190
Strong, Joseph D., Jr. *YABC 2:* 330
Stroyer, Poul *13:* 221
Strugnell, Ann *27:* 38
Struzan, Drew *117:* 6
Stubbs, William *73:* 196
Stubis, Talivaldis *5:* 182, 183; *10:* 45; *11:* 9; *18:* 304; *20:* 127

Stubley, Trevor *14:* 43; *22:* 219; *23:* 37; *28:* 61; *87:* 26
Stuck, Marion *104:* 44
Stuecklen, Karl W. *8:* 34, 65; *23:* 103
Stull, Betty *11:* 46
Stutzman, Mark *119:* 99
Stutzmann, Laura *73:* 185
Suarez, Maribel *162:* 208
Suba, Susanne *4:* 202, 203; *14:* 261; *23:* 134; *29:* 222; *32:* 30
Sueling, Barbara *98:* 185
Sueling, Gwenn *98:* 186
Sugarman, Tracy *3:* 76; *8:* 199; *37:* 181, 182
Sugimoto, Yugo *170:* 144
Sugita, Yutaka *36:* 180, 181
Suh, John *80:* 157
Sullivan, Dorothy *89:* 113
Sullivan, Edmund J. *31:* 86
Sullivan, James F. *19:* 280; *20:* 192
Sully, Tom *104:* 199, 200; *182:* 77
Sumichrast, Jozef *14:* 253; *29:* 168, 213
Sumiko *46:* 57
Summers, Leo *1:* 177; *2:* 273; *13:* 22
Summers, Mark *118:* 144
Summers, Mike *190:* 176
Sutton, Judith *94:* 164
Svarez, Juan *56:* 113
Svendsen, Mark *181:* 176
Svolinsky, Karel *17:* 104
Swain, Carol *172:* 182
Swain, Su Zan Noguchi *21:* 170
Swan, Susan *22:* 220, 221; *37:* 66; *60:* 146; *145:* 205; *181:* 168
Swann, Susan *86:* 55
Swanson, Karl *79:* 65; *89:* 186
Swayne, Sam *53:* 143, 145
Swayne, Zoa *53:* 143, 145
Swearingen, Greg *152:* 56; *165:* 135; *173:* 2
Sweat, Lynn *25:* 206; *57:* 176; *73:* 184; *168:* 178
Sweet, Darrell K. *60:* 9; *69:* 86; *74:* 15; *75:* 215; *76:* 130, 131; *81:* 96, 122; *82:* 253; *83:* 11; *84:* 14; *85:* 37; *89:* 140; *90:* 6; *91:* 137,139; *95:* 160, 161; *126:* 25; *185:* 175; *195:* 132
Sweet, Darrell K. *1:* 163; *4:* 136; *164:* 175
Sweet, Melissa *71:* 94; *72:* 172; *111:* 82; *139:* 53, 58; *141:* 88; *142:* 231; *155:* 121; *159:* 121, 122; *172:* 185; *188:* 127
Sweet, Ozzie *31:* 149, 151, 152
Sweetland, Robert *12:* 194
Swiatkowska, Gabi *132:* 43; *175:* 139; *180:* 218; *183:* 176
Swope, Martha *43:* 160; *56:* 86, 87, 89
Sylvada, Peter *154:* 174
Sylvester, Natalie G. *22:* 222
Szafran, Gene *24:* 144
Szasz, Susanne *13:* 55, 226; *14:* 48
Szekeres, Cyndy *2:* 218; *5:* 185; *8:* 85; *11:* 166; *14:* 19; *16:* 57, 159; *26:* 49, 214; *34:* 205; *60:* 150, 151, 152, 153, 154; *73:* 224; *74:* 218; *131:* 213, 215
Szpura, Beata *81:* 68; *119:* 65; *168:* 201

T

Taback, Simms *40:* 207; *52:* 120; *57:* 34; *80:* 241; *104:* 202, 203; *170:* 176, 177
Taber, Patricia *75:* 124
Taddei, Richard *112:* 13, 14
Tadgell, Nicole *150:* 77; *161:* 20; *177:* 186
Tadiello, Ed *133:* 200
Tafuri, Nancy *39:* 210; *75:* 199, 200; *92:* 75; *130:* 215, 216, 217
Tailfeathers, Gerald *86:* 85
Tait, Douglas *12:* 220; *74:* 105, 106
Takabayashi, Mari *113:* 112; *130:* 22; *156:* 169
Takahashi, Hideko *136:* 160; *187:* 6

Takakjian, Portia *15:* 274
Takashima, Shizuye *13:* 228
Talarczyk, June *4:* 173
Talbott, Hudson *84:* 240; *163:* 100
Tallarico, Tony *116:* 197
Tallon, Robert *2:* 228; *43:* 200, 201, 202, 203, 204, 205,206, 207, 209
Tamas, Szecsko *29:* 135
Tamburine, Jean *12:* 222
Tandy, H.R. *13:* 69
Tandy, Russell H. *65:* 9; *100:* 30, 131
Tang, Charles *81:* 202; *90:* 192
Tang, Susan *80:* 174; *108:* 158
Tang, You-shan *63:* 100
Tankersley, Paul *69:* 206; *133:* 219
Tannenbaum, Robert *48:* 181
Tanner, Jane *87:* 13; *97:* 37
Tanner, Tim *72:* 192; *84:* 35
Tanobe, Miyuki *23:* 221
Tarabay, Sharif *110:* 149; *113:* 123; *169:* 83
Tarkington, Booth *17:* 224, 225
Tarlow, Phyllis *61:* 198
Tate, Don *159:* 141, 191; *183:* 69; *186:* 120
Tauss, Herbert *95:* 179
Tauss, Marc *117:* 160; *126:* 155; *178:* 221
Tavares, Matt *159:* 192, 193
Taylor, Ann *41:* 226
Taylor, Dahl *129:* 157
Taylor, Geoff *93:* 156
Taylor, Isaac *41:* 228
Taylor, Mike *143:* 99, 100
Teague, Mark *83:* 6; *139:* 241; *170:* 180, 181
Teale, Edwin Way *7:* 196
Teason, James *1:* 14
Teeple, Lyn *33:* 147
Tee-Van, Helen Damrosch *10:* 176; *11:* 182
Teicher, Dick *50:* 211
Teichman, Mary *77:* 220; *124:* 208; *127:* 22
Temertey, Ludmilla *96:* 232; *104:* 43, 45; *109:* 244
Tempest, Margaret *3:* 237, 238; *88:* 200
Temple, Frances *85:* 185, 186, 187
Temple, Herbert *45:* 201
Templeton, Owen *11:* 77
ten Cate, Marijke *183:* 193
Tenggren, Gustaf *18:* 277, 278, 279; *19:* 15; *28:* 86; *YABC2:* 145
Tennent, Julie *81:* 105
Tenneson, Joyce *153:* 166
Tenney, Gordon *24:* 204
Tenniel, John *74:* 234, 235; *100:* 89; *YABC 2:* 99; *153:* 63
Tepper, Matt *116:* 80
Terkel, Ari *103:* 162
Terry, Michael *180:* 209
Terry, Will *131:* 73
Teskey, Donald *71:* 51
Thacher, Mary M. *30:* 72
Thackeray, William Makepeace *23:* 224, 228
Thamer, Katie *42:* 187
Tharlet, Eve *146:* 149
Thelwell, Norman *14:* 201
Theobalds, Prue *40:* 23
Theurer, Marilyn Churchill *39:* 195
Thiesing, Lisa *89:* 134; *95:* 202; *156:* 190; *159:* 195
Thiewes, Sam *133:* 114
Thistlethwaite, Miles *12:* 224
Thollander, Earl *11:* 47; *18:* 112; *22:* 224
Thomas, Allan *22:* 13
Thomas, Art *48:* 217
Thomas, Eric *28:* 49
Thomas, Harold *20:* 98
Thomas, Jacqui *125:* 95
Thomas, Mark *42:* 136
Thomas, Martin *14:* 255
Thomas, Middy *177:* 114
Thompson, Arthur *34:* 107
Thompson, Carol *85:* 189; *95:* 75; *102:* 86; *147:* 166; *189:* 179, 180, 181; *190:* 84
Thompson, Colin *95:* 204

Thompson, Ellen *51:* 88, 151; *60:* 33; *67:* 42; *77:* 148; *78:* 75, 219; *79:* 122, 170; *84:* 219; *85:* 97; *87:* 37; *88:* 192, 194; *89:* 80; *93:* 37; *98:* 59; *132:* 14
Thompson, George W. *22:* 18; *28:* 150; *33:* 135
Thompson, John *58:* 201; *102:* 226; *124:* 154; *128:* 228; *129:* 157; *150:* 49; *185:* 160; *191:* 192
Thompson, Julie *44:* 158
Thompson, Katherine *132:* 146
Thompson, K. Dyble *84:* 6
Thompson, Miles *152:* 77
Thompson, Sharon *74:* 113; *158:* 60; *165:* 87
Thomson, Arline K. *3:* 264
Thomson, Bill *186:* 160
Thomson, Hugh *26:* 88
Thomson, Ross *36:* 179
Thorkelson, Gregg *95:* 183, 184; *98:* 58; *165:* 30, 31
Thorn, Lori *189:* 119
Thornberg, Dan *104:* 125
Thornburgh, Rebecca McKillip *143:* 37
Thorne, Diana *25:* 212
Thornhill, Jan *77:* 213
Thorpe, Peter *58:* 109
Thorvall, Kerstin *13:* 235
Threadgall, Colin *77:* 215
Thurber, James *13:* 239, 242, 243, 245, 248, 249
Thurman, Mark *63:* 173; *168:* 116
Tibbles, Jean-Paul *115:* 200
Tibbles, Paul *45:* 23
Tibo, Gilles *67:* 207; *107:* 199, 201
Tichenor, Tom *14:* 207
Tichnor, Richard *90:* 218
Tiegreen, Alan *36:* 143; *43:* 55, 56, 58; *77:* 200; *94:* 216, 217; *121:* 54, 59
Tierney, Tom *113:* 198, 200, 201
Tilley, Debbie *102:* 134; *133:* 226; *137:* 101; *159:* 96; *190:* 211, 212
Tilney, F.C. *22:* 231
Timbs, Gloria *36:* 90
Timmins, Harry *2:* 171
Timmons, Bonnie *194:* 189
Tinkelman, Murray *12:* 225; *35:* 44
Titherington, Jeanne *39:* 90; *58:* 138; *75:* 79; *135:* 161
Tobin, Nancy *145:* 197
Toddy, Irving *172:* 144
Tokunbo, Dimitrea *181:* 183; *187:* 182, 183
Tolbert, Jeff *128:* 69
Tolford, Joshua *1:* 221
Tolkien, J.R.R. *2:* 243; *32:* 215
Tolman, Marije *195:* 43
Tolmie, Ken *15:* 292
Tomei, Lorna *47:* 168, 171
Tomes, Jacqueline *2:* 117; *12:* 139
Tomes, Margot *1:* 224; *2:* 120, 121; *16:* 207; *18:* 250; *20:* 7; *25:* 62; *27:* 78, 79; *29:* 81, 199; *33:* 82; *36:* 186, 187, 188, 189, 190; *46:* 129; *56:* 71; *58:* 183; *70:* 228; *75:* 73, 75; *80:* 80; *83:* 97; *90:* 205
Toner, Raymond John *10:* 179
Tong, Gary *66:* 215
Tongier, Stephen *82:* 32
Tooke, Susan *173:* 162
Toothill, Harry *6:* 54; *7:* 49; *25:* 219; *42:* 192
Toothill, Ilse *6:* 54
Topolski, Feliks *44:* 48
Torbert, Floyd James *22:* 226
Torgersen, Don *55:* 157
Torline, Kevin *169:* 171
Tormey, Bertram M. *75:* 3, 4
Torrecilla, Pablo *176:* 207
Torres, Leyla *156:* 199, 201
Torrey, Helen *87:* 41
Torrey, Marjorie *34:* 105
Torrey, Richard *189:* 182
Toschik, Larry *6:* 102
Totten, Bob *13:* 93

Toy, Julie *128:* 112
Trachok, Cathy *131:* 16
Tracy, Libba *82:* 24
Trago, Keith *158:* 253
Trail, Lee *55:* 157
Trang, To Ngoc *167:* 180
Trang, Winson *89:* 151
Trapani, Iza *116:* 202
Travers, Bob *49:* 100; *63:* 145
Treatner, Meryl *95:* 180
Tremain, Ruthven *17:* 238
Tresilian, Stuart *25:* 53; *40:* 212
Trez, Alain *17:* 236
Trezzo, Loretta *86:* 45
Trier, Walter *14:* 96
Trimby, Elisa *47:* 199
Trinkle, Sally *53:* 27
Triplett, Gina *182:* 193; *188:* 100
Tripp, F.J. *24:* 167
Tripp, Wallace *2:* 48; *7:* 28; *8:* 94; *10:* 54,76;
  11: 92; *31:* 170, 171; *34:* 203; *42:* 57; *60:*
  157; *73:* 182
Trivas, Irene *53:* 4; *54:* 168; *82:* 46, 101
Trnka, Jiri *22:* 151; *43:* 212, 213, 214, 215;
  YABC 1: 30, 31
Trondheim, Lewis *182:* 183
Troughton, Joanna *37:* 186; *48:* 72
Troyer, Johannes *3:* 16; *7:* 18
Trudeau, G.B. *35:* 220, 221, 222; *48:* 119,
  123, 126, 127,128, 129, 133; *168:* 189
Trueman, Matthew *165:* 208; *183:* 191
Truesdell, Sue *55:* 142; *108:* 219, 220
Tryon, Leslie *84:* 7; *139:* 214; *143:* 10; *181:*
  10
Tseng, Jean *72:* 195; *94:* 102; *119:* 126; *151:*
  106; *173:* 138, 139
Tseng, Mou-sien *72:* 195; *94:* 102; *119:* 126;
  151: 106; *173:* 138, 139
Tsinajinie, Andy *2:* 62
Tsinganos, Jim *180:* 142
Tsugami, Kyuzo *18:* 198, 199
Tucker, Ezra *156:* 31
Tuckwell, Jennifer *17:* 205
Tudor, Bethany *7:* 103
Tudor, Tasha *18:* 227; *20:* 185, 186, 187; *36:*
  111; *69:* 196, 198; *100:* 44;
  YABC 2: 46, 314; *160:* 234
Tuerk, Hanne *71:* 201
Tulloch, Maurice *24:* 79
Tunis, Edwin *1:* 218, 219; *28:* 209, 210, 211,
  212
Tunnicliffe, C.F. *62:* 176; 177; 178, 179; 181
Turkle, Brinton *1:* 211, 213; *2:* 249; *3:* 226;
  11: 3; *16:* 209; *20:* 22; *50:* 23; *67:* 50; *68:*
  65; *79:* 205, 206, 207; *128:* 47; *YABC 1:* 79
Turnbull, Christopher J. *143:* 99, 100
Turner, Gwenda *59:* 195
Turska, Krystyna *12:* 103; *31:* 173, 174, 175;
  56: 32,34; *100:* 66
Tusa, Tricia *72:* 242; *111:* 180, 181; *157:* 165;
  164: 186; *189:* 40
Tusan, Stan *6:* 58; *22:* 236, 237
Tworkov, Jack *47:* 207
Tyers, Jenny *89:* 220
Tylden-Wright, Jenny *114:* 119
Tyrol, Adelaide Murphy *103:* 27
Tyrrell, Frances *107:* 204
Tzimoulis, Paul *12:* 104

U

Uchida, Yoshiko *1:* 220
Uderzo *47:* 88
Udovic, David *189:* 185; *195:* 201
Ueno, Noriko *59:* 155
Ulm, Robert *17:* 238
Ulrich, George *73:* 15; *75:* 136, 139; *99:* 150
Ulriksen, Mark *101:* 58; *182:* 43

Unada *84:* 67
  See Gliewe, Unada
Underhill, Liz *53:* 159
Underwood, Beck *192:* 36
Underwood, Clarence *40:* 166
Unger, Jim *67:* 208
Ungerer, Tomi *5:* 188; *9:* 40; *18:* 188; *29:*
  175; *33:* 221, 222, 223, 225; *71:* 48; *106:*
  209, 210, 211, 212
Unwin, Nora S. *3:* 65, 234, 235; *4:* 237; *44:*
  173, 174; *YABC 1:* 59; *2:* 301
Upitis, Alvis *145:* 179
Urban, Helle *149:* 243
Urbanovic, Jackie *86:* 86; *189:* 186, 187
Uris, Jill *49:* 188, 197
Ursell, Martin *50:* 51
Utpatel, Frank *18:* 114
Utz, Lois *5:* 190

V

Vagin, Vladimir *66:* 10; *142:* 215
Vaillancourt, Francois *107:* 199
Vainio, Pirkko *123:* 157, 158
Valério, Geraldo *180:* 225; *194:* 116
Vallejo, Boris *62:* 130; *72:* 212; *91:* 38; *93:* 61
Van Abbe, S. *16:* 142; *18:* 282; *31:* 90; *YABC
  2:* 157, 161
Van Allsburg, Chris *37:* 205, 206; *53:* 161,
  162, 163, 165,166, 167, 168, 169, 170, 171;
  105: 215, 216, 217, 218; *156:* 176, 177, 178
Vance, James *65:* 28
Van Der Linde, Henry *99:* 17
van der Meer, Ron *98:* 204, 205
van der Meer, Atie *98:* 204, 205
Vandivert, William *21:* 175
Van Dongen, H.R. *81:* 97
Van Dusen, Chris W. *173:* 169
Van Everen, Jay *13:* 160; *YABC 1:* 121
Van Fleet, John *165:* 12, 13
Van Frankenhuyzen, Gijsbert *145:* 230; *149:*
  164; *184:* 151
van Genechten, Guido *165:* 226
van Haeringen, Annemarie *193:* 206
Van Horn, William *43:* 218
van Hout, Mies *195:* 191
van Kampen, Vlasta *194:* 217
van Lawick, Hugo *62:* 76, 79
Van Loon, Hendrik Willem *18:* 285, 289, 291
Van Munching, Paul *83:* 85
van Ommen, Sylvia *186:* 192
Van Patter, Bruce *183:* 195
Van Rynbach, Iris *102:* 192
Van Sciver, Ruth *37:* 162
VanSeveren, Joe *63:* 182
Van Stockum, Hilda *5:* 193
Van Wely, Babs *16:* 50; *79:* 16
Van Wright, Cornelius *72:* 18; *102:* 208; *116:*
  107; *152:* 236; *173:* 170, 171
Van Zyle, Jon *103:* 125; *160:* 181, 182; *176:*
  199, 200
Vardzigulyants, Ruben *90:* 54
Varga, Judy *29:* 196
Vargo, Kurt *79:* 224
Varley, Susan *61:* 199; *63:* 176, 177; *101:* 148;
  134: 220
Varon, Sara *195:* 208
Vasconcellos, Daniel *80:* 42
Vasiliu, Mircea *2:* 166, 253; *9:* 166; *13:* 58;
  68: 42
Vaughn, Frank *34:* 157
Vavra, Robert *8:* 206
Vawter, Will *17:* 163
Vayas, Diana *71:* 61
Vazquez, Carlos *125:* 184
Veeder, Larry *18:* 4

Velasquez, Eric *45:* 217; *61:* 45; *63:* 110, 111;
  88: 162; *90:* 34, 144; *94:* 213; *107:* 147;
  132: 192; *138:* 213; *159:* 126; *181:* 184;
  184: 96; *191:* 16; *192:* 234
Velasquez, Jose A. *63:* 73
Velez, Walter *71:* 75; *91:* 154; *121:* 181; *168:*
  49
Velthuijs, Max *110:* 228, 229
Vendrell, Carme Sole *42:* 205
Venezia, Mike *54:* 17
Venti, Anthony Bacon *124:* 103; *126:* 26
Venturo, Piero *61:* 194, 195
Ver Beck, Frank *18:* 16, 17
Verkaaik, Ben *110:* 209
Verling, John *71:* 27
Verney, John *14:* 225; *75:* 8
Verrier, Suzanne *5:* 20; *23:* 212
Versace, Marie *2:* 255
Verstraete, Randy *108:* 193
Vestal, H.B. *9:* 134; *11:* 101; *27:* 25; *34:* 158
Vestergaard, Hope *190:* 203
Vicatan *59:* 146
Vickrey, Robert *45:* 59, 64
Victor, Joan Berg *30:* 193
Viereck, Ellen *3:* 242; *14:* 229
Vigna, Judith *15:* 293; *102:* 194, 195, 196, 197
Vilato, Gaspar E. *5:* 41
Villiard, Paul *51:* 178
Vimnera, A. *23:* 154
Vincent, Eric *34:* 98
Vincent, Felix *41:* 237
Vincent, Gabrielle *121:* 175
Vip *45:* 164
Viskupic, Gary *83:* 48
Vitale, Stefano *109:* 71, 107; *114:* 219, 220;
  123: 106; *138:* 232; *180:* 228, 229
Vivas, Julie *51:* 67, 69; *96:* 225
Voake, Charlotte *114:* 221, 222; *180:* 232
Vo-Dinh, Mai *16:* 272; *60:* 191
Vogel, Ilse-Margret *14:* 230
Voigt, Erna *35:* 228
Vojnar, Kamil *95:* 31; *114:* 4; *115:* 62; *121:*
  90; *124:* 72; *130:* 31; *141:* 81; *146:* 196;
  150: 123; *158:* 5, 6; *158:* 154; *171:* 119,
  188; *179:* 15; *180:* 112
Vojtech, Anna *42:* 190; *108:* 222, 223; *150:*
  203; *174:* 173
von Buhler, Cynthia *149:* 237; *162:* 177; *177:*
  205; *180:* 77; *185:* 214, 215, 216
von Roehl, Angela *126:* 191
von Schmidt, Eric *8:* 62; *50:* 209, 210
von Schmidt, Harold *30:* 80
Vosburgh, Leonard *1:* 161; *7:* 32; *15:* 295,
  296; *23:* 110; *30:* 214; *43:* 181
Voss, Tom *127:* 104
Voter, Thomas W. *19:* 3, 9
Vroman, Tom *10:* 29
Vulliamy, Clara *72:* 65

W

Waber, Bernard *47:* 209, 210, 211, 212, 213,
  214; *95:* 215, 216, 217; *156:* 203, 205, 206,
  207
Wachenje, Benjamin *194:* 170
Wack, Jeff *95:* 140; *110:* 90
Wagner, John *8:* 200; *52:* 104
Wagner, Ken *2:* 59
Waide, Jan *29:* 225; *36:* 139
Wainwright, Jerry *14:* 85
Waites, Joan C. *171:* 2
Wakeen, Sandra *47:* 97
Wakiyama, Hanako *171:* 96; *192:* 236
Waldherr, Kris *81:* 186
Waldman, Bruce *15:* 297; *43:* 178
Waldman, Neil *35:* 141; *50:* 163; *51:* 180; *54:*
  78; 77; 112; *79:* 162; *82:* 174; *84:* 5, 56,
  106; *94:* 232, 233, 234; *96:* 41; *111:* 139;
  113: 9; *118:* 30; *142:* 220, 223

Waldrep, Richard *111:* 147
Walker, Brian *144:* 128
Walker, Charles *1:* 46; *4:* 59; *5:* 177; *11:* 115; *19:* 45; *34:* 74; *62:* 168; *72:* 218
Walker, Dugald Stewart *15:* 47; *32:* 202; *33:* 112
Walker, Gil *8:* 49; *23:* 132; *34:* 42
Walker, Jeff *55:* 154; *123:* 116
Walker, Jim *10:* 94
Walker, Mort *8:* 213
Walker, Norman *41:* 37; *45:* 58
Walker, Stephen *12:* 229; *21:* 174
Wallace, Beverly Dobrin *19:* 259
Wallace, Cly *87:* 93
Wallace, Ian *53:* 176, 177; *56:* 165, 166; *58:* 4; *98:* 4; *101:* 191; *112:* 124; *141:* 197, 198, 199, 200; *151:* 212
Wallace, John *105:* 228
Wallace, Nancy Elizabeth *141:* 204; *186:* 195, 197, 199
Wallenta, Adam *123:* 180
Waller, S.E. *24:* 36
Wallner, Alexandra *15:* 120; *156:* 183
Wallner, John C. *9:* 77; *10:* 188; *11:* 28; *14:* 209; *31:* 56, 118; *37:* 64; *51:* 186, 187, 188, 189, 190, 191,192, 193, 194, 195; *52:* 96; *53:* 23, 26; *71:* 99; *73:* 158; *89:* 215; *141:* 9
Wallner, John *162:* 17
Wallower, Lucille *11:* 226
Walotsky, Ron *93:* 87
Walsh, Ellen Stoll *99:* 209; *147:* 219; *194:* 194, 195, 196
Walsh, Rebecca *158:* 193
Walsh, Vivian *149:* 215; *158:* 227
Walters, Audrey *18:* 294
Walther, Tom *31:* 179
Walton, Garry *69:* 149
Walton, Tony *11:* 164; *24:* 209; *153:* 8; *177:* 73
Waltrip, Lela *9:* 195
Waltrip, Mildred *3:* 209; *37:* 211
Waltrip, Rufus *9:* 195
Wan *12:* 76
Wang, Suling *191:* 183
Warburton, Sarah *154:* 187
Wappers, G. *121:* 40
Ward, Fred *52:* 19
Ward, Helen *72:* 244; *144:* 240, 242
Ward, John *42:* 191; *96:* 54; *97:* 110; *123:* 105; *124:* 71; *173:* 66
Ward, Keith *2:* 107; *132:* 69
Ward, Leslie *34:* 126; *36:* 87
Ward, Lynd *1:* 99, 132, 133, 150; *2:* 108, 158, 196, 259; *18:* 86; *27:* 56; *29:* 79, 187, 253, 255; *36:* 199,200, 201, 202, 203, 204, 205, 206, 207, 209; *43:* 34; *56:* 28; *60:* 116; *100:* 65
Ward, Peter *37:* 116
Waring, Geoff *172:* 84
Warhola, James *92:* 5; *115:* 85, 87; *118:* 174, 175, 177; *176:* 84; *187:* 189, 190
Warner, Ben *159:* 171
Warner, Peter *14:* 87
Warnes, Tim *175:* 159
Warnick, Elsa *113:* 223
Warren, Betsy *2:* 101
Warren, Jim *85:* 81
Warren, Marion Cray *14:* 215
Warshaw, Jerry *30:* 197, 198; *42:* 165
Wasden, Kevin *102:* 162
Washington, Nevin *20:* 123
Washington, Phyllis *20:* 123
Wasserman, Amy L. *92:* 110
Waterman, Stan *11:* 76
Watkins-Pitchford, D.J. *6:* 215, 217
Watling, James *67:* 210; *78:* 112; *101:* 81; *117:* 189, 190; *127:* 119, 120
Watson, Aldren A. *2:* 267; *5:* 94; *13:* 71; *19:* 253; *32:* 220; *42:* 193, 194, 195, 196, 197, 198, 199, 200, 201; *YABC 2:* 202
Watson, G. *83:* 162

Watson, Gary *19:* 147; *36:* 68; *41:* 122; *47:* 139
Watson, J.D. *22:* 86
Watson, Karen *11:* 26
Watson, Mary *117:* 193
Watson, Richard Jesse *62:* 188, 189
Watson, Wendy *5:* 197; *13:* 101; *33:* 116; *46:* 163; *64:* 12; *74:* 242, 243; *91:* 21; *142:* 228
Watt, Mélanie *136:* 206; *193:* 211
Wattenberg, Jane *174:* 200; *185:* 46; *187:* 108
Watterson, Bill *66:* 223, 225, 226
Watts, Bernadette *4:* 227; *103:* 182, 183
Watts, James *59:* 197; *74:* 145; *86:* 124
Watts, John *37:* 149
Watts, Leslie Elizabeth *150:* 207; *165:* 106
Watts, Stan *116:* 205
Weatherby, Mark Alan *77:* 141
Webb, Jennifer *110:* 79
Webb, Lanny *142:* 175
Webb, Sophie *135:* 214
Webber, Helen *3:* 141
Webber, Irma E. *14:* 238
Weber, Erik *56:* 19, 20
Weber, Florence *40:* 153
Weber, Jill *127:* 227, 228; *189:* 163
Weber, Roland *61:* 204
Weber, Sam *190:* 227
Weber, William J. *14:* 239
Webster, Jean *17:* 241
Weeks, Sarah *162:* 39
Wegman, William *78:* 243
Wegner, Fritz *14:* 250; *20:* 189; *44:* 165; *86:* 62
Weidenear, Reynold H. *21:* 122
Weigel, Jeff *170:* 193
Weihs, Erika *4:* 21; *15:* 299; *72:* 201; *107:* 207, 208
Weil, Lisl *7:* 203; *10:* 58; *21:* 95; *22:* 188,217; *33:* 193
Weiman, Jon *50:* 162, 165; *52:* 103; *54:* 78, 79, 81; *78:* 80; *82:* 107; *93:* 82; *97:* 69; *105:* 179; *193:* 65
Weiner, Sandra *14:* 240
Weiner, Scott *55:* 27
Weinhaus, Karen Ann *53:* 90; *71:* 50; *86:* 124
Weisgard, Leonard *1:* 65; *2:* 191, 197, 204, 264, 265; *5:* 108; *21:* 42; *30:* 200, 201, 203, 204; *41:* 47; *44:* 125; *53:* 25; *85:* 196, 198, 200, 201; *100:* 139,207; *YABC 2:* 13
Weisman, David *173:* 47
Weiss, Ellen *44:* 202
Weiss, Emil *1:* 168; *7:* 60
Weiss, Harvey *1:* 145, 223; *27:* 224, 227; *68:* 214; *76:* 245, 246, 247
Weiss, Nicki *33:* 229
Weissman, Bari *49:* 72; *90:* 125; *139:* 142
Weitzman, David L. *172:* 199
Welch, Sheila Kelly *130:* 221
Welkes, Allen *68:* 218
Wellington, Monica *99:* 223; *157:* 259, 260, 261
Welliver, Norma *76:* 94
Wellner, Fred *127:* 53
Wells, Frances *1:* 183
Wells, H.G. *20:* 194, 200
Wells, Haru *53:* 120, 121
Wells, Robert E. *184:* 208
Wells, Rosemary *6:* 49; *18:* 297; *60:* 32; *66:* 203; *69:* 215, 216; *114:* 227; *118:* 149, 150; *156:* 188, 189, 190, 191
Wells, Rufus III *56:* 111, 113
Wells, Susan *22:* 43
Wendelin, Rudolph *23:* 234
Wengenroth, Stow *37:* 47
Weninger, Brigitte *189:* 192, 194
Werenskiold, Erik *15:* 6; *62:* 17
Werner, Honi *24:* 110; *33:* 41; *88:* 122
Werth, Kurt *7:* 122; *14:* 157; *20:* 214; *39:* 128
West, Harry A. *124:* 38

Westcott, Nadine Bernard *68:* 46; *84:* 49; *86:* 133; *106:* 199; *111:* 78; *113:* 111; *130:* 224; *139:* 54; *158:* 256; *194:* 199
Westerberg, Christine *29:* 226
Westerduin, Anne *105:* 229
Westerman, Johanna *162:* 206
Weston, Martha *29:* 116; *30:* 213; *33:* 85, 100; *53:* 181, 182, 183, 184; *77:* 95; *80:* 152; *119:* 196,197, 198, 199; *127:* 189; *133:* 196
Wetherbee, Margaret *5:* 3
Wexler, Jerome *49:* 73; *150:* 129
Whalley, Peter *50:* 49
Whatley, Bruce *186:* 93, 95
Wheatley, Arabelle *11:* 231; *16:* 276
Wheeler, Cindy *49:* 205
Wheeler, Dora *44:* 179
Wheelright, Rowland *15:* 81; *YABC 2:* 286
Whelan, Michael *56:* 108; *70:* 27, 29, 67, 68, 148; *74:* 18; *84:* 14; *91:* 195, 196; *95:* 147; *98:* 150, 151; *106:* 157; *113:* 218, 220; *116:* 99, 100
Whelan, Patrick *135:* 145
Whistler, Rex *16:* 75; *30:* 207, 208
White, Craig *110:* 130; *119:* 193; *130:* 33; *179:* 31
White, David Omar *5:* 56; *18:* 6
White, Joan *83:* 225
White, Martin *51:* 197; *85:* 127
Whitear *32:* 26
Whitehead, Beck *86:* 171
Whitehead, S.B. *154:* 132
Whithorne, H.S. *7:* 49
Whitney, George Gillett *3:* 24
Whitney, Jean *99:* 53
Whitson, Paul *102:* 161
Whittam, Geoffrey *30:* 191
Whyte, Mary *96:* 127
Wiberg, Harald *38:* 127; *93:* 215
Wick, Walter *77:* 128
Wickstrom, Sylvie *106:* 87; *169:* 180
Widener, Terry *105:* 230; *106:* 7; *163:* 23
Wiese, Kurt *3:* 255; *4:* 206; *14:* 17; *17:* 18, 19; *19:* 47; *24:* 152; *25:* 212; *32:* 184; *36:* 211,213, 214, 215, 216, 217, 218; *45:* 161; *100:* 92
Wiesner, David *33:* 47; *51:* 106; *57:* 67; *58:* 55; *64:* 78, 79, 81; *69:* 233; *72:* 247, 248, 249, 251,252, 253, 254; *83:* 134; *104:* 31; *117:* 197, 199, 200, 202; *139:* 223, 224; *151:* 51; *181:* 189, 190
Wiesner, William *4:* 100; *5:* 200, 201; *14:* 262
Wiggins, George *6:* 133
Wijngaard, Juan *111:* 36; *114:* 124
Wikkelsoe, Otto *45:* 25, 26
Wikland, Ilon *5:* 113; *8:* 150; *38:* 124, 125, 130; *127:* 162
Wikler, Madeline *114:* 233
Wilbur, C. Keith, M.D. *27:* 228
Wilburn, Kathy *53:* 102; *68:* 234
Wilcox, Cathy *105:* 123
Wilcox, J.A.J. *34:* 122
Wilcox, R. Turner *36:* 219
Wild, Jocelyn *46:* 220, 221, 222; *80:* 117
Wilde, George *7:* 139
Wildsmith, Brian *16:* 281, 282; *18:* 170, 171; *66:* 25; *69:* 224, 225, 227; *77:* 103; *83:* 218; *124:* 214,217, 219
Wildsmith, Mike *140:* 229
Wilhelm, Hans *58:* 189, 191; *73:* 157; *77:* 127; *135:* 229, 230, 233, 234
Wilkin, Eloise *36:* 173; *49:* 208, 209, 210
Wilkinson, Barry *50:* 213
Wilkinson, Gerald *3:* 40
Wilkon, Jozef *31:* 183, 184; *71:* 206, 207, 209; *133:* 222
Wilks, Mike *34:* 24; *44:* 203
Willems, Mo *154:* 245, 246, 247; *180:* 236, 237, 239
Willey, Bee *103:* 129; *139:* 159; *173:* 115
Willhoite, Michael A. *71:* 214
William, Maria *168:* 51

Williams, Berkeley, Jr. *64:* 75
Williams, Ferelith Eccles *22:* 238
Williams, Garth *1:* 197; *2:* 49, 270; *4:* 205; *15:* 198, 302, 304, 307; *16:* 34; *18:* 283, 298, 299, 300, 301; *29:* 177, 178, 179, 232, 233, 241, 242, 243, 244, 245, 248; *40:* 106; *66:* 229, 230, 231, 233, 234; *71:* 192; *73:* 218, 219, 220; *78:* 261; *100:* 251, 252, 255; *136:* 117; *YABC 2:* 15, 16, 19
Williams, J. Scott *48:* 28
Williams, Jennifer *102:* 201
Williams, Jenny *60:* 202; *81:* 21; *88:* 71
Williams, Kent *180:* 18
Williams, Kit *44:* 206, 207, 208, 209, 211, 212
Williams, Marcia *97:* 214; *159:* 208, 209
Williams, Maureen *12:* 238
Williams, Patrick *14:* 218
Williams, Richard *44:* 93; *72:* 229; *74:* 133; *78:* 155, 237; *91:* 178; *110:* 212; *136:* 201, 202, 203; *152:* 115
Williams, Sam *124:* 222; *153:* 11; *177:* 201, 202; *180:* 34
Williams, Sophy *135:* 236
Williams, Vera B. *53:* 186, 187, 188, 189; *102:* 201, 202, 203
Williamson, Alex *177:* 180
Williamson, Mel *60:* 9
Willingham, Fred *104:* 206; *154:* 157
Willis, Adam *181:* 75
Willmore, J.T. *54:* 113, 114
Wilsdorf, Anne *180:* 122; *189:* 124; *191:* 195
Wilson, Anne *160:* 114
Wilson, Charles Banks *17:* 92; *43:* 73
Wilson, Connie *113:* 179
Wilson, Dagmar *10:* 47
Wilson, Dawn *67:* 161; *81:* 120; *113:* 158
Wilson, Edward A. *6:* 24; *16:* 149; *20:* 220, 221; *22:* 87; *26:* 67; *38:* 212, 214, 215, 216, 217
Wilson, Forrest *27:* 231
Wilson, Gahan *35:* 234; *41:* 136
Wilson, George *76:* 87
Wilson, Helen Miranda *140:* 61
Wilson, Jack *17:* 139
Wilson, Janet *77:* 154; *96:* 114; *99:* 219, 220; *153:* 64 *106:* 122; *130:* 210; *145:* 178; *173:* 64
Wilson, John *22:* 240
Wilson, Maurice *46:* 224
Wilson, Patten *35:* 61
Wilson, Peggy *15:* 4; *84:* 20
Wilson, Phil *181:* 29
Wilson, Rowland B. *30:* 170
Wilson, Sarah *50:* 215
Wilson, Tom *33:* 232
Wilson, W.N. *22:* 26
Wilson-Max, Ken *170:* 196; *180:* 181
Wilton, Nicholas *103:* 52; *183:* 111
Wilwerding, Walter J. *9:* 202
Wimmer, Mike *63:* 6; *70:* 121; *75:* 186; *76:* 21,22, 23; *91:* 114; *97:* 45, 68; *98:* 28; *107:* 130; *146:* 21; *149:* 47; *173:* 126; *193:* 21, 25; *194:* 204, 205
Winborn, Marsha *78:* 34; *99:* 70; *192:* 20
Winch, John *165:* 233
Winchester, Linda *13:* 231
Wind, Betty *28:* 158
Windham, Kathryn Tucker *14:* 260
Windham, Sophie *184:* 212
Winfield, Alison *115:* 78
Winfield, Wayne *72:* 23
Wing, Gary *64:* 147
Wing, Ron *50:* 85
Wingerter, Linda S. *132:* 199; *174:* 181
Winick, Judd *124:* 227, 228, 229
Winslow, Will *21:* 124
Winstead, Rosie *180:* 243
Winsten, Melanie Willa *41:* 41
Winter, Jeanette *151:* 240, 241, 242; *184:* 215, 217, 218, 219

Winter, Milo *15:* 97; *19:* 221; *21:* 181, 203, 204, 205; *64:* 19; *YABC 2:* 144
Winter, Paula *48:* 227
Winter, Susan *163:* 177; *182:* 201
Winters, Greg *70:* 117
Winters, Nina *62:* 194
Wise, Louis *13:* 68
Wiseman, Ann *31:* 187
Wiseman, B. *4:* 233
Wishnefsky, Phillip *3:* 14
Wiskur, Darrell *5:* 72; *10:* 50; *18:* 246
Wisniewski, David *95:* 220, 221
Wisniewski, Robert *95:* 10; *119:* 192
Witschonke, Alan *153:* 149, 150
Witt, Dick *80:* 244
Wittmann, Patrick *162:* 204
Wittman, Sally *30:* 219
Wittner, Dale *99:* 43
Wittwer, Hala *158:* 267; *195:* 80
Woehr, Lois *12:* 5
Wohlberg, Meg *12:* 100; *14:* 197; *41:* 255
Wohnoutka, Mike *137:* 68; *190:* 199; *195:* 218
Wojtowycz, David *167:* 168
Woldin, Beth Weiner *34:* 211
Wolf, Elizabeth *133:* 151
Wolf, J. *16:* 91
Wolf, Janet *78:* 254
Wolf, Linda *33:* 163
Wolfe, Corey *72:* 213
Wolff, Ashley *50:* 217; *81:* 216; *156:* 216, 217; *170:* 57; *174:* 174; *184:* 72
Wolff, Glenn *178:* 230
Wolfsgruber, Linda *166:* 61
Wondriska, William *6:* 220
Wong, Janet S. *98:* 225; *152:* 43
Wong, Nicole *174:* 13
Wonsetler, John C. *5:* 168
Wood, Audrey *50:* 221, 222, 223; *81:* 219, 221
Wood, Don *50:* 220, 225, 226, 228, 229; *81:* 218, 220; *139:* 239, 240
Wood, Grant *19:* 198
Wood, Heather *133:* 108
Wood, Ivor *58:* 17
Wood, Muriel *36:* 119; *77:* 167; *171:* 55; *187:* 46
Wood, Myron *6:* 220
Wood, Owen *18:* 187; *64:* 202, 204, 205, 206, 208, 210
Wood, Rob *193:* 48
Wood, Ruth *8:* 11
Woodbridge, Curtis *133:* 138
Wooding, Sharon L. *66:* 237
Woodruff, Liza *132:* 239; *182:* 46, 204
Woodruff, Thomas *171:* 73
Woods, John, Jr. *109:* 142
Woodson, Jack *10:* 201
Woodson, Jacqueline *94:* 242
Woodward, Alice *26:* 89; *36:* 81
Wool, David *26:* 27
Woolley, Janet *112:* 75
Woolman, Steven *106:* 47; *163:* 73
Wooten, Vernon *23:* 70; *51:* 170
Worboys, Evelyn *1:* 166, 167
Word, Reagan *103:* 204
Wormell, Christopher *154:* 251
Worth, Jo *34:* 143
Worth, Wendy *4:* 133
Wosmek, Frances *29:* 251
Wrenn, Charles L. *38:* 96; *YABC 1:* 20, 21
Wright, Barbara Mullarney *98:* 161
Wright, Cliff *168:* 203
Wright, Dare *21:* 206
Wright-Frierson, Virginia *58:* 194; *110:* 246
Wright, George *YABC 1:* 268
Wright, Joseph *30:* 160
Wronker, Lili Cassel *3:* 247; *10:* 204; *21:* 10
Wummer, Amy *154:* 181; *168:* 150; *176:* 85
Wyant, Alexander Helwig *110:* 19
Wyatt, David *97:* 9; *101:* 44; *114:* 194; *140:* 20; *167:* 13; *188:* 48
Wyatt, Stanley *46:* 210

Wyeth, Andrew *13:* 40; *YABC 1:* 133, 134
Wyeth, Jamie *41:* 257
Wyeth, N.C. *13:* 41; *17:* 252, 253, 254, 255, 256, 257, 258, 259, 264, 265, 266, 267, 268; *18:* 181; *19:* 80, 191, 200; *21:* 57, 183; *22:* 91; *23:* 152; *24:* 28, 99; *35:* 61; *41:* 65; *100:* 206; *YABC1:* 133, 223; *2:* 53, 75, 171, 187, 317
Wyman, Cherie R. *91:* 42

X

Xuan, YongSheng *119:* 202, 207, 208; *140:* 36; *187:* 21

Y

Yaccarino, Dan *141:* 208, 209; *147:* 171; *192:* 244, 245
Yakovetic, Joe *59:* 202; *75:* 85
Yalowitz, Paul *93:* 33
Yamaguchi, Marianne *85:* 118
Yamasaki, James *167:* 93
Yang, Belle *170:* 198
Yang, Jay *1:* 8; *12:* 239
Yap, Weda *6:* 176
Yaroslava
    See Mills, Yaroslava Surmach
Yashima, Taro *14:* 84
Yates, John *74:* 249, 250
Yayo *178:* 88
Yee, Cora *166:* 233
Yee, Wong Herbert *115:* 216, 217; *172:* 204, 205; *194:* 59
Yeo, Brad *135:* 121; *192:* 106
Yerxa, Leo *181:* 195
Yezerski, Thomas F. *162:* 29
Ylla
    See Koffler, Camilla
Yohn, F.C. *23:* 128; *YABC 1:* 269
Yoo, Taeeun *191:* 198
Yorinks, Adrienne *144:* 248
Yorke, David *80:* 178
Yoshida, Toshi *77:* 231
Yoshikawa, Sachiko *168:* 104; *177:* 28; *181:* 196, 197
Youll, Paul *91:* 218
Youll, Stephen *92:* 227; *118:* 136, 137; *164:* 248
Young, Amy L. *185:* 218; *190:* 46
Young, Cybéle *167:* 9
Young, Ed *7:* 205; *10:* 206; *40:* 124; *63:* 142; *74:* 250, 251, 252, 253; *75:* 227; *81:* 159; *83:* 98; *94:* 154; *115:* 160; *137:* 162; *YABC 2:* 242; *173:* 174, 175, 176
Young, Mary O'Keefe *77:* 95; *80:* 247; *134:* 214; *140:* 213
Young, Noela *8:* 221; *89:* 231; *97:* 195
Young, Paul *190:* 222
Young, Selina *153:* 12
Yun, Cheng Mung *60:* 143

Z

Zacharow, Christopher *88:* 98
Zacks, Lewis *10:* 161
Zadig *50:* 58
Zaffo, George *42:* 208
Zagwyn, Deborah Turney *138:* 227
Zahares, Wade *193:* 219
Zaid, Barry *50:* 127; *51:* 201
Zaidenberg, Arthur *34:* 218, 219, 220
Zalben, Jane Breskin *7:* 211; *79:* 230, 231, 233; *170:* 202

Zallinger, Jean *4:* 192; *8:* 8, 129; *14:* 273; *68:* 36; *80:* 254; *115:* 219, 220, 222
Zallinger, Rudolph F. *3:* 245
Zakrajsek, Molly *177:* 146
Zappa, Ahmet *180:* 250
Zebot, George *83:* 214
Zeck, Gerry *40:* 232
Zeff, Joe *181:* 98
Zeifert, Harriet *154:* 265, 267
Zeiring, Bob *42:* 130
Zeldich, Arieh *49:* 124; *62:* 120
Zeldis, Malcah *86:* 239; *94:* 198; *146:* 265, 266
Zelinsky, Paul O. *14:* 269; *43:* 56; *49:* 218-223; *53:* 111; *68:* 195; *102:* 219, 222, 221, 222; *154:* 255, 256, 257; *171:* 141; *185:* 96
Zelvin, Diana *72:* 190; *76:* 101; *93:* 207
Zemach, Kaethe *149:* 250

Zemach, Margot *3:* 270; *8:* 201; *21:* 210, 211; *27:* 204, 205, 210; *28:* 185; *49:* 22, 183, 224; *53:* 151; *56:* 146; *70:* 245, 246; *92:* 74
Zeman, Ludmila *153* 212
Zemsky, Jessica *10:* 62
Zepelinsky, Paul *35:* 93
Zerbetz, Evon *127:* 34; *158:* 109
Zhang, Ange *101:* 190; *172:* 41
Zhang, Son Nang *163:* 113; *170:* 206
Ziegler, Jack *84:* 134
Zimdars, Berta *129:* 155
Zimet, Jay *147:* 94; *152:* 74
Zimic, Tricia *72:* 95
Zimmer, Dirk *38:* 195; *49:* 71; *56:* 151; *65:* 214; *84:* 159; *89:* 26; *147:* 224
Zimmer, Tracie Vaughn *169:* 183
Zimmerman, Andrea *192:* 49, 50
Zimmermann, H. Werner *101:* 223; *112:* 197
Zimnik, Reiner *36:* 224

Zingone, Robin *180:* 134
Zinkeisen, Anna *13:* 106
Zinn, David *97:* 97
Zoellick, Scott *33:* 231
Zollars, Jaime *190:* 190
Zonia, Dhimitri *20:* 234, 235
Zorn, Peter A., Jr. *142:* 157
Zudeck, Darryl *58:* 129; *63:* 98; *80:* 52
Zug, Mark *88:* 131
Zulewski, Tim *164:* 95
Zuma *99:* 36
Zvorykin, Boris *61:* 155
Zweifel, Francis *14:* 274; *28:* 187
Zwerger, Lisbeth *54:* 176, 178; *66:* 246, 247, 248; *130:* 230, 231, 232, 233; *181:* 92; *194:* 224, 225, 226
Zwinger, Herman H. *46:* 227
Zwolak, Paul *67:* 69, 71, 73, 74

Author Index

The following index gives the number of the volume in which an author's biographical sketch, Autobiography Feature, Brief Entry, or Obituary appears.

This index includes references to all entries in the following series, which are also published by The Gale Group.

YABC—*Yesterday's Authors of Books for Children: Facts and Pictures about Authors and Illustrators of Books for Young People from Early Times to 1960*

CLR—*Children's Literature Review: Excerpts from Reviews, Criticism, and Commentary on Books for Children*

SAAS—*Something about the Author Autobiography Series*

A

Aaron, Chester 1923- *74*
  Earlier sketch in SATA *9*
  See also SAAS *12*
Aaseng, Nate
  See Aaseng, Nathan
Aaseng, Nathan 1953- *172*
  Brief entry *38*
  Earlier sketches in SATA *51, 88*
  See also CLR *54*
  See also SAAS *12*
Abadzis, Nick 1965- *193*
Abbas, Jailan 1952- *91*
Abbey, Lynn
  See Abbey, Marilyn Lorraine
Abbey, Marilyn Lorraine 1948- *156*
Abbott, Alice
  See Borland, Kathryn Kilby
  and Speicher, Helen Ross S(mith)
Abbott, Jacob 1803-1879 .... *22*
Abbott, Manager Henry
  See Stratemeyer, Edward L.
Abbott, R(obert) Tucker 1919-1995 .... *61*
  Obituary *87*
Abbott, Sarah
  See Zolotow, Charlotte
Abbott, Tony 1952- *159*
Abdelsayed, Cindy 1962- *123*
Abdul, Raoul 1929- *12*
Abel, Raymond 1911- *12*
Abell, Kathleen 1938- *9*
Abelove, Joan *110*
Abels, Harriette S(heffer) 1926- *50*
Abercrombie, Barbara 1939- *182*
  Earlier sketch in SATA *16*
Abercrombie, Barbara Mattes
  See Abercrombie, Barbara
Abercrombie, Lynn
  See Sorrells, Walter
Abernethy, Robert G(ordon) 1927- *5*
Abisch, Roslyn Kroop 1927- *9*
Abisch, Roz
  See Abisch, Roslyn Kroop
Abodaher, David J. (Naiph) 1919- *17*
Abolafia, Yossi 1944-
  See Abulafia, Yossi
Abouzeid, Chris *175*

Abrahall, Clare Hoskyns
  See Hoskyns-Abrahall, Clare (Constance Drury)
Abrahams, Hilary (Ruth) 1938- *29*
Abrahams, Peter 1947- *194*
Abrahams, Robert David 1905-1998 .... *4*
Abrams, Joy 1941- *16*
Abrams, Lawrence F. *58*
  Brief entry *47*
Abrashkin, Raymond 1911-1960 .... *50*
Abulafia, Yossi 1944- *177*
  Brief entry *46*
  Earlier sketch in SATA *60*
Acampora, Paul *175*
Accardo, Anthony *191*
Achebe, Albert Chinualumogu
  See Achebe, Chinua
Achebe, Chinua 1930- *40*
  Brief entry *38*
  Earlier sketch in SATA *38*
  See also CLR *20*
Ackerman, Diane 1948- *102*
Ackerman, Eugene (Francis) 1888-1974 ...... *10*
Ackerman, Karen 1951- *126*
Ackerman, Susan Yoder 1945- *92*
Ackison, Wendy Wassink 1956- *103*
Ackley, Peggy Jo 1955- *58*
Ackroyd, Peter 1949- *153*
Acorn, John (Harrison) 1958- *79*
Acredolo, Linda (Potter) 1947- *159*
Acs, Laszlo (Bela) 1931- *42*
  Brief entry *32*
Acuff, Selma Boyd 1924- *45*
Ada, Alma Flor 1938- *181*
  Earlier sketches in SATA *43, 84, 143*
  See also CLR *62*
Adair, Gilbert 1944- *98*
Adair, Ian 1942- *53*
Adair, Margaret Weeks (?)-1971 .... *10*
Adam, Cornel
  See Lengyel, Cornel Adam
Adam, Mark
  See Alexander, Marc
Adam, Robert 1948- *93*
Adams, Adrienne 1906- *90*
  Earlier sketch in SATA *8*
  See also CLR *73*
Adams, Andy 1859-1935
  See YABC *1*

Adams, Barbara Johnston 1943- *60*
Adams, Bruin
  See Ellis, Edward S(ylvester)
Adams, Captain Bruin
  See Ellis, Edward S(ylvester)
Adams, Captain J. F. C.
  See Ellis, Edward S(ylvester)
Adams, Dale
  See Quinn, Elisabeth
Adams, Daniel
  See Nicole, Christopher (Robin)
Adams, Debra
  See Speregen, Devra Newberger
Adams, Douglas 1952-2001 .... *116*
  Obituary *128*
Adams, Douglas Noel
  See Adams, Douglas
Adams, Edith
  See Shine, Deborah
Adams, Florence 1932- *61*
Adams, Harriet S(tratemeyer) 1892(?)-1982 .. *1*
  Obituary *29*
Adams, Harrison
  See Rathborne, St. George (Henry)
  and Stratemeyer, Edward L.
Adams, Hazard 1926- *6*
Adams, Hazard Simeon
  See Adams, Hazard
Adams, John Anthony 1944- *67*
Adams, Laurie 1941- *33*
Adams, Lowell
  See Joseph, James (Herz)
Adams, Nicholas
  See Pine, Nicholas
Adams, Nicholas
  See Smith, Sherwood
Adams, Nicholas
  See Doyle, Debra
  and Macdonald, James D.
Adams, Pam 1919- *112*
Adams, Pamela
  See Adams, Pam
Adams, Richard (George) 1920- *69*
  Earlier sketch in SATA *7*
  See also CLR *121*
Adams, Ruth Joyce *14*
Adams, Tricia
  See Kite, Pat
Adams, William Taylor 1822-1897 .... *28*

Adam Smith, Janet (Buchanan) 1905-1999 .. *63*
Adamson, Gareth 1925-1982(?) *46*
   Obituary *30*
Adamson, George 1906-1989
   Obituary *63*
Adamson, George (Worsley) 1913-2005 ...... *30*
Adamson, Graham
   See Groom, Arthur William
Adamson, Joy(-Friederike Victoria)
   1910-1980 .... *11*
   Obituary *22*
Adamson, Wendy Writson 1942- *22*
Addison, Kenneth 1949(?)-2005 .... *187*
Addison, Kenneth L.
   See Addison, Kenneth
Addona, Angelo F. 1925- *14*
Addy, Sharon Hart 1943- *192*
   Earlier sketch in SATA *108*
Addy, Ted
   See Winterbotham, R(ussell) R(obert)
Adelberg, Doris
   See Orgel, Doris
Adelson, Leone 1908- *11*
Adinolfi, JoAnn *176*
Adkins, Jan 1944- *144*
   Earlier sketches in SATA *8, 69*
   See also CLR *77*
   See also SAAS *19*
Adler, C(arole) S(chwerdtfeger) 1932- *126*
   Earlier sketches in SATA *26, 63, 102*
   See also CLR *78*
   See also SAAS *15*
Adler, David A. 1947- *178*
   Earlier sketches in SATA *14, 70, 106, 151*
   See also CLR *108*
Adler, Irene
   See Penzler, Otto
   and Storr, Catherine (Cole)
Adler, Irving 1913- *29*
   Autobiography Feature *164*
   Earlier sketch in SATA *1*
   See also CLR *27*
   See also SAAS *15*
Adler, Larry 1939- *36*
Adler, Peggy *22*
Adler, Ruth 1915-1968 .... *1*
Adlerman, Daniel (Ezra) 1963- *163*
   Earlier sketch in SATA *96*
Adlerman, Kim
   See Adlerman, Kimberly M(arie)
Adlerman, Kimberly M(arie) 1964- *163*
   Earlier sketch in SATA *96*
Adoff, Arnold 1935- *96*
   Earlier sketches in SATA *5, 57*
   See also CLR *7*
   See also SAAS *15*
Adoff, Jaime (Levi) *163*
Adorjan, Carol (Madden) 1934- *71*
   Earlier sketch in SATA *10*
Adrian, Frances
   See Polland, Madeleine A(ngela Cahill)
Adrian, Mary
   See Jorgensen, Mary Venn
Adshead, Gladys L(ucy) 1896-1985 .... *3*
Aesop 620(?)B.C.-560(?)B.C. *64*
   See also CLR *14*
Aesop, Abraham
   See Newbery, John
Affabee, Eric
   See Stine, R.L.
Agapida, Fray Antonio
   See Irving, Washington
Agard, John 1949- *138*
Agard, Nadema 1948- *18*
Agarwal, Deepa 1947- *141*
Agee, Jon 1960- *157*
   Earlier sketch in SATA *116*
Agell, Charlotte 1959- *150*
   Earlier sketch in SATA *99*
Agent Orange
   See Moseley, James W(illett)

Aghill, Gordon
   See Garrett, (Gordon) Randall (Phillip)
   and Silverberg, Robert
Agle, Nan Hayden 1905- *3*
   See also SAAS *10*
Agnew, Edith J(osephine) 1897-1988 .... *11*
Agonito, Joseph *177*
Agonito, Rosemary 1937- *177*
Ahern, Margaret McCrohan 1921- *10*
Ahl, Anna Maria 1926- *32*
Ahlberg, Allan 1938- *165*
   Brief entry *35*
   Earlier sketches in SATA *68, 120*
   See also CLR *18*
Ahlberg, Janet 1944-1994 .... *120*
   Brief entry *32*
   Obituary *83*
   Earlier sketch in SATA *68*
   See also CLR *18*
Aichinger, Helga 1937- *4*
Aiken, Clarissa (M.) Lorenz 1899-1992 ...... *12*
   Obituary *109*
Aiken, Conrad (Potter) 1889-1973 .... *30*
   Earlier sketch in SATA *3*
Aiken, Joan (Delano) 1924-2004 .... *73*
   Autobiography Feature *109*
   Obituary *152*
   Earlier sketches in SATA *2, 30*
   See also CLR *90*
   See also SAAS *1*
Aillaud, Cindy Lou 1955- *184*
Ainsley, Alix
   See Steiner, Barbara A(nnette)
Ainsworth, Catherine Harris 1910- *56*
Ainsworth, Norma 1911-1987 .... *9*
Ainsworth, Ruth (Gallard) 1908- *73*
   Earlier sketch in SATA *7*
Ainsworth, William Harrison 1805-1882 ..... *24*
Aistrop, Jack 1916- *14*
Aitken, Amy 1952- *54*
   Brief entry *40*
Aitken, Dorothy 1916- *10*
Aitmatov, Chingiz 1928-2008 .... *56*
   See Aytmatov, Chingiz
Aitmatov, Chingiz Torekulovich
   See Aitmatov, Chingiz
Akaba, Suekichi 1910- *46*
Akers, Floyd
   See Baum, L(yman) Frank
Akib, Jamel *181*
Aks, Patricia 1926-1994 .... *68*
Alagoa, Ebiegberi Joe 1933- *108*
Alain
   See Brustlein, Daniel
Alajalov, Constantin 1900-1987
   Obituary *53*
Alan, David
   See Horsfield, Alan
Alan, Robert
   See Silverstein, Robert Alan
Alarcon, Francisco X(avier) 1954- *104*
Albert, Burton 1936- *22*
Albert, Louise 1928- *157*
Albert, Richard E. 1909-1999 .... *82*
Albert, Susan Wittig 1940- *107*
Alberts, Frances Jacobs 1907-1989 .... *14*
Albertson, Susan
   See Wojciechowski, Susan
Albion, Lee Smith *29*
Alborough, Jez 1959- *149*
   Earlier sketch in SATA *86*
Albrecht, Lillie (Vanderveer H.)
   1894-1985 .... *12*
Albyn, Carole Lisa 1955- *83*
Alchemy, Jack
   See Gershator, David
Alcock, Gudrun 1908- *56*
   Brief entry *33*

Alcock, Vivien (Dolores) 1924-2003 .... *76*
   Brief entry *38*
   Obituary *148*
   Earlier sketch in SATA *45*
   See also CLR *26*
Alcorn, John 1935- *31*
   Brief entry *30*
Alcorn, Stephen 1958- *110*
Alcott, Louisa May 1832-1888 .... *100*
   See also YABC *1*
   See also CLR *109*
Alda, Arlene 1933- *158*
   Brief entry *36*
   Earlier sketches in SATA *44, 106*
   See also CLR *93*
Alden, Isabella (Macdonald) 1841-1930 ..... *115*
   See also YABC *2*
Alden, Sue
   See Francis, Dorothy
Alderman, Clifford Lindsey 1902-1988 .... *3*
Alderson, Sue Ann 1940- *59*
   Brief entry *48*
Alding, Peter
   See Jeffries, Roderic
Aldis, Dorothy (Keeley) 1896-1966 .... *2*
Aldiss, Brian W. 1925- *34*
Aldiss, Brian Wilson
   See Aldiss, Brian W.
Aldon, Adair
   See Meigs, Cornelia Lynde
Aldous, Allan (Charles) 1911- *27*
Aldrich, Ann
   See Meaker, Marijane
Aldrich, Bess Streeter 1881-1954
   See CLR *70*
Aldrich, Thomas (Bailey) 1836-1907 .... *114*
   Earlier sketch in SATA *17*
Aldridge, (Harold Edward) James 1918- *87*
Aldridge, Josephine Haskell *14*
Aldridge, Sheila 1974- *192*
Aleas, Richard
   See Appelt, Kathi
Alegria, Malin 1974(?)- *190*
Alegria, Ricardo E(nrique) 1921- *6*
Aleksin, Anatolii Georgievich 1924- *36*
Alenov, Lydia 1948- *61*
Alex, Ben (a pseudonym) 1946- *45*
Alex, Marlee (a pseudonym) 1948- *45*
Alexander, Anna B(arbara Cooke) 1913- *1*
Alexander, Anne
   See Alexander, Anna B(arbara Cooke)
Alexander, Ellen 1938- *91*
Alexander, Frances (Laura) 1888-1979 .... *4*
Alexander, Jocelyn Anne Arundel 1930- *22*
Alexander, Linda 1935- *2*
Alexander, Lloyd 1924-2007 .... *135*
   Obituary *182*
   Earlier sketches in SATA *3, 49, 81, 129*
   See also CLR *48*
   See also SAAS *19*
Alexander, Lloyd Chudley
   See Alexander, Lloyd
Alexander, Marc 1929- *117*
Alexander, Martha 1920- *136*
   Earlier sketches in SATA *11, 70*
Alexander, Rae Pace
   See Alexander, Raymond Pace
Alexander, Raymond Pace 1898-1974 .... *22*
Alexander, Rod
   See Pellowski, Michael (Joseph)
Alexander, Sally Hobart 1943- *84*
Alexander, Sue 1933-2008 .... *136*
   Obituary *195*
   Earlier sketches in SATA *12, 89*
   See also SAAS *15*
Alexander, Vincent Arthur 1925-1980
   Obituary *23*
Alexeieff, Alexandre A. 1901-1979 .... *14*
Alger, Horatio, Jr.
   See Stratemeyer, Edward L.

Alger, Horatio, Jr. 1832-1899 16
    See also CLR 87
Alger, Leclaire (Gowans) 1898-1969 15
Aliki
    See CLR 71
    See Brandenberg, Aliki (Liacouras)
Alkema, Chester Jay 1932- 12
Al-Khalili, Jim 1962- 124
Alkiviades, Alkis 1953- 105
Alkouatli, Claire 186
Allaby, John Michael
    See Allaby, Michael
Allaby, Michael 1933- 167
Allamand, Pascale 1942- 12
Allan, Mabel Esther 1915-1998 75
    Earlier sketches in SATA 5, 32
    See also CLR 43
    See also SAAS 11
Allan, Nicholas 1956- 123
    Earlier sketch in SATA 79
Allan-Meyer, Kathleen 1918- 51
    Brief entry 46
Allard, Harry
    See Allard, Harry G(rover), Jr.
Allard, Harry G(rover), Jr. 1928- 102
    Earlier sketch in SATA 42
    See also CLR 85
Allee, Marjorie Hill 1890-1945 17
Allen, Adam
    See Epstein, Beryl (M. Williams)
    and Epstein, Samuel
Allen, Alex B.
    See Heide, Florence Parry
Allen, Allyn
    See Eberle, Irmengarde
Allen, Betsy
    See Harrison, Elizabeth (Allen) Cavanna
Allen, Bob 1961- 76
Allen, Gertrude E(lizabeth) 1888-1984 9
Allen, Grace
    See Hogarth, Grace (Weston Allen)
Allen, Jeffrey (Yale) 1948- 42
Allen, John
    See Perry, Ritchie (John Allen)
Allen, Jonathan 1957- 177
    Earlier sketch in SATA 131
Allen, Jonathan Dean
    See Allen, Jonathan
Allen, Judy (Christina) 1941- 124
    Earlier sketch in SATA 80
Allen, Kenneth S. 1913-1981 56
Allen, Leroy 1912- 11
Allen, Linda 1925- 33
Allen, Marjorie 1931- 22
Allen, Maury 1932- 26
Allen, Merritt Parmelee 1892-1954 22
Allen, Nancy Kelly 1949- 171
    Earlier sketch in SATA 127
Allen, Nina (Stroemgren) 1935- 22
Allen, Pamela (Kay) 1934- 123
    Earlier sketches in SATA 50, 81
    See also CLR 44
Allen, Rodney F. 1938-1999 27
Allen, Roger MacBride 1957- 105
Allen, Ruth
    See Peterson, Esther (Allen)
Allen, Samuel W(ashington) 1917- 9
Allen, T. D.
    See Allen, Terril Diener
Allen, Terril Diener 1908- 35
    See Allen, T. D.
Allen, Terry D.
    See Allen, Terril Diener
Allen, Thomas B. 1929- 193
    Earlier sketches in SATA 45, 140
Allen, Thomas B. 1929- 193
Allen, Thomas Benton
    See Allen, Thomas B.
Allen, Tom
    See Allen, Thomas B.

Allende, Isabel 1942- 163
    See also CLR 99
Allerton, Mary
    See Govan, (Mary) Christine Noble
Alley, Robert W.
    See Alley, R.W.
Alley, R.W. 169
Alleyn, Ellen
    See Rossetti, Christina
Allington, Richard L(loyd) 1947- 39
    Brief entry 35
Allison, Amy 1956- 138
Allison, Bob 14
Allison, Diane Worfolk 78
Allison, Jennifer 173
Allison, Linda 1948- 43
Allison, Margaret
    See Klam, Cheryl
Allman, Barbara 1950- 137
Allmendinger, David F(rederick), Jr. 1938- . 35
Allred, Alexandra Powe 1965- 144
Allred, Gordon T(hatcher) 1930- 10
Allsop, Kenneth 1920-1973 17
Allsopp, Sophie 188
Almedingen, E. M. 3
    See Almedingen, Martha Edith von
Almon, Russell
    See Clevenger, William R.
    and Downing, David A(lmon)
Almond, David 1951- 158
    Earlier sketch in SATA 114
    See also CLR 85
Almond, Linda Stevens 1881(?)-1987
    Obituary 50
Almquist, Don 1929- 11
Alphin, Elaine Marie 1955- 139
    Autobiography Feature 139
    Earlier sketches in SATA 80, 130
Alsenas, Linas 1979- 186
Alsop, Mary O'Hara 1885-1980 34
    Obituary 24
    Earlier sketch in SATA 2
    See O'Hara, Mary
Alter, Anna 1974- 135
Alter, Judith (MacBain) 1938- 101
    Earlier sketch in SATA 52
Alter, Judy
    See Alter, Judith (MacBain)
Alter, Robert Edmond 1925-1965 9
Alter, Stephen 1956- 187
Althea
    See Braithwaite, Althea
Altman, Linda Jacobs 1943- 21
Altman, Suzanne
    See Orgel, Doris
    and Schecter, Ellen
Alton, Steve 169
Altschuler, Franz 1923- 45
Altsheler, Joseph A(lexander) 1862-1919
    See YABC 1
Alvarez, John
    See del Rey, Lester
Alvarez, Joseph A. 1930- 18
Alvarez, Julia 1950- 129
al-Windawi, Thura
    See Windawi, Thura al-
Alyer, Philip A.
    See Stratemeyer, Edward L.
Amado, Elisa 193
Amann, Janet 1951- 79
Amato, Carol A. 1942- 92
Amato, Mary 1961- 178
    Earlier sketch in SATA 140
Ambrose, Stephen E. 1936-2002 138
    Earlier sketch in SATA 40
Ambrose, Stephen Edward
    See Ambrose, Stephen E.
Ambrus, Gyozo Laszlo 1935- 41
    See Ambrus, Victor G.

Ambrus, Victor G. 1
    See also SAAS 4
    See Ambrus, Gyozo Laszlo
Amend, Bill 1962- 147
Amerman, Lockhart 1911-1969 3
Ames, Evelyn 1908-1990 13
    Obituary 64
Ames, Gerald 1906-1993 11
    Obituary 74
Ames, Lee J(udah) 1921- 151
    Earlier sketch in SATA 3
Ames, Mildred 1919-1994 85
    Earlier sketches in SATA 22, 81
Amico, Tom 1960(?)- 176
Ammon, Richard 1942- 124
Amon, Aline 1928- 9
Amoss, Berthe 1925- 112
    Earlier sketch in SATA 5
Anastasio, Dina 1941- 94
    Brief entry 30
    Earlier sketch in SATA 37
Anaya, Rudolfo A. 1937-
    See CLR 129
Anaya, Rudolpho Alfonso
    See Anaya, Rudolfo A.
Anckarsvard, Karin Inez Maria 1915-1969 6
Ancona, George 1929- 192
    Earlier sketches in SATA 12, 85, 145
    See also SAAS 18
Anders, C. J.
    See Bennett, Cherie
Anders, Isabel 1946- 101
Anders, Lou 176
Andersdatter, Karla M(argaret) 1938- 34
Andersen, Bethanne 1954- 191
Andersen, Hans Christian 1805-1875 100
    See also YABC 1
    See also CLR 113
Andersen, Ted
    See Boyd, Waldo T.
Andersen, Yvonne 1932- 27
Anderson, Bernice G(oudy) 1894-1997 33
Anderson, Bob 1944- 139
    Earlier sketch in SATA 136
Anderson, Brad(ley Jay) 1924- 33
    Brief entry 31
Anderson, C. C.
    See Anderson, Catherine Corley
Anderson, C(larence) W(illiam) 1891-1971 . 11
Anderson, Catherine C.
    See Anderson, Catherine Corley
Anderson, Catherine Corley 1909-2001 72
Anderson, Clifford
    See Gardner, Richard (M.)
Anderson, Daryl Shon 1963- 93
Anderson, Dave
    See Anderson, David (Poole)
Anderson, David (Poole) 1929- 60
Anderson, Derek 1969- 169
Anderson, Eloise Adell 1927- 9
Anderson, George
    See Groom, Arthur William
Anderson, Grace Fox 1932- 43
Anderson, J(ohn) R(ichard) L(ane)
    1911-1981 15
    Obituary 27
Anderson, Jodi Lynn 182
Anderson, Joy 1928- 1
Anderson, Kevin J. 1962- 117
    Earlier sketch in SATA 74
Anderson, Kevin James
    See Anderson, Kevin J.
Anderson, Kirsty 1978- 108
Anderson, K.J.
    See Moesta, Rebecca
Anderson, Laurie Halse 1961- 186
    Earlier sketches in SATA 95, 132
    See also CLR 138
Anderson, LaVere Francis Shoenfelt
    1907-1998 27

Anderson, Leone Castell 1923- *53*
  Brief entry *49*
Anderson, Lisa G. 1963- *108*
Anderson, Lonzo *2*
  See Anderson, John L(onzo)
Anderson, Lucia (Lewis) 1922- *10*
Anderson, Madelyn Klein 1926-2005 .... *28*
Anderson, Margaret J(ean) 1931- *27*
  See also SAAS 8
Anderson, Marilyn D. 1943- *144*
Anderson, Mary 1939- *82*
  Earlier sketch in SATA 7
  See also SAAS 23
Anderson, Matthew Tobin
  See Anderson, M.T.
Anderson, Mona 1910-2004 .... *40*
Anderson, Mrs. Melvin
  See Anderson, Catherine Corley
Anderson, M.T. 1968- *182*
  Earlier sketches in SATA 97, 146
Anderson, Norman Dean 1928- *22*
Anderson, Peggy Perry 1953- *179*
  Earlier sketch in SATA 84
Anderson, Poul 1926-2001 .... *90*
  Autobiography Feature *106*
  Brief entry *39*
  See also CLR 58
Anderson, Poul William
  See Anderson, Poul
Anderson, Rachel 1943- *86*
  Earlier sketch in SATA 34
  See also SAAS 18
Anderson, Rebecca M.
  See Moesta, Rebecca
Anderson, Rebecca Moesta
  See Moesta, Rebecca
Anderson, Richard
  See Anderson, J(ohn) R(ichard) L(ane)
Anderson, Sara *173*
Anderson, (Tom) Scoular *138*
Anderson, Susan 1952- *90*
Anderson, W. B.
  See Schultz, James Willard
Anderson, Wayne 1946- *147*
  Earlier sketch in SATA 56
Andre, Evelyn M(arie) 1924- *27*
Andreasen, Dan *186*
Andreassen, Karl
  See Boyd, Waldo T.
Andreassi, K. Robert
  See DeCandido, Keith R.A.
Andree, Louise
  See Coury, Louise Andree
Andrew, Ian 1962- *166*
  Earlier sketch in SATA 116
Andrew, Ian Peter
  See Andrew, Ian
Andrew, Prudence (Hastings) 1924- *87*
Andrews, Benny 1930-2006 .... *31*
  Obituary *178*
Andrews, Eleanor Lattimore
  See Lattimore, Eleanor Frances
Andrews, Elton V.
  See Pohl, Frederik
Andrews, F(rank) Emerson 1902-1978 .... *22*
Andrews, J(ames) S(ydney) 1934- *4*
Andrews, Jan 1942- *167*
  Brief entry *49*
  Earlier sketches in SATA 58, 98
Andrews, Julie 1935- *153*
  Earlier sketch in SATA 7
  See also CLR 85
Andrews, Laura
  See Coury, Louise Andree
Andrews, Roy Chapman 1884-1960 .... *19*
Andrews, Tamra 1959- *129*
Andrews, V(irginia) C(leo) 1924(?)-1986
  Obituary *50*
Andrews, Wendy
  See Sharmat, Marjorie Weinman
Andrews, William G(eorge) 1930- *74*

Andrezel, Pierre
  See Blixen, Karen (Christentze Dinesen)
Andriani, Renee
  See Williams-Andriani, Renee
Andriola, Alfred J. 1912-1983
  Obituary *34*
Andrist, Ralph K. 1914-2004 .... *45*
Andronik, Catherine M. *189*
Andryszewski, Tricia 1956- *148*
  Earlier sketch in SATA 88
Angel, Ann 1952- *192*
Angel, Carl *178*
Angel, Marie 1923- *47*
Angeles, Peter A. 1931- *40*
Angeletti, Roberta 1964- *124*
Angeli, Marguerite (Lofft) de
  See de Angeli, Marguerite (Lofft)
Angell, Madeline 1919- *18*
Angelo, Valenti 1897- *14*
Angelou, Maya 1928- *136*
  Earlier sketch in SATA 49
  See also CLR 53
Angier, Bradford -1997 .... *12*
Angle, Paul M(cClelland) 1900-1975
  Obituary *20*
Anglund, Joan Walsh 1926- *2*
  See also CLR 94
Ango, Fan D.
  See Longyear, Barry B(rookes)
Angrist, Stanley W(olff) 1933- *4*
Anholt, Catherine 1958- *131*
  Earlier sketch in SATA 74
Anholt, Laurence 1959- *141*
  Earlier sketch in SATA 74
Anita
  See Daniel, Anita
Anmar, Frank
  See Nolan, William F(rancis)
Annett, Cora
  See Scott, Cora Annett (Pipitone)
Annie-Jo
  See Blanchard, Patricia
  and Suhr, Joanne
Annixter, Jane
  See Sturtzel, Jane Levington
Annixter, Paul
  See Sturtzel, Howard A(llison)
Anno, Mitsumasa 1926- *157*
  Earlier sketches in SATA 5, 38, 77
  See also CLR 122
Anrooy, Francine Van
  See Van Anrooy, Francine
Ansary, Mir Tamim 1948- *140*
Anstey, Caroline 1958- *81*
Antell, Will D. 1935- *31*
Anthony, Barbara
  See Barber, Antonia
Anthony, C. L.
  See Smith, Dorothy Gladys
Anthony, Edward 1895-1971 .... *21*
Anthony, John
  See Beckett, Ronald Brymer
  and Ciardi, John (Anthony)
  and Sabini, John Anthony
Anthony, Joseph Patrick 1964- *103*
Anthony, Patricia 1947- *109*
Anthony, Piers 1934- *129*
  Autobiography Feature *129*
  Earlier sketch in SATA 84
  See also CLR 118
  See also SAAS 22
Anthony, Susan C(arol) 1953- *87*
Anticaglia, Elizabeth 1939- *12*
Antilles, Kem
  See Moesta, Rebecca
Antle, Nancy 1955- *102*
Antolini, Margaret Fishback 1904-1985
  Obituary *45*
Anton, Michael J(ames) 1940- *12*
Antonacci, Robert J(oseph) 1916- *45*
  Brief entry *37*

Anvil, Christopher
  See Crosby, Harry C., Jr.
Anzaldua, Gloria (Evanjelina) 1942-2004
  Obituary *154*
Aoki, Hisako 1942- *45*
Apfel, Necia H(alpern) 1930- *51*
  Brief entry *41*
Aphrodite, J.
  See Livingston, Carole
Apikuni
  See Schultz, James Willard
Apostolina, M. *184*
Apostolina, Michael
  See Apostolina, M.
Apostolou, Christine Hale 1955- *128*
  Earlier sketch in SATA 82
  See Hale, Christy
Appel, Allen (R.) 1945- *115*
Appel, Benjamin 1907-1977 .... *39*
  Obituary *21*
Appel, Martin 1948- *45*
Appel, Martin Eliot
  See Appel, Martin
Appel, Marty
  See Appel, Martin
Appelbaum, Diana Muir Karter 1953- *132*
Appelt, Kathi 1954- *190*
  Earlier sketches in SATA 83, 129
Apperley, Dawn 1969- *135*
Appiah, Peggy 1921-2006 .... *84*
  Earlier sketch in SATA 15
  See also SAAS 19
Apple, Margot *152*
  Brief entry *42*
  Earlier sketch in SATA 64
Applebaum, Stan 1922- *45*
Applegate, K. A.
  See CLR 90
  See Applegate, Katherine (Alice)
Applegate, Katherine (Alice) 1956- *162*
  Earlier sketch in SATA 109
  See Applegate, K. A.
Appleton, Victor *67*
  Earlier sketch in SATA 1
  See Barrett, Neal, Jr.
  and Doyle, Debra
  and Macdonald, James D.
  and Stratemeyer, Edward L.
  and Vardeman, Robert E(dward)
Appleton, Victor II *67*
  Earlier sketch in SATA 1
  See Goulart, Ron(ald Joseph)
Apsler, Alfred 1907-1982 .... *10*
Aragones, Sergio 1937- *48*
  Brief entry *39*
Araujo, Frank P. 1937- *86*
Arbo, Cris 1950- *103*
Arbuckle, Dorothy Fry 1910-1982
  Obituary *33*
Arbuthnot, May Hill 1884-1969 .... *2*
Archambault, John *163*
  Earlier sketches in SATA 67, 112
Archbold, Rick 1950- *97*
Archer, Colleen Rutherford 1949- *164*
Archer, Frank
  See O'Connor, Richard
Archer, Jules 1915- *85*
  Earlier sketch in SATA 4
  See also SAAS 5
Archer, Lily 1981- *193*
Archer, Marion Fuller 1917- *11*
Archer, Nathan
  See Watt-Evans, Lawrence
Archibald, Joe
  See Archibald, Joseph S(topford)
Archibald, Joseph S(topford) 1898-1986 .... *3*
  Obituary *47*
Ard, William
  See Jakes, John
Ardagh, Philip 1961- *154*
Ardai, Charles 1969- *85*

Arden, Barbi
   See Stoutenburg, Adrien (Pearl)
Arden, William
   See Lynds, Dennis
Ardizzone, Edward (Jeffrey Irving)
   1900-1979 28
   Obituary 21
   Earlier sketch in SATA *1*
   See also CLR *3*
Ardley, Neil (Richard) 1937- 121
   Earlier sketch in SATA *43*
Arehart-Treichel, Joan 1942- 22
Arena, Felice 1968- 151
Arenella, Roy 1939- 14
Argent, Kerry 1960- 138
Argueta, Jorge 179
Arkin, Alan 1934- 59
   Brief entry 32
Arkin, Alan Wolf
   See Arkin, Alan
Arksey, Neil 158
Arlen, Leslie
   See Nicole, Christopher (Robin)
Arley, Robert
   See Jackson, Mike
Armer, Alberta (Roller) 1904-1986 9
Armer, Laura Adams 1874-1963 13
Armistead, John 1941- 130
Armitage, David 1943- 155
   Brief entry 38
   Earlier sketch in SATA *99*
Armitage, Frank
   See Carpenter, John (Howard)
Armitage, Ronda (Jacqueline) 1943- 155
   Brief entry 38
   Earlier sketches in SATA *47, 99*
Armour, Richard (Willard) 1906-1989 14
   Obituary 61
Armstrong, Alan 1939- 172
Armstrong, Alan W.
   See Armstrong, Alan
Armstrong, George D. 1927- 10
Armstrong, Gerry (Breen) 1929- 10
Armstrong, Jeannette (C.) 1948- 102
Armstrong, Jennifer 1961- 165
   Autobiography Feature 120
   Earlier sketches in SATA *77, 111*
   See also CLR *66*
   See also SAAS *24*
Armstrong, Louise 43
   Brief entry 33
Armstrong, Martin Donisthorpe
   1882-1974 115
Armstrong, Matthew 1975- 188
Armstrong, Matthew S.
   See Armstrong, Matthew
Armstrong, Ralph Richard
   See Armstrong, Richard
Armstrong, Richard 1903-1986 11
Armstrong, William H(oward) 1914-1999 4
   Obituary 111
   See also CLR *117*
   See also SAAS *7*
Armstrong-Ellis, Carey (Fraser) 1956- 145
Arndt, Ursula (Martha H.) 56
   Brief entry 39
Arneson, D(on) J(on) 1935- 37
Arnett, Caroline
   See Cole, Lois Dwight
Arnett, Jack
   See Goulart, Ron(ald Joseph)
Arnette, Robert
   See Silverberg, Robert
Arno, Enrico 1913-1981 43
   Obituary 28
Arnold, Caroline 1944- 174
   Brief entry 34
   Earlier sketches in SATA *36, 85, 131*
   See also CLR *61*
   See also SAAS *23*
Arnold, Elizabeth 1944- 164

Arnold, Elliott 1912-1980 5
   Obituary 22
Arnold, Emily 1939- 76
   Earlier sketch in SATA *50*
   See McCully, Emily Arnold
Arnold, Katya 1947- 168
   Earlier sketches in SATA *82, 115*
Arnold, Louise 175
Arnold, Marsha Diane 1948- 147
   Earlier sketch in SATA *93*
Arnold, Nick 1961- 113
Arnold, Oren 1900-1980 4
Arnold, Susan (Riser) 1951- 58
Arnold, Tedd 1949- 160
   Earlier sketches in SATA *69, 116*
Arnoldy, Julie
   See Bischoff, Julia Bristol
Arnosky, James Edward 1946- 160
   Earlier sketch in SATA *22*
   See also CLR *93*
   See Arnosky, Jim
Arnosky, Jim 189
   Earlier sketches in SATA *70, 118*
   See also CLR *93*
   See Arnosky, James Edward
Arnott, Kathleen 1914- 20
Arnov, Boris, Jr. 1926- 12
Arnow, Harriette (Louisa) Simpson
   1908-1986 42
   Obituary 47
Arnsteen, Katy Keck 1934- 68
Arnstein, Helene S(olomon) 1915- 12
Arntson, Herbert E(dward) 1911-1982 12
Aroner, Miriam 82
Aronin, Ben 1904-1980
   Obituary 25
Aronson, Marc 1950- 189
   Autobiography Feature 189
   Earlier sketches in SATA *126, 175*
Aronson, Marc Henry
   See Aronson, Marc
Aronson, Virginia 1954- 122
Arora, Shirley (Lease) 1930- 2
Arrasmith, Patrick 176
Arrigan, Mary 1943- 142
Arrington, Aileen 183
Arrington, Stephen L. 1948- 97
Arrington, Stephen Lee
   See Arrington, Stephen L.
Arrley, Richmond
   See Delany, Samuel R., Jr.
Arrowood, (McKendrick Lee) Clinton
   1939- 19
Artell, Mike 1948- 183
   Earlier sketches in SATA *89, 134*
Arthur, Robert (Andrew) 1909-1969
   See Arthur, Robert, (Jr.)
Arthur, Robert, (Jr.) 1909-1969 118
   See Arthur, Robert (Andrew)
Arthur, Ruth M(abel) 1905-1979 26
   Earlier sketch in SATA *7*
Artis, Vicki Kimmel 1945- 12
Artzybasheff, Boris (Miklailovich)
   1899-1965 14
Aruego, Ariane
   See Dewey, Ariane
Aruego, Jose 1932- 178
   Earlier sketches in SATA *6, 68, 125*
   See also CLR *5*
Aruego, Jose Espiritu
   See Aruego, Jose
Arundel, Honor (Morfydd) 1919-1973 4
   Obituary 24
   See also CLR *35*
Arundel, Jocelyn
   See Alexander, Jocelyn Anne Arundel
Arvey, Michael 1948- 79
Arzoumanian, Alik 177
Asare, Meshack (Yaw) 1945- 139
   Earlier sketch in SATA *86*

Asaro, Catherine 1955- 165
   Earlier sketch in SATA *101*
   See Asaro, Catherine Ann
Asaro, Catherine Ann 1955-
   See Asaro, Catherine
Asay, Donna Day 1945- 127
Asbjornsen, Peter Christen 1812-1885 15
   See also CLR *104*
   See Asbjornsen and Moe
Asch, Frank 1946- 154
   Earlier sketches in SATA *5, 66, 102*
Ash, Jutta 1942- 38
Ashabranner, Brent 1921- 166
   Earlier sketches in SATA *1, 67, 130*
   See also CLR *28*
   See also SAAS *14*
Ashabranner, Brent Kenneth
   See Ashabranner, Brent
Ashbless, William
   See Blaylock, James P.
   and Powers, Tim
Ashby, Gil 1958- 146
Ashby, Gwynneth 1922- 44
Ashby, Ruth 170
Ashby, Yvonne 1955- 121
Ashe, Arthur (Robert, Jr.) 1943-1993 65
   Obituary 87
Ashe, Geoffrey (Thomas) 1923- 17
   Autobiography Feature 125
Ashe, Mary Ann
   See Lewis, Mary (Christianna)
Asher, Sandra Fenichel 71
   Brief entry 34
   Earlier sketch in SATA *36*
   See also SAAS *13*
   See Asher, Sandy
Asher, Sandy 1942- 158
   Autobiography Feature 158
   Earlier sketch in SATA *118*
   See Asher, Sandra Fenichel
Asheron, Sara
   See Moore, Lilian
Ashey, Bella
   See Breinburg, Petronella
Ashford, Daisy
   See Ashford, Margaret Mary
Ashford, Jeffrey
   See Jeffries, Roderic
Ashford, Margaret Mary 1881-1972 10
Ashley, Bernard (John) 1935- 155
   Brief entry 39
   Earlier sketches in SATA *47, 79*
   See also CLR *4*
Ashley, Elizabeth
   See Salmon, Annie Elizabeth
Ashley, Ray
   See Abrashkin, Raymond
Ashman, Linda 1960- 150
Ashton, Lorayne
   See Gottfried, Theodore Mark
Ashton, Warren T.
   See Adams, William Taylor
Asimov, Isaac 1920-1992 74
   Earlier sketches in SATA *1, 26*
   See also CLR *79*
Asinof, Eliot 1919-2008 6
Asinof, Eliot Tager
   See Asinof, Eliot
Aska, Warabe 56
   See Masuda, Takeshi
Asprin, Robert L. 1946-2008 92
Asprin, Robert Lynn
   See Asprin, Robert L.
Asquith, Cynthia Mary Evelyn (Charteris)
   1887-1960 107
Asquith, Ros 153
Astley, Juliet
   See Lofts, Norah (Robinson)
Aston, Dianna Hutts 1964- 176
Aston, James
   See White, T(erence) H(anbury)

Ata, Te 1895-1995 .... *119*
Atene, Ann
  See Atene, (Rita) Anna
Atene, (Rita) Anna 1922- *12*
Atheling, William, Jr.
  See Blish, James (Benjamin)
Atkins, Catherine *160*
Atkins, Jeannine 1953- *172*
  Earlier sketch in SATA *113*
Atkinson, Allen G. 1953(?)-1987 .... *60*
  Brief entry *46*
  Obituary *55*
Atkinson, M. E.
  See Frankau, Mary Evelyn Atkinson
Atkinson, Margaret Fleming *14*
Atteberry, Kevan J. *186*
Attema, Martha 1949- *156*
  Earlier sketch in SATA *94*
Atticus
  See Davies, Hunter
  and Fleming, Ian
  and Pawle, Gerald Strachan
  and Wilson, (Thomas) Woodrow
Atwater, Florence (Hasseltine Carroll)
  1896-1979 .... *66*
  Earlier sketch in SATA *16*
  See also CLR *19*
Atwater, Montgomery Meigs 1904-1976 ...... *15*
Atwater, Richard (Tupper) 1892-1948 .... *66*
  Brief entry *27*
  Earlier sketch in SATA *54*
  See also CLR *19*
Atwater-Rhodes, Amelia 1984- *170*
  Earlier sketch in SATA *124*
Atwell, Debby 1953- *150*
  Earlier sketch in SATA *87*
Atwood, Ann (Margaret) 1913-1992 .... *7*
Atwood, Margaret 1939- *170*
  Earlier sketch in SATA *50*
Atwood, Margaret Eleanor
  See Atwood, Margaret
Aubrey, Meg Kelleher 1963- *83*
Aubry, Claude B. 1914-1984 .... *29*
  Obituary *40*
Auch, Herm *173*
Auch, Mary Jane *173*
  Earlier sketch in SATA *138*
Auch, M.J.
  See Auch, Mary Jane
Auclair, Joan 1960- *68*
Auel, Jean M(arie) 1936- *91*
Auer, Martin 1951- *77*
Augarde, Steve 1950- *159*
  Earlier sketch in SATA *25*
Augelli, John P(at) 1921- *46*
Augustine, Mildred
  See Benson, Mildred (Augustine Wirt)
Ault, Phil
  See Ault, Phillip H(alliday)
Ault, Phillip H(alliday) 1914- *23*
Ault, Rosalie Sain 1942- *38*
Ault, Roz
  See Ault, Rosalie Sain
Aung, (Maung) Htin 1909- *21*
Auntie Deb
  See Coury, Louise Andree
Auntie Louise
  See Coury, Louise Andree
Aunt Weedy
  See Alcott, Louisa May
Auseon, Andrew 1976- *166*
Austen, Carrie
  See Bennett, Cherie
Austin, Carrie
  See Seuling, Barbara
Austin, Elizabeth S. 1907-1977 .... *5*
Austin, Harry
  See McInerny, Ralph
Austin, Margot 1909(?)-1990 .... *11*
  Obituary *66*
Austin, Michael *178*

Austin, Oliver L(uther), Jr. 1903-1988 .... *7*
  Obituary *59*
Austin, Patricia 1950- *137*
Austin, R. G.
  See Gelman, Rita Golden
  and Lamb, Nancy
Austin, Virginia 1951- *152*
  Earlier sketch in SATA *80*
Auteur, Hillary
  See Gottfried, Theodore Mark
Auth, Tony *192*
  See Auth, William Anthony, Jr.
Auth, William Anthony, Jr. 1942- *51*
  See Auth, Tony
Autry, Gloria Diener
  See Allen, Terril Diener
Auvil, Peggy A 1954- *122*
Auvil, Peggy Appleby
  See Auvil, Peggy A
Aveni, Anthony F. 1938- *181*
Aveni, Anthony Francis
  See Aveni, Anthony F.
Averill, Esther (Holden) 1902-1992 .... *28*
  Obituary *72*
  Earlier sketch in SATA *1*
Avery, A. A.
  See Montgomery, Rutherford George
Avery, Al
  See Montgomery, Rutherford George
Avery, Gillian (Elise) 1926- *137*
  Autobiography Feature *137*
  Earlier sketches in SATA *7, 75*
  See also SAAS *6*
Avery, Kay 1908- *5*
Avery, Lorraine
  See Older, Effin
  and Older, Jules
Avery, Lynn
  See Cole, Lois Dwight
Avi 1937- *190*
  Earlier sketches in SATA *14, 71, 108, 156*
  See also CLR *68*
Avishai, Susan 1949- *82*
Avril, Francois 1961- *191*
Avril, Lynne
  See Cravath, Lynne W.
Awdry, Christopher Vere 1940- *67*
Awdry, Wilbert Vere 1911-1997 .... *94*
  See also CLR *23*
Axelrod, Amy *131*
Axelsen, Stephen 1953- *165*
Axton, David
  See Koontz, Dean R.
Ayars, James S(terling) 1898-1986 .... *4*
Aye, A. K.
  See Edwards, Hazel (Eileen)
Ayer, Eleanor H. 1947-1998 .... *121*
  Earlier sketch in SATA *78*
Ayer, Jacqueline 1930- *13*
Ayer, Margaret (?)-1981 .... *15*
Aylesworth, Jim 1943- *139*
  Earlier sketches in SATA *38, 89*
  See also CLR *89*
Aylesworth, Thomas G(ibbons) 1927-1995 .. *88*
  Earlier sketch in SATA *4*
  See also CLR *6*
  See also SAAS *17*
Ayliffe, Alex *190*
Aylward, Marcus
  See Alexander, Marc
Aymar, Brandt 1911- *22*
Ayme, Marcel (Andre) 1902-1967 .... *91*
  See also CLR *25*
Ayres, Becky
  See Hickox, Rebecca (Ayres)
Ayres, Katherine 1947- *187*
Ayres, Pam 1947- *90*
Ayres, Patricia Miller 1923-1985
  Obituary *46*
Aytmatov, Chingiz
  See Aitmatov, Chingiz

Ayto, Russell 1960- *166*
  Earlier sketch in SATA *111*
Azaid
  See Zaidenberg, Arthur
Azar, Penny 1952- *121*
Azarian, Mary 1940- *171*
  Earlier sketch in SATA *112*
Azore, Barbara 1934- *188*

B

Baastad, Babbis Friis
  See Friis-Baastad, Babbis Ellinor
Bab
  See Gilbert, W(illiam) S(chwenck)
Babbis, Eleanor
  See Friis-Baastad, Babbis Ellinor
Babbitt, Lucy Cullyford 1960- *85*
Babbitt, Natalie 1932- *194*
  Earlier sketches in SATA *6, 68, 106*
  See also CLR *53*
  See also SAAS *5*
Babbitt, Natalie Zane Moore
  See Babbitt, Natalie
Babcock, Chris 1963- *83*
Babcock, Dennis 1948- *22*
Babcock, Dennis Arthur
  See Babcock, Dennis
Baber, Carolyn Stonnell 1936- *96*
Baca, Ana 1967- *191*
Baca, Maria 1951- *104*
Bach, Alice (Hendricks) 1942- *93*
  Brief entry *27*
  Earlier sketch in SATA *30*
Bach, Bellamy
  See Windling, Terri
Bach, Mary 1960- *125*
Bach, Richard 1936- *13*
Bach, Richard David
  See Bach, Richard
Bache, Ellyn 1942- *124*
Bachel, Beverly K. 1957- *142*
Bachman, Fred 1949- *12*
Bachman, Richard
  See King, Stephen
Bachrach, Deborah *80*
Backus, James Gilmore 1913-1989
  Obituary *63*
Backus, Jim
  See Backus, James Gilmore
Bacmeister, Rhoda W(arner) 1893-1991 .... *11*
Bacon, Betty
  See Bacon, Elizabeth
Bacon, Elizabeth 1914-2001 .... *3*
  Obituary *131*
Bacon, Joan Chase
  See Bowden, Joan Chase
Bacon, Josephine Dodge (Daskam)
  1876-1961 .... *48*
Bacon, Margaret Frances
  Obituary *50*
  See Bacon, Peggy
Bacon, Margaret Hope 1921- *6*
Bacon, Martha Sherman 1917-1981 .... *18*
  Obituary *27*
  See also CLR *3*
Bacon, Melvin 1950- *93*
Bacon, Melvin L.
  See Bacon, Melvin
Bacon, Peggy 1895-1987 .... *2*
  See Bacon, Margaret Frances
Bacon, R(onald) L(eonard) 1924- *84*
  Earlier sketch in SATA *26*
Baden, Robert 1936- *70*
Baden-Powell, Robert (Stephenson Smyth)
  1857-1941 .... *16*
Badt, Karin L(uisa) 1963- *91*
Bae, Hyun-Joo *186*
Baehr, Kingsley M. 1937- *89*

Baehr, Patricia 1952- 65
Baehr, Patricia Goehner
  See Baehr, Patricia
Baer, Jill
  See Gilbert, (Agnes) Joan (Sewell)
Baer, Judy 1951- 71
Baer, Julie 1960- 161
Baer-Block, Roxanna 172
Baerg, Harry J(ohn) 1909-1996 12
Baeten, Lieve 1954- 83
Bagert, Brod 1947- 191
  Earlier sketch in SATA *80*
Baggette, Susan K. 1942- 126
Bagnold, Enid 1889-1981 25
  Earlier sketch in SATA *1*
Bahlke, Valerie Worth -1994 70
  Earlier sketch in SATA *8*
  See also CLR *21*
  See Worth, Valerie
Bahous, Sally 1939- 86
Bahr, Mary (Madelyn) 1946- 95
Bahr, Robert 1940- 38
Bahti, Tom 1926-1972 57
  Brief entry 31
Baicker-McKee, Carol 1958- 177
Bailey, Alice Cooper 1890-1978 12
Bailey, Anne 1958- 71
Bailey, Bernadine (Freeman) 1901-1995 14
Bailey, Carolyn Sherwin 1875-1961 14
Bailey, Debbie 1954- 123
Bailey, Donna (Veronica Anne) 1938- 68
Bailey, Jane H(orton) 1916- 12
Bailey, John (Robert) 1940- 52
Bailey, Len 193
Bailey, Linda 1948- 182
  Earlier sketch in SATA *107*
Bailey, Maralyn Collins (Harrison) 1941- 12
Bailey, Matilda
  See Radford, Ruby L(orraine)
Bailey, Maurice Charles 1932- 12
Bailey, Pearl (Mae) 1918-1990 81
Bailey, Peter 1946- 194
Bailey, Ralph Edgar 1893-1982 11
Bailey, Sheila (Lucas) 1960- 155
Baillie, Allan 1943- 151
  Earlier sketch in SATA *87*
  See also CLR *49*
  See also SAAS *21*
Baillie, Allan Stuart
  See Baillie, Allan
Baines, John (David) 1943- 71
Bains, Larry
  See Sabin, Louis
Baird, Alison 1963- 138
Baird, Bil 1904-1987 30
  Obituary 52
Baird, Thomas (P.) 1923-1990 45
  Brief entry 39
  Obituary 64
Baird, William Britton
  See Baird, Bil
Baity, Elizabeth Chesley 1907-1989 1
Baiul, Oksana 1977- 108
Bajoria, Paul 1964- 187
Bakeless, John (Edwin) 1894-1978 9
Bakeless, Katherine Little 1895-1992 9
Baker, Alan 1951- 146
  Earlier sketches in SATA *22, 93*
Baker, Augusta 1911-1998 3
Baker, Barbara 1947- 192
Baker, Betty Lou 1928-1987 73
  Obituary 54
  Earlier sketch in SATA *5*
Baker, Carin Greenberg 1959- 79
Baker, Charlotte 1910- 2
Baker, Christina
  See Kline, Christina Baker
Baker, Christopher W. 1952- 144
Baker, Deirdre 1955- 195
Baker, E.D. 190
Baker, (Mary) Elizabeth (Gillette) 1923- 7

Baker, Gayle Cunningham 1950- 39
Baker, James W. 1924- 65
  Earlier sketch in SATA *22*
Baker, James W. 1926- 122
Baker, Janice E(dla) 1941- 22
Baker, Jeanette 178
Baker, Jeannie 1950- 156
  Earlier sketches in SATA *23, 88*
  See also CLR *28*
Baker, Jeffrey J(ohn) W(heeler) 1931- 5
Baker, Jim
  See Baker, James W.
Baker, Keith 1953- 179
Baker, Ken 1962- 133
Baker, Laura Nelson 1911- 3
Baker, Margaret 1890-1965 4
Baker, Margaret J(oyce) 1918- 12
  See also SAAS *8*
Baker, Mary Gladys Steel 1892-1974 12
Baker, (Robert) Michael (Graham) 1938- 4
Baker, Nina (Brown) 1888-1957 15
Baker, Pamela J. 1947- 66
Baker, Rachel 1904-1978 2
  Obituary 26
Baker, Rosalie F. 1945- 166
Baker, Samm Sinclair 1909-1997 12
  Obituary 96
Baker, Susan (Catherine) 1942-1991 29
Balaam
  See Lamb, G(eoffrey) F(rederick)
Balan, Bruce 1959- 113
Balcavage, Dynise 1965- 137
Balch, Glenn 1902-1989 3
  Obituary 83
  See also SAAS *11*
Baldacci, David 1960- 184
Baldacci, David G.
  See Baldacci, David
  and Baldacci, David
Balderose, Nancy Ward 1952- 93
Balderson, Margaret 1935- 151
Baldry, Cherith 1947- 167
  Earlier sketch in SATA *72*
Balducci, Carolyn 1946- 5
Balducci, Carolyn Feleppa
  See Balducci, Carolyn
Baldwin, Alex
  See Griffin, W.E.B
Baldwin, Anne Norris 1938- 5
Baldwin, Clara 11
Baldwin, Gordo
  See Baldwin, Gordon C(ortis)
Baldwin, Gordon C(ortis) 1908-1983 12
Baldwin, James 1841-1925 24
Baldwin, James 1924-1987 9
  Obituary 54
Baldwin, Louis 1919- 110
Baldwin, Margaret
  See Weis, Margaret
Baldwin, Stan(ley C.) 1929- 62
  Brief entry 28
Bales, Carol Ann 1940- 57
  Brief entry 29
Balet, Jan (Bernard) 1913- 11
Balgassi, Haemi 1971- 131
Balian, Lorna 1929- 91
  Earlier sketch in SATA *9*
Balit, Christina 1961- 159
  Earlier sketch in SATA *102*
Ball, Duncan 1941- 73
Ball, Zachary
  See Janas, Frankie-Lee
  and Masters, Kelly R(ay)
Ballantine, Lesley Frost
  See Frost, Lesley
Ballantyne, R(obert) M(ichael) 1825-1894 ... 24
  See also CLR *137*
Ballard, James Graham
  See Ballard, J.G.
Ballard, Jane
  See Gorman, Carol

Ballard, J.G. 1930- 93
Ballard, John 1945- 110
Ballard, Lowell C(lyne) 1904-1986 12
  Obituary 49
Ballard, (Charles) Martin 1929- 1
Ballard, Mignon F. 1934- 64
  Brief entry 49
Ballard, Mignon Franklin
  See Ballard, Mignon F.
Ballard, Robert D(uane) 1942- 85
  See also CLR *60*
Ballard, Robin 1965- 126
Balliett, Blue 1955- 156
Ballinger, Bryan 1968- 161
Ballouhey, Pierre 1944- 90
Balogh, Penelope 1916-1975 1
  Obituary 34
Balouch, Kristen 176
Balow, Tom 1931- 12
Baltazzi, Evan S(erge) 1921- 90
Baltimore, J.
  See Catherall, Arthur
Baltzer, Hans (Adolf) 1900- 40
Bambara, Toni Cade 1939-1995 112
Bamfylde, Walter
  See Bevan, Tom
Bamman, Henry A. 1918- 12
Banat, D. R.
  See Bradbury, Ray
Bancroft, Griffing 1907-1999 6
Bancroft, Laura
  See Baum, L(yman) Frank
Bandel, Betty 1912- 47
Baner, Skulda Vanadis 1897-1964 10
Banerjee, Anjali 174
Banfill, A. Scott 1956- 98
Bang, Betsy 1912- 48
  Brief entry 37
Bang, Garrett
  See Bang, Molly
Bang, Molly 1943- 158
  Earlier sketches in SATA *24, 69, 111*
  See also CLR *8*
Bang, Molly Garrett
  See Bang, Molly
Bang-Campbell, Monika 1975(?)- 195
  Earlier sketch in SATA *140*
Banjo, The
  See Paterson, A(ndrew) B(arton)
Banke, Cecile de
  See de Banke, Cecile
Banks, Kate 1960- 172
  Earlier sketch in SATA *134*
Banks, Laura Stockton Voorhees 1908(?)-1980
  Obituary 23
Banks, Lynne Reid
  See Reid Banks, Lynne
Banks, Michael A. 1951- 101
Banks, Paul 1952- 174
Banks, Sara (Jeanne Gordon Harrell) 26
  See Harrell, Sara (Jeanne) Gordon
Bannatyne-Cugnet, Elizabeth Jo-Anne
  See Bannatyne-Cugnet, Jo
Bannatyne-Cugnet, Jo 1951- 101
Banner, Angela
  See CLR *24*
  See Maddison, Angela Mary
Bannerman, Helen (Brodie Cowan Watson)
  1862(?)-1946 19
  See also CLR *21*
Banning, Evelyn I. 1903-1993 36
Bannon, Laura (?)-1963 6
Bannor, Brett 1959- 143
Banta, Susan 181
Bantock, Nick 1950(?)- 95
Banyai, Istvan 193
Barakat, Ibtisam 1963- 186
Barasch, Lynne 1939- 186
  Earlier sketches in SATA *74, 126*
Barbalet, Margaret 1949- 77

Barbary, James
See Beeching, Jack
Barbash, Shepard 1957- 84
Barbe, Walter Burke 1926- 45
Barber, Antonia 1932- 163
Earlier sketch in SATA 29
Barber, Atiim Kiambu
See Barber, Tiki
Barber, Lynda
See Graham-Barber, Lynda
Barber, Lynda Graham
See Graham-Barber, Lynda
Barber, Richard (William) 1941- 35
Barber, Ronde 1975- 182
Barber, Tiki 1975- 182
Barbera, Joe 1911-2006 51
Obituary 179
Barbera, Joseph
See Barbera, Joe
Barbera, Joseph Roland
See Barbera, Joe
Barberis, Juan C(arlos) 1920- 61
Barbour, Karen 1956- 170
Earlier sketches in SATA 63, 121
Barbour, Ralph Henry 1870-1944 16
Barclay, Bill
See Moorcock, Michael
Barclay, Isabel
See Dobell, I(sabel) M(arian) B(arclay)
Barclay, William Ewert
See Moorcock, Michael
Bardhan-Quallen, Sudipta 168
Bardoe, Cheryl 181
Bare, Arnold Edwin 1920- 16
Bare, Colleen Stanley 32
Barenholtz, Bernard 1914-1989
Obituary 64
Bargar, Gary W. 1947-1985 63
Barger, Jan 1948- 147
Barish, Matthew 1907-2000 12
Barkan, Joanne 127
Earlier sketch in SATA 77
Barker, Albert W. 1900- 8
Barker, Carol (Minturn) 1938- 31
Barker, Cicely Mary 1895-1973 49
Brief entry 39
See also CLR 88
Barker, Melvern 1907-1989 11
Barker, S(quire) Omar 1894-1985 10
Barker, Will 1913-1983 8
Barkin, Carol 1944- 52
Earlier sketch in SATA 42
Barklem, Jill 1951- 96
See also CLR 31
Barkley, Brad 178
Barkley, James Edward 1941- 6
Barks, Carl 1901-2000 37
Barley, Janet Crane 1934- 95
Barnaby, Ralph S(tanton) 1893-1986 9
Barnard, A. M.
See Alcott, Louisa May
Barnard, Bryn 1956- 169
Earlier sketch in SATA 115
Barne, Kitty
See Barne, Marion Catherine
Barne, Marion Catherine 1883-1957 97
See Barne, Kitty
Barner, Bob 1947- 136
Earlier sketch in SATA 29
Barnes, Dawn 1957- 175
Barnes, Derrick 191
Barnes, Derrick D.
See Barnes, Derrick
Barnes, (Frank) Eric Wollencott 1907-1962 . 22
Barnes, Joyce Annette 1958- 85
Barnes, Laura T. 1958- 119
Barnes, Loutricia
See Barnes-Svarney, Patricia L(ou)
Barnes, Malcolm 1909(?)-1984
Obituary 41
Barnes, Michael 1934- 55

Barnes-Murphy, Frances 1951- 88
Barnes-Murphy, Rowan 1952- 88
Barnes-Svarney, Patricia L(ou) 1953- 67
Barnet, Nancy 1954- 84
Barnett, Ivan 1947- 70
Barnett, Lincoln (Kinnear) 1909-1979 36
Barnett, Moneta 1922-1976 33
Barnett, Naomi 1927- 40
Barney, Maginel Wright 1881(?)-1966 39
Brief entry 32
Barnhart, Clarence L(ewis) 1900-1993 48
Obituary 78
Barnouw, Adriaan Jacob 1877-1968
Obituary 27
Barnouw, Victor 1915-1989 43
Brief entry 28
Barnstone, Willis 1927- 20
Barnum, Jay Hyde 1888(?)-1962 20
Barnum, P. T., Jr.
See Stratemeyer, Edward L.
Barnum, Richard 67
Earlier sketch in SATA 1
Barnum, Theodore
See Stratemeyer, Edward L.
Baron, Kathy 1954- 90
Baron, Virginia Olsen 1931- 46
Brief entry 28
Barr, Donald 1921-2004 20
Obituary 152
Barr, George 1907-1992 2
Barr, Jene 1922-1985 16
Obituary 42
See Cohen, Jene Barr
Barr, Nevada 1952- 126
Earlier sketch in SATA 115
Barrer, Gertrude
See Barrer-Russell, Gertrude
Barrer-Russell, Gertrude 1921- 27
Barrett, Angela (Jane) 1955- 145
Earlier sketch in SATA 75
Barrett, Ethel 87
Brief entry 44
Barrett, Joyce Durham 1943- 138
Barrett, Judi
See Barrett, Judith
Barrett, Judith 1941- 26
See also CLR 98
Barrett, Robert T(heodore) 1949- 92
Barrett, Ron 1937- 14
Barrett, Susan (Mary) 1938- 113
Barrett, Tracy 1955- 156
Earlier sketches in SATA 84, 115
Barrett, William E(dmund) 1900-1986
Obituary 49
Barretta, Gene 176
Barrie, J(ames) M(atthew) 1860-1937 100
See also YABC 1
See also CLR 124
Barringer, William 1940-1996 153
Barrington, Michael
See Moorcock, Michael
Barris, George 1925- 47
Barrol, Grady
See Bograd, Larry
Barron, Rex 1951- 84
Barron, T.A. 1952- 192
Earlier sketches in SATA 83, 126
See also CLR 86
Barron, Thomas Archibald
See Barron, T.A.
Barron, Tom
See Barron, T.A.
Barrow, Lloyd H. 1942- 73
Barrows, Annie 1962- 180
Barry, Dan 1958- 177
Barry, Dana (Marie Malloy) 1949- 139
Barry, James P(otvin) 1918- 14
Barry, Katharina Watjen 1936- 4
Barry, Robert (Everett) 1931- 6
Barry, Scott 1952- 32
Barry, Sheila Anne -2003 91

Bartell, Susan S. 175
Bartenbach, Jean 1918- 40
Barth, Edna 1914-1980 7
Obituary 24
Barth, Kelly L. 1964- 152
Barthelme, Donald 1931-1989 7
Obituary 62
Barth-Grozinger, Inge 1950- 185
Bartholomew, Barbara 1941- 86
Brief entry 42
Bartholomew, Jean
See Beatty, Patricia (Robbins)
Bartlett, Alison 153
Bartlett, Philip A. 1
Bartlett, Robert Merrill 1899-1995 12
Bartoletti, Susan Campbell 1958- 173
Earlier sketches in SATA 88, 129, 135
Barton, Byron 1930- 126
Earlier sketches in SATA 9, 90
Barton, Jill(ian) 1940- 75
Barton, May Hollis 67
Earlier sketch in SATA 1
Barton, Pat 59
See Arrowsmith, Pat
Bartos-Hoeppner, Barbara 1923- 5
Bartram, Simon 156
Bartsch, Jochen 1906- 39
Baruch, Dorothy W(alter) 1899-1962 21
Barunga, Albert 1912(?)-1977 120
Baryshnikov, Mikhail 1948- 192
Bas, Rutger
See Rutgers van der Loeff-Basenau, An(na)
Maria Margaretha
Base, Graeme (Rowland) 1958- 162
Earlier sketches in SATA 67, 101
See also CLR 22
Baseman, Gary 1960- 174
Bash, Barbara 1948- 132
Bashevis, Isaac
See Singer, Isaac Bashevis
Bashevis, Yitskhok
See Singer, Isaac Bashevis
Baskin, Leonard 1922-2000 120
Brief entry 27
Earlier sketch in SATA 30
Baskin, Nora Raleigh 1961- 189
Earlier sketch in SATA 129
Bason, Lillian 1913- 20
Bass, L. G.
See Geringer, Laura
Bassett, Jeni 1959- 64
Brief entry 43
Bassett, John Keith
See Keating, Lawrence A.
Bassett, Lisa 1958- 61
Bassil, Andrea
See Nilsen, Anna
Bastyra, Judy 108
Bat-Ami, Miriam 1950- 150
Autobiography Feature 150
Earlier sketches in SATA 82, 122
Bate, Lucy 1939-1993 18
Bate, Norman (Arthur) 1916- 5
Bateman, Colin 1962- 172
Bateman, Donna M. 190
Bateman, Teresa 1957- 168
Earlier sketch in SATA 112
Bates, Amy June 189
Bates, Barbara S(nedeker) 1919- 12
Bates, Betty 19
See Bates, Elizabeth
Bates, Dianne 1948- 147
Bates, Ivan 175
Bates, Katharine Lee 1859-1929 113
See Lincoln, James
Bates, Martine
See Leavitt, Martine
Bateson, Catherine 1960- 157
Batey, Tom 1946- 52
Brief entry 41

Bath, Kevin P.
  See Bath, K.P.
Bath, K.P. 1959- 171
Batherman, Muriel
  See Sheldon, Muriel
Batson, Larry 1930- 35
Batt, Tanya Robyn 1970- 131
Battaglia, Aurelius 1910- 50
  Brief entry 33
Batten, H(arry) Mortimer 1888-1958 25
Batten, Mary 1937- 162
  Earlier sketches in SATA 5, 102
Batterberry, Ariane Ruskin 1935- 13
Batterberry, Michael Carver 1932- 32
Battle-Lavert, Gwendolyn 1951- 155
  Earlier sketch in SATA 85
  See Lavert, Gwendolyn Battle
Battles, (Roxy) Edith 1921- 7
Baudouy, Michel-Aime 1909- 7
Bauer, Caroline Feller 1935- 98
  Brief entry 46
  Earlier sketch in SATA 52
  See also SAAS 24
Bauer, Fred 1934- 36
Bauer, Helen 1900-1988 2
Bauer, Joan 1951- 160
  Earlier sketch in SATA 117
Bauer, Jutta 1955- 150
Bauer, Marion Dane 1938- 192
  Autobiography Feature 144
  Earlier sketches in SATA 20, 69, 113, 144
  See also SAAS 9
Bauer, Michael Gerard 1955(?)- 167
Bauer, Steven 1948- 125
Bauerschmidt, Marjorie 1926- 15
Baughman, Dorothy 1940- 61
Baum, Allyn Z(elton) 1924-1997 98
  Earlier sketch in SATA 20
Baum, L. Frank
  See Thompson, Ruth Plumly
Baum, L(yman) Frank 1856-1919 100
  Earlier sketch in SATA 18
  See also CLR 107
Baum, Louis 1948- 182
  Brief entry 52
  Earlier sketch in SATA 64
Baum, Louis F.
  See Baum, L(yman) Frank
Baum, Maxie 188
Baum, Willi 1931- 4
Baumann, Amy (Brown) Beeching 1922- 10
Baumann, Hans 1914- 2
  See also CLR 35
Baumann, Kurt 1935- 21
Baumgartner, Barbara 1939- 86
Baurys, Flo(rence) 1938- 122
Bausum, Ann 173
Bawden, Nina 1925- 132
  Earlier sketches in SATA 4, 72
  See also CLR 51
  See also SAAS 16
Bawden, Nina Mary Mabey
  See Bawden, Nina
Baxter, Valerie
  See Meynell, Laurence Walter
Bay, Jeanette Graham 1928- 88
Bayer, Harold
  See Gregg, Andrew K.
Bayer, Jane E. (?)-1985
  Obituary 44
Bayley, Nicola 1949- 129
  Earlier sketches in SATA 41, 69
Baylor, Byrd 1924- 136
  Earlier sketches in SATA 16, 69
  See also CLR 3
Baynes, Pauline 1922-2008 133
  Earlier sketches in SATA 19, 59
Baynes, Pauline Diana
  See Baynes, Pauline
Bayoc, Cbabi 186

BB
  See Watkins-Pitchford, Denys James
Beach, Charles
  See Reid, (Thomas) Mayne
Beach, Charles Amory 1
Beach, Edward L. 1918-2002 12
  Obituary 140
Beach, Edward Latimer
  See Beach, Edward L.
Beach, Lisa 1957- 111
Beach, Lynn
  See Lance, Kathryn
Beach, Stewart T(aft) 1899-1979 23
Beachcroft, Nina 1931- 18
Beagle, Peter S. 1939- 130
  Earlier sketch in SATA 60
Beagle, Peter Soyer
  See Beagle, Peter S.
Beaglehole, Helen 1946- 117
Beale, Fleur 107
Bealer, Alex W(inkler III) 1921-1980 8
  Obituary 22
Beales, Valerie 1915- 74
Beals, Carleton 1893-1979 12
Beals, Frank Lee 1881-1972
  Obituary 26
Beam, Matt 1970- 187
Beame, Rona 1934- 12
Beamer, (George) Charles (Jr.) 1942- 43
Bean, Jonathan 1979- 194
Bean, Normal
  See Burroughs, Edgar Rice
Beaney, Jan
  See Udall, Jan Beaney
Beaney, Jane
  See Udall, Jan Beaney
Bear, Carolyn
  See Rayban, Chloe
Bear, Greg(ory Dale) 1951- 105
  Earlier sketch in SATA 65
Bearanger, Marie
  See Messier, Claire
Beard, Charles A(ustin) 1874-1948 18
Beard, Dan(iel Carter) 1850-1941 22
Beard, Darleen Bailey 1961- 96
Bearden, Romare (Howard) 1914(?)-1988 ... 22
  Obituary 56
Beardmore, Cedric
  See Beardmore, George
Beardmore, George 1908-1979 20
Beardshaw, Rosalind 1969- 190
Beardsley, Martyn R. 1957- 150
Bearman, Jane (Ruth) 1917- 29
Beaton, Clare 1947- 125
Beatty, Elizabeth
  See Holloway, Teresa (Bragunier)
Beatty, Hetty Burlingame 1907-1971 5
Beatty, Jerome, Jr. 1918- 5
Beatty, John (Louis) 1922-1975 6
  Obituary 25
Beatty, Patricia (Robbins) 1922-1991 73
  Obituary 68
  Earlier sketches in SATA 1, 30
  See also SAAS 4
Beaty, Andrea 186
Beaty, Mary (T.) 1947- 146
Beccia, Carlyn 189
Bechard, Margaret 1953- 164
  Earlier sketch in SATA 85
Bechtel, Louise Seaman 1894-1985 4
  Obituary 43
Beck, Barbara L. 1927- 12
Beck, Ian 1947- 190
  Earlier sketch in SATA 138
  See Beck, Ian Archibald
Beck, Peggy 1949- 171
Becker, Beril 1901-1999 11
Becker, Bonny 184
Becker, Deborah Zimmett 1955- 138
Becker, Helaine 1961- 142
Becker, John (Leonard) 1901- 12

Becker, John E(mil) 1942- 148
Becker, Joyce 1936- 39
Becker, May Lamberton 1873-1958 33
Becker, Neesa 1951- 123
Becker, Shari 174
Beckett, Sheilah 1913- 33
Beckhorn, Susan Williams 1953- 189
Beckman, Delores 1914-1994 51
Beckman, Gunnel 1910- 6
  See also CLR 25
  See also SAAS 9
Beckman, Kaj
  See Beckman, Karin
Beckman, Karin 1913- 45
Beckman, Per (Frithiof) 1913- 45
Bedard, Michael 1949- 154
  Earlier sketch in SATA 93
  See also CLR 35
Beddor, Frank 194
Beddows, Eric
  See Nutt, Ken
Bedford, A. N.
  See Watson, Jane Werner
Bedford, Annie North
  See Watson, Jane Werner
Bedford, David 159
Bedoukian, Kerop 1907-1981 53
Bee, Jay
  See Brainerd, John W(hiting)
Bee, William 188
Beebe, B(urdetta) F(aye) 1
  See Johnson, B(urdetta) F(aye)
Beebe, (Charles) William 1877-1962 19
Beeby, Betty 1923- 25
Beech, Mark 1971- 191
Beech, Webb
  See Griffin, W.E.B
Beecham, Jahnna 161
Beechcroft, William
  See Hallstead, William F(inn III)
Beeching, Jack 1922- 14
Beeke, Tiphanie 163
Beeler, Janet
  See Shaw, Janet
Beeler, Nelson F(rederick) 1910-1978 13
Beere, Peter 1951- 97
Beers, Dorothy Sands 1917- 9
Beers, Lorna 1897-1989 14
Beers, V(ictor) Gilbert 1928- 130
  Earlier sketch in SATA 9
Beeton, Max
  See Redding, Robert Hull
Begay, Shonto 1954- 137
Begaye, Lisa Shook
  See Beach, Lisa
Begin, Maryjane 1963- 82
Begin-Callanan, Maryjane
  See Begin, Maryjane
Begley, Kathleen A. 1948- 21
Begley, Kathleen Anne
  See Begley, Kathleen A.
Behan, Leslie
  See Gottfried, Theodore Mark
Behler, Deborah A. 1947- 145
Behler, John L. 1943-2006 145
  Obituary 173
Behler, John Luther
  See Behler, John L.
Behn, Harry 1898-1973 2
  Obituary 34
Behnke, Frances L. 8
Behr, Joyce 1929- 15
Behrens, June York 1925- 19
Behrman, Carol H(elen) 1925- 144
  Earlier sketch in SATA 14
Beifuss, John, (Jr.) 1959- 92
Beil, Karen Magnuson 1950- 124
Beiler, Edna 1923- 61
Beinicke, Steve 1956- 69
Beirne, Barbara 1933- 71
Beiser, Arthur 1931- 22

Beiser, Germaine 1931- *11*
Belair, Richard L. 1934- *45*
Belaney, Archibald Stansfeld 1888-1938 ...... *24*
  See Grey Owl
Belbin, David 1958- *164*
  Earlier sketch in SATA *106*
Belden, Wilanne Schneider 1925- *56*
Belfrage, Sally 1936-1994 .... *65*
  Obituary *79*
Belknap, B. H.
  See Ellis, Edward S(ylvester)
Belknap, Boynton
  See Ellis, Edward S(ylvester)
Belknap, Boynton M.D.
  See Ellis, Edward S(ylvester)
Bell, Anthea 1936- *148*
  Earlier sketch in SATA *88*
Bell, Clare (Louise) 1952- *99*
Bell, Corydon Whitten 1894-1980 .... *3*
Bell, David Owen 1949- *99*
Bell, Emerson
  See Stratemeyer, Edward L.
Bell, Emily Mary
  See Cason, Mabel Earp
Bell, Frank
  See Benson, Mildred (Augustine Wirt)
Bell, Gertrude (Wood) 1911-1987 .... *12*
Bell, Hilari 1958- *151*
Bell, Jadrien
  See Golden, Christie
Bell, Janet
  See Clymer, Eleanor
Bell, Janet Cheatham 1937- *127*
Bell, Krista (Anne Blakeney) 1950- *126*
Bell, Margaret E(lizabeth) 1898-1990 .... *2*
Bell, Mary Reeves 1946- *88*
Bell, Norman (Edward) 1899- *11*
Bell, Raymond Martin 1907-1999 .... *13*
Bell, Siobhan *177*
Bell, Thelma Harrington 1896-1985 .... *3*
Bell, William 1945- *90*
  See also CLR *91*
Bellairs, John (Anthony) 1938-1991 .... *160*
  Obituary *66*
  Earlier sketches in SATA *2, 68*
  See also CLR *37*
Beller, Susan Provost 1949- *128*
  Earlier sketch in SATA *84*
  See also CLR *106*
Bellingham, Brenda 1931- *99*
  Brief entry *51*
Bello, Rosario de
  See De Bello, Rosario
Belloc, (Joseph) Hilaire (Pierre Sebastien Rene
  Swanton) 1870-1953 .... *112*
  See also YABC *1*
  See also CLR *102*
Belloc, Joseph Peter Rene Hilaire
  See Belloc, (Joseph) Hilaire (Pierre Sebastien
  Rene Swanton)
Belloc, Joseph Pierre Hilaire
  See Belloc, (Joseph) Hilaire (Pierre Sebastien
  Rene Swanton)
Belloli, Andrea P. A. 1947- *86*
Bellville, Cheryl Walsh 1944- *54*
  Brief entry *49*
Belpre, Pura 1899-1982 .... *16*
  Obituary *30*
Belting, Natalia Maree 1915-1997 .... *6*
Belton, John Raynor 1931- *22*
Belton, Sandra 1939- *186*
  Earlier sketches in SATA *85, 134*
Belton, Sandra Yvonne
  See Belton, Sandra
Belton, Sandra Yvonne
  See Belton, Sandra
Beltran, Alberto 1923- *43*
Beltran-Hernandez, Irene 1945- *74*
Belvedere, Lee
  See Grayland, Valerie (Merle Spanner)

Bemelmans, Ludwig 1898-1962 .... *100*
  Earlier sketch in SATA *15*
  See also CLR *93*
Benander, Carl D. 1941- *74*
Benary, Margot
  See Benary-Isbert, Margot
Benary-Isbert, Margot 1889-1979 .... *2*
  Obituary *21*
  See also CLR *12*
Benasutti, Marion 1908-1992 .... *6*
Benatar, Raquel 1955- *167*
Benchley, Nathaniel (Goddard) 1915-1981 .. *25*
  Obituary *28*
  Earlier sketch in SATA *3*
Benchley, Peter 1940-2006 .... *164*
  Earlier sketches in SATA *3, 89*
Benchley, Peter Bradford
  See Benchley, Peter
Bendall-Brunello, John *185*
Bender, Edna 1941- *92*
Bender, Esther 1942- *88*
Bender, Lucy Ellen 1942- *22*
Bender, Robert 1962- *160*
  Earlier sketch in SATA *79*
Bendick, Jeanne 1919- *135*
  Earlier sketches in SATA *2, 68*
  See also CLR *5*
  See also SAAS *4*
Bendick, Robert L(ouis) 1917- *11*
Benedetto, William R. 1928- *180*
Benedetto, William Ralph
  See Benedetto, William R.
Benedict, Andrew
  See Arthur, Robert, (Jr.)
Benedict, Dorothy Potter 1889-1979 .... *11*
  Obituary *23*
Benedict, Lois Trimble 1902-1967 .... *12*
Benedict, Rex 1920-1995 .... *8*
Benedict, Stewart H(urd) 1924- *26*
Beneduce, Ann Keay *128*
Benet, Laura 1884-1979 .... *3*
  Obituary *23*
Benet, Stephen Vincent 1898-1943
  See YABC *1*
Benet, Sula 1906-1982 .... *21*
  Obituary *33*
Ben-Ezer, Ehud 1936- *122*
Benezra, Barbara (Beardsley) 1921- *10*
Benham, Leslie 1922- *48*
Benham, Lois (Dakin) 1924- *48*
Benham, Mary Lile 1914-1991 .... *55*
Benjamin, E. M. J.
  See Bache, Ellyn
Benjamin, Nora
  See Kubie, Nora Gotthheil Benjamin
Benjamin, Saragail Katzman 1953- *86*
Benner, Cheryl 1962- *80*
Benner, Judith Ann 1942- *94*
Bennett, Alice
  See Ziner, Florence
Bennett, Cherie 1960- *158*
  Earlier sketch in SATA *97*
Bennett, Dorothea
  See Young, Dorothea Bennett
Bennett, Holly 1957- *181*
Bennett, Holly 1957- *181*
Bennett, James (W.) 1942- *153*
  Autobiography Feature *153*
  Earlier sketches in SATA *93, 148*
Bennett, Jay 1912- *87*
  Brief entry *27*
  Earlier sketch in SATA *41*
  See also SAAS *4*
Bennett, Jill (Crawford) 1934- *41*
Bennett, John 1865-1956
  See YABC *1*
Bennett, Penelope (Agnes) 1938- *94*
Bennett, Rachel
  See Hill, Margaret (Ohler)
Bennett, Rainey 1907-1998 .... *15*
  Obituary *111*

Bennett, Richard 1899- *21*
Bennett, Russell H(oradley) 1896- *25*
Bennett, Veronica 1953- *178*
Bennett, William (John) 1943- *102*
Benning, Elizabeth
  See Rice, Bebe Faas
Benson, Elizabeth P(olk) 1924- *65*
Benson, Kathleen 1947- *183*
  Earlier sketches in SATA *62, 111*
Benson, Linda M(aria) 1959- *84*
Benson, Mildred (Augustine Wirt)
  1905-2002 .... *100*
  Obituary *135*
  Earlier sketch in SATA *65*
  See Keene, Carolyn
Benson, Mildred Wirt
  See Benson, Mildred (Augustine Wirt)
Benson, Millie
  See Benson, Mildred (Augustine Wirt)
Benson, Patrick 1956- *147*
Benson, Sally 1900-1972 .... *35*
  Obituary *27*
  Earlier sketch in SATA *1*
Bentley, Judith (McBride) 1945- *89*
  Earlier sketch in SATA *40*
Bentley, Karen
  See Taschek, Karen
Bentley, Nancy (L.) 1946- *78*
Bentley, Nicolas Clerihew 1907-1978
  Obituary *24*
Bentley, Phyllis Eleanor 1894-1977 .... *6*
  Obituary *25*
Bentley, Roy 1947- *46*
Bentley, William (George) 1916- *84*
Benton, Jim 1963- *172*
ben Uzair, Salem
  See Horne, Richard Henry Hengist
Bercaw, Edna Coe 1961- *124*
Berck, Judith 1960- *75*
Berelson, Howard 1940- *5*
Berends, Polly Berrien 1939- *50*
  Brief entry *38*
Berenstain, Jan 1923- *135*
  Earlier sketches in SATA *12, 64, 129*
  See also CLR *19*
  See also SAAS *20*
Berenstain, Janice
  See Berenstain, Jan
Berenstain, Michael 1951- *45*
Berenstain, Mike
  See Berenstain, Michael
Berenstain, Stan 1923-2005 .... *135*
  Obituary *169*
  Earlier sketches in SATA *12, 64, 129*
  See also CLR *19*
  See also SAAS *20*
Berenstain, Stanley
  See Berenstain, Stan
Berenzy, Alix 1957- *168*
  Earlier sketch in SATA *65*
Beresford, Elisabeth 1928- *141*
  Earlier sketches in SATA *25, 86*
  See also SAAS *20*
Berg, Adriane G(ilda) 1948- *152*
Berg, Dave
  See Berg, David
Berg, David 1920-2002 .... *27*
  Obituary *137*
Berg, Elizabeth 1948- *104*
Berg, Jean Horton 1913-1995 .... *6*
Berg, Joan
  See Victor, Joan Berg
Berg, Ron 1952- *48*
Bergaust, Erik 1925-1978 .... *20*
Bergel, Colin J. 1963- *137*
Bergen, Joyce 1949- *95*
Berger, Barbara (Helen) 1945- *77*
Berger, Carin *185*
Berger, Gilda 1935- *88*
  Brief entry *42*
Berger, Josef 1903-1971 .... *36*

Berger, Melvin H. 1927- *158*
  Autobiography Feature *124*
  Earlier sketches in SATA *5, 88*
  See also CLR *32*
  See also SAAS *2*
Berger, Phil 1942-2001 .... *62*
Berger, Samantha (Allison) 1969- *140*
Berger, Terry 1933- *8*
Bergey, Alyce (Mae) 1934- *45*
Bergin, Mark 1961- *160*
  Earlier sketch in SATA *114*
Berglin, Ruth Marie 1970- *181*
Bergman, Donna 1934- *73*
Bergman, Tamar 1939- *95*
Bergsma, Jody Lynn *163*
Bergum, Constance R. 1952- *121*
Berkebile, Fred D(onovan) 1900-1978
  Obituary *26*
Berkes, Marianne *173*
Berkey, Barry Robert 1935- *24*
Berkowitz, Freda Pastor 1908-1994 .... *12*
Berkus, Clara Widess 1909- *78*
Berlan, Kathryn Hook 1946- *78*
Berlfein, Judy Reiss 1958- *79*
Berlin, Eric *195*
Berliner, Don 1930- *33*
Berliner, Franz 1930- *13*
Berlitz, Charles (L. Frambach) 1914-2003 ... *32*
  Obituary *151*
Berman, Linda 1948- *38*
Berman, Paul (Lawrence) 1949- *66*
Berna, Paul 1910-1994 .... *15*
  Obituary *78*
  See also CLR *19*
Bernadette
  See Watts, (Anna) Bernadette
Bernard, Bruce 1928-2000 .... *78*
  Obituary *124*
Bernard, George I. 1949- *39*
Bernard, Jacqueline (de Sieyes) 1921-1983 ... *8*
  Obituary *45*
Bernard, Patricia 1942- *181*
  Earlier sketch in SATA *106*
Bernard, Trish
  See Bernard, Patricia
Bernardin, James (B.) 1966- *112*
Bernardo, Anilu *184*
Bernards, Neal 1963- *71*
Bernasconi, Pablo 1973- *183*
Bernays, Anne 1930- *32*
Bernhard, Durga T. 1961- *80*
Bernhard, Emery 1950- *80*
Bernstein, Daryl (Evan) 1976- *81*
Bernstein, Joanne E(ckstein) 1943- *15*
Bernstein, Margery 1933- *114*
Bernstein, Nina 1949- *180*
Bernstein, Theodore M(enline) 1904-1979 ... *12*
  Obituary *27*
Berrien, Edith Heal
  See Heal, Edith
Berrill, Jacquelyn (Batsel) 1905- *12*
Berrington, John
  See Brownjohn, Alan
Berry, B. J.
  See Berry, Barbara J.
Berry, Barbara J. 1937- *7*
Berry, Erick
  See Best, (Evangel) Allena Champlin
Berry, James 1925- *110*
  Earlier sketch in SATA *67*
  See also CLR *22*
Berry, Jane Cobb 1915(?)-1979
  Obituary *22*
Berry, Joy
  See Berry, Joy Wilt
Berry, Joy Wilt 1944- *58*
  Brief entry *46*
Berry, Lynne *190*
Berry, William D(avid) 1926- *14*
Bersani, Shennen 1961- *164*
Berson, Harold 1926- *4*

Bertagna, Julie 1962- *151*
Bertholf, Bret *189*
Bertin, Charles-Francois
  See Berlitz, Charles (L. Frambach)
Bertolet, Paul
  See McLaughlin, Frank
Berton, Pierre (Francis de Marigny)
  1920-2004 .... *99*
  Obituary *158*
Bertrand, Cecile 1953- *76*
Bertrand, Diane Gonzales 1956- *177*
  Earlier sketch in SATA *106*
Bertrand, Lynne 1963- *164*
  Earlier sketch in SATA *81*
Beskow, Elsa (Maartman) 1874-1953 .... *20*
  See also CLR *17*
Bess, Clayton
  See CLR *39*
  See Locke, Robert
Best, (Evangel) Allena Champlin 1892-1974 . *2*
  Obituary *25*
Best, Cari 1951- *149*
  Earlier sketch in SATA *107*
Best, (Oswald) Herbert 1894-1980 .... *2*
Bestall, A(lfred) E(dmeades) 1892-1986 ...... *97*
  Obituary *48*
Betancourt, Jeanne 1941- *148*
  Brief entry *43*
  Earlier sketches in SATA *55, 96*
Beth, Mary
  See Miller, Mary Beth
Bethancourt, T. Ernesto *11*
  See also CLR *3*
  See Paisley, Tom
Bethel, Dell 1929- *52*
Bethell, Jean (Frankenberry) 1922- *8*
Bethers, Ray 1902-1973 .... *6*
Bethke, Bruce Raymond 1955- *114*
Bethlen, T.D.
  See Silverberg, Robert
Bethune, J. G.
  See Ellis, Edward S(ylvester)
Bethune, J. H.
  See Ellis, Edward S(ylvester)
Betteridge, Anne
  See Potter, Margaret (Newman)
Bettina
  See Ehrlich, Bettina Bauer
Bettmann, Otto Ludwig 1903-1998 .... *46*
Bettoli, Delana *187*
Betts, James
  See Haynes, Betsy
Betz, Eva Kelly 1897-1968 .... *10*
Bevan, Tom 1868-1930(?)
  See YABC *2*
Bewick, Thomas 1753-1828 .... *16*
Beyer, Audrey White 1916- *9*
Beyer, Paul J. III 1950- *74*
Beynon, John
  See Harris, John (Wyndham Parkes Lucas)
  Beynon
Bezencon, Jacqueline (Buxcel) 1924- *48*
Bial, Morrison David 1917- *62*
Bial, Raymond 1948- *165*
  Earlier sketches in SATA *76, 116*
Biala
  See Brustlein, Janice Tworkov
Biale, Rachel 1952- *99*
Bialk, Elisa
  See Krautter, Elisa (Bialk)
Bianchi, John 1947- *91*
Bianchi, Robert S(teven) 1943- *92*
Bianco, Margery
  See Bianco, Margery Williams
Bianco, Margery Williams 1881-1944 .... *15*
  See also CLR *19*
Bianco, Pamela 1906- *28*
Bibby, Violet 1908- *24*
Bible, Charles 1937- *13*
Bibo, Bobette
  See Gugliotta, Bobette

Bice, Clare 1909-1976 .... *22*
Bickerstaff, Isaac
  See Swift, Jonathan
Bidner, Jenni 1963- *193*
Biegel, Paul 1925- *79*
  Earlier sketch in SATA *16*
  See also CLR *27*
  See also SAAS *18*
Biemiller, Carl L(udwig), Jr.) 1912-1979 ..... *40*
  Obituary *21*
Bienenfeld, Florence L(ucille) 1929- *39*
Bierhorst, John (William) 1936- *149*
  Autobiography Feature *149*
  Earlier sketches in SATA *6, 91*
  See also SAAS *10*
Biggar, Joan R(awlins) 1936- *120*
Biggle, Lloyd, Jr. 1923-2002 .... *65*
Biggs, Brian 1968- *192*
Bilal, Abdel W(ahab) 1970- *92*
Bilbrough, Norman 1941- *111*
Bildner, Phil *173*
Bileck, Marvin 1920- *40*
Bilibin, Ivan (Iakolevich) 1876-1942 .... *61*
Bill, Alfred Hoyt 1879-1964 .... *44*
Billam, Rosemary 1952- *61*
Billings, Charlene W(interer) 1941- *41*
Billingsley, Franny 1954- *132*
Billington, Elizabeth T(hain) *50*
  Brief entry *43*
Billout, Guy (Rene) 1941- *144*
  Earlier sketch in SATA *10*
  See also CLR *33*
Bilson, Geoffrey 1938-1987 .... *99*
Binch, Caroline (Lesley) 1947- *140*
  Earlier sketch in SATA *81*
Bing, Christopher (H.) *126*
Bingham, Caroline 1962- *158*
Bingham, Jane M. 1941- *163*
Bingham, Jane Marie
  See Bingham, Jane M.
Bingham, Sam(uel A.) 1944- *96*
Bingley, Margaret (Jane Kirby) 1947- *72*
Binkley, Anne
  See Rand, Ann (Binkley)
Binzen, Bill *24*
  See Binzen, William
Birch, David (W.) 1913-1996 .... *89*
Birch, Reginald B(athurst) 1856-1943 .... *19*
Birchman, David 1949- *72*
Birchmore, Daniel A. 1951- *92*
Bird, Carmel 1940- *124*
Bird, E(lzy) J(ay) 1911- *58*
Birdsall, Jeanne 1952(?)- *170*
Birdseye, Tom 1951- *148*
  Earlier sketches in SATA *66, 98*
Birenbaum, Barbara 1941- *65*
Birmingham, Lloyd P(aul) 1924- *83*
  Earlier sketch in SATA *12*
Birmingham, Ruth
  See Sorrells, Walter
Birney, Betty G. 1947- *169*
  Earlier sketch in SATA *98*
Biro, B.
  See Biro, B(alint) S(tephen)
Biro, B(alint) S(tephen) 1921- *67*
  See Biro, Val
Biro, Val *1*
  See also CLR *28*
  See also SAAS *13*
  See Biro, B(alint) S(tephen)
Bischoff, Julia Bristol 1899-1970 .... *12*
Bishop, Bonnie 1943- *37*
Bishop, Claire Huchet 1899(?)-1993 .... *14*
  Obituary *74*
  See also CLR *80*
Bishop, Courtney
  See Ruemmler, John D(avid)
Bishop, Curtis (Kent) 1912-1967 .... *6*
Bishop, Elizabeth 1911-1979
  Obituary *24*

Bishop, Gavin 1946- *144*
  Earlier sketch in SATA 97
Bishop, Kathleen Wong 1954- *120*
Bishop, Kathy
  See Bishop, Kathleen Wong
Bishop, Nic 1955- *161*
  Earlier sketch in SATA *107*
Bisset, Donald 1910-1995 .... *86*
  Earlier sketch in SATA 7
Bisson, Terry 1942- *99*
Bisson, Terry Ballantine
  See Bisson, Terry
Bitter, Gary G(len) 1940- *22*
Bixby, William (Courtney) 1920-1986 .... *6*
  Obituary *47*
Bjoerk, Christina 1938- *99*
  Earlier sketch in SATA *67*
  See also CLR 22
Bjork, Christina
  See Bjoerk, Christina
Bjorklund, Lorence F. 1913-1978 .... *35*
  Brief entry *32*
Bjorkman, Steve *163*
Black, Algernon David 1900-1993 .... *12*
  Obituary *76*
Black, Holly 1971- *147*
Black, Irma Simonton 1906-1972 .... *2*
  Obituary *25*
Black, Mansell
  See Trevor, Elleston
Black, MaryAnn
  See Easley, MaryAnn
Black, Susan Adams 1953- *40*
Blackall, Bernie 1956- *126*
Blackall, Sophie *182*
Blackburn, Claire
  See Altman, Linda Jacobs
Blackburn, John(ny) Brewton 1952- *15*
Blackburn, Joyce Knight 1920- *29*
Blacker, Terence 1948- *194*
Blacker, Tina
  See Louise, Tina
Blackett, Veronica Heath 1927- *12*
Blackie, Jean Cutler 1943- *79*
Blacklin, Malcolm
  See Chambers, Aidan
Blacklock, Dyan 1951- *112*
Blackman, Malorie 1962- *128*
  Earlier sketch in SATA *83*
Blackton, Peter
  See Wilson, Lionel
Blackwood, Alan 1932- *70*
Blackwood, Gary L. 1945- *169*
  Earlier sketches in SATA *72, 118*
Blade, Alexander
  See Garrett, (Gordon) Randall (Phillip)
  and Hamilton, Edmond
  and Silverberg, Robert
Blades, Ann (Sager) 1947- *69*
  Earlier sketch in SATA *16*
  See also CLR *15*
Bladow, Suzanne Wilson 1937- *14*
Blaine, Chris
  See Gardner, Craig Shaw
Blaine, John
  See Goodwin, Harold L(eland)
Blaine, Marge
  See Blaine, Margery Kay
Blaine, Margery Kay 1937- *11*
Blair, Alison
  See Lerangis, Peter
Blair, Anne Denton 1914-1993 .... *46*
Blair, David Nelson 1954- *80*
Blair, Eric (Arthur) 1903-1950 .... *29*
  See Orwell, George
Blair, Jay 1953- *45*
Blair, Lucile
  See Yeakley, Marjory Hall
Blair, Margaret Whitman 1951- *124*
Blair, Mary 1911-1978 .... *195*

Blair, Pauline Hunter
  See Clarke, Pauline
Blair, Ruth Van Ness 1912-1999 .... *12*
Blair, Shannon
  See Kaye, Marilyn
Blair, Walter 1900-1992 .... *12*
  Obituary *72*
Blaisdell, Bob
  See Blaisdell, Robert
Blaisdell, Robert 1959- *105*
Blake, Bronwyn 1940- *149*
Blake, Jon 1954- *171*
  Earlier sketch in SATA *78*
Blake, Olive
  See Supraner, Robyn
Blake, Quentin (Saxby) 1932- *125*
  Earlier sketches in SATA *9, 52, 96*
  See also CLR *31*
Blake, Robert 1949- *42*
Blake, Robert J. *160*
Blake, Walker E.
  See Griffin, W.E.B
Blake, William 1757-1827 .... *30*
  See also CLR *52*
Blakely, Gloria 1950- *139*
Blakely, Roger K. 1922- *82*
Blakeney, Jay D.
  See Chester, Deborah
Blakey, Nancy 1955- *94*
Blanc, Esther S. 1913-1997 .... *66*
Blanc, Mel 1908-1989
  Obituary *64*
Blanchard, Patricia *125*
Blanchet, M(uriel) Wylie 1891-1961 .... *106*
Blanco, Richard L(idio) 1926- *63*
Bland, E.
  See Nesbit, E.
Bland, Edith Nesbit
  See Nesbit, E.
Bland, Fabian
  See Nesbit, E.
Blane, Gertrude
  See Blumenthal, Gertrude
Blank, Clarissa Mabel 1915-1965 .... *62*
Blankenship, LeeAnn 1944- *181*
Blassingame, Wyatt Rainey 1909-1985 .... *34*
  Obituary *41*
  Earlier sketch in SATA *1*
Blatchford, Claire H. 1944- *94*
Blauer, Ettagale 1940- *49*
Bledsoe, Glen L. 1951- *108*
Bledsoe, Glen Leonard
  See Bledsoe, Glen L.
Bledsoe, Karen E. 1962- *167*
  Earlier sketch in SATA *108*
Bledsoe, Karen Elizabeth
  See Bledsoe, Karen E.
Bledsoe, Lucy Jane 1957- *162*
  Earlier sketch in SATA *97*
Bleeker, Sonia *2*
  Obituary *26*
  See Zim, Sonia Bleeker
Blegen, Daniel M. 1950- *92*
Blegvad, Erik 1923- *132*
  Earlier sketches in SATA *14, 66*
Blegvad, Lenore 1926- *176*
  Earlier sketches in SATA *14, 66*
Bley, Anette 1967- *188*
Blish, James (Benjamin) 1921-1975 .... *66*
Blishen, Edward (William) 1920-1996 .... *66*
  Obituary *93*
  Earlier sketch in SATA *8*
Bliss, Corinne Demas 1947- *37*
  See Demas, Corinne
Bliss, Frederick
  See Card, Orson Scott
Bliss, Gillian
  See Paton Walsh, Jill
Bliss, Harry 1964- *156*
Bliss, Reginald
  See Wells, H(erbert) G(eorge)

Bliss, Ronald G(ene) 1942- *12*
Blitt, Barry *187*
Bliven, Bruce, Jr. 1916-2002 .... *2*
Blixen, Karen (Christentze Dinesen)
  1885-1962 .... *44*
  See Dinesen, Isak
Blizzard, Gladys S. (?)-1992 .... *79*
Blobaum, Cindy 1966- *123*
Bloch, Lucienne 1909-1999 .... *10*
Bloch, Marie Halun 1910-1998 .... *6*
  See also SAAS 9
Bloch, Robert (Albert) 1917-1994 .... *12*
  Obituary *82*
Blochman, Lawrence G(oldtree)
  1900-1975 .... *22*
Block, Francesca Lia 1962- *158*
  Earlier sketches in SATA *80, 116*
  See also CLR *116*
  See also SAAS *21*
Block, Irvin 1917- *12*
Blomgren, Jennifer (Alice) 1954- *136*
Blood, Charles Lewis 1929- *28*
Bloom, Barbara Lee 1943- *146*
Bloom, Freddy 1914-2000 .... *37*
  Obituary *121*
Bloom, Lloyd 1947- *108*
  Brief entry *43*
Bloom, Suzanne 1950- *172*
Bloomfield, Michaela 1966- *70*
Bloor, Edward 1950- *155*
  Earlier sketch in SATA *98*
Bloor, Edward William
  See Bloor, Edward
Blos, Joan W. 1928- *153*
  Autobiography Feature *153*
  Brief entry *27*
  Earlier sketches in SATA *33, 69, 109*
  See also CLR *18*
  See also SAAS *11*
Blos, Joan Winsor
  See Blos, Joan W.
Blough, Glenn O(rlando) 1907-1995 .... *1*
Blue, Rose 1931- *166*
  Autobiography Feature *117*
  Earlier sketches in SATA *5, 91, 93*
  See also SAAS *24*
Blue, Zachary
  See Stine, R.L.
Bluggage, Oranthy
  See Alcott, Louisa May
Blumberg, Leda 1956- *59*
Blumberg, Rhoda 1917- *123*
  Earlier sketches in SATA *35, 70*
  See also CLR *21*
Blume, Judy 1938- *195*
  Earlier sketches in SATA *2, 31, 79, 142*
  See also CLR *69*
Blume, Judy Sussman
  See Blume, Judy
Blume, Lesley M.M. 1975- *180*
Blumenthal, Deborah *161*
Blumenthal, Gertrude 1907-1971
  Obituary *27*
Blumenthal, Shirley 1943- *46*
Blutig, Eduard
  See Gorey, Edward (St. John)
Bly, Janet (Chester) 1945- *43*
Bly, Stephen A(rthur) 1944- *116*
  Earlier sketch in SATA *43*
Blyler, Allison Lee 1966- *74*
Blythe, Gary 1959- *185*
Blyton, Carey 1932-2002 .... *9*
  Obituary *138*
Blyton, Enid 1897-1968 .... *25*
  See also CLR *31*
Blyton, Enid Mary
  See Blyton, Enid
Bo, Ben
  See Richardson, V.A.
Boardman, Fon Wyman, Jr. 1911-2000 .... *6*

Boardman, Gwenn R. *12*
  See Petersen, Gwenn Boardman
Boase, Wendy 1944-1999 .... *28*
  Obituary *110*
Boatner, Mark Mayo III 1921- *29*
Bobbe, Dorothie de Bear 1905-1975 .... *1*
  Obituary *25*
Bober, Natalie S. 1930- *134*
  Earlier sketch in SATA *87*
  See also SAAS *23*
Bobette, Bibo
  See Gugliotta, Bobette
Bobritsky, Vladimir *47*
  Brief entry *32*
  See Bobri, Vladimir V.
Bochak, Grayce 1956- *76*
Bock, Hal
  See Bock, Harold I.
Bock, Harold I. 1939- *10*
Bock, William Sauts Netamux'we 1939- *14*
Bodanis, David *179*
Bode, Janet 1943-1999 .... *96*
  Obituary *118*
  Earlier sketch in SATA *60*
Bodecker, N(iels) M(ogens) 1922-1988 .... *73*
  Obituary *54*
  Earlier sketch in SATA *8*
Boden, Hilda
  See Bodenham, Hilda Morris
Bodenham, Hilda Morris 1901- *13*
Bodett, Tom *70*
  See Bodett, Thomas Edward
Bodie, Idella F(allaw) 1925- *89*
  Earlier sketch in SATA *12*
Bodker, Cecil 1927- *133*
  Earlier sketch in SATA *14*
  See also CLR *23*
Bodker, Cecil 1927-
  See Bodker, Cecil
Bodsworth, (Charles) Fred(erick) 1918- *27*
Boeckman, Charles 1920- *12*
Boegehold, Betty (Doyle) 1913-1985
  Obituary *42*
Boelts, Maribeth 1964- *163*
  Earlier sketch in SATA *78*
Boerst, William J. 1939- *170*
  Earlier sketch in SATA *121*
Boesch, Mark J(oseph) 1917- *12*
Boesen, Victor 1908- *16*
Bogacki, Tomek 1950- *138*
Bogaerts, Gert 1965- *80*
Bogan, Paulette 1960- *129*
Bogart, Jo Ellen 1945- *92*
  See also CLR *59*
Boggs, Ralph Steele 1901-1994 .... *7*
Bograd, Larry 1953- *89*
  Earlier sketch in SATA *33*
  See also SAAS *21*
Bogue, Gary 1938- *195*
Bogue, Gary L.
  See Bogue, Gary
Bohdal, Susi 1951- *101*
  Earlier sketch in SATA *22*
Bohlen, Nina 1931- *58*
Bohlmeijer, Arno 1956- *94*
Bohner, Charles (Henry) 1927- *62*
Bohnhoff, Maya Kaathryn 1954- *88*
Boiger, Alexandra *178*
Boissard, Janine 1932- *59*
Bojunga, Lygia
  See Nunes, Lygia Bojunga
Bojunga-Nunes, Lygia
  See Nunes, Lygia Bojunga
Boland, Janice *98*
Bolden, Tonya 1959- *188*
  Earlier sketches in SATA *79, 138*
Bolden, Tonya Wilyce
  See Bolden, Tonya
Boles, Paul Darcy 1916-1984 .... *9*
  Obituary *38*
Bolian, Polly 1925- *4*

Bollen, Roger 1941(?)- *83*
  Brief entry *29*
Bolliger, Max 1929- *7*
Bollinger, Max 1929- *167*
Bollinger, Peter *172*
Bolognese, Don(ald Alan) 1934- *129*
  Earlier sketches in SATA *24, 71*
Bolotin, Norman (Phillip) 1951- *93*
Bolton, Carole 1926- *6*
Bolton, Elizabeth
  See St. John, Nicole
Bolton, Evelyn
  See Bunting, (Anne) Eve(lyn)
Bonar, Veronica
  See Bailey, Donna (Veronica Anne)
Bond, B. J.
  See Heneghan, James
Bond, Bruce 1939- *61*
Bond, Felicia 1954- *126*
  Earlier sketch in SATA *49*
Bond, Gladys Baker 1912- *14*
Bond, Higgins 1951- *177*
  Earlier sketch in SATA *83*
Bond, J. Harvey
  See Winterbotham, R(ussell) R(obert)
Bond, (Thomas) Michael 1926- *157*
  Earlier sketches in SATA *6, 58*
  See also CLR *95*
  See also SAAS *3*
Bond, Nancy 1945- *159*
  Autobiography Feature *159*
  Earlier sketches in SATA *22, 82*
  See also CLR *11*
  See also SAAS *13*
Bond, Nancy Barbara
  See Bond, Nancy
Bond, Rebecca 1972- *130*
Bond, Ruskin 1934- *87*
  Earlier sketch in SATA *14*
Bondie, J. D.
  See Cunningham, Chet
Bondoux, Anne-Laure 1971- *175*
Bone, Ian 1956- *158*
  Earlier sketch in SATA *117*
Bonehill, Captain Ralph
  See Stratemeyer, Edward L.
Bonestell, Chesley 1888-1986
  Obituary *48*
Bonham, Barbara Thomas 1926- *7*
Bonham, Frank 1914-1989 .... *49*
  Obituary *62*
  Earlier sketch in SATA *1*
  See also SAAS *3*
Boniface, William 1963- *182*
  Earlier sketch in SATA *102*
Bonino, Louise
  See Williams, Louise Bonino
Bonk, John J. *189*
Bonn, Pat
  See Bonn, Patricia Carolyn
Bonn, Patricia Carolyn 1948- *43*
Bonner, Mary Graham 1890-1974 .... *19*
Bonner, Mike 1951- *121*
Bonners, Susan 1947- *85*
  Brief entry *48*
Bonnett-Rampersaud, Louise *173*
Bonning, Tony 1948- *169*
Bonsall, Crosby Barbara (Newell)
  1921-1995 .... *23*
  Obituary *84*
Bonsall, Joseph S. 1948- *119*
Bonsignore, Joan 1959- *140*
Bontemps, Arna(ud Wendell) 1902-1973 ..... *44*
  Obituary *24*
  Earlier sketch in SATA *2*
  See also CLR *6*
Bonzon, Paul-Jacques 1908-1978 .... *22*
Boock, Paula 1964- *134*
Booher, Dianna Daniels 1948- *33*
Book, Rick 1949- *119*

Book, Rita
  See Holub, Joan
Bookman, Charlotte
  See Zolotow, Charlotte
Boon, Debbie 1960- *103*
Boon, Emilie (Laetitia) 1958- *86*
Boone, Charles Eugene
  See Boone, Pat
Boone, Pat 1934- *7*
Boorman, Linda (Kay) 1940- *46*
Boorstin, Daniel J(oseph) 1914-2004 .... *52*
Booth, Coe *187*
Booth, Ernest Sheldon 1915-1984 .... *43*
Booth, George 1926- *191*
Booth, Graham (Charles) 1935- *37*
Bootman, Colin *159*
Borden, Louise 1949- *190*
  Autobiography Feature *141*
  Earlier sketches in SATA *68, 104, 141*
Bordier, Georgette 1924- *16*
Borgman, James
  See Borgman, Jim
Borgman, James Mark
  See Borgman, Jim
Borgman, Jim 1954- *122*
  See Borgman, James Mark
Borgo, Lacy Finn 1972- *194*
Boring, Mel 1939- *168*
  Earlier sketch in SATA *35*
Borja, Corinne 1929- *22*
Borja, Robert 1923- *22*
Borland, Hal *5*
  Obituary *24*
  See Borland, Harold Glen
Borland, Kathryn Kilby 1916- *16*
Borlenghi, Patricia 1951- *79*
Born, Adolf 1930- *49*
Bornstein, Ruth Lercher
  Autobiography Feature *107*
  See Bornstein-Lercher, Ruth
Bornstein-Lercher, Ruth 1927- *88*
  Earlier sketch in SATA *14*
  See Bornstein, Ruth Lercher
Borski, Lucia Merecka *18*
Borten, Helen Jacobson 1930- *5*
Bortolotti, Dan 1969- *157*
Borton, Elizabeth
  See Trevino, Elizabeth B(orton) de
Borton, Lady 1942- *98*
Borton de Trevino, Elizabeth
  See Trevino, Elizabeth B(orton) de
Bortstein, Larry 1942- *16*
Bortz, Alfred B(enjamin) 1944- *139*
  Earlier sketch in SATA *74*
Bortz, Fred
  See Bortz, Alfred B(enjamin)
Bosco, Jack
  See Holliday, Joseph
Boshell, Gordon 1908- *15*
Boshinski, Blanche 1922- *10*
Bosman, Paul 1929- *107*
Bosse, Malcolm (Joseph, Jr.) 1926-2002 .... *136*
  Earlier sketch in SATA *35*
Bosserman, (Charles) Phillip 1931- *84*
Bossom, Naomi 1933- *35*
Bostock, Mike 1962- *114*
Boston, L(ucy) M(aria Wood) 1892-1990 .... *19*
  Obituary *64*
  See also CLR *3*
Bostrom, Kathleen (Susan) Long 1954- *139*
Bostrom, Kathy
  See Bostrom, Kathleen (Susan) Long
Bosworth, J. Allan 1925- *19*
Bothwell, Jean (?)-1977 .... *2*
Botkin, B(enjamin) A(lbert) 1901-1975 .... *40*
Botsford, Ward 1927-2004 .... *66*
Botting, Douglas (Scott) 1934- *43*
Bottner, Barbara 1943- *170*
  Autobiography Feature *121*
  Earlier sketches in SATA *14, 93*
  See also SAAS *26*

Bottone, Frank G., Jr. 1969- *141*
Bouchard, David 1952- *117*
Boucher, (Clarence) Carter 1954- *129*
Boudelang, Bob
  See Pell, Ed(ward)
Boughton, Richard 1954- *75*
Boulet, Susan Seddon 1941- *50*
Boulle, Pierre (Francois Marie-Louis)
  1912-1994 .... *22*
  Obituary *78*
Boulton, Jane 1921- *91*
Bouma, Paddy 1947- *128*
Bour, Daniele 1939- *62*
Bourbonniere, Sylvie 1966- *182*
Bourdon, David 1934-1998 .... *46*
Bourgeois, Paulette 1951- *153*
Bourne, Lesley
  See Marshall, Evelyn
Bourne, Miriam Anne 1931-1989 .... *16*
  Obituary *63*
Boutet de Monvel, (Louis) M(aurice)
  1850(?)-1913 .... *30*
  See also CLR *32*
Bova, Ben 1932- *133*
  Earlier sketches in SATA *6, 68*
  See also CLR *96*
Bova, Benjamin William
  See Bova, Ben
Bovaird, Anne E(lizabeth) 1960- *90*
Bow, Patricia 1946- *168*
Bowden, Joan Chase 1925- *51*
  Brief entry *38*
Bowe, Julie 1962- *194*
Bowen, Alexandria Russell *97*
Bowen, Andy Russell
  See Bowen, Alexandria Russell
Bowen, Anne 1952- *170*
Bowen, Betty Morgan
  See West, Betty
Bowen, Catherine (Shober) Drinker
  1897-1973 .... *7*
Bowen, David
  See Bowen, Joshua David
Bowen, Fred 1953- *136*
Bowen, Joshua David 1930- *22*
Bowen, Rhys
  See Quin-Harkin, Janet
Bowen, Robert Sydney 1900-1977 .... *52*
  Obituary *21*
Bowermaster, Jon 1954- *135*
  Earlier sketch in SATA *77*
Bowers, Terrell L. 1945- *101*
Bowers, Terry
  See Bowers, Terrell L.
Bowers, Tim *185*
Bowie, C. W.
  See Old, Wendie C(orbin)
  and Wirths, Claudine (Turner) G(ibson)
Bowie, Jim
  See Norwood, Victor G(eorge) C(harles)
  and Stratemeyer, Edward L.
Bowkett, Stephen 1953- *67*
Bowler, Jan Brett
  See Brett, Jan
Bowler, Tim 1953- *149*
Bowman, Crystal 1951- *105*
Bowman, James Cloyd 1880-1961 .... *23*
Bowman, John S(tewart) 1931- *16*
Bowman, Kathleen (Gill) 1942- *52*
  Brief entry *40*
Bowman, Leslie
  See Bowman, Leslie W.
Bowman, Leslie W. *182*
Bowsher, Melodie *195*
Boxall, Ed *178*
Boyce, Frank Cottrell *182*
Boyce, George A(rthur) 1898- *19*
Boyd, Candy Dawson 1946- *72*
  See also CLR *50*
Boyd, Pauline
  See Schock, Pauline

Boyd, Selma
  See Acuff, Selma Boyd
Boyd, Waldo T. 1918- *18*
Boyden, Linda 1948- *143*
Boyer, Allen B. 1963- *153*
Boyer, Robert E(rnst) 1929- *22*
Boyes, Vivien 1952- *106*
Boyes, Vivien Elizabeth
  See Boyes, Vivien
Boyle, Ann (Peters) 1916- *10*
Boyle, Eleanor Vere (Gordon) 1825-1916 .... *28*
Boyle, Robert H. 1928- *65*
Boylston, Helen Dore 1895-1984 .... *23*
  Obituary *39*
Boyne, John 1971- *181*
Boynton, Sandra (Keith) 1953- *152*
  Brief entry *38*
  Earlier sketches in SATA *57, 107*
  See also CLR *105*
Boz
  See Dickens, Charles (John Huffam)
Bracken, Charles
  See Pellowski, Michael (Joseph)
Brackers de Hugo, Pierre 1960- *115*
Brackett, Dolli Tingle 1911-1993 .... *137*
Brackett, Virginia 1950- *166*
  Earlier sketch in SATA *121*
Brackett, Virginia Roberts Meredith
  See Brackett, Virginia
Bradbury, Bianca (Ryley) 1908-1982 .... *56*
  Earlier sketch in SATA *3*
Bradbury, Edward P.
  See Moorcock, Michael
Bradbury, Ray 1920- *123*
  Earlier sketches in SATA *11, 64*
Bradbury, Ray Douglas
  See Bradbury, Ray
Bradby, Marie *161*
Bradfield, Carl 1942- *91*
Bradford, Ann (Liddell) 1917- *56*
  Brief entry *38*
Bradford, Barbara Taylor 1933- *66*
Bradford, Karleen 1936- *96*
  Earlier sketch in SATA *48*
Bradford, Lois J(ean) 1936- *36*
Bradford, Richard (Roark) 1932-2002 .... *59*
  Obituary *135*
Bradley, Duane
  See Sanborn, Duane
Bradley, Kimberly Brubaker 1967- *179*
Bradley, Marion Zimmer 1930-1999 .... *139*
  Obituary *116*
  Earlier sketch in SATA *90*
  See Chapman, Lee
  and Dexter, John
  and Gardner, Miriam
  and Ives, Morgan
  and Rivers, Elfrida
Bradley, Timothy J. *193*
Bradley, Virginia 1912- *23*
Bradley, Will
  See Strickland, (William) Brad(ley)
Bradman, Tony 1954- *152*
  Earlier sketch in SATA *81*
Bradshaw, Gillian (Joan) 1949- *118*
Bradshaw, Gillian 1956- *127*
Bradshaw, Gillian Marucha
  See Bradshaw, Gillian
Bradstreet, T. J.
  See Thesman, Jean
Brady, Esther Wood 1905-1987 .... *31*
  Obituary *53*
Brady, Irene 1943- *4*
Brady, Kimberley S. 1953- *101*
Brady, Kimberley Smith
  See Brady, Kimberley S.
Brady, Lillian 1902- *28*
Bragdon, Elspeth MacDuffie 1897-1980 .... *6*
Bragdon, Lillian Jacot *24*
Brager, Bruce L. 1949- *146*
Bragg, Mabel Caroline 1870-1945 .... *24*

Bragg, Michael 1948- *46*
Bragg, Ruth Gembicki 1943- *77*
Brahm, Sumishta 1954- *58*
Brailsford, Frances
  See Wosmek, Frances
Brainerd, John W(hiting) 1918- *65*
Braithwaite, Althea 1940- *23*
  Autobiography Feature *119*
  See also SAAS *24*
Bram, Elizabeth 1948- *30*
Brancato, Robin F(idler) 1936- *97*
  See also CLR *32*
  See also SAAS *9*
Branch, Muriel Miller 1943- *152*
  Earlier sketch in SATA *94*
Brand, Christianna
  See Lewis, Mary (Christianna)
Brand, Rebecca
  See Charnas, Suzy McKee
Brande, Robin *194*
Brandel, Marc 1919- *71*
Brandenberg, Alexa (Demetria) 1966- *97*
Brandenberg, Aliki (Liacouras) 1929- *157*
  Earlier sketches in SATA *2, 35, 75, 113*
  See Aliki
Brandenberg, Franz 1932- *75*
  Earlier sketches in SATA *8, 35*
Brandenburg, Jim 1945- *87*
Brandhorst, Carl T(heodore) 1898-1988 ...... *23*
Brandis, Marianne 1938- *149*
  Earlier sketches in SATA *59, 96*
Brandon, Brumsic, Jr. 1927- *9*
Brandon, Curt
  See Bishop, Curtis (Kent)
Brandreth, Gyles 1948- *28*
Brandreth, Gyles Daubeney
  See Brandreth, Gyles
Brandt, Catharine 1905-1997 .... *40*
Brandt, Keith
  See Sabin, Louis
Brandt, Sue R(eading) 1916- *59*
Branfield, John (Charles) 1931- *11*
Branford, Henrietta 1946-1999 .... *106*
Branley, Franklyn M(ansfield) 1915-2002 .. *136*
  Earlier sketches in SATA *4, 68*
  See also CLR *13*
  See also SAAS *16*
Branscum, Robbie (Tilley) 1937-1997 .... *72*
  Obituary *96*
  Earlier sketch in SATA *23*
  See also SAAS *17*
Bransom, (John) Paul 1885-1979 .... *43*
Brashares, Ann 1967- *188*
  Earlier sketch in SATA *145*
  See also CLR *113*
Brassard, France 1963- *186*
Braswell, E.J.
  See Lynn, Tracy
Braswell, Elizabeth J.
  See Lynn, Tracy
Braswell, Liz
  See Lynn, Tracy
Bratton, Helen 1899-1986 .... *4*
Bratun, Katy 1950- *160*
  Earlier sketch in SATA *83*
Braude, Michael 1936- *23*
Braun, Lilian Jackson 1916(?)- *109*
Brautigan, Richard (Gary) 1935-1984 .... *56*
Bray, Libba *159*
Bray, Martha E.
  See Bray, Libba
Braymer, Marjorie Elizabeth 1911-1988 .... *6*
Breathed, Berke 1957- *161*
  Earlier sketch in SATA *86*
Breathed, Guy Berkeley
  See Breathed, Berke
Brecht, Edith 1895-1975 .... *6*
  Obituary *25*
Breck, Vivian
  See Breckenfeld, Vivian Gurney
Breckenfeld, Vivian Gurney 1895-1992 .... *1*

Breda, Tjalmar
See DeJong, David C(ornel)
Bredeson, Carmen 1944- 163
Earlier sketch in SATA 98
Breen, Steve 1970- 186
Breinburg, Petronella 1927- 11
See also CLR 31
Breisky, William J(ohn) 1928- 22
Brenaman, Miriam 172
Brennan, Caitlin
See Tarr, Judith
Brennan, Gale (Patrick) 1927- 64
Brief entry 53
Brennan, Herbie 1940- 183
Earlier sketch in SATA 140
Brennan, James Herbert
See Brennan, Herbie
Brennan, Jan
See Brennan, Herbie
Brennan, J.H.
See Brennan, Herbie
Brennan, Joseph Lomas 1903-2000 6
Brennan, Linda Crotta 1952- 130
Brennan, Tim
See Conroy, John Wesley
Brenner, Anita 1905-1974 56
Brenner, Barbara (Johnes) 1925- 124
Earlier sketches in SATA 4, 42, 76
See also SAAS 14
Brenner, Fred 1920- 36
Brief entry 34
Brent, Hope 1935(?)-1984
Obituary 39
Brent, Stuart 14
Breskin, Jane
See Zalben, Jane Breskin
Breslin, Theresa 128
Autobiography Feature 128
Earlier sketch in SATA 70
Breslow, Maurice 1935- 72
Breslow, Maurice A
See Breslow, Maurice
Breslow, Susan 1951- 69
Brett, Bernard 1925- 22
Brett, Grace N(eff) 1900-1975 23
Brett, Jan 1949- 171
Earlier sketches in SATA 42, 71, 130
See also CLR 27
Brett, Jan Churchill
See Brett, Jan
Brett Bowler, Jan
See Brett, Jan
Brewer, James D. 1951- 108
Brewer, Sally King 1947- 33
Brewster, Benjamin
See Folsom, Franklin (Brewster)
Brewster, Hugh 1950- 191
Earlier sketch in SATA 95
Brewster, Patience 1952- 97
Brewton, John E(dmund) 1898-1982 5
Brian, Janeen (Paulette) 1948- 141
Briant, Ed 180
Brick, John 1922-1973 10
Brickman, Robin D. 1954- 155
Bride, Nadja
See Nobisso, Josephine
Bridgers, Sue Ellen 1942- 90
Autobiography Feature 109
Earlier sketch in SATA 22
See also CLR 18
See also SAAS 1
Bridges, Laurie
See Bruck, Lorraine
Bridges, Ruby (Nell) 1954- 131
Bridges, William (Andrew) 1901-1984 5
Bridwell, Norman (Ray) 1928- 138
Earlier sketches in SATA 4, 68
See also CLR 96
Brier, Howard M(axwell) 1903-1969 8
Brierley, (Louise) 1958- 59

Briggs, Katharine Mary 1898-1980 101
Obituary 25
Briggs, Peter 1921-1975 39
Obituary 31
Briggs, Raymond 1934- 184
Earlier sketches in SATA 23, 66, 131
See also CLR 10
Briggs, Raymond Redvers
See Briggs, Raymond
Bright, Paul 1949- 182
Bright, Robert (Douglas Sr.) 1902-1988 63
Obituary 60
Earlier sketch in SATA 24
Bright, Sarah
See Shine, Deborah
Brightfield, Richard 1927- 65
Brief entry 53
Brightfield, Rick
See Brightfield, Richard
Brighton, Catherine 1943- 107
Earlier sketch in SATA 65
Brill, Marlene Targ 1945- 124
Earlier sketch in SATA 77
Brimberg, Stanlee 1947- 9
Brimner, Larry Dane 1949- 170
Autobiography Feature 112
Earlier sketch in SATA 79
Brin, David 1950- 65
Brin, Ruth Firestone 1921- 22
Brinckloe, Julie 1950- 13
Brinckloe, Julie Lorraine
See Brinckloe, Julie
Brindel, June (Rachuy) 1919- 7
Brindle, Max
See Fleischman, Sid
Brindze, Ruth 1903-1984 23
Brink, Carol Ryrie 1895-1981 100
Obituary 27
Earlier sketches in SATA 1, 31
See also CLR 30
Brinsmead, H. F.
See Brinsmead, H(esba) F(ay)
Brinsmead, H. F(ay)
See Brinsmead, H(esba) F(ay)
Brinsmead, H(esba) F(ay) 1922- 78
Earlier sketch in SATA 18
See also CLR 47
See also SAAS 5
Briquebec, John
See Rowland-Entwistle, (Arthur) Theodore
(Henry)
Brisbane, Henry R.
See Ellis, Edward S(ylvester)
Brisco, P. A.
See Matthews, Patricia
Brisco, Patty
See Matthews, Patricia
and Matthews, Clayton (Hartley)
Briscoe, Jill (Pauline) 1935- 56
Brief entry 47
Brisley, Joyce Lankester 1896-1978 22
Obituary 84
Brissenden, Connie
See Brissenden, Constance
Brissenden, Constance 1947- 150
Brisson, Pat 1951- 177
Autobiography Feature 133
Earlier sketches in SATA 67, 128, 133
Britt, Albert 1874-1969
Obituary 28
Britt, Dell 1934- 1
Brittain, Bill
See SAAS 7
See Brittain, William (E.)
Brittain, C. Dale 1948- 82
Brittain, William (E.) 1930- 76
Earlier sketch in SATA 36
See Brittain, Bill
Brittingham, Geoffrey (Hugh) 1959- 76
Britton, Kate 49
See Stegeman, Janet Allais

Britton, Louisa
See McGuire, Leslie (Sarah)
Britton, Rick 1952- 82
Bro, Margueritte (Harmon) 1894-1977 19
Obituary 27
Broach, Elise 1963- 173
Broadhead, Helen Cross 1913- 25
Brochmann, Elizabeth 1938- 41
Brock, Betty (Carter) 1923-2003 4
Obituary 150
Brock, C(harles) E(dmund) 1870-1938 42
Brief entry 32
Brock, Delia
See Ephron, Delia
Brock, Emma L(illian) 1886-1974 8
Brock, H(enry) M(atthew) 1875-1960 42
Brockett, Eleanor Hall 1913-1967 10
Brockman, C(hristian) Frank 1902-1985 26
Brockmeier, Kevin 1972- 176
Broderick, Dorothy M. 1929- 5
Brodeur, Ruth Wallace
See Wallace-Brodeur, Ruth
Brodie, Sally
See Cavin, Ruth (Brodie)
Brodsky, Beverly
See McDermott, Beverly Brodsky
Brody, Wendy
See Staub, Wendy Corsi
Broeger, Achim 1944- 31
Broekel, Rainer Lothar 1923- 38
Broekel, Ray
See Broekel, Rainer Lothar
Broekstra, Lorette 1964- 189
Earlier sketch in SATA 124
Brogden, Sherryl
See Jordan, Sherryl
Broger, Achim
See Broeger, Achim
Broida, Marian 154
Brokamp, Marilyn 1920- 10
Broman, Fred
See Moseley, James W(illett)
Bromhall, Winifred 26
Brommer, Gerald F(rederick) 1927- 28
Brondfield, Jerome 1913-1998 22
Brondfield, Jerry
See Brondfield, Jerome
Bronner, Stephen Eric 1949- 101
Bronowski, Jacob 1908-1974 55
Bronson, Alice
See Watkins, Dawn L.
Bronson, Lynn
See Lampman, Evelyn Sibley
Bronson, Wilfrid Swancourt 1894-1985
Obituary 43
Brook, Judith (Penelope) 1926- 59
Brief entry 51
Brook, Judy
See Brook, Judith (Penelope)
Brooke, L(eonard) Leslie 1862-1940 17
See also CLR 20
Brooke, William J. 1946- 139
Brooke-Haven, P.
See Wodehouse, P(elham) G(renville)
Brookins, Dana 1931- 28
Brooks, Anita 5
See Abramovitz, Anita (Zeltner Brooks)
Brooks, Bill 1939- 59
Brooks, Bruce 1950- 112
Brief entry 53
Earlier sketch in SATA 72
See also CLR 25
Brooks, Caryl 1924- 84
Brooks, Charlotte K(endrick) 1918-1998 24
Obituary 112
Brooks, Erik 1972- 182
Earlier sketch in SATA 152
Brooks, George
See Baum, L(yman) Frank

Brooks, Gwendolyn 1917-2000 6
  Obituary 123
  See also CLR 27
Brooks, Gwendolyn Elizabeth
  See Brooks, Gwendolyn
Brooks, Jerome 1931- 23
Brooks, Kevin 1959- 150
Brooks, Kevin M.
  See Brooks, Kevin
Brooks, Lester 1924- 7
Brooks, Martha 1944- 134
  Autobiography Feature 134
  Earlier sketches in SATA 68, 121
Brooks, Maurice (Graham) 1900- 45
Brooks, Polly Schoyer 1912- 12
Brooks, Ron 1948- 94
  Brief entry 33
Brooks, Ronald George
  See Brooks, Ron
Brooks, Terry 1944- 60
Brooks, Walter R(ollin) 1886-1958 17
Brooks-Hill, Helen (Mason) 1908-1994 59
Broome, Errol 1937- 158
  Earlier sketch in SATA 105
Brophy, Nannette 1963- 73
Brosnan, James Patrick 1929- 14
Brosnan, Jim
  See Brosnan, James Patrick
Brostoff, Anita 1931- 132
Brothers Grimm
  See Grimm, Jacob Ludwig Karl
  and Grimm, Wilhelm Karl
Brothers Hildebrandt, The
  See Hildebrandt, Greg
  and Hildebrandt, Tim
Broun, Emily
  See Sterne, Emma Gelders
Brouwer, S. W.
  See Brouwer, Sigmund (W.)
Brouwer, Sigmund (W.) 1959- 109
Brow, Thea 1934- 60
Brower, Millicent 8
Brower, Pauline 1929- 22
Browin, Frances Williams 1898-1986 5
Brown, Alexis
  See Baumann, Amy (Brown) Beeching
Brown, Anne Ensign 1937- 61
Brown, Beverly Swerdlow 97
Brown, Bill
  See Brown, William L(ouis)
Brown, Billye Walker
  See Cutchen, Billye Walker
Brown, Bob
  See Brown, Robert Joseph
Brown, Buck 1936- 45
Brown, Calef 179
Brown, Cassie 1919-1986 55
Brown, Charlotte Lewis 181
Brown, Conrad 1922- 31
Brown, Craig McFarland 1947- 73
Brown, David
  See Brown, David A(lan)
  and Myller, Rolf
Brown, Dee 1908-2002 110
  Obituary 141
  Earlier sketch in SATA 5
Brown, Dee Alexander
  See Brown, Dee
Brown, Don 1949- 172
Brown, Drew T. III 1955- 83
Brown, Drollene P. 1939- 53
Brown, Eleanor Frances 1908-1987 3
Brown, Elizabeth Ferguson 1937- 153
Brown, Elizabeth M(yers) 1915- 43
Brown, Fern G. 1918- 34
Brown, (Robert) Fletch 1923- 42
Brown, Fornan 1901-1996 71
  Obituary 88
Brown, George Earl 1883-1964 11
Brown, George Mackay 1921-1996 35
Brown, Irene Bennett 1932- 3

Brown, Irving
  See Adams, William Taylor
Brown, Ivor (John Carnegie) 1891-1974 5
  Obituary 26
Brown, Jane Clark 1930- 81
Brown, Janet Mitsui 87
Brown, Jo 1964- 170
Brown, Joanne 1933- 147
Brown, Joe David 1915-1976 44
Brown, Joseph E(dward) 1929- 59
  Brief entry 51
Brown, Judith Gwyn 1933- 20
Brown, Kathryn 1955- 168
  Earlier sketch in SATA 98
Brown, Kathy
  See Brown, Kathryn
Brown, Ken (James) 129
Brown, Kevin 1960- 101
Brown, Laurene Krasny 1945- 99
  Earlier sketch in SATA 54
Brown, Laurie Krasny
  See Brown, Laurene Krasny
Brown, Lloyd Arnold 1907-1966 36
Brown, Mahlon A.
  See Ellis, Edward S(ylvester)
Brown, Marc (Tolon) 1946- 145
  Earlier sketches in SATA 10, 53, 80
  See also CLR 29
Brown, Marcia (Joan) 1918- 47
  Earlier sketch in SATA 7
  See also CLR 12
Brown, Margaret Wise 1910-1952 100
  See also YABC 2
  See also CLR 107
Brown, Margery (Wheeler) 78
  Earlier sketch in SATA 5
Brown, Marion Marsh 1908-2001 6
Brown, Myra Berry 1918- 6
Brown, Palmer 1919- 36
Brown, Pamela (Beatrice) 1924-1989 5
  Obituary 61
Brown, Peter 1979- 178
Brown, Reeve Lindbergh
  See Lindbergh, Reeve
Brown, Richard E. 1946- 61
Brown, Robert Joseph 1907-1989 14
Brown, Roderick (Langmere) Haig-
  See Haig-Brown, Roderick (Langmere)
Brown, Rosalie 9
  See Moore, Rosalie (Gertrude)
Brown, Roswell
  See Webb, Jean Francis (III)
Brown, Roy (Frederick) 1921-1982 51
  Obituary 39
Brown, Ruth 1941- 170
  Earlier sketch in SATA 105
Brown, Scott 1971- 134
Brown, Sue Ellen 1954- 81
Brown, Tricia 1954- 114
Brown, Vinson 1912-1991 19
Brown, Walter R(eed) 1929- 19
Brown, Will
  See Ainsworth, William Harrison
Brown, William L(ouis) 1910-1964 5
Browne, Anthony 1946- 163
  Brief entry 44
  Earlier sketches in SATA 45, 61, 105
  See also CLR 19
Browne, Anthony Edward Tudor
  See Browne, Anthony
Browne, Dik
  See Browne, Richard Arthur Allen
Browne, Hablot Knight 1815-1882 21
Browne, Matthew
  See Rands, William Brighty
Browne, Nicki M.
  See Browne, N.M.
Browne, Nicky Matthews
  See Browne, N.M.
Browne, N.M. 1960- 167

Browne, Richard Arthur Allen 1917-1989 ... 67
  Brief entry 38
  See Browne, Dik
Browne, Vee F(rances) 1956- 90
Browning, Robert 1812-1889
  See YABC 1
  See also CLR 97
Brownjohn, Alan 1931- 6
Brownlee, Walter 1930- 62
Brownlie, Betty 1946- 159
Brownlow, Kevin 1938- 65
Brownlow, Mike 183
Brownridge, William R(oy) 1932- 94
Bruce, Dorita Fairlie 1885-1970
  Obituary 27
Bruce, (William) Harry 1934- 77
Bruce, Mary 1927- 1
Bruchac, Joseph III
  See Bruchac, Joseph
Bruchac, Joseph 1942- 176
  Autobiography Feature 176
  Earlier sketches in SATA 42, 89, 131
  See also CLR 46
Bruchac, Margaret M.
  See Bruchac, Marge
Bruchac, Marge 181
Bruck, Lorraine 1921- 55
  Brief entry 46
  See Bridges, Laurie
Bruel, Nick 166
Bruel, Robert O. 1929-2002 189
Bruemmer, Fred 1929- 47
Brugman, Alyssa (F.) 1974- 152
Brumbeau, Jeff 1955- 157
Bruna, Dick 1927- 76
  Brief entry 30
  Earlier sketch in SATA 43
  See also CLR 7
Brunhoff, Jean de 1899-1937 24
  See also CLR 116
Brunhoff, Laurent de 1925- 150
  Earlier sketches in SATA 24, 71
  See also CLR 116
Brunskill, Elizabeth Ann Flatt
  See Flatt, Lizann
Brush, Karen A(lexandra) 1960- 85
Brussel-Smith, Bernard 1914- 58
Brust, Steven 1955- 121
  Earlier sketch in SATA 86
Brust, Steven K. Zoltan
  See Brust, Steven
Brustlein, Daniel 1904- 40
Brustlein, Janice Tworkov -2000 40
  Obituary 126
Brutschy, Jennifer 1960- 84
Bryan, Ashley 1923- 178
  Earlier sketches in SATA 31, 72, 132
  See also CLR 66
Bryan, Ashley F.
  See Bryan, Ashley
Bryan, Dorothy M. 1896(?)-1984
  Obituary 39
Bryan, Jennifer 190
Bryan, Sean 192
Bryant, Bernice (Morgan) 1908-1976 11
Bryant, Jen 1960- 175
  Earlier sketch in SATA 94
Bryant, Jennifer Fisher
  See Bryant, Jen
Bryant, Laura J. 176
Brychta, Alex 1956- 21
Brynie, Faith H. 1946- 113
Brynie, Faith Hickman
  See Brynie, Faith H.
Bryson, Bernarda 1903-2004 9
  See Shahn, Bernarda Bryson
Buba, Joy Flinsch 1904- 44
Buchan, Bryan 1945- 36
Buchan, John 1875-1940
  See YABC 2

Buchan, Stuart 1942-1987
  Obituary 54
Buchanan, Debby 1952- 82
Buchanan, Deborah Leevonne
  See Buchanan, Debby
Buchanan, Jane 1956- 160
Buchanan, Paul 1959- 116
Buchanan, Sue 1939- 139
Buchheimer, Naomi Barnett
  See Barnett, Naomi
Buchignani, Walter 1965- 84
Buchmann, Stephen L. 194
Buchwald, Art 1925-2007 10
Buchwald, Arthur
  See Buchwald, Art
Buchwald, Emilie 1935- 7
Buck, Gisela 1941- 101
Buck, Lewis 1925- 18
Buck, Margaret Waring 1905-1997 3
Buck, Nola
  See Godwin, Laura
Buck, Pearl S(ydenstricker) 1892-1973 25
  Earlier sketch in SATA *1*
Buck, Siegfried 1941- 101
Buckeridge, Anthony (Malcolm)
  1912-2004 85
  Earlier sketch in SATA *6*
Buckholtz, Eileen (Garber) 1949- 54
  Brief entry 47
Buckler, Ernest 1908-1984 47
Buckless, Andrea K. 1968- 117
Buckley, Helen E(lizabeth) 1918- 90
  Earlier sketch in SATA *2*
Buckley, James, Jr. 1963- 166
  Earlier sketch in SATA *114*
Buckley, Michael 177
Buckley, Susan 184
Buckley, Susan Washburn
  See Buckley, Susan
Buckley-Archer, Linda 185
Buckmaster, Henrietta 6
  See Stephens, Henrietta Henkle
Bucks, Brad
  See Holub, Joan
Budd, E. S.
  See Sirimarco, Elizabeth
Budd, Lillian (Peterson) 1897-1989 7
Budhos, Marina 173
Buehler, Stephanie Jona 1956- 83
Buehner, Caralyn (M.) 1963- 159
  Earlier sketch in SATA *104*
Buehner, Mark 1959- 159
  Earlier sketch in SATA *104*
Buehr, Walter Franklin 1897-1971 3
Buell, Ellen Lewis
  See Cash, Ellen Lewis Buell
Buell, Janet 1952- 185
  Earlier sketch in SATA *106*
Buergel, Paul-Hermann H. 1949- 83
Buettner, Dan 1960- 95
Buff, Conrad 1886-1975 19
Buff, Mary (E. Marsh) 1890-1970 19
Buffett, Jimmy 1946- 110
  Earlier sketch in SATA *76*
Buffie, Margaret 1945- 161
  Earlier sketches in SATA *71, 107*
  See also CLR *39*
Bugbee, Emma 1888(?)-1981
  Obituary 29
Bugni, Alice 1951- 122
Buhhos, Marina Tamar
  See Budhos, Marina
Bujold, Lois McMaster 1949- 136
Bulfinch, Thomas 1796-1867 35
Bulion, Leslie 1958- 161
Bull, Angela (Mary) 1936- 45
Bull, Emma 1954- 190
  Autobiography Feature 103
  Earlier sketch in SATA *99*
Bull, Norman John 1916- 41

Bull, Peter (Cecil) 1912-1984
  Obituary 39
Bull, Schuyler M. 1974- 138
Bulla, Clyde R. 1914-2007 139
  Obituary 182
  Earlier sketches in SATA *2, 41, 91*
  See also SAAS *6*
Bullard, Lisa 1961- 142
Bullock, Kathleen (Mary) 1946- 77
Bullock, Robert (D.) 1947- 92
Bulpin, (Barbara) Vicki 92
Bumstead, Kathleen Mary 1918-1987 53
Bundles, A'Lelia Perry 1952- 76
Bunin, Catherine 1967- 30
Bunin, Sherry 1925- 30
Bunkers, Suzanne L. 1950- 136
Bunting, A. E.
  See Bunting, (Anne) Eve(lyn)
Bunting, Eve
  See Bunting, (Anne) Eve(lyn)
Bunting, (Anne) Eve(lyn) 1928- 158
  Earlier sketches in SATA *18, 64, 110*
  See also CLR *82*
  See Bunting, Eve
Bunting, Glenn (Davison) 1957- 22
Bunyan, John 1628-1688
  See CLR *124*
Burack, Sylvia K. 1916-2003 35
  Obituary 143
Burbank, Addison (Buswell) 1895-1961 37
Burch, Joann J(ohansen) 75
Burch, Robert J(oseph) 1925- 74
  Earlier sketch in SATA *1*
  See also CLR *63*
Burchard, Peter Duncan 1921- 143
  Earlier sketches in SATA *5, 74*
  See also SAAS *13*
Burchard, S. H.
  See Burchard, Sue
Burchard, Sue 1937- 22
Burckhardt, Nellie 1921- 7
Burdett, Lois 117
Burdick, Eugene (Leonard) 1918-1965 22
Burford, Eleanor
  See Hibbert, Eleanor Alice Burford
Burgan, Michael 1960- 167
  Earlier sketch in SATA *118*
Burger, Carl 1888-1967 9
Burgess, Ann Marie
  See Gerson, Noel Bertram
Burgess, Barbara Hood 1926- 69
Burgess, Em
  See Burgess, Mary Wyche
Burgess, (Frank) Gelett 1866-1951 32
  Brief entry 30
Burgess, Mark 157
Burgess, Mary Wyche 1916- 18
Burgess, Melvin 1954- 146
  Earlier sketch in SATA *96*
Burgess, Michael
  See Gerson, Noel Bertram
Burgess, Robert F(orrest) 1927- 4
Burgess, Starling
  See Tudor, Tasha
Burgess, Thornton Waldo 1874-1965 17
Burgess, Trevor
  See Trevor, Elleston
Burgwyn, Mebane Holoman 1914-1992 7
Burke, David 1927- 46
Burke, Diana G.
  See Gallagher, Diana G.
Burke, Diana Gallagher
  See Gallagher, Diana G.
Burke, Dianne O'Quinn 1940- 89
Burke, Janine 1952- 139
Burke, Jim 1973- 179
Burke, John
  See O'Connor, Richard
Burke, Katie 1953- 168
Burke, Patrick 1958- 114

Burke, Ralph
  See Garrett, (Gordon) Randall (Phillip)
  and Silverberg, Robert
Burkert, Nancy Ekholm 1933- 24
  See also SAAS *14*
Burkett, D. Brent 194
Burke-Weiner, Kimberly 1962- 95
Burks, Brian 1955- 95
Burland, Brian (Berkeley) 1931- 34
Burland, C. A.
  See Burland, Cottie (Arthur)
Burland, Cottie (Arthur) 1905-1983 5
Burleigh, Robert 1936- 193
  Earlier sketches in SATA *55, 98, 146*
Burlingame, (William) Roger 1889-1967 2
Burman, Alice Caddy 1896(?)-1977
  Obituary 24
Burman, Ben Lucien 1896-1984 6
  Obituary 40
Burn, Doris 1923- 1
Burn, Ted
  See Burn, Thomas E.
Burn, Thomas E. 1940- 150
Burnard, Damon 1963- 115
Burnett, Constance Buel 1893-1975 36
Burnett, Frances (Eliza) Hodgson
  1849-1924 100
  See also YABC *2*
  See also CLR *122*
Burnett Bossi, Lisa 193
Burney, Anton
  See Hopkins, (Hector) Kenneth
Burnford, Sheila (Philip Cochrane Every)
  1918-1984 3
  Obituary 38
  See also CLR *2*
Burnham, Gretchen
  See Sprague, Gretchen
Burnham, Nicole 1970- 161
Burnham, Niki
  See Burnham, Nicole
Burnham, Sophy 1936- 65
Burningham, John 1936- 160
  Earlier sketches in SATA *16, 59, 111*
  See also CLR *9*
Burns, Diane L. 1950- 81
  See also SAAS *24*
Burns, Eloise Wilkin
  See Wilkin, Eloise
Burns, Florence M. 1905-1988 61
Burns, Khephra 1950- 92
Burns, Loree Griffin 193
Burns, Marilyn 1941- 96
  Brief entry 33
Burns, Olive Ann 1924-1990 65
Burns, Paul C. 5
Burns, Ray
  See Burns, Raymond (Howard)
Burns, Raymond (Howard) 1924- 9
Burns, Theresa 1961- 84
Burns, William A. 1909-1999 5
Burr, Dan 1951- 65
Burr, Lonnie 1943- 47
Burrell, Roy E(ric) C(harles) 1923- 72
Burroughs, Edgar Rice 1875-1950 41
Burroughs, Jean Mitchell 1908- 28
Burroughs, Polly 1925- 2
Burroway, Janet (Gay) 1936- 23
Burstein, Chaya M(alamud) 1923- 64
Burstein, Fred 1950- 83
Burstein, John 1949- 54
  Brief entry 40
Burstein, Stanley M.
  See Burstein, Stanley Mayer
Burstein, Stanley Mayer 1941- 175
Bursztynski, Sue 1953- 114
Burt, Jesse Clifton 1921-1976 46
  Obituary 20
Burt, Olive Woolley 1894-1981 4
Burtinshaw, Julie 185
Burton, Gennett 1945- 95

Burton, Hester (Wood-Hill) 1913-2000 74
Earlier sketch in SATA 7
See also CLR 1
See also SAAS 8
Burton, Leslie
See McGuire, Leslie (Sarah)
Burton, Marilee Robin 1950- 82
Earlier sketch in SATA 46
Burton, Maurice 1898-1992 23
Burton, Rebecca 1970- 183
Burton, Robert (Wellesley) 1941- 22
Burton, Virginia Lee 1909-1968 100
Earlier sketch in SATA 2
See also CLR 11
Burton, William H(enry) 1890-1964 11
Busby, Ailie 192
Busby, Cylin 1970- 118
Busby, Edith (A. Lake) (?)-1964
Obituary 29
Buscaglia, (Felice) Leo(nardo) 1924-1998 ... 65
See also Buscaglia, Leo F.
Buscaglia, Leo F.
See Buscaglia, (Felice) Leo(nardo)
Busch, Phyllis S. 1909- 30
Bush, Anne Kelleher
See Kelleher, Anne
Bush, Catherine 1961- 128
Bushmiller, Ernie
Obituary 31
See Bushmiller, Ernest Paul
Bushnell, Jack 1952- 86
Busoni, Rafaello 1900-1962 16
Buss, Helen M.
See Clarke, Margaret
Busse, Sarah Martin 194
Busselle, Rebecca 1941- 80
Bustard, Anne 1951- 173
Butcher, Kristin 1951- 140
Butenko, Bohdan 1931- 90
Butler, Beverly Kathleen 1932- 7
Butler, Bill
See Butler, William (Arthur) Vivian
and Butler, Ernest Alton
and Butler, William Huxford
Butler, Charles 1963- 175
Earlier sketch in SATA 121
Butler, Charles Cadman
See Butler, Charles
Butler, Dori Hillestad 1965- 164
Butler, Dorothy 1925- 73
Butler, Geoff 1945- 94
Butler, M. Christina 1934- 170
Earlier sketch in SATA 72
Butler, Octavia E. 1947-2006 84
See also CLR 65
Butler, Octavia Estelle
See Butler, Octavia E.
Butler, Vivian
See Butler, William (Arthur) Vivian
Butler, William
See Butler, William (Arthur) Vivian
Butler, William (Arthur) Vivian 1927-1987 . 79
See Marric, J. J.
Butters, Dorothy Gilman 5
See Gilman, Dorothy
Butterworth, Emma Macalik 1928- 43
Butterworth, Nick 1946- 149
Earlier sketch in SATA 106
Butterworth, Oliver 1915-1990 1
Obituary 66
Butterworth, W.E.
See Griffin, W.E.B
Butterworth, William E.
See Griffin, W.E.B
Butterworth, William Edmund III
See Griffin, W.E.B
Butts, Ed 1951- 177
Butts, Edward P.
See Butts, Ed
Butts, Ellen R(ubinstein) 1942- 93

Buxton, Ralph
See Silverstein, Alvin
and Silverstein, Virginia B(arbara Opshelor)
Buzzeo, Toni 1951- 135
Byalick, Marcia 1947- 141
Earlier sketch in SATA 97
Byard, Carole (Marie) 1941- 57
Byars, Betsy 1928- 163
Autobiography Feature 108
Earlier sketches in SATA 4, 46, 80
See also CLR 72
See also SAAS 1
Byars, Betsy Cromer
See Byars, Betsy
Byfield, Barbara Ninde 1930- 8
Byman, Jeremy 1944- 129
Bynum, Janie 133
Byrd, Elizabeth 1912-1989 34
Byrd, Nicole
See Zach, Cheryl (Byrd)
Byrd, Robert (John) 1942- 158
Earlier sketches in SATA 33, 112
Byrne, Mary Gregg 1951- 162

C

C. 3. 3.
See Wilde, Oscar
Cabaniss, J(ames) Allen 1911-1997 5
Cabat, Erni 1914- 74
Cabban, Vanessa 1971- 176
Cable, Mary 1920- 9
Cabot, Meg 1967- 175
Earlier sketch in SATA 127
See also CLR 85
Cabot, Meggin
See Cabot, Meg
Cabot, Meggin Patricia
See Cabot, Meg
Cabot, Patricia
See Cabot, Meg
Cabral, O. M.
See Cabral, Olga
Cabral, Olga 1909- 46
Cabrera, Cozbi A. 1963- 177
Cabrera, Jane 1968- 182
Earlier sketches in SATA 103, 152
Cabrera, Marcela 1966- 90
Caddy, Alice
See Burman, Alice Caddy
Cade, Toni
See Bambara, Toni Cade
Cadmus and Harmonia
See Buchan, John
Cadnum, Michael 1949- 165
Earlier sketches in SATA 87, 121
See also CLR 78
Caduto, Michael J. 1955- 103
Cadwallader, Sharon 1936- 7
Cady, (Walter) Harrison 1877(?)-1970 19
Caffey, Donna (J.) 1954- 110
Cagle, Malcolm W(infield) 1918- 32
Cahn, Rhoda 1922- 37
Cahn, William 1912-1976 37
Cain, Arthur H(omer) 1913-1981 3
Cain, Christopher
See Fleming, Thomas
Cain, Sheridan 1952- 186
Caine, Geoffrey
See Walker, Robert W(ayne)
Caines, Jeannette (Franklin) 1938- 78
Brief entry 43
See also CLR 24
Cairns, Trevor 1922- 14
Calabro, Marian 1954- 79
Caldecott, Moyra 1927- 22
Caldecott, Randolph (J.) 1846-1886 100
Earlier sketch in SATA 17
See also CLR 110

Calder, Charlotte 1952- 125
Calder, David 1932-1997 105
Calder, Lyn
See Calmenson, Stephanie
Calder, Marie D(onais) 1948- 96
Calderone-Stewart, Lisa
See Calderone-Stewart, Lisa-Marie
Calderone-Stewart, Lisa-Marie 1958- 123
Caldwell, Doreen (Mary) 1942- 71
Caldwell, John C(ope) 1913-1984 7
Caletti, Deb 1963- 171
Calhoun, B. B. 1961- 98
Calhoun, Chad
See Barrett, Neal, Jr.
and Cunningham, Chet
and Goulart, Ron(ald Joseph)
Calhoun, Dia 1959- 183
Earlier sketch in SATA 129
Calhoun, Mary 2
See also CLR 42
See Wilkins, Mary Huiskamp
Calhoun, T.B.
See Bisson, Terry
Cali, Davide 1972- 190
Calif, Ruth 1922- 67
Calkins, Franklin
See Stratemeyer, Edward L.
Call, Hughie Florence 1890-1969 1
Callahan, Dorothy M(onahan) 1934- 39
Brief entry 35
Callahan, Philip Serna 1923- 25
Callan, Jamie 1954- 59
Callan, Jim 1951- 181
Callaway, Bernice (Anne) 1923- 48
Callaway, Kathy 1943- 36
Callen, Larry
See Callen, Lawrence Willard, Jr.
Callen, Lawrence Willard, Jr. 1927- 19
Calley, Karin 1965- 92
Calmenson, Stephanie 1952- 139
Brief entry 37
Earlier sketches in SATA 51, 84
Calvert, Elinor H.
See Lasell, Elinor H.
Calvert, John
See Leaf, (Wilbur) Munro
Calvert, Patricia 1931- 132
Earlier sketches in SATA 45, 69
See also SAAS 17
Camburn, Carol A.
See Camburn-Bracalente, Carol A.
Camburn-Bracalente, Carol A. 1962- 118
Cameron, Ann 1943- 129
Earlier sketches in SATA 27, 89
See also SAAS 20
Cameron, Edna M. 1905-1999 3
Cameron, Eleanor (Frances) 1912-1996 25
Obituary 93
Earlier sketch in SATA 1
See also CLR 72
See also SAAS 10
Cameron, Elizabeth
See Nowell, Elizabeth Cameron
Cameron, Elizabeth Jane 1910-1976 32
Obituary 30
Cameron, Ian
See Payne, Donald Gordon
Cameron, M(alcolm) G(ordon) Graham
See Graham-Cameron, M(alcolm) G(ordon)
Cameron, M. Graham
See Graham-Cameron, M(alcolm) G(ordon)
Cameron, Mike Graham
See Graham-Cameron, M(alcolm) G(ordon)
Cameron, Polly 1928- 2
Cameron, Scott 1962- 84
Camp, Charles L. 1893-1975
Obituary 31
Camp, Lindsay 1957- 133
Camp, Madeleine L'Engle
See L'Engle, Madeleine

Camp, Walter (Chauncey) 1859-1925
See YABC *1*
Campbell, (Elizabeth) Andrea 1963- *50*
Campbell, Ann R. 1925- *11*
Campbell, Bill 1960- *89*
Campbell, Bruce
See Epstein, Samuel
Campbell, Camilla 1905-1992 .... *26*
Campbell, Carole R. 1939- *125*
Campbell, Hope 1925- *20*
Campbell, Hugh 1930- *90*
Campbell, Jane
See Edwards, Jane Campbell
Campbell, Julie
See Tatham, Julie Campbell
Campbell, Patricia J(ean) 1930- *45*
Campbell, Patty
See Campbell, Patricia J(ean)
Campbell, Peter A. 1948- *99*
Campbell, R. W.
See Campbell, Rosemae Wells
Campbell, Robin
See Strachan, Ian
Campbell, Rod 1945- *98*
Brief entry *44*
Earlier sketch in SATA *51*
Campbell, Rosemae Wells 1909- *1*
Camper, Cathy 1956- *170*
Campion, Nardi Reeder 1917-2007 .... *22*
Campling, Elizabeth 1948- *53*
Campoy, F. Isabel 1946- *181*
Earlier sketch in SATA *143*
Camps, Luis 1928- *66*
Canales, Viola 1957- *141*
Candell, Victor 1903-1977
Obituary *24*
Canfield, Dorothea F.
See Fisher, Dorothy (Frances) Canfield
Canfield, Dorothea Frances
See Fisher, Dorothy (Frances) Canfield
Canfield, Dorothy
See Fisher, Dorothy (Frances) Canfield
Canfield, Jack 1944- *164*
Canfield, Jane White 1897-1984 .... *32*
Obituary *38*
Canfield, Muriel 1935- *94*
Caniff, Milton 1907-1988
Obituary *58*
Caniff, Milton Arthur Paul
See Caniff, Milton
Cann, Helen 1969- *179*
Earlier sketch in SATA *124*
Cann, Kate 1954- *152*
Earlier sketch in SATA *103*
Cannan, Joanna *82*
See Pullein-Thompson, Joanna Maxwell
Cannon, A(nn) E(dwards) *163*
Earlier sketch in SATA *93*
Cannon, Bettie (Waddell) 1922- *59*
Cannon, Curt
See Hunter, Evan
Cannon, Eileen E(mily) 1948- *119*
Cannon, Frank
See Mayhar, Ardath
Cannon, Janell 1957- *128*
Earlier sketch in SATA *78*
See also CLR *120*
Cannon, Marian G. 1923- *85*
Cannon, Taffy
See Cannon, Eileen E(mily)
Cantone, AnnaLaura *182*
Canusi, Jose
See Barker, S(quire) Omar
Canyon, Christopher 1966- *150*
Earlier sketch in SATA *104*
Capek, Michael 1947- *142*
Earlier sketch in SATA *96*
Capes, Bernard (Edward Joseph)
1854-1918 .... *116*
Caple, Kathy *193*

Caplin, Alfred Gerald 1909-1979
Obituary *21*
See Capp, Al
Caponigro, John Paul 1965- *84*
Capote, Truman 1924-1984 .... *91*
Capp, Al *61*
See Caplin, Alfred Gerald
Cappel, Constance 1936- *22*
Cappetta, Cynthia 1949- *125*
Cappo, Nan Willard 1955- *143*
Capps, Benjamin (Franklin) 1922- *9*
Cappy Dick
See Cleveland, George
Captain Kangaroo
See Keeshan, Robert J.
Captain Wheeler
See Ellis, Edward S(ylvester)
Captain Young of Yale
See Stratemeyer, Edward L.
Capucilli, Alyssa Satin 1957- *163*
Earlier sketch in SATA *115*
Capucine
See Mazille, Capucine
Caraher, Kim(berley Elizabeth) 1961- *105*
Caraker, Mary 1929- *74*
Caras, Roger A(ndrew) 1928-2001 .... *12*
Obituary *127*
Caravantes, Peggy 1935- *140*
Caraway, Caren 1939- *57*
Carbone, Elisa 1954- *137*
Earlier sketch in SATA *81*
See Carbone, Elisa Lynn
Carbone, Elisa Lynn *173*
See Carbone, Elisa
Carbonnier, Jeanne 1894-1974 .... *3*
Obituary *34*
Card, Orson Scott 1951- *127*
Earlier sketch in SATA *83*
See also CLR *116*
Care, Felicity
See Coury, Louise Andree
Carew, Jan 1925- *51*
Brief entry *40*
Carew, Jan Rynveld
See Carew, Jan
Carey, Bonnie
See Marshall, Bonnie C.
Carey, Charles W., Jr. 1951- *170*
Carey, Ernestine Gilbreth 1908-2006 .... *2*
Obituary *177*
Carey, Janet Lee 1959(?)- *185*
Carey, Lisa *110*
Carey, M. V.
See Carey, Mary V(irginia)
Carey, Mary V(irginia) 1925-1994 .... *44*
Brief entry *39*
Carey, Peter 1943- *94*
Carey, Peter Philip
See Carey, Peter
Carey, Valerie Scho 1949- *60*
Carheden, Goorel Kristina
See Naaslund, Goorel Kristina
Carigiet, Alois 1902-1985 .... *24*
Obituary *47*
See also CLR *38*
Carini, Edward 1923- *9*
Carkeet, David 1946- *75*
Carle, Eric 1929- *163*
Earlier sketches in SATA *4, 65, 120*
See also CLR *72*
See also SAAS *6*
Carleton, Captain L. C.
See Ellis, Edward S(ylvester)
Carleton, Captain Latham C.
See Ellis, Edward S(ylvester)
Carleton, Latham C.
See Ellis, Edward S(ylvester)
Carley, V(an Ness) Royal 1906-1976
Obituary *20*
Carling, Amelia Lau 1949- *164*
Earlier sketch in SATA *119*

Carlisle, Carolyn
See Hawes, Louise
Carlisle, Clark
See Holding, James (Clark Carlisle, Jr.)
Carlisle, Olga Andreyev 1930- *35*
Carlock, Miriam
See Eyerly, Jeannette
Carlsen, G(eorge) Robert 1917- *30*
Carlsen, Ruth C(hristoffer) 1918- *2*
Carlson, Bernice Wells 1910- *8*
Carlson, Dale (Bick) 1935- *1*
Carlson, Daniel (Bick) 1960- *27*
Carlson, Kirsten 1968- *192*
Carlson, Kirsten M.
See Carlson, Kirsten
Carlson, Laurie 1952- *173*
Earlier sketch in SATA *101*
Carlson, Laurie Winn
See Carlson, Laurie
Carlson, Melody 1956- *171*
Earlier sketch in SATA *113*
Carlson, Nancy L.
See Carlson, Nancy L(ee)
Carlson, Nancy L(ee) 1953- *144*
Brief entry *45*
Earlier sketches in SATA *56, 90*
Carlson, Natalie Savage 1906-1997 .... *68*
Earlier sketch in SATA *2*
See also SAAS *4*
Carlson, Susan Johnston 1953- *88*
Carlson, Vada F. 1897- *16*
Carlstrom, Nancy White 1948- *156*
Brief entry *48*
Earlier sketches in SATA *53, 92*
Carlton, Keith
See Robertson, Keith (Carlton)
Carlton, Susan 1960- *195*
Carlyon, Richard *55*
Carman, Patrick *161*
Carmer, Carl (Lamson) 1893-1976 .... *37*
Obituary *30*
Carmer, Elizabeth Black 1904- *24*
Carmi, Giora 1944- *149*
Earlier sketch in SATA *79*
Carmichael, Carrie *40*
See Carmichael, Harriet
Carmody, Isobelle 1958- *191*
Earlier sketch in SATA *161*
Carmody, Isobelle Jane
See Carmody, Isobelle
Carney, Mary Lou 1949- *170*
Carol, Bill J.
See Knott, William C(ecil, Jr.)
Caron, Romi
See Caron-Kyselkova', Romana
Caron-Kyselkova', Romana 1967- *94*
Caroselli, Remus F(rancis) 1916- *36*
Carpelan, Bo 1926- *8*
Carpelan, Bo Gustaf Bertelsson
See Carpelan, Bo
Carpenter, (John) Allan 1917- *81*
Earlier sketch in SATA *3*
Carpenter, Angelica Shirley 1945- *153*
Earlier sketch in SATA *71*
Carpenter, Frances 1890-1972 .... *3*
Obituary *27*
Carpenter, John (Howard) 1948- *58*
Carpenter, Johnny
See Carpenter, John (Howard)
Carpenter, Patricia (Healy Evans) 1920- *11*
Carr, Glyn
See Styles, (Frank) Showell
Carr, Harriett H(elen) 1899-1977 .... *3*
Carr, Jan 1953- *132*
Earlier sketch in SATA *89*
Carr, M. J.
See Carr, Jan
Carr, Mary Jane 1899-1988 .... *2*
Obituary *55*
Carr, Philippa
See Hibbert, Eleanor Alice Burford

Carr, Roger Vaughan 1937- 95
Carrel, Annette Felder 1929- 90
Carrick, Carol (Hatfield) 1935- 118
  Earlier sketches in SATA 7, 63
  See also SAAS 18
Carrick, Donald (F.) 1929-1989 63
  Earlier sketch in SATA 7
Carrick, Malcolm 1945- 28
Carrick, Paul 1972- 194
Carrier, Lark 1947- 71
  Brief entry 50
Carrier, Roch 1937- 166
  Earlier sketch in SATA 105
Carrighar, Sally 1898-1985 24
Carrington, G. A.
  See Cunningham, Chet
Carrington, Marsha Gray 1954- 168
  Earlier sketch in SATA 111
Carris, Joan 1938- 182
  Brief entry 42
  Earlier sketch in SATA 44
Carris, Joan Davenport
  See Carris, Joan
Carroll, Curt
  See Bishop, Curtis (Kent)
Carroll, Elizabeth
  See Barkin, Carol
  and James, Elizabeth
Carroll, Jenny
  See Cabot, Meg
Carroll, (Archer) Latrobe 1894-1996 7
Carroll, Laura
  See Parr, Lucy
Carroll, Lewis
  See CLR 108
  See Dodgson, Charles L(utwidge)
Carroll, Raymond 1924- 86
  Brief entry 47
Carruth, Hayden 1921-2008 47
Carryl, Charles E. 1841-1920 114
Carryl, Charles Edward
  See Carryl, Charles E.
Carse, Robert 1902-1971 5
Carson, J(ohn) Franklin 1920-1981 1
  Obituary 107
Carson, Mary Kay 1964- 150
Carson, Rachel
  See Carson, Rachel Louise
Carson, Rachel Louise 1907-1964 23
  See Carson, Rachel
Carson, Rosalind
  See Chittenden, Margaret
Carson, S. M.
  See Gorsline, (Sally) Marie
Carson, William C. 1928- 154
Carter, Abby 184
Carter, Alden R 1947- 137
  Earlier sketch in SATA 67
  See also CLR 22
  See also SAAS 18
Carter, Alden Richardson
  See Carter, Alden R
Carter, Andy 1948- 134
Carter, Angela 1940-1992 66
  Obituary 70
Carter, Angela Olive
  See Carter, Angela
Carter, Anne Laurel 1953- 135
Carter, Asa Earl
  See Carter, Forrest
Carter, Avis Murton
  See Allen, Kenneth S.
Carter, Bruce
  See Hough, Richard (Alexander)
Carter, Carol S(hadis) 1948- 124
Carter, David A. 1957- 170
  Earlier sketch in SATA 114
Carter, Don 1958- 192
  Earlier sketch in SATA 124
Carter, Dorothy Sharp 1921- 8
Carter, Forrest 1927(?)-1979 32

Carter, Helene 1887-1960 15
Carter, (William) Hodding, Jr. 1907-1972 2
  Obituary 27
Carter, James Earl, Jr.
  See Carter, Jimmy
Carter, Jimmy 1924- 79
Carter, Katharine J(ones) 1905-1984 2
Carter, Lin(wood Vrooman) 1930-1988 91
Carter, Mike 1936- 138
Carter, Nick
  See Avallone, Michael (Angelo, Jr.)
  and Ballard, (Willis) Todhunter
  and Crider, Bill
  and Cassiday, Bruce (Bingham)
  and Chastain, Thomas
  and Dey, Frederic (Merrill) Van Rensselaer
  and Garside, (Clifford) Jack
  and Hayes, Ralph E(ugene)
  and Henderson, M(arilyn) R(uth)
  and Lynds, Dennis
  and Lynds, Gayle (Hallenbeck)
  and Randisi, Robert J.
  and Rasof, Henry
  and Stratemeyer, Edward L.
  and Smith, Martin Cruz
  and Swain, Dwight V(reeland)
  and Vardeman, Robert E(dward)
  and Wallmann, Jeffrey M(iner)
  and White, Lionel
Carter, Peter 1929- 57
Carter, Phyllis Ann
  See Eberle, Irmengarde
Carter, Samuel (Thomson) III 1904-1988 37
  Obituary 60
Carter, William E. 1926-1983 1
  Obituary 35
Cartlidge, Michelle 1950- 96
  Brief entry 37
  Earlier sketch in SATA 49
Cartner, William Carruthers 1910- 11
Cartwright, Ann 1940- 78
Cartwright, Reg(inald Ainsley) 1938- 64
Cartwright, Sally 1923- 9
Carusone, Al 1949- 89
Carvell, Marlene 172
Carver, John
  See Gardner, Richard (M.)
Carwell, L'Ann
  See McKissack, Patricia C.
Cary
  See Cary, Louis F(avreau)
Cary, Barbara Knapp 1912(?)-1975
  Obituary 31
Cary, Kate 1967(?)- 174
Cary, Louis F(avreau) 1915- 9
Caryl, Jean
  See Kaplan, Jean Caryl Korn
Casanova, Mary 1957- 186
  Earlier sketches in SATA 94, 136
Cascone, A.G.
  See Cascone, Annette
  and Cascone, Gina
Cascone, Annette 1960- 103
Cascone, Gina 1955- 103
Case, Marshal T(aylor) 1941- 9
Case, Michael
  See Howard, Robert West
Caseley, Judith 1951- 159
  Brief entry 53
  Earlier sketch in SATA 87
Casewit, Curtis W(erner) 1922-2002 4
Casey, Barbara (Louise) 1944- 147
  Earlier sketch in SATA 79
Casey, Brigid 1950- 9
Casey, Tina 1959- 141
Cash, Ellen Lewis Buell 1905-1989
  Obituary 64
Cash, Megan Montague 160
Casilla, Robert 1959- 146
  Earlier sketch in SATA 75
Cason, Mabel Earp 1892-1965 10

Cass, Joan E(velyn) 1
Cass-Beggs, Barbara 1904- 62
Cassedy, Patrice (Rinaldo) 1953- 149
Cassedy, Sylvia 1930-1989 77
  Obituary 61
  Earlier sketch in SATA 27
  See also CLR 26
Cassel, Lili
  See Wronker, Lili Cassel
Cassels, Jean 173
Cassidy, Anne 1952- 166
Cassidy, Cathy 1962- 183
Casson, Hugh Maxwell 1910-1999 65
  Obituary 115
Cassutt, Michael 1954- 78
Cassutt, Michael Joseph
  See Cassutt, Michael
Castaldi, Elicia 194
Castaldo, Nancy Fusco 1962- 151
  Earlier sketch in SATA 93
Castaneda, Omar S. 1954- 71
Castell, Megan
  See Williams, Jeanne
Castellanos, Jane Mollie Robinson
  1913-2001 9
Castellon, Federico 1914-1971 48
Castellucci, Cecil 1969- 176
Castillo, Edmund L. 1924-2005 1
  Obituary 167
Castillo, Lauren 195
Castle, Lee
  See Ogan, George F.
  and Ogan, Margaret E. (Nettles)
Castle, Paul
  See Howard, Vernon (Linwood)
Castle, Robert
  See Hamilton, Edmond
Castrovilla, Selene 1966- 186
Caswell, Brian 1954- 171
  Earlier sketch in SATA 97
Caswell, Helen (Rayburn) 1923- 12
Catalano, Dominic 1956- 163
  Earlier sketch in SATA 76
Catalano, Grace (A.) 1961- 99
Catalanotto, Peter 1959- 195
  Autobiography Feature 113
  Earlier sketches in SATA 70, 114, 159
  See also CLR 68
  See also SAAS 25
Catanese, P.W. 1961- 179
Cate, Dick
  See Cate, Richard Edward Nelson
Cate, Richard Edward Nelson 1932- 28
Cather, Willa (Sibert) 1873-1947 30
  See also CLR 98
Catherall, Arthur 1906-1980 74
  Earlier sketch in SATA 3
  See Ruthin, Margaret
Cathon, Laura E(lizabeth) 1908-1991 27
Catlett, Elizabeth 1919(?)- 82
Catlin, Wynelle 1930- 13
Catlow, Nikalas
  See Catlow, Niki
Catlow, Niki 1975- 193
Cato, Heather 105
Cato, Sheila 114
Catran, Ken 1944- 190
Catrow, David
  See Catrow, David J. III
Catrow, David J. III 152
Catt, Louis
  See French, Vivian
Cattell, James 1954- 123
Catton, (Charles) Bruce 1899-1978 2
  Obituary 24
Catz, Max
  See Glaser, Milton
Caudell, Marian 1930- 52
Caudill, Rebecca 1899-1985 1
  Obituary 44

Cauley, Lorinda Bryan 1951- *46*
  Brief entry *43*
Caulfield, Peggy F. 1926-1987
  Obituary *53*
Cauman, Samuel 1910-1971 .... *48*
Causley, Charles (Stanley) 1917-2003 .... *66*
  Obituary *149*
  Earlier sketch in SATA *3*
  See also CLR *30*
Cavallaro, Ann (Abelson) 1918- *62*
Cavallo, Diana 1931- *7*
Cavanagh, Helen (Carol) 1939- *98*
  Brief entry *37*
  Earlier sketch in SATA *48*
Cavanah, Frances 1899-1982 .... *31*
  Earlier sketch in SATA *1*
Cavanna, Betty *30*
  Earlier sketch in SATA *1*
  See also SAAS *4*
  See Harrison, Elizabeth (Allen) Cavanna
Cavanna, Elizabeth
  See Harrison, Elizabeth (Allen) Cavanna
Cave, Kathryn 1948- *123*
  Earlier sketch in SATA *76*
Cavendish, Peter
  See Horler, Sydney
Cavin, Ruth (Brodie) 1918- *38*
Cavoukian, Raffi 1948- *68*
Cawley, Winifred 1915- *13*
Caxton, Pisistratus
  See Lytton, Edward G(eorge) E(arle) L(ytton)
  Bulwer-Lytton Baron
Cazeau, Charles J(ay) 1931- *65*
Cazet, Denys 1938- *191*
  Brief entry *41*
  Earlier sketches in SATA *52, 99, 163*
Cazzola, Gus 1934- *73*
Cebulash, Mel 1937- *91*
  Earlier sketch in SATA *10*
Ceccoli, Nicoletta *181*
Cecil, Randy 1968- *187*
Ceder, Georgiana Dorcas -1985 .... *10*
Celenza, Anna Harwell *133*
Celestino, Martha Laing
  See Laing, Martha
Cepeda, Joe *159*
Cerf, Bennett (Alfred) 1898-1971 .... *7*
Cerf, Christopher (Bennett) 1941- *2*
Cermak, Martin
  See Duchacek, Ivo D(uka)
Cerullo, Mary M. 1949- *145*
  Earlier sketch in SATA *86*
Cervon, Jacqueline
  See Moussard, Jacqueline
Cetin, Frank Stanley 1921- *2*
Chabon, Michael 1963- *145*
Chaconas, D.J.
  See Chaconas, Dori
Chaconas, Dori 1938- *175*
  Earlier sketch in SATA *145*
Chaconas, Doris J.
  See Chaconas, Dori
Chadwick, Lester *67*
  Earlier sketch in SATA *1*
Chaffee, Allen *3*
Chaffin, Lillie D(orton) 1925- *4*
Chaikin, Miriam 1924- *152*
  Earlier sketches in SATA *24, 102*
Chall, Marsha Wilson *150*
Challand, Helen J(ean) 1921- *64*
Challans, Mary 1905-1983 .... *23*
  Obituary *36*
  See Renault, Mary
Chalmers, Mary (Eileen) 1927- *6*
  See also SAAS *14*
Chamberlain, Barbara A.
  See Azore, Barbara
Chamberlain, Margaret 1954- *46*
Chamberlin, Kate 1945- *105*
Chamberlin, Mary 1960- *177*
Chamberlin, Rich *177*

Chamberlin, Richard
  See Chamberlin, Rich
Chambers, Aidan 1934- *171*
  Earlier sketches in SATA *1, 69, 108*
  See also SAAS *12*
Chambers, Bradford 1922-1984
  Obituary *39*
Chambers, Catherine E.
  See St. John, Nicole
Chambers, John W. 1933- *57*
  Brief entry *46*
Chambers, Kate
  See St. John, Nicole
Chambers, Margaret Ada Eastwood 1911- *2*
Chambers, Peggy
  See Chambers, Margaret Ada Eastwood
Chambers, Robert W(illiam) 1865-1933 .... *107*
Chambliss, Maxie *186*
Chan, Gillian 1954- *147*
  Earlier sketch in SATA *102*
Chance, James T.
  See Carpenter, John (Howard)
Chance, John T.
  See Carpenter, John (Howard)
Chance, Stephen
  See Turner, Philip (William)
Chandler, Caroline A(ugusta) 1906-1979 ..... *22*
  Obituary *24*
Chandler, David P(orter) 1933- *28*
Chandler, Edna Walker 1908-1982 .... *11*
  Obituary *31*
Chandler, Jennifer
  See Westwood, Jennifer
Chandler, Karen 1959- *122*
Chandler, Linda S(mith) 1929- *39*
Chandler, Pauline *175*
Chandler, Robert 1953- *40*
Chandler, Ruth Forbes 1894-1978 .... *2*
  Obituary *26*
Chandonnet, Ann F. 1943- *92*
Chaney, Jill 1932- *87*
Chang, Chih-Wei 1966- *111*
Chang, Cindy 1968- *90*
Chang, Margaret 1941- *71*
Chang, Margaret Scrogin
  See Chang, Margaret
Chang, Raymond 1939- *142*
  Earlier sketches in SATA *71, 142 PEN*
Chanin, Michael 1952- *84*
Channel, A. R.
  See Catherall, Arthur
Chapian, Marie 1938- *29*
Chapin, Alene Olsen Dalton 1915(?)-1986
  Obituary *47*
Chapin, Tom 1945- *83*
Chapman, Allen *67*
  Earlier sketch in SATA *1*
Chapman, Cheryl O(rth) 1948- *80*
Chapman, (Constance) Elizabeth (Mann)
  1919- *10*
Chapman, Gaynor 1935- *32*
Chapman, Gillian 1955- *120*
Chapman, Jane 1970- *176*
  Earlier sketch in SATA *122*
Chapman, Jean *104*
  Earlier sketch in SATA *34*
  See also CLR *65*
Chapman, John Stanton Higham 1891-1972
  Obituary *27*
Chapman, Lee
  See Bradley, Marion Zimmer
Chapman, Lynne F(erguson) 1963- *150*
  Earlier sketch in SATA *94*
Chapman, Maristan
  See Chapman, John Stanton Higham
Chapman, Vera (Ivy May) 1898-1996 .... *33*
Chapman, Walker
  See Silverberg, Robert
Chappell, Audrey 1954- *72*

Chappell, Warren 1904-1991 .... *68*
  Obituary *67*
  Earlier sketch in SATA *6*
  See also SAAS *10*
Chapra, Mimi *182*
Charbonneau, Eileen 1951- *118*
  Earlier sketch in SATA *84*
Charbonnet, Gabrielle 1961- *81*
Chardiet, Bernice (Kroll) 1927(?)- *27*
Charles, Donald
  See Meighan, Donald Charles
Charles, Louis
  See Stratemeyer, Edward L.
Charles, Nicholas J.
  See Kuskin, Karla
Charles, Norma *153*
Charles, Veronika Martenova *182*
Charlip, Remy 1929- *119*
  Earlier sketches in SATA *4, 68*
  See also CLR *8*
Charlot, Jean 1898-1979 .... *8*
  Obituary *31*
Charlot, Martin (Day) 1944- *64*
Charlton, Michael (Alan) 1923- *34*
Charlton-Trujillo, e.E. *189*
Charmatz, Bill 1925-2005 .... *7*
Charnas, Suzy McKee 1939- *110*
  Earlier sketch in SATA *61*
Charosh, Mannis 1906- *5*
Chartier, Normand L. 1945- *66*
Chase, Alice
  See McHargue, Georgess
Chase, Alyssa 1965- *92*
Chase, Andra 1942- *91*
Chase, Emily
  See Aks, Patricia
  and Garwood, Julie
  and Sachs, Judith
  and White, Carol
Chase, Mary (Coyle) 1907-1981 .... *17*
  Obituary *29*
Chase, Mary Ellen 1887-1973 .... *10*
Chase, Richard 1904-1988 .... *64*
  Obituary *56*
Chase, Samantha
  See Glick, Ruth (Burtnick)
Chast, Roz 1954- *97*
Chastain, Madye Lee 1908-1989 .... *4*
Chataway, Carol 1955- *140*
Chatterjee, Debjani 1952- *83*
Chauncy, Nan(cen Beryl Masterman)
  1900-1970 .... *6*
  See also CLR *6*
Chaundler, Christine 1887-1972 .... *1*
  Obituary *25*
Chbosky, Stephen 1972- *164*
Cheaney, Janie B.
  See Cheaney, J.B.
Cheaney, J.B. 1950- *188*
Chee, Cheng-Khee 1934- *79*
Cheese, Chloe 1952- *118*
Chekhonte, Antosha
  See Chekhov, Anton (Pavlovich)
Chekhov, Anton (Pavlovich) 1860-1904 .... *90*
Chelushkin, Kirill 1968- *186*
Chen, Anthony 1929- *6*
Chen, Chih-Yuan 1975- *155*
Chen, Ju-Hong 1941- *78*
Chen, Sara
  See Odgers, Sally Farrell
Chen, Tony
  See Chen, Anthony
Chen, Yong 1963- *183*
Chen, Yuan-tsung 1932- *65*
Chenault, Nell
  See Smith, Linell Nash
Chenery, Janet (Dai) 1923- *25*
Cheney, Cora 1916-1999 .... *3*
  Obituary *110*
Cheney, Glenn (Alan) 1951- *99*
Cheney, Lynne V. 1941- *152*

Cheney, Ted
  See Cheney, Theodore Albert
Cheney, Theodore A. Rees
  See Cheney, Theodore Albert
Cheney, Theodore Albert 1928- *11*
Cheng, Andrea 1957- *172*
  Earlier sketch in SATA *128*
Cheng, Christopher 1959- *173*
  Earlier sketch in SATA *106*
Cheng, Judith 1955- *36*
Cheng, Shan
  See Jiang, Cheng An
Cheripko, Jan 1951- *155*
  Earlier sketch in SATA *83*
Chermayeff, Ivan 1932- *47*
Chernenko, Dan
  See Chernenko, Dan
Chernoff, Dorothy A.
  See Ernst, (Lyman) John
Chernoff, Goldie Taub 1909- *10*
Cherry, Carolyn Janice *93*
  See Cherryh, C.J.
Cherry, Lynne 1952- *99*
  Earlier sketch in SATA *34*
Cherryh, C.J. 1942- *172*
  See Cherry, Carolyn Janice
Cherryholmes, Anne
  See Price, Olive
Cheshire, Simon *172*
Chesler, Bernice 1932-2002 .... *59*
Chess, Victoria (Dickerson) 1939- *92*
  Earlier sketch in SATA *33*
Chessa, Francesca *191*
Chester, Deborah 1957- *85*
Chester, Kate
  See Guccione, Leslie Davis
Chesterton, G(ilbert) K(eith) 1874-1936 ...... *27*
Chesworth, Michael *160*
Chetin, Helen 1922- *6*
Chetwin, Grace *86*
  Brief entry *50*
Chevalier, Christa 1937- *35*
Chevalier, Tracy 1962- *128*
Chew, Ruth 1920- *7*
Chichester Clark, Emma 1955- *156*
  Earlier sketch in SATA *117*
  See Clark, Emma Chichester
Chidsey, Donald Barr 1902-1981 .... *3*
  Obituary *27*
Chiefari, Janet D. 1942- *58*
Chien, Catia *193*
Chien-min, Lin
  See Rumford, James
Child, L. Maria
  See Child, Lydia Maria
Child, Lauren 1965- *183*
  Earlier sketches in SATA *119, 160*
Child, Lincoln 1957- *113*
Child, Lincoln B.
  See Child, Lincoln
Child, Lydia Maria 1802-1880 .... *67*
Child, Mrs.
  See Child, Lydia Maria
Child, Philip 1898-1978 .... *47*
Children's Shepherd, The
  See Westphal, Arnold Carl
Childress, Alice 1920-1994 .... *81*
  Earlier sketches in SATA *7, 48*
  See also CLR *14*
Childs, H(alla) Fay (Cochrane) 1890-1971 .... *1*
  Obituary *25*
Chilton, Charles (Frederick William)
  1917- *102*
Chima, Cinda Williams *192*
Chimaera
  See Farjeon, Eleanor
Chin, Richard (M.) 1946- *52*
Chinery, Michael 1938- *26*
Chin-Lee, Cynthia 1958- *102*
Chin-Lee D., Cynthia
  See Chin-Lee, Cynthia

Chippendale, Lisa A. *158*
Chipperfield, Joseph Eugene 1912-1980(?) .. *87*
  Earlier sketch in SATA *2*
Chisholm, P. F.
  See Finney, Patricia
Chislett, Gail (Elaine) 1948- *58*
Chittenden, Elizabeth F. 1903-1999 .... *9*
Chittenden, Margaret 1935- *28*
Chittum, Ida 1918- *7*
Chitwood, Suzanne Tanner 1958- *160*
Chmielarz, Sharon Lee 1940- *72*
Choate, Judith (Newkirk) 1940- *30*
Chocolate, Debbi 1954- *96*
Chocolate, Deborah M. Newton
  See Chocolate, Debbi
Chodos-Irvine, Margaret *152*
Choi, Sook Nyul 1937- *73*
  Autobiography Feature *126*
  See also CLR *53*
Choi, Yangsook *178*
Choldenko, Gennifer 1957- *182*
  Earlier sketch in SATA *135*
Chorao, (Ann Mc)Kay (Sproat) 1936- *162*
  Earlier sketches in SATA *8, 69*
Choron, Sandra (Zena Samelson) 1950- *146*
Chown, Marcus 1959- *137*
Choyce, Lesley 1951- *165*
  Earlier sketch in SATA *94*
Chrisman, Arthur Bowie 1889-1953 .... *124*
  See also YABC *1*
Christelow, Eileen 1943- *184*
  Autobiography Feature *120*
  Brief entry *35*
  Earlier sketches in SATA *38, 90*
Christensen, Bonnie 1951- *157*
  Earlier sketch in SATA *110*
Christensen, Gardell Dano 1907-1991 .... *1*
Christensen, Laurie
  See Steding, Laurie
Christesen, Barbara 1940- *40*
Christgau, Alice Erickson 1902-1977 .... *13*
Christian, Mary Blount 1933- *9*
Christiana, David *195*
Christie, Agatha (Mary Clarissa)
  1890-1976 .... *36*
Christie, Ann Philippa
  See Pearce, Philippa
Christie, Gregory
  See Christie, R. Gregory
Christie, Philippa *129*
  Earlier sketches in SATA *1, 67*
  See also CLR *9*
  See Pearce, Philippa
Christie, R. Gregory 1971- *185*
  Earlier sketch in SATA *127*
Christopher, John
  See CLR *2*
  See Youd, (Christopher) Samuel
Christopher, Louise
  See Hale, Arlene
Christopher, Matt(hew Frederick)
  1917-1997 .... *80*
  Obituary *99*
  Earlier sketches in SATA *2, 47*
  See also CLR *119*
  See also SAAS *9*
Christopher, Milbourne 1914(?)-1984 .... *46*
Christy, Howard Chandler 1873-1952 .... *21*
Chrustowski, Rick *176*
Chrystie, Frances N(icholson) 1904-1986 .... *60*
Chu, Daniel 1933- *11*
Chukovsky, Kornei (Ivanovich) 1882-1969 . *34*
  Earlier sketch in SATA *5*
Church, Caroline Jayne *179*
Church, Richard 1893-1972 .... *3*
Churchill, E(lmer) Richard 1937- *11*
Churchill, Elizabeth
  See Hough, Richard (Alexander)
Chute, B(eatrice) J(oy) 1913-1987 .... *2*
  Obituary *53*
Chute, Marchette (Gaylord) 1909-1994 .... *1*

Chwast, Jacqueline 1932- *6*
Chwast, Seymour 1931- *146*
  Earlier sketches in SATA *18, 96*
Ciardi, John (Anthony) 1916-1986 .... *65*
  Obituary *46*
  Earlier sketch in SATA *1*
  See also CLR *19*
  See also SAAS *26*
Ciccone, Madonna Louise Veronica
  See Madonna
Ciment, James D. 1958- *140*
Cirrone, Dorian *182*
Cisneros, Sandra 1954-
  See CLR *123*
Citra, Becky 1954- *137*
Citrin, Michael 1965(?)- *183*
Clair, Andree *19*
Clampett, Bob 1914(?)-1985
  Obituary *38*
  See Clampett, Robert
Clampett, Robert *44*
  See Clampett, Bob
Clapp, John 1968- *109*
Clapp, Patricia 1912- *74*
  Earlier sketch in SATA *4*
  See also SAAS *4*
Clare, Ellen
  See Sinclair, Olga
Clare, Helen
  See Clarke, Pauline
Claremont, Chris 1950- *87*
Claremont, Christopher Simon
  See Claremont, Chris
Clark, Ann Nolan 1896-1995 .... *82*
  Obituary *87*
  Earlier sketch in SATA *4*
  See also CLR *16*
  See also SAAS *16*
Clark, Champ 1923-2002 .... *47*
Clark, Christopher (Anthony) Stuart
  See Stuart-Clark, Christopher (Anthony)
Clark, Clara Gillow 1951- *154*
  Earlier sketch in SATA *84*
Clark, David
  See Hardcastle, Michael
Clark, David Allen
  See Ernst, (Lyman) John
Clark, Emma Chichester *69*
  See Chichester Clark, Emma
Clark, Frank J(ames) 1922- *18*
Clark, Garel
  See Garelick, May
Clark, Halsey
  See Deming, Richard
Clark, Joan
  See Benson, Mildred (Augustine Wirt)
Clark, Joan 1934- *182*
  Earlier sketches in SATA *59, 96*
Clark, Leonard 1905-1981 .... *30*
  Obituary *29*
Clark, M. R.
  See Clark, Mavis Thorpe
Clark, Margaret (D.) 1943- *126*
Clark, Margaret Goff 1913- *82*
  Earlier sketch in SATA *8*
Clark, Mary Higgins 1929- *46*
Clark, Mavis Thorpe 1909-1999 .... *74*
  Earlier sketch in SATA *8*
  See also CLR *30*
  See also SAAS *5*
Clark, Merle
  See Gessner, Lynne
Clark, Patricia Denise 1921- *117*
  See Lorrimer, Claire
Clark, Patricia Finrow 1929- *11*
Clark, Ronald William 1916-1987 .... *2*
  Obituary *52*
Clark, Sherryl 1956- *149*
Clark, Van D(eusen) 1909-1974 .... *2*
Clark, Virginia
  See Gray, Patricia (Clark)

Clark, Walter Van Tilburg 1909-1971 8
Clarke, Arthur
See Clarke, Arthur C.
Clarke, Arthur C. 1917-2008 115
Obituary 191
Earlier sketches in SATA 13, 70
See also CLR 119
Clarke, Arthur Charles
See Clarke, Arthur C.
Clarke, Clorinda 1917- 7
Clarke, Gus 1948- 134
Clarke, J.
See Clarke, Judith
Clarke, James Hall
See Rowland-Entwistle, (Arthur) Theodore
(Henry)
Clarke, Joan B. 1921- 42
Brief entry 27
Clarke, John
See Laklan, Carli
and Sontup, Dan(iel)
Clarke, Judith 1943- 164
Earlier sketches in SATA 75, 110
See also CLR 61
Clarke, Julia 1950- 138
Clarke, Kenneth 1957- 107
Clarke, Lea
See Rowland-Entwistle, (Arthur) Theodore
(Henry)
Clarke, Margaret 1941-
See CLR 99
Clarke, Mary Stetson 1911-1994 5
Clarke, Michael
See Newlon, (Frank) Clarke
Clarke, Pauline 1921- 131
See also CLR 28
See Clare, Helen
and Hunter Blair, Pauline
Clarke-Rich, Elizabeth L. 1934- 103
Clarkson, E(dith) Margaret 1915- 37
Clarkson, Ewan 1929- 9
Claudia, Susan
See Goulart, Ron(ald Joseph)
and Johnston, William
Claverie, Jean 1946- 38
Clay, Patrice 1947- 47
Clayman, Deborah Paula
See Da Costa, Deborah
Claypool, Jane 103
See Miner, Jane Claypool
Clayton, Elaine 1961- 159
Earlier sketch in SATA 94
Clayton, Lawrence (Otto, Jr.) 1945- 75
Clayton, Sandra 1951- 110
Cleary, Beverly 1916- 121
Earlier sketches in SATA 2, 43, 79
See also CLR 72
See also SAAS 20
Cleary, Beverly Atlee Bunn
See Cleary, Beverly
Cleary, Brian P. 1959- 186
Earlier sketches in SATA 93, 132
Cleaver, Bill 22
Obituary 27
See also CLR 6
See Cleaver, William J(oseph)
Cleaver, Carole 1934- 6
Cleaver, Elizabeth (Ann Mrazik)
1939-1985 23
Obituary 43
See also CLR 13
Cleaver, Hylton Reginald 1891-1961 49
Cleaver, Vera (Allen) 1919-1993 76
Earlier sketch in SATA 22
See also CLR 6
Cleishbotham, Jebediah
See Scott, Sir Walter
Cleland, Mabel
See Widdemer, Mabel Cleland
Clem, Margaret H(ollingsworth) 1923- 90

Clemens, Samuel Langhorne 1835-1910 100
See also YABC 2
See Twain, Mark
Clemens, Virginia Phelps 1941- 35
Clement, Gary 191
Clement, Janet 182
Clement, Priscilla Ferguson 1942- 171
Clement, Rod 97
Clement-Moore, Rosemary 188
Clements, Andrew 1949- 158
Earlier sketch in SATA 104
Clements, Bruce 1931- 178
Earlier sketches in SATA 27, 94
Clemesha, David 192
Clemons, Elizabeth
See Nowell, Elizabeth Cameron
Clerk, N. W.
See Lewis, C.S.
Cleveland, Bob
See Cleveland, George
Cleveland, George 1903(?)-1985
Obituary 43
Cleveland-Peck, Patricia 80
Cleven, Cathrine
See Cleven, Kathryn Seward
Cleven, Kathryn Seward 2
Clevenger, William R. 1954- 84
Clevenger, William Russell
See Clevenger, William R.
Clevin, Joergen 1920- 7
Clevin, Jorgen
See Clevin, Joergen
Clewes, Dorothy (Mary) 1907-2003 86
Obituary 138
Earlier sketch in SATA 1
Clifford, David
See Rosenberg, Eth(el) Clifford
Clifford, Eth 92
See also SAAS 22
See Rosenberg, Eth(el) Clifford
Clifford, Harold B(urton) 1893-1988 10
Clifford, Margaret Cort 1929- 1
Clifford, Martin
See Hamilton, Charles (Harold St. John)
Clifford, Mary Louise Beneway 1926- 23
Clifford, Peggy
See Clifford, Margaret Cort
Clifford, Rachel Mark
See Lewis, Brenda Ralph
Clifton, Lucille 1936- 128
Earlier sketches in SATA 20, 69
See also CLR 5
Clifton, Thelma Lucille
See Clifton, Lucille
Climo, Shirley 1928- 166
Autobiography Feature 110
Brief entry 35
Earlier sketches in SATA 39, 77
See also CLR 69
Clinton, Cathryn 1957- 136
Clinton, Dirk
See Silverberg, Robert
Clinton, Jon
See Prince, J(ack) H(arvey)
Clippinger, Carol 193
Clish, (Lee) Marian 1946- 43
Clive, Clifford
See Hamilton, Charles (Harold St. John)
Clokey, Art 1921- 59
Cloudsley-Thompson, J(ohn) L(eonard)
1921- 19
Clouse, Nancy L. 1938- 78
Clover, Peter 1952- 152
Clutha, Janet Paterson Frame
See Frame, Janet
Clymer, Eleanor 1906-2001 85
Obituary 126
Earlier sketch in SATA 9
See also SAAS 17
Clyne, Patricia (Edwards) 31

Coalson, Glo 1946- 94
Earlier sketch in SATA 26
Coates, Anna 1958- 73
Coates, Belle 1896-1986 2
Coates, Ruth Allison 1915- 11
Coats, Alice M(argaret) 1905-1976 11
Coatsworth, Elizabeth (Jane) 1893-1986 100
Obituary 49
Earlier sketches in SATA 2, 56
See also CLR 2
Cobalt, Martin
See Mayne, William (James Carter)
Cobb, Jane
See Berry, Jane Cobb
Cobb, Mary 1931- 88
Cobb, Vicki 1938- 136
Autobiography Feature 136
Earlier sketches in SATA 8, 69, 131
See also CLR 2
See also SAAS 6
Cobbett, Richard
See Pluckrose, Henry (Arthur)
Cober, Alan E(dwin) 1935-1998 7
Obituary 101
Cobham, Sir Alan
See Hamilton, Charles (Harold St. John)
Coburn, Jake 1978- 155
Cocagnac, Augustin Maurice(-Jean) 1924- 7
Cocca-Leffler, Maryann 1958- 194
Earlier sketches in SATA 80, 136
Cochran, Bill 187
Cochran, Bobbye A. 1949- 11
Cockett, Mary 3
Coddell, Esme Raji
See Codell, Esme Raji
Codell, Esme Raji 1968- 160
Cody, C. S.
See Waller, Leslie
Cody, Jess
See Cunningham, Chet
Coe, Anne (E.) 1949- 95
Coe, Douglas
See Epstein, Beryl (M. Williams)
and Epstein, Samuel
Coe, Lloyd 1899(?)-1976
Obituary 30
Coen, Rena Neumann 1925- 20
Coerr, Eleanor (Beatrice) 1922- 67
Earlier sketch in SATA 1
Cofer, Judith Ortiz 1952- 164
Earlier sketch in SATA 110
See Ortiz Cofer, Judith
Coffelt, Nancy 1961- 189
Coffey, Brian
See Koontz, Dean R.
Coffin, Geoffrey
See Mason, F(rancis) van Wyck
Coffin, M. T.
See Stanley, George Edward
Coffman, Ramon Peyton 1896-1989 4
Cogan, Karen 1954- 125
Coggins, Jack (Banham) 1911-2006 2
Cohen, Barbara 1932-1992 77
Obituary 74
Earlier sketch in SATA 10
See also SAAS 7
Cohen, Daniel (E.) 1936- 70
Earlier sketch in SATA 8
See also CLR 43
See also SAAS 4
Cohen, Deborah Bodin 1968- 180
Cohen, Jan Barger
See Barger, Jan
Cohen, Jene Barr
See Barr, Jene
Cohen, Joan Lebold 1932- 4
Cohen, Judith Love 1933- 78
Cohen, Miriam 1926-1955 155
Earlier sketches in SATA 29, 106
See also SAAS 11
Cohen, Nora 75

Cohen, Paul S. 1945- 58
Cohen, Peter Zachary 1931- 150
  Earlier sketch in SATA 4
Cohen, Robert Carl 1930- 8
Cohen, Sholom 1951- 94
Cohn, Angelo 1914-1997 19
Cohn, Diana 194
Cohn, Rachel 1968- 161
Coit, Margaret Louise 1922-2003 2
  Obituary 142
Colato Lainez, Rene 1970- 176
Colbert, Anthony 1934-2007 15
Colbert, Nancy A. 1936- 139
Colby, C(arroll) B(urleigh) 1904-1977 35
  Earlier sketch in SATA 3
Colby, Jean Poindexter 1909-1993 23
Cole, Annette
  See Steiner, Barbara A(nnette)
Cole, Babette 1949- 155
  Earlier sketches in SATA 61, 96
Cole, Betsy 1940- 83
Cole, Brock 1938- 136
  Earlier sketch in SATA 72
  See also CLR 18
Cole, Davis
  See Elting, Mary
Cole, Hannah 1954- 74
Cole, Henry 1955- 181
Cole, Jack -1974
  See Stewart, John (William)
Cole, Jackson
  See Curry, Thomas Albert
  and Germano, Peter B.
  and Heckelmann, Charles N(ewman)
  and Newton, D(wight) B(ennett)
  and Schisgall, Oscar
Cole, Jennifer
  See Zach, Cheryl (Byrd)
Cole, Joanna 1944- 168
  Brief entry 37
  Earlier sketches in SATA 49, 81, 120
  See also CLR 40
Cole, Lois Dwight 1903-1979 10
  Obituary 26
Cole, Michael 1947- 59
Cole, Sheila R. 1939- 171
  Earlier sketches in SATA 24, 95
Cole, Sheila Rotenberg
  See Cole, Sheila R.
Cole, Stephen 1971- 161
Cole, William (Rossa) 1919-2000 71
  Earlier sketch in SATA 9
  See also SAAS 9
Coleman, Andrew
  See Pine, Nicholas
Coleman, Clare
  See Bell, Clare (Louise)
  and Easton, M(alcolm) Coleman
Coleman, Janet Wyman 184
Coleman, Loren 1947- 164
Coleman, Loren Elwood, Jr.
  See Coleman, Loren
Coleman, Mary Ann 1928- 83
Coleman, Michael (Lee) 1946- 133
  Autobiography Feature 133
  Earlier sketch in SATA 108
Coleman, Rowan 187
Coleman, William L(eRoy) 1938- 49
  Brief entry 34
Coles, Robert (Martin) 1929- 23
Colfer, Eoin 1965- 148
  See also CLR 112
Colin, Ann
  See Ure, Jean
Collard, Sneed B. III 1959- 184
  Earlier sketches in SATA 84, 139
Colledge, Anne 1939- 142
Collicott, Sharleen 1937- 143
  Earlier sketch in SATA 98
Collier, Bryan 174
  Earlier sketch in SATA 126

Collier, Christopher 1930- 70
  Earlier sketch in SATA 16
  See also CLR 126
Collier, Ethel 1903-1999 22
Collier, James Lincoln 1928- 166
  Earlier sketches in SATA 8, 70
  See also CLR 126
  See also SAAS 21
Collier, Jane
  See Collier, Zena
Collier, Kristi 182
Collier, Steven 1942- 61
Collier, Zena 1926- 23
  See Collier, Jane
Collings, Gillian 1939- 102
Collington, Peter 1948- 99
  Earlier sketch in SATA 59
Collins, Ace 1953- 82
Collins, Andrew J.
  See Collins, Ace
Collins, David R(aymond) 1940-2001 121
  Earlier sketch in SATA 7
Collins, Heather 1946- 81
Collins, Hunt
  See Hunter, Evan
Collins, Michael
  See Lynds, Dennis
Collins, Michael 1930- 58
Collins, Pat(ricia) Lowery 1932- 151
  Earlier sketch in SATA 31
Collins, Paul 1954- 126
Collins, Ruth Philpott 1890-1975
  Obituary 30
Collins, Suzanne 180
Collins, Yvonne 194
Collinson, A. S.
  See Collinson, Alan S.
Collinson, Alan S. 1934- 80
Collinson, Roger (Alfred) 1936- 133
Collison, Linda 1953- 185
Collodi, Carlo
  See CLR 120
  See Lorenzini, Carlo
Colloms, Brenda 1919- 40
Colman, Hila 53
  Earlier sketch in SATA 1
  See also SAAS 14
Colman, Morris 1899(?)-1981
  Obituary 25
Colman, Penny (Morgan) 1944- 160
  Autobiography Feature 160
  Earlier sketches in SATA 77, 114
Colman, Warren (David) 1944- 67
Colombo, John Robert 1936- 50
Colon, Raul 156
Colonius, Lillian 1911-1992 3
Colorado, Antonio J.
  See Colorado (Capella), Antonio J(ulio)
Colorado (Capella), Antonio J(ulio)
  1903-1994 23
  Obituary 79
Colquhoun, Glenn 1964- 165
Colston, Fifi E. 1960- 150
Colt, Martin
  See Epstein, Beryl (M. Williams)
  and Epstein, Samuel
Colum, Padraic 1881-1972 15
  See also CLR 36
Columbus, Chris 1959- 97
Columbus, Christopher
  See Columbus, Chris
Columella
  See Moore, Clement Clarke
Colver, Anne 1908- 7
Colvin, James
  See Moorcock, Michael
Colwell, Eileen (Hilda) 1904-2002 2
Colwyn, Stewart
  See Pepper, Frank S.
Coman, Carolyn 1951- 127

Combs, Lisa M.
  See McCourt, Lisa
Combs, Robert
  See Murray, John
Comfort, Jane Levington
  See Sturtzel, Jane Levington
Comfort, Mildred Houghton 1886-1976 3
Comins, Ethel M(ae) 11
Comins, Jeremy 1933- 28
Commager, Henry Steele 1902-1998 23
  Obituary 102
Comora, Madeleine 190
Compere, Mickie
  See Davidson, Margaret
Compestine, Ying Chang 1963- 187
  Earlier sketch in SATA 140
Comport, Sally Wern 190
Compton, Patricia A. 1936- 75
Comte, The Great
  See Hawkesworth, Eric
Comus
  See Ballantyne, R(obert) M(ichael)
Comyns, Nance
  See Comyns-Toohey, Nantz
Comyns-Toohey, Nantz 1956- 86
Conan Doyle, Arthur
  See Doyle, Sir Arthur Conan
Condit, Martha Olson 1913- 28
Condon, Bill 1949- 142
Condon, Judith 83
Condon, Ken 195
Condy, Roy 1942- 96
Cone, Ferne Geller 1921- 39
Cone, Molly (Lamken) 1918- 151
  Autobiography Feature 151
  Earlier sketches in SATA 1, 28, 115
  See also SAAS 11
Cone, Patrick 1954- 89
Coney, Michael G. 1932-2005 61
  Obituary 170
Coney, Michael Greatrex
  See Coney, Michael G.
Coney, Mike
  See Coney, Michael G.
Conford, Ellen 1942- 162
  Earlier sketches in SATA 6, 68, 110
  See also CLR 71
Conger, Lesley
  See Suttles, Shirley (Smith)
Conklin, Gladys Plemon 1903- 2
Conklin, Paul S. 1929(?)-2003 43
  Brief entry 33
  Obituary 147
Conkling, Hilda 1910-1986 23
Conlan, Kathleen Elizabeth 1950- 145
Conlan, Kathy
  See Conlan, Kathleen Elizabeth
Conley-Weaver, Robyn 1963- 125
Conlon-McKenna, Marita 1956- 71
Conly, Jane Leslie 1948- 164
  Earlier sketches in SATA 80, 112
Conly, Robert Leslie 1918(?)-1973 23
  See O'Brien, Robert C.
Connell, Kirk
  See Chapman, John Stanton Higham
Connelly, Marc(us Cook) 1890-1980
  Obituary 25
Connolly, Jerome P(atrick) 1931- 8
Connolly, Pat 1943- 74
Connolly, Peter 1935- 105
  Earlier sketch in SATA 47
Conover, Chris 1950- 31
Conquest, Owen
  See Hamilton, Charles (Harold St. John)
Conrad, Joseph 1857-1924 27
Conrad, Pam 1947-1996 133
  Brief entry 49
  Obituary 90
  Earlier sketches in SATA 52, 80
  See also CLR 18
  See also SAAS 19

Conroy, Jack 19
  See Conroy, John Wesley
Conroy, John Wesley 1899-1990
  Obituary 65
  See Conroy, Jack
Conroy, Robert
  See Goldston, Robert (Conroy)
Constable, Kate 1966- 172
Constant, Alberta Wilson 1908-1981 22
  Obituary 28
Constantin, Pascale 185
Conway, Diana C(ohen) 1943- 91
Conway, Gordon
  See Hamilton, Charles (Harold St. John)
Cook, Ande 192
Cook, Bernadine 1924- 11
Cook, Fred J(ames) 1911-2003 2
  Obituary 145
Cook, Glen 1944- 171
  Earlier sketch in SATA 108
Cook, Glen Charles
  See Cook, Glen
Cook, Hugh 1956- 85
Cook, Hugh, Walter Gilbert
  See Cook, Hugh
Cook, Jean Thor 1930- 94
Cook, Joel 1934- 79
Cook, Joseph Jay 1924- 8
Cook, Lisa Broadie 157
Cook, Lyn
  See Waddell, Evelyn Margaret
Cook, Roy
  See Silverberg, Robert
Cook, Trish 175
Cooke, Ann
  See Cole, Joanna
Cooke, Arthur
  See Lowndes, Robert A(ugustine) W(ard)
Cooke, Barbara
  See Alexander, Anna B(arbara Cooke)
Cooke, David Coxe 1917- 2
Cooke, Donald Ewin 1916-1985 2
  Obituary 45
Cooke, Frank E. 1920- 87
Cooke, Jean (Isobel Esther) 1929- 74
Cooke, John Estes
  See Baum, L(yman) Frank
Cooke, Trish 1962- 129
Cookson, Catherine (McMullen) 1906-1998 .. 9
  Obituary 116
Cooley, Regina Francoise 1940- 177
Coolidge, Olivia E(nsor) 1908- 26
  Earlier sketch in SATA 1
Cooling, Wendy 169
  Earlier sketch in SATA 111
Coombs, Charles I(ra) 1914-1994 43
  Earlier sketch in SATA 3
  See also SAAS 15
Coombs, Chick
  See Coombs, Charles I(ra)
Coombs, Kate 190
Coombs, Patricia 1926- 51
  Earlier sketch in SATA 3
  See also SAAS 22
Cooney, Barbara 1917-2000 96
  Obituary 123
  Earlier sketches in SATA 6, 59
  See also CLR 23
Cooney, Caroline B. 1947- 179
  Brief entry 41
  Earlier sketches in SATA 48, 80, 113, 130
Cooney, Doug 181
Cooney, Nancy Evans 1932- 42
Coontz, Otto 1946- 33
Cooper, Ann (Catharine) 1939- 104
Cooper, Dutch
  See Kuyper, Sjoerd
Cooper, Elisha 1971- 157
  Earlier sketch in SATA 99
Cooper, Elizabeth Keyser -1992 47

Cooper, Floyd 187
  Earlier sketches in SATA 96, 144
  See also CLR 60
Cooper, Gordon 1932- 23
Cooper, Helen 1963- 169
  Earlier sketch in SATA 102
Cooper, Henry S(potswood) F(enimore), Jr.
  1933- 65
Cooper, Ilene 1948- 145
  Earlier sketches in SATA 66, 97
Cooper, James Fenimore 1789-1851 19
  See also CLR 105
Cooper, John R. 1
Cooper, Kay 1941- 11
Cooper, Lee Pelham 1926- 5
Cooper, Lester (Irving) 1919-1985 32
  Obituary 43
Cooper, Lettice (Ulpha) 1897-1994 35
  Obituary 82
Cooper, Louise 1952- 152
Cooper, M.E.
  See Lerangis, Peter
Cooper, M.E.
  See Davis, Maggie S.
Cooper, Melrose
  See Kroll, Virginia L.
Cooper, Michael L. 1950- 181
  Earlier sketches in SATA 79, 117
Cooper, Patrick 1949- 134
Cooper, Susan 1935- 151
  Earlier sketches in SATA 4, 64, 104
  See also CLR 67
  See also SAAS 6
Cooper, Susan Mary
  See Cooper, Susan
Cope, Jane U(rsula) 1949- 108
Copeland, Helen 1920- 4
Copeland, Mark 1956- 180
Copeland, Paul W. 23
Coplans, Peta 1951- 84
Copley (Diana) Heather Pickering 1918- 45
Coppard, A(lfred) E(dgar) 1878-1957
  See YABC 1
Copper, Melinda 1952- 172
Copper, Melinda McConnaughey
  See Copper, Melinda
Coralie
  See Anderson, Catherine Corley
Corbett, Grahame 43
  Brief entry 36
Corbett, Scott 1913- 42
  Earlier sketch in SATA 2
  See also CLR 1
  See also SAAS 2
Corbett, Sue 174
Corbett, W(illiam) J(esse) 1938- 102
  Brief entry 44
  Earlier sketch in SATA 50
  See also CLR 19
Corbin, Sabra Lee
  See Malvern, Gladys
Corbin, William
  See McGraw, William Corbin
Corbman, Marjorie 1987- 179
Corby, Dan
  See Catherall, Arthur
Corcoran, Barbara (Asenath) 1911- 77
  Autobiography Feature 125
  Earlier sketch in SATA 3
  See also CLR 50
  See also SAAS 20
Corcos, Lucille 1908-1973 10
Cordell, Alexander
  See Graber, Alexander
Cordell, Alexander
  See Graber, (George) Alexander
Corder, Zizou
  See Young, Louisa
Corella, Joseph
  See Odgers, Sally Farrell

Coren, Alan 1938-2007 32
  Obituary 187
Corey, Dorothy 23
Corey, Shana 1974- 133
Corfe, Thomas Howell 1928- 27
Corfe, Tom
  See Corfe, Thomas Howell
Corfield, Robin Bell 1952- 74
Corlett, William 1938-2005 46
  Brief entry 39
Cormack, M(argaret) Grant 1913- 11
Cormack, Maribelle B. 1902-1984 39
Cormier, Robert 1925-2000 83
  Obituary 122
  Earlier sketches in SATA 10, 45
  See also CLR 55
Cormier, Robert Edmund
  See Cormier, Robert
Cornelius, Carol 1942- 40
Cornelius, Kay 1933- 157
Cornell, J.
  See Cornell, Jeffrey
Cornell, James (Clayton, Jr.) 1938- 27
Cornell, Jean Gay 1920- 23
Cornell, Jeffrey 1945- 11
Cornell, Laura 189
Cornish, D.M. 1972- 185
Cornish, Sam(uel James) 1935- 23
Cornwall, Nellie
  See Sloggett, Nellie
Cornwell, Autumn 195
Corr, Christopher 1955- 189
Correy, Lee
  See Stine, G(eorge) Harry
Corrick, James A. 1945- 76
Corrigan, (Helen) Adeline 1909- 23
Corrigan, Barbara 1922- 8
Corrigan, Eireann 1977- 163
Corrin, Sara 1918- 86
  Brief entry 48
Corrin, Stephen 86
  Brief entry 48
Corsi, Wendy
  See Staub, Wendy Corsi
Cort, M. C.
  See Clifford, Margaret Cort
Cort, Margaret
  See Clifford, Margaret Cort
Corwin, Judith H(offman) 1946- 10
Cory, Rowena
  See Lindquist, Rowena Cory
Cosby, Bill
  See Cosby, William Henry, Jr.
Cosby, William Henry, Jr. 1937- 110
  Earlier sketch in SATA 66
  See Cosby, Bill
Cosentino, Ralph 169
Cosgrave, John O'Hara II 1908-1968
  Obituary 21
Cosgrove, Margaret (Leota) 1926- 47
Cosgrove, Stephen E(dward) 1945- 53
  Brief entry 40
Coskey, Evelyn 1932- 7
Cosner, Shaaron 1940- 43
Cossi, Olga 1921- 102
  Earlier sketch in SATA 67
Costabel, Eva Deutsch 1924- 45
Costabel-Deutsch, Eva
  See Costabel, Eva Deutsch
Coste, Marion 1938- 183
Costello, David 174
Costello, David F(rancis) 1904-1990 23
Cte, Genevieve 1964- 184
Cote, Nancy 182
Cott, Jonathan 1942- 23
Cottam, Clarence 1899-1974 25
Cotten, Cynthia 188
Cottle, Joan 1960- 135
Cottler, Joseph 1899-1996 22
Cottonwood, Joe 1947- 92
Cottrell, Leonard 1913-1974 24

Cottringer, Anne 1952- *150*
Earlier sketch in SATA *97*
Coulman, Valerie 1969- *161*
Couloumbis, Audrey *173*
Counsel, June 1926- *70*
Countryman, The
See Whitlock, Ralph
Courlander, Harold 1908-1996 .... *6*
Obituary *88*
Coursen, Valerie 1965(?)- *102*
Courtis, Stuart Appleton 1874-1969
Obituary *29*
Courtland, Tyler
See Stevens, Serita
Courtney, Dayle
See Goldsmith, Howard
Coury, Louise Andree 1895(?)-1983
Obituary *34*
Cousins, Linda 1946- *90*
Cousins, Lucy 1964- *172*
Cousins, Margaret 1905-1996 .... *2*
Obituary *92*
Cousteau, Jacques-Yves 1910-1997 .... *98*
Earlier sketch in SATA *38*
Couture, Christin 1951- *73*
Couvillon, Jacques *195*
Coville, Bruce 1950- *155*
Autobiography Feature *155*
Earlier sketches in SATA *32, 77, 118*
Covington, Dennis *109*
Covington, Linda
See Windsor, Linda
Cowan, Catherine *121*
Cowan, Rebecca M.
See Moesta, Rebecca
Cowan, Rebecca Moesta
See Moesta, Rebecca
Coward, Fiona 1963- *178*
Cowell, Cressida 1966- *140*
Cowen, Eve
See Werner, Herma
Cowen, Ida 1898-1993 .... *64*
Cowie, Leonard W(allace) 1919- *4*
Cowles, Kathleen
See Krull, Kathleen
Cowley, Cassia Joy
See Cowley, Joy
Cowley, Joy 1936- *164*
Cowley, (Cassia) Joy 1936- *90*
Autobiography Feature *118*
Earlier sketch in SATA *4*
See also CLR *55*
See also SAAS *26*
Cowley, Marjorie 1925- *111*
Cox, (Christopher) Barry 1931- *62*
Cox, Clinton 1934- *108*
Earlier sketch in SATA *74*
Cox, David (Dundas) 1933- *56*
Cox, Donald William 1921- *23*
Cox, Jack
See Cox, John Roberts
Cox, John Roberts 1915-1981 .... *9*
See Roberts, David
Cox, Judy 1954- *160*
Earlier sketch in SATA *117*
Cox, Palmer 1840-1924 .... *24*
See also CLR *24*
Cox, Vic 1942- *88*
Cox, Vicki 1945- *158*
Cox, Victoria
See Garretson, Victoria Diane
Cox, Wally *25*
See Cox, Wallace (Maynard)
Cox, William R(obert) 1901-1988 .... *46*
Brief entry *31*
Obituary *57*
See Ward, Jonas
Coxe, Molly 1959- *101*
Earlier sketch in SATA *69*
Coxon, Michele 1950- *158*
Earlier sketch in SATA *76*

Coy, Harold 1902-1986 .... *3*
Coy, John 1958- *171*
Earlier sketch in SATA *120*
Craats, Rennay 1973- *131*
Crabtree, Judith 1928- *98*
Earlier sketch in SATA *63*
Cracker, Edward E.B.
See Odgers, Sally Farrell
Craft, K. Y.
See Craft, Kinuko Y(amabe)
Craft, Kinuko
See Craft, Kinuko Y(amabe)
Craft, Kinuko Y(amabe) 1940- *127*
Earlier sketch in SATA *65*
Craft, Ruth 1935- *87*
Brief entry *31*
Craig, A. A.
See Anderson, Poul
Craig, Alisa
See MacLeod, Charlotte (Matilda)
Craig, Helen 1934- *94*
Earlier sketches in SATA *46, 49*
Craig, John Eland
See Chipperfield, Joseph Eugene
Craig, John Ernest 1921- *23*
Craig, Kit
See Reed, Kit
Craig, M. F.
See Craig, Mary (Francis) Shura
Craig, M. Jean *17*
Craig, M. S.
See Craig, Mary (Francis) Shura
Craig, Margaret (Maze) 1911-1964 .... *9*
Craig, Mary
See Craig, Mary (Francis) Shura
Craig, Mary Shura
See Craig, Mary (Francis) Shura
Craig, Mary (Francis) Shura 1923-1991 .... *86*
Obituary *65*
Earlier sketch in SATA *6*
See also SAAS *7*
Craig, Ruth 1922- *95*
Craik, Mrs.
See Craik, Dinah Maria (Mulock)
Craik, Dinah Maria (Mulock) 1826-1887 ..... *34*
See Craik, Mrs.
and Mulock, Dinah Maria
Crandall, Court 1965- *175*
Crandell, Rachel 1943- *152*
Crane, Barbara (Joyce) 1934- *31*
Crane, Caroline 1930- *11*
Crane, Jordan 1973- *174*
Crane, M. A.
See Wartski, Maureen (Ann Crane)
Crane, Royston Campbell 1901-1977
Obituary *22*
Crane, Stephen (Townley) 1871-1900
See YABC *2*
See also CLR *132*
Crane, Walter 1845-1915 .... *100*
Earlier sketch in SATA *18*
See also CLR *56*
Crane, William D(wight) 1892-1976 .... *1*
Cranfield, Ingrid 1945- *74*
Cranshaw, Stanley
See Fisher, Dorothy (Frances) Canfield
Crary, Elizabeth (Ann) 1942- *99*
Brief entry *43*
Crary, Margaret (Coleman) 1906-1986 .... *9*
Cravath, Lynne Avril
See Cravath, Lynne W.
Cravath, Lynne W. 1951- *182*
Earlier sketches in SATA *98, 148*
Craven, Thomas 1889-1969 .... *22*
Crawford, Charles P. 1945- *28*
Crawford, Deborah 1922- *6*
Crawford, John E(dmund) 1904-1971 .... *3*
Crawford, K(aren) Michael 1959- *155*
Crawford, Mel 1925- *44*
Brief entry *33*
Crawford, Phyllis 1899- *3*

Crawley, Dave *177*
Cray, Roberta
See Emerson, Ru
Crayder, Dorothy *7*
Crayder, Teresa
See Colman, Hila
Crayon, Geoffrey
See Irving, Washington
Craz, Albert G. 1926- *24*
Crebbin, June 1938- *169*
Earlier sketch in SATA *80*
Crecy, Jeanne
See Williams, Jeanne
Credle, Ellis 1902-1998 .... *1*
Creech, Sharon 1945- *172*
Earlier sketches in SATA *94, 139*
See also CLR *89*
Creeden, Sharon 1938- *91*
Creel, Ann Howard 1953- *187*
Creighton, (Mary) Helen 1899-1989
Obituary *64*
Creighton, Jill 1949- *96*
Crenson, Victoria 1952- *159*
Earlier sketch in SATA *88*
Cresp, Gael 1954- *119*
Crespo, George 1962- *82*
Cresswell, Helen 1934-2005 .... *79*
Obituary *168*
Earlier sketches in SATA *1, 48*
See also CLR *18*
See also SAAS *20*
Cressy, Michael 1955- *124*
Cressy, Mike
See Cressy, Michael
Cretan, Gladys (Yessayan) 1921- *2*
Cretzmeyer, Stacy (Megan) 1959- *124*
Crew, Gary 1947- *163*
Earlier sketches in SATA *75, 110*
See also CLR *42*
Crew, Helen (Cecilia) Coale 1866-1941
See YABC *2*
Crew, Linda (Jean) 1951- *137*
Earlier sketch in SATA *71*
Crews, Donald 1938- *76*
Brief entry *30*
Earlier sketch in SATA *32*
See also CLR *7*
Crews, Nina 1963- *158*
Earlier sketch in SATA *97*
Crichton, John Michael
See Crichton, Michael
Crichton, Michael 1942-2008 .... *88*
Earlier sketch in SATA *9*
Crider, Allen Billy
See Crider, Bill
Crider, Bill 1941- *99*
Crilley, Mark 1966- *148*
Autobiography Feature *148*
Earlier sketch in SATA *120*
Crimi, Carolyn 1959- *176*
Cripps, Enid Margaret
See Appiah, Peggy
Crisler, Curtis L. *188*
Crisman, Ruth 1914- *73*
Crisp, Marta Marie 1947- *128*
Crisp, Marty
See Crisp, Marta Marie
Crispin, A(nn) C(arol) 1950- *86*
Crist, James J. 1961- *168*
Cristall, Barbara *79*
Crist-Evans, Craig 1954- *153*
Crocker, Carter *193*
Crocker, Nancy 1956- *185*
Crofford, Emily (Ardell) 1927- *61*
Crofut, William E. III 1934- *23*
Croggon, Alison 1962- *194*
Croll, Carolyn 1945- *102*
Brief entry *52*
Earlier sketch in SATA *56*
Croman, Dorothy Young
See Rosenberg, Dorothy

Author Index

Cromie, Alice Hamilton 1914-2000 24
Cromie, William J(oseph) 1930- 4
Crompton, Anne Eliot 1930- 73
  Earlier sketch in SATA 23
Crompton, Richmal
  See Lamburn, Richmal Crompton
Cronbach, Abraham 1882-1965 11
Crone, Ruth 1919-2003 4
Cronin, A(rchibald) J(oseph) 1896-1981 47
  Obituary 25
Cronin, Doreen (A.) 125
  See also CLR 105
Cronin, Doreen 1966(?)- 178
  See also CLR 136
Cronin, Doreen A.
  See Cronin, Doreen
Crook, Beverly Courtney 38
  Brief entry 35
Crook, Connie Brummel 1930- 168
  Earlier sketch in SATA 98
Crook, Constance
  See Crook, Connie Brummel
Crosby, Alexander L. 1906-1980 2
  Obituary 23
Crosby, Harry C., Jr. 102
Crosby, Margaret
  See CLR 77
  See Rathmann, Peggy
Crosher, G. R. 14
Cross, Gilbert B. 1939- 60
  Brief entry 51
Cross, Gillian 1945- 178
  Autobiography Feature 178
  Earlier sketches in SATA 38, 71, 110, 165
  See also CLR 28
Cross, Gillian Clare
  See Cross, Gillian
Cross, Helen Reeder
  See Broadhead, Helen Cross
Cross, Peter 1951- 95
Cross, Tom 1954- 146
Cross, Verda 1914- 75
Cross, Wilbur Lucius III 1918- 2
Crossland, Caroline 1964- 83
Crossley-Holland, Kevin 1941- 165
  Earlier sketches in SATA 5, 74, 120
  See also CLR 84
  See also SAAS 20
Crossley-Holland, Kevin John William
  See Crossley-Holland, Kevin
Crouch, Marcus 1913-1996 4
Crout, George C(lement) 1917- 11
Crow, Donna Fletcher 1941- 40
Crow, Francis Luther
  See Luther, Frank
Crowe, Andrew 111
Crowe, John
  See Lynds, Dennis
Crowe, (Bettina) Peter Lum 1911- 6
Crowell, Grace Noll 1877-1969 34
Crowell, Pers 1910-1990 2
Crowell, Robert Leland 1909-2001 63
Crowfield, Christopher
  See Stowe, Harriet (Elizabeth) Beecher
Crowley, Arthur McBlair 1945- 38
Crowley, John 1942- 140
  Earlier sketch in SATA 65
Crownfield, Gertrude 1867-1945
  See YABC 1
Crowther, James Gerald 1899-1983 14
Crowther, Robert 1948- 163
Cruikshank, George 1792-1878 22
  See also CLR 63
Cruise, Robin 1951- 179
Crum, Shutta 192
  Earlier sketch in SATA 134
Crummel, Susan Stevens 1949- 176
  Earlier sketch in SATA 130
Crump, Fred H., Jr. 1931- 76
  Earlier sketch in SATA 11

Crump, J(ames) Irving 1887-1979 57
  Obituary 21
Crump, William D(rake) 1949- 138
Crunden, Reginald
  See Cleaver, Hylton Reginald
Crunk, T.
  See Crunk, Tony
Crunk, Tony 1956- 130
Crutcher, Chris 1946- 153
  Earlier sketches in SATA 52, 99
  See also CLR 28
Crutcher, Christopher C.
  See Crutcher, Chris
Cruz, Ray(mond) 1933- 6
Cruz Martinez, Alejandro (?)-1987 74
Crystal, Billy 1947- 154
Ctvrtek, Vaclav 1911-1976
  Obituary 27
Cuetara, Mittie 1957- 158
  Earlier sketch in SATA 106
Cuffari, Richard 1925-1978 66
  Obituary 25
  Earlier sketch in SATA 6
Cullen, Countee 1903-1946 18
Cullen, Lynn 190
Culliford, Pierre 1928-1992 40
  Obituary 74
Cullinan, Bernice E(llinger) 1926- 135
Culp, Louanna McNary 1901-1965 2
Culper, Felix
  See McCaughrean, Geraldine
Cumbaa, Stephen 1947- 72
Cumming, Peter 1951- 168
Cumming, Primrose Amy 1915- 24
Cumming, Robert 1945- 65
Cummings, Betty Sue 1918- 15
  See also SAAS 9
Cummings, Mary 1951- 185
Cummings, Parke 1902-1987 2
  Obituary 53
Cummings, Pat (Marie) 1950- 107
  Earlier sketches in SATA 42, 71
  See also CLR 48
  See also SAAS 13
Cummings, Phil 1957- 123
  Earlier sketch in SATA 74
Cummings, Priscilla 1951- 170
  Earlier sketch in SATA 129
Cummings, Richard
  See Gardner, Richard (M.)
Cummins, Maria Susanna 1827-1866
  See YABC 1
Cuneo, Mary Louise -2001 85
Cunliffe, John Arthur 1933- 86
  Earlier sketch in SATA 11
Cunliffe, Marcus (Falkner) 1922-1990 37
  Obituary 66
Cunnane, Kelly 175
Cunningham, Bob
  See May, Julian
Cunningham, Captain Frank
  See Glick, Carl (Cannon)
Cunningham, Cathy
  See Cunningham, Chet
Cunningham, Chet 1928- 23
Cunningham, Dale S(peers) 1932- 11
Cunningham, Dru 91
Cunningham, E. V.
  See Fast, Howard
Cunningham, Julia (Woolfolk) 1916- 132
  Earlier sketches in SATA 1, 26
  See also SAAS 2
Cunningham, Lawrence J. 1943- 125
Cunningham, Virginia
  See Holmgren, Virginia C(unningham)
Curiae, Amicus
  See Fuller, Edmund (Maybank)
Curie, Eve 1904-2007 1
  Obituary 188
Curlee, Lynn 1947- 190
  Earlier sketches in SATA 98, 141

Curley, Daniel 1918-1988 23
  Obituary 61
Curley, Marianne 1959- 175
  Earlier sketch in SATA 131
Currey, Anna 194
Currie, Robin 1948- 120
Currie, Stephen 1960- 132
  Earlier sketch in SATA 82
Curry, Ann (Gabrielle) 1934- 72
Curry, Jane L(ouise) 1932- 138
  Autobiography Feature 138
  Earlier sketches in SATA 1, 52, 90
  See also CLR 31
  See also SAAS 6
Curry, Peggy Simson 1911-1987 8
  Obituary 50
Curry, Tom 185
Curtis, Bruce (Richard) 1944- 30
Curtis, Chara M(ahar) 1950- 78
Curtis, Christopher Paul 1954(?)- 187
  Earlier sketches in SATA 93, 140
  See also CLR 68
Curtis, Gavin 1965- 107
Curtis, Jamie Lee 1958- 144
  Earlier sketch in SATA 95
  See also CLR 88
Curtis, Jennifer Keats 185
Curtis, Marci 160
Curtis, Patricia 1921- 101
  Earlier sketch in SATA 23
Curtis, Peter
  See Lofts, Norah (Robinson)
Curtis, Philip (Delacourt) 1920- 62
Curtis, Richard (Alan) 1937- 29
Curtis, Richard Hale
  See Deming, Richard
  and Levinson, Leonard
  and Rothweiler, Paul Roger
Curtis, Wade
  See Pournelle, Jerry (Eugene)
Curtiss, A(rlene) B. 1934- 90
Cusack, Margaret 1945- 58
Cushman, Doug 1953- 157
  Earlier sketches in SATA 65, 101
Cushman, Jerome 2
Cushman, Karen 1941- 147
  Earlier sketch in SATA 89
  See also CLR 55
Cusick, Richie Tankersley 1952- 140
  Earlier sketch in SATA 67
Cutchen, Billye Walker 1930- 15
Cutchins, Judy 1947- 59
Cutler, Daniel S(olomon) 1951- 78
Cutler, Ebbitt 1923- 9
Cutler, Ivor 1923-2006 24
  Obituary 174
Cutler, Jane 1936- 162
  Earlier sketches in SATA 75, 118
Cutler, May Ebbitt
  See Cutler, Ebbitt
Cutler, Samuel
  See Folsom, Franklin (Brewster)
Cutlip, Kimbra L(eigh-Ann) 1964- 128
Cutrate, Joe
  See Spiegelman, Art
Cutt, W(illiam) Towrie 1898-1981 16
  Obituary 85
Cuyler, Margery 1948- 195
  Earlier sketches in SATA 39, 99, 156
Cuyler, Margery Stuyvesant
  See Cuyler, Margery
Cuyler, Stephen
  See Bates, Barbara S(nedeker)
Cyrus, Kurt 1954- 179
  Earlier sketch in SATA 132
Czernecki, Stefan 1946- 178

D

Dabba Smith, Frank *174*
Dabcovich, Lydia *99*
    Brief entry *47*
    Earlier sketch in SATA *58*
Dace, Dolores B(oelens) 1929- *89*
Da Costa, Deborah *193*
Dadey, Debbie 1959- *136*
    Earlier sketch in SATA *73*
Dahl, Borghild (Margarethe) 1890-1984 .... *7*
    Obituary *37*
Dahl, Roald 1916-1990 .... *73*
    Obituary *65*
    Earlier sketches in SATA *1, 26*
    See also CLR *111*
Dahlberg, Maurine F. 1951- *171*
Dahlstedt, Marden (Stewart) 1921-1983 .... *8*
    Obituary *110*
Dain, Martin J. 1924-2000 .... *35*
Dakos, Kalli 1950- *115*
    Earlier sketch in SATA *80*
Dale, Anna 1971- *170*
Dale, Gary
    See Reece, Colleen L.
Dale, George E.
    See Asimov, Isaac
Dale, Jack
    See Holliday, Joseph
Dale, Kim 1957- *123*
Dale, Margaret J(essy) Miller 1911- *39*
Dale, Mitzi
    See Hemstock, Gillian
Dale, Norman
    See Denny, Norman (George)
Dale, Penny 1954- *151*
    Earlier sketch in SATA *70*
Daley, Michael J. *170*
Dalgliesh, Alice 1893-1979 .... *17*
    Obituary *21*
    See also CLR *62*
Dalkey, Kara 1953- *132*
Dalkey, Kara Mia
    See Dalkey, Kara
Dallas, Ruth 1919- *86*
Dalmas, John
    See Jones, John R(obert)
Dalton, Alene
    See Chapin, Alene Olsen Dalton
Dalton, Annie 1948- *140*
    Earlier sketch in SATA *40*
Dalton, Kit
    See Cunningham, Chet
Dalton, Pamela
    See Johnson, Pamela
Dalton, Sean
    See Chester, Deborah
Dalton, Sheila 1949- *108*
Daly, Jim
    See Stratemeyer, Edward L.
Daly, Jude 1951- *177*
Daly, Kathleen N(orah) *124*
    Brief entry *37*
Daly, Maureen 1921-2006 .... *129*
    Obituary *176*
    Earlier sketch in SATA *2*
    See also CLR *96*
    See also SAAS *1*
Daly, Nicholas 1946- *164*
    Earlier sketches in SATA *37, 76, 114*
    See also CLR *41*
    See Daly, Niki
Daly, Niki
    See SAAS *21*
    See Daly, Nicholas
D'Amato, Alex 1919- *20*
D'Amato, Janet (Potter) 1925- *9*
Damerow, Gail 1944- *83*
Damerow, Gail Jane
    See Damerow, Gail
D'Amico, Carmela *170*

D'Amico, Steve *170*
Damrell, Liz 1956- *77*
Damrosch, Helen
    See Tee-Van, Helen Damrosch
Dana, Barbara 1940- *22*
Dana, Richard Henry, Jr. 1815-1882 .... *26*
Danachair, Caoimhin O
    See Danaher, Kevin
Danaher, Kevin 1913-2002 .... *22*
Danakas, John 1963- *94*
Dandi
    See Mackall, Dandi Daley
D'Andrea, Kate
    See Steiner, Barbara A(nnette)
Dangerfield, Balfour
    See McCloskey, (John) Robert
Daniel, Alan 1939- *76*
    Brief entry *53*
Daniel, Anita 1893(?)-1978 .... *23*
    Obituary *24*
Daniel, Anne
    See Steiner, Barbara A(nnette)
Daniel, Becky 1947- *56*
Daniel, Claire 1949- *164*
Daniel, Colin
    See Windsor, Patricia
Daniel, Hawthorne 1890- *8*
Daniel, (Donna) Lee 1944- *76*
Daniel, Rebecca
    See Daniel, Becky
Daniels, Guy 1919-1989 .... *11*
    Obituary *62*
Daniels, Lucy
    See Oldfield, Jenny
Daniels, Max
    See Gellis, Roberta
Daniels, Olga
    See Sinclair, Olga
Daniels, Patricia 1955- *93*
Daniels, Zoe
    See Laux, Constance
Dank, Gloria Rand 1955- *56*
    Brief entry *46*
Dank, Leonard D(ewey) 1929- *44*
Dank, Milton 1920- *31*
Dann, Max 1955- *62*
Danneberg, Julie 1958- *173*
Dantz, William R.
    See Philbrick, Rodman
Danziger, Paula 1944-2004 .... *149*
    Brief entry *30*
    Obituary *155*
    Earlier sketches in SATA *36, 63, 102*
    See also CLR *20*
Darby, Gene Kegley
    See Darby, Jean (Kegley)
Darby, J. N.
    See Govan, (Mary) Christine Noble
Darby, Jean (Kegley) 1921- *68*
Darby, Patricia (Paulsen) *14*
Darby, Ray(mond) 1912-1982 .... *7*
d'Arcy, Willard
    See Cox, William R(obert)
Dare, Geena
    See McNicoll, Sylvia (Marilyn)
Darian, Shea 1959- *97*
Daringer, Helen Fern 1892-1986 .... *1*
Darke, Marjorie 1929- *87*
    Earlier sketch in SATA *16*
Darley, F(elix) O(ctavius) C(arr)
    1822-1888 .... *35*
Darling, David J. 1953- *60*
    Brief entry *44*
Darling, Kathy
    See Darling, Mary Kathleen
Darling, Lois (MacIntyre) 1917-1989 .... *3*
    Obituary *64*
Darling, Louis, (Jr.) 1916-1970 .... *3*
    Obituary *23*
Darling, Mary Kathleen 1943- *124*
    Earlier sketches in SATA *9, 79*

Darling, Sandra Louise Woodward
    See Day, Alexandra
Darnell, K(athryn) L(ynne) 1955- *150*
Darroll, Sally
    See Odgers, Sally Farrell
Darrow, Sharon *181*
Darrow, Whitney, (Jr.) 1909-1999 .... *13*
    Obituary *115*
Darwin, Len
    See Darwin, Leonard
Darwin, Leonard 1916- *24*
Dasent, Sir George Webbe 1817-1896 .... *62*
    Brief entry *29*
Dash, Joan 1925- *142*
Daskam, Josephine Dodge
    See Bacon, Josephine Dodge (Daskam)
D'ath, Justin 1953- *174*
    Earlier sketch in SATA *106*
Dauer, Rosamond 1934- *23*
Daugherty, Charles Michael 1914- *16*
Daugherty, James (Henry) 1889-1974 .... *13*
    See also CLR *78*
Daugherty, Richard D(eo) 1922- *35*
Daugherty, Sonia Medwedeff (?)-1971
    Obituary *27*
d'Aulaire, Edgar Parin 1898-1986 .... *66*
    Obituary *47*
    Earlier sketch in SATA *5*
    See also CLR *21*
d'Aulaire, Ingri (Mortenson Parin)
    1904-1980 .... *66*
    Obituary *24*
    Earlier sketch in SATA *5*
    See also CLR *21*
Dave, Dave
    See Berg, David
Daveluy, Paule Cloutier 1919- *11*
Davenier, Christine 1961- *179*
    Earlier sketch in SATA *127*
Davenport, John 1960- *156*
Daves, Michael 1938- *40*
David, A. R.
    See David, A(nn) Rosalie
David, A(nn) Rosalie 1946- *103*
David, Jonathan
    See Ames, Lee J(udah)
David, Lawrence 1963- *165*
    Earlier sketch in SATA *111*
David, Peter 1956- *72*
David, Peter Allen
    See David, Peter
David, Rosalie
    See David, A(nn) Rosalie
Davidson, Alice Joyce 1932- *54*
    Brief entry *45*
Davidson, Basil 1914- *13*
Davidson, (Marie) Diane 1924- *91*
Davidson, Hugh
    See Hamilton, Edmond
Davidson, Jessica 1915-1986 .... *5*
Davidson, Judith 1953- *40*
Davidson, Lionel 1922- *87*
Davidson, Margaret 1936- *5*
Davidson, Marion
    See Garis, Howard R(oger)
Davidson, Mary R. 1885-1973 .... *9*
Davidson, Mary S. 1940- *61*
Davidson, Mickie
    See Davidson, Margaret
Davidson, Nicole
    See Jensen, Kathryn
Davidson, R.
    See Davidson, Raymond
Davidson, Raymond 1926- *32*
Davidson, Rosalie 1921- *23*
Davie, Helen K(ay) 1952- *148*
    Earlier sketch in SATA *77*
Davies, Andrew (Wynford) 1936- *27*
Davies, Bettilu D(onna) 1942- *33*
Davies, Hunter 1936- *55*
    Brief entry *45*

Davies, Jacqueline 1962- *186*
  Earlier sketch in SATA *155*
Davies, Joan 1934- *50*
  Brief entry *47*
Davies, Nicola 1958- *182*
  Earlier sketches in SATA *99, 150*
Davies, Peter J(oseph) 1937- *52*
Davies, Sumiko 1942- *46*
Davis, (A.) Aubrey 1949- *153*
Davis, Barbara Steincrohn
  See Davis, Maggie S.
Davis, Bette J. 1923- *15*
Davis, Burke 1913- *4*
Davis, Christopher 1928- *6*
Davis, D(elbert) Dwight 1908-1965 .... *33*
Davis, Daniel S(heldon) 1936- *12*
Davis, David R. 1948- *106*
Davis, Donald 1944- *169*
  Earlier sketch in SATA *93*
Davis, Donald D.
  See Davis, Donald
Davis, Emma
  See Davis, Maggie S.
Davis, Gibbs 1953- *102*
  Brief entry *41*
  Earlier sketch in SATA *46*
Davis, Grania 1943- *88*
  Brief entry *50*
Davis, H(arold) L(enoir) 1896-1960 .... *114*
Davis, Hubert J(ackson) 1904-1997 .... *31*
Davis, James Robert 1945- *32*
  See Davis, Jim
Davis, Jenny 1953- *74*
Davis, Jim
  See Davis, James Robert
Davis, Julia 1900(?)-1993 .... *6*
  Obituary *75*
Davis, Karen (Elizabeth) 1944- *109*
Davis, Katie 1959(?)- *152*
Davis, Lambert *176*
Davis, Leslie
  See Guccione, Leslie Davis
Davis, Louise Littleton 1921- *25*
Davis, Maggie S. 1943- *57*
Davis, Marguerite 1889- *34*
Davis, Mary L(ee) 1935- *9*
Davis, Mary Octavia 1901-1976 .... *6*
Davis, Nelle 1958- *73*
Davis, Ossie 1917-2005 .... *81*
  See also CLR *56*
Davis, Paxton 1925-1994 .... *16*
Davis, Robert 1881-1949
  See YABC *1*
Davis, Robin W(orks) 1962- *87*
Davis, Russell Gerard 1922- *3*
Davis, Tim(othy N.) 1957- *94*
Davis, Verne Theodore 1889-1973 .... *6*
Davis, Yvonne 1927- *115*
Davol, Marguerite W. 1928- *146*
  Earlier sketch in SATA *82*
DaVolls, Andy (P.) 1967- *85*
DaVolls, Linda 1966- *85*
Davys, Sarah
  See Manning, Rosemary (Joy)
Dawes, Claiborne 1935- *111*
Dawson, Elmer A. *67*
  Earlier sketch in SATA *1*
Dawson, Imogen (Zoe) 1948- *126*
  Earlier sketch in SATA *90*
Dawson, Mary 1919- *11*
Day, A(rthur) Grove 1904-1994 .... *59*
Day, Alexandra 1941- *169*
  Earlier sketches in SATA *67, 97*
  See also CLR *22*
  See also SAAS *19*
Day, Beth (Feagles) 1924- *33*
Day, Donna
  See Asay, Donna Day
Day, Edward C. 1932- *72*
Day, Jon 1936(?)- *79*
Day, Karen *187*

Day, Larry 1956- *181*
Day, Nancy 1953- *140*
Day, Nancy Raines 1951- *148*
  Earlier sketch in SATA *93*
Day, Shirley 1962- *94*
Day, Thomas 1748-1789
  See YABC *1*
Day, Trevor 1955- *124*
Dazey, Agnes J(ohnston) *2*
Dazey, Frank M. *2*
Deacon, Alexis 1978- *139*
Deacon, Eileen
  See Geipel, Eileen
Deacon, Richard
  See McCormick, (George) Donald (King)
Deadman, Ronald 1919-1988(?)
  Obituary *56*
Deak, Erzsi 1959- *152*
Dean, Anabel 1915- *12*
Dean, Carolee 1962- *148*
Dean, David 1976- *192*
Dean, Karen Strickler 1923- *49*
Dean, Ruth (Brigham) 1947- *145*
Dean, Zoey
  See Bennett, Cherie
de Angeli, Marguerite (Lofft) 1889-1987 ... *100*
  Obituary *51*
  Earlier sketches in SATA *1, 27*
  See also CLR *1*
Deans, Karen *195*
Deans, Sis Boulos 1955- *136*
  Earlier sketch in SATA *78*
DeArmand, Frances Ullmann 1904(?)-1984 . *10*
  Obituary *38*
DeArmond, Dale 1914- *70*
DeArmond, Dale Burlison
  See DeArmond, Dale
Deary, Terry 1946- *171*
  Brief entry *41*
  Earlier sketches in SATA *51, 101*
Deaver, Julie Reece 1953- *68*
de Banke, Cecile 1889-1965 .... *11*
De Bello, Rosario 1923- *89*
Debon, Nicolas *186*
  Earlier sketch in SATA *151*
de Bono, Edward 1933- *66*
de Brissac, Malcolm
  See Dickinson, Peter (Malcolm de Brissac)
de Brunhoff, Jean
  See Brunhoff, Jean de
De Brunhoff, Laurent
  See Brunhoff, Laurent de
De Bruyn, Monica G. 1952- *13*
De Bruyn, Monica Jean Grembowicz
  See De Bruyn, Monica G.
DeBry, Roger K. 1942- *91*
de Camp, Catherine Crook 1907-2000 .... *83*
  Earlier sketch in SATA *12*
de Camp, L(yon) Sprague 1907-2000 .... *83*
  Earlier sketch in SATA *9*
DeCandido, Keith R.A. *112*
Dechausay, Sonia E. *94*
Decker, C.B. *172*
Decker, Cynthia B.
  See Decker, C.B.
Decker, Duane 1910-1964 .... *5*
DeClements, Barthe (Faith) 1920- *131*
  Earlier sketches in SATA *35, 71*
  See also CLR *23*
de Conte, Sieur Louis
  See Clemens, Samuel Langhorne
Dedman, Stephen *108*
Dee, Catherine 1964- *138*
Dee, Ruby *77*
  See Wallace, Ruby Ann
Deedy, John 1923- *24*
Deegan, Paul Joseph 1937- *48*
  Brief entry *38*
Deem, James M. 1950- *191*
  Autobiography Feature *191*
  Earlier sketches in SATA *75, 134*

Deem, James Morgan
  See Deem, James M.
Deeter, Catherine 1947- *137*
DeFelice, Cynthia 1951- *165*
  Earlier sketches in SATA *79, 121*
DeFelice, Cynthia C.
  See DeFelice, Cynthia
Defoe, Daniel 1660(?)-1731 .... *22*
  See also CLR *61*
DeFord, Deborah H. *123*
deFrance, Anthony
  See DiFranco, Anthony (Mario)
Degen, Bruce 1945- *147*
  Brief entry *47*
  Earlier sketches in SATA *57, 97*
DeGering, Etta (Belle) Fowler 1898-1996 ..... *7*
De Goldi, Kate
  See De Goldi, Kathleen Domenica
De Goldi, Kathleen Domenica 1959- *123*
de Goursac, Olivier 1959- *184*
De Grazia, Ted *39*
  See De Grazia, Ettore
deGroat, Diane 1947- *169*
  Earlier sketches in SATA *31, 90*
deGros, J. H.
  See Villiard, Paul
de Grummond, Lena Young *62*
  Earlier sketch in SATA *6*
de Hamel, Joan Littledale 1924- *86*
De Haven, Tom 1949- *72*
de Hugo, Pierre
  See Brackers de Hugo, Pierre
Deiss, Joseph Jay 1915- *12*
de Jenkins, Lyll Becerra 1925-1997 .... *102*
DeJong, David C(ornel) 1905-1967 .... *10*
de Jong, Dola 1911-2003 .... *7*
  Obituary *149*
  See de Jong, Dorothea Rosalie
DeJong, Meindert 1906-1991 .... *2*
  Obituary *68*
  See also CLR *73*
DeJonge, Joanne E. 1943- *56*
Deka, Connie
  See Laux, Constance
de Kay, Ormonde (Jr.) 1923-1998 .... *7*
  Obituary *106*
de Kiriline, Louise
  See Lawrence, Louise de Kiriline
Dekker, Carl
  See Laffin, John (Alfred Charles)
  and Lynds, Dennis
deKruif, Paul (Henry) 1890-1971 .... *50*
  Earlier sketch in SATA *5*
Delacre, Lulu 1957- *156*
  Earlier sketch in SATA *36*
DeLaCroix, Alice 1940- *195*
  Earlier sketch in SATA *75*
de la Cruz, Melissa 1971- *179*
De la Garza, Phyllis 1942- *169*
De Lage, Ida 1918- *11*
de la Mare, Walter (John) 1873-1956 .... *16*
  See also CLR *23*
Delaney, Harry 1932- *3*
Delaney, Joseph 1945- *172*
Delaney, M.C.
  See Delaney, Michael
Delaney, Michael 1955- *180*
  Earlier sketch in SATA *96*
Delaney, Michael Clark
  See Delaney, Michael
Delaney, Ned *28*
  See Delaney, Thomas Nicholas III
Delano, Hugh 1933- *20*
Delany, Samuel R., Jr. 1942- *92*
Delany, Samuel Ray
  See Delany, Samuel R., Jr.
De La Ramee, Marie Louise 1839-1908 ...... *20*
  See Ouida
de la Roche, Mazo 1879-1961 .... *64*
De La Roche Saint Andre, Anne 1950- *75*
Delaune, (Jewel) Lynn (de Grummond) *7*

DeLaurentis, Louise Budde 1920- 12
del Barco, Lucy Salamanca 1900(?)-1989
    Obituary 64
Delderfield, Eric R(aymond) 1909-1995 14
Delderfield, Ronald Frederick 1912-1972 20
DeLeeuw, Adele (Louise) 1899-1988 30
    Obituary 56
    Earlier sketch in SATA *1*
De Leon, Nephtali 1945- 97
Delessert, Etienne 1941- 179
    Brief entry 27
    Earlier sketches in SATA *46, 130*
    See also CLR *81*
Delgado, James P. 1958- 122
de Lint, Charles 1951- 157
    Earlier sketch in SATA *115*
de Lint, Charles Henri Diederick Hofsmit
    See de Lint, Charles
Delmar, Roy
    See Wexler, Jerome (LeRoy)
Deloria, Vine, Jr. 1933-2005 21
    Obituary 171
Deloria, Vine Victor, Jr.
    See Deloria, Vine, Jr.
del Rey, Lester 1915-1993 22
    Obituary 76
Delrio, Martin
    See Doyle, Debra
    and Macdonald, James D.
Delton, Judy 1931-2001 77
    Obituary 130
    Earlier sketch in SATA *14*
    See also SAAS *9*
Delulio, John 1938- 15
Delving, Michael
    See Williams, Jay
de Marcken, Gail 186
Demarest, Chris L. 1951- 175
    Brief entry 44
    Earlier sketches in SATA *45, 82, 128*
Demarest, Christopher Lynn
    See Demarest, Chris L.
Demarest, Doug
    See Barker, Will
De Mari, Silvana 1953- 193
Demas, Corinne
    See Bliss, Corinne Demas
Demas, Vida 1927- 9
DeMatteis, J.M. 1953- 180
DeMatteis, John Marc
    See DeMatteis, J.M.
De Mejo, Oscar 1911-1992 40
Demers, Dominique 1956- 177
de Messieres, Nicole 1930- 39
Demi
    See Hitz, Demi
Demijohn, Thom
    See Disch, Thomas M.
    and Sladek, John
Deming, Richard 1915-1983 24
    See Queen, Ellery
Deming, Sarah 191
de Monfreid, Dorothee 1973- 189
Demuth, Patricia Brennan 1948- 84
    Brief entry 51
Dendinger, Roger E. 1952- 158
Denenberg, Barry 175
Dengler, Marianna (Herron) 1935- 103
Dengler, Sandy 1939- 54
    Brief entry 40
Denim, Sue
    See Pilkey, Dav
Denise, Christopher 1968- 193
    Earlier sketch in SATA *147*
Denman, K.L. 1957- 186
Denmark, Harrison
    See Zelazny, Roger
Dennard, Deborah 1953- 136
    Earlier sketch in SATA *78*
Denney, Diana 1910-2000 25
    Obituary 120

Dennis, Morgan 1891(?)-1960 18
Dennis, Wesley 1903-1966 18
Denniston, Elinore 1900-1978
    Obituary 24
Denny, Norman (George) 1901-1982 43
Denslow, Sharon Phillips 1947- 142
    Earlier sketch in SATA *68*
Denslow, W(illiam) W(allace) 1856-1915 16
    See also CLR *15*
Dent, Grace 1973- 187
Denton, Kady MacDonald 181
    Earlier sketches in SATA *66, 110*
    See also CLR *71*
Denton, Terry 1950- 186
Denver, Walt
    See Redding, Robert Hull
    and Sherman, Jory (Tecumseh)
Denzel, Justin F(rancis) 1917-1999 46
    Brief entry 38
Denzer, Ann Wiseman
    See Wiseman, Ann (Sayre)
DePalma, Mary Newell 1961- 185
    Earlier sketch in SATA *139*
dePaola, Thomas Anthony 1934- 155
    Earlier sketches in SATA *11, 59, 108*
    See dePaola, Tomie
dePaola, Tomie
    See CLR *81*
    See also SAAS *15*
    See dePaola, Thomas Anthony
deParrie, Paul 1949- 74
DePauw, Linda Grant 1940- 24
DeRan, David 1946- 76
Derby, Ken 1956- 181
Derby, Kenneth R.
    See Derby, Ken
Derby, Pat 1942- 172
Derby, Sally 1934- 189
    Earlier sketches in SATA *89, 132*
de Regniers, Beatrice Schenk (Freedman)
    1914-2000 68
    Obituary 123
    Earlier sketch in SATA *2*
    See also SAAS *6*
Dereske, Jo 1947- 72
Derleth, August (William) 1909-1971 5
Derman, Martha (Winn) 74
Derman, Sarah Audrey 1915- 11
DeRoberts, Lyndon
    See Silverstein, Robert Alan
de Roo, Anne Louise 1931-1997 84
    Earlier sketch in SATA *25*
    See also CLR *63*
deRosa, Dee 70
Derrick, Lionel
    See Cunningham, Chet
Derrickson, Jim 1959- 141
Derry Down Derry
    See Lear, Edward
Dervaux, Isabelle 1961- 106
Derwent, Lavinia 14
Desai, Anita 1937- 126
    Earlier sketch in SATA *63*
DeSaix, Deborah Durland 188
De Saulles, Tony 1958- 119
Desbarats, Peter 1933- 39
de Selincourt, Aubrey 1894-1962 14
Deshpande, Chris 1950- 69
Desimini, Lisa 1964- 148
    Earlier sketch in SATA *86*
Desjarlais, John 1953- 71
Desjarlais, John J.
    See Desjarlais, John
Desmoinaux, Christel 1967- 149
    Earlier sketch in SATA *103*
Desmond, Adrian J(ohn) 1947- 51
Desmond, Alice Curtis 1897-1990 8
Desnoettes, Caroline 183
DeSpain, Pleasant 1943- 87
Desputeaux, Helene 1959- 95

Dessen, Sarah 1970- 172
    Earlier sketch in SATA *120*
Detine, Padre
    See Olsen, Ib Spang
de Trevino, Elizabeth B.
    See Trevino, Elizabeth B(orton) de
de Trevino, Elizabeth Borton
    See Trevino, Elizabeth B(orton) de
Detwiler, Susan Dill 1956- 58
Deuker, Carl 1950- 150
    Earlier sketch in SATA *82*
Deutsch, Babette 1895-1982 1
    Obituary 33
Deutsch, Eva Costabel
    See Costabel, Eva Deutsch
Deutsch, Helen 1906-1992 76
Deutsch, Kurt
    See Singer, Kurt D.
De Valera, Sinead 1879(?)-1975
    Obituary 30
Devaney, John 1926-1994 12
de Varennes, Monique 1947- 168
de Varona, Frank J. 1943- 83
Devereux, Frederick L(eonard), Jr.
    1914-1993 9
Devi, Nila
    See Woody, Regina Jones
deVinck, Christopher 1951- 85
DeVita, James 195
DeVito, Cara 1956- 80
Devlin, Dorothy Wende
    See Devlin, Wende
Devlin, Harry 1918-2001 136
    Earlier sketches in SATA *11, 74*
Devlin, Wende 1918-2002 74
    Earlier sketch in SATA *11*
Devon, Paddie 1953- 92
Devons, Sonia 1974- 72
Devorah-Leah 111
de Vos, Gail 1949- 122
DeVries, Douglas 1933- 122
De Waard, E(lliott) John 1935- 7
Dewan, Ted 1961- 157
    Earlier sketch in SATA *108*
Dewdney, Anna 184
Dewdney, Selwyn (Hanington) 1909-1979 ... 64
DeWeese, Gene
    See DeWeese, Thomas Eugene
DeWeese, Jean
    See DeWeese, Thomas Eugene
DeWeese, Thomas Eugene 1934- 46
    Brief entry 45
Dewey, Ariane 1937- 178
    Earlier sketches in SATA *7, 109*
Dewey, Jennifer (Owings) 1941- 103
    Brief entry 48
    Earlier sketch in SATA *58*
Dewey, Kenneth Francis 1940- 39
De Wire, Elinor 1953- 180
deWit, Dorothy (May Knowles) 1916-1980 . 39
    Obituary 28
Dexter, Alison 1966- 125
Dexter, John
    See Bradley, Marion Zimmer
Deyneka, Anita 1943- 24
Deyrup, Astrith Johnson 1923- 24
Dhami, Narinder 1958- 152
Dhondy, Farrukh 1944- 152
    Earlier sketch in SATA *65*
    See also CLR *41*
Diakite, Baba Wague 1961- 174
Diakite, Penda 1993(?)- 174
Diamond, Arthur 1957- 76
Diamond, Donna 1950- 69
    Brief entry 30
    Earlier sketch in SATA *35*
Diamond, Petra
    See Sachs, Judith
Diamond, Rebecca
    See Sachs, Judith
Dias, Earl Joseph 1916- 41

Dias, Ron 1937- *71*
Diaz, David 1959(?)- *189*
  Earlier sketches in SATA *96, 150*
  See also CLR *65*
Dibley, Glin *188*
DiCamillo, Kate 1964- *163*
  Earlier sketch in SATA *121*
  See also CLR *117*
Di Certo, J(oseph) J(ohn) 1933- *60*
DiCianni, Ron 1952- *107*
Dick, Trella Lamson 1889-1974 .... *9*
Dickens, Charles (John Huffam)
  1812-1870 .... *15*
  See also CLR *95*
Dickens, Frank
  See Huline-Dickens, Frank William
Dickens, Monica (Enid) 1915-1992 .... *4*
  Obituary *74*
Dickerson, Roy Ernest 1886-1965
  Obituary *26*
Dickinson, Emily (Elizabeth) 1830-1886 ..... *29*
Dickinson, Mary 1949- *48*
  Brief entry *41*
Dickinson, Mary-Anne
  See Rodda, Emily
Dickinson, Peter (Malcolm de Brissac)
  1927- *150*
  Earlier sketches in SATA *5, 62, 95*
  See also CLR *125*
Dickinson, Susan 1931- *8*
Dickinson, Terence 1943- *102*
Dickinson, W(illiam) Croft 1897-1963 .... *13*
Dickson, Gordon R. 1923-2001 .... *77*
Dickson, Gordon Rupert
  See Dickson, Gordon R.
Dickson, Helen
  See Reynolds, Helen Mary Greenwood Camp-
  bell
Dickson, Naida 1916- *8*
Diehn, Gwen 1943- *80*
Dierssen, Andreas 1962- *190*
Dieterich, Michele M. 1962- *78*
Dietz, David H(enry) 1897-1984 .... *10*
  Obituary *41*
Dietz, Lew 1907-1997 .... *11*
  Obituary *95*
Diffily, Deborah *159*
Di Fiori, Larry
  See Di Fiori, Lawrence
Di Fiori, Lawrence 1934- *130*
DiFranco, Anthony (Mario) 1945- *42*
Digby, Anne 1935- *72*
Digges, Jeremiah
  See Berger, Josef
Digman, Kristina 1959- *176*
D'Ignazio, Fred(erick) 1949- *39*
  Brief entry *35*
Di Grazia, Thomas (?)-1983 .... *32*
Dijkstra, Lida 1961- *195*
Dikty, Julian May
  See May, Julian
Dillard, Annie 1945- *140*
  Earlier sketch in SATA *10*
Dillard, Kristine 1964- *113*
Dillard, Polly Hargis 1916- *24*
Diller, Harriett 1953- *78*
Dillon, Barbara 1927- *44*
  Brief entry *39*
Dillon, Diane 1933- *194*
  Earlier sketches in SATA *15, 51, 106*
  See also CLR *44*
Dillon, Diane Claire
  See Dillon, Diane
Dillon, Eilis 1920-1994 .... *74*
  Autobiography Feature *105*
  Obituary *83*
  Earlier sketch in SATA *2*
  See also CLR *26*
Dillon, Jana (a pseudonym) 1952- *117*

Dillon, Leo 1933- *194*
  Earlier sketches in SATA *15, 51, 106*
  See also CLR *44*
Dillon, Sharon Saseen
  See Saseen, Sharon (Dillon)
Dils, Tracey E. 1958- *83*
Dilson, Jesse 1914-1988 .... *24*
Dinan, Carolyn *59*
  Brief entry *47*
Dines, Carol 1956- *175*
Dines, (Harry) Glen 1925-1996 .... *7*
Dinesen, Isak
  See Blixen, Karen (Christentze Dinesen)
Dinessi, Alex
  See Schembri, Jim
Dinneen, Betty 1929- *61*
Dinnerstein, Harvey 1928- *42*
Dinsdale, Tim(othy Kay) 1924-1987 .... *11*
Diop, Birago (Ismael) 1906-1989
  Obituary *64*
Diouf, Sylviane A. *168*
Diouf, Sylviane Anna
  See Diouf, Sylviane A.
DiPucchio, Kelly *159*
Dirk
  See Gringhuis, Richard H.
Dirks, Wilhelmina 1916- *59*
Dirks, Willy
  See Dirks, Wilhelmina
Dirtmeister
  See Tomecek, Steve
DiSalvo, DyAnne 1960- *144*
  Earlier sketch in SATA *59*
DiSalvo-Ryan, DyAnne
  See DiSalvo, DyAnne
Disch, Thomas M. 1940-2008 .... *92*
  Obituary *195*
  See also CLR *18*
  See also SAAS *15*
  See Disch, Tom
Disch, Thomas Michael
  See Disch, Thomas M.
Disch, Tom
  See Disch, Thomas M.
Disher, Garry 1949- *125*
  Earlier sketch in SATA *81*
Disney, Walt(er Elias) 1901-1966 .... *28*
  Brief entry *27*
Ditchfield, Christin 1973- *189*
DiTerlizzi, Tony 1969- *154*
Divakaruni, Chitra Banerjee 1956- *160*
Di Valentin, Maria (Amelia) Messuri
  1911-1985 .... *7*
Divine, Arthur Durham 1904-1987
  Obituary *52*
Divine, David
  See Divine, Arthur Durham
Dixon, Ann R. 1954- *127*
  Earlier sketch in SATA *77*
Dixon, Ann Renee
  See Dixon, Ann R.
Dixon, Dougal 1947- *190*
  Earlier sketches in SATA *45, 127*
Dixon, Franklin W. *100*
  Earlier sketches in SATA *1, 67*
  See also CLR *61*
  See Barrett, Neal, Jr.
  and Goulart, Ron(ald Joseph)
  and Lantz, Francess L(in)
  and Lerangis, Peter
  and McFarlane, Leslie (Charles)
  and Stanley, George Edward
  and Stratemeyer, Edward L.
Dixon, Jeanne 1936- *31*
Dixon, Paige
  See Corcoran, Barbara (Asenath)
Dixon, Peter L(ee) 1931- *6*
Dixon, Rachel 1952- *74*
Djoleto, (Solomon Alexander) Amu 1929- ... *80*
d'lacey, Chris 1949- *165*

Doak, Annie
  See Dillard, Annie
Doane, Pelagie 1906-1966 .... *7*
Dobell, I(sabel) M(arian) B(arclay)
  1909-1998 .... *11*
Dobie, J(ames) Frank 1888-1964 .... *43*
Dobkin, Alexander 1908-1975
  Obituary *30*
Dobler, Lavinia G. 1910- *6*
Dobrin, Arnold 1928- *4*
Dobson, Jill 1969- *140*
Dobson, Julia 1941- *48*
Dobson, Mary 1954- *117*
Dockery, Wallene T. 1941- *27*
Dockray, Tracy 1962- *139*
Dockrey, Karen 1955- *103*
Doctor, Bernard
  See Doctor, Bernard Aquina
Doctor, Bernard Aquina 1950- *81*
Doctor X
  See Nourse, Alan E(dward)
Dodd, Ed(ward Benton) 1902-1991 .... *4*
  Obituary *68*
Dodd, Lynley (Stuart) 1941- *132*
  Earlier sketches in SATA *35, 86*
  See also CLR *62*
Dodd, Marty 1921- *142*
Dodd, Quentin 1972- *137*
Dodds, Bill 1952- *78*
Dodds, Dayle Ann 1952- *150*
  Earlier sketch in SATA *75*
Doder, Joshua
  See Lacey, Josh
Dodge, Bertha S(anford) 1902-1995 .... *8*
Dodge, Fremont
  See Grimes, Lee
Dodge, Gil
  See Hano, Arnold
Dodge, Mary (Elizabeth) Mapes
  1831(?)-1905 .... *100*
  Earlier sketch in SATA *21*
  See also CLR *62*
Dodgson, Charles L(utwidge) 1832-1898 ... *100*
  See also YABC *2*
  See also CLR *2*
  See Carroll, Lewis
Dodson, Kenneth MacKenzie 1907-1999 ..... *11*
Dodson, Susan 1941- *50*
  Brief entry *40*
Dogyear, Drew
  See Gorey, Edward (St. John)
Doherty, Berlie 1943- *111*
  Earlier sketch in SATA *72*
  See also CLR *21*
  See also SAAS *16*
Doherty, Charles Hugh 1913- *6*
Doherty, Craig A. 1951- *169*
  Earlier sketch in SATA *83*
Doherty, Katherine M(ann) 1951- *83*
Doherty, Kieran 1945- *164*
Dokey, Cameron 1956- *97*
Dolan, Edward F(rancis), Jr. 1924- *94*
  Brief entry *31*
  Earlier sketch in SATA *45*
Dolan, Ellen M(eara) 1929-1998 .... *88*
Dolan, Sean J. 1958- *74*
Dolce, J. Ellen 1948- *75*
Dolch, Edward William 1889-1961 .... *50*
Dolch, Marguerite Pierce 1891-1978 .... *50*
Dollar, Diane (Hills) 1933- *57*
Dolson, Hildegarde *5*
  See Lockridge, Hildegarde (Dolson)
Domanska, Janina 1913(?)-1995 .... *68*
  Obituary *84*
  Earlier sketch in SATA *6*
  See also CLR *40*
  See also SAAS *18*
Dominguez, Angel 1953- *76*
Domino, John
  See Averill, Esther (Holden)
Domjan, Joseph (Spiri) 1907-1992 .... *25*

Domm, Jeffrey C. 1958- 84
Donahue, Dorothy 178
Donald, Rhonda Lucas 1962- 147
Donalds, Gordon
    See Shirreffs, Gordon D(onald)
Donaldson, Bryna
    See Stevens, Bryna
Donaldson, Gordon 1913-1993 64
    Obituary 76
Donaldson, Joan 1953- 78
Donaldson, Julia 1948- 180
    Earlier sketches in SATA 82, 132
Donaldson, Stephen R. 1947- 121
Donaldson, Stephen Reeder
    See Donaldson, Stephen R.
Doner, Kim 1955- 91
Doney, Todd L. W. 1959- 104
Dong-Sung, Kim 1970- 195
Dong-Sung Kim
    See Dong-Sung, Kim
Donkin, Nance (Clare) 1915- 95
Donna, Natalie 1934-1979 9
Donnelly, Elfie 1950-
    See CLR 104
Donnelly, Jennifer 1963- 154
Donnelly, Matt 1972- 148
Donnio, Sylviane 188
Donoghue, Emma 1969- 101
Donoughue, Carol 1935- 139
Donovan, Frank (Robert) 1906-1975
    Obituary 30
Donovan, John 1928-1992 72
    Brief entry 29
    See also CLR 3
Donovan, Mary Lee 1961- 86
Donovan, William
    See Berkebile, Fred D(onovan)
Donze, Mary Terese 1911- 89
Doob, Leonard W(illiam) 1909-2000 8
Dooley, Norah 1953- 74
Dooling, Michael 1958- 105
Dor, Ana
    See Ceder, Georgiana Dorcas
Dore, (Louis Christophe Paul) Gustave
    1832-1883 19
Doremus, Robert 1913- 30
Doren, Marion (Walker) 1928- 57
Dorenkamp, Michelle 1957- 89
Dorflinger, Carolyn 1953- 91
Dorfman, Joaquin 1979- 180
Dorfman, Joaquin Emiliano
    See Dorfman, Joaquin
Dorian, Edith M(cEwen) 1900-1983 5
Dorian, Harry
    See Hamilton, Charles (Harold St. John)
Dorian, Marguerite 7
Dorin, Patrick C(arberry) 1939- 59
    Brief entry 52
Dorman, Brandon 194
Dorman, Michael 1932- 7
Dorman, N. B. 1927- 39
Dorris, Michael 1945-1997 75
    Obituary 94
    See also CLR 58
Dorris, Michael A.
    See Dorris, Michael
Dorris, Michael Anthony
    See Dorris, Michael
Dorritt, Susan
    See Schlein, Miriam
Dorros, Alex 1991- 194
Dorros, Arthur 1950- 168
    Earlier sketches in SATA 78, 122
    See also CLR 42
    See also SAAS 20
Dorros, Arthur M.
    See Dorros, Arthur
Dorson, Richard M(ercer) 1916-1981 30
Doss, Helen (Grigsby) 1918- 20
Doss, Margot Patterson 6

Dothers, Anne
    See Chess, Victoria (Dickerson)
Dotlich, Rebecca Kai 1951- 182
Dottig
    See Grider, Dorothy
Dotts, Maryann J. 1933- 35
Doty, Jean Slaughter 1929- 28
Doty, Roy 1922- 28
Doubtfire, Dianne (Abrams) 1918- 29
Doucet, Sharon Arms 1951- 144
    Autobiography Feature 144
    Earlier sketch in SATA 125
Dougherty, Charles 1922- 18
Dougherty, Terri (L.) 1964- 146
Doughty, Rebecca 1955- 174
Douglas, Blaise 1960- 101
Douglas, Carole Nelson 1944- 73
Douglas, Garry
    See Kilworth, Garry
Douglas, James McM.
    See Griffin, W.E.B
Douglas, Kathryn
    See Ewing, Kathryn
Douglas, Leonard
    See Bradbury, Ray
Douglas, Lola
    See Zeises, Lara M.
Douglas, Marjory Stoneman 1890-1998 10
Douglas, Michael
    See Bright, Robert (Douglas Sr.)
Douglas, Michael
    See Crichton, Michael
Douglas, Shirley Stewart
    See Tepper, Sheri S.
Douglass, Barbara 1930- 40
Douglass, Frederick 1817(?)-1895 29
Douglass, Keith
    See Cunningham, Chet
Douty, Esther M(orris) 1909-1978 8
    Obituary 23
Dow, Emily R. 1904-1987 10
Dow, Vicki
    See McVey, Vicki
Dowd, John David 1945- 78
Dowdell, Dorothy (Florence) Karns 1910- ... 12
Dowden, Anne Ophelia Todd 1907-2007 7
    Obituary 180
    See also SAAS 10
Dowdey, Landon Gerald 1923- 11
Dowdy, Mrs. Regera
    See Gorey, Edward (St. John)
Dowell, Frances O'Roark 157
Dower, Laura 185
Dowling, Terry 1947- 101
Downer, Ann 1960- 155
Downer, Marion 1892(?)-1971 25
Downes, Belinda 1962- 180
Downey, Fairfax D(avis) 1893-1990 3
    Obituary 66
Downey, Lynn 1961- 185
Downham, Jenny 192
Downie, John 1931- 87
Downie, Mary Alice 1934- 171
    Earlier sketches in SATA 13, 87
Downie, Mary Alice Dawe
    See Downie, Mary Alice
Downing, David A(lmon) 1958- 84
Downing, Johnette 184
Downing, Julie 1956- 148
    Earlier sketch in SATA 81
Downing, Paula E. 1951- 80
Downing, Warwick 1931- 138
Downing, Wick
    See Downing, Warwick
Dowswell, Paul 1957- 184
Doyle, A. Conan
    See Doyle, Sir Arthur Conan
Doyle, Sir Arthur Conan 1859-1930 24
    See also CLR 106
    See Conan Doyle, Arthur

Doyle, Brian 1935- 156
    Earlier sketches in SATA 67, 104
    See also CLR 22
    See also SAAS 16
Doyle, Charlotte 1937- 178
    Earlier sketch in SATA 94
Doyle, Charlotte Lackner
    See Doyle, Charlotte
Doyle, Conan
    See Doyle, Sir Arthur Conan
Doyle, Debra 1952- 165
    Earlier sketch in SATA 105
    See Appleton, Victor
Doyle, Donovan
    See Boegehold, Betty (Doyle)
Doyle, John
    See Graves, Robert
Doyle, Malachy 1954- 165
    Earlier sketch in SATA 120
    See also CLR 83
Doyle, Richard 1824-1883 21
Doyle, Sir A. Conan
    See Doyle, Sir Arthur Conan
Dr. A
    See Asimov, Isaac
    and Silverstein, Alvin
    and Silverstein, Virginia B(arbara Opshelor)
Dr. Alphabet
    See Morice, Dave
Dr. Fred
    See Bortz, Alfred B(enjamin)
Dr. Laura
    See Schlessinger, Laura (Catherine)
Dr. Seuss
    See CLR 100
    See Geisel, Theodor Seuss
    and LeSieg, Theo.
    and Seuss, Dr.
    and Stone, Rosetta
Dr. Zed
    See Penrose, Gordon
Drabble, Margaret 1939- 48
Drackett, Phil(ip Arthur) 1922- 53
Draco, F.
    See Davis, Julia
Dracup, Angela 1943- 74
Dragisic, Patricia 116
Dragonwagon, Crescent 1952- 186
    Autobiography Feature 186
    Earlier sketches in SATA 11, 41, 75, 133
    See also SAAS 14
Drake, David 1945- 85
Drake, David Allen
    See Drake, David
Drake, Frank
    See Hamilton, Charles (Harold St. John)
Drake, Jane 1954- 82
Drakeford, Dale B 1952- 113
Drakeford, Dale Benjamin
    See Drakeford, Dale B
Draper, Hastings
    See Jeffries, Roderic
Draper, Sharon
    See Draper, Sharon M.
Draper, Sharon M. 1948- 195
    Autobiography Feature 146
    Earlier sketches in SATA 98, 146
    See also CLR 57
Draper, Sharon Mills
    See Draper, Sharon M.
Drapier, M. B.
    See Swift, Jonathan
Drawson, Blair 1943- 126
    Earlier sketch in SATA 17
Dray, Matt 1967- 177
Dray, Matthew Frederick
    See Dray, Matt
Dresang, Eliza (Carolyn Timberlake) 1941- . 19
Drescher, Henrik 1955- 172
    Earlier sketches in SATA 67, 105
    See also CLR 20

Drescher, Joan E(lizabeth) 1939- *137*
  Earlier sketch in SATA *30*
Dressen-McQueen, Stacey *191*
Dreves, Veronica R. 1927-1986
  Obituary *50*
Drew, Patricia (Mary) 1938- *15*
Drewery, Mary 1918- *6*
Drewery, Melanie 1970- *165*
Drewry, Henry N(athaniel) 1924- *138*
Dreyer, Ellen *177*
Drial, J. E.
  See Laird, Jean E(louise)
Drimmer, Frederick 1916-2000 .... *60*
  Obituary *124*
Driskill, J. Lawrence 1920- *90*
Driskill, Larry
  See Driskill, J. Lawrence
Driving Hawk, Virginia
  See Sneve, Virginia Driving Hawk
Dron, Laura
  See Matthews, L.S.
Drucker, Malka 1945- *111*
  Brief entry *29*
  Earlier sketch in SATA *39*
Drucker, Olga Levy 1927- *79*
Druitt, Tobias
  See Purkiss, Diane
Drummond, V(iolet) H(ilda) 1911-2000 .... *6*
Drummond, Walter
  See Silverberg, Robert
Drury, Clare Marie
  See Hoskyns-Abrahall, Clare (Constance Drury)
Drury, Roger W(olcott) 1914-1996 .... *15*
Druse, Eleanor
  See King, Stephen
Dryden, Pamela
  See St. John, Nicole
D.T., Hughes
  See Hughes, Dean
Duane, Diane (Elizabeth) 1952- *145*
  Brief entry *46*
  Earlier sketches in SATA *58, 95*
Dubanevich, Arlene 1950- *56*
Dubelaar, Thea 1947- *60*
du Blane, Daphne
  See Groom, Arthur William
Duble, Kathleen Benner 1958- *164*
Du Bois, Shirley Graham 1907(?)-1977 .... *24*
  See Graham, Shirley
Du Bois, W(illiam) E(dward) B(urghardt) 1868-1963 .... *42*
du Bois, William Pene
  See Pene du Bois, William (Sherman)
Duboise, Novella 1911-1999 .... *88*
Dubosarsky, Ursula 1961- *193*
  Earlier sketches in SATA *107, 147*
DuBose, LaRocque (Russ) 1926- *2*
Dubrovin, Vivian 1931- *139*
  Earlier sketch in SATA *65*
DuBurke, Randy *172*
Ducey, Jean Sparks 1915- *93*
Duchacek, Ivo D(uka) 1913-1988
  Obituary *55*
Du Chaillu, Paul (Belloni) 1835(?)-1903 ..... *26*
Ducharme, Dede Fox
  See Ducharme, Lilian Fox
Ducharme, Lilian Fox 1950- *122*
Ducornet, Erica 1943- *7*
  See Ducornet, Rikki
Ducornet, Rikki
  See Ducornet, Erica
Duden, Jane 1947- *136*
Duder, Tessa 1940- *117*
  Earlier sketch in SATA *80*
  See also CLR *43*
  See also SAAS *23*
Dudley, Helen
  See Hope Simpson, Jacynth
Dudley, Martha Ward 1909(?)-1985
  Obituary *45*

Dudley, Nancy
  See Cole, Lois Dwight
Dudley, Robert
  See Baldwin, James
Dudley, Ruth H(ubbell) 1905-2001 .... *11*
Dudley-Smith, T.
  See Trevor, Elleston
Due, Linnea A. 1948- *64*
Dueck, Adele 1955- *97*
Dueland, Joy V(ivian) *27*
Duerr, Gisela 1968- *89*
Duey, Kathleen 1950- *132*
Dufault, Joseph Ernest Nephtali
  See James, Will(iam Roderick)
Duff, Annis (James) 1904(?)-1986
  Obituary *49*
Duff, Maggie
  See Duff, Margaret K(app)
Duff, Margaret K(app) 1916-2003 .... *37*
  Obituary *144*
Duffey, Betsy (Byars) 1953- *131*
  Earlier sketch in SATA *80*
Duffie, Charles 1960- *144*
Duffield, Katy S. 1961- *147*
Duffy, Carol Ann 1955- *165*
  Earlier sketch in SATA *95*
Dugan, Jack
  See Griffin, W.E.B
Dugan, John Kevin
  See Griffin, W.E.B
Dugan, Michael (Gray) 1947- *15*
Duggan, Alfred Leo 1903-1964 .... *25*
Duggan, Maurice (Noel) 1922-1974 .... *40*
  Obituary *30*
Duggleby, John 1952- *94*
Dugin, Andrej 1955- *77*
Dugina, Olga 1964- *77*
du Jardin, Rosamond Neal 1902-1963 .... *2*
Duka, Ivo
  See Duchacek, Ivo D(uka)
Duke, Kate 1956- *192*
  Earlier sketches in SATA *90, 148*
  See also CLR *51*
Duke, Will
  See Gault, William Campbell
Dulac, Edmund 1882-1953 .... *19*
Dumas, Alexandre (pere) 1802-1870 .... *18*
  See also CLR *134*
Dumas, Jacqueline 1946- *55*
Dumas, Philippe 1940- *119*
  Earlier sketch in SATA *52*
du Maurier, Daphne 1907-1989 .... *27*
  Obituary *60*
Dumbleton, Mike 1948- *124*
  Earlier sketch in SATA *73*
Dunbar, Fiona 1961- *167*
Dunbar, Joyce 1944- *162*
  Earlier sketches in SATA *76, 112*
Dunbar, Paul Laurence 1872-1906 .... *34*
Dunbar, Polly 1980(?)- *181*
Dunbar, Robert E(verett) 1926- *32*
Duncan, Alexandra
  See Moore, Ishbel (Lindsay)
Duncan, Alice Faye 1967- *168*
  Earlier sketch in SATA *95*
Duncan, Gregory
  See McClintock, Marshall
Duncan, Jane
  See Cameron, Elizabeth Jane
Duncan, Julia K. *1*
  See Benson, Mildred (Augustine Wirt)
Duncan, Lois 1934- *141*
  Autobiography Feature *141*
  Earlier sketches in SATA *1, 36, 75, 133*
  See also CLR *129*
  See also SAAS *2*
Duncan, Norman 1871-1916
  See YABC *1*
Duncan, Terence
  See Nolan, William F(rancis)

Duncombe, Frances (Riker) 1900-1994 .... *25*
  Obituary *82*
Dunham, Montrew 1919- *162*
Dunham, Montrew Goetz
  See Dunham, Montrew
Dunkle, Clare B. 1964- *155*
Dunlap, Julie 1958- *84*
Dunleavy, Deborah 1951- *133*
Dunlop, Agnes M. R. (?)-1982 .... *87*
  See Kyle, Elisabeth
Dunlop, Eileen (Rhona) 1938- *76*
  Earlier sketch in SATA *24*
  See also SAAS *12*
Dunn, Anne M. 1940- *107*
Dunn, Harvey T(homas) 1884-1952 .... *34*
Dunn, Herb
  See Gutman, Dan
Dunn, John M. (III) 1949- *93*
Dunn, Judy
  See Spangenberg, Judith Dunn
Dunn, Mary Lois 1930- *6*
Dunnahoo, Terry Janson 1927- *7*
Dunne, Jeanette 1952- *72*
Dunne, Kathleen 1933- *126*
Dunne, Marie
  See Clark, Ann Nolan
Dunne, Mary Collins 1914- *11*
Dunne, Mary Jo
  See Dunne, Mary Collins
Dunnett, Kaitlyn
  See Emerson, Kathy Lynn
Dunnett, Margaret (Rosalind) 1909-1977 ..... *42*
Dunnick, Regan *178*
Dunrea, Olivier 1953- *160*
  Brief entry *46*
  Earlier sketches in SATA *59, 118*
Dunrea, Olivier Jean-Paul Dominique
  See Dunrea, Olivier
Dunton, Dorothy 1912- *92*
Dupasquier, Philippe 1955- *151*
  Earlier sketch in SATA *86*
DuPrau, Jeanne 1944- *144*
Dupuy, T(revor) N(evitt) 1916-1995 .... *4*
  Obituary *86*
DuQuette, Keith 1960- *155*
  Earlier sketch in SATA *90*
Duran, Gloria 1924- *171*
Duran, Gloria Bradley
  See Duran, Gloria
Duranceau, Suzanne 1952- *162*
Durango, Julia 1967- *173*
Durant, Alan 1958- *165*
  Earlier sketch in SATA *121*
Durant, John 1902- *27*
Durbin, William 1951- *174*
  Earlier sketch in SATA *143*
Durell, Ann 1930- *66*
Durkee, Sarah *173*
Durrant, Lynda 1954- *148*
  Earlier sketch in SATA *96*
Durrell, Gerald (Malcolm) 1925-1995 .... *8*
  Obituary *84*
Durrell, Julie 1955- *94*
Durrett, Deanne 1940- *144*
  Earlier sketch in SATA *92*
Du Soe, Robert C. 1892-1958
  See YABC *2*
Dussling, Jennifer 1970- *143*
  Earlier sketch in SATA *96*
DuTemple, Lesley A. 1952- *113*
Dutton, Sandra *191*
Dutz
  See Davis, Mary Octavia
Duval, Katherine
  See James, Elizabeth
Duval, Kathy 1946- *181*
Duvall, Aimee
  See Thurlo, Aimee
  and Thurlo, David
Duvall, Evelyn Millis 1906- *9*
Duvall, Jill D(onovan) 1932- *102*

Duvoisin, Roger (Antoine) 1904-1980 30
   Obituary 23
   Earlier sketch in SATA 2
   See also CLR 23
Dwiggins, Don(ald J.) 1913-1988 4
   Obituary 60
Dwight, Allan
   See Cole, Lois Dwight
Dwyer, Deanna
   See Koontz, Dean R.
Dwyer, K.R.
   See Koontz, Dean R.
Dyck, Peter J. 1914- 75
Dyer, James (Frederick) 1934- 37
Dyer, Jane 191
   Earlier sketch in SATA 147
Dyess, John (Foster) 1939- 76
Dygard, Thomas J. 1931-1996 97
   Obituary 92
   Earlier sketch in SATA 24
   See also SAAS 15
Dyke, John 1935- 35

E

E. V. L.
   See Lucas, E(dward) V(errall)
Eagar, Frances (Elisabeth Stuart)
   1940-1978 11
   Obituary 55
Eager, Edward (McMaken) 1911-1964 17
   See also CLR 43
Eager, George 1921- 56
   See Eager, George B.
Eager, George B.
   See Eager, George
Eagle, Ellen 1953- 61
Eagle, Kin
   See Adlerman, Daniel (Ezra)
   and Adlerman, Kimberly M(arie)
Eagle, Mike 1942- 11
Earle, Olive L(ydia) 1888-1982 7
Earle, William
   See Johns, W(illiam) E(arle)
Earls, Nick 1963- 156
   Earlier sketch in SATA 95
Early, Jack
   See Scoppettone, Sandra
Early, Jon
   See Johns, W(illiam) E(arle)
Early, Margaret 1951- 72
Earnshaw, Brian 1929- 17
Earnshaw, Micky
   See Earnshaw, Spencer Wright
Earnshaw, Spencer Wright 1939- 88
Easley, MaryAnn 94
Eastman, Charles A(lexander) 1858-1939
   See YABC 1
Eastman, P(hilip) D(ey) 1909-1986 33
   Obituary 46
Easton, Kelly 1960- 192
   Earlier sketch in SATA 141
Eastwick, Ivy (Ethel) O(live) 3
Eaton, Anne T(haxter) 1881-1971 32
Eaton, Anthony 1971- 167
Eaton, George L.
   See Verral, Charles Spain
Eaton, Janet
   See Givens, Janet E(aton)
Eaton, Jeanette 1886-1968 24
Eaton, Tom 1940- 22
Ebel, Alex 1927- 11
Eber, Dorothy (Margaret) Harley 1930- 27
Eberhart, Sheri S.
   See Tepper, Sheri S.
Eberle, Irmengarde 1898-1979 2
   Obituary 23
Eble, Diane 1956- 74
Eboch, Chris 113

Echlin, Kim 1955- 166
Eckblad, Edith Berven 1923- 23
Ecke, Wolfgang 1927-1983
   Obituary 37
Eckert, Allan W. 1931- 91
   Brief entry 27
   Earlier sketch in SATA 29
   See also SAAS 21
Eckert, Horst 1931- 72
   Earlier sketch in SATA 8
   See Janosch
Ecklar, Julia (Marie) 1964- 112
Eddings, David (Carroll) 1931- 91
Ede, Janina 1937- 33
Edell, Celeste 12
Edelman, Lily (Judith) 1915-1981 22
Edelson, Edward 1932- 51
Edens, Cooper 1945- 166
   Earlier sketches in SATA 49, 112
Edens, (Bishop) David 1926- 39
Edey, Maitland A(rmstrong) 1910-1992 25
   Obituary 71
Edgeworth, Maria 1768-1849 21
Edgy, Wardore
   See Gorey, Edward (St. John)
Edison, Theodore
   See Stratemeyer, Edward L.
Edler, Tim(othy) 1948- 56
Edmiston, Jim 1948- 80
Edmonds, I(vy) G(ordon) 1917- 8
Edmonds, Walter D(umaux) 1903-1998 27
   Obituary 99
   Earlier sketch in SATA 1
   See also SAAS 4
Edmund, Sean
   See Pringle, Laurence
Edsall, Marian (Stickney) 1920- 8
Edwards, Al
   See Nourse, Alan E(dward)
Edwards, Anne 1927- 35
Edwards, Audrey 1947- 52
   Brief entry 31
Edwards, Becky (Jane) 1966- 125
Edwards, Bertram
   See Edwards, Herbert Charles
Edwards, Bronwen Elizabeth
   See Rose, Wendy
Edwards, Cecile Pepin 1916- 25
Edwards, Dorothy 1914-1982 88
   Obituary 31
   Earlier sketch in SATA 4
Edwards, F. E.
   See Nolan, William F(rancis)
Edwards, Frank B. 1952- 93
Edwards, Gunvor 32
Edwards, Harvey 1929- 5
Edwards, Hazel (Eileen) 1945- 135
Edwards, Herbert Charles 1912- 12
Edwards, Jane Campbell 1932- 10
Edwards, Julia
   See Stratemeyer, Edward L.
Edwards, Julie
   See Andrews, Julie
Edwards, Julie Andrews
   See Andrews, Julie
Edwards, Linda Strauss 1948- 49
   Brief entry 42
Edwards, Margaret (Alexander) 1902-1988
   Obituary 56
Edwards, Michelle 1955- 152
   Earlier sketch in SATA 70
Edwards, Monica le Doux Newton
   1912-1998 12
Edwards, Olwen
   See Gater, Dilys
Edwards, Page (Lawrence, Jr.) 1941-1999 ... 59
Edwards, Pamela Duncan 189
Edwards, R. T.
   See Goulart, Ron(ald Joseph)
Edwards, Sally (Cary) 1929- 7

Edwards, Samuel
   See Gerson, Noel Bertram
Edwards, Wallace 1957(?)- 170
Egan, E(dward) W(elstead) 1922- 35
Egan, Kerry 175
Egan, Lorraine Hopping 1960- 134
   Earlier sketch in SATA 91
Egan, Tim 1957- 191
   Earlier sketches in SATA 89, 155
Egermeier, Elsie E(milie) 1890-1986 65
Eggenberger, David 1918- 6
Eggleston, Edward 1837-1902 27
Egielski, Richard 1952- 163
   Earlier sketches in SATA 11, 49, 106
   See also CLR 28
Egypt, Ophelia Settle 1903-1984 16
   Obituary 38
Ehlert, Lois 1934- 172
   Earlier sketches in SATA 35, 69, 128
   See also CLR 28
Ehlert, Lois Jane
   See Ehlert, Lois
Ehling, Katalin Olah 1941- 93
Ehrenfreund, Norbert 1921- 86
Ehrenhaft, Daniel 1970- 185
Ehrhardt, Karen 1963- 184
Ehrlich, Amy 1942- 132
   Earlier sketches in SATA 25, 65, 96
Ehrlich, Bettina Bauer 1903-1985 1
Ehrlich, H. M.
   See Ziefert, Harriet
Eichenberg, Fritz 1901-1990 50
   Earlier sketch in SATA 9
Eichler, Margrit 1942- 35
Eichner, James A. 1927- 4
Eidson, Thomas 1944- 112
Eifert, Virginia (Louise) S(nider) 1911-1966 . 2
Eige, (Elizabeth) Lillian 1915- 65
Eiken, J. Melia 1967- 125
Einsel, Naiad 10
Einsel, Walter 1926- 10
Einzig, Susan 1922- 43
Eiseman, Alberta 1925- 15
Eisenberg, Azriel (Louis) 1903-1985 12
Eisenberg, Lisa 1949- 155
   Brief entry 50
   Earlier sketch in SATA 57
Eisenberg, Phyllis Rose 1924- 41
Eisner, Vivienne
   See Margolis, Vivienne
Eisner, Will 1917-2005 165
   Earlier sketch in SATA 31
Eisner, William Erwin
   See Eisner, Will
Eitzen, Allan 1928- 9
Eitzen, Ruth (Carper) 1924- 9
Ekwensi, C. O. D.
   See Ekwensi, Cyprian
Ekwensi, Cyprian 1921-2007 66
Ekwensi, Cyprian Odiatu Duaka
   See Ekwensi, Cyprian
Elam, Richard M(ace, Jr.) 1920- 9
Elborn, Andrew
   See Clements, Andrew
   and Clements, Andrew
Elboz, Stephen 1956- 152
Eldin, Peter 1939- 154
Eldon, Kathy 1946- 107
Elfman, Blossom 1925- 8
Elgin, Kathleen 1923- 39
Elia
   See Lamb, Charles
Eliot, A. D.
   See Jewett, (Theodora) Sarah Orne
Eliot, Alice
   See Jewett, (Theodora) Sarah Orne
Eliot, Anne
   See Cole, Lois Dwight
Eliot, Dan
   See Silverberg, Robert
Elish, Dan 1960- 129
   Earlier sketch in SATA 68

Elisha, Ron 1951- *104*
Elisofon, Eliot 1911-1973
   Obituary *21*
Elkeles, Simone *187*
Elkin, Benjamin 1911-1995 .... *3*
Elkins, Dov Peretz 1937- *5*
Ellacott, S(amuel) E(rnest) 1911- *19*
Elleman, Barbara 1934- *147*
Ellen, Jaye
   See Nixon, Joan Lowery
Eller, Scott
   See Holinger, William (Jacques)
   and Shepard, Jim
Ellestad, Myrvin
   See Ellestad, Myrvin H.
Ellestad, Myrvin H. 1921- *120*
Elliot, David 1952- *122*
Elliott, Bruce
   See Field, Edward
Elliott, David 1947- *163*
Elliott, Don
   See Silverberg, Robert
Elliott, Elizabeth Shippen Green
   See Green, Elizabeth Shippen
Elliott, Janice 1931-1995 .... *119*
Elliott, Joey
   See Houk, Randy
Elliott, Louise *111*
Elliott, Odette 1939- *75*
Elliott, Patricia 1946- *176*
Elliott, Sarah M(cCarn) 1930- *14*
Elliott, (Robert) Scott 1970- *153*
Elliott, William
   See Bradbury, Ray
Ellis, (Mary) Amabel (Nassau Strachey)
   Williams
   See Williams-Ellis, (Mary) Amabel (Nassau
   Strachey)
Ellis, Anyon
   See Rowland-Entwistle, (Arthur) Theodore
   (Henry)
Ellis, Carson 1975- *190*
Ellis, Carson Friedman
   See Ellis, Carson
Ellis, Deborah 1960- *187*
   Earlier sketch in SATA *129*
Ellis, E. S.
   See Ellis, Edward S(ylvester)
Ellis, Edward S(ylvester) 1840-1916
   See YABC *1*
Ellis, Ella Thorp 1928- *127*
   Earlier sketch in SATA *7*
   See also SAAS *9*
Ellis, Harry Bearse 1921-2004 .... *9*
Ellis, Herbert
   See Wilson, Lionel
Ellis, Mel(vin Richard) 1912-1984 .... *7*
   Obituary *39*
Ellis, Richard 1938- *130*
Ellis, Sarah 1952- *179*
   Earlier sketches in SATA *68, 131*
   See also CLR *42*
Ellison, Emily *114*
Ellison, Lucile Watkins 1907(?)-1979 ...... *50*
   Obituary *22*
Ellison, Virginia H(owell) 1910- *4*
Ellsberg, Edward 1891-1983 .... *7*
Ellsworth, Mary Ellen (Tressel) 1940- *146*
Elmer, Robert 1958- *154*
   Earlier sketch in SATA *99*
Elmore, (Carolyn) Patricia 1933- *38*
   Brief entry *35*
El-Moslimany, Ann P(axton) 1937- *90*
Elschner, Geraldine 1954- *183*
Elspeth
   See Bragdon, Elspeth MacDuffie
Elster, Jean Alicia 1953- *150*
Elting, Mary 1906- *88*
   Earlier sketch in SATA *2*
   See also SAAS *20*
Elvgren, Jennifer Riesmeyer *179*

Elwart, Joan Potter 1927- *2*
Elwood, Ann 1931- *55*
   Brief entry *52*
Elwood, Roger 1943-2007 .... *58*
Elya, Susan M(iddleton) 1955- *159*
   Earlier sketch in SATA *106*
Elzbieta *88*
Ember, Kathi *190*
Emberley, Barbara A(nne) 1932- *146*
   Earlier sketches in SATA *8, 70*
   See also CLR *5*
Emberley, Ed(ward Randolph) 1931- *146*
   Earlier sketches in SATA *8, 70*
   See also CLR *81*
Emberley, Michael 1960- *189*
   Earlier sketches in SATA *34, 80, 119*
Embry, Margaret Jacob 1919-1975 .... *5*
Emecheta, Buchi 1944- *66*
Emecheta, Florence Onye Buchi
   See Emecheta, Buchi
Emerson, Alice B. *67*
   Earlier sketch in SATA *1*
   See Benson, Mildred (Augustine Wirt)
Emerson, Kathy Lynn 1947- *63*
Emerson, Ru 1944- *107*
   Earlier sketch in SATA *70*
Emerson, Sally 1952- *111*
Emerson, William K(eith) 1925- *25*
Emert, Phyllis R(aybin) 1947- *93*
Emery, Anne (McGuigan) 1907- *33*
   Earlier sketch in SATA *1*
Emmens, Carol Ann 1944- *39*
Emmett, Jonathan 1965- *188*
   Earlier sketch in SATA *138*
Emmons, Della (Florence) Gould 1890-1983
   Obituary *39*
Emory, Jerry 1957- *96*
Emrich, Duncan (Black Macdonald)
   1908-1970(?) *11*
Emshwiller, Carol 1921- *174*
   Autobiography Feature *174*
Emshwiller, Carol Fries
   See Emshwiller, Carol
Emslie, M. L.
   See Simpson, Myrtle L(illias)
Ende, Michael (Andreas Helmuth)
   1929-1995 .... *130*
   Brief entry *42*
   Obituary *86*
   Earlier sketch in SATA *61*
   See also CLR *138*
Enderle, Dotti 1954- *145*
Enderle, Judith (Ann) Ross 1941- *89*
   Autobiography Feature *114*
   Earlier sketch in SATA *38*
   See also SAAS *26*
Enell, Trinka (Gochenour) 1951- *79*
Enfield, Carrie
   See Smith, Susan Vernon
Engdahl, Sylvia Louise 1933- *4*
   Autobiography Feature *122*
   See also CLR *2*
   See also SAAS *5*
Engel, Diana 1947- *70*
Engelbreit, Mary 1952- *169*
Engelhart, Margaret S. 1924- *59*
Engelmann, Kim (V.) 1959- *87*
England, George Allan 1877-1936 .... *102*
Englart, Mindi Rose 1965- *146*
Engle, Eloise
   See Paananen, Eloise (Katherine)
Engle, Margarita 1951- *193*
Englebert, Victor 1933- *8*
English, James W(ilson) 1915- *37*
Engstrom, Elizabeth 1951- *110*
Enright, D(ennis) J(oseph) 1920-2002 .... *25*
   Obituary *140*
Enright, Dominique *194*
Enright, Elizabeth (Wright) 1909-1968 .... *9*
   See also CLR *4*
Ensor, Barbara *180*

Ensor, Robert (T.) 1922- *93*
Enthoven, Sam 1974- *187*
Entwistle, (Arthur) Theodore (Henry) Rowland
   See Rowland-Entwistle, (Arthur) Theodore
   (Henry)
Enys, Sarah L.
   See Sloggett, Nellie
Epanya, Christian A(rthur Kingue) 1956- *91*
Ephraim, Shelly S(chonebaum) 1952- *97*
Ephron, Delia 1944- *65*
   Brief entry *50*
Epler, Doris M. 1928- *73*
Epple, Anne Orth 1927- *20*
Epstein, Anne Merrick 1931- *20*
Epstein, Beryl (M. Williams) 1910- *31*
   Earlier sketch in SATA *1*
   See also CLR *26*
   See also SAAS *17*
Epstein, Perle S(herry) 1938- *27*
Epstein, Rachel S. 1941- *102*
Epstein, Samuel 1909-2000 .... *31*
   Earlier sketch in SATA *1*
   See also CLR *26*
   See also SAAS *17*
Erdman, Loula Grace 1905(?)-1976 .... *1*
Erdoes, Richard 1912- *33*
   Brief entry *28*
Erdogan, Buket *187*
Erdrich, Karen Louise
   See Erdrich, Louise
Erdrich, Louise 1954- *141*
   Earlier sketch in SATA *94*
Erickson, Betty J. 1923- *97*
Erickson, Betty Jean
   See Erickson, Betty J.
Erickson, John R. 1943- *136*
   Earlier sketch in SATA *70*
Erickson, Jon 1948- *141*
Erickson, Phoebe *59*
Erickson, Russell E(verett) 1932- *27*
Erickson, Sabra Rollins 1912-1995 .... *35*
Erickson, Walter
   See Fast, Howard
Ericson, Walter
   See Fast, Howard
Ericsson, Jennifer A. *170*
Erikson, Mel 1937- *31*
Ering, Timothy Basil *176*
Erlanger, Baba
   See Trahey, Jane
Erlbach, Arlene 1948- *160*
   Earlier sketches in SATA *78, 115*
Erlbruch, Wolf 1948- *181*
Erlich, Lillian (Feldman) 1910-1983 .... *10*
Ermatinger, James W. 1959- *170*
Ernest, William
   See Berkebile, Fred D(onovan)
Ernst, (Lyman) John 1940- *39*
Ernst, Kathleen
   See Ernst, Kathleen A.
Ernst, Kathleen A. 1959- *162*
Ernst, Kathryn (Fitzgerald) 1942- *25*
Ernst, Lisa Campbell 1957- *154*
   Brief entry *44*
   Earlier sketches in SATA *55, 95*
Erskine, Kathryn *193*
Ervin, Janet Halliday 1923- *4*
Erwin, Will
   See Eisner, Will
Esbaum, Jill *174*
Esbensen, Barbara J(uster) 1925-1996 .... *97*
   Brief entry *53*
   Earlier sketch in SATA *62*
Eschbacher, Roger *160*
Escriva, Vivi *182*
Eseki, Bruno
   See Mphahlele, Ezekiel

Eshmeyer, R. E. 29
See Eschmeyer, R(einhart) E(rnst)
Eskridge, Ann E. 1949- 84
Espeland, Pamela (Lee) 1951- 128
Brief entry 38
Earlier sketch in SATA 52
Espriella, Don Manuel Alvarez
See Southey, Robert
Espy, Willard R(ichardson) 1910-1999 38
Obituary 113
Essrig, Harry 1912- 66
Estep, Irene Compton 5
Esterl, Arnica 1933- 77
Estes, Eleanor (Ruth) 1906-1988 91
Obituary 56
Earlier sketch in SATA 7
See also CLR 70
Estoril, Jean
See Allan, Mabel Esther
Estrada, Pau 1961- 74
Etchemendy, Nancy 1952- 166
Earlier sketch in SATA 38
Etchemendy, Nancy Elise Howell
See Etchemendy, Nancy
Etchison, Birdie L(ee) 1937- 38
Etchison, Craig 1945- 133
Etherington, Frank 1945- 58
Eton, Robert
See Meynell, Laurence Walter
Ets, Marie Hall 1893-1984 2
See also CLR 33
Ettlinger, Doris 1950- 173
Eunson, (John) Dale 1904-2002 5
Obituary 132
Evan, Frances Y. 1951- 167
Evanoff, Vlad 1916- 59
Evans, Cambria 1981- 178
Evans, Douglas 1953- 144
Earlier sketch in SATA 93
Evans, Eva (Knox) 1905-1998 27
Evans, Freddi Williams 1957- 134
Evans, Greg 1947- 143
Earlier sketch in SATA 73
Evans, Hubert Reginald 1892-1986 118
Obituary 48
Evans, Katherine (Floyd) 1901-1964 5
Evans, Larry
See Evans, Laurence Chubb
Evans, Laurence Chubb 1939- 88
Evans, Lawrence Watt
See Watt-Evans, Lawrence
Evans, Lezlie 180
Evans, Mari 1923- 10
Evans, Mark 19
Evans, Nancy 1950- 65
Evans, Patricia Healy
See Carpenter, Patricia (Healy Evans)
Evans, (Alice) Pearl 1927- 83
Evans, Shane W. 189
Evans, Shirlee 1931- 58
Evans, Tabor
See Cameron, Lou
and Knott, William C(ecil, Jr.)
and Wallmann, Jeffrey M(iner)
and Whittington, Harry (Benjamin)
Evarts, Esther
See Benson, Sally
Evarts, Hal G., (Jr.) 1915-1989 6
Everett, Gail
See Hale, Arlene
Evernden, Margery 1916- 5
Eversole, Robyn 1971- 74
Eversole, Robyn H.
See Eversole, Robyn
Eversole, Robyn Harbert
See Eversole, Robyn
Evslin, Bernard 1922-1993 83
Brief entry 28
Obituary 77
Earlier sketch in SATA 45

Ewart, Claire 1958- 145
Earlier sketch in SATA 76
Ewen, David 1907-1985 4
Obituary 47
Ewing, Juliana (Horatia Gatty) 1841-1885 ... 16
See also CLR 78
Ewing, Kathryn 1921- 20
Eyerly, Jeannette 1908-2008 86
Earlier sketch in SATA 4
See also SAAS 10
Eyerly, Jeannette Hyde
See Eyerly, Jeannette
Eyre, Dorothy
See McGuire, Leslie (Sarah)
Eyre, Frank 1910-1988
Obituary 62
Eyre, Katherine Wigmore 1901-1970 26
Ezzell, Marilyn 1937- 42
Brief entry 38

F

Fabe, Maxene 1943- 15
Faber, Doris (Greenberg) 1924- 78
Earlier sketch in SATA 3
Faber, Harold 1919- 5
Fabre, Jean Henri (Casimir) 1823-1915 22
Facklam, Margery (Metz) 1927- 132
Earlier sketches in SATA 20, 85
Fadiman, Clifton (Paul) 1904-1999 11
Obituary 115
Fagan, Cary 1957- 186
Fahs, Sophia Blanche Lyon 1876-1978 102
Failing, Barbara Larmon 182
Fair, David 1952- 96
Fair, Sylvia 1933- 13
Fairfax-Lucy, Brian (Fulke Cameron-Ramsay)
1898-1974 6
Obituary 26
Fairfield, Flora
See Alcott, Louisa May
Fairlie, Gerard 1899-1983
Obituary 34
Fairman, Joan A(lexandra) 1935- 10
Faithfull, Gail 1936- 8
Falcone, L(ucy) M. 1951- 155
Falconer, Ian 1959- 179
Earlier sketch in SATA 125
See also CLR 90
Falconer, James
See Kirkup, James
Falconer, Lee N.
See May, Julian
Falkner, Leonard 1900-1977 12
Fall, Andrew
See Arthur, Robert, (Jr.)
Fall, Thomas
See Snow, Donald Clifford
Faller, Regis 1968- 187
Falls, C(harles) B(uckles) 1874-1960 38
Brief entry 27
Falstein, Louis 1909-1995 37
Fancher, Lou 1960- 177
Fanelli, Sara 1969- 126
Earlier sketch in SATA 89
Fanning, Leonard M(ulliken) 1888-1967 5
Faralla, Dana 1909- 9
Faralla, Dorothy W.
See Faralla, Dana
Farb, Peter 1929-1980 12
Obituary 22
Farber, Norma 1909-1984 75
Obituary 38
Earlier sketch in SATA 25
Fardell, John 1967- 195
Farish, Terry 1947- 146
Earlier sketch in SATA 82
Farjeon, (Eve) Annabel 1919-2004 11
Obituary 153

Farjeon, Eleanor 1881-1965 2
See also CLR 34
Farley, Carol (J.) 1936- 137
Earlier sketch in SATA 4
Farley, Terri 165
Farley, Walter (Lorimer) 1915-1989 132
Earlier sketches in SATA 2, 43
Farlow, James O(rville, Jr.) 1951- 75
Farmer, Nancy 1941- 161
Earlier sketches in SATA 79, 117
Farmer, Patti 1948- 79
Farmer, Penelope (Jane) 1939- 105
Brief entry 39
Earlier sketch in SATA 40
See also CLR 8
See also SAAS 22
Farmer, Peter 1950- 38
Farmer, Philip Jose 1918- 93
Farnham, Burt
See Clifford, Harold B(urton)
Farnsworth, Bill 1958- 186
Earlier sketches in SATA 84, 135
Farquhar, Margaret C(utting) 1905-1988 13
Farquharson, Alexander 1944- 46
Farquharson, Martha
See Finley, Martha
Farr, Diana (Pullein-Thompson) 82
See Pullein-Thompson, Diana
Farr, Finis (King) 1904-1982 10
Farrar, Jill
See Morris, Jill
Farrar, Susan Clement 1917- 33
Farrell, Ben
See Cebulash, Mel
Farrell, Patrick
See Odgers, Sally Farrell
Farrell, Sally
See Odgers, Sally Farrell
Farrer, Vashti 167
Farrington, Benjamin 1891-1974
Obituary 20
Farrington, S(elwyn) Kip, Jr. 1904-1983 20
Farshtey, Greg(ory T.) 1965- 148
Farthing, Alison 1936- 45
Brief entry 36
Farthing-Knight, Catherine 1933- 92
Fassler, Joan (Grace) 1931- 11
Fast, Howard 1914-2003 7
Autobiography Feature 107
Fast, Howard Melvin
See Fast, Howard
Fasulo, Michael 1963- 83
Fatchen, Max 1920- 84
Earlier sketch in SATA 20
See also SAAS 20
Fate, Marilyn
See Collins, Paul
Father Goose
See Ghigna, Charles
Fatigati, (Frances) Evelyn 1948- 24
Fatio, Louise 1904-1993 6
Fatus, Sophie 1957- 182
Faulhaber, Martha 1926- 7
Faulkner, Anne Irvin 1906- 23
Faulkner, Frank
See Ellis, Edward S(ylvester)
Faulkner, Nancy
See Faulkner, Anne Irvin
Faulknor, Cliff(ord Vernon) 1913- 86
Favole, Robert J(ames) 1950- 125
Fax, Elton Clay 1909-1993 25
Faxon, Lavinia
See Russ, Lavinia (Faxon)
Feagles, Anita M(acRae) 1927- 9
Feagles, Elizabeth
See Day, Beth (Feagles)
Feague, Mildred H. 1915- 14
Fearnley, Jan 1965- 153
Fearrington, Ann (Peyton) 1945- 146
Fecher, Constance
See Heaven, Constance (Christina)

Feder, Chris Welles 1938- 81
Feder, Harriet K. 1928- 73
Feder, Paula (Kurzband) 1935- 26
Federici, Debbie 1965- 175
Federici, Debbie Tanner
  See Federici, Debbie
Feelings, Muriel (Lavita Grey) 1938- 16
  See also CLR 5
  See also SAAS 8
Feelings, Thomas 1933-2003 8
  Obituary 148
  See Feelings, Tom
Feelings, Tom 69
  See also CLR 58
  See also SAAS 19
  See Feelings, Thomas
Fehler, Gene 1940- 74
Fehrenbach, T(heodore) R(eed, Jr.) 1925- 33
Feiffer, Jules 1929- 157
  Earlier sketches in SATA 8, 61, 111
Feiffer, Jules Ralph
  See Feiffer, Jules
Feiffer, Kate 1964- 170
Feig, Barbara Krane 1937- 34
Feikema, Feike
  See Manfred, Frederick (Feikema)
Feil, Hila 1942- 12
Feilen, John
  See May, Julian
Feinberg, Barbara Jane 1938- 58
  See Feinberg, Barbara Silberdick
Feinberg, Barbara Silberdick 123
  See Feinberg, Barbara Jane
Feinstein, John 1956- 195
  Earlier sketch in SATA 163
Feldman, Anne (Rodgers) 1939- 19
Feldman, Elane 79
Felin, M. Sindy 194
Felix
  See Vincent, Felix
Fell, Derek 1939- 167
Fell, Derek John
  See Fell, Derek
Fellows, Muriel H. 10
Fellows, Stan 1957- 177
Fellows, Stanley
  See Fellows, Stan
Felsen, Henry Gregor 1916-1995 1
  See also SAAS 2
Felstead, Cathie 1954- 192
Feltenstein, Arlene (H.) 1934- 119
Felton, Harold William 1902-1991 1
Felton, Ronald Oliver 1909- 3
Felts, Shirley 1934- 33
Fenderson, Lewis H., Jr. 1907-1983 47
  Obituary 37
Fenner, Carol (Elizabeth) 1929-2002 89
  Obituary 132
  Earlier sketch in SATA 7
  See also SAAS 24
Fenner, Phyllis R(eid) 1899-1982 1
  Obituary 29
Fensham, Elizabeth 169
Fenten, Barbara D(oris) 1935- 26
Fenten, D(onald) X. 1932- 4
Fenton, Carroll Lane 1900-1969 5
Fenton, Edward 1917-1995 7
  Obituary 89
Fenton, Mildred Adams 1899-1995 21
Fenwick, Patti
  See Grider, Dorothy
Feravolo, Rocco Vincent 1922- 10
Ferber, Brenda A. 1967- 184
Ferber, Edna 1887-1968 7
Fergus, Charles 114
Ferguson, Alane 1957- 182
  Earlier sketch in SATA 85
Ferguson, Bob
  See Ferguson, Robert Bruce
Ferguson, Cecil 1931- 45
Ferguson, Robert Bruce 1927-2001 13

Ferguson, Sarah 1959- 180
  Earlier sketches in SATA 66, 110
Ferguson, Sarah Margaret
  See Ferguson, Sarah
Ferguson, Walter (W.) 1930- 34
Fergusson, Erna 1888-1964 5
Fermi, Laura 1907-1977 6
  Obituary 28
Fern, Eugene A. 1919-1987 10
  Obituary 54
Fernandes, Eugenie 1943- 139
  Earlier sketch in SATA 77
Fernandez, Laura 1960- 171
Ferrari, Maria 123
Ferreiro, Carmen 1958- 158
Ferrell, Nancy Warren 1932- 70
Ferrier, Lucy
  See Penzler, Otto
Ferris, Helen Josephine 1890-1969 21
Ferris, James Cody 1
  See McFarlane, Leslie (Charles)
Ferris, Jean 1939- 149
  Brief entry 50
  Earlier sketches in SATA 56, 105
Ferris, Jeri Chase 1937- 84
Ferry, Charles 1927- 92
  Earlier sketch in SATA 43
  See also CLR 34
  See also SAAS 20
Fetz, Ingrid 1915- 30
Feydy, Anne Lindbergh
  Brief entry 32
  See Sapieyevski, Anne Lindbergh
Fiammenghi, Gioia 1929- 66
  Earlier sketch in SATA 9
Fiarotta, Noel 15
  See Ficarotta, Noel
Fiarotta, Phyllis 15
  See Ficarotta, Phyllis
Fichter, George S. 1922-1993 7
Ficocelli, Elizabeth 189
Fidler, Kathleen (Annie) 1899-1980 87
  Obituary 45
  Earlier sketch in SATA 3
Fiedler, Jean(nette Feldman) 4
Fiedler, Joseph Daniel 159
Fiedler, Lisa 185
Field, Dorothy 1944- 97
Field, Edward 1924- 109
  Earlier sketch in SATA 8
Field, Elinor Whitney 1889-1980
  Obituary 28
Field, Eugene 1850-1895 16
Field, Gans T.
  See Wellman, Manly Wade
Field, James 1959- 113
Field, Peter
  See Drago, Harry Sinclair
  and Dresser, Davis
  and Mann, E(dward) B(everly)
Field, Rachel (Lyman) 1894-1942 15
  See also CLR 21
Fielding, Kate
  See Oldfield, Jenny
Fields, Bryan W. 1958(?)- 188
Fields, Terri 1948- 191
Fields, T.S.
  See Fields, Terri
Fienberg, Anna 1956- 183
  Earlier sketch in SATA 112
Fife, Dale (Odile Hollerbach) 1901- 18
Fighter Pilot, A
  See Johnston, H(ugh) A(nthony) S(tephen)
Figler, Jeanie 1949- 123
Figley, Marty Rhodes 1948- 158
  Earlier sketch in SATA 88
Figueredo, D(anilo) H. 1951- 155
Figueroa, Pablo 1938- 9
Fijan, Carol 1918- 12
Filderman, Diane E(lizabeth) 1959- 87
Files, Meg 1946- 107

Fillmore, Parker H(oysted) 1878-1944
  See YABC 1
Filstrup, Chris
  See Filstrup, E(dward) Christian
Filstrup, E(dward) Christian 1942- 43
Filstrup, Janie
  See Merrill, Jane
Finchler, Judy 1943- 93
Finder, Martin
  See Salzmann, Siegmund
Findlay, Jamieson 1958- 169
Findon, Joanne 1957- 161
Fine, Anne 1947- 160
  Earlier sketches in SATA 29, 72, 111
  See also CLR 25
  See also SAAS 15
Fine, Edith Hope 169
Fine, Howard 1961- 181
Fine, Jane
  See Ziefert, Harriet
Finger, Charles J(oseph) 1869(?)-1941 42
Fink, William B(ertrand) 1916- 22
Finke, Blythe Foote 1922- 26
Finkel, George (Irvine) 1909-1975 8
Finkelstein, Norman H. 1941- 137
  Earlier sketch in SATA 73
Finkelstein, Norman Henry
  See Finkelstein, Norman H.
Finlay, Alice Sullivan 1946- 82
Finlay, Winifred Lindsay Crawford
  (McKissack) 1910-1989 23
Finlayson, Ann 1925- 8
Finley, Martha 1828-1909 43
Finley, Mary Peace 1942- 83
Finney, Jack 109
  See Finney, Walter Braden
Finney, Patricia 1958- 163
Finney, Shan 1944- 65
Firer, Ben Zion
  See Firer, Benzion
Firer, Benzion 1914- 64
Fireside, Bryna J. 1932- 73
Firmin, Charlotte 1954- 29
Firmin, Peter 1928- 58
  Earlier sketch in SATA 15
Firth, Barbara 179
Fischbach, Julius 1894-1988 10
Fischer, John
  See Fluke, Joanne
Fischer, R.J.
  See Fluke, Joanne
Fischer, Scott M. 1971- 195
Fischer-Nagel, Andreas 1951- 56
Fischer-Nagel, Heiderose 1956- 56
Fischler, Shirley (Walton) 66
Fischler, Stan(ley I.) 66
  Brief entry 36
Fishback, Margaret
  See Antolini, Margaret Fishback
Fishbone, Greg R. 195
Fisher, Aileen (Lucia) 1906-2002 73
  Obituary 143
  Earlier sketches in SATA 1, 25
  See also CLR 49
Fisher, Barbara 1940- 44
  Brief entry 34
Fisher, Carolyn 1968- 154
Fisher, Catherine 1957- 155
Fisher, Chris 1958- 80
Fisher, Clavin C(argill) 1912- 24
Fisher, Cynthia 195
Fisher, Dorothy (Frances) Canfield 1879-1958
  See YABC 1
  See also CLR 71
Fisher, Gary L. 1949- 86
Fisher, John (Oswald Hamilton) 1909- 15
Fisher, Laura Harrison 1934- 5

Fisher, Leonard Everett 1924- *176*
  Autobiography Feature *122*
  Earlier sketches in SATA *4, 34, 73, 120*
  See also CLR *18*
  See also SAAS *1*
Fisher, Lois I. 1948- *38*
  Brief entry *35*
Fisher, Margery (Turner) 1913-1992 .... *20*
  Obituary *74*
Fisher, Marshall Jon 1963- *113*
Fisher, Nikki
  See Strachan, Ian
Fisher, Robert (Tempest) 1943- *47*
Fisher, Suzanne
  See Staples, Suzanne Fisher
Fisher, Valorie *177*
Fishman, Cathy Goldberg 1951- *106*
Fisk, Nicholas *25*
  See Higginbottom, David
Fisk, Pauline 1948- *160*
  Earlier sketch in SATA *66*
Fiske, Tarleton
  See Bloch, Robert (Albert)
Fisscher, Catharina G. M. 1958- *142*
Fisscher, Tiny
  See Fisscher, Catharina G. M.
Fitch, Clarke
  See Sinclair, Upton
Fitch, John IV
  See Cormier, Robert
Fitch, Sheree 1956- *178*
  Earlier sketch in SATA *108*
Fitschen, Dale 1937- *20*
Fitzalan, Roger
  See Trevor, Elleston
Fitzgerald, Captain Hugh
  See Baum, L(yman) Frank
FitzGerald, Cathleen 1932-1987
  Obituary *50*
Fitzgerald, Dawn *175*
Fitzgerald, Edward Earl 1919-2001 .... *20*
Fitzgerald, F(rancis) A(nthony) 1940- *15*
Fitzgerald, John D(ennis) 1907(?)-1988 .... *20*
  Obituary *56*
  See also CLR *1*
Fitzgerald, Merni Ingrassia 1955- *53*
Fitzgibbon, Terry 1948- *121*
Fitzhardinge, Joan Margaret 1912- *73*
  Earlier sketch in SATA *2*
  See Phipson, Joan
Fitzhugh, Louise (Perkins) 1928-1974 .... *45*
  Obituary *24*
  Earlier sketch in SATA *1*
  See also CLR *72*
Fitzhugh, Percy Keese 1876-1950 .... *65*
Fitzpatrick, Marie-Louise 1962- *189*
  Earlier sketch in SATA *125*
FitzRalph, Matthew
  See McInerny, Ralph
Fitz-Randolph, Jane (Currens) 1915- *51*
Fitzsimons, Cecilia 1952- *97*
Fitzsimons, Cecilia A.L.
  See Fitzsimons, Cecilia
Flack, Marjorie 1897-1958 .... *100*
  See also YABC *2*
  See also CLR *28*
Flack, Naomi John White -1999 .... *40*
  Brief entry *35*
Flake, Sharon G. *166*
Flanagan, John 1944- *180*
Flanagan, John Anthony
  See Flanagan, John
Flannery, Kate
  See De Goldi, Kathleen Domenica
Flatt, Lizann 1966- *88*
Fleagle, Gail S(hatto) 1940- *117*
Fleetwood, Jenni 1947- *80*
Fleischer, Jane
  See Oppenheim, Joanne
Fleischhauer-Hardt, Helga 1936- *30*

Fleischman, Albert Sidney
  See Fleischman, Sid
Fleischman, John 1948- *145*
Fleischman, Paul 1952- *156*
  Brief entry *32*
  Earlier sketches in SATA *39, 72, 110*
  See also CLR *66*
  See also SAAS *20*
Fleischman, Sid 1920- *185*
  Earlier sketches in SATA *8, 59, 96, 148*
  See also CLR *15*
Fleischner, Jennifer 1956- *188*
  Earlier sketch in SATA *93*
Fleisher, Paul 1948- *132*
  Earlier sketch in SATA *81*
Fleisher, Robbin 1951-1977 .... *52*
  Brief entry *49*
Fleishman, Seymour 1918- *66*
  Brief entry *32*
Fleming, A. A.
  See Arthur, Robert, (Jr.)
Fleming, Alice Mulcahey 1928- *9*
Fleming, Candace 1962- *190*
  Earlier sketches in SATA *94, 143*
Fleming, Denise 1950- *173*
  Earlier sketches in SATA *81, 126*
Fleming, Elizabeth P. 1888-1985
  Obituary *48*
Fleming, Ian 1908-1964 .... *9*
Fleming, Ian Lancaster
  See Fleming, Ian
Fleming, Ronald Lee 1941- *56*
Fleming, Sally
  See Walker, Sally M(acArt)
Fleming, Stuart
  See Knight, Damon (Francis)
Fleming, Susan 1932- *32*
Fleming, Thomas 1927- *8*
Fleming, Thomas James
  See Fleming, Thomas
Fleming, Virginia (Edwards) 1923- *84*
Flesch, Y.
  See Flesch, Yolande (Catarina)
Flesch, Yolande (Catarina) 1950- *55*
Fletcher, Charlie May Hogue 1897-1977 .... *3*
Fletcher, Colin 1922-2007 .... *28*
Fletcher, Dirk
  See Cunningham, Chet
Fletcher, George U.
  See Pratt, (Murray) Fletcher
Fletcher, Helen Jill 1910- *13*
Fletcher, Ralph 1953- *195*
  Earlier sketches in SATA *105, 149*
  See also CLR *104*
Fletcher, Ralph J.
  See Fletcher, Ralph
Fletcher, Richard E. 1917(?)-1983
  Obituary *34*
Fletcher, Rick
  See Fletcher, Richard E.
Fletcher, Susan 1951- *181*
  Earlier sketches in SATA *70, 110*
Fletcher, Susan Clemens
  See Fletcher, Susan
Fleur, Paul
  See Pohl, Frederik
Flexner, James Thomas 1908-2003 .... *9*
Flinn, Alex 1966- *159*
Flint, Helen 1952- *102*
Flint, Russ 1944- *74*
Flitner, David P(erkins), Jr. 1949- *7*
Floca, Brian *190*
  Earlier sketch in SATA *155*
Floethe, Louise Lee 1913-1988 .... *4*
Floethe, Richard 1901-1998 .... *4*
Floherty, John Joseph 1882-1964 .... *25*
Flood, Bo
  See Flood, Nancy Bo
Flood, Nancy Bo 1945- *130*
Flood, Pansie Hart 1964- *140*
Flood, William 1942- *129*

Flooglebuckle, Al
  See Spiegelman, Art
Flora, James (Royer) 1914-1998 .... *30*
  Obituary *103*
  Earlier sketch in SATA *1*
  See also SAAS *6*
Flores-Galbis, Enrique 1952- *186*
Florian, Douglas 1950- *177*
  Earlier sketches in SATA *19, 83, 125*
Flory, Jane Trescott 1917- *22*
Flournoy, Valerie 1952- *95*
Flournoy, Valerie Rose
  See Flournoy, Valerie
Flowerdew, Phyllis -1994 .... *33*
Flowers, Pam 1946- *136*
Flowers, Sarah 1952- *98*
Floyd, Gareth 1940- *62*
  Brief entry *31*
Fluchere, Henri 1914-1991 .... *40*
Fluke, Joanne 1943- *88*
Flutsztejn-Gruda, Ilona 1930- *170*
Flynn, Barbara 1928- *9*
Flynn, Jackson
  See Bensen, Donald R.
  and Shirreffs, Gordon D(onald)
Flynn, Nicholas
  See Odgers, Sally Farrell
Flynn, Rachel 1953- *171*
  Earlier sketch in SATA *109*
Flynn, Warren (G.) 1950- *154*
Fodor, R(onald) V(ictor) 1944- *25*
Fogelin, Adrian 1951- *175*
  Earlier sketch in SATA *129*
Foley, (Anna) Bernice Williams 1902-1987 . *28*
Foley, Greg E. 1969- *190*
Foley, June 1944- *44*
Foley, (Mary) Louise Munro 1933- *106*
  Brief entry *40*
  Earlier sketch in SATA *54*
Foley, Rae
  See Denniston, Elinore
Folke, Will
  See Bloch, Robert (Albert)
Follett, Helen Thomas 1884(?)-1970
  Obituary *27*
Folsom, Franklin (Brewster) 1907-1995 .... *5*
  Obituary *88*
Folsom, Michael (Brewster) 1938-1990 .... *40*
  Obituary *88*
Fontenot, Mary Alice 1910- *91*
  Earlier sketch in SATA *34*
Fontes, Justine *172*
Fontes, Ron 1952- *183*
Foon, Dennis 1951- *119*
Fooner, Michael *22*
Foote, Timothy (Gilson) 1926- *52*
Forberg, Ati *22*
  See Forberg, Beate Gropius
Forbes, Anna 1954- *101*
Forbes, Bryan 1926- *37*
Forbes, Cabot L.
  See Hoyt, Edwin P(almer), Jr.
Forbes, Esther 1891-1967 .... *100*
  Earlier sketch in SATA *2*
  See also CLR *27*
Forbes, Graham B. *1*
Forbes, Kathryn
  See McLean, Kathryn (Anderson)
Forbes, Robert
  See Arthur, Robert, (Jr.)
Ford, Albert Lee
  See Stratemeyer, Edward L.
Ford, Barbara *56*
  Brief entry *34*
Ford, Brian J(ohn) 1939- *49*
Ford, Carolyn (Mott) 1938- *98*
Ford, Christine 1953- *176*
Ford, David
  See Baldacci, David
  and Baldacci, David

Ford, David B.
See Baldacci, David
Ford, David Baldacci
See Baldacci, David
Ford, Elbur
See Hibbert, Eleanor Alice Burford
Ford, Ellen 1949- 89
Ford, George (Jr.) 31
Ford, Hilary
See Youd, (Christopher) Samuel
Ford, Hildegarde
See Morrison, Velma Ford
Ford, Jerome W. 1949- 78
Ford, Jerry
See Ford, Jerome W.
Ford, Juwanda G(ertrude) 1967- 102
Ford, Marcia
See Radford, Ruby L(orraine)
Ford, Nancy K(effer) 1906-1961
Obituary 29
Ford, Peter 1936- 59
Ford, S. M.
See Uhlig, Susan
Forde, Catherine 1961- 170
Foreman, Michael 1938- 184
Earlier sketches in SATA 2, 73, 129, 135
See also CLR 32
See also SAAS 21
Foreman, Wilmoth 1939- 153
Forest, Dial
See Gault, William Campbell
Forest, Heather 1948- 185
Earlier sketch in SATA 120
Forester, C(ecil) S(cott) 1899-1966 13
Forman, Brenda 1936- 4
Forman, James
See Forman, James D.
Forman, James D. 1932- 70
Earlier sketch in SATA 8
Forman, James Douglas
See Forman, James D.
Forman, Ruth 1970- 186
Forrest, Elizabeth
See Salsitz, Rhondi Vilott
Forrest, Mary
See Pausacker, Jenny
Forrest, Sybil
See Markun, Patricia Maloney
Forrestal, Elaine 1941- 165
Earlier sketch in SATA 117
Forrester, Frank H. 1919(?)-1986
Obituary 52
Forrester, Helen 48
See Bhatia, Jamunadevi
Forrester, Jade
See Pausacker, Jenny
Forrester, Marian
See Schachtel, Roger
Forrester, Sandra 1949- 166
Earlier sketch in SATA 90
Forrester, Victoria 1940- 40
Brief entry 35
Forsee, (Frances) Aylesa -1986 1
Forsey, Chris 1950- 59
Forshay-Lunsford, Cin 1965- 60
Forster, E(dward) M(organ) 1879-1970 57
Forsyth, Kate 1966- 154
Fort, Paul
See Stockton, Francis Richard
Forte, Maurizio 1961- 110
Fortey, Richard 1946- 109
Fortey, Richard A.
See Fortey, Richard
Fortey, Richard Alan
See Fortey, Richard
Forth, Melissa D(eal) 96
Fortnum, Peggy 26
See Nuttall-Smith, Margaret Emily Noel
Fortune, Eric 182
Forward, Robert L(ull) 1932-2002 82
Foster, Alan Dean 1946- 70

Foster, Brad W. 1955- 34
Foster, Doris Van Liew 1899-1993 10
Foster, E(lizabeth) C(onnell) 1902- 9
Foster, Elizabeth 1902- 12
Foster, Elizabeth 1905-1963 10
Foster, F. Blanche 1919- 11
Foster, G(eorge) Allen 1907-1969 26
Foster, Genevieve (Stump) 1893-1979 2
Obituary 23
See also CLR 7
Foster, Hal
See Foster, Harold (Rudolf)
Foster, Harold (Rudolf) 1892-1982 31
See Foster, Hal
Foster, Jeanne
See Williams, Jeanne
Foster, John
See Foster, John L(ouis)
and Furcolo, Foster
Foster, John (Thomas) 1925- 8
Foster, John L(ouis) 1941- 102
Foster, Laura Louise (James) 1918- 6
Foster, Leila Merrell 1929- 73
Foster, Lynne 1937- 74
Foster, Margaret Lesser 1899(?)-1979
Obituary 21
Foster, Marian Curtis 1909-1978 23
Foster, Sally 58
Foulds, E. V.
See Foulds, Elfrida Vipont
Foulds, Elfrida Vipont 1902-1992 52
See Vipont, Elfrida
Fountas, Angela Jane 180
Fourie, Corlia 1944- 91
Fourth Brother, The
See Aung, (Maung) Htin
Fowke, Edith (Margaret) 1913-1996 14
Fowles, John 1926-2005 22
Obituary 171
Fowles, John Robert
See Fowles, John
Fox, Aileen 1907-2005 58
Obituary 170
Fox, Aileen Mary
See Fox, Aileen
Fox, Annie 1950- 175
Fox, Charles Philip 1913-2003 12
Obituary 150
Fox, Christyan 188
Fox, Diane 188
Fox, Eleanor
See St. John, Wylly Folk
Fox, Fontaine Talbot, Jr. 1884-1964
Obituary 23
Fox, Fred 1903(?)-1981
Obituary 27
Fox, Freeman
See Hamilton, Charles (Harold St. John)
Fox, Geoffrey 1941- 73
Fox, Grace
See Anderson, Grace Fox
Fox, Helen 1962- 181
Fox, Larry 30
Fox, Lorraine 1922-1976 27
Earlier sketch in SATA 11
Fox, Louisa
See Kroll, Virginia L.
Fox, Mary Virginia 1919- 152
Brief entry 39
Earlier sketches in SATA 44, 88
Fox, Mem 103
See also CLR 23
See Fox, Merrion Frances
Fox, Merrion Frances 1946- 155
Earlier sketch in SATA 51
See also CLR 80
See Fox, Mem
Fox, Michael W(ilson) 1937- 15
Fox, Paula 1923- 167
Earlier sketches in SATA 17, 60, 120
See also CLR 96

Fox, Robert J. 1927- 33
Foyt, Victoria 187
Fradin, Dennis
See Fradin, Dennis Brindell
Fradin, Dennis Brindell 1945- 185
Earlier sketches in SATA 29, 90, 135
Fradin, Judith Bloom 1945- 185
Earlier sketches in SATA 90, 152
Frailey, Paige (Menefee) 1965- 82
Frame, Janet 1924-2004 119
Frame, Paul 1913-1994 60
Brief entry 33
Obituary 83
Frances, Miss
See Horwich, Frances R(appaport)
Franchere, Ruth 18
Francis, Charles
See Holme, Bryan
Francis, Dee
See Haas, Dorothy F.
Francis, Dorothy 1926- 127
Earlier sketch in SATA 10
Francis, Dorothy B.
See Francis, Dorothy
Francis, Dorothy Brenner
See Francis, Dorothy
Francis, Jaye
See Pausacker, Jenny
Francis, Pamela (Mary) 1926- 11
Franck, Eddie
See Cooke, Frank E.
Franco, Betsy 188
Earlier sketch in SATA 150
Franco, Eloise (Bauder) 1910- 62
Franco, Johan (Henri Gustave) 1908-1988 ... 62
Franco, Marjorie 38
Francois, Andre 1915-2005 25
Francoise
See Seignobosc, Francoise
Frank, Anne(lies Marie) 1929-1945 87
Brief entry 42
See also CLR 101
Frank, Daniel B. 1956- 55
Frank, Emily R.
See Frank, E.R.
Frank, E.R. 1967- 157
Frank, Helene
See Vautier, Ghislaine
Frank, Hillary 1976- 148
Frank, Josette 1893-1989 10
Obituary 63
Frank, Lucy 1947- 166
Earlier sketch in SATA 94
Frank, Mary 1933- 34
Frank, R., Jr.
See Ross, Frank (Xavier), Jr.
Frankau, Mary Evelyn Atkinson 1899-1974 .. 4
Frankel, Alona 1937- 66
Frankel, Bernice 9
Frankel, Edward 1910- 44
Frankel, Ellen 1951- 78
Frankel, Julie 1947- 40
Brief entry 34
Frankenberg, Robert 1911- 22
Franklin, Cheryl J. 1955- 70
Franklin, Harold 1926- 13
Franklin, Kristine L. 1958- 124
Earlier sketch in SATA 80
Franklin, Lance
See Lantz, Francess L(in)
Franklin, Madeleine
See L'Engle, Madeleine
Franklin, Madeleine L'Engle
See L'Engle, Madeleine
Franklin, Madeleine L'Engle Camp
See L'Engle, Madeleine
Franklin, Max
See Deming, Richard
Franklin, Steve
See Stevens, Franklin
Franson, Leanne R. 1963- 111

Franson, Scott E. 1966- *192*
Franzen, Nils-Olof 1916- *10*
Frascino, Edward *48*
    Brief entry *33*
    See also SAAS *9*
Frasconi, Antonio 1919- *131*
    Earlier sketches in SATA *6, 53*
    See also SAAS *11*
Fraser, Betty
    See Fraser, Elizabeth Marr
Fraser, Elizabeth Marr 1928- *31*
Fraser, Eric (George) 1902-1983 .... *38*
Fraser, Mary Ann 1959- *137*
    Earlier sketch in SATA *76*
    See also SAAS *23*
Fraser, Wynnette (McFaddin) 1925- *90*
Frasier, Debra 1953- *182*
    Earlier sketches in SATA *69, 112*
Fraustino, Lisa Rowe 1961- *146*
    Autobiography Feature *146*
    Earlier sketch in SATA *84*
Frazee, Marla 1958- *187*
    Earlier sketches in SATA *105, 151*
Frazetta, Frank 1928- *58*
Frazier, Craig 1955- *177*
Frazier, Neta (Osborn) Lohnes 1890-1990 ..... *7*
Frederic, Mike
    See Cox, William R(obert)
Fredericks, Anthony D. 1947- *113*
Freed, Alvyn M. 1913-1993 .... *22*
Freedman, Benedict 1919- *27*
Freedman, Claire *185*
Freedman, Deborah 1960- *191*
Freedman, Jeff 1953- *90*
Freedman, Nancy 1920- *27*
Freedman, Russell 1929- *175*
    Earlier sketches in SATA *16, 71, 123*
    See also CLR *71*
Freedman, Russell Bruce
    See Freedman, Russell
Freeman, Barbara C(onstance) 1906- *28*
Freeman, Bill
    See Freeman, William Bradford
Freeman, Don 1908-1978 .... *17*
    See also CLR *90*
Freeman, Ira Maximilian 1905-1987 .... *21*
Freeman, Lucy (Greenbaum) 1916-2004 ...... *24*
Freeman, Mae (Blacker) 1907- *25*
Freeman, Marcia S. 1937- *102*
Freeman, Martha 1956- *152*
    Earlier sketch in SATA *101*
Freeman, Nancy 1932- *61*
Freeman, Peter J.
    See Calvert, Patricia
Freeman, Sarah (Caroline) 1940- *66*
Freeman, Tor 1977- *164*
Freeman, VicToria
    See Freeman, Tor
Freeman, William Bradford 1938- *58*
    Brief entry *48*
Fregosi, Claudia (Anne Marie) 1946- *24*
French, Allen 1870-1946
    See YABC *1*
French, Dorothy Kayser 1926- *5*
French, Fiona 1944- *132*
    Earlier sketches in SATA *6, 75*
    See also CLR *37*
    See also SAAS *21*
French, Jackie *186*
    Autobiography Feature *139*
    Earlier sketches in SATA *108, 139*
    See French, Jackie Anne
    and French, Jacqueline Anne
French, Kathryn
    See Mosesson, Gloria R(ubin)
French, Martin *176*
French, Michael 1944- *49*
    Brief entry *38*
French, Paul
    See Asimov, Isaac

French, Simon 1957- *147*
    Earlier sketch in SATA *86*
French, Vivian *165*
Frenette, Liza *126*
Freschet, Gina 1960- *175*
    Earlier sketch in SATA *139*
Frewer, Glyn (M.) 1931- *11*
Frey, Darcy *98*
Freymann, Saxton 1958(?)- *178*
Freymann-Weyr, (Rhoda) Garret (Michaela)
    1965- *145*
Frick, C. H.
    See Irwin, Constance (H.) Frick
Frick, Constance
    See Irwin, Constance (H.) Frick
Fricke, Aaron 1962- *89*
Fridell, Ron 1943- *124*
Friedlander, Joanne K(ohn) 1930- *9*
Friedman, Aimee 1979- *189*
Friedman, D. Dina 1957- *180*
Friedman, Debra 1955- *150*
Friedman, Estelle (Ehrenwald) 1920- *7*
Friedman, Frieda 1905- *43*
Friedman, Ina R(osen) 1926- *136*
    Brief entry *41*
    Earlier sketch in SATA *49*
Friedman, Jerrold David
    See Gerrold, David
Friedman, Judi 1935- *59*
Friedman, Laurie 1964- *179*
    Earlier sketch in SATA *138*
Friedman, Marvin 1930- *42*
    Brief entry *33*
Friedman, Robin 1968- *162*
Friedmann, Stan 1953- *80*
Friedrich, Otto (Alva) 1929-1995 .... *33*
Friedrich, Priscilla 1927- *39*
Friend, Catherine 1957(?)- *194*
Friend, David Michael 1975- *195*
Friend, Natasha 1972- *184*
Friendlich, Dick
    See Friendlich, Richard J.
Friendlich, Richard J. 1909- *11*
Friermood, Elisabeth Hamilton 1903-1992 .... *5*
Friesen, Bernice (Sarah Anne) 1966- *105*
Friesen, Gayle 1960- *109*
Friesner, Esther M. 1951- *168*
    Earlier sketch in SATA *71*
Friis-Baastad, Babbis Ellinor 1921-1970 .... *7*
Frimmer, Steven 1928- *31*
Frischmuth, Barbara 1941- *114*
Friskey, Margaret (Richards) 1901-1995 .... *5*
Fritts, Mary Bahr
    See Bahr, Mary (Madelyn)
Fritz, Jean (Guttery) 1915- *163*
    Autobiography Feature *122*
    Earlier sketches in SATA *1, 29, 72, 119*
    See also CLR *96*
    See also SAAS *2*
Froehlich, Margaret W(alden) 1930- *56*
Frois, Jeanne 1953- *73*
Froissart, Jean 1338(?)-1410(?) *28*
Froman, Elizabeth Hull 1920-1975 .... *10*
Froman, Robert (Winslow) 1917- *8*
Fromm, Lilo 1928- *29*
Frommer, Harvey 1937- *41*
Frost, A(rthur) B(urdett) 1851-1928 .... *19*
Frost, Elizabeth
    See Frost-Knappman, Elizabeth
Frost, Erica
    See Supraner, Robyn
Frost, Helen 1949- *194*
    Autobiography Feature *194*
    Earlier sketches in SATA *157, 183*
Frost, Helen Marie
    See Frost, Helen
Frost, Lesley 1899-1983 .... *14*
    Obituary *34*
Frost, Robert 1874-1963 .... *14*
    See also CLR *67*

Frost, Robert Lee
    See Frost, Robert
Frost, Shelley 1960- *138*
Frost-Knappman, Elizabeth 1943- *179*
Froud, Brian 1947- *150*
Fry, Annette R(iley) *89*
Fry, Christopher 1907-2005 .... *66*
Fry, Edward Bernard 1925- *35*
Fry, Rosalie Kingsmill 1911-1992 .... *3*
    See also SAAS *11*
Fry, Virginia Lynn 1952- *95*
Frye, Sally
    See Moore, Elaine
Fuchs, Bernie 1932- *162*
    Earlier sketch in SATA *95*
Fuchs, Erich 1916- *6*
Fuchshuber, Annegert 1940- *43*
Fuerst, Jeffrey B. 1956- *143*
Fuertes, Gloria 1918-1998 .... *115*
Fuge, Charles 1966- *144*
    Earlier sketch in SATA *74*
Fujikawa, Gyo 1908-1998 .... *76*
    Brief entry *30*
    Obituary *110*
    Earlier sketch in SATA *39*
    See also CLR *25*
    See also SAAS *16*
Fujita, Tamao 1905-1999 .... *7*
Fujiwara, Kim 1957- *81*
Fujiwara, Michiko 1946- *15*
Fuka, Vladimir 1926-1977
    Obituary *27*
Fulcher, Jennifer
    See Westwood, Jennifer
Fuller, Catherine Leuthold 1916- *9*
Fuller, Edmund (Maybank) 1914- *21*
Fuller, Iola
    See McCoy, Iola Fuller
Fuller, John G(rant, Jr.) 1913-1990 .... *65*
Fuller, Kathleen
    See Gottfried, Theodore Mark
Fuller, Lois Hamilton 1915- *11*
Fuller, Margaret
    See Ossoli, Sarah Margaret (Fuller)
Fuller, Maud
    See Petersham, Maud (Sylvia Fuller)
Fuller, Roy (Broadbent) 1912-1991 .... *87*
Fuller, Sarah Margaret
    See Ossoli, Sarah Margaret (Fuller)
Fuller, Sarah Margaret
    See Ossoli, Sarah Margaret (Fuller)
Fults, John Lee 1932- *33*
Funk, Thompson 1911- *7*
Funk, Tom
    See Funk, Thompson
Funke, Cornelia 1958- *174*
    Earlier sketch in SATA *154*
Funke, Cornelia Caroline
    See Funke, Cornelia
Funke, Lewis 1912-1992 .... *11*
Fuqua, Jonathon Scott 1966- *141*
Furbee, Mary R.
    See Furbee, Mary Rodd
Furbee, Mary Rodd 1954- *138*
Furchgott, Terry 1948- *29*
Furlong, Monica (Mavis) 1930-2003 .... *86*
    Obituary *142*
Furman, Gertrude Lerner Kerman 1909- *21*
Furniss, Tim 1948- *49*
Furrow, Robert 1985- *172*
Furukawa, Toshi 1924- *24*
Fusillo, Archimede 1962- *137*
Futcher, Jane P. 1947- *76*
Futehali, Zahida
    See Whitaker, Zai
Fyleman, Rose (Amy) 1877-1957 .... *21*
Fyson, J(enny) G(race) 1904- *42*

G

Gaan, Margaret 1914- *65*
Gaber, Susan 1956- *169*
  Earlier sketch in SATA *115*
Gaberman, Judie Angell 1937- *78*
  Earlier sketch in SATA *22*
  See also CLR *33*
Gabhart, Ann
  See Gabhart, Ann H.
Gabhart, Ann H. 1947- *75*
Gable, Brian 1949- *195*
Gabler, Mirko 1951- *77*
Gabriel, Adriana
  See Rojany, Lisa
Gabrys, Ingrid Schubert
  See Schubert-Gabrys, Ingrid
Gackenbach, Dick 1927- *79*
  Brief entry *30*
  Earlier sketch in SATA *48*
Gadd, Jeremy 1949- *116*
Gaddis, Vincent H. 1913-1997 .... *35*
Gadler, Steve J. 1905-1985 .... *36*
Gaeddert, Lou Ann (Bigge) 1931- *103*
  Earlier sketch in SATA *20*
Gaeddert, Louann
  See Gaeddert, Lou Ann (Bigge)
Gaer, Joseph 1897-1969 .... *118*
Gaer, Yossef
  See Gaer, Joseph
Gaetz, Dayle Campbell 1947- *138*
Gaffney, Timothy R. 1951- *170*
  Earlier sketch in SATA *69*
Gaffron, Norma (Bondeson) 1931- *97*
Gag, Flavia 1907-1979
  Obituary *24*
Gag, Wanda (Hazel) 1893-1946 .... *100*
  See also YABC *1*
  See also CLR *4*
Gage, Brian *162*
Gage, Wilson
  See Steele, Mary Q(uintard Govan)
Gagliano, Eugene M. 1946- *150*
Gagliardo, Ruth Garver 1895(?)-1980
  Obituary *22*
Gagnon, Cecile 1936- *58*
Gaiman, Neil 1960- *146*
  Earlier sketch in SATA *85*
  See also CLR *109*
Gaiman, Neil Richard
  See Gaiman, Neil
Gainer, Cindy 1962- *74*
Gaines, Ernest J. 1933- *86*
  See also CLR *62*
Gaines, Ernest James
  See Gaines, Ernest J.
Gaither, Gloria 1942- *127*
Gal, Laszlo 1933- *96*
  Brief entry *32*
  Earlier sketch in SATA *52*
  See also CLR *61*
Galbraith, Kathryn O(sebold) 1945- *85*
Galdone, Paul 1907(?)-1986 .... *66*
  Obituary *49*
  Earlier sketch in SATA *17*
  See also CLR *16*
Galinsky, Ellen 1942- *23*
Gall, Chris 1961- *176*
Gallagher, Diana G. 1946- *153*
Gallagher, Lurlene Nora
  See McDaniel, Lurlene
Gallant, Roy A(rthur) 1924- *110*
  Earlier sketches in SATA *4, 68*
  See also CLR *30*
Gallardo, Evelyn 1948- *78*
Gallaz, Christophe 1948- *162*
  See also CLR *126*
Gallego Garcia, Laura 1977- *173*
Gallico, Paul (William) 1897-1976 .... *13*
Gallo, Donald R. 1938- *112*
  Autobiography Feature *104*

Gallo, Donald Robert
  See Gallo, Donald R.
Galloway, Owateka (S.) 1981- *121*
Galloway, Priscilla 1930- *112*
  Earlier sketch in SATA *66*
Gallup, Joan 1957- *128*
Galouchko, Annouchka Gravel 1960- *95*
Galt, Thomas Franklin, Jr. 1908-1989 .... *5*
Galt, Tom
  See Galt, Thomas Franklin, Jr.
Galvin, Matthew R. 1950- *93*
Galvin, Matthew Reppert
  See Galvin, Matthew R.
Gamble, Kim 1952- *183*
  Earlier sketches in SATA *81, 124*
Gambrell, Jamey *82*
Gamerman, Martha 1941- *15*
Gammell, Stephen 1943- *128*
  Earlier sketches in SATA *53, 81*
  See also CLR *83*
Ganly, Helen (Mary) 1940- *56*
Gannett, Ruth Chrisman (Arens)
  1896-1979 .... *33*
Gannett, Ruth Stiles 1923- *3*
Gannon, Robert Haines 1931- *8*
Gano, Lila 1949- *76*
Gans, Roma 1894-1996 .... *45*
  Obituary *93*
Gant, Matthew
  See Hano, Arnold
Gantner, Susan (Verble) 1939- *63*
Gantos, Jack 1951- *169*
  Earlier sketches in SATA *20, 81, 119*
  See also CLR *85*
Gantos, John Bryan, Jr.
  See Gantos, Jack
Ganz, Yaffa 1938- *61*
  Brief entry *52*
Garafano, Marie 1942- *84*
Garant, Andre J. 1968- *123*
Garbe, Ruth Moore
  See Moore, Ruth (Ellen)
Garber, Esther
  See Lee, Tanith
Garcia, Yolanda P. 1952- *113*
Garcia, Yolanda Pacheco
  See Garcia, Yolanda P.
Gard, Janice
  See Latham, Jean Lee
Gard, Joyce
  See Reeves, Joyce
Gard, Robert Edward 1910-1992 .... *18*
  Obituary *74*
Gard, (Sanford) Wayne 1899-1986
  Obituary *49*
Gardam, Jane 1928- *130*
  Brief entry *28*
  Earlier sketches in SATA *39, 76*
  See also CLR *12*
  See also SAAS *9*
Gardam, Jane Mary
  See Gardam, Jane
Gardella, Tricia 1944- *96*
Garden, Nancy 1938- *147*
  Autobiography Feature *147*
  Earlier sketches in SATA *12, 77, 114*
  See also CLR *51*
  See also SAAS *8*
Gardiner, John Reynolds 1944-2006 .... *64*
  Obituary *174*
Gardiner, Lindsey 1971- *144*
Gardner, Craig Shaw 1949- *99*
Gardner, Dic
  See Gardner, Richard (M.)
Gardner, Graham *159*
Gardner, Hugh 1910-1986
  Obituary *49*
Gardner, Jane Mylum 1946- *83*
Gardner, Jeanne LeMonnier 1925- *5*
Gardner, John, Jr. 1933-1982 .... *40*
  Obituary *31*

Gardner, John Champlin, Jr.
  See Gardner, John, Jr.
Gardner, Lyn *192*
Gardner, Martin 1914- *142*
  Earlier sketch in SATA *16*
Gardner, Miriam
  See Bradley, Marion Zimmer
Gardner, Richard (M.) 1931- *24*
Gardner, Richard A(lan) 1931-2003 .... *13*
  Obituary *144*
Gardner, Sally *177*
Gardner, Sandra 1940- *70*
Gardner, Scot 1968- *143*
Gardner, Sheldon 1934- *33*
Gardner, Ted
  See Gardner, Theodore Roosevelt II
Gardner, Theodore Roosevelt
  See Gardner, Theodore Roosevelt II
Gardner, Theodore Roosevelt II 1934- *84*
Garelick, May 1910-1989 .... *19*
Garfield, James B. 1881-1984 .... *6*
  Obituary *38*
Garfield, Leon 1921-1996 .... *76*
  Obituary *90*
  Earlier sketches in SATA *1, 32*
  See also CLR *21*
Garfinkle, Debra L.
  See Garfinkle, D.L.
Garfinkle, D.L. *187*
Garis, Howard R(oger) 1873-1962 .... *13*
Garland, Mark 1953- *79*
Garland, Mark A.
  See Garland, Mark
Garland, Michael 1952- *168*
Garland, Sarah 1944- *135*
  Earlier sketch in SATA *62*
Garland, Sherry 1948- *145*
  Autobiography Feature *145*
  Earlier sketches in SATA *73, 114*
Garner, Alan 1934- *69*
  Autobiography Feature *108*
  Earlier sketch in SATA *18*
  See also CLR *130*
Garner, David 1958- *78*
Garner, Eleanor Ramrath 1930- *122*
Garner, James Finn 1960(?)- *92*
Garnet, A. H.
  See Slote, Alfred
Garnett, Eve C. R. 1900-1991 .... *3*
  Obituary *70*
Garofoli, Viviana 1970- *186*
Garou, Louis P.
  See Bowkett, Stephen
Garraty, John A. 1920-2007 .... *23*
  Obituary *189*
Garraty, John Arthur
  See Garraty, John A.
Garren, Devorah-Leah
  See Devorah-Leah
Garret, Maxwell R. 1917- *39*
Garretson, Victoria Diane 1945- *44*
Garrett, Helen 1895- *21*
Garrett, Richard 1920- *82*
Garrigue, Sheila 1931- *21*
Garrison, Barbara 1931- *163*
  Earlier sketch in SATA *19*
Garrison, Frederick
  See Sinclair, Upton
Garrison, Mary 1952- *146*
Garrison, Peter
  See Gardner, Craig Shaw
Garrison, Webb B(lack) 1919-2000 .... *25*
Garrity, Jennifer Johnson 1961- *124*
Garrity, Linda K. 1947- *128*
Garst, Doris Shannon 1894-1981 .... *1*
Garst, Shannon
  See Garst, Doris Shannon
Garth, Will
  See Hamilton, Edmond
  and Kuttner, Henry
Garthwaite, Marion H(ook) 1893-1981 .... *7*

Garton, Malinda D(ean) (?)-1976
  Obituary 26
Garvie, Maureen 1944- 175
Garvie, Maureen McCallum
  See Garvie, Maureen
Garza, Carmen Lomas 1948- 182
Garza, Xavier 184
Gascoigne, Bamber 1935- 62
Gaskins, Pearl Fuyo 1957- 134
Gasperini, Jim 1952- 54
  Brief entry 49
Gater, Dilys 1944- 41
Gates, Doris 1901-1987 34
  Obituary 54
  Earlier sketch in SATA *1*
  See also SAAS *1*
Gates, Frieda 1933- 26
Gates, Susan 1950- 153
Gates, Viola R. 1931- 101
Gathorne-Hardy, Jonathan G. 1933- 124
  Earlier sketch in SATA *26*
Gatti, Anne 1952- 103
Gatty, Juliana Horatia
  See Ewing, Juliana (Horatia Gatty)
Gauch, Patricia Lee 1934- 80
  Earlier sketch in SATA *26*
  See also CLR *56*
  See also SAAS *21*
Gaudasinska, Elzbieta 1943- 190
Gaul, Randy 1959- 63
Gault, Clare 1925- 36
Gault, Frank 1926-1982 36
  Brief entry 30
Gault, William Campbell 1910-1995 8
Gauthier, Gail 1953- 160
  Earlier sketch in SATA *118*
Gaver, Becky
  See Gaver, Rebecca
Gaver, Rebecca 1952- 20
Gavin, Jamila 1941- 125
  Earlier sketch in SATA *96*
Gay, Amelia
  See Hogarth, Grace (Weston Allen)
Gay, Francis
  See Gee, H(erbert) L(eslie)
Gay, Kathlyn 1930- 144
  Earlier sketch in SATA *9*
Gay, Marie-Louise 1952- 179
  Earlier sketches in SATA *68, 126*
  See also CLR *27*
  See also SAAS *21*
Gay, Michel 1947- 162
Gay, Zhenya 1906-1978 19
Gaze, Gillian
  See Barklem, Jill
Gear, Kathleen M. O'Neal
  See Gear, Kathleen O'Neal
Gear, Kathleen O'Neal 1954- 166
  Earlier sketch in SATA *71*
Gear, W. Michael 1955- 166
  Earlier sketch in SATA *71*
Geary, Rick 1946- 142
Geason, Susan 1946- 122
Gedalof, Robin
  See McGrath, Robin
Gedge, Pauline (Alice) 1945- 101
Gee, H(erbert) L(eslie) 1901-1977
  Obituary 26
Gee, Maurice 1931- 101
  Earlier sketch in SATA *46*
  See also CLR *56*
Gee, Maurice Gough
  See Gee, Maurice
Geehan, Wayne (E.) 1947- 107
Geer, Charles 1922- 42
  Brief entry 32
Geeslin, Campbell 1925- 163
  Earlier sketch in SATA *107*
Gehman, Mary W. 1923- 86
Gehr, Mary 1910(?)-1997 32
  Obituary 99

Geipel, Eileen 1932- 30
Geis, Alissa Imre 1976- 189
Geis, Darlene Stern 1918(?)-1999 7
  Obituary 111
Geisel, Helen 1898-1967 26
Geisel, Theodor Seuss 1904-1991 100
  Obituary 67
  Earlier sketches in SATA *1, 28, 75*
  See also CLR *100*
  See Dr. Seuss
Geisert, Arthur 1941- 171
  Brief entry 52
  Earlier sketches in SATA *56, 92, 133*
  See also CLR *87*
  See also SAAS *23*
Geisert, Arthur Frederick
  See Geisert, Arthur
Geisert, Bonnie 1942- 165
  Earlier sketch in SATA *92*
Geist, Ken 191
Geldart, William 1936- 15
Gelinas, Paul J. 1904-1996 10
Gellis, Roberta 1927- 128
Gellis, Roberta Leah Jacobs
  See Gellis, Roberta
Gellman, Marc 112
Gelman, Amy 1961- 72
Gelman, Jan 1963- 58
Gelman, Rita Golden 1937- 131
  Brief entry 51
  Earlier sketch in SATA *84*
Gelman, Steve 1934- 3
Gemming, Elizabeth 1932- 11
Gendel, Evelyn W. 1916(?)-1977
  Obituary 27
Gennaro, Joseph F(rancis), Jr. 1924- 53
Gentile, Petrina 1969- 91
Gentle, Mary 1956- 48
Gentleman, David (William) 1930- 7
Geoghegan, Adrienne 1962- 143
George, Barbara
  See Katz, Bobbi
George, Emily
  See Katz, Bobbi
George, Gail
  See Katz, Bobbi
George, Jean
  See George, Jean Craighead
George, Jean Craighead 1919- 170
  Earlier sketches in SATA *2, 68, 124*
  See also CLR *136*
George, John L(othar) 1916- 2
George, Kristine O'Connell 1954- 156
  Earlier sketch in SATA *110*
George, Lindsay Barrett 1952- 155
  Earlier sketch in SATA *95*
George, S(idney) C(harles) 1898- 11
George, Sally
  See Orr, Wendy
George, Twig C. 1950- 114
George, W(illiam) Lloyd 1900(?)-1975
  Obituary 30
Georgiou, Constantine 1927- 7
Georgiou, Theo
  See Odgers, Sally Farrell
Geraghty, Paul 1959- 130
Gerard, Jean Ignace Isidore 1803-1847 45
Geras, Adele 1944- 180
  Autobiography Feature 180
  Earlier sketches in SATA *23, 87, 129, 173*
  See also SAAS *21*
Geras, Adele Daphne Weston
  See Geras, Adele
Gerber, Merrill Joan 1938- 170
  Autobiography Feature 170
  Earlier sketches in SATA *64, 127*
Gerber, Perren 1933- 104
Gerberg, Mort 1931- 64
Gergely, Tibor 1900-1978 54
  Obituary 20

Geringer, Laura 1948- 164
  Earlier sketches in SATA *29, 94*
Gerler, William R(obert) 1917-1996 47
Gerrard, Jean 1933- 51
Gerrard, Roy 1935-1997 90
  Brief entry 45
  Obituary 99
  Earlier sketch in SATA *47*
  See also CLR *23*
Gerritsen, Paula 1956- 177
Gerrold, David 1944- 144
  Earlier sketch in SATA *66*
Gershator, David 1937- 180
Gershator, Phillis 1942- 188
  Earlier sketches in SATA *90, 158*
Gershon, Dann 1955- 187
Gershon, Gina 1962- 187
Gerson, Corinne 1927- 37
Gerson, Mary-Joan 136
  Earlier sketch in SATA *79*
Gerson, Noel Bertram 1914-1988 22
  Obituary 60
Gerstein, Mordicai 1935- 178
  Brief entry 36
  Earlier sketches in SATA *47, 81, 142*
  See also CLR *102*
Gertridge, Allison 1967- 132
Gervais, Bernadette 1959- 80
Gervay, Susanne 183
Gesner, Clark 1938-2002 40
  Obituary 143
Gessner, Lynne 1919- 16
Geter, Tyrone 150
Getz, David 1957- 91
Getzinger, Donna 1968- 128
Gevirtz, Eliezer 1950- 49
Gevry, Claudine 188
Gewe, Raddory
  See Gorey, Edward (St. John)
Ghan, Linda (R.) 1947- 77
Ghent, Natale 1962- 148
Gherman, Beverly 1934- 123
  Earlier sketch in SATA *68*
Ghigna, Charles 1946- 153
  Earlier sketch in SATA *108*
Giacobbe, Beppe 1953- 174
Giambastiani, Kurt R. A. 1958- 141
Giannini, Enzo 1946- 68
Gibbons, Alan 1953- 124
Gibbons, Faye 1938- 103
  Earlier sketch in SATA *65*
Gibbons, Gail 1944- 160
  Earlier sketches in SATA *23, 72, 104*
  See also CLR *8*
  See also SAAS *12*
Gibbons, Gail Gretchen
  See Gibbons, Gail
Gibbons, Kaye 1960- 117
Gibbs, Adrea 1960- 126
Gibbs, Alonzo (Lawrence) 1915-1992 5
Gibbs, (Cecilia) May 1877-1969
  Obituary 27
Gibbs, Tony
  See Gibbs, Wolcott, Jr.
Gibbs, Wolcott, Jr. 1935- 40
Giblin, James Cross 1933- 122
  Earlier sketches in SATA *33, 75*
  See also CLR *29*
  See also SAAS *12*
Gibson, Andrew (William) 1949- 72
Gibson, Betty 1911- 75
Gibson, Jo
  See Fluke, Joanne
Gibson, William 1914-2008 66
Gibson, William Ford
  See Gibson, William
Gidal, Nachum
  See Gidal, Tim Nachum
Gidal, Sonia (Epstein) 1922- 2
Gidal, Tim Nachum 1909-1996 2

Gidalewitsch, Nachum
    See Gidal, Tim Nachum
Gideon, Melanie 1963- 175
Giegling, John A(llan) 1935- 17
Gifaldi, David 1950- 76
Giff, Patricia Reilly 1935- 160
    Earlier sketches in SATA 33, 70, 121
Giffard, Hannah 1962- 83
Gifford, Griselda 1931- 171
    Earlier sketch in SATA 42
Gifford, Kerri 1961- 91
Gifford, Peggy 1952- 191
Gilbert, Ann
    See Taylor, Ann
Gilbert, Anne Yvonne 1951- 128
    See Gilbert, Yvonne
Gilbert, Barbara Snow 1954- 97
Gilbert, Catherine
    See Murdock, Catherine Gilbert
Gilbert, Frances
    See Collings, Gillian
Gilbert, Harriett 1948- 30
Gilbert, (Agnes) Joan (Sewell) 1931- 10
Gilbert, John (Raphael) 1926- 36
Gilbert, Nan
    See Gilbertson, Mildred Geiger
Gilbert, Roby Goodale 1966- 90
Gilbert, Ruth Gallard Ainsworth
    See Ainsworth, Ruth (Gallard)
Gilbert, Sara (Dulaney) 1943- 82
    Earlier sketch in SATA 11
Gilbert, Sheri L. 157
Gilbert, Suzie 1956- 97
Gilbert, W(illiam) S(chwenck) 1836-1911 ... 36
Gilbert, Yvonne 185
    See Gilbert, Anne Yvonne
Gilbertson, Mildred Geiger 1908-1988 2
Gilbreath, Alice 1921- 12
Gilbreth, Frank B(unker), Jr. 1911-2001 2
Gilchrist, Jan Spivey 1949- 130
    Earlier sketch in SATA 72
Gilden, Mel 1947- 97
Giles, Gail 152
Gilfond, Henry 2
Gilge, Jeanette 1924- 22
Gili, Phillida 1944- 70
Gill, Derek (Lewis Theodore) 1919-1997 9
Gill, Margery Jean 1925- 22
Gill, Shelley 176
Gill, Stephen 1932- 63
Gillespie, Carol Ann 1951- 158
Gillett, Mary (Bledsoe) 7
Gillette, Henry Sampson 1915- 14
Gillette, J(an) Lynett 1946- 103
Gilley, Jeremy 1969- 174
Gillham, Bill
    See Gillham, W(illiam) E(dwin) C(harles)
Gillham, W(illiam) E(dwin) C(harles)
    1936- 42
Gilliam, Stan 1946- 39
    Brief entry 35
Gilliland, Alexis A(rnaldus) 1931- 72
Gilliland, (Cleburne) Hap 1918- 92
Gilliland, Judith Heide 180
Gillmor, Don 1954- 127
Gilman, Esther 1925- 15
Gilman, Laura Anne 178
Gilman, Phoebe 1940-2002 104
    Obituary 141
    Earlier sketch in SATA 58
Gilmore, Iris 1900-1982 22
Gilmore, Kate 1931- 87
Gilmore, Mary (Jean Cameron) 1865-1962 . 49
Gilmore, Susan 1954- 59
Gilpin, Stephen 177
Gilroy, Beryl (Agatha) 1924- 80
Gilson, Barbara
    See Gilson, Charles James Louis
Gilson, Charles James Louis 1878-1943
    See YABC 2

Gilson, Jamie 1933- 176
    Brief entry 34
    Earlier sketches in SATA 37, 91
Ginsburg, Mirra 1909-2000 92
    Earlier sketch in SATA 6
    See also CLR 45
Giovanni, Nikki 1943- 107
    Earlier sketch in SATA 24
    See also CLR 73
Giovanni, Yolanda Cornelia
    See Giovanni, Nikki
Giovanni, Yolande Cornelia
    See Giovanni, Nikki
Giovanni, Yolande Cornelia, Jr.
    See Giovanni, Nikki
Giovanopoulos, Paul (Arthur) 1939- 7
Gipson, Fred(erick Benjamin) 1908-1973 2
    Obituary 24
Girard, Linda (Walvoord) 1942- 41
Girion, Barbara 1937- 78
    Earlier sketch in SATA 26
    See also SAAS 14
Girouard, Patrick 1957- 155
Girzone, Joseph F. 1930- 76
Girzone, Joseph Francis
    See Girzone, Joseph F.
Gise, Joanne
    See Mattern, Joanne
Gittings, Jo (Grenville) Manton 1919- 3
Gittings, Robert (William Victor) 1911-1992 . 6
    Obituary 70
Givens, Janet E(aton) 1932- 60
Givner, Joan 1936- 171
Givner, Joan Mary
    See Givner, Joan
Gladstone, Eve
    See Werner, Herma
Gladstone, Gary 1935- 12
Gladstone, M(yron) J. 1923- 37
Glanville, Brian (Lester) 1931- 42
Glanzman, Louis S. 1922- 36
Glaser, Byron 1954- 154
Glaser, Dianne E(lizabeth) 1937- 50
    Brief entry 31
Glaser, Isabel Joshlin 1929- 94
Glaser, Milton 1929- 151
    Earlier sketch in SATA 11
Glaser, Shirley 151
Glaspell, Susan 1882(?)-1948
    See YABC 2
Glass, Andrew 1949- 150
    Brief entry 46
    Earlier sketch in SATA 90
Glass, Linzi 175
Glass, Linzi Alex
    See Glass, Linzi
Glasscock, Amnesia
    See Steinbeck, John (Ernst)
Glassman, Bruce 1961- 76
Glauber, Uta (Heil) 1936- 17
Glazer, Thomas (Zachariah) 1914-2003 9
Glazer, Tom
    See Glazer, Thomas (Zachariah)
Gleasner, Diana (Cottle) 1936- 29
Gleason, Judith 1929- 24
Gleason, Katherine (A.) 1960- 104
Gleeson, Libby 1950- 142
    Autobiography Feature 142
    Earlier sketches in SATA 82, 118
Gleiter, Jan 1947- 111
Gleitzman, Morris 1953- 156
    Earlier sketch in SATA 88
    See also CLR 88
Glen, Maggie 1944- 88
Glendinning, Richard 1917-1988 24
Glendinning, Sally
    See Glendinning, Sara W(ilson)
Glendinning, Sara W(ilson) 1913-1993 24
Glenn, John W. 195

Glenn, Mel 1943- 93
    Brief entry 45
    Earlier sketch in SATA 51
    See also CLR 51
Glenn, Patricia Brown 1953- 86
Glenn, Sharlee 159
Glenn, Sharlee Mullins
    See Glenn, Sharlee
Glennon, Karen M. 1946- 85
Gles, Margaret Breitmaier 1940- 22
Glick, Carl (Cannon) 1890-1971 14
Glick, Ruth (Burtnick) 1942- 125
Glick, Virginia Kirkus 1893-1980
    Obituary 23
Gliewe, Unada (Grace) 1927- 3
Glimmerveen, Ulco 1958- 85
Glines, Carroll V(ane), Jr. 1920- 19
Gliori, Debi 1959- 189
    Earlier sketches in SATA 72, 138
Globe, Leah Ain 1900- 41
Glori Ann
    See Blakely, Gloria
Glovach, Linda 1947- 105
    Earlier sketch in SATA 7
Glover, Denis (James Matthews) 1912-1980 . 7
Glubok, Shirley (Astor) 146
    Autobiography Feature 146
    Earlier sketches in SATA 6, 68
    See also CLR 1
    See also SAAS 7
Gluck, Felix 1923-1981
    Obituary 25
Glyman, Caroline A. 1967- 103
Glynne-Jones, William 1907-1977 11
Gobbato, Imero 1923- 39
Gobbletree, Richard
    See Quackenbush, Robert M(ead)
Goble, Dorothy 26
Goble, Paul 1933- 131
    Earlier sketches in SATA 25, 69
    See also CLR 21
Goble, Warwick (?)-1943 46
Godden, (Margaret) Rumer 1907-1998 36
    Obituary 109
    Earlier sketch in SATA 3
    See also CLR 20
    See also SAAS 12
Gode, Alexander
    See Gode von Aesch, Alexander (Gottfried
    Friedrich)
Gode von Aesch, Alexander (Gottfried
    Friedrich) 1906-1970 14
Godfrey, Jane
    See Bowden, Joan Chase
Godfrey, Martyn
    See Godfrey, Martyn N.
    and Godfrey, Martyn N.
Godfrey, Martyn N. 1949-2000 95
    See also CLR 57
    See Godfrey, Martyn
Godfrey, William
    See Youd, (Christopher) Samuel
Godkin, Celia (Marilyn) 1948- 145
    Earlier sketch in SATA 66
Godon, Ingrid 1958- 186
Godwin, Laura 1956- 179
Godwin, Sam
    See Pirotta, Saviour
Goedecke, Christopher (John) 1951- 81
Goekler, Susan
    See Wooley, Susan Frelick
Goertzen, Glenda 172
Goettel, Elinor 1930- 12
Goetz, Delia 1898-1996 22
    Obituary 91
Goffe, Toni 1936- 61
Goffstein, Brooke
    See Goffstein, M(arilyn) B(rooke)
Goffstein, M(arilyn) B(rooke) 1940- 70
    Earlier sketch in SATA 8
    See also CLR 3

Goforth, Ellen
  See Francis, Dorothy
Gogol, Sara 1948-2004 80
Goh, Chan Hon 1969- 145
Going, Kelly L.
  See Going, K.L.
Going, Kelly Louise
  See Going, K.L.
Going, K.L. 156
Golann, Cecil Paige 1921-1995 11
Golbin, Andree 1923- 15
Gold, Alison Leslie 1945- 104
Gold, Bernice 150
Gold, Phyllis 21
  See Goldberg, Phyllis
Gold, Robert S(tanley) 1924- 63
Gold, Sharlya 9
Gold, Susan
  See Gold, Susan Dudley
Gold, Susan Dudley 1949- 147
Goldberg, Grace 1956- 78
Goldberg, Herbert S. 1926- 25
Goldberg, Jacob 1943- 94
Goldberg, Jake
  See Goldberg, Jacob
Goldberg, Jan 123
  See Curran, Jan Goldberg
Goldberg, Stan J. 1939- 26
Goldberg, Susan 1948- 71
Goldberg, Whoopi 1955- 119
Goldblatt, Stacey 1969(?)- 191
Golden, Christie 1963- 167
  Earlier sketch in SATA *116*
Goldentyer, Debra 1960- 84
Goldfeder, Cheryl
  See Pahz, Cheryl Suzanne
Goldfeder, James
  See Pahz, James Alon
Goldfeder, Jim
  See Pahz, James Alon
Goldfinger, Jennifer P. 1963- 185
Goldfrank, Helen Colodny 1912- 6
Goldin, Augusta 1906-1999 13
Goldin, Barbara Diamond 1946- 129
  Autobiography Feature 129
  Earlier sketch in SATA *92*
  See also SAAS 26
Goldin, David 1963- 101
Golding, Julia 1969- 188
Golding, Theresa Martin 1960- 150
Golding, William 1911-1993
  See CLR *130*
Golding, William Gerald
  See Golding, William
Goldman, Alex J. 1917- 65
Goldman, E(leanor) M(aureen) 1943- 103
Goldman, Elizabeth 1949- 90
Goldring, Ann 1937- 149
Goldsborough, June 1923- 19
Goldsmith, Connie 1945- 147
Goldsmith, Howard 1943- 108
  Earlier sketch in SATA *24*
Goldsmith, John Herman Thorburn 1903-1987
  Obituary 52
Goldsmith, Oliver 1730(?)-1774 26
Goldsmith, Ruth M. 1919- 62
Goldstein, Nathan 1927- 47
Goldstein, Philip 1910-1997 23
Goldston, Robert (Conroy) 1927- 6
Goldstone, Bruce 183
Goldstone, Lawrence A.
  See Treat, Lawrence
Golembe, Carla 1951- 79
Golenbock, Peter 1946- 99
Goll, Reinhold W(eimar) 1897-1993 26
Gollub, Matthew 1960- 134
  Earlier sketch in SATA *83*
Gomes, Filomena 1965- 183
Gomez, Elena 191
Gomez, Elizabeth 133

Gomez-Freer, Elizabeth
  See Gomez, Elizabeth
Gomi, Taro 1945- 103
  Earlier sketch in SATA *64*
  See also CLR *57*
Gondosch, Linda 1944- 58
Gonyea, Mark 194
Gonzalez, Catherine Troxell 1917-2000 87
Gonzalez, Christina
  See Gonzalez, Maya Christina
Gonzalez, Gloria 1940- 23
Gonzalez, Julie 1958- 174
Gonzalez, Maya
  See Gonzalez, Maya Christina
Gonzalez, Maya Christina 1964- 175
  Earlier sketch in SATA *115*
Gonzalez, Rigoberto 1970- 147
Goobie, Beth 1959- 128
Good, Alice 1950- 73
Goodall, Daphne Machin
  See Machin Goodall, Daphne (Edith)
Goodall, Jane 1934- 111
Goodall, John S(trickland) 1908-1996 66
  Obituary 91
  Earlier sketch in SATA *4*
  See also CLR *25*
Goodbody, Slim
  See Burstein, John
Goode, Diane 1949- 170
  Earlier sketches in SATA *15, 84, 114*
Goode, Diane Capuozzo
  See Goode, Diane
Goode, Stephen Ray 1943- 55
  Brief entry 40
Goodenow, Earle 1913- 40
Goodhart, Pippa 1958- 153
Goodhue, Thomas W. 1949- 143
Goodin, Sallie (Brown) 1953- 74
Goodman, Alison 1966- 111
Goodman, Deborah Lerme 1956- 50
  Brief entry 49
Goodman, Elaine 1930- 9
Goodman, Joan Elizabeth 1950- 162
  Earlier sketches in SATA *50, 94*
Goodman, Susan E. 1952- 181
Goodman, Walter 1927-2002 9
Goodrich, Samuel Griswold 1793-1860 23
Goodsell, Jane Neuberger 1921(?)-1988
  Obituary 56
GoodWeather, Hartley
  See King, Thomas
Goodweather, Hartley
  See King, Thomas
Goodwin, Hal
  See Goodwin, Harold L(eland)
Goodwin, Harold L(eland) 1914-1990 51
  Obituary 65
  Earlier sketch in SATA *13*
Goodwin, William 1943- 117
Goor, Nancy (Ruth Miller) 1944- 39
  Brief entry 34
Goor, Ron(ald Stephen) 1940- 39
  Brief entry 34
Goossen, Agnes
  See Epp, Margaret A(gnes)
Goossens, Philippe 1963- 195
Gootman, Marilyn E. 1944- 179
Gopnik, Adam 1956- 171
Gorbachev, Valeri 1944- 184
  Autobiography Feature 143
  Earlier sketches in SATA *98, 143*
Gordion, Mark
  See Turtledove, Harry
Gordon, Ad
  See Hano, Arnold
Gordon, Amy 1949- 156
  Earlier sketch in SATA *115*
Gordon, Bernard Ludwig 1931- 27
Gordon, Colonel H. R.
  See Ellis, Edward S(ylvester)

Gordon, David 180
  See Garrett, (Gordon) Randall (Phillip)
Gordon, Donald
  See Payne, Donald Gordon
Gordon, Dorothy 1893-1970 20
Gordon, Esther S(aranga) 1935- 10
Gordon, Frederick 1
Gordon, Gaelyn 1939-1997
  See CLR *75*
Gordon, Gary
  See Edmonds, I(vy) G(ordon)
Gordon, Hal
  See Goodwin, Harold L(eland)
Gordon, Jeffie Ross
  See Enderle, Judith (Ann) Ross
  and Gordon, Stephanie Jacob
Gordon, John
  See Gesner, Clark
Gordon, John (William) 1925- 84
Gordon, Lew
  See Baldwin, Gordon C(ortis)
Gordon, Margaret (Anna) 1939- 9
Gordon, Mike 1948- 101
Gordon, Mildred 1912-1979
  Obituary 24
Gordon, Selma
  See Lanes, Selma Gordon
Gordon, Sheila 1927- 88
  See also CLR *27*
Gordon, Shirley 1921- 48
  Brief entry 41
Gordon, Sol 1923- 11
Gordon, Stephanie Jacob 1940- 89
  Autobiography Feature 114
  Earlier sketch in SATA *64*
  See also SAAS 26
Gordon, Stewart
  See Shirreffs, Gordon D(onald)
Gordons, The
  See Gordon, Mildred
  and Gordon, Gordon
Gore, Leonid 185
Gorelick, Molly C(hernow) 1920-2003 9
  Obituary 153
Gorey, Edward (St. John) 1925-2000 70
  Brief entry 27
  Obituary 118
  Earlier sketch in SATA *29*
  See also CLR *36*
Gorham, Charles Orson 1868-1936 36
Gorham, Michael
  See Folsom, Franklin (Brewster)
Gorman, Carol 187
  Earlier sketch in SATA *150*
Gorman, Jacqueline Laks 1955- 148
Gormley, Beatrice 1942- 127
  Brief entry 35
  Earlier sketch in SATA *39*
Gorog, Judith (Katharine Allen) 1938- 75
  Earlier sketch in SATA *39*
Gorrell, Gena K. 1946- 170
Gorsline, Douglas (Warner) 1913-1985 11
  Obituary 43
Gorsline, (Sally) Marie 1928- 28
Gorsline, S. M.
  See Gorsline, (Sally) Marie
Gorton, Kaitlyn
  See Emerson, Kathy Lynn
Gorton, Kathy Lynn
  See Emerson, Kathy Lynn
Goryan, Sirak
  See Saroyan, William
Goscinny, Rene 1926-1977 47
  Brief entry 39
  See also CLR *37*
Goss, Clay(ton E.) 1946- 82
Goss, Gary 1947- 124
Goss, Mini 1963- 186

Gottesman, S. D.
See Kornbluth, C(yril) M.
and Lowndes, Robert A(ugustine) W(ard)
and Pohl, Frederik
Gottfried, Ted
See Gottfried, Theodore Mark
Gottfried, Theodore Mark 1928- 150
Earlier sketch in SATA 85
Gottlieb, Gerald 1923- 7
Gottlieb, William P. 1917-2006 24
Gottlieb, William Paul
See Gottlieb, William P.
Goudey, Alice E(dwards) 1898-1993 20
Goudge, Eileen 1950- 88
Goudge, Elizabeth (de Beauchamp)
1900-1984 2
Obituary 38
See also CLR 94
Gough, Catherine 24
See Mulgan, Catherine
Gough, Philip 1908- 45
Gough, Sue 1940- 106
Goulart, Ron(ald Joseph) 1933- 138
Earlier sketch in SATA 6
See Appleton, Victor II
and Dixon, Franklin W.
and Hope, Laura Lee
and Keene, Carolyn
Gould, Alberta 1945- 96
Gould, Chester 1900-1985 49
Obituary 43
Gould, Jean R(osalind) 1909-1993 11
Obituary 77
Gould, Lilian 6
Gould, Marilyn 1928- 76
Earlier sketch in SATA 15
Gould, Robert 154
Gould, Steven 1955- 95
Gould, Steven Charles
See Gould, Steven
Gourley, Catherine 1950- 190
Earlier sketch in SATA 95
Gourse, Leslie 1939-2004 89
Govan, (Mary) Christine Noble 1898-1985 ... 9
Gove, Doris 1944- 72
Govenar, Alan 1952- 189
Govenar, Alan Bruce
See Govenar, Alan
Govern, Elaine 1939- 26
Gowen, L. Kris 1968- 156
Graaf, Peter
See Youd, (Christopher) Samuel
Graber, Alexander 1914-1997 98
Earlier sketch in SATA 7
Graber, (George) Alexander 1914-1997 98
Graber, Janet 1942- 170
Graber, Richard (Fredrick) 1927- 26
Grabianski, Janusz 1928-1976 39
Obituary 30
Graboff, Abner 1919-1986 35
Grace, Fran(ces Jane) 45
Grace, N.B.
See Harper, Suzanne
Grace, Theresa
See Mattern, Joanne
Gracza, Margaret Young 1928- 56
Graduate of Oxford, A
See Ruskin, John
Grady, Denise 1952- 189
Graeber, Charlotte Towner 106
Brief entry 44
Earlier sketch in SATA 56
Graeme, Roderic
See Jeffries, Roderic
Graf, Michael
See Graf, Mike
Graf, Mike 1960- 164
Graff, Lisa 1981- 188
Graff, Polly Anne Colver
See Colver, Anne
Graff, (S.) Stewart 1908- 9

Graham, Ada 1931- 11
Graham, Alastair 1945- 74
Graham, Arthur Kennon
See Harrison, David L.
Graham, Bob 1942- 187
Earlier sketches in SATA 63, 101, 151
See also CLR 31
Graham, Brenda Knight 1942- 32
Graham, Charlotte
See Bowden, Joan Chase
Graham, Eleanor 1896-1984 18
Obituary 38
Graham, Ennis
See Molesworth, Mary Louisa
Graham, Frank, Jr. 1925- 11
Graham, Georgia 1959- 190
Graham, Ian 1953- 112
Graham, John 1926-2007 11
Graham, Kennon
See Harrison, David L.
Graham, Larry
See Graham, Lawrence
Graham, Lawrence 1962- 63
Graham, Lawrence Otis
See Graham, Lawrence
Graham, Linda
See Graham-Barber, Lynda
Graham, Lorenz (Bell) 1902-1989 74
Obituary 63
Earlier sketch in SATA 2
See also CLR 10
See also SAAS 5
Graham, Margaret Bloy 1920- 11
Graham, Robin Lee 1949- 7
Graham, Shirley 1896(?)-1977
See Du Bois, Shirley Graham
Graham-Barber, Lynda 1944- 159
Earlier sketch in SATA 42
Graham-Cameron, M.
See Graham-Cameron, M(alcolm) G(ordon)
Graham-Cameron, M(alcolm) G(ordon)
1931- 53
Brief entry 45
Graham-Cameron, Mike
See Graham-Cameron, M(alcolm) G(ordon)
Grahame, Kenneth 1859-1932 100
See also YABC 1
See also CLR 135
Gralley, Jean 166
Gramatky, Hardie 1907-1979 30
Obituary 23
Earlier sketch in SATA 1
See also CLR 22
Grambling, Lois G. 1927- 148
Earlier sketch in SATA 71
Grambo, Rebecca L(ynn) 1963- 109
Grammer, June Amos 1927- 58
Grand, Samuel 1912-1988 42
Grandits, John 1949- 192
GrandPre, Mary 1954- 184
Grandville, J. J.
See Gerard, Jean Ignace Isidore
Grandville, Jean Ignace Isidore Gerard
See Gerard, Jean Ignace Isidore
Granfield, Linda 1950- 160
Earlier sketch in SATA 96
Grange, Peter
See Nicole, Christopher (Robin)
Granger, Margaret Jane 1925(?)-1977
Obituary 27
Granger, Michele 1949- 88
Granger, Peggy
See Granger, Margaret Jane
Granowsky, Alvin 1936- 101
Granstaff, Bill 1925- 10
Granstrom, Brita 1969- 167
Earlier sketch in SATA 111
Grant, Bruce 1893-1977 5
Obituary 25
Grant, Cynthia D. 1950- 147
Earlier sketches in SATA 33, 77

Grant, Eva 1907-1996 7
Grant, Evva H. 1913-1977
Obituary 27
Grant, Gordon 1875-1962 25
Grant, Gwen(doline Ellen) 1940- 47
Grant, Katie M.
See Grant, K.M.
Grant, K.M. 175
Grant, (Alice) Leigh 1947- 10
Grant, Matthew G.
See May, Julian
Grant, Maxwell
See Gibson, Walter B(rown)
and Lynds, Dennis
Grant, Melvyn 183
Grant, Myrna (Lois) 1934- 21
Grant, Neil 1938- 154
Earlier sketch in SATA 14
Grant, Nicholas
See Nicole, Christopher (Robin)
Grant, Richard 1948- 80
Grant, Skeeter
See Spiegelman, Art
Grater, Michael 1923- 57
Gravel, Fern
See Hall, James Norman
Gravelle, Karen 1942- 166
Earlier sketch in SATA 78
Graves, Charles Parlin 1911-1972 4
Graves, Keith 191
Earlier sketch in SATA 156
Graves, Robert 1895-1985 45
Graves, Robert von Ranke
See Graves, Robert
Graves, Valerie
See Bradley, Marion Zimmer
Gravett, Emily 1972(?)- 189
Gray, Betsy
See Poole, Gray Johnson
Gray, Caroline
See Nicole, Christopher (Robin)
Gray, Dianne E. 183
Gray, Elizabeth Janet
See Vining, Elizabeth Gray
Gray, Genevieve S(tuck) 1920-1995 4
Gray, Harold (Lincoln) 1894-1968 33
Brief entry 32
Gray, Jenny
See Gray, Genevieve S(tuck)
Gray, John Lee
See Jakes, John
Gray, Judith A. 1949- 93
Gray, Judith Anne
See Gray, Judith A.
Gray, Keith 151
Gray, Kes 1960- 153
Gray, Les 1929- 82
Gray, Libba Moore 1937- 83
Gray, Luli 1945- 149
Earlier sketch in SATA 90
Gray, Marian
See Pierce, Edith Gray
Gray, Nicholas Stuart 1922-1981 4
Obituary 27
Gray, Nigel 1941- 104
Earlier sketch in SATA 33
Gray, (Lucy) Noel (Clervaux) 1898-1983 47
Gray, Patricia (Clark) 7
Gray, Patsey
See Gray, Patricia (Clark)
Gray, Rita 184
Graydon, Shari 1958- 158
Grayland, V. Merle
See Grayland, Valerie (Merle Spanner)
Grayland, Valerie (Merle Spanner) 7
Grayson, Devin (Kalile) 1970- 119
Grayson, Kristine
See Rusch, Kristine Kathryn
Grayson, Paul 1946- 79
Graystone, Lynn
See Brennan, Joseph Lomas

Great Comte, The
  See Hawkesworth, Eric
Greaves, Margaret 1914-1995 87
  Earlier sketch in SATA 7
Greaves, Nick 1955- 77
Gree, Alain 1936- 28
Green, Adam
  See Weisgard, Leonard (Joseph)
Green, Anne Canevari 1943- 62
Green, Brian
  See Card, Orson Scott
Green, Cliff(ord) 1934- 126
Green, Connie Jordan 1938- 80
Green, D.
  See Casewit, Curtis W(erner)
Green, Elizabeth Shippen 1871-1954 139
Green, Hannah
  See Greenberg, Joanne (Goldenberg)
Green, Jane 1937- 9
Green, John 1977(?)- 170
Green, Mary Moore 1906- 11
Green, Morton 1937- 8
Green, Norma B(erger) 1925- 11
Green, Phyllis 1932- 20
Green, Roger (Gilbert) Lancelyn 1918-1987 . 2
  Obituary 53
Green, (James Le)Roy 1948- 89
Green, Sheila Ellen 1934- 148
  Earlier sketches in SATA 8, 87
Green, Timothy 1953- 91
Greenaway, Kate 1846-1901 100
  See also YABC 2
  See also CLR 111
Greenbank, Anthony Hunt 1933- 39
Greenberg, David 1954- 171
Greenberg, David T.
  See Greenberg, David
Greenberg, Harvey R. 1935- 5
Greenberg, Jan 1942- 125
  Earlier sketch in SATA 61
Greenberg, Joanne (Goldenberg) 1932- 25
Greenberg, Melanie Hope 1954- 72
Greenberg, Polly 1932- 52
  Brief entry 43
Greenblat, Rodney Alan 1960- 106
Greenburg, Dan 1936- 175
  Earlier sketch in SATA 102
Greene, Bette 1934- 161
  Earlier sketches in SATA 8, 102
  See also CLR 2
  See also SAAS 16
Greene, Carla 1916- 67
  Earlier sketch in SATA 1
Greene, Carol 102
  Brief entry 44
  Earlier sketch in SATA 66
Greene, Constance C(larke) 1924- 72
  Earlier sketch in SATA 11
  See also CLR 62
  See also SAAS 11
Greene, Edgar
  See Papademetriou, Lisa
Greene, Ellin 1927- 23
Greene, Graham 1904-1991 20
Greene, Graham Henry
  See Greene, Graham
Greene, Jacqueline Dembar 1946- 131
  Earlier sketch in SATA 76
Greene, Laura Offenhartz 1935- 38
Greene, Meg
  See Malvasi, Meg Greene
Greene, Michele 1962- 178
Greene, Michele Dominguez
  See Greene, Michele
Greene, Rhonda Gowler 1955- 160
  Earlier sketch in SATA 101
Greene, Stephanie 1953- 173
  Earlier sketch in SATA 127
Greene, Wade 1933- 11
Greene, Yvonne
  See Flesch, Yolande (Catarina)

Greenfeld, Howard (Scheinman) 1928- 140
  Earlier sketch in SATA 19
Greenfeld, Josh(ua Joseph) 1928- 62
Greenfield, Eloise 1929- 155
  Earlier sketches in SATA 19, 61, 105
  See also CLR 38
  See also SAAS 16
Greenhaus, Thelma Nurenberg 1903-1984
  Obituary 45
Greenhut, Josh
  See Mercer, Sienna
Greenhut, Josh
  See Mercer, Sienna
Greening, Hamilton
  See Hamilton, Charles (Harold St. John)
Greenlaw, M. Jean 1941- 107
Greenleaf, Barbara Kaye 1942- 6
Greenleaf, Peter 1910-1997 33
Greenlee, Sharon 1935- 77
Greeno, Gayle 1949- 81
Greenseid, Diane 1948- 178
  Earlier sketch in SATA 93
Greenspun, Adele Aron 1938- 142
  Earlier sketch in SATA 76
Greenstein, Elaine 1959- 150
  Earlier sketch in SATA 82
Greenwald, Sheila
  See Green, Sheila Ellen
Greenwood, Barbara 1940- 129
  Earlier sketch in SATA 90
Greenwood, Pamela D. 1944- 115
Greer, Richard
  See Garrett, (Gordon) Randall (Phillip)
  and Silverberg, Robert
Gregg, Andrew K. 1929- 81
Gregg, Charles T(hornton) 1927- 65
Gregg, Walter H(arold) 1919- 20
Gregor, Arthur 1923- 36
Gregor, Lee
  See Pohl, Frederik
Gregori, Leon 1919- 15
Gregorian, Joyce Ballou 1946-1991 30
  Obituary 83
Gregorich, Barbara 1943- 184
  Earlier sketch in SATA 66
Gregorowski, Christopher 1940- 30
Gregory, Diana (Jean) 1933- 49
  Brief entry 42
Gregory, Harry
  See Gottfried, Theodore Mark
Gregory, Jean
  See Ure, Jean
Gregory, Kristiana 1951- 136
  Earlier sketch in SATA 74
Gregory, Nan 1944- 192
  Earlier sketch in SATA 148
Gregory, Philippa 1954- 122
Gregory, Stephen
  See Penzler, Otto
Gregory, Valiska 1940- 82
Greif, Jean-Jacques 1944- 195
Greisman, Joan Ruth 1937- 31
Grendon, Stephen
  See Derleth, August (William)
Grenville, Pelham
  See Wodehouse, P(elham) G(renville)
Gretz, Susanna 1937- 7
Gretzer, John 18
Grewdead, Roy
  See Gorey, Edward (St. John)
Grey, Carol
  See Lowndes, Robert A(ugustine) W(ard)
Grey, Christopher 191
Grey, Christopher Peter
  See Grey, Christopher
Grey, Jerry 1926- 11
Grey, Mini 166
Greybeard the Pirate
  See Macintosh, Brownie

Grey Owl
  See CLR 32
  See Belaney, Archibald Stansfeld
Gri
  See Denney, Diana
Gribbin, John 1946- 159
Gribbin, John R.
  See Gribbin, John
Grice, Frederick 1910-1983 6
Grider, Dorothy 1915- 31
Gridley, Marion E(leanor) 1906-1974 35
  Obituary 26
Grieco-Tiso, Pina 1954- 108
Grieder, Walter 1924- 9
Griego, Tony A. 1955- 77
Griese, Arnold A(lfred) 1921- 9
Griessman, Annette 1962- 170
  Earlier sketch in SATA 116
Grieve, James 1934- 146
Grifalconi, Ann 1929- 133
  Earlier sketches in SATA 2, 66
  See also CLR 35
  See also SAAS 16
Griffin, Adele 1970- 195
  Earlier sketches in SATA 105, 153
Griffin, Elizabeth May 1985- 89
Griffin, Gillett Good 1928- 26
Griffin, Judith Berry 34
Griffin, Kitty 1951- 137
Griffin, Peni R. 1961- 193
  Earlier sketches in SATA 67, 99
Griffin, Peni Rae Robinson
  See Griffin, Peni R.
Griffin, Steven A. 1953- 89
Griffin, Steven Arthur
  See Griffin, Steven A.
Griffin, W.E.B 1929- 5
Griffith, Connie 1946- 89
Griffith, Gershom 1960- 85
Griffith, Helen V(irginia) 1934- 87
  Autobiography Feature 107
  Earlier sketch in SATA 39
Griffith, Jeannette
  See Eyerly, Jeannette
Griffiths, Andy 1961- 152
Griffiths, G(ordon) D(ouglas) 1910-1973
  Obituary 20
Griffiths, Helen 1939- 86
  Earlier sketch in SATA 5
  See also CLR 75
  See also SAAS 5
Grigson, Jane (McIntire) 1928-1990 63
Grimes, Lee 1920- 68
Grimes, Nikki 1950- 174
  Earlier sketches in SATA 93, 136
  See also CLR 42
Grimly, Gris 186
Grimm, Jacob Ludwig Karl 1785-1863 22
  See also CLR 112
  See Grimm Brothers
Grimm, Wilhelm Karl 1786-1859 22
  See also CLR 112
  See Grimm Brothers
Grimm, William C(arey) 1907-1992 14
Grimm and Grim
  See Grimm, Jacob Ludwig Karl
  and Grimm, Wilhelm Karl
Grimm Brothers
  See CLR 112
  See Grimm, Jacob Ludwig Karl
  and Grimm, Wilhelm Karl
Grimsdell, Jeremy 1942- 83
Grimshaw, Nigel (Gilroy) 1925- 23
Grimsley, Gordon
  See Groom, Arthur William
Grindley, (Jane) Sally 1953- 148
Gringhuis, Dirk
  See Gringhuis, Richard H.
Gringhuis, Richard H. 1918-1974 6
  Obituary 25

Grinnell, David
　　See Wollheim, Donald A(llen)
Grinnell, George Bird 1849-1938 .... *16*
Grinspoon, David
　　See Grinspoon, David H.
Grinspoon, David H. 1959- *156*
Grinspoon, David Harry
　　See Grinspoon, David H.
Gripe, Maria 1923- *74*
　　Earlier sketch in SATA *2*
　　See also CLR *5*
Gripe, Maria Kristina
　　See Gripe, Maria
Groch, Judith (Goldstein) 1929- *25*
Grode, Redway
　　See Gorey, Edward (St. John)
Groener, Carl
　　See Lowndes, Robert A(ugustine) W(ard)
Groening, Matt 1954- *116*
　　Earlier sketch in SATA *81*
Grohmann, Susan 1948- *84*
Grohskopf, Bernice *7*
Grol, Lini R(icharda) 1913- *9*
Grollman, Earl A. 1925- *22*
Groom, Arthur William 1898-1964 .... *10*
Grooms, Duffy 1964- *169*
Gross, Alan 1947- *54*
　　Brief entry *43*
Gross, Ernie 1913- *67*
Gross, Philip 1952- *164*
　　Earlier sketch in SATA *84*
Gross, Philip John
　　See Gross, Philip
Gross, Ruth Belov 1929- *33*
Gross, Sarah Chokla 1906-1976 .... *9*
　　Obituary *26*
Grosser, Morton 1931- *74*
Grosser, Vicky 1958- *83*
Grossman, Bill 1948- *126*
　　Earlier sketch in SATA *72*
Grossman, Nancy 1940- *29*
Grossman, Patricia 1951- *73*
Grossman, Robert 1940- *11*
Grote, JoAnn A. 1951- *113*
Groten, Dallas 1951- *64*
Groth, John (August) 1908-1988 .... *21*
　　Obituary *56*
Groth-Fleming, Candace
　　See Fleming, Candace
Grove, Vicki 1948- *151*
　　Autobiography Feature *151*
　　Earlier sketch in SATA *122*
Grover, Lorie Ann 1964- *168*
Grover, Wayne 1934- *69*
Groves, Georgina
　　See Symons, (Dorothy) Geraldine
Groves, Maketa 1950- *107*
Groves, Seli *77*
Grubb, Lisa *160*
Gruber, Michael 1940- *173*
Gruber, Terry (deRoy) 1953- *66*
Gruelle, John (Barton) 1880-1938 .... *35*
　　Brief entry *32*
　　See Gruelle, Johnny
Gruelle, Johnny
　　See CLR *34*
　　See Gruelle, John (Barton)
Gruenberg, Sidonie Matsner 1881-1974 .... *2*
　　Obituary *27*
Gruhzit-Hoyt, Olga (Margaret) 1922- *127*
　　Earlier sketch in SATA *16*
Grummer, Arnold E(dward) 1923- *49*
Grunewalt, Pine
　　See Kunhardt, Edith
Grunwell, Jeanne Marie 1971- *147*
Grupper, Jonathan *137*
Gryski, Camilla 1948- *72*
Guarino, Dagmar
　　See Guarino, Deborah
Guarino, Deborah 1954- *68*
Guay, Georgette (Marie Jeanne) 1952- *54*

Guback, Georgia *88*
Guccione, Leslie Davis 1946- *111*
　　Earlier sketch in SATA *72*
Guck, Dorothy 1913-2002 .... *27*
Guerny, Gene
　　See Gurney, Gene
Guest, Elissa Haden 1953- *125*
Guest, Jacqueline 1952- *135*
Guevara, Susan *167*
　　Earlier sketch in SATA *97*
Gugler, Laurel Dee *95*
Gugliotta, Bobette 1918-1994 .... *7*
Guianan, Eve 1965- *102*
Guiberson, Brenda Z. 1946- *124*
　　Earlier sketch in SATA *71*
Guibert, Emmanuel 1964- *181*
Guile, Melanie 1949- *152*
　　Earlier sketch in SATA *104*
Guillaume, Jeanette G. Flierl 1899-1990 .... *8*
Guillot, Rene 1900-1969 .... *7*
　　See also CLR *22*
Guisewite, Cathy (Lee) 1950- *57*
Gulbis, Stephen 1959- *142*
Gulley, Judie 1942- *58*
Gump, P. Q.
　　See Card, Orson Scott
Gump, P.Q.
　　See Card, Orson Scott
Gundrey, Elizabeth 1924- *23*
Gunn, James E. 1923- *35*
Gunn, James Edwin
　　See Gunn, James E.
Gunn, Robin Jones 1955- *84*
Gunning, Monica Olwen 1930- *161*
Gunston, Bill
　　See Gunston, William Tudor
Gunston, William Tudor 1927- *9*
Gunterman, Bertha Lisette 1886(?)-1975
　　Obituary *27*
Gunther, John 1901-1970
Guravich, Dan 1918- *74*
Gurko, Leo 1914- *9*
Gurko, Miriam 1910(?)-1988 .... *9*
　　Obituary *58*
Gurney, Gene 1924- *65*
Gurney, James 1958- *120*
　　Earlier sketch in SATA *76*
Gurney, John Steven 1962- *143*
　　Earlier sketch in SATA *75*
Gustafson, Sarah R.
　　See Riedman, Sarah R(egal)
Gustafson, Scott 1956- *34*
Gustavson, Adam *176*
Guthrie, A(lfred) B(ertram), Jr. 1901-1991 .. *62*
　　Obituary *67*
Guthrie, Anne 1890-1979 .... *28*
Guthrie, Donna W. 1946- *105*
　　Earlier sketch in SATA *63*
Gutierrez, Akemi *172*
Gutman, Bill *128*
　　Brief entry *43*
　　Earlier sketch in SATA *67*
Gutman, Dan 1955- *188*
　　Earlier sketches in SATA *77, 139*
Gutman, Naham 1899(?)-1981
　　Obituary *25*
Gutmann, Bessie Pease 1876-1960 .... *73*
Guy, Geoffrey 1942- *153*
Guy, Ginger Foglesong 1954- *171*
Guy, Rosa (Cuthbert) 1925- *122*
　　Earlier sketches in SATA *14, 62*
　　See also CLR *137*
Guy, Susan 1948- *149*
Guymer, (Wilhelmina) Mary 1909- *50*
Guzman, Lila 1952- *168*
Guzman, Rick 1957- *168*
Gwaltney, Doris 1932- *181*
Gwynne, Fred(erick Hubbard) 1926-1993 .... *41*
　　Brief entry *27*
　　Obituary *75*

Gwynne, Oscar A.
　　See Ellis, Edward S(ylvester)
Gwynne, Oswald A.
　　See Ellis, Edward S(ylvester)

H

Haab, Sherri 1964- *169*
　　Earlier sketch in SATA *91*
Haar, Jaap ter
　　See CLR *15*
　　See ter Haar, Jaap
Haarsma, P.J. *183*
Haas, Carolyn Buhai 1926- *43*
Haas, Dan 1957- *105*
Haas, Dorothy F. *46*
　　Brief entry *43*
　　See also SAAS *17*
Haas, Irene 1929- *96*
　　Earlier sketch in SATA *17*
Haas, James E(dward) 1943- *40*
Haas, (Katherine) Jessie 1959- *135*
　　Autobiography Feature *135*
　　Earlier sketch in SATA *98*
Haas, Merle S. 1896(?)-1985
　　Obituary *41*
Habenstreit, Barbara 1937- *5*
Haber, Karen 1955- *78*
Haber, Louis 1910-1988 .... *12*
Hacker, Randi 1951- *185*
Hacker, Randi Dawn
　　See Hacker, Randi
Hackett, John Winthrop 1910-1997 .... *65*
Hacks, Peter 1928-2003
　　Obituary *151*
Haddix, Margaret Peterson 1964- *187*
　　Earlier sketches in SATA *94, 125*
Haddon, Mark 1962- *155*
Hader, Berta (Hoerner) 1891(?)-1976 .... *16*
Hader, Elmer (Stanley) 1889-1973 .... *16*
Hadithi, Mwenye
　　See Hobson, Bruce
Hadley, Franklin
　　See Winterbotham, R(ussell) R(obert)
Hadley, Lee 1934-1995 .... *89*
　　Brief entry *38*
　　Obituary *86*
　　Earlier sketch in SATA *47*
　　See also CLR *40*
　　See Irwin, Hadley
Haeffele, Deborah 1954- *76*
Haenel, Wolfram 1956- *89*
　　See also CLR *64*
Hafner, Marylin 1925- *179*
　　Earlier sketches in SATA *7, 121*
Haft, Erin
　　See Ehrenhaft, Daniel
Hager, Alan 1940- *176*
Hager, Alice Rogers 1894-1969
　　Obituary *26*
Hager, Betty 1923- *89*
Hager, Sarah *171*
Hager, Thomas 1953- *119*
Hager, Tom
　　See Hager, Thomas
Hagerup, Klaus 1946- *186*
Haggard, H(enry) Rider 1856-1925 .... *16*
Haggerty, James J(oseph) 1920- *5*
Hagon, Priscilla
　　See Allan, Mabel Esther
Hague, (Susan) Kathleen 1949- *49*
　　Brief entry *45*
Hague, Michael 1948- *185*
　　Brief entry *32*
　　Earlier sketches in SATA *48, 80, 129*
Hague, Michael R.
　　See Hague, Michael
Hahn, Emily 1905-1997 .... *3*
　　Obituary *96*

Hahn, Hannelore 8
Hahn, James (Sage) 1947- 9
Hahn, (Mona) Lynn 1949- 9
Hahn, Mary Downing 1937- 157
    Autobiography Feature 157
    Brief entry 44
    Earlier sketches in SATA 50, 81, 138
    See also SAAS 12
Hahn, Michael T. 1953- 92
Haig-Brown, Roderick (Langmere)
    1908-1976 12
    See also CLR 31
Haight, Anne Lyon 1895-1977
    Obituary 30
Haight, Rip
    See Carpenter, John (Howard)
Haight, Sandy 1949- 79
Haij, Vera
    See Jansson, Tove (Marika)
Haines, Gail Kay 1943- 11
Haines, Margaret Ann Beck
    See Beck, Peggy
Haining, Peter 1940-2007 14
    Obituary 188
Haining, Peter Alexander
    See Haining, Peter
Hains, Harriet
    See Watson, Carol
Hajdusiewicz, Babs Bell 163
Hakim, Joy 1931- 173
    Earlier sketch in SATA 83
Halacy, D(aniel) S(tephen), Jr. 1919-2002 ... 36
    See Halacy, Dan
Halacy, Dan
    See SAAS 8
    See Halacy, D(aniel) S(tephen), Jr.
Halam, Ann
    See Jones, Gwyneth A(nn)
Haldane, Roger John 1945- 13
Hale, Arlene 1924-1982 49
Hale, Bruce 1957- 123
Hale, Christy 179
    See Apostolou, Christine Hale
Hale, Edward Everett 1822-1909 16
Hale, Glenn
    See Walker, Robert W(ayne)
Hale, Helen
    See Mulcahy, Lucille Burnett
Hale, Irina 1932- 26
Hale, Kathleen 1898-2000 66
    Obituary 121
    Earlier sketch in SATA 17
Hale, Linda (Howe) 1929- 6
Hale, Lucretia P.
    See Hale, Lucretia Peabody
Hale, Lucretia Peabody 1820-1900 26
    See also CLR 105
Hale, Marian 194
Hale, Nancy 1908-1988 31
    Obituary 57
Hale, Shannon 158
Haley, Gail E(inhart) 1939- 161
    Autobiography Feature 161
    Brief entry 28
    Earlier sketches in SATA 43, 78, 136
    See also CLR 21
    See also SAAS 13
Haley, Neale 52
Hall, Adam
    See Trevor, Elleston
Hall, Adele 1910- 7
Hall, Anna Gertrude 1882-1967 8
Hall, Barbara 1960- 68
Hall, Becky 1950- 186
Hall, Beverly B. 1918- 95
Hall, Borden
    See Yates, Raymond F(rancis)
Hall, Brian P(atrick) 1935- 31
Hall, Cameron
    See del Rey, Lester

Hall, Caryl
    See Hansen, Caryl (Hall)
Hall, Donald 1928- 97
    Earlier sketch in SATA 23
Hall, Donald Andrew, Jr.
    See Hall, Donald
Hall, Douglas 1931- 43
Hall, Elizabeth 1929- 77
Hall, Elvajean 1910-1984 6
Hall, Francie 1940- 166
Hall, James Norman 1887-1951 21
Hall, Jesse
    See Boesen, Victor
Hall, Katy
    See McMullan, Kate
Hall, Kirsten Marie 1974- 67
Hall, Lynn 1937- 79
    Earlier sketches in SATA 2, 47
    See also SAAS 4
Hall, Malcolm 1945- 7
Hall, Marjory
    See Yeakley, Marjory Hall
Hall, Melanie W. 1949- 169
    Earlier sketches in SATA 78, 116
Hall, Patricia 1940- 136
Hall, Rosalys Haskell 1914- 7
Hall, Willis 1929-2005 66
Hallard, Peter
    See Catherall, Arthur
Hallas, Richard
    See Knight, Eric
Hall-Clarke, James
    See Rowland-Entwistle, (Arthur) Theodore
    (Henry)
Hallensleben, Georg 1958- 173
Haller, Dorcas Woodbury 1946- 46
Hallett, Mark 1947- 83
Halliburton, Richard 1900-1939(?) 81
Halliburton, Warren J. 1924- 19
Halliday, Brett
    See Dresser, Davis
    and Johnson, (Walter) Ryerson
    and Terrall, Robert
Halliday, William R(oss) 1926- 52
Hallin, Emily Watson 1916-1995 6
Hallinan, P(atrick) K(enneth) 1944- 39
    Brief entry 37
Hallman, Ruth 1929- 43
    Brief entry 28
Hallowell, Tommy
    See Hill, Thomas
Hall-Quest, (Edna) Olga W(ilbourne)
    1899-1986 11
    Obituary 47
Halls, Kelly Milner 1957- 131
Hallstead, William F(inn III) 1924- 11
Hallward, Michael 1889-1982 12
Halperin, Michael 156
Halperin, Wendy Anderson 1952- 125
    Earlier sketch in SATA 80
Halpin, Brendan 1968- 193
Halpin, Marlene 1927- 88
Halsell, Grace (Eleanor) 1923-2000 13
Halsey, Megan 185
Halsted, Anna Roosevelt 1906-1975
    Obituary 30
Halter, Jon C(harles) 1941- 22
Halvorson, Marilyn 1948- 123
Hamalian, Leo 1920- 41
Hamberger, John 1934- 14
Hamblin, Dora Jane 1920- 36
Hambly, Barbara 1951- 108
Hambly, Barbara Joan
    See Hambly, Barbara
Hamer, Martyn
    See Eldin, Peter
Hamerstrom, Frances 1907-1998 24
Hamil, Thomas Arthur 1928- 14
Hamill, Ethel
    See Webb, Jean Francis (III)
Hamilton, (John) Alan 1943- 66

Hamilton, Alice
    See Cromie, Alice Hamilton
Hamilton, Anita 1919- 92
Hamilton, Buzz
    See Hemming, Roy G.
Hamilton, Carol (Jean Barber) 1935- 94
Hamilton, Charles (Harold St. John)
    1876-1961 13
Hamilton, Charles 1913-1996 65
    Obituary 93
Hamilton, Clive
    See Lewis, C.S.
Hamilton, Dorothy (Drumm) 1906-1983 12
    Obituary 35
Hamilton, Edith 1867-1963 20
Hamilton, Edmond 1904-1977 118
Hamilton, (Muriel) Elizabeth (Mollie)
    1906- 23
Hamilton, Emma Walton 1962- 177
Hamilton, Franklin
    See Silverberg, Robert
Hamilton, Gail
    See Corcoran, Barbara (Asenath)
    and Dodge, Mary Abigail
Hamilton, Kersten 1958- 134
Hamilton, Martha 1953- 183
    Earlier sketch in SATA 123
Hamilton, Mary (E.) 1927- 55
Hamilton, Mollie
    See Kaye, M.M.
Hamilton, Morse 1943-1998 101
    Earlier sketch in SATA 35
Hamilton, Peter F. 1960- 109
Hamilton, Priscilla
    See Gellis, Roberta
Hamilton, Ralph
    See Stratemeyer, Edward L.
Hamilton, Virginia 1936-2002 123
    Obituary 132
    Earlier sketches in SATA 4, 56, 79
    See also CLR 127
Hamilton, Virginia Esther
    See Hamilton, Virginia
Hamilton-Paterson, James 1941- 82
Hamlet, Ova
    See Lupoff, Richard A(llen)
Hamley, Dennis 1935- 69
    Earlier sketch in SATA 39
    See also CLR 47
    See also SAAS 22
Hamlin, Peter J. 1970- 84
Hamm, Diane Johnston 1949- 78
Hammer, Charles 1934- 58
Hammer, Richard 1928- 6
Hammerman, Gay M(orenus) 1926- 9
Hammond, Andrew 1970- 181
Hammond, Ralph
    See Hammond Innes, Ralph
Hammond, Winifred G(raham) 1899-1992 ... 29
    Obituary 107
Hammond Innes, Ralph 1913-1998 116
Hammontree, Marie (Gertrude) 1913- 13
Hample, Zack 1977- 161
Hampshire, Joyce Gregorian
    See Gregorian, Joyce Ballou
Hampshire, Susan 1942- 98
Hampson, (Richard) Denman 1929- 15
Hampson, Frank 1918(?)-1985
    Obituary 46
Hampton, Wilborn 156
Hamre, Leif 1914- 5
Hamsa, Bobbie 1944- 52
    Brief entry 38
Han, Jenny 1981- 175
Han, Lu
    See Stickler, Soma Han
Han, Soma
    See Stickler, Soma Han
Han, Suzanne Crowder 1953- 89
Hancock, Mary A. 1923- 31
Hancock, Sibyl 1940- 9

Hand, Elizabeth 1957- 167
  Earlier sketch in SATA *118*
Handford, Martin (John) 1956- 64
  See also CLR 22
Handforth, Thomas (Schofield) 1897-1948 .. 42
Handler, Daniel
  See Snicket, Lemony
Handville, Robert (Tompkins) 1924- 45
Hane, Roger 1940-1974
  Obituary 20
Hanel, Wolfram
  See Haenel, Wolfram
Haney, Lynn 1941- 23
Hanff, Helene 1916-1997 97
  Earlier sketch in SATA *11*
Hanley, Boniface Francis 1924- 65
Hanlon, Emily 1945- 15
Hann, Jacquie 1951- 19
Hann, Judith 1942- 77
Hanna, Bill
  See Hanna, William (Denby)
Hanna, Cheryl 1951- 84
Hanna, Jack (Bushnell) 1947- 74
Hanna, Nell(ie L.) 1908- 55
Hanna, Paul R(obert) 1902-1988 9
Hanna, William (Denby) 1910-2001 51
  Obituary 126
Hannam, Charles 1925- 50
Hannan, Peter 1954- 187
Hannigan, Katherine 170
Hannon, Ezra
  See Hunter, Evan
Hann-Syme, Marguerite 127
Hano, Arnold 1922- 12
Hano, Renee Roth
  See Roth-Hano, Renee
Hanover, Terri
  See Huff, Tanya
Hansen, Ann Larkin 1958- 96
Hansen, Brooks 1965- 104
Hansen, Caryl (Hall) 1929- 39
Hansen, Ian V. 1929- 113
Hansen, Jennifer 1972- 156
Hansen, Joyce 1942- 172
  Autobiography Feature 172
  Brief entry 39
  Earlier sketches in SATA *46, 101*
  See also CLR 21
  See also SAAS 15
Hansen, Joyce Viola
  See Hansen, Joyce
Hansen, Mark Victor 112
Hansen, Ron(ald Thomas) 1947- 56
Hanser, Richard (Frederick) 1909-1981 13
Hanson, Joan 1938- 8
Hanson, Joseph E. 1894(?)-1971
  Obituary 27
Hanson, Mary Elizabeth 188
Hanson, Warren 1949- 155
Hansson, Gunilla 1939- 64
Harald, Eric
  See Boesen, Victor
Harcourt, Ellen Knowles 1890(?)-1984
  Obituary 36
Hard, Charlotte (Ann) 1969- 98
Hardcastle, Michael 1933- 47
  Brief entry 38
Harding, Lee 1937- 32
  Brief entry 31
Hardt, Helga Fleischhauer
  See Fleischhauer-Hardt, Helga
Hardwick, Richard Holmes, Jr. 1923- 12
Hardy, Alice Dale 67
  Earlier sketch in SATA *1*
Hardy, David A(ndrews) 1936- 9
Hardy, Jon 1958- 53
Hardy, LeAnne 1951- 154
Hardy, Stuart
  See Schisgall, Oscar
Hare, Norma Q(uarles) 1924- 46
  Brief entry 41

Harel, Nira 1936- 154
Harford, Henry
  See Hudson, W(illiam) H(enry)
Hargrave, Leonie
  See Disch, Thomas M.
Hargreaves, (Charles) Roger 1935-1988
  Obituary 56
Hargrove, James 1947- 57
  Brief entry 50
Hargrove, Jim
  See Hargrove, James
Hariton, Anca I. 1955- 79
Hark, Mildred
  See McQueen, Mildred Hark
Harkaway, Hal
  See Stratemeyer, Edward L.
Harkins, Philip 1912-1997 6
  Obituary 129
Harlan, Elizabeth 1945- 41
  Brief entry 35
Harlan, Glen
  See Cebulash, Mel
Harlan, Judith 1949- 135
  Earlier sketch in SATA *74*
  See also CLR 81
Harland, Richard 1947- 152
Harlee, J. V.
  See Leese, Jennifer L.B.
Harler, Ann
  See Van Steenwyk, Elizabeth (Ann)
Harley, Avis 183
Harley, Bill 1954- 87
Harlow, Joan Hiatt 1932- 157
Harman, Fred 1902(?)-1982
  Obituary 30
Harman, Hugh 1903-1982
  Obituary 33
Harmelink, Barbara (Mary) 9
Harmer, Mabel 1894-1992 45
Harmon, Dan
  See Harmon, Daniel E(lton)
Harmon, Daniel E(lton) 1949- 157
Harmon, Margaret 1906- 20
Harmon, Michael 1969- 189
Harmon, William (Ruth) 1938- 65
Harnan, Terry 1920- 12
Harness, Cheryl 1951- 178
  Earlier sketch in SATA *131*
Harnett, Cynthia (Mary) 1893-1981 5
  Obituary 32
Harper, Anita 1943- 41
Harper, Betty 1946- 126
Harper, Charise
  See Harper, Charise Mericle
Harper, Charise Mericle 179
Harper, Elaine
  See Hallin, Emily Watson
Harper, Ellen
  See Noble, Marty
Harper, Jamie 174
Harper, Jessica (R.) 1949- 148
Harper, Jo 1932- 169
  Earlier sketch in SATA *97*
Harper, Mary Wood
  See Dixon, Jeanne
Harper, Piers 1966- 161
  Earlier sketch in SATA *105*
Harper, Suzanne 194
Harper, Wilhelmina 1884-1973 4
  Obituary 26
Harrah, Madge 1931- 154
Harrah, Michael 1940- 41
Harrah, Monique
  See Harrah, Madge
Harrar, George E. 1949- 124
Harrell, Beatrice Orcutt 1943- 93
Harrell, Janice 1945- 70
Harries, Joan 1922- 39
Harrill, Ronald 1950- 90
Harrington, Denis J(ames) 1932- 88
Harrington, Janice N. 1956- 187

Harrington, Lyn 5
  See Harrington, Evelyn Davis
Harris, Alan 1944- 71
Harris, Aurand 1915-1996 37
  Obituary 91
Harris, Bob
  See Harris, Robert J.
Harris, Carol Flynn 1933- 135
Harris, Catherine
  See Ainsworth, Catherine Harris
Harris, Christie
  See Harris, Christie (Lucy) Irwin
Harris, Christie (Lucy) Irwin 1907-2002 74
  Autobiography Feature 116
  Earlier sketch in SATA *6*
  See also CLR 47
  See also SAAS 10
Harris, Christine 1955- 105
Harris, Colver
  See Colver, Anne
Harris, David 1942- 118
Harris, David William
  See Harris, David
Harris, Dorothy Joan 1931- 153
  Earlier sketch in SATA *13*
Harris, Geraldine (Rachel) 1951- 54
Harris, Jacqueline L. 1929- 62
Harris, Janet 1932-1979 4
  Obituary 23
Harris, Jesse
  See Standiford, Natalie
Harris, Joan 1946- 146
Harris, Joel Chandler 1848-1908 100
  See also YABC 1
  See also CLR 128
Harris, John (Wyndham Parkes Lucas) Beynon
  1903-1969 118
  See Wyndham, John
Harris, Johnson
  See Harris, John (Wyndham Parkes Lucas)
  Beynon
Harris, Jonathan 1921-1997 52
Harris, Larry Vincent 1939- 59
Harris, Lavinia
  See St. John, Nicole
Harris, Leon A., Jr. 1926-2000 4
Harris, Lorle K(empe) 1912-2001 22
Harris, Marilyn
  See Springer, Marilyn Harris
Harris, Mark Jonathan 1941- 84
  Earlier sketch in SATA *32*
Harris, Mary K(athleen) 1905-1966 119
Harris, Robert J. 1955- 195
Harris, Robie H. 1940- 147
  Brief entry 53
  Earlier sketch in SATA *90*
Harris, Robin
  See Shine, Deborah
Harris, Rosemary (Jeanne) 82
  Earlier sketch in SATA *4*
  See also CLR 30
  See also SAAS 7
Harris, Ruth Elwin 1935- 164
Harris, Sherwood 1932- 25
Harris, Steven Michael 1957- 55
Harris, Trudy 1949- 191
  Earlier sketch in SATA *128*
Harris-Filderman, Diane
  See Filderman, Diane E(lizabeth)
Harrison, C(hester) William 1913-1994 35
Harrison, Carol
  See Harrison, Carol Thompson
Harrison, Carol Thompson 113
Harrison, David L. 1937- 186
  Earlier sketches in SATA *26, 92, 150*
Harrison, Deloris 1938- 9
Harrison, Edward Hardy 1926- 56
Harrison, Elizabeth (Allen) Cavanna
  1909-2001 142
  See Cavanna, Betty
Harrison, Harry 1925- 4

Harrison, Harry Max
  See Harrison, Harry
Harrison, Mette Ivie 1970- *149*
Harrison, Michael 1939- *106*
Harrison, Molly (Hodgett) 1909-2002 .... *41*
Harrison, Sarah 1946- *63*
Harrison, Ted
  See Harrison, Edward Hardy
Harsh, Fred (T.) 1925- *72*
Harshaw, Ruth H(etzel) 1890-1968 .... *27*
Harshman, Marc 1950- *109*
  Earlier sketch in SATA *71*
Hart, Alison
  See Leonhardt, Alice
Hart, Bruce 1938-2006 .... *57*
  Brief entry *39*
Hart, Carole 1943- *57*
  Brief entry *39*
Hart, Carolyn 1936- *74*
Hart, Carolyn G.
  See Hart, Carolyn
Hart, Carolyn Gimpel
  See Hart, Carolyn
Hart, Jan Siegel 1940- *79*
Hart, Joyce 1954- *148*
Hart, Karen *185*
Hart, Lenore *171*
Hart, Philip S. 1944- *180*
Hart, Virginia 1949- *83*
Harte, (Francis) Bret(t) 1836(?)-1902 .... *26*
Harter, Debbie 1963- *107*
Hartfield, Claire 1957- *147*
Hartinger, Brent 1964- *174*
  Earlier sketch in SATA *145*
Hartland, Jessie *171*
Hartley, Ellen (Raphael) 1915-1980 .... *23*
Hartley, Fred Allan III 1953- *41*
Hartley, William B(rown) 1913-1980 .... *23*
Hartling, Peter
  See CLR *29*
  See Hartling, Peter
Hartling, Peter 1933- *66*
  See Hartling, Peter
Hartman, Evert 1937- *38*
  Brief entry *35*
Hartman, Jane E(vangeline) 1928- *47*
Hartman, Louis F(rancis) 1901-1970 .... *22*
Hartman, Rachel *174*
Hartman, Victoria 1942- *91*
Hartnett, Sonya 1968- *176*
  Earlier sketches in SATA *93, 130*
Hartshorn, Ruth M. 1928- *11*
Hartung, Susan Kathleen *192*
  Earlier sketch in SATA *150*
Hartwig, Manfred 1950- *81*
Harvey, Brett 1936- *61*
Harvey, Edith 1908(?)-1972
  Obituary *27*
Harvey, Gill *189*
Harvey, Karen D. 1935- *88*
Harvey, Roland 1945- *179*
  Earlier sketches in SATA *71, 123*
Harvey-Fitzhenry, Alyxandra 1974- *189*
Harwick, B. L.
  See Keller, Beverly L(ou)
Harwin, Brian
  See Henderson, LeGrand
Harwood, Pearl Augusta (Bragdon)
  1903-1998 .... *9*
Haseley, Dennis 1950- *157*
  Brief entry *44*
  Earlier sketches in SATA *57, 105*
Hashmi, Kerri 1955- *108*
Haskell, Arnold L(ionel) 1903-1981(?) *6*
Haskins, James
  See Haskins, James S.
Haskins, James S. 1941-2005 .... *132*
  Autobiography Feature *132*
  Earlier sketches in SATA *9, 69, 105*
  See also CLR *39*
  See Haskins, Jim

Haskins, Jim
  See SAAS *4*
  See Haskins, James S.
Hasler, Eveline 1933- *181*
Hasler, Joan 1931- *28*
Hass, Robert 1941- *94*
Hassall, Joan 1906-1988 .... *43*
  Obituary *56*
Hassett, Ann 1958- *162*
Hassett, John *162*
Hassler, Jon 1933-2008 .... *19*
  Obituary *191*
Hassler, Jon Francis
  See Hassler, Jon
Hastings, Beverly
  See Barkin, Carol
  and James, Elizabeth
Hastings, Graham
  See Jeffries, Roderic
Hastings, Ian 1912- *62*
Hastings, Victor
  See Disch, Thomas M.
Hatch, Lynda S. 1950- *90*
Hathaway, Barbara *164*
Hathorn, Libby 1943- *156*
  Autobiography Feature *156*
  Earlier sketches in SATA *74, 120*
  See Hathorn, Elizabeth Helen
Hatkoff, Craig 1954- *192*
Hatlo, Jimmy 1898-1963
  Obituary *23*
Haugaard, Erik Christian 1923- *68*
  Earlier sketch in SATA *4*
  See also CLR *11*
  See also SAAS *12*
Haugaard, Kay *117*
Haugen, Hayley Mitchell 1968- *172*
Haugen, Tormod 1945- *66*
Hauman, Doris 1898-1984 .... *32*
Hauman, George 1890-1961 .... *32*
Hauptly, Denis J(ames) 1945- *57*
Hauser, Jill Frankel 1950- *127*
Hauser, Margaret L(ouise) 1909- *10*
Hausherr, Rosmarie 1943- *86*
Hausman, Gerald 1945- *180*
  Earlier sketches in SATA *13, 90, 132*
  See also CLR *89*
Hausman, Gerry
  See Hausman, Gerald
Hauth, Katherine B. 1940- *99*
Hautman, Pete 1952- *173*
  Earlier sketches in SATA *82, 128*
Hautman, Peter Murray
  See Hautman, Pete
Hautzig, Deborah 1956- *106*
  Earlier sketch in SATA *31*
Hautzig, Esther Rudomin 1930- *148*
  Earlier sketches in SATA *4, 68*
  See also CLR *22*
  See also SAAS *15*
Havel, Geoff 1955- *152*
Havel, Jennifer
  See Havill, Juanita
Havelin, Kate 1961- *143*
Havighurst, Walter (Edwin) 1901-1994 .... *1*
  Obituary *79*
Haviland, Virginia 1911-1988 .... *6*
  Obituary *54*
Havill, Juanita 1949- *155*
  Earlier sketch in SATA *74*
Hawes, Judy 1913- *4*
Hawes, Louise 1943- *180*
  Earlier sketch in SATA *60*
Hawke, Rosanne 1953- *165*
  Earlier sketch in SATA *124*
Hawke, Rosanne Joy
  See Hawke, Rosanne
Hawkes, Kevin (Cliff) 1959- *150*
  Earlier sketch in SATA *78*
Hawkes, Nigel 1943- *119*
Hawkesworth, Eric 1921- *13*

Hawkins, Arthur 1903-1985 .... *19*
Hawkins, Colin 1945- *162*
  Earlier sketch in SATA *112*
Hawkins, Jacqui *162*
  Earlier sketch in SATA *112*
Hawkins, Jimmy 1941- *188*
Hawkins, Laura 1951- *74*
Hawkins, (Helena Ann) Quail 1905-2002 ...... *6*
  Obituary *141*
Hawkinson, John (Samuel) 1912-1994 .... *4*
Hawkinson, Lucy (Ozone) 1924-1971 .... *21*
Hawks, Robert 1961- *85*
Hawley, Mabel C. *67*
  Earlier sketch in SATA *1*
Hawthorne, Captain R. M.
  See Ellis, Edward S(ylvester)
Hawthorne, Nathaniel 1804-1864
  See YABC *2*
  See also CLR *103*
Hay, Jeff T. *154*
Hay, John 1915- *13*
Hay, Timothy
  See Brown, Margaret Wise
Hayashi, Leslie Ann 1954- *115*
Hayashi, Nancy 1939- *186*
  Earlier sketch in SATA *80*
Haycak, Cara 1961- *180*
Haycock, Kate 1962- *77*
Haycraft, Howard 1905-1991 .... *6*
  Obituary *70*
Haycraft, Molly Costain 1911- *6*
Hayden, Gwendolen Lampshire 1904- *35*
Hayden, Robert C(arter), Jr. 1937- *47*
  Brief entry *28*
Hayden, Robert E(arl) 1913-1980 .... *19*
  Obituary *26*
Hayden, Torey L. 1951- *163*
  Earlier sketch in SATA *65*
Hayden, Torey Lynn
  See Hayden, Torey L.
Hayes, Carlton J(oseph) H(untley)
  1882-1964 .... *11*
Hayes, Daniel 1952- *109*
  Earlier sketch in SATA *73*
Hayes, Geoffrey 1947- *91*
  Earlier sketch in SATA *26*
Hayes, Joe 1945- *131*
  Earlier sketch in SATA *88*
Hayes, John F. 1904-1980 .... *11*
Hayes, Rosemary *158*
Hayes, Sheila 1937- *51*
  Brief entry *50*
Hayes, Will *7*
Hayes, William D(imitt) 1913-1976 .... *8*
Haynes, Betsy 1937- *94*
  Brief entry *37*
  Earlier sketch in SATA *48*
  See also CLR *90*
Haynes, David 1955- *97*
Haynes, Linda
  See Swinford, Betty (June Wells)
Haynes, Mary 1938- *65*
Haynes, Max 1956- *72*
Hays, H(offmann) R(eynolds) 1904-1980 .... *26*
Hays, Thomas Anthony 1957- *84*
Hays, Tony
  See Hays, Thomas Anthony
Hays, Wilma Pitchford 1909- *28*
  Earlier sketch in SATA *1*
  See also CLR *59*
  See also SAAS *3*
Hayward, Linda 1943- *185*
  Brief entry *39*
  Earlier sketch in SATA *101*
Haywood, Carolyn 1898-1990 .... *75*
  Obituary *64*
  Earlier sketches in SATA *1, 29*
  See also CLR *22*
Hazell, Rebecca (Eileen) 1947- *141*
Hazen, Barbara Shook 1930- *178*
  Earlier sketches in SATA *27, 90*

Head, Gay
　See Hauser, Margaret L(ouise)
Head, Tom 1978- 167
Headley, Elizabeth
　See Harrison, Elizabeth (Allen) Cavanna
Headley, Justina Chen 1968- 176
Headstrom, (Birger) Richard 1902-1985 8
Heady, Eleanor B(utler) 1917-1979 8
Heagy, William D. 1964- 76
Heal, Edith 1903-1995 7
Heal, Gillian 1934- 89
Heale, Jay (Jeremy Peter Wingfield) 1937- .. 84
Healey, Brooks
　See Albert, Burton
Healey, Larry 1927- 44
　Brief entry 42
Heap, Sue 1954- 187
　Earlier sketch in SATA 150
Heaps, Willard A(llison) 1908-1987 26
Hearn, Diane Dawson 1952- 79
Hearn, Emily
　See Valleau, Emily
Hearn, Julie 1958- 152
Hearn, Lian
　See Rubinstein, Gillian
Hearn, Sneed
　See Gregg, Andrew K.
Hearne, Betsy 1942- 146
　Earlier sketches in SATA 38, 95
Heath, Charles D(ickinson) 1941- 46
Heath, Veronica
　See Blackett, Veronica Heath
Heaven, Constance (Christina) 1911- 7
Hebert-Collins, Sheila 1948- 111
Hecht, George J(oseph) 1895-1980
　Obituary 22
Hecht, Henri Joseph 1922- 9
Hechtkopf, Henryk 1910- 17
Heck, Bessie (Mildred) Holland 1911-1995 . 26
Heck, Ed 1963- 173
Heckert, Connie K(aye Delp) 1948- 82
Hedderwick, Mairi 1939- 145
　Earlier sketches in SATA 30, 77
Hedges, Sid(ney) G(eorge) 1897-1974 28
Hedrick, Irene Hope 1920- 175
Heelan, Jamee Riggio 1965- 146
Heerboth, Sharon
　See Leon, Sharon
Heffernan, John 1949- 168
　Earlier sketch in SATA 121
Heffron, Dorris 1944- 68
Hefter, Richard 1942- 31
Hegarty, Reginald Beaton 1906-1973 10
Hehenberger, Shelly 1968- 126
Heidbreder, Robert K. 1947- 130
Heide, Florence Parry 1919- 192
　Earlier sketches in SATA 32, 69, 118
　See also CLR 60
　See also SAAS 6
Heiderstadt, Dorothy 1907-2001 6
Heidi Louise
　See Erdrich, Louise
Heidler, David S(tephen) 1955- 132
Heidler, Jeanne T. 1956- 132
Heilbroner, Joan Knapp 1922- 63
Heilbrun, Lois Hussey 1922(?)-1987
　Obituary 54
Heiligman, Deborah 1958- 193
　Earlier sketches in SATA 90, 144
Heilman, Joan Rattner 50
Heimann, Rolf 1940- 164
　Earlier sketch in SATA 120
Hein, Lucille Eleanor 1915-1994 20
Heine, Helme 1941- 135
　Earlier sketch in SATA 67
　See also CLR 18
Heinlein, Robert A. 1907-1988 69
　Obituary 56
　Earlier sketch in SATA 9
　See also CLR 75

Heinlein, Robert Anson
　See Heinlein, Robert A.
Heins, Ethel L(eah) 1918-1997 101
Heins, Paul 1909- 13
Heintze, Carl 1922- 26
Heinz, Bill
　See Heinz, W.C.
Heinz, Brian J. 1946- 181
　Earlier sketch in SATA 95
Heinz, Brian James
　See Heinz, Brian J.
Heinz, W.C. 1915-2008 26
Heinz, Wilfred Charles
　See Heinz, W.C.
Heinzen, Mildred
　See Masters, Mildred
Heisel, Sharon E(laine) 1941- 125
　Earlier sketch in SATA 84
Heitzmann, William Ray 1948- 73
Heitzmann, Wm. Ray
　See Heitzmann, William Ray
Helakoski, Leslie 178
Helberg, Shirley Adelaide Holden 1919- ... 138
Helfer, Andrew 187
Helfer, Ralph 1937- 177
Helfman, Elizabeth S(eaver) 1911-2001 3
Helfman, Harry Carmozin 1910-1995 3
Helgerson, Joseph 1950- 181
Hellard, Susan 182
Hellberg, Hans-Eric 1927- 38
Heller, Linda 1944- 46
　Brief entry 40
Heller, Mike
　See Hano, Arnold
Heller, Ruth M. 1924- 112
　Earlier sketch in SATA 66
Hellman, Hal
　See Hellman, Harold
Hellman, Harold 1927- 4
Helman, Andrea (Jean) 1946- 160
　Earlier sketch in SATA 107
Helmer, Diana Star 1962- 86
Helmer, Marilyn 160
　Earlier sketch in SATA 112
Helps, Racey 1913-1971 2
　Obituary 25
Helquist, Brett 187
　Earlier sketch in SATA 146
Helweg, Hans H. 1917- 50
　Brief entry 33
Helyar, Jane Penelope Josephine 1933- 138
　Autobiography Feature 138
　Earlier sketch in SATA 82
　See Poole, Josephine
Hemmant, Lynette 1938- 69
Hemming, Roy G. 1928-1995 11
　Obituary 86
Hemphill, Helen 1955- 179
Hemphill, Kris (Harrison) 1963- 118
Hemphill, Martha Locke 1904-1973 37
Hemphill, Stephanie 190
Hemstock, Gillian 1956- 173
Henba, Bobbie 1926- 87
Henbest, Nigel 1951- 55
　Brief entry 52
Henderley, Brooks 1
Henderson, Aileen Kilgore 1921- 178
Henderson, Aileen Mary
　See Fox, Aileen
Henderson, Gordon 1950- 53
Henderson, Kathy 1949- 155
　Brief entry 53
　Earlier sketches in SATA 55, 95
Henderson, LeGrand 1901-1965 9
Henderson, Nancy Wallace 1916- 22
Henderson, Zenna (Chlarson) 1917-1983 5
Hendrickson, Walter Brookfield, Jr. 1936- 9
Hendry, Diana 1941- 106
　Earlier sketch in SATA 68
Hendry, Frances Mary 1941- 171
　Earlier sketch in SATA 110

Hendry, Linda (Gail) 1961- 83
Heneghan, James 1930- 160
　Earlier sketches in SATA 53, 97
Henkes, Kevin 1960- 154
　Earlier sketches in SATA 43, 76, 108
　See also CLR 108
Hennessy, Barbara G.
　See Hennessy, B.G.
Hennessy, Barbara Gulbrandsen
　See Hennessy, B.G.
Hennessy, B.G. 1951- 175
Henney, Carolee Wells 1928- 102
Henriod, Lorraine 1925- 26
Henriquez, Emile F. 1937- 170
　Earlier sketch in SATA 89
Henry, April 1959- 174
Henry, Ernest 1948- 107
Henry, Joanne Landers 1927- 6
Henry, Maeve 1960- 75
Henry, Marguerite 1902-1997 100
　Obituary 99
　See also CLR 4
　See also SAAS 7
Henry, Marie H. 1935- 65
Henry, Marilyn 1939- 117
Henry, Marion
　See del Rey, Lester
Henry, O.
　See Porter, William Sydney
Henry, Oliver
　See Porter, William Sydney
Henry, T. E.
　See Rowland-Entwistle, (Arthur) Theodore
　(Henry)
Henschel, Elizabeth Georgie 56
Henson, James Maury
　See Henson, Jim
Henson, Jim 1936-1990 43
　Obituary 65
Henstra, Friso 1928- 73
　Earlier sketch in SATA 8
　See also SAAS 14
Hentoff, Nat(han Irving) 1925- 133
　Brief entry 27
　Earlier sketches in SATA 42, 69
　See also CLR 52
Henty, G(eorge) A(lfred) 1832-1902 64
　See also CLR 76
Heo, Yumi 1964- 146
　Earlier sketch in SATA 94
Hepler, Heather 177
Herald, Kathleen
　See Peyton, Kathleen Wendy (Herald)
Herb, Angela M. 1970- 92
Herbert, Cecil
　See Hamilton, Charles (Harold St. John)
Herbert, Don 1917-2007 2
　Obituary 184
Herbert, Donald Jeffrey
　See Herbert, Don
Herbert, Frank 1920-1986 37
　Obituary 47
　Earlier sketch in SATA 9
Herbert, Frank Patrick
　See Herbert, Frank
Herbert, Helen (Jean) 1947- 57
Herbert, Janis 1956- 139
Herbert, Wally 1934-2007 23
Herbert, Walter William
　See Herbert, Wally
Herbst, Judith 1947- 74
Herda, D.J. 1948- 80
Herge
　See CLR 114
　See Remi, Georges
Heritage, Martin
　See Horler, Sydney
Herkimer, L(awrence) R(ussell) 1925(?)- 42
Herlihy, Dirlie Anne 1935- 73
Herman, Charlotte 1937- 99
　Earlier sketch in SATA 20

Hermanson, Dennis (Everett) 1947- *10*
Hermes, Jules 1962- *92*
Hermes, Patricia 1936- *191*
  Earlier sketches in SATA *31, 78, 141*
Hermes, Patricia Mary
  See Hermes, Patricia
Hernandez, Natalie Nelson 1929- *123*
Herndon, Ernest *91*
Herold, Ann Bixby 1937- *72*
Herrera, Juan Felipe 1948- *127*
Herrick, Steven 1958- *156*
  Earlier sketch in SATA *103*
Herriman, George (Joseph) 1880-1944 .... *140*
Herriot, James 1916-1995 .... *135*
  Earlier sketch in SATA *86*
  See also CLR *80*
  See Wight, James Alfred
Herrmanns, Ralph 1933- *11*
Herrold, Tracey
  See Dils, Tracey E.
Herron, Edward A(lbert) 1912- *4*
Herschler, Mildred Barger *130*
Hersey, John 1914-1993 .... *25*
  Obituary *76*
Hersey, John Richard
  See Hersey, John
  and Hersey, John
Hershberger, Priscilla (Gorman) 1951- *81*
Hershenhorn, Esther 1945- *151*
Hershey, Kathleen M. 1934- *80*
Hershey, Mary *173*
Hersom, Kathleen 1911- *73*
Hertz, Grete Janus 1915- *23*
Herzig, Alison Cragin 1935- *87*
Herzog, Brad 1968- *131*
Heslewood, Juliet 1951- *82*
Hess, Lilo 1916- *4*
Hess, Paul 1961- *134*
Hesse, Hermann 1877-1962 .... *50*
Hesse, Karen 1952- *158*
  Autobiography Feature *113*
  Earlier sketches in SATA *74, 103*
  See also CLR *54*
  See also SAAS *25*
Hest, Amy 1950- *193*
  Earlier sketches in SATA *55, 82, 129*
Heuer, Kenneth John 1927- *44*
Heuman, William 1912-1971 .... *21*
Heuston, Kimberley 1960- *167*
Heuston, Kimberley Burton
  See Heuston, Kimberley
Hewes, Agnes Danforth 1874-1963 .... *35*
Hewett, Anita 1918-1989 .... *13*
Hewett, Joan 1930- *140*
  Earlier sketch in SATA *81*
Hewett, Richard 1929- *81*
Hewitson, Jennifer 1961- *97*
Hewitt, Margaret 1961- *84*
Hewitt, Sally 1949- *127*
Hext, Harrington
  See Phillpotts, Eden
Hey, Nigel S(tewart) 1936- *20*
Heyduck-Huth, Hilde 1929- *8*
Heyer, Carol 1950- *130*
  Earlier sketch in SATA *74*
Heyer, Marilee 1942- *102*
  Earlier sketch in SATA *64*
Heyerdahl, Thor 1914-2002 .... *52*
  Earlier sketch in SATA *2*
Heyes, (Nancy) Eileen 1956- *150*
  Earlier sketch in SATA *80*
Heyliger, William 1884-1955
  See YABC *1*
Heyman, Ken(neth Louis) 1930- *114*
  Earlier sketch in SATA *34*
Heyward, (Edwin) DuBose 1885-1940 .... *21*
Heywood, Karen 1946- *48*
Hezlep, William (Earl) 1936- *88*
Hibbert, Christopher 1924- *4*

Hibbert, Eleanor Alice Burford 1906-1993 .... *2*
  Obituary *74*
  See Holt, Victoria
Hickman, Estella (Lee) 1942- *111*
Hickman, Janet 1940- *127*
  Earlier sketch in SATA *12*
Hickman, Martha Whitmore 1925- *26*
Hickman, Pamela 1958- *186*
  Earlier sketch in SATA *128*
Hickock, Will
  See Harrison, C(hester) William
Hickok, Lorena A. 1893-1968 .... *20*
Hickox, Rebecca (Ayres) *116*
Hicks, Barbara Jean 1953- *165*
Hicks, Betty *191*
Hicks, Clifford B. 1920- *50*
Hicks, Eleanor B.
  See Coerr, Eleanor (Beatrice)
Hicks, Harvey
  See Stratemeyer, Edward L.
Hicks, Peter 1952- *111*
Hicyilmaz, Gaye 1947- *157*
  Earlier sketch in SATA *77*
Hieatt, Constance B(artlett) 1928- *4*
Hiebert, Ray Eldon 1932- *13*
Higdon, Hal 1931- *4*
Higginbottom, David 1923- *87*
  See Fisk, Nicholas
Higginbottom, J(effrey) Winslow 1945- *29*
Higgins, Joanna 1945- *125*
Higgins, Simon (Richard) 1958- *105*
Higginsen, Vy *79*
High, Linda Oatman 1958- *188*
  Autobiography Feature *188*
  Earlier sketches in SATA *94, 145*
High, Philip E. 1914- *119*
High, Philip Empson
  See High, Philip E.
Higham, David (Michael) 1949- *50*
Higham, Jon Atlas
  See Higham, Jonathan Huw
Higham, Jonathan Huw 1960- *59*
Highet, Helen
  See MacInnes, Helen (Clark)
Hightman, Jason 1971(?)- *189*
Hightman, J.P.
  See Hightman, Jason
Hightower, Florence Cole 1916-1981 .... *4*
  Obituary *27*
Highwater, Jamake (Mamake)
  1942(?)-2001 .... *69*
  Brief entry *30*
  Earlier sketch in SATA *32*
  See also CLR *17*
Hilb, Nora 1953- *178*
Hildebrandt, Greg 1939- *172*
  Brief entry *33*
  Earlier sketch in SATA *55*
Hildebrandt, Tim 1939-2006 .... *55*
  Brief entry *33*
Hildebrandt, Timothy
  See Hildebrandt, Tim
Hildebrandts, The
  See Hildebrandt, Greg
  and Hildebrandt, Tim
Hilder, Rowland 1905-1993 .... *36*
  Obituary *77*
Hildick, E. W.
  See SAAS *6*
  See Hildick, (Edmund) Wallace
Hildick, (Edmund) Wallace 1925-2001 .... *68*
  Earlier sketch in SATA *2*
  See Hildick, E. W.
Hilgartner, Beth 1957- *58*
Hill, Alexis
  See Craig, Mary (Francis) Shura
  and Glick, Ruth (Burtnick)
Hill, Anthony R. 1942- *164*
  Earlier sketch in SATA *91*
Hill, Anthony Robert
  See Hill, Anthony R.

Hill, David 1942- *152*
  Earlier sketch in SATA *103*
Hill, Donna (Marie) 1921- *124*
  Earlier sketch in SATA *24*
Hill, Douglas 1935-2007 .... *78*
  Earlier sketch in SATA *39*
Hill, Douglas Arthur
  See Hill, Douglas
Hill, Elizabeth Starr 1925- *143*
  Earlier sketch in SATA *24*
Hill, Eric 1927- *133*
  Brief entry *53*
  Earlier sketch in SATA *66*
  See also CLR *13*
Hill, Gordon
  See Eldin, Peter
Hill, Grace Brooks *67*
  Earlier sketch in SATA *1*
Hill, Grace Livingston 1865-1947
  See YABC *2*
Hill, Helen M(orey) 1915- *27*
Hill, John
  See Koontz, Dean R.
Hill, Johnson
  See Kunhardt, Edith
Hill, Judy I. R.
  See Roberts, Judy I.
Hill, Kathleen Louise 1917- *4*
Hill, Kay
  See Hill, Kathleen Louise
Hill, Kirkpatrick 1938- *188*
  Earlier sketches in SATA *72, 126*
Hill, Laban Carrick *170*
Hill, Lee Sullivan 1958- *96*
Hill, Lorna 1902-1991 .... *12*
Hill, Margaret (Ohler) 1915- *36*
Hill, Meg
  See Hill, Margaret (Ohler)
Hill, Meredith
  See Craig, Mary (Francis) Shura
Hill, Monica
  See Watson, Jane Werner
Hill, Pamela Smith 1954- *112*
Hill, Ralph Nading 1917-1987 .... *65*
Hill, Robert W(hite) 1919-1982 .... *12*
  Obituary *31*
Hill, Ruth A.
  See Viguers, Ruth Hill
Hill, Ruth Livingston
  See Munce, Ruth Hill
Hill, Stuart 1958- *186*
Hill, Susan 1942- *183*
Hill, Susan Elizabeth
  See Hill, Susan
Hill, Susanna Leonard 1965- *193*
Hill, Thomas 1960- *82*
Hillcourt, William 1900-1992 .... *27*
Hillenbrand, Will 1960- *147*
  Earlier sketch in SATA *84*
Hiller, Ilo (Ann) 1938- *59*
Hillerman, Tony 1925-2008 .... *6*
Hillert, Margaret 1920- *91*
  Earlier sketch in SATA *8*
Hilliard, Richard *183*
Hillman, Elizabeth 1942- *75*
Hillman, John 1952- *120*
Hillman, Martin
  See Hill, Douglas
Hillman, Priscilla 1940- *48*
  Brief entry *39*
Hills, C.A.R. 1955- *39*
Hills, Charles Albert Reis
  See Hills, C.A.R.
Hills, Tad *173*
Hilton, Irene Pothus -1979 .... *7*
Hilton, James 1900-1954 .... *34*
Hilton, Margaret Lynette 1946- *105*
  Earlier sketch in SATA *68*
  See Hilton, Nette

Hilton, Nette
  See CLR 25
  See also SAAS 21
  See Hilton, Margaret Lynette
Hilton, Ralph 1907-1982 8
Hilton, Suzanne 1922- 4
Hilton-Bruce, Anne
  See Hilton, Margaret Lynette
Him, George 1937-1982
  Obituary 30
Himelblau, Linda -2005 179
Himelstein, Shmuel 1940- 83
Himler, Ann 1946- 8
Himler, Ronald 1937- 183
  Earlier sketches in SATA 6, 92, 137
Himler, Ronald Norbert
  See Himler, Ronald
Himmelman, John C(arl) 1959- 159
  Earlier sketches in SATA 47, 94
Hinckley, Helen
  See Jones, Helen Hinckley
Hind, Dolores (Ellen) 1931- 53
  Brief entry 49
Hindin, Nathan
  See Bloch, Robert (Albert)
Hindley, Judy 1940- 179
  Earlier sketch in SATA 120
Hinds, P(atricia) Mignon 98
Hines, Anna Grossnickle 1946- 141
  Brief entry 45
  Earlier sketches in SATA 51, 95
  See also SAAS 16
Hines, Gary (Roger) 1944- 136
  Earlier sketch in SATA 74
Hinojosa, Maria (de Lourdes) 1961- 88
Hinton, Nigel 1941- 166
Hinton, Sam 1917- 43
Hinton, S.E. 1950- 160
  Earlier sketches in SATA 19, 58, 115
  See also CLR 23
Hinton, Susan Eloise
  See Hinton, S.E.
Hintz, Martin 1945- 128
  Brief entry 39
  Earlier sketch in SATA 47
Hintz, Stephen V. 1975- 129
Hippopotamus, Eugene H.
  See Kraus, (Herman) Robert
Hirano, Cathy 1957- 68
Hirsch, Karen 1941- 61
Hirsch, Odo 157
  Earlier sketch in SATA 111
Hirsch, Phil 1926- 35
Hirsch, S. Carl 1913-1990 2
  See also SAAS 7
Hirschfelder, Arlene B. 1943- 138
  Earlier sketch in SATA 80
Hirschi, Ron 1948- 192
  Earlier sketches in SATA 56, 95
Hirschmann, Linda (Ann) 1941- 40
Hirsh, Marilyn 1944-1988 7
  Obituary 58
Hirshberg, Al(bert Simon) 1909-1973 38
Hiscock, Bruce 1940- 137
  Earlier sketch in SATA 57
Hiser, Constance 1950- 71
Hiser, Iona Seibert -1998 4
Hislop, Julia Rose Catherine 1962- 74
Hissey, Jane 1952- 130
  Autobiography Feature 130
  Earlier sketches in SATA 58, 103
Hissey, Jane Elizabeth
  See Hissey, Jane
Hitchcock, Alfred (Joseph) 1899-1980 27
  Obituary 24
Hite, Sid 1954- 175
  Earlier sketches in SATA 75, 136
Hitte, Kathryn 1919- 16

Hitz, Demi 1942- 152
  Earlier sketches in SATA 11, 66, 102
  See also CLR 58
  See Demi
Hitzeroth, Deborah L. 1961- 78
Hnizdovsky, Jacques 1915- 32
Ho, Louise 185
Ho, Minfong 1951- 151
  Earlier sketches in SATA 15, 94
  See also CLR 28
Hoagland, Edward (Morley) 1932- 51
Hoare, Robert J(ohn) 1921-1975 38
Hoban, Lillian 1925-1998 69
  Obituary 104
  Earlier sketch in SATA 22
  See also CLR 67
Hoban, Russell 1925- 136
  Earlier sketches in SATA 1, 40, 78
  See also CLR 139
Hoban, Russell Conwell
  See Hoban, Russell
Hoban, Tana 1917(?)-2006 104
  Obituary 173
  Earlier sketches in SATA 22, 70
  See also CLR 76
  See also SAAS 12
Hobart, Lois (Elaine) 7
Hobbie, Holly 1944- 178
  See also CLR 88
Hobbie, Jocelyn 190
Hobbs, Leigh 1953- 166
Hobbs, Valerie 1941- 193
  Autobiography Feature 145
  Earlier sketches in SATA 93, 145
Hobbs, Will 1947- 177
  Autobiography Feature 127
  Earlier sketches in SATA 72, 110
  See also CLR 59
Hobbs, William Carl
  See Hobbs, Will
Hoberman, Mary Ann 1930- 158
  Earlier sketches in SATA 5, 72, 111
  See also CLR 22
  See also SAAS 18
Hobson, Bruce 1950- 62
Hobson, Burton (Harold) 1933- 28
Hobson, Laura Z(ametkin) 1900-1986 52
Hobson, Sally 1967- 172
  Earlier sketch in SATA 84
Hoce, Charley E. 174
Hochschild, Arlie Russell 1940- 11
Hockaby, Stephen
  See Mitchell, Gladys (Maude Winifred)
Hockenberry, Hope
  See Newell, Hope Hockenberry
Hodge, Deborah 1954- 163
  Earlier sketch in SATA 122
Hodge, P. W.
  See Hodge, Paul W(illiam)
Hodge, Paul W(illiam) 1934- 12
Hodgell, P(atricia) C(hristine) 1951- 42
Hodges, C. Walter 1909-2004 2
  Obituary 158
Hodges, Carl G. 1902-1964 10
Hodges, Cyril Walter
  See Hodges, C. Walter
Hodges, Elizabeth Jamison 1
Hodges, Margaret 1911-2005 167
  Obituary 172
  Earlier sketches in SATA 1, 33, 75, 117
  See also SAAS 9
Hodges, Margaret Moore
  See Hodges, Margaret
Hodgetts, Blake Christopher 1967- 43
Hodgson, Harriet (W.) 1935- 84
Hoehne, Marcia 1951- 89
Hoellwarth, Cathryn Clinton
  See Clinton, Cathryn
Hoestlandt, Jo 1948- 94
Hoestlandt, Jocelyne
  See Hoestlandt, Jo

Hoexter, Corinne K. 1927- 6
Hoeye, Michael 1947- 136
Hoff, Carol 1900-1979 11
Hoff, Mary (King) 1956- 157
  Earlier sketch in SATA 74
Hoff, Syd(ney) 1912-2004 138
  Obituary 154
  Earlier sketches in SATA 9, 72
  See also CLR 83
  See also SAAS 4
Hoffman, Edwin D. 49
Hoffman, Elizabeth P(arkinson) 1921-2003
  Obituary 153
Hoffman, Mary (Margaret) 1945- 144
  Earlier sketches in SATA 59, 97
  See also SAAS 24
  See Lassiter, Mary
Hoffman, Mat 1972- 150
Hoffman, Nina Kiriki 1955- 160
Hoffman, Phyllis M(iriam) 1944- 4
Hoffman, Rosekrans 1926- 15
Hoffmann, E(rnst) T(heodor) A(madeus)
  1776-1822 27
  See also CLR 133
Hoffmann, Felix 1911-1975 9
Hoffmann, Heinrich 1809-1894
  See CLR 122
Hoffmann, Margaret Jones 1910- 48
Hoffmann, Peggy
  See Hoffmann, Margaret Jones
Hofher, Catherine Baxley 1954- 130
Hofher, Cathy
  See Hofher, Catherine Baxley
Hofmeyr, Dianne (Louise) 138
Hofsepian, Sylvia A. 1932- 74
Hofsinde, Robert 1902-1973 21
Hogan, Bernice Harris 1929- 12
Hogan, Inez 1895-1973 2
Hogan, James P(atrick) 1941- 81
Hogan, Jamie 192
Hogan, Linda 1947- 132
Hogarth, Burne 1911-1996 89
  Earlier sketch in SATA 63
Hogarth, Grace (Weston Allen) 1905-1995 .. 91
Hogarth, Jr.
  See Kent, Rockwell
Hogarth, (Arthur) Paul 1917-2001 41
Hogg, Garry 1902-1976 2
Hogg, Gary 1957- 172
  Earlier sketch in SATA 105
Hogner, Dorothy Childs 4
Hogner, Nils 1893-1970 25
Hogrogian, Nonny 1932- 74
  Autobiography Feature 127
  Earlier sketch in SATA 7
  See also CLR 95
  See also SAAS 1
Hoh, Diane 1937- 102
  Brief entry 48
  Earlier sketch in SATA 52
Hoke, Helen
  Obituary 65
  See Watts, Helen L. Hoke
Hoke, John (Lindsay) 1925- 7
Hokenson, Terry 1948- 193
Hol, Coby 1943- 126
Holabird, Katharine 1948- 135
  Earlier sketch in SATA 62
Holaday, Bobbie 1922- 153
Holbeach, Henry
  See Rands, William Brighty
Holberg, Ruth L(angland) 1889-1984 1
Holbrook, Kathy 1963- 107
Holbrook, Peter
  See Glick, Carl (Cannon)
Holbrook, Sabra
  See Erickson, Sabra Rollins
Holbrook, Sara 131
Holbrook, Stewart Hall 1893-1964 2
Holcomb, Jerry (Leona) Kimble 1927- 113

Holcomb, Nan
  See McPhee, Norma H.
Holden, Elizabeth Rhoda
  See Lawrence, Louise
Holding, James (Clark Carlisle, Jr.)
  1907-1997 3
  See Queen, Ellery
Holeman, Linda 1949- 136
  Autobiography Feature 136
  Earlier sketch in SATA *102*
Holinger, William (Jacques) 1944- 90
Holisher, Desider 1901-1972 6
Holl, Adelaide Hinkle 1910- 8
Holl, Kristi D(iane) 1951- 51
Holland, Gay W. 1941- 128
Holland, Isabelle (Christian) 1920-2002 70
  Autobiography Feature 103
  Obituary 132
  Earlier sketch in SATA *8*
  See also CLR *57*
Holland, Janice 1913-1962 18
Holland, John L(ewis) 1919- 20
Holland, Joyce
  See Morice, Dave
Holland, Julia 1954- 106
Holland, Lynda (H.) 1959- 77
Holland, Lys
  See Gater, Dilys
Holland, Marion 1908-1989 6
  Obituary 61
Hollander, John 1929- 13
Hollander, Nicole 1940(?)- 101
Hollander, Paul
  See Silverberg, Robert
Hollander, Phyllis 1928- 39
Hollander, Zander 1923- 63
Holldobler, Turid 1939- 26
Holliday, Joe
  See Holliday, Joseph
Holliday, Joseph 1910- 11
Holling, Holling C(lancy) 1900-1973 15
  Obituary 26
  See also CLR *50*
Hollingsworth, Alvin C(arl) 1930- 39
Hollingsworth, Mary 1947- 166
  Earlier sketch in SATA *91*
Holloway, Teresa (Bragunier) 1906- 26
Holm, (Else) Anne (Lise) 1922-1998 1
  See also CLR *75*
  See also SAAS *7*
Holm, Jennifer L. 1968(?)- 183
  Earlier sketches in SATA *120, 163*
Holm, Matthew 1974- 174
Holm, Sharon Lane 1955- 114
  Earlier sketch in SATA *78*
Holman, Felice 1919- 82
  Earlier sketch in SATA *7*
  See also SAAS *17*
Holm and Hamel
  See Holm, Jennifer L.
Holme, Bryan 1913-1990 26
  Obituary 66
Holmes, Barbara Ware 1945- 127
  Earlier sketch in SATA *65*
Holmes, Elizabeth 1957- 191
Holmes, Elizabeth Ann
  See Holmes, Elizabeth
Holmes, John
  See Souster, (Holmes) Raymond
Holmes, Marjorie (Rose) 1910-2002 43
Holmes, Martha 1961- 72
Holmes, Mary Z(astrow) 1943- 80
Holmes, Oliver Wendell 1809-1894 34
Holmes, Peggy 1898- 60
Holmes, Raymond
  See Souster, (Holmes) Raymond
Holmes, Rick
  See Hardwick, Richard Holmes, Jr.
Holmes, Sara Lewis 186
Holmgren, Helen Jean 1930- 45

Holmgren, Sister George Ellen
  See Holmgren, Helen Jean
Holmgren, Virginia C(unningham) 1909- 26
Holmquist, Eve 1921- 11
Holt, Kimberly Willis 1960- 179
  Earlier sketch in SATA *122*
Holt, Margaret 1937- 4
Holt, Margaret Van Vechten (Saunders)
  1899-1963 32
Holt, Michael (Paul) 1929- 13
Holt, Rackham
  See Holt, Margaret Van Vechten (Saunders)
Holt, Rochelle L. 41
  See DuBois, Rochelle (Lynn) Holt
Holt, Stephen
  See Thompson, Harlan (Howard)
Holt, Victoria
  See Hibbert, Eleanor Alice Burford
Holton, Leonard
  See Wibberley, Leonard (Patrick O'Connor)
Holtze, Sally Holmes 1952- 64
Holtzman, Jerome 1926-2008 57
  Obituary 194
Holub, Joan 1956- 149
  Earlier sketch in SATA *99*
Holub, Josef 1926- 175
Holubitsky, Katherine 1955- 165
  Earlier sketch in SATA *121*
Holyer, Erna Maria 1925- 22
Holyer, Ernie
  See Holyer, Erna Maria
Holz, Loretta (Marie) 1943- 17
Homel, David 1952- 97
Homze, Alma C. 1932- 17
Honey, Elizabeth 1947- 137
  Autobiography Feature 137
  Earlier sketch in SATA *112*
Honeycutt, Natalie 1945- 97
Hong, Lily Toy 1958- 76
Hong, Maxine Ting Ting
  See Kingston, Maxine Hong
Honig, Donald 1931- 18
Honness, Elizabeth H. 1904- 2
Hoobler, Dorothy 1941- 161
  Earlier sketches in SATA *28, 109*
Hoobler, Thomas 161
  Earlier sketches in SATA *28, 109*
Hood, Joseph F. 1925- 4
Hood, Robert E. 1926- 21
Hood, Sarah
  See Killough, (Karen) Lee
Hook, Brendan 1963- 105
Hook, Frances 1912-1983 27
Hook, Geoffrey R(aynor) 1928- 103
Hook, Jeff
  See Hook, Geoffrey R(aynor)
Hook, Martha 1936- 27
Hooker, Richard
  See Heinz, W.C.
Hooker, Ruth 1920-1998 21
hooks, bell 1952(?)- 170
  Earlier sketch in SATA *115*
Hooks, William H(arris) 1921- 94
  Earlier sketch in SATA *16*
Hoon, Patricia Easterly 1954- 90
Hooper, Byrd
  See St. Clair, Byrd Hooper
Hooper, Mary 1948- 160
Hooper, Maureen Brett 1927- 76
Hooper, Meredith 1939- 159
  Earlier sketches in SATA *28, 101*
Hooper, Meredith Jean
  See Hooper, Meredith
Hooper, Patricia 1941- 95
Hoopes, Lyn Littlefield 1953- 49
  Brief entry 44
Hoopes, Ned E(dward) 1932- 21
Hoopes, Roy 1922- 11
Hoose, Phillip M. 1947- 137

Hoover, H(elen) M(ary) 1935- 132
  Brief entry 33
  Earlier sketches in SATA *44, 83*
  See also SAAS *8*
Hoover, Helen (Drusilla Blackburn)
  1910-1984 12
  Obituary 39
Hope, Christopher 1944- 62
Hope, Christopher David Tully
  See Hope, Christopher
Hope, Laura Lee 67
  Earlier sketch in SATA *1*
  See Goulart, Ron(ald Joseph)
  and Stanley, George Edward
Hope Simpson, Jacynth 1930- 12
Hopf, Alice (Martha) L(ightner) 1904-1988 ... 5
  Obituary 55
Hopkins, A. T.
  See Turngren, Annette
Hopkins, C. M.
  See Hopkins, Cathy
Hopkins, Cathy 1953- 165
Hopkins, Cathy M.
  See Hopkins, Cathy
Hopkins, Clark 1895-1976
  Obituary 34
Hopkins, Ellen L. 1955- 128
Hopkins, Jackie
  See Hopkins, Jackie Mims
Hopkins, Jackie Mims 1952- 178
  Earlier sketch in SATA *92*
Hopkins, Joseph G(erard) E(dward) 1909- ... 11
Hopkins, (Hector) Kenneth 1914-1988
  Obituary 58
Hopkins, Lee Bennett 1938- 168
  Earlier sketches in SATA *3, 68, 125*
  See also CLR *44*
  See also SAAS *4*
Hopkins, Lyman
  See Folsom, Franklin (Brewster)
Hopkins, Marjorie 1911-1999 9
Hopkins, Mary R(ice) 1956- 97
Hopkinson, Amanda 1948- 84
Hopkinson, Deborah 1952- 180
  Autobiography Feature 180
  Earlier sketches in SATA *76, 108, 159*
  See also CLR *118*
Hopman, Philip 1961- 177
Hoppe, Joanne 1932- 42
Hoppe, Matthias 1952- 76
Hopper, Nancy J. 1937- 38
  Brief entry 35
Hopping, Lorraine Jean
  See Egan, Lorraine Hopping
Horacek, Petr 163
Horenstein, Henry 1947- 108
Horgan, Paul (George Vincent O'Shaughnessy)
  1903-1995 13
  Obituary 84
Horlak, E.E.
  See Tepper, Sheri S.
Horler, Sydney 1888-1954 102
Horn, Sandra Ann 1944- 154
Hornblow, Arthur, Jr. 1893-1976 15
Hornblow, Leonora 1920-2005 18
  Obituary 171
Hornblow, Leonora Schinasi
  See Hornblow, Leonora
Horne, Constance 1927- 149
Horne, Richard 1960-2007 169
  Obituary 180
  Earlier sketch in SATA *111*
Horne, Richard Henry Hengist
  1802(?)-1884 29
Horner, Althea (Jane) 1926- 36
Horner, Dave 1934- 12
Horner, Jack
  See Horner, John R(obert)
Horner, John R(obert) 1946- 106
Hornik, Laurie Miller 159

Horniman, Joanne 1951- 167
Earlier sketch in SATA 98
Hornos, Axel 1907-1994 20
Hornstein, Reuben Aaron 1912- 64
Horowitz, Anthony 1955- 195
Earlier sketch in SATA 137
Horowitz, Dave 1973(?)- 172
Horowitz, Ruth 1957- 136
Horrocks, Anita 1958- 169
Horse, Harry
See Horne, Richard
Horsfield, Alan 1939- 153
Hort, Lenny 179
Horton, James O. 1943- 173
Horton, James Oliver
See Horton, James O.
Horton, Madelyn (Stacey) 1962- 77
Horvath, Betty 1927- 4
Horvath, David 1972(?)- 192
Horvath, Polly 1957- 194
Earlier sketches in SATA 85, 140
See also CLR 90
Horwich, Frances R(appaport) 1908-2001 11
Obituary 130
Horwitz, Elinor Lander 45
Brief entry 33
Horwood, William 1944- 85
Hosford, Dorothy (Grant) 1900-1952 22
Hosford, Jessie 1892-1990 5
Hoshi, Shin'ichi 1926- 101
Hoshino, Felicia 1968- 189
Hoskyns-Abrahall, Clare (Constance
Drury) 13
Hosler, Danamarie 1978- 184
Hossack, Sylvia 1939- 83
Hossack, Sylvie Adams
See Hossack, Sylvia
Hosseini, Khaled 1965- 156
Hossell, Karen Price
See Price, Karen
Hosta, Dar 192
Hostetler, Marian 1932- 91
Houck, Carter 1924- 22
Hough, (Helen) Charlotte 1924- 9
Hough, Judy Taylor 1932- 63
Brief entry 51
Earlier sketch in SATA 56
Hough, Richard (Alexander) 1922-1999 17
Houghton, Eric 1930- 7
Houk, Randy 1944- 97
Houlehen, Robert J. 1918- 18
Household, Geoffrey (Edward West)
1900-1988 14
Obituary 59
Housman, Laurence 1865-1959 25
Houston, Dick 1943- 74
Houston, Gloria 138
Autobiography Feature 138
Earlier sketch in SATA 81
Houston, James A(rchibald) 1921-2005 74
Obituary 163
Earlier sketch in SATA 13
See also CLR 3
See also SAAS 17
Houston, James D. 1933- 78
Houston, Jeanne Toyo Wakatsuki
See Houston, Jeanne Wakatsuki
Houston, Jeanne Wakatsuki 1934- 168
Autobiography Feature 168
Earlier sketch in SATA 78
Houston, Juanita C. 1921- 129
Houton, Kathleen
See Kilgore, Kathleen
Houts, Amy F. 164
Hovey, Kate 158
Howard, Alan 1922- 45
Howard, Alyssa
See Buckholtz, Eileen (Garber)
and Glick, Ruth (Burtnick)
and Titchener, Louise
Howard, Arthur 1948- 165

Howard, Arthur Charles
See Howard, Arthur
Howard, Elizabeth Fitzgerald 1927- 119
Earlier sketch in SATA 74
Howard, Ellen 1943- 184
Earlier sketches in SATA 67, 99
Howard, Jane R(uble) 1924- 87
Howard, Norman Barry 1949- 90
Howard, P. M.
See Howard, Pauline Rodriguez
Howard, Paul 1967- 190
Earlier sketch in SATA 118
Howard, Pauline Rodriguez 1951- 124
Howard, Prosper
See Hamilton, Charles (Harold St. John)
Howard, Robert West 1908-1988 5
Howard, Todd 1964- 135
Howard, Tristan
See Currie, Stephen
Howard, Vernon (Linwood) 1918-1992 40
Obituary 73
Howard, Warren F.
See Pohl, Frederik
Howarth, Daniel 188
Howarth, David (Armine) 1912-1991 6
Obituary 68
Howarth, Lesley 1952- 94
Howe, Deborah 1946-1978 29
Howe, James 1946- 161
Earlier sketches in SATA 29, 71, 111
See also CLR 9
Howe, John F. 1957- 79
Howe, Norma 1930- 126
Howell, Pat 1947- 15
Howell, S.
See Styles, (Frank) Showell
Howell, Virginia
See Ellison, Virginia H(owell)
Howes, Barbara 1914-1996 5
Howie, Diana 1945- 122
Howie, Diana Melson
See Howie, Diana
Howker, Janni 1957- 72
Brief entry 46
See also CLR 14
See also SAAS 13
Howland, Ethan 1963- 131
Hoy, Linda 1946- 65
Hoy, Nina
See Roth, Arthur J(oseph)
Hoyle, Geoffrey 1942- 18
Hoyt, Ard 190
Hoyt, Edwin P(almer), Jr. 1923- 28
Hoyt, Erich 1950- 140
Earlier sketch in SATA 65
Hoyt, Olga
See Gruhzit-Hoyt, Olga (Margaret)
Hrdlitschka, Shelley 1956- 167
Earlier sketch in SATA 111
Hrdlitschka, Shelley Joanne
See Hrdlitschka, Shelley
Htin Aung, U.
See Aung, (Maung) Htin
Hu, Ying-Hwa 173
Huang, Benrei 1959- 86
Hubalek, Linda K. 1954- 111
Hubbard, Margaret Ann
See Priley, Margaret (Ann) Hubbard
Hubbard, Michelle Calabro 1953- 122
Hubbard, Patricia 1945- 124
Hubbard, Woodleigh Marx 160
Earlier sketch in SATA 98
Hubbell, Patricia 1928- 186
Earlier sketches in SATA 8, 132
Hubery, Julia 195
Hubley, Faith Elliot 1924-2001 48
Obituary 133
Hubley, John 1914-1977 48
Obituary 24
Huck, Charlotte S. 1922- 136
Earlier sketch in SATA 82

Hudak, Michal 1956- 143
Hudson, Cheryl Willis 1948- 160
Earlier sketch in SATA 81
Hudson, Jan 1954-1990 77
See also CLR 40
Hudson, Jeffrey
See Crichton, Michael
Hudson, (Margaret) Kirsty 1947- 32
Hudson, Margaret
See Shuter, Jane (Margaret)
Hudson, W(illiam) H(enry) 1841-1922 35
Hudson, Wade 1946- 162
Earlier sketch in SATA 74
Huelsmann, Eva 1928- 16
Huff, Barbara A. 1929- 67
Huff, Tanya 1957- 171
Earlier sketch in SATA 85
Huff, Tanya Sue
See Huff, Tanya
Huff, T.S.
See Huff, Tanya
Huff, Vivian 1948- 59
Huffaker, Sandy 1943- 10
Huffman, Tom 24
Huggins, Nathan Irvin 1927-1989 63
Huggins, Peter 178
Hughes, Carol 1955- 108
Hughes, Dean 1943- 139
Earlier sketches in SATA 33, 77
See also CLR 76
Hughes, Eden
See Griffin, W.E.B
Hughes, Edward James
See Hughes, Ted
Hughes, (James Mercer) Langston
1902-1967 33
Earlier sketch in SATA 4
See also CLR 17
Hughes, Libby 71
Hughes, Matilda
See MacLeod, Charlotte (Matilda)
Hughes, Monica 1925-2003 162
Earlier sketches in SATA 15, 70, 119
See also CLR 60
See also SAAS 11
Hughes, Monica Ince
See Hughes, Monica
Hughes, Richard (Arthur Warren)
1900-1976 8
Obituary 25
Hughes, Sara
See Saunders, Susan
Hughes, Shirley 1927- 159
Earlier sketches in SATA 16, 70, 110
See also CLR 15
Hughes, Ted 1930-1998 49
Brief entry 27
Obituary 107
See also CLR 131
See Hughes, Edward James
Hughes, Thomas 1822-1896 31
Hughes, Virginia
See Campbell, Hope
Hughes, Walter (Llewellyn) 1910-1993 26
Hughey, Roberta 1942- 61
Hugo, Pierre Brackers de
See Brackers de Hugo, Pierre
Hugo, Victor (Marie) 1802-1885 47
Huline-Dickens, Frank William 1931- 34
Huling, Jan 172
Huliska-Beith, Laura 175
Hull, Eleanor (Means) 1913- 21
Hull, Eric Traviss
See Harnan, Terry
Hull, H. Braxton
See Jacobs, Helen Hull
Hull, Jesse Redding
See Hull, Jessie Redding
Hull, Jessie Redding 1932- 51
Hull, Katharine 1921-1977 23
Hull, Lise (E.) 1954- 148

Hull, Maureen 1949- 142
Hulme, Joy N. 1922- 161
　Earlier sketches in SATA 74, 112
Hults, Dorothy Niebrugge 1898-2000 6
Humble, Richard 1945- 60
Hume, Lachie 189
Hume, Lotta Carswell 7
Hume, Ruth Fox 1922-1980 26
　Obituary 22
Hume, Stephen Eaton 1947- 136
Hummel, Berta 1909-1946 43
Hummel, Sister Maria Innocentia
　See Hummel, Berta
Humphrey, Carol Sue 1956- 167
Humphrey, Henry (III) 1930- 16
Humphrey, Kate
　See Forsyth, Kate
Humphrey, Sandra McLeod 1936- 95
Humphreys, Martha 1943- 71
Humphreys, Susan L.
　See Lowell, Susan
Hundal, Nancy 1957- 128
Huneck, Stephen 1949- 183
　Earlier sketch in SATA 129
Hungerford, Hesba Fay
　See Brinsmead, H(esba) F(ay)
Hungerford, Pixie
　See Brinsmead, H(esba) F(ay)
Hunkin, Timothy Mark Trelawney 1950- 53
Hunt, Angela Elwell 1957- 159
　Earlier sketch in SATA 75
Hunt, Francesca
　See Holland, Isabelle (Christian)
Hunt, Irene 1907-2001 91
　Earlier sketch in SATA 2
　See also CLR 1
Hunt, Janie Louise 1963- 102
Hunt, Jonathan 1966- 84
Hunt, Joyce 1927- 31
Hunt, Linda 1940- 39
Hunt, Lisa B(ehnke) 1967- 84
Hunt, Mabel Leigh 1892-1971 1
　Obituary 26
Hunt, Morton M(agill) 1920- 22
Hunt, Nigel
　See Greenbank, Anthony Hunt
Hunt, Peter (Leonard) 1945- 76
Hunter, Anne B. 1966- 118
Hunter, Bernice Thurman 1922-2002 85
　Brief entry 45
Hunter, Bobbi Dooley 1945- 89
Hunter, Captain Marcy
　See Ellis, Edward S(ylvester)
Hunter, Chris
　See Fluke, Joanne
Hunter, Clingham M.D.
　See Adams, William Taylor
Hunter, Edith Fisher 1919- 31
Hunter, Erin
　See Cary, Kate
Hunter, Evan 1926-2005 25
　Obituary 167
　See McBain, Ed
Hunter, George E.
　See Ellis, Edward S(ylvester)
Hunter, Hilda 1921- 7
Hunter, Jana
　See Hunter, Jana Novotny
Hunter, Jana Novotny 190
Hunter, Jim 1939- 65
Hunter, Kristin
　See Lattany, Kristin (Elaine Eggleston) Hunter
Hunter, Leigh
　See Etchison, Birdie L(ee)
Hunter, Lieutenant Ned
　See Ellis, Edward S(ylvester)
Hunter, Mel 1927-2004 39

Hunter, Mollie 1922- 139
　Autobiography Feature 139
　Earlier sketches in SATA 54, 106
　See also CLR 25
　See also SAAS 7
　See McIlwraith, Maureen Mollie Hunter
Hunter, Ned
　See Ellis, Edward S(ylvester)
Hunter, Norman (George Lorimer)
　1899-1995 84
　Earlier sketch in SATA 26
Hunter, Ryan Ann
　See Greenwood, Pamela D.
　and Macalaster, Elizabeth G.
Hunter, Sara Hoagland 1954- 98
Hunter Blair, Pauline 3
　See Clarke, Pauline
Huntington, Amy 1956- 180
　Earlier sketch in SATA 138
Huntington, Geoffrey 145
Huntington, Harriet E(lizabeth) 1909- 1
Huntsberry, William E(mery) 1916- 5
Hurd, Clement (G.) 1908-1988 64
　Obituary 54
　Earlier sketch in SATA 2
　See also CLR 49
Hurd, Edith Thacher 1910-1997 64
　Obituary 95
　Earlier sketch in SATA 2
　See also CLR 49
　See also SAAS 13
Hurd, (John) Thacher 1949- 94
　Autobiography Feature 123
　Brief entry 45
　Earlier sketch in SATA 46
Hurley, Jo
　See Dower, Laura
Hurlimann, Bettina 39
　Obituary 34
　See Huerlimann, Bettina
Hurlimann, Ruth 32
　Brief entry 31
　See Huerlimann, Ruth
Hurmence, Belinda 1921- 77
　See also CLR 25
　See also SAAS 20
Hurst, Carol Otis 1933-2007 185
　Earlier sketch in SATA 130
Hurt-Newton, Tania 1968- 84
Hurwin, Davida Wills 1950- 180
Hurwitz, Johanna 1937- 175
　Earlier sketches in SATA 20, 71, 113
　See also SAAS 18
Hurwood, Bernhardt J. 1926-1987 12
　Obituary 50
Husain, Shahrukh 1950- 108
Huser, Glen 1943- 151
Hutchens, Paul 1902-1977 31
Hutchins, Carleen Maley 1911- 9
Hutchins, Hazel J. 1952- 175
　Brief entry 51
　Earlier sketches in SATA 81, 135
　See also SAAS 24
Hutchins, Pat 1942- 178
　Earlier sketches in SATA 15, 70, 111
　See also CLR 20
　See also SAAS 16
Hutchins, Ross Elliott 1906- 4
Hutchison, Linda 1942- 152
Huthmacher, J. Joseph 1929- 5
Hutto, Nelson (Allen) 1904-1985 20
Hutton, Kathryn 1915- 89
Hutton, Warwick 1939-1994 20
　Obituary 83
　See also SAAS 17
Huxley, Aldous (Leonard) 1894-1963 63
Huxley, Elspeth (Josceline Grant)
　1907-1997 62
　Obituary 95
Hyde, Catherine R.
　See Hyde, Catherine Ryan

Hyde, Catherine Ryan 1955- 141
Hyde, Dayton O(gden) 9
Hyde, Hawk
　See Hyde, Dayton O(gden)
Hyde, Jeannette
　See Eyerly, Jeannette
Hyde, Margaret O. 1917- 139
　Earlier sketches in SATA 1, 42, 76
　See also CLR 23
　See also SAAS 8
Hyde, Margaret Oldroyd
　See Hyde, Margaret O.
Hyde, Shelley
　See Reed, Kit
Hyde, Wayne Frederick 1922- 7
Hylander, Clarence J(ohn) 1897-1964 7
Hyman, Robin P(hilip) 1931- 12
Hyman, Trina Schart 1939-2004 95
　Obituary 158
　Earlier sketches in SATA 7, 46
　See also CLR 50
Hymes, Lucia M(anley) 1907-1998 7
Hyndman, Jane Andrews Lee 1912-1978 46
　Obituary 23
　Earlier sketch in SATA 1
Hyndman, Robert Utley 1906-1973 18
Hynes, Pat 98

I

Iannone, Jeanne 7
　See Balzano, Jeanne (Koppel)
Ibatoulline, Bagram 1965(?)- 174
Ibbitson, John Perrie 1955- 102
Ibbotson, Eva 1925- 156
　Earlier sketches in SATA 13, 103
Ibbotson, M. C(hristine) 1930- 5
Icenoggle, Jodi 1967- 168
Icenoggle, Jodi O.
　See Icenoggle, Jodi
Ichikawa, Satomi 1949- 146
　Brief entry 36
　Earlier sketches in SATA 47, 78
　See also CLR 62
Ignoffo, Matthew 1945- 92
Igus, Toyomi 1953- 112
　Earlier sketch in SATA 76
Ihimaera, Witi (Tame) 1944- 148
Ikeda, Daisaku 1928- 77
Ilowite, Sheldon A. 1931- 27
Ilsey, Dent
　See Chapman, John Stanton Higham
Ilsley, Dent
　See Chapman, John Stanton Higham
Ilsley, Velma (Elizabeth) 1918- 12
Imai, Ayano 1980- 190
Imai, Miko 1963- 90
Imershein, Betsy 1953- 62
Immel, Mary Blair 1930- 28
Immell, Myra H. 1941- 92
Impey, Rose 1947- 152
　Earlier sketch in SATA 69
Ingelow, Jean 1820-1897 33
Ingermanson, Randall 1958- 134
Ingermanson, Randy
　See Ingermanson, Randall
Ingersoll, Norman 1928- 79
Ingham, Colonel Frederic
　See Hale, Edward Everett
Ingman, Bruce 1963- 182
　Earlier sketch in SATA 134
Ingman, Nicholas 1948- 52
Ingold, Jeanette 128
Ingpen, Robert 1936- 166
　Earlier sketch in SATA 109
Ingpen, Robert Roger
　See Ingpen, Robert
Ingraham, Erick 1950- 145
Ingraham, Leonard W(illiam) 1913-2003 4

Ingram, Scott 1948- 167
  Earlier sketch in SATA 92
Ingram, W. Scott
  See Ingram, Scott
Ingrams, Doreen 1906-1997 97
  Earlier sketch in SATA 20
Ingrid, Charles
  See Salsitz, Rhondi Vilott
Ingves, Gunilla (Anna Maria Folkesdotter)
  1939- 101
Inkpen, Mick 1952- 154
  Earlier sketch in SATA 99
Innes, (Ralph) Hammond
  See Hammond Innes, Ralph
Innes, Ralph Hammond
  See Hammond Innes, Ralph
Innocenti, Roberto 1940- 159
  Earlier sketch in SATA 96
  See also CLR 126
Innocenti and Gallaz
  See Gallaz, Christophe
  and Innocenti, Roberto
Inyart, Gene 6
  See Namovicz, Gene Inyart
Ionesco, Eugene 1912-1994 7
  Obituary 79
Ipcar, Dahlov (Zorach) 1917- 147
  Autobiography Feature 147
  Earlier sketches in SATA 1, 49
  See also SAAS 8
Ireland, Karin 151
  Earlier sketch in SATA 101
Ironside, Jetske 1940- 60
Irvin, Fred 1914- 15
Irvine, Georgeanne 1955- 72
Irvine, Joan 1951- 80
Irving, Alexander
  See Hume, Ruth Fox
Irving, Robert
  See Adler, Irving
Irving, Washington 1783-1859
  See YABC 2
  See also CLR 97
Irwin, Ann(abelle Bowen) 1915-1998 89
  Brief entry 38
  Obituary 106
  Earlier sketch in SATA 44
  See also CLR 40
  See Irwin, Hadley
Irwin, Constance (H.) Frick 1913-1995 6
Irwin, Hadley
  See CLR 40
  See also SAAS 14
  See Hadley, Lee
  and Irwin, Ann(abelle Bowen)
Irwin, Keith Gordon 1885-1964 11
Isaac, Joanne 1934- 21
Isaacs, Anne 1949- 185
  Earlier sketch in SATA 90
Isaacs, Jacob
  See Kranzler, George G(ershon)
Isaacson, Philip M(arshal) 1924- 87
Isadora, Rachel 1953(?)- 165
  Brief entry 32
  Earlier sketches in SATA 54, 79, 121
  See also CLR 7
Isbell, Rebecca T(emple) 1942- 125
Isham, Charlotte H(ickock) 1912- 21
Ishida, Jui 176
Ish-Kishor, Judith 1892-1972 11
Ish-Kishor, Sulamith 1896-1977 17
Ishmael, Woodi 1914-1995 31
  Obituary 109
Isle, Sue 1963- 105
Israel, Elaine 1945- 12
Israel, Marion Louise 1882-1973
  Obituary 26
Iterson, S(iny) R(ose) Van
  See Van Iterson, S(iny) R(ose)
Ivanko, John D. 1966- 111

Ivanko, John Duane
  See Ivanko, John D.
Iversen, Jeremy 1980(?)- 174
Iversen, Jeremy Watt
  See Iversen, Jeremy
Iverson, Carol (L.) 1941- 145
Iverson, Diane 1950- 122
Iverson, Eric G.
  See Turtledove, Harry
Ivery, Martha M. 1948- 124
Ives, David 1951- 173
Ives, Morgan
  See Bradley, Marion Zimmer
Iwai, Melissa 183
Iwamatsu, Jun Atsushi 1908-1994 81
  Earlier sketch in SATA 14
  See Yashima, Taro
Iwasaki (Matsumoto), Chihiro 1918-1974
  See CLR 18

J

Jablonski, Carla 184
Jac, Lee
  See Morton, Lee Jack, Jr.
Jacka, Martin 1943- 72
Jackson, Alison 1953- 160
  Earlier sketches in SATA 73, 108
Jackson, Anne 1896(?)-1984
  Obituary 37
Jackson, C(aary) Paul 1902-1991 6
Jackson, Caary
  See Jackson, C(aary) Paul
Jackson, Charlotte E. (Cobden) 1903(?)-1989
  Obituary 62
Jackson, Dave
  See Jackson, J. David
Jackson, Ellen B. 1943- 167
  Earlier sketches in SATA 75, 115
Jackson, Garnet Nelson 1944- 87
Jackson, Geoffrey (Holt Seymour) 1915-1987
  Obituary 53
Jackson, Gina
  See Fluke, Joanne
Jackson, Guida M. 1930- 71
Jackson, J. David 1944- 91
Jackson, Jacqueline 1928- 65
Jackson, Jacqueline Dougan
  See Jackson, Jacqueline
Jackson, Jesse 1908-1983 29
  Obituary 48
  Earlier sketch in SATA 2
  See also CLR 28
Jackson, Marjorie 1928- 127
Jackson, Melanie 1956- 141
Jackson, Mike 1946- 91
Jackson, Neta J. 1944- 91
Jackson, O. B.
  See Jackson, C(aary) Paul
Jackson, Rob 1961- 176
Jackson, Robert B(lake) 1926- 8
Jackson, Robert Bradley
  See Jackson, Rob
Jackson, Sally
  See Kellogg, Jean (Defrees)
Jackson, Shirley 1919-1965 2
Jackson, Woody 1948- 92
Jacob, Helen Pierce 1927- 21
Jacobin
  See Bisson, Terry
Jacobs, Deborah Lynn 187
Jacobs, Flora Gill 1918-2006 5
  Obituary 178
Jacobs, Francine 1935- 150
  Brief entry 42
  Earlier sketch in SATA 43
Jacobs, Frank 1929- 30
Jacobs, Helen Hull 1908-1997 12
Jacobs, Joseph 1854-1916 25

Jacobs, Judy 1952- 69
Jacobs, Laurie A. 1956- 89
Jacobs, Leah
  See Gellis, Roberta
Jacobs, Leland Blair 1907-1992 20
  Obituary 71
Jacobs, Linda
  See Altman, Linda Jacobs
Jacobs, Lou(is), Jr. 1921- 2
Jacobs, Shannon K. 1947- 77
Jacobs, Susan 30
  See Quinn, Susan
Jacobs, William Jay 1933- 89
  Earlier sketch in SATA 28
Jacobsen, Laura 177
Jacobson, Daniel 1923- 12
Jacobson, Jennifer
  See Jacobson, Jennifer Richard
Jacobson, Jennifer Richard 1958- 170
Jacobson, Morris K(arl) 1906- 21
Jacobson, Rick 170
Jacopetti, Alexandra 14
  See Hart, Alexandra
Jacques, Brian 1939- 176
  Earlier sketches in SATA 62, 95, 138
  See also CLR 21
Jacques, Robin 1920-1995 32
  Brief entry 30
  Obituary 86
  See also SAAS 5
Jaekel, Susan M. 1948- 89
Jaffe, Michele 179
Jaffe, Michele Sharon
  See Jaffe, Michele
Jaffee, Al(lan) 1921- 66
  Earlier sketch in SATA 37
Jagendorf, Moritz (Adolf) 1888-1981 2
  Obituary 24
Jahn, Michael
  See Jahn, (Joseph) Michael
Jahn, (Joseph) Michael 1943- 28
Jahn, Mike
  See Jahn, (Joseph) Michael
Jahn-Clough, Lisa 1967- 193
  Earlier sketches in SATA 88, 152
Jahsmann, Allan Hart 1916- 28
Jakes, John 1932- 62
Jakes, John William
  See Jakes, John
James, Andrew
  See Kirkup, James
James, Ann 1952- 168
  Earlier sketches in SATA 82, 117
James, Betsy 183
James, Brian 1976- 140
James, Bronte
  See Nash, Renea Denise
James, Captain Lew
  See Stratemeyer, Edward L.
James, Charlie 1961- 185
James, Curtis E. 182
James, Dynely
  See Mayne, William (James Carter)
James, Edwin
  See Gunn, James E.
James, Elizabeth 1942- 97
  Earlier sketches in SATA 39, 45, 52
James, Emily
  See Standiford, Natalie
James, Gordon C. 1973- 195
James, Harry Clebourne 1896-1978 11
James, J. Alison 1962- 146
  Earlier sketch in SATA 83
James, Josephine
  See Sterne, Emma Gelders
James, Mary
  See Meaker, Marijane
James, Philip
  See del Rey, Lester
  and Moorcock, Michael
James, Robin 1953- 50

James, Robin Irene
  See James, Robin
James, Tegan
  See Odgers, Sally Farrell
James, T.F.
  See Fleming, Thomas
James, Will(iam Roderick) 1892-1942 19
Jameson, W. C. 1942- 93
Jamieson, Ian R.
  See Goulart, Ron(ald Joseph)
Jamiolkowski, Raymond M. 1953- 81
Jane, Mary Childs 1909- 6
Jane, Pamela 158
Janeczko, Paul B(ryan) 1945- 155
  Earlier sketches in SATA 53, 98
  See also CLR 47
  See also SAAS 18
Janes, Edward C. 1908- 25
Janes, J(oseph) Robert 1935- 148
  Brief entry 50
  Earlier sketch in SATA 101
Janeway, Elizabeth (Hall) 1913-2005 19
Janger, Kathleen N. 1940- 66
Janice
  See Brustlein, Janice Tworkov
Janisch, Heinz 1960- 181
Janosch
  See CLR 26
  See Eckert, Horst
Janover, Caroline (Davis) 1943- 141
  Earlier sketch in SATA 89
Janovitz, Marilyn 194
Jansen, Jared
  See Cebulash, Mel
Janson, Dora Jane (Heineberg) 1916- 31
Janson, H(orst) W(oldemar) 1913-1982 9
Jansson, Tove (Marika) 1914-2001 41
  Earlier sketch in SATA 3
  See also CLR 125
Janus, Grete
  See Hertz, Grete Janus
Jaques, Faith 1923-1997 97
  Earlier sketches in SATA 21, 69
Jaquith, Priscilla 1908- 51
Jaramillo, Mari-Luci 1928- 139
Jarman, Julia 1946- 133
Jarman, Rosemary Hawley 1935- 7
Jarrell, Mary Von Schrader 1914- 35
Jarrell, Randall 1914-1965 7
  See also CLR 111
Jarrett, Roxanne
  See Werner, Herma
Jarrow, Gail 1952- 185
  Earlier sketch in SATA 84
Jarvis, E.K.
  See Ellison, Harlan
  and Silverberg, Robert
Jarvis, Robin 1963- 181
Jaskol, Julie 1958- 127
Jasner, W. K.
  See Watson, Jane Werner
Jassem, Kate
  See Oppenheim, Joanne
Jauss, Anne Marie 1902(?)-1991 10
  Obituary 69
Javernick, Ellen 1938- 89
Jayne, Lieutenant R. H.
  See Ellis, Edward S(ylvester)
Jaynes, Clare
  See Mayer, Jane Rothschild
Jeake, Samuel, Jr.
  See Aiken, Conrad (Potter)
Jean-Bart, Leslie 1954- 121
Jeapes, Ben 1965- 174
Jefferds, Vincent H(arris) 1916- 59
  Brief entry 49
Jefferies, (John) Richard 1848-1887 16
Jeffers, Dawn 189
Jeffers, Oliver 1977- 175

Jeffers, Susan 1942- 137
  Earlier sketches in SATA 17, 70, 129
  See also CLR 30
Jefferson, Sarah
  See Farjeon, (Eve) Annabel
Jeffries, Roderic 1926- 4
Jeffries, Roderic Graeme
  See Jeffries, Roderic
Jenkin-Pearce, Susie 1943- 80
Jenkins, A.M. 174
Jenkins, Amanda McRaney
  See Jenkins, A.M.
Jenkins, Debra Reid
  See Reid Jenkins, Debra
Jenkins, Emily 1967- 174
  Earlier sketch in SATA 144
Jenkins, Jean 98
Jenkins, Jerry B. 1949- 149
Jenkins, Jerry Bruce
  See Jenkins, Jerry B.
Jenkins, Leonard 189
Jenkins, Marie M(agdalen) 1909- 7
Jenkins, Patrick 1955- 72
Jenkins, Steve 1952- 188
  Earlier sketch in SATA 154
Jenkins, William A(twell) 1922-1998 9
Jenkyns, Chris 1924- 51
Jennings, Coleman A(lonzo) 1933- 64
Jennings, Dana Andrew 1957- 93
Jennings, Elizabeth (Joan) 1926-2001 66
Jennings, Gary 1928-1999 9
  Obituary 117
Jennings, Gary Gayne
  See Jennings, Gary
Jennings, Patrick 1962- 160
  Earlier sketch in SATA 96
Jennings, Paul 1943- 165
  Earlier sketch in SATA 88
  See also CLR 40
Jennings, Richard W. 1945- 185
  Earlier sketch in SATA 136
Jennings, Robert
  See Hamilton, Charles (Harold St. John)
Jennings, S. M.
  See Meyer, Jerome Sydney
Jennings, Sharon 1954- 95
Jennings, Sharon Elizabeth
  See Jennings, Sharon
Jennison, C. S.
  See Starbird, Kaye
Jennison, Keith Warren 1911-1995 14
Jensen, Kathryn 1949- 81
Jensen, Kristine Mary 1961- 78
Jensen, Niels 1927- 25
Jensen, Vickie (Dee) 1946- 81
Jensen, Virginia Allen 1927- 8
Jenson-Elliott, Cynthia L(ouise) 1962- 143
Jeram, Anita 1965- 154
  Earlier sketches in SATA 71, 102
Jerman, Jerry 1949- 89
Jernigan, E. Wesley 1940- 85
Jernigan, Gisela (Evelyn) 1948- 85
Jeschke, Susan 1942- 42
  Brief entry 27
Jessel, Camilla (Ruth) 1937- 143
  Earlier sketch in SATA 29
Jessell, Tim 177
Jessey, Cornelia
  See Sussman, Cornelia Silver
Jewel
  See Kilcher, Jewel
Jewell, Nancy 1940- 109
  Brief entry 41
Jewett, Eleanore Myers 1890-1967 5
Jewett, (Theodora) Sarah Orne 1849-1909 ... 15
Jezard, Alison 1919- 57
  Brief entry 34
Jiang, Cheng An 1943- 109
Jiang, Ji-li 1954- 101
Jiang, Zheng An
  See Jiang, Cheng An

Jiler, John 1946- 42
  Brief entry 35
Jimenez, Francisco 1943- 108
Jinks, Catherine 1963- 155
  Earlier sketch in SATA 94
Jobb, Jamie 1945- 29
Jobling, Curtis 131
Jocelyn, Ann Henning 1948- 92
Jocelyn, Marthe 1956- 163
  Earlier sketch in SATA 118
Joerns, Consuelo 44
  Brief entry 33
Joey D
  See Macaulay, Teresa (E.)
Johansen, Krista V.
  See Johansen, K.V.
Johansen, K.V 1968- 186
Johansen, K.V. 1968- 186
  Earlier sketch in SATA 129
Johansson, Philip 163
John, Joyce 59
Johns, Avery
  See Cousins, Margaret
Johns, Elizabeth 1943- 88
Johns, Janetta
  See Quin-Harkin, Janet
Johns, Linda 1945- 173
Johns, W(illiam) E(arle) 1893-1968 55
Johns, Captain W. E.
  See Johns, W(illiam) E(arle)
Johnson, A.
  See Johnson, Annabell (Jones)
Johnson, A. E.
  See Johnson, Annabell (Jones)
  and Johnson, Edgar (Raymond)
Johnson, Angela 1961- 188
  Earlier sketches in SATA 69, 102, 150
  See also CLR 33
Johnson, Annabel
  See Johnson, Annabell (Jones)
Johnson, Annabell (Jones) 1921- 72
  Earlier sketch in SATA 2
  See Johnson, Annabel
Johnson, Art 1946- 123
Johnson, Benjamin F., of Boone
  See Riley, James Whitcomb
Johnson, Bettye 1858-1919
  See Rogers, Bettye
Johnson, Caryn
  See Goldberg, Whoopi
Johnson, Caryn E.
  See Goldberg, Whoopi
Johnson, Caryn Elaine
  See Goldberg, Whoopi
Johnson, Charles R. 1925- 11
Johnson, Charlotte Buel 46
  See von Wodtke, Charlotte Buel Johnson
Johnson, Chuck
  See Johnson, Charles R.
Johnson, Crockett
  See CLR 98
  See Leisk, David (Johnson)
Johnson, D(ana) William 1945- 23
Johnson, Daniel Shahid 1954- 73
Johnson, David
  See Johnson, David A.
Johnson, David A. 1951- 191
Johnson, D.B. 1944- 183
  Earlier sketch in SATA 146
Johnson, Dinah 130
  See Johnson, Dianne
Johnson, Dolores 1949- 69
Johnson, Donald B.
  See Johnson, D.B.
Johnson, Dorothy M(arie) 1905-1984 6
  Obituary 40
Johnson, E(ugene) Harper 44
Johnson, Edgar (Raymond) 1912-1990 72
  Earlier sketch in SATA 2
Johnson, Eleanor Murdock 1892-1987
  Obituary 54

Johnson, Elizabeth 1911-1984 7
Obituary 39
Johnson, Eric W(arner) 1918-1994 ....
Obituary 82
Earlier sketch in SATA 8
Johnson, Evelyne 1922- 20
Johnson, Fred 19(?)-1982 63
Johnson, Gaylord 1884-1972 7
Johnson, Gerald White 1890-1980 19
Obituary 28
Johnson, Harper
See Johnson, E(ugene) Harper
Johnson, Harriett 1908-1987
Obituary 53
Johnson, James Ralph 1922- 1
Johnson, James Weldon 1871-1938 31
See also CLR 32
Johnson, Jane 1951- 48
Johnson, Joan J. 1942- 59
Johnson, John E(mil) 1929- 34
Johnson, Johnny 1901-1995
See Johnson, (Walter) Ryerson
Johnson, Kathleen Jeffrie 1950- 186
Johnson, La Verne B(ravo) 1925- 13
Johnson, Layne 187
Johnson, Lee Kaiser 1962- 78
Johnson, Lissa H(alls) 1955- 65
Johnson, Lois Smith 1894-1993 6
Johnson, Lois Walfrid 1936- 130
Earlier sketches in SATA 22, 91
Johnson, Margaret S(weet) 1893-1964 35
Johnson, Marguerite Annie
See Angelou, Maya
Johnson, Mary Frances K. 1929(?)-1979
Obituary 27
Johnson, Maud Battle 1918(?)-1985
Obituary 46
Johnson, Meredith Merrell 1952- 104
Johnson, Milton 1932- 31
Johnson, Neil 1954- 135
Earlier sketch in SATA 73
Johnson, Pamela 1949- 71
Johnson, Patricia Polin 1956- 84
Johnson, Paul Brett 1947- 132
Earlier sketch in SATA 83
Johnson, Rebecca L. 1956- 147
Earlier sketch in SATA 67
Johnson, Rick L. 1954- 79
Johnson, (Walter) Ryerson 1901-1995 10
Obituary 106
See Halliday, Brett
Johnson, Scott 1952- 119
Earlier sketch in SATA 76
Johnson, Sherrie 1948- 87
Johnson, Shirley K(ing) 1927- 10
Johnson, Siddie Joe 1905-1977
Obituary 20
Johnson, Spencer 1938- 145
Brief entry 38
Johnson, Stacie
See Myers, Walter Dean
Johnson, Stephen T. 1964- 189
Earlier sketches in SATA 84, 141
Johnson, Steve 1960- 177
Johnson, Sue Kaiser 1963- 78
Johnson, Sylvia A. 166
Brief entry 52
Earlier sketch in SATA 104
Johnson, William R. 38
Johnson, William Weber 1909-1992 7
Johnston, Agnes Christine
See Dazey, Agnes J(ohnston)
Johnston, Annie Fellows 1863-1931 37
Johnston, Dorothy Grunbock 1915-1979 54
Johnston, Ginny 1946- 60
Johnston, H(ugh) A(nthony) S(tephen)
1913-1967 14
Johnston, Janet 1944- 71
Johnston, Jeffry W. 188
Johnston, Johanna 1914(?)-1982 12
Obituary 33

Johnston, Julie 1941- 110
Autobiography Feature 128
Earlier sketch in SATA 78
See also CLR 41
See also SAAS 24
Johnston, Lynn 1947- 118
Johnston, Lynn Beverley
See Johnston, Lynn
Johnston, Mark 194
Johnston, Norma 29
See St. John, Nicole
Johnston, Portia
See Takakjian, Portia
Johnston, Susan Taylor 1942- 128
Earlier sketch in SATA 83
See Johnston, Tony
Johnston, Tim(othy Patrick) 1962- 146
Johnston, Tony 180
Earlier sketch in SATA 8
See Johnston, Susan Taylor
Joinson, Carla 160
Jolin, Paula 186
Jonas, Ann 1932- 135
Brief entry 42
Earlier sketch in SATA 50
See also CLR 74
Jonell, Lynne 109
Jones, Adrienne 1915-2000 82
Earlier sketch in SATA 7
See also SAAS 10
Jones, Annabel
See Lewis, Mary (Christianna)
Jones, Betty Millsaps 1940- 54
Jones, Carol 1942- 153
Earlier sketch in SATA 79
Jones, Carrie 1971- 191
Jones, Charles M(artin) 1912-2002 53
Obituary 133
See Jones, Chuck
Jones, Charlotte Foltz 1945- 122
Earlier sketch in SATA 77
Jones, Chuck
See Jones, Charles M(artin)
Jones, Constance 112
Jones, Constance A.
See Jones, Constance
Jones, Diana Wynne 1934- 160
Earlier sketches in SATA 9, 70, 108
See also CLR 120
See also SAAS 7
Jones, Douglas C(lyde) 1924-1998 52
Jones, Elizabeth McDavid 155
Jones, Elizabeth Orton 1910-2005 18
Obituary 164
Jones, Evan 1915-1996 3
Jones, Geraldine
See McCaughrean, Geraldine
Jones, Gillingham
See Hamilton, Charles (Harold St. John)
Jones, Gwyneth A(nn) 1952- 159
Jones, Harold 1904-1992 14
Obituary 72
Jones, Helen Hinckley 1903-1991 26
Jones, Helen L(ouise) 1903-1973
Obituary 22
Jones, Hettie 1934- 42
Brief entry 27
Jones, Hortense P. 1918- 9
Jones, J. Sydney 1948- 101
Jones, Jasmine
See Papademetriou, Lisa
Jones, Jennifer (Berry) 1947- 90
Jones, Jessie Mae Orton 1887(?)-1983
Obituary 37
Jones, John R(obert) 1926- 76
Jones, Jon Sydney
See Jones, J. Sydney
Jones, Kimberly K. 1957- 187
Jones, Marcia Thornton 1958- 115
Earlier sketch in SATA 73
Jones, Martha T(annery) 1931- 130

Jones, Mary Alice 1898(?)-1980 6
Jones, McClure 34
Jones, Noah Z. 182
Jones, Patrick 1961- 136
Jones, Penelope 1938- 31
Jones, Rebecca C(astaldi) 1947- 99
Earlier sketch in SATA 33
Jones, Robin D(orothy) 1959- 80
Jones, Sanford W.
See Thorn, John
Jones, Sylvie 185
Jones, Sylvie Michelle
See Jones, Sylvie
Jones, Terence Graham Parry 1942- 127
See Jones, Terry
and Monty Python
Jones, Terry 67
Brief entry 51
See Jones, Terence Graham Parry
Jones, Tim Wynne
See Wynne-Jones, Tim
Jones, Traci L. 186
Jones, V(ictoria) M(ary) 1958- 147
Jones, Veda Boyd 1948- 119
Jones, Volcano
See Mitchell, Adrian
Jones, Weyman (B.) 1928- 4
See also SAAS 11
Jones, William Glynne
See Glynne-Jones, William
Jonk, Clarence 1906-1987 10
Jonsberg, Barry 1951- 168
Joos, Francoise 1956- 78
Joos, Frederic 1953- 78
Joosse, Barbara M. 1949- 164
Earlier sketches in SATA 52, 96
Joosse, Barbara Monnot
See Joosse, Barbara M.
Jordan, Alexis Hill
See Glick, Ruth (Burtnick)
and Titchener, Louise
Jordan, Anne Devereaux 1943- 80
Jordan, Chris
See Philbrick, Rodman
Jordan, Deloris 191
Jordan, Don
See Howard, Vernon (Linwood)
Jordan, Hope Dahle 1905-1995 15
Jordan, Jael (Michal) 1949- 30
Jordan, June 1936-2002 136
Earlier sketch in SATA 4
See also CLR 10
Jordan, June Meyer
See Jordan, June
Jordan, Lee
See Scholefield, Alan
Jordan, Martin George 1944- 84
Jordan, Robert 1948-2007 95
See Rigney, James Oliver, Jr.
Jordan, Robert K.
See Jordan, Robert
Jordan, Rosa 1939- 191
Jordan, Roslyn M. 189
Jordan, Sherryl 1949- 122
Earlier sketch in SATA 71
See also SAAS 23
Jordan, Shirley 1930- 154
Jordan, Tanis 1946- 84
Jorgensen, Mary Venn -1995 36
Jorgensen, Norman 1954- 157
Jorgenson, Ivar
See Silverberg, Robert
Jorisch, Stephane 178
Joseph, Anne
See Coates, Anna
Joseph, James (Herz) 1924- 53
Joseph, Joan 1939- 34
Joseph, Joseph M(aron) 1903-1979 22
Joseph, Patrick
See O'Malley, Kevin

Josephs, Rebecca
  See Talbot, Toby
Josh
  See Clemens, Samuel Langhorne
Joshua, Peter
  See Stone, Peter
Joslin, Mary 1953- 176
Joslin, Sesyle 2
  See Hine, Sesyle Joslin
Joyce, Bill
  See Joyce, William
Joyce, J(ames) Avery 1902-1987 11
  Obituary 50
Joyce, Peter 1937- 127
Joyce, William 1957- 118
  Brief entry 46
  Earlier sketch in SATA 72
  See also CLR 26
Joyner, Jerry 1938- 34
Juan, Ana 1961- 179
Jubert, Herve 185
Juby, Susan 1969- 156
Jucker, Sita 1921- 5
Judah, Aaron 1923- 118
Judd, Cyril
  See Kornbluth, C(yril) M.
  and Merril, Judith
  and Pohl, Frederik
Judd, Denis (O'Nan) 1938- 33
Judd, Frances K. 1
  See Benson, Mildred (Augustine Wirt)
Jude, Conny 81
Judge, Lita 192
Judson, Clara Ingram 1879-1960 38
  Brief entry 27
Judy, Stephen
  See Tchudi, Stephen N.
Judy, Stephen N.
  See Tchudi, Stephen N.
Juhasz, Victor 1954- 177
Jukes, Mavis 1947- 111
  Brief entry 43
  Earlier sketch in SATA 72
  See also SAAS 12
Jules, Jacqueline 1956- 183
  Earlier sketch in SATA 148
Julian, Jane
  See Wiseman, David
Jumpp, Hugo
  See MacPeek, Walter G.
Jungman, Ann 165
Jupo, Frank J. 1904-1981 7
Jurmain, Suzanne 1945- 169
  Earlier sketch in SATA 72
Jurmain, Suzanne Tripp
  See Jurmain, Suzanne
Juster, Norton 1929- 132
  Earlier sketch in SATA 3
  See also CLR 112
Justus, May 1898-1989 1
  Obituary 106
Juvenilia
  See Taylor, Ann

K

Kaaberbol, Lene
  See Kaaberbol, Lene
Kaaberbol, Lene 1960- 159
Kabdebo, Tamas
  See Kabdebo, Thomas
Kabdebo, Thomas 1934- 10
Kabibble, Osh
  See Jobb, Jamie
Kacer, Kathy 1954- 184
  Earlier sketch in SATA 142
Kaczman, James 156
Kadair, Deborah Ousley 184
Kadesch, Robert R(udstone) 1922- 31

Kadohata, Cynthia 1956(?)- 180
  Earlier sketch in SATA 155
  See also CLR 121
Kaempfert, Wade
  See del Rey, Lester
Kaestner, Erich 1899-1974 14
  See also CLR 4
  See Kastner, Erich
Kahl, Jonathan (D.) 1959- 77
Kahl, M(arvin) P(hilip) 1934- 37
Kahl, Virginia (Caroline) 1919-2004 48
  Brief entry 38
  Obituary 158
Kahn, Joan 1914-1994 48
  Obituary 82
Kahn, Katherine Janus 1942- 167
  Earlier sketch in SATA 90
Kahn, Peggy
  See Katz, Bobbi
Kahn, Roger 1927- 37
Kahukiwa, Robyn 1940- 134
Kains, Josephine
  See Goulart, Ron(ald Joseph)
Kaizuki, Kiyonori 1950- 72
Kakimoto, Kozo 1915- 11
Kalashnikoff, Nicholas 1888-1961 16
Kalb, Jonah 1926- 23
Kalbacken, Joan 1925- 96
Kalechofsky, Roberta 1931- 92
Kaler, James Otis 1848-1912 15
Kalish, Claire M. 1947- 92
Kallen, Stuart A(rnold) 1955- 126
  Earlier sketch in SATA 86
Kallevig, Christine Petrell 1955- 164
Kalman, Bobbie 1947- 63
Kalman, Maira 1949- 137
  Earlier sketch in SATA 96
  See also CLR 32
Kalnay, Francis 1899-1992 7
Kaloustian, Rosanne 1955- 93
Kalow, Gisela 1946- 32
Kalstein, Dave 175
Kamen, Gloria 1923- 98
  Earlier sketch in SATA 9
Kamerman, Sylvia E.
  See Burack, Sylvia K.
Kamm, Josephine (Hart) 1905-1989 24
Kammerman, Sylvia K.
  See Burack, Sylvia K.
Kandel, Michael 1941- 93
Kandell, Alice S. 1938- 35
Kane, Bob 1916-1998 120
Kane, Henry Bugbee 1902-1971 14
Kane, L. A.
  See Mannetti, Lisa
Kane, Robert W. 1910- 18
Kane, Wilson
  See Bloch, Robert (Albert)
Kanefield, Teri 1960- 135
Kaner, Etta 1947- 126
Kanetzke, Howard W(illiam) 1932- 38
Kann, Elizabeth 180
Kann, Victoria 180
Kanoza, Muriel Canfield
  See Canfield, Muriel
Kantner, Seth 1965- 179
Kanzawa, Toshiko
  See Furukawa, Toshi
Kanzler, John 1963- 188
Kaplan, Andrew 1960- 78
Kaplan, Anne Bernays
  See Bernays, Anne
Kaplan, Bess 1927- 22
Kaplan, Boche 1926- 24
Kaplan, Elizabeth 1956- 83
Kaplan, Elizabeth A.
  See Kaplan, Elizabeth
Kaplan, Irma 1900- 10
Kaplan, Jean Caryl Korn 1926- 10
Kaplow, Robert 1954- 70

Karageorge, Michael
  See Anderson, Poul
Karas, G. Brian 1957- 178
Karas, George Brian
  See Karas, G. Brian
Karasz, Ilonka 1896-1981
  Obituary 29
Karen, Ruth 1922-1987 9
  Obituary 54
Kark, Nina Mary
  See Bawden, Nina
Karl, Herb 1938- 73
Karl, Jean E(dna) 1927-2000 122
  Earlier sketch in SATA 34
  See also SAAS 10
Karlin, Bernie 1927- 68
Karlin, Eugene 1918- 10
Karlin, Nurit 103
  Earlier sketch in SATA 63
Karnes, Frances A. 1937- 110
Karp, Naomi J. 1926- 16
Karpinski, J. Rick
  See Karpinski, John Eric
Karpinski, John Eric 1952- 81
Karpinski, Rick
  See Karpinski, John Eric
Karr, Kathleen 1946- 127
  Earlier sketch in SATA 82
Karr, Phyllis Ann 1944- 119
Karwoski, Gail 1949- 127
Karwoski, Gail Langer
  See Karwoski, Gail
Kashiwagi, Isami 1925- 10
Kaslik, Ibi 185
  See Kaslik, Ibolya Emma
Kassem, Lou 1931- 62
  Brief entry 51
Kastel, Warren
  See Silverberg, Robert
Kastner, Erich
  See Kaestner, Erich
Kastner, Jill (Marie) 1964- 117
  Earlier sketch in SATA 70
Kasuya, Masahiro 1937- 51
Kasza, Keiko 1951- 191
  Earlier sketch in SATA 124
Kataphusin
  See Ruskin, John
Katchen, Carole 1944- 9
Kathryn
  See Searle, Kathryn Adrienne
Katona, Robert 1949- 21
Katsarakis, Joan Harries
  See Harries, Joan
Katz, Alan 185
Katz, Avner 1939- 103
Katz, Bobbi 1933- 179
  Earlier sketch in SATA 12
Katz, Fred(eric Phillip) 1938- 6
Katz, Jane B(resler) 1934- 33
Katz, Karen 1947- 195
  Earlier sketch in SATA 158
Katz, Marjorie P.
  See Weiser, Marjorie P(hillis) K(atz)
Katz, Susan 1945- 156
Katz, Welwyn Wilton 1948- 96
  Autobiography Feature 118
  Earlier sketch in SATA 62
  See also CLR 45
Katz, William 1940- 98
Katz, William Loren 1927- 13
Kaufman, Bel 57
Kaufman, Jeff 1955- 84
Kaufman, Joe 1911-2001 33
Kaufman, Joseph
  See Kaufman, Joe
Kaufman, Mervyn D. 1932- 4
Kaufmann, Angelika 1935- 15
Kaufmann, John 1931- 18
Kaula, Edna Mason 1906-1987 13

Kaur Khalsa, Dayal
  See Khalsa, Dayal Kaur
Kavaler, Lucy 1930- 23
Kavanagh, Jack 1920- 85
Kavanagh, P(atrick) J(oseph Gregory)
  1931- 122
Kavanaugh, Ian
  See Webb, Jean Francis (III)
Kay, Alan N. 1965- 144
Kay, Elizabeth 1949- 165
Kay, Guy Gavriel 1954- 167
  Earlier sketch in SATA 121
Kay, Helen
  See Goldfrank, Helen Colodny
Kay, Jackie 1961- 165
  Earlier sketch in SATA 97
Kay, Jacqueline Margaret
  See Kay, Jackie
Kay, Mara 13
Kay, Verla 1946- 120
Kaye, Danny 1913-1987
  Obituary 50
Kaye, Geraldine (Hughesdon) 1925- 85
  Earlier sketch in SATA 10
Kaye, Judy
  See Baer, Judy
Kaye, Marilyn 1949- 110
  Earlier sketch in SATA 56
Kaye, Mary Margaret
  See Kaye, M.M.
Kaye, M.M. 1908-2004 62
  Obituary 152
Kaye, Mollie
  See Kaye, M.M.
Kaye, Peggy 1948- 143
Keach, James P. 1950- 125
Keams, Geri 1951- 117
Keane, Bil 1922- 4
Keaney, Brian 1954- 188
  Earlier sketch in SATA 106
Kearney, Meg 1964- 178
Kearny, Jillian
  See Goulart, Ron(ald Joseph)
Keating, Bern
  See Keating, Leo Bernard
Keating, Frank 1944- 143
Keating, Lawrence A. 1903-1966 23
Keating, Leo Bernard 1915- 10
Keats, Emma 1899(?)-1979(?) 68
Keats, Ezra Jack 1916-1983 57
  Obituary 34
  Earlier sketch in SATA 14
  See also CLR 35
Keefer, Catherine
  See Ogan, George F.
  and Ogan, Margaret E. (Nettles)
Keefer, Janice Kulyk 132
  See Kulyk Keefer, Janice
Keegan, Marcia 1943- 104
  Earlier sketch in SATA 9
Keehn, Sally M. 1947- 165
  Earlier sketch in SATA 87
Keel, Frank
  See Keeler, Ronald F(ranklin)
Keeler, Patricia 183
Keeler, Patricia A.
  See Keeler, Patricia
Keeler, Ronald F(ranklin) 1913-1983 47
Keely, Jack 1951- 119
Keen, Martin L. 1913-1992 4
Keenan, Sheila 1953- 95
Keene, Ann T(odd) 1940- 86
Keene, Carolyn 100
  Earlier sketch in SATA 65
  See also CLR 118
  See Benson, Mildred (Augustine Wirt)
  and Goulart, Ron(ald Joseph)
  and Lerangis, Peter
  and McFarlane, Leslie (Charles)
  and Stanley, George Edward
  and Stratemeyer, Edward L.

Keens-Douglas, Richardo 1953- 154
  Earlier sketch in SATA 95
Keep, Linda Lowery
  See Lowery, Linda
Keep, Richard 1949- 170
Keep, Richard Cleminson
  See Keep, Richard
Keeping, Charles (William James)
  1924-1988 69
  Obituary 56
  Earlier sketch in SATA 9
  See also CLR 34
Keeshan, Robert J. 1927-2004 32
  Obituary 151
Kehlenbeck, Angela 1959- 186
Kehret, Peg 1936- 149
  Autobiography Feature 149
  Earlier sketches in SATA 73, 108
Keillor, Garrison 1942- 58
Keillor, Gary Edward
  See Keillor, Garrison
Keir, Christine
  See Pullein-Thompson, Christine
Keister, Douglas 1948- 88
Keith, Doug 1952- 81
Keith, Eros 1942- 52
Keith, Hal 1934- 36
Keith, Harold (Verne) 1903-1998 74
  Earlier sketch in SATA 2
Keith, Robert
  See Applebaum, Stan
Keleinikov, Andrei 1924- 65
Kelemen, Julie 1959- 78
Kelen, Emery 1896-1978 13
  Obituary 26
Kelleam, Joseph E(veridge) 1913-1975 31
Kelleher, Anne 1959- 97
Kelleher, Annette 1950- 122
Kelleher, Daria Valerian 1955- 79
Kelleher, Victor (Michael Kitchener)
  1939- 129
  Brief entry 52
  Earlier sketch in SATA 75
  See also CLR 36
Keller, Beverly L(ou) 91
  Earlier sketch in SATA 13
Keller, Charles 1942- 82
  Earlier sketch in SATA 8
Keller, Debra 1958- 94
Keller, Dick 1923- 36
Keller, Emily 96
Keller, Gail Faithfull
  See Faithfull, Gail
Keller, Holly 1942- 157
  Brief entry 42
  Earlier sketches in SATA 76, 108
  See also CLR 45
Keller, Irene (Barron) 1927-2002 36
  Obituary 139
Kelley, Ellen A. 185
Kelley, Ellen Chavez
  See Kelley, Ellen A.
Kelley, Gary 1945- 183
Kelley, Leo P(atrick) 1928- 32
  Brief entry 31
Kelley, Patrick (G.) 1963- 129
Kelley, Patte 1947- 93
Kelley, True 1946- 179
Kelley, True (Adelaide) 1946- 130
  Brief entry 39
  Earlier sketches in SATA 41, 92
Kelley, True Adelaide
  See Kelley, True
Kellin, Sally Moffet 1932- 9
Kelling, Furn L. 1914-2000 37
Kellogg, Gene
  See Kellogg, Jean (Defrees)
Kellogg, Jean (Defrees) 1916-1978 10
Kellogg, Steven 1941- 177
  Earlier sketches in SATA 8, 57, 130
  See also CLR 6

Kellogg, Steven Castle
  See Kellogg, Steven
Kellow, Kathleen
  See Hibbert, Eleanor Alice Burford
Kelly, C. M. O.
  See Gibbs, (Cecilia) May
Kelly, Clint 1950- 140
Kelly, Eric P(hilbrook) 1884-1960
  See YABC 1
Kelly, Fiona
  See Coleman, Michael (Lee)
  and Hendry, Frances Mary
  and Oldfield, Jenny
  and Welford, Sue
Kelly, Irene 1957- 147
Kelly, Jeff
  See Kelly, Jeffrey
Kelly, Jeffrey 1946- 65
Kelly, Joanne (W.) 1934- 87
Kelly, Kate 1958- 91
Kelly, Kathleen M. 1964- 71
Kelly, Katy 1955- 169
Kelly, Lauren
  See Oates, Joyce Carol
Kelly, Laurene 1954- 123
Kelly, Martha Rose 1914-1983 37
Kelly, Marty
  See Kelly, Martha Rose
Kelly, Mij 166
Kelly, Ralph
  See Geis, Darlene Stern
Kelly, Regina Z(immerman) 1898-1986 5
Kelly, Rosalie (Ruth) 43
Kelly, Tom 1961- 191
Kelly, Walt(er Crawford) 1913-1973 18
Kelsey, Alice Geer 1896-1982 1
Kelsey, Elin 159
Kemnitz, Thomas Milton, Jr. 1984- 152
Kemnitz, Tom, Jr.
  See Kemnitz, Thomas Milton, Jr.
Kemp, Gene 1926- 75
  Earlier sketch in SATA 25
  See also CLR 29
Kempner, Mary Jean 1913-1969 10
Kempter, Christa 1945- 187
Kempton, Jean Welch 1914- 10
Kenah, Katharine 1949- 182
Kenda, Margaret 1942- 71
Kendall, Carol (Seeger) 1917- 74
  Earlier sketch in SATA 11
  See also SAAS 7
Kendall, Katherine
  See Applegate, Katherine (Alice)
Kendall, Lace
  See Stoutenburg, Adrien (Pearl)
Kendall, Martha E. 87
Kendall, Russ 1957- 83
Kenealy, James P. 1927- 52
  Brief entry 29
Kenealy, Jim
  See Kenealy, James P.
Kennaway, Adrienne 1945- 171
  Earlier sketch in SATA 60
Kennedy, Brendan 1970- 57
Kennedy, Dana Forrest 1917- 74
Kennedy, Dorothy M(intzlaff) 1931- 53
Kennedy, Doug 1963- 189
  Earlier sketch in SATA 122
Kennedy, Frances 1937- 192
Kennedy, John Fitzgerald 1917-1963 11
Kennedy, Joseph Charles 1929- 130
  Autobiography Feature 130
  Earlier sketches in SATA 14, 86
  See Kennedy, X. J.
Kennedy, Kim 189
Kennedy, Pamela (J.) 1946- 87
Kennedy, Paul E(dward) 1929- 113
  Earlier sketch in SATA 33
Kennedy, Richard (Pitt) 1910-1989
  Obituary 60
Kennedy, (Jerome) Richard 1932- 22

Kennedy, Robert 1938- 63
Kennedy, T.A. 1953- 42
  Brief entry 35
Kennedy, Teresa
  See Kennedy, T.A.
Kennedy, Teresa A.
  See Kennedy, T.A.
Kennedy, William 1928- 57
Kennedy, William Joseph
  See Kennedy, William
Kennedy, X. J.
  See CLR 27
  See also SAAS 22
  See Kennedy, Joseph Charles
Kennell, Ruth Epperson 1893-1977 6
  Obituary 25
Kennemore, Tim 1957- 133
Kennen, Ally 190
Kennett, David 1959- 121
Kenny, Ellsworth Newcomb 1909-1971
  Obituary 26
Kenny, Herbert Andrew 1912-2002 13
Kenny, Jude
  See Daly, Jude
Kenny, Kathryn
  See Bowden, Joan Chase
  and Krull, Kathleen
  and Sanderlin, Owenita (Harrah)
  and Stack, Nicolete Meredith
Kenny, Kevin
  See Krull, Kathleen
Kensinger, George
  See Fichter, George S.
Kensington, Kathryn Wesley
  See Rusch, Kristine Kathryn
Kent, Alexander
  See Reeman, Douglas Edward
Kent, David
  See Lambert, David (Compton)
Kent, Deborah Ann 1948- 155
  Brief entry 41
  Earlier sketches in SATA 47, 104
Kent, Jack
  See Kent, John Wellington
Kent, John Wellington 1920-1985 24
  Obituary 45
Kent, Lisa 1942- 90
Kent, Mallory
  See Lowndes, Robert A(ugustine) W(ard)
Kent, Margaret 1894- 2
Kent, Rockwell 1882-1971 6
Kent, Rose 188
Kent, Sherman 1903-1986 20
  Obituary 47
Kenward, Jean 1920- 42
Kenworthy, Leonard S. 1912-1991 6
Kenyon, Karen (Smith) 1938- 145
Kenyon, Kate
  See Adorjan, Carol (Madden)
  and Ransom, Candice F.
Kenyon, Ley 1913-1990 6
Keown, Elizabeth 78
Kepes, Juliet A(ppleby) 1919-1999 13
Kerby, Mona 1951- 75
Kerigan, Florence 1896-1984 12
Kerley, Barbara 1960- 191
  Earlier sketch in SATA 138
Kerman, Gertrude
  See Furman, Gertrude Lerner Kerman
Kerns, Thelma 1929- 116
Kerr, Anne Louise
  See Mackey, Weezie Kerr
Kerr, Bob 1951- 120
Kerr, Jessica 1901-1991 13
Kerr, (Anne-)Judith 1923-1970 24
Kerr, M. E.
  See Meaker, Marijane
Kerr, P.B.
  See Kerr, Philip
Kerr, Philip 1956- 168
Kerr, Phyllis Forbes 1942- 72

Kerr, Tom 1950- 77
Kerrin, Jessica Scott 174
Kerry, Frances
  See Kerigan, Florence
Kerry, Lois
  See Duncan, Lois
Kershen, (L.) Michael 1982- 82
Kerven, Rosalind 1954- 83
Ker Wilson, Barbara 1929- 121
  Earlier sketches in SATA 20, 70
  See also SAAS 18
Keselman, Gabriela 1953- 128
Kesey, Ken 1935-2001 66
  Obituary 131
Kesey, Ken Elton
  See Kesey, Ken
Kesler, Jay 1935- 65
Kessel, Joyce Karen 1937- 41
Kessler, Cristina 190
Kessler, Ethel 1922- 44
  Brief entry 37
Kessler, Leonard P. 1921- 14
Kest, Kristin 1967- 168
  Earlier sketch in SATA 118
Kesteven, G. R.
  See Crosher, G. R.
Ketcham, Hank
  See Ketcham, Henry King
Ketcham, Henry King 1920-2001 28
  Brief entry 27
  Obituary 128
Ketcham, Sallie 1963- 124
Ketchum, Liza 1946- 132
  See Murrow, Liza Ketchum
Ketner, Mary Grace 1946- 75
Kettelkamp, Larry (Dale) 1933- 2
  See also SAAS 3
Ketteman, Helen 1945- 167
  Earlier sketches in SATA 73, 115
Kettle, Peter
  See Glover, Denis (James Matthews)
Kevles, Bettyann Holtzmann 1938- 23
Key, Alexander (Hill) 1904-1979 8
  Obituary 23
Key, Samuel M.
  See de Lint, Charles
Key, Watt 1970- 189
Keyes, Daniel 1927- 37
Keyes, Fenton 1915-1999 34
Keyes, Greg 1963- 116
Keyes, J. Gregory
  See Keyes, Greg
Keyser, Marcia 1933- 42
Keyser, Sarah
  See McGuire, Leslie (Sarah)
Khalsa, Dayal Kaur 1943-1989 62
  See also CLR 30
  See Kaur Khalsa, Dayal
Khan, Rukhsana 1962- 165
  Earlier sketch in SATA 118
Khanshendel, Chiron
  See Rose, Wendy
Kheirabadi, Masoud 1951- 158
Khemir, Sabiha 87
Kherdian, David 1931- 74
  Autobiography Feature 125
  Earlier sketch in SATA 16
  See also CLR 24
Khing, T.T. 1933- 192
Kibbe, Pat (Hosley) 60
Kidd, Diana 1933-2000 150
Kidd, Richard 1952-2008 152
  Obituary 194
Kidd, Ronald 1948- 173
  Earlier sketches in SATA 42, 92
Kiddell, John 1922- 3
Kiddell-Monroe, Joan 1908-1972 55
Kidwell, Carl 1910- 43
Kiefer, Irene 1926- 21
Kiefer, Kathleen Balmes 1957- 142

Kierstead, Vera M.
  See Kierstead-Farber, Vera M.
Kierstead-Farber, Vera M. 1913- 121
Kierstead-Farber, Vera May
  See Kierstead-Farber, Vera M.
Kiesel, Stanley 1925- 35
Kiesler, Kate (A.) 1971- 152
  Earlier sketch in SATA 90
Kihn, Greg 1952- 110
Kikukawa, Cecily H(arder) 1919- 44
  Brief entry 35
Kilcher, Jewel 1974- 109
Kile, Joan 1940- 78
Kilgore, Kathleen 1946- 42
Kilian, Crawford 1941- 35
Killdeer, John
  See Mayhar, Ardath
Killien, Christi 1956- 73
Killilea, Marie (Lyons) 1913-1991 2
Killingback, Julia 1944- 63
Killough, (Karen) Lee 1942- 64
Kilreon, Beth
  See Walker, Barbara (Jeanne) K(erlin)
Kilworth, Garry 1941- 94
Kilworth, Garry D.
  See Kilworth, Garry
Kilworth, Garry Douglas
  See Kilworth, Garry
Kim, Helen 1899-1970 98
Kimball, Gayle 1943- 90
Kimball, Violet T(ew) 1932- 126
Kimball, Yeffe 1914-1978 37
Kimber, Murray 1964- 171
Kimble, Warren 176
Kimbrough, Emily 1899-1989 2
  Obituary 59
Kimeldorf, Martin 1948- 121
Kimeldorf, Martin R.
  See Kimeldorf, Martin
Kimenye, Barbara 1940(?)- 121
Kimmel, Elizabeth Cody 170
Kimmel, Eric A. 1946- 176
  Earlier sketches in SATA 13, 80, 125
Kimmel, Margaret Mary 1938- 43
  Brief entry 33
Kimmelman, Burt 1947- 180
Kimmelman, Leslie (Grodinsky) 1958- 156
  Earlier sketch in SATA 85
Kincaid, Jamaica 1949-
  See CLR 63
Kincher, Jonni 1949- 79
Kindl, Patrice 1951- 128
  Earlier sketch in SATA 82
  See also CLR 132
Kindred, Wendy (Good) 1937- 7
Kines, Pat Decker 1937- 12
King, Adam
  See Hoare, Robert J(ohn)
King, Alison
  See Martini, Teri
King, (Maria) Anna 1964- 72
King, Billie Jean 1943- 12
King, Christopher (L.) 1945- 84
King, (David) Clive 1924- 144
  Earlier sketch in SATA 28
King, Colin 1943- 76
King, Cynthia 1925- 7
King, Daniel (John) 1963- 130
King, Elizabeth 1953- 83
King, Frank O. 1883-1969
  Obituary 22
King, Frank R. 1904-1999 127
King, Jane
  See Currie, Stephen
King, Jeanette (Margaret) 1959- 105
King, Larry L. 1929- 66
King, Laurie R. 1952- 88
King, Marian 1900(?)-1986 23
  Obituary 47
King, Martin Luther, Jr. 1929-1968 14
King, Mary Ellen 1958- 93

King, Paul
  See Drackett, Phil(ip Arthur)
King, Paula
  See Downing, Paula E.
King, Stephen 1947- 161
  Earlier sketches in SATA *9, 55*
  See also CLR *124*
King, Stephen Edwin
  See King, Stephen
King, Stephen Michael 157
King, Steve
  See King, Stephen
King, Thomas 1943- 96
King, Thomas Hunt
  See King, Thomas
King, Tony 1947- 39
Kingman, Dong (Moy Shu) 1911-2000 44
Kingman, Lee 67
  Earlier sketch in SATA *1*
  See also SAAS *3*
  See Natti, (Mary) Lee
Kingsland, Leslie William 1912- 13
Kingsley, Charles 1819-1875
  See YABC *2*
  See also CLR *77*
Kingsley, Emily Perl 1940- 33
Kingsley, Kaza 193
King-Smith, Dick 1922- 192
  Brief entry 38
  Earlier sketches in SATA *47, 80, 135*
  See also CLR *40*
Kingston, Maxine Hong 1940- 53
Kingston, Maxine Ting Ting Hong
  See Kingston, Maxine Hong
Kinney, C. Cle(land) 1915- 6
Kinney, Harrison 1921- 13
Kinney, Jean Stout 1912- 12
Kinney, Jeff 1971- 187
Kinsey, Elizabeth
  See Clymer, Eleanor
Kinsey, Helen 1948- 82
Kinsey-Warnock, Natalie 1956- 167
  Earlier sketches in SATA *71, 116*
Kinzel, Dorothy 1950- 57
Kinzel, Dottie
  See Kinzel, Dorothy
Kipling, (Joseph) Rudyard 1865-1936 100
  See also YABC *2*
  See also CLR *65*
Kippax, Frank
  See Needle, Jan
Kirby, David K. 1944- 78
Kirby, David Kirk
  See Kirby, David K.
Kirby, Margaret
  See Bingley, Margaret (Jane Kirby)
Kirby, Susan E. 1949- 62
Kirk, Connie Ann 1957- 167
Kirk, Daniel 1952- 153
  Earlier sketch in SATA *107*
Kirk, David 1955- 161
  Earlier sketch in SATA *117*
Kirk, Heather 1949- 166
Kirk, Ruth (Kratz) 1925- 5
Kirkham, Dinah
  See Card, Orson Scott
Kirkland, Will
  See Hale, Arlene
Kirkpatrick, Katherine (Anne) 1964- 113
Kirkup, James 1918- 12
Kirkus, Virginia
  See Glick, Virginia Kirkus
Kirkwood, Kathryn
  See Fluke, Joanne
Kirshenbaum, Binnie 79
Kirshner, David S. 1958- 123
Kish, Eleanor M(ary) 1924- 73
Kish, Ely
  See Kish, Eleanor M(ary)
Kishida, Eriko 1929- 12
Kisinger, Grace Gelvin (Maze) 1913-1965 .. 10

Kissin, Eva H. 1923- 10
Kissinger, Rosemary K.
  See Updyke, Rosemary K.
Kistler, John M. 1967- 160
Kitamura, Satoshi 1956- 143
  Earlier sketches in SATA *62, 98*
  See also CLR *60*
Kitchen, Bert
  See Kitchen, Herbert Thomas
Kitchen, Herbert Thomas 1940- 70
Kite, L. Patricia
  See Kite, Pat
Kite, Pat 1940- 78
Kitt, Tamara
  See de Regniers, Beatrice Schenk (Freedman)
Kittinger, Jo S(usenbach) 1955- 148
  Earlier sketch in SATA *96*
Kituomba
  See Odaga, Asenath (Bole)
Kitzinger, Sheila 1929- 57
Kiwak, Barbara 1966- 103
Kjelgaard, James Arthur 1910-1959 17
  See also CLR *81*
  See Kjelgaard, Jim
Kjelgaard, Jim
  See Kjelgaard, James Arthur
Kjelle, Marylou Morano 1954- 146
Klagsbrun, Francine (Lifton) 36
Klaits, Barrie 1944- 52
Klam, Cheryl 191
Klaperman, Gilbert 1921- 33
Klaperman, Libby Mindlin 1921-1982 33
  Obituary 31
Klass, David 1960- 142
  Earlier sketch in SATA *88*
Klass, Morton 1927-2001 11
Klass, Sheila Solomon 1927- 99
  Autobiography Feature 126
  Earlier sketch in SATA *45*
  See also SAAS *26*
Klause, Annette Curtis 1953- 175
  Earlier sketch in SATA *79*
  See also CLR *104*
Klaveness, Jan O'Donnell 1939- 86
Kleberger, Ilse 1921- 5
Kleeberg, Irene (Flitner) Cumming 1932- 65
Klein, Aaron E. 1930-1998 45
  Brief entry 28
Klein, Bill 1945- 89
Klein, David 1919-2001 59
Klein, Frederick C. 1938- 154
Klein, Gerda Weissmann 1924- 44
Klein, H(erbert) Arthur 8
Klein, James 1932- 115
Klein, Leonore (Glotzer) 1916- 6
Klein, Mina C(ooper) 1906-1979 8
Klein, Norma 1938-1989 57
  Earlier sketch in SATA *7*
  See also CLR *19*
  See also SAAS *1*
Klein, Rachel S. 1953- 105
Klein, Robin 1936- 164
  Brief entry 45
  Earlier sketches in SATA *55, 80*
  See also CLR *21*
Klemin, Diana 65
Klemm, Barry 1945- 104
Klemm, Edward G., Jr. 1910-2001 30
Klemm, Roberta K(ohnhorst) 1884-1975 30
Kleven, Elisa 1958- 173
  Earlier sketch in SATA *76*
  See also CLR *85*
Klevin, Jill Ross 1935- 39
  Brief entry 38
Kliban, B(ernard) 1935-1990 35
  Obituary 66
Klimowicz, Barbara 1927- 10
Kline, Christina Baker 1964- 101
Kline, James
  See Klein, James

Kline, Jim
  See Kline, Jim
Kline, Lisa Williams 1954- 143
Kline, Suzy 1943- 193
  Autobiography Feature 193
  Brief entry 48
  Earlier sketches in SATA *67, 99, 152*
Kliros, Thea 1935- 106
Klise, Kate 181
Klise, M. Sarah 1961- 180
  Earlier sketch in SATA *128*
Klots, Alexander Barrett 1903-1989
  Obituary 62
Klug, Ron(ald) 1939- 31
Knaak, Richard A. 1961- 166
  Earlier sketch in SATA *86*
Knaak, Richard Allen
  See Knaak, Richard A.
Knapp, Edward
  See Kunhardt, Edith
Knapp, Ron 1952- 34
Knebel, Fletcher 1911-1993 36
  Obituary 75
Kneeland, Linda Clarke 1947- 94
Knickerbocker, Diedrich
  See Irving, Washington
Knifesmith
  See Cutler, Ivor
Knigge, Robert (R.) 1921(?)-1987 50
Knight, Anne (Katherine) 1946- 34
Knight, Brenda 112
Knight, Christopher G. 1943- 96
Knight, Damon (Francis) 1922-2002 9
  Obituary 139
Knight, David C(arpenter) 1925-1984 14
  See also CLR *38*
Knight, Eric 1897-1943 18
Knight, Eric Mowbray
  See Knight, Eric
Knight, Francis Edgar 1905- 14
Knight, Frank
  See Knight, Francis Edgar
Knight, Hilary 1926- 132
  Earlier sketches in SATA *15, 69*
Knight, Joan (MacPhail) 159
  Earlier sketch in SATA *82*
Knight, Joan
  See Knight, Joan (MacPhail)
Knight, Kathryn Lasky
  See Lasky, Kathryn
Knight, Mallory T.
  See Hurwood, Bernhardt J.
Knight, Ruth Adams 1898-1974
  Obituary 20
Knight, Theodore O. 1946- 77
Knobloch, Dorothea 1951- 88
Knoepfle, John (Ignatius) 1923- 66
Knott, Bill
  See Knott, William C(ecil, Jr.)
Knott, William C(ecil, Jr.) 1927- 3
  See Knott, Bill
  and Mitchum, Hank
  and Sharpe, Jon
Knotts, Howard (Clayton, Jr.) 1922- 25
Knowles, Anne 1933- 37
Knowles, John 1926-2001 89
  Obituary 134
  Earlier sketch in SATA *8*
  See also CLR *98*
Knox, Calvin M.
  See Silverberg, Robert
Knox, (Mary) Eleanor Jessie 1909-2000 59
  Earlier sketch in SATA *30*
Knox, Elizabeth 1959- 176
Knox, Elizabeth Fiona
  See Knox, Elizabeth
Knox, James
  See Brittain, William (E.)
Knox, Jolyne 1937- 76
Knudsen, James 1950- 42
Knudsen, Michelle 171

Knudson, R. R.
See SAAS 18
See Knudson, Rozanne
Knudson, Richard L(ewis) 1930- 34
Knudson, Rozanne 1932-2008 79
Earlier sketch in SATA 7
See Knudson, R. R.
Knutson, Barbara 1959-2005 166
Knutson, Kimberley 115
Knye, Cassandra
See Disch, Thomas M.
Koch, Dorothy Clarke 1924- 6
Koch, Kenneth 1925-2002 65
Koch, Kenneth Jay
See Koch, Kenneth
Koch, Phyllis (Mae) McCallum 1911- 10
Kocsis, J. C.
See Paul, James
Koda-Callan, Elizabeth 1944- 140
Earlier sketch in SATA 67
Koehler, Phoebe 1955- 85
Koehler-Pentacoff, Elizabeth 1957- 160
Earlier sketch in SATA 96
Koehn, Ilse
See Van Zwienen, Ilse Charlotte Koehn
Koeller, Carol 192
Koenig, Viviane 1950- 80
Koering, Ursula 1921-1976 64
Koerner, W(illiam) H(enry) D(avid)
1878-1938 21
Koertge, Ronald 1940- 131
Earlier sketches in SATA 53, 92
Koestler-Grack, Rachel A. 1973- 156
Koff, Richard Myram 1926- 62
Koffinke, Carol 1949- 82
Kogan, Deborah 50
See Kogan Ray, Deborah
Kogan Ray, Deborah 1940- 161
See Kogan, Deborah
and Ray, Deborah
Kogawa, Joy Nozomi 1935- 99
Kogler, Jennifer Anne 1982(?)- 174
Kohl, Herbert 1937- 47
Kohl, Herbert R.
See Kohl, Herbert
Kohl, MaryAnn F(aubion) 1947- 144
Earlier sketch in SATA 74
Kohler, Julilly H(ouse) 1908-1976
Obituary 20
Kohn, Bernice 4
See Hunt, Bernice (Kohn)
Kohn, Rita (T.) 1933- 89
Kohner, Frederick 1905-1986 10
Obituary 48
Koide, Tan 1938-1986 50
Koike, Kay 1940- 72
Koja, Kathe 1960- 155
Kolb, Larry J. 1953- 175
Kolba, St. Tamara 22
Kolibalova, Marketa
See Kolibalova, Marketa
Kolibalova, Marketa 1953- 126
Koller, Jackie French 1948- 157
Earlier sketches in SATA 72, 109
See also CLR 68
Kolodny, Nancy J. 1946- 76
Komaiko, Leah 1954- 164
Earlier sketch in SATA 97
Komisar, Lucy 1942- 9
Komoda, Beverly 1939- 25
Komoda, Kiyo 1937- 9
Kompaneyets, Marc 1974- 169
Komroff, Manuel 1890-1974 2
Obituary 20
Konigsburg, E.L. 1930- 194
Earlier sketches in SATA 4, 48, 94, 126
See also CLR 81
Konigsburg, Elaine Lobl
See Konigsburg, E.L.

Koning, Hans 1921-2007
Obituary 182
See Koningsberger, Hans
Koningsberger, Hans 5
See Koning, Hans
Konkle, Janet Everest 1917- 12
Kono, Erin Eitter 1973- 177
Konzak, Burt 1946- 151
Koob, Theodora (J. Foth) 1918- 23
Kooiker, Leonie
See Kooyker-Romijn, Johanna Maria
Koons, James
See Pernu, Dennis
Koontz, Dean
See Koontz, Dean R.
Koontz, Dean R. 1945- 165
Earlier sketch in SATA 92
Koontz, Dean Ray
See Koontz, Dean R.
Koontz, Robin Michal 1954- 136
Earlier sketch in SATA 70
Kooyker, Leonie
See Kooyker-Romijn, Johanna Maria
Kooyker-Romijn, Johanna Maria 1927- 48
See Kooyker, Leonie
Kooyker-Romyn, Johanna Maria
See Kooyker-Romijn, Johanna Maria
Kopelke, Lisa 1963- 154
Kopper, Lisa (Esther) 1950- 105
Brief entry 51
Koppes, Steven N. 1957- 169
Koppes, Steven Nelson
See Koppes, Steven N.
Korach, Mimi 1922- 9
Koralek, Jenny 1934- 140
Earlier sketch in SATA 71
Korczak, Janusz 65
See Goldszmit, Henryk
Koren, Edward (Benjamin) 1935- 148
Earlier sketch in SATA 5
Korinets, Iurii Iosifovich
See Korinetz, Yuri (Iosifovich)
Korinetz, Yuri (Iosifovich) 1923- 9
See also CLR 4
Korman, Bernice 1937- 78
Korman, Gordon 1963- 167
Brief entry 41
Earlier sketches in SATA 49, 81, 119
See also CLR 25
Korman, Gordon Richard
See Korman, Gordon
Korman, Justine 1958- 70
Kornblatt, Marc 1954- 147
Earlier sketch in SATA 84
Kornprobst, Jacques 1937- 177
Korte, Gene J. 1950- 74
Korty, Carol 1937- 15
Koscielniak, Bruce 1947- 153
Earlier sketches in SATA 67, 99
Koshin, Alexander (A.) 1952- 86
Kositsky, Lynne 1947- 158
Koskenmaki, Rosalie
See Maggio, Rosalie
Koss, Amy Goldman 1954- 158
Earlier sketch in SATA 115
Kossin, Sandy (Sanford) 1926- 10
Kossman, Nina 1959- 84
Kostick, Conor 1964- 186
Kotzwinkle, William 1938- 146
Earlier sketches in SATA 24, 70
See also CLR 6
Kouhi, Elizabeth 1917- 54
Brief entry 49
Kouts, Anne 1945- 8
Koutsky, Jan Dale 1955- 146
Kovacs, Deborah 1954- 132
Earlier sketch in SATA 79
Kovalski, Maryann 1951- 175
Earlier sketches in SATA 58, 97
See also CLR 34
See also SAAS 21

Kowalski, Kathiann M. 1955- 151
Earlier sketch in SATA 96
Kraft, Betsy Harvey 1937- 157
Kraft, Erik P. 193
Krahn, Fernando 1935- 49
Brief entry 31
See also CLR 3
Krakauer, Hoong Yee Lee 1955- 86
Krakauer, Jon 1954- 108
Kramer, George
See Heuman, William
Kramer, Nora 1896(?)-1984 26
Obituary 39
Kramer, Remi (Thomas) 1935- 90
Krantz, Hazel (Newman) 12
Kranzler, George G(ershon) 1916- 28
Kranzler, Gershon
See Kranzler, George G(ershon)
Krasilovsky, Phyllis 1926- 38
Earlier sketch in SATA 1
See also CLR 83
See also SAAS 5
Krasne, Betty
See Levine, Betty K(rasne)
Krasner, Steven 1953- 154
Krasno, Rena 1923- 104
Kratman, Tom 175
Kraus, Joanna Halpert 1937- 87
Kraus, (Herman) Robert 1925-2001 93
Obituary 130
Earlier sketches in SATA 4, 65
See also SAAS 11
Krauss, Ruth (Ida) 1911-1993 30
Obituary 75
Earlier sketch in SATA 1
See also CLR 42
Krautter, Elisa (Bialk) 1912(?)-1990 1
Obituary 65
Krautwurst, Terry 1946- 79
Kray, Robert Clement 1930- 82
Krech, Bob 1956- 185
Krech, Robert
See Krech, Bob
Kredel, Fritz 1900-1973 17
Kreikemeier, Gregory Scott 1965- 85
Kreloff, Elliot 189
Krementz, Jill 1940- 134
Earlier sketches in SATA 17, 71
See also CLR 5
See also SAAS 8
Kremer, Marcie
See Sorenson, Margo
Krenina, Katya 1968- 101
Krensky, Stephen 1953- 188
Brief entry 41
Earlier sketches in SATA 47, 93, 136
Krensky, Stephen Alan
See Krensky, Stephen
Kresh, Paul 1919-1997 61
Obituary 94
Kress, Nancy 1948- 147
Autobiography Feature 147
Earlier sketch in SATA 85
Kricher, John C. 1944- 113
Krieger, Melanie 96
Krinitz, Esther Nisenthal 1927-2001 194
Kripke, Dorothy Karp 30
Krisher, Trudy 1946- 160
Earlier sketch in SATA 86
Krisher, Trudy B.
See Krisher, Trudy
Krishnaswami, Uma 1956- 182
Earlier sketch in SATA 144
Kristof, Jane 1932- 8
Kroeber, Theodora (Kracaw) 1897-1979 1
Kroeger, Mary Kay 1950- 92
Krohn, Katherine E(lizabeth) 1961- 125
Earlier sketch in SATA 84
Kroll, Francis Lynde 1904-1973 10

Kroll, Steven 1941- *135*
   Autobiography Feature *135*
   Earlier sketches in SATA *19, 66, 125*
   See also SAAS *7*
Kroll, Virginia L. 1948- *168*
   Earlier sketches in SATA *76, 114*
Kroll, Virginia Louisa
   See Kroll, Virginia L.
Kromhout, Rindert 1958- *189*
Krommes, Beth 1956- *181*
   Earlier sketch in SATA *128*
Kronenwetter, Michael 1943- *62*
Kroniuk, Lisa
   See Berton, Pierre (Francis de Marigny)
Kropp, Paul (Stephan) 1948- *38*
   Brief entry *34*
   See also CLR *96*
Krosoczka, Jarrett J. 1977- *155*
Krovatin, Christopher 1985- *171*
Kruess, James
   See CLR *9*
   See Kruss, James
Kruglik, Gerald *187*
Krull, Kathleen 1952- *184*
   Autobiography Feature *106*
   Brief entry *39*
   Earlier sketches in SATA *52, 80, 149*
   See also CLR *44*
Krumgold, Joseph (Quincy) 1908-1980 .... *48*
   Obituary *23*
   Earlier sketch in SATA *1*
Krupinski, Loretta 1940- *161*
   Earlier sketches in SATA *67, 102*
Krupnick, Karen 1947- *89*
Krupp, E(dwin) C(harles) 1944- *123*
   Earlier sketch in SATA *53*
Krupp, Robin Rector 1946- *53*
Krush, Beth 1918- *18*
Krush, Joe 1918- *18*
   See Krush, Joseph P.
Kruss, James 1926-1997 .... *8*
   See Kruess, James
Krykorka, Vladyana 1945- *96*
Kubie, Eleanor Gottheil
   See Kubie, Nora Gottheil Benjamin
Kubie, Nora Benjamin
   See Kubie, Nora Gottheil Benjamin
Kubie, Nora Gottheil Benjamin 1899-1988 . *39*
   Obituary *59*
Kubinyi, Laszlo 1937- *94*
   Earlier sketch in SATA *17*
Kudlinski, Kathleen V. 1950- *150*
Kuenstler, Morton 1927- *10*
Kuh, Charlotte 1892(?)-1985
   Obituary *43*
Kuharski, Janice 1947- *128*
Kuijer, Guus 1942- *179*
Kujoth, Jean Spealman 1935-1975
   Obituary *30*
Kuklin, Susan 1941- *163*
   Earlier sketches in SATA *63, 95*
   See also CLR *51*
Kulikov, Boris 1966- *170*
Kulka, Joe *188*
Kulling, Monica 1952- *89*
Kullman, Harry 1919-1982 .... *35*
Kumin, Maxine 1925- *12*
Kumin, Maxine Winokur
   See Kumin, Maxine
Kunhardt, Dorothy (Meserve) 1901-1979 .... *53*
   Obituary *22*
Kunhardt, Edith 1937- *67*
Kunjufu, Jawanza 1953- *73*
Kunstler, Morton
   See Kuenstler, Morton
Kuntz, J(ohn) L. 1947- *91*
Kuntz, Jerry 1956- *133*
Kupferberg, Herbert 1918-2001 .... *19*
Kuratomi, Chizuko 1939- *12*
   See also CLR *32*
Kurczok, Belinda 1978- *121*

Kurelek, William 1927-1977 .... *8*
   Obituary *27*
   See also CLR *2*
Kurian, George 1928- *65*
Kurjian, Judi(th M.) 1944- *127*
Kurland, Gerald 1942- *13*
Kurland, Michael 1938- *118*
   Earlier sketch in SATA *48*
Kurland, Michael Joseph
   See Kurland, Michael
Kuroi, Ken 1947- *120*
Kurokawa, Mitsuhiro 1954- *88*
Kurten, Bjorn (Olof) 1924-1988 .... *64*
Kurtz, Jane 1952- *139*
   Earlier sketch in SATA *91*
   See also CLR *123*
Kurtz, Katherine 1944- *182*
   Earlier sketches in SATA *76, 126*
Kurtz, Katherine Irene
   See Kurtz, Katherine
Kurz, Rudolf 1952- *95*
Kushner, Donn (J.) 1927- *52*
   See also CLR *55*
Kushner, Ellen 1955- *98*
Kushner, Ellen Ruth
   See Kushner, Ellen
Kushner, Jill Menkes 1951- *62*
Kushner, Lawrence 1943- *169*
   Earlier sketch in SATA *83*
Kushner, Tony 1956- *160*
Kuskin, Karla 1932- *164*
   Earlier sketches in SATA *2, 68, 111*
   See also CLR *4*
   See also SAAS *3*
Kuskin, Karla Seidman
   See Kuskin, Karla
Kusugak, Michael 1948- *143*
Kusugak, Michael Arvaarluk
   See Kusugak, Michael
Kuttner, Paul 1922- *18*
Kuyper, Sjoerd 1952- *177*
Kuzma, Kay 1941- *39*
Kvale, Velma R(uth) 1898-1979 .... *8*
Kvasnosky, Laura McGee 1951- *182*
   Earlier sketches in SATA *93, 142*
Kwasney, Michelle D. 1960- *162*
Kyle, Benjamin
   See Gottfried, Theodore Mark
Kyle, Elisabeth
   See Dunlop, Agnes M. R.
Kyte, Kathy S. 1946- *50*
   Brief entry *44*

L

L., Barry
   See Longyear, Barry B(rookes)
L., Tommy
   See Lorkowski, Thomas V(incent)
Labouisse, Eve Curie
   See Curie, Eve
Labouisse, Eve Denise
   See Curie, Eve
Lace, William W. 1942- *126*
Lacey, Josh 1968- *187*
Lachner, Dorothea
   See Knobloch, Dorothea
Lachtman, Ofelia Dumas 1919- *179*
Lackey, Mercedes R. 1950- *127*
   Earlier sketch in SATA *81*
Lackey, Mercedes Ritchie
   See Lackey, Mercedes R.
Lacoe, Addie *78*
Lacome, Julie 1961- *174*
   Earlier sketch in SATA *80*
Lacy, Leslie Alexander 1937- *6*
Ladd, Cheryl (Jean) 1951- *113*
Ladd, Louise 1943- *97*

Ladd, Veronica
   See Miner, Jane Claypool
Laden, Nina 1962- *148*
   Earlier sketch in SATA *85*
Lader, Lawrence 1919-2006 .... *6*
   Obituary *178*
LaDoux, Rita C. 1951- *74*
Lady, A
   See Taylor, Ann
Lady Mears
   See Tempest, Margaret Mary
Lady of Quality, A
   See Bagnold, Enid
La Farge, Oliver 1901-1963 .... *19*
La Farge, Oliver Hazard Perry
   See La Farge, Oliver
La Farge, Phyllis *14*
LaFaye, A. 1970- *156*
   Earlier sketch in SATA *105*
LaFaye, Alexandria R.T.
   See LaFaye, A.
LaFevers, R.L. *191*
LaFevers, Robin L.
   See LaFevers, R.L.
Laffin, John (Alfred Charles) 1922- *31*
LaFontaine, Bruce 1948- *176*
   Earlier sketch in SATA *114*
La Fontaine, Jean de 1621-1695 .... *18*
Lager, Claude
   See Lapp, Christiane (Germain)
Lager, Marilyn 1939- *52*
Lagercrantz, Rose (Elsa) 1947- *39*
Lagerloef, Selma (Ottiliana Lovisa)
   See Lagerlof, Selma (Ottiliana Lovisa)
Lagerlof, Selma (Ottiliana Lovisa)
   1858-1940 .... *15*
   See also CLR *7*
   See Lagerloef, Selma (Ottiliana Lovisa)
Laguna, Sofie 1968- *158*
LaHaye, Tim F. 1926- *149*
LaHaye, Timothy F.
   See LaHaye, Tim F.
Laiken, Deirdre S(usan) 1948- *48*
   Brief entry *40*
Laimgruber, Monika 1946- *11*
Lain, Anna
   See Lamb, Nancy
Laing, Alexander (Kinnan) 1903-1976 .... *117*
Laing, Martha 1951- *39*
Laird, Christa 1944- *108*
   Autobiography Feature *120*
   See also SAAS *26*
Laird, Elizabeth (Mary Risk) 1943- *159*
   Earlier sketches in SATA *77, 114*
   See also CLR *65*
Laird, Jean E(louise) 1930- *38*
Laite, Gordon 1925- *31*
Lake, Harriet
   See Taylor, Paula (Wright)
Lakin, Patricia 1944- *190*
Laklan, Carli 1907-1988 .... *5*
Laliberte, Louise-Andree 1958- *169*
Lalicki, Barbara *61*
Lalicki, Tom 1949- *186*
Lally, Soinbhe 1945- *119*
LaMarche, Jim *162*
Lamb, Albert *187*
Lamb, Beatrice Pitney 1904-1997 .... *21*
Lamb, Charles 1775-1834 .... *17*
Lamb, Elizabeth Searle 1917- *31*
Lamb, G(eoffrey) F(rederick) *10*
Lamb, Harold (Albert) 1892-1962 .... *53*
Lamb, Lynton (Harold) 1907-1977 .... *10*
Lamb, Mary Ann 1764-1847 .... *17*
Lamb, Nancy 1939- *80*
Lamb, Robert (Boyden) 1941- *13*
Lamba, Marie *195*
Lambert, David (Compton) 1932- *84*
   Brief entry *49*
Lambert, Janet 1895(?)-1973 .... *25*
Lambert, Martha L. *113*

Lambert, Saul 1928- *23*
Lambert, Stephen *174*
Lamburn, Richmal Crompton 1890-1969 .... *5*
  See Crompton, Richmal
Lamensdorf, Len 1930- *120*
Lamensdorf, Leonard
  See Lamensdorf, Len
Laminack, Lester L. 1956- *163*
  Earlier sketch in SATA *120*
Lamorisse, Albert (Emmanuel) 1922-1970 ... *23*
Lampert, Emily 1951- *52*
  Brief entry *49*
Lamplugh, Lois 1921- *17*
Lampman, Evelyn Sibley 1907-1980 .... *87*
  Obituary *23*
  Earlier sketch in SATA *4*
Lamprey, Louise 1869-1951
  See YABC 2
Lampton, Chris
  See Lampton, Christopher F.
Lampton, Christopher
  See Lampton, Christopher F.
Lampton, Christopher F. *67*
  Brief entry *47*
Lamstein, Sarah 1943- *174*
  Earlier sketch in SATA *126*
Lamstein, Sarah Marwil
  See Lamstein, Sarah
Lanagan, Margo 1960- *163*
Lancaster, Bruce 1896-1963 .... *9*
Lancaster, Matthew 1973(?)-1983
  Obituary *45*
Lance, Kathryn 1943- *76*
Land, Barbara (Neblett) 1923- *16*
Land, Jane
  See Borland, Kathryn Kilby
  and Speicher, Helen Ross S(mith)
Land, Myrick (Ebben) 1922-1998 .... *15*
Land, Ross
  See Borland, Kathryn Kilby
  and Speicher, Helen Ross S(mith)
Landau, Elaine 1948- *141*
  Earlier sketches in SATA *10, 94*
Landau, Jacob 1917- *38*
Landeck, Beatrice 1904-1978 .... *15*
Landin, Les 1923- *2*
Landis, J(ames) D(avid) 1942- *60*
  Brief entry *52*
Landis, James D.
  See Landis, J(ames) D(avid)
Landis, Jill Marie 1948- *101*
Landmann, Bimba 1968- *176*
Landon, Dena 1978(?)- *168*
Landon, Lucinda 1950- *56*
  Brief entry *51*
Landon, Margaret (Dorothea Mortenson)
  1903-1993 .... *50*
Landshoff, Ursula 1908-1989 .... *13*
Landstrom, Lena 1943- *146*
Landstrom, Olof 1943- *146*
Lane, Carolyn 1926-1993 .... *10*
Lane, Connie
  See Laux, Constance
Lane, Dakota 1959- *166*
  Earlier sketch in SATA *105*
Lane, Jerry
  See Martin, Patricia Miles
Lane, John (Richard) 1932- *15*
Lane, Margaret 1907-1994 .... *65*
  Brief entry *38*
  Obituary *79*
Lane, Rose Wilder 1887-1968 .... *29*
  Brief entry *28*
Lanes, Selma Gordon 1929- *3*
Lanfredi, Judy 1964- *83*
Lang, Andrew 1844-1912 .... *16*
  See also CLR *101*
Lang, Aubrey *169*
Lang, Paul 1948- *83*
Lang, Susan S. 1950- *68*

Lang, T.T.
  See Taylor, Theodore
Langdo, Bryan 1973- *191*
  Earlier sketch in SATA *138*
Lange, John
  See Crichton, Michael
Lange, Karen E. *190*
Lange, Suzanne 1945- *5*
Langley, Andrew 1949- *166*
  Earlier sketch in SATA *104*
Langley, Charles P(itman) III 1949- *103*
Langley, Jonathan 1952- *122*
Langley, Noel 1911-1980
  Obituary *25*
Langley, Wanda *173*
Langner, Nola *8*
  See Malone, Nola Langner
Langone, John (Michael) 1929- *46*
  Brief entry *38*
Langreuter, Jutta 1944- *122*
Langrish, Katherine *177*
Langsen, Richard C. 1953- *95*
Langstaff, John 1920-2005 .... *68*
  Obituary *172*
  Earlier sketch in SATA *6*
  See also CLR *3*
Langstaff, John Meredith
  See Langstaff, John
Langstaff, Launcelot
  See Irving, Washington
Langston, Laura 1958- *186*
Langton, Jane (Gillson) 1922- *140*
  Autobiography Feature *140*
  Earlier sketches in SATA *3, 68, 129*
  See also CLR *33*
  See also SAAS *5*
Lanier, Sidney 1842-1881 .... *18*
Lanier, Sterling E. 1927-2007 .... *109*
Lanier, Sterling Edmund
  See Lanier, Sterling E.
Lanino, Deborah 1964- *123*
Lankford, Mary D. 1932- *112*
  Earlier sketch in SATA *77*
Lannin, Joanne 1951- *121*
Lannin, Joanne A.
  See Lannin, Joanne
Lansdale, Joe R. 1951- *116*
Lansdale, Joe Richard
  See Lansdale, Joe R.
Lansing, Alfred 1921-1975 .... *35*
Lansing, Karen E. 1954- *71*
Lansky, Vicki 1942- *177*
Lantier-Sampon, Patricia 1952- *92*
Lantz, Fran
  See Lantz, Francess L(in)
Lantz, Francess L(in) 1952-2004 .... *153*
  Autobiography Feature *153*
  Obituary *159*
  Earlier sketches in SATA *63, 109*
  See Dixon, Franklin W.
Lantz, Paul 1908- *45*
Lantz, Walter 1900-1994 .... *37*
  Obituary *79*
Lanza, Barbara 1945- *101*
Lapp, Christiane (Germain) 1948- *74*
Lappin, Peter 1911-1999 .... *32*
Larbalestier, Justine *178*
Lardy, Philippe 1963- *168*
LaReau, Jenna *181*
LaReau, Kara *181*
Larios, Julie 1949- *178*
Larios, Julie Hofstrand
  See Larios, Julie
Larkin, Amy
  See Burns, Olive Ann
Larkin, Maia
  See Wojciechowska, Maia (Teresa)
Laroche, Giles 1956- *126*
  Earlier sketch in SATA *71*
LaRochelle, David 1960- *171*
  Earlier sketch in SATA *115*

Larom, Henry V. 1903(?)-1975
  Obituary *30*
LaRose, Linda *125*
Larrabee, Lisa 1947- *84*
Larrecq, John M(aurice) 1926-1980 .... *44*
  Obituary *25*
Larrick (Crosby), Nancy 1910-2004 .... *4*
Larsen, Anita 1942- *78*
Larsen, Egon 1904- *14*
Larsen, Rebecca 1944- *54*
Larson, Eve
  See St. John, Wylly Folk
Larson, Gary 1950- *57*
Larson, Ingrid D(ana) 1965- *92*
Larson, Jean Russell 1930- *121*
Larson, Kirby 1954- *181*
  Earlier sketch in SATA *96*
Larson, Norita D(ittberner) 1944- *29*
Larson, William H. 1938- *10*
Larsson, Carl (Olof) 1853-1919 .... *35*
LaSalle, Charles A.
  See Ellis, Edward S(ylvester)
LaSalle, Charles E.
  See Ellis, Edward S(ylvester)
Lasell, Elinor H. 1929- *19*
Lasell, Fen H.
  See Lasell, Elinor H.
Lasenby, Jack 1931- *172*
  Earlier sketches in SATA *65, 103*
Laser, Michael 1954- *117*
Lash, Joseph P. 1909-1987 .... *43*
Lasher, Faith B. 1921- *12*
Lasker, David 1950- *38*
Lasker, Joe *83*
  See also SAAS *17*
  See Lasker, Joseph Leon
Lasker, Joseph Leon 1919- *9*
  See Lasker, Joe
Laski, Marghanita 1915-1988 .... *55*
Laskin, Pamela L. 1954- *75*
Lasky, Kathryn 1944- *157*
  Earlier sketches in SATA *13, 69, 112*
  See also CLR *11*
Lasky Knight, Kathryn
  See Lasky, Kathryn
Lass, Bonnie *131*
Lassalle, C. E.
  See Ellis, Edward S(ylvester)
Lassiter, Mary *59*
  See Hoffman, Mary (Margaret)
Lassiter, Rhiannon 1977- *157*
Latham, Barbara 1896- *16*
Latham, Frank B(rown) 1910-2000 .... *6*
Latham, Jean Lee 1902-1995 .... *68*
  Earlier sketch in SATA *2*
  See also CLR *50*
Latham, Mavis
  See Clark, Mavis Thorpe
Latham, Philip
  See Richardson, Robert S(hirley)
Lathrop, Dorothy P(ulis) 1891-1980 .... *14*
  Obituary *24*
Lathrop, Francis
  See Leiber, Fritz (Reuter, Jr.)
Latimer, Jim 1943- *80*
Latta, Rich
  See Latta, Richard
Latta, Richard 1946- *113*
Latta, Sara L. 1960- *174*
Lattany, Kristin
  See Lattany, Kristin (Elaine Eggleston) Hunter
Lattany, Kristin (Eggleston) Hunter 1931- . *154*
  Autobiography Feature *154*
  Earlier sketch in SATA *132*
Lattany, Kristin (Elaine Eggleston) Hunter
  1931- *132*
  Earlier sketch in SATA *12*
  See also CLR *3*
  See also SAAS *10*
  See Hunter, Kristin

Lattimore, Eleanor Frances 1904-1986 7
  Obituary 48
Lattin, Ann
  See Cole, Lois Dwight
Lauber, Patricia (Grace) 1924- 138
  Earlier sketches in SATA *1, 33, 75*
  See also CLR *16*
Laugesen, Mary E(akin) 1906-1995 5
Laughbaum, Steve 1945- 12
Laughlin, Florence Young 1910-2001 3
Laughlin, Rosemary 1941- 123
Laure, Ettagale
  See Blauer, Ettagale
Laure, Jason 1940- 50
  Brief entry 44
Laurence, Ester Hauser 1935- 7
Laurence, Jean Margaret Wemyss
  See Laurence, Margaret
Laurence, Margaret 1926-1987
  Obituary 50
Laurie, Rona 1916- 55
Laurin, Anne
  See McLaurin, Anne
Lauritzen, Jonreed 1902-1979 13
Lauscher, Hermann
  See Hesse, Hermann
Lauture, Denize 1946- 86
Laux, Connie
  See Laux, Constance
Laux, Constance 1952- 97
Laux, Dorothy 1920- 49
Lavallee, Barbara 1941- 166
  Earlier sketch in SATA *74*
Lavender, David (Sievert) 1910-2003 97
  Obituary 145
  Earlier sketch in SATA *64*
Lavender, William D. 1921- 143
Laverne, Christine 175
Lavert, Gwendolyn Battle 1951- 131
  See Battle-Lavert, Gwendolyn
Laverty, Donald
  See Blish, James (Benjamin)
  and Knight, Damon (Francis)
Lavigne, Louis-Dominique 107
Lavine, David 1928- 31
Lavine, Sigmund Arnold 1908-1986 82
  Earlier sketch in SATA *3*
  See also CLR *35*
Lavond, Paul Dennis
  See Kornbluth, C(yril) M.
  and Lowndes, Robert A(ugustine) W(ard)
  and Pohl, Frederik
Lawhead, Stephen R. 1950- 109
Lawhead, Steve
  See Lawhead, Stephen R.
Lawlor, Laurie 1953- 137
  Earlier sketch in SATA *80*
Lawlor, William
  See Lawlor, William T.
Lawlor, William T. 1951- 183
Lawrence, Ann (Margaret) 1942-1987 41
  Obituary 54
Lawrence, Iain 1955- 183
  Earlier sketch in SATA *135*
Lawrence, J. T.
  See Rowland-Entwistle, (Arthur) Theodore
  (Henry)
Lawrence, Jerome 1915-2004 65
Lawrence, John 1933- 30
Lawrence, Josephine 1890(?)-1978
  Obituary 24
Lawrence, Louise 1943- 119
  Earlier sketches in SATA *38, 78*
Lawrence, Louise de Kiriline 1894-1992 13
Lawrence, Lynn
  See Garland, Sherry
Lawrence, Margery H. 1889-1969 120
Lawrence, Michael 1943- 132
Lawrence, Mildred Elwood 1907-1997 3
Lawrence, R(onald) D(ouglas) 1921- 55
Lawrinson, Julia 1969- 141

Lawson, Amy
  See Gordon, Amy
Lawson, Carol (Antell) 1946- 42
Lawson, Don(ald Elmer) 1917-1990 9
Lawson, Joan 1906- 55
Lawson, Julie 1947- 126
  Earlier sketch in SATA *79*
  See also CLR *89*
Lawson, Marion Tubbs 1896-1994 22
Lawson, Robert 1892-1957 100
  See also YABC *2*
  See also CLR *73*
Lawton, Clive A. 1951- 145
Laxdal, Vivienne 1962- 112
Laybourn, Emma 193
Laycock, George (Edwin) 1921- 5
Layne, Laura
  See Knott, William C(ecil, Jr.)
Layne, Steven L. 171
Layton, Neal 1971- 187
  Earlier sketch in SATA *152*
Layton, Neal Andrew
  See Layton, Neal
Lazare, Gerald John 1927- 44
Lazare, Jerry
  See Lazare, Gerald John
Lazarevich, Mila 1942- 17
Lazarus, Keo Felker 1913-1993 21
  Obituary 129
Lea, Alec 1907- 19
Lea, Joan
  See Neufeld, John (Arthur)
Leach, Maria 1892-1977 39
  Brief entry 28
Leacock, Elspeth 1946- 131
Leacroft, Helen (Mabel Beal) 1919- 6
Leacroft, Richard (Vallance Becher) 1914- 6
Leaf, Margaret P. 1909(?)-1988
  Obituary 55
Leaf, (Wilbur) Munro 1905-1976 20
  See also CLR *25*
Leaf, VaDonna Jean 1929- 26
Leah, Devorah
  See Devorah-Leah
Leakey, Richard E(rskine Frere) 1944- 42
Leander, Ed
  See Richelson, Geraldine
Lear, Edward 1812-1888 100
  Earlier sketch in SATA *18*
  See also CLR *75*
Lears, Laurie 1955- 127
Leasor, James 1923-2007 54
Leasor, Thomas James
  See Leasor, James
Leavitt, Jerome E(dward) 1916- 23
Leavitt, Martine 1953- 170
LeBar, Mary E(velyn) 1910-1982 35
LeBlanc, Annette M. 1965- 68
LeBlanc, L(ee) 1913- 54
LeBox, Annette 1943- 145
Lebrun, Claude 1929- 66
Le Cain, Errol (John) 1941-1989 68
  Obituary 60
  Earlier sketch in SATA *6*
Lecourt, Nancy (Hoyt) 1951- 73
Ledbetter, Suzann 1953- 119
Leder, Jane Mersky 1945- 61
  Brief entry 51
Lederer, Muriel 1929- 48
Lederer, William J(ulius) 1912- 62
Lee, Amanda
  See Baggett, Nancy
  and Buckholtz, Eileen (Garber)
  and Glick, Ruth (Burtnick)
Lee, Benjamin 1921- 27
Lee, Betsy 1949- 37
Lee, Carol
  See Fletcher, Helen Jill
Lee, Carol Ann 1969- 185
Lee, Chinlun 182

Lee, Cora
  See Anderson, Catherine Corley
Lee, Dennis (Beynon) 1939- 102
  Earlier sketch in SATA *14*
  See also CLR *3*
Lee, Dom 1959- 146
  Autobiography Feature 121
  Earlier sketch in SATA *83*
  See also SAAS *26*
Lee, Doris Emrick 1905-1983 44
  Obituary 35
Lee, Edward
  See Lee, J. Edward
Lee, Elizabeth Rogers 1940- 90
Lee, Harper 1926- 11
Lee, Hector Viveros 1962- 115
Lee, Howard N.
  See Goulart, Ron(ald Joseph)
Lee, Huy Voun 1969- 129
Lee, J. Edward 1953- 130
Lee, Jeanne M. 1943- 138
Lee, John R(obert) 1923-1976 27
Lee, Jordan
  See Scholefield, Alan
Lee, Joseph Edward
  See Lee, J. Edward
Lee, Julian
  See Latham, Jean Lee
Lee, Linda
  See Eyerly, Jeannette
Lee, Liz
  See Lee, Elizabeth Rogers
Lee, Lucy
  See Talbot, Charlene Joy
Lee, Lyn 1953- 128
Lee, Manning de Villeneuve 1894-1980 37
  Obituary 22
Lee, Marian
  See Clish, (Lee) Marian
Lee, Marie G. 1964- 178
  Earlier sketches in SATA *81, 130*
Lee, Marie Myung-Ok
  See Lee, Marie G.
Lee, Mary Price 1934- 82
  Earlier sketch in SATA *8*
Lee, Mildred 6
  See also SAAS *12*
  See Scudder, Mildred Lee
Lee, Nelle Harper
  See Lee, Harper
Lee, Richard S. 1927- 82
Lee, Robert C. 1931- 20
Lee, Robert E(dwin) 1918-1994 65
  Obituary 82
Lee, Robert J. 1921- 10
Lee, Roy
  See Hopkins, Clark
Lee, Sally 1943- 67
Lee, Suzy 193
Lee, Tammie
  See Townsend, Thomas L.
Lee, Tanith 1947- 185
  Earlier sketches in SATA *8, 88, 134*
Leech, Ben
  See Bowkett, Stephen
Leeds, Constance 188
Leedy, Loreen 1959- 175
  Brief entry 50
  Earlier sketches in SATA *54, 84, 128*
Leedy, Loreen Janelle
  See Leedy, Loreen
Lee-Hostetler, Jeri 1940- 63
Leekley, Thomas B(riggs) 1910-2001 23
Leeming, Jo Ann
  See Leeming, Joseph
Leeming, Joseph 1897-1968 26
Leemis, Ralph B. 1954- 72
Leese, Jennifer L.B. 1970- 163
Leeson, Muriel 1920- 54
Leeson, R. A.
  See Leeson, Robert (Arthur)

Leeson, Robert (Arthur) 1928- 76
Earlier sketch in SATA *42*
Lee Tae-Jun 1904-1956(?) *194*
Lee-Tai, Amy 1964- *189*
Leffland, Ella 1931- *65*
Lefler, Irene (Whitney) 1917- *12*
LeFrak, Karen *182*
Le Gallienne, Eva 1899-1991 .... *9*
Obituary *68*
Legg, Gerald 1947- *143*
Legg, Sarah Martha Ross Bruggeman (?)-1982
Obituary *40*
LeGrand
See Henderson, LeGrand
Le Guin, Ursula K. 1929- *194*
Earlier sketches in SATA *4, 52, 99, 149*
See also CLR *91*
Le Guin, Ursula Kroeber
See Le Guin, Ursula K.
Legum, Colin 1919-2003 .... *10*
Lehman, Barbara 1963- *170*
Earlier sketch in SATA *115*
Lehman, Bob *91*
Lehman, Elaine *91*
Lehmann, Debra Lynn
See Vanasse, Deb
Lehn, Cornelia 1920- *46*
Lehne, Judith Logan 1947- *93*
Lehr, Delores 1920- *10*
Lehr, Norma 1930- *71*
Leiber, Fritz (Reuter, Jr.) 1910-1992 .... *45*
Obituary *73*
Leibold, Jay 1957- *57*
Brief entry *52*
Leichman, Seymour 1933- *5*
Leigh, Nila K. 1981- *81*
Leigh, Tom 1947- *46*
Leigh-Pemberton, John 1911-1997 .... *35*
Leighton, Clare (Veronica Hope)
1899-1989 .... *37*
Leighton, Margaret (Carver) 1896-1987 .... *1*
Obituary *52*
Leiner, Al(an) 1938- *83*
Leiner, Katherine 1949- *93*
Leipold, L. Edmond 1902-1983 .... *16*
Leisk, David (Johnson) 1906-1975 .... *30*
Obituary *26*
Earlier sketch in SATA *1*
See also CLR *98*
See Johnson, Crockett
Leister, Mary 1917- *29*
Leitch, Patricia 1933- *98*
Earlier sketch in SATA *11*
Leitner, Isabella 1924- *86*
Leland, Bob 1956- *92*
Leland, Robert E.
See Leland, Bob
Lematre, Pascal 1967- *176*
Lember, Barbara Hirsch 1941- *92*
LeMieux, A.C. 1954- *125*
Earlier sketch in SATA *90*
See LeMieux, Anne
LeMieux, Anne
See LeMieux, A.C.
LeMieux, Anne Connelly
See LeMieux, A.C.
Lemieux, Michele 1955- *139*
Lemke, Horst 1922- *38*
Lenanton, Carola Mary Anima Oman
See Oman, Carola (Mary Anima)
Lenard, Alexander 1910-1972
Obituary *21*
L'Engle, Madeleine 1918-2007 .... *128*
Obituary *186*
Earlier sketches in SATA *1, 27, 75*
See also CLR *57*
See also SAAS *15*
L'Engle, Madeleine Camp Franklin
See L'Engle, Madeleine
Lengyel, Cornel Adam 1915- *27*

Lengyel, Emil 1895-1985 .... *3*
Obituary *42*
Lennon, John (Ono) 1940-1980 .... *114*
Leno, Jay 1950- *154*
LeNoir, Janice 1941- *89*
Lens, Sidney 1912-1986 .... *13*
Obituary *48*
Lenski, Lois 1893-1974 .... *100*
Earlier sketches in SATA *1, 26*
See also CLR *26*
Lent, Blair *133*
Earlier sketch in SATA *2*
Lent, Henry Bolles 1901-1973 .... *17*
Lent, John 1948- *108*
Leodhas, Sorche Nic
See Alger, Leclaire (Gowans)
Leokum, Arkady 1916(?)- *45*
Leon, Sharon 1959- *79*
Leonard, Alison 1944- *70*
Leonard, Constance (Brink) 1923- *42*
Brief entry *40*
Leonard, Dutch
See Leonard, Elmore
Leonard, Elmore 1925- *163*
Leonard, Elmore John, Jr.
See Leonard, Elmore
Leonard, Jonathan N(orton) 1903-1975 .... *36*
Leonard, Laura 1923- *75*
Leong, Gor Yun
See Ellison, Virginia H(owell)
Leonhardt, Alice 1950- *152*
Lerangis, Peter 1955- *171*
Earlier sketch in SATA *72*
See Dixon, Franklin W.
and Keene, Carolyn
Lerner, Aaron 1920-2007 .... *35*
Obituary *179*
Lerner, Aaron Bunsen
See Lerner, Aaron
Lerner, Carol 1927- *86*
Earlier sketch in SATA *33*
See also CLR *34*
See also SAAS *12*
Lerner, Gerda 1920- *65*
Lerner, Harriet 1944- *101*
Lerner, Marguerite Rush 1924-1987 .... *11*
Obituary *51*
Lerner, Sharon (Ruth) 1938-1982 .... *11*
Obituary *29*
Leroe, Ellen W(hitney) 1949- *99*
Brief entry *51*
Earlier sketch in SATA *61*
Leroux, Gaston 1868-1927 .... *65*
Leroux-Hugon, Helene 1955- *132*
LeRoy, Gen *52*
Brief entry *36*
Lerrigo, Marion Olive 1898-1968
Obituary *29*
LeShan, Eda J(oan) 1922-2002 .... *21*
See also CLR *6*
LeSieg, Theo.
See Dr. Seuss
and Geisel, Theodor Seuss
and Seuss, Dr.
and Stone, Rosetta
Lesinski, Jeanne M. 1960- *120*
Leslie, Robert Franklin 1911-1990 .... *7*
Leslie, Roger 1961- *168*
Leslie, Roger James
See Leslie, Roger
Leslie, Sarah
See McGuire, Leslie (Sarah)
LeSourd, Catherine
See Marshall, (Sarah) Catherine (Wood)
Lessac, Frane
See Lessac, Frane
Lessac, Frane 1954- *148*
Earlier sketch in SATA *61*
Lessem, Dino Don
See Lessem, Don

Lessem, Don 1951- *182*
Earlier sketches in SATA *97, 155*
Lesser, Margaret 1899(?)-1979
Obituary *22*
Lesser, Rika 1953- *53*
Lester, Alison 1952- *129*
Earlier sketches in SATA *50, 90*
Lester, Helen 1936- *189*
Earlier sketches in SATA *46, 92, 145*
Lester, Julius 1939- *157*
Earlier sketches in SATA *12, 74, 112*
See also CLR *41*
Lester, Julius Bernard
See Lester, Julius
Lester, Mike 1955- *131*
Le Sueur, Meridel 1900-1996 .... *6*
Lethcoe, Jason *191*
Le Tord, Bijou 1945- *95*
Earlier sketch in SATA *49*
Letts, Billie 1938- *121*
Leuck, Laura 1962- *192*
Earlier sketches in SATA *85, 146*
Leutscher, Alfred (George) 1913- *23*
Levai, Blaise 1919- *39*
Levenkron, Steven 1941- *86*
Leverich, Kathleen 1948- *103*
LeVert, (William) John 1946- *55*
Levete, Sarah 1961- *153*
Levin, Betty 1927- *137*
Earlier sketches in SATA *19, 84*
See also SAAS *11*
Levin, Ira 1929-2007 .... *66*
Obituary *187*
Levin, Ira Marvin
See Levin, Ira
Levin, Ira Marvin
See Levin, Ira
Levin, Marcia Obrasky 1918- *13*
Levin, Meyer 1905-1981 .... *21*
Obituary *27*
Levin, Miriam (Ramsfelder) 1962- *97*
Levine, Abby 1943- *54*
Brief entry *52*
Levine, Betty K(rasne) 1933- *66*
Levine, David 1926- *43*
Brief entry *35*
Levine, Edna S(imon) *35*
Levine, Ellen 1939- *190*
Levine, Evan 1962- *77*
Earlier sketch in SATA *74*
Levine, Gail Carson 1947- *195*
Earlier sketches in SATA *98, 161*
See also CLR *85*
Levine, I(srael) E. 1923-2003 .... *12*
Obituary *146*
Levine, Joan Goldman *11*
Levine, Joseph 1910- *33*
Levine, Marge 1934- *81*
Levine, Rhoda *14*
Levine, Sarah 1970- *57*
Levine, Shar 1953- *131*
Levine-Freidus, Gail
See Provost, Gail Levine
Levinson, Nancy Smiler 1938- *140*
Earlier sketches in SATA *33, 80*
Levinson, Riki *99*
Brief entry *49*
Earlier sketch in SATA *52*
Levithan, David 1972- *166*
Levitin, Sonia 1934- *192*
Autobiography Feature *131*
Earlier sketches in SATA *4, 68, 119, 131*
See also CLR *53*
See also SAAS *2*
Levitt, Sidney (Mark) 1947- *68*
Levon, O. U.
See Kesey, Ken
Levoy, Myron *49*
Brief entry *37*
Levy, Barrie *112*

Levy, Constance 1931- *140*
  Earlier sketch in SATA *73*
  See also SAAS *22*
Levy, Elizabeth 1942- *169*
  Earlier sketches in SATA *31, 69, 107*
  See also SAAS *18*
Levy, Janice *172*
Levy, Marilyn 1937- *67*
Levy, Nathan 1945- *63*
Levy, Robert 1945- *82*
Lewees, John
  See Stockton, Francis Richard
Lewin, Betsy 1937- *169*
  Autobiography Feature *115*
  Earlier sketches in SATA *32, 90*
Lewin, Hugh 1939- *72*
  Brief entry *40*
  See also CLR *9*
Lewin, Ted 1935- *195*
  Autobiography Feature *115*
  Earlier sketches in SATA *21, 76, 119, 165*
Lewis, Alice C. 1936- *46*
Lewis, Alice Hudson 1895(?)-1971
  Obituary *29*
Lewis, Amanda 1955- *80*
Lewis, Anthony 1927- *27*
Lewis, Anthony 1966- *120*
Lewis, Barbara A. 1943- *73*
Lewis, Beverly 1949- *80*
Lewis, Brenda Ralph 1932- *72*
Lewis, Brian 1963- *128*
Lewis, Claudia (Louise) 1907-2001 .... *5*
Lewis, Clive Staples
  See Lewis, C.S.
Lewis, C.S. 1898-1963 .... *100*
  Earlier sketch in SATA *13*
  See also CLR *109*
Lewis, Cynthia Copeland 1960- *111*
Lewis, E. M. *123*
  Earlier sketch in SATA *20*
Lewis, Earl Bradley
  See Lewis, E.B.
Lewis, E.B. 1956- *168*
  Earlier sketches in SATA *93, 124*
Lewis, Elizabeth Foreman 1892-1958 .... *121*
  See also YABC *2*
Lewis, Francine
  See Wells, Helen
Lewis, Hilda (Winifred) 1896-1974
  Obituary *20*
Lewis, J. Patrick 1942- *162*
  Earlier sketches in SATA *69, 104*
Lewis, Jack P(earl) 1919- *65*
Lewis, Jean 1924- *61*
Lewis, Joseph Anthony
  See Lewis, Anthony
Lewis, Julinda
  See Lewis-Ferguson, Julinda
Lewis, Kevin *173*
Lewis, Kim 1951- *136*
  Earlier sketch in SATA *84*
Lewis, Linda (Joy) 1946- *67*
Lewis, Lucia Z.
  See Anderson, Lucia (Lewis)
Lewis, Marjorie 1929- *40*
  Brief entry *35*
Lewis, Mary (Christianna) 1907(?)-1988 ..... *64*
  Obituary *56*
  See Brand, Christianna
Lewis, Mervyn
  See Frewer, Glyn (M.)
Lewis, Michael
  See Untermeyer, Louis
Lewis, Naomi *144*
  Earlier sketch in SATA *76*
Lewis, Paeony 1960- *173*
Lewis, Paul
  See Gerson, Noel Bertram
Lewis, Richard 1935- *3*
Lewis, Rob 1962- *72*

Lewis, Roger
  See Zarchy, Harry
Lewis, Shannon
  See Llywelyn, Morgan
Lewis, Shari 1934-1998 .... *35*
  Brief entry *30*
  Obituary *104*
Lewis, Sylvan R.
  See Aronson, Virginia
Lewis, Thomas P(arker) 1936- *27*
Lewis, Wendy A. 1966- *150*
Lewis-Ferguson, Julinda 1955- *85*
Lewison, Wendy Cheyette *177*
Lewiton, Mina 1904-1970 .... *2*
Lew-Vriethoff, Joanne *186*
Lexau, Joan M. *130*
  Earlier sketches in SATA *1, 36*
Ley, Willy 1906-1969 .... *2*
Leydon, Rita (Floden) 1949- *21*
Leyland, Eric (Arthur) 1911- *37*
L'Hommedieu, Dorothy Keasley 1885-1961
  Obituary *29*
Li, Xiao Jun 1952- *86*
Liatsos, Sandra Olson 1942- *103*
Libby, Alisa M. *189*
Libby, Barbara M. *153*
Libby, Bill
  See Libby, William M.
Libby, William M. 1927-1984 .... *5*
  Obituary *39*
Liberty, Gene 1924- *3*
Lichtenheld, Tom *152*
Lichtman, Wendy 1946- *193*
Liddell, Kenneth 1912-1975 .... *63*
Lidz, Jane *120*
Lieberman, E(dwin) James 1934- *62*
Liebers, Arthur 1913-1984 .... *12*
Lieblich, Irene 1923- *22*
Liers, Emil E(rnest) 1890-1975 .... *37*
Lies, Brian 1963- *190*
  Earlier sketch in SATA *131*
Liestman, Vicki 1961- *72*
Lietz, Gerald S. 1918- *11*
Life, Kay (Guinn) 1930- *83*
Lifton, Betty Jean *118*
  Earlier sketch in SATA *6*
Lifton, Robert Jay 1926- *66*
Lightburn, Ron 1954- *91*
Lightburn, Sandra 1955- *91*
Lightner, A. M.
  See Hopf, Alice (Martha) L(ightner)
Lightner, Alice
  See Hopf, Alice (Martha) L(ightner)
Lignell, Lois 1911- *37*
Liles, Maurine Walpole 1935- *81*
Lillegard, Dee *184*
Lilley, Stephen R. 1950- *97*
Lilley, Stephen Ray
  See Lilley, Stephen R.
Lillington, Kenneth (James) 1916-1998 .... *39*
Lilly, Nate *182*
Lilly, Ray
  See Curtis, Richard (Alan)
Lim, John 1932- *43*
Liman, Ellen (Fogelson) 1936- *22*
Limb, Sue 1946- *158*
Limburg, Peter R(ichard) 1929- *13*
Lin, Grace 1974- *162*
  Earlier sketch in SATA *111*
Lincoln, C(harles) Eric 1924-2000 .... *5*
Lincoln, Hazel *187*
Lincoln, James
  See Bates, Katharine Lee
Lindbergh, Anne *81*
  See Sapieyevski, Anne Lindbergh
Lindbergh, Anne Morrow 1906-2001 .... *33*
  Obituary *125*
Lindbergh, Anne Spencer Morrow
  See Lindbergh, Anne Morrow
Lindbergh, Charles A(ugustus, Jr.)
  1902-1974 .... *33*

Lindbergh, Reeve 1945- *163*
  Earlier sketch in SATA *116*
Lindblom, Steven (Winther) 1946- *94*
  Brief entry *39*
  Earlier sketch in SATA *42*
Linde, Gunnel 1924- *5*
Lindenbaum, Pija 1955- *183*
  Earlier sketches in SATA *77, 144*
Lindgren, Astrid (Anna Emilia Ericsson)
  1907-2002 .... *38*
  Obituary *128*
  Earlier sketch in SATA *2*
  See also CLR *119*
Lindgren, Barbro 1937- *120*
  Brief entry *46*
  Earlier sketch in SATA *63*
  See also CLR *86*
Lindman, Maj (Jan) 1886-1972 .... *43*
Lindop, Edmund 1925- *5*
Lindquist, Jennie Dorothea 1899-1977 .... *13*
Lindquist, Rowena Cory 1958- *98*
Lindquist, Willis 1908-1988 .... *20*
Lindsay, Norman Alfred William
  1879-1969 .... *67*
  See also CLR *8*
Lindsay, (Nicholas) Vachel 1879-1931 .... *40*
Lindsey, Kathleen D(orothy) 1949- *153*
Line, David
  See Davidson, Lionel
Line, Les 1935- *27*
Lines, Kathleen Mary 1902-1988
  Obituary *61*
Linfield, Esther *40*
Lingard, Joan (Amelia) 1932- *130*
  Autobiography Feature *130*
  Earlier sketches in SATA *8, 74, 114*
  See also CLR *89*
  See also SAAS *5*
Link, Martin 1934- *28*
Linn, Margot
  See Ziefert, Harriet
Linnea, Sharon 1956- *82*
Lion, Melissa 1976- *176*
Lionni, Leo(nard) 1910-1999 .... *72*
  Obituary *118*
  Earlier sketch in SATA *8*
  See also CLR *71*
Lipinsky de Orlov, Lino S. 1908- *22*
Lipkind, William 1904-1974 .... *15*
Lipman, David 1931-2008 .... *21*
Lipman, Matthew 1923- *14*
Lippincott, Bertram 1898(?)-1985
  Obituary *42*
Lippincott, Gary A. 1953- *119*
  Earlier sketch in SATA *73*
Lippincott, Joseph W(harton) 1887-1976 ..... *17*
Lippincott, Sarah Lee 1920- *22*
Lippman, Peter J. 1936- *31*
Lipsyte, Robert 1938- *161*
  Earlier sketches in SATA *5, 68, 113*
  See also CLR *76*
Lipsyte, Robert Michael
  See Lipsyte, Robert
Lisandrelli, Elaine Slivinski 1951- *94*
Lisker, Sonia O. 1933- *44*
Lisle, Holly 1960- *98*
Lisle, Janet Taylor 1947- *150*
  Brief entry *47*
  Earlier sketches in SATA *59, 96*
  See also SAAS *14*
Lisle, Rebecca *162*
Lisle, Seward D.
  See Ellis, Edward S(ylvester)
Lisowski, Gabriel 1946- *47*
  Brief entry *31*
Liss, Howard 1922-1995 .... *4*
  Obituary *84*
Lisson, Deborah 1941- *110*
  Earlier sketch in SATA *71*
List, Ilka Katherine 1935- *6*
Liston, Robert A. 1927- *5*

Litchfield, Ada B(assett) 1916-1999 5
Litchfield, Jo 1973- 116
Lithgow, John (Arthur) 1945- 145
Litowinsky, Olga (Jean) 1936- 26
Littke, Lael J. 1929- 140
  Earlier sketches in SATA 51, 83
Little, A. Edward
  See Klein, Aaron E.
Little, Douglas 1942- 96
Little, (Flora) Jean 1932- 149
  Earlier sketches in SATA 2, 68, 106
  See also CLR 4
  See also SAAS 17
Little, Lessie Jones 1906-1986 60
  Obituary 50
Little, Mary E. 1912-1999 28
Littlechild, George 1958- 85
Littledale, Freya (Lota) 1929-1992 74
  Earlier sketch in SATA 2
Littlefield, Bill 1948- 83
Littlefield, Holly 1963- 97
Littlesugar, Amy 1953- 176
  Earlier sketch in SATA 122
Littleton, Mark R. 1950- 142
  Earlier sketch in SATA 89
Littman, Sarah Darer 175
Litty, Julie 1971- 181
Lively, Penelope 1933- 164
  Earlier sketches in SATA 7, 60, 101
  See also CLR 7
Lively, Penelope Margaret
  See Lively, Penelope
Liverakos, L.A.
  See Gilman, Laura Anne
Liversidge, (Henry) Douglas 1913- 8
Livesey, Claire (Warner) 1927- 127
Livingston, Carole 1941- 42
Livingston, (M.) Irene 1932- 150
Livingston, Myra Cohn 1926-1996 68
  Obituary 92
  Earlier sketch in SATA 5
  See also CLR 7
  See also SAAS 1
Livingston, Richard R(oland) 1922- 8
Livo, Norma J. 1929- 76
Ljungkvist, Laura 180
Llerena Aguirre, Carlos 1952- 19
Llerena Aguirre, Carlos Antonio
  See Llerena Aguirre, Carlos
Llewellyn, Claire 1954- 143
  Earlier sketch in SATA 77
Llewellyn, Grace 1964- 110
Llewellyn, Richard
  See Llewellyn Lloyd, Richard Dafydd Vivian
Llewellyn, Sam 1948- 185
  Earlier sketch in SATA 95
Llewellyn Lloyd, Richard Dafydd Vivian
  1906-1983 11
  Obituary 37
  See Llewellyn, Richard
Llewelyn, T. Harcourt
  See Hamilton, Charles (Harold St. John)
Lloyd, Alan
  See Lloyd, A.R.
Lloyd, Alan Richard
  See Lloyd, A.R.
Lloyd, A.R. 1927- 168
  Earlier sketch in SATA 97
Lloyd, David
  See Lloyd, David T.
Lloyd, David T. 1954- 167
Lloyd, E. James
  See James, Elizabeth
Lloyd, Errol 1943- 22
Lloyd, Hugh
  See Fitzhugh, Percy Keese
Lloyd, James
  See James, Elizabeth
Lloyd, Megan 1958- 189
  Earlier sketches in SATA 77, 117

Lloyd, Norman 1909-1980
  Obituary 23
Lloyd, (Mary) Norris 1908-1993 10
  Obituary 75
Lloyd, Sam 183
Lloyd-Jones, Sally 1960- 179
Lloyd Webber, Andrew 1948- 56
  See Webber, Andrew Lloyd
Llywelyn, Morgan 1937- 109
Lo, Ginnie 165
Lo, Virginia M.
  See Lo, Ginnie
Lobato, Jose Bento Monteiro 1882-1948 ... 114
Lobel, Anita (Kempler) 1934- 162
  Earlier sketches in SATA 6, 55, 96
Lobel, Arnold (Stark) 1933-1987 55
  Obituary 54
  Earlier sketch in SATA 6
  See also CLR 5
Lobel, Gillian 181
Lobsenz, Amelia 12
Lobsenz, Norman M(itchell) 1919- 6
Lochak, Michele 1936- 39
Lochlons, Colin
  See Jackson, C(aary) Paul
Locke, Clinton W. 1
Locke, Elsie (Violet) 1912-2001 87
Locke, Lucie 1904-1989 10
Locke, Robert 1944- 63
  See Bess, Clayton
Locker, Thomas 1937- 109
  Earlier sketch in SATA 59
  See also CLR 14
Lockhart, E.
  See Jenkins, Emily
Lockridge, Hildegarde (Dolson)
  1908-1981 121
  See Dolson, Hildegarde
Lockwood, Mary
  See Spelman, Mary
Lodge, Bernard 1933- 107
  Earlier sketch in SATA 33
Lodge, Jo 1966- 173
  Earlier sketch in SATA 112
Loeb, Jeffrey 1946- 57
Loeb, Robert H., Jr. 1917- 21
Loefgren, Ulf 1931- 3
Loehfelm, Bill 1969- 153
Loehr, Mallory 184
Loehr, Patrick 1968(?)- 194
Loeper, John J(oseph) 1929- 118
  Earlier sketch in SATA 10
Loescher, Ann Dull 1942- 20
Loescher, Gil(burt Damian) 1945- 20
Loewer, Jean Jenkins
  See Jenkins, Jean
Loewer, (Henry) Peter 1934- 98
LoFaro, Jerry 1959- 77
Lofo
  See Heimann, Rolf
Lofting, Hugh (John) 1886-1947 100
  Earlier sketch in SATA 15
  See also CLR 19
Lofts, Norah (Robinson) 1904-1983 8
  Obituary 36
Logan, Jake
  See Knott, William C(ecil, Jr.)
  and Krepps, Robert W(ilson)
  and Pearl, Jacques Bain
  and Riefe, Alan
  and Rifkin, Shepard
  and Smith, Martin Cruz
Logan, Mark
  See Nicole, Christopher (Robin)
Logan, Rochelle 1954- 169
Logston, Anne 1962- 112
Logue, Christopher 1926- 23
Logue, Mary 1952- 161
  Earlier sketch in SATA 112
Logue, Mary Louise
  See Logue, Mary

Loh, Morag 1935- 73
Lohans, Alison 1949- 101
Loizeaux, William 185
Loken, Newton Clayton 1919- 26
Lomas, Steve
  See Brennan, Joseph Lomas
Lomask, Milton (Nachman) 1909-1991 20
Lombard, Jenny 178
Lombino, Salvatore
  See Hunter, Evan
LoMonaco, Palmyra 1932- 102
London, Jack 1876-1916 18
  See also CLR 108
  See London, John Griffith
London, Jane
  See Geis, Darlene Stern
London, Jonathan (Paul) 1947- 157
  Earlier sketches in SATA 74, 113
Lonergan, (Pauline) Joy (MacLean) 1909- ... 10
Lonette, Reisie (Dominee) 1924- 43
Long, Cathryn J. 1946- 89
Long, Earlene (Roberta) 1938- 50
Long, Emmett
  See Leonard, Elmore
Long, Ethan 1968(?)- 182
Long, Helen Beecher 1
Long, Judith Elaine 1953- 20
Long, Judy
  See Long, Judith Elaine
Long, Kim 1949- 69
Long, Laura Mooney 1892-1967
  Obituary 29
Long, Loren 1966(?)- 188
  Earlier sketch in SATA 151
Long, Melinda 1960- 152
Long, Sylvia 1948- 179
  Earlier sketch in SATA 120
Longbeard, Frederick
  See Longyear, Barry B(rookes)
Longfellow, Henry Wadsworth 1807-1882 ... 19
  See also CLR 99
Longfellow, Layne (A.) 1937- 102
Longman, Harold S. 1919- 5
Longsworth, Polly 1933- 28
Longtemps, Kenneth 1933- 17
Longway, A. Hugh
  See Lang, Andrew
Longyear, Barry B(rookes) 1942- 117
Look, Lenore 180
Loomans, Diane 1955- 90
Loomis, Christine 160
  Earlier sketch in SATA 113
Loomis, Jennifer A. 1942- 101
Loomis, Robert D. 5
Lopez, Angelo (Cayas) 1967- 83
Lopez, Barry (Holstun) 1945- 67
Lopez, Jack 1950- 178
Lopez, Loretta 1963- 190
Lopez, Lorraine M. 1956- 181
Lopshire, Robert M(artin) 1927- 6
Loraine, Connie
  See Reece, Colleen L.
Lorbiecki, Marybeth 1959- 172
  Earlier sketch in SATA 121
Lord, Athena V. 1932- 39
Lord, Beman 1924-1991 5
  Obituary 69
Lord, Bette Bao 1938- 58
Lord, Cynthia 182
Lord, (Doreen Mildred) Douglas 1904- 12
Lord, John Vernon 1939- 21
Lord, Nancy
  See Titus, Eve
Lord, Patricia C. 1927-1988
  Obituary 58
Lord, Walter 1917-2002 3
Lorde, Diana
  See Reno, Dawn E(laine)
Lorenz, Albert 1941- 115

Lorenzini, Carlo 1826-1890 .... *100*
　Earlier sketch in SATA 29
　See Collodi, Carlo
Lorey, Dean 1967- *193*
Lorimer, Janet 1941- *60*
Loring, Emilie (Baker) 1864(?)-1951 .... *51*
Lorkowski, Thomas V(incent) 1950- *92*
Lorkowski, Tom
　See Lorkowski, Thomas V(incent)
Lorraine, Walter (Henry) 1929- *16*
Lorrimer, Claire
　See Clark, Patricia Denise
Loss, Joan 1933- *11*
Lothrop, Harriet Mulford Stone 1844-1924 . *20*
Lottridge, Celia Barker 1936- *157*
　Earlier sketch in SATA *112*
LoTurco, Laura 1963- *84*
Lotz, Wolfgang 1912-1981 .... *65*
Louie, Ai-Ling 1949- *40*
　Brief entry *34*
Louis, Catherine 1963- *186*
Louis, Pat
　See Francis, Dorothy
Louisburgh, Sheila Burnford
　See Burnford, Sheila (Philip Cochrane Every)
Louise, Anita
　See Riggio, Anita
Louise, Tina 1934- *191*
Lourie, Helen
　See Storr, Catherine (Cole)
Lourie, Peter 1952- *183*
　Earlier sketches in SATA *82, 142*
Lourie, Peter King
　See Lourie, Peter
Love, Ann 1947- *168*
　Earlier sketch in SATA *79*
Love, D. Anne 1949- *180*
　Earlier sketches in SATA *96, 145*
Love, Douglas 1967- *92*
Love, Judith Dufour
　See Love, Judy
Love, Judy *188*
Love, Katherine (Isabel) 1907- *3*
Love, Kathleen Ann
　See Love, Ann
Love, Sandra (Weller) 1940- *26*
Lovejoy, Jack 1937- *116*
Lovelace, Delos Wheeler 1894-1967 .... *7*
Lovelace, Maud Hart 1892-1980 .... *2*
　Obituary *23*
Lovell, Ingraham
　See Bacon, Josephine Dodge (Daskam)
Loverseed, Amanda (Jane) 1965- *75*
Lovett, Margaret (Rose) 1915- *22*
Low, Alice 1926- *156*
　Earlier sketches in SATA *11, 76*
Low, Elizabeth Hammond 1898-1991 .... *5*
Low, Joseph 1911-2007 .... *14*
Low, Penelope Margaret
　See Lively, Penelope
Low, William *177*
Lowe, Jay, Jr.
　See Loeper, John J(oseph)
Lowell, Pamela *187*
Lowell, Susan 1950- *127*
　Earlier sketch in SATA *81*
Lowenstein, Dyno 1914-1996 .... *6*
Lowenstein, Sallie 1949- *116*
Lowery, Linda 1949- *151*
　Earlier sketch in SATA *74*
Lowitz, Anson C. 1901(?)-1978 .... *18*
Lowitz, Sadyebeth Heath 1901-1969 .... *17*
Lowndes, Robert A(ugustine) W(ard)
　1916-1998 .... *117*
Lowrey, Janette Sebring 1892-1986 .... *43*
Lowry, Lois 1937- *177*
　Autobiography Feature *127*
　Earlier sketches in SATA *23, 70, 111*
　See also CLR *72*
　See also SAAS *3*

Lowry, Lois Hammersberg
　See Lowry, Lois
Lowry, Peter 1953- *7*
Lowther, George F. 1913-1975
　Obituary *30*
Loyie, Larry 1933- *150*
Lozansky, Edward D. 1941- *62*
Lozier, Herbert 1915- *26*
Lubar, David 1954- *190*
　Earlier sketch in SATA *133*
Lubell, Cecil 1912-2000 .... *6*
Lubell, Winifred (A. Milius) 1914- *6*
Lubin, Leonard
　See Lubin, Leonard B.
Lubin, Leonard B. 1943-1994 .... *45*
　Brief entry *37*
Lubka, S. Ruth 1948- *154*
Lubner, Susan *185*
Luby, Thia 1954- *124*
Lucado, Max (Lee) 1955- *104*
Lucas, Cedric 1962- *101*
Lucas, E(dward) V(errall) 1868-1938 .... *20*
Lucas, Eileen 1956- *113*
　Earlier sketch in SATA *76*
Lucas, George 1944- *56*
Lucas, Jerry 1940- *33*
Lucas, Margeaux *186*
Lucas, Victoria
　See Plath, Sylvia
Lucashenko, Melissa 1967- *104*
Luccarelli, Vincent 1923- *90*
Luce, Celia (Geneva Larsen) 1914- *38*
Luce, Willard (Ray) 1914-1990 .... *38*
Lucht, Irmgard 1937- *82*
Luckett, Dave 1951- *167*
　Earlier sketch in SATA *106*
Luckhardt, Mildred Corell 1898-1990 .... *5*
Ludden, Allen (Ellsworth) 1918(?)-1981
　Obituary *27*
Ludel, Jacqueline 1945- *64*
Ludlow, Geoffrey
　See Meynell, Laurence Walter
Ludlum, Mabel Cleland
　See Widdemer, Mabel Cleland
Ludwig, Helen *33*
Ludwig, Lyndell 1923- *63*
Ludwig, Trudy 1959- *166*
Lueders, Edward (George) 1923- *14*
Luenn, Nancy 1954- *79*
　Earlier sketch in SATA *51*
Lufkin, Raymond H. 1897- *38*
Lugard, Flora Louisa Shaw 1852-1929 .... *21*
Luger, Harriett Mandelay 1914- *23*
Luhrmann, Winifred B(ruce) 1934- *11*
Luis, Earlene W. 1929- *11*
Luke, Pauline *178*
Luke, Pauline R.
　See Luke, Pauline
Lum, Peter
　See Crowe, (Bettina) Peter Lum
Lumry, Amanda (R.) *159*
Lund, Deb *157*
Lund, Doris Herold 1919- *12*
Lung, Chang
　See Jordan, Robert
Lunge-Larsen, Lise 1955- *184*
　Earlier sketch in SATA *138*
Lunn, Carolyn (Kowalczyk) 1960- *67*
Lunn, Janet (Louise Swoboda) 1928- *110*
　Earlier sketches in SATA *4, 68*
　See also CLR *18*
　See also SAAS *12*
Lunsford, Cin Forshay
　See Forshay-Lunsford, Cin
Lupica, Mike *177*
　See Lupica, Michael
Lupoff, Dick
　See Lupoff, Richard A(llen)
Lupoff, Richard A(llen) 1935- *60*
Lurie, Alison 1926- *112*
　Earlier sketch in SATA *46*

Lurie, Morris 1938- *72*
Lussert, Anneliese 1929- *101*
Lusted, Marcia Amidon 1962- *143*
Lustig, Arnost 1926- *56*
Lustig, Loretta 1944- *46*
Luthardt, Kevin 1973- *172*
Luther, Frank 1905-1980
　Obituary *25*
Luther, Rebekah (Lyn) S(tiles) 1960- *90*
Luttmann, Gail
　See Damerow, Gail
Luttrell, Guy L. 1938- *22*
Luttrell, Ida (Alleene) 1934- *91*
　Brief entry *35*
　Earlier sketch in SATA *40*
Luttrell, William (J. III) 1954- *149*
Lutz, John 1939- *180*
Lutz, John Thomas
　See Lutz, John
Lutz, Norma Jean 1943- *122*
Lutzeier, Elizabeth 1952- *72*
Lutzker, Edythe 1904-1991 .... *5*
Luxbacher, Irene M. 1970- *153*
Luzadder, Patrick 1954- *89*
Luzzati, Emanuele 1921-2007 .... *7*
Luzzatto, Paola Caboara 1938- *38*
Lybbert, Tyler 1970- *88*
Lydon, Michael 1942- *11*
Lyfick, Warren
　See Reeves, Lawrence F.
Lyle, Katie Letcher 1938- *8*
Lynch, Chris 1962- *171*
　Earlier sketches in SATA *95, 131*
　See also CLR *58*
Lynch, Lorenzo 1932- *7*
Lynch, Marietta 1947- *29*
Lynch, P(atrick) J(ames) 1962- *122*
　Earlier sketch in SATA *79*
Lynch, Patricia (Nora) 1898-1972 .... *9*
Lynds, Dennis 1924-2005 .... *47*
　Brief entry *37*
Lyne, Alison Davis *188*
Lyngseth, Joan
　See Davies, Joan
Lynn, Elizabeth A(nne) 1946- *99*
Lynn, Mary
　See Brokamp, Marilyn
Lynn, Patricia
　See Watts, Mabel Pizzey
Lynn, Tracy *175*
Lyon, Elinor 1921-2008 .... *6*
　Obituary *192*
Lyon, Elinor Bruce
　See Lyon, Elinor
Lyon, George Ella 1949- *148*
　Autobiography Feature *148*
　Earlier sketches in SATA *68, 119*
Lyon, Lyman R.
　See de Camp, L(yon) Sprague
Lyons, Dorothy M(arawee) 1907-1997 .... *3*
Lyons, Grant 1941- *30*
Lyons, Marcus
　See Blish, James (Benjamin)
Lyons, Mary E. 1947- *195*
　Autobiography Feature *195*
　Earlier sketches in SATA *93, 142*
Lyons, Mary Evelyn
　See Lyons, Mary E.
Lystad, Mary (Hanemann) 1928- *11*
Lytle, Elizabeth Stewart 1949- *79*
Lytle, Robert A. 1944- *119*
Lyttle, Richard B(ard) 1927- *23*
Lytton, Edward G(eorge) E(arle) L(ytton)
　Bulwer-Lytton Baron 1803-1873 .... *23*

M

Ma, Wenhai 1954- 84
Maar, Leonard (Frank, Jr.) 1927- 30
Maartens, Maretha 1945- 73
Maas, Selve -1997 14
Maass, Robert 195
Mabie, Grace
See Mattern, Joanne
Mac
See MacManus, Seumas
and Maccari, Ruggero
Macalaster, Elizabeth G. 1951- 115
MacAlister, Katie 159
MacAllan, Andrew
See Leasor, James
MacAodhagain, Eamon
See Egan, E(dward) W(elstead)
MacArthur-Onslow, Annette Rosemary
1933- 26
Macaulay, David (Alexander) 1946- 137
Brief entry 27
Earlier sketches in SATA 46, 72
See also CLR 14
Macaulay, Teresa (E.) 1947- 95
Macavinta, Courtney 176
MacBeth, George (Mann) 1932-1992 4
Obituary 70
MacBride, Roger Lea 1929-1995 85
MacCarter, Don 1944- 91
MacClintock, Dorcas 1932- 8
MacCready, Robin Merrow 1959(?)- 190
MacCullough, Carolyn 174
MacDonald, Alan 1958- 192
MacDonald, Amy 1951- 156
Autobiography Feature 156
Earlier sketches in SATA 76, 136
MacDonald, Anne Elizabeth Campbell Bard
-1958
See MacDonald, Betty
MacDonald, Anson
See Heinlein, Robert A.
MacDonald, Betty 1908-1958
See YABC 1
See MacDonald, Anne Elizabeth Campbell
Bard
Macdonald, Blackie
See Emrich, Duncan (Black Macdonald)
Macdonald, Caroline 1948- 86
Obituary 111
See also CLR 60
Macdonald, Dwight 1906-1982 29
Obituary 33
MacDonald, George 1824-1905 100
Earlier sketch in SATA 33
See also CLR 67
MacDonald, Golden
See Brown, Margaret Wise
Macdonald, Guy 195
Macdonald, James D. 1954- 165
Earlier sketches in SATA 81, 114
See Appleton, Victor
Macdonald, Marcia
See Hill, Grace Livingston
MacDonald, Margaret Read 1940- 194
Earlier sketches in SATA 94, 164
Macdonald, Marianne 1934- 113
Macdonald, Mary
See Gifford, Griselda
Macdonald, Maryann 1947- 189
Earlier sketch in SATA 72
Macdonald, Shelagh 1937- 25
MacDonald, Suse 1940- 193
Brief entry 52
Earlier sketches in SATA 54, 109
Macdonald, Zillah K(atherine) 1885-1979 ... 11
MacDonnell, Megan
See Stevens, Serita
MacDougal, John
See Blish, James (Benjamin)
Mace, Elisabeth 1933- 27

Mace, Varian 1938- 49
MacEwen, Gwendolyn (Margaret)
1941-1987 50
Obituary 55
Macfarlan, Allan A. 1892-1982 35
MacFarlane, Iris 1922- 11
MacGill-Callahan, Sheila 1926-2000 78
MacGregor, Carol Lynn 153
MacGregor, Ellen 1906-1954 39
Brief entry 27
MacGregor-Hastie, Roy (Alasdhair Niall)
1929- 3
MacGrory, Yvonne 1948- 142
Machado, Ana Maria 1941- 150
MacHale, D.J. 1956- 175
MacHale, Donald James
See MacHale, D.J.
Machetanz, Frederick 1908- 34
Machin Goodall, Daphne (Edith) 37
Macht, Norm
See Macht, Norman L.
Macht, Norman L. 1929- 122
Macht, Norman Lee
See Macht, Norman L.
MacInnes, Helen (Clark) 1907-1985 22
Obituary 44
Macintosh, Brownie 1950- 98
MacIntyre, Elisabeth 1916- 17
Mack, Jeff 194
Mack, L.V.
See Kimmelman, Burt
Mack, Stan(ley) 17
Mack, Todd 168
Mack, Tracy 1968- 183
Earlier sketch in SATA 128
Mackall, Dandi D.
See Mackall, Dandi Daley
Mackall, Dandi Daley 1949- 182
Earlier sketches in SATA 118, 177
Mackay, Claire 1930- 97
Autobiography Feature 124
Earlier sketch in SATA 40
See also CLR 43
Mackay, Constance D'Arcy (?)-1966 125
Mackay, Donald 1914-2005 81
Obituary 173
Mackay, Donald Alexander
See Mackay, Donald
MacKaye, Percy (Wallace) 1875-1956 32
Mackel, Kathryn 1950- 162
Mackel, Kathy
See Mackel, Kathryn
MacKellar, William 1914- 4
Macken, Walter 1915-1967 36
MacKenzie, Jill (Kelly) 1947- 75
Mackey, Ernan
See McInerny, Ralph
Mackey, Weezie Kerr 188
Mackie, Maron
See McNeely, Jeannette
Mackin, Edward
See McInerny, Ralph
MacKinnon, Bernie 1957- 69
MacKinnon Groomer, Vera 1915- 57
MacKinstry, Elizabeth 1879-1956 42
Mackler, Carolyn 1973- 156
MacLachlan, Patricia 1938- 168
Brief entry 42
Earlier sketches in SATA 62, 107
See also CLR 14
MacLane, Jack
See Crider, Bill
MacLean, Alistair (Stuart) 1922(?)-1987 23
Obituary 50
Maclean, Art
See Shirreffs, Gordon D(onald)
MacLean, Christine Kole 177
MacLean, Glynne 1964- 150
MacLeod, Beatrice 1910- 162
Earlier sketch in SATA 10

MacLeod, Beatrice Beach
See MacLeod, Beatrice
MacLeod, Charlotte (Matilda) 1922-2005 28
Obituary 160
MacLeod, Doug 1959- 60
MacLeod, Elizabeth 184
Earlier sketch in SATA 158
MacLeod, Ellen Jane (Anderson) 1916- 14
MacManus, James
See MacManus, Seumas
MacManus, Seumas 1869-1960 25
MacMaster, Eve (Ruth) B(owers) 1942- 46
MacMillan, Annabelle
See Quick, Annabelle
MacMillan, Dianne M(arie) 1943- 125
Earlier sketch in SATA 84
Macnaughton, Tina 182
Macneill, Janet
See McNeely, Jeannette
MacPeek, Walter G. 1902-1973 4
Obituary 25
MacPhail, Catherine 1946- 130
MacPherson, Margaret 1908-2001 9
See also SAAS 4
MacPherson, Thomas George 1915-1976
Obituary 30
MacPherson, Winnie 1930- 107
MacRae, Tom 1980- 181
Macrae, Travis
See Feagles, Anita M(acRae)
MacRaois, Cormac 1944- 72
Macumber, Mari
See Sandoz, Mari(e Susette)
Macy, Sue 1954- 134
Earlier sketch in SATA 88
Madaras, Lynda 1947- 151
Madden, Don 1927- 3
Madden, Kerry 1961- 168
Madden-Lunsford, Kerry
See Madden, Kerry
Maddern, Eric 1950- 166
Maddigan, Beth 1967- 174
Maddison, Angela Mary 1923- 10
See Banner, Angela
Maddock, Reginald (Bertram) 1912-1994 15
Madenski, Melissa (Ann) 1949- 77
Madian, Jon 1941- 9
Madison, Alan 182
Madison, Arnold 1937- 6
Madison, Winifred 5
Madonna 1958- 149
Madsen, Gunnar 171
Madsen, Ross Martin 1946- 82
Madsen, Susan A. 1954- 90
Madsen, Susan Arrington
See Madsen, Susan A.
Maestro, Betsy (Crippen) 1944- 106
Brief entry 30
Earlier sketch in SATA 59
See also CLR 45
Maestro, Giulio 1942- 106
Earlier sketches in SATA 8, 59
See also CLR 45
Maeterlinck, Maurice 1862-1949 66
Magee, Doug 1947- 78
Magee, Wes 1939- 64
Maggio, Rosalie 1943- 69
Magid, Ken(neth Marshall) 65
Magnus, Erica 1946- 77
Magoon, Scott 182
Magorian, James 1942- 92
Earlier sketch in SATA 32
Magorian, Michelle 1947- 128
Earlier sketch in SATA 67
Magorian, Michelle Jane
See Magorian, Michelle
Magovern, Peg 103
Maguire, Anne
See Nearing, Penny

Maguire, Gregory 1954- *129*
　Earlier sketches in SATA *28, 84*
　See also SAAS *22*
Maguire, Gregory Peter
　See Maguire, Gregory
Maguire, Jack 1920-2000 .... *74*
Maguire, Jesse
　See Smith, Sherwood
Maguire, Jessie
　See Smith, Sherwood
Maher, Ramona 1934- *13*
Mahlqvist, (Karl) Stefan *30*
　See Maehlqvist, (Karl) Stefan
Mahon, Julia C(unha) 1916- *11*
Mahood, Kenneth 1930- *24*
Mahy, Margaret 1936- *171*
　Earlier sketches in SATA *14, 69, 119*
　See also CLR *78*
Mahy, Margaret May
　See Mahy, Margaret
Maiden, Cecil (Edward) 1902-1981 .... *52*
Maidoff, Ilka
　See List, Ilka Katherine
Maifair, Linda Lee 1947- *83*
Maik, Henri
　See Hecht, Henri Joseph
Maillu, David G(ian) 1939- *111*
Maine, Trevor
　See Catherall, Arthur
Mains, Randolph P. 1946- *80*
Maione, Heather *189*
Maiorano, Robert 1946- *43*
Maisner, Heather 1947- *89*
Maison, Della
　See Katz, Bobbi
Maitland, Antony Jasper 1935- *25*
Maitland, Barbara *102*
Mai-Wyss, Tatjana 1972- *187*
Major, Kevin (Gerald) 1949- *134*
　Earlier sketches in SATA *32, 82*
　See also CLR *11*
Majure, Janet 1954- *96*
Makhijani, Pooja *188*
Makie, Pam 1943- *37*
Makowski, Silk
　See Makowski, Silvia Ann
Makowski, Silvia Ann 1940- *101*
Malam, John 1957- *152*
　Earlier sketch in SATA *89*
Maland, Nick *195*
Malcolm, Dan
　See Silverberg, Robert
Malcolm, Jahnna N.
　See Beecham, Jahnna
Malcolmson, Anne
　See von Storch, Anne B.
Malcolmson, David 1899-1978 .... *6*
Maletta, Dr. Arlene
　See Feltenstein, Arlene (H.)
Mali, Jane Lawrence 1937-1995 .... *51*
　Brief entry *44*
　Obituary *86*
Malkin, Nina 1959(?)- *179*
Mallett, Jerry J. 1939- *76*
Mallory, Kenneth 1945- *185*
　Earlier sketch in SATA *128*
Mallowan, Agatha Christie
　See Christie, Agatha (Mary Clarissa)
Malmberg, Carl 1904-1979 .... *9*
Malmgren, Dallin 1949- *65*
Malo, John W. 1911-2000 .... *4*
Malone, James Hiram 1930- *84*
Malone, Nola Langner 1930-2003
　Obituary *151*
　See Langner, Nola
Malone, Patricia 1932- *155*
Malone, Peter 1953- *191*
Maloney, Pat
　See Markun, Patricia Maloney
Malory, Sir Thomas 1410(?)-1471(?) *59*
　Brief entry *33*

Maltese, Michael 1909(?)-1981
　Obituary *24*
Malvasi, Meg Greene *143*
Malvern, Corinne 1905-1956 .... *34*
Malvern, Gladys (?)-1962 .... *23*
Mama G.
　See Davis, Grania
Mammano, Julie (Lynn) 1962- *107*
Mamonova, Tatyana 1943- *93*
Manchel, Frank 1935- *10*
Manchester, William (Raymond)
　1922-2004 .... *65*
Mandel, Brett H. 1969- *108*
Mandel, Peter 1957- *87*
Mandel, Sally (Elizabeth) 1944- *64*
Mandell, Muriel (Hortense Levin) 1921- *63*
Manders, John 1957- *175*
Manes, Stephen 1949- *99*
　Brief entry *40*
　Earlier sketch in SATA *42*
Manfred, Frederick (Feikema) 1912-1994 .... *30*
Mangin, Marie France 1940- *59*
Mangione, Jerre *6*
　Obituary *104*
　See Mangione, Gerlando
Mango, Karin N. 1936- *52*
Mangurian, David 1938- *14*
Mania, Cathy 1950- *102*
Mania, Robert 1952- *102*
Mania, Robert C., Jr.
　See Mania, Robert
Maniatty, Taramesha 1978- *92*
Maniscalco, Joseph 1926- *10*
Manley, Deborah 1932- *28*
Manley, Seon 1921- *15*
　See also CLR *3*
　See also SAAS *2*
Mann, Elizabeth 1948- *153*
Mann, Josephine
　See Pullein-Thompson, Josephine (Mary
　Wedderburn)
Mann, Kenny 1946- *91*
Mann, Pamela 1946- *91*
Mann, Patrick
　See Waller, Leslie
Mann, Peggy *6*
　See Houlton, Peggy Mann
Mannetti, Lisa 1953- *57*
　Brief entry *51*
Mannheim, Grete (Salomon) 1909-1986 ...... *10*
Manniche, Lise 1943- *31*
Manning, Jane K. *185*
Manning, Mick 1959- *176*
Manning, Rosemary (Joy) 1911-1988 .... *10*
　See Davys, Sarah
　and Voyle, Mary
Manning, Sarra *162*
Manning-Sanders, Ruth (Vernon)
　1895(?)-1988 .... *73*
　Obituary *57*
　Earlier sketch in SATA *15*
Mannion, Diane
　See Paterson, Diane
Mannis, Celeste Davidson *173*
Mannon, Warwick
　See Hopkins, (Hector) Kenneth
Mansir, A. Richard 1932- *170*
Manson, Ainslie Kertland 1938- *115*
Manson, Beverlie 1945- *57*
　Brief entry *44*
Manthorpe, Helen 1958- *122*
Mantinband, Gerda (B.) 1917- *74*
Manton, Jo
　See Gittings, Jo (Grenville) Manton
Manuel, Lynn 1948- *179*
　Earlier sketch in SATA *99*
Manushkin, Fran 1942- *166*
　Earlier sketches in SATA *7, 54, 93*
Manushkin, Frances
　See Manushkin, Fran

Man Without a Spleen, A
　See Chekhov, Anton (Pavlovich)
Manzano, Sonia 1950- *167*
Mapes, Mary A.
　See Ellison, Virginia H(owell)
Maple, Marilyn 1931- *80*
Mappin, Strephyn 1956- *109*
Mara, Barney
　See Roth, Arthur J(oseph)
Mara, Jeanette
　See Cebulash, Mel
Marais, Josef 1905-1978
　Obituary *24*
Marasmus, Seymour
　See Rivoli, Mario
Marbach, Ethel
　See Pochocki, Ethel (Frances)
Marcal, Annette B.
　See Callaway, Bernice (Anne)
Marcelino
　See Agnew, Edith J(osephine)
Marcellino, Fred 1939-2001 .... *118*
　Obituary *127*
　Earlier sketch in SATA *68*
March, Carl
　See Fleischman, Sid
Marchant, Bessie 1862-1941
　See YABC *2*
Marchant, Catherine
　See Cookson, Catherine (McMullen)
Marcher, Marion Walden 1890-1987 .... *10*
Marchesi, Stephen 1951- *114*
Marchesi, Steve
　See Marchesi, Stephen
　and Older, Effin
　and Older, Jules
Marchetta, Melina 1965- *170*
Marciano, John Bemelmans 1970- *167*
　Earlier sketch in SATA *118*
　See also CLR *93*
Marco, Lou
　See Gottfried, Theodore Mark
Marcus, Leonard S. 1950- *187*
　Earlier sketch in SATA *133*
Marcus, Paul 1953- *82*
Marcus, Rebecca B(rian) 1907- *9*
Marcuse, Aida E. 1934- *89*
Marek, Margot L. 1934(?)-1987
　Obituary *54*
Margaret, Karla
　See Andersdatter, Karla M(argaret)
Margolin, Harriet
　See Ziefert, Harriet
Margolis, Jeffrey A. 1948- *108*
Margolis, Leslie *187*
Margolis, Richard J(ules) 1929-1991 .... *86*
　Obituary *67*
　Earlier sketch in SATA *4*
Margolis, Vivienne 1922- *46*
Mariana
　See Foster, Marian Curtis
Marie, Geraldine 1949- *61*
Mariner, Scott
　See Pohl, Frederik
Marino, Dorothy Bronson 1912- *14*
Marino, Jan 1936- *114*
Marino, Nick
　See Deming, Richard
Marino, Peter 1960- *179*
Mario, Anna
　See Odgers, Sally Farrell
Marion, Henry
　See del Rey, Lester
Maris, Ron *71*
　Brief entry *45*
Mark, Jan 1943-2006 .... *164*
　Obituary *173*
　Earlier sketches in SATA *22, 69, 114*
　See also CLR *11*
Mark, Janet Marjorie
　See Mark, Jan

Mark, Joan T. 1937- *122*
Mark, Pauline (Dahlin) 1913-1997 .... *14*
Mark, Polly
  See Mark, Pauline (Dahlin)
Mark, Ted
  See Gottfried, Theodore Mark
Markel, Michelle *169*
Marker, Sherry 1941- *76*
Markert, Jennifer 1965- *83*
Markert, Jenny
  See Markert, Jennifer
Markham, Lynne 1947- *102*
Markham, Marion M. 1929- *60*
Markham, Wendy
  See Staub, Wendy Corsi
Markins, W. S.
  See Jenkins, Marie M(agdalen)
Markle, Sandra L. 1946- *185*
  Brief entry *41*
  Earlier sketches in SATA *57, 92, 148*
Markle, Sandra Lee
  See Markle, Sandra L.
Marko, Katherine D(olores) *28*
Markoosie
  See Patsauq, Markoosie
Marks, Alan 1957- *187*
  Earlier sketches in SATA *77, 151*
Marks, Burton 1930- *47*
  Brief entry *43*
Marks, Graham *158*
Marks, Hannah K.
  See Trivelpiece, Laurel
Marks, J.
  See Highwater, Jamake (Mamake)
Marks, J(ames) M(acdonald) 1921- *13*
Marks, Laurie J. 1957- *68*
Marks, Margaret L. 1911(?)-1980
  Obituary *23*
Marks, Mickey Klar -1986 .... *12*
Marks, Peter
  See Smith, Robert Kimmel
Marks, Rita 1938- *47*
Marks, Stan(ley) *14*
Marks-Highwater, J.
  See Highwater, Jamake (Mamake)
Markun, Patricia Maloney 1924- *15*
Markusen, Bruce (Stanley Rodriguez)
  1965- *141*
Marley, Louise 1952- *173*
  Earlier sketch in SATA *120*
Marlin, Hilda
  See Van Stockum, Hilda
Marlow, Max
  See Nicole, Christopher (Robin)
Marlow, Susan K. 1953- *178*
Marlowe, Amy Bell *67*
  Earlier sketch in SATA *1*
Marlowe, Jack
  See Deary, Terry
Marney, Dean 1952- *90*
Marokvia, Artur 1909- *31*
Marokvia, Mireille 1908-2008 .... *5*
Marokvia, Mireille Journet
  See Marokvia, Mireille
Marol, Jean-Claude 1946- *125*
Marr, John S(tuart) 1940- *48*
Marr, Melissa 1972- *189*
Marric, J. J.
  See Butler, William (Arthur) Vivian
    and Creasey, John
Marrin, Albert 1936- *193*
  Brief entry *43*
  Earlier sketches in SATA *53, 90, 126*
  See also CLR *53*
Marriott, Alice Lee 1910-1992 .... *31*
  Obituary *71*
Marriott, Janice 1946- *134*
Marriott, Pat(ricia) 1920- *35*
Marroquin, Patricio
  See Markun, Patricia Maloney

Mars, W. T.
  See Mars, Witold Tadeusz J.
Mars, Witold Tadeusz J. 1912-1985 .... *3*
Marsden, Carolyn 1950- *175*
  Earlier sketch in SATA *140*
Marsden, John 1950- *146*
  Earlier sketches in SATA *66, 97*
  See also CLR *34*
  See also SAAS *22*
Marsh, Carole 1946- *127*
Marsh, Dave 1950- *66*
Marsh, J. E.
  See Marshall, Evelyn
Marsh, James 1946- *73*
Marsh, Jean
  See Marshall, Evelyn
Marsh, Joan F. 1923- *83*
Marsh, Paul
  See Hopkins, (Hector) Kenneth
Marsh, Valerie 1954- *89*
Marshall, Anthony D(ryden) 1924- *18*
Marshall, Bonnie C. 1941- *141*
  Earlier sketch in SATA *18*
Marshall, Bridget M(ary) 1974- *103*
Marshall, (Sarah) Catherine (Wood)
  1914-1983 .... *2*
  Obituary *34*
Marshall, Douglas
  See McClintock, Marshall
Marshall, Edmund
  See Hopkins, (Hector) Kenneth
Marshall, Edward
  See Marshall, James
Marshall, Evelyn 1897-1991 .... *11*
Marshall, Felicity 1950- *116*
Marshall, Garry 1934- *60*
Marshall, H. H.
  See Jahn, (Joseph) Michael
Marshall, James 1942-1992 .... *75*
  Earlier sketches in SATA *6, 51*
  See also CLR *21*
Marshall, James Edward
  See Marshall, James
Marshall, James Vance
  See Payne, Donald Gordon
Marshall, Janet (Perry) 1938- *97*
Marshall, Jeff
  See Laycock, George (Edwin)
Marshall, Kim
  See Marshall, Michael (Kimbrough)
Marshall, Michael (Kimbrough) 1948- *37*
Marshall, Percy
  See Young, Percy M(arshall)
Marshall, S(amuel) L(yman) A(twood)
  1900-1977 .... *21*
Marsoli, Lisa Ann 1958- *101*
  Brief entry *53*
Marsten, Richard
  See Hunter, Evan
Marston, Elsa 1933- *156*
Marston, Hope Irvin 1935- *127*
  Earlier sketch in SATA *31*
Marszalek, John F. 1939- *167*
Marszalek, John Francis, Jr.
  See Marszalek, John F.
Marszalek, John Francis 1939-
  See Marszalek, John F.
Martchenko, Michael 1942- *154*
  Earlier sketches in SATA *50, 95*
Martel, Aimee
  See Thurlo, Aimee
    and Thurlo, David
Martel, Suzanne 1924- *99*
Martignoni, Margaret E. 1908(?)-1974
  Obituary *27*
Martin, Ann M. 1955- *192*
  Brief entry *41*
  Earlier sketches in SATA *44, 70, 126*
  See also CLR *32*

Martin, Bill, Jr. *67*
  Brief entry *40*
  See also CLR *97*
  See Martin, William Ivan, Jr.
Martin, Charles E(lmer) *70*
  Earlier sketch in SATA *69*
  See Mastrangelo, Charles E(lmer)
Martin, Christopher
  See Hoyt, Edwin P(almer), Jr.
Martin, Claire 1933- *76*
Martin, David Stone 1913-1992 .... *39*
Martin, Del 1921-2008 .... *47*
  See Martin, Dorothy
    and Martin, Dorothy L.
Martin, Donald
  See Honig, Donald
Martin, Dorothy
  See Martin, Del
Martin, Dorothy L.
  See Martin, Del
Martin, Eugene *1*
Martin, Eva M. 1939- *65*
Martin, Frances M(cEntee) 1906-1998 .... *36*
Martin, Francesca 1947- *101*
Martin, Fred 1948- *119*
Martin, Fredric
  See Christopher, Matt(hew Frederick)
Martin, George Raymond Richard
  See Martin, George R.R.
Martin, George R.R. 1948- *118*
Martin, J(ohn) P(ercival) 1880(?)-1966 .... *15*
Martin, Jacqueline Briggs 1945- *188*
  Earlier sketches in SATA *98, 149*
Martin, Jane Read 1957- *84*
Martin, Jeremy
  See Levin, Marcia Obrasky
Martin, Les
  See Schulman, L(ester) M(artin)
Martin, Linda 1961- *82*
Martin, Lynne 1923- *21*
Martin, Marcia
  See Levin, Marcia Obrasky
Martin, Marvin 1926- *126*
Martin, Melanie
  See Pellowski, Michael (Joseph)
Martin, Nancy
  See Salmon, Annie Elizabeth
Martin, Patricia Miles 1899-1986 .... *43*
  Obituary *48*
  Earlier sketch in SATA *1*
Martin, Peter
  See Chaundler, Christine
Martin, Rafe 1946- *175*
Martin, Rene 1891-1977 .... *42*
  Obituary *20*
Martin, Rupert (Claude) 1905- *31*
Martin, S. R.
  See Mappin, Strephyn
Martin, Stefan 1936- *32*
Martin, Vicky
  See Storey, Victoria Carolyn
Martin, Webber
  See Silverberg, Robert
Martin, Wendy
  See Martini, Teri
Martin, William Ivan, Jr. 1916-2004 .... *145*
  Earlier sketch in SATA *40*
  See Martin, Bill, Jr.
Martineau, Diane 1940- *178*
Martineau, Harriet 1802-1876
  See YABC *2*
Martinet, Jeanne 1958- *80*
Martinez, Agnes *167*
Martinez, Arturo O. 1933- *192*
Martinez, Ed(ward) 1954- *98*
Martinez, Elizabeth Coonrod 1954- *85*
Martinez, Victor 1954- *95*
Martini, Teri 1930- *3*
Martini, Therese
  See Martini, Teri
Martino, Alfred C. 1964- *174*

Martinson, Janis
  See Herbert, Janis
Marton, Jirina 1946- *144*
  Earlier sketch in SATA *95*
Marton, Pierre
  See Stone, Peter
Martson, Del
  See Lupoff, Richard A(llen)
Martyr, Paula (Jane) *57*
  See Lawford, Paula Jane
Maruki, Toshi 1912-2000 .... *112*
  See also CLR *19*
Marvin, Isabel R(idout) 1924- *84*
Marx, Patricia Windschill 1948- *160*
  Earlier sketch in SATA *112*
Marx, Robert F(rank) 1936- *24*
Marx, Trish
  See Marx, Patricia Windschill
Marzani, Carl (Aldo) 1912-1994 .... *12*
Marzollo, Jean 1942- *190*
  Autobiography Feature *190*
  Earlier sketches in SATA *29, 77, 130*
  See also SAAS *15*
Masefield, John (Edward) 1878-1967 .... *19*
Masoff, Joy 1951- *118*
Mason, Adrienne 1962- *163*
Mason, Cherie *170*
Mason, Edwin A. 1905-1979
  Obituary *32*
Mason, Ernst
  See Pohl, Frederik
Mason, F(rancis) van Wyck 1901-1978 .... *3*
  Obituary *26*
Mason, Frank W.
  See Mason, F(rancis) van Wyck
Mason, George Frederick 1904-2000 .... *14*
Mason, Miriam E(vangeline) 1900-1973 .... *2*
  Obituary *26*
Mason, Prue *195*
Mason, Simon 1962- *178*
Mason, Tally
  See Derleth, August (William)
Mason, Van Wyck
  See Mason, F(rancis) van Wyck
Mass, Wendy 1967- *158*
Mass, William
  See Gibson, William
Masselman, George 1897-1971 .... *19*
Massie, Dianne Redfield 1938- *125*
  Earlier sketch in SATA *16*
Massie, Elizabeth *108*
Masson, Sophie 1959- *179*
  Earlier sketch in SATA *133*
Masters, Anthony (Richard) 1940-2003 ...... *112*
  Obituary *145*
Masters, Kelly R(ay) 1897-1987 .... *3*
Masters, Mildred 1932- *42*
Masters, William
  See Cousins, Margaret
Masters, Zeke
  See Bensen, Donald R.
  and Goulart, Ron(ald Joseph)
Matas, Carol 1949- *194*
  Autobiography Feature *112*
  Earlier sketch in SATA *93*
  See also CLR *52*
Matchette, Katharine E. 1941- *38*
Math, Irwin 1940- *42*
Mathabane, Mark 1960- *123*
Mather, Kirtley F(letcher) 1888-1978 .... *65*
Mathers, Petra 1945- *176*
  Earlier sketch in SATA *119*
  See also CLR *76*
Matheson, Richard (Christian) 1953- *119*
Matheson, Shirlee Smith 1942- *155*
Mathews, Ellie 1946(?)- *193*
Mathews, Janet 1914-1992 .... *41*
Mathews, Judith *80*
  See Goldberger, Judith M.
Mathews, Louise
  See Tooke, Louise Mathews

Mathiesen, Egon 1907-1976
  Obituary *28*
Mathieu, Joe 1949- *185*
  Brief entry *36*
  Earlier sketches in SATA *43, 94*
Mathieu, Joseph P.
  See Mathieu, Joe
Mathis, Sharon Bell 1937- *58*
  Earlier sketch in SATA *7*
  See also CLR *3*
  See also SAAS *3*
Matlin, Marlee 1965- *181*
Matlin, Marlee Beth
  See Matlin, Marlee
Matloff, Gregory 1945- *73*
Matott, Justin 1961- *109*
Matranga, Frances Carfi 1922- *78*
Matray, James I. 1948- *161*
Matray, James Irving
  See Matray, James I.
Matson, Emerson N(els) 1926- *12*
Matsui, Tadashi 1926- *8*
Matsuno, Masako *6*
  See Kobayashi, Masako Matsuno
Matsuoka, Mei 1981- *192*
Matte, (Encarnacion) L'Enc 1936- *22*
Mattern, Joanne 1963- *122*
Matheson, Jenny *180*
Matthews, Aline
  See De Wire, Elinor
Matthews, Andrew 1948- *138*
Matthews, Caitlin 1952- *122*
Matthews, Downs 1925- *71*
Matthews, Elizabeth 1978- *194*
Matthews, Ellen
  See Bache, Ellyn
Matthews, Ellen 1950- *28*
Matthews, Harold Downs
  See Matthews, Downs
Matthews, Jacklyn Meek
  See Meek, Jacklyn O'Hanlon
Matthews, John (Kentigern) 1948- *116*
Matthews, Laura S.
  See Matthews, L.S.
Matthews, Liz
  See Pellowski, Michael (Joseph)
Matthews, L.S. *183*
Matthews, Morgan
  See Pellowski, Michael (Joseph)
Matthews, Nicola
  See Browne, N.M.
Matthews, Patricia 1927-2006 .... *28*
Matthews, Patricia Anne
  See Matthews, Patricia
Matthews, Tina 1961- *190*
Matthews, Tom L.
  See Lalicki, Tom
Matthews, William Henry III 1919- *45*
  Brief entry *28*
Matthiessen, Peter 1927- *27*
Mattingley, Christobel (Rosemary) 1931- *85*
  Earlier sketch in SATA *37*
  See also CLR *24*
  See also SAAS *18*
Matulay, Laszlo 1912- *43*
Matus, Greta 1938- *12*
Maugham, W. S.
  See Maugham, W(illiam) Somerset
Maugham, W(illiam) Somerset 1874-1965 .. *54*
Maugham, William Somerset
  See Maugham, W(illiam) Somerset
Maurer, Diane Philippoff
  See Maurer-Mathison, Diane V(ogel)
Maurer, Diane Vogel
  See Maurer-Mathison, Diane V(ogel)
Maurer-Mathison, Diane V(ogel) 1944- *89*
Mauser, Pat Rhoads
  See McCord, Patricia
Mauser, Patricia Rhoads *37*
  See McCord, Patricia
Maves, Mary Carolyn 1916- *10*

Maves, Paul B(enjamin) 1913-1994 .... *10*
Mavor, Salley 1955- *125*
Mawicke, Tran 1911- *15*
Max 1906-1989
  See Diop, Birago (Ismael)
Max, Peter 1939- *45*
Maxon, Anne
  See Best, (Evangel) Allena Champlin
Maxwell, Arthur S. 1896-1970 .... *11*
Maxwell, Edith 1923- *7*
Maxwell, Gavin 1914-1969 .... *65*
Maxwell, Katie
  See MacAlister, Katie
Maxwell, William (Keepers, Jr.) 1908-2000
  Obituary *128*
Maxwell-Hyslop, Miranda 1968- *154*
May, Charles Paul 1920- *4*
May, Elaine Tyler 1947- *120*
May, J. C.
  See May, Julian
May, Julian 1931- *11*
May, Robert Lewis 1905-1976
  Obituary *27*
May, Robert Stephen 1929-1996 .... *46*
May, Robin
  See May, Robert Stephen
Mayall, Beth *171*
Mayberry, Florence V(irginia) Wilson *10*
Maybury, Richard J. 1946- *72*
Maybury, Rick
  See Maybury, Richard J.
Mayer, Agatha
  See Maher, Ramona
Mayer, Albert Ignatius, Jr. 1906-1994
  Obituary *29*
Mayer, Ann M(argaret) 1938- *14*
Mayer, Danuta 1958- *117*
Mayer, Jane Rothschild 1903-2001 .... *38*
Mayer, Marianna 1945- *132*
  Earlier sketches in SATA *32, 83*
Mayer, Mercer 1943- *137*
  Earlier sketches in SATA *16, 32, 73, 129*
  See also CLR *11*
Mayerson, Charlotte Leon *36*
Mayerson, Evelyn Wilde 1935- *55*
Mayfield, Katherine 1958- *118*
Mayfield, Sue 1963- *146*
  Earlier sketch in SATA *72*
Mayhar, Ardath 1930- *38*
Mayhew, James (John) 1964- *149*
  Earlier sketch in SATA *85*
Maynard, Olga 1920- *40*
Mayne, William (James Carter) 1928- *122*
  Earlier sketches in SATA *6, 68*
  See also CLR *123*
  See also SAAS *11*
Maynes, J. O. Rocky, Jr.
  See Maynes, J. Oscar, Jr.
Maynes, J. Oscar, Jr. 1929- *38*
Mayo, Gretchen Will 1936- *163*
  Earlier sketch in SATA *84*
Mayo, Margaret 1935- *165*
  Earlier sketches in SATA *38, 96*
Mayo, Margaret Mary
  See Mayo, Margaret
Mays, Lucinda L(a Bella) 1924- *49*
Mays, (Lewis) Victor (Jr.) 1927- *5*
Mazer, Anne 1953- *192*
  Earlier sketches in SATA *67, 105*
Mazer, Harry 1925- *167*
  Earlier sketches in SATA *31, 67, 105*
  See also CLR *16*
  See also SAAS *11*
Mazer, Norma Fox 1931- *168*
  Earlier sketches in SATA *24, 67, 105*
  See also CLR *23*
  See also SAAS *1*
Mazille, Capucine 1953- *96*
Mazza, Adriana 1928- *19*
Mazzio, Joann 1926- *74*
Mbugua, Kioi Wa 1962- *83*

McAfee, Carol 1955- 81
McAllister, Amanda
  See Dowdell, Dorothy (Florence) Karns
  and Hager, Jean
  and Meaker, Eloise
McAllister, Angela 182
McAllister, Margaret I. 1956- 169
  Earlier sketch in SATA 117
McAllister, M.I.
  See McAllister, Margaret I.
McArthur, Nancy 96
McAvoy, Jim 1972- 142
McBain, Ed
  See Hunter, Evan
McBain, Georgina 189
McBratney, Sam 1943- 164
  Earlier sketch in SATA 89
  See also CLR 44
McBrier, Michael
  See Older, Effin
  and Older, Jules
McCafferty, Jim 1954- 84
McCaffery, Janet 1936- 38
McCaffrey, Anne 1926- 152
  Autobiography Feature 152
  Earlier sketches in SATA 8, 70, 116
  See also CLR 130
  See also SAAS 11
McCaffrey, Anne Inez
  See McCaffrey, Anne
McCaffrey, Mary
  See Szudek, Agnes S(usan) P(hilomena)
McCain, Becky Ray 1954- 138
McCain, Murray (David, Jr.) 1926-1981 7
  Obituary 29
McCall, Edith (Sansom) 1911- 6
McCall, Virginia Nielsen 1909-2000 13
McCall, Wendell
  See Pearson, Ridley
McCallum, Phyllis
  See Koch, Phyllis (Mae) McCallum
McCallum, Stephen 1960- 91
McCampbell, Darlene Z. 1942- 83
McCann, Edson
  See del Rey, Lester
  and Pohl, Frederik
McCann, Gerald 1916- 41
McCann, Helen 1948- 75
McCannon, Dindga 41
McCants, William D. 1961- 82
McCarter, Neely Dixon 1929- 47
McCarthy, Agnes 1933- 4
McCarthy, Colin (John) 1951- 77
McCarthy, Meghan 168
McCarthy, Ralph F. 1950- 139
McCarthy-Tucker, Sherri N. 1958- 83
McCarty, Peter 1966- 182
McCarty, Rega Kramer 1904-1986 10
McCaslin, Nellie 1914-2005 12
McCaughrean, Geraldine 1951- 173
  Earlier sketches in SATA 87, 139
  See also CLR 38
McCaughren, Tom 1936- 75
McCauley, Adam 1965- 128
McCay, (Zenas) Winsor 1869-1934 134
  Earlier sketch in SATA 41
McClafferty, Carla Killough 1958- 137
McClary, Jane Stevenson 1919-1990
  Obituary 64
McCleery, Patsy R. 1925- 133
  Earlier sketch in SATA 88
McClintock, Barbara 1955- 146
  Earlier sketches in SATA 57, 95
McClintock, Marshall 1906-1967 3
McClintock, May Garelick
  See Garelick, May
McClintock, Mike
  See McClintock, Marshall
McClintock, Norah 178
McClintock, Theodore 1902-1971 14
McClinton, Leon 1933- 11

McCloskey, Kevin 1951- 79
McCloskey, (John) Robert 1914-2003 100
  Obituary 146
  Earlier sketches in SATA 2, 39
  See also CLR 7
McCloy, James F(loyd) 1941- 59
McClung, Robert M(arshall) 1916- 135
  Earlier sketches in SATA 2, 68
  See also CLR 11
  See also SAAS 15
McClure, Gillian Mary 1948- 31
McColley, Kevin 1961- 80
  See also SAAS 23
McConduit, Denise Walter 1950- 89
McConnell, James Douglas Rutherford
  1915-1988 40
  Obituary 56
McCord, Anne 1942- 41
McCord, David (Thompson Watson)
  1897-1997 18
  Obituary 96
  See also CLR 9
McCord, Jean 1924- 34
McCord, Pat Mauser
  See McCord, Patricia
McCord, Patricia 1943- 159
  See Mauser, Patricia Rhoads
McCord, Patricia Sue Rhoads Mauser
  See McCord, Patricia
McCormick, Brooks
  See Adams, William Taylor
McCormick, Dell J. 1892-1949 19
McCormick, (George) Donald (King)
  1911-1998 14
McCormick, Edith (Joan) 1934- 30
McCormick, Kimberly A. 1960- 153
McCormick, Patricia 1956- 181
  Earlier sketch in SATA 128
McCourt, Edward (Alexander) 1907-1972
  Obituary 28
McCourt, Lisa 1964- 159
  Earlier sketch in SATA 117
McCourt, Malachy 1931- 126
McCoy, Iola Fuller 3
McCoy, J(oseph) J(erome) 1917- 8
McCoy, Karen Kawamoto 1953- 82
McCoy, Lois (Rich) 1941- 38
McCrady, Lady 1951- 16
McCrea, James (Craig, Jr.) 1920- 3
McCrea, Ruth (Pirman) 1921- 3
McCreigh, James
  See Pohl, Frederik
McCrumb, Sharyn 1948- 109
McCue, Lisa 1959- 177
  Earlier sketch in SATA 65
McCue, Lisa Emiline
  See McCue, Lisa
McCullen, Andrew
  See Arthur, Robert, (Jr.)
McCullers, (Lula) Carson (Smith)
  1917-1967 27
McCulloch, Derek (Ivor Breashur) 1897-1967
  Obituary 29
McCulloch, John Tyler
  See Burroughs, Edgar Rice
McCulloch, Sarah
  See Ure, Jean
McCullough, David 1933- 62
McCullough, David Gaub
  See McCullough, David
McCullough, Frances Monson 1938- 8
McCullough, Sharon Pierce 1943- 131
McCully, Emily Arnold 134
  Autobiography Feature 134
  Earlier sketches in SATA 5, 110
  See also CLR 46
  See also SAAS 7
  See Arnold, Emily
McCune, Dan
  See Haas, Dorothy F.
McCunn, Ruthanne Lum 1946- 63

McCurdy, Michael (Charles) 1942- 147
  Earlier sketches in SATA 13, 82
McCutcheon, Elsie (Mary Jackson) 1937- ... 60
McCutcheon, John 1952- 97
McDaniel, Becky Bring 1953- 61
McDaniel, Lurlene 1944- 146
  Earlier sketch in SATA 71
McDaniels, Pellom III 1968- 121
McDaniels, Preston 1952- 192
McDearmon, Kay 20
McDermott, Beverly Brodsky 1941- 11
McDermott, Eleni 156
McDermott, Gerald (Edward) 1941- 163
  Earlier sketches in SATA 16, 74
  See also CLR 9
McDermott, Michael 1962- 76
McDevitt, Jack 1935- 155
  Earlier sketch in SATA 94
McDevitt, John Charles
  See McDevitt, Jack
McDole, Carol
  See Farley, Carol (J.)
McDonald, Collin 1943- 79
McDonald, Gerald D(oan) 1905-1970 3
McDonald, Jamie
  See Heide, Florence Parry
McDonald, Janet 1953-2007 148
McDonald, Jill (Masefield) 1927-1982 13
  Obituary 29
McDonald, Joyce 1946- 164
  Earlier sketch in SATA 101
McDonald, Lucile Saunders 1898-1992 10
McDonald, Mary Ann 1956- 84
McDonald, Megan 1959- 151
  Autobiography Feature 151
  Earlier sketches in SATA 67, 99, 148
  See also CLR 94
McDonald, Meme 1954- 112
McDonald, Mercedes 1956- 169
  Earlier sketch in SATA 97
McDonell, Chris 1960- 138
McDonnell, Christine 1949- 115
  Earlier sketch in SATA 34
McDonnell, Flora (Mary) 1963- 146
  Earlier sketch in SATA 90
McDonnell, Kathleen 1947- 186
McDonnell, Lois Eddy 1914-2001 10
McDonnell, Patrick 1956- 179
McDonough, Yona Zeldis 1957- 73
McElligott, Matt(hew) 1968- 135
McElmeel, Sharron L. 1942- 128
McElmurry, Jill 159
McElrath, William N. 1932- 65
McElrath-Eslick, Lori 1960- 96
McEntee, Dorothy (Layng) 1902- 37
McEwen, Katherine 183
McEwen, Robert (Lindley) 1926-1980
  Obituary 23
McFadden, Kevin Christopher
  See Pike, Christopher
McFall, Christie 1918- 12
McFall, Gardner 1952- 183
McFarlan, Donald M(aitland) 1915- 59
McFarland, Henry "Hammer"
  See McFarland, Henry O.
McFarland, Henry O. 1934- 143
McFarland, Kenton D(ean) 1920- 11
McFarland, Martha
  See Smith-Ankrom, M. E.
McFarlane, Leslie (Charles) 1902-1977 31
  See Dixon, Franklin W.
  and Ferris, James Cody
  and Keene, Carolyn
  and Rockwood, Roy
McFarlane, Peter (William) 1940- 95
McFarlane, Sheryl P. 1954- 86
McFarlane, Todd 1961- 117
McGaw, Jessie Brewer 1913-1997 10
McGee, Barbara 1943- 6
McGee, Marni 163
McGiffin, (Lewis) Lee (Shaffer) 1908-1978 ... 1

McGill, Alice *159*
McGill, Ormond 1913- *92*
McGinley, Jerry 1948- *116*
McGinley, Phyllis 1905-1978 .... *44*
  Obituary *24*
  Earlier sketch in SATA *2*
McGinnis, Lila S(prague) 1924- *44*
McGinty, Alice B. 1963- *134*
McGivern, Justin 1985- *129*
McGivern, Maureen Daly
  See Daly, Maureen
McGivern, Maureen Patricia Daly
  See Daly, Maureen
McGough, Elizabeth (Hemmes) 1934- *33*
McGovern, Ann 1930- *132*
  Earlier sketches in SATA *8, 69, 70*
  See also CLR *50*
  See also SAAS *17*
McGowen, Thomas E. 1927- *109*
  Earlier sketch in SATA *2*
McGowen, Tom
  See McGowen, Thomas E.
McGrady, Mike 1933- *6*
McGrath, Barbara Barbieri 1953- *169*
  Earlier sketch in SATA *108*
McGrath, Robin 1949- *121*
McGrath, Thomas (Matthew) 1916-1990 ..... *41*
  Obituary *66*
McGraw, Eloise Jarvis 1915-2000 .... *67*
  Obituary *123*
  Earlier sketch in SATA *1*
  See also SAAS *6*
McGraw, William Corbin 1916-1999 .... *3*
McGreal, Elizabeth
  See Yates, Elizabeth
McGregor, Barbara 1959- *82*
McGregor, Craig 1933- *8*
McGregor, Iona 1929- *25*
McGrory, Anik *193*
McGuffey, Alexander Hamilton 1816-1896 . *60*
McGuigan, Mary Ann 1949- *106*
McGuire, Edna 1899- *13*
McGuire, Leslie (Sarah) 1945- *94*
  Brief entry *45*
  Earlier sketch in SATA *52*
McGuire, Robert *187*
McGuirk, Leslie (A.) 1960- *152*
McGurk, Slater
  See Roth, Arthur J(oseph)
McHargue, Georgess 1941- *77*
  Earlier sketch in SATA *4*
  See also CLR *2*
  See also SAAS *5*
McHenry, E.B. 1963(?)- *193*
McHugh, (Berit) Elisabet 1941- *55*
  Brief entry *44*
McIlvaine, Jane
  See McClary, Jane Stevenson
McIlwraith, Maureen Mollie Hunter *2*
  See Hunter, Mollie
McInerney, Judith W(hitelock) 1945- *49*
  Brief entry *46*
McInerny, Ralph 1929- *93*
McInerny, Ralph Matthew
  See McInerny, Ralph
McKaughan, Larry (Scott) 1941- *75*
McKay, Donald 1895- *45*
McKay, Hilary (Jane) 1959- *145*
  Earlier sketch in SATA *92*
  See also SAAS *23*
McKay, Lawrence, Jr. 1948- *114*
McKay, Robert W. 1921- *15*
McKay, Sharon E. 1954- *165*
McKay, Simon
  See Nicole, Christopher (Robin)
McKeating, Eileen 1957- *81*
McKee, David (John) 1935- *158*
  Earlier sketches in SATA *70, 107*
  See also CLR *38*
McKee, Tim 1970- *111*

McKeever, Marcia
  See Laird, Jean E(louise)
McKelvey, Carole A. 1942- *78*
McKelvy, Charles 1950- *124*
McKendrick, Melveena (Christine) 1941- *55*
McKendry, Joe 1972- *170*
McKenna, Colleen O'Shaughnessy 1948- .. *136*
  Earlier sketch in SATA *76*
McKenzie, Dorothy Clayton 1910-1981
  Obituary *28*
McKenzie, Ellen Kindt 1928- *80*
McKernan, Victoria 1957- *171*
McKie, Robin *112*
McKillip, Patricia A. 1948- *174*
  Earlier sketches in SATA *30, 80, 126*
McKillip, Patricia Anne
  See McKillip, Patricia A.
McKim, Audrey Margaret 1909-1999 .... *47*
McKimmie, Chris *194*
McKinley, Jennifer Carolyn Robin
  See McKinley, Robin
McKinley, Robin 1952- *195*
  Brief entry *32*
  Earlier sketches in SATA *50, 89, 130*
  See also CLR *127*
McKinney, Barbara Shaw 1951- *116*
McKinney, Nadine 1938- *91*
McKinty, Adrian *186*
McKissack, Fredrick L. 1939- *162*
  Brief entry *53*
  Earlier sketches in SATA *73, 117*
  See also CLR *55*
McKissack, Fredrick Lemuel
  See McKissack, Fredrick L.
McKissack, Patricia C. 1944- *195*
  Earlier sketches in SATA *51, 73, 117, 162*
  See also CLR *129*
McKissack, Patricia L'Ann Carwell
  See McKissack, Patricia C.
McKissack and McKissack
  See McKissack, Fredrick L.
  and McKissack, Patricia C.
McKown, Robin (?)-1976 .... *6*
McKy, Katie 1956- *184*
McLaren, Clemence 1938- *158*
  Earlier sketch in SATA *105*
McLaughlin, Frank 1934- *73*
McLaurin, Anne 1953- *27*
McLean, Andrew 1946- *172*
  Earlier sketch in SATA *113*
McLean, J. Sloan
  See Gillette, Virginia M(ary)
  and Wunsch, Josephine (McLean)
McLean, Janet 1946- *113*
McLean, Kathryn (Anderson) 1909-1966 .... *9*
McLean, Virginia Overton 1946- *90*
McLean-Carr, Carol 1948- *122*
McLeish, Kenneth 1940-1997 .... *35*
McLenighan, Valjean 1947- *46*
  Brief entry *40*
McLennan, Connie *171*
McLennan, Will
  See Wisler, G(ary) Clifton
McLeod, Bob 1951- *173*
McLeod, Chum 1955- *95*
McLeod, Emilie Warren 1926-1982 .... *23*
  Obituary *31*
McLeod, Kirsty
  See Hudson, (Margaret) Kirsty
McLeod, Margaret Vail
  See Holloway, Teresa (Bragunier)
McLerran, Alice 1933- *137*
  Earlier sketch in SATA *68*
McLimans, David 1949- *182*
McLoughlin, John C. 1949- *47*
McManus, Patrick F. 1933- *46*
McManus, Patrick Francis
  See McManus, Patrick F.
McMeekin, Clark
  See McMeekin, Isabel McLennan
McMeekin, Isabel McLennan 1895-1973 .... *3*

McMenemy, Sarah 1965- *156*
McMillan, Bruce 1947- *192*
  Earlier sketches in SATA *22, 70, 129*
  See also CLR *47*
McMillan, Naomi
  See Grimes, Nikki
McMorey, James L.
  See Moyer, Terry J.
McMorrow, Annalisa 1969- *104*
McMullan, Jim 1934- *150*
  Earlier sketch in SATA *87*
McMullan, K. H.
  See McMullan, Kate
McMullan, Kate 1947- *189*
  Brief entry *48*
  Earlier sketches in SATA *52, 87, 132*
McMullan, Kate Hall
  See McMullan, Kate
McMurtrey, Martin A(loysius) 1921- *21*
McNabb, Linda 1963- *147*
McNair, Kate *3*
McNair, Sylvia 1924-2002 .... *74*
McNamara, Margaret C(raig) 1915-1981
  Obituary *24*
McNaught, Harry *32*
McNaughton, Colin 1951- *134*
  Earlier sketches in SATA *39, 92*
  See also CLR *54*
McNaughton, Janet 1953- *162*
  Earlier sketch in SATA *110*
McNeal, Laura *194*
McNeal, Tom *194*
McNeely, Jeannette 1918- *25*
McNeer, May (Yonge) 1902-1994 .... *81*
  Earlier sketch in SATA *1*
McNeese, Tim 1953- *139*
McNeill, Janet *97*
  Earlier sketch in SATA *1*
  See Alexander, Janet
McNicholas, Shelagh *191*
McNickle, (William) D'Arcy 1904-1977
  Obituary *22*
McNicoll, Sylvia (Marilyn) 1954- *113*
  See also CLR *99*
McNulty, Faith 1918-2005 .... *168*
  Earlier sketches in SATA *12, 84, 139*
McPhail, David 1940- *183*
  Brief entry *32*
  Earlier sketches in SATA *47, 81, 140*
McPhail, David M.
  See McPhail, David
McPhail, David Michael
  See McPhail, David
McPhee, Norma H. 1928- *95*
McPhee, Richard B(yron) 1934- *41*
McPherson, James M. 1936- *141*
  Earlier sketch in SATA *16*
McPherson, James Munro
  See McPherson, James M.
McQueen, Lucinda 1950- *58*
  Brief entry *48*
McQueen, Mildred Hark 1908-1978 .... *12*
McRae, Russell (William) 1934- *63*
McShean, Gordon 1936- *41*
Mc Swigan, Marie 1907-1962 .... *24*
McTavish, Sandy
  See Eyerly, Jeannette
McVeity, Jen *148*
McVey, Vicki 1946- *80*
McVicker, Charles (Taggart) 1930- *39*
McVicker, Chuck
  See McVicker, Charles (Taggart)
McWhirter, A(lan) Ross 1925-1975 .... *37*
  Obituary *31*
McWhirter, Norris (Dewar) 1925-2004 .... *37*
McWilliams, Karen 1943- *65*
Mdurvwa, Hajara E. 1962- *92*
Meacham, Margaret 1952- *95*
Meachum, Virginia 1918- *133*
  Earlier sketch in SATA *87*

Mead, Alice 1952- *146*
Earlier sketch in SATA *94*
Mead, Margaret 1901-1978
Obituary *20*
Mead, Russell (M., Jr.) 1935- *10*
Mead, Stella (?)-1981
Obituary *27*
Meade, Ellen *5*
See Roddick, Ellen
Meade, Marion 1934- *127*
Earlier sketch in SATA *23*
Meader, Stephen W(arren) 1892-1977 .... *1*
Meadmore, Susan
See Sallis, Susan (Diana)
Meadow, Charles T(roub) 1929- *23*
Meadowcroft, Enid LaMonte
See Wright, Enid Meadowcroft (LaMonte)
Meadows, Graham (W.) 1934- *161*
Meaker, M. J.
See Meaker, Marijane
Meaker, Marijane 1927- *160*
Autobiography Feature *111*
Earlier sketches in SATA *20, 61, 99*
See also CLR *29*
See also SAAS *1*
Meaker, Marijane Agnes
See Meaker, Marijane
Means, Florence Crannell 1891-1980 .... *1*
Obituary *25*
See also CLR *56*
Mearian, Judy Frank 1936- *49*
Mecca, Judy Truesdell 1955- *127*
Mechling, Lauren 1978(?)- *194*
Medary, Marjorie 1890-1980 .... *14*
Meddaugh, Susan 1944- *176*
Earlier sketches in SATA *29, 84, 125*
Medearis, Angela Shelf 1956- *123*
Earlier sketch in SATA *72*
Medearis, Mary 1915- *5*
Medina, Jane 1953- *167*
Earlier sketch in SATA *122*
Medina, Nico 1982- *193*
Medlicott, Mary 1946- *88*
Mee, Charles L., Jr. 1938- *72*
Earlier sketch in SATA *8*
Meek, Jacklyn O'Hanlon 1933- *51*
Brief entry *34*
Meek, S(terner St.) P(aul) 1894-1972
Obituary *28*
Meeker, Clare Hodgson 1952- *96*
Meeker, Oden 1919(?)-1976 .... *14*
Meeker, Richard
See Brown, Fornan
Meeks, Esther MacBain *1*
Meggs, Libby Phillips 1943- *130*
Mehdevi, Alexander (Sinclair) 1947- *7*
Mehdevi, Anne (Marie) Sinclair 1947- *8*
Meidell, Sherry 1951- *73*
Meier, Minta 1906- *55*
Meighan, Donald Charles 1929- *30*
Meigs, Cornelia Lynde 1884-1973 .... *6*
See also CLR *55*
Meilach, Dona Z(weigoron) 1926- *34*
Meilman, Philip W(arren) 1951- *79*
Meinstereifel, Ronald L. 1960- *134*
Meisel, Paul *184*
Melcher, Daniel 1912-1985
Obituary *43*
Melcher, Frederic Gershom 1879-1963
Obituary *22*
Melcher, Marguerite Fellows 1879-1969 ...... *10*
Melendez, Francisco 1964- *72*
Melin, Grace Hathaway 1892-1973 .... *10*
Mellersh, H(arold) E(dward) L(eslie)
1897- *10*
Melling, David *186*
Melmoth, Sebastian
See Wilde, Oscar
Melnikoff, Pamela (Rita) *97*

Meltzer, Milton 1915- *128*
Autobiography Feature *124*
Earlier sketches in SATA *1, 50, 80*
See also CLR *13*
See also SAAS *1*
Melville, Anne
See Potter, Margaret (Newman)
Melville, Herman 1819-1891 .... *59*
Melwood, Mary
See Lewis, E. M.
Melzack, Ronald 1929- *5*
Memling, Carl 1918-1969 .... *6*
Menchin, Scott *188*
Mendel, Jo
See Bond, Gladys Baker
and Gilbertson, Mildred Geiger
Mendelson, Steven T. 1958-1995 .... *86*
Mendelson-Stevens, Serita Deborah
See Stevens, Serita
Mendes, Valerie 1939- *157*
Mendez, Raymond A. 1947- *66*
Mendonca, Susan
Brief entry *45*
See Smith, Susan Vernon
Mendoza, George 1934- *41*
Brief entry *39*
See also SAAS *7*
Menendez, Shirley (C.) 1937- *146*
Meng, Cece *194*
Meng, Heinz (Karl) 1924- *13*
Mennen, Ingrid 1954- *85*
Menotti, Gian Carlo 1911-2007 .... *29*
Obituary *180*
Menuhin, Sir Yehudi 1916-1999 .... *40*
Obituary *113*
Menville, Douglas 1935- *64*
Menzel, Barbara Jean 1946- *63*
Mercati, Cynthia *164*
Mercati, Cynthia J.
See Mercati, Cynthia
Mercer, Charles (Edward) 1917-1988 .... *16*
Obituary *61*
Mercer, Sienna *192*
Meredith, Arnold
See Hopkins, (Hector) Kenneth
Meredith, David William
See Miers, Earl Schenck
Meringoff, Laurene Krasny
See Brown, Laurene Krasny
Meriwether, Louise 1923- *52*
Brief entry *31*
Merlin, Arthur
See Blish, James (Benjamin)
Merlin, Christina
See Heaven, Constance (Christina)
Merriam, Eve 1916-1992 .... *73*
Earlier sketches in SATA *3, 40*
See also CLR *14*
Merrill, Jane 1946- *42*
Merrill, Jane Merrill
See Merrill, Jane
Merrill, Jean (Fairbanks) 1923- *82*
Earlier sketch in SATA *1*
See also CLR *52*
Merrill, Phil
See Merrill, Jane
Merriman, Alex
See Silverberg, Robert
Merriman, Rachel 1971- *149*
Earlier sketch in SATA *98*
Merrit, Elizabeth
See Goudge, Eileen
Merski, Patricia K.
See Merski, P.K.
Merski, P.K. *172*
Mertz, Barbara
See Peters, Elizabeth
Mertz, Barbara Gross
See Peters, Elizabeth
Meschel, Susan V. 1936- *83*
Messenger, Charles (Rynd Milles) 1942- *59*

Messick, Dale 1906-2005 .... *64*
Brief entry *48*
Messier, Claire 1956- *103*
Messieres, Nicole de
See de Messieres, Nicole
Messmer, Otto 1892(?)-1983 .... *37*
Mesta, Gabriel
See Moesta, Rebecca
Metcalf, Doris H(unter) *91*
Metcalf, Suzanne
See Baum, L(yman) Frank
Metos, Thomas H(arry) 1932- *37*
Metter, Bert(ram Milton) 1927- *56*
Metzenthen, David 1958- *167*
Earlier sketch in SATA *106*
Meunier, Brian 1954- *195*
Meyer, Barbara 1939- *77*
Meyer, Carolyn 1935- *142*
Autobiography Feature *142*
Earlier sketches in SATA *9, 70, 118*
See also SAAS *9*
Meyer, Carolyn Mae
See Meyer, Carolyn
Meyer, Edith Patterson 1895-1993 .... *5*
Meyer, F(ranklyn) E(dward) 1932- *9*
Meyer, Jean Shepherd *11*
Meyer, Jerome Sydney 1895-1975 .... *3*
Obituary *25*
Meyer, June
See Jordan, June
Meyer, Kerstin 1966- *190*
Meyer, L. A.
See Meyer, Louis A(lbert), Jr.
Meyer, Louis A(lbert), Jr. 1942- *144*
Earlier sketch in SATA *12*
Meyer, Renate 1930- *6*
Meyer, Stephenie 1973- *193*
Meyer, Susan E. 1940- *64*
Meyers, Susan 1942- *164*
Earlier sketches in SATA *19, 108*
Meynell, Laurence Walter 1899-1989
Obituary *61*
Meynier, Yvonne (Pollet) 1908- *14*
Mezey, Robert 1935- *33*
Micale, Albert 1913- *22*
Michael, James
See Scagnetti, Jack
Michael, Livi 1960- *172*
Michael, Manfred
See Winterfeld, Henry
Michael, Olivia
See Michael, Livi
Michaels, Barbara
See Peters, Elizabeth
Michaels, Jamie *195*
Michaels, Joanne Louise
See Teitelbaum, Michael
Michaels, Kristin
See Williams, Jeanne
Michaels, Molly
See Untermeyer, Louis
Michaels, Neal
See Teitelbaum, Michael
Michaels, Rune *194*
Michaels, Ski
See Pellowski, Michael (Joseph)
Michaels, Steve 1955- *71*
Michaels, William M. 1917- *77*
Michel, Anna 1943- *49*
Brief entry *40*
Michel, Francois 1948- *82*
Michelin, Linda *183*
Michelson, Richard *173*
Micich, Paul *74*
Micklish, Rita 1931- *12*
Micklos, John, Jr. 1956- *173*
Earlier sketch in SATA *129*
Micklos J., John, Jr. 1956-
See Micklos, John, Jr.
Micucci, Charles (Patrick, Jr.) 1959- *144*
Earlier sketch in SATA *82*

Middleton, Haydn 1955- *152*
Earlier sketch in SATA *85*
Miers, Earl Schenck 1910-1972 .... *1*
Obituary *26*
Migdale, Lawrence 1951- *89*
Mikaelsen, Ben 1952- *173*
Earlier sketches in SATA *73, 107*
Mikaelsen, Benjamin John
See Mikaelsen, Ben
Miklowitz, Gloria D. 1927- *129*
Earlier sketches in SATA *4, 68*
See also SAAS *17*
Mikolaycak, Charles 1937-1993 .... *78*
Obituary *75*
Earlier sketch in SATA *9*
See also SAAS *4*
Mild, Warren (Paul) 1922- *41*
Milelli, Pascal 1965- *135*
Miles, Betty 1928- *78*
Earlier sketch in SATA *8*
See also SAAS *9*
Miles, Miska
See Martin, Patricia Miles
Miles, (Mary) Patricia 1930- *29*
Miles, Patricia A.
See Martin, Patricia Miles
Miles, Victoria 1966- *188*
Milgrim, David *187*
Earlier sketch in SATA *158*
Milgrom, Harry 1912-1978 .... *25*
Milhous, Katherine 1894-1977 .... *15*
Milich, Zoran *174*
Milios, Rita 1949- *79*
Militant
See Sandburg, Carl (August)
Millais, Raoul 1901- *77*
Millar, Barbara F. 1924- *12*
Millar, Margaret (Ellis Sturm) 1915-1994 .... *61*
Obituary *79*
Millbank, Captain H. R.
See Ellis, Edward S(ylvester)
Millen, C(ynthia) M. 1955- *114*
Miller, Albert G(riffith) 1905-1982 .... *12*
Obituary *31*
Miller, Alice Ann 1958- *150*
Miller, Alice P(atricia McCarthy) *22*
Miller, Debbie 1951- *160*
Earlier sketch in SATA *103*
Miller, Debbie S.
See Miller, Debbie
Miller, Deborah Uchill 1944- *61*
Miller, Don 1923- *15*
Miller, Doris R.
See Mosesson, Gloria R(ubin)
Miller, Eddie
See Miller, Edward
Miller, Edna Anita 1920- *29*
Miller, Edward 1905-1974 .... *8*
Miller, Edward 1964- *183*
Miller, Elizabeth 1933- *41*
Miller, Ellanita 1957- *87*
Miller, Eugene 1925- *33*
Miller, Frances A. 1937- *52*
Brief entry *46*
Miller, Helen M(arkley) -1984 .... *5*
Miller, Helen Topping 1884-1960
Obituary *29*
Miller, Jane (Judith) 1925-1989 .... *15*
Miller, Jewel 1956- *73*
Miller, John
See Samachson, Joseph
Miller, Judi *117*
Miller, Kate 1948- *193*
Miller, Kirsten 1973- *185*
Miller, Louise (Rolfe) 1940- *76*
Miller, M. L. *85*
Miller, Madge 1918- *63*
Miller, Margaret J.
See Dale, Margaret J(essy) Miller
Miller, Marilyn (Jean) 1925- *33*
Miller, Marvin *65*

Miller, Mary
See Northcott, (William) Cecil
Miller, Mary Beth 1942- *9*
Miller, Mary Beth 1964- *185*
Miller, Maryann 1943- *73*
Miller, Natalie 1917-1976 .... *35*
Miller, Robert H. 1944- *91*
Miller, Ron 1947- *185*
Miller, Ruth White
See White, Ruth C.
Miller, Sandra
See Miller, Sandy
Miller, Sandra Peden
See Miller, Sandy
Miller, Sandy 1948- *41*
Brief entry *35*
Miller, Sarah 1969- *175*
Miller, Virginia
See Austin, Virginia
Miller, William R. 1959- *116*
Milligan, Bryce 1953- *170*
Milligan, Spike
See CLR *92*
See Milligan, Terence Alan
Milligan, Terence Alan 1918-2002 .... *29*
Obituary *134*
See Milligan, Spike
Millington, Ada
See Deyneka, Anita
Millman, Isaac 1933- *140*
Mills, Adam
See Stanley, George Edward
Mills, Claudia 1954- *191*
Brief entry *41*
Earlier sketches in SATA *44, 89, 145*
Mills, Elaine (Rosemary) 1941- *72*
Mills, Joyce C. 1944- *102*
Mills, Judith Christine 1956- *130*
Mills, Yaroslava Surmach 1925- *35*
Millspaugh, Ben P. 1936- *77*
Millstead, Thomas E. *30*
Milne, A. A. 1882-1956 .... *100*
See also YABC *1*
See also CLR *108*
Milne, Alan Alexander
See Milne, A. A.
Milne, Lorus J. *5*
See also CLR *22*
See also SAAS *18*
Milne, Margery *5*
See also CLR *22*
See also SAAS *18*
Milne, Terry
See Milne, Theresa Ann
Milne, Theresa Ann 1964- *84*
Milnes, Irma McDonough 1924- *101*
Milonas, Rolf
See Myller, Rolf
Milord, Susan 1954- *147*
Earlier sketch in SATA *74*
Milotte, Alfred G(eorge) 1904-1989 .... *11*
Obituary *62*
Milstein, Linda 1954- *80*
Milton, Ann *134*
Milton, Hilary (Herbert) 1920- *23*
Milton, John R(onald) 1924- *24*
Milton, Joyce 1946- *101*
Brief entry *41*
Earlier sketch in SATA *52*
Milverton, Charles A.
See Penzler, Otto
Minahan, John A. 1956- *92*
Minar, Barbra (Goodyear) 1940- *79*
Minard, Rosemary 1939- *63*
Minarik, Else Holmelund 1920- *127*
Earlier sketch in SATA *15*
See also CLR *33*
Miner, Jane Claypool 1933- *38*
Brief entry *37*
See Claypool, Jane
Miner, Lewis S. 1909-1971 .... *11*

Mines, Jeanette 1948- *61*
Mines, Jeanette Marie
See Mines, Jeanette
Minier, Nelson
See Stoutenburg, Adrien (Pearl)
Minnitt, Ronda Jacqueline
See Armitage, David
Minor, Wendell G. 1944- *164*
Earlier sketches in SATA *78, 109*
Minter, Daniel 1961- *176*
Mintonye, Grace *4*
Miranda, Anne 1954- *109*
Earlier sketch in SATA *71*
Mirocha, Paul *192*
Mirsky, Jeannette 1903-1987 .... *8*
Obituary *51*
Mirsky, Reba Paeff 1902-1966 .... *1*
Misako Rocks! *192*
Mishica, Clare 1960- *91*
Miskovits, Christine 1939- *10*
Miss Frances
See Horwich, Frances R(appaport)
Miss Read
See Saint, Dora Jessie
Mister Rogers
See Rogers, Fred McFeely
Mitchard, Jacquelyn 1956- *168*
Earlier sketch in SATA *98*
Mitchell, Adrian 1932-2008 .... *166*
Earlier sketch in SATA *104*
Mitchell, Allison
See Griffin, W.E.B
Mitchell, Betty Jo
See Mitchell, B.J.
Mitchell, B.J. 1931- *120*
Mitchell, Clyde
See Ellison, Harlan
and Silverberg, Robert
Mitchell, Cynthia 1922- *29*
Mitchell, (Sibyl) Elyne (Keith) 1913- *10*
Mitchell, Gladys (Maude Winifred)
1901-1983 .... *46*
Obituary *35*
Mitchell, Jay
See Roberson, Jennifer
Mitchell, Joyce Slayton 1933- *142*
Brief entry *43*
Earlier sketch in SATA *46*
Mitchell, K. L.
See Lamb, Elizabeth Searle
Mitchell, Kathy 1948- *59*
Mitchell, Lori 1961- *128*
Mitchell, Margaree King 1953- *84*
Mitchell, Marianne 1947- *145*
Mitchell, Rhonda *89*
Mitchell, Todd 1974- *191*
Mitchell, Yvonne 1925-1979
Obituary *24*
Mitchelson, Mitch
See Mitchelson, Peter Richard
Mitchelson, Peter Richard 1950- *104*
Mitchison, Naomi (Margaret Haldane)
1897-1999 .... *24*
Obituary *112*
Mitchnik, Helen 1901-1982 .... *41*
Brief entry *35*
Mitchum, Hank
See Knott, William C(ecil, Jr.)
and Murray, Stuart A. P.
and Newton, D(wight) B(ennett)
and Sherman, Jory (Tecumseh)
Mitgutsch, Ali 1935- *76*
Mitsuhashi, Yoko *45*
Brief entry *33*
Mitton, Jacqueline 1948- *162*
Earlier sketches in SATA *66, 115*
Mitton, Simon 1946- *66*
Mitton, Tony 1951- *149*
Earlier sketch in SATA *104*
Miura, Taro 1968- *181*
Mizner, Elizabeth Howard 1907- *27*

Mizumura, Kazue *18*
Mlynowski, Sarah 1977(?)- *180*
Mobin-Uddin, Asma *172*
Mobley, Joe A. 1945- *91*
Moche, Dinah (Rachel) L(evine) 1936- *44*
    Brief entry *40*
Mochi, Ugo (A.) 1889-1977 .... *38*
Mochizuki, Ken 1954- *146*
    Earlier sketch in SATA *81*
    See also SAAS *22*
Modarressi, Mitra 1967- *126*
Modell, Frank B. 1917- *39*
    Brief entry *36*
Modesitt, Jeanne 1953- *143*
    Earlier sketch in SATA *92*
Modesitt, L.E., Jr. 1943- *164*
    Earlier sketch in SATA *91*
Modesitt, Leland Exton, Jr.
    See Modesitt, L.E., Jr.
Modrell, Dolores 1933- *72*
Moe, Barbara 1937- *20*
Moe, Jorgen (Ingebretsen) 1813-1882
    See CLR *104*
    See Asbjørnsen and Moe
Moed-Kass, Pnina *169*
Moerbeek, Kees 1955- *98*
Moeri, Louise 1924- *93*
    Earlier sketch in SATA *24*
    See also SAAS *10*
Moesta, Rebecca 1956- *182*
Moffett, Jami 1952- *84*
Moffett, Martha (Leatherwood) 1934- *8*
Mogensen, Suzanne A(ncher) 1946- *129*
Mohn, Peter B(urnet) 1934- *28*
Mohn, Viola Kohl 1914- *8*
Mohr, Nicholasa 1938- *97*
    Autobiography Feature *113*
    Earlier sketch in SATA *8*
    See also CLR *22*
    See also SAAS *8*
Mok, Esther 1953- *93*
Molan, Christine 1943- *84*
Molarsky, Osmond 1909- *16*
Moldon, Peter L(eonard) 1937- *49*
Mole, John 1941- *103*
    Earlier sketch in SATA *36*
    See also CLR *61*
Molesworth, Mary Louisa 1839-1921 .... *98*
Molin, Charles
    See Mayne, William (James Carter)
Molina, Silvia 1946- *97*
Molk, Laurel 1957- *162*
    Earlier sketch in SATA *92*
Mollel, Tololwa M. 1952- *88*
Molloy, Anne Baker 1907-1999 .... *32*
Molloy, Michael (John) 1940- *162*
Molloy, Paul (George) 1924- *5*
Moloney, James 1954- *144*
    Autobiography Feature *144*
    Earlier sketch in SATA *94*
Momaday, N. Scott 1934- *48*
    Brief entry *30*
Momaday, Navarre Scott
    See Momaday, N. Scott
Monaco, Octavia 1963- *169*
Monagle, Bernie 1957- *121*
Moncure, Jane Belk 1926- *23*
Monjo, F(erdinand) N(icholas III)
    1924-1978 .... *16*
    See also CLR *2*
Monk, Isabell 1952- *136*
Monks, Lydia *189*
Monroe, Lyle
    See Heinlein, Robert A.
Monroe, Marion
    Obituary *34*
    See Cox, Marion Monroe
Monsell, Helen Albee 1895-1971 .... *24*
Monson-Burton, Marianne 1975- *139*
Montana, Bob 1920-1975
    Obituary *21*

Montecalvo, Janet *177*
Montenegro, Laura Nyman 1953- *95*
Montero, Gloria 1933- *109*
Montes, Marisa 1951- *144*
Montgomerie, Norah (Mary) 1913- *26*
Montgomery, Constance
    See Cappel, Constance
Montgomery, Elizabeth Rider *34*
    Obituary *41*
    Earlier sketch in SATA *3*
    See Julesberg, Elizabeth Rider Montgomery
Montgomery, Hugh (Edward) 1962- *146*
Montgomery, L(ucy) M(aud) 1874-1942 .... *100*
    See also YABC *1*
    See also CLR *91*
Montgomery, Raymond A. (Jr.) 1936- *39*
Montgomery, Rutherford George 1894-1985 . *3*
Montgomery, Sy 1958- *184*
    Autobiography Feature *132*
    Earlier sketches in SATA *114, 132*
Montgomery, Vivian *36*
Monthei, Betty *179*
Montijo, Rhode *179*
Montileaux, Donald F. 1948- *183*
Montpetit, Charles 1958- *101*
Montresor, Beni 1926-2001 .... *38*
    Earlier sketch in SATA *3*
    See also SAAS *4*
Montserrat, Pep *181*
Monty Python
    See Chapman, Graham
    and Cleese, John (Marwood)
    and Gilliam, Terry
    and Idle, Eric
    and Jones, Terence Graham Parry
    and Palin, Michael
Moodie, Craig 1956- *172*
Moodie, Fiona 1952- *133*
Moody, Minerva
    See Alcott, Louisa May
Moody, Ralph Owen 1898-1982 .... *1*
Moon, Carl 1879(?)-1948 .... *25*
Moon, Grace (Purdie) 1877(?)-1947 .... *25*
Moon, Lily
    See Warnes, Tim
Moon, Nicola 1952- *147*
    Earlier sketch in SATA *96*
Moon, Pat 1946- *113*
Moon, Sheila 1910-1991 .... *5*
    Obituary *114*
Moon, Sheila Elizabeth
    See Moon, Sheila
Mooney, Bel 1946- *95*
Mooney, Bill 1936- *122*
Mooney, Elizabeth C(omstock) 1918-1986
    Obituary *48*
Mooney, William
    See Mooney, Bill
Moor, Emily
    See Deming, Richard
Moorcock, Michael 1939- *166*
    Earlier sketch in SATA *93*
    See Bradbury, Edward P.
Moorcock, Michael John
    See Moorcock, Michael
Moore, Anne Carroll 1871-1961 .... *13*
Moore, Cheri
    See Ladd, Cheryl (Jean)
Moore, Clement Clarke 1779-1863 .... *18*
Moore, Cyd 1957- *186*
    Earlier sketches in SATA *83, 133*
Moore, Don W. 1905(?)-1986
    Obituary *48*
Moore, Elaine 1944- *86*
Moore, Eva 1942- *103*
    Earlier sketch in SATA *20*
Moore, Ishbel (Lindsay) 1954- *140*
Moore, Jack (William) 1941- *46*
    Brief entry *32*
Moore, Janet Gaylord 1905-1992 .... *18*
Moore, Jim 1946- *42*

Moore, John Travers 1908- *12*
Moore, Lilian 1909-2004 .... *137*
    Obituary *155*
    Earlier sketch in SATA *52*
    See also CLR *15*
Moore, Liz
    See Moore, M. Elizabeth
Moore, M. Elizabeth 1959- *156*
Moore, Margaret R(umberger) 1903- *12*
Moore, Margie *176*
Moore, Marianne (Craig) 1887-1972 .... *20*
Moore, Patrick (Alfred Caldwell) 1923- *49*
    Brief entry *39*
    See also SAAS *8*
Moore, Patrick 1959- *184*
Moore, Perry *193*
Moore, Peter 1963- *175*
Moore, Peter G.
    See Moore, Peter
Moore, Ray (S.) 1905(?)-1984
    Obituary *37*
Moore, Regina
    See Dunne, Mary Collins
Moore, Ruth (Ellen) 1908-1989 .... *23*
Moore, Ruth Nulton 1923- *38*
Moore, S(arah) E. *23*
Moore, Sarah Margaret
    See Hodges, Margaret
Moore, Tara 1950- *61*
Moore, Yvette 1958- *154*
    Earlier sketches in SATA *69, 70*
Moores, Dick
    See Moores, Richard (Arnold)
Moores, Richard (Arnold) 1909-1986
    Obituary *48*
Mooser, Stephen 1941- *75*
    Earlier sketch in SATA *28*
Mora, Francisco X(avier) 1952- *90*
Mora, Pat 1942- *186*
    Earlier sketches in SATA *92, 134*
    See also CLR *58*
Mora, Patricia
    See Mora, Pat
Morales, Yuyi *180*
    Earlier sketch in SATA *154*
Moran, Tom 1943- *60*
Moranville, Sharelle Byars *152*
Moray Williams, Ursula 1911-2006 .... *142*
    Obituary *177*
    Earlier sketch in SATA *73*
    See also SAAS *9*
    See Williams, Ursula Moray
Mordvinoff, Nicolas 1911-1973 .... *17*
More, Caroline
    See Cone, Molly (Lamken)
    and Strachan, Margaret Pitcairn
Moreno, Rene King *190*
Moreton, Andrew Esq.
    See Defoe, Daniel
Morey, Charles
    See Fletcher, Helen Jill
Morey, Walt(er Nelson) 1907-1992 .... *51*
    Obituary *70*
    Earlier sketch in SATA *3*
    See also SAAS *9*
Morgan, Alfred P(owell) 1889-1972 .... *33*
Morgan, Alison (Mary) 1930- *85*
    Earlier sketch in SATA *30*
Morgan, Anne 1954- *121*
Morgan, Douglas
    See Macdonald, James D.
Morgan, Ellen
    See Bumstead, Kathleen Mary
Morgan, Geoffrey 1916- *46*
Morgan, Helen (Gertrude Louise)
    1921-1990 .... *29*
Morgan, Jane
    See Cooper, James Fenimore
    and Franklin, Jane (Morgan)
    and Moren, Sally M(oore)
Morgan, Lenore H. 1908-1976 .... *8*

Morgan, Mary 1957- *114*
  Earlier sketch in SATA *81*
Morgan, Michaela *180*
  See Basile, Gloria Vitanza
Morgan, Nicola 1961- *161*
Morgan, Nina 1953- *110*
Morgan, Pierr 1952- *122*
  Earlier sketch in SATA *77*
Morgan, Robin (Evonne) 1941- *80*
Morgan, Roxanne
  See Gentle, Mary
Morgan, Sarah (Nicola) 1959- *68*
Morgan, Shirley *10*
  See Kiepper, Shirley Morgan
Morgan, Stacy T(owle) 1959- *104*
Morgan, Stevie
  See Davies, Nicola
Morgan, Tom 1942- *42*
Morgan, Wendy
  See Staub, Wendy Corsi
Morgan-Vanroyen, Mary
  See Morgan, Mary
Morgenstern, Susie Hoch 1945- *133*
Mori, Hana 1909-1990(?) *88*
Mori, Kyoko 1957- *122*
  Autobiography Feature *126*
  See also CLR *64*
  See also SAAS *26*
Moriarty, Jaclyn *162*
Moriarty, William J. 1930- *127*
Morice, Dave 1946- *93*
Morin, Isobel V. 1928- *110*
Morine, Hoder
  See Conroy, John Wesley
Morley, Wilfred Owen
  See Lowndes, Robert A(ugustine) W(ard)
Morningstar, Mildred (Whaley) 1912-1997 .. *61*
  Obituary *114*
Morozumi, Atsuko *110*
Morpurgo, Michael 1943- *184*
  Earlier sketches in SATA *93, 143*
  See also CLR *51*
Morrah, Dave
  See Morrah, David Wardlaw, Jr.
Morrah, David Wardlaw, Jr. 1914-1991 .... *10*
Morreale-de la Garza, Phyllis
  See De la Garza, Phyllis
Morressy, John 1930-2006 .... *23*
Morrill, Leslie H(olt) 1934-2003 .... *48*
  Brief entry *33*
  Obituary *148*
  See also SAAS *22*
Morris, Chris(topher Crosby) 1946- *66*
Morris, Deborah 1956- *91*
Morris, Desmond 1928- *14*
Morris, Desmond John
  See Morris, Desmond
Morris, Don 1954- *83*
Morris, Gerald 1963- *150*
  Earlier sketch in SATA *107*
Morris, Gerald Paul
  See Morris, Gerald
Morris, Gilbert (Leslie) 1929- *104*
Morris, Jackie *151*
Morris, Janet (Ellen) 1946- *66*
Morris, Jay
  See Tatham, Julie Campbell
Morris, (Margaret) Jean 1924- *98*
Morris, Jeffrey B(randon) 1941- *92*
Morris, Jennifer E. 1969- *179*
Morris, Jill 1936- *165*
  Earlier sketch in SATA *119*
Morris, Juddi *85*
Morris, Judy K. 1936- *61*
Morris, Oradel Nolen *128*
Morris, Robert A(da) 1933- *7*
Morris, William 1913-1994 .... *29*
Morrison, Bill 1935- *66*
  Brief entry *37*
Morrison, Chloe Anthony Wofford
  See Morrison, Toni

Morrison, Dorothy Nafus *29*
Morrison, Frank 1971- *185*
Morrison, Gordon 1944- *183*
  Earlier sketches in SATA *87, 128*
Morrison, Joan 1922- *65*
Morrison, Lillian 1917- *108*
  Earlier sketch in SATA *3*
Morrison, Lucile Phillips 1896- *17*
Morrison, Martha A. 1948- *77*
Morrison, Meighan 1966- *90*
Morrison, Richard
  See Lowndes, Robert A(ugustine) W(ard)
Morrison, Robert
  See Lowndes, Robert A(ugustine) W(ard)
Morrison, Roberta
  See Webb, Jean Francis (III)
Morrison, Susan Dudley
  See Gold, Susan Dudley
Morrison, Taylor 1971- *187*
  Earlier sketches in SATA *95, 159*
Morrison, Toni 1931- *144*
  Earlier sketch in SATA *57*
  See also CLR *99*
Morrison, Velma Ford 1909- *21*
Morrison, Wilbur Howard 1915- *64*
Morrison, William
  See Samachson, Joseph
Morriss, James E(dward) 1932- *8*
Morrissey, Dean *183*
Morrow, Barbara Olenyik 1952- *167*
Morrow, Betty
  See Bacon, Elizabeth
Morse, Carol
  See Yeakley, Marjory Hall
Morse, Dorothy B(ayley) 1906-1979
  Obituary *24*
Morse, Flo 1921- *30*
Morse, Tony 1953- *129*
Mort, Vivian
  See Cromie, Alice Hamilton
Mortensen, Denise Dowling *179*
Mortimer, Anne 1958- *116*
Mortimer, Mary H.
  See Coury, Louise Andree
Morton, Alexandra (Hubbard) 1957- *144*
Morton, Anthony
  See Arthur, Robert, (Jr.)
Morton, Jane 1931- *50*
Morton, Joseph C. 1932- *156*
Morton, Lee Jack, Jr. 1928- *32*
Morton, Miriam 1918(?)-1985 .... *9*
  Obituary *46*
Mosatche, Harriet (S.) 1949- *122*
Moscow, Alvin 1925- *3*
Mosel, Arlene (Tichy) 1921-1996 .... *7*
Moseley, James W(illett) 1931- *139*
Moseng, Elisabeth 1967- *90*
Moser, Barry 1940- *185*
  Earlier sketches in SATA *56, 79, 138*
  See also CLR *49*
  See also SAAS *15*
Moser, Don(ald Bruce) 1932- *31*
Moser, Laura *194*
Moser, Lisa *192*
Moses, Sheila P. 1961- *168*
Moses, Will 1956- *178*
  Earlier sketch in SATA *120*
Mosesson, Gloria R(ubin) *24*
Mosher, Richard 1949- *120*
Moskin, Marietta D(unston) 1928- *23*
Moskof, Martin Stephen 1930- *27*
Mosley, Francis 1957- *57*
Moss, Don(ald) 1920- *11*
Moss, Elaine (Dora) 1924- *57*
  Brief entry *31*
Moss, Jeff(rey) 1942-1998 .... *73*
  Obituary *106*
Moss, Marissa 1959- *163*
  Earlier sketches in SATA *71, 104*
  See also CLR *134*

Moss, Miriam 1955- *140*
  Earlier sketch in SATA *76*
Moss, Thylias 1954- *108*
Moss, Thylias Rebecca Brasier
  See Moss, Thylias
Most, Bernard 1937- *134*
  Brief entry *40*
  Earlier sketches in SATA *48, 91*
Mosz, Gosia 1972- *194*
Mott, Evelyn Clarke 1962- *133*
  Earlier sketch in SATA *75*
Motz, Lloyd 1909-2004 .... *20*
Mould, Edwin
  See Whitlock, Ralph
Mouly, Francoise *155*
Mountain, Robert
  See Montgomery, Raymond A. (Jr.)
Mountfield, David
  See Grant, Neil
Mourlevat, Jean-Claude 1952- *187*
Moussard, Jacqueline 1924- *24*
Mowat, Claire 1933- *123*
Mowat, Claire Angel Wheeler
  See Mowat, Claire
Mowat, Farley 1921- *55*
  Earlier sketch in SATA *3*
  See also CLR *20*
Mowat, Farley McGill
  See Mowat, Farley
Mowll, Joshua 1970(?)- *188*
Mowry, Jess 1960- *131*
  Autobiography Feature *131*
  Earlier sketch in SATA *109*
  See also CLR *65*
Moxley, Sheila 1966- *96*
Moyer, Terry J. 1937- *94*
Moyes, Patricia *63*
  See Haszard, Patricia Moyes
Moyler, Alan (Frank Powell) 1926- *36*
Mozelle, Shirley *179*
Mozley, Charles 1915- *43*
  Brief entry *32*
Mphahlele, Es'kia -2008
  See Mphahlele, Ezekiel
Mphahlele, Ezekiel 1919-2008 .... *119*
  See Mphahlele, Es'kia
Mr. McGillicuddy
  See Abisch, Roslyn Kroop
Mr. Sniff
  See Abisch, Roslyn Kroop
Mr. Tivil
  See Lorkowski, Thomas V(incent)
Mr. Wizard
  See Herbert, Don
Mrs. Fairstar
  See Horne, Richard Henry Hengist
Muchamore, Robert 1972- *175*
Muchmore, Jo Ann 1937- *103*
Mude, O.
  See Gorey, Edward (St. John)
Mudgeon, Apeman
  See Mitchell, Adrian
Mueller, Jorg 1942- *67*
  See also CLR *43*
Mueller, Virginia 1924- *28*
Muggs
  See Watkins, Lois
Muir, Diana
  See Appelbaum, Diana Muir Karter
Muir, Frank (Herbert) 1920-1998 .... *30*
Muir, Helen 1937- *65*
Mukerji, Dhan Gopal 1890-1936 .... *40*
  See also CLR *10*
Mulcahy, Lucille Burnett *12*
Mulford, Philippa G. 1948- *112*
  Earlier sketch in SATA *43*
Mulford, Philippa Greene
  See Mulford, Philippa G.
Mulila, Vigad G.
  See Maillu, David G(ian)
Mull, Brandon 1974- *190*

Mullen, Michael 1937- *122*
Muller, Billex
   See Ellis, Edward S(ylvester)
Muller, Jorg
   See Mueller, Jorg
Muller, (Lester) Robin 1953- *86*
Mullin, Caryl Cude 1969- *130*
Mullins, Edward S(wift) 1922- *10*
Mullins, Hilary 1962- *84*
Mulock, Dinah Maria
   See Craik, Dinah Maria (Mulock)
Mulvihill, William Patrick 1923- *8*
Mumford, Ruth
   See Dallas, Ruth
Mumy, Bill 1954- *112*
Mun
   See Leaf, (Wilbur) Munro
Munari, Bruno 1907-1998 .... *15*
   See also CLR 9
Munce, Ruth Hill 1898- *12*
Mundy, Simon 1954- *64*
Mundy, Simon Andrew James Hainault
   See Mundy, Simon
Munger, Nancy *170*
Munowitz, Ken 1935-1977 .... *14*
Munoz, William 1949- *92*
   Earlier sketch in SATA *42*
Munro, Alice 1931- *29*
Munro, Alice Anne
   See Munro, Alice
Munro, Eleanor 1928- *37*
Munro, Roxie 1945- *184*
   Earlier sketches in SATA *58, 136*
Munsch, Bob
   See Munsch, Robert (Norman)
Munsch, Robert (Norman) 1945- *120*
   Brief entry *48*
   Earlier sketches in SATA *50, 83*
   See also CLR 19
Munsinger, Lynn 1951- *177*
   Earlier sketches in SATA *33, 94*
Munson, Derek 1970- *139*
Munson, R. W.
   See Karl, Jean E(dna)
Munson-Benson, Tunie 1946- *15*
Munsterberg, Peggy 1921- *102*
Muntean, Michaela *182*
Munthe, Nelly 1947- *53*
Munves, James (Albert) 1922- *30*
Munzer, Martha E. 1899-1999 .... *4*
Murawski, Darlyne A. *193*
Murch, Mel
   See Manes, Stephen
Murdoch, David H(amilton) 1937- *96*
Murdoch, Patricia 1957- *192*
Murdock, Catherine Gilbert *185*
Murhall, J(acqueline) J(ane) 1964- *143*
Murphy, Barbara Beasley 1933- *130*
   Earlier sketch in SATA *5*
Murphy, Claire Rudolf 1951- *137*
   Earlier sketch in SATA *76*
Murphy, E(mmett) Jefferson 1926- *4*
Murphy, Jill (Frances) 1949- *142*
   Earlier sketches in SATA *37, 70*
   See also CLR 39
Murphy, Jim 1947- *185*
   Brief entry *32*
   Earlier sketches in SATA *37, 77, 124*
   See also CLR 53
Murphy, Joseph E., Jr. 1930- *65*
Murphy, Kelly 1977- *190*
   Earlier sketch in SATA *143*
Murphy, Louise 1943- *155*
Murphy, Pat
   See Murphy, E(mmett) Jefferson
Murphy, Patricia J. 1963- *132*
Murphy, Rita *180*
Murphy, Robert (William) 1902-1971 .... *10*
Murphy, Shirley Rousseau 1928- *126*
   Earlier sketches in SATA *36, 71*
   See also SAAS 18

Murphy, Stuart J. 1942- *157*
   Earlier sketch in SATA *115*
Murphy, Tim
   See Murphy, Jim
Murphy, Tom *191*
   See Murphy, Thomas Basil, Jr.
Murray, John 1923- *39*
Murray, Kirsty 1960- *165*
   Earlier sketch in SATA *108*
Murray, Marguerite 1917- *63*
Murray, Marian *5*
Murray, Martine 1965- *125*
Murray, (Judith) Michele (Freedman)
   1933-1974 .... *7*
Murray, Ossie 1938- *43*
Murray, Peter
   See Hautman, Pete
Murrow, Liza Ketchum 1946- *78*
   See Ketchum, Liza
Musgrave, Florence 1902-1999 .... *3*
Musgrove, Margaret W(ynkoop) 1943- *124*
   Earlier sketch in SATA *26*
Mussey, Virginia Howell
   See Ellison, Virginia H(owell)
Mussey, Virginia T.H.
   See Ellison, Virginia H(owell)
Mutel, Cornelia F. 1947- *74*
Muth, Jon J. *165*
Mutz
   See Kuenstler, Morton
Mwangi, Meja 1948- *174*
My Brother's Brother
   See Chekhov, Anton (Pavlovich)
Myers, Anna *160*
Myers, Arthur 1917- *91*
   Earlier sketch in SATA *35*
Myers, Bernice *81*
   Earlier sketch in SATA *9*
Myers, Caroline Elizabeth Clark
   1887-1980 .... *28*
Myers, Christopher 1975- *183*
   See also CLR 97
Myers, Edward 1950- *172*
   Earlier sketch in SATA *96*
Myers, Elisabeth P(erkins) 1918- *36*
Myers, (Mary) Hortense (Powner)
   1913-1987 .... *10*
Myers, Jack 1913-2006 .... *83*
   Obituary *178*
Myers, Jack Edgar
   See Myers, Jack
Myers, Lou 1915-2005 .... *81*
   Obituary *171*
Myers, Louis
   See Myers, Lou
Myers, R.E. 1924- *119*
Myers, Robert Eugene
   See Myers, R.E.
Myers, Tim 1953- *176*
   Earlier sketch in SATA *147*
Myers, Timothy Joseph
   See Myers, Tim
Myers, Walter Dean 1937- *193*
   Brief entry *27*
   Earlier sketches in SATA *41, 71, 109, 157*
   See also CLR 110
   See also SAAS 2
   See Myers, Walter M.
Myers, Walter M.
   See Myers, Walter Dean
Myller, Rolf 1926-2006 .... *27*
   Obituary *175*
Myra, Harold L(awrence) 1939- *46*
   Brief entry *42*
Myracle, Lauren 1969- *162*
Myrus, Donald (Richard) 1927- *23*
Mysterious Traveler, The
   See Arthur, Robert, (Jr.)

N

Na, An *149*
Naaslund, Goorel Kristina 1940- *170*
Nadel, Laurie 1948- *74*
Naden, Corinne J. 1930- *166*
   Earlier sketch in SATA *79*
Nadimi, Suzan *188*
Nagel, Andreas Fischer
   See Fischer-Nagel, Andreas
Nagel, Heiderose Fischer
   See Fischer-Nagel, Heiderose
Nagle, Shane *176*
Naidoo, Beverley 1943- *180*
   Earlier sketches in SATA *63, 135*
   See also CLR 29
Naipaul, Shivadhar Srinivasa
   See Naipaul, Shiva
Nakae, Noriko 1940- *59*
Nakatani, Chiyoko 1930-1981 .... *55*
   Brief entry *40*
   See also CLR 30
Nally, Susan W. 1947- *90*
Namioka, Lensey 1929- *157*
   Autobiography Feature *116*
   Earlier sketches in SATA *27, 89*
   See also CLR 48
   See also SAAS 24
Nanji, Shenaaz 1954- *131*
Nanogak Agnes 1925- *61*
Napier, Mark
   See Laffin, John (Alfred Charles)
Napoli, Donna Jo 1948- *190*
   Earlier sketches in SATA *92, 137*
   See also CLR 51
   See also SAAS 23
Narahashi, Keiko 1959- *115*
   Earlier sketch in SATA *79*
Narayan, Rasipuram Krishnaswami
   See Narayan, R.K.
Narayan, R.K. 1906-2001 .... *62*
Nascimbene, Yan 1949- *173*
   Earlier sketch in SATA *133*
Nash, Bruce M(itchell) 1947- *34*
Nash, Frederic Ogden
   See Nash, Ogden
Nash, Linell
   See Smith, Linell Nash
Nash, Mary (Hughes) 1925- *41*
Nash, Ogden 1902-1971 .... *46*
   Earlier sketch in SATA *2*
Nash, Renea Denise 1963- *81*
Nast, Elsa Ruth
   See Watson, Jane Werner
Nast, Thomas 1840-1902 .... *51*
   Brief entry *33*
Nastick, Sharon 1954- *41*
Natarajan, Srividya *187*
Nathan, Adele (Gutman) 1900(?)-1986
   Obituary *48*
Nathan, Amy *155*
   Earlier sketch in SATA *104*
Nathan, Dorothy (Goldeen) (?)-1966 .... *15*
Nathan, Robert (Gruntal) 1894-1985 .... *6*
   Obituary *43*
Nathanson, Laura Walther 1941- *57*
Natti, Susanna 1948- *125*
   Earlier sketch in SATA *32*
Nau, Thomas *186*
Naughtie, Eleanor
   See Updale, Eleanor
Naughton, Bill
   See Naughton, William John (Francis)
Naughton, James Franklin 1957- *85*
Naughton, Jim
   See Naughton, James Franklin
Naughton, William John (Francis)
   1910-1992 .... *86*
   See Naughton, Bill
Navarra, John Gabriel 1927- *8*
Naylor, Penelope 1941- *10*

Naylor, Phyllis 1933- *152*
   Autobiography Feature *152*
   Earlier sketches in SATA *12, 66, 102*
   See also CLR *135*
   See also SAAS *10*
Naylor, Phyllis Reynolds 1933-
   See Naylor, Phyllis
Nazarian, Nikki
   See Nichols, Cecilia Fawn
Nazaroff, Alexander I(vanovich) 1898-1981 .. *4*
Neal, Harry Edward 1906-1993 .... *5*
   Obituary *76*
Neal, Michael
   See Teitelbaum, Michael
Nearing, Penny 1916- *47*
   Brief entry *42*
Nebel, Gustave E. *45*
   Brief entry *33*
Nebel, Mimouca
   See Nebel, Gustave E.
Nee, Kay Bonner *10*
Needham, Kate 1962- *95*
Needle, Jan 1943- *98*
   Earlier sketch in SATA *30*
   See also CLR *43*
   See also SAAS *23*
Needleman, Jacob 1934- *6*
Neel, David 1960- *82*
Neel, Preston 1959- *93*
Negri, Rocco 1932- *12*
Negrin, Fabian 1963- *189*
Neier, Aryeh 1937- *59*
Neigoff, Anne *13*
Neigoff, Mike 1920- *13*
Neilson, Frances Fullerton (Jones)
   1910-2001 .... *14*
Neimark, Anne E. 1935- *145*
   Earlier sketch in SATA *4*
Neimark, Paul G. 1934- *80*
   Brief entry *37*
Neitzel, Shirley 1941- *134*
   Earlier sketch in SATA *77*
Nell
   See Hanna, Nell(ie L.)
Nelscott, Kris
   See Rusch, Kristine Kathryn
Nelson, Blake 1960- *177*
Nelson, Catherine Chadwick 1926- *87*
Nelson, Cordner (Bruce) 1918- *54*
   Brief entry *29*
Nelson, Drew 1952- *77*
Nelson, Esther L. 1928- *13*
Nelson, Jim A.
   See Stotter, Mike
Nelson, Julie L. 1970- *117*
Nelson, Kadir *181*
   Earlier sketch in SATA *154*
Nelson, Kris
   See Rusch, Kristine Kathryn
Nelson, Lawrence E(rnest) 1928-1977
   Obituary *28*
Nelson, Marilyn 1946- *180*
   Autobiography Feature *180*
   Earlier sketch in SATA *151*
   See Waniek, Marilyn Nelson
Nelson, Mary Carroll 1929- *23*
Nelson, O. Terry 1941- *62*
Nelson, Peter N. 1953- *73*
Nelson, Richard K(ing) 1941- *65*
Nelson, Robin Laura 1971- *141*
Nelson, Roy Paul 1923- *59*
Nelson, S.D. *181*
Nelson, Sharlene (P.) 1933- *96*
Nelson, Suzanne 1976- *184*
Nelson, Ted (W.) 1931- *96*
Nelson, Theresa 1948- *143*
   Autobiography Feature *143*
   Earlier sketch in SATA *79*
Nemeth, Sally *187*
Nerlove, Miriam 1959- *53*
   Brief entry *49*

Nesbit, E. 1858-1924 .... *100*
   See also YABC *1*
   See also CLR *70*
Nesbit, Edith
   See Nesbit, E.
Nesbit, Troy
   See Folsom, Franklin (Brewster)
Nespojohn, Katherine V(eronica) 1912-1975 . *7*
Ness, Evaline (Michelow) 1911-1986 .... *26*
   Obituary *49*
   Earlier sketch in SATA *1*
   See also CLR *6*
   See also SAAS *1*
Nestor, Larry 1940- *149*
Nestor, William P(rodromos) 1947- *49*
Nethery, Mary *93*
Neubecker, Robert *170*
Neuberger, Julia (Babette Sarah) 1950- *142*
   Earlier sketch in SATA *78*
Neufeld, John (Arthur) 1938- *131*
   Autobiography Feature *131*
   Earlier sketches in SATA *6, 81*
   See also CLR *52*
   See also SAAS *3*
Neuhaus, David 1958- *83*
Neumeyer, Peter F(lorian) 1929- *13*
Neurath, Marie (Reidemeister) 1898-1986 ..... *1*
Neuschwander, Cindy 1953- *157*
   Earlier sketch in SATA *107*
Neusner, Jacob 1932- *38*
Neville, Charles
   See Bodsworth, (Charles) Fred(erick)
Neville, Emily Cheney 1919- *1*
   See also SAAS *2*
Neville, Mary
   See Woodrich, Mary Neville
Nevins, Albert (Francis) J(erome)
   1915-1997 .... *20*
Nevius, Carol 1955- *186*
Newberger, Devra
   See Speregen, Devra Newberger
Newberry, Clare Turlay 1903-1970 .... *1*
   Obituary *26*
Newbery, John 1713-1767 .... *20*
Newbery, Linda 1952- *184*
   Earlier sketch in SATA *142*
Newcomb, Ellsworth
   See Kenny, Ellsworth Newcomb
Newcombe, Jack *45*
   Brief entry *33*
   See Newcombe, Eugene A.
Newcome, Robert 1955- *91*
Newcome, Zita 1959- *88*
Newell, Crosby
   See Bonsall, Crosby Barbara (Newell)
Newell, Edythe W(eatherford) 1910-1989 .... *11*
Newell, Hope Hockenberry 1896-1965 .... *24*
Newfeld, Frank 1928- *26*
Newgarden, Mark 1959- *194*
Newlon, (Frank) Clarke 1905(?)-1982 .... *6*
   Obituary *33*
Newman, Barbara Johansen *191*
Newman, Daisy 1904-1994 .... *27*
   Obituary *78*
Newman, Gerald 1939- *46*
   Brief entry *42*
Newman, Jerry 1935- *82*
Newman, Leslea 1955- *134*
   Earlier sketches in SATA *71, 128*
Newman, Margaret
   See Potter, Margaret (Newman)
Newman, Marjorie *146*
Newman, Matthew (Harrison) 1955- *56*
Newman, Nanette 1934- *162*
Newman, Robert (Howard) 1909-1988 .... *87*
   Obituary *60*
   Earlier sketch in SATA *4*
Newman, Shirlee P(etkin) *144*
   Earlier sketches in SATA *10, 90*
Newsom, Carol 1948- *92*
   Earlier sketch in SATA *40*

Newsom, Tom 1944- *80*
Newth, Mette 1942- *140*
Newton, David E(dward) 1933- *67*
Newton, James R(obert) 1935- *23*
Newton, Robert 1965- *191*
Newton, Suzanne 1936- *77*
   Earlier sketch in SATA *5*
Ney, John 1923- *43*
   Brief entry *33*
Nez, John *155*
Ng, Franklin *82*
Nguyen, Vincent *187*
Nichol, B(arrie) P(hillip) 1944-1988 .... *66*
Nicholas, Louise D.
   See Watkins, Dawn L.
Nicholls, Judith (Ann) 1941- *61*
Nichols, Cecilia Fawn 1906-1987 .... *12*
Nichols, Grace 1950- *164*
   Earlier sketch in SATA *98*
Nichols, Janet (Louise) 1952- *67*
Nichols, Judy 1947- *124*
Nichols, Leigh
   See Koontz, Dean R.
Nichols, Paul
   See Hawks, Robert
Nichols, Peter
   See Youd, (Christopher) Samuel
Nichols, (Joanna) Ruth 1948- *15*
Nicholson, C. R.
   See Nicole, Christopher (Robin)
Nicholson, Christina
   See Nicole, Christopher (Robin)
Nicholson, Joyce Thorpe 1919- *35*
Nicholson, Lois P. 1949- *88*
Nicholson, Robin
   See Nicole, Christopher (Robin)
Nicholson, William *180*
Nicholson, William 1872-1949
   See CLR *76*
Nickel, Barbara 1966- *188*
Nickell, Joe 1944- *167*
   Earlier sketch in SATA *73*
Nickelsburg, Janet 1893-1983 .... *11*
Nickerson, Elizabeth *14*
   See Nickerson, Betty
Nickl, Barbara (Elisabeth) 1939- *56*
Nicklaus, Carol *62*
   Brief entry *33*
Nickle, John *181*
Nickless, Will 1902-1979(?) *66*
Nic Leodhas, Sorche
   See Alger, Leclaire (Gowans)
Nicol, Ann
   See Turnbull, Ann
Nicolas
   See Mordvinoff, Nicolas
Nicolay, Helen 1866-1954
   See YABC *1*
Nicole, Christopher (Robin) 1930- *5*
Nicoll, Helen 1937- *87*
Nicolson, Cynthia Pratt 1949- *141*
Ni Dhuibhne, Eilis 1954- *91*
Niehaus, Paddy Bouma
   See Bouma, Paddy
Nields, Nerissa 1967- *166*
Nielsen, Kay (Rasmus) 1886-1957 .... *16*
   See also CLR *16*
Nielsen, Laura F(arnsworth) 1960- *93*
Nielsen, Nancy J. 1951- *77*
Nielsen, Susin 1964- *195*
Nielsen, Virginia
   See McCall, Virginia Nielsen
Nielsen-Fernlund, Susin
   See Nielsen, Susin
Niemann, Christoph 1970- *191*
Nieuwsma, Milton J(ohn) 1941- *142*
Nightingale, Sandy 1953- *76*
Nikolajeva, Maria 1952- *127*
Nikola-Lisa, W. 1951- *180*
   Earlier sketch in SATA *71*

Niland, Deborah 1951- 172
　Earlier sketch in SATA 27
Niland, Kilmeny 75
Nilsen, Anna 1948- 174
　Earlier sketch in SATA 96
Nilsson, Eleanor 1939- 117
　Earlier sketch in SATA 81
　See also SAAS 23
Nilsson, Per 1954- 159
Nimmo, Jenny 1944- 144
　Earlier sketch in SATA 87
　See also CLR 44
Niven, Larry 1938- 171
　Earlier sketch in SATA 95
　See Niven, Laurence VanCott
Niven, Laurence VanCott
　See Niven, Larry
Nivola, Claire A. 1947- 140
　Earlier sketch in SATA 84
Nix, Garth 1963- 143
　Earlier sketch in SATA 97
　See also CLR 68
Nixon, Hershell Howard 1923- 42
Nixon, Joan Lowery 1927-2003 115
　Obituary 146
　Earlier sketches in SATA 8, 44, 78
　See also CLR 24
　See also SAAS 9
Nixon, K.
　See Nixon, Kathleen Irene (Blundell)
Nixon, Kathleen Irene (Blundell)
　1894-1988(?) 14
　Obituary 59
Nobisso, Josephine 1953- 121
　Earlier sketch in SATA 78
Noble, Iris (Davis) 1922-1986 5
　Obituary 49
Noble, Marty 1947- 125
　Earlier sketch in SATA 97
Noble, Trinka Hakes 1944- 123
　Brief entry 37
Noda, Takayo 1961- 168
Nodelman, Perry 1942- 101
Nodset, Joan L.
　See Lexau, Joan M.
Noel Hume, Ivor 1927- 65
Noestlinger, Christine
　See Nostlinger, Christine
Noguere, Suzanne 1947- 34
Nolan, Dennis 1945- 166
　Brief entry 34
　Earlier sketches in SATA 42, 92
Nolan, Han 1956- 157
　Earlier sketch in SATA 109
Nolan, Janet 1956- 191
　Earlier sketch in SATA 145
Nolan, Jeannette Covert 1897-1974 2
　Obituary 27
Nolan, Paul T(homas) 1919- 48
Nolan, William F(rancis) 1928- 88
　Brief entry 28
Nolen, Jerdine 1953- 157
　Earlier sketch in SATA 105
Noll, Sally 1946- 82
Noonan, Brandon 1979- 184
Noonan, Diana 1960- 146
Noonan, Julia 1946- 148
　Earlier sketches in SATA 4, 95
Norac, Carl 1960- 166
Norcross, John
　See Conroy, John Wesley
Nordan, Robert W(arren) 1934-2004 133
Nordhoff, Charles Bernard 1887-1947 23
Nordlicht, Lillian 29
Nordstrom, Ursula 1910-1988 3
　Obituary 57
Nordtvedt, Matilda 1926- 67
Norling, Beth 1969- 149
Norman, Charles 1904-1996 38
　Obituary 92

Norman, Howard
　See Norman, Howard A.
Norman, Howard A. 1949- 81
Norman, James
　See Schmidt, James Norman
Norman, Jay
　See Arthur, Robert, (Jr.)
Norman, Lilith 1927- 120
　Earlier sketch in SATA 86
Norman, Mary 1931- 36
Norman, Steve
　See Pashko, Stanley
Norment, Lisa 1966- 91
Norris, Gunilla Brodde 1939- 20
North, Andrew
　See Norton, Andre
North, Anthony
　See Koontz, Dean R.
North, Captain George
　See Stevenson, Robert Louis (Balfour)
North, Captain George
　See Stevenson, Robert Louis (Balfour)
North, Howard
　See Trevor, Elleston
North, Joan 1920- 16
North, Milou
　See Erdrich, Louise
North, Robert
　See Withers, Carl A.
North, Sara
　See Bonham, Barbara Thomas
　and Hager, Jean
North, Sterling 1906-1974 45
　Obituary 26
　Earlier sketch in SATA 1
Northcott, (William) Cecil 1902-1987
　Obituary 55
Northeast, Brenda V(ictoria) 1948- 106
Northmore, Elizabeth Florence 1906-1974 . 122
Norton, Alice Mary 43
　Earlier sketch in SATA 1
　See Norton, Andre
Norton, Andre 1912-2005 91
　See also CLR 50
　See Norton, Alice Mary
Norton, Browning
　See Norton, Frank R. B(rowning)
Norton, Frank R. B(rowning) 1909-1989 10
Norton, Mary 1903-1992 60
　Obituary 72
　Earlier sketch in SATA 18
　See also CLR 6
Nosredna, Trebor
　See Anderson, Bob
Nostlinger, Christine 1936- 162
　Brief entry 37
　Earlier sketch in SATA 64
　See also CLR 12
Nourse, Alan E(dward) 1928-1992 48
　See also CLR 33
Novak, Matt 1962- 165
　Brief entry 52
　Earlier sketches in SATA 60, 104
Novelli, Luca 1947- 61
Nowell, Elizabeth Cameron 12
Noyes, Deborah 1965- 194
　Earlier sketch in SATA 145
Nugent, Nicholas 1949- 73
Numeroff, Laura Joffe 1953- 142
　Earlier sketches in SATA 28, 90
　See also CLR 85
Nunes, Lygia Bojunga 1932- 154
　Earlier sketch in SATA 75
　See Bojunga, Lygia
Nunn, Laura (Donna) Silverstein 1968- 124
Nurenberg, Thelma
　See Greenhaus, Thelma Nurenberg
Nurnberg, Maxwell 1897-1984 27
　Obituary 41
Nussbaumer, Paul (Edmund) 1934- 16

Nutt, Ken 1951- 163
　Earlier sketch in SATA 97
Nuygen, Mathieu 1967- 80
Nuzum, K.A. 195
Nyberg, (Everett Wayne) Morgan 1944- 87
Nyce, (Nellie) Helene von Strecker
　1885-1969 19
Nyce, Vera 1862-1925 19
Nye, Naomi Shihab 1952- 147
　Earlier sketch in SATA 86
　See also CLR 59
Nye, Robert 1939- 6
Nyikos, Stacy A. 1969- 164
Nystrom, Carolyn 1940- 130
　Earlier sketch in SATA 67

O

Oakes, Elizabeth H. 1964- 132
Oakes, Vanya 1909-1983 6
　Obituary 37
Oakley, Don(ald G.) 1927- 8
Oakley, Graham 1929- 84
　Earlier sketch in SATA 30
　See also CLR 7
Oakley, Helen (McKelvey) 1906- 10
Oana, Katherine 1929- 53
　Brief entry 37
Oates, Eddie H. 1943- 88
Oates, Joyce Carol 1938- 159
Oates, Stephen B(aery) 1936- 59
Obed, Ellen Bryan 1944- 74
Oberle, Joseph 1958- 69
Oberman, Sheldon 1949-2004 85
　Autobiography Feature 114
　Obituary 153
　See also CLR 54
　See also SAAS 26
Obligado, Lilian (Isabel) 1931- 61
　Brief entry 45
Obrant, Susan 1946- 11
O'Brian, E.G.
　See Clarke, Arthur C.
O'Brien, Anne Sibley 1952- 80
　Brief entry 48
　Earlier sketch in SATA 53
O'Brien, E.G.
　See Clarke, Arthur C.
O'Brien, Esse Forrester 1895(?)-1975
　Obituary 30
O'Brien, Patrick 1960- 193
O'Brien, Robert C.
　See CLR 2
　See Conly, Robert Leslie
O'Brien, Thomas C(lement) 1938- 29
O'Callaghan, Julie 1954- 113
O'Callahan, Jay 1938- 88
O'Carroll, Ryan
　See Markun, Patricia Maloney
Ochiltree, Dianne 1953- 117
Ockham, Joan Price
　See Price, Joan
O'Connell, Margaret F(orster) 1935-1977 30
　Obituary 30
O'Connell, Peg
　See Ahern, Margaret McCrohan
O'Connell, Rebecca 1968- 130
O'Connor, Barbara 1950- 193
　Earlier sketch in SATA 154
O'Connor, Francine M(arie) 1930- 90
O'Connor, Genevieve A. 1914- 75
O'Connor, George 183
O'connor, Ian 1965- 188
O'Connor, Jane 1947- 186
　Brief entry 47
　Earlier sketches in SATA 59, 103, 150
O'Connor, Karen 1938- 89
　Earlier sketch in SATA 34

O'Connor, Patrick
  See Wibberley, Leonard (Patrick O'Connor)
O'Connor, Richard 1915-1975
  Obituary 21
O'Conor, Jane 1958- 78
Odaga, Asenath (Bole) 1937- 130
  Earlier sketch in SATA 67
  See also SAAS 19
O Danachair, Caoimhin
  See Danaher, Kevin
Odanaka, Barbara 159
O'Daniel, Janet 1921- 24
O'Day, Cathy
  See Crane, Barbara (Joyce)
O'Dell, Scott 1898-1989 134
  Earlier sketches in SATA *12, 60*
  See also CLR *126*
Odenwald, Robert P(aul) 1899-1965 .... *11*
Odgers, Sally
  See Odgers, Sally Farrell
Odgers, Sally Farrell 1957- 139
  Earlier sketch in SATA 72
O'Donnell, Dick
  See Lupoff, Richard A(llen)
  and Thompson, Don(ald Arthur)
Odriozola, Elena 186
Oechsli, Kelly 1918-1999 5
Oesterle, Virginia Rorby
  See Rorby, Ginny
Ofek, Uriel 1926- 36
  See also CLR 28
Offenbacher, Ami 1958- 91
Offit, Sidney 1928- 10
Ofosu-Appiah, L(awrence) H(enry) 1920- ... 13
Ogan, George F. 1912-1983 13
Ogan, M. G.
  See Ogan, George F.
  and Ogan, Margaret E. (Nettles)
Ogan, Margaret E. (Nettles) 1923-1979 13
Ogburn, Charlton (Jr.) 1911-1998 3
  Obituary 109
Ogburn, Jacqueline K. 162
Ogilvie, Elisabeth May 1917-2006 40
  Brief entry 29
  Obituary 176
Ogilvy, Gavin
  See Barrie, J(ames) M(atthew)
Ogilvy, Ian 1943- 177
Ogilvy, Ian Raymond
  See Ogilvy, Ian
Ogle, Lucille Edith 1904-1988
  Obituary 59
Ogletree, Charles J. 1952- 175
O'Green, Jennifer
  See Roberson, Jennifer
O'Green, Jennifer Roberson
  See Roberson, Jennifer
O'Hagan, Caroline 1946- 38
O'Hanlon, Jacklyn
  See Meek, Jacklyn O'Hanlon
O'Hara, Elizabeth
  See Ni Dhuibhne, Eilis
O'Hara, Kenneth
  See Morris, (Margaret) Jean
O'Hara, Mary
  See Alsop, Mary O'Hara
O'Hara (Alsop), Mary
  See Alsop, Mary O'Hara
O'Hare, Jeff(rey A.) 1958- 105
Ohi, Ruth 1964- 95
Ohiyesa
  See Eastman, Charles A(lexander)
Ohlsson, Ib 1935- 7
Ohmi, Ayano 1959- 115
Ohtomo, Yasuo 1946- 37
o huigin, sean 1942- 138
  See also CLR 75
Oiseau
  See Moseley, James W(illett)
Oke, Janette 1935- 97

O'Keefe, Susan Heyboer 176
  Earlier sketch in SATA 133
O'Keeffe, Frank 1938- 99
O'Kelley, Mattie Lou 1908-1997 97
  Earlier sketch in SATA 36
Okimoto, Jean Davies 1942- 103
  Earlier sketch in SATA 34
Okomfo, Amasewa
  See Cousins, Linda
Olaleye, Isaac O. 1941- 96
  See also SAAS 23
Olcott, Frances Jenkins 1872(?)-1963 19
Old, Wendie C(orbin) 1943- 154
Old Boy
  See Hughes, Thomas
Oldenburg, E(gbert) William 1936-1974 35
Older, Effin 1942- 114
Older, Jules 1940- 156
  Earlier sketch in SATA 114
Oldfield, Jenny 1949- 140
Oldfield, Margaret J(ean) 1932- 56
Oldfield, Pamela 1931- 86
Oldham, June 70
Oldham, Mary 1944- 65
Olds, Elizabeth 1896-1991 3
  Obituary 66
Olds, Helen Diehl 1895-1981 9
  Obituary 25
Oldstyle, Jonathan
  See Irving, Washington
O'Leary, Brian (Todd) 1940- 6
O'Leary, Patsy B(aker) 1937- 97
Oliphant, B.J.
  See Tepper, Sheri S.
Oliver, Burton
  See Burt, Olive Woolley
Oliver, Chad
  See Oliver, Symmes C(hadwick)
Oliver, John Edward 1933- 21
Oliver, Marilyn Tower 1935- 89
Oliver, Narelle 1960- 152
Oliver, Shirley (Louise Dawkins) 1958- 74
Oliver, Symmes C(hadwick) 1928-1993 101
  See Oliver, Chad
Oliviero, Jamie 1950- 84
Olmsted, Lorena Ann 1890-1989 13
Olney, Ross R. 1929- 13
Olschewski, Alfred (Erich) 1920- 7
Olsen, Barbara 148
Olsen, Carol 1945- 89
Olsen, Ib Spang 1921- 81
  Earlier sketch in SATA 6
Olsen, Violet (Mae) 1922-1991 58
Olson, Arielle North 1932- 67
Olson, Gene 1922- 32
Olson, Gretchen 187
Olson, Helen Kronberg 48
Olson, Kay Melchisedech 1948- 175
Olson, Marianne
  See Mitchell, Marianne
Olson-Brown, Ellen 1967- 183
Olugebefola, Ademole 1941- 15
Oluonye, Mary N(kechi) 1955- 111
Om
  See Gorey, Edward (St. John)
O'Malley, Kevin 1961- 191
  Earlier sketch in SATA 157
Oman, Carola (Mary Anima) 1897-1978 35
O'Mara, Carmel 1965- 166
O'Mara-Horwitz, Carmel
  See O'Mara, Carmel
O'Meara, Walter (Andrew) 1897-1989 65
Ommanney, F(rancis) D(ownes) 1903-1980 . 23
O Mude
  See Gorey, Edward (St. John)
Oneal, Elizabeth 1934- 82
  Earlier sketch in SATA 30
  See Oneal, Zibby
O'Neal, Reagan
  See Jordan, Robert

O'Neal, Regan
  See Jordan, Robert
Oneal, Zibby
  See CLR 13
  See Oneal, Elizabeth
O'Neill, Amanda 1951- 111
O'Neill, Gerard K(itchen) 1927-1992 65
O'Neill, Judith (Beatrice) 1930- 34
O'Neill, Mary L(e Duc) 1908(?)-1990 2
  Obituary 64
O'Neill, Reagan
  See Jordan, Robert
Onslow, Annette Rosemary MacArthur
  See MacArthur-Onslow, Annette Rosemary
Onslow, John 1906-1985
  Obituary 47
Onyefulu, Ifeoma 1959- 157
  Earlier sketches in SATA 81, 115
Opie, Iona (Margaret Balfour) 1923- 118
  Earlier sketches in SATA 3, 63
  See also SAAS 6
Opie, Peter (Mason) 1918-1982 118
  Obituary 28
  Earlier sketches in SATA 3, 63
Oppel, Kenneth 1967- 153
  Earlier sketch in SATA 99
Oppenheim, Joanne 1934- 174
  Earlier sketches in SATA 5, 82, 136
Oppenheim, Shulamith Levey 1928- 177
Oppenheimer, Joan L(etson) 1925- 28
Oppong, Joseph Ransford 1953- 160
Optic, Oliver
  See Adams, William Taylor
  and Stratemeyer, Edward L.
Oram, Hiawyn 1946- 101
  Earlier sketch in SATA 56
Orbach, Ruth Gary 1941- 21
Orczy, Emma
  See Orczy, Baroness Emmuska
Orczy, Emma Magdalena Rosalia Maria Josefa
  See Orczy, Baroness Emmuska
Orczy, Emmuska
  See Orczy, Baroness Emmuska
Orczy, Baroness Emmuska 1865-1947 40
  See Orczy, Emma
Orde, A.J.
  See Tepper, Sheri S.
O'Reilly, Jackson
  See Jordan, Robert
Orenstein, Denise Gosliner 1950- 157
Orgel, Doris 1929- 148
  Earlier sketches in SATA 7, 85
  See also CLR 48
  See also SAAS 19
Oriolo, Joe
  See Oriolo, Joseph D.
Oriolo, Joseph D. 1913-1985
  Obituary 46
Orleans, Ilo 1897-1962 10
Orlev, Uri 1931- 135
  Earlier sketch in SATA 58
  See also CLR 30
  See also SAAS 19
Ormai, Stella 57
  Brief entry 48
Ormerod, Jan 1946- 132
  Brief entry 44
  Earlier sketches in SATA 55, 70
  See also CLR 20
Ormes, Jackie
  See Ormes, Zelda J.
Ormes, Zelda J. 1914-1986
  Obituary 47
Ormondroyd, Edward 1925- 14
Ormsby, Virginia H(aire) 1906-1990 11
Orona-Ramirez, Kristy 1964- 189
Orozco, Jose-Luis 1948- 179
Orr, Katherine S(helley) 1950- 72
Orr, Wendy 1953- 141
  Earlier sketch in SATA 90

Orris
    See Ingelow, Jean
Orth, Richard
    See Gardner, Richard (M.)
Ortiz Cofer, Judith
    See Cofer, Judith Ortiz
Orwell, George
    See CLR 68
    See Blair, Eric (Arthur)
Orwin, Joanna 1944- 141
Osborn, Elinor 1939- 145
Osborn, Lois D(orothy) 1915- 61
Osborne, Charles 1927- 59
Osborne, Chester G(orham) 1915-1987 11
Osborne, David
    See Silverberg, Robert
Osborne, George
    See Silverberg, Robert
Osborne, Leone Neal 1914-1996 2
Osborne, Mary Pope 1949- 144
    Earlier sketches in SATA *41, 55, 98*
    See also CLR 88
Osceola
    See Blixen, Karen (Christentze Dinesen)
Osgood, William E(dward) 1926- 37
O'Shaughnessy, Darren
    See Shan, Darren
O'Shaughnessy, Ellen Cassels 1937- 78
O'Shea, Catherine Patricia Shiels
    See O'Shea, Pat
O'Shea, Pat 1931-2007 87
    See also CLR 18
Osmond, Edward 1900- 10
Ossoli, Sarah Margaret (Fuller) 1810-1850 .. 25
    See Fuller, Margaret
Ostendorf, (Arthur) Lloyd, (Jr.) 1921-2000 .. 65
    Obituary 125
Ostow, Micol 1976- 170
Otfinoski, Steven 1949- 116
    Earlier sketch in SATA *56*
Otis, James
    See Kaler, James Otis
O'Toole, Thomas 1941- 71
O'Trigger, Sir Lucius
    See Horne, Richard Henry Hengist
Otten, Charlotte
    See Otten, Charlotte F.
Otten, Charlotte F. 1926- 98
Otten, Charlotte Fennema
    See Otten, Charlotte F.
Ottley, Matt 1962- 171
    Earlier sketch in SATA *102*
Ottley, Reginald Leslie 1909-1985 26
    See also CLR 16
Otto, Margaret Glover 1909-1976
    Obituary 30
Otto, Svend
    See Soerensen, Svend Otto
Oughton, Jerrie (Preston) 1937- 131
    Earlier sketch in SATA *76*
Oughton, (William) Taylor 1925- 104
Ouida
    See De La Ramee, Marie Louise
Ousley, Odille 1896-1976 10
Outcalt, Todd 1960- 123
Overmyer, James E. 1946- 88
Overton, Jenny (Margaret Mary) 1942- 52
    Brief entry 36
Owen, Ann
    See Qualey, Marsha
Owen, Annie 1949- 75
Owen, Caroline Dale
    See Snedeker, Caroline Dale (Parke)
Owen, Clifford
    See Hamilton, Charles (Harold St. John)
Owen, Dilys
    See Gater, Dilys
Owen, (Benjamin) Evan 1918-1984 38

Owen, (John) Gareth 1936-2002 162
    Earlier sketch in SATA *83*
    See also CLR 31
    See also SAAS 14
Owen, James A. 185
Owens, Bryant 1968- 116
Owens, Dana Elaine
    See Queen Latifah
Owens, Gail 1939- 54
Owens, Mary Beth 191
Owens, Thomas S(heldon) 1960- 86
Owens, Tom
    See Owens, Thomas S(heldon)
Oxenbury, Helen 1938- 149
    Earlier sketches in SATA *3, 68*
    See also CLR 70
Oxendine, Bess Holland 1933- 90
Oz, Frank (Richard) 1944- 60
Ozer, Jerome S. 1927- 59

P

Pace, Lorenzo 1943- 131
Pace, Mildred Mastin 1907- 46
    Brief entry 29
Pachter, Hedwig (?)-1988 63
Pack, Janet 1952- 77
Pack, Robert 1929- 118
Packard, Edward 1931- 148
    Earlier sketches in SATA *47, 90*
Packer, Kenneth L. 1946- 116
Packer, Vin
    See Meaker, Marijane
Pad, Peter
    See Stratemeyer, Edward L.
Page, Eileen
    See Heal, Edith
Page, Eleanor
    See Coerr, Eleanor (Beatrice)
Page, Jake 1936- 81
Page, James Keena, Jr.
    See Page, Jake
Page, Lou Williams 1912-1997 38
Page, Mary
    See Heal, Edith
Page, Robin 1943- 154
Pagnucci, Susan 1944- 90
Pahlen, Kurt 1907-2003
    Obituary 147
Pahz, Cheryl
    See Pahz, Cheryl Suzanne
Pahz, Cheryl Suzanne 1949- 11
Pahz, James Alon 1943- 11
Paice, Margaret 1920- 10
Paige, Harry W(orthington) 1922- 41
    Brief entry 35
Paige, Richard
    See Koontz, Dean R.
Paige, Robin
    See Albert, Susan Wittig
Paine, Penelope Colville 1946- 87
Paine, Roberta M. 1925- 13
Paisley, Tom 1932- 78
    See Bethancourt, T. Ernesto
Palatini, Margie 174
    Earlier sketch in SATA *134*
Palazzo, Anthony D.
    See Palazzo, Tony
Palazzo, Tony 1905-1970 3
Palder, Edward L. 1922- 5
Palecek, Josef 1932- 56
Palecek, Libuse 1937- 89
Palen, Debbie 195
Palin, Michael 1943- 67
    See Monty Python
Palin, Michael Edward
    See Palin, Michael
Palladini, David (Mario) 1946- 40
    Brief entry 32

Pallas, Norvin 1918-1983 23
Pallister, John C(lare) 1891-1980
    Obituary 26
Pallotta, Gerard Larry
    See Pallotta, Jerry
Pallotta, Jerry 1953- 186
Pallotta-Chiarolli, Maria 1960- 117
Palmer, Bernard (Alvin) 1914-1998 26
Palmer, C. Everard 1930- 14
Palmer, (Ruth) Candida 1926- 11
Palmer, Cyril Everard
    See Palmer, C. Everard
Palmer, Don
    See Benson, Mildred (Augustine Wirt)
Palmer, Hap 1942- 68
Palmer, Heidi 1948- 15
Palmer, Helen Marion
    See Geisel, Helen
Palmer, Jessica 1953- 120
Palmer, Judd 1972- 153
Palmer, Juliette 1930- 15
Palmer, Kate Salley 1946- 97
Palmer, Maria
    See Strachan, Ian
Palmer, Maria
    See Brennan, Herbie
Palmer, Robin 1909-2000 43
Paltrowitz, Donna 1950- 61
    Brief entry 50
Paltrowitz, Donna Milman
    See Paltrowitz, Donna
Paltrowitz, Stuart 1946- 61
    Brief entry 50
Pamintuan, Macky 178
Panagopoulos, Janie Lynn 149
Panati, Charles 1943- 65
Panchyk, Richard 1970- 138
Panetta, George 1915-1969 15
Panetta, Joseph N. 1953- 96
Panik, Sharon 1952- 82
Panowski, Eileen Thompson 1920- 49
Pansy
    See Alden, Isabella (Macdonald)
Pantell, Dora (Fuchs) 39
Panter, Carol 1936- 9
Paolini, Christopher 1983- 157
    See also CLR 102
Papademetriou, Lisa 175
Paparone, Pam 185
Paparone, Pamela
    See Paparone, Pam
Papas, Bill
    See Papas, William
Papas, William 1927-2000 50
Papashvily, George 1898-1978 17
Papashvily, Helen (Waite) 1906-1996 17
Pape, D. L.
    See Pape, Donna (Lugg)
Pape, Donna (Lugg) 1930- 82
    Earlier sketch in SATA *2*
Paperny, Myra (Green) 1932- 51
    Brief entry 33
Paradis, Adrian A(lexis) 1912- 67
    Earlier sketch in SATA *1*
    See also SAAS 8
Paradis, Marjorie Bartholomew
    1886(?)-1970 17
Paradiz, Valerie 1963- 176
Parenteau, Shirley Laurolyn 1935- 47
    Brief entry 40
Parish, Margaret (Cecile) 1927-1988 73
    See Parish, Peggy
Parish, Margaret Holt
    See Holt, Margaret
Parish, Peggy 17
    Obituary 59
    See also CLR 22
    See Parish, Margaret (Cecile)

Park, Barbara 1947- *123*
  Brief entry *35*
  Earlier sketches in SATA *40, 78*
  See also CLR *34*
Park, Bill
  See Park, W(illiam) B(ryan)
Park, Frances 1955- *171*
Park, Ginger *173*
Park, Janie Jaehyun *150*
Park, Jordan
  See Kornbluth, C(yril) M.
  and Pohl, Frederik
Park, Linda Sue 1960- *173*
  Earlier sketch in SATA *127*
  See also CLR *84*
Park, Nick 1958- *113*
Park, (Rosina) Ruth (Lucia) 1923(?)- *93*
  Earlier sketch in SATA *25*
  See also CLR *51*
Park, W(illiam) B(ryan) 1936- *22*
Parke, Marilyn 1928- *82*
Parker, Barbara Keevil 1938- *157*
Parker, Daniel
  See Ehrenhaft, Daniel
Parker, Elinor Milnor 1906- *3*
Parker, Julie F. 1961- *92*
Parker, Kim 1963- *174*
Parker, Kristy 1957- *59*
Parker, Lois M(ay) 1912-1996 .... *30*
Parker, Margot M. 1937- *52*
Parker, Marjorie Blain 1960- *145*
Parker, Mary Jessie 1948- *71*
Parker, Nancy Winslow 1930- *132*
  Earlier sketches in SATA *10, 69*
  See also SAAS *20*
Parker, Richard 1915-1990 .... *14*
Parker, Robert
  See Boyd, Waldo T.
Parker, Toni Trent 1947-2005 .... *142*
  Obituary *169*
Parker-Rees, Guy *193*
Parkes, Lucas
  See Harris, John (Wyndham Parkes Lucas)
  Beynon
Parkhill, John
  See Cox, William R(obert)
Parkins, David 1955- *176*
Parkinson, Ethelyn M(inerva) 1906-1999 ..... *11*
Parkinson, Kathy *71*
  See Parkinson, Kathryn N.
Parkinson, Siobhan
  See Parkinson, Siobhan
Parkinson, Siobhan 1954- *178*
Parks, Deborah A. 1948- *133*
  Earlier sketch in SATA *91*
Parks, Edd Winfield 1906-1968 .... *10*
Parks, Gordon 1912-2006 .... *108*
  Obituary *175*
  Earlier sketch in SATA *8*
Parks, Gordon Roger Alexander
  See Parks, Gordon
Parks, Peggy J. 1951- *143*
Parks, PJ
  See Parks, Peggy J.
Parks, Rosa 1913-2005 .... *83*
  Obituary *169*
Parks, Rosa Louise Lee
  See Parks, Rosa
Parks, Van Dyke 1943- *62*
Parley, Peter
  See Goodrich, Samuel Griswold
Parlin, John
  See Graves, Charles Parlin
Parme, Fabrice 1966- *191*
Parnall, Peter 1936- *69*
  Earlier sketch in SATA *16*
  See also SAAS *11*
Parotti, Phillip (Elliott) 1941- *109*
Parr, Ann 1943- *144*
Parr, Danny
  See Parr, Ann

Parr, Letitia (Evelyn) 1906-1985(?) *37*
Parr, Lucy 1924- *10*
Parr, Todd *179*
  Earlier sketch in SATA *134*
Parrish, Anne 1888-1957 .... *27*
Parrish, Mary
  See Cousins, Margaret
Parrish, Maxfield
  See Parrish, (Frederick) Maxfield
Parrish, (Frederick) Maxfield 1870-1966 ..... *14*
Parry, Marian 1924- *13*
Parson Lot
  See Kingsley, Charles
Parsons, Alexandra 1947- *92*
Parsons, Ellen
  See Dragonwagon, Crescent
Parsons, Martin 1951- *116*
Parsons, Martin Leslie
  See Parsons, Martin
Parsons, Tom
  See MacPherson, Thomas George
Parsons-Yazzi, Evangeline *172*
Partch, Virgil Franklin II 1916-1984 .... *39*
  Obituary *39*
Parton, Dolly 1946- *94*
Parton, Dolly Rebecca
  See Parton, Dolly
Partridge, Benjamin W., Jr. 1915-2005 .... *28*
  Obituary *163*
Partridge, Benjamin Waring, Jr.
  See Partridge, Benjamin W., Jr.
Partridge, Cora Cheney
  See Cheney, Cora
Partridge, Elizabeth *134*
Partridge, Jenny (Lilian) 1947- *52*
  Brief entry *37*
Pasachoff, Naomi 1947- *147*
Pascal, David 1918- *14*
Pascal, Francine 1938- *143*
  Brief entry *37*
  Earlier sketches in SATA *51, 80*
  See also CLR *25*
Paschal, Nancy
  See Trotter, Grace V(iolet)
Paschkis, Julie 1957- *177*
Pascudniak, Pascal
  See Lupoff, Richard A(llen)
Pashko, Stanley 1913-1982 .... *29*
Passailaigue, Thomas E.
  See Paisley, Tom
Pateman, Robert 1954- *84*
Patent, Dorothy Hinshaw 1940- *162*
  Autobiography Feature *162*
  Earlier sketches in SATA *22, 69, 120*
  See also CLR *19*
  See also SAAS *13*
Paterson, A(ndrew) B(arton) 1864-1941 .... *97*
Paterson, Banjo
  See Paterson, A(ndrew) B(arton)
Paterson, Diane 1946- *177*
  Brief entry *33*
  Earlier sketch in SATA *59*
Paterson, John (Barstow) 1932- *114*
Paterson, Katherine 1932- *133*
  Earlier sketches in SATA *13, 53, 92*
  See also CLR *127*
Paterson, Katherine Womeldorf
  See Paterson, Katherine
Patience, John 1949- *90*
Patneaude, David 1944- *159*
  Earlier sketch in SATA *85*
Paton, Alan 1903-1988 .... *11*
  Obituary *56*
Paton, Alan Stewart
  See Paton, Alan
Paton, Jane (Elizabeth) 1934- *35*
Paton, Priscilla 1952- *98*
Paton Walsh, Gillian
  See Paton Walsh, Jill

Paton Walsh, Jill 1937- *190*
  Autobiography Feature *190*
  Earlier sketches in SATA *4, 72, 109*
  See also CLR *65*
  See also SAAS *3*
  See Paton Walsh, Gillian
  and Walsh, Jill Paton
Patrick, Susan
  See Clark, Patricia Denise
Patron, Susan 1948- *182*
  Earlier sketch in SATA *76*
Patsauq, Markoosie 1942-
  See CLR *23*
Patschke, Steve 1955- *125*
Patten, Brian 1946- *152*
  Earlier sketch in SATA *29*
Patterson, Charles 1935- *59*
Patterson, Geoffrey 1943- *54*
  Brief entry *44*
Patterson, James 1947- *164*
Patterson, James B.
  See Patterson, James
Patterson, Lillie G. -1999 .... *88*
  Earlier sketch in SATA *14*
Patterson, Nancy Ruth 1944- *148*
  Earlier sketch in SATA *72*
Pattison, Darcy (S.) 1954- *126*
  Earlier sketch in SATA *72*
Pattou, Edith *164*
Patz (Blaustein), Nancy *154*
Paul, Aileen 1917- *12*
Paul, Ann Whitford 1941- *168*
  Earlier sketches in SATA *76, 110*
Paul, David (Tyler) 1934-1988
  Obituary *56*
Paul, Dominique 1973- *184*
Paul, Elizabeth
  See Crow, Donna Fletcher
Paul, Hamish Vigne Christie 1951- *151*
  See also CLR *87*
Paul, James 1936- *23*
Paul, Korky
  See Paul, Hamish Vigne Christie
Paul, Robert
  See Roberts, John G(aither)
Paul, Tessa 1944- *103*
Pauli, Hertha (Ernestine) 1909-1973 .... *3*
  Obituary *26*
Paull, Grace A. 1898- *24*
Paulsen, Gary 1939- *189*
  Earlier sketches in SATA *22, 50, 54, 79, 111,
  158*
  See also CLR *82*
Paulson, Jack
  See Jackson, C(aary) Paul
Pauquet, Gina Ruck
  See Ruck-Pauquet, Gina
Pausacker, Jenny 1948- *72*
  See also SAAS *23*
Pausewang, Gudrun 1928- *165*
  Earlier sketch in SATA *104*
Pavel, Frances 1907- *10*
Paver, Michelle *170*
Paxton, Tom *70*
  See Paxton, Thomas R.
Paye, Won-Ldy *185*
Payne, Alan
  See Jakes, John
Payne, Bernal C., Jr. 1941- *60*
Payne, C. Douglas
  See Payne, C.D.
Payne, C.D. 1949- *133*
Payne, C.F. 1956- *179*
Payne, Chris Fox
  See Payne, C.F.
Payne, Donald Gordon 1924- *37*
Payne, Emmy
  See West, Emily Govan
Payne, Nina *135*
Payne, Rachel Ann
  See Jakes, John

Payson, Dale 1943- 9
Payzant, Charles 18
Paz, A.
    See Pahz, James Alon
Paz, Zan
    See Pahz, Cheryl Suzanne
Peace, Mary
    See Finley, Mary Peace
Peacock, Shane 1957- 192
Peake, Mervyn 1911-1968 23
Peale, Norman Vincent 1898-1993 20
    Obituary 78
Pearce, Ann Philippa
    See Pearce, Philippa
Pearce, Jacqueline 1962- 146
Pearce, Margaret 104
Pearce, Philippa 1920-2006
    Obituary 179
    See Christie, Philippa
Peare, Catherine Owens 1911- 9
Pearsall, Shelley 1966- 190
Pearson, Gayle 1947- 119
    Earlier sketch in SATA 53
Pearson, Jean Mary
    See Gardam, Jane
Pearson, Kit 1947- 77
    Autobiography Feature 117
    See also CLR 26
Pearson, Mary E. 1955- 134
Pearson, Ridley 1953- 182
Pearson, Susan 1946- 166
    Brief entry 27
    Earlier sketches in SATA 39, 91
Pearson, Tracey Campbell 1956- 155
    Earlier sketch in SATA 64
Pease, (Clarence) Howard 1894-1974 2
    Obituary 25
Peavy, Linda 1943- 54
Peck, Anne Merriman 1884-1976 18
Peck, Beth 1957- 190
    Earlier sketch in SATA 79
Peck, Jan 159
Peck, Jeanie J. 1967- 147
Peck, Marshall III 1951- 92
Peck, Richard 1934- 190
    Autobiography Feature 110
    Earlier sketches in SATA 18, 55, 97, 110, 158
    See also CLR 15
    See also SAAS 2
Peck, Richard Wayne
    See Peck, Richard
Peck, Robert Newton 1928- 156
    Autobiography Feature 108
    Earlier sketches in SATA 21, 62, 111
    See also CLR 45
    See also SAAS 1
Peck, Sylvia 1953- 133
Peck-Whiting, Jeanie J.
    See Peck, Jeanie J.
Pedersen, Janet 193
Pederson, Sharleen
    See Collicott, Sharleen
Peebles, Anne
    See Galloway, Priscilla
Peek, Merle 1938- 39
Peel, John 1954- 79
Peel, Norman Lemon
    See Hirsch, Phil
Peeples, Edwin A(ugustus, Jr.) 1915-1994 6
Peers, Judi 1956- 119
Peers, Judith May West
    See Peers, Judi
Peet, Bill
    See CLR 12
    See Peet, William Bartlett
Peet, Creighton B. 1899-1977 30
Peet, Mal 171
Peet, Malcolm
    See Peet, Mal

Peet, William Bartlett 1915-2002 78
    Obituary 137
    Earlier sketches in SATA 2, 41
    See Peet, Bill
Peguero, Leone 116
Pelaez, Jill 1924- 12
Pelham, David 1938- 70
Pell, Ed(ward) 1950- 157
Pelletier, Andrew T. 195
Pelletier, Andrew Thomas
    See Pelletier, Andrew T.
Pellowski, Anne 1933- 20
Pellowski, Michael (Joseph) 1949- 151
    Brief entry 48
    Earlier sketch in SATA 88
Pellowski, Michael Morgan
    See Pellowski, Michael (Joseph)
Pelta, Kathy 1928- 18
Peltier, Leslie C(opus) 1900-1980 13
Pemberton, Bonnie 191
Pemberton, John Leigh
    See Leigh-Pemberton, John
Pembury, Bill
    See Groom, Arthur William
Pemsteen, Hans
    See Manes, Stephen
Pendennis, Arthur Esquir
    See Thackeray, William Makepeace
Pender, Lydia Podger 1907- 61
Pendery, Rosemary (Schmitz) 7
Pendle, Alexy 1943- 29
Pendle, George 1906-1977
    Obituary 28
Pendleton, Don
    See Cunningham, Chet
    and Garside, (Clifford) Jack
    and Jagninski, Tom
    and Krauzer, Steven M(ark)
    and Obstfeld, Raymond
Pendziwol, Jean E. 1965- 177
Pene du Bois, William (Sherman)
    1916-1993 68
    Obituary 74
    Earlier sketch in SATA 4
    See also CLR 1
Penn, Ruth Bonn
    See Rosenberg, Eth(el) Clifford
Pennac, Daniel 1944- 155
Pennage, E. M.
    See Finkel, George (Irvine)
Penner, Fred 1946- 169
    Earlier sketch in SATA 67
Penner, Frederick Ralph Cornelius
    See Penner, Fred
Penney, Grace Jackson 1904-2000 35
Penney, Ian 1960- 76
Penney, Sue 1957- 152
    Earlier sketch in SATA 102
Pennington, Eunice 1923- 27
Pennington, Lillian Boyer 1904- 45
Pennypacker, Sara 1951- 187
Penrose, Gordon 1925- 66
Penson, Mary E. 1917- 78
Penzler, Otto 1942- 38
Pepe, Phil 1935- 20
Pepe, Philip
    See Pepe, Phil
Peppe, Rodney (Darrell) 1934- 74
    Earlier sketch in SATA 4
    See also SAAS 10
Pepper, Frank S. 1910-1988
    Obituary 61
Percy, Charles Henry
    See Smith, Dorothy Gladys
Percy, Rachel 1930- 63
Perdrizet, Marie-Pierre 1952- 79
Perenyi, Constance 1954- 93
Perenyi, Constance Marie
    See Perenyi, Constance
Perera, Hilda 1926- 105
Perera, Thomas Biddle 1938- 13

Peretti, Frank E. 1951- 141
    Earlier sketch in SATA 80
Perez, Lana
    See Perez, Marlene
Perez, Lucia Angela 1973- 182
Perez, Marlene 170
Pericoli, Matteo 1968- 178
Perkins, Al(bert Rogers) 1904-1975 30
Perkins, Lucy Fitch 1865-1937 72
Perkins, Lynne Rae 172
    Earlier sketch in SATA 131
Perkins, (Richard) Marlin 1905-1986 21
    Obituary 48
Perkins, Mitali 1963- 188
    Earlier sketch in SATA 88
Perks, Anne-Marie 1955- 122
Perl, Erica S. 188
Perl, Lila 72
    Earlier sketch in SATA 6
Perl, Susan 1922-1983 22
    Obituary 34
Perlman, Rhea 1948- 183
Perlmutter, O(scar) William 1920-1975 8
Pernu, Dennis 1970- 87
Perrault, Charles 1628-1703 25
    See also CLR 134
Perret, Delphine 1980- 190
Perret, Gene (Richard) 1937- 76
Perrine, Mary 1913-1976 2
Perrins, Lesley 1953- 56
Perrow, Angeli 1954- 121
Perry, Andrea 1956- 190
    Earlier sketch in SATA 148
Perry, Barbara Fisher
    See Fisher, Barbara
Perry, Elizabeth 1959- 174
Perry, Elizabeth Goodwin
    See Perry, Elizabeth
Perry, Marie Fritz 165
Perry, Patricia 1949- 30
Perry, Phyllis J(ean) 1933- 152
    Earlier sketches in SATA 60, 101
Perry, Ritchie (John Allen) 1942- 105
Perry, Roger 1933- 27
Perry, Steve(n Carl) 1947- 76
Pershall, Mary K. 1951- 172
    Earlier sketch in SATA 70
Pershing, Marie
    See Schultz, Pearle Henriksen
Perske, Robert 1927- 57
Persun, Morgan Reed
    See Watkins, Dawn L.
Petach, Heidi 149
Peter
    See Stratemeyer, Edward L.
Peters, Alexander
    See Hollander, Zander
Peters, Andrew Fusek 1965- 169
    Earlier sketch in SATA 107
Peters, Caroline
    See Betz, Eva Kelly
Peters, David
    See David, Peter
Peters, Elizabeth 1927- 49
Peters, Emma
    See Price, Karen
Peters, Gabriel
    See Matott, Justin
Peters, Julie Anne 1952- 128
    Earlier sketch in SATA 82
Peters, Linda
    See Catherall, Arthur
Peters, Lisa Westberg 1951- 161
    Earlier sketches in SATA 74, 115
Peters, Patricia 1953- 84
Peters, Russell M. 1929- 78
Peters, S. H.
    See Porter, William Sydney
    and Proffitt, Nicholas
Petersen, David 1946- 109
    Earlier sketch in SATA 62

Petersen, Gwenn Boardman 1924- *61*
See Boardman, Gwenn R.
Petersen, P(eter) J(ames) 1941- *118*
Brief entry *43*
Earlier sketches in SATA *48, 83*
Petersen, Palle 1943- *85*
Petersham, Maud (Sylvia Fuller)
1890-1971 .... *17*
See also CLR *24*
Petersham, Miska 1888-1960 .... *17*
See also CLR *24*
Peterson, Cris 1952- *174*
Earlier sketches in SATA *84, 145*
Peterson, Dawn 1934- *86*
Peterson, Esther (Allen) 1934- *35*
Peterson, Hans 1922- *8*
Peterson, Harold L(eslie) 1922-1978 .... *8*
Peterson, Helen Stone 1910- *8*
Peterson, Jean Sunde 1941- *108*
Peterson, Jeanne Whitehouse 1939- *159*
See Whitehouse, Jeanne
Peterson, Kathleen B. 1951- *119*
Peterson, Lorraine 1940- *56*
Brief entry *44*
Peterson, Shelley 1952- *146*
Petie, Haris *10*
See Petty, Roberta
Petricic, Dusan 1946- *176*
Petrides, Heidrun 1944- *19*
Petrie, Catherine 1947- *52*
Brief entry *41*
Petrone, Valeria *186*
Petrosino, Tamara *193*
Petroski, Catherine (Ann Groom) 1939- *48*
Petrovich, Michael B(oro) 1922- *40*
Petrovskaya, Kyra
See Wayne, Kyra Petrovskaya
Petruccio, Steven James 1961- *67*
Petry, Ann (Lane) 1908-1997 .... *5*
Obituary *94*
See also CLR *12*
Pettit, Jayne 1932- *108*
Petty, J.T. 1977- *189*
Pevsner, Stella *131*
Earlier sketches in SATA *8, 77*
See also SAAS *14*
Peyo
See Culliford, Pierre
Peyton, K. M.
See CLR *3*
See also SAAS *17*
See Peyton, Kathleen Wendy (Herald)
Peyton, Kathleen Wendy (Herald) 1929- *157*
Earlier sketches in SATA *15, 62*
See Peyton, K. M.
Pfanner, (Anne) Louise 1955- *68*
Pfeffer, Susan Beth 1948- *180*
Earlier sketches in SATA *4, 83*
See also CLR *11*
See also SAAS *17*
Pfeffer, Wendy 1929- *142*
Earlier sketch in SATA *78*
Pfeiffer, Janet (B.) 1949- *96*
Pfister, Marcus *150*
Earlier sketch in SATA *83*
See also CLR *42*
Pfitsch, Patricia Curtis 1948- *148*
Pflieger, Pat 1955- *84*
Pham, LeUyen 1973- *175*
Phelan, Mary Kay 1914- *3*
Phelan, Matt 1970- *172*
Phelan, Terry Wolfe 1941- *56*
Phelps, Ethel Johnston 1914-1984 .... *35*
Philbrick, Rodman 1951- *163*
Earlier sketch in SATA *122*
See Philbrick, W. R.
Philbrick, W. R. *163*
See Philbrick, Rodman
Philbrick, W. Rodman
See Philbrick, Rodman
Philbrook, Clem(ent E.) 1917- *24*

Phillips, Aileen Paul
See Paul, Aileen
Phillips, Betty Lou
See Phillips, Elizabeth Louise
Phillips, Bob 1940- *95*
Phillips, Douglas A. 1949- *161*
Phillips, Elizabeth Louise *58*
Brief entry *48*
Phillips, Irv(ing W.) 1905-2000 .... *11*
Obituary *125*
Phillips, Jack
See Sandburg, Carl (August)
Phillips, Leon
See Gerson, Noel Bertram
Phillips, Loretta (Hosey) 1893-1987 .... *10*
Phillips, Louis 1942- *102*
Earlier sketch in SATA *8*
Phillips, Mary Geisler 1881-1964 .... *10*
Phillips, Michael
See Nolan, William F(rancis)
Phillips, (Woodward) Prentice 1894-1981 .... *10*
Phillips, Suzanne *192*
Phillpotts, Eden 1862-1960 .... *24*
Phin
See Thayer, Ernest Lawrence
Phipson, Joan
See CLR *5*
See also SAAS *3*
See Fitzhardinge, Joan Margaret
Phiz
See Browne, Hablot Knight
Phleger, Fred B. 1909-1993 .... *34*
Phleger, Marjorie Temple 1908(?)-1986 .... *1*
Obituary *47*
Piaget, Jean 1896-1980
Obituary *23*
Piatti, Celestino 1922- *16*
Picard, Barbara Leonie 1917- *89*
Earlier sketch in SATA *2*
See also SAAS *10*
Pichon, Liz *174*
Pickard, Charles 1932- *36*
Pickering, James Sayre 1897-1969 .... *36*
Obituary *28*
Pickering, Jimmy *195*
Pickering, Robert B. 1950- *93*
Pielichaty, Helena 1955- *142*
Pienkowski, Jan (Michal) 1936- *131*
Earlier sketches in SATA *6, 58*
See also CLR *6*
Pierce, Edith Gray 1893-1977 .... *45*
Pierce, Katherine
See St. John, Wylly Folk
Pierce, Meredith Ann 1958- *127*
Brief entry *48*
Earlier sketch in SATA *67*
See also CLR *20*
Pierce, Ruth (Ireland) 1936- *5*
Pierce, Sharon
See McCullough, Sharon Pierce
Pierce, Tamora 1954- *187*
Brief entry *49*
Earlier sketches in SATA *51, 96, 153*
Pierce, Terry *178*
Pierik, Robert 1921- *13*
Piers, Robert
See Anthony, Piers
Pig, Edward
See Gorey, Edward (St. John)
Pike, Bob
See Pike, Robert W(ilson)
Pike, Christopher 1954(?)- *156*
Earlier sketch in SATA *68*
See also CLR *29*
Pike, Deborah 1951- *89*
Pike, E(dgar) Royston 1896-1980 .... *22*
Obituary *56*
Pike, R. William 1956- *92*
Pike, Robert W(ilson) 1931- *102*
Pilarski, Laura 1926- *13*

Pilgrim, Anne
See Allan, Mabel Esther
Pilkey, Dav 1966- *166*
Earlier sketches in SATA *68, 115*
See also CLR *48*
Pilkey, David Murray, Jr.
See Pilkey, Dav
Pilkington, Francis Meredyth 1907- *4*
Pilkington, Roger (Windle) 1915-2003 .... *10*
Obituary *144*
Pin, Isabel 1975- *183*
Pinchot, David 1914(?)-1983
Obituary *34*
Pincus, Harriet 1938- *27*
Pinczes, Elinor J(ane) 1940- *81*
Pine, Nicholas 1951- *91*
Pine, Tillie S(chloss) 1896-1999 .... *13*
Pini, Richard (Alan) 1950- *89*
Pini, Wendy 1951- *89*
Pinkerton, Kathrene Sutherland (Gedney)
1887-1967
Obituary *26*
Pinkett, Jada
See Smith, Jada Pinkett
Pinkney, Andrea Davis 1963- *160*
Earlier sketch in SATA *113*
Pinkney, (Jerry) Brian 1961- *148*
Earlier sketch in SATA *74*
See also CLR *54*
Pinkney, Gloria Jean 1941- *85*
Pinkney, J. Brian
See Pinkney, (Jerry) Brian
Pinkney, Jerry 1939- *151*
Brief entry *32*
Earlier sketches in SATA *41, 71, 107*
See also CLR *43*
See also SAAS *12*
Pinkney, John *97*
Pinkney, Sandra L. *193*
Earlier sketch in SATA *128*
Pinkwater, D. Manus
See Pinkwater, Daniel Manus
Pinkwater, Daniel
See Pinkwater, Daniel Manus
Pinkwater, Daniel M.
See Pinkwater, Daniel Manus
Pinkwater, Daniel Manus 1941- *158*
Earlier sketches in SATA *8, 46, 76, 114*
See also CLR *4*
See also SAAS *3*
Pinkwater, Jill *188*
Pinkwater, Manus
See Pinkwater, Daniel Manus
Pinner, Joma
See Werner, Herma
Pioneer
See Yates, Raymond F(rancis)
Piowaty, Kim Kennelly 1957- *49*
Piper, Roger
See Fisher, John (Oswald Hamilton)
Pirner, Connie White 1955- *72*
Piro, Richard 1934- *7*
Pirot, Alison Lohans
See Lohans, Alison
Pirotta, Saviour *184*
Pirsig, Robert M(aynard) 1928- *39*
Pita
See Rendon, Maria
Pitcher, C.
See Pitcher, Caroline
Pitcher, Caroline 1948- *128*
Pitcher, Caroline Nell
See Pitcher, Caroline
Pitman, (Isaac) James 1901-1985
Obituary *46*
Pitre, Felix 1949- *84*
Pitrone, Jean Maddern 1920- *4*
Pittman, Helena Clare 1945- *71*
Pitz, Henry C(larence) 1895-1976 .... *4*
Obituary *24*
Pitzer, Susanna 1958- *181*

Piven, Hanoch 1963- *173*
Pixley, Marcella *194*
Pizer, Vernon 1918- *21*
Place, Marian T(empleton) 1910- *3*
Place, Robin (Mary) 1926- *71*
Plaidy, Jean
    See Hibbert, Eleanor Alice Burford
Plain, Belva 1919- *62*
Plaine, Alfred R. 1898(?)-1981
    Obituary *29*
Plath, Sylvia 1932-1963 .... *96*
Platt, Chris 1959- *185*
Platt, Kin 1911- *86*
    Earlier sketch in SATA *21*
    See also SAAS *17*
Platt, Randall 1948- *95*
Platt, Randall Beth
    See Platt, Randall
Platt, Richard 1953- *166*
    Earlier sketch in SATA *120*
Playfellow, Robin
    See Ellis, Edward S(ylvester)
Playsted, James
    See Wood, James Playsted
Plecas, Jennifer 1966- *149*
    Earlier sketch in SATA *84*
Plimpton, George 1927-2003 .... *10*
    Obituary *150*
Plimpton, George Ames
    See Plimpton, George
Plomer, William Charles Franklin
    1903-1973 .... *24*
Plotz, Helen Ratnoff 1913-2000 .... *38*
Plourde, Lynn 1955- *168*
    Earlier sketch in SATA *122*
Plowden, David 1932- *52*
Plowden, Martha Ward 1948- *98*
Plowhead, Ruth Gipson 1877-1967 .... *43*
Plowman, Stephanie 1922- *6*
Pluckrose, Henry (Arthur) 1931- *141*
    Earlier sketch in SATA *13*
Plum, J.
    See Wodehouse, P(elham) G(renville)
Plum, Jennifer
    See Kurland, Michael
Plumb, Charles P. 1900(?)-1982
    Obituary *29*
Plume, Ilse *170*
    Brief entry *43*
Plumme, Don E.
    See Katz, Bobbi
Plummer, Margaret 1911- *2*
Plum-Ucci, Carol *184*
Pochocki, Ethel (Frances) 1925- *76*
Podendorf, Illa (E.) 1903(?)-1983 .... *18*
    Obituary *35*
Podwal, Mark 1945- *160*
    Earlier sketch in SATA *101*
Podwal, Mark H.
    See Podwal, Mark
Poe, Edgar Allan 1809-1849 .... *23*
Poe, Ty (Christopher) 1975- *94*
Pogany, William Andrew 1882-1955 .... *44*
    See Pogany, Willy
Pogany, Willy
    Brief entry *30*
    See Pogany, William Andrew
Pohl, Frederik 1919- *24*
Pohlmann, Lillian (Grenfell) 1902-1997 .... *11*
Pohrt, Tom 1953- *195*
    Earlier sketches in SATA *67, 152*
Pointon, Robert
    See Rooke, Daphne (Marie)
Points, Larry G. 1945- *177*
    Earlier sketch in SATA *133*
Points, Larry Gene
    See Points, Larry G.
Pokeberry, P.J.
    See Mitchell, B.J.
POLA
    See Watson, Pauline

Polacco, Patricia 1944- *180*
    Earlier sketches in SATA *74, 123*
    See also CLR *40*
Polacco, Patricia Ann
    See Polacco, Patricia
Polak, Monique 1960- *178*
Polatnick, Florence T. 1923- *5*
Polder, Markus
    See Kruss, James
Polese, Carolyn 1947- *58*
Polese, James 1914- *87*
Polette, Nancy (Jane) 1930- *42*
Polhamus, Jean Burt 1928- *21*
Policoff, Stephen Phillip 1948- *77*
Polikoff, Barbara G. 1929- *162*
    Earlier sketch in SATA *77*
Polikoff, Barbara Garland
    See Polikoff, Barbara G.
Polisar, Barry Louis 1954- *134*
    Earlier sketch in SATA *77*
Politi, Leo 1908-1996 .... *47*
    Obituary *88*
    Earlier sketch in SATA *1*
    See also CLR *29*
Polking, Kirk 1925- *5*
Pollack, Jill S. 1963- *88*
Pollack, Merrill S. 1924-1988
    Obituary *55*
Polland, Barbara K(ay) 1939- *44*
Polland, Madeleine A(ngela Cahill) 1918- ... *68*
    Earlier sketch in SATA *6*
    See also SAAS *8*
Pollema-Cahill, Phyllis 1958- *123*
Pollock, Bruce 1945- *46*
Pollock, Mary
    See Blyton, Enid
Pollock, Penny 1935- *137*
    Brief entry *42*
    Earlier sketch in SATA *44*
Pollowitz, Melinda Kilborn 1944- *26*
Polner, Murray 1928- *64*
Polonsky, Arthur 1925- *34*
Polseno, Jo *17*
Pomaska, Anna 1946- *117*
Pomerantz, Charlotte 1930- *177*
    Earlier sketches in SATA *20, 80*
Pomeroy, Pete
    See Roth, Arthur J(oseph)
Pond, Alonzo W(illiam) 1894-1986 .... *5*
Pontiflet, Ted 1932- *32*
Poole, Gray Johnson 1906- *1*
Poole, Josephine *5*
    See also SAAS *2*
    See Helyar, Jane Penelope Josephine
Poole, (Jane Penelope) Josephine
    See Helyar, Jane Penelope Josephine
Poole, Lynn 1910-1969 .... *1*
Poole, Peggy 1925- *39*
Poortvliet, Rien 1932- *65*
    Brief entry *37*
Pope, Elizabeth Marie 1917-1992 .... *38*
    Brief entry *36*
Pope, Kevin 1958- *183*
Popescu, Christine
    See Pullein-Thompson, Christine
Poploff, Michelle 1956- *67*
Popp, K. Wendy *91*
Poppel, Hans 1942- *71*
Portal, Colette 1936- *6*
Porte, Barbara Ann 1943- *152*
    Brief entry *45*
    Earlier sketches in SATA *57, 93*
Porter, A(nthony) P(eyton) 1945- *68*
Porter, Connie (Rose) 1959(?)- *129*
    Earlier sketch in SATA *81*
Porter, Donald Clayton
    See Gerson, Noel Bertram
Porter, Eleanor H(odgman) 1868-1920
    See CLR *110*
Porter, Gene(va Grace) Stratton
    See Stratton-Porter, Gene(va Grace)

Porter, Janice Lee 1953- *108*
    Earlier sketch in SATA *68*
Porter, Katherine Anne 1890-1980 .... *39*
    Obituary *23*
Porter, Kathryn
    See Swinford, Betty (June Wells)
Porter, Pamela 1956- *193*
Porter, Sheena 1935- *24*
    See also SAAS *10*
Porter, Sue
    See Limb, Sue
Porter, Sue 1951- *76*
Porter, Tracey *191*
Porter, William Sydney 1862-1910
    See YABC *2*
    See Henry, O.
Portis, Antoinette *189*
Porto, Tony 1960- *153*
Portteus, Eleanora Marie Manthei (?)-1983
    Obituary *36*
Posada, Mia *187*
Posell, Elsa Z(eigerman) -1995 .... *3*
Posten, Margaret L(ois) 1915- *10*
Posthuma, Sieb 1960- *150*
Potok, Chaim 1929-2002 .... *106*
    Obituary *134*
    Earlier sketch in SATA *33*
    See also CLR *92*
Potok, Herbert Harold -2002
    See Potok, Chaim
Potok, Herman Harold
    See Potok, Chaim
Potter, Beatrix 1866-1943 .... *132*
    Earlier sketch in SATA *100*
    See also YABC *1*
    See also CLR *73*
Potter, Giselle *187*
    Earlier sketch in SATA *150*
Potter, Helen Beatrix
    See Potter, Beatrix
Potter, Margaret (Newman) 1926-1998 .... *21*
    Obituary *104*
    See Betteridge, Anne
Potter, Marian 1915- *9*
Potter, Miriam Clark 1886-1965 .... *3*
Poulin, Stephane 1961- *98*
    See also CLR *28*
Poulton, Kimberly 1957(?)- *136*
Pournelle, Jerry (Eugene) 1933- *161*
    Earlier sketches in SATA *26, 91*
Povelite, Kay 1955- *102*
Pow, Tom 1950- *163*
Powe-Allred, Alexandra
    See Allred, Alexandra Powe
Powell, A. M.
    See Morgan, Alfred P(owell)
Powell, Consie *174*
Powell, E. Sandy 1947- *72*
Powell, E.S.
    See Powell, E. Sandy
Powell, Pamela 1960- *78*
Powell, Patricia Hruby 1951- *136*
Powell, Randy 1956- *118*
Powell, Richard Stillman
    See Barbour, Ralph Henry
Powell, Robert (Stephenson Smyth) Baden
    See Baden-Powell, Robert (Stephenson
    Smyth)
Powell, Stephanie 1953- *93*
Power, Margaret (M.) 1945- *125*
    Earlier sketch in SATA *75*
Powers, Anne
    See Schwartz, Anne Powers
Powers, Bill 1931- *52*
    Brief entry *31*
Powers, Daniel 1959- *164*
Powers, Jessica Lynn
    See Powers, J.L.
Powers, J.L. 1974- *195*
Powers, Margaret
    See Heal, Edith

Powers, Tim 1952- 107
Powers, Timothy Thomas
    See Powers, Tim
Powledge, Fred 1935- 37
Poydar, Nancy 190
Poynter, Margaret 1927- 27
Prachaticka, Marketa
    See Kolibalova, Marketa
Prachatika, Marketa
    See Kolibalova, Marketa
Prager, Arthur 44
Prager, Ellen J. 1962- 136
Prange, Beckie 172
Prap, Lila 1955- 177
Praprotnik-Zupancic, Lilijana
    See Prap, Lila
Pratchett, Terence David John
    See Pratchett, Terry
Pratchett, Terry 1948- 185
    Earlier sketches in SATA 82, 139
    See also CLR 64
Prater, John 1947- 149
    Earlier sketches in SATA 72, 103
Prato, Rodica 184
Pratt, (Murray) Fletcher 1897-1956 102
Pratt, Kristin Joy 1976- 87
Pratt, Pierre 1962- 166
    Earlier sketch in SATA 95
Preiss, Byron 1953-2005 166
    Brief entry 42
    Earlier sketch in SATA 47
Preiss, Byron Cary
    See Preiss, Byron
Preller, James 1961- 88
Prelutsky, Jack 1940- 171
    Earlier sketches in SATA 22, 66, 118
    See also CLR 115
Prentice, Amy
    See Kaler, James Otis
Prescott, Casey
    See Morris, Chris(topher Crosby)
Presnall, Judith (Ann) Janda 1943- 96
Pressler, Mirjam 1940- 155
Preston, Douglas 1956- 113
Preston, Edna Mitchell 40
Preston, Lillian Elvira 1918- 47
Preussler, Otfried 1923- 24
Prevert, Jacques (Henri Marie) 1900-1977
    Obituary 30
Prevost, Guillaume 1964- 192
Price, Beverley Joan 1931- 98
Price, Charlie 187
Price, Christine (Hilda) 1928-1980 3
    Obituary 23
Price, Garrett 1896-1979
    Obituary 22
Price, Jennifer
    See Hoover, Helen (Drusilla Blackburn)
Price, Joan 1931- 124
Price, Jonathan (Reeve) 1941- 46
Price, Karen 1957- 125
Price, Kathy Z. 1957- 172
Price, Lucie Locke
    See Locke, Lucie
Price, Olive 1903-1991 8
Price, Susan 1955- 128
    Earlier sketches in SATA 25, 85
Price, Willard 1887-1983 48
    Brief entry 38
Price-Groff, Claire 127
Priceman, Marjorie 1958- 168
    Earlier sketches in SATA 81, 120
Prichard, Katharine Susannah 1883-1969 66
Prideaux, Tom 1908-1993 37
    Obituary 76
Priestley, Alice 1962- 95
Priestley, Lee (Shore) 1904-1999 27
Priestly, Doug 1954- 122
Priestly, Douglas Michael
    See Priestly, Doug
Prieto, Mariana Beeching 1912-1999 8

Priley, Margaret (Ann) Hubbard 1909-1992
    Obituary 130
Primavera, Elise 1954- 185
    Brief entry 48
    Earlier sketches in SATA 58, 109
Prime, Derek (James) 1931- 34
Prince, Alison (Mary) 1931- 86
    Earlier sketch in SATA 28
Prince, April Jones 1975- 180
Prince, J(ack) H(arvey) 1908- 17
Prince, Joshua 188
Prince, Maggie 102
Pringle, Eric 138
Pringle, Laurence 1935- 154
    Earlier sketches in SATA 4, 68, 104
    See also CLR 57
    See also SAAS 6
Pringle, Laurence Patrick
    See Pringle, Laurence
Prinz, Yvonne 1960- 175
Prior, Natalie Jane 1963- 106
Pritchett, Elaine H(illyer) 1920- 36
Pritchett, Laura 1971- 178
Pritchett, Laura Rose
    See Pritchett, Laura
Pritts, Kim Derek 1953- 83
Prochazkova, Iva 1953- 68
Proctor, Everitt
    See Montgomery, Rutherford George
Proeysen, Alf 1914-1970
    See CLR 24
    See Proysen, Alf
Professor Scribbler
    See Hollingsworth, Mary
Proimos, James 1955- 173
Prose, Francine 1947- 149
    Earlier sketch in SATA 101
Protopopescu, Orel 186
Protopopescu, Orel Odinov
    See Protopopescu, Orel
Provensen, Alice 1918- 147
    Earlier sketches in SATA 9, 70
    See also CLR 11
Provensen, Martin (Elias) 1916-1987 70
    Obituary 51
    Earlier sketch in SATA 9
    See also CLR 11
Provenzo, Eugene (F., Jr.) 1949- 142
    Earlier sketch in SATA 78
Provist, d'Alain 1906-1989
    See Diop, Birago (Ismael)
Provost, Gail Levine 1944- 65
Provost, Gary (Richard) 1944-1995 66
Proysen, Alf 67
    See Proeysen, Alf
Pruett, Candace (J.) 1968- 157
Pryor, Bonnie H. 1942- 69
Pryor, Boori (Monty) 1950- 112
Pryor, Helen Brenton 1897-1972 4
Pryor, Michael 1957- 153
Pucci, Albert John 1920- 44
Pudney, John (Sleigh) 1909-1977 24
Pugh, Ellen (Tiffany) 1920- 7
Pullein-Thompson, Christine 1925-2005 82
    Obituary 172
    Earlier sketch in SATA 3
Pullein-Thompson, Diana 3
    See Farr, Diana (Pullein-Thompson)
Pullein-Thompson, Josephine (Mary
    Wedderburn) 82
    Earlier sketch in SATA 3
Pullen, Zachary 189
Pullman, Philip 1946- 150
    Earlier sketches in SATA 65, 103
    See also CLR 84
    See also SAAS 17
Pullman, Philip Nicholas
    See Pullman, Philip
Pulver, Harry, Jr. 1960- 129
Pulver, Robin 1945- 133
    Earlier sketch in SATA 76

Puner, Helen W(alker) 1915-1989 37
    Obituary 63
Purdy, Carol 1943- 120
    Earlier sketch in SATA 66
Purdy, Susan G(old) 1939- 8
Purkiss, Diane 1961- 194
Purmell, Ann 1953- 147
Purnell, Idella 1901-1982 120
Purscell, Phyllis 1934- 7
Purtill, Richard L. 1931- 53
Pushker, Gloria 1927- 162
    Earlier sketch in SATA 75
Pushker, Gloria Teles
    See Pushker, Gloria
Pushkin, Aleksandr Sergeevich
    See Pushkin, Alexander (Sergeyevich)
Pushkin, Alexander (Sergeyevich)
    1799-1837 61
    See Pushkin, Aleksandr Sergeevich
Putnam, Alice 1916- 61
Putnam, Arthur Lee
    See Alger, Horatio, Jr.
Putnam, Peter B(rock) 1920-1998 30
    Obituary 106
Puttock, Simon 178
Puybaret, Eric 1976- 195
Pyle, Howard 1853-1911 100
    Earlier sketch in SATA 16
    See also CLR 117
Pyle, Katharine 1863-1938 66
Pyne, Mable Mandeville 1903-1969 9
Pyrnelle, Louise-Clarke 1850-1907 114

                        Q

Quackenbush, Robert M(ead) 1929- 133
    Autobiography Feature 133
    Earlier sketches in SATA 7, 70
    See also CLR 122
    See also SAAS 7
Qualey, Marsha 1953- 124
    Earlier sketch in SATA 79
Qualls, Sean 177
Quammen, David 1948- 7
Quark, Jason
    See Eldin, Peter
Quarles, Benjamin (Arthur) 1904-1996 12
Quatermass, Martin
    See Carpenter, John (Howard)
Quattlebaum, Mary 1958- 185
    Earlier sketches in SATA 88, 134
Quay, Emma 173
    Earlier sketch in SATA 119
Queen, Ellery
    See Deming, Richard
    and Dannay, Frederic
    and Davidson, Avram (James)
    and Fairman, Paul W.
    and Flora, Fletcher
    and Holding, James (Clark Carlisle, Jr.)
    and Hoch, Edward D.
    and Kane, Henry
    and Lee, Manfred B.
    and Marlowe, Stephen
    and Powell, (Oval) Talmage
    and Sheldon, Walter J(ames)
    and Sturgeon, Theodore (Hamilton)
    and Tracy, Don(ald Fiske)
    and Vance, Jack
Queen Latifah 1970- 185
Quennell, Marjorie Courtney 1884-1972 29
Quentin
    See Sheldon, David
Quentin, Brad
    See Bisson, Terry
Quest, (Edna) Olga W(ilbourne) Hall
    See Hall-Quest, (Edna) Olga W(ilbourne)
Quick, Annabelle 1922-1986 2

Quigg, Jane (Hulda) (?)-1986
  Obituary 49
Quill, Monica
  See McInerny, Ralph
Quin-Harkin, Janet 1941- 165
  Earlier sketches in SATA 18, 90, 119
Quin-Harkin, Janet Elizabeth
  See Quin-Harkin, Janet
Quinlan, Susan E. 1954- 88
Quinlan, Susan Elizabeth
  See Quinlan, Susan E.
Quinn, Elisabeth 1881-1962 22
Quinn, Pat 1947- 130
Quinn, Patrick 1950- 73
Quinn, Rob 1972- 138
Quinn, Theodora K.
  See Kroeber, Theodora (Kracaw)
Quinn, Vernon
  See Quinn, Elisabeth
Quintano, D.M.
  See Sheldon, Dyan
Quirk, Anne (E.) 1956- 99
Quixley, Jim 1931- 56
Quyth, Gabriel
  See Jennings, Gary

R

Ra, Carol F. 1939- 76
Raab, Evelyn 1951- 129
Rabb, Margo 1972- 188
Rabb, M.E.
  See Rabb, Margo
Rabe, Berniece (Louise) 1928- 148
  Autobiography Feature 148
  Earlier sketches in SATA 7, 77
  See also SAAS 10
Rabe, Olive H(anson) (?)-1968 13
Rabin, Staton 1958- 162
  Earlier sketch in SATA 84
Rabinowich, Ellen 1946- 29
Rabinowitz, Sandy 1954- 52
  Brief entry 39
Rachlin, Carol K(ing) 1919- 64
Rachlin, Harvey 1951- 47
Rachlin, Harvey Brant
  See Rachlin, Harvey
Rachlin, Nahid 64
Rachlis, Eugene (Jacob) 1920-1986
  Obituary 50
Rackham, Arthur 1867-1939 100
  Earlier sketch in SATA 15
  See also CLR 57
Raczka, Bob 1963- 191
  Earlier sketch in SATA 163
Radencich, Marguerite C. 1952-1998 79
Radford, Ruby L(orraine) 1891-1971 6
Radin, Ruth Yaffe 1938- 107
  Brief entry 52
  Earlier sketch in SATA 56
Radlauer, David 1952- 28
Radlauer, Edward 1921- 15
Radlauer, Ruth Shaw 1926- 98
  Earlier sketch in SATA 15
Radley, Gail 1951- 112
  Earlier sketch in SATA 25
Radunsky, Vladimir 177
Rae, Gwynedd 1892-1977 37
Raebeck, Lois 1921- 5
Rael, Elsa Okon 1927-
  See CLR 84
Raffi
  See Cavoukian, Raffi
Raftery, Gerald (Bransfield) 1905-1986 11
Ragan-Reid, Gale 1956- 90
Rahaman, Vashanti 1953- 98
Rahn, Joan Elma 1929- 27
Rai, Bali 1971- 152
Raible, Alton (Robert) 1918- 35

Raiff, Stan 1930- 11
Raines, Shirley C(arol) 1945- 128
Rainey, W. B.
  See Blassingame, Wyatt Rainey
Rake, Jody 1961- 157
Rallison, Janette 1966- 183
Ralston, Jan
  See Dunlop, Agnes M. R.
Rama, Sue 190
Ramal, Walter
  See de la Mare, Walter (John)
Ramanujan, A(ttipat) K(rishnaswami)
  1929-1993 86
Rame, David
  See Divine, Arthur Durham
Ramirez, Orlando L. 1972- 194
Ramstad, Ralph L. 1919- 115
Rana, Indi
  See Rana, Indira Higham
Rana, Indira Higham 1944- 82
Ranadive, Gail 1944- 10
Rand, Ann (Binkley) 30
Rand, Gloria 1925- 156
  Earlier sketch in SATA 101
Rand, Paul 1914-1996 6
Randall, Carrie
  See Ransom, Candice F.
Randall, David 1972- 167
Randall, Florence Engel 1917-1997 5
Randall, Janet
  See Young, Janet Randall
  and Young, Robert W(illiam)
Randall, Robert
  See Garrett, (Gordon) Randall (Phillip)
  and Silverberg, Robert
Randall, Ruth (Elaine) Painter 1892-1971 3
Randell, Beverley
  See Price, Beverley Joan
Randle, Kristen D. 1952- 92
  Autobiography Feature 119
  See also SAAS 24
Randle, Kristen Downey
  See Randle, Kristen D.
Randolph, Boynton M.D.
  See Ellis, Edward S(ylvester)
Randolph, Ellen
  See Rawn, Melanie
Randolph, Geoffrey
  See Ellis, Edward S(ylvester)
Randolph, J. H.
  See Ellis, Edward S(ylvester)
Randolph, Lieutenant J. H.
  See Ellis, Edward S(ylvester)
Rands, William Brighty 1823-1882 17
Raney, Ken 1953- 74
Rankin, Joan 1940- 148
  Earlier sketch in SATA 88
Rankin, Laura 1953(?)- 176
Ranney, Agnes V. 1916-1985 6
Ransom, Candice F. 1952- 183
  Brief entry 49
  Earlier sketches in SATA 52, 89, 135
Ransom, Jeanie Franz 1957- 187
Ransome, Arthur (Michell) 1884-1967 22
  See also CLR 8
Ransome, James E. 1961- 178
  Earlier sketches in SATA 76, 123
  See also CLR 86
Rant, Tol E.
  See Longyear, Barry B(rookes)
Raphael, Elaine 23
  See Bolognese, Elaine (Raphael Chionchio)
Raposo, Joseph Guilherme 1938-1989
  Obituary 61
Rapp, Adam 1968(?)- 148
Rappaport, Doreen 151
Rappaport, Eva 1924- 6
Rappoport, Ken 1935- 167
  Earlier sketch in SATA 89
Rarick, Carrie 1911-2002 41

Raschka, Chris 1959- 166
  Earlier sketches in SATA 80, 117
Raschka, Christopher
  See Raschka, Chris
Rascol, Sabina I. 159
Rash, Andy 162
Raskin, Edith Lefkowitz 1908-1987 9
Raskin, Ellen 1928-1984 139
  Earlier sketches in SATA 2, 38
  See also CLR 12
Raskin, Joseph 1897-1982 12
  Obituary 29
Rathjen, Carl Henry 1909-1984 11
Rathmann, Peggy 1953- 157
  Earlier sketch in SATA 94
  See Crosby, Margaret
Ratliff, Thomas M. 1948- 118
Ratner, Sue Lynn
  See Alexander, Sue
Rattigan, Jama Kim 1951- 99
Ratto, Linda Lee 1952- 79
Rattray, Simon
  See Trevor, Elleston
Ratz de Tagyos, Paul 1958- 76
Rau, Dana Meachen 1971- 167
  Earlier sketch in SATA 94
Rau, Margaret 1913- 168
  Earlier sketch in SATA 9
  See also CLR 8
Rauch, Mabel Thompson 1888-1972
  Obituary 26
Raucher, Herman 1928- 8
Raum, Elizabeth 1949- 155
Raven, Margot Theis 184
RavenWolf, Silver 1956- 155
Ravielli, Anthony 1916-1997 3
  Obituary 95
Ravilious, Robin 1944- 77
Rawding, F(rederick) W(illiam) 1930- 55
Rawlings, Marjorie Kinnan 1896-1953 100
  See also YABC 1
  See also CLR 63
Rawlinson, Julia 175
Rawls, (Woodrow) Wilson 1913-1984 22
  See also CLR 81
Rawlyk, George Alexander 1935- 64
Rawn, Melanie 1954- 98
Rawn, Melanie Robin
  See Rawn, Melanie
Rawson, Katherine 1955- 190
Ray, Carl 1943-1978 63
Ray, Deborah
  See Kogan Ray, Deborah
Ray, Delia 1963- 179
  Earlier sketch in SATA 70
Ray, Irene
  See Sutton, Margaret Beebe
Ray, Jane 1960- 152
  Earlier sketch in SATA 72
Ray, JoAnne 1935- 9
Ray, Mary (Eva Pedder) 1932- 127
  Earlier sketch in SATA 2
Ray, Mary Lyn 1946- 154
  Earlier sketch in SATA 90
Rayban, Chloe 1944- 167
Rayevsky, Robert 1955- 190
  Earlier sketch in SATA 81
Raymond, James Crossley 1917-1981
  Obituary 29
Raymond, Robert
  See Alter, Robert Edmond
Rayner, Hugh 151
Rayner, Mary 1933- 87
  Earlier sketch in SATA 22
  See also CLR 41
Rayner, Shoo
  See Rayner, Hugh
Rayner, William 1929- 55
  Brief entry 36
Raynor, Dorka 28
Rayson, Steven 1932- 30

Razzell, Arthur (George) 1925- *11*
Razzell, Mary (Catherine) 1930- *102*
Razzi, James 1931- *10*
Read, Elfreida 1920- *2*
Read, Nicholas 1956- *146*
Read, Piers Paul 1941- *21*
Reade, Deborah 1949- *69*
Reader, Dennis 1929- *71*
Reading, Richard P(atrick) 1962- *161*
Readman, Jo 1958- *89*
Ready, Kirk L(ewis) 1943- *39*
Reaney, James 1926-2008 .... *43*
Reaney, James Crerar
    See Reaney, James
Reardon, Joyce
    See Pearson, Ridley
Reaver, Chap 1935-1993 .... *69*
    Obituary *77*
Reaver, Herbert R.
    See Reaver, Chap
Reaves, J. Michael
    See Reaves, (James) Michael
Reaves, (James) Michael 1950- *99*
Reber, Deborah *189*
Recorvits, Helen *191*
Redding, Robert Hull 1919- *2*
Redekopp, Elsa *61*
Redlich, Ben 1977- *181*
Redsand, Anna 1948- *184*
Redway, Ralph
    See Hamilton, Charles (Harold St. John)
Redway, Ridley
    See Hamilton, Charles (Harold St. John)
Reece, Colleen L. 1935- *116*
Reece, Gabrielle 1970- *108*
Reed, Betty Jane 1921- *4*
Reed, E.
    See Evans, Mari
Reed, Gwendolyn E(lizabeth) 1932- *21*
Reed, Kit 1932- *184*
    Autobiography Feature *184*
    Earlier sketches in SATA *34, 116*
Reed, Lynn Rowe *171*
Reed, Neil 1961- *99*
Reed, Talbot Baines 1852-1893
    See CLR *76*
Reed, Thomas (James) 1947- *34*
Reed, William Maxwell 1871-1962 .... *15*
Reeder, Carolyn 1937- *97*
    Earlier sketch in SATA *66*
    See also CLR *69*
Reeder, Colin (Dawson) 1938- *74*
Reeder, Colonel Red
    See Reeder, Russell P(otter), Jr.
Reeder, Russell P(otter), Jr. 1902-1998 .... *4*
    Obituary *101*
Reeder, Stephanie Owen 1951- *102*
Reed-Jones, Carol 1955- *112*
Reef, Catherine 1951- *189*
    Earlier sketches in SATA *73, 128*
Reekie, Jocelyn (Margaret) 1947- *145*
Reeman, Douglas Edward 1924- *63*
    Brief entry *28*
Rees, Celia 1949- *124*
Rees, David (Bartlett) 1936-1993 .... *69*
    Obituary *76*
    Earlier sketch in SATA *36*
    See also SAAS *5*
Rees, Douglas 1947- *169*
Rees, Ennis (Samuel, Jr.) 1925- *3*
Rees, (George) Leslie (Clarence)
    1905-2000 .... *105*
    Obituary *135*
Reese, Bob
    See Reese, Robert A.
Reese, Della 1931(?)- *114*
Reese, Lyn *64*
    See Reese, Carolyn Johnson
Reese, Robert A. 1938- *60*
    Brief entry *53*
Reese, (John) Terence 1913-1996 .... *59*

Reeve, Joel
    See Cox, William R(obert)
Reeve, Kirk 1934- *117*
Reeve, Philip *170*
Reeve, Rosie *188*
Reeve, Rosie *186*
Reeves, Faye Couch 1953- *76*
Reeves, James *15*
    See Reeves, John Morris
Reeves, Jeni 1947- *111*
Reeves, John Morris 1909-1978 .... *87*
    See Reeves, James
Reeves, Joyce 1911- *17*
Reeves, Lawrence F. 1926- *29*
Reeves, Ruth Ellen
    See Ranney, Agnes V.
Regan, Dian Curtis 1950- *149*
    Autobiography Feature *149*
    Earlier sketches in SATA *75, 133*
Regehr, Lydia 1903-1991 .... *37*
Reger, James P. 1952- *106*
Reggiani, Renee 1925- *18*
Rehm, Karl M. 1935- *72*
Reich, Ali
    See Katz, Bobbi
Reich, Susanna 1954- *113*
Reiche, Dietlof 1941- *159*
Reichert, Edwin C(lark) 1909-1988
    Obituary *57*
Reichert, Mickey Zucker
    See Reichert, Miriam Zucker
Reichert, Miriam Zucker 1962- *85*
Reichert, Renee *172*
Reichhold, Jane(t E.) 1937- *147*
Reid, Alastair 1926- *46*
Reid, Barbara 1922- *21*
Reid, Barbara (Jane) 1957- *93*
    See also CLR *64*
Reid, Desmond
    See Moorcock, Michael
    and McNeilly, Wilfred (Glassford)
Reid, Eugenie Chazal 1924- *12*
Reid, John Calvin *21*
Reid, (Thomas) Mayne 1818-1883 .... *24*
Reid, Meta Mayne 1905-1991 .... *58*
    Brief entry *36*
Reid, Robin (Nicole) 1969- *145*
Reid Banks, Lynne 1929- *165*
    Earlier sketches in SATA *22, 75, 111*
    See also CLR *86*
    See Banks, Lynne Reid
Reider, Katja 1960- *126*
Reid Jenkins, Debra 1955- *87*
Reiff, Stephanie Ann 1948- *47*
    Brief entry *28*
Reig, June 1933- *30*
Reigot, Betty Polisar 1924- *55*
    Brief entry *41*
Reilly, Joan *195*
Reim, Melanie (K.) 1956- *104*
Reinach, Jacquelyn (Krasne) 1930-2000 .... *28*
Reiner, Carl 1922- *151*
Reiner, William B(uck) 1910-1976 .... *46*
    Obituary *30*
Reinfeld, Fred 1910-1964 .... *3*
Reinhardt, Dana 1971- *175*
Reinhart, Matthew 1971- *161*
Reiniger, Lotte 1899-1981 .... *40*
    Obituary *33*
Reinsma, Carol 1949- *91*
Reinstedt, Randall A. 1935- *101*
Reinstedt, Randy
    See Reinstedt, Randall A.
Reisberg, Mira 1955- *82*
Reisberg, Veg
    See Reisberg, Mira
Reiser, Lynn 1944- *180*
    Earlier sketches in SATA *81, 138*
Reiser, Lynn Whisnant
    See Reiser, Lynn
Reisgies, Teresa (Maria) 1966- *74*

Reiss, Johanna (de Leeuw) 1929(?)- *18*
    See also CLR *19*
Reiss, John J. *23*
Reiss, Kathryn 1957- *144*
    Earlier sketch in SATA *76*
Reit, Seymour Victory 1918-2001 .... *21*
    Obituary *133*
Reit, Sy
    See Reit, Seymour Victory
Relf, Patricia 1954- *134*
    Earlier sketch in SATA *71*
Remi, Georges 1907-1983 .... *13*
    Obituary *32*
    See Herge
Remington, Frederic S(ackrider)
    1861-1909 .... *41*
Remkiewicz, Frank 1939- *152*
    Earlier sketch in SATA *77*
Remy, Georges
    See Remi, Georges
Renaud, Bernadette 1945- *66*
Renault, Mary
    See Challans, Mary
Rendell, Joan *28*
Rendina, Laura (Jones) Cooper 1902- *10*
Rendon, Marcie R. 1952- *97*
Rendon, Maria 1965- *116*
Renee, Janina 1956- *140*
Renfro, Ed 1924- *79*
Renick, Marion (Lewis) 1905-1983 .... *1*
Renken, Aleda 1907- *27*
Renlie, Frank H. 1936- *11*
Rennert, Richard Scott 1956- *67*
Rennison, Louise 1951- *149*
Reno, Dawn E(laine) 1953- *130*
Rensie, Willis
    See Eisner, Will
Renton, Cam
    See Armstrong, Richard
Renvoize, Jean *5*
Resau, Laura 1973- *190*
Resciniti, Angelo G. 1952- *75*
Resnick, Michael David
    See Resnick, Mike
Resnick, Mike 1942- *159*
    Earlier sketches in SATA *38, 106*
Resnick, Seymour 1920- *23*
Retla, Robert
    See Alter, Robert Edmond
Reuter, Bjarne (B.) 1950- *142*
    Earlier sketch in SATA *68*
Reuter, Carol (Joan) 1931- *2*
Revena
    See Wright, Betty Ren
Revsbech, Vicki
    See Liestman, Vicki
Rex, Adam *186*
Rex, Michael *191*
Rey, H(ans) A(ugusto) 1898-1977 .... *100*
    Earlier sketches in SATA *1, 26, 69*
    See also CLR *93*
Rey, Margret (Elisabeth) 1906-1996 .... *86*
    Obituary *93*
    Earlier sketch in SATA *26*
    See also CLR *93*
Reyher, Becky
    See Reyher, Rebecca Hourwich
Reyher, Rebecca Hourwich 1897-1987 .... *18*
    Obituary *50*
Reynold, Ann
    See Bernardo, Anilu
Reynolds, Adrian 1963- *192*
Reynolds, C. Buck 1957- *107*
Reynolds, Dickson
    See Reynolds, Helen Mary Greenwood Campbell
Reynolds, Helen Mary Greenwood Campbell
    1884-1969
    Obituary *26*
Reynolds, Jan 1956- *180*

Reynolds, John
    See Whitlock, Ralph
Reynolds, Madge
    See Whitlock, Ralph
Reynolds, Malvina 1900-1978 .... *44*
    Obituary *24*
Reynolds, Marilyn 1935- *121*
    See also SAAS *23*
Reynolds, Marilyn M.
    See Reynolds, Marilyn
Reynolds, Marilynn 1940- *141*
    Earlier sketch in SATA *80*
Reynolds, Pamela 1923- *34*
Reynolds, Peter H. 1961- *128*
Reynolds, Peter J. 1961- *179*
Reynolds, Susan *179*
Rhine, Richard
    See Silverstein, Alvin
    and Silverstein, Virginia B(arbara Opshelor)
Rhoades, Diane 1952- *90*
Rhodes, Bennie (Loran) 1927- *35*
Rhodes, Donna McKee 1962- *87*
Rhodes, Frank Harold Trevor 1926- *37*
Rhue, Morton
    See Strasser, Todd
Rhyne, Nancy 1926- *66*
Rhynes, Martha E. 1939- *141*
Ribbons, Ian 1924- *37*
    Brief entry *30*
    See also SAAS *3*
Ricciuti, Edward R(aphael) 1938- *10*
Rice, Alice (Caldwell) Hegan 1870-1942 ..... *63*
Rice, Bebe Faas 1932- *89*
Rice, Charles D(uane) 1910-1971
    Obituary *27*
Rice, Dale R. 1948- *42*
Rice, Dale Richard
    See Rice, Dale R.
Rice, Dick
    See Rice, R. Hugh
Rice, Earle (Wilmont), Jr. 1928- *151*
    Earlier sketch in SATA *92*
Rice, Edward 1918-2001 .... *47*
    Brief entry *42*
Rice, Elizabeth 1913-1976 .... *2*
Rice, Eve 1951- *91*
    Earlier sketch in SATA *34*
Rice, Eve Hart
    See Rice, Eve
Rice, Inez 1907- *13*
Rice, James 1934- *93*
    Earlier sketch in SATA *22*
Rice, John F. 1958- *82*
Rice, R. Hugh 1929- *115*
Rice, Richard H.
    See Rice, R. Hugh
Rich, Barbara
    See Graves, Robert
Rich, Elaine Sommers 1926- *6*
Rich, Josephine Bouchard 1912- *10*
Rich, Louise Dickinson 1903-1991 .... *54*
    Obituary *67*
Richard, Adrienne 1921- *5*
    See also SAAS *9*
Richard, James Robert
    See Bowen, Robert Sydney
Richards, Chuck 1957- *170*
Richards, Frank
    See Hamilton, Charles (Harold St. John)
Richards, Hilda
    See Hamilton, Charles (Harold St. John)
Richards, Jackie 1925- *102*
Richards, Jean 1940- *135*
Richards, Justin *169*
Richards, Kay
    See Baker, Susan (Catherine)
Richards, Laura E(lizabeth Howe) 1850-1943
    See YABC *1*
    See also CLR *54*
Richards, Leigh
    See King, Laurie R.

Richards, Marlee
    See Brill, Marlene Targ
Richards, Norman 1932- *48*
Richards, R(onald) C(harles) W(illiam)
    1923- *59*
    Brief entry *43*
Richards, Walter Alden (Jr.) 1907-1988
    Obituary *56*
Richardson, Andrew (William) 1986- *120*
Richardson, Carol 1932- *58*
Richardson, Frank Howard 1882-1970
    Obituary *27*
Richardson, Grace Lee
    See Dickson, Naida
Richardson, Jean (Mary) *59*
Richardson, Judith Benet 1941- *77*
Richardson, Nigel 1957- *187*
Richardson, Robert S(hirley) 1902-1981 .... *8*
Richardson, Sandy 1949- *116*
Richardson, V.A. *189*
Richardson, Willis 1889-1977 .... *60*
Richelson, Geraldine 1922- *29*
Richemont, Enid 1940- *82*
Richler, Mordecai 1931-2001 .... *98*
    Brief entry *27*
    Earlier sketch in SATA *44*
    See also CLR *17*
Richman, Sophia 1941- *142*
Rich-McCoy, Lois
    See McCoy, Lois (Rich)
Richmond, Robin 1951- *75*
Richoux, Pat(ricia) 1927- *7*
Richter, Alice 1941- *30*
Richter, Conrad (Michael) 1890-1968 .... *3*
Richter, Hans Peter 1925-1993 .... *6*
    See also CLR *21*
    See also SAAS *11*
Richter, Jutta 1955- *184*
Rickard, Graham 1949- *71*
Rico, Don(ato) 1917-1985
    Obituary *43*
Riddell, Chris 1962- *166*
    Earlier sketch in SATA *114*
Riddell, Christopher Barry
    See Riddell, Chris
Riddell, Edwina 1955- *82*
Ridden, Brian (John) 1934- *123*
Riddle, Tohby 1965- *151*
    Earlier sketch in SATA *74*
Riddles, Libby 1956- *140*
Rideout, Sandy *194*
Ridge, Antonia (Florence) (?)-1981 .... *7*
    Obituary *27*
Ridge, Martin 1923-2003 .... *43*
Ridley, Philip *171*
    Earlier sketch in SATA *88*
Ridlon, Marci *22*
    See Balterman, Marcia Ridlon
Riedman, Sarah R(egal) 1902-1995 .... *1*
Riehecky, Janet 1953- *164*
Ries, Lori *185*
Riesenberg, Felix, Jr. 1913-1962 .... *23*
Rieu, E(mile) V(ictor) 1887-1972 .... *46*
    Obituary *26*
Riffenburgh, Beau 1955- *175*
Rigg, Sharon
    See Creech, Sharon
Riggio, Anita 1952- *148*
    Earlier sketch in SATA *73*
Riggs, Shannon *190*
Riggs, Sidney Noyes 1892-1975
    Obituary *28*
Riggs, Stephanie 1964- *138*
Riglietti, Serena 1969- *189*
Rigney, James Oliver, Jr.
    See Jordan, Robert
Rikhoff, Jean 1928- *9*
Rikki
    See Ducornet, Erica
Riley, James A. 1939- *97*
Riley, James Whitcomb 1849-1916 .... *17*

Riley, Jocelyn 1949- *60*
    Brief entry *50*
Riley, Jocelyn Carol
    See Riley, Jocelyn
Riley, Linda Capus 1950- *85*
Riley, Martin 1948- *81*
Rimbauer, Steven
    See Pearson, Ridley
Rimes, (Margaret) LeAnn 1982- *154*
Rinaldi, Ann 1934- *161*
    Brief entry *50*
    Earlier sketches in SATA *51, 78, 117*
    See also CLR *46*
Rinard, Judith E(llen) 1947- *140*
    Earlier sketch in SATA *44*
Rinder, Lenore 1949- *92*
Ring, Elizabeth 1920- *79*
Ringdahl, Mark
    See Longyear, Barry B(rookes)
Ringgold, Faith 1930- *187*
    Earlier sketches in SATA *71, 114*
    See also CLR *30*
Ringi, Kjell (Arne Soerensen) 1939- *12*
Rinkoff, Barbara Jean (Rich) 1923-1975 .... *4*
    Obituary *27*
Rinn, Miriam 1946- *127*
Riordan, James 1936- *95*
Riordan, Rick *174*
Rios, Tere
    See Versace, Marie Teresa Rios
Ripken, Cal, Jr. 1960- *114*
Ripken, Calvin Edward, Jr.
    See Ripken, Cal, Jr.
Ripley, Catherine 1957- *82*
Ripley, Elizabeth Blake 1906-1969 .... *5*
Ripper, Charles L(ewis) 1929- *3*
Ripper, Chuck
    See Ripper, Charles L(ewis)
Riq
    See Atwater, Richard (Tupper)
Rish, David 1955- *110*
Riskind, Mary 1944- *60*
Rissinger, Matt 1956- *93*
Rissman, Art
    See Sussman, Susan
Rissman, Susan
    See Sussman, Susan
Ritchie, Barbara Gibbons *14*
Ritter, Felix
    See Kruss, James
Ritter, John H. 1951- *137*
    Earlier sketch in SATA *129*
Ritter, Lawrence S(tanley) 1922-2004 .... *58*
    Obituary *152*
Ritthaler, Shelly 1955- *91*
Ritts, Paul 1920(?)-1980
    Obituary *25*
Ritz, Karen 1957- *80*
Rivera, Geraldo (Miguel) 1943- *54*
    Brief entry *28*
Rivers, Elfrida
    See Bradley, Marion Zimmer
Rivers, Karen 1970- *131*
Riverside, John
    See Heinlein, Robert A.
Rivkin, Ann 1920- *41*
Rivoli, Mario 1943- *10*
Roach, Marilynne K. 1946- *9*
Roach, Marilynne Kathleen
    See Roach, Marilynne K.
Roach, Portia
    See Takakjian, Portia
Robb, Don 1937- *194*
Robb, Laura 1937- *95*
Robbrecht, Thierry 1960- *182*
Robbins, Frank 1917-1994(?) *42*
    Brief entry *32*
Robbins, Ken 1945- *147*
    Brief entry *53*
    Earlier sketch in SATA *94*

Robbins, Raleigh
    See Hamilton, Charles (Harold St. John)
Robbins, Ruth 1917(?)- *14*
Robbins, Tony
    See Pashko, Stanley
Robbins, Wayne
    See Cox, William R(obert)
Robel, S. L.
    See Fraustino, Lisa Rowe
Roberson, Jennifer 1953- *72*
Roberson, John R(oyster) 1930- *53*
Robert, Adrian
    See St. John, Nicole
Roberts, Bethany *133*
Roberts, Bruce (Stuart) 1930- *47*
    Brief entry *39*
Roberts, Charles G(eorge) D(ouglas)
    1860-1943 .... *88*
    Brief entry *29*
    See also CLR *33*
Roberts, David *191*
    See Cox, John Roberts
Roberts, Diane 1937- *184*
Roberts, Elizabeth 1944- *80*
Roberts, Elizabeth Madox 1886-1941 .... *33*
    Brief entry *27*
    See also CLR *100*
Roberts, Jim
    See Bates, Barbara S(nedeker)
Roberts, John G(aither) 1913-1993 .... *27*
Roberts, Judy I. 1957- *93*
Roberts, Katherine 1962- *152*
Roberts, M. L.
    See Mattern, Joanne
Roberts, Nancy Correll 1924- *52*
    Brief entry *28*
Roberts, Priscilla 1955- *184*
Roberts, Terence
    See Sanderson, Ivan T(erence)
Roberts, Willo Davis 1928-2004 .... *150*
    Autobiography Feature *150*
    Obituary *160*
    Earlier sketches in SATA *21, 70, 133*
    See also CLR *95*
    See also SAAS *8*
Robertson, Barbara (Anne) 1931- *12*
Robertson, Don 1929-1999 .... *8*
    Obituary *113*
Robertson, Dorothy Lewis 1912- *12*
Robertson, Ellis
    See Ellison, Harlan
    and Silverberg, Robert
Robertson, James I., Jr. 1930- *182*
Robertson, James Irvin
    See Robertson, James I., Jr.
Robertson, Janet (E.) 1935- *68*
Robertson, Jennifer Sinclair 1942-1998 .... *12*
Robertson, Jenny
    See Robertson, Jennifer Sinclair
Robertson, Keith (Carlton) 1914-1991 .... *85*
    Obituary *69*
    Earlier sketch in SATA *1*
    See also SAAS *15*
Robertson, Stephen
    See Walker, Robert W(ayne)
Robertus, Polly M. 1948- *73*
Robeson, Kenneth
    See Dent, Lester
    and Goulart, Ron(ald Joseph)
Robeson, Kenneth
    See Johnson, (Walter) Ryerson
Robinet, Harriette Gillem 1931- *104*
    Earlier sketch in SATA *27*
    See also CLR *64*
Robins, Deri 1958- *166*
    Earlier sketch in SATA *117*
Robins, Patricia
    See Clark, Patricia Denise
Robins, Rollo, Jr.
    See Ellis, Edward S(ylvester)

Robins, Seelin
    See Ellis, Edward S(ylvester)
Robinson, Adjai 1932- *8*
Robinson, Aminah Brenda Lynn 1940- *159*
    Earlier sketch in SATA *77*
Robinson, Barbara (Webb) 1927- *84*
    Earlier sketch in SATA *8*
Robinson, C(harles) A(lexander), Jr.
    1900-1965 .... *36*
Robinson, Charles 1870-1937 .... *17*
Robinson, Charles 1931- *6*
Robinson, Dorothy W. 1929- *54*
Robinson, Eve
    See Tanselle, Eve
Robinson, Glen 1953- *92*
Robinson, Glendal P.
    See Robinson, Glen
Robinson, Jan M. 1933- *6*
Robinson, Jean O. 1934- *7*
Robinson, Joan (Mary) G(ale Thomas)
    1910-1988 .... *7*
Robinson, Kim Stanley 1952- *109*
Robinson, Lee 1948- *110*
Robinson, Lloyd
    See Silverberg, Robert
Robinson, Lynda S(uzanne) 1951- *107*
Robinson, Marileta 1942- *32*
Robinson, Maudie Millian Oller 1914- *11*
Robinson, Maurice R(ichard) 1895-1982
    Obituary *29*
Robinson, Nancy K(onheim) 1942-1994 ...... *91*
    Brief entry *31*
    Obituary *79*
    Earlier sketch in SATA *32*
Robinson, Ray(mond Kenneth) 1920- *23*
Robinson, Shari
    See McGuire, Leslie (Sarah)
Robinson, Sharon 1950- *162*
Robinson, Spider 1948- *118*
Robinson, Sue
    See Robinson, Susan Maria
Robinson, Susan Maria 1955- *105*
Robinson, Suzanne
    See Robinson, Lynda S(uzanne)
Robinson, T(homas) H(eath) 1869-1950 ...... *17*
Robinson, (Wanda) Veronica 1926- *30*
Robinson, W(illiam) Heath 1872-1944 .... *17*
Robison, Bonnie 1924- *12*
Robison, Nancy L(ouise) 1934- *32*
Robles, Harold E. 1948- *87*
Robottom, John 1934- *7*
Robson, Eric 1939- *82*
Rocco, John 1967- *188*
Roche, A. K.
    See Abisch, Roslyn Kroop
    and Kaplan, Boche
Roche, Denis (Mary) 1967- *99*
Roche, Luane 1937- *170*
Roche, P(atricia) K. 1935- *57*
    Brief entry *34*
Roche, Terry
    See Poole, Peggy
Rochman, Hazel 1938- *105*
Rock, Lois
    See Joslin, Mary
Rock, Maxine 1940- *108*
Rocker, Fermin 1907- *40*
Rocklin, Joanne 1946- *134*
    Earlier sketch in SATA *86*
Rockwell, Anne F. 1934- *194*
    Earlier sketches in SATA *33, 71, 114, 162*
    See also SAAS *19*
Rockwell, Anne Foote
    See Rockwell, Anne F.
Rockwell, Bart
    See Pellowski, Michael (Joseph)
Rockwell, Harlow 1910-1988 .... *33*
    Obituary *56*
Rockwell, Lizzy 1961- *185*
Rockwell, Norman (Percevel) 1894-1978 .... *23*

Rockwell, Thomas 1933- *70*
    Earlier sketch in SATA *7*
    See also CLR *6*
Rockwood, Joyce 1947- *39*
Rockwood, Roy *67*
    Earlier sketch in SATA *1*
    See McFarlane, Leslie (Charles)
    and Stratemeyer, Edward L.
Rodanas, Kristina 1952- *155*
Rodari, Gianni 1920-1980
    See CLR *24*
Rodd, Kathleen Tennant *57*
    Obituary *55*
    See Rodd, Kylie Tennant
Rodda, Emily 1948- *146*
    Earlier sketch in SATA *97*
    See also CLR *32*
Roddenberry, Eugene Wesley 1921-1991 ..... *45*
    Obituary *69*
    See Roddenberry, Gene
Roddenberry, Gene
    Obituary *69*
    See Roddenberry, Eugene Wesley
Roddie, Shen *153*
Roddy, Lee 1921- *57*
Rodenas, Paula *73*
Rodgers, Frank 1944- *69*
Rodgers, Mary 1931- *130*
    Earlier sketch in SATA *8*
    See also CLR *20*
Rodman, Emerson
    See Ellis, Edward S(ylvester)
Rodman, Eric
    See Silverberg, Robert
Rodman, Maia
    See Wojciechowska, Maia (Teresa)
Rodman, Mary Ann *185*
Rodman, (Cary) Selden 1909-2002 .... *9*
Rodowsky, Colby 1932- *164*
    Earlier sketches in SATA *21, 77, 120*
    See also SAAS *22*
Rodowsky, Colby F.
    See Rodowsky, Colby
Rodriguez, Alejo 1941- *83*
Rodriguez, Alex 1975- *189*
Rodriguez, Christina 1981- *177*
Rodriguez, Luis J. 1954- *125*
Rodriguez, Rachel *180*
Rodriguez, Rachel Victoria
    See Rodriguez, Rachel
Roeder, Virginia Marsh 1926- *98*
Roehrig, Catharine H. 1949- *67*
Roennfeldt, Robert 1953- *78*
Roessel-Waugh, C. C.
    See Waugh, Carol-Lynn Rossel
    and Waugh, Charles G(ordon)
Roets, Lois F. 1937- *91*
Roever, J(oan) M(arilyn) 1935- *26*
Rofes, Eric 1954-2006 .... *52*
Rofes, Eric Edward 1954-2006
    See Rofes, Eric
Roffey, Maureen 1936- *33*
Rogak, Lisa 1962- *80*
Rogak, Lisa Angowski
    See Rogak, Lisa
Rogasky, Barbara 1933- *144*
    Earlier sketch in SATA *86*
Rogers, (Thomas) Alan (Stinchcombe)
    1937- *81*
    Earlier sketch in SATA *2*
Rogers, Bettye 1858-1919 .... *103*
Rogers, Cindy 1950- *89*
Rogers, Emma 1951- *74*
Rogers, Frances 1888-1974 .... *10*
Rogers, Fred McFeely 1928-2003 .... *33*
    Obituary *138*
Rogers, Hal
    See Sirimarco, Elizabeth
Rogers, Jean 1919- *55*
    Brief entry *47*

Rogers, Matilda 1894-1976 .... *5*
   Obituary *34*
Rogers, Pamela 1927- *9*
Rogers, Paul 1950- *98*
   Earlier sketch in SATA *54*
Rogers, Robert
   See Hamilton, Charles (Harold St. John)
Rogers, Sherry *193*
Rogers, W(illiam) G(arland) 1896-1978 .... *23*
Rohan, M. S.
   See Rohan, Michael Scott
Rohan, Michael Scott 1951- *98*
Rohan, Mike Scott
   See Rohan, Michael Scott
Rohmann, Eric 1957- *171*
   See also CLR *100*
Rohmer, Harriet 1938- *56*
Rohrer, Doug 1962- *89*
Rojan
   See Rojankovsky, Feodor (Stepanovich)
Rojankovsky, Feodor (Stepanovich)
   1891-1970 .... *21*
Rojany, Lisa *94*
Rokeby-Thomas, Anna E(lma) 1911- *15*
Roland, Albert 1925-2002 .... *11*
Roland, Mary
   See Lewis, Mary (Christianna)
Roleff, Tamara L. 1959- *143*
Rolerson, Darrell A(llen) 1946- *8*
Roll, Winifred 1909-1998 .... *6*
Rollins, Charlemae Hill 1897-1979 .... *3*
   Obituary *26*
Rollock, Barbara T(herese) 1924- *64*
Romack, Janice Reed
   See LeNoir, Janice
Romain, Trevor *134*
Romanenko, Vitaliy 1962- *101*
Romano, Louis G. 1921- *35*
Romano, Melora A. 1966- *118*
Romano, Ray 1957- *170*
Romano, Raymond
   See Romano, Ray
Romijn, Johanna Maria Kooyker
   See Kooyker-Romijn, Johanna Maria
Romyn, Johanna Maria Kooyker
   See Kooyker-Romijn, Johanna Maria
Rong, Yu 1970- *174*
Rongen, Bjoern 1906- *10*
Rongen, Bjorn
   See Rongen, Bjoern
Ronson, Mark
   See Alexander, Marc
Rood, Ronald (N.) 1920- *12*
Rook, Sebastian
   See Jeapes, Ben
Rooke, Daphne (Marie) 1914- *12*
Roop, Connie 1951- *167*
   Brief entry *49*
   Earlier sketches in SATA *54, 116*
Roop, Constance Betzer
   See Roop, Connie
Roop, Peter 1951- *167*
   Brief entry *49*
   Earlier sketches in SATA *54, 116*
Roop, Peter G.
   See Roop, Peter
Roop, Peter Geiger
   See Roop, Peter
Roos, Stephen 1945- *128*
   Brief entry *41*
   Earlier sketches in SATA *47, 77*
Roose-Evans, James 1927- *65*
Roosevelt, (Anna) Eleanor 1884-1962 .... *50*
Root, Barry *182*
Root, Betty *84*
Root, Kimberly Bulcken *192*
Root, Phyllis 1949- *184*
   Brief entry *48*
   Earlier sketches in SATA *55, 94, 145*
Root, Shelton L., Jr. 1923-1986
   Obituary *51*

Roper, Laura (Newbold) Wood 1911-2003 .. *34*
   Obituary *150*
Roper, Robert 1946- *142*
   Earlier sketch in SATA *78*
Roraback, Robin (Ellan) 1964- *111*
Rorby, Ginny 1944- *94*
Rorer, Abigail 1949- *85*
Rosamel, Godeleine de 1968- *151*
Roscoe, D(onald) T(homas) 1934- *42*
Rose, Anne *8*
Rose, Deborah Lee 1955- *185*
   Earlier sketches in SATA *71, 124*
Rose, Elizabeth (Jane Pretty) 1933- *68*
   Brief entry *28*
Rose, Florella
   See Carlson, Vada F.
Rose, Gerald (Hembdon Seymour) 1935- *68*
   Brief entry *30*
Rose, Malcolm 1953- *168*
   Earlier sketch in SATA *107*
Rose, Nancy A.
   See Sweetland, Nancy A(nn)
Rose, Ted 1940- *93*
Rose, Wendy 1948- *12*
Rosen, Lillian (Diamond) 1928- *63*
Rosen, Marvin 1933- *161*
Rosen, Michael 1946- *181*
   Brief entry *40*
   Earlier sketches in SATA *48, 84, 137*
   See also CLR *45*
Rosen, Michael J(oel) 1954- *86*
Rosen, Michael Wayne
   See Rosen, Michael
Rosen, Sidney 1916- *1*
Rosen, Winifred 1943- *8*
Rosenbaum, Maurice 1907- *6*
Rosenberg, Amye 1950- *74*
Rosenberg, Dorothy 1906- *40*
Rosenberg, Eth(el) Clifford 1915- *3*
   See Clifford, Eth
Rosenberg, Jane 1949- *58*
Rosenberg, Liz 1958- *129*
   Earlier sketch in SATA *75*
Rosenberg, Maxine B(erta) 1939- *93*
   Brief entry *47*
   Earlier sketch in SATA *55*
Rosenberg, Nancy (Sherman) 1931- *4*
Rosenberg, Sharon 1942- *8*
Rosenberry, Vera 1948- *144*
   Earlier sketch in SATA *83*
Rosenblatt, Arthur
   See Rosenblatt, Arthur S.
Rosenblatt, Arthur S. 1938- *68*
   Brief entry *45*
Rosenblatt, Lily 1956- *90*
Rosenbloom, Joseph 1928- *21*
Rosenblum, Richard 1928- *11*
Rosenburg, John M. 1918- *6*
Rosenfeld, Dina 1962- *99*
Rosenthal, Amy Krouse 1965- *177*
Rosenthal, Betsy R. 1957- *178*
Rosenthal, Harold 1914-1999 .... *35*
Rosenthal, M(acha) L(ouis) 1917-1996 ... *59*
Rosenthal, Marc 1949- *193*
Rosenthal, Mark A(lan) 1946- *64*
Rosman, Steven M 1956- *81*
Rosman, Steven Michael
   See Rosman, Steven M
Rosoff, Meg 1956- *160*
Ross, Alan
   See Warwick, Alan R(oss)
Ross, Christine 1950- *172*
   Earlier sketch in SATA *83*
Ross, Clare *111*
   Earlier sketch in SATA *48*
   See Romano, Clare
Ross, Dana Fuller
   See Cockrell, Amanda
   and Gerson, Noel Bertram
Ross, Dave *32*
   See Ross, David

Ross, David 1896-1975 .... *49*
   Obituary *20*
Ross, David 1949- *133*
   See Ross, Dave
Ross, Deborah J.
   See Wheeler, Deborah
Ross, Diana
   See Denney, Diana
Ross, Edward S(hearman) 1915- *85*
Ross, Eileen 1950- *115*
Ross, Frank (Xavier), Jr. 1914- *28*
Ross, Jane 1961- *79*
Ross, John 1921- *45*
Ross, Judy 1942- *54*
Ross, Katharine Reynolds
   See Ross, Kathy
Ross, Kathy 1948- *169*
   Earlier sketch in SATA *89*
Ross, Kent 1956- *91*
Ross, Lillian Hammer 1925- *72*
Ross, Michael Elsohn 1952- *170*
   Earlier sketches in SATA *80, 127*
Ross, Pat(ricia Kienzle) 1943- *53*
   Brief entry *48*
Ross, Ramon R(oyal) 1930- *62*
Ross, Stewart 1947- *134*
   Earlier sketch in SATA *92*
   See also SAAS *23*
Ross, Tom 1958- *84*
Ross, Tony 1938- *176*
   Earlier sketches in SATA *17, 65, 130*
Ross, Wilda 1915- *51*
   Brief entry *39*
Rossel, Seymour 1945- *28*
Rossell, Judith 1953- *187*
Rossel-Waugh, C. C.
   See Waugh, Carol-Lynn Rossel
Rossetti, Christina 1830-1894 .... *20*
   See also CLR *115*
Rossetti, Christina Georgina
   See Rossetti, Christina
Rossi, Joyce 1943- *116*
Rossotti, Hazel Swaine 1930- *95*
Rostkowski, Margaret I. 1945- *59*
Roth, Arnold 1929- *21*
Roth, Arthur J(oseph) 1925-1993 .... *43*
   Brief entry *28*
   Obituary *75*
   See also SAAS *11*
Roth, David 1940- *36*
Roth, Julie Jersild *180*
Roth, Matthue 1978(?)- *174*
Roth, Roger *190*
Roth, Susan L. *181*
   Earlier sketch in SATA *134*
Rothberg, Abraham 1922- *59*
Roth-Hano, Renee 1931- *85*
Rothkopf, Carol Z. 1929- *4*
Rothman, Joel 1938- *7*
Rotner, Shelley 1951- *169*
   Earlier sketch in SATA *76*
Rottman, S(usan) L(ynn) 1970- *157*
   Earlier sketch in SATA *106*
Roueche, Berton 1911-1994 .... *28*
Roughsey, Dick 1921(?)-1985 .... *35*
   See also CLR *41*
Roughsey, Goobalathaldin
   See Roughsey, Dick
Rounds, Glen (Harold) 1906-2002 .... *112*
   Obituary *141*
   Earlier sketches in SATA *8, 70*
Rourke, Constance Mayfield 1885-1941
   See YABC *1*
Rowan, Deirdre
   See Williams, Jeanne
Rowe, Jennifer
   See Rodda, Emily
Rowe, John A. 1949- *146*
Rowe, Viola Carson 1903-1969
   Obituary *26*
Rowh, Mark 1952- *90*

Rowland, Florence Wightman 1900-1997 8
    Obituary 108
Rowland-Entwistle, (Arthur) Theodore (Henry)
    1925- 94
    Earlier sketch in SATA 31
Rowling, J.K. 1965- 174
    Earlier sketch in SATA 109
    See also CLR 112
Rowling, Joanne Kathleen
    See Rowling, J.K.
Rowsome, Frank (Howard), Jr. 1914-1983 .. 36
Roy, Gabrielle 1909-1983 104
Roy, Jacqueline 1954- 74
Roy, Jennifer
    See Roy, Jennifer Rozines
Roy, Jennifer Rozines 1967- 178
Roy, Jessie Hailstalk 1895-1986
    Obituary 51
Roy, Liam
    See Scarry, Patricia (Murphy)
Roy, Ron(ald) 1940- 110
    Brief entry 35
    Earlier sketch in SATA 40
Roybal, Laura 1956- 85
Roybal, Laura Husby
    See Roybal, Laura
Royds, Caroline 1953- 55
Royston, Angela 1945- 169
    Earlier sketch in SATA 120
Rozakis, Laurie E. 1952- 84
Rubel, Nicole 1953- 181
    Earlier sketches in SATA 18, 95, 135
Rubin, Eva Johanna 1925- 38
Rubin, Susan Goldman 1939- 182
    Earlier sketches in SATA 84, 132
Rubin, Vicky 1964- 193
Rubinetti, Donald 1947- 92
Rubinstein, Gillian 1942- 158
    Autobiography Feature 116
    Earlier sketches in SATA 68, 105
    See also CLR 35
    See also SAAS 25
Rubinstein, Gillian Margaret
    See Rubinstein, Gillian
Rubinstein, Patricia (Giulia Caulfield Kate)
    -2003 29
    Obituary 149
    See Forest, Antonia
Rubinstein, Robert E(dward) 1943- 49
Rublowsky, John M(artin) 1928- 62
Rubright, Lynn 1936- 171
Ruby, Laura 181
    Earlier sketch in SATA 155
Ruby, Lois 1942- 184
    Autobiography Feature 105
    Brief entry 34
    Earlier sketches in SATA 35, 95
Ruby, Lois F.
    See Ruby, Lois
Ruchlis, Hy(man) 1913-1992 3
    Obituary 72
Rucker, Mike 1940- 91
Ruckman, Ivy 1931- 93
    Earlier sketch in SATA 37
Ruck-Pauquet, Gina 1931- 40
    Brief entry 37
Ruditis, Paul 190
Rudley, Stephen 1946- 30
Rudolph, Marguerita 1908- 21
Rudomin, Esther
    See Hautzig, Esther Rudomin
Rue, Leonard Lee III 1926- 142
    Earlier sketch in SATA 37
Rueda, Claudia 183
Ruedi, Norma Paul
    See Ainsworth, Norma
Ruelle, Karen Gray 1957- 126
    Earlier sketch in SATA 84
Ruemmler, John D(avid) 1948- 78
Ruepp, Krista 1947- 143
Ruffell, Ann 1941- 30

Ruffins, Reynold 1930- 125
    Earlier sketch in SATA 41
Rugoff, Milton 1913- 30
Ruhen, Olaf 1911-1989 17
Rukeyser, Muriel 1913-1980
    Obituary 22
Rumbaut, Hendle 1949- 84
Rumford, James 1948- 193
    Earlier sketch in SATA 116
Rumsey, Marian (Barritt) 1928- 16
Rumstuckle, Cornelius
    See Brennan, Herbie
Runnerstroem, Bengt Arne 1944- 75
Runyan, John
    See Palmer, Bernard (Alvin)
Runyon, Catherine 1947- 62
Ruoff, A. LaVonne Brown 1930- 76
Rupp, Rebecca 185
Rusch, Kris
    See Rusch, Kristine Kathryn
Rusch, Kristine Kathryn 1960- 113
Rush, Alison 1951- 41
Rush, Peter 1937- 32
Rushdie, Ahmed Salman
    See Rushdie, Salman
Rushdie, Salman 1947-
    See CLR 125
Rushford, Patricia H(elen) 1943- 134
Rushmore, Helen 1898-1994 3
Rushmore, Robert (William) 1926-1986 8
    Obituary 49
Ruskin, Ariane
    See Batterberry, Ariane Ruskin
Ruskin, John 1819-1900 24
Russ, Lavinia (Faxon) 1904-1992 74
Russell, Charlotte
    See Rathjen, Carl Henry
Russell, Ching Yeung 1946- 107
Russell, Don(ald Bert) 1899-1986
    Obituary 47
Russell, Franklin (Alexander) 1926- 11
Russell, Gertrude Barrer
    See Barrer-Russell, Gertrude
Russell, Helen Ross 1915- 8
Russell, James 1933- 53
Russell, Jim
    See Russell, James
Russell, Joan Plummer 1930- 139
Russell, P(hilip) Craig 1951- 162
    Earlier sketch in SATA 80
Russell, Patrick
    See Sammis, John
Russell, Paul (Gary) 1942- 57
Russell, Sarah
    See Laski, Marghanita
Russell, Sharman Apt 1954- 123
Russell, Solveig Paulson 1904-1985 3
Russo, Marisabina 1950- 188
    Earlier sketches in SATA 106, 151
Russo, Monica J. 1950- 83
Russo, Susan 1947- 30
Russon, Penni 1974- 179
Rutgers van der Loeff, An
    See Rutgers van der Loeff-Basenau, An(na)
    Maria Margaretha
Rutgers van der Loeff-Basenau, An(na) Maria
    Margaretha 1910- 22
Ruth, Rod 1912-1987 9
Rutherford, Douglas
    See McConnell, James Douglas Rutherford
Rutherford, Meg 1932- 34
Ruthin, Margaret 4
    See Catherall, Arthur
Rutledge, Jill Zimmerman 1951- 155
Rutz, Viola Larkin 1932- 12
Ruurs, Margriet 1952- 147
    Earlier sketch in SATA 97
Ruzicka, Rudolph 1883-1978
    Obituary 24
Ruzzier, Sergio 1966- 159

Ryan, Betsy
    See Ryan, Elizabeth (Anne)
Ryan, Cheli Duran 20
Ryan, Darlene 1958- 176
Ryan, Elizabeth (Anne) 1943- 30
Ryan, Jeanette
    See Mines, Jeanette
Ryan, John (Gerald Christopher) 1921- 22
Ryan, Margaret 1950- 166
    Earlier sketch in SATA 78
Ryan, Mary E. 1953- 61
Ryan, Mary Elizabeth
    See Ryan, Mary E.
Ryan, Pam Munoz 1951- 134
Ryan, Patrick 1957- 138
Ryan, Peter (Charles) 1939- 15
Ryan-Lush, Geraldine 1949- 89
Rybakov, Anatoli (Naumovich) 1911-1998 .. 79
    Obituary 108
    See Rybakov, Anatolii (Naumovich)
Rybakov, Anatolii (Naumovich)
    See Rybakov, Anatoli (Naumovich)
Rybolt, Thomas R. 1954- 62
Rybolt, Thomas Roy
    See Rybolt, Thomas R.
Rybolt, Tom
    See Rybolt, Thomas R.
Rydberg, Ernest E(mil) 1901-1993 21
Rydberg, Lou(isa Hampton) 1908- 27
Rydell, Katy 1942- 91
Rydell, Wendell
    See Rydell, Wendy
Rydell, Wendy 4
Ryden, Hope 91
    Earlier sketch in SATA 8
Ryder, Joanne (Rose) 1946- 163
    Brief entry 34
    Earlier sketches in SATA 65, 122
    See also CLR 37
Ryder, Pamela
    See Lamb, Nancy
Rye, Anthony
    See Youd, (Christopher) Samuel
Rylant, Cynthia 1954- 195
    Brief entry 44
    Earlier sketches in SATA 50, 76, 112, 160
    See also CLR 86
    See also SAAS 13
Rymer, Alta May 1925- 34

S

S. L. C.
    See Clemens, Samuel Langhorne
S., Svend Otto
    See Soerensen, Svend Otto
Saaf, Donald W(illiam) 1961- 124
Saal, Jocelyn
    See Sachs, Judith
Sabbeth, Carol (Landstrom) 1957- 125
Saberhagen, Fred 1930-2007 89
    Obituary 184
    Earlier sketch in SATA 37
Saberhagen, Fred T.
    See Saberhagen, Fred
Saberhagen, Fred Thomas
    See Saberhagen, Fred
Saberhagen, Frederick Thomas
    See Saberhagen, Fred
Sabin, Edwin L(egrand) 1870-1952
    See YABC 2
Sabin, Francene 27
Sabin, Lou
    See Sabin, Louis
Sabin, Louis 1930- 27
Sabre, Dirk
    See Laffin, John (Alfred Charles)
Sabuda, Robert (James) 1965- 120
    Earlier sketch in SATA 81

Sabuda, Robert 1965- 170
Sabuda, Robert James
    See Sabuda, Robert
Sachar, Louis 1954- 154
    Brief entry 50
    Earlier sketches in SATA 63, 104
    See also CLR 79
Sachs, Elizabeth-Ann 1946- 48
Sachs, Judith 1947- 52
    Brief entry 51
Sachs, Marilyn 1927- 164
    Autobiography Feature 110
    Earlier sketches in SATA 3, 68
    See also CLR 2
    See also SAAS 2
Sachs, Marilyn Stickle
    See Sachs, Marilyn
Sackett, S(amuel) J(ohn) 1928- 12
Sackson, Sid 1920- 16
Sacre, Antonio 1968- 152
Saddler, Allen
    See Richards, R(onald) C(harles) W(illiam)
Saddler, K. Allen
    See Richards, R(onald) C(harles) W(illiam)
Sadie, Stanley 1930-2005 14
Sadie, Stanley John
    See Sadie, Stanley
Sadiq, Nazneen 1944- 101
Sadler, Catherine Edwards 1952- 60
    Brief entry 45
Sadler, Marilyn (June) 1950- 79
Sadler, Mark
    See Lynds, Dennis
Saffer, Barbara 144
Sagan, Carl 1934-1996 58
    Obituary 94
Sagan, Carl Edward
    See Sagan, Carl
Sage, Juniper
    See Brown, Margaret Wise
    and Hurd, Edith Thacher
Sagsoorian, Paul 1923- 12
Said, S.F. 1967- 174
Saidman, Anne 1952- 75
Saint, Dora Jessie 1913- 10
St. Anthony, Jane 175
St. Antoine, Sara L. 1966- 84
St. Clair, Byrd Hooper 1905-1976
    Obituary 28
Saint-Exupery, Antoine de 1900-1944 20
    See also CLR 10
Saint-Exupery, Antoine Jean Baptiste Marie
    Roger de
    See Saint-Exupery, Antoine de
St. George, Judith 1931- 161
    Earlier sketches in SATA 13, 99
    See also CLR 57
    See also SAAS 12
St. James, Blakely
    See Gottfried, Theodore Mark
    and Platt, Charles
St. James, Blakely
    See Griffin, W.E.B
St. James, Sierra
    See Rallison, Janette
Saint James, Synthia 1949- 152
    Earlier sketch in SATA 84
St. John, Nicole 143
    Autobiography Feature 143
    Earlier sketch in SATA 89
    See also CLR 46
    See also SAAS 7
    See Johnston, Norma
St. John, Patricia Mary 1919-1993
    Obituary 79
St. John, Philip
    See del Rey, Lester
St. John, Wylly Folk 1908-1985 10
    Obituary 45
St. Max, E. S.
    See Ellis, Edward S(ylvester)

St. Meyer, Ned
    See Stratemeyer, Edward L.
St. Mox, E. A.
    See Ellis, Edward S(ylvester)
St. Myer, Ned
    See Stratemeyer, Edward L.
St. Tamara
    See Kolba, St. Tamara
Saito, Michiko
    See Fujiwara, Michiko
Sakaki, Ichiro 1969- 192
Sakers, Don 1958- 72
Sakharnov, S.
    See Sakharnov, Svyatoslav
Sakharnov, Svyatoslav 1923- 65
Sakharnov, Svyatoslav Vladimirovich
    See Sakharnov, Svyatoslav
Saksena, Kate 148
Sakurai, Gail 1952- 153
    Earlier sketch in SATA 87
Salamanca, Lucy
    See del Barco, Lucy Salamanca
Salassi, Otto R(ussell) 1939-1993 38
    Obituary 77
Salat, Cristina 82
Saldana, Rene, Jr. 186
Saldutti, Denise 1953- 39
Sale, Tim 1956- 153
Salem, Kay 1952- 92
Salerno, Steven 176
Salinger, J.D. 1919- 67
    See also CLR 18
Salinger, Jerome David
    See Salinger, J.D.
Salisbury, Graham 1944- 195
    Earlier sketches in SATA 76, 108, 161
Salisbury, Joyce E(llen) 1944- 138
Salkey, (Felix) Andrew (Alexander)
    1928-1995 118
    Earlier sketch in SATA 35
Salley, Coleen 166
Sallis, Susan (Diana) 1929- 55
Salmon, Annie Elizabeth 1899- 13
Salonen, Roxane Beauclair 1968- 184
Salsi, Lynn 1947- 130
Salsitz, R. A. V.
    See Salsitz, Rhondi Vilott
Salsitz, Rhondi Vilott 115
    See Salsitz, R. A. V.
Salten, Felix
    See Salzmann, Siegmund
Salter, Cedric
    See Knight, Francis Edgar
Saltman, Judith 1947- 64
Saltzberg, Barney 1955- 194
    Earlier sketch in SATA 135
Saltzman, David (Charles Laertes)
    1967-1990 86
Salvadori, Mario (George) 1907-1997 97
    Earlier sketch in SATA 40
Salwood, F.K.
    See Kilworth, Garry
Salzer, L. E.
    See Wilson, Lionel
Salzman, Marian 1959- 77
Salzmann, Siegmund 1869-1945 25
    See Salten, Felix
Samachson, Dorothy (Mirkin) 1914-1997 3
Samachson, Joseph 1906-1980 3
    Obituary 52
Sammis, John 1942- 4
Sampson, Emma (Keats) Speed 1868-1947 . 68
Sampson, Fay (Elizabeth) 1935- 151
    Brief entry 40
    Earlier sketch in SATA 42
Sampson, Michael 1952- 143
    Earlier sketch in SATA 95
Samson, Anne S(tringer) 1933- 2
Samson, Joan 1937-1976 13
Samson, Suzanne M. 1959- 91
Samuels, Charles 1902-1982 12

Samuels, Cynthia K(alish) 1946- 79
Samuels, Gertrude 1910(?)-2003 17
    Obituary 147
Sanborn, Duane 1914-1996 38
Sancha, Sheila 1924- 38
Sanchez, Alex 1957- 151
Sanchez, Sonia 1934- 136
    Earlier sketch in SATA 22
    See also CLR 18
Sanchez-Silva, Jose Maria 1911- 132
    Earlier sketch in SATA 16
    See also CLR 12
Sand, George X. 45
Sandak, Cass R(obert) 1950-2001 51
    Brief entry 37
Sandberg, (Karin) Inger 1930- 15
Sandberg, Karl C. 1931- 35
Sandberg, Lasse (E. M.) 1924- 15
Sandburg, Carl (August) 1878-1967 8
    See also CLR 67
Sandburg, Charles
    See Sandburg, Carl (August)
Sandburg, Charles A.
    See Sandburg, Carl (August)
Sandburg, Helga 1918- 3
    See also SAAS 10
Sandell, Lisa Ann 1977- 175
Sander, Heather L. 1947- 157
Sanderlin, George 1915- 4
Sanderlin, Owenita (Harrah) 1916- 11
Sanders, Betty Jane
    See Monthei, Betty
Sanders, Nancy I. 1960- 141
    Earlier sketch in SATA 90
Sanders, Scott Russell 1945- 109
    Earlier sketch in SATA 56
Sanders, Winston P.
    See Anderson, Poul
Sanderson, Irma 1912- 66
Sanderson, Ivan T(erence) 1911-1973 6
Sanderson, Margaret Love
    See Keats, Emma
    and Sampson, Emma (Keats) Speed
Sanderson, Ruth 1951- 172
    Earlier sketches in SATA 41, 109
Sanderson, Ruth L.
    See Sanderson, Ruth
Sandin, Joan 1942- 153
    Earlier sketches in SATA 12, 94
Sandison, Janet
    See Cameron, Elizabeth Jane
Sandler, Martin W. 160
Sandom, J. Gregory
    See Welsh, T.K.
Sandom, J.G.
    See Welsh, T.K.
Sandoz, Mari(e Susette) 1900-1966 5
Sanford, Agnes (White) 1897-1976 61
Sanford, Doris 1937- 69
Sanger, Marjory Bartlett 1920- 8
San Jose, Christine 1929- 167
Sankey, Alice (Ann-Susan) 1910- 27
San Souci, Daniel 192
    Earlier sketch in SATA 96
San Souci, Robert D. 1946- 158
    Earlier sketches in SATA 40, 81, 117
    See also CLR 43
Santamaria, Benjamin 1955- 184
Santat, Dan 188
Santesson, Hans Stefan 1914(?)-1975
    Obituary 30
Santiago, Esmeralda 1948- 129
Santos, Helen
    See Griffiths, Helen
Santrey, Louis
    See Sabin, Louis
Santucci, Barbara 1948- 130
Sapergia, Barbara 1943- 181

Sapieyevski, Anne Lindbergh 1940-1993 78
  Earlier sketch in SATA 35
  See Feydy, Anne Lindbergh
  and Lindbergh, Anne
Saport, Linda 1954- 123
Sapp, Allen 1929- 151
Sarac, Roger
  See Caras, Roger A(ndrew)
Sarah, Duchess of York
  See Ferguson, Sarah
Sarasin, Jennifer
  See Sachs, Judith
Sardinha, Rick 192
Sarg, Anthony Frederick
  See Sarg, Tony
Sarg, Tony 1882-1942
  See YABC 1
Sargent, Pamela 1948- 78
  Earlier sketch in SATA 29
Sargent, Robert 1933- 2
Sargent, Sarah 1937- 44
  Brief entry 41
Sargent, Shirley 1927-2004 11
Sarnoff, Jane 1937- 10
Saroyan, William 1908-1981 23
  Obituary 24
Sarton, Eleanor May
  See Sarton, May
Sarton, May 1912-1995 36
  Obituary 86
Sasaki, Chris 182
Saseen, Sharon (Dillon) 1949- 59
Sasek, Miroslav 1916-1980 16
  Obituary 23
  See also CLR 4
Sasso, Sandy Eisenberg 1947- 162
  Earlier sketches in SATA 86, 116
Sathre, Vivian 1952- 133
  Earlier sketch in SATA 79
Satterfield, Charles
  See del Rey, Lester
  and Pohl, Frederik
Sattgast, L. J.
  See Sattgast, Linda J.
Sattgast, Linda J. 1953- 91
Sattler, Helen Roney 1921-1992 74
  Earlier sketch in SATA 4
  See also CLR 24
Sauer, Julia Lina 1891-1983 32
  Obituary 36
Sauerwein, Leigh 1944- 155
Saul, Carol P. 1947- 117
  Earlier sketch in SATA 78
Saul, John III
  See Saul, John
Saul, John 1942- 98
Saul, John W.
  See Saul, John
Saul, John W. III
  See Saul, John
Saul, John Woodruff III
  See Saul, John
Saul, (Ellen) Wendy 1946- 42
Saulnier, Karen Luczak 1940- 80
Saunders, Caleb
  See Heinlein, Robert A.
Saunders, Dave 1939- 85
Saunders, Julie 1939- 85
Saunders, (William) Keith 1910-1994 12
Saunders, Rubie (Agnes) 1929- 21
Saunders, Susan 1945- 96
  Brief entry 41
  Earlier sketch in SATA 46
Saunders-Smith, Gail 1952- 169
Sauvain, Philip Arthur 1933- 111
Savadier, Elivia 1950- 164
  Earlier sketch in SATA 79
Savage, Alan
  See Nicole, Christopher (Robin)
Savage, Blake
  See Goodwin, Harold L(eland)

Savage, Candace (M.) 1949- 142
Savage, Deborah 1955- 76
Savage, Jeff 1961- 97
Savage, Katharine James 1905-1989
  Obituary 61
Savage, Stephen 1965- 194
Savage, Thomas 1915-2003
  Obituary 147
Savageau, Cheryl 1950- 96
Savery, Constance (Winifred) 1897-1999 1
Saville, Andrew
  See Taylor, Andrew
Saville, (Leonard) Malcolm 1901-1982 23
  Obituary 31
Saviozzi, Adriana
  See Mazza, Adriana
Savitt, Sam 1917(?)-2000 8
  Obituary 126
Savitz, Harriet May 1933- 72
  Earlier sketch in SATA 5
  See also SAAS 26
Sawicki, Mary 1950- 90
Sawyer, (Frederick) Don(ald) 1947- 72
Sawyer, Kem Knapp 1953- 84
Sawyer, Robert J. 1960- 149
  Earlier sketch in SATA 81
Sawyer, Robert James
  See Sawyer, Robert J.
Sawyer, Ruth 1880-1970 17
  See also CLR 36
Saxby, H.M.
  See Saxby, (Henry) Maurice
Saxby, (Henry) Maurice 1924- 71
Saxon, Andrew
  See Arthur, Robert, (Jr.)
Saxon, Antonia
  See Sachs, Judith
Say, Allen 1937- 161
  Earlier sketches in SATA 28, 69, 110
  See also CLR 135
Sayers, Frances Clarke 1897-1989 3
  Obituary 62
Sayles, Elizabeth 1956- 163
  Earlier sketch in SATA 108
Saylor-Marchant, Linda 1963- 82
Sayre, April Pulley 1966- 191
  Earlier sketches in SATA 88, 131
Sazer, Nina 1949- 13
Scabrini, Janet 1953- 13
Scagell, Robin 1946- 107
Scagnetti, Jack 1924- 7
Scamander, Newt
  See Rowling, J.K.
Scamell, Ragnhild 1940- 180
  Earlier sketch in SATA 77
Scanlon, Marion Stephany 11
Scannel, John Vernon
  See Scannell, Vernon
Scannell, Vernon 1922-2007 59
  Obituary 188
Scarborough, Elizabeth 171
  See Scarborough, Elizabeth Ann
Scarborough, Elizabeth Ann 1947- 171
  Earlier sketch in SATA 98
  See Scarborough, Elizabeth
Scarf, Maggi
  See Scarf, Maggie
Scarf, Maggie 1932- 5
Scariano, Margaret M. 1924- 86
Scarlett, Susan
  See Streatfeild, Noel
Scarry, Huck
  See Scarry, Richard McClure, Jr.
Scarry, Patricia (Murphy) 1924- 2
Scarry, Patsy
  See Scarry, Patricia (Murphy)
Scarry, Richard (McClure) 1919-1994 75
  Obituary 90
  Earlier sketches in SATA 2, 35
  See also CLR 41
Scarry, Richard McClure, Jr. 1953- 35

Schachner, Judith Byron 1951- 178
  Earlier sketch in SATA 88
Schachner, Judy
  See Schachner, Judith Byron
Schachtel, Roger 1949- 38
Schachtel, Roger Bernard
  See Schachtel, Roger
Schade, Susan 189
Schaedler, Sally 116
Schaefer, Carole Lexa 173
Schaefer, Jack (Warner) 1907-1991 66
  Obituary 65
  Earlier sketch in SATA 3
Schaefer, Lola M. 1950- 183
  Earlier sketches in SATA 91, 144
Schaeffer, Mead 1898- 21
Schaeffer, Susan Fromberg 1941- 22
Schaer, Brigitte 1958- 112
Schaller, George
  See Schaller, George B.
Schaller, George B. 1933- 30
Schaller, George Beals
  See Schaller, George B.
Schanzer, Rosalyn (Good) 1942- 138
  Earlier sketch in SATA 77
Schatell, Brian 66
  Brief entry 47
Schechter, Betty (Goodstein) 1921- 5
Schechter, Simone
  See Elkeles, Simone
Schecter, Ellen 1944- 85
Scheeder, Louis 1946- 141
Scheer, Julian (Weisel) 1926-2001 8
Scheffer, Victor B(lanchard) 1906- 6
Scheffler, Axel 1957- 180
Scheffler, Ursel 1938- 81
Scheffrin-Falk, Gladys 1928- 76
Scheidl, Gerda Marie 1913- 85
Scheier, Michael 1943- 40
  Brief entry 36
Schell, Mildred 1922- 41
Schell, Orville (Hickok) 1940- 10
Scheller, Melanie 1953- 77
Schellie, Don 1932- 29
Schembri, Jim 1962- 124
Schembri, Pamela 1969- 195
Schemm, Mildred Walker 1905-1998 21
  Obituary 103
  See Walker, Mildred
Schenker, Dona 1947- 133
  Earlier sketch in SATA 68
Scher, Paula 1948- 47
Scherer, Jeffrey 194
Scherf, Margaret 1908-1979 10
Schermer, Judith (Denise) 1941- 30
Schertle, Alice 1941- 192
  Earlier sketches in SATA 36, 90, 145
Schick, Alice 1946- 27
Schick, Eleanor 1942- 144
  Earlier sketches in SATA 9, 82
Schick, Joel 1945- 31
  Brief entry 30
Schields, Gretchen 1948- 75
Schiff, Ken(neth Roy) 1942- 7
Schiller, Andrew 1919- 21
Schiller, Barbara (Heyman) 1928- 21
Schiller, Pamela (Byrne) 127
Schindel, John 1955- 115
  Earlier sketch in SATA 77
Schindelman, Joseph 1923- 67
  Brief entry 32
Schindler, S.D. 1952- 171
  Brief entry 50
  Earlier sketches in SATA 75, 118
Schindler, Steven D.
  See Schindler, S.D.
Schinto, Jeanne 1951- 93
Schisgall, Oscar 1901-1984 12
  Obituary 38
Schlaepfer, Gloria G. 1931- 154

Schlee, Ann 1934- *44*
   Brief entry *36*
Schleichert, Elizabeth 1945- *77*
Schlein, Miriam 1926-2004 .... *130*
   Obituary *159*
   Earlier sketches in SATA *2, 87*
   See also CLR *41*
Schlesinger, Arthur M., Jr. 1917-2007 .... *61*
   Obituary *181*
   See Schlesinger, Arthur Meier
Schlesinger, Arthur Meier 1888-1965
Schlessinger, Laura (Catherine) 1947- *160*
   Earlier sketch in SATA *110*
Schlitz, Laura Amy *184*
Schloat, G. Warren, Jr. 1914-2000 .... *4*
Schmid, Eleonore 1939- *126*
   Earlier sketches in SATA *12, 84*
Schmiderer, Dorothy 1940- *19*
Schmidt, Annie M. G. 1911-1995 .... *67*
   Obituary *91*
   See also CLR *22*
Schmidt, Diane 1953- *70*
Schmidt, Elizabeth 1915- *15*
Schmidt, Gary D. 1957- *193*
   Earlier sketches in SATA *93, 135*
Schmidt, James Norman 1912-1983 .... *21*
Schmidt, Karen Lee 1953- *185*
   Earlier sketch in SATA *94*
Schmidt, Lynette 1952- *76*
Schneider, Antonie 1954- *167*
   Earlier sketch in SATA *89*
Schneider, Christine M. 1972(?)- *171*
   Earlier sketch in SATA *120*
Schneider, Dick
   See Schneider, Richard H.
Schneider, Elisa
   See Kleven, Elisa
Schneider, Herman 1905-2003 .... *7*
   Obituary *148*
Schneider, Howie -2007 .... *181*
Schneider, Laurie
   See Adams, Laurie
Schneider, Nina 1913-2007 .... *2*
   Obituary *186*
Schneider, Nina Zimet
   See Schneider, Nina
Schneider, Rex 1937- *44*
Schneider, Richard H. 1922- *171*
Schneider, Richard Henry
   See Schneider, Richard H.
Schneider, Robyn 1986- *187*
Schnirel, James R. 1931- *14*
Schnitter, Jane T. 1958- *88*
Schnitzlein, Danny *134*
Schnur, Steven 1952- *144*
   Earlier sketch in SATA *95*
Schnurre, Wolfdietrich 1920-1989
   Obituary *63*
Schoberle, Cecile 1949- *80*
Schock, Pauline 1928- *45*
Schoell, William 1951- *160*
Schoen, Barbara (Taylor) 1924-1993 .... *13*
Schoenherr, Ian *177*
Schoenherr, John (Carl) 1935- *66*
   Earlier sketch in SATA *37*
   See also SAAS *13*
Schofield, Sandy
   See Rusch, Kristine Kathryn
Scholastica, Sister Mary
   See Jenkins, Marie M(agdalen)
Scholefield, A. T.
   See Scholefield, Alan
Scholefield, Alan 1931- *66*
Scholefield, Edmund O.
   See Griffin, W.E.B
Scholey, Arthur 1932- *28*
Scholz, Jackson Volney 1897-1986
   Obituary *49*
Schone, Virginia *22*

Schongut, Emanuel 1936- *184*
   Brief entry *36*
   Earlier sketch in SATA *52*
Schoonover, Frank (Earle) 1877-1972 .... *24*
Schoor, Gene 1921- *3*
Schories, Pat 1952- *164*
   Earlier sketch in SATA *116*
Schorr, Melissa 1972- *194*
Schorr, Melissa Robin
   See Schorr, Melissa
Schott, Jane A. 1946- *172*
Schotter, Roni *190*
   Earlier sketches in SATA *105, 149*
Schraff, Anne E(laine) 1939- *92*
   Earlier sketch in SATA *27*
Schram, Peninnah 1934- *119*
Schrank, Joseph 1900-1984
   Obituary *38*
Schrecengost, Maity 1938- *118*
Schrecengost, S. Maitland
   See Schrecengost, Maity
Schreck, Karen
   See Schreck, Karen Halvorsen
Schreck, Karen Halvorsen 1962- *185*
Schrecker, Judie 1954- *90*
Schreiber, Elizabeth Anne (Ferguson)
   1947- *13*
Schreiber, Ralph W(alter) 1942- *13*
Schreiner, Samuel A(gnew), Jr. 1921- *70*
Schroeder, Alan 1961- *98*
   Earlier sketch in SATA *66*
Schroeder, Binette
   See Nickl, Barbara (Elisabeth)
Schroeder, Russell (K.) 1943- *146*
Schroeder, Ted 1931(?)-1973
   Obituary *20*
Schubert, Dieter 1947- *101*
   Earlier sketch in SATA *62*
Schubert, Leda 1950(?)- *181*
Schubert-Gabrys, Ingrid 1953- *101*
   Earlier sketch in SATA *62*
Schuelein-Steel, Danielle
   See Steel, Danielle
Schuelein-Steel, Danielle Fernande
   See Steel, Danielle
Schuerger, Michele R. *110*
Schuett, Stacey 1960- *168*
   Earlier sketch in SATA *75*
Schulke, Flip Phelps Graeme 1930- *57*
Schulman, Arlene 1961- *105*
Schulman, Janet 1933- *137*
   Earlier sketch in SATA *22*
Schulman, L(ester) M(artin) 1934- *13*
Schulte, Elaine L(ouise) 1934- *36*
Schultz, Betty K(epka) 1932- *125*
Schultz, Gwendolyn *21*
Schultz, James Willard 1859-1947
   See YABC *1*
Schultz, Pearle Henriksen 1918- *21*
Schulz, Charles M. 1922-2000 .... *10*
   Obituary *118*
Schulz, Charles Monroe
   See Schulz, Charles M.
Schumacher, Julie 1958- *191*
Schumaker, Ward 1943- *96*
Schuman, Michael A. 1953- *134*
   Earlier sketch in SATA *85*
Schur, Maxine
   See Schur, Maxine Rose
Schur, Maxine Rose 1948- *135*
   Autobiography Feature *135*
   Brief entry *49*
   Earlier sketches in SATA *53, 98*
Schurfranz, Vivian 1925- *13*
Schutzer, A. I. 1922- *13*
Schuyler, Pamela R. 1948- *30*
Schwabach, Karen *185*
Schwager, Tina 1964- *110*
Schwandt, Stephen (William) 1947- *61*
Schwark, Mary Beth 1954- *51*

Schwartz, Alvin 1927-1992 .... *56*
   Obituary *71*
   Earlier sketch in SATA *4*
   See also CLR *89*
Schwartz, Amy 1954- *189*
   Brief entry *41*
   Earlier sketches in SATA *47, 83, 131*
   See also CLR *25*
   See also SAAS *18*
Schwartz, Anne Powers 1913-1987 .... *10*
Schwartz, Carol 1954- *77*
Schwartz, Charles W(alsh) 1914- *8*
Schwartz, David M. 1951- *110*
   Earlier sketch in SATA *59*
Schwartz, David Martin
   See Schwartz, David M.
Schwartz, Elizabeth Reeder 1912- *8*
Schwartz, Ellen 1949- *117*
Schwartz, Jerome L.
   See Lawrence, Jerome
Schwartz, Joel L. 1940- *54*
   Brief entry *51*
Schwartz, Joyce R. 1950- *93*
Schwartz, Julius 1907-2004 .... *45*
Schwartz, Perry 1942- *75*
Schwartz, Sheila (Ruth) 1929- *27*
Schwartz, Stephen (Lawrence) 1948- *19*
Schwartz, Virginia Frances 1950- *184*
   Earlier sketch in SATA *131*
Schwarz, (Silvia Tessa) Viviane 1977- *141*
Schweitzer, Byrd Baylor
   See Baylor, Byrd
Schweitzer, Iris *59*
   Brief entry *36*
Schweninger, Ann 1951- *168*
   Earlier sketches in SATA *29, 98*
Schwerin, Doris H(alpern) 1922- *64*
Scieszka, Jon 1954- *160*
   Earlier sketches in SATA *68, 105*
   See also CLR *107*
Scillian, Devin *128*
Scioscia, Mary (Hershey) 1926- *63*
Scofield, Penrod 1933- *62*
   Obituary *78*
Scoggin, Margaret C(lara) 1905-1968 .... *47*
   Brief entry *28*
Scoltock, Jack 1942- *141*
   Earlier sketch in SATA *72*
Scoppettone, Sandra 1936- *92*
   Earlier sketch in SATA *9*
   See Early, Jack
Scot, Michael
   See Rohan, Michael Scott
Scot-Bernard, P.
   See Bernard, Patricia
Scotland, Jay
   See Jakes, John
Scott, Alastair
   See Allen, Kenneth S.
Scott, Ann Herbert 1926- *140*
   Autobiography Feature *140*
   Brief entry *29*
   Earlier sketches in SATA *56, 94*
Scott, Bill
   See Scott, William N(eville)
Scott, Bill 1920(?)-1985
   Obituary *46*
Scott, Cora Annett (Pipitone) 1931- *11*
Scott, Dan
   See Barker, S(quire) Omar
Scott, Elaine 1940- *164*
   Earlier sketches in SATA *36, 90*
Scott, Elizabeth *194*
Scott, Jack Denton 1915-1995 .... *83*
   Earlier sketch in SATA *31*
   See also CLR *20*
   See also SAAS *14*
Scott, Jane (Harrington) 1931- *55*
Scott, Jessica
   See De Wire, Elinor
Scott, John 1912-1976 .... *14*

Scott, John Anthony 1916- 23
Scott, John M(artin) 1913- 12
Scott, Mary
    See Mattern, Joanne
Scott, Melissa 1960- 109
Scott, Richard
    See Rennert, Richard Scott
Scott, Roney
    See Gault, William Campbell
Scott, Sally 1909-1978 43
Scott, Sally 1948- 44
Scott, Sally Elisabeth
    See Scott, Sally
Scott, W. N.
    See Scott, William N(eville)
Scott, Sir Walter 1771-1832
    See YABC 2
Scott, Warwick
    See Trevor, Elleston
Scott, William N(eville) 1923- 87
Scotti, Anna
    See Coates, Anna
Scotton, Rob 1960- 177
Scribner, Charles, Jr. 1921-1995 13
    Obituary 87
Scribner, Joanne L. 1949- 33
Scribner, Kimball 1917- 63
Scrimger, Richard 1957- 164
    Earlier sketch in SATA *119*
Scrimsher, Lila Gravatt 1897-1974
    Obituary 28
Scroder, Walter K. 1928- 82
Scroggs, Kirk 187
Scruggs, Sandy 1961- 89
Scudder, Brooke 1959- 154
Scull, Marie-Louise 1943-1993 77
Scuro, Vincent 1951- 21
Seabrooke, Brenda 1941- 148
    Earlier sketches in SATA *30, 88*
Seaman, Augusta Huiell 1879-1950 31
Seamands, Ruth 1916- 9
Searcy, Margaret Zehmer 1926- 54
    Brief entry 39
Searight, Mary W(illiams) 1918- 17
Searle, Kathryn Adrienne 1942- 10
Searle, Ronald (William Fordham) 1920- 70
    Earlier sketch in SATA *42*
Sears, Stephen W. 1932- 4
Sebastian, Lee
    See Silverberg, Robert
Sebestyen, Igen
    See Sebestyen, Ouida
Sebestyen, Ouida 1924- 140
    Earlier sketch in SATA *39*
    See also CLR *17*
    See also SAAS *10*
Sebrey, Mary Ann 1951- 62
Sechrist, Elizabeth Hough 1903-1991 2
Sedges, John
    See Buck, Pearl S(ydenstricker)
Sedgwick, Marcus 1968- 160
Seed, Cecile Eugenie 1930- 86
    See Seed, Jenny
Seed, Jenny 8
    See also CLR *76*
    See Seed, Cecile Eugenie
Seed, Sheila Turner 1937(?)-1979
    Obituary 23
Seeger, Elizabeth 1889-1973
    Obituary 20
Seeger, Laura Vaccaro 172
Seeger, Pete 1919- 139
    Earlier sketch in SATA *13*
Seeger, Peter R.
    See Seeger, Pete
Seeley, Laura L. 1958- 71
Seever, R.
    See Reeves, Lawrence F.
Sefozo, Mary 1925- 82
Sefton, Catherine
    See Waddell, Martin

Segal, John 178
Segal, Joyce 1940- 35
Segal, Lore 1928- 163
    Earlier sketches in SATA *4, 66*
    See also SAAS *11*
Segal, Lore Groszmann
    See Segal, Lore
Segar, E(lzie) C(risler) 1894-1938 61
Segovia, Andres 1893(?)-1987
    Obituary 52
Seguin, Marilyn W(eymouth) 1951- 91
Seguin-Fontes, Marthe 1924- 109
Seibold, J. Otto 1960- 149
    Earlier sketch in SATA *83*
    See also SAAS *22*
Seidel, Ross 95
Seidelman, James Edward 1926- 6
Seiden, Art(hur) 107
    Brief entry 42
Seidler, Ann (G.) 1925- 131
Seidler, Tor 1952- 149
    Brief entry 46
    Earlier sketches in SATA *52, 98*
Seidman, Laurence Ivan 1925- 15
Seigel, Kalman 1917-1998 12
    Obituary 103
Seignobosc, Francoise 1897-1961 21
Seinfeld, Jerry 1954- 146
Seitz, Jacqueline 1931- 50
Seixas, Judith S. 1922- 17
Sejima, Yoshimasa 1913- 8
Selberg, Ingrid (Maria) 1950- 68
Selden, George
    See CLR *8*
    See Thompson, George Selden
Selden, Neil R(oy) 1931- 61
Self, Margaret Cabell 1902-1996 24
Selfors, Suzanne 1963- 193
Selick, Henry 1952- 183
Selig, Sylvie 1942- 13
Selkirk, Jane
    See Chapman, John Stanton Higham
Sellers, Naomi
    See Flack, Naomi John White
Selman, LaRue W. 1927- 55
Selsam, Millicent E(llis) 1912-1996 29
    Obituary 92
    Earlier sketch in SATA *1*
    See also CLR *1*
Seltzer, Meyer 1932- 17
Seltzer, Richard 1946- 41
Seltzer, Richard Warren, Jr.
    See Seltzer, Richard
Selvadurai, Shyam 1965(?)- 171
Selway, Martina 1940- 169
    Earlier sketch in SATA *74*
Selzer, Adam 1980- 192
Selznick, Brian 1966- 171
    Earlier sketches in SATA *79, 117*
Semel, Nava 1954- 107
Semloh
    See Holmes, Peggy
Sendak, Jack 1924(?)-1995 28
Sendak, Maurice 1928- 165
    Earlier sketches in SATA *1, 27, 113*
    See also CLR *131*
Sendak, Maurice Bernard
    See Sendak, Maurice
Sender, Ruth M(insky) 1926- 62
Sengler, Johanna 1924- 18
Senisi, Ellen B. 1951- 116
Senisi, Ellen Babinec
    See Senisi, Ellen B.
Senn, J(oyce) A(nn) 1941- 115
Senn, Steve 1950- 60
    Brief entry 48
Serage, Nancy 1924- 10
Seredy, Kate 1899-1975 1
    Obituary 24
    See also CLR *10*
Serfozo, Mary 1925- 194

Seroff, Victor I(lyitch) 1902-1979 12
    Obituary 26
Serraillier, Ian (Lucien) 1912-1994 73
    Obituary 83
    Earlier sketch in SATA *1*
    See also CLR *2*
    See also SAAS *3*
Serros, Michele 175
Serros, Michele M.
    See Serros, Michele
Servello, Joe 1932- 10
Service, Pamela F. 1945- 64
Service, Robert
    See Service, Robert W(illiam)
Service, Robert W(illiam) 1874(?)-1958 20
    See Service, Robert
Serwadda, W(illiam) Moses 1931- 27
Serwer-Bernstein, Blanche L(uria)
    1910-1997 10
Sescoe, Vincent E. 1938- 123
Seth, Mary
    See Lexau, Joan M.
Seton, Anya 1904(?)-1990 3
    Obituary 66
Seton, Ernest (Evan) Thompson 1860-1946 . 18
    See also CLR *59*
Seton-Thompson, Ernest
    See Seton, Ernest (Evan) Thompson
Seuling, Barbara 1937- 193
    Earlier sketches in SATA *10, 98, 145*
    See also SAAS *24*
Seuss, Dr.
    See Dr. Seuss
    and Geisel, Theodor Seuss
    and LeSieg, Theo.
    and Stone, Rosetta
Severn, Bill
    See Severn, William Irving
Severn, David
    See Unwin, David S(torr)
Severn, William Irving 1914- 1
Sewall, Marcia 1935- 119
    Earlier sketches in SATA *37, 69*
Seward, Prudence 1926- 16
Sewell, Anna 1820-1878 100
    Earlier sketch in SATA *24*
    See also CLR *17*
Sewell, Helen (Moore) 1896-1957 38
Sexton, Anne (Harvey) 1928-1974 10
Seymour, Alta Halverson 10
Seymour, Jane 1951- 139
Seymour, Tres 1966- 164
    Earlier sketch in SATA *82*
Sfar, Joann 1971- 182
Shachtman, Tom 1942- 49
Shackleton, C.C.
    See Aldiss, Brian W.
Shader, Rachel
    See Sofer, Barbara
Shadow, Jak
    See Sutherland, Jon
Shadyland, Sal
    See Cooper, Louise
Shafer, Audrey 183
Shafer, Robert E(ugene) 1925- 9
Shaffer, Terea 1968- 79
Shahan, Sherry 1949- 134
    Earlier sketch in SATA *92*
Shahn, Ben(jamin) 1898-1969
    Obituary 21
Shahn, Bernarda Bryson
    See Bryson, Bernarda
Shaik, Fatima 114
Shalant, Phyllis 1949- 150
Shan, Darren 1972- 168
    Earlier sketch in SATA *129*
Shanberg, Karen
    See Shragg, Karen (I.)
Shane, Harold Gray 1914-1993 36
    Obituary 76
Shange, Ntozake 1948- 157

Shanks, Ann Zane (Kushner) 10
Shannon, David 1959- 152
  Earlier sketch in SATA 107
  See also CLR 87
Shannon, George (William Bones) 1952- ... 143
  Earlier sketches in SATA 35, 94
Shannon, Jacqueline 63
Shannon, Margaret
  See Silverwood, Margaret Shannon
Shannon, Monica 1905(?)-1965 28
Shannon, Terry 21
  See Mercer, Jessie
Shannon, Terry Miller 1951- 148
Shapiro, Irwin 1911-1981 32
Shapiro, Jody Fickes 1940- 193
Shapiro, Karen Jo 1964- 186
Shapiro, Milton J. 1926- 32
Shapiro, Tricia
  See Andryszewski, Tricia
Shapp, Charles M(orris) 1906-1989
  Obituary 61
Shapp, Martha Glauber 1910- 3
Sharenow, Robert 193
Sharfman, Amalie 14
Sharma, Partap 1939- 15
Sharma, Rashmi
  See Singh, Rashmi Sharma
Sharman, Alison
  See Leonard, Alison
Sharmat, Marjorie Weinman 1928- 133
  Earlier sketches in SATA 4, 33, 74
Sharmat, Mitchell 1927- 127
  Earlier sketch in SATA 33
Sharp, Anne Wallace 1947- 144
Sharp, Luke
  See Alkiviades, Alkis
Sharp, Margery 1905-1991 29
  Obituary 67
  Earlier sketch in SATA 1
  See also CLR 27
Sharp, Zerna A. 1889-1981
  Obituary 27
Sharpe, Jon
  See Duncan, Alice
  and Knott, William C(ecil, Jr.)
  and Messman, Jon
Sharpe, Mitchell R(aymond) 1924- 12
Sharpe, Susan 1946- 71
Sharratt, Nick 1962- 153
  Earlier sketch in SATA 104
Shasha, Mark 1961- 80
Shattuck, Roger 1923-2005 64
  Obituary 174
Shattuck, Roger Whitney
  See Shattuck, Roger
Shaw, Arnold 1909-1989 4
  Obituary 63
Shaw, Carolyn V. 1934- 91
Shaw, Charles (Green) 1892-1974 13
Shaw, Evelyn S. 1927- 28
Shaw, Flora Louisa
  See Lugard, Flora Louisa Shaw
Shaw, Janet 1937- 146
  Earlier sketch in SATA 61
  See also CLR 96
Shaw, Janet Beeler
  See Shaw, Janet
Shaw, Lisa
  See Rogak, Lisa
Shaw, Margret 1940- 68
Shaw, Mary 1965- 180
Shaw, Nancy 1946- 162
  Earlier sketch in SATA 71
Shaw, Ray 7
Shaw, Richard 1923- 12
Shawn, Frank S.
  See Goulart, Ron(ald Joseph)
Shay, Art
  See Shay, Arthur
Shay, Arthur 1922- 4

Shay, Lacey
  See Shebar, Sharon Sigmond
Shea, Bob 188
Shea, George 1940- 54
  Brief entry 42
Shea, Pegi Deitz 1960- 172
  Earlier sketches in SATA 77, 137
Shearer, John 1947- 43
  Brief entry 27
  See also CLR 34
Shearer, Ted 1919- 43
Shearing, Leonie 1972- 184
Sheban, Chris 182
Shebar, Sharon Sigmond 1945- 36
Shecter, Ben 1935- 16
Shedd, Warner 1934- 147
  Earlier sketch in SATA 87
Sheedy, Alexandra Elizabeth 1962- 39
  Earlier sketch in SATA 19
Sheehan, Ethna 1908-2000 9
Sheehan, Patty 1945- 77
Sheehan, Sean 1951- 154
  Earlier sketch in SATA 86
Sheen, Barbara 1949- 143
Shefelman, Janice Jordan 1930- 129
  Earlier sketch in SATA 58
Shefelman, Tom (Whitehead) 1927- 58
Sheffer, H. R.
  See Abels, Harriette S(heffer)
Sheffield, Charles 1935-2002 109
Sheffield, Janet N. 1926- 26
Sheikh, Nazneen
  See Sadiq, Nazneen
Shekerjian, Regina Tor 16
Shelby, Anne 1948- 85
  Autobiography Feature 121
  See also SAAS 26
Sheldon, Ann
  See Antle, Nancy
Sheldon, Ann 67
  Earlier sketch in SATA 1
Sheldon, Aure 1917-1976 12
Sheldon, David 185
Sheldon, Dyan 181
Sheldon, John
  See Bloch, Robert (Albert)
Sheldon, Muriel 1926- 45
  Brief entry 39
Shell, Barry 1951- 176
Shelley, Frances
  See Wees, Frances Shelley
Shelley, Mary Wollstonecraft (Godwin)
  1797-1851 29
  See also CLR 133
Shelton, William Roy 1919-1995 5
  Obituary 129
Shemie, Bonnie (Jean Brenner) 1949- 96
Shemin, Margaretha (Hoeneveld) 1928- 4
Shen, Michele 1953- 173
Shenker, Michele
  See Shen, Michele
Shenton, Edward 1895-1977 45
Shepard, Aaron 1950- 187
  Earlier sketches in SATA 75, 113
Shepard, Ernest Howard 1879-1976 100
  Obituary 24
  Earlier sketches in SATA 3, 33
  See also CLR 27
Shepard, James R.
  See Shepard, Jim
Shepard, Jim 1956- 164
  Earlier sketch in SATA 90
Shepard, Mary
  See Knox, (Mary) Eleanor Jessie
Shephard, Esther 1891-1975 5
  Obituary 26
Shepherd, Donna Walsh
  See Walsh Shepherd, Donna
Shepherd, Elizabeth 4
Shepherd, Irana 173

Shepherd, Roni
  See Shepherd, Irana
Sheppard, Kate 195
Shepperson, Rob 178
Sherburne, Zoa (Lillian Morin) 1912-1995 3
  See also SAAS 18
Sherlock, Patti 71
Sherman, D(enis) R(onald) 1934- 48
  Brief entry 29
Sherman, Diane (Finn) 1928- 12
Sherman, Elizabeth
  See Friskey, Margaret (Richards)
Sherman, Harold (Morrow) 1898-1987 37
  Obituary 137
Sherman, Josepha 163
  Earlier sketch in SATA 75
Sherman, Michael
  See Lowndes, Robert A(ugustine) W(ard)
Sherman, Nancy
  See Rosenberg, Nancy (Sherman)
Sherman, Pat 174
Sherman, Peter Michael
  See Lowndes, Robert A(ugustine) W(ard)
Sherrard, Valerie (Anne) 1957- 141
Sherrod, Jane
  See Singer, Jane Sherrod
Sherry, Clifford J. 1943- 84
Sherry, (Dulcie) Sylvia 1932- 122
  Earlier sketch in SATA 8
Sherwan, Earl 1917- 3
Sherwood, Jonathan
  See London, Jonathan (Paul)
Sheth, Kashmira 186
Shetterly, Will 1955- 78
  Autobiography Feature 106
Shetterly, William Howard
  See Shetterly, Will
Shiefman, Vicky 1942- 22
Shields, Brenda Desmond (Armstrong)
  1914- 37
Shields, Carol Diggory 174
Shields, Charles 1944- 10
Shiels, Barbara
  See Adams, Barbara Johnston
Shiffman, Lena 1957- 101
Shiina, Makoto 1944- 83
Shimin, Symeon 1902-1984 13
Shimko, Bonnie 1941- 191
Shine, Andrea 1955- 104
Shine, Deborah 1932- 71
Shinn, Everett 1876-1953 21
Shinn, Sharon 1957- 164
  Earlier sketch in SATA 110
Shippen, Katherine B(inney) 1892-1980 1
  Obituary 23
  See also CLR 36
Shippey, T. A. 1943- 143
Shippey, Thomas Alan
  See Shippey, T. A.
Shipton, Eric Earle 1907-1977 10
Shiraz, Yasmin 173
Shirer, William L(awrence) 1904-1993 45
  Obituary 78
Shirley, Gayle C 1955- 96
Shirley, Gayle Corbett
  See Shirley, Gayle C
Shirley, Jean 1919- 70
Shirreffs, Gordon D(onald) 1914-1996 11
  See Gordon, Stewart
Shirts, Morris A(lpine) 1922- 63
Shlichta, Joe 1968- 84
Shmurak, Carole B. 1944- 118
Sholokhov, Mikhail (Aleksandrovich)
  1905-1984
  Obituary 36
Shore, Diane Z. 179
Shore, Diane ZuHone
  See Shore, Diane Z.
Shore, June Lewis 30
Shore, Nancy 1960- 124
Shore, Robert 1924- 39

Short, Michael 1937- 65
Short, Roger
    See Arkin, Alan
Shortall, Leonard W. 19
Shortt, Tim(othy Donald) 1961- 96
Shotwell, Louisa Rossiter 1902-1993 3
Shoup, Barbara 1947- 156
    Earlier sketch in SATA 86
    See also SAAS 24
Shoveller, Herb 184
Showalter, Jean B(reckinridge) 12
Showell, Ellen Harvey 1934- 33
Showers, Paul C. 1910-1999 92
    Obituary 114
    Earlier sketch in SATA 21
    See also CLR 6
    See also SAAS 7
Shpakow, Tanya 1959(?)- 94
Shpitalnik, Vladimir 1964- 83
Shragg, Karen (I.) 1954- 142
Shreeve, Elizabeth 1956- 156
Shreve, Susan
    See Shreve, Susan Richards
Shreve, Susan Richards 1939- 152
    Brief entry 41
    Earlier sketches in SATA 46, 95
Shriver, Jean Adair 1932- 75
Shriver, Maria 1955- 134
Shriver, Maria Owings
    See Shriver, Maria
Shrode, Mary
    See Hollingsworth, Mary
Shtainmets, Leon 32
Shub, Elizabeth 1915(?)-2004 5
Shuken, Julia 1948- 84
Shulevitz, Uri 1935- 165
    Earlier sketches in SATA 3, 50, 106
    See also CLR 61
Shulman, Alix Kates 1932- 7
Shulman, Dee 1957- 146
Shulman, Irving 1913-1995 13
Shulman, Mark 1962- 184
Shulman, Max 1919-1988
    Obituary 59
Shulman, Milton 1913-2004
    Obituary 154
Shulman, Neil B(arnett) 1945- 89
Shumsky, Zena
    See Collier, Zena
Shura, Mary Francis
    See Craig, Mary (Francis) Shura
Shusterman, Neal 1962- 140
    Autobiography Feature 140
    Earlier sketches in SATA 85, 121
Shuter, Jane (Margaret) 1955- 151
    Earlier sketch in SATA 90
Shuttlesworth, Dorothy Edwards 3
Shwartz, Susan (Martha) 1949- 94
Shyer, Christopher 1961- 98
Shyer, Marlene Fanta 13
Siberell, Anne 29
Sibley, Don 1922- 12
Siburt, Ruth 1951- 121
Siculan, Daniel 1922- 12
Siddon, Barbara
    See Bradford, Barbara Taylor
Sidgwick, Ethel 1877-1970 116
Sidjakov, Nicolas 1924- 18
Sidman, Joyce 1956- 181
    Earlier sketch in SATA 145
Sidney, Frank
    See Warwick, Alan R(oss)
Sidney, Margaret
    See Lothrop, Harriet Mulford Stone
Siebert, Diane 1948- 189
Siegal, Aranka 1930- 88
    Brief entry 37
Siegel, Beatrice 36
Siegel, Helen
    See Siegl, Helen
Siegel, Robert 1939- 39

Siegel, Robert Harold
    See Siegel, Robert
Siegel, Siena Cherson 1967(?)- 185
Siegelson, Kim L. 1962- 114
Sieger, Ted 1958- 189
Siegl, Helen 1924- 34
Siepmann, Mary Aline
    See Wesley, Mary (Aline)
Sierra, Judy 1945- 195
    Earlier sketches in SATA 104, 162
Sieswerda, Paul L. 1942- 147
Sievert, Terri
    See Dougherty, Terri (L.)
Silas
    See McCay, (Zenas) Winsor
Silcock, Sara Lesley 1947- 12
Silin-Palmer, Pamela 184
Sill, Cathryn 1953- 141
    Earlier sketch in SATA 74
Sill, John 1947- 140
    Earlier sketch in SATA 74
Sillitoe, Alan 1928- 61
Sills, Leslie (Elka) 1948- 129
Silly, E. S.
    See Kraus, (Herman) Robert
Silsbe, Brenda 1953- 73
Silva, Joseph
    See Goulart, Ron(ald Joseph)
Silver, Ruth
    See Chew, Ruth
Silverberg, Robert 1935- 91
    Autobiography Feature 104
    Earlier sketch in SATA 13
    See also CLR 59
Silverman, Erica 1955- 165
    Earlier sketches in SATA 78, 112
Silverman, Janis L. 1946- 127
Silverman, Mel(vin Frank) 1931-1966 9
Silverman, Robin L. 1954- 96
Silverman, Robin Landew
    See Silverman, Robin L.
Silverstein, Alvin 1933- 124
    Earlier sketches in SATA 8, 69
    See also CLR 25
Silverstein, Herma 1945- 106
Silverstein, Robert Alan 1959- 124
    Earlier sketch in SATA 77
Silverstein, Shel 1932-1999 92
    Brief entry 27
    Obituary 116
    Earlier sketch in SATA 33
    See also CLR 96
Silverstein, Sheldon Allan
    See Silverstein, Shel
Silverstein, Virginia B(arbara Opshelor)
    1937- 124
    Earlier sketches in SATA 8, 69
    See also CLR 25
Silverthorne, Elizabeth 1930- 35
Silverwood, Margaret Shannon 1966- 137
    Earlier sketch in SATA 83
Silvey, Diane F. 1946- 135
Sim, David 1951- 162
Sim, Dorrith M. 1931- 96
Simak, Clifford D(onald) 1904-1988
    Obituary 56
Simard, Remy 1959- 168
Simmie, Lois (Ann) 1932- 106
Simmonds, Posy 1945- 130
    See also CLR 23
Simmons, Andra 1939- 141
Simmons, Elly 1955- 134
Simmons, Michael 1970- 185
Simms, Laura 1947- 117
Simner, Janni Lee 113
Simon, Charlie May
    See Fletcher, Charlie May Hogue
Simon, Francesca 1955- 111
Simon, Gabriel 1972- 118
Simon, Hilda Rita 1921- 28
    See also CLR 39

Simon, Howard 1903-1979 32
    Obituary 21
Simon, Joe
    See Simon, Joseph H.
Simon, Joseph H. 1913- 7
Simon, Martin P(aul William) 1903-1969 12
Simon, Mina Lewiton
    See Lewiton, Mina
Simon, Norma (Feldstein) 1927- 129
    Earlier sketches in SATA 3, 68
Simon, Seymour 1931- 138
    Earlier sketches in SATA 4, 73
    See also CLR 63
Simon, Shirley (Schwartz) 1921- 11
Simon, Solomon 1895-1970 40
Simonetta, Linda 1948- 14
Simonetta, Sam 1936- 14
Simons, Barbara B(rooks) 1934- 41
Simont, Marc 1915- 126
    Earlier sketches in SATA 9, 73
Simpson, Colin 1908-1983 14
Simpson, Harriette
    See Arnow, Harriette (Louisa) Simpson
Simpson, Jacynth Hope
    See Hope Simpson, Jacynth
Simpson, Lesley 1963- 150
Simpson, Margaret 1943- 128
Simpson, Myrtle L(illias) 1931- 14
Sims, Blanche 168
    Earlier sketch in SATA 75
Sims, Blanche L.
    See Sims, Blanche
Simundsson, Elva 1950- 63
Sinclair, Clover
    See Gater, Dilys
Sinclair, Emil
    See Hesse, Hermann
Sinclair, Jeff 1958- 77
Sinclair, Olga 1923- 121
Sinclair, Rose
    See Smith, Susan Vernon
Sinclair, Upton 1878-1968 9
Sinclair, Upton Beall
    See Sinclair, Upton
Singer, A.L.
    See Lerangis, Peter
Singer, Arthur 1917-1990 64
Singer, Isaac
    See Singer, Isaac Bashevis
Singer, Isaac Bashevis 1904-1991 27
    Obituary 68
    Earlier sketch in SATA 3
    See also CLR 1
Singer, Jane Sherrod 1917-1985 4
    Obituary 42
Singer, Julia 1917- 28
Singer, Kurt D. 1911-2005 38
    Obituary 172
Singer, Marilyn 1948- 158
    Autobiography Feature 158
    Brief entry 38
    Earlier sketches in SATA 48, 80, 125
    See also CLR 48
    See also SAAS 13
Singer, Muff 1942-2005 104
    Obituary 160
Singer, Nicky 1956- 194
Singer, Susan (Mahler) 1941- 9
Singh, Rashmi Sharma 1952- 90
Singleton, Linda Joy 1957- 166
    Earlier sketch in SATA 88
Singleton, L.J.
    See Singleton, Linda Joy
Sinykin, Sheri(l Terri) Cooper 1950- 142
    Autobiography Feature 142
    Earlier sketches in SATA 72, 133
Sipiera, Paul P., (Jr.) 1948- 144
    Earlier sketch in SATA 89
Siracusa, Catherine (Jane) 1947- 82
Sirett, Dawn (Karen) 1966- 88
Sirimarco, Elizabeth 1966- 158

Sirof, Harriet 1930- 94
  Earlier sketch in SATA 37
Sirois, Allen L. 1950- 76
Sirvaitis (Chernyaev), Karen (Ann) 1961- ... 79
Sis, Peter 1949- 192
  Earlier sketch in SATA 149
  See also CLR 110
Sisson, Rosemary Anne 1923- 11
Sister Mary Terese
  See Donze, Mary Terese
Sita, Lisa 1962- 87
Sitomer, Alan Lawrence 174
Sitomer, Harry 1903-1985 31
Sitomer, Mindel 1903-1987 31
Sittenfeld, Curtis 1975(?)- 164
Sive, Helen R(obinson) 1951- 30
Sivulich, Sandra (Jeanne) Stroner 1941- 9
Siy, Alexandra 193
Skarmeta, Antonio 1940- 57
Skelly, James R(ichard) 1927- 17
Skelton, Matthew 1971- 185
Skinner, Constance Lindsay 1877-1939
  See YABC 1
Skinner, Cornelia Otis 1901-1979 2
Skipper, G. C. 1939- 46
  Brief entry 38
Sklansky, Amy E(dgar) 1971- 145
Skofield, James 95
  Brief entry 44
Skold, Betty Westrom 1923- 41
Skorpen, Liesel Moak 1935- 3
Skott, Maria
  See Nikolajeva, Maria
Skrypuch, Marsha Forchuk 1954- 134
Skultety, Nancy Laney 1960- 175
Skurzynski, Gloria 1930- 145
  Autobiography Feature 145
  Earlier sketches in SATA 8, 74, 122
  See also SAAS 9
Skurzynski, Gloria Joan
  See Skurzynski, Gloria
Skutch, Robert 1925- 89
Skye, Maggie
  See Werner, Herma
Skye, Obert 170
Slack, Michael 1969- 189
Slackman, Charles B. 1934- 12
Slade, Arthur G. 1967- 149
  Earlier sketch in SATA 106
Slade, Arthur Gregory
  See Slade, Arthur G.
Slade, Christian 1974- 193
Slade, Richard 1910-1971 9
Slangerup, Erik Jon 1969- 130
Slate, Joseph 1928- 174
  Earlier sketches in SATA 38, 122
Slate, Joseph Frank
  See Slate, Joseph
Slater, Dashka 1963- 179
Slater, Ray
  See Lansdale, Joe R.
Slaughter, Hope 1940- 84
Slaughter, Jean
  See Doty, Jean Slaughter
Slaughter, Tom 1955- 152
Slavicek, Louise Chipley 1956- 144
Slavin, Bill 1959- 148
  Earlier sketch in SATA 76
Slaymaker, Melissa Eskridge 1958- 158
Sleator, William 1945- 161
  Earlier sketches in SATA 3, 68, 118
  See also CLR 128
Sleator, William Warner III
  See Sleator, William
Slegers, Liesbet 1975- 154
Sleigh, Barbara 1906-1982 86
  Obituary 30
  Earlier sketch in SATA 3

Slepian, Jan 1921- 85
  Brief entry 45
  Earlier sketch in SATA 51
  See also SAAS 8
Slepian, Janice B.
  See Slepian, Jan
Slicer, Margaret O. 1920- 4
Slier, Debby
  See Shine, Deborah
Sloan, Brian 1966- 172
Sloan, Carolyn 1937- 116
  Earlier sketch in SATA 58
Sloan, Glenna (Davis) 1930- 120
Sloane, Eric 1910(?)-1985 52
  Obituary 42
Sloane, Todd 1955- 88
Sloat, Teri 1948- 164
  Earlier sketches in SATA 70, 106
Slobodkin, Florence Gersh 1905-1994 5
  Obituary 107
Slobodkin, Louis 1903-1975 26
  Earlier sketch in SATA 1
Slobodkina, Esphyr 1908-2002 1
  Obituary 135
  See also SAAS 8
Sloggett, Nellie 1851-1923 44
Sloss, Lesley Lord 1965- 72
Slote, Alfred 1926- 72
  Earlier sketch in SATA 8
  See also CLR 4
  See also SAAS 21
Slote, Elizabeth 1956- 80
Small, David 1945- 183
  Brief entry 46
  Earlier sketches in SATA 50, 95, 126
  See also CLR 53
Small, Ernest
  See Lent, Blair
Small, Mary 1932- 165
Small, Terry 1942- 75
Smallcomb, Pam 1954- 159
Smalls, Irene
  See Smalls-Hector, Irene
Smalls-Hector, Irene 1950- 146
  Earlier sketch in SATA 73
  See also CLR 103
Smallwood, Norah (Evelyn) 1910(?)-1984
  Obituary 41
Smaridge, Norah (Antoinette) 1903-1994 6
Smee, Nicola 1948- 167
  Earlier sketch in SATA 76
Smiley, Virginia Kester 1923- 2
Smith, Alexander McCall 1948- 179
  Earlier sketch in SATA 73
Smith, Anne Warren 1938- 41
  Brief entry 34
Smith, Barry (Edward Jervis) 1943- 75
Smith, Beatrice S(chillinger) 12
Smith, Betsy Covington 1937- 55
  Earlier sketch in SATA 43
Smith, Betty (Wehner) 1904-1972 6
Smith, Bradford 1909-1964 5
Smith, Brenda 1946- 82
Smith, C. Pritchard
  See Hoyt, Edwin P(almer), Jr.
Smith, Caesar
  See Trevor, Elleston
Smith, Charles R., (Jr.) 1969- 159
Smith, Craig 1955- 172
  Earlier sketches in SATA 81, 117
Smith, Cynthia Leitich 1967- 152
Smith, Datus C(lifford), Jr. 1907-1999 13
  Obituary 116
Smith, Debra 1955- 89
Smith, Derek 1943- 141
Smith, Dick King
  See King-Smith, Dick
Smith, Dodie
  See Smith, Dorothy Gladys

Smith, Doris Buchanan 1934-2002 75
  Obituary 140
  Earlier sketch in SATA 28
  See also SAAS 10
Smith, Dorothy Gladys 1896-1990 82
  Obituary 65
  See Smith, Dodie
Smith, Dorothy Stafford 1905- 6
Smith, E(lmer) Boyd 1860-1943
  See YABC 1
Smith, E(dric) Brooks 1917- 40
Smith, Emma 1923- 52
  Brief entry 36
Smith, (Katherine) Eunice (Young)
  1902-1993 5
Smith, Frances C(hristine) 1904-1986 3
Smith, Gary R. 1932- 14
Smith, Geof 1969- 102
Smith, George Harmon 1920- 5
Smith, Gordon 1951- 184
Smith, Greg Leitich 152
Smith, H(arry) Allen 1907-1976
  Obituary 20
Smith, Helene 1937- 142
Smith, Howard E(verett), Jr. 1927- 12
Smith, Hugh L(etcher) 1921-1968 5
Smith, Imogene Henderson 1922- 12
Smith, Jacqueline B. 1937- 39
Smith, Jada Pinkett 1971- 161
Smith, James D. 1955- 176
Smith, James Noel 1950- 193
Smith, Janet (Buchanan) Adam
  See Adam Smith, Janet (Buchanan)
Smith, Janice Lee 1949- 155
  Earlier sketch in SATA 54
Smith, Jean
  See Smith, Frances C(hristine)
Smith, Jean Pajot 1945- 10
Smith, Jeff(rey Alan) 1960- 161
  Earlier sketch in SATA 93
Smith, Jeff Allen
  See Smith, Jeff(rey Alan)
Smith, Jenny 1963- 90
Smith, Jessie
  See Kunhardt, Edith
Smith, Jessie Willcox 1863-1935 21
  See also CLR 59
Smith, Joan (Mary) 1933- 54
  Brief entry 46
Smith, Johnston
  See Crane, Stephen (Townley)
Smith, Jos A. 1936- 181
  Earlier sketches in SATA 73, 120
Smith, Joseph Arthur
  See Smith, Jos A.
Smith, Judie R. 1936- 80
Smith, Lafayette
  See Higdon, Hal
Smith, Lane 1959- 179
  Earlier sketches in SATA 76, 131
  See also CLR 47
Smith, Lee
  See Albion, Lee Smith
Smith, Lendon H(oward) 1921- 64
Smith, Lillian H(elena) 1887-1983
  Obituary 32
Smith, Linda 1949- 177
Smith, Linell Nash 1932- 2
Smith, Lucia B. 1943- 30
Smith, Maggie 1965- 190
Smith, Marion Hagens 1913- 12
Smith, Marion Jaques 1899-1987 13
Smith, Mary Ellen 10
Smith, Marya 1945- 78
Smith, Mike
  See Smith, Mary Ellen
Smith, Nancy Covert 1935- 12
Smith, Norman F. 1920- 70
  Earlier sketch in SATA 5
Smith, Patricia Clark 1943- 96

Smith, Pauline C.
  See Arthur, Robert, (Jr.)
Smith, Pauline C(oggeshall) 1908-1994 .... *27*
Smith, Philip Warren 1936- *46*
Smith, R. Alexander McCall
  See Smith, Alexander McCall
Smith, Rebecca 1946- *123*
Smith, Robert Kimmel 1930- *77*
  Earlier sketch in SATA *12*
Smith, Robert Paul 1915-1977 .... *52*
  Obituary *30*
Smith, Roland 1951- *193*
  Earlier sketches in SATA *115, 161*
Smith, Rosamond
  See Oates, Joyce Carol
Smith, Ruth Leslie 1902- *2*
Smith, Samantha 1972-1985
  Obituary *45*
Smith, Sandra Lee 1945- *75*
Smith, Sarah Stafford
  See Smith, Dorothy Stafford
Smith, Sharon 1947- *82*
Smith, Sherri L. 1971- *156*
Smith, Sherwood 1951- *140*
  Earlier sketch in SATA *82*
Smith, Shirley Raines
  See Raines, Shirley C(arol)
Smith, Susan Carlton 1923- *12*
Smith, Susan Mathias 1950- *43*
  Brief entry *35*
Smith, Susan Vernon 1950- *48*
  See Mendonca, Susan
Smith, Tim(othy R.) 1945- *151*
Smith, Ursula 1934- *54*
Smith, Vian (Crocker) 1920-1969 .... *11*
Smith, Wanda VanHoy 1926- *65*
Smith, Ward
  See Goldsmith, Howard
Smith, William A. 1918- *10*
Smith, William Jay 1918- *154*
  Autobiography Feature *154*
  Earlier sketches in SATA *2, 68*
  See also SAAS *22*
Smith, Winsome 1935- *45*
Smith, Z.Z.
  See Westheimer, David
Smith-Ankrom, M. E. 1942- *130*
Smith-Griswold, Wendy 1955- *88*
Smith-Rex, Susan J. 1950- *94*
Smithsen, Richard
  See Pellowski, Michael (Joseph)
Smits, Teo
  See Smits, Theodore R(ichard)
Smits, Theodore R(ichard) 1905-1996 .... *45*
  Brief entry *28*
Smolinski, Dick 1932- *86*
Smothers, Ethel Footman 1944- *149*
  Earlier sketch in SATA *76*
Smucker, Barbara 1915-2003 .... *130*
  Earlier sketches in SATA *29, 76*
  See also CLR *10*
  See also SAAS *11*
Smucker, Barbara Claassen
  See Smucker, Barbara
Smyth, Iain 1959- *105*
Snedeker, Caroline Dale (Parke) 1871-1956
  See YABC *2*
Sneed, Brad *191*
Snell, Nigel (Edward Creagh) 1936- *57*
  Brief entry *40*
Snellgrove, L(aurence) E(rnest) 1928- *53*
Snelling, Dennis (Wayne) 1958- *84*
Sneve, Virginia Driving Hawk 1933- *95*
  Earlier sketch in SATA *8*
  See also CLR *2*
Snicket, Lemony 1970- *187*
  Earlier sketch in SATA *126*
  See also CLR *79*
Sniegoski, Thomas E. *195*
Sniegoski, Tom
  See Sniegoski, Thomas E.

Snodgrass, Mary Ellen 1944- *75*
Snodgrass, Quentin Curtius
  See Clemens, Samuel Langhorne
Snodgrass, Thomas Jefferson
  See Clemens, Samuel Langhorne
Snook, Barbara (Lillian) 1913-1976 .... *34*
Snow, Alan 1959- *190*
Snow, Donald Clifford 1917-1979 .... *16*
Snow, Dorothea J(ohnston) 1909- *9*
Snow, Richard F(olger) 1947- *52*
  Brief entry *37*
Snyder, Anne 1922-2001 .... *4*
  Obituary *125*
Snyder, Bernadette McCarver 1930- *97*
Snyder, Carol 1941- *35*
Snyder, Gerald S(eymour) 1933- *48*
  Brief entry *34*
Snyder, Jerome 1916-1976
  Obituary *20*
Snyder, Midori 1954- *106*
Snyder, Paul A. 1946- *125*
Snyder, Zilpha Keatley 1927- *163*
  Autobiography Feature *163*
  Earlier sketches in SATA *1, 28, 75, 110*
  See also CLR *121*
  See also SAAS *2*
Snyderman, Reuven K. 1922- *5*
So, Meilo *162*
Sobel, June 1950- *149*
Soble, Jennie
  See Cavin, Ruth (Brodie)
Sobol, Donald J. 1924- *132*
  Earlier sketches in SATA *1, 31, 73*
  See also CLR *4*
Sobol, Harriet Langsam 1936- *47*
  Brief entry *34*
Sobol, Rose 1931- *76*
Sobott-Mogwe, Gaele 1956- *97*
Soderlind, Arthur E(dwin) 1920- *14*
Soentpiet, Chris K. 1970- *159*
  Earlier sketch in SATA *97*
Soerensen, Svend Otto 1916- *67*
Sofer, Barbara 1949- *109*
Sofer, Rachel
  See Sofer, Barbara
Softly, Barbara Frewin 1924- *12*
Soglow, Otto 1900-1975
  Obituary *30*
Sohl, Frederic J(ohn) 1916- *10*
Sohr, Daniel 1973- *190*
Sokol, Bill
  See Sokol, William
Sokol, William 1923- *37*
Sokolov, Kirill 1930- *34*
Solbert, Romaine G. 1925- *2*
Solbert, Ronni
  See Solbert, Romaine G.
Solheim, James *133*
Solomon, Heather M. *188*
Solomon, Joan 1930- *51*
  Brief entry *40*
Solomons, Ikey Esquir
  See Thackeray, William Makepeace
Solonevich, George 1915-2003 .... *15*
Solot, Mary Lynn 1939- *12*
Somerlott, Robert 1928-2001 .... *62*
Somervill, Barbara A(nn) 1948- *140*
Sommer, Angela
  See Sommer-Bodenburg, Angela
Sommer, Carl 1930- *175*
  Earlier sketch in SATA *126*
Sommer, Elyse 1929- *7*
Sommer, Robert 1929- *12*
Sommer-Bodenburg, Angela 1948- *113*
  Earlier sketch in SATA *63*
Sommerdorf, Norma 1926- *131*
Sommerdorf, Norma Jean
  See Sommerdorf, Norma
Sommerfelt, Aimee 1892-1975 .... *5*
Son, John *160*
Sones, Sonya *131*

Sonneborn, Ruth (Cantor) 1899-1974 .... *4*
  Obituary *27*
Sonnenblick, Jordan 1969- *185*
Sonnenmark, Laura A. 1958- *73*
Sopko, Eugen 1949- *58*
Sorel, Edward 1929- *126*
  Brief entry *37*
  Earlier sketch in SATA *65*
Sorensen, Henri 1950- *115*
  Earlier sketch in SATA *77*
Sorensen, Svend Otto
  See Soerensen, Svend Otto
Sorensen, Virginia 1912-1991 .... *2*
  Obituary *72*
  See also SAAS *15*
Sorenson, Jane 1926- *63*
Sorenson, Margo 1946- *96*
Sorley Walker, Kathrine *41*
Sorra, Kristin *185*
Sorrells, Walter *177*
Sorrentino, Joseph N. 1937- *6*
Sortor, June Elizabeth 1939- *12*
Sortor, Toni
  See Sortor, June Elizabeth
Soskin, V. H.
  See Ellison, Virginia H(owell)
Soto, Gary 1952- *174*
  Earlier sketches in SATA *80, 120*
  See also CLR *38*
Sotomayor, Antonio 1902-1985 .... *11*
Souci, Robert D. San
  See San Souci, Robert D.
Soudley, Henry
  See Wood, James Playsted
Souhami, Jessica *176*
Soule, Gardner (Bosworth) 1913-2000 .... *14*
Soule, Jean Conder 1919- *10*
Souster, (Holmes) Raymond 1921- *63*
South, Sheri Cobb 1959- *82*
Southall, Ivan 1921-2008 .... *134*
  Autobiography Feature *134*
  Earlier sketches in SATA *3, 68*
  See also CLR *2*
  See also SAAS *3*
Southall, Ivan Francis
  See Southall, Ivan
Southey, Robert 1774-1843 .... *54*
Southgate, Vera *54*
Sovak, Jan 1953- *115*
Sowden, Celeste
  See Walters, Celeste
Sowter, Nita *69*
Spafford, Suzy 1945- *160*
Spagnoli, Cathy 1950- *134*
  Earlier sketch in SATA *79*
Spain, Sahara Sunday 1991- *133*
Spain, Susan Rosson *185*
Spalding, Andrea 1944- *150*
  Earlier sketch in SATA *101*
Spanfeller, James J(ohn) 1930- *19*
  See Spanfeller, Jim
Spanfeller, Jim
  See SAAS *8*
  See Spanfeller, James J(ohn)
Spangenberg, Judith Dunn 1942- *5*
Spanyol, Jessica 1965- *137*
Spar, Jerome 1918- *10*
Sparks, Barbara 1942- *78*
Sparks, Beatrice (Mathews) 1918- *44*
  Brief entry *28*
  See also CLR *139*
Sparks, Mary W. 1920- *15*
Spaulding, Douglas
  See Bradbury, Ray
Spaulding, Leonard
  See Bradbury, Ray
Spaulding, Norma *107*
Speare, Elizabeth George 1908-1994 .... *62*
  Obituary *83*
  Earlier sketch in SATA *5*
  See also CLR *8*

Spearing, Judith (Mary Harlow) 1922- 9
Spears, Rick 182
Speck, Nancy 1959- 104
Specking, Inez 1890-1960(?) 11
Speed, Nell
    See Keats, Emma
    and Sampson, Emma (Keats) Speed
Speed, Nell (Ewing) 1878-1913 68
Speer, Bonnie Stahlman 1929- 113
Speer-Lyon, Tammie L. 1965- 89
Speicher, Helen Ross S(mith) 1915- 8
Speir, Nancy 1958- 81
Spellman, John W(illard) 1934- 14
Spellman, Roger G.
    See Cox, William R(obert)
Spelman, Cornelia Maude 1946- 144
    Earlier sketch in SATA 96
Spelman, Mary 1934- 28
Spelvin, George
    See Lerangis, Peter
    and Phillips, David Atlee
Spence, Cynthia
    See Eble, Diane
Spence, Eleanor (Rachel) 1928- 21
    See also CLR 26
Spence, Geraldine 1931- 47
Spencer, Ann 1918- 10
Spencer, Cornelia
    See Yaukey, Grace S(ydenstricker)
Spencer, Donald D(ean) 1931- 41
Spencer, Elizabeth 1921- 14
Spencer, Leonard G.
    See Garrett, (Gordon) Randall (Phillip)
    and Silverberg, Robert
Spencer, William 1922- 9
Spencer, Zane A(nn) 1935- 35
Sper, Emily 1957- 142
Speregen, Devra Newberger 1964- 84
Sperling, Dan(iel Lee) 1949- 65
Sperry, Armstrong W. 1897-1976 1
    Obituary 27
Sperry, Raymond
    See Garis, Howard R(oger)
Sperry, Raymond, Jr. 1
Spetter, Jung-Hee 1969- 134
Spicer, Dorothy Gladys -1975 32
Spiegel, Beth 184
Spiegelman, Art 1948- 158
    Earlier sketch in SATA 109
Spiegelman, Judith M. 5
Spielberg, Steven 1947- 32
Spier, Peter (Edward) 1927- 54
    Earlier sketch in SATA 4
    See also CLR 5
Spilhaus, Athelstan (Frederick) 1911-1998 .. 13
    Obituary 102
Spilka, Arnold 1917- 6
Spillane, Frank Morrison
    See Spillane, Mickey
Spillane, Mickey 1918-2006 66
    Obituary 176
    See Spillane, Frank Morrison
Spinelli, Eileen 1942- 186
    Earlier sketches in SATA 38, 101, 150
Spinelli, Jerry 1941- 195
    Earlier sketches in SATA 39, 71, 110, 158
    See also CLR 82
Spink, Reginald (William) 1905-1994 11
Spinka, Penina Keen 1945- 72
Spinner, Stephanie 1943- 132
    Earlier sketches in SATA 38, 91
Spinossimus
    See White, William, Jr.
Spiotta-DiMare, Loren 173
Spires, Ashley 1978- 183
Spires, Elizabeth 1952- 111
    Earlier sketch in SATA 71
Spirin, Gennadii
    See Spirin, Gennady
Spirin, Gennadij
    See Spirin, Gennady

Spirin, Gennady 1948- 134
    Earlier sketch in SATA 95
    See also CLR 88
Spivak, Dawnine 101
Spizman, Robyn Freedman 194
Spohn, David 1948- 72
Spohn, Kate 1962- 147
    Earlier sketch in SATA 87
Spollen, Christopher 1952- 12
Spooner, Michael (Tim) 1954- 92
Spowart, Robin 1947- 177
    Earlier sketch in SATA 82
Sprague, Gretchen 1926-2003 27
Sprengel, Artie
    See Lerangis, Peter
Sprigge, Elizabeth (Miriam Squire)
    1900-1974 10
Spring, (Robert) Howard 1889-1965 28
Springer, Margaret 1941- 78
Springer, Marilyn Harris 1931- 47
Springer, Nancy 1948- 172
    Earlier sketches in SATA 65, 110
Springstubb, Tricia 1950- 78
    Brief entry 40
    Earlier sketch in SATA 46
Spudvilas, Anne 1951- 94
Spurll, Barbara 1952- 78
Spurr, Elizabeth 172
Spykman, E(lizabeth) C(hoate) 1896-1965 .. 10
    See also CLR 35
Spyri, Johanna (Heusser) 1827-1901 100
    Earlier sketch in SATA 19
    See also CLR 115
Squires, Phil
    See Barker, S(quire) Omar
Srba, Lynne 98
Sreenivasan, Jyotsna 1964- 101
S-Ringi, Kjell
    See Ringi, Kjell (Arne Soerensen)
Stacey, Cherylyn 1945- 96
Stacy, Donald
    See Pohl, Frederik
Stadtler, Bea 1921- 17
Stafford, Jean 1915-1979
    Obituary 22
Stafford, Liliana 1950- 141
Stafford, Paul 1966- 116
Stahl, Ben(jamin) 1910-1987 5
    Obituary 54
Stahl, Hilda 1938-1993 48
    Obituary 77
Stahler, David, Jr. 162
Stainton, Sue 187
Stair, Gobin (John) 1912- 35
Stalder, Valerie 27
Stamaty, Mark Alan 1947- 12
Stambler, Irwin 1924- 5
Standiford, Natalie 1961- 169
    Earlier sketch in SATA 81
Stanek, Lou Willett 1931- 63
Stang, Judit 1921-1977 29
Stang, Judy
    See Stang, Judit
Stangl, (Mary) Jean 1928- 67
Stanhope, Eric
    See Hamilton, Charles (Harold St. John)
Stankevich, Boris 1928- 2
Stanley, Diane 1943- 164
    Brief entry 32
    Earlier sketches in SATA 37, 80, 115
    See also CLR 46
    See also SAAS 15
Stanley, George Edward 1942- 157
    Earlier sketches in SATA 53, 111
    See Dixon, Franklin W.
    and Hope, Laura Lee
    and Keene, Carolyn
Stanley, Jerry 1941- 127
    Earlier sketch in SATA 79
Stanley, Mandy 165

Stanley, Robert
    See Hamilton, Charles (Harold St. John)
Stanley, Sanna 1962- 145
Stanli, Sue
    See Meilach, Dona Z(weigoron)
Stanstead, John
    See Groom, Arthur William
Stanton, Karen 1960- 190
Stanton, Schuyler
    See Baum, L(yman) Frank
Staples, Suzanne Fisher 1945- 151
    Earlier sketches in SATA 70, 105
    See also CLR 137
Stapleton, Marjorie (Winifred) 1932- 28
Stapp, Arthur D(onald) 1906-1972 4
Starbird, Kaye 1916- 6
    See also CLR 60
Stark, Evan 1942- 78
Stark, James
    See Goldston, Robert (Conroy)
Stark, Ulf 1944- 124
Starke, Ruth (Elaine) 1946- 129
Starkey, Marion L(ena) 1901-1991 13
Starr, Ward
    See Manes, Stephen
Starret, William
    See McClintock, Marshall
Starr Taylor, Bridget 1959- 99
Stasiak, Krystyna 49
Staub, Frank 1949- 116
Staub, Frank Jacob
    See Staub, Frank
Staub, Wendy Corsi 1964- 114
Stauffacher, Sue 1961- 155
Stauffer, Don
    See Berkebile, Fred D(onovan)
Staunton, Schuyler
    See Baum, L(yman) Frank
Staunton, Ted 1956- 167
    Earlier sketch in SATA 112
Stead, Rebecca 1968(?)- 188
Steadman, Ralph 1936- 123
    Earlier sketch in SATA 32
Steadman, Ralph Idris
    See Steadman, Ralph
Stearman, Kaye 1951- 118
Stearns, Monroe (Mather) 1913-1987 5
    Obituary 55
Steckler, Arthur 1921-1985 65
Steding, Laurie 1953- 119
Steel, Danielle 1947- 66
Steel, Danielle Fernande
    See Steel, Danielle
Steele, Addison II
    See Lupoff, Richard A(llen)
Steele, Alexander 1958- 116
Steele, Henry Maxwell
    See Steele, Max
Steele, Mary 1930- 94
Steele, Mary Q(uintard Govan) 1922-1992 .. 51
    Obituary 72
    Earlier sketch in SATA 3
Steele, Max 1922-2005 168
    Earlier sketch in SATA 10
Steele, Philip 1948- 140
    Earlier sketch in SATA 81
Steele, William O(wen) 1917-1979 51
    Obituary 27
    Earlier sketch in SATA 1
Steelhammer, Ilona 1952- 98
Steelsmith, Shari 1962- 72
Stefanik, Alfred T. 1939- 55
Steffanson, Con
    See Cassiday, Bruce (Bingham)
    and Goulart, Ron(ald Joseph)
Steffens, Bradley 1955- 166
    Earlier sketch in SATA 77
Steffensmeier, Alexander 1977- 195
Stegeman, Janet Allais 1923- 53
    Brief entry 49
    See Britton, Kate

Steggall, Susan 1967- *182*
Steig, William 1907-2003 .... *111*
    Obituary *149*
    Earlier sketches in SATA *18, 70*
    See also CLR *103*
Steig, William H.
    See Steig, William
Stein, David Ezra *180*
Stein, M(eyer) L(ewis) 1920- *6*
Stein, Mathilde 1969- *195*
Stein, Mini *2*
Stein, R(ichard) Conrad 1937- *154*
    Earlier sketches in SATA *31, 82*
Stein, Wendy 1951- *77*
Steinbeck, John (Ernst) 1902-1968 .... *9*
Steinberg, Alfred 1917-1995 .... *9*
Steinberg, Fannie 1899-1990 .... *43*
Steinberg, Fred J. 1933- *4*
Steinberg, Phillip Orso 1921- *34*
Steinberg, Rafael (Mark) 1927- *45*
Steinberg, Saul 1914-1999 .... *67*
Steincrohn, Maggie
    See Davis, Maggie S.
Steiner, Barbara A(nnette) 1934- *83*
    Earlier sketch in SATA *13*
    See also SAAS *13*
Steiner, Charlotte 1900-1981 .... *45*
Steiner, George 1929- *62*
Steiner, Joan *110*
Steiner, Jorg
    See Steiner, Jorg
Steiner, Jorg 1930- *35*
Steiner, K. Leslie
    See Delany, Samuel R., Jr.
Steiner, Stan(ley) 1925-1987 .... *14*
    Obituary *50*
Steinhardt, Bernice *193*
Steins, Richard 1942- *79*
Stem, Jacqueline 1931- *110*
Stemple, Jason *179*
Steneman, Shep 1945- *132*
Stengel, Joyce A. 1938- *158*
Stephanie, Gordon
    See Gordon, Stephanie Jacob
Stephens, Alice Barber 1858-1932 .... *66*
Stephens, Casey
    See Wagner, Sharon B.
Stephens, J.B.
    See Lynn, Tracy
Stephens, Mary Jo 1935- *8*
Stephens, Rebecca 1961- *141*
Stephens, Reed
    See Donaldson, Stephen R.
Stephens, Suzanne
    See Kirby, Susan E.
Stephens, William M(cLain) 1925- *21*
Stephensen, A. M.
    See Manes, Stephen
Stephenson, Lynda 1941- *179*
Stephenson, Lynda A.
    See Stephenson, Lynda
Stepp, Ann 1935- *29*
Stepto, Michele 1946- *61*
Steptoe, Javaka 1971- *151*
Steptoe, John (Lewis) 1950-1989 .... *63*
    Earlier sketch in SATA *8*
    See also CLR *12*
Sterling, Brett
    See Bradbury, Ray
    and Hamilton, Edmond
    and Samachson, Joseph
Sterling, Dorothy 1913-2008 .... *83*
    Autobiography Feature *127*
    Earlier sketch in SATA *1*
    See also CLR *1*
    See also SAAS *2*
Sterling, Philip 1907-1989 .... *8*
    Obituary *63*
Sterling, Shirley (Anne) 1948- *101*
Stern, Ellen Norman 1927- *26*
Stern, Judith M. 1951- *75*

Stern, Madeleine
    See Stern, Madeleine B.
Stern, Madeleine B. 1912-2007 .... *14*
Stern, Madeleine Bettina
    See Stern, Madeleine B.
Stern, Maggie 1953- *156*
Stern, Philip Van Doren 1900-1984 .... *13*
    Obituary *39*
Stern, Simon 1943- *15*
Sterne, Emma Gelders 1894- *6*
Steurt, Marjorie Rankin 1888-1978 .... *10*
Stevens, Bryna 1924- *65*
Stevens, Carla M(cBride) 1928- *13*
Stevens, Chambers 1968- *128*
Stevens, Diane 1939- *94*
Stevens, Franklin 1933- *6*
Stevens, Greg
    See Cook, Glen
Stevens, Gwendolyn 1944- *33*
Stevens, Jan Romero 1953- *95*
Stevens, Janet 1953- *193*
    Earlier sketches in SATA *90, 148*
Stevens, Kathleen 1936- *49*
Stevens, Leonard A. 1920- *67*
Stevens, Lucile Vernon 1899-1994 .... *59*
Stevens, Margaret Dean
    See Aldrich, Bess Streeter
Stevens, Patricia Bunning 1931- *27*
Stevens, Peter
    See Geis, Darlene Stern
Stevens, Serita 1949- *70*
Stevens, Serita Deborah
    See Stevens, Serita
Stevens, Serita Mendelson
    See Stevens, Serita
Stevens, Shira
    See Stevens, Serita
Stevenson, Anna (M.) 1905- *12*
Stevenson, Augusta 1869(?)-1976 .... *2*
    Obituary *26*
Stevenson, Burton Egbert 1872-1962 .... *25*
Stevenson, Drew 1947- *60*
Stevenson, Harvey 1960- *148*
    Earlier sketch in SATA *80*
Stevenson, James 1929- *195*
    Brief entry *34*
    Earlier sketches in SATA *42, 71, 113, 161*
    See also CLR *17*
Stevenson, Janet 1913- *8*
Stevenson, Robert Louis (Balfour)
    1850-1894 .... *100*
    See also YABC *2*
    See also CLR *107*
Stevenson, Sucie
    See Stevenson, Sucie
Stevenson, Sucie 1956- *194*
    Earlier sketch in SATA *104*
Stewart, A(gnes) C(harlotte) *15*
Stewart, Amber *181*
Stewart, Chantal 1945- *173*
    Earlier sketch in SATA *121*
Stewart, Charles
    See Zurhorst, Charles (Stewart, Jr.)
Stewart, Eleanor
    See Porter, Eleanor H(odgman)
Stewart, Elisabeth J(ane) 1927- *93*
Stewart, Elizabeth Laing 1907- *6*
Stewart, Gail B. 1949- *141*
Stewart, George Rippey 1895-1980 .... *3*
    Obituary *23*
Stewart, Jennifer J(enkins) 1960- *128*
Stewart, Joel *151*
Stewart, John (William) 1920- *14*
    See Cole, Jack
Stewart, Mary (Florence Elinor) 1916- *12*
Stewart, Mary Rainbow
    See Stewart, Mary (Florence Elinor)
Stewart, Melissa 1968- *167*
    Earlier sketch in SATA *111*
Stewart, Paul 1955- *163*
    Earlier sketch in SATA *114*

Stewart, Robert Neil 1891-1972 .... *7*
Stewart, Sarah *143*
Stewart, Scott
    See Zaffo, George J.
Stewart, W(alter) P. 1924- *53*
Stewart, Whitney 1959- *167*
    Earlier sketch in SATA *92*
Stewig, John Warren 1937- *162*
    Earlier sketches in SATA *26, 110*
Stickler, Soma Han 1942- *128*
Stidworthy, John 1943- *63*
Stiegemeyer, Julie *180*
Stiles, Martha Bennett *108*
    Earlier sketch in SATA *6*
Still, James 1906-2001 .... *29*
    Obituary *127*
Stille, Darlene R. 1942- *170*
    Earlier sketch in SATA *126*
Stille, Darlene Ruth
    See Stille, Darlene R.
Stillerman, Marci *104*
Stillerman, Robbie 1947- *12*
Stilley, Frank 1918- *29*
Stilton, Geronimo *158*
Stimpson, Gerald
    See Mitchell, Adrian
Stine, Catherine *165*
Stine, G(eorge) Harry 1928-1997 .... *136*
    Earlier sketch in SATA *10*
Stine, Jovial Bob
    See Stine, R.L.
Stine, R.L. 1943- *194*
    Earlier sketches in SATA *31, 76, 129*
    See also CLR *111*
Stine, Robert Lawrence
    See Stine, R.L.
Stinetorf, Louise (Allender) 1900-1992 .... *10*
Stinson, Kathy 1952- *98*
Stirling, Arthur
    See Sinclair, Upton
Stirling, Ian 1941- *77*
Stirling, Nora B(romley) 1900-1997 .... *3*
Stirnweis, Shannon 1931- *10*
Stobbs, William 1914-2000 .... *17*
    Obituary *120*
Stock, Carolmarie 1951- *75*
Stock, Catherine 1952- *158*
    Earlier sketches in SATA *65, 114*
Stockdale, Susan 1954- *98*
Stockham, Peter (Alan) 1928- *57*
Stockton, Francis Richard 1834-1902 .... *44*
    See Stockton, Frank R.
Stockton, Frank R.
    Brief entry *32*
    See Stockton, Francis Richard
Stockwell-Moniz, Marc J. 1954- *164*
Stoddard, Edward G. 1923- *10*
Stoddard, Hope 1900-1987 .... *6*
Stoddard, Sandol 1927- *98*
    See Warburg, Sandol Stoddard
Stoehr, Shelley 1969- *107*
Stoeke, Janet Morgan 1957- *136*
    Earlier sketch in SATA *90*
Stohner, Anu 1952- *179*
Stoiko, Michael 1919- *14*
Stojic, Manya 1967- *156*
Stoker, Abraham 1847-1912 .... *29*
    See Stoker, Bram
Stoker, Bram
    See Stoker, Abraham
Stokes, Cedric
    See Beardmore, George
Stokes, Jack (Tilden) 1923- *13*
Stokes, Olivia Pearl 1916- *32*
Stolz, Mary 1920-2006 .... *133*
    Obituary *180*
    Earlier sketches in SATA *10, 71*
    See also SAAS *3*
Stolz, Mary Slattery
    See Stolz, Mary

Stone, Alan
    See Svenson, Andrew E(dward)
Stone, David K(arl) 1922- 9
Stone, David Lee 1978- 166
Stone, Eugenia 1879-1971 7
Stone, Gene
    See Stone, Eugenia
Stone, Helen V(irginia) 6
Stone, Idella Purnell
    See Purnell, Idella
Stone, Ikey
    See Purnell, Idella
Stone, Irving 1903-1989 3
    Obituary 64
Stone, Jeff 178
Stone, Jon 1931-1997 39
    Obituary 95
Stone, Josephine Rector
    See Dixon, Jeanne
Stone, Lesley
    See Trevor, Elleston
Stone, Peter 1930-2003 65
    Obituary 143
Stone, Phoebe 134
Stone, Raymond 1
Stone, Rosetta
    See Dr. Seuss
    and Geisel, Theodor Seuss
    and LeSieg, Theo.
    and Seuss, Dr.
Stone, Tanya Lee 182
Stonehouse, Bernard 1926- 140
    Earlier sketches in SATA 13, 80
Stones, (Cyril) Anthony 1934- 72
Stong, Phil(ip Duffield) 1899-1957 32
Stoops, Erik D(aniel) 1966- 142
    Earlier sketch in SATA 78
Stoppelmoore, Cheryl Jean
    See Ladd, Cheryl (Jean)
Stops, Sue 1936- 86
Storace, Patricia 193
Storad, Conrad J. 1957- 119
Storey, Margaret 1926- 9
Storey, Victoria Carolyn 1945- 16
Storme, Peter
    See Stern, Philip Van Doren
Storr, Catherine (Cole) 1913-2001 87
    Obituary 122
    Earlier sketch in SATA 9
Story, Josephine
    See Loring, Emilie (Baker)
Stotko, Mary-Ann 1960- 154
Stott, Dorothy (M.) 1958- 99
    Earlier sketch in SATA 67
Stott, Dot
    See Stott, Dorothy (M.)
Stotter, Mike 1957- 108
Stout, William 1949- 132
Stoutenburg, Adrien (Pearl) 1916-1982 3
Stoutland, Allison 1963- 130
Stover, Allan C(arl) 1938- 14
Stover, Jill (Griffin) 1958- 82
Stover, Marjorie Filley 1914- 9
Stowe, Harriet (Elizabeth) Beecher 1811-1896
    See YABC 1
    See also CLR 131
Stowe, Leland 1899-1994 60
    Obituary 78
Stowe, Rosetta
    See Ogan, George F.
    and Ogan, Margaret E. (Nettles)
Stower, Adam 195
Strachan, Ian 1938- 85
Strachan, Linda 167
Strachan, Margaret Pitcairn 1908-1998 14
Strahinich, H. C.
    See Strahinich, Helen C.
Strahinich, Helen C. 1949- 78
Strait, Treva Adams 1909-2002 35
Strand, Mark 1934- 41

Strange, Philippa
    See Coury, Louise Andree
Stranger, Joyce
    See SAAS 24
    See Wilson, Joyce M(uriel Judson)
Strangis, Joel 1948- 124
Strannigan, Shawn 1956- 93
Strannigan, Shawn Alyne
    See Strannigan, Shawn
Strasser, Todd 1950- 153
    Earlier sketches in SATA 41, 45, 71, 107
    See also CLR 11
Stratemeyer, Edward L. 1862-1930 100
    Earlier sketches in SATA 1, 67
    See Adams, Harrison
    and Appleton, Victor
    and Dixon, Franklin W.
    and Keene, Carolyn
    and Rockwood, Roy
    and Young, Clarence
Stratford, Philip 1927- 47
Stratton, Allan 1951- 178
Stratton, J. M.
    See Whitlock, Ralph
Stratton, Thomas
    See Coulson, Robert S(tratton)
    and DeWeese, Thomas Eugene
Stratton-Porter, Gene(va Grace) 1863-1924 15
    See also CLR 87
    See Porter, Gene(va Grace) Stratton
Strauss, Gwen 1963- 77
Strauss, Joyce 1936- 53
Strauss, Linda Leopold 1942- 127
Strauss, Susan (Elizabeth) 1954- 75
Strayer, E. Ward
    See Stratemeyer, Edward L.
Streano, Vince(nt Catello) 1945- 20
Streatfeild, Mary Noel
    See Streatfeild, Noel
Streatfeild, Noel 1897(?)-1986 20
    Obituary 48
    See also CLR 83
Street, Janet Travell 1959- 84
Street, Julia Montgomery 1898-1993 11
Streissguth, Thomas 1958- 116
Strelkoff, Tatiana 1957- 89
Stren, Patti 1949- 88
    Brief entry 41
    See also CLR 5
Strete, Craig Kee 1950- 96
    Earlier sketch in SATA 44
Stretton, Barbara (Humphrey) 1936- 43
    Brief entry 35
Strickland, (William) Brad(ley) 1947- 142
    Earlier sketches in SATA 83, 137
Strickland, Craig (A.) 1956- 102
Strickland, Dorothy S(alley) 1933- 89
Strickland, Michael R. 1965- 144
    Earlier sketch in SATA 83
Strickland, Tessa 173
Striegel, Jana 1955- 140
Striegel-Wilson, Jana
    See Striegel, Jana
Striker, Lee
    See Clark, Margaret (D.)
Striker, Susan 1942- 63
Stringer, Lauren 1957- 183
    Earlier sketch in SATA 129
Stroeyer, Poul 1923- 13
Stromoski, Rick 1958- 111
Strong, Charles
    See Epstein, Beryl (M. Williams)
    and Epstein, Samuel
Strong, David
    See McGuire, Leslie (Sarah)
Strong, Jeremy 1949- 175
    Earlier sketches in SATA 36, 105
Strong, J.J.
    See Strong, Jeremy
Strong, Pat
    See Hough, Richard (Alexander)

Strong, Stacie 1965- 74
Stroud, Bettye 1939- 165
    Earlier sketch in SATA 96
Stroud, Jonathan 1970- 159
    Earlier sketch in SATA 102
    See also CLR 134
Stroyer, Poul
    See Stroeyer, Poul
Strug, Kerri 1977- 108
Stryer, Andrea Stenn 1938- 192
Stryker, Daniel
    See Morris, Chris(topher Crosby)
    and Stump, Jane Barr
Stuart, David
    See Hoyt, Edwin P(almer), Jr.
Stuart, Derek
    See Foster, John L(ouis)
Stuart, Forbes 1924- 13
Stuart, Ian
    See MacLean, Alistair (Stuart)
Stuart, Jesse (Hilton) 1906-1984 2
    Obituary 36
Stuart, Ruth McEnery 1849(?)-1917 116
Stuart, Sheila
    See Baker, Mary Gladys Steel
Stuart-Clark, Christopher (Anthony) 1940- 32
Stubis, Talivaldis 1926- 5
Stubley, Trevor (Hugh) 1932- 22
Stucky, Naomi R. 1922- 72
Stucley, Elizabeth
    See Northmore, Elizabeth Florence
Stultifer, Morton
    See Curtis, Richard (Alan)
Sture-Vasa, Mary
    See Alsop, Mary O'Hara
Sturges, Philemon 174
Sturtevant, Katherine 1950- 180
    Earlier sketch in SATA 130
Sturton, Hugh
    See Johnston, H(ugh) A(nthony) S(tephen)
Sturtzel, Howard A(llison) 1894-1985 1
Sturtzel, Jane Levington 1903-1996 1
Stutley, D(oris) J(ean) 1959- 142
Stutson, Caroline 1940- 104
Stuve-Bodeen, Stephanie 1965- 158
    Earlier sketch in SATA 114
Stux, Erica 1929- 140
Styles, (Frank) Showell 1908- 10
Stynes, Barbara White 133
Suba, Susanne 4
Subond, Valerie
    See Grayland, Valerie (Merle Spanner)
Sudbery, Rodie 1943- 42
Suen, Anastasia 1956(?)- 157
Sufrin, Mark 1925- 76
Sugarman, Joan G. 1917- 64
Sugarman, Tracy 1921- 37
Sugita, Yutaka 1930- 36
Suhl, Yuri (Menachem) 1908-1986 8
    Obituary 50
    See also CLR 2
    See also SAAS 1
Suhr, Joanne 129
Suid, Murray 1942- 27
Sullivan, George (Edward) 1927- 147
    Earlier sketches in SATA 4, 89
Sullivan, Jody
    See Rake, Jody
Sullivan, Kathryn A. 1954- 141
Sullivan, Mary Ann 1954- 63
Sullivan, Mary W(ilson) 1907- 13
Sullivan, Pat
    See Messmer, Otto
Sullivan, Paul 1939- 106
Sullivan, Sarah G. 1953- 179
Sullivan, Silky
    See Makowski, Silvia Ann
Sullivan, Sue
    See Sullivan, Susan E.
Sullivan, Susan E. 1962- 123
Sullivan, Thomas Joseph, Jr. 1947- 16

Sullivan, Tom
  See Sullivan, Thomas Joseph, Jr.
Sully, Tom 1959- *104*
Sumichrast, Jozef 1948- 29
Sumiko
  See Davies, Sumiko
Summerforest, Ivy B.
  See Kirkup, James
Summers, Barbara 1944- *182*
Summers, James L(evingston) 1910-1973 57
  Brief entry 28
Summertree, Katonah
  See Windsor, Patricia
Sun, Chyng Feng 1959- 90
Sunderlin, Sylvia (S.) 1911-1997 28
  Obituary 99
Sung, Betty Lee 26
Supeene, Shelagh Lynne 1952- *153*
Supraner, Robyn 1930- *101*
  Earlier sketch in SATA *20*
Supree, Burt(on) 1941-1992 73
Surface, Mary Hall 1958- *126*
Surge, Frank 1931- *13*
Susac, Andrew 1929- 5
Susi, Geraldine Lee 1942- 98
Sussman, Cornelia Silver 1914-1999 59
Sussman, Irving 1908-1996 59
Sussman, Susan 1942- 48
Sutcliff, Rosemary 1920-1992 78
  Obituary 73
  Earlier sketches in SATA *6, 44*
  See also CLR *138*
Sutcliffe, Jane 1957- *138*
Sutherland, Colleen 1944- 79
Sutherland, Efua (Theodora Morgue)
  1924-1996 25
Sutherland, Jon 1958- *167*
Sutherland, Jonathan D.
  See Sutherland, Jon
Sutherland, Jonathan David
  See Sutherland, Jon
Sutherland, Margaret 1941- *15*
Sutherland, Zena Bailey 1915-2002 37
  Obituary 137
Suttles, Shirley (Smith) 1922- 21
Sutton, Ann (Livesay) 1923- 31
Sutton, Eve(lyn Mary) 1906-1992 26
Sutton, Felix 1910(?)-1973 31
Sutton, Jane 1950- 52
  Brief entry 43
Sutton, Larry M(atthew) 1931- 29
Sutton, Margaret Beebe 1903-2001 .... *1*
  Obituary 131
Sutton, Myron Daniel 1925- 31
Sutton, Roger 1956- 93
Suzanne, Jamie
  See Hawes, Louise
  and Lantz, Francess L(in)
  and Singleton, Linda Joy
  and Zach, Cheryl (Byrd)
Suzuki, David T(akayoshi) 1936- *138*
Svendsen, Mark 1962- *181*
  Earlier sketch in SATA *120*
Svendsen, Mark Nestor
  See Svendsen, Mark
Svenson, Andrew E(dward) 1910-1975 2
  Obituary 26
Swaab, Neil 1978- *191*
Swain, Carol 1962- *172*
Swain, Gwyneth 1961- *134*
  Earlier sketch in SATA *84*
Swain, Ruth
  See Swain, Ruth Freeman
Swain, Ruth Freeman 1951- *161*
  Earlier sketch in SATA *119*
Swain, Su Zan (Noguchi) 1916- 21
Swallow, Pamela Curtis *178*
Swamp, Jake 1941- 98
Swan, Susan 1944- *108*
  Earlier sketch in SATA *22*
Swann, Brian (Stanley Frank) 1940- *116*

Swann, E. L.
  See Lasky, Kathryn
Swann, Ruth Rice 1920- 84
Swanson, Helen M(cKendry) 1919- 94
Swanson, June 1931- 76
Swanson, Wayne 1942- *167*
Swarthout, Glendon (Fred) 1918-1992 26
Swarthout, Kathryn 1919- 7
Swayne, Sam(uel F.) 1907- 53
Swayne, Zoa (Lourana) 1905- 53
Sweat, Lynn 1934- *168*
  Earlier sketch in SATA *57*
Swede, George 1940- 67
Sweeney, James B(artholomew) 1910-1999 . 21
Sweeney, Joyce 1955- *167*
  Earlier sketches in SATA *65, 68, 108*
Sweeney, Joyce Kay
  See Sweeney, Joyce
Sweeney, Karen O'Connor
  See O'Connor, Karen
Sweeney, Matthew (Gerard) 1952- *156*
Sweet, Melissa 1956- *172*
Sweet, Sarah C.
  See Jewett, (Theodora) Sarah Orne
Sweetland, Nancy A(nn) 1934- 48
Swenson, Allan A(rmstrong) 1933- 21
Swenson, May 1919-1989 .... *15*
Swentzell, Rina 1939- 79
Swiatkowska, Gabi 1971(?)- *180*
Swift, Bryan
  See Knott, William C(ecil, Jr.)
Swift, David
  See Kaufmann, John
Swift, Hildegarde Hoyt 1890(?)-1977
  Obituary 20
Swift, Jonathan 1667-1745 19
  See also CLR *53*
Swift, Merlin
  See Leeming, Joseph
Swiger, Elinor Porter 1927- 8
Swinburne, Laurence (Joseph) 1924- 9
Swinburne, Stephen R. 1952- *188*
  Earlier sketch in SATA *150*
Swinburne, Steve
  See Swinburne, Stephen R.
Swindells, Robert (Edward) 1939- *150*
  Brief entry 34
  Earlier sketches in SATA *50, 80*
  See also SAAS *14*
Swinford, Betty (June Wells) 1927- 58
Swinford, Bob
  See Swinford, Betty (June Wells)
Swithen, John
  See King, Stephen
Switzer, Ellen 1923- 48
Swope, Sam *156*
Swope, Samuel
  See Swope, Sam
Sybesma, Jetske
  See Ironside, Jetske
Sydney, Frank
  See Warwick, Alan R(oss)
Sylvester, Natalie G(abry) 1922- 22
Syme, (Neville) Ronald 1913-1992 87
  Earlier sketch in SATA *2*
Symes, R. F. 77
Symes, Ruth Louise 1962- *179*
Symons, (Dorothy) Geraldine 1909- 33
Symons, Stuart
  See Stanley, George Edward
Symynkywicz, Jeffrey B. 1954- 87
Symynkywicz, Jeffrey Bruce
  See Symynkywicz, Jeffrey B.
Synge, (Phyllis) Ursula 1930- 9
Sypher, Lucy Johnston 1907- 7
Szasz, Suzanne (Shorr) 1915-1997 .... *13*
  Obituary 99
Szekeres, Cyndy 1933- *157*
  Autobiography Feature *157*
  Earlier sketches in SATA *5, 60, 131*
  See also SAAS *13*

Szekessy, Tanja 98
Szpura, Beata 1961- 93
Szudek, Agnes S(usan) P(hilomena) 57
  Brief entry 49
Szulc, Tad 1926-2001 26
Szydlow, Jarl
  See Szydlowski, Mary Vigliante
Szydlowski, Mary Vigliante 1946- 94
Szymanski, Lois 1957- 91

T

Taback, Simms 1932- *170*
  Brief entry 36
  Earlier sketches in SATA *40, 104*
  See also CLR *100*
Taber, Gladys (Bagg) 1899-1980
  Obituary 22
Tabor, Nancy Maria Grande 1949- *161*
  Earlier sketch in SATA *89*
Tabrah, Ruth Milander 1921- *14*
Tackach, James 1953- *123*
Tackach, James M.
  See Tackach, James
Tadgell, Nicole 1969- *177*
Tafuri, Nancy 1946- *192*
  Autobiography Feature *192*
  Earlier sketches in SATA *39, 75, 130*
  See also CLR *74*
  See also SAAS *14*
Tagg, Christine Elizabeth 1962- *138*
Tagliaferro, Linda *173*
Taha, Karen T(erry) 1942- *156*
  Earlier sketch in SATA *71*
Tai, Sharon O. 1963- *153*
Tait, Douglas 1944- *12*
Takabayashi, Mari 1960- *156*
  Earlier sketch in SATA *115*
Takahashi, Rumiko 1957- *163*
Takakjian, Portia 1930- *15*
Takashima, Misako
  See Misako Rocks!
Takashima, Shizuye 1928- *13*
Takayama, Sandi 1962- *106*
Takeda, Pete(r M.) 1964- *148*
Tal, Eve 1947- *176*
Talbert, Marc (Alan) 1953- *154*
  Autobiography Feature *154*
  Earlier sketches in SATA *68, 99*
Talbot, Charlene Joy 1928- *10*
Talbot, Toby 1928- *14*
Talbott, Hudson 1949- *131*
  Earlier sketch in SATA *84*
Taliaferro, Dorothy L.
  See Martin, Del
Talifero, Gerald 1950- 75
Talker, T.
  See Rands, William Brighty
Tallarico, Tony 1933- *116*
Tallcott, Emogene *10*
Tallis, Robyn
  See Coville, Bruce
  and Doyle, Debra
  and Macdonald, James D.
  and Smith, Sherwood
  and Zambreno, Mary Frances
Tallon, Robert 1939- 43
  Brief entry 28
Talmadge, Marian 14
Tamar, Erika 1934- *150*
  Earlier sketches in SATA *62, 101*
Tamarin, Alfred H. 1913-1980 .... *13*
Tamburine, Jean 1930- *12*
Tames, Richard (Lawrence) 1946- *102*
  Earlier sketch in SATA *67*
Tamminga, Frederick W(illiam) 1934- 66
Tammuz, Benjamin 1919-1989
  Obituary 63
Tan, Amy 1952- 75

Tan, Amy Ruth
  See Tan, Amy
Tanaka, Beatrice 1932- 76
Tanaka, Shelley 136
Tang, Charles 1948- 81
Tang, Greg 172
Tang, You-Shan 1946- 53
Tania B.
  See Blixen, Karen (Christentze Dinesen)
Tankard, Jeremy 1973- 191
Tannen, Mary 1943- 37
Tannenbaum, Beulah Goldstein 1916- 3
Tannenbaum, D(onald) Leb 1948- 42
Tanner, Jane 1946- 74
Tanner, Louise S(tickney) 1922-2000 9
Tanobe, Miyuki 1937- 23
Tanselle, Eve 1933- 125
Tapio, Pat Decker
  See Kines, Pat Decker
Tapp, Kathy Kennedy 1949- 88
  Brief entry 50
Tarbescu, Edith 1939- 107
Tarkington, (Newton) Booth 1869-1946 17
Tarpley, Natasha A(nastasia) 1971- 147
Tarr, Judith 1955- 149
  Earlier sketch in SATA 64
Tarry, Ellen 1906- 16
  See also CLR 26
  See also SAAS 16
Tarshis, Jerome 1936- 9
Tarshis, Lauren 187
Tarsky, Sue 1946- 41
Taschek, Karen 1956- 185
Tashjian, Janet 1956- 151
  Earlier sketch in SATA 102
Tashjian, Virginia A. 1921-2008 3
Tasker, James 1908- 9
Tate, Don(ald E.) 159
Tate, Eleanora E. 1948- 191
  Earlier sketches in SATA 38, 94
  See also CLR 37
Tate, Eleanora Elaine
  See Tate, Eleanora E.
Tate, Ellalice
  See Hibbert, Eleanor Alice Burford
Tate, Joan 1922- 86
  Earlier sketch in SATA 9
  See also SAAS 20
Tate, Mary Anne
  See Hale, Arlene
Tate, Nikki 134
Tate, Richard
  See Masters, Anthony (Richard)
Tate, Suzanne 1930- 91
Tatham, Betty 142
Tatham, Campbell
  See Elting, Mary
Tatham, Julie
  See Tatham, Julie Campbell
Tatham, Julie Campbell 1908-1999 80
Tavares, Matt 159
Tavares, Victor 1971- 176
Taves, Isabella 1915- 27
Taylor, Alastair 1959- 130
Taylor, Andrew 1951- 70
Taylor, Andrew John Robert
  See Taylor, Andrew
Taylor, Ann 1782-1866 41
  Brief entry 35
Taylor, Audilee Boyd 1931- 59
Taylor, Barbara J. 1927- 10
Taylor, Ben
  See Strachan, Ian
Taylor, Carl 1937- 14
Taylor, Cheryl Munro 1957- 96
Taylor, Cora (Lorraine) 1936- 103
  Earlier sketch in SATA 64
  See also CLR 63
Taylor, Dave 1948- 78
Taylor, David
  See Taylor, Dave

Taylor, David 1900-1965 10
Taylor, Debbie A. 1955- 169
Taylor, Elizabeth 1912-1975 13
Taylor, Florance Walton 9
Taylor, Florence M(arian Tompkins)
  1892-1983 9
Taylor, G(raham) P(eter) 1959(?)- 156
Taylor, Gage 1942-2000 87
Taylor, Graham
  See Taylor, G(raham) P(eter)
Taylor, Herb(ert Norman, Jr.) 1942-1987 22
  Obituary 54
Taylor, J. David
  See Taylor, Dave
Taylor, Jane 1783-1824 41
  Brief entry 35
Taylor, Jerry D(uncan) 1938- 47
Taylor, John Robert
  See Taylor, Andrew
Taylor, Judy
  See Hough, Judy Taylor
Taylor, Kenneth N. 1917-2005 26
Taylor, Kenneth Nathaniel
  See Taylor, Kenneth N.
Taylor, Kim 180
Taylor, L(ester) B(arbour), Jr. 1932- 27
Taylor, Lois Dwight Cole
  See Cole, Lois Dwight
Taylor, Louise Todd 1939- 47
Taylor, Margaret 1950- 106
Taylor, Mark 1927- 32
  Brief entry 28
Taylor, Mildred D. 1943- 135
  See also CLR 90
  See also SAAS 5
Taylor, Mildred Delois
  See Taylor, Mildred D.
Taylor, Paula (Wright) 1942- 48
  Brief entry 33
Taylor, Robert Lewis 1912-1998 10
Taylor, Sean 1965- 192
Taylor, Sydney (Brenner) 1904(?)-1978 28
  Obituary 26
  Earlier sketch in SATA 1
Taylor, Theodore 1921-2006 128
  Obituary 177
  Earlier sketches in SATA 5, 54, 83
  See also CLR 30
  See also SAAS 4
Taylor, William 1938- 164
  Earlier sketches in SATA 78, 113
  See also CLR 63
Tazewell, Charles 1900-1972 74
Tchana, Katrin
  See Tchana, Katrin Hyman
Tchana, Katrin H.
  See Tchana, Katrin Hyman
Tchana, Katrin Hyman 1963- 177
  Earlier sketch in SATA 125
Tchekhov, Anton
  See Chekhov, Anton (Pavlovich)
Tchen, Richard 120
Tchudi, Stephen N. 1942- 55
Teague, Bob
  See Teague, Robert
Teague, Mark 1963- 170
  Earlier sketches in SATA 68, 99
Teague, Mark Christopher
  See Teague, Mark
Teague, Robert 1929- 32
  Brief entry 31
Teal, Val 1902-1997 10
  Obituary 114
Teal, Valentine M.
  See Teal, Val
Teale, Edwin Way 1899-1980 7
  Obituary 25
Teasdale, Sara 1884-1933 32
Tebbel, John (William) 1912-2004 26
Teensma, Lynne Bertrand
  See Bertrand, Lynne

Tee-Van, Helen Damrosch 1893-1976 10
  Obituary 27
Tegner, Bruce 1928- 62
Teitelbaum, Michael 1953- 116
  Earlier sketch in SATA 59
Tejima
  See Tejima, Keizaburo
Tejima, Keizaburo 1931- 139
  See also CLR 20
Telander, Todd (G.) 1967- 88
Teleki, Geza 1943- 45
Telemaque, Eleanor Wong 1934- 43
Telescope, Tom
  See Newbery, John
Tellis, Annabel 1967- 191
Temkin, Sara Anne Schlossberg 1913-1996 . 26
Temko, Florence 13
Tempest, Margaret Mary 1892-1982
  Obituary 33
Templar, Maurice
  See Groom, Arthur William
Temple, Arthur
  See Northcott, (William) Cecil
Temple, Charles 1947- 79
Temple, Frances (Nolting) 1945-1995 85
Temple, Herbert 1919- 45
Temple, Paul
  See McConnell, James Douglas Rutherford
Temple, William F(rederick) 1914-1989 107
Tenggren, Gustaf 1896-1970 18
  Obituary 26
Tennant, Kylie 6
  See Rodd, Kylie Tennant
Tennant, Veronica 1947- 36
Tenneshaw, S.M.
  See Beaumont, Charles
  and Garrett, (Gordon) Randall (Phillip)
  and Silverberg, Robert
Tenniel, John 1820-1914 74
  Brief entry 27
  See also CLR 18
Tepper, Sheri S. 1929- 113
Terada, Alice M. 1928- 90
Terban, Marvin 1940- 54
  Brief entry 45
ter Haar, Jaap 1922- 6
  See Haar, Jaap ter
Terhune, Albert Payson 1872-1942 15
Terkel, Susan N(eiburg) 1948- 103
  Earlier sketch in SATA 59
Terlouw, Jan (Cornelis) 1931- 30
Terrell, John Upton 1900-1988
  Obituary 60
Terris, Susan 1937- 77
  Earlier sketch in SATA 3
Terry, Luther L(eonidas) 1911-1985 11
  Obituary 42
Terry, Margaret
  See Dunnahoo, Terry Janson
Terry, Walter 1913-1982 14
Terzian, James P. 1915- 14
Tessendorf, K(enneth) C(harles) 1925-2003 . 75
  Obituary 142
Tessler, Stephanie Gordon
  See Gordon, Stephanie Jacob
Tester, Sylvia Root 1939- 64
  Brief entry 37
Tether, (Cynthia) Graham 1950- 46
  Brief entry 36
Tetzner, Lisa 1894-1963 169
Thach, James Otis 1969- 195
Thacher, Mary McGrath 1933- 9
Thackeray, William Makepeace 1811-1863 .. 23
Thaler, Michael C.
  See Thaler, Mike
Thaler, Mike 1936- 93
  Brief entry 47
  Earlier sketch in SATA 56
Thaler, Shmuel 1958- 126
  Earlier sketch in SATA 72
Thamer, Katie 1955- 42

Thane, Elswyth 1900-1984(?) *32*
Tharp, Louise (Marshall) Hall 1898-1992 ...... *3*
  Obituary *129*
Tharp, Tim 1957- *189*
Thayer, Jane
  See Woolley, Catherine
Thayer, Marjorie 1908-1992 .... *74*
  Brief entry *37*
Thayer, Peter
  See Wyler, Rose
Thelwell, Norman 1923-2004 .... *14*
Themerson, Stefan 1910-1988 .... *65*
Thermes, Jennifer 1966- *155*
Theroux, Paul 1941- *109*
  Earlier sketch in SATA *44*
Theroux, Paul Edward
  See Theroux, Paul
Thesman, Jean *124*
  Earlier sketch in SATA *74*
The Tjong-Khing
  See Khing, T.T.
Thieda, Shirley Ann 1943- *13*
Thiele, Colin 1920-2006 .... *125*
  Earlier sketches in SATA *14, 72*
  See also CLR *27*
  See also SAAS *2*
Thiele, Colin Milton
  See Thiele, Colin
Thiesing, Lisa 1958- *159*
  Earlier sketch in SATA *95*
Thimmesh, Catherine *189*
Thiry, Joan (Marie) 1926- *45*
Thistlethwaite, Miles 1945- *12*
Thollander, Earl 1922- *22*
Thomas, Abigail 1941- *112*
Thomas, Andrea
  See Hill, Margaret (Ohler)
Thomas, Art(hur Lawrence) 1952- *48*
  Brief entry *38*
Thomas, Carroll
  See Ratliff, Thomas M.
  and Shmurak, Carole B.
Thomas, Dylan (Marlais) 1914-1953 .... *60*
Thomas, Egbert S.
  See Ellis, Edward S(ylvester)
Thomas, Estelle Webb 1899-1982 .... *26*
Thomas, Frances 1943- *171*
  Earlier sketch in SATA *92*
Thomas, H. C.
  See Keating, Lawrence A.
Thomas, Ianthe 1951- *139*
  Brief entry *42*
  See also CLR *8*
Thomas, Jane Resh 1936- *171*
  Earlier sketches in SATA *38, 90*
Thomas, Jerry D. 1959- *91*
Thomas, J.F.
  See Fleming, Thomas
Thomas, Joan Gale
  See Robinson, Joan (Mary) G(ale Thomas)
Thomas, Joyce Carol 1938- *137*
  Autobiography Feature *137*
  Earlier sketches in SATA *40, 78, 123*
  See also CLR *19*
  See also SAAS *7*
Thomas, Lowell Jackson, Jr. 1923- *15*
Thomas, Margaret
  See Thomas, Peggy
Thomas, Meredith 1963- *119*
Thomas, Michael
  See Wilks, Michael Thomas
Thomas, Middy 1931- *191*
Thomas, Patricia J. 1934- *51*
Thomas, Peggy *174*
Thomas, Rob 1965- *97*
Thomas, Scott 1959- *147*
Thomas, Velma Maia 1955- *171*
Thomas, Vernon (Arthur) 1934- *56*

Thomas, Victoria
  See DeWeese, Thomas Eugene
  and Kugi, Constance Todd
Thomasma, Kenneth R. 1930- *90*
Thomassie, Tynia 1959- *92*
Thompson, Brenda 1935- *34*
Thompson, Carol 1951- *189*
  Earlier sketch in SATA *85*
Thompson, China
  See Lewis, Mary (Christianna)
Thompson, Colin (Edward) 1942- *163*
  Earlier sketch in SATA *95*
Thompson, David H(ugh) 1941- *17*
Thompson, Eileen
  See Panowski, Eileen Thompson
Thompson, George Selden 1929-1989 .... *73*
  Obituary *63*
  Earlier sketch in SATA *4*
  See Selden, George
Thompson, Harlan (Howard) 1894-1987 ...... *10*
  Obituary *53*
  See Holt, Stephen
Thompson, Hilary 1943- *56*
  Brief entry *49*
Thompson, Julian F(rancis) 1927- *155*
  Brief entry *40*
  Earlier sketches in SATA *55, 99*
  See also CLR *24*
  See also SAAS *13*
Thompson, K(athryn Carolyn) Dyble
  1952- *82*
Thompson, Kay 1912(?)-1998 .... *16*
  See also CLR *22*
Thompson, Lauren 1962- *174*
  Earlier sketch in SATA *132*
Thompson, Lauren Stevens
  See Thompson, Lauren
Thompson, Megan Lloyd
  See Lloyd, Megan
Thompson, Richard 1951- *184*
Thompson, Ruth Plumly 1891-1976 .... *66*
Thompson, Sharon 1952- *119*
Thompson, Sharon Elaine
  See Thompson, Sharon
Thompson, Stith 1885-1976 .... *57*
  Obituary *20*
Thompson, Vivian L(aubach) 1911- *3*
Thomson, Bill 1963- *187*
Thomson, Celia
  See Lynn, Tracy
Thomson, David (Robert Alexander)
  1914-1988 .... *40*
  Obituary *55*
Thomson, Pat 1939- *122*
  Earlier sketch in SATA *77*
Thomson, Peggy 1922- *31*
Thomson, Sarah L. *178*
Thon, Melanie Rae 1957- *132*
Thong, Roseanne *174*
Thorburn, John
  See Goldsmith, John Herman Thorburn
Thorn, John 1947- *59*
Thorndyke, Helen Louise *67*
  Earlier sketch in SATA *1*
  See Benson, Mildred (Augustine Wirt)
Thorne, Ian
  See May, Julian
Thorne, Jean Wright
  See May, Julian
Thornhill, Jan 1955- *148*
  Earlier sketch in SATA *77*
Thornton, Hall
  See Silverberg, Robert
Thornton, W. B.
  See Burgess, Thornton Waldo
Thornton, Yvonne S(hirley) 1947- *96*
Thorpe, E(ustace) G(eorge) 1916- *21*
Thorpe, J. K.
  See Nathanson, Laura Walther
Thorvall, Kerstin 1925- *13*

Thorvall-Falk, Kerstin
  See Thorvall, Kerstin
Thrasher, Crystal (Faye) 1921- *27*
Threadgall, Colin 1941- *77*
Three Little Pigs
  See Lantz, Francess L(in)
Thum, Gladys 1920- *26*
Thum, Marcella *28*
  Earlier sketch in SATA *3*
Thundercloud, Katherine
  See Witt, Shirley Hill
Thurber, James (Grover) 1894-1961 .... *13*
Thurlo, Aimee *161*
Thurlo, David *161*
Thurman, Judith 1946- *33*
Thurman, Mark (Gordon Ian) 1948- *63*
Thwaite, Ann (Barbara Harrop) 1932- *14*
Tibbetts, Peggy *127*
Tibbles, Jean-Paul 1958- *115*
Tibo, Gilles 1951- *107*
  Earlier sketch in SATA *67*
Tiburzi, Bonnie 1948- *65*
Ticheburn, Cheviot
  See Ainsworth, William Harrison
Tichenor, Tom 1923-1992 .... *14*
Tichnor, Richard 1959- *90*
Tichy, William 1924- *31*
Tickle, Jack
  See Chapman, Jane
Tiegreen, Alan F. 1935- *94*
  Brief entry *36*
Tierney, Frank M. 1930- *54*
Tierney, Tom 1928- *113*
Tiffault, Benette W. 1955- *77*
Tiller, Ruth L. 1949- *83*
Tilley, Debbie *190*
Tilly, Nancy 1935- *62*
Tilton, Madonna Elaine 1929- *41*
Tilton, Rafael
  See Tilton, Madonna Elaine
Timberlake, Amy *156*
Timberlake, Carolyn
  See Dresang, Eliza (Carolyn Timberlake)
Timmers, Leo 1970- *190*
Timmins, William F(rederick) *10*
Tinbergen, Niko(laas) 1907-1988
  Obituary *60*
Tincknell, Cathy *194*
Tiner, John Hudson 1944- *32*
Tingle, Dolli (?)-
  See Brackett, Dolli Tingle
Tingle, Rebecca *174*
Tingum, Janice 1958- *91*
Tinkelman, Murray 1933- *12*
Tinkham, Kelly A. *188*
Tinkle, (Julien) Lon 1906-1980 .... *36*
Tinling, Marion (Rose) 1904- *140*
Tipene, Tim 1972- *141*
Tippett, James S(terling) 1885-1958 .... *66*
Tirone Smith, Mary-Ann 1944- *143*
Titlebaum, Ellen *195*
Titler, Dale M(ilton) 1926- *35*
  Brief entry *28*
Titmarsh, Michael Angelo
  See Thackeray, William Makepeace
Titus, Eve 1922- *2*
Tjong Khing, The 1933- *76*
Tobias, Katherine
  See Gottfried, Theodore Mark
Tobias, Tobi 1938- *82*
  Earlier sketch in SATA *5*
  See also CLR *4*
Todd, Anne Ophelia
  See Dowden, Anne Ophelia Todd
Todd, Barbara 1961- *173*
Todd, Barbara K(eith) 1917- *10*
Todd, Chuck *195*
Todd, H(erbert) E(atton) 1908-1988 .... *84*
  Earlier sketch in SATA *11*
Todd, Loreto 1942- *30*
Todd, Pamela 1950- *124*

Todd, Peter
  See Hamilton, Charles (Harold St. John)
Toews, Miriam 1964- 165
Tofel, Richard J. 1957- 140
Toft, Kim Michelle 1960- 170
Tokunbo, Dimitrea 187
Tolan, Stephanie S. 1942- 142
  Earlier sketches in SATA *38, 78*
Toland, John (Willard) 1912-2004 38
Tolbert, Steve 1944- 143
Tolkien, John Ronald Reuel
  See Tolkien, J.R.R
Tolkien, J.R.R 1892-1973 100
  Obituary 24
  Earlier sketches in SATA *2, 32*
  See also CLR *56*
Toll, Emily
  See Cannon, Eileen E(mily)
Toll, Nelly S. 1935- 78
Tolland, W. R.
  See Heitzmann, William Ray
Tolles, Martha 1921- 76
  Earlier sketch in SATA *8*
Tolliver, Ruby C(hangos) 1922- 110
  Brief entry 41
  Earlier sketch in SATA *55*
Tolmie, Kenneth Donald 1941- 15
Tolstoi, Lev
  See Tolstoy, Leo (Nikolaevich)
Tolstoy, Leo (Nikolaevich) 1828-1910 26
  See Tolstoi, Lev
Tolstoy, Count Leo
  See Tolstoy, Leo (Nikolaevich)
Tomalin, Ruth 29
Tomaselli, Rosa
  See Pausacker, Jenny
Tomecek, Steve 172
Tomes, Margot (Ladd) 1917-1991 70
  Brief entry 27
  Obituary 69
  Earlier sketch in SATA *36*
Tomey, Ingrid 1943- 77
Tomfool
  See Farjeon, Eleanor
Tomkins, Jasper
  See Batey, Tom
Tomline, F. Latour
  See Gilbert, W(illiam) S(chwenck)
Tomlinson, Heather 192
Tomlinson, Jill 1931-1976 3
  Obituary 24
Tomlinson, Reginald R(obert) 1885-1979(?)
  Obituary 27
Tomlinson, Theresa 1946- 165
  Earlier sketch in SATA *103*
  See also CLR *60*
Tompert, Ann 1918- 139
  Earlier sketches in SATA *14, 89*
Toner, Raymond John 1908-1986 10
Tong, Gary S. 1942- 66
Tong, Paul 188
Took, Belladonna
  See Chapman, Vera (Ivy May)
Tooke, Louise Mathews 1950- 38
Tooke, Susan 173
Toonder, Martin
  See Groom, Arthur William
Toothaker, Roy Eugene 1928- 18
Tooze, Ruth (Anderson) 1892-1972 4
Topek, Susan Remick 1955- 78
Topping, Audrey R(onning) 1928- 14
Tor, Regina
  See Shekerjian, Regina Tor
Torbert, Floyd James 1922- 22
Torgersen, Don Arthur 1934- 55
  Brief entry 41
Torley, Luke
  See Blish, James (Benjamin)
Torres, Andres Segovia
  See Segovia, Andres
Torres, Daniel 1958- 102

Torres, John A. 1965- 163
  Earlier sketch in SATA *94*
Torres, John Albert
  See Torres, John A.
Torres, Laura 1967- 146
  Earlier sketch in SATA *87*
Torres, Leyla 1960- 155
Torrey, Rich
  See Torrey, Richard
Torrey, Richard 189
Torrie, Malcolm
  See Mitchell, Gladys (Maude Winifred)
Toten, Teresa 1955- 99
Totham, Mary
  See Breinburg, Petronella
Touponce, William F. 1948- 114
Tournier, Michel 1924- 23
Tournier, Michel Edouard
  See Tournier, Michel
Towle, Wendy 1963- 79
Towne, Mary
  See Spelman, Mary
Townley, Rod
  See Townley, Roderick
Townley, Roderick 1942- 177
Townsend, Brad W. 1962- 91
Townsend, John Rowe 1922- 132
  Autobiography Feature 132
  Earlier sketches in SATA *4, 68*
  See also CLR *2*
  See also SAAS *2*
Townsend, Michael 1981- 194
Townsend, Sue 93
  Brief entry 48
  Earlier sketch in SATA *55*
  See Townsend, Susan Lilian
Townsend, Thomas L. 1944- 59
Townsend, Tom
  See Townsend, Thomas L.
Townson, Hazel 134
Toye, William Eldred 1926- 8
Traherne, Michael
  See Watkins-Pitchford, Denys James
Trahey, Jane 1923-2000 36
  Obituary 120
Trapani, Iza 1954- 116
  Earlier sketch in SATA *80*
Trapp, Maria Augusta von 16
  See von Trapp, Maria Augusta
Travers, P(amela) L(yndon) 1899-1996 100
  Obituary 90
  Earlier sketches in SATA *4, 54*
  See also CLR *93*
  See also SAAS *2*
Travis, Lucille 133
  Earlier sketch in SATA *88*
Treadgold, Mary 1910- 49
Trease, (Robert) Geoffrey 1909-1998 60
  Obituary 101
  Earlier sketch in SATA *2*
  See also CLR *42*
  See also SAAS *6*
Treat, Lawrence 1903-1998 59
Tredez, Alain 1926- 17
Tredez, Denise 1930- 50
Treece, Henry 1912-1966 2
  See also CLR *2*
Tregarthen, Enys
  See Sloggett, Nellie
Tregaskis, Richard 1916-1973 3
  Obituary 26
Treherne, Katie Thamer 1955- 76
Trell, Max 1900-1996 14
  Obituary 108
Tremain, Ruthven 1922- 17
Trembath, Don 1963- 168
  Earlier sketch in SATA *96*
Tremens, Del
  See MacDonald, Amy
Trent, Robbie 1894-1988 26

Trent, Timothy
  See Malmberg, Carl
Treseder, Terry Walton 1956- 68
Tresilian, (Cecil) Stuart 1891-(?) 40
Tresselt, Alvin 1916-2000 7
  See also CLR *30*
Trevino, Elizabeth B(orton) de 1904- 29
  Earlier sketch in SATA *1*
  See also SAAS *5*
Trevor, Elleston 1920-1995 28
  See Hall, Adam
Trevor, Frances
  See Teasdale, Sara
Trevor, Glen
  See Hilton, James
Trevor, (Lucy) Meriol 1919-2000 113
  Obituary 122
  Earlier sketch in SATA *10*
Trewellard, J.M. 195
Trewellard, Juliet
  See Trewellard, J.M.
Trez, Alain
  See Tredez, Alain
Trez, Denise
  See Tredez, Denise
Trezise, Percy (James) 1923-
  See CLR *41*
Triggs, Tony D. 1946- 70
Trimble, Marshall I(ra) 1939- 93
Trimby, Elisa 1948- 47
  Brief entry 40
Tring, A. Stephen
  See Meynell, Laurence Walter
Tripp, Eleanor B(aldwin) 1936- 4
Tripp, Janet 1942- 108
Tripp, Jenny 188
Tripp, John
  See Moore, John Travers
Tripp, Nathaniel 1944- 101
Tripp, Paul 1916-2002 8
  Obituary 139
Tripp, Valerie 1951- 168
  Earlier sketch in SATA *78*
Tripp, Wallace (Whitney) 1940- 31
Trivelpiece, Laurel 1926- 56
  Brief entry 46
Trivett, Daphne Harwood 1940- 22
Trivizas, Eugene 1946- 84
Trnka, Jiri 1912-1969 43
  Brief entry 32
Trollope, Anthony 1815-1882 22
Trost, Lucille W(ood) 1938- 149
  Earlier sketch in SATA *12*
Trott, Betty 1933- 91
Trotter, Deborah W. 184
Trotter, Grace V(iolet) 1900-1991 10
Trottier, Maxine 1950- 175
  Earlier sketch in SATA *131*
Troughton, Joanna (Margaret) 1947- 37
Trout, Kilgore
  See Farmer, Philip Jose
Trout, Richard E. 123
Trudeau, Garretson Beekman
  See Trudeau, G.B.
Trudeau, Garry
  See Trudeau, G.B.
Trudeau, Garry B.
  See Trudeau, G.B.
Trudeau, G.B. 1948- 168
  Earlier sketch in SATA *35*
  See Trudeau, Garry B.
Trueit, Trudi
  See Trueit, Trudi Strain
Trueit, Trudi Strain 1963- 179
Trueman, Matthew 183
Trueman, Terry 1947- 178
  Earlier sketch in SATA *132*
Truesdell, Judy
  See Mecca, Judy Truesdell
Truesdell, Sue
  See Truesdell, Susan G.

Truesdell, Susan G. *108*
  Brief entry *45*
Trumbauer, Lisa (Trutkoff) 1963- *149*
Truss, Jan 1925- *35*
Truss, Lynne 1955(?)- *194*
Tryon, Leslie *194*
  Earlier sketch in SATA *139*
Tubb, Jonathan N. 1951- *78*
Tubby, I. M.
  See Kraus, (Herman) Robert
Tucker, Caroline
  See Nolan, Jeannette Covert
Tudor, Edward
  See Browne, Anthony
Tudor, Tasha 1915-2008 .... *160*
  Earlier sketches in SATA *20, 69*
  See also CLR *13*
Tuerk, Hanne 1951- *71*
Tulloch, Richard 1949- *180*
  Earlier sketch in SATA *76*
Tulloch, Richard George
  See Tulloch, Richard
Tulloch, Shirley *169*
Tully, John (Kimberley) 1923- *14*
Tumanov, Vladimir A. 1961- *138*
Tung, Angela 1972- *109*
Tunis, Edwin (Burdett) 1897-1973 .... *28*
  Obituary *24*
  Earlier sketch in SATA *1*
  See also CLR *2*
Tunis, John R(oberts) 1889-1975 .... *37*
  Brief entry *30*
Tunnell, Michael
  See Tunnell, Michael O('Grady)
Tunnell, Michael O('Grady) 1950- *157*
  Earlier sketch in SATA *103*
Tunnicliffe, C(harles) F(rederick)
  1901-1979 .... *62*
Turck, Mary C. 1950- *144*
Turk, Hanne
  See Tuerk, Hanne
Turk, Ruth 1917- *82*
Turkle, Brinton 1915- *79*
  Earlier sketch in SATA *2*
Turlington, Bayly 1919-1977 .... *5*
  Obituary *52*
Turnbull, Agnes Sligh 1888-1982 .... *14*
Turnbull, Ann 1943- *160*
  Earlier sketch in SATA *18*
Turnbull, Ann Christine
  See Turnbull, Ann
Turner, Alice K. 1940- *10*
Turner, Ann 1945- *188*
  Autobiography Feature *188*
  Earlier sketches in SATA *14, 77, 113, 178*
Turner, Ann Warren
  See Turner, Ann
Turner, Bonnie 1932- *75*
Turner, Elizabeth 1774-1846
  See YABC *2*
Turner, Glennette Tilley 1933- *183*
  Earlier sketch in SATA *71*
Turner, Josie
  See Crawford, Phyllis
Turner, Megan Whalen 1965- *174*
  Earlier sketch in SATA *94*
Turner, Philip (William) 1925- *83*
  Earlier sketch in SATA *11*
  See also CLR *89*
  See also SAAS *6*
Turner, Robyn 1947- *77*
Turner, Sheila R.
  See Seed, Sheila Turner
Turngren, Annette 1902(?)-1980
  Obituary *23*
Turngren, Ellen (?)-1964 .... *3*
Turska, Krystyna (Zofia) 1933- *31*
  Brief entry *27*
Turteltaub, H.N.
  See Turtledove, Harry

Turtledove, Harry 1949- *166*
  Earlier sketch in SATA *116*
Turtledove, Harry Norman
  See Turtledove, Harry
Tusa, Tricia 1960- *111*
  Earlier sketch in SATA *72*
Tusiani, Joseph 1924- *45*
Twain, Mark
  See CLR *66*
  See Clemens, Samuel Langhorne
Tweit, Susan J 1956- *94*
Tweit, Susan Joan
  See Tweit, Susan J
Tweton, D. Jerome 1933- *48*
Twinem, Neecy 1958- *92*
Tworkov, Jack 1900-1982 .... *47*
  Obituary *31*
Tyche
  See Papademetriou, Lisa
Tyers, Jenny 1969- *89*
Tyers, Kathy 1952- *82*
Tyler, Anne 1941- *173*
  Earlier sketches in SATA *7, 90*
Tyler, Linda
  See Tyler, Linda W(agner)
Tyler, Linda W(agner) 1952- *65*
Tyler, Vicki 1952- *64*
Tyne, Joel
  See Schembri, Jim
Tyrrell, Frances 1959- *107*

U

Ubell, Earl 1926-2007 .... *4*
  Obituary *182*
Uchida, Yoshiko 1921-1992 .... *53*
  Obituary *72*
  Earlier sketch in SATA *1*
  See also CLR *56*
  See also SAAS *1*
Udall, Jan Beaney 1938- *10*
Uden, (Bernard Gilbert) Grant 1910- *26*
Uderzo, Albert 1927-
  See CLR *37*
Udovic, David 1950- *189*
Udry, Janice May 1928- *152*
  Earlier sketch in SATA *4*
Uegaki, Chieri 1969- *153*
Ueno, Noriko
  See Nakae, Noriko
Uhlberg, Myron *174*
Uhlig, Richard 1970- *195*
Uhlig, Susan 1955- *129*
Ulam, S(tanislaw) M(arcin) 1909-1984 .... *51*
Ullman, James Ramsey 1907-1971 .... *7*
Ulm, Robert 1934-1977 .... *17*
Ulmer, Louise 1943- *53*
Ulyatt, Kenneth 1920- *14*
Umansky, Kaye 1946- *188*
  Earlier sketch in SATA *158*
Unada
  See Gliewe, Unada (Grace)
Uncle Carter
  See Boucher, (Clarence) Carter
Uncle Eric
  See Maybury, Richard J.
Uncle Gus
  See Rey, H(ans) A(ugusto)
Uncle Mac
  See McCulloch, Derek (Ivor Breashur)
Uncle Ray
  See Coffman, Ramon Peyton
Uncle Shelby
  See Silverstein, Shel
Underhill, Alice Mertie (Waterman)
  1900-1971 .... *10*
Underhill, Liz 1948- *53*
  Brief entry *49*
Unger, Harlow G. 1931- *75*

Unger, Jim 1937- *67*
Ungerer, (Jean) Thomas 1931- *106*
  Earlier sketches in SATA *5, 33*
  See Ungerer, Tomi
Ungerer, Tomi 1931-
  See CLR *77*
  See Ungerer, (Jean) Thomas
Unkelbach, Kurt 1913-1992 .... *4*
Unnerstad, Edith (Totterman) 1900-1982 .... *3*
  See also CLR *36*
Unobagha, Uzo *139*
Unrau, Ruth 1922- *9*
Unstead, R(obert) J(ohn) 1915-1988 .... *12*
  Obituary *56*
Unsworth, Walt(er) 1928- *4*
Untermeyer, Bryna Ivens 1909-1985 .... *61*
Untermeyer, Louis 1885-1977 .... *37*
  Obituary *26*
  Earlier sketch in SATA *2*
Unwin, David S(torr) 1918- *14*
Unwin, Nora S(picer) 1907-1982 .... *3*
  Obituary *49*
Unzner, Christa 1958- *141*
  Earlier sketch in SATA *80*
Unzner-Fischer, Christa
  See Unzner, Christa
Updale, Eleanor 1953- *175*
Updyke, Rosemary K. 1924- *103*
Upitis, Alvis *109*
Urban, Helle (Denise) 1957- *149*
Urbanovic, Jackie *189*
Ure, Jean 1943- *192*
  Autobiography Feature *192*
  Earlier sketches in SATA *48, 78, 129*
  See also CLR *34*
  See also SAAS *14*
U'Ren, Andrea 1968- *142*
Uris, Leon 1924-2003 .... *49*
  Obituary *146*
Uris, Leon Marcus
  See Uris, Leon
Ursu, Anne *177*
Ury, Allen B. 1954- *98*
Uschan, Michael V. 1948- *129*
Usher, Margo Scegge
  See McHargue, Georgess
Uslan, Michael E. 1951- *169*
Uston, Ken(neth Senzo) 1935-1987 .... *65*
Uttley, Alice Jane (Taylor) 1884-1976 .... *88*
  Obituary *26*
  Earlier sketch in SATA *3*
  See Uttley, Alison
Uttley, Alison
  See Uttley, Alice Jane (Taylor)
Utz, Lois (Marie) 1932-1986 .... *5*
  Obituary *50*

V

Vaeth, J(oseph) Gordon 1921- *17*
Vagin, Vladimir (Vasilevich) 1937- *142*
Vail, Rachel 1966- *163*
  Earlier sketch in SATA *94*
Vainio, Pirkko 1957- *123*
  Earlier sketch in SATA *76*
Valen, Nanine 1950- *21*
Valencak, Hannelore *42*
  See Mayer, Hannelore Valencak
Valens, Amy 1946- *70*
Valens, E(vans) G(ladstone), Jr. 1920-1992 ... *1*
Valentine, Johnny *72*
Valerio, Geraldo 1970- *180*
Valgardson, W(illiam) D(empsey) 1939- *151*
  Earlier sketch in SATA *101*
Valleau, Emily 1925- *51*
Van Abbe, Salaman 1883-1955 .... *18*
Van Allsburg, Chris 1949- *156*
  Earlier sketches in SATA *37, 53, 105*
  See also CLR *113*

Van Anrooy, Francine 1924- 2
Van Anrooy, Frans
    See Van Anrooy, Francine
Vanasse, Deb 1957- 170
Vance, Eleanor Graham 1908-1985 11
Vance, Gerald
    See Garrett, (Gordon) Randall (Phillip)
    and Silverberg, Robert
Vance, Marguerite 1889-1965 29
VanCleave, Janice 1942- 116
    Autobiography Feature 123
    Earlier sketch in SATA 75
Vandenburg, Mary Lou 1943- 17
Vander Boom, Mae M. 14
Vander-Els, Betty 1936- 63
van der Heide, Iris 1970- 183
van der Linde, Laurel 1952- 78
van der Meer, Ron 1945- 98
Van der Veer, Judy 1912-1982 4
    Obituary 33
Vanderwerff, Corrine 1939- 117
Vander Zee, Ruth 159
Vande Velde, Vivian 1951- 141
    Earlier sketches in SATA 62, 95
Vandivert, Rita (Andre) 1905-1986 21
Van Draanen, Wendelin 122
Van Dusen, Chris 173
Van Duyn, Janet 1910- 18
Van Dyne, Edith
    See Baum, L(yman) Frank
    and Sampson, Emma (Keats) Speed
    and van Zantwijk, Rudolf (Alexander
    Marinus)
Vane, Mitch
    See Vane, Mitchelle
Vane, Mitchelle 176
van Frankenhuyzen, Gijsbert 1951- 132
Van Genechten, Guido 1957- 165
van Haeringen, Annemarie 193
Van Hook, Beverly H. 1941- 99
Van Horn, William 1939- 43
van Hout, Mies 1962- 178
Van Iterson, S(iny) R(ose) 26
Van Kampen, Vlasta 1943- 163
    Earlier sketch in SATA 54
Van Laan, Nancy 1939- 105
van Lawick-Goodall, Jane
    See Goodall, Jane
Van Leeuwen, Jean 1937- 141
    Autobiography Feature 141
    Earlier sketches in SATA 6, 82, 132
    See also SAAS 8
van Lhin, Erik
    See del Rey, Lester
Van Loon, Hendrik Willem 1882-1944 18
van Ommen, Sylvia 1978- 186
VanOosting, James 1951- 170
Van Orden, M(erton) D(ick) 1921- 4
Van Patter, Bruce 183
Van Rensselaer, Alexander (Taylor Mason)
    1892-1962 14
Van Riper, Guernsey, Jr. 1909-1995 3
van Rossum, Heleen 1962- 174
Van Rynbach, Iris 1952- 102
Vansant, Rhonda Joy Edwards 1950- 92
Van Steenwyk, Elizabeth (Ann) 1928- 89
    Earlier sketch in SATA 34
Van Stockum, Hilda 1908-2006 5
    Obituary 179
van Straaten, Harmen 1961- 195
Van Tuyl, Barbara 1940- 11
van Vogt, A(lfred) E(lton) 1912-2000 14
    Obituary 124
Van Woerkom, Dorothy (O'Brien)
    1924-1996 21
Van Wormer, Joe
    See Van Wormer, Joseph Edward
Van Wormer, Joseph Edward 1913-1998 35
Van Wright, Cornelius 173

Van Zwienen, Ilse Charlotte Koehn
    1929-1991 34
    Brief entry 28
    Obituary 67
Van Zyle, Jon 1942- 176
    Earlier sketch in SATA 84
Varela, Barry 180
Varga, Judy
    See Stang, Judit
Varley, Dimitry V. 1906-1984 10
Varley, Susan 1961- 134
    Earlier sketch in SATA 63
Varon, Sara 195
Vasileva, Tatiana
    See Wassiljewa, Tatjana
Vasiliev, Valery 1949- 80
Vasilieva, Tatiana
    See Wassiljewa, Tatjana
Vasiliu, Mircea 1920- 2
Vass, George 1927- 57
    Brief entry 31
Vaughan, Carter A.
    See Gerson, Noel Bertram
Vaughan, Harold Cecil 1923- 14
Vaughan, Marcia (K.) 1951- 159
    Earlier sketch in SATA 60, 95
Vaughan, Richard 1947- 87
Vaughan, Sam(uel) 1928- 14
Vaughn, Ruth 1935- 14
Vaught, Susan 1965- 195
Vautier, Ghislaine 1932- 53
Vavra, Robert James 1935- 8
Vecsey, George Spencer 1939- 9
Vedral, Joyce L(auretta) 1943- 65
Vega, Denise B. 174
    See Vega, Denise
Veglahn, Nancy (Crary) 1937- 5
Vejjajiva, Jane 1963- 189
Velasquez, Eric 192
Velasquez, Gloria (Louise) 1949- 113
    See Velasquez(-Trevino), Gloria (Louise)
Velthuijs, Max 1923-2005 110
    Obituary 160
    Earlier sketch in SATA 53
Venable, Alan (Hudson) 1944- 8
Venezia, Mike 1945- 150
Ventura, Anthony
    See Pellowski, Michael (Joseph)
Ventura, Piero (Luigi) 1937- 61
    Brief entry 43
    See also CLR 16
Vequin, Capini
    See Quinn, Elisabeth
Verba, Joan Marie 1953- 78
Verboven, Agnes 1951- 103
verDorn, Bethea (Stewart) 1952- 76
Verissimo, Erico (Lopes) 1905-1975 113
Verne, Jules (Gabriel) 1828-1905 21
    See also CLR 88
Verner, Gerald 1897(?)-1980
    Obituary 25
Verney, John 1913-1993 14
    Obituary 75
Verniero, Joan C. 1949- 181
Vernon, (Elda) Louise A(nderson) 1914- 14
Vernon, Rosemary
    See Smith, Susan Vernon
Vernor, D.
    See Casewit, Curtis W(erner)
Verr, Harry Coe
    See Kunhardt, Edith
Verral, Charles Spain 1904-1990 11
    Obituary 65
Verrone, Robert J. 1935(?)-1984
    Obituary 39
Versace, Marie Teresa Rios 1917- 2
Vertreace, Martha M(odena) 1945- 78
Vesey, A(manda) 1939- 62
Vesey, Mark (David) 1958- 123
Vesey, Paul
    See Allen, Samuel W(ashington)

Vestergaard, Hope 178
Vestly, Anne-Cath(arina) 1920- 14
    See also CLR 99
Vevers, (Henry) Gwynne 1916-1988 45
    Obituary 57
Viator, Vacuus
    See Hughes, Thomas
Vicar, Henry
    See Felsen, Henry Gregor
Vick, Helen Hughes 1950- 88
Vicker, Angus
    See Felsen, Henry Gregor
Vickers, Sheena 1960- 94
Vickery, Kate
    See Kennedy, T.A.
Victor, Edward 1914- 3
Victor, Joan Berg 1942- 30
Vidrine, Beverly Barras 1938- 188
    Earlier sketch in SATA 103
Viereck, Ellen K. 1928- 14
Viereck, Phillip 1925- 3
Viertel, Janet 1915- 10
Vigliante, Mary
    See Szydlowski, Mary Vigliante
Vigna, Judith 1936- 102
    Earlier sketch in SATA 15
Viguers, Ruth Hill 1903-1971 6
Villareal, Ray 187
Villasenor, Edmundo
    See Villasenor, Victor
Villasenor, Victor 1940- 171
Villasenor, Victor E. 1940-
    See Villasenor, Victor
Villasenor, Victor Edmundo
    See Villasenor, Victor
Villiard, Paul 1910-1974 51
    Obituary 20
Villiers, Alan (John) 1903-1982 10
Vilott, Rhondi
    See Salsitz, Rhondi Vilott
Vincent, Eric Douglas 1953- 40
Vincent, Erin 1969- 188
Vincent, Felix 1946- 41
Vincent, Gabrielle 1928-2000 121
    Earlier sketch in SATA 61
    See also CLR 13
Vincent, Mary Keith
    See St. John, Wylly Folk
Vincent, William R.
    See Heitzmann, William Ray
Vinegar, Tom
    See Gregg, Andrew K.
Vinest, Shaw
    See Longyear, Barry B(rookes)
Vinge, Joan (Carol) D(ennison) 1948- 113
    Earlier sketch in SATA 36
Vining, Elizabeth Gray 1902-1999 6
    Obituary 117
    See Gray, Elizabeth Janet
Vinson, Kathryn 1911-1995 21
Vinton, Iris 1906(?)-1988 24
    Obituary 55
Viola, Herman J(oseph) 1938- 126
Viorst, Judith 1931- 172
    Earlier sketches in SATA 7, 70, 123
    See also CLR 90
Vip
    See Partch, Virgil Franklin II
Vipont, Charles
    See Foulds, Elfrida Vipont
Vipont, Elfrida
    See Foulds, Elfrida Vipont
Viscott, David S(even) 1938-1996 65
Visser, W(illem) F(rederik) H(endrik)
    1900-1968 10
Vitale, Stefano 1958- 180
    Earlier sketch in SATA 114
Vivas, Julie 1947- 96
Vivelo, Jackie 1943- 63
Vivelo, Jacqueline J.
    See Vivelo, Jackie

Vivelo, Jacqueline Jean
See Vivelo, Jackie
Vizzini, Ned 1981- 179
Earlier sketch in SATA 125
Vlahos, Olivia 1924- 31
Vlasic, Bob
See Hirsch, Phil
Voake, Charlotte 180
Earlier sketch in SATA 114
Voake, Steve 1961- 178
Vo-Dinh, Mai 1933- 16
Vogel, Carole Garbuny 1951- 105
Earlier sketch in SATA 70
Vogel, Ilse-Margret 1918- 14
Vogel, John H., Jr. 1950- 18
Vogt, Esther Loewen 1915-1999 14
Vogt, Gregory L. 94
Vogt, Marie Bollinger 1921- 45
Voight, Virginia Frances 1909-1989 8
Voigt, Cynthia 1942- 160
Brief entry 33
Earlier sketches in SATA 48, 79, 116
See also CLR 48
Voigt, Erna 1925- 35
Voigt-Rother, Erna
See Voigt, Erna
Vojtech, Anna 1946- 108
Earlier sketch in SATA 42
Vollstadt, Elizabeth Weiss 1942- 121
Volponi, Paul 175
Volting, Dr. R.E.
See Lerangis, Peter
Von Ahnen, Katherine 1922- 93
von Buhler, Cynthia 185
Vondra, J. Gert
See Vondra, Josef
Vondra, Josef 1941- 121
Vondra, Josef Gert
See Vondra, Josef
Von Gunden, Kenneth 1946- 113
Von Hagen, Victor Wolfgang 1908-1985 29
von Klopp, Vahrah
See Malvern, Gladys
von Schmidt, Eric 1931-2007 50
Brief entry 36
Obituary 181
von Storch, Anne B. 1910- 1
von Ziegesar, Cecily 1970- 161
Vos, Ida 1931-2006 121
Earlier sketch in SATA 69
See also CLR 85
Vosburgh, Leonard (W.) 1912- 15
Voyle, Mary
See Manning, Rosemary (Joy)
Vrettos, Adrienne Maria 187
Vriens, Jacques 1946- 151
Vugteveen, Verna Aardema 107
Obituary 119
Earlier sketches in SATA 4, 68
See also CLR 17
See also SAAS 8
See Aardema, Verna
Vulture, Elizabeth T.
See Gilbert, Suzie
Vuong, Lynette Dyer 1938- 110
Earlier sketch in SATA 60

W

Waas, Uli
See Waas-Pommer, Ulrike
Waas-Pommer, Ulrike 1949- 85
Waber, Bernard 1924- 155
Brief entry 40
Earlier sketches in SATA 47, 95
See also CLR 55
Wachtel, Shirley Russak 1951- 88
Wachter, Oralee (Roberts) 1935- 61
Brief entry 51

Waddell, Evelyn Margaret 1918- 10
Waddell, Martin 1941- 129
Autobiography Feature 129
Earlier sketches in SATA 43, 81, 127
See also CLR 31
See also SAAS 15
Waddy, Lawrence (Heber) 1914- 91
Wade, Mary Dodson 1930- 151
Earlier sketch in SATA 79
Wade, Suzanne
See Kirby, Susan E.
Wade, Theodore E., Jr. 1936- 37
Wademan, Peter John 1946- 122
Wademan, Spike
See Wademan, Peter John
Wadsworth, Ginger 1945- 157
Earlier sketch in SATA 103
Wagenheim, Kal 1935- 21
Wagner, Michele R. 1975- 157
Wagner, Sharon B. 1936- 4
Wagoner, David (Russell) 1926- 14
Wahl, Jan (Boyer) 1933- 132
Earlier sketches in SATA 2, 34, 73
See also SAAS 3
Wahl, Mats 1945- 186
Waide, Jan 1952- 29
Wainscott, John Milton 1910-1981 53
Wainwright, Richard M. 1935- 91
Wainwright, Ruth
See Symes, Ruth Louise
Wait, Lea 1946- 137
Waite, Judy 174
Waite, Judy Bernard
See Bernard, Patricia
Waite, Michael P(hillip) 1960- 101
Waite, P(eter) B(usby) 1922- 64
Waites, Joan C. 187
Waitley, Douglas 1927- 30
Wakefield, Jean L.
See Laird, Jean E(louise)
Wakin, Daniel (Joseph) 1961- 84
Wakin, Edward 1927- 37
Wakiyama, Hanako 1966- 192
Walck, Henry Z. 1908(?)-1984
Obituary 40
Walden, Amelia Elizabeth 3
Walden, Mark 188
Waldherr, Kris 1963- 76
Waldman, Bruce 1949- 15
Waldman, Neil 1947- 142
Earlier sketches in SATA 51, 94
Waldron, Ann Wood 1924- 16
Waldron, Kathleen Cook 176
Walgren, Judy 1963- 118
Walker, Addison
See Walker, (Addison) Mort
Walker, Alice 1944- 31
Walker, Alice Malsenior
See Walker, Alice
Walker, Barbara (Jeanne) K(erlin) 1921- 80
Earlier sketch in SATA 4
Walker, Barbara M(uhs) 1928- 57
Walker, (James) Braz(elton) 1934-1983 45
Walker, David G(ordon) 1926- 60
Walker, David Harry 1911-1992 8
Obituary 71
Walker, Diana 1925- 9
Walker, Diane Marie Catherine
See Walker, Kate
Walker, Dick
See Pellowski, Michael (Joseph)
Walker, Frank 1931-2000 36
Walker, Holly Beth
See Bond, Gladys Baker
Walker, Kate 1950- 165
Earlier sketch in SATA 82
Walker, Kathrine Sorley
See Sorley Walker, Kathrine
Walker, Lou Ann 1952- 66
Brief entry 53

Walker, Louise Jean 1891-1976
Obituary 35
Walker, Mary Alexander 1927- 61
Walker, Mildred
See Schemm, Mildred Walker
Walker, (Addison) Mort 1923- 8
Walker, Pamela 1948- 142
Earlier sketch in SATA 24
Walker, Paul Robert 1953- 154
Walker, Robert W(ayne) 1948- 66
Walker, Sally M(acArt) 1954- 135
Walker, Stephen J. 1951- 12
Walker-Blondell, Becky 1951- 89
Wallace, Barbara Brooks 1922- 136
Earlier sketches in SATA 4, 78
See also SAAS 17
Wallace, Beverly Dobrin 1921- 19
Wallace, Bill 1947- 169
Brief entry 47
Earlier sketches in SATA 53, 101
Wallace, Daisy
See Cuyler, Margery
Wallace, Ian 1950- 141
Earlier sketches in SATA 53, 56
See also CLR 37
Wallace, John 1966- 155
Earlier sketch in SATA 105
Wallace, John A(dam) 1915-2004 3
Obituary 155
Wallace, Karen 1951- 188
Earlier sketches in SATA 83, 139
Wallace, Nancy Elizabeth 1948- 186
Earlier sketch in SATA 141
Wallace, Nigel
See Hamilton, Charles (Harold St. John)
Wallace, Paula S. 153
Wallace, Rich 1957- 158
Earlier sketch in SATA 117
Wallace, Robert 1932-1999 47
Brief entry 37
Wallace, William Keith
See Wallace, Bill
Wallace-Brodeur, Ruth 1941- 169
Brief entry 41
Earlier sketches in SATA 51, 88
Wallenta, Adam 1974- 123
Waller, Leslie 1923-2007 20
Walley, Byron
See Card, Orson Scott
Wallis, Diz 1949- 77
Wallis, G. McDonald
See Campbell, Hope
Wallner, Alexandra 1946- 156
Brief entry 41
Earlier sketches in SATA 51, 98
Wallner, John C. 1945- 133
Earlier sketches in SATA 10, 51
Wallower, Lucille 11
Walrod, Amy 1973(?)- 182
Walsh, Ann 1942- 176
Earlier sketch in SATA 62
Walsh, Ellen Stoll 1942- 194
Earlier sketches in SATA 49, 99, 147
Walsh, George Johnston 1889-1981 53
Walsh, Gillian Paton
See Paton Walsh, Jill
Walsh, Jill Paton
See CLR 128
See Paton Walsh, Jill
Walsh, Joanna 1970- 182
Walsh, Lawrence 1942- 170
Walsh, Marissa 1972- 195
Walsh, Marissa Mitzy
See Walsh, Marissa
Walsh, Mary Caswell 1949- 118
Walsh, Suella 170
Walsh, V. L.
See Walsh, Vivian
Walsh, Vivian 1960- 120
Walsh Shepherd, Donna 1948- 78
Walter, Frances V. 1923- 71

Walter, Mildred Pitts 1922- 133
  Brief entry 45
  Earlier sketch in SATA 69
  See also CLR 61
  See also SAAS 12
Walter, Villiam Christian
  See Andersen, Hans Christian
Walter, Virginia 134
  See Walter, Virginia A.
Walters, Audrey 1929- 18
Walters, Celeste 1938- 126
Walters, Eric (Robert) 1957- 155
  Earlier sketch in SATA 99
Walters, Helen B. (?)-1987
  Obituary 50
Walters, Hugh
  See Hughes, Walter (Llewellyn)
Walther, Thomas A. 1950- 31
Walther, Tom
  See Walther, Thomas A.
Waltner, Elma 1912-1987 40
Waltner, Willard H. 1909- 40
Walton, Darwin McBeth 1926- 119
Walton, Fiona L. M. 1959- 89
Walton, Richard J. 1928- 4
Walton, Rick 1957- 151
  Earlier sketch in SATA 101
Waltrip, Lela (Kingston) 1904-1995 9
Waltrip, Mildred 1911- 37
Waltrip, Rufus (Charles) 1898-1988 9
Walworth, Nancy Zinsser 1917- 14
Wangerin, Walter, Jr. 1944- 98
  Brief entry 37
  Earlier sketch in SATA 45
Waniek, Marilyn Nelson 1946- 60
  See Nelson, Marilyn
Wannamaker, Bruce
  See Moncure, Jane Belk
Warbler, J. M.
  See Cocagnac, Augustin Maurice(-Jean)
Warburg, Sandol Stoddard 14
  See Stoddard, Sandol
Ward, E. D.
  See Gorey, Edward (St. John)
  and Lucas, E(dward) V(errall)
Ward, Ed
  See Stratemeyer, Edward L.
Ward, Helen 1962- 144
  Earlier sketch in SATA 72
Ward, Jay 1920-1989
  Obituary 63
Ward, Jennifer 1963- 146
Ward, John (Stanton) 1917- 42
Ward, Jonas
  See Ard, William (Thomas)
  and Cox, William R(obert)
  and Garfield, Brian (Francis Wynne)
Ward, Lynd (Kendall) 1905-1985 36
  Obituary 42
  Earlier sketch in SATA 2
Ward, Martha (Eads) 5
Ward, Melanie
  See Curtis, Richard (Alan)
  and Lynch, Marilyn
Ward, Nick 1955- 190
Ward, Tom
  See Stratemeyer, Edward L.
Wardell, Dean
  See Prince, J(ack) H(arvey)
Wardlaw, Lee 1955- 115
  Earlier sketch in SATA 79
Ware, Cheryl 1963- 101
Ware, Chris 1967- 140
Ware, Leon (Vernon) 1909-1976 4
Wargin, Kathy-jo 1965- 145
Warhola, James 1955- 187
Warner, Frank A. 67
  Earlier sketch in SATA 1
Warner, Gertrude Chandler 1890-1979 9
  Obituary 73
Warner, J(ohn) F. 1929- 75

Warner, Lucille Schulberg 30
Warner, Matt
  See Fichter, George S.
Warner, Oliver (Martin Wilson) 1903-1976 . 29
Warner, Sally 1946- 131
Warner, Sunny (B.) 1931- 108
Warnes, Tim 1971- 166
  Earlier sketch in SATA 116
Warnes, Timothy
  See Warnes, Tim
Warnick, Elsa 1942- 113
Warren, Andrea 1946- 98
Warren, Betsy
  See Warren, Elizabeth Avery
Warren, Billy
  See Warren, William Stephen
Warren, Cathy 1951- 62
  Brief entry 46
Warren, Elizabeth
  See Supraner, Robyn
Warren, Elizabeth Avery 1916- 46
  Brief entry 38
Warren, Jackie M. 1953- 135
Warren, Joshua P(aul) 1976- 107
Warren, Joyce W(illiams) 1935- 18
Warren, Mary Phraner 1929- 10
Warren, Robert Penn 1905-1989 46
  Obituary 63
Warren, Scott S. 1957- 79
Warren, William Stephen 1882-1968 9
Warrick, Patricia Scott 1925- 35
Warriner, John 1907(?)-1987
  Obituary 53
Warsh
  See Warshaw, Jerry
Warshaw, Jerry 1929- 30
Warshaw, Mary 1931- 89
Warshofsky, Fred 1931- 24
Warshofsky, Isaac
  See Singer, Isaac Bashevis
Wartski, Maureen (Ann Crane) 1940- 50
  Brief entry 37
Warwick, Alan R(oss) 1900-1973 42
Wa-sha-quon-asin
  See Belaney, Archibald Stansfeld
Wa-Sha-Quon-Asin
  See Belaney, Archibald Stansfeld
Washburn, Bradford 1910-2007 38
  Obituary 181
Washburn, Henry Bradford, Jr.
  See Washburn, Bradford
Washburn, Jan(ice) 1926- 63
Washburn, Lucia 193
Washburne, Carolyn Kott 1944- 86
Washburne, Heluiz Chandler 1892-1970 10
  Obituary 26
Washington, Booker T(aliaferro)
  1856-1915 28
Washington, Donna L. 1967- 159
  Earlier sketch in SATA 98
Wasserstein, Wendy 1950-2006 94
  Obituary 174
Wassiljewa, Tatjana 1928- 106
Watanabe, Shigeo 1928- 131
  Brief entry 32
  Earlier sketch in SATA 39
  See also CLR 8
Waters, John F(rederick) 1930- 4
Waters, Tony 1958- 75
Waterton, Betty (Marie) 1923- 99
  Brief entry 34
  Earlier sketch in SATA 37
Watkins, Dawn L. 126
Watkins, Gloria Jean
  See hooks, bell
Watkins, Lois 1930- 88
Watkins, Peter 1934- 66
Watkins, Yoko Kawashima 1933- 93

Watkins-Pitchford, Denys James
  1905-1990 87
  Obituary 66
  Earlier sketch in SATA 6
  See also SAAS 4
Watling, James 1933- 117
  Earlier sketch in SATA 67
Watson, Aldren A(uld) 1917- 42
  Brief entry 36
Watson, Amy Zakrzewski 1965- 76
Watson, B. S.
  See Teitelbaum, Michael
Watson, Carol 1949- 78
Watson, C.G. 193
Watson, Clyde 1947- 68
  Earlier sketch in SATA 5
  See also CLR 3
Watson, Helen Orr 1892-1978
  Obituary 24
Watson, James 1936- 106
  Earlier sketch in SATA 10
Watson, Jane Werner 1915- 54
  Earlier sketch in SATA 3
Watson, John H.
  See Farmer, Philip Jose
Watson, Mary 1953- 117
Watson, N. Cameron 1955- 81
Watson, Nancy Dingman 32
Watson, Pauline 1925- 14
Watson, Richard F.
  See Silverberg, Robert
Watson, Richard Jesse 1951- 62
Watson, Sally (Lou) 1924- 3
Watson, Wendy (McLeod) 1942- 142
  Earlier sketches in SATA 5, 74
Watson Taylor, Elizabeth 1915- 41
Watt, Melanie 1975- 193
  Earlier sketch in SATA 136
Watt, Thomas 1935- 4
Wattenberg, Jane 174
Watterson, Bill 1958- 66
Watt-Evans, Lawrence 1954- 121
Watts, (Anna) Bernadette 1942- 103
  Earlier sketch in SATA 4
Watts, Ephraim
  See Horne, Richard Henry Hengist
Watts, Franklin (Mowry) 1904-1978 46
  Obituary 21
Watts, Irene N(aemi) 1931- 111
  Earlier sketch in SATA 56
Watts, Isaac 1674-1748 52
Watts, James K(ennedy) M(offitt) 1955- 59
Watts, Jeri Hanel 1957- 170
Watts, Julia 1969- 103
Watts, Leander 1956- 146
Watts, Leslie Elizabeth 1961- 168
Watts, Mabel Pizzey 1906-1994 11
Watts, Nigel 1957-1999 121
Waugh, C. C. Roessel
  See Waugh, Carol-Lynn Rossel
  and Waugh, Charles G(ordon)
Waugh, Carol-Lynn Rossel 1947- 41
Waugh, Dorothy -1996 11
Waugh, Sylvia 1935- 169
Waugh, Virginia
  See Sorensen, Virginia
Wax, Wendy A. 1963- 163
  Earlier sketch in SATA 73
Wayland, April Halprin 1954- 143
  Earlier sketch in SATA 78
  See also SAAS 26
Wayland, Patrick
  See O'Connor, Richard
Wayne, (Anne) Jenifer 1917-1982 32
Wayne, Kyra Petrovskaya 1918- 8
Wayne, Richard
  See Decker, Duane
Wayshak, Deborah Noyes
  See Noyes, Deborah
Waystaff, Simon
  See Swift, Jonathan

Weales, Gerald (Clifford) 1925- *11*
Weary, Ogdred
    See Gorey, Edward (St. John)
Weatherford, Carole Boston 1956- *181*
    Earlier sketch in SATA *138*
Weatherly, Lee 1967- *192*
Weatherly, Myra 1926- *130*
Weatherly, Myra S.
    See Weatherly, Myra
Weaver, Harriett E. 1908-1993 .... *65*
Weaver, John L. 1949- *42*
Weaver, Robyn
    See Conley-Weaver, Robyn
Weaver, Robyn M.
    See Conley-Weaver, Robyn
Weaver, Ward
    See Mason, F(rancis) van Wyck
Weaver, Will 1950- *161*
    Earlier sketches in SATA *88, 109*
Weaver, William Weller
    See Weaver, Will
Weaver-Gelzer, Charlotte 1950- *79*
Webb, Christopher
    See Wibberley, Leonard (Patrick O'Connor)
Webb, Jacqueline
    See Pearce, Margaret
Webb, Jacquelyn
    See Pearce, Margaret
    and Pearce, Margaret
Webb, Jean Francis (III) 1910-1991 .... *35*
Webb, Kaye 1914- *60*
Webb, Lois Sinaiko 1922- *82*
Webb, Margot 1934- *67*
Webb, Sharon 1936- *41*
Webb, Sophie 1958- *135*
Webber, Andrew Lloyd
    See Lloyd Webber, Andrew
Webber, Desiree Morrison 1956- *170*
Webber, Irma E(leanor Schmidt)
    1904-1995 .... *14*
Weber, Alfons 1921- *8*
Weber, Bruce 1942- *120*
    Earlier sketch in SATA *73*
Weber, Debora 1955- *58*
Weber, EdNah New Rider 1919(?)- *168*
Weber, Jill 1950- *127*
Weber, Judith E(ichler) 1938- *64*
Weber, Ken(neth J.) 1940- *90*
Weber, Lenora Mattingly 1895-1971 .... *2*
    Obituary *26*
Weber, Michael 1945- *87*
Weber, Sandra 1961- *158*
Weber, William J(ohn) 1927- *14*
Webster, Alice Jane Chandler 1876-1916 ..... *17*
Webster, David 1930- *11*
Webster, Frank V. *67*
    Earlier sketch in SATA *1*
Webster, Gary
    See Garrison, Webb B(lack)
Webster, James 1925-1981 .... *17*
    Obituary *27*
Webster, Jean
    See Webster, Alice Jane Chandler
Wechsler, Doug *189*
Wechsler, Herman J. 1904-1976
    Obituary *20*
Wechter, Nell (Carolyn) Wise 1913-1989 .. *127*
    Earlier sketch in SATA *60*
Weck, Thomas L. 1942- *62*
Wedd, Kate
    See Gregory, Philippa
Weddle, Ethel Harshbarger 1897-1996 .... *11*
Weeks, Sarah *194*
    Earlier sketch in SATA *158*
Weems, David B(urnola) 1922- *80*
Wees, Frances Shelley 1902-1982 .... *58*
Weevers, Peter 1944- *59*
Wegen, Ronald 1946-1985 .... *99*
Wegman, William (George) 1943- *135*
    Earlier sketches in SATA *78, 129*
Wegner, Fritz 1924- *20*

Weidhorn, Manfred 1931- *60*
Weidt, Maryann N. 1944- *85*
Weigel, Jeff 1958- *170*
Weigelt, Udo 1960- *168*
Weihs, Erika 1917- *107*
    Earlier sketch in SATA *15*
Weik, Mary Hays 1898(?)-1979 .... *3*
    Obituary *23*
Weil, Ann Yezner 1908-1969 .... *9*
Weil, Lisl 1910- *7*
Weilerstein, Sadie Rose 1894-1993 .... *3*
    Obituary *75*
Weill, Cynthia 1959- *167*
Wein, Elizabeth E(ve) 1964- *151*
    Earlier sketch in SATA *82*
Weinberg, Larry
    See Weinberg, Lawrence (E.)
Weinberg, Lawrence (E.) *92*
    Brief entry *48*
Weinberger, Tanya 1939- *84*
Weiner, Sandra 1922- *14*
Weingarten, Violet (Brown) 1915-1976 .... *3*
    Obituary *27*
Weingartner, Charles 1922- *5*
Weinheimer, Beckie 1958- *186*
Weinstein, Nina 1951- *73*
Weir, Bob 1947- *76*
Weir, Diana (R.) Loiewski 1958- *111*
Weir, Joan S(herman) 1928- *99*
Weir, LaVada *2*
Weir, Rosemary (Green) 1905-1994 .... *21*
Weir, Wendy 1949- *76*
Weis, Margaret 1948- *164*
    Earlier sketches in SATA *38, 92*
Weisberger, Bernard A(llen) 1922- *21*
Weiser, Marjorie P(hillis) K(atz) 1934- *33*
Weisgard, Leonard (Joseph) 1916-2000 .... *85*
    Obituary *122*
    Earlier sketches in SATA *2, 30*
    See also SAAS *19*
Weiss, Adelle 1920- *18*
Weiss, Ann E(dwards) 1943- *69*
    Earlier sketch in SATA *30*
    See also SAAS *13*
Weiss, Edna
    See Barth, Edna
Weiss, Ellen 1953- *44*
Weiss, Harvey 1922- *76*
    Earlier sketches in SATA *1, 27*
    See also CLR *4*
    See also SAAS *19*
Weiss, Jaqueline Shachter 1926- *65*
Weiss, Malcolm E. 1928- *3*
Weiss, Margaret Edith
    See Weis, Margaret
Weiss, Miriam
    See Schlein, Miriam
Weiss, Mitch 1951- *183*
    Earlier sketch in SATA *123*
Weiss, Nicki 1954- *86*
    Earlier sketch in SATA *33*
Weiss, Renee Karol 1923- *5*
Weissberger, Ela 1930- *181*
Weissberger, Ela Stein
    See Weissberger, Ela
Weissenborn, Hellmuth 1898-1982
    Obituary *31*
Weitzman, David L. 1936- *172*
    Earlier sketch in SATA *122*
Wekesser, Carol A. 1963- *76*
Welber, Robert *26*
Welch, Amanda (Jane) 1945- *75*
Welch, D'Alte Aldridge 1907-1970
    Obituary *27*
Welch, Jean-Louise
    See Kempton, Jean Welch
Welch, Pauline
    See Bodenham, Hilda Morris
Welch, Ronald
    See Felton, Ronald Oliver
Welch, Sheila Kelly 1945- *130*

Welch, Willy 1952- *93*
Weldin, Frauke 1969- *188*
Welford, Sue 1942- *75*
Weller, George 1907-2002 .... *31*
    Obituary *140*
Weller, George Anthony
    See Weller, George
Welling, Peter J. 1947- *135*
Wellington, Monica 1957- *157*
    Earlier sketches in SATA *67, 99*
Wellman, Alice 1900-1984 .... *51*
    Brief entry *36*
Wellman, Manly Wade 1903-1986 .... *6*
    Obituary *47*
Wellman, Paul I. 1898-1966 .... *3*
Wellman, Paul Iselin
    See Wellman, Paul I.
Wellman, Sam(uel) 1939- *122*
Wells, H(erbert) G(eorge) 1866-1946 .... *20*
    See also CLR *133*
Wells, Helen
    See Campbell, Hope
Wells, Helen 1910-1986 .... *49*
    Earlier sketch in SATA *2*
Wells, J. Wellington
    See de Camp, L(yon) Sprague
Wells, June
    See Swinford, Betty (June Wells)
Wells, Robert
    See Welsch, Roger L(ee)
Wells, Robert E. *184*
Wells, Rosemary 1943- *156*
    Earlier sketches in SATA *18, 69, 114*
    See also CLR *69*
    See also SAAS *1*
Wells, Susan (Mary) 1951- *78*
Wels, Byron G(erald) 1924-1993 .... *9*
Welsbacher, Anne 1955- *89*
Welsch, Roger L(ee) 1936- *82*
Welsh, David
    See Hills, C.A.R.
Welsh, Mary Flynn 1910(?)-1984
    Obituary *38*
Welsh, T.K. 1956- *184*
Weltner, Linda R(iverly) 1938- *38*
Welton, Jude 1955- *143*
    Earlier sketch in SATA *79*
Welty, S. F.
    See Welty, Susan F.
Welty, Susan F. 1905- *9*
Wemmlinger, Raymond *190*
Wendelin, Rudolph 1910-2000 .... *23*
Weninger, Brigitte 1960- *189*
Wentworth, Robert
    See Hamilton, Edmond
Werlin, Nancy 1961- *161*
    Earlier sketches in SATA *87, 119*
Werner, Elsa Jane
    See Watson, Jane Werner
Werner, Herma 1926- *47*
    Brief entry *41*
Werner, Jane
    See Watson, Jane Werner
Werner, K.
    See Casewit, Curtis W(erner)
Wersba, Barbara 1932- *58*
    Autobiography Feature *103*
    Earlier sketch in SATA *1*
    See also CLR *78*
    See also SAAS *2*
Werstein, Irving 1914(?)-1971 .... *14*
Werth, Kurt 1896-1983 .... *20*
Wesley, Alison
    See Barnes, Michael
Wesley, Kathryn
    See Rusch, Kristine Kathryn
Wesley, Mary (Aline) 1912-2002 .... *66*
Wesley, Valerie Wilson 1947- *168*
    Earlier sketch in SATA *106*
West, Andrew
    See Arthur, Robert, (Jr.)

West, Anna 1938- 40
West, Barbara
    See Price, Olive
West, Betty 1921- 11
West, Bruce 1951- 63
West, C. P.
    See Wodehouse, P(elham) G(renville)
West, Dorothy
    See Benson, Mildred (Augustine Wirt)
West, Emily Govan 1919- 38
West, Emmy
    See West, Emily Govan
West, James
    See Withers, Carl A.
West, Jerry
    See Svenson, Andrew E(dward)
West, (Mary) Jessamyn 1902-1984
    Obituary 37
West, John
    See Arthur, Robert, (Jr.)
West, Owen
    See Koontz, Dean R.
Westall, Robert (Atkinson) 1929-1993 69
    Obituary 75
    Earlier sketch in SATA 23
    See also CLR 13
    See also SAAS 2
Westaway, Jane 1948- 121
Westcott, Nadine Bernard 1949- 130
Westera, Marleen 1962- 187
Westerberg, Christine 1950- 29
Westerduin, Anne 1945- 105
Westerfeld, Scott 161
Westervelt, Virginia Veeder 1914-2005 10
Westheimer, David 1917-2005 14
    Obituary 170
Westheimer, David Kaplan
    See Westheimer, David
Westmacott, Mary
    See Christie, Agatha (Mary Clarissa)
Westman, Barbara 70
Westman, Paul (Wendell) 1956- 39
Westmoreland, William C. 1914-2005 63
Westmoreland, William Childs
    See Westmoreland, William C.
Weston, Allen
    See Hogarth, Grace (Weston Allen)
    and Norton, Andre
Weston, Carol 1956- 135
Weston, Carrie 190
Weston, John (Harrison) 1932- 21
Weston, Martha 1947- 119
    Earlier sketch in SATA 53
Westphal, Arnold Carl 1897- 57
Westrup, Hugh 102
Westwood, Jennifer 1940-2008 10
    Obituary 192
Wexler, Jerome (LeRoy) 1923- 14
Weyland, Jack 1940- 81
Weyn, Suzanne 1955- 164
    Earlier sketches in SATA 63, 101
Weyr, Garret
    See Freymann-Weyr, (Rhoda) Garret
    (Michaela)
Wezyk, Joanna 1966- 82
Whaley, Joyce Irene 1923- 61
Whalin, W. Terry 1953- 93
Wharf, Michael
    See Weller, George
Wharmby, Margot 63
Wharton, Edith (Newbold Jones) 1862-1937
    See CLR 136
Whatley, Bruce 1954- 177
Wheatley, Arabelle 1921- 16
Wheatley, Nadia 1949- 147
Wheeler, Cindy 1955- 49
    Brief entry 40
Wheeler, Deborah 1947- 83
Wheeler, Janet D. 1
Wheeler, Jill C. 1964- 136
    Earlier sketch in SATA 86

Wheeler, Jody 1952- 148
    Earlier sketch in SATA 84
Wheeler, Lisa 1963- 162
Wheeler, Opal 1898- 23
Whelan, Elizabeth M(urphy) 1943- 14
Whelan, Gloria 1923- 178
    Earlier sketches in SATA 85, 128
    See also CLR 90
Whelan, Gloria Ann
    See Whelan, Gloria
Whipple, A(ddison) B(eecher) C(olvin)
    1918- 64
Whipple, Cal
    See Whipple, A(ddison) B(eecher) C(olvin)
Whisp, Kennilworthy
    See Rowling, J.K.
Whistler, Reginald John 1905-1944 30
Whistler, Rex
    See Whistler, Reginald John
Whitaker, Zai 183
Whitcher, Susan (Godsil) 1952- 96
Whitcomb, Jon 1906-1988 10
    Obituary 56
Whitcomb, Laura 171
White, Anne Terry 1896-1980 2
White, Bessie (Felstiner) 1892(?)-1986
    Obituary 50
White, Carolyn 1948- 130
White, Dale
    See Place, Marian T(empleton)
White, Dori 1919- 10
White, E. B. 1899-1985 100
    Obituary 44
    Earlier sketches in SATA 2, 29
    See also CLR 107
White, Eliza Orne 1856-1947
    See YABC 2
White, Elwyn Brooks
    See White, E. B.
White, Florence M(eiman) 1910- 14
White, Laurence B(arton), Jr. 1935- 10
White, Lee 176
White, Martin 1943- 51
White, Nancy 1942- 126
White, Ramy Allison 67
    Earlier sketch in SATA 1
White, Robb 1909-1990 83
    Earlier sketch in SATA 1
    See also CLR 3
    See also SAAS 1
White, Ruth C. 1942- 186
    Autobiography Feature 186
    Earlier sketches in SATA 39, 117, 165
White, T(erence) H(anbury) 1906-1964 12
    See also CLR 139
White, Tekla N. 1934- 115
White, Timothy (Thomas Anthony)
    1952-2002 60
White, Tom 1923- 148
White, William, Jr. 1934- 16
Whitehead, Don(ald) F. 1908-1981 4
Whitehead, Jenny 1964- 191
Whitehead, Kathy 1957- 176
Whitehouse, Arch
    See Whitehouse, Arthur George Joseph
Whitehouse, Arthur George Joseph
    1895-1979 14
    Obituary 23
Whitehouse, Elizabeth S(cott) 1893-1968 35
Whitehouse, Jeanne 29
    See Peterson, Jeanne Whitehouse
Whitelaw, Nancy 1933- 166
    Earlier sketch in SATA 76
Whitesel, Cheryl Aylward 162
Whitinger, R. D.
    See Place, Marian T(empleton)
Whitley, Mary Ann
    See Sebrey, Mary Ann
Whitley, Peggy 1938- 140
Whitlock, Pamela 1921(?)-1982
    Obituary 31

Whitlock, Ralph 1914-1995 35
Whitman, Alice
    See Marker, Sherry
Whitman, Sylvia (Choate) 1961- 135
    Earlier sketch in SATA 85
Whitman, Walt(er) 1819-1892 20
Whitmore, Arvella 1922- 125
Whitney, Alex(andra) 1922- 14
Whitney, David C(harles) 1921- 48
    Brief entry 29
Whitney, Kim Ablon 162
Whitney, Phyllis A. 1903-2008 30
    Obituary 189
    Earlier sketch in SATA 1
    See also CLR 59
Whitney, Phyllis Ayame
    See Whitney, Phyllis A.
Whitney, Phyllis Ayame
    See Whitney, Phyllis A.
Whitney, Sharon 1937- 63
Whitney, Thomas P. 1917-2007 25
    Obituary 189
Whitney, Thomas Porter
    See Whitney, Thomas P.
Whittington, Mary K(athrine) 1941- 75
Whitworth, John 1945- 123
Whybrow, Ian 132
Whyte, Mal(colm Kenneth, Jr.) 1933- 62
Whyte, Mary 1953- 148
    Earlier sketch in SATA 94
Whyte, Ron 1942(?)-1989
    Obituary 63
Whytock, Cherry 177
Wiater, Stanley 1953- 84
Wibbelsman, Charles J(oseph) 1945- 59
Wibberley, Leonard (Patrick O'Connor)
    1915-1983 45
    Obituary 36
    Earlier sketch in SATA 2
    See also CLR 3
    See Holton, Leonard
Wiberg, Harald (Albin) 1908- 93
    Brief entry 40
Wick, Walter 1953- 148
Wickens, Elaine 86
Wicker, Ireene 1905(?)-1987
    Obituary 55
Wickstrom, Sylvie 1960- 169
Widdemer, Mabel Cleland 1902-1964 5
Widener, Terry 1950- 105
Widerberg, Siv 1931- 10
Wiebe, Rudy 1934- 156
Wiebe, Rudy Henry
    See Wiebe, Rudy
Wieler, Diana (Jean) 1961- 109
Wiener, Lori 1956- 84
Wier, Ester (Alberti) 1910-2000 3
Wiese, Kurt 1887-1974 36
    Obituary 24
    Earlier sketch in SATA 3
    See also CLR 86
Wiesel, Elie 1928- 56
Wiesel, Eliezer
    See Wiesel, Elie
Wiesner, David 1956- 181
    Earlier sketches in SATA 72, 117, 139
    See also CLR 84
Wiesner, Portia
    See Takakjian, Portia
Wiesner, William 1899-1984 5
Wiggers, Raymond 1952- 82
Wiggin, Eric E. 1939- 167
    Earlier sketch in SATA 88
Wiggin, Eric Ellsworth 1939-
    See Wiggin, Eric E.
Wiggin (Riggs), Kate Douglas (Smith)
    1856-1923
    See YABC 1
    See also CLR 52
Wiggins, VeraLee (Chesnut) 1928-1995 89

Wight, James Alfred 1916-1995 .... *55*
  Brief entry *44*
  See Herriot, James
Wignell, Edel 1936- *69*
Wijnberg, Ellen *85*
Wikland, Ilon 1930- *93*
  Brief entry *32*
Wikler, Madeline 1943- *114*
Wilber, Donald N(ewton) 1907-1997 .... *35*
Wilbur, C. Keith 1923- *27*
Wilbur, Frances 1921- *107*
Wilbur, Richard 1921- *108*
  Earlier sketch in SATA *9*
Wilbur, Richard Purdy
  See Wilbur, Richard
Wilburn, Kathy 1948- *68*
Wilcox, Charlotte 1948- *72*
Wilcox, R(uth) Turner 1888-1970 .... *36*
Wilcox, Roger
  See Collins, Paul
Wild, Jocelyn 1941- *46*
Wild, Kate 1954- *192*
Wild, Margaret 1948- *151*
Wild, Robin (Evans) 1936- *46*
Wild, Robyn 1947- *117*
Wilde, D. Gunther
  See Hurwood, Bernhardt J.
Wilde, Oscar 1854(?)-1900 .... *24*
  See also CLR *114*
Wilde, Oscar Fingal O'Flahertie Willis
  See Wilde, Oscar
Wilder, Buck
  See Smith, Tim(othy R.)
Wilder, Laura (Elizabeth) Ingalls
  1867-1957 .... *100*
  Earlier sketches in SATA *15, 29*
  See also CLR *111*
Wildsmith, Brian 1930- *124*
  Earlier sketches in SATA *16, 69*
  See also CLR *52*
  See also SAAS *5*
Wiles, Deborah *171*
Wilhelm, Doug 1952- *190*
Wilhelm, Hans 1945- *135*
  Earlier sketch in SATA *58*
  See also CLR *46*
  See also SAAS *21*
Wilkie, Katharine E(lliott) 1904-1980 .... *31*
Wilkin, Eloise 1904-1987 .... *49*
  Obituary *54*
Wilkins, Frances 1923- *14*
Wilkins, Kim *147*
Wilkins, Marilyn (Ruth) 1926- *30*
Wilkins, Marne
  See Wilkins, Marilyn (Ruth)
Wilkins, Mary Huiskamp 1926- *139*
  Earlier sketch in SATA *84*
  See Calhoun, Mary
Wilkins, Mary Huiskamp Calhoun
  See Wilkins, Mary Huiskamp
Wilkins, Rose *180*
Wilkinson, (Thomas) Barry 1923- *50*
  Brief entry *32*
Wilkinson, Beth 1925- *80*
Wilkinson, Brenda 1946- *91*
  Earlier sketch in SATA *14*
  See also CLR *20*
Wilkinson, (John) Burke 1913-2000 .... *4*
Wilkinson, Sylvia 1940- *56*
  Brief entry *39*
Wilkon, Jozef 1930- *133*
  Earlier sketches in SATA *31, 71*
Wilkowski, Sue *193*
Wilks, Michael Thomas 1947- *44*
Wilks, Mike
  See Wilks, Michael Thomas
Will
  See Lipkind, William

Willard, Barbara (Mary) 1909-1994 .... *74*
  Earlier sketch in SATA *17*
  See also CLR *2*
  See also SAAS *5*
Willard, Mildred Wilds 1911-1978 .... *14*
Willard, Nancy 1936- *191*
  Brief entry *30*
  Earlier sketches in SATA *37, 71, 127*
  See also CLR *5*
Willcox, Isobel 1907-1996 .... *42*
Willems, Mo *180*
  Earlier sketch in SATA *154*
  See also CLR *114*
Willett, Edward (C.) 1959- *115*
Willey, Bee *184*
Willey, Margaret 1950- *86*
Willey, Robert
  See Ley, Willy
Willhoite, Michael A. 1946- *71*
William, Kate
  See Armstrong, Jennifer
Williams, Arlene *171*
Williams, Barbara 1925- *107*
  Earlier sketch in SATA *11*
  See also CLR *48*
  See also SAAS *16*
Williams, Barbara 1937- *62*
Williams, Beryl
  See Epstein, Beryl (M. Williams)
Williams, Brian (Peter) 1943- *54*
Williams, Carol Lynch 1959- *110*
Williams, Charles
  See Collier, James Lincoln
Williams, Clyde C. 1881-1974 .... *8*
  Obituary *27*
Williams, Coe
  See Harrison, C(hester) William
Williams, Colleen Madonna Flood 1963- .. *156*
Williams, Cynthia G. 1958- *123*
Williams, Dar 1967- *168*
Williams, Donna Reilly 1945- *83*
Williams, Dorothy
  See Williams, Marcia
Williams, Dorothy Snowden
  See Williams, Dar
Williams, Eric (Ernest) 1911-1983 .... *14*
  Obituary *38*
Williams, Ferelith Eccles *22*
  See Eccles Williams, Ferelith
Williams, Frances B.
  See Browin, Frances Williams
Williams, Garth (Montgomery) 1912-1996 .. *66*
  Obituary *90*
  Earlier sketch in SATA *18*
  See also CLR *57*
  See also SAAS *7*
Williams, Guy R(ichard) 1920- *11*
Williams, Hawley
  See Heyliger, William
Williams, Helen 1948- *77*
Williams, J. R.
  See Williams, Jeanne
Williams, J. Walker
  See Wodehouse, P(elham) G(renville)
Williams, Jay 1914-1978 .... *41*
  Obituary *24*
  Earlier sketch in SATA *3*
  See also CLR *8*
Williams, Jeanne 1930- *5*
Williams, Jenny 1939- *60*
Williams, Karen Lynn 1952- *99*
  Earlier sketch in SATA *66*
Williams, Kit 1946(?)- *44*
  See also CLR *4*
Williams, Laura E. *180*
Williams, Laura Ellen
  See Williams, Laura E.
Williams, L.E.
  See Williams, Laura Ellen
Williams, Leslie 1941- *42*
Williams, Linda 1948- *59*

Williams, Louise Bonino 1904(?)-1984
  Obituary *39*
Williams, Lynn
  See Hale, Arlene
Williams, Marcia 1945- *159*
  Earlier sketch in SATA *97*
  See Williams, Marcia Dorothy
Williams, Marcia Dorothy *71*
  See Williams, Marcia
Williams, Margery
  See Bianco, Margery Williams
Williams, Mark
  See Arthur, Robert, (Jr.)
Williams, Mark London 1959- *140*
Williams, Maureen 1951- *12*
Williams, Michael
  See St. John, Wylly Folk
Williams, Patrick J.
  See Griffin, W.E.B
Williams, Pete
  See Faulknor, Cliff(ord Vernon)
Williams, S. P.
  See Hart, Virginia
Williams, Sam *177*
  Earlier sketch in SATA *124*
Williams, Selma R(uth) 1925- *14*
Williams, Sherley Anne 1944-1999 .... *78*
  Obituary *116*
Williams, Sheron 1955- *77*
Williams, Shirley
  See Williams, Sherley Anne
Williams, Slim
  See Williams, Clyde C.
Williams, Sophy 1965- *135*
Williams, Susan
  See Beckhorn, Susan Williams
Williams, Suzanne (Bullock) 1953- *71*
Williams, Ursula Moray *3*
  See Moray Williams, Ursula
Williams, Vera B(aker) 1927- *102*
  Brief entry *33*
  Earlier sketch in SATA *53*
  See also CLR *9*
Williams-Andriani, Renee 1963- *98*
Williams-Ellis, (Mary) Amabel (Nassau
  Strachey) 1894-1984 .... *29*
  Obituary *41*
Williams-Garcia, Rita 1957- *160*
  Earlier sketch in SATA *98*
  See also CLR *36*
Williamson, Gwyneth 1965- *109*
Williamson, Henry (William) 1895-1977 ...... *37*
  Obituary *30*
Williamson, Joanne S(mall) 1926- *122*
  Earlier sketch in SATA *3*
Willis, Charles
  See Clarke, Arthur C.
Willis, Connie 1945- *110*
  See also CLR *66*
Willis, Jeanne 1959- *195*
  Earlier sketches in SATA *61, 123*
Willis, Jeanne Mary
  See Willis, Jeanne
Willis, Meredith Sue 1946- *101*
Willis, Nancy Carol 1952- *139*
  Earlier sketch in SATA *93*
Willis, Paul J. 1955- *113*
Willms, Russ *95*
Willoughby, Lee Davis
  See Avallone, Michael (Angelo, Jr.)
  and Brandner, Gary (Phil)
  and Deming, Richard
  and DeAndrea, William L(ouis)
  and Laymon, Richard (Carl)
  and Streib, Dan(iel Thomas)
  and Toombs, John
  and Webb, Jean Francis (III)
Willson, Robina Beckles *27*
  See Beckles Willson, Robina (Elizabeth)
Wilma, Dana
  See Faralla, Dana

Wilsdorf, Anne 1954- *191*
Wilson, April *80*
Wilson, Barbara Ker
  See Ker Wilson, Barbara
Wilson, Beth P(ierre) *8*
Wilson, Budge 1927- *55*
  See Wilson, Marjorie
Wilson, Carletta 1951- *81*
Wilson, Carter 1941- *6*
Wilson, Charles Morrow 1905-1977 .... *30*
Wilson, Christopher B. 1910(?)-1985
  Obituary *46*
Wilson, Darryl B(abe) 1939- *90*
Wilson, Diane Lee *172*
Wilson, Dirk
  See Pohl, Frederik
Wilson, Dorothy Clarke 1904-2003 .... *16*
Wilson, Edward A(rthur) 1886-1970 .... *38*
Wilson, Ellen (Janet Cameron) (?)-1976 ...... *9*
  Obituary *26*
Wilson, Eric (H.) 1940- *34*
  Brief entry *32*
Wilson, Erica *51*
Wilson, Forrest 1918- *27*
Wilson, Gahan 1930- *35*
  Brief entry *27*
Wilson, Gina 1943- *85*
  Brief entry *34*
  Earlier sketch in SATA *36*
Wilson, (Leslie) Granville 1912- *14*
Wilson, Hazel (Hutchins) 1898-1992 .... *3*
  Obituary *73*
Wilson, J(erry) M. 1964- *121*
Wilson, Jacqueline 1945- *153*
  Brief entry *52*
  Earlier sketches in SATA *61, 102*
Wilson, John 1922- *22*
Wilson, John 1951- *182*
Wilson, John Alexander
  See Wilson, John
Wilson, Johnniece Marshall 1944- *75*
Wilson, Jonathan 1950- *181*
Wilson, Joyce M(uriel Judson) *84*
  Earlier sketch in SATA *21*
  See Stranger, Joyce
Wilson, Karma *174*
Wilson, Leslie 1952- *166*
Wilson, Linda Miller 1936- *116*
Wilson, Lionel 1924-2003 .... *33*
  Brief entry *31*
  Obituary *144*
Wilson, Marjorie
  Brief entry *51*
  See Wilson, Budge
Wilson, Maurice (Charles John) 1914- *46*
Wilson, Nancy Hope 1947- *138*
  Earlier sketch in SATA *81*
Wilson, Nathan D.
  See Wilson, N.D.
Wilson, N.D. 1978- *194*
Wilson, Nick
  See Ellis, Edward S(ylvester)
Wilson, Phil 1948- *181*
Wilson, Ron(ald William) 1941- *38*
Wilson, Sarah 1934- *142*
  Earlier sketch in SATA *50*
Wilson, Tom 1931- *33*
  Brief entry *30*
Wilson, Troy 1970- *169*
Wilson, Walt(er N.) 1939- *14*
Wilson-Max, Ken 1965- *170*
  Earlier sketch in SATA *93*
Wilton, Elizabeth 1937- *14*
Wilton, Hal
  See Pepper, Frank S.
Wilwerding, Walter Joseph 1891-1966 .... *9*
Wimmer, Mike 1961- *194*
  Earlier sketch in SATA *70*
Winborn, Marsha (Lynn) 1947- *75*
Winch, John 1944- *165*
  Earlier sketch in SATA *117*

Winchester, James H(ugh) 1917-1985 .... *30*
  Obituary *45*
Winchester, Stanley
  See Youd, (Christopher) Samuel
Windawi, Thura al- 1983(?)- *165*
Winders, Gertrude Hecker -1987 .... *3*
Windham, Basil
  See Wodehouse, P(elham) G(renville)
Windham, Kathryn T(ucker) 1918- *14*
Windham, Sophie *184*
Windling, Terri 1958- *151*
Windrow, Martin
  See Windrow, Martin Clive
Windrow, Martin C.
  See Windrow, Martin Clive
Windrow, Martin Clive 1944- *68*
Windsor, Claire
  See Hamerstrom, Frances
Windsor, Linda 1950- *124*
Windsor, Patricia 1938- *78*
  Earlier sketch in SATA *30*
  See also SAAS *19*
Wineman-Marcus, Irene 1952- *81*
Winer, Yvonne 1934- *120*
Winerip, Michael *175*
Winfield, Arthur M.
  See Stratemeyer, Edward L.
Winfield, Edna
  See Stratemeyer, Edward L.
Winfield, Julia
  See Armstrong, Jennifer
Wing, Natasha (Lazutin) 1960- *82*
Winick, Judd 1970- *124*
Winks, Robin William 1930-2003 .... *61*
Winn, Alison
  See Wharmby, Margot
Winn, Chris 1952- *42*
Winn, Janet Bruce 1928- *43*
Winn, Marie 1936(?)- *38*
Winnick, Karen B(eth) B(inkoff) 1946- *51*
Winslow, Barbara 1947- *91*
Winstead, Rosie *180*
Winston, Clara 1921-1983 .... *54*
  Obituary *39*
Winston, Richard 1917-1979 .... *54*
Winter, Janet 1926- *126*
Winter, Jeanette 1939- *184*
  Earlier sketch in SATA *151*
Winter, Jonah 1962- *179*
Winter, Milo (Kendall) 1888-1956 .... *21*
Winter, Paula Cecelia 1929- *48*
Winter, R. R.
  See Winterbotham, R(ussell) R(obert)
Winter, Susan *182*
Winterbotham, R(ussell) R(obert)
  1904-1971 .... *10*
Winterbotham, Russ
  See Winterbotham, R(ussell) R(obert)
Winterfeld, Henry 1901-1990 .... *55*
Winters, J. C.
  See Cross, Gilbert B.
Winters, Jon
  See Cross, Gilbert B.
Winters, Katherine 1936- *153*
  Earlier sketch in SATA *103*
Winters, Kay
  See Winters, Katherine
Winters, Nina 1944- *62*
Winters, Paul A. 1965- *106*
Winterson, Jeanette 1959- *190*
Winterton, Gayle
  See Adams, William Taylor
Winthrop, Elizabeth *164*
  Autobiography Feature *116*
  Earlier sketches in SATA *8, 76*
  See also CLR *89*
  See Mahony, Elizabeth Winthrop
Winton, Ian (Kenneth) 1960- *76*
Winton, Tim 1960- *98*
Wintz-Litty, Julie
  See Litty, Julie

Wirt, Ann
  See Benson, Mildred (Augustine Wirt)
Wirt, Mildred A.
  See Benson, Mildred (Augustine Wirt)
Wirtenberg, Patricia Z. 1932-2007 .... *10*
Wirtenberg, Patricia Zarrella
  See Wirtenberg, Patricia Z.
Wirth, Beverly 1938- *63*
Wirths, Claudine (Turner) G(ibson)
  1926-2000 .... *104*
  Earlier sketch in SATA *64*
Wise, Bill 1958- *191*
Wise, Lenny
  See Wise, Leonard
Wise, Leonard 1940- *167*
Wise, Leonard A.
  See Wise, Leonard
Wise, Leonard Allan
  See Wise, Leonard
Wise, William 1923- *163*
  Earlier sketch in SATA *4*
Wise, Winifred E. *2*
Wiseman, Ann (Sayre) 1926- *31*
Wiseman, B(ernard) 1922-1995 .... *4*
Wiseman, David 1916- *43*
  Brief entry *40*
Wishinsky, Frieda 1948- *166*
  Earlier sketches in SATA *70, 112*
Wisler, G(ary) Clifton 1950- *103*
  Brief entry *46*
  Earlier sketch in SATA *58*
Wismer, Donald (Richard) 1946- *59*
Wisner, Bill
  See Wisner, William L.
Wisner, William L. 1914(?)-1983 .... *42*
Wisnewski, David 1953-2002
  See Wisniewski, David
Wisniewski, David 1953-2002 .... *95*
  Obituary *139*
  See also CLR *51*
Wister, Owen 1860-1938 .... *62*
Witham, (Phillip) Ross 1917- *37*
Withers, Carl A. 1900-1970 .... *14*
Withers, Pam 1956- *182*
Withrow, Sarah 1966- *124*
Witt, Dick 1948- *80*
Witt, Shirley Hill 1934- *17*
Wittanen, Etolin 1907- *55*
Wittels, Harriet Joan 1938- *31*
Wittig, Susan
  See Albert, Susan Wittig
Wittlinger, Ellen 1948- *189*
  Autobiography Feature *128*
  Earlier sketches in SATA *83, 122*
Wittman, Sally (Anne Christensen) 1941- *30*
Witty, Paul 1898-1976 .... *50*
  Obituary *30*
Wodehouse, P(elham) G(renville)
  1881-1975 .... *22*
Wodge, Dreary
  See Gorey, Edward (St. John)
Woelfle, Gretchen 1945- *145*
Wohlberg, Meg 1905-1990 .... *41*
  Obituary *66*
Wohlrabe, Raymond A. 1900-1977 .... *4*
Wohnoutka, Mike *195*
Wojciechowska, Maia (Teresa) 1927-2002 ... *83*
  Autobiography Feature *104*
  Obituary *134*
  Earlier sketches in SATA *1, 28*
  See also CLR *1*
  See also SAAS *1*
Wojciechowski, Susan *126*
  Earlier sketch in SATA *78*
Wojnarowski, Adrian 1970- *190*
Wolcott, Patty 1929- *14*
Wold, Allen L. 1943- *64*
Wold, Jo Anne 1938- *30*
Woldin, Beth Weiner 1955- *34*
Wolf, Allan 1963- *192*

Wolf, Bernard 1930- *102*
    Brief entry *37*
Wolf, Erica (Van Varick) 1978- *156*
Wolf, Gita 1956- *101*
Wolf, Janet 1957- *78*
Wolf, J.M.
    See Wolf, Joan M.
Wolf, Joan M. 1966- *193*
Wolf, Sallie 1950- *80*
Wolfe, Art 1952- *76*
Wolfe, Burton H. 1932- *5*
Wolfe, Gene 1931- *165*
    Earlier sketch in SATA *118*
Wolfe, Gene Rodman
    See Wolfe, Gene
Wolfe, Louis 1905-1985 .... *8*
    Obituary *133*
Wolfe, Rinna (Evelyn) 1925- *38*
Wolfenden, George
    See Beardmore, George
Wolfer, Dianne 1961- *167*
    Autobiography Feature *117*
    Earlier sketch in SATA *104*
Wolff, Alexander (Nikolaus) 1957- *137*
    Earlier sketch in SATA *63*
Wolff, Ashley 1956- *155*
    Earlier sketches in SATA *50, 81*
Wolff, Diane 1945- *27*
Wolff, Ferida 1946- *164*
    Earlier sketch in SATA *79*
Wolff, Jennifer Ashley
    See Wolff, Ashley
Wolff, Robert Jay 1905-1977 .... *10*
Wolff, Sonia
    See Levitin, Sonia
Wolff, Virginia Euwer 1937- *137*
    Earlier sketch in SATA *78*
    See also CLR *62*
Wolfman, Judy 1933- *138*
Wolfson, Evelyn 1937- *62*
Wolitzer, Hilma 1930- *31*
Wolkoff, Judie (Edwards) *93*
    Brief entry *37*
Wolkstein, Diane 1942- *138*
    Earlier sketches in SATA *7, 82*
Wollheim, Donald A(llen) 1914-1990
    Obituary *69*
Wolny, P.
    See Janeczko, Paul B(ryan)
Wolters, Richard A. 1920-1993 .... *35*
Wondriska, William 1931- *6*
Wong, Jade Snow 1922-2006 .... *112*
    Obituary *175*
Wong, Janet S. 1962- *148*
    Earlier sketch in SATA *98*
    See also CLR *94*
Wood, Anne (Savage) 1937- *64*
Wood, Audrey *139*
    Brief entry *44*
    Earlier sketches in SATA *50, 81*
    See also CLR *26*
Wood, Catherine
    See Etchison, Birdie L(ee)
Wood, David 1944- *87*
Wood, Don 1945- *50*
    Brief entry *44*
    See also CLR *26*
Wood, Douglas 1951- *180*
    Earlier sketches in SATA *81, 132*
Wood, Douglas Eric
    See Wood, Douglas
Wood, Edgar A(llardyce) 1907-1998 .... *14*
Wood, Esther
    See Brady, Esther Wood
Wood, Frances Elizabeth *34*
Wood, Frances M. 1951- *97*
Wood, James Playsted 1905- *1*
Wood, Jenny 1955- *88*
Wood, John Norris 1930- *85*

Wood, June Rae 1946- *120*
    Earlier sketch in SATA *79*
    See also CLR *82*
Wood, Kerry
    See Wood, Edgar A(llardyce)
Wood, Kim Marie *134*
Wood, Laura N.
    See Roper, Laura (Newbold) Wood
Wood, Linda C(arol) 1945- *59*
Wood, Marcia 1956- *80*
Wood, Marcia Mae
    See Wood, Marcia
Wood, Nancy
    See Wood, Nancy C.
Wood, Nancy C. 1936- *178*
    Earlier sketch in SATA *6*
Wood, Nuria
    See Nobisso, Josephine
Wood, Owen 1929- *64*
Wood, Phyllis Anderson 1923- *33*
    Brief entry *30*
Wood, Richard 1949- *110*
Wood, Tim(othy William Russell) 1946- *88*
Wood, Wallace 1927-1981
    Obituary *33*
Woodard, Carol 1929- *14*
Woodburn, John Henry 1914- *11*
Woodbury, David Oakes 1896-1981 .... *62*
Woodford, Peggy 1937- *25*
Woodhouse, Barbara (Blackburn)
    1910-1988 .... *63*
Woodhull, Ann Love *194*
Wooding, Chris 1977- *166*
Wooding, Sharon
    See Wooding, Sharon L(ouise)
Wooding, Sharon L(ouise) 1943- *66*
Woodman, Allen 1954- *76*
Woodrich, Mary Neville 1915- *2*
Woodruff, Elvira 1951- *162*
    Earlier sketches in SATA *70, 106*
Woodruff, Joan Leslie 1953- *104*
Woodruff, Liza 1971(?)- *182*
Woodruff, Marian
    See Goudge, Eileen
Woodruff, Noah 1977- *86*
Woods, George A(llan) 1926-1988 .... *30*
    Obituary *57*
Woods, Geraldine 1948- *111*
    Brief entry *42*
    Earlier sketch in SATA *56*
Woods, Harold 1945- *56*
    Brief entry *42*
Woods, Lawrence
    See Lowndes, Robert A(ugustine) W(ard)
Woods, Margaret 1921- *2*
Woods, Nat
    See Stratemeyer, Edward L.
Woodson, Jack
    See Woodson, John Waddie Jr.
Woodson, Jacqueline 1964- *189*
    Earlier sketches in SATA *94, 139*
    See also CLR *49*
Woodson, Jacqueline Amanda
    See Woodson, Jacqueline
Woodson, John Waddie Jr. 1913- *10*
Woodtor, Dee
    See Woodtor, Delores Parmer
Woodtor, Dee Parmer 1945(?)-2002
    See Woodtor, Delores Parmer
Woodtor, Delores Parmer 1945-2002 .... *93*
Wood-Trost, Lucille
    See Trost, Lucille W(ood)
Woodward, (Landon) Cleveland 1900-1986 . *10*
    Obituary *48*
Woodworth, Chris 1957- *168*
Woodworth, Viki 1952- *127*
Woody, Regina Jones 1894-1983 .... *3*
Woog, Adam 1953- *125*
    Earlier sketch in SATA *84*
Wooldridge, Connie Nordhielm 1950- *143*
    Earlier sketch in SATA *92*

Wooldridge, Frosty 1947- *140*
Wooldridge, Rhoda 1906-1988 .... *22*
Wooley, Susan Frelick 1945- *113*
Woolf, Paula 1950- *104*
Woolfe, Angela 1976- *169*
Woolley, Catherine 1904-2005 .... *3*
    Obituary *166*
Woolman, Steven 1969-2004 .... *163*
    Earlier sketch in SATA *90*
Woolsey, Janette 1904-1989 .... *3*
    Obituary *131*
Worcester, Donald E(mmet) 1915- *18*
Word, Reagan 1944- *103*
Work, Virginia 1946- *57*
    Brief entry *45*
Worline, Bonnie Bess 1914- *14*
Wormell, Christopher 1955- *154*
    Earlier sketch in SATA *103*
Wormell, Mary 1959- *96*
Wormser, Richard 1933- *106*
    Autobiography Feature *118*
    See also SAAS *26*
Wormser, Sophie 1897-1979 .... *22*
Worth, Richard 1945- *59*
    Brief entry *46*
Worth, Valerie 1933-1994 .... *81*
    See Bahlke, Valerie Worth
Wortis, Avi
    See Avi
Wortis, Edward Irving
    See Avi
Wosmek, Frances 1917- *29*
Woychuk, Denis 1953- *71*
Wrede, Patricia C(ollins) 1953- *146*
    Earlier sketch in SATA *67*
Wriggins, Sally Hovey 1922- *17*
Wright, Alexandra 1979- *103*
Wright, Betty Ren *109*
    Brief entry *48*
    Earlier sketch in SATA *63*
Wright, Cliff 1963- *168*
    Earlier sketch in SATA *76*
Wright, Courtni
    See Wright, Courtni C(rump)
Wright, Courtni C(rump) 1950- *84*
Wright, Courtni Crump
    See Wright, Courtni C(rump)
Wright, Dare 1914(?)-2001 .... *21*
    Obituary *124*
Wright, David K. 1943- *112*
    Earlier sketch in SATA *73*
Wright, Elinor
    See Lyon, Elinor
Wright, Enid Meadowcroft (LaMonte)
    1898-1966 .... *3*
Wright, Esmond 1915-2003 .... *10*
Wright, Frances Fitzpatrick 1897-1982 .... *10*
Wright, J. B.
    See Barkan, Joanne
Wright, Judith 1915-2000 .... *14*
    Obituary *121*
Wright, Judith Arundell
    See Wright, Judith
Wright, Katrina
    See Gater, Dilys
Wright, Kenneth
    See del Rey, Lester
Wright, Kit 1944- *87*
Wright, Leslie B(ailey) 1959- *91*
Wright, Nancy Means *38*
Wright, R(obert) H(amilton) 1906- *6*
Wright, Rachel *134*
Wright, Susan Kimmel 1950- *97*
Wrightfrierson
    See Wright-Frierson, Virginia (Marguerite)
Wright-Frierson, Virginia (Marguerite)
    1949- *110*
    Earlier sketch in SATA *58*

Wrightson, (Alice) Patricia 1921- *112*
  Earlier sketches in SATA *8, 66*
  See also CLR *14*
  See also SAAS *4*
Wroble, Lisa A. 1963- *134*
Wrongo, I.B.
  See Katz, Alan
Wronker, Lili
  See Wronker, Lili Cassel
Wronker, Lili Cassel 1924- *10*
Wryde, Dogear
  See Gorey, Edward (St. John)
Wu, Elizabeth
  See Wu, Liz
Wu, Liz *184*
Wu, Norbert 1961- *155*
  Earlier sketch in SATA *101*
Wulffson, Don 1943- *155*
  Earlier sketches in SATA *32, 88*
Wulffson, Don L.
  See Wulffson, Don
Wunderli, Stephen 1958- *79*
Wunsch, Josephine (McLean) 1914- *64*
Wuorio, Eva-Lis 1918- *34*
  Brief entry *28*
Wurts, Janny 1953- *98*
Wyatt, B. D.
  See Robinson, Spider
Wyatt, David 1968- *185*
Wyatt, Jane
  See Bradbury, Bianca (Ryley)
Wyatt, Melissa 1963- *177*
Wyeth, Betsy James 1921- *41*
Wyeth, N(ewell) C(onvers) 1882-1945 .... *17*
  See also CLR *106*
Wyler, Rose 1909-2000 .... *18*
  Obituary *121*
Wylie, Betty Jane *48*
Wylie, Laura
  See Matthews, Patricia
Wylie, Laurie
  See Matthews, Patricia
Wyllie, Stephen *86*
Wyman, Andrea *75*
Wyman, Carolyn 1956- *83*
Wymer, Norman (George) 1911- *25*
Wynard, Talbot
  See Hamilton, Charles (Harold St. John)
Wyndham, John
  See Harris, John (Wyndham Parkes Lucas)
  Beynon
Wyndham, Lee
  See Hyndman, Jane Andrews Lee
Wyndham, Robert
  See Hyndman, Robert Utley
Wynne-Jones, Tim 1948- *186*
  Autobiography Feature *136*
  Earlier sketches in SATA *67, 96, 136*
  See also CLR *58*
Wynne-Jones, Timothy
  See Wynne-Jones, Tim
Wynter, Edward (John) 1914- *14*
Wynyard, Talbot
  See Hamilton, Charles (Harold St. John)
Wyss, Johann David Von 1743-1818 .... *29*
  Brief entry *27*
  See also CLR *92*
Wyss, Thelma Hatch 1934- *140*
  Earlier sketch in SATA *10*

X

Xavier, Father
  See Hurwood, Bernhardt J.
Xuan, YongSheng 1952- *116*
  Autobiography Feature *119*

Y

Yaccarino, Dan *192*
  Earlier sketch in SATA *141*
Yadin, (Rav-Aloof) Yigael 1917-1984 .... *55*
Yaffe, Alan
  See Yorinks, Arthur
Yagher, Kevin 1962- *143*
Yakovetic, (Joseph Sandy) 1952- *59*
Yakovetic, Joe
  See Yakovetic, (Joseph Sandy)
Yamada, Utako 1963- *188*
Yamaguchi, Marianne (Illenberger) 1936- *7*
Yamaka, Sara 1978- *92*
Yamanaka, Lois-Ann 1961- *166*
Yancey, Diane 1951- *138*
  Earlier sketch in SATA *81*
Yancey, Richard *193*
Yancey, Rick
  See Yancey, Richard
Yang, Belle 1960- *170*
Yang, James 1960- *190*
Yang, Jay 1941- *12*
Yang, Mingyi 1943- *72*
Yarbrough, Camille 1938- *79*
  See also CLR *29*
Yarbrough, Ira 1910(?)-1983
  Obituary *35*
Yaroslava
  See Mills, Yaroslava Surmach
Yarrow, Peter 1938- *195*
Yashima, Taro
  See CLR *4*
  See Iwamatsu, Jun Atsushi
Yates, Elizabeth 1905-2001 .... *68*
  Obituary *128*
  Earlier sketch in SATA *4*
  See also SAAS *6*
Yates, Janelle K(aye) 1957- *77*
Yates, John 1939- *74*
Yates, Philip 1958- *149*
  Earlier sketch in SATA *92*
Yates, Raymond F(rancis) 1895-1966 .... *31*
Yaukey, Grace S(ydenstricker) 1899-1994 ... *80*
  Earlier sketch in SATA *5*
Ye, Ting-xing 1952- *106*
Yeahpau, Thomas M. 1975- *187*
Yeakley, Marjory Hall 1908- *21*
Yeatman, Linda 1938- *42*
Yee, Brenda Shannon *133*
Yee, Lisa 1959- *160*
Yee, Paul (R.) 1956- *143*
  Earlier sketches in SATA *67, 96*
  See also CLR *44*
Yee, Wong Herbert 1953- *172*
  Earlier sketches in SATA *78, 115*
Yeh, Chun-Chan 1914- *79*
  See Ye Junjian
Ye Junjian
  See Yeh, Chun-Chan
Yenawine, Philip 1942- *85*
Yensid, Retlaw
  See Disney, Walt(er Elias)
Yeo, Wilma (Lethem) 1918-1994 .... *81*
  Earlier sketch in SATA *24*
Yeoman, John 1934- *80*
  Earlier sketch in SATA *28*
  See also CLR *46*
Yep, Laurence 1948- *176*
  Earlier sketches in SATA *7, 69, 123*
  See also CLR *132*
Yep, Laurence Michael
  See Yep, Laurence
Yepsen, Roger B(ennet), Jr. 1947- *59*
Yerian, Cameron John *21*
Yerian, Margaret A. *21*
Yerxa, Leo 1947- *181*
Yetska
  See Ironside, Jetske
Yezerski, Thomas F. 1969- *190*
Yin *194*

Ylvisaker, Anne 1965(?)- *172*
Yoder, Carolyn P(atricia) 1953- *149*
Yoder, Dorothy Meenen 1921- *96*
Yoder, Dot
  See Yoder, Dorothy Meenen
Yoder, Walter D. 1933- *88*
Yolen, Jane 1939- *194*
  Autobiography Feature *111*
  Earlier sketches in SATA *4, 40, 75, 112, 158*
  See also CLR *44*
  See also SAAS *1*
Yolen, Jane Hyatt
  See Yolen, Jane
Yonge, Charlotte (Mary) 1823-1901 .... *17*
Yoo, Paula 1969(?)- *174*
Yoo, Taeeun *191*
Yorinks, Adrienne 1956- *171*
Yorinks, Arthur 1953- *144*
  Earlier sketches in SATA *33, 49, 85*
  See also CLR *20*
York, Alison
  See Nicole, Christopher (Robin)
York, Andrew
  See Nicole, Christopher (Robin)
York, Carol Beach 1928- *77*
  Earlier sketch in SATA *6*
York, Rebecca
  See Buckholtz, Eileen (Garber)
  and Glick, Ruth (Burtnick)
York, Simon
  See Heinlein, Robert A.
Yoshida, Toshi 1911- *77*
Yoshikawa, Sachiko *181*
Yost, Edna 1889-1971
  Obituary *26*
Youd, C. S.
  See SAAS *6*
  See Youd, (Christopher) Samuel
Youd, (Christopher) Samuel 1922- *135*
  Brief entry *30*
  Earlier sketch in SATA *47*
  See Christopher, John
  and Youd, C. S.
Young, Amy L. *185*
Young, Bob
  See Young, Robert W(illiam)
  and Young, James Robert
Young, Carol 1945- *102*
Young, Catherine
  See Olds, Helen Diehl
Young, Clarence *67*
  Earlier sketch in SATA *1*
  See Stratemeyer, Edward L.
Young, Collier
  See Bloch, Robert (Albert)
Young, Dan 1952- *126*
Young, Dianne 1959- *88*
Young, Dorothea Bennett 1924- *31*
Young, Ed 1931- *173*
  Earlier sketches in SATA *10, 74, 122*
  See also CLR *27*
Young, Ed Tse-chun
  See Young, Ed
Young, Edward
  See Reinfeld, Fred
Young, Elaine L.
  See Schulte, Elaine L(ouise)
Young, James
  See Graham, Ian
Young, Jan
  See Young, Janet Randall
Young, Janet 1957- *188*
Young, Janet Randall 1919-1994 .... *3*
Young, Janet Ruth
  See Young, Janet
Young, Jeff C. 1948- *132*
Young, John
  See Macintosh, Brownie
Young, Judy 1956- *155*
Young, Judy (Elaine) Dockrey 1949- *72*

Young, Karen Romano 1959- 168
  Earlier sketch in SATA *116*
Young, Ken 1956- 86
Young, Lois Horton 1911-1981 26
Young, Louisa *161*
Young, Louise B. 1919- 64
Young, Margaret B(uckner) 1922- 2
Young, Mary 1940- 89
Young, Miriam 1913-1974 7
Young, Noela 1930- 89
Young, (Rodney Lee) Patrick (Jr.) 1937- 22
Young, Percy M(arshall) 1912-2004 31
  Obituary *154*
Young, Richard Alan 1946- 72
Young, Robert W(illiam) 1916-1969 3
Young, Ross B. 1955- 150
Young, Ruth 1946- 67
Young, Sara
  See Pennypacker, Sara
Young, Scott A. 1918-2005 5
Young, Scott Alexander
  See Young, Scott A.
Young, Vivien
  See Gater, Dilys
Younger, Barbara 1954- 108
Youngs, Betty 1934-1985 53
  Obituary 42
Younkin, Paula 1942- 77
Yount, Lisa (Ann) 1944- 124
  Earlier sketch in SATA *74*
Yourgrau, Barry 179
Yuditskaya, Tatyana 1964- 75
Yumoto, Kazumi 1959- 153

Z

Zach, Cheryl (Byrd) 1947- 98
  Brief entry 51
  Earlier sketch in SATA *58*
  See also SAAS *24*
Zacharias, Gary L. 1946- 153
Zaffo, George J. (?)-1984 42
Zagarenski, Pamela 1969(?)- 183
Zagwyn, Deborah Turney 1953- 138
  Earlier sketch in SATA *78*
Zahares, Wade 193
Zahn, Timothy 1951- 156
  Earlier sketch in SATA *91*
Zaid, Barry 1938- 51
Zaidenberg, Arthur 1908(?)-1990 34
  Obituary 66
Zalben, Jane Breskin 1950- 170
  Earlier sketches in SATA *7, 79, 120*
  See also CLR *84*
Zallinger, Jean (Day) 1918- 115
  Earlier sketches in SATA *14, 80*
Zallinger, Peter Franz 1943- 49
Zambreno, Mary Frances 1954- 140
  Earlier sketch in SATA *75*
Zanderbergen, George
  See May, Julian
Zappa, Ahmet 1974- 180
Zappa, Ahmet Emuukha Rodan
  See Zappa, Ahmet
Zappler, Lisbeth 1930- 10
Zarchy, Harry 1912-1987 34
Zarin, Cynthia 1959- 192
  Earlier sketch in SATA *108*
Zaring, Jane (Thomas) 1936- 40
Zarins, Joyce Audy 57
  See dos Santos, Joyce Audy
Zaslavsky, Claudia 1917- 36
Zaugg, Sandra L. 1938- 118

Zaugg, Sandy
  See Zaugg, Sandra L.
Zaunders, Bo 1939- 137
Zawadzki, Marek 1958- 97
Zebra, A.
  See Scoltock, Jack
Zebrowski, George 1945- 67
Zebrowski, George T.
  See Zebrowski, George
Zeck, Gerald Anthony 1939- 40
Zeck, Gerry
  See Zeck, Gerald Anthony
Zed, Dr.
  See Penrose, Gordon
Zei, Alki 1925- 24
  See also CLR *6*
Zeier, Joan T(heresa) 1931- 81
Zeinert, Karen 1942-2002 137
  Earlier sketch in SATA *79*
Zeises, Lara M. 1976- 184
  Earlier sketch in SATA *145*
Zelazny, Roger 1937-1995 57
  Brief entry 39
Zelazny, Roger Joseph
  See Zelazny, Roger
Zeldis, Malcah 1931- 146
  Earlier sketch in SATA *86*
Zelinsky, Paul O. 1953- 154
  Brief entry 33
  Earlier sketches in SATA *49, 102*
  See also CLR *55*
Zellan, Audrey Penn 22
  See Penn, Audrey
Zemach, Harve 3
  See Fischtrom, Harvey
Zemach, Kaethe 1958- 149
  Brief entry 39
  Earlier sketch in SATA *49*
Zemach, Margot 1931-1989 70
  Obituary 59
  Earlier sketch in SATA *21*
Zemach-Bersin, Kaethe
  See Zemach, Kaethe
Zeman, Ludmila 1947- 153
Zephaniah, Benjamin 1958- 189
  Earlier sketches in SATA *86, 140*
Zephaniah, Benjamin Obadiah Iqbal
  See Zephaniah, Benjamin
Zephaniah, Benjamin Pbadiah Iqubal
  See Zephaniah, Benjamin
Zephaniah, Benjamin Pbadiah Iqubal
  See Zephaniah, Benjamin
Zerman, Melvyn Bernard 1930- 46
Zettner, Pat 1940- 70
Zevin, Gabrielle 176
Zhang, Christopher Zhong-Yuan 1954- 91
Zhang, Song Nan 1942- 170
  Earlier sketch in SATA *85*
Ziefert, Harriet 1941- 154
  Earlier sketch in SATA *101*
Ziegler, Jack (Denmore) 1942- 60
Ziemienski, Dennis (Theodore) 1947- 10
Ziliox, Marc
  See Fichter, George S.
Zillah
  See Macdonald, Zillah K(atherine)
Zim, Herbert S(pencer) 1909-1994 30
  Obituary 85
  Earlier sketch in SATA *1*
  See also CLR *2*
  See also SAAS *2*
Zima, Gordon 1920- 90
Zimelman, Nathan 1921- 65
  Brief entry 37
Zimmer, Dirk 1943- 147
  Earlier sketch in SATA *65*

Zimmer, Tracie Vaughn 169
Zimmerman, Andrea 1950- 192
  Earlier sketch in SATA *123*
Zimmerman, Andrea Griffing
  See Zimmerman, Andrea
Zimmerman, H. Werner 1951- 101
Zimmerman, Heinz Werner
  See Zimmerman, H. Werner
Zimmerman, Naoma 1914-2004 10
Zimmermann, Arnold E. 1909- 58
Zimmett, Debbie
  See Becker, Deborah Zimmett
Zimmy
  See Stratemeyer, Edward L.
Zimnik, Reiner 1930- 36
  See also CLR *3*
Zindel, Bonnie 1943- 34
Zindel, Lizabeth 187
Zindel, Paul 1936-2003 102
  Obituary 142
  Earlier sketches in SATA *16, 58*
  See also CLR *85*
Ziner, Feenie
  See Ziner, Florence
Ziner, Florence 1921- 5
Zingara, Professor
  See Leeming, Joseph
Zinger, Yitskhok
  See Singer, Isaac Bashevis
Zion, Eugene 1913-1975 18
Zion, Gene
  See Zion, Eugene
Zoehfeld, Kathleen Weidner 1954- 193
Zohorsky, Janet R. 1958- 148
Zolkower, Edie Stoltz 171
Zolkowski, Cathy (A.) 1969- 121
Zollars, Jaime 191
Zolotow, Charlotte 1915- 138
  Earlier sketches in SATA *1, 35, 78*
  See also CLR *77*
Zolotow, Charlotte Gertrude Shapiro
  See Zolotow, Charlotte
Zolotow, Ellen
  See Dragonwagon, Crescent
Zonderman, Jon 1957- 92
Zonia, Dhimitri 1921- 20
Zonta, Pat 1951- 143
Zubrowski, Bernard 1939- 90
  Earlier sketch in SATA *35*
Zubrowski, Bernie
  See Zubrowski, Bernard
Zucker, Miriam S.
  See Reichert, Miriam Zucker
Zuckerman, Linda 190
Zudeck, Darryl 1961- 61
Zupa, G. Anthony
  See Zeck, Gerald Anthony
Zupancic, Lilijana Praprotnik
  See Prap, Lila
Zurbo, Matt(hew) 1967- 98
Zurhorst, Charles (Stewart, Jr.) 1913-1989 .. 12
Zurlo, Tony 1941- 145
Zuromskis, Diane
  See Stanley, Diane
Zuromskis, Diane Stanley
  See Stanley, Diane
Zusak, Markus 1975- 149
Zwahlen, Diana 1947- 88
Zweifel, Frances W. 1931- 14
Zwerger, Lisbeth 1954- 194
  Earlier sketches in SATA *66, 130*
  See also CLR *46*
  See also SAAS *13*
Zwinger, Ann (H.) 1925- 46
Zymet, Cathy Alter 1965- 121

DATE DUE

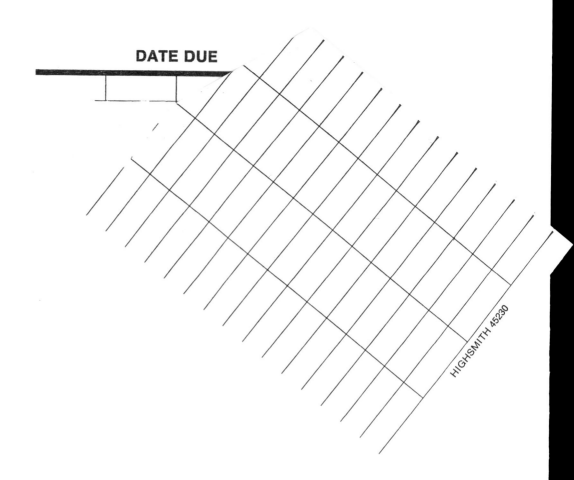

HIGHSMITH 45230